1956	1958	1960	1962	1964	1966	1968	1970	1972	1974	1976	1978	1980	1982
437.5	467.2	526.4	585.6	663.6	787.8	910.0	1038.5	1238.3	1500.0	1825.3	2294.7	2789.5	3255.0
271.7	296.2	331.7	363.3	411.4	480.9	558.0	648.5	770.6	933.4	1151.9	1428.5	1757.1	2077.3
72.0	64.5	78.9	88.1	102.1	131.3	141.2	152.4	207.6	249.4	292.0	438.0	479.3	517.2
91.4	106.0	111.6	130.1	143.2	171.8	209.4	233.8	263.5	317.9	383.0	453.6	566.2	680.5
2.4	0.5	4.2	4.1	6.9	3.9	1.4	4.0	−3.4	−0.8	−1.6	−25.4	−13.1	−20.0
391.1	415.2	470.8	526.4	598.6	712.2	821.6	931.8	1111.8	1137.5	1620.1	2032.4	2446.6	2828.1
395.6	416.8	474.9	530.1	602.7	711.0	823.2	930.9	1111.2	1342.1	1611.8	2027.4	2439.3	2864.3
244.5	259.5	296.4	327.1	370.7	442.7	524.3	617.2	725.1	890.2	1059.3	1336.1	1651.8	1925.8
14.2	15.4	17.1	18.8	19.6	20.8	20.9	21.4	23.4	24.3	22.3	22.1	30.0	38.8
6.9	9.5	10.6	14.2	17.4	22.4	27.1	39.1	47.9	70.8	85.5	115.0	181.8	271.1
48.5	43.5	53.8	63.3	76.5	93.2	98.8	83.6	112.1	115.8	163.3	216.6	201.1	209.7
45.8	50.1	50.7	51.2	59.0	63.9	74.3	78.4	95.9	113.1	132.2	166.6	174.1	176.3
36.6	28.6	46.2	55.8	64.4	71.7	77.8	91.2	106.9	127.8	149.2	171.0	200.5	222.4
339.6	369.0	411.5	456.7	514.6	603.9	712.0	838.8	992.7	1222.6	1474.8	1837.7	2307.9	2775.3
303.0	350.5	365.4	405.1	462.5	537.5	625.0	735.7	869.1	1071.6	1302.5	1608.3	2009.0	2421.2
1801.0	1898.0	2022.0	2171.0	2410.0	2734.0	3114.0	3587.0	4140.0	5010.0	5972.0	7224.0	8822.0	10,426.0
8.5	8.6	7.3	8.3	8.8	8.3	8.4	9.4	8.9	10.6	9.4	8.9	10.0	11.2

1956	1958	1960	1962	1964	1966	1968	1970	1972	1974	1976	1978	1980	1982
2255.8	2279.7	2501.8	2715.2	2998.6	3399.1	3652.7	3771.9	4105.0	4319.6	4540.9	5015.0	5161.7	5189.3
1.9	−1.0	2.5	6.1	5.8	6.5	4.8	0.2	5.3	−0.5	5.3	5.6	−0.2	−1.9
27.2	28.9	29.6	30.2	31.0	32.4	34.8	38.8	41.8	49.3	56.9	65.2	82.4	96.5
1.5	2.8	1.7	1.0	1.3	2.9	4.2	5.7	3.2	11.0	5.8	7.6	13.5	6.2
136.0	138.4	140.7	145.2	160.3	172.0	197.4	214.4	249.2	274.2	306.2	357.3	408.5	474.8
2.73	1.57	3.21	2.71	3.5	5.11	5.66	7.17	4.44	10.51	5.05	7.94	13.35	12.24
3.77	3.83	4.82	4.5	4.5	5.63	5.63	7.91	5.72	8.03	6.84	9.06	15.27	14.86
168.9	174.9	180.7	186.5	191.9	196.6	200.7	205.1	209.9	213.9	218.0	222.6	227.7	232.2
66.6	67.6	69.6	70.6	73.1	75.8	78.7	82.8	87.0	91.9	96.2	102.3	106.9	110.2
63.8	63.0	65.8	66.7	69.3	72.9	75.9	78.7	82.2	86.8	88.8	96.0	99.3	99.5
2.8	4.6	3.9	3.9	3.8	2.9	2.8	4.1	4.9	5.2	7.4	6.2	7.6	10.7
4.1	6.8	5.5	5.5	5.2	3.8	3.6	4.9	5.6	5.6	7.7	6.1	7.1	9.7
0.1	2.8	1.7	4.6	3.4	4.1	3.4	2.0	3.2	−1.6	3.1	1.1	−0.2	−0.8
5.3	4.2	4.4	4.5	5.2	5.6	5.1	4.0	4.3	5.5	5.4	5.4	4.8	3.5
2.94	3.0	2.91	2.85	3.0	3.1	3.18	3.39	2.85	9.25	13.1	14.95	37.42	31.83
3.9	−2.8	0.3	−7.1	−5.9	−3.7	−25.2	−2.8	−23.4	−6.1	−73.7	−59.2	−73.8	−128.0
272.7	279.7	290.5	302.9	316.1	328.5	368.7	380.9	435.9	483.9	629.0	776.6	909.1	1137.3
2.7	0.8	2.8	3.4	6.8	3.0	0.6	2.3	−5.8	2.0	4.3	−15.1	2.3	−5.5

(Continued in back of book)

EIGHTEENTH EDITION

Economics

Principles, Problems, and Policies

The McGraw-Hill Economics Series

ESSENTIALS OF ECONOMICS

Brue, McConnell, and Flynn
Essentials of Economics
Second Edition

Mandel
Economics: The Basics
First Edition

Schiller
Essentials of Economics
Seventh Edition

PRINCIPLES OF ECONOMICS

Colander
Economics, Microeconomics, and Macroeconomics
Seventh Edition

Frank and Bernanke
Principles of Economics, Principles of Microeconomics, Principles of Macroeconomics
Fourth Edition

Frank and Bernanke
Brief Editions: Principles of Economics, Principles of Microeconomics, and Principles of Macroeconomics
First Edition

McConnell, Brue, and Flynn
Economics, Microeconomics, and Macroeconomics
Eighteenth Edition

McConnell, Brue, and Flynn
Brief Editions: Microeconomics and Macroeconomics
First Edition

Miller
Principles of Microeconomics
First Edition

Samuelson and Nordhaus
Economics, Microeconomics, and Macroeconomics
Eighteenth Edition

Schiller
The Economy Today, The Micro Economy Today, and The Macro Economy Today
Eleventh Edition

Slavin
Economics, Microeconomics, and Macroeconomics
Ninth Edition

ECONOMICS OF SOCIAL ISSUES

Guell
Issues in Economics Today
Fourth Edition

Sharp, Register, and Grimes
Economics of Social Issues
Eighteenth Edition

ECONOMETRICS

Gujarati and Porter
Basic Econometrics
Fifth Edition

Gujarati and Porter
Essentials of Econometrics
Fourth Edition

MANAGERIAL ECONOMICS

Baye
Managerial Economics and Business Strategy
Sixth Edition

Brickley, Smith, and Zimmerman
Managerial Economics and Organizational Architecture
Fifth Edition

Thomas and Maurice
Managerial Economics
Ninth Edition

INTERMEDIATE ECONOMICS

Bernheim and Whinston
Microeconomics
First Edition

Dornbusch, Fischer, and Startz
Macroeconomics
Tenth Edition

Frank
Microeconomics and Behavior
Seventh Edition

ADVANCED ECONOMICS

Romer
Advanced Macroeconomics
Third Edition

MONEY AND BANKING

Cecchetti
Money, Banking, and Financial Markets
Second Edition

URBAN ECONOMICS

O'Sullivan
Urban Economics
Seventh Edition

LABOR ECONOMICS

Borjas
Labor Economics
Fifth Edition

McConnell, Brue, and Macpherson
Contemporary Labor Economics
Eighth Edition

PUBLIC FINANCE

Rosen and Gayer
Public Finance
Eighth Edition

Seidman
Public Finance
First Edition

ENVIRONMENTAL ECONOMICS

Field and Field
Environmental Economics: An Introduction
Fifth Edition

INTERNATIONAL ECONOMICS

Appleyard, Field, and Cobb
International Economics
Sixth Edition

King and King
International Economics, Globalization, and Policy: A Reader
Fifth Edition

Pugel
International Economics
Fourteenth Edition

Instructors teaching a concise and digitally integrated principles course welcome the Brief Editions

The Brief Editions of *Microeconomics* and *Macroeconomics* simplify the core concepts and remodel the examples presented in *Economics*, 18e. Not just cut-and-paste books, the Brief Editions are concise, highly integrated principles textbooks distinct in purpose, style, and coverage from *Economics*, 18e.

Microeconomics, Brief Edition

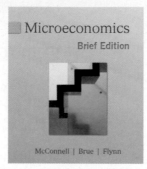

Go to **www.mcconnellbriefmicro1e.com** for sample chapters, the text preface, and more information.

Macroeconomics, Brief Edition

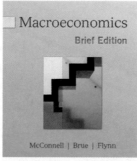

Go to **www.mcconnellbriefmacro1e.com** for sample chapters, the text preface, and more information.

For instructors teaching a one-semester Micro-Macro survey course, we present *Essentials of Economics, 2e*

Go to **www.brue2e.com** for sample chapters, the text preface, and more information.

EIGHTEENTH EDITION

Economics

Principles, Problems, and Policies

Campbell R. McConnell

University of Nebraska

Stanley L. Brue

Pacific Lutheran University

Sean M. Flynn

Vassar College

McGraw-Hill Irwin

Boston   Burr Ridge, IL   Dubuque, IA   New York   San Francisco   St. Louis
Bangkok   Bogotá   Caracas   Kuala Lumpur   Lisbon   London   Madrid   Mexico City
Milan   Montreal   New Delhi   Santiago   Seoul   Singapore   Sydney   Taipei   Toronto

To **Mem** and to **Terri** and **Craig**, and to **past instructors**

McGraw-Hill
Irwin

ECONOMICS: PRINCIPLES, PROBLEMS, AND POLICIES

Published by McGraw-Hill/Irwin, a business unit of The McGraw-Hill Companies, Inc., 1221
Avenue of the Americas, New York, NY, 10020. Copyright © 2009, 2008, 2005, 2002, 1999, 1996,
1993, 1990, 1987, 1984, 1981, 1978, 1975, 1972, 1969, 1966, 1963, 1960 by
The McGraw-Hill Companies, Inc.

Some ancillaries, including electronic and print components, may not be available to customers
outside the United States.

This book is printed on acid-free paper.

1 2 3 4 5 6 7 8 9 0 WCK/WCK 0 9 8

ISBN   978-0-07-337569-4
MHID   0-07-337569-1

Publisher: *Douglas Reiner*
Developmental editor: *Elizabeth Clevenger*
Developmental editor: *Anne Hilbert*
Editorial coordinator: *Noelle Fox*
Senior marketing manager: *Jennifer Lambert*
Senior marketing manager: *Melissa Larmon*
Senior project manager: *Harvey Yep*
Lead production supervisor: *Michael R. McCormick*
Interior designer: *Cara Hawthorne*
Senior photo research coordinator: *Lori Kramer*
Photo researcher: *Keri Johnson*
Senior media project manager: *Kerry Bowler*
Cover design: *Cara Hawthorne*
Cover image: *© David Churchill/Arcaid/Corbis*
Typeface: *10/12 Janson Text 55 Roman*
Compositor: *Aptara, Inc.*
Printer: *Quebecor World Versailles Inc.*

Library of Congress Cataloging-in-Publication Data

McConnell, Campbell R.
    Economics: principles, problems, and policies / Campbell R. McConnell, Stanley L. Brue,
Sean M. Flynn. — 18th ed.
    p. cm. — (The McGraw-Hill series in economics)
    Includes index.
    ISBN-13: 978-0-07-337569-4 (alk. paper)
    ISBN-10: 0-07-337569-1 (alk. paper)
    1. Economics. I. Brue, Stanley L., 1945- II. Flynn, Sean Masaki. III. Title.
HB171.5.M47 2009
330—dc22

                              2008037520

www.mhhe.com

About the Authors

Campbell R. McConnell earned his Ph.D. from the University of Iowa after receiving degrees from Cornell College and the University of Illinois. He taught at the University of Nebraska–Lincoln from 1953 until his retirement in 1990. He is also coauthor of *Contemporary Labor Economics*, eighth edition, and *Essentials of Economics*, second edition (both The McGraw-Hill Companies), and has edited readers for the principles and labor economics courses. He is a recipient of both the University of Nebraska Distinguished Teaching Award and the James A. Lake Academic Freedom Award and is past president of the Midwest Economics Association. Professor McConnell was awarded an honorary Doctor of Laws degree from Cornell College in 1973 and received its Distinguished Achievement Award in 1994. His primary areas of interest are labor economics and economic education. He has an extensive collection of jazz recordings and enjoys reading jazz history.

Stanley L. Brue did his undergraduate work at Augustana College (South Dakota) and received its Distinguished Achievement Award in 1991. He received his Ph.D. from the University of Nebraska–Lincoln. He is a professor at Pacific Lutheran University, where he has been honored as a recipient of the Burlington Northern Faculty Achievement Award. Professor Brue has also received the national Leavey Award for excellence in economic education. He has served as national president and chair of the Board of Trustees of Omicron Delta Epsilon International

Economics Honorary. He is coauthor of *Economic Scenes*, fifth edition (Prentice-Hall), *Contemporary Labor Economics*, eighth edition, *Essentials of Economics*, second edition (both The McGraw-Hill Companies), and *The Evolution of Economic Thought*, seventh edition (South-Western). For relaxation, he enjoys international travel, attending sporting events, and skiing with family and friends.

Sean M. Flynn did his undergraduate work at the University of Southern California before completing his Ph.D. at U.C. Berkeley, where he served as the Head Graduate Student Instructor for the Department of Economics after receiving the Outstanding Graduate Student Instructor Award. He teaches at Vassar College in Poughkeepsie, New York, and is also the author of *Economics for Dummies* (Wiley) and *Essentials of Economics*, second edition (The McGraw-Hill Companies). His research interests include finance and behavioral economics. An accomplished martial artist, he has represented the United States in international aikido tournaments and is the author of *Understanding Shodokan Aikido* (Shodokan Press). Other hobbies include running, travel, and ethnic food.

List of Key Graphs

Preface

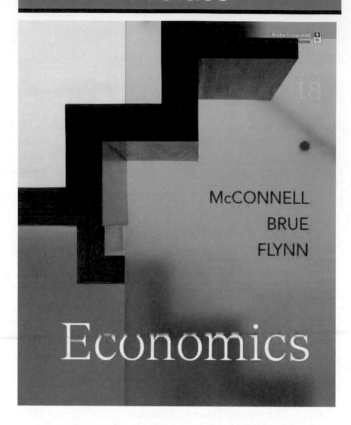

McCONNELL
BRUE
FLYNN

Economics

Welcome to the eighteenth edition of *Economics*, the best-selling economics textbook in the world. An estimated 14 million students have used *Economics* or its companion editions, *Macroeconomics* and *Microeconomics*. *Economics* has been adapted into Australian and Canadian editions and translated into Italian, Russian, Chinese, French, Spanish, Portuguese, and other languages. We are pleased that *Economics* continues to meet the market test: nearly one out of four U.S. students in principles courses used the seventeenth edition.

A Note about the Cover and New Coauthor

In the tradition of the previous two covers, the cover for this edition includes a photograph of steps. The new edition's cover is a metaphor for the step-by-step approach that we use to present basic economic principles. It also represents the simplicity, beauty, and power of basic economic models. We have chosen a highly modern photo to reflect the addition of our new coauthor, Sean M. Flynn, who has helped modernize the content of the book from cover to cover. Sean did his undergraduate work at USC, received his Ph.D. from U.C. Berkeley (in 2002), teaches principles at Vassar, and is the author of *Economics for Dummies*. We

are greatly pleased to have Sean working on the text since he shares our commitment to present economics in a way that is understandable to all.

Fundamental Objectives

We have three main goals for *Economics*:

- Help the beginning student master the principles essential for understanding the economizing problem, specific economic issues, and the policy alternatives.
- Help the student understand and apply the economic perspective and reason accurately and objectively about economic matters.
- Promote a lasting student interest in economics and the economy.

What's New and Improved?

One of the benefits of writing a successful text is the opportunity to revise—to delete the outdated and install the new, to rewrite misleading or ambiguous statements, to introduce more relevant illustrations, to improve the organizational structure, and to enhance the learning aids.

This is the most significant revision of *Economics* since the fourteenth edition. It has greatly benefited from the addition of our new coauthor. The more significant changes include the following.

Micro First Organization

Perhaps most noticeably, we changed the book's organization to micro first in keeping with how contemporary economists view the direction of linkage between the two parts of the subject. All the new principles texts introduced during the past two decades have been organized as micro-first texts and colleges have increasingly changed their course numbering (sequencing) to micro first.

As it relates to the actual principles course, however, this change in ordering is mainly symbolic. Micro and macro courses are still taught separately and independently, with no prerequisite on either. Also, students increasingly use the split micro and macro versions of our main text, even in schools that adopt our book for all sections of both micro and macro principles. We therefore think that most instructors will find it relatively easy to make the transition to the new ordering.

Fully Updated, Totally Contemporary Macroeconomics

We recast the entire macro analysis in terms of the modern, dominant paradigm of macroeconomics, using economic growth as the central backdrop and viewing business fluctuations as significant and costly variations in the rate of growth. In this paradigm, business cycles result from demand shocks (or, less often, supply shocks) in conjunction with inflexible short-run product prices and wages. The degree of price and wage stickiness decreases with time. In our models, the *immediate short run* is a period in which the price level and wages are not only sticky, but stuck; the *short run* is a period in which product prices are flexible and wages are not; and the *long run* is a period in which both prices and wages are fully flexible. Each of these three periods—and thus each of the models based on them—is relevant to understanding the actual macro economy and its occasional difficulties.

New Chapter 23 introduces the macro framework in a lively, intuitive way, using an example of a hypothetical single-firm economy. It also makes a clear, critical distinction between the broader concept of financial investment and the narrower subset of investment called economic investment in a way that allows us to use both ideas. A chapter on the measurement of nominal and real GDP follows. With real GDP clearly defined and measured, we present a chapter on economic growth. This early placement of the growth chapter allows students to understand the importance of economic growth and the factors that drive it. This growth chapter is followed by a chapter that introduces business fluctuations along the economy's growth path and the problems of unemployment and inflation that may result.

Following this set of core beginning chapters, we immediately begin to build models of the economy for the immediate short run and the short run. Students are therefore quickly introduced to models in which recessions and inflation can occur. This approach allows us to use the short-run AD-AS model to address fiscal policy and monetary policy relatively earlier in the macro. Students are made fully aware from the start of the macro that the rate of economic growth is fundamentally important for standards of living. Yet, the quick introduction of sticky price models enables students to understand demand shocks, recession, stimulatory fiscal policy, Fed monetary policy actions, and other topics that dominate the news about the macro economy.

Because Chapter 5 provides an early introduction to international trade and international finance, we are able to integrate the global economy from the start of the macro analysis. Then, after eventually developing the long-run AD-AS model, we directly link this long-run analysis back to our earlier discussions of growth. We finish the macro with two chapters that provide further analysis of international trade, balance of payments, exchange rates, and trade imbalances. The macro ends with a bonus Web chapter on

the requisites for, and impediments to, economic growth in developing nations.

Although the framework in which the macro is built is extensively revised, the revisions were made to preserve the main elements of the chapters in the previous edition. We simply have wrapped the macroeconomics analysis into a modern package of growth, expectations, shocks, price stickiness, time horizons, and international linkages.

Our macro content is also fully modern in terms of its coverage of contemporary problems and policies. For example, we cover the mortgage debt crisis, the recent economic slowdown, the Fed's reductions of the Federal funds rate, the Fed's term auction facility, the stimulus tax package of 2008, and more.

Four New Chapters

Four chapters—two micro and two macro—are new to the print version of *Economics*. Our common purpose for all four chapters is to incorporate contemporary analytical themes and address current economic issues.

Chapter 15: Natural Resource and Energy Economics. This new micro chapter—brought from our Web site for the seventeenth edition—is now in Part 3 (Microeconomics of Resource Markets). This chapter addresses the question of whether the world is becoming overpopulated and rapidly running out of resources. It covers topics such as declining fertility rates, the optimal rate of resource extraction, resource substitution, resource sustainability, oil prices, and alternative energy sources. An understanding of the basic economic principles of natural resource economics will be critical to future voters and leaders. This micro treatment of natural resource and energy topics is particularly timely since many students are regularly exposed to alarmist views on these subjects.

Chapter 22: Immigration. This new micro chapter covers the economics of immigration—both legal and illegal—in an analytical and balanced way. Students are highly interested in this subject, yet often lack the economic knowledge and tools to grasp the issues and debates. This chapter provides that basic economic understanding. The chapter also serves as a timely application of the economic principles developed in the prior chapters on resource markets.

Chapter 23: An Introduction to Macroeconomics. As previously noted, this new chapter introduces the revised macroeconomic content in an interesting, concise way. It motivates the study of macroeconomics and establishes the analytical framework to the subject that we use throughout the macro portion of the book.

Chapter 34: Financial Economics. This new macro chapter examines ideas such as compound interest, present value, arbitrage, risk, diversification, and the risk-return relationship. Students need a better grounding in such ideas to truly understand the modern economy. In view of the problems in the financial markets over the recent past, we think that integrating financial economics more directly in the macro principles course makes good sense. For many students, this course will be their only (classroom!) opportunity to learn that promises of high, unguaranteed returns reflect high, uninsured risk. Even if instructors cannot find time to assign and cover the entire chapter, they may want to discuss the beginning portion, which addresses the time value of money and provides easy-to-understand real-world examples of present value.

To make room for our four new chapters, we had to make certain accommodations. Specifically, we moved our micro chapter "Technology, R & D, and Efficiency" to the book's Web site, where it joins the chapter "The Economics of Developing Countries." Both chapters are available free to students for full-color viewing and can be printed for off-computer study. Furthermore, these chapters are fully supported by all the supplementary materials such as the *Study Guide* and Test Banks. Instructors who wish to cover the R&D chapter, rather than, for example, the new resource chapter, can easily make the substitution.

We also deleted the chapter "Labor Market Issues and Institutions: Unions, Discrimination, and Immigration." The core of the union content is now is an appendix to the wage determination chapter; the discrimination material is consolidated and placed in the chapter "Income Inequality, Poverty, and Discrimination," and the immigration content now is part of the full new chapter on this subject.

Also, we deleted the mainly macro chapter on the balance of payments, exchanges rates, and trade deficits from the *micro* split version of *Economics*. It continues to be in *Economics* and the macro split.

Our explicit discussion of Keynesian versus Classical macroeconomics in the chapter on macro theories and issues has been deleted since we integrated the graphical analysis into earlier chapters. Finally, we have deleted the lengthy historical discussions of the gold standard and the Bretton Woods System from the chapter on exchange rates and placed it as supplemental material for the chapter at our Web site. Other, lesser deletions or abridgements have occurred throughout the book.

Three New Appendixes

Three additional chapter appendixes are available for optional assignment in this edition. All are supported by the supplementary materials. The concise new appendixes are:

Chapter 3: Additional Examples of Supply and Demand. At the end of Chapter 3 we provide several additional examples of supply and demand, including concrete examples of simultaneous shifts in supply and demand curves. Products covered include lettuce, corn and ethanol, pink salmon, gasoline, and sushi. We also use the Olympic Games to illustrate examples of preset prices, shortages, and surpluses.

Chapter 11: Additional Game Theory Applications. We placed several applications of game theory in a new appendix at the end of the micro chapter on monopolistic competition and oligopoly. Instructors who like to stress game theory in dealing with oligopoly now have strong backup support from the textbook for their efforts. The appendix discusses concepts such as dominant strategies, Nash equilibrium, repeated games, and first-mover advantages.

Chapter 13: Labor Unions and Their Impacts. This compact appendix covers union membership, the decline of unions, collective bargaining, and the economic effects of unions.

New (or Relocated) "Consider This" and "Last Word" Boxes

Our "Consider This" boxes are used to provide analogies, examples, or stories that help drive home central economic ideas in a student-oriented, real-world manner. For instance, the idea of trade secrets is described with the legend of "cat gut" and violin strings, while McDonald's "McHits" and "McMisses" demonstrate the idea of consumer sovereignty. These brief vignettes, each accompanied by a photo, illustrate key points in a lively, colorful, and easy-to-remember way.

New or relocated "Consider This" boxes include such disparate topics as an economic comparison of the two Koreas (Chapter 2), "buying American" (Chapter 5), the prisoner's dilemma (Chapter 11), government policies and birth rates (Chapter 15), turning

CONSIDER THIS . . .

Did Gates, Winfrey, and Rodriguez Make Bad Choices?

Opportunity costs come into play in decisions well beyond simple buying decisions. Consider the different choices people make with respect to college. College graduates usually earn about 50 percent more during their lifetimes than persons with just high school diplomas. For most capable students, "Go to college, stay in college, and earn a degree" is very sound advice.

Yet Microsoft cofounder Bill Gates and talk show host Oprah Winfrey* both dropped out of college, and baseball star Alex Rodriguez ("A-Rod") never even bothered to start classes. What were they thinking? Unlike most students, Gates faced enormous opportunity costs for staying in college. He had a vision for his company, and his starting work young helped ensure Microsoft's success. Similarly, Winfrey landed a spot in local television news when she was a teenager, eventually producing and starring in the *Oprah Winfrey Show* when she was 32 years old. Getting a degree in her twenties might have interrupted the string of successes that made her famous talk show possible. And Rodriguez knew that professional athletes have short careers. Therefore, going to college directly after high school would have taken away four years of his peak earning potential.

So Gates, Winfrey, and Rodriguez understood opportunity costs and made their choices accordingly. The size of opportunity costs greatly matters in making individual decisions.

*Winfrey eventually went back to school and earned a degree from Tennessee State University when she was in her thirties.

LAST Word

Pitfalls to Sound Economic Reasoning

Because They Affect Us So Personally, We Often Have Difficulty Thinking Accurately and Objectively About Economic Issues.

Here are some common pitfalls to avoid in successfully applying the economic perspective.

Biases Most people bring a bundle of biases and preconceptions to the field of economics. For example, some might think that corporate profits are excessive or that lending money is always superior to borrowing money. Others might believe that government is necessarily less efficient than businesses or that more government regulation is always better than less. Biases cloud thinking and interfere with objective analysis. All of us must be willing to shed biases and preconceptions that are not supported by facts.

Loaded Terminology The

media is sometimes emotionally biased, or loaded. The writer or spokesperson may have a cause to promote or an ax to grind and may slant comments accordingly. High profits may be labeled "obscene," low wages may be called "exploitive," or self-interested behavior may be "greed." Government workers may be referred to as "mindless bureaucrats" and those favoring stronger government regulations may be called "socialists." To objectively analyze economic issues, you must be prepared to reject or discount such terminology.

Fallacy of Composition Another pitfall in economic thinking is the assumption that what is true for one individual or part of a whole is necessarily true for the group of individuals or the whole. This is a logical fallacy called the *fallacy of composition*; the assumption is not correct. A statement that is true for an individual or part is not necessarily valid for the larger group or whole. You may see the action better if you leap to your feet to

entrails into oil (Chapter 15), putting corn in our gas tanks (Chapter 19), consumption inequality (Chapter 20), the cancer fight that is going nuclear (Chapter 21), the contributions of past immigrants to the U.S. economy (Chapter 22), patent reform in India (Chapter 25), and the relative returns on standard versus ethical investing (Chapter 34).

Our "Last Word" pieces are lengthier applications and case studies located toward the end of chapters. New or relocated Last Words include those on fair trade products (Chapter 5); insights from behavioral economics (Chapter 7); the link between economic growth and environmental protection (Chapter 15); past and current, and proposed U.S. immigration laws (Chapter 22); the role of inventory management in moderating recessions (Chapter 23); the Fed's response to the mortgage debt crisis (Chapter 33); the relative performance of index funds versus actively managed funds (Chapter 34); and Bastiat's "Petition of the Candlemakers" (Chapter 37).

Contemporary Discussions and Examples

The eighteenth edition refers to and discusses many current topics. Examples include the cost of the war in Iraq; surpluses and shortages of tickets at the Olympics; the myriad impacts of ethanol subsides; offshoring of American jobs; trade adjustment assistance; the additions of countries to the European Union and to the euro zone; normal trade relations status; aspects of behavioral economics; game theory; the most rapidly expanding and disappearing U.S. jobs; oil and gasoline prices; climate change; The Food, Conservation, and Energy Act of 2008; consumption versus income inequality; prescription drug coverage under Medicare; Health Savings Accounts (HSAs); comprehensive immigration reform; China's rapid growth rate; the business downturn of late

2007 and early 2008; the stimulus package of 2008; Federal budget deficits; the mortgage debt crisis; recent Fed monetary policy; the Fed's new term auction facility; the Taylor rule; U.S. trade deficits, and many more.

Distinguishing Features

Comprehensive Explanations at an Appropriate Level *Economics* is comprehensive, analytical, and challenging yet fully accessible to a wide range of students. The thoroughness and accessibility enable instructors to select topics for special classroom emphasis with confidence that students can read and comprehend other independently assigned material in the book. Where needed, an extra sentence of explanation is provided. Brevity at the expense of clarity is false economy.

Fundamentals of the Market System Many economies throughout the world are still making difficult transitions from planning to markets while a handful of other countries such as Venezuela seem to be trying to reestablish government-controlled, centrally planned economies. Our detailed description of the institutions and operation of the market system in Chapter 2 is therefore even more relevant than before. We pay particular attention to property rights, entrepreneurship, freedom of enterprise and choice, competition, and the role of profits because these concepts are often misunderstood by beginning students worldwide.

Early and Full Integration of International Economics We give the principles and institutions of the global economy early treatment. Chapter 5 examines the growth of world trade and its major participants, specialization and comparative advantage, the foreign exchange market, tariffs and subsidies, and various trade agreements. This strong introduction to international economics permits "globalization" of later discussions in both the micro and the macro chapters. Then, we delve into the more difficult, graphical analysis of international trade and finance in Chapters 37 and 38.

Early and Extensive Treatment of Government Government is an integral component of modern capitalism. This book introduces the economic functions of government early and accords them systematic treatment in Chapter 4. Chapter 16 examines public goods and externalities in further detail, and Chapter 17 looks at salient facets of public choice theory and taxation. Both the micro and the macro sections of the text include issue- and policy-oriented chapters.

Stress on the Theory of the Firm We have given much attention to microeconomics in general and to the theory of the firm in particular, for two reasons. First, the concepts of microeconomics are difficult for most beginning students; abbreviated expositions usually compound these difficulties by raising more questions than they answer. Second, we wanted to couple analysis of the various market structures with a discussion of the impact of each market arrangement on price, output levels, resource allocation, and the rate of technological advance.

Step-by-Step, Two-Path Macro As in the previous edition, our macro continues to be distinguished by a systematic step-by-step approach in developing ideas and building models. Explicit assumptions about price and wage stickiness are posited and then systematically peeled away, yielding new models and extensions, all in the broader context of growth, expectations, shocks, and degrees of price and wage stickiness over time.

In crafting this step-by-step macro approach, we took care to preserve the "two-path macro" that many instructors appreciated. Instructors who so choose can bypass the immediate short-run model (Chapter 28) and can proceed without loss of continuity directly to the short-run AD-AS model (Chapter 29), fiscal policy, money and banking, monetary policy, and the long-run analysis.

Emphasis on Technological Change and Economic Growth This edition continues to emphasize economic growth. Chapter 1 uses the production possibilities curve to show the basic ingredients of growth. Chapter 25 explains how growth is measured and presents the facts of growth. It also discusses the causes of growth, looks at productivity growth, and addresses some controversies surrounding economic growth. Chapter 25's Last Word examines the rapid economic growth in China. Chapter 39Web focuses on developing countries and the growth obstacles they confront. Chapter 11Web provides an explicit and cohesive discussion of the microeconomics of technological advance, including topics such as invention, innovation, and diffusion; start-up firms; R&D decision making; market structure and R&D effort; and creative destruction.

Focus on Economic Policy and Issues For many students, the micro chapters on antitrust, agriculture, income inequality, health care, and immigration, along with the macro chapters on fiscal policy and monetary policy, are where the action is centered. We guide that action along logical lines through the application of appropriate analytical tools. In the micro, we favor inclusiveness; instructors can effectively choose two or three chapters from Part 5.

Integrated Text and Web Site *Economics* and its Web site are highly integrated through in-text Web buttons, Web-based end-of-chapter questions, bonus Web chapters, multiple-choice self-tests at the Web site, math notes, and other features. Our Web site is part and parcel of our student learning package, customized to the book.

The in-text Web buttons (or indicators) merit special mention. Three differing colors of rectangular indicators appear throughout the book, informing readers that complementary content on a subject can be found at our Web site, **www.mcconnell18e.com**. The indicator types are:

Worked Problems Written by Norris Peterson of Pacific Lutheran University (WA), these pieces consist of side-by-side computational questions and computational procedures used to derive the answers. In essence, they extend the textbook's explanation involving computations—for example, of real GDP, real GDP per capita, the unemployment rate, the inflation rate, per-unit production costs, economic profit, and more. From a student's perspective, they provide "cookbook" help for problem solving.

> **WORKED PROBLEMS**
> **W 1.1**
> Budget lines

Interactive Graphs These pieces (developed under the supervision of Norris Peterson) depict 30 major graphs and instruct students to shift the curves, observe the outcomes, and derive relevant generalizations. This hands-on graph work will greatly reinforce the graphs and their meaning.

> **INTERACTIVE GRAPHS**
> **G 1.1**
> Production possibilities curve

Origin of the Ideas These pieces, written by Randy Grant of Linfield College (OR), are brief histories of 70 major ideas identified in the book. They identify the particular economists who developed ideas such as opportunity costs, equilibrium price, the multiplier, comparative advantage, and elasticity.

> **ORIGIN OF THE IDEA**
> **O 1.1**
> Origin of the term "Economics"

Organizational Alternatives

Although instructors generally agree on the content of principles of economics courses, they sometimes differ on how to arrange the material. *Economics* includes 10 parts, and thus provides considerable organizational flexibility.

We chose to move from microeconomics to macroeconomics because this is consistent with how contemporary economists view the direction of linkage between the two components. The introductory material of Part 1, however, can be followed immediately by the macroanalysis of Parts 6 and 7. Similarly, the two-path macro enables covering the full aggregate expenditures model or advancing directly from the basic macro relationships chapter to the AD-AS model.

Some instructors will prefer to intersperse the microeconomics of Parts 3 and 4 with the problems chapters of Part 5. Chapter 19 on agriculture may follow Chapter 9 on pure competition; Chapter 18 on antitrust and regulation may follow Chapters 10, 11, and 11Web on imperfect competition models and technological advance. Chapter 22 on immigration may follow Chapter 13 on wages; and Chapter 20 on income inequality may follow Chapters 13 and 14 on distributive shares of national income.

Instructors who teach the typical two-semester course and feel comfortable with the book's organization will find that, by putting Parts 1 to 5 in the first semester and Parts 6 to 10 in the second, the material is divided logically between the two semesters.

Pedagogical Aids

Economics is highly student-oriented. The "To the Student" statement at the beginning of Part 1 details the book's many pedagogical aids. The eighteenth edition is also accompanied by a variety of high-quality supplements that help students master the subject and help instructors implement customized courses.

Supplements for Students and Instructors

Study Guide
One of the world's leading experts on economic education, William Walstad of the University of Nebraska–Lincoln, prepared the eighteenth edition of the *Study Guide*. Many students find the *Study Guide* indispensable. Each chapter contains an introductory statement, a checklist of behavioral objectives, an outline, a list of important terms, fill-in questions, problems and projects, objective questions, and discussion questions.

The *Guide* comprises a superb "portable tutor" for the principles student. Separate *Study Guides* are available for the macro and micro paperback editions of the text.

Premium Content
The Premium Content, available at the Online Learning Center, offers a range of dynamic study aids to the student. Narrated PowerPoint presenta-

tions enable students to see key concepts and hear the explanation simultaneously. The Solman Videos, a set of more than 250 minutes of video created by Paul Solman of *The News Hour with Jim Lehrer*, cover core economic concepts such as elasticity, deregulation, and perfect competition. These study aids plus pre- and post-tests and chapter quizzes can be purchased and downloaded to an iPod, MP3 player, or desktop computer. Premium Content enables the student to study and self-test on his or her computer or on the go.

McGraw-Hill Connect Economics
Connect Economics is a complete, online supplement system that duplicates and expands upon the textbook's end-of-chapter material and test banks. Nearly all the questions

from the text, including the numerous graphing exercises, are presented in an autogradable format and tied to the text's learning objectives. Instructors may edit existing questions and author entirely new problems. Connect Economics can be used for student practice, homework, quizzes, and formal examinations. Detailed grade reports enable instructors to see how each student performs on a particular problem, a full assignment, and in the context of the overall class. The Connect Economics grade reports can be easily integrated with WebCT and Blackboard. Connect Economics is also available with an integrated online version of the textbook. With a single access code, students can read the eBook, work through practice problems, do homework, and take exams.

CourseSmart eTextbook
For roughly half the cost of a print book, you can reduce your impact on the

environment by buying McConnell, Brue, and Flynn's *Economics*, 18e eText. CourseSmart eTextbooks, available in a standard online reader, retain the exact content and look of the print text, plus offer the advantage of digital navigation to which students are accustomed. Students can search the text, highlight, take notes, and use e-mail tools to share notes with their classmates. CourseSmart also includes tech support in case help is ever needed. To buy *Economics*, 18e as an eText, or to learn more about this digital solution, visit **www.Course Smart.com** and search by title, author, or ISBN.

Instructor's Manual
Shawn D. Knabb of Western Washington University revised and updated the *Instructor's Manual*.

The revised *Instructor's Manual* includes:
- Chapter summaries.
- Listings of "what's new" in each chapter.
- Teaching tips and suggestions.
- Learning objectives.
- Chapter outlines.
- Data and visual aid sources with suggestions for classroom use.
- Extra questions and problems.
- End-of-chapter correlation guides mapping content to the learning objectives and important AACSB and Bloom's Taxonomy standards.

The *Instructor's Manual* is available on the instructor's side of the Online Learning Center.

Three Test Banks
Test Bank I contains about 6650 multiple-choice and true-false questions, most of which were written by the text authors. Randy Grant revised Test Bank I for the eighteenth edition. Test Bank II contains around 6300 multiple-choice and true-false questions, updated by Michael Youngblood of Rock Valley College. All Test Bank I and II questions are organized by learning objective, topic, AACSB Assurance of Learning, and Bloom's Taxonomy guidelines. Test Bank III, written by William Walstad, contains more than 600 pages of short-answer questions and problems created in the style of the book's end-of-chapter questions. Test Bank III can be used to construct student assignments or design essay and problem exams. Suggested answers to the essay and problem questions are included. In all, more than 14,000 questions give instructors maximum testing flexibility while ensuring the fullest possible text correlation.

Test Banks I and II are available through EZ Test Online as well as in MS Word. EZ Test allows professors to created customized tests that contain both questions that they select from the test banks as well as questions that they craft themselves. Test Bank III is available in MS Word on the password-protected instructor's side of the Online Learning Center, and on the Instructor Resource CD, both of which we will describe shortly.

PowerPoint Presentations
Nora Underwood of the University of Central Florida updated the *PowerPoint Presentations* for the eighteenth edition. Each chapter, including the Web chapters, is accompanied by a concise yet thorough tour of the key concepts. Instructors can use the slides in the classroom while students can use the slides to study. Students can view a second, distinct set of slides—the *Narrated PowerPoint Presentations*—on the site or download the material to their video iPod. The content is correlated to the Learning Objectives. This exceptional study aid, updated by Darlene DeVera of Deanza College, is a part of the Premium Content package.

Digital Image Library
Every graph and table in the text is available on the instructor's side of the Web site and on the Instructor's Resource CD-ROM.

Online Learning Center (www.mcconnell18e.com)
The Web site accompanying this book is a central resource for students and instructors alike. The optional Web Chapters: "Technology, R&D, and Efficiency," "The Economics of Developing Countries," and Chapter 38 Web supplement: "Previous International Exchange-Rate Systems" are posted as full-color PDF files. As previously mentioned, the three in-text Web buttons alert the students to points in the book where they can springboard to the Web site to get more information. Students can test their knowledge of a chapter's concepts with the self-graded multiple choice quiz and review PowerPoint presentations.

The password-protected Instructor Center houses the Instructor's Manual, all three Test Banks, and links to EZ Test Online, PowerPoint Presentations, and Digital Image Library.

Instructor's Resource CD-ROM
This CD contains all three test banks, PowerPoint presentations, and the Digital Image Library featuring all of the tables and figures from the text.

Classroom Performance Systems by eInstruction
This is a revolutionary system that brings ultimate interactivity to the classroom. CPS is a wireless response system that gives you immediate feedback from every student in the class. CPS units include easy-to-use software for creating and delivering questions and assessments to your class. With CPS you can ask subjective and objective questions. Then every student responds with an individual, wireless response pad, providing instant results. CPS is the perfect

tool for engaging students while gathering important assessment data.

Instructors can access eInstruction questions in two formats—CPS and PowerPoint. Motivate student preparation, interactivity, and active learning with these lecture formatted questions.

Assurance of Learning Ready
Assurance of learning is an important element of many accreditation standards. *Economics*, 18e is designed specifically to support your assurance of learning initiatives. Each chapter in the book begins with a list of numbered learning objectives which appear throughout the chapter, as well as in the end-of-chapter problems and exercises. Every test bank question is also linked to one of these objectives, in addition to level of difficulty, topic area, Bloom's Taxonomy level, and AACSB skill area. EZ Test, McGraw-Hill's easy-to-use test bank software, can search the test bank by these and other categories, providing an engine for targeted Assurance of Learning analysis and assessment.

AACSB Statement
The McGraw-Hill Companies is a proud corporate member of AACSB International. Understanding the importance and value of AACSB accreditation, *Economics*, 18e has sought to recognize the curricula guidelines detailed in the AACSB standards for business accreditation by connecting end-of-chapter questions in *Economics*, 18e and the accompanying test banks to the general knowledge and skill guidelines found in the AACSB standards.

The statements contained in *Economics*, 18e are provided only as a guide for the users of this text. The AACSB leaves content coverage and assessment within the purview of individual schools, the mission of the school, and the faculty. While *Economics*, 18e and the teaching package make no claim of any specific AACSB qualification or evaluation, we have, within *Economics*, 18e labeled selected questions according to the six general knowledge and skills areas.

Acknowledgments

We give special thanks to Norris Peterson of Pacific Lutheran University and Randy Grant of Linfield College, who created the "button" content on our Web site. We again thank James Reese of the University of South Carolina at Spartanburg, who wrote the original Internet exercises. Although many of those questions were replaced or modified in the typical course of revision, several remain virtually unchanged. We also thank Nora Underwood at the University of Central Florida for updating the PowerPoint slides for the eighteenth edition and Darlene DeVera of Deanza College for the Narrated PowerPoint presentations. Shawn Knabb of Western Washington University deserves a great thanks for updating the *Instructor's Manual* as well as for accuracy checking the many parts making up 18e and the ancillies. Thanks to Mohammad Bajwa of Northampton Community College, who accuracy checked both Test Banks I and II, and to Benjamin Pappas, who updated the art in both Test banks. Finally, we thank William Walstad and Tom Barbiero (the coauthor of our Canadian edition) for their helpful ideas and insights.

We are greatly indebted to an all-star group of professionals at McGraw-Hill—in particular Douglas Reiner, Elizabeth Clevenger, Harvey Yep, Jennifer Lambert, Melissa Larmon, and Brent Gordon—for their publishing and marketing expertise.

We thank Keri Johnson for her selection of the Consider This and Last Word photos and Cara Hawthorne for the design.

The eighteenth edition has benefited from a number of perceptive formal reviews. The contributors, listed at the end of the Preface, were a rich source of suggestions for this revision. To each of you, and others we may have inadvertently overlooked, thank you for your considerable help in improving *Economics*.

Stanley L. Brue
Sean M. Flynn
Campbell R. McConnell

Contributors

Homer Guevara, *Northwest Vista College*
Gus Herring, *Brookhaven College*
John Heywood, *University of Wisconsin–Milwaukee*
Charles Hiatt, *Central Florida Community College–Ocala*
George E. Hoffer, *Virginia Commonwealth University*
Adora D. Holstein, *Robert Morris University*
Jack W. Hou, *California State University, Long Beach*
Jim H. Hubert, *Seattle Central Community College*
George Jakubson, *Cornell University–Ithaca*
Vincent Jackson, *Florida Community College, Jacksonville*
Wayne Joerding, *Washington State University*
Barbara John, *University of Dayton*
Simran Kahai, *John Carroll University*
Yvan J. Kelly, *Flagler College*
Kamau Kinuthia, *American River College*
Mary Beth Klinger, *College of Southern Maryland*
Shawn Knabb, *Western Washington University*
Heather Kohls, *Marquette University*
Maria Cornachione Kula, *Roger Williams University*
Theodore A. Labay, *Bishop State Community College*
Carsten Lange, *California State Polytechnic University, Pomona*
Ron Laschever, *University of Illinois–Urbana Champaign*
Fritz Laux, *Northeastern State University*
Marc Law, *University of Vermont*
Shu Lin, *Florida Atlantic University–Boca Raton*
KT Magnusson, *Salt Lake Community College*
Murir Mahmud, *Dixie State College*
Paula Manns, *Atlantic Cape Community College*
Evelina Mengova, *California State University, Fullerton*
Babu Nahata, *University of Louisville*
Gerald Nyambane, *Davenport University*
Victor Oguledo, *Florida A&M*
Glenda Orosco, *Oklahoma State University, Okmulgee*
Joan Osborne, *Palo Alto College*
Michel-Ange Pantal, *University of Missouri, Columbia*
Charles J. Parker, *Wayne State College*
Nathan Perry, *University of Utah–Salt Lake City*
Mary Anne Pettit, *Southern Illinois University*
Diana Petersdorf, *University of Wisconsin, Stout*
Chirinjev Peterson, *Greenville Technical College*
John Pharr, *Cedar Valley College*
James Ragan, *Kansas State University*
Brian Rosario, *University of California, Davis*
Marina Rosser, *James Madison University*
Nicole Cornell Sadowski, *York College of Pennsylvania*
Allen R. Sanderson, *University of Chicago*
David P. Schutte, *Mountain View College*
Gerald Scott, *Florida Atlantic University–Boca Raton*
Timothy Shaughnessy, *Louisiana State University–Shreveport*

John Shea, *University of Maryland–College Park*
Curtis Simon, *Clemson University*
Virginia Shingleton, *Valparaiso University*
Tom Sweeney, *Des Moines Area Community College*
Regina Tawah, *Bowie State University*
Manjuri Talukdar, *Northern Illinois University*
Henry Terrell, *University of Maryland–College Park*
Mary Thompson, *Belmont University*
Wendine Thompson-Dawson, *Monmouth College*
Ross D. Weiner, *The City College of New York*
William Wood, *James Madison University*
J. Christopher M. Wreh, *North Central Texas College*
Jay Zagorsky, *Boston University*
Inske Zandvliet, *Brookhaven College*
Michael Zerbe, *Stark State College of Technology*

User Survey Respondents

Deergha Adhikari, *University of Louisiana at Lafayette*
Douglas K. Adie, *Ohio University*
Charles Anderson, *Kean University*
Ali Ataiifar, *Delaware County Community College*
Wendy Bailey, *Troy University*
Mohammad Bajwa, *Northampton Community College*
Robert Berger, *Flagler College*
Gale Blalock, *University of Evansville*
Martin Bookbinder, *Passaic County College*
Jonathan Bricker, *Asheville Buncombe Technical Community College*
Lindsay Calkins, *John Carroll University*
Gary E. Clayton, *Northern Kentucky University*
Jane Cline, *Forsyth Technical Community College*
Ana Carolina Corrales, *Miami Dade College North*
Morassa Danai, *California State University, Fullerton*
James Davis, *Santa Rosa Junior College*
Tanya Downing, *Cuesta College*
James Fallon, *Gwynedd Mercy College*
Jeff Foran, *Miami-Dade College Wolfson*
David Foster, *Grayson County College*
Arthur Friedberg, *Mohawk Valley Community College*
Mark Friedman, *Middlesex Community College*
Anthony A. Gabb, *St. John's University*
Leticia Garcia, *Elgin Community College*
Anthony J. Greco, *University of Louisiana, Lafayette*
Paul L. Hettler, *California University of Pennsylvania*
John G. Kamiru, *Norfolk State University*
Reza Karim, *Des, Moines Area Community College*
Frances F. Lea, *Germanna Community College*
Sarah Leahy, *Brookdale Community College*
Judy Lee, *Leeward Community College*

Phillip K. Letting, *Harrisburg Area Community College*

Melissa Lind, *University of Texas Arlington*

Glenn Lowell, *Utah Valley State College Orem*

Zagros Madjd-Sadjadi, *Winston-Salem State University*

Susan McElroy, *University of Texas at Dallas*

Meghan Millea, *Mississippi State University*

Ilir Miteza, *University of Michigan, Dearborn*

Darrell Neron, *Peirce College*

Robert Newman, *University of Texas at San Antonio*

Ifeakandu Okoye, *Florida A&M University*

Mary Ellen McGowan Overbay, *Seton Hall University*

Steve Peng, *Ohio University–Zanesville*

Marilyn Pugh, *University of Maryland University College*

Manuel C. Rios, *Laredo Community College*

Henry Ryder, *Gloucester County College*

David Schaffer, *University of Wisconsin, Eau Claire*

Terri A. Sexton, *California State University, Sacramento*

David Shorow, *Richland College*

Carl Simkonis, *Northern Kentucky University*

Macki Sissoko, *Norfolk State University*

Noel Smith, *Palm Beach Community College–South*

Richard Snyder, *Florida State University*

Mike Toma, *Armstrong Atlantic State University*

Michael Twomey, *University of Michigan, Dearborn*

Lawrence Waldman, *Central New Mexico Community College*

Thomas Wier, *Northeastern State University*

Mahmut Yasar, *University of Texas at Arlington*

Edward Zajicek, *Winston-Salem State University*

Inske Zandvliet, *Brookhaven College*

Brief Contents

Contents

PART ONE

Introduction to Economics and
the Economy

This book and its ancillaries contain several features designed to help you learn economics:

- *Web buttons (indicators)* A glance through the book reveals many pages with rectangular icons in the margins. These "buttons" alert you to helpful learning aids available with the book. The blue green button denotes "Interactive Graphs" found at the text's Web site, **www.mcconnell18e.com**. Brief exercises have you interact with the graphs, for example, by clicking on a specific curve and dragging it to a new location. These exercises will enhance your understanding of the underlying concepts. The blue button symbolizes "Worked Problems." Numeric problems are presented and then solved, side-by-side, step-by-step. Seeing how the problems are worked will help you solve similar problems on quizzes and exams. The green button stands for "Origin of the Idea." Each of these pieces traces a particular idea to the person or persons who first developed it.

INTERACTIVE GRAPHS
G 3.1
Supply and demand

WORKED PROBLEMS
W 2.1
Least-cost production

ORIGIN OF THE IDEA
O 1.4
Ceteris paribus

After reading a chapter, thumb back through it to note the Web buttons and their associated numbers. On the home page of our Internet site select Student Edition and use the pull-down list under "Choose one" to find the Web button content for each chapter.

- *Other Internet aids* Our Internet site contains many other aids. In the Student Edition you will find self-testing multiple-choice quizzes, PowerPoint presentations, and much more. For those of you with a very strong mathematics background, be sure to note the "See the Math" section on the Web site. There you will find nearly 50 notes that develop the algebra and, in a few cases, the calculus that underlie the economic concepts.

- *Appendix on graphs* Be assured, however, that you will need only basic math skills to do well in the principles course. In particular, you will need to be comfortable with basic graphical analysis and a few quantitative concepts. The appendix at the end of Chapter 1 reviews graphs and slopes of curves. You may want to read it before starting Chapter 1.

- *Reviews* Each chapter contains two to four Quick Reviews and an end-of-chapter summary. These reviews will help you focus on essential ideas and study for exams.

- *Key terms and Key Graphs* Key terms are set in boldface type within the chapters, listed at the end of each chapter, and again defined in the glossary at the end of the book. Graphs with special relevance are labeled Key Graphs, and each includes a multiple-choice Quick Quiz. Your instructor may or may not emphasize all of these figures, but you should pay special attention to those that are discussed in class; you can be certain there will be exam questions on them.

- *Consider This and Last Word boxes* Many chapters include a Consider This box. These brief pieces provide commonplace analogies, examples, and stories that help you understand and remember central economic ideas. Each chapter concludes with a Last Word box. Some of them are revealing applications of economic ideas; others are short case studies. While it is tempting to ignore in-text boxes, don't. Most are fun to read, and all will improve your grasp of economics.

- *Questions* A comprehensive list of study questions is located at the end of each chapter. Each question is keyed to a particular learning objective (LO) in the list of LOs at the beginning of the chapter. Several of the questions are designated Key Questions and therefore are particularly important. At the Internet site is a multiple-choice quiz for each chapter.

- *Study Guide* We enthusiastically recommend the *Study Guide* accompanying this text. This "portable tutor" contains not only a broad sampling of various kinds of questions but a host of useful learning aids. Software-driven tutorials (*Connect for Economics*, for example) are also available with the text.

Our two main goals are to help you understand and apply economics and help you improve your analytical skills. An understanding of economics will enable you to comprehend a whole range of economic, social, and political problems that otherwise would seem puzzling and perplexing. Also, your study will enhance reasoning skills that are highly prized in the workplace.

Good luck with your study. We think it will be well worth your time and effort.

IN THIS CHAPTER YOU WILL LEARN:

1 The definition of economics and the features of the economic perspective.

2 The role of economic theory in economics.

3 The distinction between microeconomics and macroeconomics.

4 The categories of scarce resources and the nature of the economizing problem.

5 About production possibilities analysis, increasing opportunity costs, and economic growth.

6 (Appendix) About graphs, curves, and slopes as they relate to economics.

1

Limits, Alternatives, and Choices

(An appendix on understanding graphs follows this chapter. If you need a quick review of this mathematical tool, you might benefit by reading the appendix first.) People's wants are numerous and varied. Biologically, people need only air, water, food, clothing, and shelter. But in modern society people also desire goods and services that provide a more comfortable or affluent standard of living. We want bottled water, soft drinks, and fruit juices, not just water from the creek. We want salads, burgers, and pizzas, not just berries and nuts. We want jeans, suits, and coats, not just woven reeds. We want apartments, condominiums, or houses, not just mud huts. And, as the saying goes, "that is not the half of it." We also want flat-panel TVs, Internet service, education, homeland security, cell phones, health care, and much more.

Fortunately, society possesses productive resources, such as labor and managerial talent, tools and machinery, and land and mineral deposits. These resources, employed in the economic system (or simply the economy), help us produce goods and services that satisfy many of our economic wants.

But the blunt reality is that our economic wants far exceed the productive capacity of our scarce (limited) resources. We are forced to make choices. This unyielding truth underlies the definition of **economics,** which is the social science concerned with how individuals, institutions, and society make optimal (best) choices under conditions of scarcity.

The Economic Perspective

Economists view things from a unique perspective. This **economic perspective,** or economic way of thinking, has several critical and closely interrelated features.

Scarcity and Choice

From our definition of economics, we can easily see why economists view the world through the lens of scarcity. Scarce economic resources mean limited goods and services. Scarcity restricts options and demands choices.

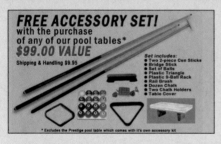
Free for All?

Free products are seemingly everywhere. Sellers offer free software, free cell phones, and free checking accounts. Dentists give out free toothbrushes. At state visitor centers, there are free brochures and maps.

Does the presence of so many free products contradict the economist's assertion "There is no free lunch"? No! Resources are used to produce each of these products, and because those resources have alternative uses, society gives up something else to get the "free" good. Where resources are used to produce goods or services, there is no free lunch.

So why are these goods offered for free? In a word: marketing! Firms sometimes offer free products to entice people to try them, hoping they will then purchase those goods later. The free software may eventually entice you to buy the producer's upgraded software. In other instances, the free brochures contain advertising for shops and restaurants, and that free e-mail program is filled with ads. In still other cases, the product is free only in conjunction with a larger purchase. To get the free bottle of soda, you must buy the large pizza. To get the free cell phone, you need to sign up for a year's worth of cell phone service.

So "free" products may or may not be truly free to individuals. They are never free to society.

Because we "can't have it all," we must decide what we will have and what we must forgo.

At the core of economics is the idea that "there is no free lunch." You may be treated to lunch, making it "free" from your perspective, but someone bears a cost. Because all resources are either privately or collectively owned by members of society, ultimately society bears the cost. Scarce inputs of land, equipment, farm labor, the labor of cooks and waiters, and managerial talent are required. Because society could have used these resources to produce something else, it sacrifices those other goods and services in making the lunch available. Economists call such sacrifices **opportunity costs:** To obtain more of one thing, society forgoes the opportunity of getting the next best thing. That sacrifice is the opportunity cost of the choice.

Purposeful Behavior

Economics assumes that human behavior reflects "rational self-interest." Individuals look for and pursue opportunities to increase their **utility**—the pleasure, happiness, or satisfaction obtained from consuming a good or service. They allocate their time, energy, and money to maximize their satisfaction. Because they weigh costs and benefits, their economic decisions are "purposeful" or "rational," not "random" or "chaotic."

Consumers are purposeful in deciding what goods and services to buy. Business firms are purposeful in deciding what products to produce and how to produce them. Government entities are purposeful in deciding what public services to provide and how to finance them.

"Purposeful behavior" does not assume that people and institutions are immune from faulty logic and therefore are perfect decision makers. They sometimes make mistakes. Nor does it mean that people's decisions are unaffected by emotion or the decisions of those around them. "Purposeful behavior" simply means that people make decisions with some desired outcome in mind.

Rational self-interest is not the same as selfishness. In the economy, increasing one's own wage, rent, interest, or profit normally requires identifying and satisfying *somebody else's* wants! Also, people make personal sacrifices to others. They contribute time and money to charities because they derive pleasure from doing so. Parents help pay for their children's education for the same reason. These self-interested, but unselfish, acts help maximize the givers'

Fast-Food Lines

The economic perspective is useful in analyzing all sorts of behaviors. Consider an everyday example: the behavior of fast-food customers. When customers enter the restaurant, they go to the shortest line, believing that line will minimize their time cost of obtaining food. They are acting purposefully; time is limited, and people prefer using it in some way other than standing in line.

If one fast-food line is temporarily shorter than other lines, some people will move to that line. These movers apparently view the time saving from the shorter line (marginal benefit) as exceeding the cost of moving from their present line (marginal cost). The line switching tends to equalize line lengths. No further movement of customers between lines occurs once all lines are about equal.

Fast-food customers face another cost-benefit decision when a clerk opens a new station at the counter. Should they move to the new station or stay put? Those who shift to the new line decide that the time saving from the move exceeds the extra cost of physically moving. In so deciding, customers must also consider just how quickly they can get to the new station compared with others who may be contemplating the same move. (Those who hesitate in this situation are lost!)

Customers at the fast-food establishment do not have perfect information when they select lines. Thus, not all decisions turn out as expected. For example, you might enter a short line and find someone in front of you is ordering hamburgers and fries for 40 people in the Greyhound bus parked out back (and the employee is a trainee)! Nevertheless, at the time you made your decision, you thought it was optimal.

Finally, customers must decide what food to order when they arrive at the counter. In making their choices, they again compare marginal costs and marginal benefits in attempting to obtain the greatest personal satisfaction for their expenditure.

Economists believe that what is true for the behavior of customers at fast-food restaurants is true for economic behavior in general. Faced with an array of choices, consumers, workers, and businesses rationally compare marginal costs and marginal benefits in making decisions.

satisfaction as much as any personal purchase of goods or services. Self-interested behavior is simply behavior designed to increase personal satisfaction, however it may be derived.

Marginal Analysis: Benefits and Costs

The economic perspective focuses largely on **marginal analysis**—comparisons of marginal benefits and marginal costs, usually for decision making. To economists, "marginal" means "extra," "additional," or "a change in." Most choices or decisions involve changes in the status quo, meaning the existing state of affairs.

Should you attend school for another year? Should you study an extra hour for an exam? Should you supersize your fries? Similarly, should a business expand or reduce its output? Should government increase or decrease its funding for a missile defense system?

Each option involves marginal benefits and, because of scarce resources, marginal costs. In making choices rationally, the decision maker must compare those two amounts. Example: You and your fiancée are shopping for an engagement ring. Should you buy a $\frac{1}{2}$-carat diamond, a $\frac{5}{8}$-carat diamond, a $\frac{3}{4}$ carat diamond, a 1-carat diamond, or something even larger? The marginal cost of a larger-size diamond is the added expense beyond the cost of the smaller-size diamond. The marginal benefit is the perceived lifetime pleasure (utility) from the larger-size stone. If the marginal benefit of

ORIGIN OF THE IDEA

O 1.3

Marginal analysis

the larger diamond exceeds its marginal cost (and you can afford it), buy the larger stone. But if the marginal cost is more than the marginal benefit, buy the smaller diamond instead, even if you can afford the larger stone!

In a world of scarcity, the decision to obtain the marginal benefit associated with some specific option always includes the marginal cost of forgoing something else. The money spent on the larger-size diamond means forgoing some other product. An opportunity cost—the value of the next best thing forgone—is always present whenever a choice is made. **(Key Question 3)**

Theories, Principles, and Models

Like the physical and life sciences, as well as other social sciences, economics relies on the **scientific method**. That procedure consists of several elements:

- Observing real-world behavior and outcomes.
- Based on those observations, formulating a possible explanation of cause and effect (hypothesis).

- Testing this explanation by comparing the outcomes of specific events to the outcome predicted by the hypothesis.
- Accepting, rejecting, and modifying the hypothesis, based on these comparisons.
- Continuing to test the hypothesis against the facts. As favorable results accumulate, the hypothesis evolves into a theory. A very well-tested and widely accepted theory is referred to as an economic law or an **economic principle**—a statement about economic behavior or the economy that enables prediction of the probable effects of certain actions. Combinations of such laws or principles are incorporated into models, which are simplified representations of how something works, such as a market or segment of the economy.

Economists develop theories of the behavior of individuals (consumers, workers) and institutions (businesses, governments) engaged in the production, exchange, and consumption of goods and services. Theories, principles, and models are "purposeful simplifications." The full scope of economic reality itself is too complex and bewildering to be understood as a whole. In developing theories, principles, and models economists remove the clutter and simplify.

Economic principles and models are highly useful in analyzing economic behavior and understanding how the economy operates. They are the tools for ascertaining cause and effect (or action and outcome) within the economic system. Good theories do a good job of explaining and predicting. They are supported by facts concerning how individuals and institutions actually behave in producing, exchanging, and consuming goods and services.

There are some other things you should know about economic principles.

- *Generalizations* Economic principles are generalizations relating to economic behavior or to the economy itself. Economic principles are expressed as the tendencies of typical or average consumers, workers, or business firms. For example, economists say that consumers buy more of a particular product when its price falls. Economists recognize that some consumers may increase their purchases by a large amount, others by a small amount, and a few not at all. This "price-quantity" principle, however, holds for the typical consumer and for consumers as a group.
- *Other-Things-Equal Assumption* In constructing their theories, economists use the *ceteris paribus* or

other-things-equal assumption—the assumption that factors other than those being considered do not change. They assume that all variables except those under immediate consideration are held constant for a particular analysis. For example, consider the relationship between the price of Pepsi and the amount of it purchased. Assume that of all the factors that might influence the amount of Pepsi purchased (for example, the price of Pepsi, the price of Coca-Cola, and consumer incomes and preferences), only the price of Pepsi varies. This is helpful because the economist can then focus on the relationship between the price of Pepsi and purchases of Pepsi in isolation without being confused by changes in other variables.

ORIGIN OF THE IDEA
O 1.4
Ceteris paribus

- *Graphical Expression* Many economic models are expressed graphically. Be sure to read the special appendix at the end of this chapter as a review of graphs.

Microeconomics and Macroeconomics

Economists develop economic principles and models at two levels.

Microeconomics

Microeconomics is the part of economics concerned with individual units such as a person, a household, a firm, or an industry. At this level of analysis, the economist observes the details of an economic unit, or very small segment of the economy, under a figurative microscope. In microeconomics we look at decision making by individual customers, workers, households, and business firms. We measure the price of a specific product, the number of workers employed by a single firm, the revenue or income of a particular firm or household, or the expenditures of a specific firm, government entity, or family. In microeconomics, we examine the sand, rock, and shells, not the beach.

Macroeconomics

Macroeconomics examines either the economy as a whole or its basic subdivisions or aggregates, such as the government, household, and business sectors. An **aggregate** is a collection of specific economic units treated as if they were one unit. Therefore, we might lump together the millions of consumers in the U.S. economy and treat them as if they were one huge unit called "consumers."

In using aggregates, macroeconomics seeks to obtain an overview, or general outline, of the structure of the economy and the relationships of its major aggregates. Macroeconomics speaks of such economic measures as total output, total employment, total income, aggregate expenditures, and the general level of prices in analyzing various economic problems. No or very little attention is given to specific units making up the various aggregates.

Figuratively, macroeconomics looks at the beach, not the pieces of sand, the rocks, and the shells.

The micro–macro distinction does not mean that economics is so highly compartmentalized that every topic can be readily labeled as either micro or macro; many topics and subdivisions of economics are rooted in both. Example: While the problem of unemployment is usually treated as a macroeconomic topic (because unemployment relates to aggregate production), economists recognize that the decisions made by *individual* workers on how long to search for jobs and the way *specific* labor markets encourage or impede hiring are also critical in determining the unemployment rate. **(Key Question 5)**

Positive and Normative Economics

Both microeconomics and macroeconomics contain elements of positive economics and normative economics. **Positive economics** focuses on facts and cause-and-effect relationships. It includes description, theory development, and theory testing (theoretical economics). Positive economics avoids value judgments, tries to establish scientific statements about economic behavior, and deals with what the economy is actually like. Such scientific-based analysis is critical to good policy analysis.

Economic policy, on the other hand, involves **normative economics,** which incorporates value judgments about what the economy should be like or what particular policy actions should be recommended to achieve a desirable goal (policy economics). Normative economics looks at the desirability of certain aspects of the economy. It underlies expressions of support for particular economic policies.

Positive economics concerns *what is*, whereas normative economics embodies subjective feelings about *what ought to be*. Examples: Positive statement: "The unemployment rate in France is higher than that in the United States." Normative statement: "France ought to undertake policies to make its labor market more flexible to reduce unemployment rates." Whenever words such as "ought"

or "should" appear in a sentence, you are very likely encountering a normative statement.

Most of the disagreement among economists involves normative, value-based policy questions. Of course, economists sometime disagree about which theories or models best represent the economy and its parts, but they agree on a full range of economic principles. Most economic controversy thus reflects differing opinions or value judgments about what society should be like.

QUICK REVIEW 1.1

- Economics examines how individuals, institutions, and society make choices under conditions of scarcity.
- The economic perspective stresses (a) resource scarcity and the necessity of making choices, (b) the assumption of purposeful (or rational) behavior, and (c) comparisons of marginal benefit and marginal cost.
- In choosing among alternatives, people incur opportunity costs—the value of their next-best option.
- Economists use the scientific method to establish economic theories—cause-effect generalizations about the economic behavior of individuals and institutions.
- Microeconomics focuses on specific decision-making units of the economy, macroeconomics examines the economy as a whole.
- Positive economics deals with factual statements ("what is"); normative economics involves value judgments ("what ought to be").

Individuals' Economizing Problem

A close examination of the **economizing problem**—the need to make choices because economic wants exceed economic means—will enhance your understanding of economic models and the difference between microeconomic and macroeconomic analysis. Let's first build a microeconomic model of the economizing problem faced by an individual.

Limited Income

We all have a finite amount of income, even the wealthiest among us. Even Donald Trump must decide how to spend his money! And the majority of us have much more limited means. Our income comes to us in the form of wages, interest, rent, and profit, although we may also receive money from government programs or family members. As Global Perspective 1.1 shows, the average income of Americans in 2006 was $44,970. In the poorest nations, it was less than $500.

GLOBAL PERSPECTIVE 1.1

Average Income, Selected Nations

Average income (total income/population) and therefore typical individual budget constraints vary greatly among nations.

Country	Per Capita Income, 2006 (U.S. dollars, based on exchange rates)
Switzerland	$57,230
United States	44,970
Japan	38,410
France	36,550
South Korea	17,690
Mexico	7,870
Brazil	4,730
China	2,010
Pakistan	770
Nigeria	640
Rwanda	250
Liberia	140

Source: World Bank, **www.worldbank.org.**

Unlimited Wants

For better or worse, most people have virtually unlimited wants. We desire various goods and services that provide utility. Our wants extend over a wide range of products, from *necessities* (for example, food, shelter, and clothing) to *luxuries* (for example, perfumes, yachts, and sports cars). Some wants such as basic food, clothing, and shelter have biological roots. Other wants, for example, specific kinds of food, clothing, and shelter, arise from the conventions and customs of society.

Over time, as new and improved products are introduced, economic wants tend to change and multiply. Only recently have people wanted iPods, Internet service, digital cameras, or camera phones because those products did not exist a few decades ago. Also, the satisfaction of certain wants may trigger others: the acquisition of a Ford Focus or a Honda Civic has been known to whet the appetite for a Lexus or a Mercedes.

Services, as well as goods, satisfy our wants. Car repair work, the removal of an inflamed appendix, legal and accounting advice, and haircuts all satisfy human wants.

Actually, we buy many goods, such as automobiles and washing machines, for the services they render. The differences between goods and services are often smaller than they appear to be.

For most people, the desires for goods and services cannot be fully satisfied. Bill Gates may have all that he wants for himself, but his massive charitable giving suggests that he keenly wants better health care for the world's poor. Our desires for a particular good or service can be satisfied; over a short period of time we can surely get enough toothpaste or pasta. And one appendectomy is plenty. But our broader desire for more goods and services and higher-quality goods and services seems to be another story.

Because we have only limited income (usually through our work) but seemingly insatiable wants, it is in our self-interest to economize: to pick and choose goods and services that maximize our satisfaction.

A Budget Line

We can clarify the economizing problem facing consumers by visualizing a **budget line** (or, more technically, a *budget constraint*). It is a schedule or curve that shows various combinations of two products a consumer can purchase with a specific money income. Although we assume two products, the analysis generalizes to the full range of products available to an individual consumer.

To understand the idea of a budget line, suppose that you received a Barnes & Noble (or Borders) gift card as a birthday present. The $120 card is soon to expire. You take the card to the store and confine your purchase decisions to two alternatives: DVDs and paperback books. DVDs are $20 each and paperback books are $10 each. Your purchase options are shown in the table in Figure 1.1.

At one extreme, you might spend all of your $120 "income" on 6 DVDs at $20 each and have nothing left to spend on books. Or, by giving up 2 DVDs and thereby gaining $40, you can have 4 DVDs at $20 each and 4 books at $10 each. And so on to the other extreme, at which you could buy 12 books at $10 each, spending your entire gift card on books with nothing left to spend on DVDs.

The graph in Figure 1.1 shows the budget line. Note that the graph is not restricted to whole units of DVDs and books as is the table. Every point on the graph represents a possible combination of DVDs and books, including fractional quantities. The slope of the graphed budget line measures the ratio of the price of books (P_b) to the price of DVDs (P_{dvd}); more precisely, the slope is $P_b/P_{dvd} = \$-10/\$+20 = -\frac{1}{2}$, or $-.5$. So you must forgo

FIGURE 1.1 A consumer's budget line. The budget line (or budget constraint) shows all the combinations of any two products that can be purchased, given the prices of the products and the consumer's money income.

The Budget Line: Whole-Unit Combinations of DVDs and Paperback Books Attainable with an Income of $120		
Units of DVDs (Price = $20)	Units of Books (Price = $10)	Total Expenditure
6	0	($120 = $120 + $0)
5	2	($120 = $100 + $20)
4	4	($120 = $80 + $40)
3	6	($120 = $60 + $60)
2	8	($120 = $40 + $80)
1	10	($120 = $20 + $100)
0	12	($120 = $0 + $120)

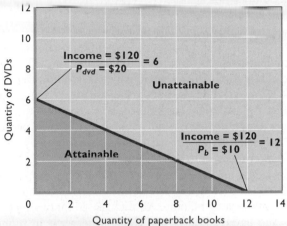

$$\frac{\text{Income} = \$120}{P_{dvd} = \$20} = 6$$

Unattainable

$$\frac{\text{Income} = \$120}{P_b = \$10} = 12$$

Attainable

Quantity of DVDs (vertical axis) — *Quantity of paperback books* (horizontal axis)

1 DVD (measured on the vertical axis) to buy 2 books (measured on the horizontal axis). This yields a slope of $-\frac{1}{2}$ or -.5.

The budget line illustrates several ideas.

Attainable and Unattainable Combinations

All the combinations of DVDs and books on or inside the budget line are *attainable* from the $120 of money income. You can afford to buy, for example, 3 DVDs at $20 each and 6 books at $10 each. You also can obviously afford to buy 2 DVDs and 5 books, if so desired, and not use up the value on the gift card. But to achieve maximum utility you will want to spend the full $120.

In contrast, all combinations beyond the budget line are *unattainable*. The $120 limit simply does not allow you to purchase, for example, 5 DVDs at $20 each and 5 books at $10 each. That $150 expenditure would clearly exceed the $120 limit. In Figure 1.1 the attainable combinations are on and within the budget line; the unattainable combinations are beyond the budget line.

Trade-Offs and Opportunity Costs

The budget line in Figure 1.1 illustrates the idea of trade-offs arising from limited income. To obtain more DVDs, you have to give up some books. For example, to obtain the first DVD, you trade off 2 books. So the opportunity cost of the first DVD is 2 books. To obtain the second DVD the opportunity cost is also 2 books. The straight-line budget constraint, with its constant slope, indicates constant opportunity cost. That is, the opportunity cost of 1 extra DVD remains the same (= 2 books) as more DVDs are

ORIGIN OF THE IDEA
O 1.5
Opportunity costs

CONSIDER THIS . . .

Did Gates, Winfrey, and Rodriguez Make Bad Choices?

Opportunity costs come into play in decisions well beyond simple buying decisions. Consider the different choices people make with respect to college. College graduates usually earn about 50 percent more during their lifetimes than persons with just high school diplomas. For most capable students, "Go to college, stay in college, and earn a degree" is very sound advice.

Yet Microsoft cofounder Bill Gates and talk show host Oprah Winfrey* both dropped out of college, and baseball star Alex Rodriguez ("A-Rod") never even bothered to start classes. What were they thinking? Unlike most students, Gates faced enormous opportunity costs for staying in college. He had a vision for his company, and his starting work young helped ensure Microsoft's success. Similarly, Winfrey landed a spot in local television news when she was a teenager, eventually producing and starring in the *Oprah Winfrey Show* when she was 32 years old. Getting a degree in her twenties might have interrupted the string of successes that made her famous talk show possible. And Rodriguez knew that professional athletes have short careers. Therefore, going to college directly after high school would have taken away four years of his peak earning potential.

So Gates, Winfrey, and Rodriguez understood opportunity costs and made their choices accordingly. The size of opportunity costs greatly matters in making individual decisions.

*Winfrey eventually went back to school and earned a degree from Tennessee State University when she was in her thirties.

purchased. And, in reverse, the opportunity cost of 1 extra book does not change (= $\frac{1}{2}$ DVD) as more books are bought.

Choice Limited income forces people to choose what to buy and what to forgo to fulfill wants. You will select the combination of DVDs and paperback books that you think is "best." That is, you will evaluate your marginal benefits and marginal costs (here, product price) to make choices that maximize your satisfaction. Other people, with the same $120 gift card, would undoubtedly make different choices.

Income Changes The location of the budget line varies with money income. An increase in money income shifts the budget line to the right; a decrease in money income shifts it to the left. To verify this, recalculate the table in Figure 1.1, assuming the card value (income) is (a) $240 and (b) $60, and plot the new budget lines in the graph. No wonder people like to have more income: That shifts their budget lines outward and enables them to buy more goods and services. But even with more income, people will still face spending trade-offs, choices, and opportunity costs. **(Key Question 7)**

> **WORKED PROBLEMS**
>
> **W 1.1**
> Budget lines

> **QUICK REVIEW 1.2**
>
> - Because wants exceed incomes, individuals face an economizing problem; they must decide what to buy and what to forgo.
> - A budget line (budget constraint) shows the various combinations of two goods that a consumer can purchase with a specific money income.
> - Straight-line budget constraints imply constant opportunity costs associated with obtaining more of either of the two goods.

Society's Economizing Problem

Society must also make choices under conditions of scarcity. It, too, faces an economizing problem. Should it devote more of its limited resources to the criminal justice system (police, courts, and prisons) or to education (teachers, books, and schools)? If it decides to devote more resources to both, what other goods and services does it forgo? Health care? Energy development?

Scarce Resources

Society has limited or scarce **economic resources,** meaning all natural, human, and manufactured resources that go into the production of goods and services. This includes the entire set of factory and farm buildings and all the equipment, tools, and machinery used to produce manufactured goods and agricultural products; all transportation and communication facilities; all types of labor; and land and mineral resources.

Resource Categories

Economists classify economic resources into four general categories.

Land Land means much more to the economist than it does to most people. To the economist **land** includes all natural resources ("gifts of nature") used in the production process, such as arable land, forests, mineral and oil deposits, and water resources.

Labor The resource **labor** consists of the physical and mental talents of individuals used in producing goods and services. The services of a logger, retail clerk, machinist, teacher, professional football player, and nuclear physicist all fall under the general heading "labor."

Capital For economists, **capital** (or capital goods) includes all manufactured aids used in producing consumer goods and services. Included are all factory, storage, transportation, and distribution facilities, as well as tools and machinery. Economists refer to the purchase of capital goods as **investment.**

Capital goods differ from consumer goods because consumer goods satisfy wants directly, whereas capital goods do so indirectly by aiding the production of consumer goods. Note that the term "capital" as used by economists refers not to money but to tools, machinery, and other productive equipment. Because money produces nothing, economists do not include it as an economic resource. Money (or money capital or financial capital) is simply a means for purchasing capital goods.

Entrepreneurial Ability Finally, there is the special human resource, distinct from labor, called **entrepreneurial ability.** The entrepreneur performs several functions:

- The entrepreneur takes the initiative in combining the resources of land, labor, and capital to produce a good or a service. Both a sparkplug and a catalyst, the entrepreneur is the driving force behind production and the agent who combines the other resources in what is hoped will be a successful business venture.

- The entrepreneur makes the strategic business decisions that set the course of an enterprise.
- The entrepreneur is an innovator. He or she commercializes new products, new production techniques, or even new forms of business organization.
- The entrepreneur is a risk bearer. The entrepreneur has no guarantee of profit. The reward for the entrepreneur's time, efforts, and abilities may be profits or losses. The entrepreneur risks not only his or her invested funds but those of associates and stockholders as well.

Because land, labor, capital, and entrepreneurial ability are combined to produce goods and services, they are called the **factors of production,** or simply "inputs."

Production Possibilities Model

Society uses its scarce resources to produce goods and services. The alternatives and choices it faces can best be understood through a macroeconomic model of production possibilities. To keep things simple, let's initially assume:

- *Full employment* The economy is employing all its available resources.
- *Fixed resources* The quantity and quality of the factors of production are fixed.
- *Fixed technology* The state of technology (the methods used to produce output) is constant.
- *Two goods* The economy is producing only two goods: pizzas and industrial robots. Pizzas symbolize **consumer goods,** products that satisfy our wants directly; industrial robots (for example, the kind used to weld automobile frames) symbolize **capital goods,** products that satisfy our wants indirectly by making possible more efficient production of consumer goods.

Production Possibilities Table

A production possibilities table lists the different combinations of two products that can be produced with a specific set of resources, assuming full employment. Table 1.1 presents a simple, hypothetical economy that is producing pizzas and industrial robots; the data are, of course, hypothetical. At alternative A, this economy would be devoting all its available resources to the production of industrial robots (capital goods); at alternative E, all resources would go to pizza production (consumer goods). Those alternatives are unrealistic extremes; an economy typically produces both capital goods and consumer goods, as in B, C, and D. As we move from alternative A to E, we increase the production of pizzas at the expense of the production of industrial robots.

Because consumer goods satisfy our wants directly, any movement toward E looks tempting. In producing more pizzas, society increases the current satisfaction of its wants. But there is a cost: More pizzas mean fewer industrial robots. This shift of resources to consumer goods catches up with society over time because the stock of capital goods does not expand at the current rate, with the result that some potential for greater future production is lost. By moving toward alternative E, society chooses "more now" at the expense of "much more later."

By moving toward A, society chooses to forgo current consumption, thereby freeing up resources that can be used to increase the production of capital goods. By building up its stock of capital this way, society will have greater future production and, therefore, greater future consumption. By moving toward A, society is choosing "more later" at the cost of "less now."

Generalization: At any point in time, a fully employed economy must sacrifice some of one good to obtain more of another good. Scarce resources prohibit such an economy from having more of both goods. Society must choose among alternatives. There is no such thing as a free pizza, or a free industrial robot. Having more of one thing means having less of something else.

Production Possibilities Curve

The data presented in a production possibilities table are shown graphically as a **production possibilities curve.** Such a curve displays the different combinations of goods and services that society can produce in a fully employed economy, assuming a fixed availability of supplies of resources and constant technology. We arbitrarily represent the economy's output of capital goods (here, industrial robots) on the vertical axis and the output of consumer goods (here, pizzas) on the horizontal axis, as shown in **Figure 1.2 (Key Graph).**

Each point on the production possibilities curve represents some maximum output of the two products.

INTERACTIVE GRAPHS

G 1.1

Production possibilities curve

TABLE 1.1 **Production Possibilities of Pizzas and Industrial Robots**

Type of Product	Production Alternatives				
	A	B	C	D	E
Pizzas (in hundred thousands)	0	1	2	3	4
Robots (in thousands)	10	9	7	4	0

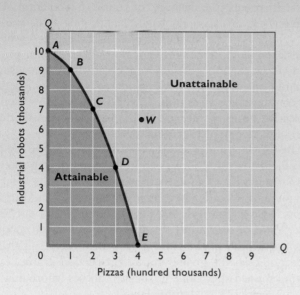

FIGURE 1.2 **The production possibilities curve.** Each point on the production possibilities curve represents some maximum combination of two products that can be produced if resources are fully employed. When an economy is operating on the curve, more industrial robots means fewer pizzas, and vice versa. Limited resources and a fixed technology make any combination of industrial robots and pizzas lying outside the curve (such as at *W*) unattainable. Points inside the curve are attainable, but they indicate that full employment is not being realized.

QUICK QUIZ FOR FIGURE 1.2

1. Production possibilities curve *ABCDE* is bowed out from the origin because:
  a. the marginal benefit of pizzas declines as more pizzas are consumed.
  b. the curve gets steeper as we move from *E* to *A*.
  c. it reflects the law of increasing opportunity costs.
  d. resources are scarce.

2. The marginal opportunity cost of the second unit of pizza is:
  a. 2 units of robots.
  b. 3 units of robots.
  c. 7 units of robots.
  d. 9 units of robots.

3. The total opportunity cost of 7 units of robots is:
  a. 1 unit of pizza.
  b. 2 units of pizza.
  c. 3 units of pizza.
  d. 4 units of pizza.

4. All points on this production possibilities curve necessarily represent:
  a. society's optimal choice.
  b. less than full use of resources.
  c. unattainable levels of output.
  d. full employment.

Answers: 1. c; 2. a; 3. b; 4. d

The curve is a "constraint" because it shows the limit of attainable outputs. Points on the curve are attainable as long as the economy uses all its available resources. Points lying inside the curve are also attainable, but they reflect less total output and therefore are not as desirable as points on the curve. Points inside the curve imply that the economy could have more of both industrial robots and pizzas if it achieved full employment of its resources. Points lying beyond the production possibilities curve, like *W*, would represent a greater output than the output at any point on the curve. Such points, however, are unattainable with the current availability of resources and technology.

Law of Increasing Opportunity Costs

Figure 1.2 clearly shows that more pizzas means fewer industrial robots. The number of units of industrial robots that must be given up to obtain another unit of pizzas, of course, is the opportunity cost of that unit of pizzas.

In moving from alternative A to alternative B in Table 1.1, the cost of 1 additional unit of pizzas is 1 fewer unit of industrial robots. But when additional units are considered—B to C, C to D, and D to E—an important economic principle is revealed: For society, the opportunity cost of each additional unit of pizzas is greater than the opportunity cost of the preceding one. When we move from A to B, just

1 unit of industrial robots is sacrificed for 1 more unit of pizzas; but in going from B to C we sacrifice 2 additional units of industrial robots for 1 more unit of pizzas; then 3 more of industrial robots for 1 more of pizzas; and finally 4 for 1. Conversely, confirm that as we move from E to A, the cost of an additional unit of industrial robots (on average) is $\frac{1}{4}, \frac{1}{3}, \frac{1}{2}$, and 1 unit of pizzas, respectively, for the four successive moves.

Our example illustrates the **law of increasing opportunity costs.** As the production of a particular good increases, the opportunity cost of producing an additional unit rises.

Shape of the Curve
The law of increasing opportunity costs is reflected in the shape of the production possibilities curve: The curve is bowed out from the origin of the graph. Figure 1.2 shows that when the economy moves from *A* to *E*, it must give up successively larger amounts of industrial robots (1, 2, 3, and 4) to acquire equal increments of pizzas (1, 1, 1, and 1). This is shown in the slope of the production possibilities curve, which becomes steeper as we move from *A* to *E*.

Economic Rationale
The economic rationale for the law of increasing opportunity costs is that economic resources are not completely adaptable to alternative uses. Many resources are better at producing one type of good than at producing others. Some land is highly suited to growing the ingredients necessary for pizza production, but as pizza production expands society has to start using land that is less bountiful for farming. Other land is rich in mineral deposits and therefore well-suited to producing the materials needed to make industrial robots. As society steps up the production of robots, it must use land that is less and less adaptable to making their components.

If we start at *A* and move to *B* in Figure 1.2, we can shift resources whose productivity is relatively high in pizza production and low in industrial robots. But as we move from *B* to *C*, *C* to *D*, and so on, resources highly productive

> **WORKED PROBLEMS**
>
> **W 1.2**
> Production possibilities

of pizzas become increasingly scarce. To get more pizzas, resources whose productivity in industrial robots is relatively great will be needed. Increasingly more of such resources, and hence greater sacrifices of industrial robots, will be needed to achieve each 1-unit increase in pizzas. This lack of perfect flexibility, or interchangeability, on the part of resources is the cause of increasing opportunity costs for society. **(Key Question 10)**

Optimal Allocation
Of all the attainable combinations of pizzas and industrial robots on the curve in Figure 1.2, which is optimal (best)? That is, what specific quantities of resources should be allocated to pizzas and what specific quantities should be allocated to industrial robots in order to maximize satisfaction?

Recall that economic decisions center on comparisons of marginal benefit (MB) and marginal cost (MC). Any economic activity should be expanded as long as marginal benefit exceeds marginal cost and should be reduced if marginal cost exceeds marginal benefit. The optimal amount of the activity occurs where MB = MC. Society needs to make a similar assessment about its production decision.

Consider pizzas. We already know from the law of increasing opportunity costs that the marginal costs of additional units of pizza will rise as more units are produced. At the same time, we need to recognize that the extra or marginal benefits that come from producing and consuming pizza decline with each successive unit of pizza. Consequently, each successive unit of pizza brings with it both increasing marginal costs and decreasing marginal benefits.

The optimal quantity of pizza production is indicated by point *e* at the intersection of the MB and MC curves: 200,000 units in Figure 1.3. Why is this amount the optimal quantity? If only 100,000 units of pizzas were produced, the marginal benefit of an extra unit of pizza (point *a*) would

FIGURE 1.3 Optimal output: MB = MC. Achieving the optimal output requires the expansion of a good's output until its marginal benefit (MB) and marginal cost (MC) are equal. No resources beyond that point should be allocated to the product. Here, optimal output occurs at point *e*, where 200,000 units of pizzas are produced.

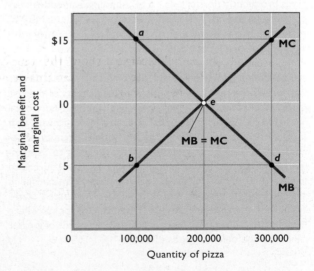

exceed its marginal cost (point *b*). In money terms, MB is $15, while MC is only $5. When society gains something worth $15 at a marginal cost of only $5, it is better off. In Figure 1.3, net gains can continue to be realized until pizza-product production has been increased to 200,000.

CONSIDER THIS . . .

The Economics of War

Production possibilities analysis is helpful in assessing the costs and benefits of waging the broad war on terrorism, including the wars in Afghanistan and Iraq. At the end of 2007, the estimated cost of those efforts exceeded $400 billion.

If we categorize all U.S. production as either "defense goods" or "civilian goods," we can measure them on the axes of a production possibilities diagram such as that shown in Figure 1.2. The opportunity cost of using more resources for defense goods is the civilian goods sacrificed. In a fully employed economy, more defense goods are achieved at the opportunity cost of fewer civilian goods—health care, education, pollution control, personal computers, houses, and so on. The cost of war and defense is the other goods forgone. The benefits of these activities are numerous and diverse but clearly include the gains from protecting against future loss of American lives, assets, income, and well-being.

Society must assess the marginal benefit (MB) and marginal cost (MC) of additional defense goods to determine their optimal amounts—where to locate on the defense goods–civilian goods production possibilities curve. Although estimating marginal benefits and marginal costs is an imprecise art, the MB-MC framework is a useful way of approaching choices. An optimal allocation of resources requires that society expand production of defense goods until MB = MC.

The events of September 11, 2001, and the future threats they foreshadowed increased the marginal benefits of defense goods, as perceived by Americans. If we label the horizontal axis in Figure 1.3 "defense goods" and draw in a rightward shift of the MB curve, you will see that the optimal quantity of defense goods rises. In view of the concerns relating to September 11, the United States allocated more of its resources to defense. But the MB-MC analysis also reminds us we can spend too much on defense, as well as too little. The United States should not expand defense goods beyond the point where MB = MC. If it does, it will be sacrificing civilian goods of greater value than the defense goods obtained.

In contrast, the production of 300,000 units of pizzas is excessive. There the MC of an added unit is $15 (point *c*) and its MB is only $5 (point *d*). This means that 1 unit of pizza is worth only $5 to society but costs it $15 to obtain. This is a losing proposition for society!

So resources are being efficiently allocated to any product when the marginal benefit and marginal cost of its output are equal (MB = MC). Suppose that by applying the same analysis to industrial robots, we find that the optimal (MB = MC) output of robots is 7000. This would mean that alternative *C* (200,000 units of pizzas and 7000 units of industrial robots) on the production possibilities curve in Figure 1.2 would be optimal for this economy. **(Key Question 11)**

QUICK REVIEW 1.3

- Economists categorize economic resources as land, labor, capital, and entrepreneurial ability.
- The production possibilities curve illustrates several ideas: (a) scarcity of resources is implied by the area of unattainable combinations of output lying outside the production possibilities curve; (b) choice among outputs is reflected in the variety of attainable combinations of goods lying along the curve; (c) opportunity cost is illustrated by the downward slope of the curve; (d) the law of increasing opportunity costs is implied by the bowed-outward shape of the curve.
- A comparison of marginal benefits and marginal costs is needed to determine the best or optimal output mix on a production possibilities curve.

Unemployment, Growth, and the Future

In the depths of the Great Depression of the 1930s, one-quarter of U.S. workers were unemployed and one-third of U.S. production capacity was idle. The United States has suffered a number of considerably milder downturns since then, one occurring in 2001. In that year total production fell one-half a percentage point and unemployment increased by about 2 million workers.

Almost all nations have experienced widespread unemployment and unused production capacity from business downturns at one time or another. Since 1995, for example, several nations—including Argentina, Japan, Mexico, Germany, and South Korea—have had economic downturns and unemployment.

How do these realities relate to the production possibilities model? Our analysis and conclusions change if we

FIGURE 1.4 Unemployment and the production possibilities curve. Any point inside the production possibilities curve, such as U, represents unemployment or a failure to achieve full employment. The arrows indicate that by realizing full employment, the economy could operate on the curve. This means it could produce more of one or both products than it is producing at point U.

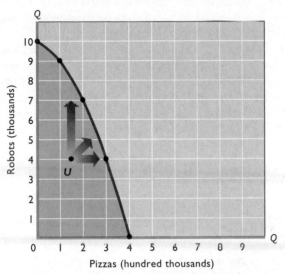

relax the assumption that all available resources are fully employed. The five alternatives in Table 1.1 represent maximum outputs; they illustrate the combinations of pizzas and industrial robots that can be produced when the economy is operating at full employment. With unemployment, this economy would produce less than each alternative shown in the table.

Graphically, we represent situations of unemployment by points inside the original production possibilities curve (reproduced here in Figure 1.4). Point U is one such point. Here the economy is falling short of the various maximum combinations of pizzas and industrial robots represented by the points on the production possibilities curve. The arrows in Figure 1.4 indicate three possible paths back to full employment. A move toward full employment would yield a greater output of one or both products.

A Growing Economy

When we drop the assumptions that the quantity and quality of resources and technology are fixed, the production possibilities curve shifts positions and the potential maximum output of the economy changes.

Increases in Resource Supplies
Although resource supplies are fixed at any specific moment, they change over time. For example, a nation's growing population brings about increases in the supplies of labor and entrepreneurial ability. Also, labor quality usually

improves over time via more education and training. Historically, the economy's stock of capital has increased at a significant, though unsteady, rate. And although some of our energy and mineral resources are being depleted, new sources are also being discovered. The development of irrigation programs, for example, adds to the supply of arable land.

The net result of these increased supplies of the factors of production is the ability to produce more of both consumer goods and capital goods. Thus, 20 years from now, the production possibilities may supersede those shown in Table 1.1. The new production possibilities might look like those in the table in Figure 1.5. The greater abundance of resources will result in a greater potential output of one or both products at each alternative. The economy will have achieved economic growth in the form of expanded potential output. Thus, when an increase in the quantity or quality of resources occurs, the production possibilities curve shifts outward and to the right, as illustrated by the move from the inner curve to curve $A'B'C'D'E'$ in Figure 1.5. This sort of

FIGURE 1.5 Economic growth and the production possibilities curve. The increase in supplies of resources, improvements in resource quality, and technological advances that occur in a dynamic economy move the production possibilities curve outward and to the right, allowing the economy to have larger quantities of both types of goods.

Type of Product	Production Alternatives				
	A'	B'	C'	D'	E'
Pizzas (in hundred thousands)	0	2	4	6	8
Robots (in thousands)	14	12	9	5	0

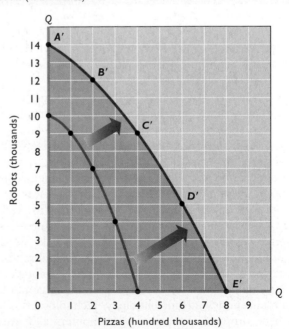

Because They Affect Us So Personally, We Often Have Difficulty Thinking Accurately and Objectively About Economic Issues.

Here are some common pitfalls to avoid in successfully applying the economic perspective.

Biases Most people bring a bundle of biases and preconceptions to the field of economics. For example, some might think that corporate profits are excessive or that lending money is always superior to borrowing money. Others might believe that government is necessarily less efficient than businesses or that more government regulation is always better than less. Biases cloud thinking and interfere with objective analysis. All of us must be willing to shed biases and preconceptions that are not supported by facts.

Loaded Terminology The economic terminology used in newspapers and broadcast media is sometimes emotionally biased, or loaded. The writer or spokesperson may have a cause to promote or an ax to grind and may slant comments accordingly. High profits may be labeled "obscene," low wages may be called "exploitive," or self-interested behavior may be "greed." Government workers may be referred to as "mindless bureaucrats" and those favoring stronger government regulations may be called "socialists." To objectively analyze economic issues, you must be prepared to reject or discount such terminology.

Fallacy of Composition Another pitfall in economic thinking is the assumption that what is true for one individual or part of a whole is necessarily true for a group of individuals or the whole. This is a logical fallacy called the *fallacy of composition;* the assumption is not correct. A statement that is valid for an individual or part is not necessarily valid for the larger group or whole. You may see the action better if you leap to your feet to see an outstanding play at a football game. But if all the

shift represents growth of economic capacity, which, when used, means **economic growth:** a larger total output.

Advances in Technology
An advancing technology brings both new and better goods and improved ways of producing them. For now, let's think of technological advance as being only improvements in the methods of production, for example, the introduction of computerized systems to manage inventories and schedule production. These advances alter our previous discussion of the economizing problem by allowing society to produce more goods with available resources. As with increases in resource supplies, technological advances make possible the production of more industrial robots and more pizzas.

A real-world example of improved technology is the recent surge of new technologies relating to computers, communications, and biotechnology. Technological advances have dropped the prices of computers and greatly increased their speed. Improved software has greatly increased the everyday usefulness of computers. Cellular phones and the Internet have increased communications capacity, enhancing production and improving the efficiency of markets. Advances in biotechnology have resulted in important agricultural and medical discoveries. These and other new and improved technologies have contributed to U.S. economic growth (outward shifts of the nation's production possibilities curve.)

Conclusion: Economic growth is the result of (1) increases in supplies of resources, (2) improvements in resource quality, and (3) technological advances. The consequence of growth is that a full-employment economy can enjoy a greater output of both consumption goods and capital goods. Whereas static, no-growth economies must sacrifice some of one good to obtain more of another, dynamic, growing economies can have larger quantities of both goods. **(Key Question 13)**

spectators leap to their feet at the same time, nobody—including you—will have a better view than when all remained seated.

Here are two economic examples: An individual stockholder can sell shares of, say, Google stock without affecting the price of the stock. The individual's sale will not noticeably reduce the share price because the sale is a negligible fraction of the total shares of Google being bought and sold. But if all the Google shareholders decide to sell their shares the same day, the market will be flooded with shares and the stock price will fall precipitously. Similarly, a single cattle ranch can increase its revenue by expanding the size of its livestock herd. The extra cattle will not affect the price of cattle when they are brought to market. But if all ranchers as a group expand their herds, the total output of cattle will increase so much that the price of cattle will decline when the cattle are sold. If the price reduction is relatively large, ranchers as a group might find that their income has fallen despite their having sold a greater number of cattle because the fall in price overwhelms the increase in quantity.

Post Hoc Fallacy You must think very carefully before concluding that because event A precedes event B, A is the cause of B. This kind of faulty reasoning is known as the *post hoc, ergo propter hoc*, or "after this, therefore because of this," fallacy. Noneconomic example: A professional football team hires a new coach and the team's record improves. Is the new coach the cause? Maybe. Perhaps the presence of more experienced and talented players or an easier schedule is the true cause. The rooster crows before dawn but does not cause the sunrise.

Economic example: Many people blamed the Great Depression of the 1930s on the stock market crash of 1929. But the crash did not cause the Great Depression. The same severe weaknesses in the economy that caused the crash caused the Great Depression. The depression would have occurred even without the preceding stock market crash.

Correlation but Not Causation Do not confuse correlation, or connection, with causation. Correlation between two events or two sets of data indicates only that they are associated in some systematic and dependable way. For example, we may find that when variable X increases, Y also increases. But this correlation does not necessarily mean that there is causation—that increases in X cause increases in Y. The relationship could be purely coincidental or dependent on some other factor, Z, not included in the analysis.

Here is an example: Economists have found a positive correlation between education and income. In general, people with more education earn higher incomes than those with less education. Common sense suggests education is the cause and higher incomes are the effect; more education implies a more knowledgeable and productive worker, and such workers receive larger salaries.

But might the relationship be explainable in other ways? Are education and income correlated because the characteristics required for succeeding in education—ability and motivation—are the same ones required to be a productive and highly paid worker? If so, then people with those traits will probably both obtain more education and earn higher incomes. But greater education will not be the sole cause of the higher income.

Present Choices and Future Possibilities

An economy's current choice of positions on its production possibilities curve helps determine the future location of that curve. Let's designate the two axes of the production possibilities curve as "goods for the future" and "goods for the present," as in Figure 1.6. Goods for the future are such things as capital goods, research and education, and preventive medicine. They increase the quantity and quality of property resources, enlarge the stock of technological information, and improve the quality of human resources. As we have already seen, goods for the future such as capital goods are the ingredients of economic growth. Goods for the present are consumer goods such as food, clothing, and entertainment.

Now suppose there are two hypothetical economies, Presentville and Futureville, that are initially identical in every respect except one: Presentville's current choice of positions on its production possibilities curve strongly favors present goods over future goods. Point P in Figure 1.6a indicates that choice. It is located quite far down the curve to the right, indicating a high priority for goods for the present, at the expense of fewer goods for the future. Futureville, in contrast, makes a current choice that stresses larger amounts of future goods and smaller amounts of present goods, as shown by point F in Figure 1.6b.

Now, other things equal, we can expect the future production possibilities curve of Futureville to be farther to the right than Presentville's curve. By currently choosing an output more favorable to technological advances and to increases in the quantity and quality of resources, Futureville will achieve greater economic

FIGURE 1.6 Present choices and future locations of production possibilities curves. A nation's current choice favoring "present goods," as made by Presentville in (a), will cause a modest outward shift of the production possibilities curve in the future. A nation's current choice favoring "future goods," as made by Futureville in (b), will result in a greater outward shift of the curve in the future.

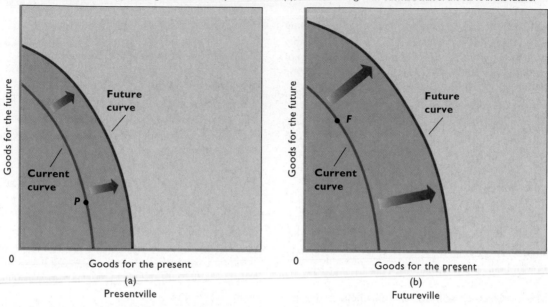

(a)
Presentville

(b)
Futureville

growth than Presentville. In terms of capital goods, Futureville is choosing to make larger current additions to its "national factory" by devoting more of its current output to capital than Presentville. The payoff from this choice for Futureville is greater future production capacity and economic growth. The opportunity cost is fewer consumer goods in the present for Futureville to enjoy.

Is Futureville's choice thus necessarily "better" than Presentville's? That, we cannot say. The different outcomes simply reflect different preferences and priorities in the two countries. But each country will have to live with the economic consequences of its choice. **(Key Question 14)**

A Qualification: International Trade

Production possibilities analysis implies that an individual nation is limited to the combinations of output indicated by its production possibilities curve. But we must modify this principle when international specialization and trade exist.

You will see in later chapters that an economy can circumvent, through international specialization and trade, the output limits imposed by its domestic production possibilities curve. International specialization means directing domestic resources to output that a nation is highly efficient at producing. International trade involves the exchange of these goods for goods produced abroad.

Specialization and trade enable a nation to get more of a desired good at less sacrifice of some other good. Rather than sacrifice three units of robots to get a third unit of pizza, as in Table 1.1, a nation might be able to obtain the third unit of pizza by trading only two units of robots for it. Specialization and trade have the same effect as having more and better resources or discovering improved production techniques; both increase the quantities of capital and consumer goods available to society. Expansion of domestic production possibilities and international trade are two separate routes for obtaining greater output.

QUICK REVIEW 1.4

- Unemployment causes an economy to operate at a point inside its production possibilities curve.

- Increases in resource supplies, improvements in resource quality, and technological advance cause economic growth, which is depicted as an outward shift of the production possibilities curve.

- An economy's present choice of capital and consumer goods helps determine the future location of its production possibilities curve.

- International specialization and trade enable a nation to obtain more goods than its production possibilities curve indicates.

Summary

1. Economics is the social science that examines how individuals, institutions, and society make optimal choices under conditions of scarcity. Central to economics is the idea of opportunity cost: the value of the good, service, or time forgone to obtain something else.

2. The economic perspective includes three elements: scarcity and choice, purposeful behavior, and marginal analysis. It sees individuals and institutions making rational decisions based on comparisons of marginal costs and marginal benefits.

3. Economists employ the scientific method, in which they form and test hypotheses of cause-and-effect relationships to generate theories, laws, and principles. Economists often combine theories into representations called models.

4. Microeconomics examines the decision making of specific economic units or institutions. Macroeconomics looks at the economy as a whole or its major aggregates.

5. Positive economic analysis deals with facts; normative economics reflects value judgments.

6. Individuals face an economizing problem. Because their wants exceed their incomes, they must decide what to purchase and what to forgo. Society also faces an economizing problem. Societal wants exceed the available resources necessary to fulfill them. Society therefore must decide what to produce and what to forgo.

7. Graphically, a budget line (or budget constraint) illustrates the economizing problem for individuals. The line shows the various combinations of two products that a consumer can purchase with a specific money income, given the prices of the two products.

8. Economic resources are inputs into the production process and can be classified as land, labor, capital, or entrepreneurial ability. Economic resources are also known as factors of production or inputs.

9. Economists illustrate society's economizing problem through production possibilities analysis. Production possibilities tables and curves show the different combinations of goods and services that can be produced in a fully employed economy, assuming that resource quantity, resource quality, and technology are fixed.

10. An economy that is fully employed and thus operating on its production possibilities curve must sacrifice the output of some types of goods and services to increase the production of others. The gain of one type of good or service is always accompanied by an opportunity cost in the form of the loss of some of the other type.

11. Because resources are not equally productive in all possible uses, shifting resources from one use to another creates increasing opportunity costs. The production of additional units of one product requires the sacrifice of increasing amounts of the other product.

12. The optimal (best) point on the production possibilities curve represents the most desirable mix of goods and is determined by expanding the production of each good until its marginal benefit (MB) equals its marginal cost (MC).

13. Over time, technological advances and increases in the quantity and quality of resources enable the economy to produce more of all goods and services, that is, to experience economic growth. Society's choice as to the mix of consumer goods and capital goods in current output is a major determinant of the future location of the production possibilities curve and thus of the extent of economic growth.

14. International trade enables nations to obtain more goods from their limited resources than their production possibilities curve indicates.

Terms and Concepts

economics	macroeconomics	capital
economic perspective	aggregate	investment
opportunity cost	positive economics	entrepreneurial ability
utility	normative economics	factors of production
marginal analysis	economizing problem	consumer goods
scientific method	budget line	capital goods
economic principle	economic resources	production possibilities curve
other-things-equal assumption	land	law of increasing opportunity costs
microeconomics	labor	economic growth

Study Questions

1. What is an opportunity cost? How does the idea relate to the definition of economics? Which of the following decisions would entail the greater opportunity cost: Allocating a square block in the heart of New York City for a surface parking lot or allocating a square block at the edge of a typical suburb for such a lot? Explain. **LO1**

2. What is meant by the term "utility" and how does the idea relate to purposeful behavior? **LO2**

3. **KEY QUESTION** Cite three examples of recent decisions that you made in which you, at least implicitly, weighed marginal cost and marginal benefit. **LO1**

4. What are the key elements of the scientific method and how does this method relate to economic principles and laws? **LO2**

5. **KEY QUESTION** Indicate whether each of the following statements applies to microeconomics or macroeconomics: **LO3**
   a. The unemployment rate in the United States was 4.9 percent in January 2008.
   b. A U.S. software firm discharged 15 workers last month and transferred the work to India.
   c. An unexpected freeze in central Florida reduced the citrus crop and caused the price of oranges to rise.
   d. U.S. output, adjusted for inflation, grew by 2.2 percent in 2007.
   e. Last week Wells Fargo Bank lowered its interest rate on business loans by one-half of 1 percentage point.
   f. The consumer price index rose by 2.8 percent in 2007.

6. State (a) a positive economic statement of your choice, and then (b) a normative economic statement relating to your first statement. **LO2**

7. **KEY QUESTION** Suppose you won $15 on a lotto ticket at the local 7-Eleven and decided to spend all the winnings on candy bars and bags of peanuts. The price of candy bars is $.75 and the price of peanuts is $1.50. **LO4**
   a. Construct a table showing the alternative combinations of the two products that are available.
   b. Plot the data in your table as a budget line in a graph. What is the slope of the budget line? What is the opportunity cost of one more candy bar? Of one more bag of peanuts? Do these opportunity costs rise, fall, or remain constant as each additional unit of the product is purchased?
   c. How, in general, would you decide which of the available combinations of candy bars and bags of peanuts to buy?
   d. Suppose that you had won $30 on your ticket, not $15. Show the $30 budget line in your diagram. Why would this budget line be preferable to the old one?

8. What are economic resources? What categories do economists use to classify them? Why are resources also called factors of production? Why are they called inputs? **LO4**

9. Why is money not considered to be a capital resource in economics? Why is entrepreneurial ability considered a category of economic resource, distinct from labor? What are the major functions of the entrepreneur? **LO4**

10. **KEY QUESTION** Below is a production possibilities table for consumer goods (automobiles) and capital goods (forklifts): **LO5**

Type of Production	Production Alternatives				
	A	B	C	D	E
Automobiles	0	2	4	6	8
Forklifts	30	27	21	12	0

   a. Show these data graphically. Upon what specific assumptions is this production possibilities curve based?
   b. If the economy is at point C, what is the cost of one more automobile? Of one more forklift? Explain how the production possibilities curve reflects the law of increasing opportunity costs.
   c. If the economy characterized by this production possibilities table and curve were producing 3 automobiles and 20 fork lifts, what could you conclude about its use of its available resources?
   d. What would production at a point outside the production possibilities curve indicate? What must occur before the economy can attain such a level of production?

11. **KEY QUESTION** Specify and explain the typical shapes of marginal-benefit and marginal-cost curves. How are these curves used to determine the optimal allocation of resources to a particular product? If current output is such that marginal cost exceeds marginal benefit, should more or fewer resources be allocated to this product? Explain. **LO5**

12. Explain how (if at all) each of the following events affects the location of a country's production possibilities curve: **LO5**
   a. The quality of education increases.
   b. The number of unemployed workers increases.
   c. A new technique improves the efficiency of extracting copper from ore.
   d. A devastating earthquake destroys numerous production facilities.

13. **KEY QUESTION** Referring to the table in question 10, suppose improvement occurs in the technology of producing forklifts but not in the technology of producing automobiles. Draw the new production possibilities curve. Now assume that a technological advance occurs in producing automobiles but not in producing forklifts. Draw the new production possibilities curve. Now draw a production possibilities curve that reflects technological improvement in the production of both goods. **LO5**

14. **KEY QUESTION** On average, households in China save 40 percent of their annual income each year, whereas households in the United States save less than 5 percent. Production possibilities are growing at roughly 9 percent annually in China and 3.5 percent in the United States. Use graphical analysis of "present goods" versus "future goods" to explain the differences in growth rates. **LO5**

15. Suppose that, on the basis of a nation's production possibilities curve, an economy must sacrifice 10,000 pizzas domestically to get the 1 additional industrial robot it desires but that it can get the robot from another country in exchange for 9000 pizzas. Relate this information to the following statement: "Through international specialization and trade, a nation can reduce its opportunity cost of obtaining goods and thus 'move outside its production possibilities curve.'" **LO5**

16. **LAST WORD** Studies indicate that married men on average earn more income than unmarried men of the same age and education level. Why must we be cautious in concluding that marriage is the cause and higher income is the effect?

Web-Based Questions

1. **NORMATIVE ECONOMICS—REPUBLICANS VERSUS DEMOCRATS** Visit both the Republicans' **www.rnc.org** and the Democrats' **www.democrats.org** Web sites. Identify an economic issue that both parties address and compare and contrast their views on that issue. Generally speaking, how much of the disagreement is based on normative economics compared to positive economics? Give an example of loaded terminology from each site.

2. **MORE LABOR RESOURCES—WHAT IS THE EVIDENCE FOR THE UNITED STATES AND JAPAN?** Go to the Bureau of Labor Statistics' Web site at **www.bls.gov** and select Get Detailed Statistics. Look for Labor Force Statistics from the Current Population Survey and click the Most Requested Statistics icon. Find U.S. civilian employment data for the last 10 years. How many more workers were there at the end of the 10-year period than at the beginning? Next, return to the Detailed Statistics page. Use the Most Requested Statistics icon next to Foreign Labor Statistics (it's under Productivity and Technology) to find total employment growth in Japan over the last 10 years. In which of the two countries did "more labor resources" have the greatest impact in shifting the nation's production possibilities curve outward over the 10-year period?

FURTHER TEST YOUR KNOWLEDGE AT
www.mcconnell18e.com

Graphs and Their Meaning

If you glance quickly through this text, you will find many graphs. Some seem simple, while others seem more formidable. All are included to help you visualize and understand economic relationships. Physicists and chemists sometimes illustrate their theories by building arrangements of multicolored wooden balls, representing protons, neutrons, and electrons, that are held in proper relation to one another by wires or sticks. Economists most often use graphs to illustrate their models. By understanding these "pictures," you can more readily comprehend economic relationships. Most of our principles or models explain relationships between just two sets of economic facts, which can be conveniently represented with two-dimensional graphs.

Construction of a Graph

A *graph* is a visual representation of the relationship between two variables. The table in Figure 1 is a hypothetical illustration showing the relationship between income and consumption for the economy as a whole. Without even studying economics, we would logically expect that people would buy more goods and services when their incomes go up. Thus, it is not surprising to find in the table that total consumption in the economy increases as total income increases.

The information in the table is expressed graphically in Figure 1. Here is how it is done: We want to show visually how consumption changes as income changes. We therefore represent income on the **horizontal axis** of the graph and consumption on the **vertical axis.**

Now we arrange the vertical and horizontal scales of the graph to reflect the ranges of values of consumption and income and mark the scales in convenient increments. As you can see, the values marked on the scales cover all the values in the table. The increments on both scales are $100.

Because the graph has two dimensions, each point within it represents an income value and its associated consumption value. To find a point that represents one of the five income-consumption combinations in the table in Figure 1, we draw straight lines from the appropriate values on the vertical and horizontal axes. For example, to plot point *c* (the $200 income–$150 consumption point), we draw straight lines up from the horizontal (income) axis at $200 and across from the vertical (consumption) axis at $150. These lines intersect at point *c*, which represents this particular income-consumption combination. You should verify that the other income-consumption combinations shown in the table are properly located in the graph in Figure 1. Finally, by assuming that the same general relationship between income and consumption prevails for all other incomes, we draw a line or smooth curve to connect these points. That line or curve represents the income-consumption relationship.

If the curve is a straight line, as in Figure 1, we say the relationship is *linear*. (It is permissible, and even customary, to call straight lines in graphs "curves.")

FIGURE 1 Graphing the direct relationship between consumption and income. Two sets of data that are positively or directly related, such as consumption and income, graph as an upsloping line.

Income per Week	Consumption per Week	Point
$ 0	$ 50	a
100	100	b
200	150	c
300	200	d
400	250	e

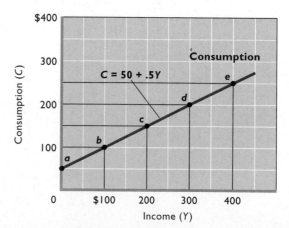

Direct and Inverse Relationships

The line in Figure 1 slopes upward to the right, so it depicts a **direct relationship** between income and consumption. By a **direct relationship** (or positive relationship) we mean that two variables—in this case, consumption and income—change in the *same* direction. An increase in consumption is associated with an increase in income; a decrease in consumption accompanies a decrease in income. When two sets of data are positively or directly related, they always graph as an *upsloping* line, as in Figure 1.

In contrast, two sets of data may be inversely related. Consider the table in Figure 2, which shows the relationship between the price of basketball tickets and game attendance at Gigantic State University (GSU). Here we have an **inverse relationship** (or negative relationship) because the two variables change in *opposite* directions. When ticket prices decrease, attendance increases. When ticket prices increase, attendance decreases. The six data points in the table in Figure 2 are plotted in the graph. Observe that an inverse relationship always graphs as a *downsloping* line.

Dependent and Independent Variables

Although it is not always easy, economists seek to determine which variable is the "cause" and which is the "effect." Or, more formally, they seek the independent variable and the dependent variable. The **independent variable** is the cause or source; it is the variable that changes first. The **dependent variable** is the effect or outcome; it is the variable that changes because of the change in the independent variable. As in our income-consumption example, income generally is the independent variable and consumption the dependent variable. Income causes consumption to be what it is rather than the other way around. Similarly, ticket prices (set in advance of the season and printed on the ticket) determine attendance at GSU basketball games; attendance at games does not determine the printed ticket prices for those games. Ticket price is the independent variable and the quantity of tickets purchased is the dependent variable.

You may recall from your high school courses that mathematicians put the independent variable (cause) on the horizontal axis and the dependent variable (effect) on the vertical axis. Economists are less tidy; their graphing of independent and dependent variables is more arbitrary. Their conventional graphing of the income-consumption relationship is consistent with mathematical presentation, but economists put price and cost data on the vertical axis. Hence, economists' graphing of GSU's ticket price–attendance data differs from normal mathematical procedure. This does not present a problem, but we want you to be aware of this fact to avoid possible confusion.

Other Things Equal

Our simple two-variable graphs purposely ignore many other factors that might affect the amount of consump-

FIGURE 2 Graphing the inverse relationship between ticket prices and game attendance. Two sets of data that are negatively or inversely related, such as ticket price and the attendance at basketball games, graph as a downsloping line.

Ticket Price	Attendance, Thousands	Point
$50	0	a
40	4	b
30	8	c
20	12	d
10	16	e
0	20	f

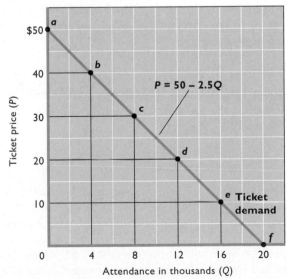

tion occurring at each income level or the number of people who attend GSU basketball games at each possible ticket price. When economists plot the relationship between any two variables, they employ the *ceteris paribus* (other-things-equal) assumption. Thus, in Figure 1 all factors other than income that might affect the amount of consumption are presumed to be constant or unchanged. Similarly, in Figure 2 all factors other than ticket price that might influence attendance at GSU basketball games are assumed constant. In reality, "other things" are not equal; they often change, and when they do, the relationship represented in our two tables and graphs will change. Specifically, the lines we have plotted would shift to new locations.

Consider a stock market "crash." The dramatic drop in the value of stocks might cause people to feel less wealthy and therefore less willing to consume at each level of income. The result might be a downward shift of the consumption line. To see this, you should plot a new consumption line in Figure 1, assuming that consumption is, say, $20 less at each income level. Note that the relationship remains direct; the line merely shifts downward to reflect less consumption spending at each income level.

Similarly, factors other than ticket prices might affect GSU game attendance. If GSU loses most of its games, attendance at GSU games might be less at each ticket price. To see this, redraw Figure 2 assuming that 2000 fewer fans attend GSU games at each ticket price. **(Key Appendix Question 2)**

Slope of a Line

Lines can be described in terms of their slopes. The **slope of a straight line** is the ratio of the vertical change (the rise or drop) to the horizontal change (the run) between any two points of the line.

Positive Slope
Between point *b* and point *c* in Figure 1, the rise or vertical change (the change in consumption) is +$50 and the run or horizontal change (the change in income) is +$100. Therefore:

$$\text{Slope} = \frac{\text{vertical change}}{\text{horizontal change}} = \frac{+50}{+100} = \frac{1}{2} = .5$$

Note that our slope of $\frac{1}{2}$ or .5 is positive because consumption and income change in the same direction; that is, consumption and income are directly or positively related.

The slope of .5 tells us there will be a $1 increase in consumption for every $2 increase in income. Similarly, it

indicates that for every $2 decrease in income there will be a $1 decrease in consumption.

Negative Slope
Between any two of the identified points in Figure 2, say, point *c* and point *d*, the vertical change is −10 (the drop) and the horizontal change is +4 (the run). Therefore:

$$\text{Slope} = \frac{\text{vertical change}}{\text{horizontal change}} = \frac{-10}{+4}$$

$$= -2\frac{1}{2} = -2.5$$

This slope is negative because ticket price and attendance have an inverse relationship.

Note that on the horizontal axis attendance is stated in thousands of people. So the slope of −10/+4 or −2.5 means that lowering the price by $10 will increase attendance by 4000 people. This is the same as saying that a $2.50 price reduction will increase attendance by 1000 persons.

Slopes and Measurement Units
The slope of a line will be affected by the choice of units for either variable. If, in our ticket price illustration, we had chosen to measure attendance in individual people, our horizontal change would have been 4000 and the slope would have been

$$\text{Slope} = \frac{-10}{+4000} = \frac{-1}{+400} = -.0025$$

The slope depends on the way the relevant variables are measured.

Slopes and Marginal Analysis
Recall that economics is largely concerned with changes from the status quo. The concept of slope is important in economics because it reflects marginal changes—those involving 1 more (or 1 less) unit. For example, in Figure 1 the .5 slope shows that $.50 of extra or marginal consumption is associated with each $1 change in income. In this example, people collectively will consume $.50 of any $1 increase in their incomes and reduce their consumption by $.50 for each $1 decline in income.

Infinite and Zero Slopes
Many variables are unrelated or independent of one another. For example, the quantity of wristwatches purchased is not related to the price of bananas. In Figure 3a we represent the price of bananas on the vertical axis and the quantity of watches demanded on

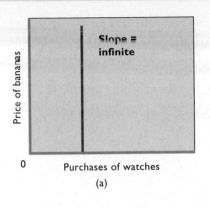

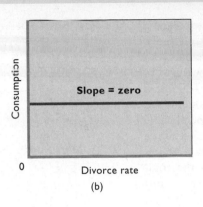

FIGURE 3 Infinite and zero slopes. (a) A line parallel to the vertical axis has an infinite slope. Here, purchases of watches remain the same no matter what happens to the price of bananas. (b) A line parallel to the horizontal axis has a slope of zero. In this case, consumption remains the same no matter what happens to the divorce rate. In both (a) and (b), the two variables are totally unrelated to one another.

the horizontal axis. The graph of their relationship is the line parallel to the vertical axis, indicating that the same quantity of watches is purchased no matter what the price of bananas. The slope of such a line is *infinite*.

Similarly, aggregate consumption is completely unrelated to the nation's divorce rate. In Figure 3b we put consumption on the vertical axis and the divorce rate on the horizontal axis. The line parallel to the horizontal axis represents this lack of relatedness. This line has a slope of *zero*.

Vertical Intercept

A line can be located on a graph (without plotting points) if we know its slope and its vertical intercept. The **vertical intercept** of a line is the point where the line meets the vertical axis. In Figure 1 the intercept is $50. This intercept means that if current income were zero, consumers would still spend $50. They might do this through borrowing or by selling some of their assets. Similarly, the $50 vertical intercept in Figure 2 shows that at a $50 ticket price, GSU's basketball team would be playing in an empty arena.

Equation of a Linear Relationship

If we know the vertical intercept and slope, we can describe a line succinctly in equation form. In its general form, the equation of a straight line is

$$y = a + bx$$

where y = dependent variable
a = vertical intercept
b = slope of line
x = independent variable

For our income-consumption example, if C represents consumption (the dependent variable) and Y represents income (the independent variable), we can write $C = a + bY$.

By substituting the known values of the intercept and the slope, we get

$$C = 50 + .5Y$$

This equation also allows us to determine the amount of consumption C at any specific level of income. You should use it to confirm that at the $250 income level, consumption is $175.

When economists reverse mathematical convention by putting the independent variable on the vertical axis and the dependent variable on the horizontal axis, then y stands for the independent variable, rather than the dependent variable in the general form. We noted previously that this case is relevant for our GSU ticket price–attendance data. If P represents the ticket price (independent variable) and Q represents attendance (dependent variable), their relationship is given by

$$P = 50 - 2.5Q$$

where the vertical intercept is 50 and the negative slope is $-2\frac{1}{2}$, or -2.5. Knowing the value of P lets us solve for Q, our dependent variable. You should use this equation to predict GSU ticket sales when the ticket price is $15. **(Key Appendix Question 3)**

Slope of a Nonlinear Curve

We now move from the simple world of linear relationships (straight lines) to the more complex world of nonlinear relationships. The slope of a straight line is the same at all its points. The slope of a line representing a nonlinear relationship changes from one point to another. Such lines are always referred to as *curves*.

Consider the downsloping curve in Figure 4. Its slope is negative throughout, but the curve flattens as we move down along it. Thus, its slope constantly changes; the curve has a different slope at each point.

To measure the slope at a specific point, we draw a straight line tangent to the curve at that point. A line is *tangent at a point* if it touches, but does not intersect, the curve at that point. Thus line *aa* is tangent to the curve in Figure 4 at point *A*. The slope of the curve at that point is equal to the slope of the tangent line. Specifically, the total vertical change (drop) in the tangent line *aa* is −20 and the total horizontal change (run) is +5. Because the slope of the tangent line *aa* is −20/+5, or −4, the slope of the curve at point *A* is also −4.

> **INTERACTIVE GRAPHS**
>
> **G 1.3**
>
> Curves and slopes

Line *bb* in Figure 4 is tangent to the curve at point *B*. Following the same procedure, we find the slope at *B* to be −5/+15, or −$\frac{1}{3}$. Thus, in this flatter part of the curve, the slope is less negative. **(Key Appendix Question 7)**

FIGURE 4 Determining the slopes of curves.
The slope of a nonlinear curve changes from point to point on the curve. The slope at any point (say, *B*) can be determined by drawing a straight line that is tangent to that point (line *bb*) and calculating the slope of that line.

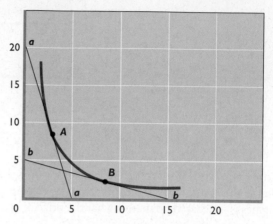

Appendix Summary

1. Graphs are a convenient and revealing way to represent economic relationships.

2. Two variables are positively or directly related when their values change in the same direction. The line (curve) representing two directly related variables slopes upward.

3. Two variables are negatively or inversely related when their values change in opposite directions. The curve representing two inversely related variables slopes downward.

4. The value of the dependent variable (the "effect") is determined by the value of the independent variable (the "cause").

5. When the "other factors" that might affect a two-variable relationship are allowed to change, the graph of the relationship will likely shift to a new location.

6. The slope of a straight line is the ratio of the vertical change to the horizontal change between any two points. The slope of an upsloping line is positive; the slope of a downsloping line is negative.

7. The slope of a line or curve depends on the units used in measuring the variables. It is especially relevant for economics because it measures marginal changes.

8. The slope of a horizontal line is zero; the slope of a vertical line is infinite.

9. The vertical intercept and slope of a line determine its location; they are used in expressing the line—and the relationship between the two variables—as an equation.

10. The slope of a curve at any point is determined by calculating the slope of a straight line tangent to the curve at that point.

Appendix Terms and Concepts

horizontal axis

vertical axis

direct relationship

inverse relationship

independent variable

dependent variable

slope of a straight line

vertical intercept

Appendix Study Questions

1. Briefly explain the use of graphs as a way to represent economic relationships. What is an inverse relationship? How does it graph? What is a direct relationship? How does it graph? Graph and explain the relationships you would expect to find between (*a*) the number of inches of rainfall per month and the sale of umbrellas, (*b*) the amount of tuition and the level of enrollment at a university, and (*c*) the popularity of an entertainer and the price of her concert tickets.

   In each case cite and explain how variables other than those specifically mentioned might upset the expected relationship. Is your graph in previous part *b* consistent with the fact that, historically, enrollments and tuition have both increased? If not, explain any difference. **LO6**

2. **KEY APPENDIX QUESTION** Indicate how each of the following might affect the data shown in the table and graph in Figure 2 of this appendix: **LO6**
   a. GSU's athletic director schedules higher-quality opponents.
   b. An NBA team locates in the city where GSU plays.
   c. GSU contracts to have all its home games televised.

3. **KEY APPENDIX QUESTION** The following table contains data on the relationship between saving and income. Rearrange these data into a meaningful order and graph them on the accompanying grid. What is the slope of the line? The vertical intercept? Interpret the meaning of both the slope and the intercept. Write the equation that represents this line. What would you predict saving to be at the $12,500 level of income? **LO6**

Income per Year	Saving per Year
$15,000	$1,000
0	−500
10,000	500
5,000	0
20,000	1,500

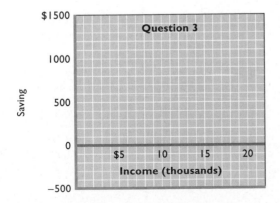

4. Construct a table from the data shown on the graph below. Which is the dependent variable and which the independent variable? Summarize the data in equation form. **LO6**

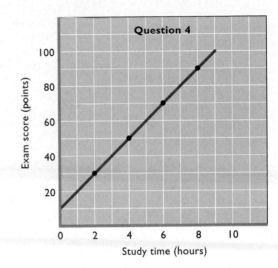

5. Suppose that when the interest rate on loans is 16 percent, businesses find it unprofitable to invest in machinery and equipment. However, when the interest rate is 14 percent, $5 billion worth of investment is profitable. At 12 percent interest, a total of $10 billion of investment is profitable. Similarly, total investment increases by $5 billion for each successive 2-percentage-point decline in the interest rate. Describe the relevant relationship between the interest rate and investment in words, in a table, on a graph, and as an equation. Put the interest rate on the vertical axis and investment on the horizontal axis. In your equation use the form $i = a + bI$, where i is the interest rate, a is the vertical intercept, b is the slope of the line (which is negative), and I is the level of investment. Comment on the advantages and disadvantages of the verbal, tabular, graphical, and equation forms of description. **LO6**

6. Suppose that $C = a + bY$, where $C =$ consumption, $a =$ consumption at zero income, $b =$ slope, and $Y =$ income. **LO6**
   a. Are C and Y positively related or are they negatively related?
   b. If graphed, would the curve for this equation slope upward or slope downward?
   c. Are the variables C and Y inversely related or directly related?
   d. What is the value of C if $a = 10$, $b = .50$, and $Y = 200$?
   e. What is the value of Y if $C = 100$, $a = 10$, and $b = .25$?

7. **KEY APPENDIX QUESTION** The accompanying graph shows curve XX' and tangents at points A, B, and C. Calculate the slope of the curve at these three points. **LO6**

8. In the accompanying graph, is the slope of curve AA' positive or negative? Does the slope increase or decrease as we move along the curve from A to A'? Answer the same two questions for curve BB'. **LO6**

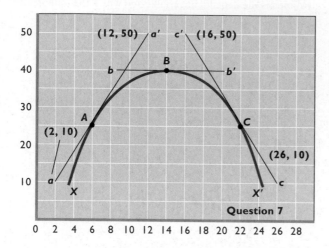

Question 7

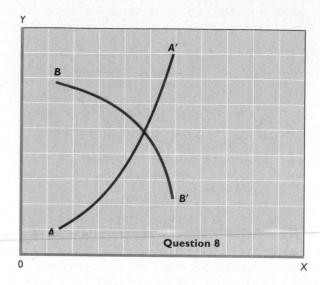

Question 8

The Market System and the Circular Flow

You are at the mall. Suppose you were assigned to compile a list of all the individual goods and services there, including the different brands and variations of each type of product. That task would be daunting and the list would be long! And even though a single shopping mall contains a remarkable quantity and variety of goods, it is only a tiny part of the national economy.

Who decided that the particular goods and services available at the mall and in the broader economy should be produced? How did the producers determine which technology and types of resources to use in producing these particular goods? Who will obtain these products? What accounts for the new and improved products among these goods? This chapter will answer these and related questions.

Economic Systems

Every society needs to develop an **economic system**—a particular set of institutional arrangements and a coordinating mechanism—to respond to the economizing problem. The economic system has to determine what goods are produced, how they are produced, who gets them, how to accommodate change, and how to promote technological progress.

Economic systems differ as to (1) who owns the factors of production and (2) the method used to motivate, coordinate, and direct economic activity. Economic systems have two polar extremes: the command system and the market system.

The Command System

The **command system** is also known as *socialism* or *communism*. In that system, government owns most property resources and economic decision making occurs through a central economic plan. A central planning board appointed by the government makes nearly all the major decisions concerning the use of resources, the composition and distribution of output, and the organization of production. The government owns most of the business firms, which produce according to government directives. The central planning board determines production goals for each enterprise and specifies the amount of resources to be allocated to each enterprise so that it can reach its production goals. The division of output between capital and consumer goods is centrally decided, and capital goods are allocated among industries on the basis of the central planning board's long-term priorities.

A pure command economy would rely exclusively on a central plan to allocate the government-owned property resources. But, in reality, even the preeminent command economy—the Soviet Union—tolerated some private ownership and incorporated some markets before its collapse in 1992. Recent reforms in Russia and most of the eastern European nations have to one degree or another transformed their command economies to capitalistic, market-oriented systems. China's reforms have not gone as far, but they have greatly reduced the reliance on central planning. Although government ownership of resources and capital in China is still extensive, the nation has increasingly relied on free markets to organize and coordinate its economy. North Korea and Cuba are the last prominent remaining examples of largely centrally planned economies. Other countries using mainly the command system include Turkmenistan, Laos, Belarus, Libya, Myanmar, and Iran. Later in this chapter, we will explore the main reasons for the general demise of the command systems.

The Market System

The polar alternative to the command system is the **market system**, or *capitalism*. The system is characterized by the private ownership of resources and the use of markets and prices to coordinate and direct economic activity. Participants act in their own self-interest. Individuals and businesses seek to achieve their economic goals through their own decisions regarding work, consumption, or production. The system allows for the private ownership of capital, communicates through prices, and coordinates economic activity through *markets*—places where buyers and sellers come together. Goods and services are produced and resources are supplied by whoever is willing and able to do so. The result is competition among independently acting buyers and sellers of each product and resource. Thus, economic decision making is widely dispersed. Also, the high potential monetary rewards create powerful incentives for existing firms to innovate and entrepreneurs to pioneer new products and processes.

In *pure* capitalism—or *laissez-faire* capitalism—government's role would be limited to protecting private property and establishing an environment appropriate to the operation of the market system. The term "laissez-faire" means "let it be," that is, keep government from interfering with the economy. The idea is that such interference will disturb the efficient working of the market system.

ORIGIN OF THE IDEA

O 2.1

Laissez-faire

But in the capitalism practiced in the United States and most other countries, government plays a substantial role in the economy. It not only provides the rules for economic activity but also promotes economic stability and growth, provides certain goods and services that would otherwise be underproduced or not produced at all, and modifies the distribution of income. The government, however, is not the dominant economic force in deciding what to produce, how to produce it, and who will get it. That force is the market.

Characteristics of the Market System

An examination of some of the key features of the market system in detail will be very instructive.

Private Property

In a market system, private individuals and firms, not the government, own most of the property resources (land and capital). It is this extensive private ownership of capital that gives capitalism its name. This right of **private property,** coupled with the freedom to negotiate binding legal contracts, enables individuals and businesses to obtain, use, and dispose of property resources as they see fit. The right of property owners to designate who will receive their property when they die helps sustain the institution of private property.

Property rights encourage investment, innovation, exchange, maintenance of property, and economic growth. Nobody would stock a store, build a factory, or clear land for farming if someone else, or the government itself, could take that property for his or her own benefit.

Property rights also extend to intellectual property through patents, copyrights, and trademarks. Such long-term protection encourages people to write books, music, and computer programs and to invent new products and production processes without fear that others will steal them and the rewards they may bring.

Moreover, property rights facilitate exchange. The title to an automobile or the deed to a cattle ranch assures the buyer that the seller is the legitimate owner. Also, property rights encourage owners to maintain or improve their property so as to preserve or increase its value. Finally, property rights enable people to use their time and resources to produce more goods and services, rather than using them to protect and retain the property they have already produced or acquired.

Freedom of Enterprise and Choice

Closely related to private ownership of property is freedom of enterprise and choice. The market system requires that various economic units make certain choices, which are expressed and implemented in the economy's markets:

- **Freedom of enterprise** ensures that entrepreneurs and private businesses are free to obtain and use economic resources to produce their choice of goods and services and to sell them in their chosen markets.

- **Freedom of choice** enables owners to employ or dispose of their property and money as they see fit. It also allows workers to try to enter any line of work for which they are qualified. Finally, it ensures that consumers are free to buy the goods and services that best satisfy their wants and that their budgets allow.

These choices are free only within broad legal limitations, of course. Illegal choices such as selling human organs or buying illicit drugs are punished through fines and imprisonment. (Global Perspective 2.1 reveals that the degree of economic freedom varies greatly from economy to economy.)

Self-Interest

In the market system, **self-interest** is the motivating force of the various economic units as they express their free choices. Self-interest simply means that each economic

ORIGIN OF THE IDEA

O 2.2

Self-interest

unit tries to achieve its own particular goal, which usually requires delivering something of value to others. Entrepreneurs try to maximize profit or minimize loss. Property owners try to get the highest price for the sale or rent of their resources. Workers try to maximize their utility (satisfaction) by finding jobs that offer the best combination of wages, hours, fringe benefits, and working conditions. Consumers try to obtain the products they want at the

GLOBAL PERSPECTIVE 2.1

Index of Economic Freedom, Selected Economies

The Index of Economic Freedom measures economic freedom using 10 broad categories such as trade policy, property rights, and government intervention, with each category containing more than 50 specific criteria. The index then ranks 157 economies according to their degree of economic freedom. A few selected rankings for 2008 are listed below.

FREE

1 Hong Kong

3 Ireland

5 United States

MOSTLY FREE

20 Belgium

31 Spain

48 France

MOSTLY UNFREE

101 Brazil

126 China

134 Russia

REPRESSED

148 Venezuela

156 Cuba

157 North Korea

Source: Used by permission of The Heritage Foundation (**www.heritage.org**) and *The Wall Street Journal.*

lowest possible price and apportion their expenditures to maximize their utility. The motive of self-interest gives direction and consistency to what might otherwise be a chaotic economy.

Competition

The market system depends on **competition** among economic units. The basis of this competition is freedom of choice exercised in pursuit of a monetary return. Very broadly defined, competition requires

- Two or more buyers and two or more sellers acting independently in a particular product or resource market. (Usually there are many more than two buyers or sellers.)
- Freedom of sellers and buyers to enter or leave markets, on the basis of their economic self-interest.

Competition among buyers and sellers diffuses economic power within the businesses and households that make up the economy. When there are many buyers and sellers acting independently in a market, no single buyer or seller can dictate the price of the product or resource because others can undercut that price.

Competition also implies that producers can enter or leave an industry; no insurmountable barriers prevent an industry's expanding or contracting. This freedom of an industry to expand or contract provides the economy with the flexibility needed to remain efficient over time. Freedom of entry and exit enables the economy to adjust to changes in consumer tastes, technology, and resource availability.

The diffusion of economic power inherent in competition limits the potential abuse of that power. A producer that charges more than the competitive market price will lose sales to other producers. An employer who pays less than the competitive market wage rate will lose workers to other employers. A firm that fails to exploit new technology will lose profits to firms that do. Competition is the basic regulatory force in the market system.

Markets and Prices

We may wonder why an economy based on self-interest does not collapse in chaos. If consumers want breakfast cereal but businesses choose to produce running shoes and resource suppliers decide to make computer software, production would seem to be deadlocked by the apparent inconsistencies of free choices.

In reality, the millions of decisions made by households and businesses are highly coordinated with one another by markets and prices, which are key components of the market system. They give the system its ability to coordinate millions of daily economic decisions. A **market**

is an institution or mechanism that brings buyers ("demanders") and sellers ("suppliers") into contact. A market system conveys the decisions made by buyers and sellers of products and resources. The decisions made on each side of the market determine a set of product and resource prices that guide resource owners, entrepreneurs, and consumers as they make and revise their choices and pursue their self-interest.

Just as competition is the regulatory mechanism of the market system, the market system itself is the organizing and coordinating mechanism. It is an elaborate communication network through which innumerable individual free choices are recorded, summarized, and balanced. Those who respond to market signals and heed market dictates are rewarded with greater profit and income; those who do not respond to those signals and choose to ignore market dictates are penalized. Through this mechanism society decides what the economy should produce, how production can be organized efficiently, and how the fruits of production are to be distributed among the various units that make up the economy.

> ### QUICK REVIEW 2.1
>
> - The market system rests on the private ownership of property and on freedom of enterprise and freedom of choice.
> - The market system permits consumers, resource suppliers, and businesses to pursue and further their self-interest.
> - Competition diffuses economic power and limits the actions of any single seller or buyer.
> - The coordinating mechanism of capitalism is a system of markets and prices.

Technology and Capital Goods

In the market system, competition, freedom of choice, self-interest, and personal reward provide the opportunity and motivation for technological advance. The monetary rewards for new products or production techniques accrue directly to the innovator. The market system therefore encourages extensive use and rapid development of complex capital goods: tools, machinery, large-scale factories, and facilities for storage, communication, transportation, and marketing.

Advanced technology and capital goods are important because the most direct methods of production are often the least efficient. The only way to avoid that inefficiency is to rely on capital goods. It would be ridiculous for a farmer to go at production with bare hands. There are huge benefits to be derived from creating and using such capital equipment as plows, tractors, and storage bins. The more efficient production means much more abundant output.

Specialization

The extent to which market economies rely on **specialization** is extraordinary. Specialization is the use of resources of an individual, firm, region, or nation to produce one or a few goods or services rather than the entire range of goods and services. Those goods and services are then exchanged for a full range of desired products. The majority of consumers produce virtually none of the goods and services they consume, and they consume little or nothing of the items they produce. The person working nine to five installing windows in commercial aircraft may rarely fly. Many farmers sell their milk to the local dairy and then buy margarine at the local grocery store. Society learned long ago that self-sufficiency breeds inefficiency. The jack-of-all-trades may be a very colorful individual but is certainly not an efficient producer.

Division of Labor

Human specialization—called the **division of labor**—contributes to a society's output in several ways:

- *Specialization makes use of differences in ability.* Specialization enables individuals to take advantage of existing differences in their abilities and skills. If Peyton is strong, athletic, and good at throwing a football and Beyonce is beautiful, agile, and can sing, their distribution of talents can be most efficiently used if Peyton plays professional football and Beyonce records songs and gives concerts.

ORIGIN OF THE IDEA

O 2.3

Specialization: division of labor

- *Specialization fosters learning by doing.* Even if the abilities of two people are identical, specialization may still be advantageous. By devoting time to a single task, a person is more likely to develop the skills required and to improve techniques than by working at a number of different tasks. You learn to be a good lawyer by studying and practicing law.
- *Specialization saves time.* By devoting time to a single task, a person avoids the loss of time incurred in shifting from one job to another. Also, time is saved by not "fumbling around" with a task that one is not trained to do.

For all these reasons, specialization increases the total output society derives from limited resources.

Geographic Specialization

Specialization also works on a regional and international basis. It is conceivable that oranges could be grown in Nebraska, but because of the unsuitability of the land, rainfall, and temperature, the costs would be very high. And it is conceivable that wheat could be grown in Florida, but such production would be costly for similar geographical reasons. So Nebraskans produce products—wheat in particular—for which their resources are best suited, and Floridians do the same, producing oranges and other citrus fruits. By specializing, both economies produce more than is needed locally. Then, very sensibly, Nebraskans and Floridians swap some of their surpluses—wheat for oranges, oranges for wheat.

Similarly, on an international scale, the United States specializes in producing such items as commercial aircraft and computers, which it sells abroad in exchange for video recorders from Japan, bananas from Honduras, and woven baskets from Thailand. Both human specialization and geographic specialization are needed to achieve efficiency in the use of limited resources.

Use of Money

A rather obvious characteristic of any economic system is the extensive use of money. Money performs several functions, but first and foremost it is a **medium of exchange.** It makes trade easier.

Specialization requires exchange. Exchange can, and sometimes does, occur through **barter**—swapping goods for goods, say, wheat for oranges. But barter poses serious problems because it requires a *coincidence of wants* between the buyer and the seller. In our example, we assumed that Nebraskans had excess wheat to trade and wanted oranges. And we assumed that Floridians had excess oranges to trade and wanted wheat. So an exchange occurred. But if such a coincidence of wants is missing, trade is stymied.

Suppose that Nebraska has no interest in Florida's oranges but wants potatoes from Idaho. And suppose that Idaho wants Florida's oranges but not Nebraska's wheat. And, to complicate matters, suppose that Florida wants some of Nebraska's wheat but none of Idaho's potatoes. We summarize the situation in Figure 2.1.

In none of the cases shown in the figure is there a coincidence of wants. Trade by barter clearly would be difficult. Instead, people in each state use **money,** which is simply a convenient social invention to facilitate exchanges of goods and services. Historically, people have used cattle, cigarettes, shells, stones, pieces of metal, and many other commodities, with varying degrees of success, as a medium of exchange. But to serve as money, an item needs to pass only one test: It must be generally acceptable to sellers in exchange for their goods and services. Money is socially defined; whatever society accepts as a medium of exchange *is* money.

Today, most economies use pieces of paper as money. The use of paper dollars (currency) as a medium of exchange is what enables Nebraska, Florida, and Idaho to overcome their trade stalemate, as demonstrated in Figure 2.1.

FIGURE 2.1 **Money facilitates trade when wants do not coincide.** The use of money as a medium of exchange permits trade to be accomplished despite a noncoincidence of wants. (1) Nebraska trades the wheat that Florida wants for money from Floridians; (2) Nebraska trades the money it receives from Florida for the potatoes it wants from Idaho; (3) Idaho trades the money it receives from Nebraska for the oranges it wants from Florida.

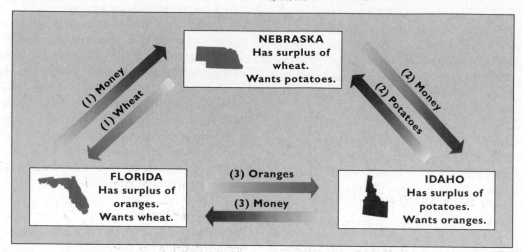

On a global basis different nations have different currencies, and that complicates specialization and exchange. But markets in which currencies are bought and sold make it possible for U.S. residents, Japanese, Germans, Britons, and Mexicans, through the swapping of dollars, yen, euros, pounds, and pesos, one for another, to exchange goods and service without resorting to barter.

Active, but Limited, Government

An active, but limited, government is the final characteristic of market systems in modern advanced industrial economies. Although a market system promotes a high degree of efficiency in the use of its resources, it has certain inherent shortcomings, called "market failures." We will discover in subsequent chapters that government can increase the overall effectiveness of the economic system in several ways.

QUICK REVIEW 2.2

- The market systems of modern industrial economies are characterized by extensive use of technologically advanced capital goods. Such goods help these economies achieve greater efficiency in production.
- Specialization is extensive in market systems; it enhances efficiency and output by enabling individuals, regions, and nations to produce the goods and services for which their resources are best suited.
- The use of money in market systems facilitates the exchange of goods and services that specialization requires.

Five Fundamental Questions

The key features of the market system help explain how market economies respond to five fundamental questions:

- What goods and services will be produced?
- How will the goods and services be produced?
- Who will get the goods and services?
- How will the system accommodate change?
- How will the system promote progress?

These five questions highlight the economic choices underlying the production possibilities curve discussed in Chapter 1. They reflect the reality of scarce resources in a world of unlimited wants. All economies, whether market or command, must address these five questions.

What Will Be Produced?

How will a market system decide on the specific types and quantities of goods to be produced? The simple answer is this: The goods and services produced at a continuing profit will be produced, and those produced at a continuing loss will not. Profits and losses are the difference between the total revenue (TR) a firm receives from the sale of its products and the total opportunity cost (TC) of producing those products. (For economists, economic costs include not only wage and salary payments to labor, and interest and rental payments for capital and land, but also payments to the entrepreneur for organizing and combining the other resources to produce a commodity.)

Continuing economic profit (TR > TC) in an industry results in expanded production and the movement of resources toward that industry. Existing firms grow and new firms enter. The industry expands. Continuing losses (TC > TR) in an industry leads to reduced production and the exit of resources from that industry. Some existing firms shrink in size; others go out of business. The industry contracts. In the market system, consumers are sovereign (in command). **Consumer sovereignty** is crucial in determining the types and quantities of goods produced. Consumers spend their income on the goods they are most willing and able to buy. Through these **"dollar votes"** they register their wants in the market. If the dollar votes for a certain product are great enough to create a profit, businesses will produce that product and offer it for sale. In contrast, if the dollar votes do not create sufficient revenues to cover costs, businesses will not produce the product. So the consumers are sovereign. They collectively direct resources to industries that are meeting consumer wants and away from industries that are not meeting consumer wants.

The dollar votes of consumers determine not only which industries will continue to exist but also which products will survive or fail. Only profitable industries, firms, and products survive. So firms are not as free to produce whatever products they wish as one might otherwise think. Consumers' buying decisions make the production of some products profitable and the production of other products unprofitable, thus restricting the choice of businesses in deciding what to produce. Businesses must match their production choices with consumer choices or else face losses and eventual bankruptcy.

The same holds true for resource suppliers. The employment of resources derives from the sale of the goods and services that the resources help produce. Autoworkers are employed because automobiles are sold. There are few remaining professors of early Latin because there are few people desiring to learn the Latin language. Resource suppliers, desiring to earn income, are not truly free to allocate their resources to the production of goods that consumers do not value highly. Consumers register their preferences in the market; producers and resource suppliers, prompted by their own self-interest, respond appropriately. **(Key Question 8)**

How Will the Goods and Services Be Produced?

What combinations of resources and technologies will be used to produce goods and services? How will the production be organized? The answer: In combinations and ways that minimize the cost per unit of output. Because competition eliminates high-cost producers, profitability requires that firms produce their output at minimum cost per unit. Achieving this least-cost production necessitates, for example, that firms use the right mix of labor and capital, given the prices and productivity of those resources. It also means locating production facilities optimally to hold down production and transportation expenses.

Least-cost production also means that firms must employ the most economically efficient technique of production in producing their output. The most efficient production technique depends on

- The available technology, that is, the various combinations of resources that will produce the desired results.
- The prices of the needed resources.

A technique that requires just a few inputs of resources to produce a specific output may be highly inefficient economically if those resources are valued very highly in the

CONSIDER THIS . . .

McHits and McMisses

McDonald's has introduced several new menu items over the decades. Some have been profitable "hits," while others have been "misses." Ultimately, consumers decide whether a menu item is profitable and therefore whether it stays on the McDonald's menu.

- Hulaburger (1962)—McMiss
- Filet-O-Fish (1963)—McHit
- Strawberry shortcake (1966)—McMiss
- Big Mac (1968)—McHit
- Hot apple pie (1968)—McHit
- Egg McMuffin (1975)—McHit
- Drive-thru (1975)—McHit
- Chicken McNuggets (1983)—McHit
- Extra Value Meal (1991)—McHit
- McLean Deluxe (1991)—McMiss
- Arch Deluxe (1996)—McMiss
- 55-cent special (1997)—McMiss
- Big Xtra (1999)—McHit

Source: "Polishing the Golden Arches," *Forbes,* June 15, 1998, pp. 42–43, updated.

TABLE 2.1 **Three Techniques for Producing $15 Worth of Bar Soap**

		Units of Resource					
		Technique 1		Technique 2		Technique 3	
Resource	Price per Unit of Resource	Units	Cost	Units	Cost	Units	Cost
Labor	$2	4	$ 8	2	$ 4	1	$ 2
Land	1	1	1	3	3	4	4
Capital	3	1	3	1	3	2	6
Entrepreneurial ability	3	1	3	1	3	1	3
Total cost of $15 worth of bar soap			$15		$13		$15

market. Economic efficiency requires obtaining a particular output of product with the least input of scarce resources, when both output and resource inputs are measured in dollars and cents. The combination of resources that will produce, say, $15 worth of bathroom soap at the lowest possible cost is the most efficient.

Suppose there are three possible techniques for producing the desired $15 worth of bars of soap. Suppose also that the quantity of each resource required by each production technique and the prices of the required resources are as shown in Table 2.1. By multiplying the required quantities of each resource by its price in each of the three techniques, we can determine the total cost of producing $15 worth of soap by means of each technique.

Technique 2 is economically the most efficient, because it is the least costly. It enables society to obtain $15 worth of output by using a smaller amount of resources— $13 worth—than the $15 worth required by the two other techniques.

WORKED PROBLEMS

W 2.1

Least-cost production

Competition will dictate that producers use technique 2. Thus, the question of how goods will be produced is answered. They will be produced in a least-cost way.

A change in either technology or resource prices, however, may cause a firm to shift from the technology it is using. If the price of labor falls to $.50, technique 1 becomes more desirable than technique 2. Firms will find they can lower their costs by shifting to a technology that uses more of the resource whose price has fallen. Exercise: Would a new technique involving 1 unit of labor, 4 of land, 1 of capital, and 1 of entrepreneurial ability be preferable to the techniques listed in Table 2.1, assuming the resource prices shown there? **(Key Question 9)**

Who Will Get the Output?

The market system enters the picture in two ways when determining the distribution of total output. Generally, any product will be distributed to consumers on the basis of their ability and willingness to pay its existing market price. If the price of some product, say, a small sailboat, is $3000, then buyers who are willing and able to pay that price will "sail, sail away." Consumers who are unwilling or unable to pay the price will be "sitting on the dock of the bay."

The ability to pay the prices for sailboats and other products depends on the amount of income that consumers have, along with the prices of, and preferences for, various goods. If consumers have sufficient income and want to spend their money on a particular good, they can have it. And the amount of income they have depends on (1) the quantities of the property and human resources they supply and (2) the prices those resources command in the resource market. Resource prices (wages, interest, rent, profit) are crucial in determining the size of each person's income and therefore each person's ability to buy part of the economy's output. If a lawyer earning $200 an hour and a recreational worker earning $10 an hour both work the same number of hours each year, the lawyer will be able to take possession of 20 times as much of society's output as the recreational worker that year.

How Will the System Accommodate Change?

Market systems are dynamic: Consumer preferences, technology, and supplies of resources all change. This means that the particular allocation of resources that is now the most efficient for a specific pattern of consumer tastes, range of technological alternatives, and amount of available resources will become obsolete and inefficient as consumer preferences change, new techniques of production are discovered, and resource supplies change over time. Can the market economy adjust to such changes?

Suppose consumer tastes change. For instance, assume that consumers decide they want more fruit juice and less milk than the economy currently provides. Those changes in consumer tastes will be communicated to producers through an increase in spending on fruit and a decline in spending on milk. Other things equal, prices and profits in the fruit juice industry will rise and those in the milk industry will fall. Self-interest will induce existing competitors to expand output and entice new competitors to enter the prosperous fruit industry and will in time force firms to scale down—or even exit—the depressed milk industry.

The higher prices and greater economic profit in the fruit-juice industry will not only induce that industry to expand but will also give it the revenue needed to obtain the resources essential to its growth. Higher prices and profits will permit fruit producers to attract more resources from less urgent alternative uses. The reverse occurs in the milk industry, where fewer workers and other resources are employed. These adjustments in the economy are appropriate responses to the changes in consumer tastes. This is consumer sovereignty at work.

The market system is a gigantic communications system. Through changes in prices and profits, it communicates changes in such basic matters as consumer tastes and elicits appropriate responses from businesses and resource suppliers. By affecting price and profits, changes in consumer tastes direct the expansion of some industries and the contraction of others. Those adjustments are conveyed to the resource market. As expanding industries employ more resources and contracting industries employ fewer, the resulting changes in resource prices (wages and salaries, for example) and income flows guide resources from the contracting industries to the expanding industries.

This directing or guiding function of prices and profits is a core element of the market system. Without such a system, a government planning board or some other administrative agency would have to direct businesses and resources into the appropriate industries. A similar analysis shows that the system can and does adjust to other fundamental changes—for example, to changes in technology and in the prices of various resources.

How Will the System Promote Progress?

Society desires economic growth (greater output) and higher standards of living (greater income per person). How does the market system promote technological improvements and capital accumulation, both of which contribute to a higher standard of living for society?

Technological Advance

The market system provides a strong incentive for technological advance and enables better products and processes to supplant inferior ones. An entrepreneur or firm that introduces a popular new product will gain revenue and economic profit at the expense of rivals. Firms that are highly profitable one year may find they are in financial trouble just a few years later.

Technological advance also includes new and improved methods that reduce production or distribution costs. By passing part of its cost reduction on to the consumer through a lower product price, a firm can increase sales and obtain economic profit at the expense of rival firms.

Moreover, the market system promotes the *rapid spread* of technological advance throughout an industry. Rival firms must follow the lead of the most innovative firm or else suffer immediate losses and eventual failure. In some cases, the result is **creative destruction:** The creation of new products and production methods completely destroys the market positions of firms that are wedded to existing products and older ways of doing business. Example: The advent of compact discs largely demolished long-play vinyl records, and iPods and other digital technologies are now supplanting CDs.

Capital Accumulation

Most technological advances require additional capital goods. The market system provides the resources necessary to produce those goods through increased dollar votes for capital goods. That is, the market system acknowledges dollar voting for capital goods as well as for consumer goods.

But who will register votes for capital goods? Answer: Entrepreneurs and owners of businesses. As receivers of profit income, they often use part of that income to purchase capital goods. Doing so yields even greater profit income in the future if the technological innovation is successful. Also, by paying interest or selling ownership shares, the entrepreneur and firm can attract some of the income of households as saving to increase their dollar votes for the production of more capital goods. **(Key Question 10)**

QUICK REVIEW 2.3

- The output mix of the market system is determined by profits, which in turn depend heavily on consumer preferences. Economic profits cause industries to expand; losses cause industries to contract.

- Competition forces industries to use the least costly production methods.

- Competitive markets reallocate resources in response to changes in consumer tastes, technological advances, and changes in availability of resources.

- In a market economy, consumer income and product prices determine how output will be distributed.

- Competitive markets create incentives for technological advance and capital accumulation, both of which contribute to increases in standards of living.

The "Invisible Hand"

In his 1776 book *The Wealth of Nations*, Adam Smith first noted that the operation of a market system creates a curious unity between private interests and social interests. Firms and resource suppliers, seeking to further their own self-interest and operating within the framework of a highly competitive market system, will simultaneously, as though guided by an **"invisible hand,"** promote the public or social interest. For example, we have seen that in a competitive environment, businesses seek to build new and improved products to increase profits. Those enhanced products increase society's well-being. Businesses also use the least costly combination of resources to produce a specific output because doing so is in their self-interest. To act otherwise would be to forgo profit or even to risk business failure. But, at the same time, to use scarce resources in the least costly way is clearly in the social interest as well. It "frees up" resources to produce something else that society desires.

Self-interest, awakened and guided by the competitive market system, is what induces responses appropriate to the changes in society's wants. Businesses seeking to make higher profits and to avoid losses, and resource suppliers pursuing greater monetary rewards, negotiate changes in the allocation of resources and end up with the output that society wants. Competition controls or guides self-interest such that self-interest automatically and quite unintentionally furthers the best interest of society. The invisible hand ensures that when firms maximize their profits and resource suppliers maximize their incomes, these groups also help maximize society's output and income.

Of the various virtues of the market system, three merit reemphasis:

- *Efficiency* The market system promotes the efficient use of resources by guiding them into the production of the goods and services most wanted by society. It forces the use of the most efficient techniques in organizing resources for production, and it encourages the development and adoption of new and more efficient production techniques.
- *Incentives* The market system encourages skill acquisition, hard work, and innovation. Greater work skills and effort mean greater production and higher incomes, which usually translate into a higher standard of living. Similarly, the assuming of risks by entrepreneurs can result in substantial profit incomes. Successful innovations generate economic rewards.
- *Freedom* The major noneconomic argument for the market system is its emphasis on personal freedom.

In contrast to central planning, the market system coordinates economic activity without coercion. The market system permits—indeed, it thrives on—freedom of enterprise and choice. Entrepreneurs and workers are free to further their own self-interest, subject to the rewards and penalties imposed by the market system itself.

Of course, no economic system, including the market system, is flawless. In Chapter 4 we will explain several well-known shortcomings of the market system and examine the government policies that try to remedy them.

The Demise of the Command Systems

Our discussion of how a market system answers the five fundamental questions provides insights on why command systems of the Soviet Union, eastern Europe, and China (prior to its market reforms) failed. Those systems encountered two insurmountable problems.

The Coordination Problem

The first difficulty was the coordination problem. The central planners had to coordinate the millions of individual decisions by consumers, resource suppliers, and businesses. Consider the setting up of a factory to produce tractors. The central planners had to establish a realistic annual production target, for example, 1000 tractors. They then had to make available all the necessary inputs—labor, machinery, electric power, steel, tires, glass, paint, transportation—for the production and delivery of those 1000 tractors.

Because the outputs of many industries serve as inputs to other industries, the failure of any single industry to achieve its output target caused a chain reaction of repercussions. For example, if iron mines, for want of machinery or labor or transportation, did not supply the steel industry with the required inputs of iron ore, the steel mills were unable to fulfill the input needs of the many industries that depended on steel. Those steel-using industries (such as tractor, automobile, and transportation) were unable to fulfill their planned production goals. Eventually the chain reaction spread to all firms that used steel as an input and from there to other input buyers or final consumers.

The coordination problem became more difficult as the economies expanded. Products and production processes grew more sophisticated and the number of industries requiring planning increased. Planning techniques that worked for the simpler economy proved highly inadequate and inefficient for the larger economy. Bottlenecks and production stoppages became the norm, not the exception. In trying to cope, planners further suppressed product variety, focusing on one or two products in each product category.

A lack of a reliable success indicator added to the coordination problem in the Soviet Union and China (prior to its market reforms). We have seen that market economies rely on profit as a success indicator. Profit depends on consumer demand, production efficiency, and product quality. In contrast, the major success indicator for the command economies usually was a quantitative production target that the central planners assigned. Production costs, product quality, and product mix were secondary considerations. Managers and workers often sacrificed product quality and variety because they were being awarded bonuses for meeting quantitative, not qualitative, targets. If meeting production goals meant sloppy assembly work and little product variety, so be it.

It was difficult at best for planners to assign quantitative production targets without unintentionally producing distortions in output. If the plan specified a production target for producing nails in terms of *weight* (tons of nails), the enterprise made only large nails. But if it specified the target as a *quantity* (thousands of nails), the firm made all small nails, and lots of them! That is precisely what happened in the centrally planned economies.

The Incentive Problem

The command economies also faced an incentive problem. Central planners determined the output mix. When they misjudged how many automobiles, shoes, shirts, and chickens were wanted at the government-determined prices, persistent shortages and surpluses of those products arose. But as long as the managers who oversaw the production of those goods were rewarded for meeting their assigned production goals, they had no incentive to adjust production in response to the shortages and surpluses. And there were no fluctuations in prices and profitability to signal that more or less of certain products was desired. Thus, many products were unavailable or in short supply, while other products were overproduced and sat for months or years in warehouses.

The command systems of the Soviet Union and China before its market reforms also lacked entrepreneurship. Central planning did not trigger the profit motive, nor did it reward innovation and enterprise. The route for getting ahead was through participation in the political hierarchy of the Communist Party. Moving up the hierarchy meant better housing, better access to health care, and the right

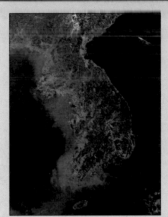

The Two Koreas

North Korea is one of the few command economies still standing. After the Second World War, the Korean peninsula was divided into North Korea and South Korea. North Korea, under the influence of the Soviet Union, established a command economy that emphasized government ownership and central government planning. South Korea, protected by the United States, established a market economy based upon private ownership and the profit motive. Today, the differences in the economic outcomes of the two systems are striking:

	North Korea	South Korea
GDP	$40 billion*	$1.2 trillion*
GDP per capita	$1,800*	$24,500*
Exports	$1.3 billion	$326 billion
Imports	$2.7 billion	$309.3 billion
Agriculture as % of GDP	30 percent	3 percent

*Based on purchasing power equivalencies to the U.S. dollar.
Source: CIA World Fact Book, 2008, **www.cia.gov.**

to shop in special stores. Meeting production targets and maneuvering through the minefields of party politics were measures of success in "business." But a definition of business success based solely on political savvy was not conducive to technological advance, which is often disruptive to existing products, production methods, and organizational structures.

The Circular Flow Model

The dynamic market economy creates continuous, repetitive flows of goods and services, resources, and money. The **circular flow diagram,** shown in **Figure 2.2 (Key Graph),** illustrates those flows. Observe that in the diagram we group private decision makers into *businesses* and *households* and group markets into the *resource market* and the *product market*.

ORIGIN OF THE IDEA

O 2.4
Circular flow diagram

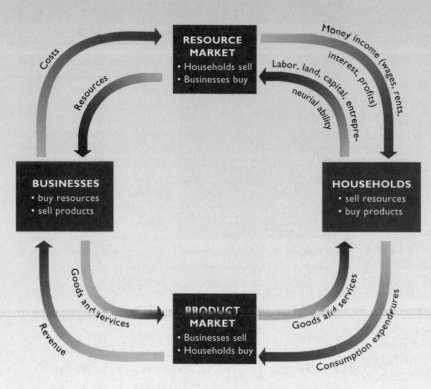

FIGURE 2.2 The circular flow diagram. Resources flow from households to businesses through the resource market, and products flow from businesses to households through the product market. Opposite these real flows are monetary flows. Households receive income from businesses (their costs) through the resource market, and businesses receive revenue from households (their expenditures) through the product market.

QUICK QUIZ FOR FIGURE 2.2

1. The resource market is the place where:
   a. households sell products and businesses buy products.
   b. businesses sell resources and households sell products.
   c. households sell resources and businesses buy resources (or the services of resources).
   d. businesses sell resources and households buy resources (or the services of resources).

2. Which of the following would be determined in the product market?
   a. a manager's salary.
   b. the price of equipment used in a bottling plant.
   c. the price of 80 acres of farmland.
   d. the price of a new pair of athletic shoes.

3. In this circular flow diagram:
   a. money flows counterclockwise.
   b. resources flow counterclockwise.
   c. goods and services flow clockwise.
   d. households are on the selling side of the product market.

4. In this circular flow diagram:
   a. households spend income in the product market.
   b. firms sell resources to households.
   c. households receive income through the product market.
   d. households produce goods.

Answers: 1. c; 2. d; 3. b; 4. a

Resource Market

The upper part of the circular flow diagram represents the **resource market:** the place where resources or the services of resource suppliers are bought and sold. In the resource market, households sell resources and businesses buy them. Households (that is, people) own all economic resources either directly as workers or entrepreneurs or indirectly through their ownership of busi-ness corporations. They sell their resources to businesses, which buy them because they are necessary for produc-ing goods and services. The funds that businesses pay for resources are costs to businesses but are flows of wage, rent, interest, and profit income to the house-holds. Productive resources therefore flow from house-holds to businesses, and money flows from businesses to households.

Economist Donald Boudreaux Marvels at the Way the Market System Systematically and Purposefully Arranges the World's Tens of Billions of Individual Resources.

In *The Future and Its Enemies*, Virginia Postrel notes the astonishing fact that if you thoroughly shuffle an ordinary deck of 52 playing cards, chances are practically 100 percent that the resulting arrangement of cards has never before existed. *Never.* Every time you shuffle a deck, you produce an arrangement of cards that exists for the first time in history.

The arithmetic works out that way. For a very small number of items, the number of possible arrangements is small. Three items, for example, can be arranged only six different ways. But the number of possible arrangements grows very large very quickly. The number of different ways to arrange five items is 120 . . . for ten items it's 3,628,800 . . . for fifteen items it's 1,307,674,368,000.

The number of different ways to arrange 52 items is 8.066×10^{67}. This is a *big* number. No human can comprehend its enormousness. By way of comparison, the number of possible ways to arrange a mere 20 items is 2,432,902,008,176,640,000—a number larger than the total number of seconds that have elapsed since the beginning of time ten billion years ago—and this number is Lilliputian compared to 8.066×10^{67}.

What's the significance of these facts about numbers? Consider the number of different resources available in the world—my labor, your labor, your land, oil, tungsten, cedar, coffee beans, chickens, rivers, the Empire State Building, [Microsoft] Windows, the wharves at Houston, the classrooms at Oxford, the airport at Miami, and on and on and on. No one can possibly count all of the different productive resources available for our use. But we can be sure that this number is at least in the tens of billions.

When you reflect on how incomprehensibly large is the number of ways to arrange a deck containing a mere 52 cards, the mind boggles at the number of different ways to arrange all the world's resources.

If our world were random—if resources combined together haphazardly, as if a giant took them all into his hands and tossed them down like so many [cards]—it's a virtual certainty that the resulting combination of resources would be useless. Unless this chance arrangement were quickly rearranged according to some productive logic, nothing worthwhile would be produced. We would all starve to death. Because only a tiny fraction of possible arrangements serves human ends, any arrangement will be useless if it is chosen randomly or with inadequate knowledge of how each and every resource might be productively combined with each other.

And yet, we witness all around us an arrangement of resources that's productive and serves human goals. Today's arrangement of resources might not be perfect, but it is vastly superior to most of the trillions upon trillions of other possible arrangements.

How have we managed to get one of the minuscule number of arrangements that works? The answer is private property—a social institution that encourages mutual accommodation.

Private property eliminates the possibility that resource arrangements will be random, for each resource owner chooses a course of action only if it promises rewards to the owner that exceed the rewards promised by all other available courses.

[The result] is a breathtakingly complex and productive arrangement of countless resources. This arrangement emerged over time (and is still emerging) as the result of billions upon billions of individual, daily, small decisions made by people seeking to better employ their resources and labor in ways that other people find helpful.

Source: Abridged from Donald J. Boudreaux, "Mutual Accommodation," *Ideas on Liberty,* May 2000, pp. 4–5. Reprinted with permission. Used by permission of The Freeman.

Product Market

Next consider the lower part of the diagram, which represents the **product market:** the place where goods and services produced by businesses are bought and sold. In the product market, businesses combine resources to produce and sell goods and services. Households use the (limited) income they have received from the sale of resources to buy goods and services. The monetary flow of consumer spending on goods and services yields sales revenues for businesses. Businesses compare those revenues to their costs in determining profitability and whether or not a particular good or service should continue to be produced.

The circular flow model depicts a complex, interrelated web of decision making and economic activity involving businesses and households. For the economy, it is the circle of life. Businesses and households are both buyers and sellers. Businesses buy resources and sell products. Households buy products and sell resources. As shown in Figure 2.2, there is a counterclockwise *real flow* of economic resources and finished goods and services and a clockwise *money flow* of income and consumption expenditures.

Summary

1. The market system and the command system are the two broad types of economic systems used to address the economizing problem. In the market system (or capitalism), private individuals own most resources, and markets coordinate most economic activity. In the command system (or socialism or communism), government owns most resources and central planners coordinate most economic activity.

2. The market system is characterized by the private ownership of resources, including capital, and the freedom of individuals to engage in economic activities of their choice to advance their material well-being. Self-interest is the driving force of such an economy and competition functions as a regulatory or control mechanism.

3. In the market system, markets, prices, and profits organize and make effective the many millions of individual economic decisions that occur daily.

4. Specialization, use of advanced technology, and the extensive use of capital goods are common features of market systems. Functioning as a medium of exchange, money eliminates the problems of bartering and permits easy trade and greater specialization, both domestically and internationally.

5. Every economy faces five fundamental questions: (a) What goods and services will be produced? (b) How will the goods and services be produced? (c) Who will get the goods and services? (d) How will the system accommodate change? (e) How will the system promote progress?

6. The market system produces products whose production and sale yield total revenue sufficient to cover total cost. It does not produce products for which total revenue continuously falls short of total cost. Competition forces firms to use the lowest-cost production techniques.

7. Economic profit (total revenue minus total cost) indicates that an industry is prosperous and promotes its expansion. Losses signify that an industry is not prosperous and hasten its contraction.

8. Consumer sovereignty means that both businesses and resource suppliers are subject to the wants of consumers. Through their dollar votes, consumers decide on the composition of output.

9. The prices that a household receives for the resources it supplies to the economy determine that household's income. This income determines the household's claim on the economy's output. Those who have income to spend get the products produced in the market system.

10. By communicating changes in consumer tastes to entrepreneurs and resource suppliers, the market system prompts appropriate adjustments in the allocation of the economy's resources. The market system also encourages technological advance and capital accumulation, both of which raise a nation's standard of living.

11. Competition, the primary mechanism of control in the market economy, promotes a unity of self-interest and social interests. As directed by an invisible hand, competition harnesses the self-interest motives of businesses and resource supplier to further the social interest.

12. The command systems of the Soviet Union and pre-reform China met their demise because of coordination difficulties under central planning and the lack of a profit incentive. The coordination problem resulted in bottlenecks, inefficiencies, and a focus on a limited number of products. The incentive problem discouraged product improvement, new product development, and entrepreneurship.

13. The circular flow model illustrates the flows of resources and products from households to businesses and from businesses to households, along with the corresponding monetary flows. Businesses are on the buying side of the resource market and the selling side of the product market. Households are on the selling side of the resource market and the buying side of the product market.

Terms and Concepts

economic system	competition	consumer sovereignty
command system	market	dollar votes
market system	specialization	creative destruction
private property	division of labor	"invisible hand"
freedom of enterprise	medium of exchange	circular flow diagram
freedom of choice	barter	resource market
self-interest	money	product market

Study Questions

1. Contrast how a market system and a command economy try to cope with economic scarcity. **LO1**

2. How does self-interest help achieve society's economic goals? Why is there such a wide variety of desired goods and services in a market system? In what way are entrepreneurs and businesses at the helm of the economy but commanded by consumers? **LO2**

3. Why is private property, and the protection of property rights, so critical to the success of the market system? **LO2**

4. What are the advantages of using capital in the production process? What is meant by the term "division of labor"? What are the advantages of specialization in the use of human and material resources? Explain why exchange is the necessary consequence of specialization. **LO2**

5. What problem does barter entail? Indicate the economic significance of money as a medium of exchange. What is meant by the statement "We want money only to part with it"? **LO2**

6. Evaluate and explain the following statements: **LO2**
   a. The market system is a profit-and-loss system.
   b. Competition is the disciplinarian of the market economy.

7. In the 1990s thousands of "dot-com" companies emerged with great fanfare to take advantage of the Internet and new information technologies. A few, like Yahoo, eBay, and Amazon, have generally thrived and prospered, but many others struggled and eventually failed. Explain these varied outcomes in terms of how the market system answers the question "What goods and services will be produced?" **LO3**

8. **KEY QUESTION** With current technology, suppose a firm is producing 400 loaves of banana bread daily. Also assume that the least-cost combination of resources in producing those loaves is 5 units of labor, 7 units of land, 2 units of capital, and 1 unit of entrepreneurial ability, selling at prices of $40, $60, $60, and $20, respectively. If the firm can sell these 400 loaves at $2 per unit, will it continue to produce banana bread? If this firm's situation is typical for the other makers of banana bread, will resources flow to or away from this bakery good? **LO3**

9. **KEY QUESTION** Assume that a business firm finds that its profit is greatest when it produces $40 worth of product A. Suppose also that each of the three techniques shown in the table below will produce the desired output: **LO3**
   a. With the resource prices shown, which technique will the firm choose? Why? Will production using that technique entail profit or loss? What will be the amount of that profit or loss? Will the industry expand or contract? When will that expansion or contraction end?
   b. Assume now that a new technique, technique 4, is developed. It combines 2 units of labor, 2 of land, 6 of capital, and 3 of entrepreneurial ability. In view of the resource prices in the table, will the firm adopt the new technique? Explain your answer.
   c. Suppose that an increase in the labor supply causes the price of labor to fall to $1.50 per unit, all other resource prices remaining unchanged. Which technique will the producer now choose? Explain.
   d. "The market system causes the economy to conserve most in the use of resources that are particularly scarce in supply. Resources that are scarcest relative to the demand for them have the highest prices. As a result, producers use these resources as sparingly as is possible." Evaluate this statement. Does your answer to part c, above, bear out this contention? Explain.

		Resource Units Required		
Resource	Price per Unit of Resource	Technique 1	Technique 2	Technique 3
Labor	$3	5	2	3
Land	4	2	4	2
Capital	2	2	4	5
Entrepreneurial ability	2	4	2	4

10. **KEY QUESTION** Some large hardware stores such as Home Depot boast of carrying as many as 20,000 different products

in each store. What motivated the producers of those individual products to make them and offer them for sale? How did the producers decide on the best combinations of resources to use? Who made those resources available, and why? Who decides whether these particular hardware products should continue to be produced and offered for sale? **LO3**

11. What is meant by the term "creative destruction"? How does the emergence of MP3 (iPod) technology relate to this idea? **LO3**

12. In a sentence, describe the meaning of the phrase "invisible hand." **LO4**

13. In market economies, firms rarely worry about the availability of inputs to produce their products, whereas in command economies input availability is a constant concern. Why the difference? **LO4**

14. Distinguish between the resource market and the product market in the circular flow model. In what way are businesses and households both sellers and buyers in this model? What are the flows in the circular flow model? **LO5**

15. **LAST WORD** What explains why millions of economic resources tend to get arranged logically and productively rather than haphazardly and unproductively?

Web-Based Questions

1. **DIAMONDS—INTERESTED IN BUYING ONE?** Go to the Internet auction site eBay at **www.ebay.com** and select the category Jewelry and Watches, followed by Loose Diamonds and Gemstones, and then Diamonds, Natural. How many natural diamonds are for sale at the moment? Note the wide array of sizes and prices of the diamonds. In what sense is there competition among the sellers in this market? How does that competition influence prices? In what sense is there competition among buyers? How does that competition influence prices?

2. **BARTER AND THE IRS** Bartering occurs when goods or services are exchanged without the exchange of money. For some, barter's popularity is that it enables them to avoid paying taxes to the government. How might such avoidance occur? Does the Internal Revenue Service (IRS), **www.irs.ustreas.gov** treat barter as taxable or nontaxable income? (Type "bartering income" in the site's search tool.) How is the value of a barter transaction determined? What are some IRS barter examples? What does the IRS require of the members of so-called barter exchanges?

FURTHER TEST YOUR KNOWLEDGE AT
www.mcconnell18e.com

1 What demand is and what affects it.

2 What supply is and what affects it.

3 How supply and demand together determine market equilibrium.

4 How changes in supply and demand affect equilibrium prices and quantities.

5 What government-set prices are and how they can cause product surpluses and shortages.

6 (Appendix) How supply and demand analysis can add insights on actual-economy situations.

Demand, Supply, and Market Equilibrium

ORIGIN OF THE IDEA
O 3.1
Demand and supply

According to an old joke, if you teach a parrot to say "demand and supply," you have an economist. There is an element of truth in this quip. The tools of demand and supply can take us far in understanding how individual markets work.

Markets

Markets bring together buyers ("demanders") and sellers ("suppliers"), and they exist in many forms. The corner gas station, an e-commerce site, the local music store, a farmer's roadside stand—all are familiar markets. The New York Stock Exchange and the Chicago Board of Trade are markets where buyers and sellers of stocks and bonds and farm commodities from all over the world communicate with one another to buy and sell. Auctioneers bring together potential buyers and sellers of art, livestock, used farm equipment, and, sometimes, real estate. In labor markets, new college graduates "sell" and employers "buy" specific labor services.

Some markets are local; others are national or international. Some are highly personal, involving face-to-face contact between demander and supplier; others are faceless, with buyer and seller never seeing or knowing each other.

To keep things simple, we will focus in this chapter on markets consisting of large numbers of independently acting buyers and sellers of standardized products. These are the highly competitive markets such as a central grain exchange, a stock market, or a market for foreign currencies in which the price is "discovered" through the interacting decisions of buyers and sellers. All such markets involve demand, supply, price, and quantity.

Demand

Demand is a schedule or a curve that shows the various amounts of a product that consumers are willing and able to purchase at each of a series of possible prices during a specified period of time.[1] Demand shows the quantities of a product that will be purchased at various possible prices, *other things equal*. Demand can easily be shown in table form. The table in Figure 3.1 is a hypothetical **demand schedule** for a *single consumer* purchasing bushels of corn.

The table reveals the relationship between the various prices of corn and the quantity of corn a particular consumer would be willing and able to purchase at each of these prices. We say "willing and able" because willingness alone is not effective in the market. You may be willing to buy a plasma television set, but if that willingness is not backed by the necessary dollars, it will not be effective and, therefore, will not be reflected in the market. In the table in Figure 3.1, if the price of corn were $5 per bushel, our consumer would be willing and able to buy 10 bushels per week; if it were $4, the consumer would be willing and able to buy 20 bushels per week; and so forth.

The table does not tell us which of the five possible prices will actually exist in the corn market. That depends

---

[1]This definition obviously is worded to apply to product markets. To adjust it to apply to resource markets, substitute the word "resource" for "product" and the word "businesses" for "consumers."

FIGURE 3.1 An individual buyer's demand for corn. Because price and quantity demanded are inversely related, an individual's demand schedule graphs as a downsloping curve such as *D*. Other things equal, consumers will buy more of a product as its price declines and less of the product as its price rises. (Here and in later figures, *P* stands for price and *Q* stands for quantity demanded or supplied.)

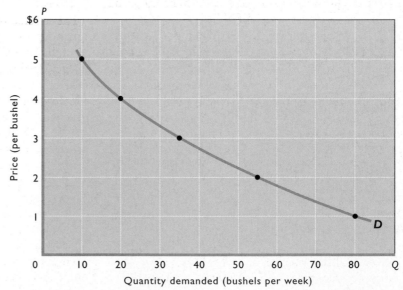

Demand for Corn	
Price per Bushel	Quantity Demanded per Week
$5	10
4	20
3	35
2	55
1	80

on the interaction between demand and supply. Demand is simply a statement of a buyer's plans, or intentions, with respect to the purchase of a product.

To be meaningful, the quantities demanded at each price must relate to a specific period—a day, a week, a month. Saying "A consumer will buy 10 bushels of corn at $5 per bushel" is meaningless. Saying "A consumer will buy 10 bushels of corn per week at $5 per bushel" is meaningful. Unless a specific time period is stated, we do not know whether the demand for a product is large or small.

Law of Demand

A fundamental characteristic of demand is this: Other things equal, as price falls, the quantity demanded rises, and as price rises, the quantity demanded falls. In short, there is a negative or *inverse* relationship between price and quantity demanded. Economists call this inverse relationship the **law of demand.**

ORIGIN OF THE IDEA
O 3.2
Law of demand

The other-things-equal assumption is critical here. Many factors other than the price of the product being considered affect the amount purchased. For example, the quantity of Nikes purchased will depend not only on the price of Nikes but also on the prices of such substitutes as Reeboks, Adidas, and New Balances. The law of demand in this case says that fewer Nikes will be purchased if the price of Nikes rises and if the prices of Reeboks, Adidas, and New Balances all remain constant. In short, if the *relative price* of Nikes rises, fewer Nikes will be bought. However, if the price of Nikes and the prices of all other competing shoes increase by some amount—say, $5—consumers might buy more, less, or the same number of Nikes.

Why the inverse relationship between price and quantity demanded? Let's look at three explanations, beginning with the simplest one:

- The law of demand is consistent with common sense. People ordinarily *do* buy more of a product at a low price than at a high price. Price is an obstacle that deters consumers from buying. The higher that obstacle, the less of a product they will buy; the lower the price obstacle, the more they will buy. The fact that businesses have "sales" is evidence of their belief in the law of demand.

- In any specific time period, each buyer of a product will derive less satisfaction (or benefit, or utility) from each successive unit of the product consumed. The second Big Mac will yield less satisfaction to the consumer than the first, and the third still less than

ORIGIN OF THE IDEA
O 3.3
Diminishing marginal utility

the second. That is, consumption is subject to **diminishing marginal utility.** And because successive units of a particular product yield less and less marginal utility, consumers will buy additional units only if the price of those units is progressively reduced.

- We can also explain the law of demand in terms of income and substitution effects. The **income effect** indicates that a lower price increases the purchasing power of a buyer's money income, enabling the buyer to purchase more of the product than before. A higher price has the opposite effect. The **substitution effect** suggests that at a lower price buyers have the incentive to substitute what is now a less expensive product for similar products that are now *relatively* more expensive. The product whose price has fallen is now "a better deal" relative to the other products.

For example, a decline in the price of chicken will increase the purchasing power of consumer incomes, enabling people to buy more chicken (the income effect). At a lower price,

ORIGIN OF THE IDEA
O 3.4
Income and substitution effects

chicken is relatively more attractive and consumers tend to substitute it for pork, lamb, beef, and fish (the substitution effect). The income and substitution effects combine to make consumers able and willing to buy more of a product at a low price than at a high price.

The Demand Curve

The inverse relationship between price and quantity demanded for any product can be represented on a simple graph, in which, by convention, we measure *quantity demanded* on the horizontal axis and *price* on the vertical axis. In the graph in Figure 3.1 we have plotted the five price-quantity data points listed in the accompanying table and connected the points with a smooth curve, labeled *D*. Such a curve is called a **demand curve.** Its downward slope reflects the law of demand—people buy more of a product, service, or resource as its price falls. The relationship between price and quantity demanded is inverse (or negative).

The table and graph in Figure 3.1 contain exactly the same data and reflect the same relationship between price and quantity demanded. But the graph shows that relationship much more simply and clearly than a table or a description in words.

Market Demand

So far, we have concentrated on just one consumer. But competition requires that more than one buyer be present in each market. By adding the quantities demanded by all consumers at each of the various possible prices, we can get from *individual* demand to *market* demand. If there are just three buyers in the market, as represented in the table in Figure 3.2, it is relatively easy to determine the total quantity demanded at each price. Figure 3.2 shows the graphical summing procedure: At each price we sum horizontally the quantities demanded by Joe, Jen, and Jay to obtain the total quantity demanded at that price; we then plot the price and the total quantity demanded as one point on the market demand curve.

Competition, of course, ordinarily entails many more than three buyers of a product. To avoid hundreds or thousands or millions of additions, we suppose that all the buyers in a market are willing and able to buy the same amounts at each of the possible prices. Then we just multiply those amounts by the number of buyers to obtain the market demand. That is how we arrived at the demand schedule and demand curve D_1 in Figure 3.3 for a market of 200 corn buyers, each with a demand as shown in the table in Figure 3.1.

In constructing a demand curve such as D_1 in Figure 3.3, economists assume that price is the most important influence on the amount of any product purchased. But economists know that other factors can and do affect purchases. These factors, called **determinants of demand,** are assumed to be constant when a demand curve like D_1 is drawn. They are the "other things equal" in the relationship between price and quantity demanded. When any of these determinants changes, the demand curve will shift to the right or left. For this reason, determinants of demand are sometimes referred to as *demand shifters*.

The basic determinants of demand are (1) consumers' tastes (preferences), (2) the number of buyers in the market, (3) consumers' incomes, (4) the prices of related goods, and (5) consumer expectations.

Change in Demand

A change in one or more of the determinants of demand will change the demand data (the demand schedule) in the table accompanying Figure 3.3 and therefore the location of the demand curve there. A change in the demand schedule or, graphically, a shift in the demand curve is called a *change in demand*.

If consumers desire to buy more corn at each possible price than is reflected in column 2 in the table in Figure 3.3, that *increase in demand* is shown as a shift of the demand curve to the right, say, from D_1 to D_2. Conversely, a *decrease in demand* occurs when consumers buy less corn

FIGURE 3.2 Market demand for corn, three buyers. The market demand curve D is the horizontal summation of the individual demand curves (D_1, D_2, and D_3) of all the consumers in the market. At the price of $3, for example, the three individual curves yield a total quantity demanded of 100 bushels.

Market Demand for Corn, Three Buyers							
Price per Bushel	Quantity Demanded						Total Quantity Demanded per Week
	Joe		Jen		Jay		
$5	10	+	12	+	8	=	30
4	20	+	23	+	17	=	60
3	35	+	39	+	26	=	100
2	55	+	60	+	39	=	154
1	80	+	87	+	54	=	221

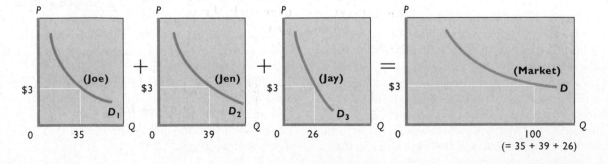

FIGURE 3.3 Changes in the demand for corn. A change in one or more of the determinants of demand causes a change in demand. An increase in demand is shown as a shift of the demand curve to the right, as from D_1 to D_2. A decrease in demand is shown as a shift of the demand curve to the left, as from D_1 to D_3. These changes in demand are to be distinguished from a change in quantity demanded, which is caused by a change in the price of the product, as shown by a movement from, say, point *a* to point *b* on fixed demand curve D_1.

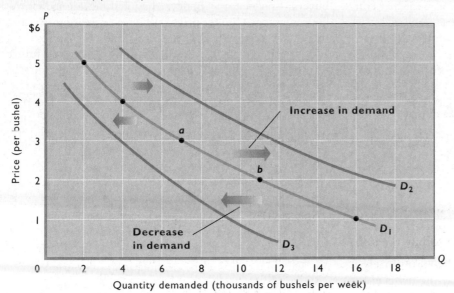

Market Demand for Corn, 200 Buyers, (D_1)	
(1) Price per Bushel	(2) Total Quantity Demanded per Week
$5	2,000
4	4,000
3	7,000
2	11,000
1	16,000

at each possible price than is indicated in column 2. The leftward shift of the demand curve from D_1 to D_3 in Figure 3.3 shows that situation.

Now let's see how changes in each determinant affect demand.

Tastes A favorable change in consumer tastes (preferences) for a product—a change that makes the product more desirable—means that more of it will be demanded at each price. Demand will increase; the demand curve will shift rightward. An unfavorable change in consumer preferences will decrease demand, shifting the demand curve to the left.

New products may affect consumer tastes; for example, the introduction of digital cameras greatly decreased the demand for film cameras. Consumers' concern over the health hazards of cholesterol and obesity have increased the demand for broccoli, low-calorie beverages, and fresh fruit while decreasing the demand for beef, veal, eggs, and whole milk. Over the past several years, the demand for coffee drinks and table wine has greatly increased, driven by a change in tastes. So, too, has the demand for DVDs and iPhones.

Number of Buyers An increase in the number of buyers in a market is likely to increase product demand; a decrease in the number of buyers will probably decrease demand. For example, the rising number of older per-

sons in the United States in recent years has increased the demand for motor homes, medical care, and retirement communities. Large-scale immigration from Mexico has greatly increased the demand for a range of goods and services in the Southwest, including Mexican food products in local grocery stores. Improvements in communications have given financial markets international range and have thus increased the demand for stocks and bonds. International trade agreements have reduced foreign trade barriers to American farm commodities, increasing the number of buyers and therefore the demand for those products.

In contrast, emigration (out-migration) from many small rural communities has reduced the population and thus the demand for housing, home appliances, and auto repair in those towns.

Income How changes in income affect demand is a more complex matter. For most products, a rise in income causes an increase in demand. Consumers typically buy more steaks, furniture, and electronic equipment as their incomes increase. Conversely, the demand for such products declines as their incomes fall. Products whose demand varies *directly* with money income are called *superior goods*, or **normal goods.**

Although most products are normal goods, there are some exceptions. As incomes increase beyond some point, the demand for used clothing, retread tires, and third-hand automobiles may decrease, because the higher incomes enable consumers to buy new versions of those products. Rising incomes may also decrease the demand for soy-enhanced hamburger. Similarly, rising incomes may cause the demand for charcoal grills to decline as wealthier consumers switch to gas grills. Goods whose demand varies *inversely* with money income are called **inferior goods.**

Prices of Related Goods

A change in the price of a related good may either increase or decrease the demand for a product, depending on whether the related good is a substitute or a complement:

- A **substitute good** is one that can be used in place of another good.
- A **complementary good** is one that is used together with another good.

Substitutes

Häagen-Dazs ice cream and Ben & Jerry's ice cream are substitute goods or, simply, *substitutes*. When two products are substitutes, an increase in the price of one will increase the demand for the other. Conversely, a decrease in the price of one will decrease the demand for the other. For example, when the price of Häagen-Dazs ice cream rises, consumers will buy less of it and increase their demand for Ben & Jerry's ice cream. When the price of Colgate toothpaste declines, the demand for Crest decreases. So it is with other product pairs such as Nikes and Reeboks, Budweiser and Miller beer, or Chevrolets and Fords. They are *substitutes in consumption*.

Complements

Because complementary goods (or, simply, *complements*) are used together, they are typically demanded jointly. Examples include computers and software, cell phones and cellular service, and snowboards and lift tickets. If the price of a complement (for example, lettuce) goes up, the demand for the related good (salad dressing) will decline. Conversely, if the price of a complement (for example, tuition) falls, the demand for a related good (textbooks) will increase.

Unrelated Goods

The vast majority of goods are not related to one another and are called *independent goods*. Examples are butter and golf balls, potatoes and automobiles, and bananas and wristwatches. A change in the price of one has little or no effect on the demand for the other.

Consumer Expectations

Changes in consumer expectations may shift demand. A newly formed expectation of higher future prices may cause consumers to buy now in order to "beat" the anticipated price rises, thus increasing current demand. That is often what happens in so-called hot real estate markets. Buyers rush in because they think the price of new homes will continue to escalate rapidly. Some buyers fear being "priced out of the market" and therefore not obtaining the home they desire. Other buyers—speculators—believe they will be able to sell the houses later at a higher price. Whichever their motivation, these buyers increase the current demand for houses.

Similarly, a change in expectations concerning future income may prompt consumers to change their current spending. For example, first-round NFL draft choices may splurge on new luxury cars in anticipation of a lucrative professional football contract. Or workers who become fearful of losing their jobs may reduce their demand for, say, vacation travel.

In summary, an *increase* in demand—the decision by consumers to buy larger quantities of a product at each possible price—may be caused by

- A favorable change in consumer tastes.
- An increase in the number of buyers.
- Rising incomes if the product is a normal good.
- Falling incomes if the product is an inferior good.
- An increase in the price of a substitute good.
- A decrease in the price of a complementary good.
- A new consumer expectation that either prices or income will be higher in the future.

You should "reverse" these generalizations to explain a *decrease* in demand. Table 3.1 provides additional illustrations of the determinants of demand. **(Key Question 3)**

TABLE 3.1 Determinants of Demand: Factors That Shift the Demand Curve

Determinant	Examples
Change in buyer tastes	Physical fitness rises in popularity, increasing the demand for jogging shoes and bicycles; cell phone popularity rises, reducing the demand for traditional land phones.
Change in number of buyers	A decline in the birthrate reduces the demand for children's toys.
Change in income	A rise in incomes increases the demand for normal goods such as restaurant meals, sports tickets, and necklaces while reducing the demand for inferior goods such as cabbage, turnips, and inexpensive wine.
Change in the prices of related goods	A reduction in airfares reduces the demand for bus transportation (substitute goods); a decline in the price of DVD players increases the demand for DVD movies (complementary goods).
Change in consumer expectations	Inclement weather in South America creates an expectation of higher future prices of coffee beans, thereby increasing today's demand for coffee beans.

Changes in Quantity Demanded

A *change in demand* must not be confused with a *change in quantity demanded*. A **change in demand** is a shift of the demand curve to the right (an increase in demand) or to the left (a decrease in demand). It occurs because the consumer's state of mind about purchasing the product has been altered in response to a change in one or more of the determinants of demand. Recall that "demand" is a schedule or a curve; therefore, a "change in demand" means a change in the schedule and a shift of the curve.

In contrast, a **change in quantity demanded** is a movement from one point to another point—from one price-quantity combination to another—on a fixed demand schedule or demand curve. The cause of such a change is an increase or decrease in the price of the product under consideration. In the table in Figure 3.3, for example, a decline in the price of corn from $5 to $4 will increase the quantity of corn demanded from 2000 to 4000 bushels.

In Figure 3.3 the shift of the demand curve D_1 to either D_2 or D_3 is a change in demand. But the movement from point *a* to point *b* on curve D_1 represents a change in quantity demanded: Demand has not changed; it is the entire curve, and it remains fixed in place.

QUICK REVIEW 3.1

- Demand is a schedule or a curve showing the amount of a product that buyers are willing and able to purchase, in a particular time period, at each possible price in a series of prices.
- The law of demand states that, other things equal, the quantity of a good purchased varies inversely with its price.
- The demand curve shifts because of changes in (a) consumer tastes, (b) the number of buyers in the market, (c) consumer income, (d) the prices of substitute or complementary goods, and (e) consumer expectations.
- A change in demand is a shift of the demand curve; a change in quantity demanded is a movement from one point to another on a fixed demand curve.

Supply

Supply is a schedule or curve showing the various amounts of a product that producers are willing and able to make available for sale at each of a series of possible prices during a specific period.[2] The table in Figure 3.4 is a hypothetical

---

[2]This definition is worded to apply to product markets. To adjust it to apply to resource markets, substitute "resource" for "product" and "owners" for "producers."

supply schedule for a single producer of corn. It shows the quantities of corn that will be supplied at various prices, other things equal.

Law of Supply

The table in Figure 3.4 shows a positive or direct relationship that prevails between price and quantity supplied. As price rises, the quantity supplied rises; as price falls, the quantity supplied falls. This relationship is called the **law of supply**. A supply schedule tells us that, other things equal, firms will produce and offer for sale more of their product at a high price than at a low price. This, again, is basically common sense.

Price is an obstacle from the standpoint of the consumer, who is on the paying end. The higher the price, the less the consumer will buy. But the supplier is on the receiving end of the product's price. To a supplier, price represents *revenue*, which serves as an incentive to produce and sell a product. The higher the price, the greater this incentive and the greater the quantity supplied.

Consider a farmer who is deciding on how much corn to plant. As corn prices rise, as shown in the table in Figure 3.4, the farmer finds it profitable to plant more corn. And the higher corn prices enable the farmer to cover the increased costs associated with more intensive cultivation and the use of more seed, fertilizer, and pesticides. The overall result is more corn.

Now consider a manufacturer. Beyond some quantity of production, manufacturers usually encounter increases in *marginal cost*—the added cost of producing one more unit of output. Certain productive resources—in particular, the firm's plant and machinery—cannot be expanded quickly, so the firm uses more of other resources such as labor to produce more output. But as labor becomes more abundant relative to the fixed plant and equipment, the additional workers have relatively less space and access to equipment. For example, the added workers may have to wait to gain access to machines. As a result, each added worker produces less added output, and the marginal cost of successive units of output rises accordingly. The firm will not produce the more costly units unless it receives a higher price for them. Again, price and quantity supplied are directly related.

The Supply Curve

As with demand, it is convenient to represent individual supply graphically. In Figure 3.4, curve S is the **supply curve** that corresponds with the price–quantity supplied data in the accompanying table. The upward slope of the curve reflects the law of supply—producers offer more of

FIGURE 3.4 An individual producer's supply of corn. Because price and quantity supplied are directly related, the supply curve for an individual producer graphs as an upsloping curve. Other things equal, producers will offer more of a product for sale as its price rises and less of the product for sale as its price falls.

Supply of Corn	
Price per Bushel	Quantity Supplied per Week
$5	60
4	50
3	35
2	20
1	5

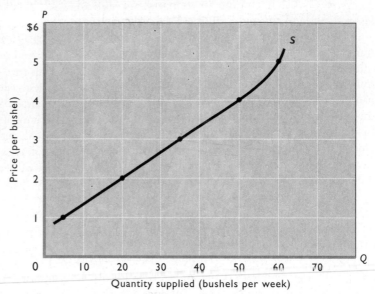

Quantity supplied (bushels per week)

a good, service, or resource for sale as its price rises. The relationship between price and quantity supplied is positive, or direct.

Market Supply

Market supply is derived from individual supply in exactly the same way that market demand is derived from individual demand. We sum the quantities supplied by each producer at each price. That is, we obtain the market supply curve by "horizontally adding" the supply curves of the individual producers. The price–quantity supplied data in the table accompanying Figure 3.5 are for an assumed 200 identical producers in the market, each willing to supply corn according to the supply schedule shown in Figure 3.4. Curve S_1 in Figure 3.5 is a graph of the market supply data. Note that the values of the axes in Figure 3.5 are the same as those used in our graph of market demand (Figure 3.3). The only difference is that we change the label on the horizontal axis from "quantity demanded" to "quantity supplied."

Determinants of Supply

In constructing a supply curve, we assume that price is the most significant influence on the quantity supplied of any product. But other factors (the "other things equal") can and do affect supply. The supply curve is drawn on the assumption that these other things are fixed and do not change. If one of them does change, a *change in supply* will occur, meaning that the entire supply curve will shift.

The basic **determinants of supply** are (1) resource prices, (2) technology, (3) taxes and subsidies, (4) prices of other goods, (5) producer expectations, and (6) the number of sellers in the market. A change in any one or more of these determinants of supply, or *supply shifters*, will move the supply curve for a product either right or left. A shift to the *right*, as from S_1 to S_2 in Figure 3.5, signifies an *increase* in supply: Producers supply larger quantities of the product at each possible price. A shift to the *left*, as from S_1 to S_3, indicates a *decrease* in supply: Producers offer less output at each price.

Changes in Supply

Let's consider how changes in each of the determinants affect supply. The key idea is that costs are a major factor underlying supply curves; anything that affects costs (other than changes in output itself) usually shifts the supply curve.

Resource Prices The prices of the resources used in the production process help determine the costs of production incurred by firms. Higher *resource* prices raise production costs and, assuming a particular *product* price, squeeze profits. That reduction in profits reduces the incentive for firms to supply output at each product price. For example, an increase in the prices of sand, crushed rock, and Portland cement will increase the cost of producing concrete and reduce its supply.

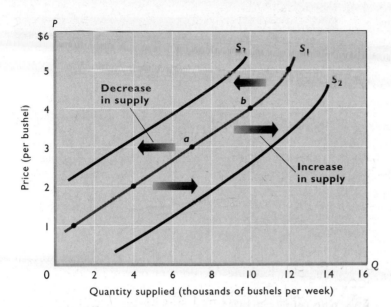

FIGURE 3.5 Changes in the supply of corn. A change in one or more of the determinants of supply causes a change in supply An increase in supply is shown as a rightward shift of the supply curve, as from S_1 to S_2. A decrease in supply is depicted as a leftward shift of the curve, as from S_1 to S_3. In contrast, a change in the *quantity supplied* is caused by a change in the product's price and is shown by a movement from one point to another, as from *b* to *a* on fixed supply curve S_1.

Market Supply of Corn, 200 Producers, (S_1)	
(1) Price per Bushel	(2) Total Quantity Supplied per Week
$5	12,000
4	10,000
3	7,000
2	4,000
1	1,000

In contrast, lower *resource* prices reduce production costs and increase profits. So when resource prices fall, firms supply greater output at each product price. For example, a decrease in the price of flat-panel glass will increase the supply of big-screen television sets.

Technology Improvements in technology (techniques of production) enable firms to produce units of output with fewer resources. Because resources are costly, using fewer of them lowers production costs and increases supply. Example: Technological advances in producing flat-panel computer monitors have greatly reduced their cost. Thus, manufacturers will now offer more such monitors than previously at the various prices; the supply of flat-panel monitors has increased.

Taxes and Subsidies Businesses treat most taxes as costs. An increase in sales or property taxes will increase production costs and reduce supply. In contrast, subsidies are "taxes in reverse." If the government subsidizes the production of a good, it in effect lowers the producers' costs and increases supply.

Prices of Other Goods Firms that produce a particular product, say, soccer balls, can sometimes use their plant and equipment to produce alternative goods, say, basketballs and volleyballs. The higher prices of these "other goods" may entice soccer ball producers to switch production to those other goods in order to increase profits. This *substitution in production* results in a

decline in the supply of soccer balls. Alternatively, when the prices of basketballs and volleyballs decline relative to the price of soccer balls, producers of those goods may decide to produce more soccer balls instead, increasing their supply.

Producer Expectations Changes in expectations about the future price of a product may affect the producer's current willingness to supply that product. It is difficult, however, to generalize about how a new expectation of higher prices affects the present supply of a product. Farmers anticipating a higher wheat price in the future might withhold some of their current wheat harvest from the market, thereby causing a decrease in the current supply of wheat. In contrast, in many types of manufacturing industries, newly formed expectations that price will increase may induce firms to add another shift of workers or to expand their production facilities, causing current supply to increase.

Number of Sellers Other things equal, the larger the number of suppliers, the greater the market supply. As more firms enter an industry, the supply curve shifts to the right. Conversely, the smaller the number of firms in the industry, the less the market supply. This means that as firms leave an industry, the supply curve shifts to the left. Example: The United States and Canada have imposed restrictions on haddock fishing to replenish dwindling stocks. As part of that policy, the Federal government has bought the boats of some of the haddock fishers as a way of putting

TABLE 3.2 **Determinants of Supply: Factors That Shift the Supply Curve**

Determinant	Examples
Change in resource prices	A decrease in the price of microchips increases the supply of computers; an increase in the price of crude oil reduces the supply of gasoline.
Change in technology	The development of more effective wireless technology increases the supply of cell phones.
Changes in taxes and subsidies	An increase in the excise tax on cigarettes reduces the supply of cigarettes; a decline in subsidies to state universities reduces the supply of higher education.
Change in prices of other goods	An increase in the price of cucumbers decreases the supply of watermelons.
Change in producer expectations	An expectation of a substantial rise in future log prices decreases the supply of logs today.
Change in number of suppliers	An increase in the number of tatoo parlors increases the supply of tatoos; the formation of women's professional basketball leagues increases the supply of women's professional basketball games.

them out of business and decreasing the catch. The result has been a decline in the market supply of haddock.

Table 3.2 is a checklist of the determinants of supply, along with further illustrations. **(Key Question 6)**

Changes in Quantity Supplied

The distinction between a *change in supply* and a *change in quantity supplied* parallels the distinction between a change in demand and a change in quantity demanded. Because supply is a schedule or curve, a **change in supply** means a change in the schedule and a shift of the curve. An increase in supply shifts the curve to the right; a decrease in supply shifts it to the left. The cause of a change in supply is a change in one or more of the determinants of supply.

In contrast, a **change in quantity supplied** is a movement from one point to another on a fixed supply curve. The cause of such a movement is a change in the price of the specific product being considered.

Consider supply curve S_1 in Figure 3.5. A decline in the price of corn from \$4 to \$3 decreases the quantity of corn supplied per week from 10,000 to 7000 bushels. This movement from point *b* to point *a* along S_1 is a change in quantity supplied, not a change in supply. Supply is the full schedule of prices and quantities shown, and this schedule does not change when the price of corn changes.

Market Equilibrium

With our understanding of demand and supply, we can now show how the decisions of buyers of corn interact with the decisions of sellers to determine the equilibrium price and quantity of corn. In the table in Figure 3.6, columns 1 and 2 repeat the market supply of corn (from the table in Figure 3.5), and columns 2 and 3 repeat the market demand for corn (from the table in Figure 3.3). We assume this is a competitive market so that neither buyers nor sellers can set the price.

Equilibrium Price and Quantity

We are looking for the equilibrium price and equilibrium quantity. The **equilibrium price** (or *market-clearing price*) is the price where the intentions of buyers and sellers match. It is the price where quantity demanded equals quantity supplied. The table in Figure 3.6 reveals that at \$3, *and only at that price*, the number of bushels of corn that sellers wish to sell (7000) is identical to the number consumers want to buy (also 7000). At \$3 and 7000 bushels of corn, there is neither a shortage nor a surplus of corn. So 7000 bushels of corn is the **equilibrium quantity:** the quantity demanded and quantity supplied at the equilibrium price in a competitive market.

INTERACTIVE GRAPHS

G 3.1

Supply and demand

Graphically, the equilibrium price is indicated by the intersection of the supply curve and the demand curve in **Figure 3.6 (Key Graph).** (The horizontal axis now measures both quantity demanded and quantity supplied.) With neither a shortage nor a surplus at \$3, the market is in equilibrium, meaning "in balance" or "at rest."

Competition among buyers and among sellers drives the price to the equilibrium price; once there, it remains unless it is subsequently disturbed by changes in demand or supply (shifts of the curves). To better understand the

key graph

FIGURE 3.6 Equilibrium price and quantity. The intersection of the downsloping demand curve *D* and the upsloping supply curve *S* indicates the equilibrium price and quantity, here $3 and 7000 bushels of corn. The shortages of corn at below-equilibrium prices (for example, 7000 bushels at $2) drive up price. The higher prices increase the quantity supplied and reduce the quantity demanded until equilibrium is achieved. The surpluses caused by above-equilibrium prices (for example, 6000 bushels at $4) push price down. As price drops, the quantity demanded rises and the quantity supplied falls until equilibrium is established. At the equilibrium price and quantity, there are neither shortages nor surpluses of corn.

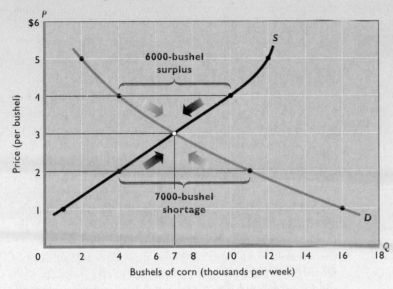

Market Supply of and Demand for Corn			
(1) Total Quantity Supplied per Week	**(2)** Price per Bushel	**(3)** Total Quantity Demanded per Week	**(4)** Surplus (+) or Shortage (−)*
12,000	$5	2,000	+10,000 ↓
10,000	4	4,000	+6,000 ↓
7,000	**3**	**7,000**	**0**
4,000	2	11,000	−7,000 ↑
1,000	1	16,000	−15,000 ↑

*Arrows indicate the effect on price.

QUICK QUIZ FOR FIGURE 3.6

1. Demand curve *D* is downsloping because
   a. producers offer less of a product for sale as the price of the product falls.
   b. lower prices of a product create income and substitution effects that lead consumers to purchase more of it.
   c. the larger the number of buyers in a market, the lower the product price.
   d. price and quantity demanded are directly (positively) related.

2. Supply curve *S*
   a. reflects an inverse (negative) relationship between price and quantity supplied.
   b. reflects a direct (positive) relationship between price and quantity supplied.
   c. depicts the collective behavior of buyers in this market.

   d. shows that producers will offer more of a product for sale at a low product price than at a high product price.

3. At the $3 price:
   a. quantity supplied exceeds quantity demanded.
   b. quantity demanded exceeds quantity supplied.
   c. the product is abundant and a surplus exists.
   d. there is no pressure on price to rise or fall.

4. At price $5 in this market:
   a. there will be a shortage of 10,000 units.
   b. there will be a surplus of 10,000 units.
   c. quantity demanded will be 12,000 units.
   d. quantity demanded will equal quantity supplied.

Answers: 1. b; 2. b; 3. d; 4. b

uniqueness of the equilibrium price, let's consider other prices. At any above-equilibrium price, quantity supplied exceeds quantity demanded. For example, at the $4 price, sellers will offer 10,000 bushels of corn, but buyers will purchase only 4000. The $4 price encourages sellers to offer lots of corn but discourages many consumers from buying it. The result is a **surplus** (or *excess supply*) of 6000 bushels. If corn sellers produced them all, they would find themselves with 6000 unsold bushels of corn.

Surpluses drive prices down. Even if the $4 price existed temporarily, it could not persist. The large surplus would prompt competing sellers to lower the price to encourage buyers to take the surplus off their hands. As the price fell, the incentive to produce corn would decline and the incentive for consumers to buy corn would increase. As shown in Figure 3.6, the market would move to its equilibrium at $3.

Any price below the $3 equilibrium price would create a shortage; quantity demanded would exceed quantity supplied. Consider a $2 price, for example. We see both from column 2 of the table and from the demand curve in Figure 3.6 that quantity demanded exceeds quantity supplied at that price. The result is a **shortage** (or *excess demand*) of 7000 bushels of corn. The $2 price discourages sellers from devoting resources to corn and encourages

---

CONSIDER THIS . . .

Ticket Scalping: A Bum Rap!

Ticket prices for athletic events and musical concerts are usually set far in advance of the events. Sometimes the original ticket price is too low to be the equilibrium price. Lines form at the ticket window and a severe shortage of tickets occurs at the printed price. What happens next? Buyers who are willing to pay more than the original price bid up the ticket price in resale ticket markets.

Tickets sometimes get resold for much greater amounts than the original price—market transactions known as "scalping." For example, an original buyer may resell a $75 ticket to a concert for $200, $250, or more. Reporters sometimes denounce scalpers for "ripping off" buyers by charging "exorbitant" prices.

But is scalping really a rip-off? We must first recognize that such ticket resales are voluntary transactions. If both buyer and seller did not expect to gain from the exchange, it would not occur! The seller must value the $200 more than seeing the event, and the buyer must value seeing the event at $200 or more. So there are no losers or victims here: Both buyer and seller benefit from the transaction. The scalping market simply redistributes assets (game or concert tickets) from those who would rather have the money (and the other things that the money can buy) to those who would rather have the tickets.

Does scalping impose losses or injury on the sponsors of the event? If the sponsors are injured, it is because they initially priced tickets below the equilibrium level. Perhaps they did this to create a long waiting line and the attendant news media publicity. Alternatively, they may have had a genuine desire to keep tickets affordable for lower-income, ardent fans. In either case, the event sponsors suffer an opportunity cost in the form of less ticket revenue than they might have otherwise received. But such losses are self-inflicted and separate and distinct from the fact that some tickets are later resold at a higher price.

So is ticket scalping undesirable? Not on economic grounds! It is an entirely voluntary activity that benefits both sellers and buyers.

---

consumers to desire more bushels than are available. The $2 price cannot persist as the equilibrium price. Many consumers who want to buy corn at this price will not obtain it. They will express a willingness to pay more than $2 to get corn. Competition among these buyers will drive up the price, eventually to the $3 equilibrium level. Unless disrupted by changes of supply or demand, this $3 price of corn will continue to prevail.

Rationing Function of Prices

The ability of the competitive forces of supply and demand to establish a price at which selling and buying decisions are consistent is called the rationing function of prices. In our case, the equilibrium price of $3 clears the market, leaving no burdensome surplus for sellers and no inconvenient shortage for potential buyers. And it is the combination of freely made individual decisions that sets this market-clearing price. In effect, the market outcome says that all buyers who are willing and able to pay $3 for a bushel of corn will obtain it; all buyers who cannot or will not pay $3 will go without corn. Similarly, all producers who are willing and able to offer corn for sale at $3 a bushel will sell it; all producers who cannot or will not sell for $3 per bushel will not sell their product. **(Key Question 8)**

Efficient Allocation

A competitive market such as that we have described not only rations goods to consumers but also allocates society's resources efficiently to the particular product. Competition among corn producers forces them to use the best technology and right mix of productive resources. Otherwise, their costs will be too high relative to the market price and they will be unprofitable. The result is **productive efficiency:** the production of any particular good in the least costly way. When society produces corn at the lowest achievable per-unit cost, it is expending the least-valued combination of resources to produce that product and therefore is making available more-valued resources to produce other desired goods. Suppose society has only $100 worth of resources available. If it can produce a bushel of corn using $3 of those resources, then it will have available $97 of resources remaining to produce other goods. This is clearly better than producing the corn for $5 and having only $95 of resources available for the alternative uses.

Competitive markets also produce **allocative efficiency:** the *particular mix* of goods and services most highly valued by society (minimum-cost production assumed). For example, society wants land suitable for growing corn used for that purpose, not to grow dandelions. It wants diamonds to be used for jewelry, not crushed up and used as an additive to give concrete more sparkle. It wants MP3 players and iPods, not cassette players and tapes. Moreover, society does not want to devote all its resources to corn, diamonds, and portable digital music players. It wants to assign some resources to wheat, gasoline, and cell phones. Competitive markets make those allocatively efficient assignments.

The equilibrium price and quantity in competitive markets usually produce an assignment of resources that is "right" from an economic perspective. Demand essentially reflects the marginal benefit (MB) of the good, based on the utility received. Supply reflects the marginal cost (MC) of producing the good. The market ensures that firms produce all units of goods for which MB exceeds MC and no units for which MC exceeds MB. At the intersection of the demand and supply curves, MB equals MC and allocative efficiency results. As economists say, there is neither an "underallocaton of resources" nor an "overallocation of resources" to the product.

Changes in Supply, Demand, and Equilibrium

We know that demand might change because of fluctuations in consumer tastes or incomes, changes in consumer expectations, or variations in the prices of related goods. Supply might change in response to changes in resource prices, technology, or taxes. What effects will such changes in supply and demand have on equilibrium price and quantity?

Changes in Demand Suppose that the supply of some good (for example, health care) is constant and demand increases, as shown in Figure 3.7a. As a result, the new intersection of the supply and demand curves is at higher values on both the price and the quantity axes. Clearly, an increase in demand raises both equilibrium price and equilibrium quantity. Conversely, a decrease in demand such as that shown in Figure 3.7b reduces both equilibrium price and equilibrium quantity. (The value of graphical analysis is now apparent: We need not fumble with columns of figures to determine the outcomes; we need only compare the new and the old points of intersection on the graph.)

Changes in Supply What happens if the demand for some good (for example, flash drives) is constant but supply increases, as in Figure 3.7c? The new intersection of supply and demand is located at a lower equilibrium price but at a higher equilibrium quantity. An increase in supply reduces equilibrium price but increases equilibrium quantity. In contrast, if supply decreases, as in Figure 3.7d, the equilibrium price rises while the equilibrium quantity declines.

Complex Cases When both supply and demand change, the effect is a combination of the individual effects.

Supply Increase; Demand Decrease What effect will a supply increase and a demand decrease for some good (for example, apples) have on equilibrium price? Both changes decrease price, so the net result is a price drop greater than that resulting from either change alone.

What about equilibrium quantity? Here the effects of the changes in supply and demand are opposed: the increase in supply increases equilibrium quantity, but the decrease in demand reduces it. The direction of the change in quantity depends on the relative sizes of the changes in supply and demand. If the increase in supply is larger than the decrease in demand, the equilibrium quantity will increase. But if the decrease in demand is greater than the increase in supply, the equilibrium quantity will decrease.

Supply Decrease; Demand Increase A decrease in supply and an increase in demand for some good (for example, gasoline) both increase price. Their combined effect is an increase in equilibrium price greater than that caused by either change separately. But their effect on equilibrium quantity is again indeterminate, depending on the relative sizes of the changes in supply and demand. If the decrease in supply is larger than the increase in demand, the equilibrium quantity will decrease. In contrast, if the increase in demand is greater than the decrease in supply, the equilibrium quantity will increase.

Supply Increase; Demand Increase What if supply and demand both increase for some good (for example, cell phones)? A supply increase drops equilibrium price, while a demand increase boosts it. If the increase in supply is greater than the increase in demand, the equilibrium price will fall. If the opposite holds, the equilibrium price will rise.

The effect on equilibrium quantity is certain: The increases in supply and in demand each raises equilibrium quantity. Therefore, the equilibrium quantity will increase by an amount greater than that caused by either change alone.

Supply Decrease; Demand Decrease What about decreases in both supply and demand for some good (for example, new homes)? If the decrease in supply is greater

FIGURE 3.7 Changes in demand and supply and the effects on price and quantity. The increase in demand from D_1 to D_2 in (a) increases both equilibrium price and equilibrium quantity. The decrease in demand from D_3 to D_4 in (b) decreases both equilibrium price and equilibrium quantity. The increase in supply from S_1 to S_2 in (c) decreases equilibrium price and increases equilibrium quantity. The decline in supply from S_3 to S_4 in (d) increases equilibrium price and decreases equilibrium quantity. The boxes in the top right corners summarize the respective changes and outcomes. The upward arrows in the boxes signify increases in equilibrium price (P) and equilibrium quantity (Q); the downward arrows signify decreases in these items.

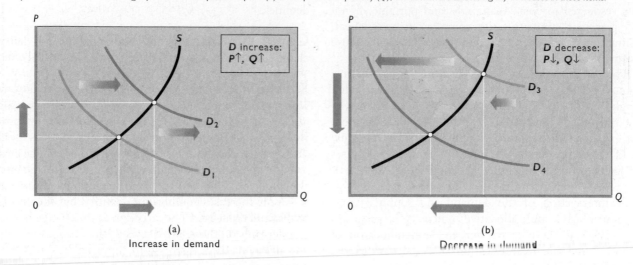

(a)
Increase in demand

(b)
Decrease in demand

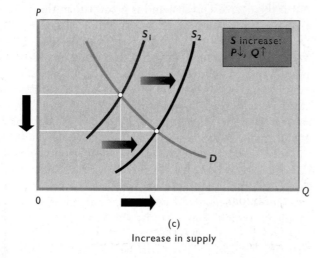

(c)
Increase in supply

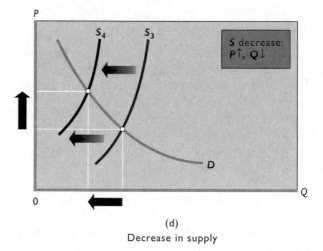

(d)
Decrease in supply

than the decrease in demand, equilibrium price will rise. If the reverse is true, equilibrium price will fall. Because decreases in supply and in demand each reduces equilibrium quantity, we can be sure that equilibrium quantity will fall.

Table 3.3 summarizes these four cases. To understand them fully, you should draw supply and demand diagrams for each case to confirm the effects listed in this table.

Special cases arise when a decrease in demand and a decrease in supply, or an increase in demand and an increase in supply, exactly cancel out. In both cases, the net effect on equilibrium price will be zero; price will not change. **(Key Question 9)**

The optional appendix accompanying this chapter provides examples of situations in which both supply and demand change over the same period of time.

TABLE 3.3 Effects of Changes in Both Supply and Demand

Change in Supply	Change in Demand	Effect on Equilibrium Price	Effect on Equilibrium Quantity
1. Increase	Decrease	Decrease	Indeterminate
2. Decrease	Increase	Increase	Indeterminate
3. Increase	Increase	Indeterminate	Increase
4. Decrease	Decrease	Indeterminate	Decrease

CONSIDER THIS . . .

Salsa and Coffee Beans

If you forget the other-things-equal assumption, you can encounter situations that *seem* to be in conflict with the laws of demand and supply. For example, suppose salsa manufacturers sell 1 million bottles of salsa at $4 a bottle in one year; 2 million bottles at $5 in the next year; and 3 million at $6 in the year thereafter. Price and quantity purchased vary directly, and these data seem to be at odds with the law of demand.

But there is no conflict here; the data do not refute the law of demand. The catch is that the law of demand's other-things-equal assumption has been violated over the three years in the example. Specifically, because of changing tastes and rising incomes, the demand for salsa has increased sharply, as in Figure 3.7a. The result is higher prices *and* larger quantities purchased.

Another example: The price of coffee beans occasionally shoots upward at the same time that the quantity of coffee beans harvested declines. These events seemingly contradict the direct relationship between price and quantity denoted by supply. The catch again is that the other-things-equal assumption underlying the upsloping supply curve is violated. Poor coffee harvests decrease supply, as in Figure 3.7d, increasing the equilibrium price of coffee and reducing the equilibrium quantity.

The laws of demand and supply are not refuted by observations of price and quantity made over periods of time in which either demand or supply curves shift.

Application: Government-Set Prices

Prices in most markets are free to rise or fall to their equilibrium levels, no matter how high or low those levels might be. However, government sometimes concludes that supply and demand will produce prices that are unfairly high for buyers or unfairly low for sellers. So government may place legal limits on how high or low a price or prices may go. Is that a good idea?

Price Ceilings on Gasoline

A **price ceiling** sets the maximum legal price a seller may charge for a product or service. A price at or below the ceiling is legal; a price above it is not. The rationale for establishing price ceilings (or ceiling prices) on specific products is that

they purportedly enable consumers to obtain some "essential" good or service that they could not afford at the equilibrium price. Examples are rent controls and usury laws, which specify maximum "prices" in the forms of rent and interest that can be charged to borrowers.

Graphical Analysis We can easily show the effects of price ceilings graphically. Suppose that rapidly rising world income boosts the purchase of automobiles and shifts the demand for gasoline to the right so that the equilibrium or market price reaches $3.50 per gallon, shown as P_0 in Figure 3.8. The rapidly rising price of gasoline greatly burdens low- and moderate-income households, which pressure government to "do something." To keep gasoline affordable for these households, the government imposes a ceiling price P_c of $3 per gallon. To impact the market, a price ceiling must be below the equilibrium price. A ceiling price of $4, for example, would have had no immediate effect on the gasoline market.

What are the effects of this $3 ceiling price? The rationing ability of the free market is rendered ineffective. Because the ceiling price P_c is below the market-clearing price P_0, there is a lasting shortage of gasoline. The quantity of gasoline demanded at P_c is Q_d and the quantity supplied is only Q_s; a persistent excess demand or shortage of amount $Q_d - Q_s$ occurs.

The price ceiling P_c prevents the usual market adjustment in which competition among buyers bids up price, inducing more production and rationing some buyers out of the market. That process would continue until the shortage disappeared at the equilibrium price and quantity, P_0 and Q_0.

By preventing these market adjustments from occurring, the price ceiling poses problems born of the market disequilibrium.

FIGURE 3.8 A price ceiling. A price ceiling is a maximum legal price such as P_c. When the ceiling price is below the equilibrium price, a persistent product shortage results. Here that shortage is shown by the horizontal distance between Q_d and Q_s.

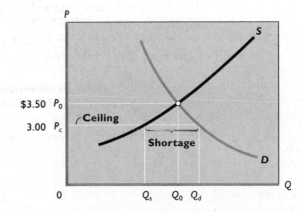

A Legal Market for Human Organs?

A Legal Market Might Eliminate the Present Shortage of Human Organs for Transplant. But There Are Many Serious Objections to "Turning Human Body Parts into Commodities" for Purchase and Sale.

It has become increasingly commonplace in medicine to transplant kidneys, lungs, livers, eye corneas, pancreases, and hearts from deceased individuals to those whose organs have failed or are failing. But surgeons and many of their patients face a growing problem: There are shortages of donated organs available for transplant. Not everyone who needs a transplant can get one. In 2007 there were 97,000 Americans on the waiting list for transplants. Indeed, an inadequate supply of donated organs causes an estimated 6000 deaths in the United States each year.

Why Shortages? Seldom do we hear of shortages of desired goods in market economies. What is different about organs for transplant? One difference is that no legal market exists for human organs. To understand this situation, observe the demand curve D_1 and supply curve S_1 in the accompanying figure. The downward slope of the demand curve tells us that if there were a market for human organs, the quantity of organs demanded would be greater at lower prices than at higher prices. Vertical supply curve S_1 represents the fixed quantity of human organs now donated via consent before death. Because the price of these donated organs is in effect zero, quantity demanded Q_3 exceeds quantity supplied Q_1. The shortage of $Q_3 - Q_1$ is rationed through a waiting list of those in medical need of transplants. Many people die while still on the waiting list.

Use of a Market A market for human organs would increase the incentive to donate organs. Such a market might work like this: An individual might specify in a legal document that he or she is willing to sell one or more usable human organs upon death or near-death. The person could specify where the money from the sale would go, for example, to family, a church, an educational institution, or a charity. Firms would then emerge to purchase organs and resell them where needed for profit. Under such a system, the supply curve of usable organs would take on the normal

Rationing Problem How will the available supply Q_s be apportioned among buyers who want the greater amount Q_d? Should gasoline be distributed on a first-come, first-served basis, that is, to those willing and able to get in line the soonest and stay in line? Or should gas stations distribute it on the basis of favoritism? Since an unregulated shortage does not lead to an equitable distribution of gasoline, the government must establish some formal system for rationing it to consumers. One option is to issue ration coupons, which authorize bearers to purchase a fixed amount of gasoline per month. The rationing system might entail first the printing of coupons for Q_s gallons of gasoline and then the equal distribution of the coupons among consumers so that the wealthy family of four and the poor family of four both receive the same number of coupons.

Black Markets But ration coupons would not prevent a second problem from arising. The demand curve in Figure 3.8 reveals that many buyers are willing to pay more than the ceiling price P_c. And, of course, it is more profitable for gasoline stations to sell at prices above the ceiling. Thus, despite a sizable enforcement bureaucracy that would have to accompany the price controls, *black markets* in which gasoline is illegally bought and sold at prices above the legal limits will flourish. Counterfeiting of ration coupons will also be a problem. And since the price of gasoline is now "set by government," government might face political pressure to set the price even lower.

Rent Controls

About 200 cities in the United States, including New York City, Boston, and San Francisco, have at one time or another enacted rent controls: maximum rents established by law (or, more recently, have set maximum rent increases for existing tenants). Such laws are well intended. Their goals are to protect low-income families from escalating rents caused by perceived housing shortages and to make housing more affordable to the poor.

upward slope of typical supply curves. The higher the expected price of an organ, the greater the number of people who would be willing to have their organs sold at death. Suppose that the supply curve is S_2 in the figure. At the equilibrium price P_1, the number of organs made available for transplant (Q_2) would equal the number purchased for transplant (also Q_2). In this generalized case, the shortage of organs would be eliminated and, of particular importance, the number of organs available for transplanting would rise from Q_1 to Q_2. This means more lives would be saved and enhanced than under the present donor system.

Objections In view of this positive outcome, why is there no such market for human organs? Critics of market-based solutions have two main objections. The first is a moral objection: Critics feel that turning human organs into commodities commercializes human beings and diminishes the special nature of human life. They say there is something unseemly about selling and buying body organs as if they were bushels of wheat or ounces of gold. (There is, however, a market for blood!) Moreover, critics note that the market would ration the available organs (as represented by Q_2 in the figure)

to people who either can afford them (at P_1) or have health insurance for transplants. The poor and uninsured would be left out.

Second, a health-cost objection suggests that a market for body organs would greatly increase the cost of health care. Rather than obtaining freely donated (although "too few") body organs, patients or their insurance companies would have to pay market prices for them, further increasing the cost of medical care.

Rebuttal Supporters of market-based solutions to organ shortages point out that the laws against selling organs are simply driving the market underground. Worldwide, an estimated $1 billion-per-year illegal market in human organs has emerged. As in other illegal markets, the unscrupulous tend to thrive. This fact is dramatized by the accompanying photo, in which four Pakistani villagers show off their scars after they each sold a kidney to pay off debt. Supporters say that legalization of the market for human organs would increase organ supply from legal sources, drive down the price of organs, and reduce the abuses such as those now taking place in illegal markets.

What have been the actual economic effects? On the demand side, it is true that as long as rents are below equilibrium, more families are willing to consume rental housing; the quantity of rental housing demanded increases at the lower price. But a large problem occurs on the supply side. Price controls make it less attractive for landlords to offer housing on the rental market. In the short run, owners may sell their rental units or convert them to condominiums. In the long run, low rents make it unprofitable for owners to repair or renovate their rental units. (Rent controls are one cause of the many abandoned apartment buildings found in larger cities.) Also, insurance companies, pension funds, and other potential new investors in housing will find it more profitable to invest in office buildings, shopping malls, or motels, where rents are not controlled.

In brief, rent controls distort market signals and thus resources are misallocated: Too few resources are allocated to rental housing and too many to alternative uses. Ironically, although rent controls are often legislated to

lessen the effects of perceived housing shortages, controls in fact are a primary cause of such shortages. For that reason, most American cities either have abandoned or are in the process of dismantling rent controls.

Price Floors on Wheat
A **price floor** is a minimum price fixed by the government. A price at or above the price floor is legal; a price below it is not. Price floors above equilibrium prices are usually invoked when society feels that the free functioning of the market system has not provided a sufficient income for certain groups of resource suppliers or producers. Supported prices for agricultural products and current minimum wages are two examples of price (or wage) floors. Let's look at the former.

Suppose the equilibrium price for wheat is $2 per bushel and, because of that low price, many farmers have extremely low incomes. The government decides to help out by establishing a legal price floor or price support of $3 per bushel.

FIGURE 3.9 **A price floor.** A price floor is a minimum legal price such as P_f. When the price floor is above the equilibrium price, a persistent product surplus results. Here that surplus is shown by the horizontal distance between Q_s and Q_d.

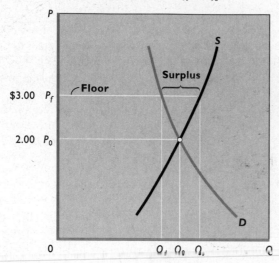

What will be the effects? At any price above the equilibrium price, quantity supplied will exceed quantity demanded—that is, there will be a persistent excess supply or surplus of the product. Farmers will be willing to produce and offer for sale more than private buyers are willing to purchase at the price floor. As we saw with a price ceiling, an imposed legal price disrupts the rationing ability of the free market.

Graphical Analysis
Figure 3.9 illustrates the effect of a price floor graphically. Suppose that S and D are the supply and demand curves for wheat. Equilibrium price and quantity are P_0 and Q_0, respectively. If the government imposes a price floor of P_f, farmers will produce Q_s but private buyers will purchase only Q_d. The surplus is the excess of Q_s over Q_d.

The government may cope with the surplus resulting from a price floor in two ways:

- It can restrict supply (for example, by instituting acreage allotments by which farmers agree to take a certain amount of land out of production) or increase demand (for example, by researching new uses for the product involved). These actions may reduce the difference between the equilibrium price and the price floor and that way reduce the size of the resulting surplus.

- If these efforts are not wholly successful, then the government must purchase the surplus output at the $3 price (thereby subsidizing farmers) and store or otherwise dispose of it.

Additional Consequences Price floors such as P_f in Figure 3.9 not only disrupt the rationing ability of prices but distort resource allocation. Without the price floor, the $2 equilibrium price of wheat would cause financial losses and force high-cost wheat producers to plant other crops or abandon farming altogether. But the $3 price floor allows them to continue to grow wheat and remain farmers. So society devotes too many of its scarce resources to wheat production and too few to producing other, more valuable, goods and services. It fails to achieve allocative efficiency.

That's not all. Consumers of wheat-based products pay higher prices because of the price floor. Taxpayers pay higher taxes to finance the government's purchase of the surplus. Also, the price floor causes potential environmental damage by encouraging wheat farmers to bring hilly, erosion-prone "mar-

> **INTERACTIVE GRAPHS**
> **G 3.2**
> Price floors and ceilings

ginal land" into production. The higher price also prompts imports of wheat. But, since such imports would increase the quantity of wheat supplied and thus undermine the price floor, the government needs to erect tariffs (taxes on imports) to keep the foreign wheat out. Such tariffs usually prompt other countries to retaliate with their own tariffs against U.S. agricultural or manufacturing exports.

So it is easy to see why economists "sound the alarm" when politicians advocate imposing price ceilings or price floors such as price controls, rent controls, interest-rate lids, or agricultural price supports. In all these cases, good intentions lead to bad economic outcomes. Government-controlled prices cause shortages or surpluses, distort resource allocation, and produce negative side effects. **(Key Question 14)**

> **QUICK REVIEW 3.3**
>
> - In competitive markets, prices adjust to the equilibrium level at which quantity demanded equals quantity supplied.
> - The equilibrium price and quantity are those indicated by the intersection of the supply and demand curves for any product or resource.
> - An increase in demand increases equilibrium price and quantity; a decrease in demand decreases equilibrium price and quantity.
> - An increase in supply reduces equilibrium price but increases equilibrium quantity; a decrease in supply increases equilibrium price but reduces equilibrium quantity.
> - Over time, equilibrium price and quantity may change in directions that seem at odds with the laws of demand and supply because the other-things-equal assumption is violated.
> - Government-controlled prices in the form of ceilings and floors stifle the rationing function of prices, distort resource allocations, and cause negative side effects.

Summary

1. Demand is a schedule or curve representing the willingness of buyers in a specific period to purchase a particular product at each of various prices. The law of demand implies that consumers will buy more of a product at a low price than at a high price. So, other things equal, the relationship between price and quantity demanded is negative or inverse and is graphed as a downsloping curve.

2. Market demand curves are found by adding horizontally the demand curves of the many individual consumers in the market.

3. Changes in one or more of the determinants of demand (consumer tastes, the number of buyers in the market, the money incomes of consumers, the prices of related goods, and consumer expectations) shift the market demand curve. A shift to the right is an increase in demand; a shift to the left is a decrease in demand. A change in demand is different from a change in the quantity demanded, the latter being a movement from one point to another point on a fixed demand curve because of a change in the product's price.

4. Supply is a schedule or curve showing the amounts of a product that producers are willing to offer in the market at each possible price during a specific period. The law of supply states that, other things equal, producers will offer more of a product at a high price than at a low price. Thus, the relationship between price and quantity supplied is positive or direct, and supply is graphed as an upsloping curve.

5. The market supply curve is the horizontal summation of the supply curves of the individual producers of the product.

6. Changes in one or more of the determinants of supply (resource prices, production techniques, taxes or subsidies, the prices of other goods, producer expectations, or the number of sellers in the market) shift the supply curve of a product. A shift to the right is an increase in supply; a shift to the left is a decrease in supply. In contrast, a change in the price of the product being considered causes a change in the quantity supplied, which is shown as a movement from one point to another point on a fixed supply curve.

7. The equilibrium price and quantity are established at the intersection of the supply and demand curves. The interaction of market demand and market supply adjusts the price to the point at which the quantities demanded and supplied are equal. This is the equilibrium price. The corresponding quantity is the equilibrium quantity.

8. The ability of market forces to synchronize selling and buying decisions to eliminate potential surpluses and shortages is known as the rationing function of prices. The equilibrium quantity in competitive markets reflects both productive efficiency (least-cost production) and allocative efficiency (the right amount of the product relative to other products).

9. A change in either demand or supply changes the equilibrium price and quantity. Increases in demand raise both equilibrium price and equilibrium quantity; decreases in demand lower both equilibrium price and equilibrium quantity. Increases in supply lower equilibrium price and raise equilibrium quantity; decreases in supply raise equilibrium price and lower equilibrium quantity.

10. Simultaneous changes in demand and supply affect equilibrium price and quantity in various ways, depending on their direction and relative magnitudes (see Table 3.3).

11. A price ceiling is a maximum price set by government and is designed to help consumers. Effective price ceilings produce persistent product shortages, and if an equitable distribution of the product is sought, government must ration the product to consumers.

12. A price floor is a minimum price set by government and is designed to aid producers. Effective price floors lead to persistent product surpluses; the government must either purchase the product or eliminate the surplus by imposing restrictions on production or increasing private demand.

13. Legally fixed prices stifle the rationing function of prices and distort the allocation of resources.

Terms and Concepts

demand

demand schedule

law of demand

diminishing marginal utility

income effect

substitution effect

demand curve

determinants of demand

normal goods

inferior goods

substitute good

complementary good

change in demand

change in quantity demanded

supply

supply schedule

law of supply

supply curve

determinants of supply

change in supply

change in quantity supplied

equilibrium price

equilibrium quantity

surplus

shortage

productive efficiency

allocative efficiency

price ceiling

price floor

Study Questions

1. Explain the law of demand. Why does a demand curve slope downward? How is a market demand curve derived from individual demand curves? **LO1**

2. What are the determinants of demand? What happens to the demand curve when any of these determinants change? Distinguish between a change in demand and a change in the quantity demanded, noting the cause(s) of each. **LO1**

3. **KEY QUESTION** What effect will each of the following have on the demand for small automobiles such as the Mini Cooper and Smart car? **LO1**
   a. Small automobiles become more fashionable.
   b. The price of large automobiles rises (with the price of small autos remaining the same).
   c. Income declines and small autos are an inferior good.
   d. Consumers anticipate that the price of small autos will greatly come down in the near future.
   e. The price of gasoline substantially drops.

4. Explain the law of supply. Why does the supply curve slope upward? How is the market supply curve derived from the supply curves of individual producers? **LO2**

5. What are the determinants of supply? What happens to the supply curve when any of these determinants changes? Distinguish between a change in supply and a change in the quantity supplied, noting the cause(s) of each. **LO2**

6. **KEY QUESTION** What effect will each of the following have on the supply of *auto* tires? **LO2**
   a. A technological advance in the methods of producing tires.
   b. A decline in the number of firms in the tire industry.
   c. An increase in the prices of rubber used in the production of tires.
   d. The expectation that the equilibrium price of auto tires will be lower in the future than currently.
   e. A decline in the price of the large tires used for semi trucks and earth-hauling rigs (with no change in the price of auto tires).
   f. The levying of a per-unit tax on each auto tire sold.
   g. The granting of a 50-cent-per-unit subsidy for each auto tire produced.

7. "In the corn market, demand often exceeds supply and supply sometimes exceeds demand." "The price of corn rises and falls in response to changes in supply and demand." In which of these two statements are the terms "supply" and "demand" used correctly? Explain. **LO2**

8. **KEY QUESTION** Suppose the total demand for wheat and the total supply of wheat per month in the Kansas City grain market are as shown in the accompanying table. **LO3**
   a. What is the equilibrium price? What is the equilibrium quantity? Fill in the surplus-shortage column and use it to explain why your answers are correct.
   b. Graph the demand for wheat and the supply of wheat. Be sure to label the axes of your graph correctly. Label equilibrium price *P* and equilibrium quantity *Q*.

Thousands of Bushels Demanded	Price per Bushel	Thousands of Bushels Supplied	Surplus (+) or Shortage (−)
85	$3.40	72	_____
80	3.70	73	_____
75	4.00	75	_____
70	4.30	77	_____
65	4.60	79	_____
60	4.90	81	_____

   c. Why will $3.40 not be the equilibrium price in this market? Why not $4.90? "Surpluses drive prices up; shortages drive them down." Do you agree?

9. **KEY QUESTION** How will each of the following changes in demand and/or supply affect equilibrium price and equilibrium quantity in a competitive market; that is, do price and quantity rise, fall, or remain unchanged, or are the answers indeterminate because they depend on the magnitudes of the shifts? Use supply and demand diagrams to verify your answers. **LO4**
   a. Supply decreases and demand is constant.
   b. Demand decreases and supply is constant.
   c. Supply increases and demand is constant.
   d. Demand increases and supply increases.
   e. Demand increases and supply is constant.
   f. Supply increases and demand decreases.
   g. Demand increases and supply decreases.
   h. Demand decreases and supply decreases.

10. In 2001 an outbreak of foot-and-mouth disease in Europe led to the burning of millions of cattle carcasses. What impact do you think this had on the supply of cattle hides, hide prices, the supply of leather goods, and the price of leather goods? **LO4**

11. Use two market diagrams to explain how an increase in state subsidies to public colleges might affect tuition and enrollments in both public and private colleges. **LO4**

12. Critically evaluate: "In comparing the two equilibrium positions in Figure 3.7b, I note that a smaller amount is actually demanded at a lower price. This refutes the law of demand." **LO4**

13. For each stock in the stock market, the number of shares sold daily equals the number of shares purchased. That is, the quantity of each firm's shares demanded equals the quantity supplied. So, if this equality always occurs, why do the prices of stock shares ever change? **LO4**

14. **KEY QUESTION** Refer to the table in question 8. Suppose that the government establishes a price ceiling of $3.70 for wheat. What might prompt the government to establish this price ceiling? Explain carefully the main effects. Demonstrate your answer graphically. Next, suppose that the government establishes a price floor of $4.60 for wheat.

What will be the main effects of this price floor? Demonstrate your answer graphically. **LO5**

15. What do economists mean when they say that "price floors and ceilings stifle the rationing function of prices and distort resource allocation"? **LO5**

16. **ADVANCED ANALYSIS** Assume that demand for a commodity is represented by the equation $P = 10 - .2Q_d$ and supply by the equation $P = 2 + .2Q_s$, where Q_d and Q_s are quantity demanded and quantity supplied, respectively, and P is price. Using the equilibrium condition $Q_s = Q_d$, solve the equations to determine equilibrium price. Now determine equilibrium quantity. Graph the two equations to substantiate your answers. **LO4**

17. **LAST WORD** What is the current overall number of American candidates waiting for an organ transplant? (For the answer, visit the United Network for Organ Sharing Web site, **www.unos.org.**) For what transplant organ is the waiting list the longest? (Select Data and "At a glance.") Do you favor the establishment of a legal market for transplant organs? Why or why not?

Web-Based Questions

1. **FARM COMMODITY PRICES—SUPPLY AND DEMAND IN ACTION** The U.S. Department of Agriculture, **www.nass.usda.gov,** publishes charts on the prices of farm products. Go to the USDA home page and select Charts and Maps and then Agricultural Prices (under Economics). Choose three farm products and determine whether their prices (as measured by "prices received by farmers") have generally increased, decreased, or stayed the same over the past three years. In which of the three cases, if any, do you think that supply has increased more rapidly than demand? In which of the three cases, if any, do you think that demand has increased more rapidly than supply? Explain your reasoning.

2. **CHANGES IN DEMAND—BABY DIAPERS AND RETIREMENT VILLAGES** Other things equal, an increase in the number of buyers for a product or service will increase demand. Baby diapers and retirement villages are two products designed for different population groups. The U.S. Census Bureau Web site, **www.census.gov/ipc/www/idb,** provides population pyramids (graphs that show the distribution of population by age and sex) for countries for 2000, 2025, and 2050. View the population pyramids for Mexico, Japan, and the United States by selecting International Data Base and then Population Pyramids. Which country do you think will have the greatest percentage increase in demand for baby diapers between 2000 and 2050? For retirement villages? Which country do you think will have the greatest absolute increase in demand for baby diapers? For retirement villages?

FURTHER TEST YOUR KNOWLEDGE AT
www.mcconnell18e.com

Additional Examples of Supply and Demand

Our discussion has clearly demonstrated that supply and demand analysis is a powerful tool for understanding equilibrium prices and quantities. The information provided is fully sufficient for moving forward in the book, but you may find that additional examples of supply and demand are helpful. This optional appendix provides several concrete illustrations of changes in supply and demand.

Your instructor may assign all, some, or none of this appendix, depending on time availability and personal preferences.

Changes in Supply and Demand

As Figure 3.6 of this chapter demonstrates, changes in supply and demand cause changes in price, quantity, or both. The following applications illustrate this fact in several real-world markets. The simplest situations are those in which either supply changes while demand remains constant or demand changes while supply remains constant. Let's consider two such simple cases first, before looking at more complex applications.

Lettuce

Every now and then we hear on the news that extreme weather has severely reduced the size of some crop such as lettuce, oranges, or cherries. Suppose, for example, that a severe freeze destroys a sizable portion of the lettuce crop. This unfortunate situation implies a significant decline in supply, which we represent as a leftward shift of the supply curve from S_1 to S_2 in Figure 1. At each price, consumers desire as much lettuce as before, so the freeze does not affect the demand for lettuce. That is, demand curve D_1 does not shift.

What are the consequences of the reduced supply of lettuce for equilibrium price and quantity? As shown in Figure 1, the leftward shift of the supply curve disrupts the previous equilibrium in the market for lettuce and drives the equilibrium price upward upward from P_1 to P_2. Consumers respond to that price hike by reducing the quantity of lettuce demanded from Q_1 to Q_2. Equilibrium in the market is restored, now at P_2 and Q_2.

Consumers who are willing and able to pay price P_2 obtain lettuce; consumers unwilling or unable to pay that price do not. Some consumers continue to buy as much lettuce as before, even at the higher price. Others buy

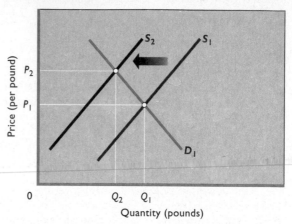

FIGURE 1 The market for lettuce. The decrease in the supply of lettuce, shown here by the shift from S_1 to S_2, increases the equilibrium price of lettuce from P_1 to P_2 and reduces the equilibrium quantity from Q_1 to Q_2.

some lettuce but not as much as before, and still others opt out of the market completely. The latter two groups use the money they would have spent on lettuce to obtain other products, say, carrots, whose price has not gone up.

Corn and Ethanol

Between the beginning of 2006 and the middle of 2007, the price of corn doubled. Did people suddenly demand more corn flakes? Not hardly! The demand for cereals, beef, and other food products that use corn as inputs was relatively stable. Instead, the driving force was a rapid increase in the price of oil and gasoline (one of our following examples). This increase boosted the demand for ethanol, an alcohol-like substance that is blended with conventional gasoline. In the United States, producers refine ethanol mainly from corn, although ethanol can also be refined from sugar and other agricultural commodities. So the increase in the demand for ethanol drove up the demand for corn and raised its equilibrium price.

We depict this situation in Figure 2 as the rightward shift of the demand curve from D_1 to D_2. This demand increase upped the equilibrium price of corn, in this case from P_1 to P_2. Producers responded accordingly by increasing the quantity of corn supplied, as from Q_1 to Q_2. At the higher price and quantity, the market achieved a new equilibrium.

FIGURE 2 The market for corn. The increase in the demand for corn, shown here by the shift from D_1 to D_2, increases the equilibrium price of corn from P_1 to P_2 and expands the equilibrium quantity from Q_1 to Q_2.

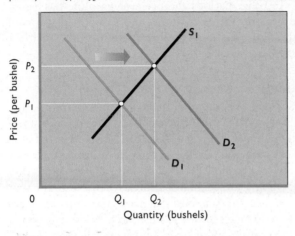

FIGURE 3 The market for pink salmon. In the last several decades, the supply of pink salmon has increased and the demand for pink salmon has decreased. As a result, the price of pink salmon has declined, as from P_1 to P_2. Because supply has increased by more than demand has decreased, the equilibrium quantity of pink salmon has increased, as from Q_1 to Q_2.

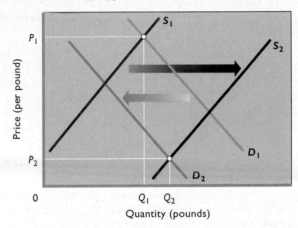

Notice that the demand for corn, the price of corn, and the quantity of corn demanded and supplied all increased. But in the period depicted, the supply of corn—the entire curve S_1—remained securely fixed in place. Eventually, of course, the potential for high profits will encourage farmers to plant more corn and therefore shift the supply curve rightward. Depending on what happens to demand, the price of corn may drop closer to P_1.

The rapid rise in the price of corn had a host of other effects that are easily understood through demand and supply analysis. The costs of producing corn-fed beef went up, which reduced the supply of beef and upped the price of hamburger and steak. The higher corn price caused a jump in the price of farm land in the Corn Belt. Further, the price of corn syrup (fructose) used in soft drinks rocketed and led some soft-drink makers to use cane sugar instead of corn syrup in the production process. In Mexico, large numbers of angry people gathered in cities to protest the higher price of tortillas, which are made from corn and consumed in large quantities by many Mexicans.

Pink Salmon

Now let's see what happens when both supply and demand change at the same time. Several decades ago, people who caught salmon earned as much as $1 for each pound of pink salmon—the type used mainly for canning—brought to the buyer. In Figure 3 that price is represented as P_1, at the intersection of supply curve S_1 and demand curve D_1. The corresponding quantity of pink salmon is shown as Q_1 pounds.

As time passed, supply and demand changed in the market for pink salmon. On the supply side, improved technology in the form of larger, more efficient fishing boats greatly increased the catch and lowered the cost of obtaining it. Also, high profits at price P_1 encouraged many new fishers to enter the industry. As a result of these changes, the supply of pink salmon greatly increased and the supply curve shifted to the right, as from S_1 to S_2 in Figure 3.

Over the same years, the demand for pink salmon declined, as represented by the leftward shift from D_1 to D_2 in Figure 3. That decrease was caused by increases in consumer income and reductions of the price of substitute products. As buyers' incomes rose, consumers shifted demand away from canned fish and toward higher-quality fresh or frozen fish, including more-valued Atlantic, Chinook, Sockeye, and Coho salmon. Moreover, the emergence of fish farming, in which salmon are raised in ocean net pens, lowered the prices of these substitute species. That, too, reduced the demand for pink salmon.

The altered supply and demand reduced the price of pink salmon to as low as $.10 per pound, as represented by the drop in price from P_1 to P_2 in Figure 3. Both the supply increase and the demand decrease helped reduce the equilibrium price. However, in this particular case the equilibrium quantity of pink salmon increased, as represented by the move from Q_1 to Q_2. Both shifts of the curves reduced the equilibrium price, but equilibrium quantity increased because the increase in supply exceeded the decrease in demand.

Gasoline

The price of gasoline has increased rapidly in the United States over the past several years. For example, the average price of a gallon of gasoline rose from around $2 in 2004 to about $3 in 2007. What caused this 50 percent rise in the price of gasoline? How would we diagram this increase?

We begin in Figure 4 with the price of a gallon of gasoline at P_1, representing the $2 price. Simultaneous supply and demand factors disturbed this equilibrium. Supply uncertainties relating to Middle East politics and warfare and expanded demand for oil by fast-growing countries such as China pushed up the price of a barrel of oil from $37 in 2004 to $80 in 2007. Oil is the main input for producing gasoline, so any sustained rise in its price boosts the per-unit cost of producing gasoline. Such cost rises decrease the supply of gasoline, as represented by the leftward shift of the supply curve from S_1 to S_2 in Figure 4. At times refinery breakdowns in the United States also contributed to this reduced supply.

While the supply of gasoline declined between 2004 and 2007, the demand for gasoline increased, as depicted by the rightward shift of the demand curve from D_1 to D_2. Incomes in general were rising over these years because the U.S. economy was rapidly expanding. Rising incomes raise demand for all normal goods, including gasoline. An increased number of low-gas-mileage SUVs and light trucks on the road also contributed to growing gas demand.

The combined decline in gasoline supply and increase in gasoline demand boosted the price of gasoline from $2 to $3, as represented by the rise from P_1 to P_2 in Figure 4. Because the demand increase outweighed the supply decrease, the equilibrium quantity expanded, here from Q_1 to Q_2.

In other periods the price of gasoline has *declined* as the demand for gasoline has increased. Test your understanding of the analysis by explaining how such a price decrease could occur.

Sushi

Sushi bars are springing up like Starbucks in American cities (well, maybe not that fast!). Consumption of this raw-fish delicacy from Japan has soared in the United States in recent years. Nevertheless, the price of sushi has remained relatively constant.

Supply and demand analysis helps explain this circumstance of increased quantity and constant price. A change in tastes has increased the U.S. demand for sushi. Many consumers of sushi find it highly tasty when they try it. And, as implied by the growing number of sushi bars in the United States, the supply of sushi has also expanded.

We represent these supply and demand changes in Figure 5 as the rightward shift of the demand curve from D_1 to D_2 and the rightward shift of the supply curve from S_1 to S_2. Observe that the equilibrium quantity of sushi increases from Q_1 to Q_2 and equilibrium price remains constant at P_1. The increase in supply, which-taken alone would reduce price, has perfectly offset the increase in demand, which taken alone would raise price. The price of sushi does not change, but the equilibrium quantity greatly

FIGURE 4 The market for gasoline. An increase in the demand for gasoline, as shown by the shift from D_1 to D_2, coupled with a decrease in supply, as shown by the shift from S_1 to S_2, boosts equilibrium price (here from P_1 to P_2). In this case, equilibrium quantity increases from Q_1 Q_2 because the increase in demand outweighs the decrease in supply.

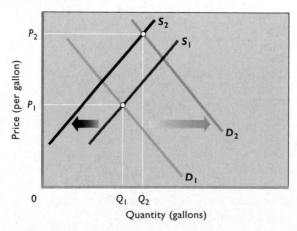

FIGURE 5 The market for sushi. Equal increases in the demand for sushi, as from D_1 to D_2, and in the supply of sushi, as from S_1 to S_2, expand the equilibrium quantity of sushi (here from Q_1 to Q_2) while leaving the price of sushi unchanged at P_1.

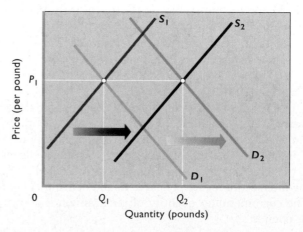

rises. That happens because both the increase in demand and the increase in supply expand purchases and sales.

Simultaneous increases in demand and supply can cause price to either rise, fall, or remain constant, depending on the relative magnitudes of the supply and demand increases. In this case, price remained constant.

Preset Prices

In the body of this chapter, we saw that an effective government-imposed price ceiling (legal maximum price) causes quantity demanded to exceed quantity supplied—a shortage. An effective government-imposed price floor (legal minimum price) causes quantity supplied to exceed quantity demanded—a surplus. Put simply: Shortages result when prices are set below, and surpluses result when prices are set above, equilibrium prices.

We now want to establish that shortages and surpluses can occur in markets other than those in which government imposes price floors and ceilings. Such market imbalances happen when the seller or sellers set prices in advance of sales and the prices selected turn out to be below or above equilibrium prices. Consider the following two examples.

Olympic Figure Skating Finals

Tickets for the women's figure skating championship at the Olympics are among the world's "hottest tickets." The popularity of this event and the high incomes of buyers translate into tremendous ticket demand. The Olympic officials set the price for the tickets in advance. Invariably, the price, although high, is considerably below the equilibrium price that would equate quantity demanded and quantity supplied. A severe shortage of tickets therefore occurs in this *primary market*—the market involving the official ticket office.

The shortage, in turn, creates a *secondary market* in which buyers bid for tickets held by initial purchasers rather than the original seller. Scalping tickets—selling them above the ticket price—may be legal or illegal, depending on local laws.

Figure 6 shows how the shortage in the primary ticket market looks in terms of supply and demand analysis. Demand curve D represents the strong demand for tickets and supply curve S represents the supply of tickets. The supply curve is vertical because a fixed number of tickets are printed to match the capacity of the arena. At the printed ticket price of P_1, the quantity of tickets demanded, Q_2, exceeds the quantity supplied, Q_1. The

FIGURE 6 The market for tickets to the Olympic women's figure skating finals. The demand curve D and supply curve S for the Olympic women's figure skating finals produce an equilibrium price that is above the P_1 price printed on the ticket. At price P_1 the quantity of tickets demanded, Q_2, greatly exceeds the quantity of tickets available (Q_1). The resulting shortage of ab (= Q_2Q_1) gives rise to a legal or illegal secondary market.

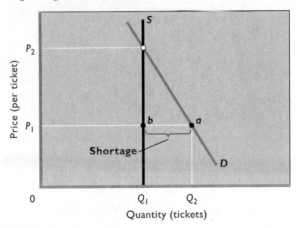

result is a shortage of ab—the horizontal distance between Q_2 and Q_1 in the primary market.

If the printed ticket price had been the higher equilibrium price P_2, no shortage of tickets would have occurred. But at the lower price P_1, a shortage and secondary ticket market will emerge among those buyers willing to pay more than the printed ticket price and those sellers willing to sell their purchased tickets for more than the printed price. Wherever there are shortages and secondary markets, it is safe to assume that price was set below the equilibrium price.

Olympic Curling Preliminaries

Contrast the shortage of tickets for the women's figure skating finals at the Olympics to the surplus of tickets for one of the preliminary curling matches. For the uninitiated, curling is a sport in which participants slide a heavy round object called a "stone" down the ice toward a target while teammates called "sweepers" use brooms to alter the course of the stone when desired.

Curling is a popular spectator sport in a few nations such as Canada, but it does not draw many fans in most countries. So the demand for tickets to most of the preliminary curling events is not very strong. We demonstrate this weak demand as D in Figure 7. As in our previous example, the supply of tickets is fixed by the size of the arena and is shown as vertical line S.

FIGURE 7 The market for tickets to the Olympic curling preliminaries. The demand curve *D* and supply curve *S* for the Olympic curling preliminaries produce an equilibrium price below the P_1 price printed on the ticket. At price P_1 the quantity of tickets demanded is less than the quantity of tickets available. The resulting surplus of *ba* (= Q_1Q_2) means the event is not sold out.

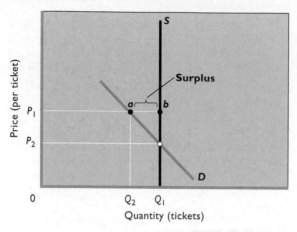

We represent the printed ticket price as P_1 in Figure 7. In this case the printed price is much higher than the equilibrium price of P_2. At the printed ticket price, quantity supplied is Q_1 and quantity demanded is Q_2. So a surplus of tickets of *ba* (= Q_1Q_2) occurs. No ticket scalping occurs and there are numerous empty seats. Only if the Olympic officials had priced the tickets at the lower price P_2 would the event have been a sellout. (Actually, the Olympic officials try to adjust to demand realities for curling contests by holding them in smaller ice arenas than used for figure skating and by charging less for tickets. Nevertheless, the stands are rarely full for the preliminary contests, which compete against final events in other winter Olympic sports.)

Appendix Summary

1. A decrease in the supply of a product increases its equilibrium price and reduces its equilibrium quantity. In contrast, an increase in the demand for a product boosts both its equilibrium price and its equilibrium quantity.

2. Simultaneous changes in supply and demand affect equilibrium price and quantity in various ways, depending on the relative magnitudes of the changes in supply and demand. Equal increases in supply and demand, for example, leave equilibrium price unchanged.

3. Sellers set prices of some items such as tickets in advance of the event. These items are sold in the primary market that involves the original seller and buyers. If preset prices turn out to be below the equilibrium prices, shortages occur and scalping in legal or illegal secondary markets arises. The prices in the secondary market then rise above the preset prices. In contrast, surpluses occur when the preset prices happen to exceed the equilibrium prices.

Appendix Study Questions

1. Suppose the supply of apples sharply increases because of perfect weather conditions throughout the growing season. Assuming no change in demand, explain the effect on the equilibrium price and quantity of apples. Explain why quantity demanded increases even though demand does not change. **LO6**

2. Assume the demand for lumber suddenly rises because of a rapid growth of demand for new housing. Assume no change in supply. Why does the equilibrium price of lumber rise? What would happen if the price did not rise under the demand and supply circumstances described? **LO6**

3. Suppose both the demand for olives and the supply of olives decline by equal amounts over some time period. Use graphical analysis to show the effect on equilibrium price and quantity. **LO6**

4. Assume that both the supply of bottled water and the demand for bottled water rise during the summer but that supply increases more rapidly than demand. What can you conclude about the directions of the impacts on equilibrium price and equilibrium quantity? **LO6**

5. Why are shortages or surpluses more likely with preset prices, such as those on tickets, than flexible prices, such as those on gasoline? **LO6**

6. Use the table below to answer the questions that follow:
   LO6
   a. If this table reflects the supply of and demand for tickets to a particular World Cup soccer game, what is the stadium capacity?
   b. If the preset ticket price is $45, would we expect to see a secondary market for tickets? Explain why or why not.

Quantity Demanded, Thousands	Price	Quantity Supplied, Thousands
80	$25	60
75	35	60
70	45	60
65	55	60
60	65	60
55	75	60
50	85	60

Would the price of a ticket in the secondary market be higher than, the same as, or lower than the price in the primary (original) market?
   c. Suppose for some other World Cup game the quantities of tickets demanded are 20,000 lower at each ticket price than shown in the table. If the ticket price remains $45, would the event be a sellout? Explain why or why not.

7. Most scalping laws make it illegal to sell—but not to buy—tickets at prices above those printed on the tickets. Assuming that is the case, use supply and demand analysis to explain why the equilibrium ticket price in an illegal secondary market tends to be higher than in a legal secondary market. **LO6**

8. Go to the Web site of the Energy Information Administration, **www.eia.doe.gov,** and follow the links to find the current retail price of gasoline. How does the current price of regular gasoline compare with the price a year ago? What must have happened to either supply, demand, or both to explain the observed price change? **LO6**

IN THIS CHAPTER YOU WILL LEARN:

1 Important facts about U.S. households and U.S. businesses.

2 Why the corporate form of business organization dominates sales and profits.

3 The problem that arises when corporate owners (principals) and their managers (agents) have different interests.

4 About the economic role of government in the economy.

5 The categories of government spending and the sources of government revenues.

The U.S. Economy: Private and Public Sectors

We now move from the general characteristics of the market economy, including the role of supply and demand, to specific information about the world's largest economy. Each year, the value of U.S. output exceeds that of Japan, Germany, the United Kingdom, and France—combined! For descriptive convenience, we will divide the economy into two sectors: the *private sector,* which includes *households* and *businesses,* and the *public sector,* or simply *government.*

This chapter builds on the simple circular flow diagram of Chapter 2 (Figure 2.2, p. 40) by providing institutional detail about the households and businesses listed in that diagram and by also adding and examining the role of government in the economy's flow of goods and services. The chapter answers some very important questions: What types of income do households receive and how do they dispose of it? What are the types of business enterprises and why has the corporate form of business dominated?

Households as Income Receivers

Recall that households are a key element in the circular flow diagram. The U.S. economy currently has about 114 million households, which, by definition, consist of one or more persons occupying a housing unit. Households are both the ultimate suppliers of all economic resources *and* the major spenders in the economy. We can categorize the income received by households by how it was earned and by how it was divided among households.

The Functional Distribution of Income

The **functional distribution of income** indicates how the nation's income is apportioned among wages, rents, interest, and profits, that is, according to the function performed by the income receiver. Wages are paid to labor; rents and interest are paid to owners of property resources; and profits are paid to the owners of corporations and unincorporated businesses.

Figure 4.1 shows the functional distribution of U.S. income earned in 2007. The largest source of income for households is the wages and salaries paid to workers. Notice that the bulk of total U.S. income (71 percent) goes to labor, not to capital. Proprietors' income—the income of doctors, lawyers, small-business owners, farmers, and owners of other unincorporated enterprises—also has a "wage" element. Some of this income is payment for one's own labor and some of it is profit from one's own business.

The other three types of income are self-evident: Some households own corporate stock and receive dividend incomes on their holdings. Many households also own bonds and savings accounts that yield interest income. And some households receive rental income by providing buildings and natural resources (including land) to businesses and other individuals.

The Personal Distribution of Income

The **personal distribution of income** indicates how the nation's total income is divided among individual households. In Figure 4.2 households are divided into five

FIGURE 4.1 The functional distribution of U.S. income, 2007. Seventy-one percent of U.S. income is received as wages and salaries. Income to property owners—corporate profit, interest, and rents—accounts for about 20 percent of total income.

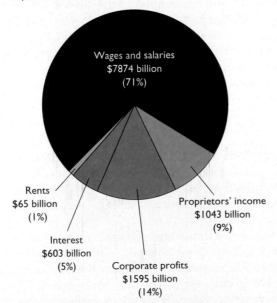

Wages and salaries
$7874 billion
(71%)

Rents
$65 billion
(1%)

Interest
$603 billion
(5%)

Corporate profits
$1595 billion
(14%)

Proprietors' income
$1043 billion
(9%)

Source: Bureau of Economic Analysis, **www.bea.gov.**

FIGURE 4.2 The personal distribution of income among U.S. households, 2006. Personal income is unequally distributed in the United States, with the top 20 percent of households receiving about one-half of the total income. In an equal distribution, all five vertical bars would be as high as the horizontal line drawn at 20 percent; then each 20 percent of families would receive 20 percent of the nation's total income.

Numbers do not add to 100 percent due to rounding.

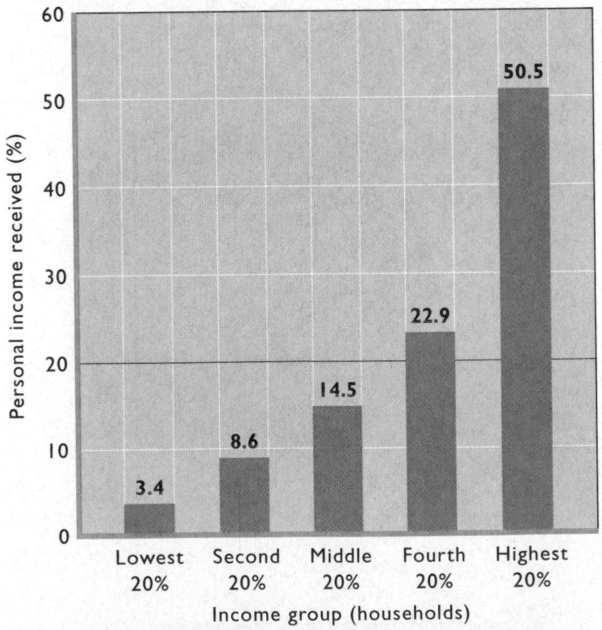

Personal income received (%) vs. Income group (households)

- Lowest 20%: 3.4
- Second 20%: 8.6
- Middle 20%: 14.5
- Fourth 20%: 22.9
- Highest 20%: 50.5

Source: Bureau of the Census, **www.census.gov.**

73

numerically equal groups or quintiles; the heights of the bars show the percentage of total income received by each group. In 2006 the poorest 20 percent of all households received 3.4 percent of total personal income and the richest 20 percent received 50.5 percent. Taxes, noncash transfer (for example, food stamps), and the movement of households among categories over time lessen the income inequality shown in Figure 4.2. Nevertheless, even with these things considered, the United States clearly has considerable income inequality. **(Key Question 2)**

Households as Spenders

How do households dispose of their income? Part of it flows to government as taxes and the rest is divided between personal savings and personal consumption expenditures. In 2007, households disposed of their total personal income as shown in Figure 4.3.

Personal Taxes

In 2007, U.S. households paid $1483 billion in personal taxes (mainly income taxes and property taxes), or 13 percent of their $11,260 billion of income. Personal taxes of which the personal income tax is the major component, have risen in relative terms since the Second World War.

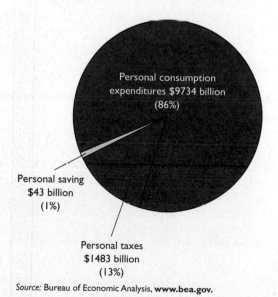

FIGURE 4.3 The disposition of household income, 2007. Households apportion their income among taxes, saving, and consumption, with most going to consumption. (The way income is defined in this figure differs slightly from that used in Figure 4.1, accounting for the quantitative discrepancies between the "total income" amounts in the two figures.)

Personal consumption expenditures $9734 billion (86%)

Personal saving $43 billion (1%)

Personal taxes $1483 billion (13%)

Source: Bureau of Economic Analysis, **www.bea.gov.**

In 1941, households paid just 3 percent of their total income in personal taxes.

Personal Saving

Economists define "saving" as that part of after-tax income that is not spent; hence, households have just two choices about what to do with their income after taxes—use it to consume, or save it. Saving is the portion of income that is not paid in taxes or used to purchase consumer goods but instead flows into bank accounts, insurance policies, bonds and stocks, mutual funds, and other financial assets.

U.S. households typically save about 3 percent of their income each year. Reasons for saving center on *security* and *speculation.* Households save to provide a nest egg for coping with unforeseen contingencies (sickness, accident, and unemployment), for retirement from the workforce, for financing the education of children, or simply for financial security. They may also channel part of their income to purchase stocks, speculating that their investments will increase in value.

The desire to save is not enough in itself, however. You must be able to save, and that depends on the size of your income. If your income is low, you may not be able to save any money at all. If your income is very, very low, you may *dissave*—that is, spend more than your after-tax income. You do this by borrowing or by digging into savings you may have accumulated in years when your income was higher.

Of course, some high-income people also dissave. That is how large fortunes are squandered. But overall, both saving and consumption vary directly with income; as households garner more income, they usually save more and consume more. In fact, the top 10 percent of income receivers account for most of the personal saving in the U.S. economy.

As shown in Figure 4.3, personal saving was $43 billion in 2007. This amounted to less the one percent of household income.

Personal Consumption Expenditures

As Figure 4.3 shows, 86 percent of the total income of households flows back into the business sector as personal consumption expenditures—money spent on consumer goods.

Figure 4.4 shows how consumers divide their expenditures among durable goods, nondurable goods, and services. Eleven percent of consumer expenditures are on **durable goods**—products that have expected lives of three years or more. Such goods include automobiles,

FIGURE 4.4 The composition of consumer expenditures, 2007. Consumers divide their spending among durable goods (goods that have expected lives of three years or more), nondurable goods, and services. About 60 percent of consumer spending is for services.

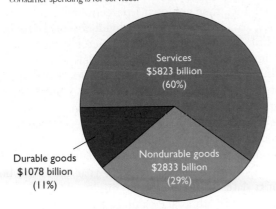

Services
$5823 billion
(60%)

Durable goods
$1078 billion
(11%)

Nondurable goods
$2833 billion
(29%)

Source: Bureau of Economic Analysis, **www.bea.gov.**

furniture, and personal computers. Another 29 percent of consumer expenditures are on **nondurable goods**—products that have lives of less than three years. Included are such goods as food, clothing, and gasoline. About 60 percent of consumer expenditures are on **services**—the work done for consumers by lawyers, barbers, doctors, lodging personnel, and so on. This high percentage is the reason that the United States is often referred to as a *service-oriented economy.*

QUICK REVIEW 4.1

- The functional distribution of income indicates how income is apportioned among wages, rents, interest, and profits; the personal distribution of income indicates how income is divided among families.
- Wages and salaries are the major component of the functional distribution of income. The personal distribution of income reveals considerable inequality.
- About 86 percent of household income is consumed; the rest is saved or paid in taxes.
- Consumer spending is directed to durable goods, nondurable goods, and services, with 60 percent going to services.

The Business Population

Businesses constitute the second major part of the private sector. Like households, they are a major element in the circular flow diagram that we discussed in Chapter 2.

In discussing businesses, it will be useful to distinguish among a plant, a firm, and an industry:

- A **plant** is a physical establishment—a factory, farm, mine, store, or warehouse—that performs one or more functions in fabricating and distributing goods and services.
- A **firm** is an organization that employs resources to produce goods and services for profit and operates one or more plants.
- An **industry** is a group of firms that produce the same, or similar, products.

The organizational structures of firms are often complex and varied. *Multiplant firms* may be organized horizontally, with several plants performing much the same function. Examples are the multiple bottling plants of Coca-Cola and the many individual Wal-Mart stores. Firms also may be *vertically integrated,* meaning they own plants that perform different functions in the various stages of the production process. For example, oil companies such as Shell own oil fields, refineries, and retail gasoline stations. Some firms are *conglomerates,* so named because they have plants that produce products in several industries. For example, Pfizer makes not only prescription medicines (Lipitor, Viagra) but also chewing gum (Trident, Dentyne), razors (Schick), cough drops (Halls), breath mints (Clorets, Certs), and antacids (Rolaids).

Legal Forms of Businesses

The business population is extremely diverse, ranging from giant corporations such as ExxonMobil, with 2007 sales of $347 billion and thousands of employees, to neighborhood specialty shops with one or two employees and sales of only $200 to $300 per day. There are three major legal forms of businesses:

- A **sole proprietorship** is a business owned and operated by one person. Usually, the proprietor (the owner) personally supervises its operation.
- The **partnership** form of business organization is a natural outgrowth of the sole proprietorship. In a partnership, two or more individuals (the partners) agree to own and operate a business together. Usually they pool their financial resources and business skills. Consequently, they share the risks and the profits or losses.
- A **corporation** is a legal creation that can acquire resources, own assets, produce and sell products, incur debts, extend credit, sue and be sued, and perform the functions of any other type of enterprise. A corporation is distinct and separate from the individual stockholders who own it. Hired managers run most corporations.

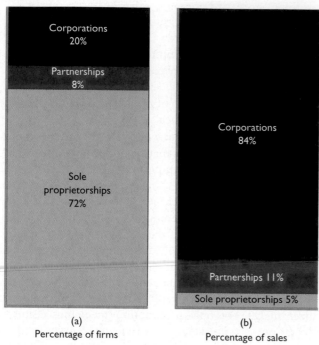

FIGURE 4.5 The business population and shares of domestic output. (a) Sole proprietorships dominate the business population numerically, but (b) corporations account for about 84 percent of total sales (output).

Source: U.S. Census Bureau, **www.census.gov.** Latest data.

Figure 4.5a shows how the business population is distributed among the three major forms. About 72 percent of U.S. firms are sole proprietorships. These firms are so numerous mainly because they are easy to set up and organize. The proprietor is his or her own boss and has substantial freedom of action. Partnerships constitute 8 percent of all U.S. business enterprises. The other 20 percent are corporations.

But as Figure 4.5b shows, sole proprietorships account for only 5 percent of total sales (output value) and partnerships only 11 percent. The remainder—an amazing 84 percent—accrues to corporations.

Advantages of Corporations

Certain advantages of the corporate form of business enterprise have catapulted it into a dominant sales and profit position in the United States. The corporation is by far the most effective form of business organization for raising money to finance the expansion of its facilities and capabilities. The corporation employs unique methods of finance—the selling of stocks (equity financing) and bonds (debt financing)—that enable it to pool the financial resources of large numbers of people.

A common **stock** represents a share in the ownership of a corporation. The purchaser of a stock certificate has the right to vote for corporate officers and to share in dividends. If you buy 1000 of the 100,000 shares issued by OutTell, Inc., then you own 1 percent of the company, are entitled to 1 percent of any dividends declared by the board of directors, and control 1 percent of the votes in the annual election of corporate officials.

In contrast, a corporate **bond** does not bestow any corporate ownership on the purchaser. A bond purchaser is simply lending money to a corporation. A bond is an IOU, in acknowledgment of a loan, whereby the corporation promises to pay the holder a fixed amount set forth on the bond at some specified future date and other fixed amounts (interest payments) every year up to the bond's maturity date. For example, you might purchase a 10-year OutTell bond with a face value of $1000 and a 5 percent rate of interest. This means that in exchange for your $1000, OT promises you a $50 interest payment for each of the next 10 years and then repays your $1000 principal at the end of that period.

Financing through sales of stocks and bonds also provides other advantages to those who purchase these *corporate securities.* An individual investor can spread risks by buying the securities of several corporations. And it is usually easy for holders of corporate securities to sell their holdings. Organized stock exchanges and bond markets simplify the transfer of securities from sellers to buyers. This "ease of sale" increases the willingness of savers to make financial investments in corporate securities. Besides, corporations have easier access to bank credit than do other types of business organizations. Corporations are better risks and are more likely to become profitable clients of banks.

Corporations provide **limited liability** to owners (stockholders), who risk only what they paid for their stock. Their personal assets are not at stake if the corporation defaults on its debts. Creditors can sue the corporation as a legal entity but cannot sue the owners of the corporation as individuals.

Because of their ability to attract financial capital, successful corporations can easily expand the scope of their operations and realize the benefits of expansion. For example, they can take advantage of mass-production technologies and division of labor. A corporation can hire specialists in production, accounting, and marketing functions and thus improve efficiency.

Unlike sole proprietorships and partnerships, the corporation has a life independent of its owners and its officers. As a legal entity, corporations are immortal. The transfer of corporate ownership through inheritance or

The World's 10 Largest Corporations

Five of the world's 10 largest corporations, based on dollar revenue in 2007, were headquartered in the United States.

Wal-Mart (U.S.)	$351 billion
ExxonMobil (U.S.)	$347 billion
Shell (U.K./Netherlands)	$319 billion
BP (U.K.)	$274 billion
General Motors (U.S.)	$207 billion
Toyota (Japan)	$205 billion
Chevron (U.S.)	$201 billion
DaimlerChrysler (Germany)	$190 billion
ConocoPhillips (U.S.)	$172 billion
Total (France)	$168 billion

Source: "The World's 10 Largest Corporations," *Fortune Global 500, 2007.* **www.fortune.com.** © 2007 Time Inc. All rights reserved.

the sale of stock does not disrupt the continuity of the corporation. Corporations have permanence that lends itself to long-range planning and growth. This permanence and growth explains why virtually all the nation's largest business enterprises are corporations.

The Principal-Agent Problem

Many of the world's corporations are extremely large. In 2007, 351 of the world's largest corporations had annual sales of more than $20 billion; 121 firms had sales exceeding $50 billion; and 30 firms had sales greater than $100 billion. U.S.-based Wal-Mart alone had sales of $351 billion in 2007. Global Perspective 4.1 lists the world's 10 largest corporations, by annual sales.

But large size creates a potential problem. In sole proprietorships and partnerships, the owners of the real and financial assets of the firm enjoy direct control of those assets. But ownership of large corporations is spread over tens or hundreds of thousands of stockholders. The owners of a corporation usually do not manage it—they hire others to do so.

That practice can create a **principal-agent problem.** The *principals* are the stockholders who own the corporation and who hire executives as their *agents* to run the

ORIGIN OF THE IDEA

O 4.1
Principal-agent problem

business on their behalf. But the interests of these managers (the agents) and the wishes of the owners (the principals) do not always coincide. The owners typically want maximum company profit and stock price. However, the agent may want the power, prestige, and pay that often accompany control over a large enterprise, independent of its profitability and stock price.

So a conflict of interest may develop. For example, executives may build expensive office buildings, enjoy

CONSIDER THIS . . .

Unprincipled Agents

In the 1990s many corporations addressed the principal-agent problem by providing a substantial part of executive pay either as shares of the firm's stock or as stock options. Stock options are contracts that allow executives or other key employees to buy shares of their employers' stock at fixed, lower prices when the stock prices rise. The intent was to align the interest of the executives and other key employees more closely with those of the broader corporate owners. By pursuing high profits and share prices, the executives would enhance their own wealth as well as that of all the stockholders.

This "solution" to the principal-agent problem had an unexpected negative side effect. It prompted a few unscrupulous executives to inflate their firms' share prices by hiding costs, overstating revenues, engaging in deceptive transactions, and, in general, exaggerating profits. These executives then sold large quantities of their inflated stock, making quick personal fortunes. In some cases, "independent" outside auditing firms turned out to be not so independent because they held valuable consulting contracts with the firms being audited.

When the stock-market bubble of the late 1990s burst, many instances of business manipulations and fraudulent accounting were exposed. Several executives of large U.S. firms were indicted and a few large firms collapsed, among them Enron (energy trading), WorldCom (communications), and Arthur Andersen (accounting and business consulting). General stockholders of those firms were left holding severely depressed or even worthless stock.

In 2002 Congress strengthened the laws and penalties against executive misconduct. Also, corporations have improved their accounting and auditing procedures. But seemingly endless revelations of executive wrongdoings make clear that the principal-agent problem is not an easy problem to solve.

excessive perks such as corporate jets, and pay too much to acquire other corporations. Consequently, the firm's costs will be excessive and the executives will fail to maximize profit and the stock price for the owners. **(Key Question 4)**

The Public Sector: Government's Role

The economic activities of the *public sector*—Federal, state, and local government—are extensive. We begin by discussing the economic functions of governments. What is government's role in the economy?

Providing the Legal Structure

Government provides the legal framework and the services needed for a market economy to operate effectively. The legal framework sets the legal status of business enterprises, ensures the rights of private ownership, and allows the making and enforcement of contracts. Government also establishes the legal "rules of the game" that control relationships among businesses, resource suppliers, and consumers. Discrete units of government referee economic relationships, seek out foul play, and impose penalties.

Government intervention is presumed to improve the allocation of resources. By supplying a medium of exchange, ensuring product quality, defining ownership rights, and enforcing contracts, the government increases the volume and safety of exchange. This widens the market and fosters greater specialization in the use of land, labor, capital, and

entrepreneurial resources. Such specialization promotes a more efficient allocation of resources.

Like the optimal amount of any "good," the optimal amount of regulation is that at which the marginal benefit and marginal cost are equal. Thus, there can be either too little regulation (MB exceeds MC) or too much regulation (MB is less than MC). The task is to decide wisely on the right amount.

Maintaining Competition

Competition is the basic regulatory mechanism in the market system. It is the force that subjects producers and resource suppliers to the dictates of consumer sovereignty. With competition, buyers are the boss, the market is their agent, and businesses are their servants.

It is a different story where a single seller—a **monopoly**—controls an industry. By controlling supply, a monopolist can charge a higher-than-competitive price. Producer sovereignty then supplants consumer sovereignty. In the United States, government has attempted to control monopoly through *regulation* and through *antitrust*.

A few industries are natural monopolies—industries in which technology is such that only a single seller can achieve the lowest possible costs. In some cases government has allowed these monopolies to exist but has also created public commissions to regulate their prices and set their service standards. Examples of *regulated monopolies* are some firms that provide local electricity, telephone, and transportation services.

In nearly all markets, however, efficient production can best be attained with a high degree of competition. The Federal government has therefore enacted a series of antitrust (antimonopoly) laws, beginning with the Sherman Act of 1890, to prohibit certain monopoly abuses and, if necessary, break monopolists up into competing firms. Under these laws, for example, in 2000 Microsoft was found guilty of monopolizing the market for operating systems for personal computers. Rather than breaking up Microsoft, however, the government imposed a series of prohibitions and requirements that collectively limited Microsoft's ability to engage in anticompetitive actions.

Redistributing Income

The market system is impersonal and may distribute income more inequitably than society desires. It yields very large incomes to those whose labor, by virtue of inherent ability and acquired education and skills, commands high wages. Similarly, those who, through hard work or inheritance, possess valuable capital and land receive large property incomes.

But many other members of society have less productive ability, have received only modest amounts of education and training, and have accumulated or inherited no property resources. Moreover, some of the elderly, the physically and mentally disabled, and the poorly educated earn small incomes or, like the unemployed, no income at all. Thus society chooses to redistribute a part of total income through a variety of government policies and programs. They are:

- *Transfer payments* *Transfer payments*, for example, in the form of welfare checks and food stamps, provide relief to the destitute, the dependent, the disabled, and older citizens; unemployment compensation payments provide aid to the unemployed.
- *Market intervention* Government also alters the distribution of income through *market intervention*, that is, by acting to modify the prices that are or would be established by market forces. Providing farmers with above-market prices for their output and requiring that firms pay minimum wages are illustrations of government interventions designed to raise the income of specific groups.
- *Taxation* The government uses the personal income tax to take a larger proportion of the income of the rich than of the poor, thus narrowing the after-tax income difference between high-income and low-income earners.

The *extent* to which government should redistribute income is subject to lively debate. Redistribution involves both benefits and costs. The purported benefits are greater "fairness" or "economic justice"; the purported costs are reduced incentives to work, save, invest, and produce, and therefore a loss of total output and income.

Reallocating Resources

Market failure occurs when the competitive market system (1) produces the "wrong" amounts of certain goods and services or (2) fails to allocate any resources whatsoever to the production of certain goods and services whose output is economically justified. The first type of failure results from what economists call *externalities* or *spillovers* and the second type involves *public goods*. Government can take actions to try to address both kinds of market failure.

Externalities
When we say that competitive markets automatically bring about the efficient use of resources, we assume that all the benefits and costs for each product are fully reflected in the market demand and supply curves. That is not always the case. In some markets certain benefits or costs may escape the buyer or seller.

An **externality** occurs when some of the costs or the benefits of a good are passed on to or "spill over to" someone other than the immediate buyer or seller. Such spillovers are called externalities because they are benefits or costs that accrue to some third party that is *external* to the market transaction.

ORIGIN OF THE IDEA

O 4.2
Externalities

Negative Externalities
Production or consumption costs inflicted on a third party without compensation are called **negative externalities.** Environmental pollution is an example. When a chemical manufacturer or a meat-packing plant dumps its wastes into a lake or river, swimmers, fishers, and boaters—and perhaps those who drink the water—suffer external costs. When a petroleum refinery pollutes the air with smoke or a paper mill creates obnoxious odors, the community experiences external costs for which it is not compensated.

What are the economic effects? Recall that costs determine the position of the firm's supply curve. When a firm avoids some costs by polluting, its supply curve lies farther to the right than it does when the firm bears the full costs of production. As a result, the price of the product is too low and the output of the product is too large to achieve allocative efficiency. A market failure occurs in the form of an overallocation of resources to the production of the good.

Correcting for Negative Externalities
Some externalities get resolved via private negotiations between those creating the externalities and those affected by them. But when the externalities are widespread and negotiation between parties is unrealistic, government can play an important role. For example, it can do two things to correct the overallocation of resources associated with negative externalities. Both solutions are designed to internalize external costs, that is, to make the offending firm pay the costs rather than shift them to others:

- *Legislation* In cases of air and water pollution, the most direct action is legislation prohibiting or limiting the pollution. Such legislation forces potential polluters to pay for the proper disposal of industrial wastes—here, by installing smoke-abatement equipment or water-purification facilities. The idea is to force potential offenders, under the threat of legal action, to bear *all* the costs associated with production.
- *Specific taxes* A less direct action is based on the fact that taxes are a cost and therefore a determinant of a

firm's supply curve. Government might levy a *specific tax*—that is, a tax confined to a particular product—on each unit of the polluting firm's output. The amount of this tax would roughly equal the estimated dollar value of the negative externality arising from the production of each unit of output. Through this tax, government would impose a cost on the offending firm equivalent to the spillover cost the firm is avoiding. This would shift the firm's supply curve to the left, reducing equilibrium output and eliminating the overallocation of resources.

Positive Externalities Sometimes externalities appear as benefits to other producers or consumers. These uncompensated spillovers accruing to third parties or the community at large are called **positive externalities.** Immunization against measles and polio results in direct benefits to the immediate consumer of those vaccines. But it also results in widespread substantial external benefits to the entire community.

Education is another example of positive externalities. Education benefits individual consumers: Better-educated people generally achieve higher incomes than less-well-educated people. But education also provides benefits to society, in the form of a more versatile and more productive labor force, on the one hand, and smaller outlays for crime prevention, law enforcement, and welfare programs, on the other.

External benefits mean that the market demand curve, which reflects only private benefits, understates total benefits. The demand curve for the product lies farther to the left than it would if the market took all benefits into account. As a result, a smaller amount of the product will be produced, or, alternatively, there will be an *underallocation* of resources to the product—again a market failure.

Correcting for Positive Externalities How might government deal with the underrallocation of resources resulting from positive externalities? The answer is either to subsidize consumers (to increase demand), to subsidize producers (to increase supply), or, in the extreme, to have government produce the product:

- *Subsidize consumers* To correct the underallocation of resources to higher education, the U.S. government provides low-interest loans to students so that they can afford more education. Those loans increase the demand for higher education.
- *Subsidize suppliers* In some cases government finds it more convenient and administratively simpler to correct an underallocation by subsidizing suppliers. For example, in higher education, state governments

provide substantial portions of the budgets of public colleges and universities. Such subsidies lower the costs of producing higher education and increase its supply. Publicly subsidized immunization programs, hospitals, and medical research are other examples.

- *Provide goods via government* A third policy option may be appropriate where positive externalities are extremely large: Government may finance or, in the extreme, own and operate the industry that is involved. Examples are the U.S. Postal Service and Federal air traffic control systems.

Public Goods and Services

Certain goods called *private goods* are produced through the competitive market system. Examples are the wide variety of items sold in stores. Private goods have two characteristics—*rivalry* and *excludability*. "Rivalry" means that when one person buys and consumes a product, it is not available for purchase and consumption by another person. What Joan gets, Jane cannot have. *Excludability* means that buyers who are willing and able to pay the market price for the product obtain its benefits, but those unable or unwilling to pay that price do not. This characteristic enables profitable production by a private firm.

Certain other goods and services called **public goods** have the opposite characteristics—*nonrivalry* and *nonexcludability*. Everyone can simultaneously obtain the benefit from a public good such as a global positioning system, national defense, street lighting, and environmental protection. One person's benefit does not reduce the benefit available to others. More important, there is no effective way of excluding individuals from the benefit of the good once it comes into existence. The inability to exclude creates a **free-rider problem,** in which people can receive benefits from a public good without having to pay for it. As a result, goods and services subject to free riding will typically be unprofitable for any private firm that decides to produce and sell them.

An example of a public good is the war on terrorism. This public good is thought to be economically justified by the majority of Americans because the benefits are perceived as exceeding the costs. Once the war efforts are undertaken, however, the benefits accrue to all Americans (nonrivalry). And there is no practical way to exclude any American from receiving those benefits (nonexcludability).

No private firm will undertake the war on terrorism because the benefits cannot be profitably sold (due to the free-rider problem). So here we have a service that yields substantial benefits but to which the market system will not allocate sufficient resources. Like national defense in general, the pursuit of the war on terrorism is a public good. Society signals its desire for such goods by voting for particular political candidates who support their provision. Because of the free-rider problem, the public sector provides these goods and finances them through compulsory charges in the form of taxes.

Quasi-Public Goods Government provides many goods that fit the economist's definition of a public good. However, it also provides other goods and services that could be produced and delivered in such a way that exclusion would be possible. Such goods, called **quasi-public goods,** include education, streets and highways, police and fire protection, libraries and museums, preventive medicine, and sewage disposal. They could all be priced and provided by private firms through the market system. But, as we noted earlier, because they all have substantial positive externalities, they would be underproduced by the market system. Therefore, government often provides them to avoid the underallocation of resources that would otherwise occur.

The Reallocation Process How are resources reallocated from the production of private goods to the production of public and quasi-public goods? If the resources of the economy are fully employed, government must free up resources from the production of private goods and make them available for producing public and quasi-public goods. It does so by reducing private demand for them. And it does that by levying taxes on households and businesses, taking some of their income out of the circular flow. With lower incomes and hence less purchasing power, households and businesses must curtail their consumption and investment spending. As a result, the private demand for goods and services declines, as does the private demand for resources. So by diverting purchasing power from private spenders to government, taxes remove resources from private use.

Government then spends the tax proceeds to provide public and quasi-public goods and services. Taxation releases resources from the production of private consumer goods (food, clothing, television sets) and private investment goods (printing presses, boxcars, warehouses). Government shifts those resources to the production of public and quasi-public goods (post offices, submarines, parks), changing the composition of the economy's total output. **(Key Questions 9 and 10)**

Promoting Stability

Macroeconomic stability is said to exist when an economy's output matches its production capacity, its labor

Street Entertainers

Street entertainers are often found in tourist areas of major cities. Some entertainers are highly creative and talented; others "need more practice." But, regardless of talent level, these entertainers illuminate the concepts of free riders and public goods.

Most street entertainers have a hard time earning a living from their activities (unless event organizers pay them) because they have no way of excluding nonpayers from the benefits of their entertainment. They essentially are providing public, not private, goods and must rely on voluntary payments.

The result is a significant free-rider problem. Only a few in the audience put money in the container or instrument case, and many who do so contribute only token amounts. The rest are free riders who obtain the benefits of the street entertainment and retain their money for purchases that *they* initiate.

Street entertainers are acutely aware of the free-rider problem, and some have found creative ways to lessen it. For example, some entertainers involve the audience directly in the act. This usually creates a greater sense of audience willingness (or obligation) to contribute money at the end of the performance.

"Pay for performance" is another creative approach to lessening the free-rider problem. A good example is the street entertainer painted up to look like a statue. When people drop coins into the container, the "statue" makes a slight movement. The greater the contributions, the greater the movement. But these human "statues" still face a free-rider problem: Nonpayers also get to enjoy the acts.

Finally, because talented street entertainers create a festive street environment, cities or retailers sometimes hire them to perform. The "free entertainment" attracts crowds of shoppers, who buy goods from nearby retailers. In these instances the cities or retailers use tax revenue or commercial funds to pay the entertainers, in the former case validating them as public goods.

resources are fully employed, and inflation is low and stable. (Inflation is a general increase in the level of prices.) In such circumstances, the economy's total spending matches its production capacity. Government and the nation's central bank (the Federal Reserve in the United States) promote full employment and price stability through prudent *fiscal policy* (government taxing and spending policy) and *monetary policy* (central bank interest rate policy). But sometimes unexpected shocks occur to the economy that cause total spending either to fall far below production capacity or to surge way above it, resulting in widespread unemployment or inflation. Government may try to address these problems by altering its fiscal policy or monetary policy.

- *Unemployment* When private sector spending is too low, resulting in unemployment, government may try to increase total spending (private + public) by raising its own spending or by lowering tax rates to encourage greater private spending. Also, the nation's central bank may take monetary actions to lower interest rates, thereby encouraging more private borrowing and spending.

- *Inflation* Inflation is a general increase in the level of prices. Prices of goods and services rise when the amount of spending in the economy expands more rapidly than the supply of goods and services. This can happen when the nation's central bank allows interest rates to remain too low for the economic circumstances. In such situations, the central bank can act to lower inflation by increasing the interest rate so as to dampen private borrowing and spending. The government may also try to reduce total spending by cutting its own expenditures or boosting tax rates to reduce private spending.

Government's Role: A Qualification

Government does not have an easy task in performing the aforementioned economic functions. In a democracy, government undertakes its economic role in the context of politics. To serve the public, politicians need to get elected. To stay elected, officials (presidents, senators, representatives, mayors, council members, school board members) need to satisfy their particular constituencies. At best, the political realities complicate government's role in the economy; at worst, they produce undesirable economic outcomes.

In the political context, overregulation can occur in some cases; underregulation, in others. Income can be redistributed to such an extent that incentives to work, save, and invest suffer. Some public goods and quasi-public goods can be produced not because their benefits exceed their costs but because their benefits accrue to firms located in states served by powerful elected officials. Inefficiency can easily creep into government activities because of the lack of a profit incentive to hold down costs. Policies to correct negative externalities can be politically

blocked by the very parties that are producing the spillovers. In short, the economic role of government, although critical to a well-functioning economy, is not always perfectly carried out.

The Circular Flow Revisited

In Figure 4.6 we integrate government into the circular flow model first shown in Figure 2.2. Here flows (1) through (4) are the same as the corresponding flows in that figure. Flows (1) and (2) show business expenditures for the resources provided by households. These expenditures are costs to businesses but represent wage, rent, interest, and profit income to households. Flows (3) and (4) show household expenditures for the goods and services produced by businesses.

Now consider what happens when we add government. Flows (5) through (8) illustrate that government makes purchases in both product and resource markets. Flows (5) and (6) represent government purchases of such products as paper, computers, and military hardware from private businesses. Flows (7) and (8) represent government purchases of resources. The Federal government employs and pays salaries to members of Congress, the armed forces, Justice Department lawyers, meat inspectors, and so on. State and local governments hire and pay teachers, bus drivers, police, and firefighters. The Federal government might also lease or purchase land to expand a military base and a city might buy land on which to build a new elementary school.

Government then provides public goods and services to both households and businesses, as shown by flows

FIGURE 4.6 **The circular flow and the public sector.** Government buys products from the product market and employs resources from the resource market to provide public goods and services to households and businesses. Government finances its expenditures through the net taxes (taxes minus transfer payments) it receives from households and businesses.

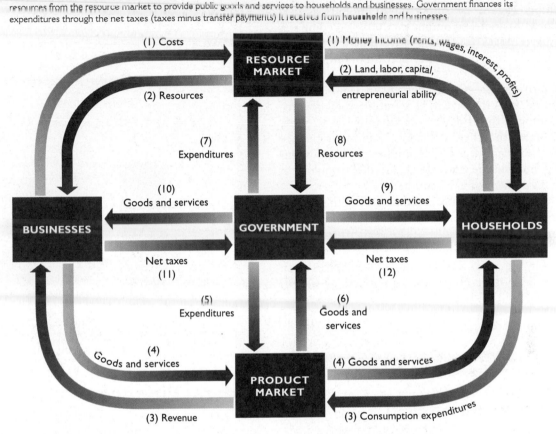

(9) and (10). To finance those public goods and services, businesses and households are required to pay taxes, as shown by flows (11) and (12). These flows are labeled as *net* taxes to indicate that they also include "taxes in reverse" in the form of transfer payments to households and subsidies to businesses. Thus, flow (11) entails various subsidies to farmers, shipbuilders, and airlines as well as income, sales, and excise taxes paid by businesses to government. Most subsidies to business are "concealed" in the form of low-interest loans, loan guarantees, tax concessions, or public facilities provided at prices below their cost. Similarly, flow (12) includes both taxes (personal income taxes, payroll taxes) collected by government directly from households and transfer payments such as welfare payments and Social Security benefits paid by government.

Government Finance

How large is the U.S. public sector? What are the main expenditure categories of Federal, state, and local governments? How are these expenditures financed?

Government Purchases and Transfers

We can get an idea of the size of government's economic role by examining government purchases of goods and services and government transfer payments. There is a significant difference between these two kinds of outlays:

- **Government purchases** are *exhaustive;* the products purchased directly absorb (require the use of) resources and are part of the domestic output. For example, the purchase of a missile absorbs the labor of physicists and engineers along with steel, explosives, and a host of other inputs.

- **Transfer payments** are *nonexhaustive;* they do not directly absorb resources or create output. Social Security benefits, welfare payments, veterans' benefits, and unemployment compensation are examples of transfer payments. Their key characteristic is that recipients make no current contribution to domestic output in return for them.

Federal, state, and local governments spent $4413 billion in 2007. Of that total, government purchases were \$2671 billion and government transfers were \$1742 billion. Figure 4.7 shows these amounts as percentages of U.S. domestic output for 2007 and compares them to percentages for 1960. Government purchases have declined from about 22 to 19 percent of output since 1960. But transfer payments have more than doubled as a percentage of output—from 5 percent in 1960 to about 13 percent in 2007. Relative to U.S. output, total government spending is thus higher today than it was 47 years ago. This means that the tax revenues required to finance government expenditures are also higher. Today, government spending and the tax revenues needed to finance it are about 32 percent of U.S. output.

In 2007 the so-called Tax Freedom Day in the United States was April 30. On that day the average worker had earned enough (from the start of the year) to pay his or her share of the taxes required to finance government spending for the year. Tax Freedom Day arrives even later in several other countries, as implied in Global Perspective 4.2.

FIGURE 4.7 Government purchases, transfers, and total spending as percentages of U.S. output, 1960 and 2007. Government purchases have declined as a percentage of U.S. output since 1960. Transfer payments, however, have increased by more than this drop, raising total government spending (purchases plus transfers) from 27 percent of U.S. GDP in 1960 to about 32 percent today.

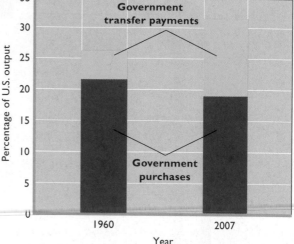

Source: Compiled from Bureau of Economic Analysis data, **www.bea.gov.**

GLOBAL PERSPECTIVE 4.2

Total Tax Revenue as a Percentage of Total Output, Selected Nations*

A nation's "tax burden" is its tax revenue from all levels of government as a percentage of its total output (GDP). Among the world's industrialized nations, South Korea, Japan, United States have the lowest tax burdens.

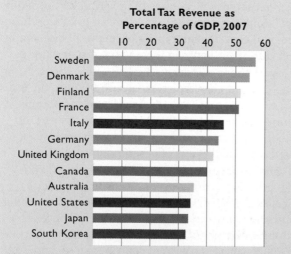

*Includes government nontax revenue from fees, charges, fines and sales of government property.

Source: Organization for Economic Cooperation and Development. **www.oecd.org.**

Federal Finance

Now let's look separately at each of the Federal, state, and local units of government in the United States and compare their expenditures and taxes. Figure 4.8 tells the story for the Federal government.

Federal Expenditures

Four areas of Federal spending stand out: (1) pensions and income security, (2) national defense, (3) health, and (4) interest on the public debt. The *pensions and income security* category includes the many income-maintenance programs for the aged, persons with disabilities or handicaps, the unemployed, the retired, and families with no breadwinner. This category—dominated by the \$461 billion pension portion of the Social Security program—accounts for 34 percent of total Federal expenditures. (This chapter's Last Word examines the impact of the aging U.S. population on the future financing of this area of Federal spending.) *National defense* accounts for about 21 percent of the Federal budget, underscoring the high cost of military preparedness. *Health* reflects the cost of government health programs for the retired (Medicare) and poor (Medicaid). *Interest on the public debt* is a substantial amount because the public debt itself is large.

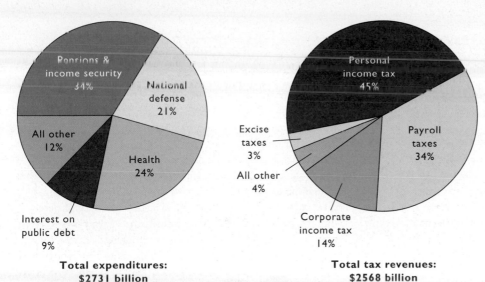

FIGURE 4.8 **Federal expenditures and tax revenues, 2007.** Federal expenditures are dominated by spending for pensions and income security, health, and national defense. A full 79 percent of federal tax revenue is derived from just two sources: the personal income tax and payroll taxes. The $163 billion difference between expenditures and revenues reflects a budget deficit.

Total expenditures:
$2731 billion

Total tax revenues:
$2568 billion

Source: U.S. Treasury, *Combined Statement of Receipts, Outlays, and Balances, 2007,* **fms.treas.gov.**

Federal Tax Revenues

The revenue side of Figure 4.8 shows that the personal income tax, payroll taxes, and the corporate income tax are the basic revenue sources, accounting respectively for 45, 34, and 14 cents of each dollar collected.

Personal Income Tax The **personal income tax** is the kingpin of the Federal tax system and merits special comment. This tax is levied on *taxable income,* that is, on the incomes of households and unincorporated businesses after certain exemptions ($3500 for each household member) and deductions (business expenses, charitable contributions, home mortgage interest payments, certain state and local taxes) are taken into account.

The Federal personal income tax is a *progressive tax,* meaning that people with higher incomes pay a larger percentage of their incomes as taxes than do people with lower incomes. The progressivity is achieved by applying higher tax rates to successive layers or brackets of income.

Columns 1 and 2 in Table 4.1 show the mechanics of the income tax for a married couple filing a joint return in 2008. Note that a 10 percent tax rate applies to all taxable income up to $16,050 and a 15 percent rate applies to additional income up to $65,100. The rates on additional layers of income then go up to 25, 28, 33, and 35 percent.

The tax rates shown in column 2 in Table 4.1 are marginal tax rates. A **marginal tax rate** is the rate at which the tax is paid on each *additional* unit of taxable income. Thus, if a couple's taxable income is $80,000, they will pay the marginal rate of 10 percent on each dollar from $1 to $16,050, 15 percent on each dollar from

TABLE 4.1 Federal Personal Income Tax Rates, 2008*

(1) Total Taxable Income	(2) Marginal Tax Rate, %	(3) Total Tax on Highest Income In Bracket	(4) Average Tax Rate on Highest Income in Bracket, % (3) ÷ (1)
$1–$16,050	10.0	$ 1605	10
$16,051–$65,100	15.0	8963	14
$65,101–$131,450	25.0	25,550	19
$131,451–$200,300	28.0	44,828	22
$200,301–$357,700	33.0	96,770	27
Over $357,700	35.0		

*For a married couple filing a joint return.

$16,501 to $65,100, and 25 percent on each dollar from $65,101 to $80,000. You should confirm that their total income tax is $12,688.

The marginal tax rates in column 2 overstate the personal income tax bite because the rising rates in that column apply only to the income within each successive tax bracket. To get a better idea of the tax burden, we must consider average tax rates. The **average tax rate** is the total tax paid divided by total taxable income. The couple in our previous example is in the 25 percent tax bracket because they pay a top marginal tax rate of 25 percent on the highest dollar of their income. But their *average* tax rate is 16 percent (= $12,688/$80,000).

WORKED PROBLEMS

W 4.1

Taxes and Progressivity

There Is a Severe Long-Run Shortfall in Social Security Funding Because Expected Future Outlays to Retirees Greatly Exceed Expected Future Revenues.

The Social Security program (excluding Medicare) has grown from less than one-half of 1 percent of U.S. GDP in 1950 to 4.3 percent of GDP today. That percentage is projected to grow to 6 percent of GDP in 2030 and slightly higher thereafter.

The $461 billion Social Security program is largely an annual "pay-as-you-go" plan, meaning that most of the current revenues from the 12.4 percent Social Security tax (the rate when the 2.9 percent Medicare tax is excluded) are paid out to current Social Security retirees. In anticipation of the large benefits owed to the baby boomers when they retire, however, the Social Security Administration has been placing an excess of current revenues over current payouts into a trust fund consisting of U.S. Treasury securities. But the accumulation of money in the Social Security trust fund will be greatly inadequate for paying the retirement benefits promised to all future retirees.

In 2017 Social Security retirement revenues will fall below Social Security retirement benefits and the system will begin dipping into the trust fund to make up the difference. The trust fund will be exhausted in 2041, after which the annual tax revenues will cover only 75 percent of the promised benefits. The Federal government faces a several-trillion-dollar shortfall of long-run revenues for funding Social Security.

As shown in the accompanying figure, the problem is one of demographics. The percentage of the American population age 62 or older will rise substantially over the next several decades, with the greatest increases for those age 75 and older. High fertility rates during the "baby boom" (1946–1964), declining birthrates thereafter, and rising life expectancies have combined to produce an aging population. In the future, more people will be receiving Social Security benefits for longer periods and each person's benefits will be paid for by fewer workers. The number of workers per Social Security beneficiary was 5:1 in 1960. Today it is 3:1, and by 2040 it will be only 2:1.

There is no easy way to restore long-run balance to Social Security funding. Either benefits must be reduced or revenues must be increased. The Social Security Administration concludes that bringing projected Social Security revenues and payments into balance over the next 75 years would require a 12 percent permanent reduction in Social Security benefits, a 14 percent permanent increase in tax revenues, or some combination of the two.*

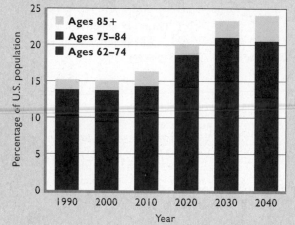

A tax whose average rate rises as income increases is a progressive tax. Such a tax claims both a larger absolute amount and a larger proportion of income as income rises. Thus we can say that the Federal personal income tax is progressive. **(Key Question 15)**

Payroll Taxes Social Security contributions are **payroll taxes**—taxes based on wages and salaries—used to finance two compulsory Federal programs for retired workers: Social Security (an income-enhancement program) and Medicare (which pays for medical services). Employers and employees pay these taxes equally. Enlargements in, and extensions of, the Social Security programs, plus growth of the labor force, have resulted in significant increases in these payroll taxes in recent years. In 2008, employees and employers each paid 7.65 percent on the first $102,000 of an employee's annual earnings and 1.45 percent on all additional earnings.

Corporate Income Tax The Federal government also taxes corporate income. The **corporate income tax** is levied on a corporation's profit—the difference between its total revenue and its total expenses. For almost all corporations, the tax rate is 35 percent.

Excise Taxes Taxes on commodities or on purchases take the form of **sales and excise taxes.** The difference

Several ideas have been offered to improve the financial outlook of Social Security. These ideas include increasing the retirement age, subjecting a larger portion of total earnings to the Social Security tax, and reducing benefits for wealthy retirees.

Other ideas are more novel. For example, one suggestion is to boost the trust fund by investing all or part of it in corporate stocks and bonds. The Federal government would own the stock investments, and an appointed panel would oversee the direction of those investments. The presumed higher returns on the investments relative to the lower returns on U.S. securities would stretch out the life of the trust fund. Nevertheless, a substantial increase in the payroll tax would still be needed to cover the shortfalls after the trust fund is exhausted.

Another option is to increase the payroll tax immediately—perhaps by as much as 1.5 percentage points—and allocate the new revenues to individual accounts. Government would control the accumulations in the accounts, but individuals could direct their investments to a restricted list of broad stock or bond funds. When they retire, recipients could convert these individual account balances to annuities—securities paying monthly payments for life. That annuity income would supplement reduced monthly benefits from the pay-as-you-go system when the trust fund is exhausted.

A different route is to place half the payroll tax into accounts that individuals, not the government, would own, maintain, and bequeath. Individuals could invest these funds in

bank certificates of deposit or in approved stock and bond funds and draw upon the accounts when they reach retirement age. A flat monthly benefit would supplement the accumulations in the private accounts. The personal security accounts would be phased in over time, so those individuals now receiving or about to receive Social Security benefits would continue to receive benefits.

These general ideas do not exhaust the possible reforms since the variations on each plan are nearly endless. Reaching consensus on Social Security reform will be difficult because every citizen has a direct economic stake in the outcome and little agreement is present among them on the proper magnitude of the benefits, how the program should be structured, and how we should pay for the projected funding shortfall. Nevertheless, society will eventually need to confront the problem of trillions of dollars of unfunded Social Security liabilities.[†]

---

*Social Security Board of Trustees. "Status of the Social Security and Medicare Programs: A Summary of the 2008 Annual Reports," **www.ssa.gov.**

[†]Medicare (the health insurance that accompanies Social Security) is also severely underfunded. To bring projected Medicare revenues and expenditures into long-run balance would require an immediate increase in the Medicare payroll tax by 122 percent, a 51 percent reduction of Medicare payments from their projected levels, or some combination of each. The total funding shortfall through 2080 for Social Security and Medicare (including its prescription drug benefit) was $24 trillion in 2007.

---

between the two is mainly one of coverage. Sales taxes fall on a wide range of products, whereas excises are levied individually on a small, select list of commodities. As Figure 4.8 suggests, the Federal government collects excise taxes (on the sale of such commodities as alcoholic beverages, tobacco, and gasoline) but does not levy a general sales tax; sales taxes are, however, the primary revenue source of most state governments.

State and Local Finance

State and local governments have different mixes of revenues and expenditures than the Federal government has.

State Finances

The primary source of tax revenue for state governments is sales and excise taxes, which account for about 47 percent of all their tax revenue. State personal income taxes, which have much lower rates than the Federal income tax, are the second most important source of state tax revenue. They bring in about 35 percent of total state tax revenue. Corporate income taxes and license fees account for most of the remainder of state tax revenue.

Education expenditures account for about 36 percent of all state spending. State expenditures on public welfare are next in relative weight, at about 28 percent of the total. States also spend heavily on health and hospitals (7 percent), highway maintenance and construction (7 percent), and public safety (4 percent). That leaves about 18 percent of all state spending for a variety of other purposes.

These tax and expenditure percentages combine data from all the states, so they reveal little about the finances of individual states. States vary significantly in the taxes levied. Thus, although personal income taxes are a major source of revenue for all state governments combined, seven states do not levy a personal income tax. Also, there are great variations in the sizes of tax revenues and disbursements among the states, both in the aggregate and as percentages of personal income.

Thirty-nine states augment their tax revenues with state-run lotteries to help close the gap between their tax receipts and expenditures. Individual states also receive large intergovernmental grants from the Federal government. In fact, about 24 percent of their total revenue is in that form. States also take in revenue from miscellaneous sources such as state-owned utilities and liquor stores.

Local Finances

The local levels of government include counties, municipalities, townships, and school districts as well as cities and towns. Local governments obtain about 72 percent of their tax revenue from **property taxes.** Sales and excise taxes contribute about 16 percent of all local government tax revenue.

About 44 percent of local government expenditures go to education. Welfare, health, and hospitals (12 percent); public safety (11 percent); housing, parks, and sewerage (8 percent); and streets and highways (4 percent) are also major spending categories.

The tax revenues of local government cover less than one-half of their expenditures. The remaining revenue comes from intergovernmental grants from the Federal and state governments. Also, local governments receive considerable amounts of proprietary income, for example, revenue from government-owned utilities providing water, electricity, natural gas, and transportation.

QUICK REVIEW 4.4

- As percentages of GDP, government purchases are 19 percent; government transfers, 13 percent; and the two combined, 32 percent.
- Income security and national defense are the main categories of Federal spending; personal income, payroll, and corporate income taxes are the primary sources of Federal revenue.
- States rely on sales and excise taxes for revenue; their spending is largely for education and public welfare.
- Education is the main expenditure for local governments, most of whose revenue comes from property taxes.

Summary

1. The functional distribution of income shows how society's total income is divided among wages, rents, interest, and profit; the personal distribution of income shows how total income is divided among individual households.

2. Households use all their income for paying personal taxes, for saving, and for buying consumer goods. Nearly about 60 percent of their consumption expenditures are for services.

3. Sole proprietorships are firms owned and usually operated by single individuals. Partnerships are firms owned and usually operated by just a handful of individuals. Corporations—the dominant form of business organization—are legal entities, distinct and separate from the individuals who own them. They often have thousands, or even millions, of owners—the stockholders.

4. Corporations finance their operations and purchases of new plant and equipment partly through the issuance of stocks and bonds. Stocks are ownership shares of a corporation, and bonds are promises to repay a loan, usually at a set rate of interest.

5. A principal-agent problem may occur in corporations when the agents (managers) hired to represent the interest of the principals (stockholders) pursue their own objectives to the detriment of the objectives of the principals.

6. Government improves the operation of the market system by (a) providing an appropriate legal and social framework and (b) acting to maintain competition.

7. Government alters the distribution of income through the tax-transfer system and through market intervention.

8. Externalities, or spillovers, cause the equilibrium output of certain goods to vary from the socially efficient output. Negative externalities result in an overallocation of resources, which can be corrected by legislation or by specific taxes. Positive externalities are accompanied by an underallocation of resources, which can be corrected by government subsidies to consumers or producers.

9. Only government is willing to provide public goods, which can be consumed by all simultaneously (nonrivalry) and

entail benefits from which nonpaying consumers (free riders) cannot be excluded (nonexcludability). Because doing so is not profitable, private firms will not produce public goods. Quasi-public goods have some of the characteristics of public goods and some of the characteristics of private goods; government provides them because the private sector would underallocate resources to their production.

10. To try to stabilize the economy, the government adjusts its spending and taxes, and the nation's central bank (the Federal Reserve in the United States) uses monetary actions to alter interest rates.

11. Government purchases exhaust (use up or absorb) resources; transfer payments do not. Government purchases have declined from about 22 percent of domestic output in 1960 to 19 percent today. Transfer payments, however, have grown rapidly. As a percentage of GDP, total government spending (purchases plus transfers) now stands at about 32 percent, up from 27 percent in 1960.

12. The main categories of Federal spending are pensions and income security, national defense, health, and interest on the public debt; Federal revenues come primarily from personal income taxes, payroll taxes, and corporate income taxes.

13. States derive their revenue primarily from sales and excise taxes and personal income taxes; major state expenditures go to education, public welfare, health and hospitals, and highways. Local communities derive most of their revenue from property taxes; education is their most important expenditure.

14. State and local tax revenues are supplemented by sizable revenue grants from the Federal government.

Terms and Concepts

functional distribution of income	stock	government purchases
personal distribution of income	bond	transfer payments
durable goods	limited liability	personal income tax
nondurable goods	principal-agent problem	marginal tax rate
services	monopoly	average tax rate
plant	externality	payroll taxes
firm	negative externalities	corporate income tax
industry	positive externalities	sales and excise taxes
sole proprietorship	public goods	property taxes
partnership	free-rider problem	
corporation	quasi-public goods	

Study Questions

1. Distinguish between the functional distribution and personal distribution of income. Which is being referred to in each of the following statements? "The combined share of wage income and proprietary income has remained remarkably stable at about 80 percent since the Second World War." "The relative income of the richest households is higher today than in 1970." **LO1**

2. **KEY QUESTION** Assume that the five residents of Econoville receive incomes of $50, $75, $125, $250, and $500. Present the resulting distribution of income as a graph similar to Figure 4.2. Compare the incomes of the lowest fifth and the highest fifth of the income receivers. **LO1**

3. Distinguish between a plant, a firm, and an industry. Contrast a vertically integrated firm, a horizontally integrated firm, and a conglomerate. Cite an example of a horizontally integrated firm from which you have recently made a purchase. **LO1**

4. **KEY QUESTION** What are the three major legal forms of business organization? Which form is the most prevalent in terms of numbers? Why do you think that is so? Which form is dominant in terms of total sales? What major advantages of this form of business organization gave rise to its dominance? **LO2**

5. What is the principal-agent problem as it relates to managers and stockholders? How did firms try to solve it in the 1990s? In what way did the "solution" backfire on some firms? **LO3**

6. Identify and briefly describe the main economic functions of government. What function do you think is the most controversial? Explain why. **LO4**

7. What divergences arise between equilibrium output and efficient output when (*a*) negative externalities and (*b*) positive

externalities are present? How might government correct these divergences? Cite an example (other than the text examples) of an external cost and an external benefit. **LO4**

8. Explain why zoning laws, which allow certain land uses only in specific locations, might be justified in dealing with a problem of negative externalities. Explain why tax breaks to businesses that set up in areas of high unemployment might be justified in view of positive externalities. Explain why excise taxes on beer might be justified in dealing with a problem of external costs. **LO4**

9. **KEY QUESTION** What are the two characteristics of public goods? Explain the significance of each for public provision as opposed to private provision. What is the free-rider problem as it relates to public goods? Is U.S. border patrol a public good or a private good? Why? How about satellite TV? Explain. **LO4**

10. **KEY QUESTION** Draw a production possibilities curve with public goods on the vertical axis and private goods on the horizontal axis. Assuming the economy is initially operating *on the curve*, indicate how the production of public goods might be increased. How might the output of public goods be increased if the economy is initially operating at a point *inside the curve?* **LO4**

11. Use the distinction between the characteristics of private and public goods to determine whether the following should be produced through the market system or provided by government: (*a*) French fries, (*b*) airport screening, (*c*) court systems, (*d*) mail delivery, and (*e*) medical care. State why you answered as you did in each case. **LO4**

12. Use the circular flow diagram to show how each of the following government actions simultaneously affects the allocation of resources and the distribution of income: **LO4**
   a. The construction of a new high school.
   b. A 2-percentage-point reduction of the corporate income tax.
   c. An expansion of preschool programs for disadvantaged children.
   d. The levying of an excise tax on polluters.

13. What do economists mean when they say government purchases are "exhaustive" expenditures whereas government transfer payments are "nonexhaustive" expenditures? Cite an example of a government purchase and a government transfer payment. **LO5**

14. What is the most important source of revenue and the major type of expenditure at the Federal level? At the state level? At the local level? **LO5**

15. **KEY QUESTION** Suppose in Fiscalville there is no tax on the first $10,000 of income, but a 20 percent tax on earnings between $10,000 and $20,000 and a 30 percent tax on income between $20,000 and $30,000. Any income above $30,000 is taxed at 40 percent. If your income is $50,000, how much will you pay in taxes? Determine your marginal and average tax rates. Is this a progressive tax? Explain. **LO5**

16. **LAST WORD** What do economists mean when they refer to Social Security as a pay-as-you-go plan? What is the Social Security trust fund? What is the nature of the long-run fiscal imbalance in the Social Security retirement system? What are the broad options for addressing this problem?

Web-Based Questions

1. **PERSONAL DISTRIBUTION OF INCOME—WHAT IS THE TREND?** Visit the U.S. Census Bureau Web site at **www.census.gov** and in order select Income, Historical Income Tables, Households, and Table H-2. Since 1970, how has the share of aggregate household income received by the lowest and highest income quintiles (fifths) changed?

2. **STATE TAXES AND EXPENDITURES PER CAPITA— WHERE DOES YOUR STATE RANK?** Go to the Census

Bureau site, **www.census.gov/govs/www/state.html**, and select years in descending order until you find a table that ranks the states by tax revenue and expenditures per capita. Where does your home state rank in each category? Where does the state in which you are attending college, if different, rank? Speculate as to why a large gap separates the high-ranking and low-ranking states.

**FURTHER TEST YOUR KNOWLEDGE AT
www.mcconnell18e.com**

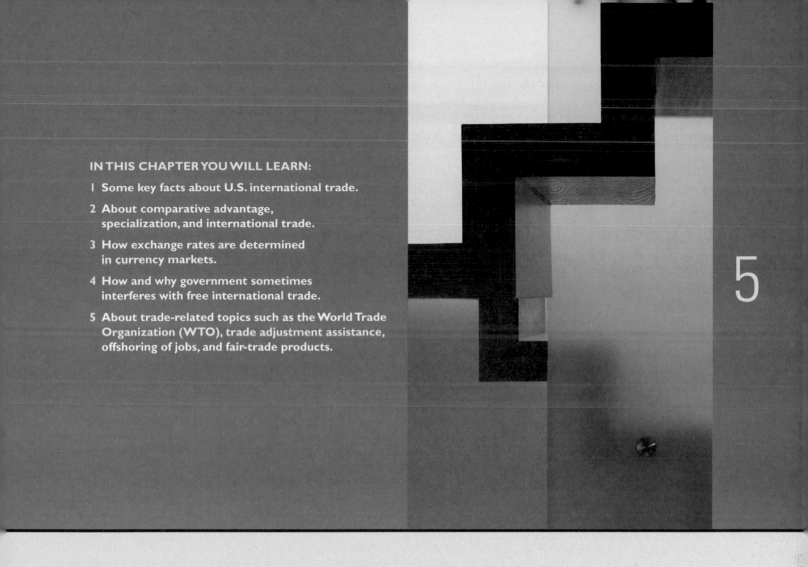

IN THIS CHAPTER YOU WILL LEARN:

1 Some key facts about U.S. international trade.

2 About comparative advantage, specialization, and international trade.

3 How exchange rates are determined in currency markets.

4 How and why government sometimes interferes with free international trade.

5 About trade-related topics such as the World Trade Organization (WTO), trade adjustment assistance, offshoring of jobs, and fair-trade products.

5

The United States in the Global Economy

Backpackers in the wilderness like to think they are "leaving the world behind," but, like Atlas, they carry the world on their shoulders. Much of their equipment is imported—knives from Switzerland, rain gear from South Korea, cameras from Japan, aluminum pots from England, sleeping bags from China, and compasses from Finland. Moreover, they may have driven to the trailheads in Japanese-made Toyotas or German-made BMWs, sipping coffee from Brazil or snacking on bananas from Honduras.

International trade and the global economy affect all of us daily, whether we are hiking in the wilderness, driving our cars, listening to music, or working at our jobs. We cannot "leave the world behind." We are enmeshed in a global web of economic relationships—trading of goods and services, multinational corporations, cooperative ventures among the world's firms, and ties among the world's financial markets. That web is so complex that it is difficult to determine just what is—or isn't—an American product. A Finnish company owns Wilson sporting goods; a Swiss company owns Gerber baby food; and a London-incorporated South African company owns Miller Brewing. The Chrysler PT Cruiser is assembled in Mexico. Many "U.S." products such as Boeing aircraft contain numerous components from abroad, and, conversely, many "foreign" products such as Airbus planes contain numerous U.S.-produced parts.

International Linkages

Several economic flows link the U.S. economy and the economies of other nations. As identified in Figure 5.1, these flows are:

- **Goods and services flows** or simply **trade flows.** The United States exports goods and services to other nations and imports goods and services from them.
- **Capital and labor flows** or simply **resource flows.** U.S. firms establish production facilities—new capital—in foreign countries, and foreign firms establish production facilities in the United States. Labor also moves between nations. Each year many foreigners immigrate to the United States and some Americans move to other nations.
- **Information and technology flows.** The United States transmits information to other nations about U.S. products, prices, interest rates, and investment opportunities and receives such information from abroad. Firms in other countries use technology created in the United States, and U.S. businesses incorporate technology developed abroad.
- **Financial flows.** Money is transferred between the United States and other countries for several purposes, for example, paying for imports, buying foreign assets, paying interest on debt, purchasing foreign currencies by tourists, and providing foreign aid.

The United States and World Trade

Our main goal in this chapter is to examine trade flows and the financial flows that pay for them. What is the extent and pattern of international trade, and how much has that trade grown? Who are the major participants?

Volume and Pattern

Table 5.1 suggests the importance of world trade for selected countries. Many countries, with restricted resources and limited domestic markets, cannot efficiently produce the variety of goods their citizens want. So they must import goods from other nations. That, in turn, means that they must export, or sell abroad, some of their own products. For such countries, exports may run from 25 to 50 percent or more of their gross domestic product (GDP)—the market value of all goods and services produced in an economy. Other countries, the United States, for example, have rich and diversified resource bases and large internal markets. Although the total volume of trade is huge in the United States, it constitutes a smaller percentage of GDP than it does in a number of other nations.

Volume For the United States and for the world as a whole, the volume of international trade has been increasing

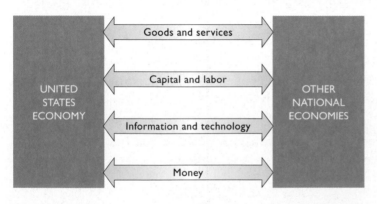

FIGURE 5.1 International linkages. The U.S. economy is intertwined with other national economies through goods and services flows (trade flows), capital and labor flows (resource flows), information and technology flows, and financial flows.

TABLE 5.1 **Exports of Goods and Services as a Percentage of GDP, Selected Countries, 2007**

Country	Exports as Percentage of GDP
Belgium	91
Netherlands	75
Germany	47
South Korea	45
Canada	35
Italy	29
France	27
New Zealand	27
Spain	26
United Kingdom	25
Japan	18
United States	12

Source: Derived by authors from IMF, *International Financial Statistics,* 2008.

both absolutely and relative to their GDPs. A comparison of the boxed data in Figure 5.2 reveals substantial growth in the dollar amount of U.S. exports and imports over the past several decades. The graph shows the rapid growth of U.S. exports and imports of goods and services as percentages of GDP. On a national income account basis, U.S.

exports and imports were 12 and 17 percent of GDP, respectively, in 2007.

Even so, the United States now accounts for a diminished percentage of total world trade. In 1950, it supplied about 33 percent of the world's total exports, compared with about 9 percent today. World trade has increased more rapidly for other nations than it has for the United States. But in terms of absolute volumes of imports and exports, the United States is still the world's leading trading nation.

Dependence The United States is almost entirely dependent on other countries for bananas, cocoa, coffee, spices, tea, raw silk, nickel, tin, natural rubber, and diamonds. Imported goods compete with U.S. goods in many of our domestic markets: Japanese cameras and cars, French and Italian wines, and Swiss and Austrian snow skis are a few examples. Even the "great American pastime" of baseball relies heavily on imported gloves and baseballs.

On the export side, many U.S. industries depend on sales abroad for their profitability. For example almost all segments of U.S. agriculture rely to one degree or another on exports. In fact, exports of rice, wheat, cotton, and tobacco vary from one-fourth to more than one-half of the total output of those crops. The U.S. computer, chemical, semiconductor, aircraft, automobile, machine tool, and coal industries,

FIGURE 5.2 **U.S. trade as percentage of GDP.** U.S. imports and exports have increased in volume and have greatly increased as a percentage of GDP since 1975.

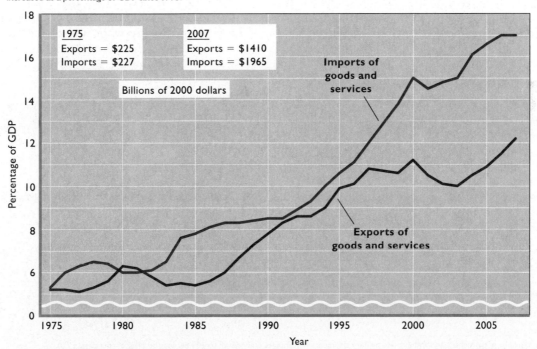

Source: Bureau of Economic Analysis, **www.bea.gov.** Data are from the national income accounts and are adjusted for inflation (2000 dollars).

TABLE 5.2 Principal U.S. Exports and Imports of Goods, 2007 (in Billions of Dollars)

Exports	Amount	Imports	Amount
Chemicals	$94.1	Petroleum	$331.0
Agricultural products	77.6	Automobiles	133.8
Consumer durables	70.9	Metals	115.7
Semiconductors	50.2	Household appliances	112.1
Aircraft	48.6	Computers	104.0
Fuels and lubricants	47.7	Consumer electronics	94.7
Automobiles	43.6	Clothing	86.3
Computers	42.9	Chemicals	56.2
Generating equipment	41.5	Generating equipment	55.0
Medical equipment	32.0	Aircraft	34.4

Source: Consolidated by authors from data provided by the Bureau of Economic Analysis, www.bea.gov.

among many others, sell significant portions of their output in international markets. Table 5.2 shows some of the major commodity exports and imports of the United States.

Trade Patterns The following facts will give you an overview of U.S. international trade:

- A *trade deficit* occurs when imports exceed exports. The United States has a trade deficit in goods. In 2007, U.S. imports of goods exceeded U.S. exports of goods by $816 billion.
- A *trade surplus* occurs when exports exceed imports. The United States has a trade surplus in services. U.S. firms and citizens collectively sell (export) more transportation, banking, legal and other services

abroad than they purchase (import) from foreign firms and citizens. In 2007, these U.S. exports of services exceeded U.S. imports of services by $107 billion.
- The United States imports some of the same categories of goods that it exports, specifically, automobiles, computers, semiconductors, and telecommunications equipment (see Table 5.2).
- About half of U.S. export and import trade is with other industrially advanced countries. The remainder is with developing countries, including members of the Organization of Petroleum Exporting Countries (OPEC).
- Canada is the United States' most important trading partner quantitatively. In 2007, 22 percent of U.S.

TABLE 5.3 U.S. Exports and Imports of Goods by Area, 2007*

Exports to	Billions of Dollars	Percentage of Total	Imports from	Billions of Dollars	Percentage of Total
Canada	$250	22	Canada	$317	16
European Union	242	21	European Union	356	18
Germany	49	4	Germany	94	5
United Kingdom	49	4	United Kingdom	56	3
France	27	2	France	42	2
All other EU	117	10	All other EU	164	8
Mexico	136	12	Mexico	214	11
China	65	6	China	322	16
Japan	61	5	Japan	146	7
OPEC countries	49	4	OPEC countries	174	9
All other	346	30	All other	436	22
Total	$1149	100	Total	$1965	100

*Data are on a balance of payments basis and exclude military shipments. Percentages do not sum to 100 percent because of rounding.
Source: Bureau of Economic Analysis, www.bea.gov.

exported goods were sold to Canadians, who in turn provided 16 percent of the U.S. imports of goods (see Table 5.3).

- The United States has sizable trade deficits with China and Japan. In 2007, U.S. imported goods from China exceeded exported goods to China by $257 billion, and U.S. imported goods from Japan exceeded U.S. exported goods to Japan by $85 billion (see Table 5.3).

- The U.S. dependence on foreign oil is reflected in its trade with members of OPEC. In 2007, the United States imported $174 billion of goods (mainly oil) from OPEC members, while exporting $49 billion of goods to those countries (see Table 5.3).

- In terms of volume, the most significant U.S. export of *services* is airline transportation provided by U.S. carriers for foreign passengers.

Financial Linkages International trade requires complex financial linkages among nations. How does a nation such as the United States obtain more goods from others than it provides to them? How does the United States finance its trade deficits, such as its 2007 goods and services deficit of $709 billion (= +$107 billion in services − $816 billion in goods) in 2007? The answer is by either borrowing from foreigners or selling real assets (for example, factories, real estate) to them. In terms of borrowing, the United States is the world's largest borrower of foreign funds, which can be used to purchase foreign goods. In terms of selling real assets, the countries with which the United States has large trade deficits end up holding large numbers of U.S. dollars (since, for instance, Sony is paid in dollars when it sells a television set in the United State). Many of these U.S. dollars are then used to buy U.S. real assets, thereby transferring ownership of those assets from U.S. citizens to foreign citizens.

Rapid Trade Growth

Several factors have propelled the rapid growth of international trade since the Second World War.

Transportation Technology High transportation costs are a barrier to any type of trade, particularly among traders who are distant from one another. But improvements in transportation have shrunk the globe and have fostered world trade. Container ships deliver self-contained box cars of goods to ports, which off-load them to waiting trucks and trains. We now routinely transport oil in massive tankers, significantly lowering the cost of transportation per barrel. Grain is loaded onto oceangoing ships at modern,

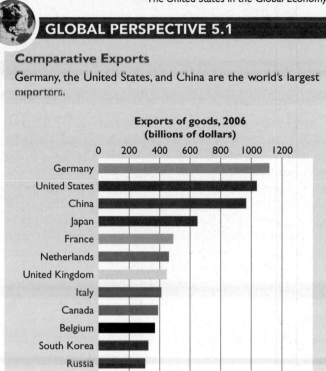

GLOBAL PERSPECTIVE 5.1

Comparative Exports

Germany, the United States, and China are the world's largest exporters.

**Exports of goods, 2006
(billions of dollars)**

Germany
United States
China
Japan
France
Netherlands
United Kingdom
Italy
Canada
Belgium
South Korea
Russia
Mexico
Taiwan
Saudi Arabia

Source: Data used with permission of World Trade Organization, **www.wto.org.**

efficient grain silos at Great Lakes and coastal ports. Natural gas flows through large-diameter pipelines from exporting to importing countries—for instance, from Russia to Germany and from Canada to the United States.

Communications Technology Dramatic improvements in communications technology have also advanced world trade. Computers, the Internet, telephones, and fax (facsimile) machines now directly link traders around the world, enabling exporters to access overseas markets and to carry out trade deals. A distributor in New York can get a price quote on 1000 woven baskets in Thailand as quickly as a quotation on 1000 laptop computers in Texas. Money moves around the world in the blink of an eye. Exchange rates, stock prices, and interest rates flash onto computer screens nearly simultaneously in Los Angeles, London, and Lisbon.

General Decline in Tariffs *Tariffs* are excise taxes (duties) on imported products. They have had their ups and downs over the years, but since 1940 they have generally fallen. A glance ahead to Figure 5.4, page 103, shows that U.S. tariffs as a percentage of imports (on which duties are levied) are now about 5 percent, down from 37 percent in 1940. Many nations still maintain barriers to free trade, but, on average, tariffs have fallen significantly, thus increasing international trade.

Participants in International Trade

All the nations of the world participate to some extent in international trade. Global Perspective 5.1 lists the top participants in world trade *by total dollar volume* (as opposed to *percentage of GDP*, as in Table 5.1). Observe that Germany, the United States, China, and Japan had combined exports of $3.6 trillion in 2006. This amounted to 31 percent of total world exports that year. Along with Germany, other western European nations such as France, Britain, and Italy are major exporters. So, too, are the east and southeast Asian countries of South Korea, Taiwan, and Singapore, whose combined exports exceed those individually of France, Britain, or Italy.

China, with its increased reliance on the market system and its reintegration of Hong Kong, has quickly emerged as a major international trader. In 1990 its exports were about $60 billion. In 2006 they were nearly $969 billion.

QUICK REVIEW 5.1

- Four main categories of economic flows link nations: goods and services flows, capital and labor flows, information and technology flows, and financial flows.
- World trade has increased globally and nationally. In terms of volume, the United States is the world's leading international trader. But with exports and imports of only about 12 to 17 percent of GDP, the United States is not as dependent on international trade as some other nations.
- Advances in transportation and communications technology and declines in tariffs have all helped expand world trade.
- Nearly all nations participate in world trade, but the United States, China, Japan, the western European nations, and Canada dominate world trade by volume.

Specialization and Comparative Advantage

Given the presence of an *open economy*—one that includes the international sector—the United States produces more of certain goods (exports) and fewer of other goods (imports) than it would otherwise. Thus U.S. labor and other resources are shifted toward export industries and away from import industries. For example, the United States uses more resources to make commercial aircraft and to grow wheat and less to make autos and clothing. So we ask: "Do shifts of resources like these make economic sense? Do they enhance U.S. total output and thus the U.S. standard of living?"

The answers are affirmative. Specialization and international trade increase the productivity of a nation's resources and allow for greater total output than would otherwise be possible. This idea is not new. Adam Smith had this to say in 1776:

> It is the maxim of every prudent master of a family, never to attempt to make at home what it will cost him more to make than to buy. The taylor does not attempt to make his own shoes, but buys them of the shoemaker. The shoemaker does not attempt to make his own clothes, but employs a taylor. The farmer attempts to make neither the one nor the other, but employs those different artificers....
>
> What is prudence in the conduct of every private family, can scarce be folly in that of a great kingdom. If a foreign country can supply us with a commodity cheaper than we can make it, better buy it of them with some part of the produce of our own industry, employed in a way in which we have some advantage.[1]

Nations specialize and trade for the same reasons as individuals: Specialization and exchange result in greater overall output and income.

In the early 1800s British economist David Ricardo expanded on Smith's idea by observing that it pays for a person or a country to specialize and trade even if some potential trading partner is more productive in *all* economic activities. We demonstrate Ricardo's basic principle in the Consider This box to the right. You should read it before plunging into the more elaborate analysis of comparative advantage.

Comparative Advantage: Production Possibilities Analysis

The simple example in the Consider This box shows that specialization is economically desirable because it results in more efficient production. Now let's put specialization into the context of trading nations and use the familiar concept of the production possibilities table for our analysis.

Assumptions and Comparative Costs

Suppose the production possibilities for one product in Mexico and for one product in the United States are as shown in Tables 5.4 and 5.5. Both tables reflect constant costs. Each country must give up a constant amount of one product to secure a certain increment of the other product.

---

[1]Adam Smith, *The Wealth of Nations* (New York: Modern Library, 1937), p. 424. (Originally published in 1776.)

TABLE 5.4 Mexico's Production Possibilities Table (in Tons)

Product	Production Alternatives				
	A	B	C	D	E
Avocados	0	20	24	40	60
Soybeans	15	10	9	5	0

TABLE 5.5 U.S. Production Possibilities Table (in Tons)

Product	Production Alternatives				
	R	S	T	U	V
Avocados	0	30	33	60	90
Soybeans	30	20	19	10	0

(This assumption simplifies our discussion without impairing the validity of our conclusions. Later we will allow for increasing costs.)

Also for simplicity, suppose that the labor forces in the United States and Mexico are of equal size. If the United States and Mexico use their entire (equal-size) labor forces

A CPA and House Painter

Suppose that Madison, a certified public accountant (CPA), is a swifter painter than Mason, the professional painter she is thinking of hiring. Also assume that Madison can earn $50 per hour as an accountant but would have to pay Mason $15 per hour. And suppose that Madison would need 30 hours to paint her house but Mason would need 40 hours.

Should Madison take time from her accounting to paint her own house, or should she hire the painter? Madison's opportunity cost of painting her house is $1500 (= 30 hours of sacrificed CPA time × $50 per CPA hour). The cost of hiring Mason is only $600 (= 40 hours of painting × $15 per hour of painting). Although Madison is better at both accounting and painting, she will get her house painted at lower cost by specializing in accounting and using some of her earnings from accounting to hire a house painter.

Similarly, Mason can reduce his cost of obtaining accounting services by specializing in painting and using some of his income to hire Madison to prepare his income tax forms. Suppose Mason would need 10 hours to prepare his tax return, while Madison could handle the task in 2 hours. Mason would sacrifice $150 of income (= 10 hours of painting time × $15 per hour) to do something he could hire Madison to do for $100 (= 2 hours of CPA time × $50 per CPA hour). By using Madison to prepare his tax return, Mason lowers the cost of getting his tax return prepared.

What is true for our CPA and house painter is also true for nations. Specializing enables nations to reduce the cost of obtaining the goods and services they desire.

to produce avocados, the United States can produce 90 tons compared with Mexico's 60 tons. Similarly, the United States can produce 30 tons of soybeans compared to Mexico's 15 tons. So output per worker in the United States exceeds that in Mexico in producing both goods, perhaps because of better technology. The United States has an *absolute advantage* (relative to Mexico) in producing both soybeans or avocados.

But gains from specialization and trade between the United States and Mexico are possible even under these circumstances. Specialization and trade are mutually "profitable" to the two nations if the comparative costs of producing the two products *within* the two nations differ. What are the comparative costs of avocados and soybeans in Mexico? By comparing production alternatives A and B in Table 5.4, we see that 5 tons of soybeans (= 15 − 10) must be sacrificed to produce 20 tons of avocados (= 20 − 0). Or, more simply, in Mexico it costs 1 ton of soybeans (S) to produce 4 tons of avocados (A); that is, 1S ≡ 4A. (The "≡" sign simply signifies "equivalent to.") Because we assumed constant costs, this domestic opportunity cost will not change as Mexico expands the output of either product. This is evident from production possibilities B and C, where we see that 4 more tons of avocados (= 24 − 20) cost 1 unit of soybeans (= 10 − 9).

Similarly, in Table 5.5, comparing U.S. production alternatives R and S reveals that in the United States it costs 10 tons of soybeans (= 30 − 20) to obtain 30 tons of avocados (= 30 − 0). That is, the domestic comparative-cost ratio for the two products in the United States is 1S ≡ 3A. Comparing production alternatives S and T reinforces this conclusion: an extra 3 tons of avocados (= 33 − 30) comes at the sacrifice of 1 ton of soybeans (= 20 − 19).

The comparative costs of the two products within the two nations are obviously different. Economists say that the United States has a domestic comparative advantage or, simply, a **comparative advantage** over Mexico in soybeans. The United States must forgo only 3 tons of avocados to get 1 ton of soybeans, but Mexico must forgo 4 tons of avocados to get 1 ton of soybeans. In terms of domestic opportunity costs, soybeans are relatively cheaper in the United States. A nation has a comparative advantage in some product when it can produce that product at a lower domestic opportunity cost than can a potential

TABLE 5.6 Comparative-Advantage Example: A Summary

Soybeans	Avocados
Mexico: Must give up 4 tons of avocados to get 1 ton of soybeans	*Mexico:* Must give up $\frac{1}{4}$ ton of soybeans to get 1 ton of avocados
United States: Must give up 3 tons of avocados to get 1 ton of soybeans	*United States:* Must give up $\frac{1}{3}$ ton of soybeans to get 1 ton of avocados
Comparative advantage: United States	*Comparative advantage:* Mexico

trading partner. Mexico, in contrast, has a comparative advantage in avocados. While 1 ton of avocados costs $\frac{1}{3}$ ton of soybeans in the United States, it costs only $\frac{1}{4}$ ton of soybeans in Mexico. Comparatively speaking, avocados are cheaper in Mexico. We summarize the situation in Table 5.6. Be sure to give it a close look.

Because of these differences in domestic opportunity costs, if both nations specialize, each according to its comparative advantage, each can achieve a larger total output with the same total input of resources. Together they will be using their scarce resources more efficiently.

> **ORIGIN OF THE IDEA**
>
> **O 5.1**
>
> Absolute and comparative advantage

Terms of Trade The United States can shift production between soybeans and avocados at the rate of 1S for 3A. Thus, the United States would specialize in soybeans only if it could obtain *more than* 3 tons of avocados for 1 ton of soybeans by trading with Mexico. Similarly, Mexico can shift production at the rate of 4A for 1S. So it would be advantageous to Mexico to specialize in avocados if it could get 1 ton of soybeans for *less than* 4 tons of avocados.

Suppose that through negotiation the two nations agree on an exchange rate of 1 ton of soybeans for $3\frac{1}{2}$ tons of avocados. These **terms of trade** are mutually beneficial to both countries, since each can "do better" through such trade than through domestic production alone. The

United States can get $3\frac{1}{2}$ tons of avocados by sending 1 ton of soybeans to Mexico, while it can get only 3 tons of avocados by shifting its own resources domestically from soybeans to avocados. Mexico can obtain 1 ton of soybeans at a lower cost of $3\frac{1}{2}$ tons of avocados through trade with the United States, compared to the cost of 4 tons if Mexico produced the ton of soybeans itself.

Gains from Specialization and Trade Let's pinpoint the gains in total output from specialization and trade. Suppose that, before specialization and trade, production alternative C in Table 5.4 and alternative T in 5.5 were the optimal product mixes for the two countries. That is, Mexico preferred 24 tons of avocados and 9 tons of soybeans (Table 5.4) and the United States preferred 33 tons of avocados and 19 tons of soybeans (Table 5.5) to all other available domestic alternatives. These outputs are shown in column 1 in Table 5.7.

Now assume that both nations specialize according to their comparative advantage, with Mexico producing 60 tons of avocados and no soybeans (alternative E) and the United States producing no avocados and 30 tons of soybeans (alternative R). These outputs are shown in column 2 in Table 5.7. Using our 1S ≡ $3\frac{1}{2}$ A terms of trade, assume that Mexico exchanges 35 tons of avocados for 10 tons of U.S. soybeans. Column 3 in Table 5.7 shows the quantities exchanged in this trade, with a minus sign indicating exports and a plus sign indicating imports. As shown in column 4, after the trade Mexico has 25 tons of avocados and 10 tons of soybeans, while the United States has 35 tons of avocados and 20 tons of soybeans. Compared with their optimum product mixes before specialization and trade (column 1), *both* nations now enjoy more avocados and more soybeans! Specifically, Mexico has gained 1 ton of avocados and 1 ton of soybeans. The United States has gained 2 tons of avocados and 1 ton of soybeans. These gains are shown in column 5.

Specialization based on comparative advantage improves global resource allocation. The same total inputs of world resources and technology result in a larger global output.

TABLE 5.7 Specialization According to Comparative Advantage and the Gains from Trade (in Tons)

Country	(1) Outputs before Specialization	(2) Outputs after Specialization	(3) Amounts Traded	(4) Outputs Available after Trade	(5) Gains from Specialization and Trade (4) − (1)
Mexico	24 avocados	60 avocados	−35 avocados	25 avocados	1 avocados
	9 soybeans	0 soybeans	+10 soybeans	10 soybeans	1 soybeans
United States	33 avocados	0 avocados	+35 avocados	35 avocados	2 avocados
	19 soybeans	30 soybeans	−10 soybeans	20 soybeans	1 soybeans

If Mexico and the United States allocate all their resources to avocados and soybeans, respectively, the same total inputs of resources can produce more output between them, indicating that resources are being allocated more efficiently.

Through specialization and international trade a nation can overcome the production constraints imposed by its domestic production possibilities table and curve. Our discussion of Tables 5.4, 5.5, and 5.7 has shown just

WORKED PROBLEMS

W 5.1

Gains from specialization

how this is done. The domestic production possibilities data (Tables 5.4 and 5.5) of the two countries have not changed, meaning that neither nation's production possibilities curve has shifted. But specialization and trade mean that citizens of both countries can enjoy increased consumption (column 5 of Table 5.7). **(Key Question 4)**

The Foreign Exchange Market

Buyers and sellers, whether individuals, firms, or nations, use money to buy products or to pay for the use of resources. Within the domestic economy, prices are stated in terms of the domestic currency and buyers use that currency to purchase domestic products. In Mexico, for example, buyers have pesos, and that is what sellers want.

International markets are different. Sellers set their prices in terms of their domestic currencies, but buyers often possess entirely different currencies. How many dollars does it take to buy a truckload of Mexican avocados selling for 3000 pesos, a German automobile selling for 50,000 euros, or a Japanese motorcycle priced at 300,000 yen? Producers in Mexico, Germany, and Japan want payment in pesos, euros, and yen, respectively, so that they can pay their wages, rent, interest, dividends, and taxes.

A **foreign exchange market,** a market in which various national currencies are exchanged for one another, serves this need. The equilibrium prices in such currency markets are called **exchange rates.** An exchange rate is the rate at which the currency of one nation can be exchanged for the currency of another nation. (See Global Perspective 5.2.)

The market price or exchange rate of a nation's currency is an unusual price; it links all domestic prices with all foreign prices. Exchange rates enable consumers in one country to translate prices of foreign goods into units of their own currency: They need only multiply the foreign product price by the exchange rate. If the U.S. dollar = yen exchange rate is $.01 (1 cent) per yen, a Sony television set priced at ¥20,000 will cost $200 (= 20,000 × $.01) in the United States. If the exchange rate rises to $.02 (2 cents)

GLOBAL PERSPECTIVE 5.2

Exchange Rates: Foreign Currency per U.S. Dollar

The amount of foreign currency that a dollar will buy varies greatly from nation to nation and fluctuates in response to supply and demand changes in the foreign exchange market. The amounts shown here are for January 2008. (You can easily update these exchange rates via *The Wall Street Journal.*)

$1 Will Buy

39.17 Indian rupees
.51 British pound
1.01 Canadian dollars
10.94 Mexican pesos
1.12 Swiss francs
.68 European euro
109.87 Japanese yen
937.38 South Korean won
6.42 Swedish kronors

per yen, the television will cost $400 (= 20,000 × $.02) in the United States. Similarly, all other Japanese products would double in price to U.S. buyers in response to the altered exchange rate.

Dollar-Yen Market

How does the foreign exchange market work? Let's look briefly at the market for dollars and yen. U.S. firms exporting goods to Japan want payment in dollars, not yen; but the Japanese importers of those U.S. goods possess yen, not dollars. So the Japanese importers supply their yen in exchange for dollars in the foreign exchange market. At the same time, there are U.S. importers of Japanese goods who need to pay the Japanese exporters in yen, not dollars. These importers go to the foreign exchange market as demanders of yen. We then have a market in which the "price" is in dollars and the "product" is yen.

Figure 5.3 shows the supply of yen (by Japanese importers) and the demand for yen (by U.S. importers). The intersection of demand curve D_y and supply curve S_y

INTERACTIVE GRAPHS

G 5.1

Exchange rates

establishes the equilibrium dollar price of yen. Here the equilibrium price of 1 yen—the dollar-yen exchange rate — is 1 cent per yen, or $.01 = ¥1. At this price, the market for yen clears; there is neither a shortage nor a surplus of yen.

FIGURE 5.3 **The market for yen.** U.S. imports from Japan create a demand D_y for yen, while U.S. exports to Japan (Japan's imports) create a supply S_y of yen. The dollar price of 1 yen—the exchange rate—is determined at the intersection of the supply and demand curves. In this case the equilibrium price is $.01, meaning that 1 cent will buy 1 yen.

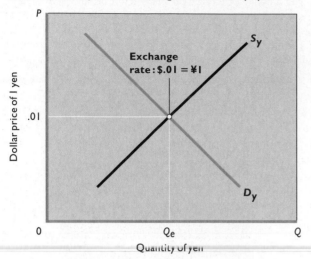

The equilibrium $.01 price of 1 yen means that $1 will buy 100 yen or ¥100 worth of Japanese goods. Conversely, 100 yen will buy $1 worth of U.S. goods.

Changing Rates: Depreciation and Appreciation

What might cause the exchange rate to change? The determinants of the demand for and supply of yen are similar to the determinants of demand and supply for almost any product. In the United States, several things might increase the demand for—and therefore the dollar price of—yen. Incomes might rise in the United States, enabling residents to buy not only more domestic goods but also more Sony televisions, Nikon cameras, and Nissan automobiles from Japan. So people in the United States would need more yen, and the demand for yen would increase. Or a change in people's tastes might enhance their preferences for Japanese goods. When gas prices soared in the 1970s, many auto buyers in the United States shifted their demand from gas-guzzling domestic cars to gas-efficient Japanese compact cars. The result was an increased demand for yen.

The point is that an increase in the U.S. demand for Japanese goods will increase the demand for yen and raise the dollar price of yen. Suppose the dollar price of yen rises from $.01 = ¥1 to $.02 = ¥1. When the dollar price of yen increases, we say a **depreciation** of the dollar relative to the yen has occurred. It then takes more dollars (pennies in this case) to buy a single yen. Alternatively

stated, the *international value of the dollar* has declined. A depreciated dollar buys fewer yen and therefore fewer Japanese goods; the yen and all Japanese goods have become more expensive to U.S. buyers. Result: Consumers in the United States shift their expenditures from Japanese goods to now less expensive American goods. The Ford Taurus becomes relatively more attractive than the Honda Accord to U.S. consumers. Conversely, because each yen buys more dollars—that is, because the international value of the yen has increased—U.S. goods become cheaper to people in Japan and U.S. exports to Japan rise.

If the opposite event occurred—if the Japanese demanded more U.S. goods—then they would supply more yen to pay for these goods. The increase in the supply of yen relative to the demand for yen would decrease the equilibrium price of yen in the foreign exchange market. For example, the dollar price of yen might decline from $.01 = ¥1 to $.005 = ¥1. A decrease in the dollar price of yen is called an **appreciation** of the dollar relative to the yen. It means that the international value of the dollar has increased. It then takes fewer dollars (or pennies) to buy a single yen; the dollar is worth more because it can purchase more yen and therefore more Japanese goods. Each Sony PlayStation becomes less expensive in terms of dollars, so people in the United States purchase more of them. In general, U.S. imports rise. Meanwhile, because it takes more yen to get a dollar, U.S. exports to Japan fall.

The central point is this : When the dollar depreciates (dollar price of foreign currencies rises), U.S. exports rise and U.S. imports fall; when the dollar appreciates (dollar price of foreign currencies falls), U.S. exports fall and U.S. imports rise. **(Key Question 6)**

QUICK REVIEW 5.2

- A country has a comparative advantage when it can produce a product at a lower domestic opportunity cost than a potential trading partner can.
- Specialization based on comparative advantage increases the total output available for nations that trade with one another.
- The foreign exchange market is a market in which national currencies are exchanged.
- An appreciation of the dollar is an increase in the international value of the dollar relative to the currency of some other nation; after appreciation a dollar buys more units of that currency. A depreciation of the dollar is a decrease in the international value of the dollar relative to some other currency; after depreciation a dollar buys fewer units of that currency.

Government and Trade

If people and nations benefit from specialization and international exchange, why do governments sometimes try to restrict the free flow of imports or encourage exports? What kinds of world trade barriers can governments erect, and why would they do so?

Trade Impediments and Subsidies

There are four means by which governments commonly interfere with free trade:

- **Protective tariffs** are excise taxes or duties placed on imported goods. Protective tariffs are designed to shield domestic producers from foreign competition. They impede free trade by causing a rise in the prices of imported goods, thereby shifting demand toward domestic products. An excise tax on imported shoes, for example, would make domestically produced shoes more attractive to consumers.
- **Import quotas** are limits on the quantities or total value of specific items that may be imported. Once a quota is "filled," further imports of that product are choked off. Import quotas are more effective than tariffs in retarding international commerce. With a tariff, a product can go on being imported in large quantities; with an import quota, however, all imports are prohibited once the quota is filled.
- **Nontariff barriers** (and, implicitly, *nonquota* barriers) include onerous licensing requirements, unreasonable standards pertaining to product quality, or simply bureaucratic hurdles and delays in customs procedures. Some nations require that importers of foreign goods obtain licenses and then restrict the number of licenses issued. Although many nations carefully inspect imported agricultural products to prevent the introduction of potentially harmful insects, some countries use lengthy inspections to impede imports.
- **Export subsidies** consist of government payments to domestic producers of export goods. By reducing production costs, the subsidies enable producers to charge lower prices and thus to sell more exports in world markets. Two examples: Some European governments have heavily subsidized Airbus Industries, a European firm that produces commercial aircraft, to help Airbus compete against the American firm Boeing. The United States and other nations have subsidized domestic farmers to boost the domestic food supply. Such subsidies have lowered the market price of food and have artificially lowered export prices on agricultural produce.

Why Government Trade Interventions?

In view of the benefits of free trade, what accounts for the impulse to impede imports and boost exports through government policy? There are several reasons—some legitimate, most not.

Misunderstanding the Gains from Trade It
is a commonly accepted myth that the greatest benefit to be derived from international trade is greater domestic employment in the export sector. This suggests that exports are "good" because they increase domestic employment, whereas imports are "bad" because they deprive people of jobs at home. Actually, the true benefit created by international trade is the overall increase in output obtained through specialization and exchange. A nation can fully employ its resources, including labor, with or without international trade. International trade, however, enables society to use its resources in ways that increase its total output and therefore its overall well being.

A nation does not need international trade to operate *on* its production possibilities curve. A closed (nontrading) national economy can have full employment without international trade. However, through world trade an economy can reach a point of consumption *beyond* its domestic production possibilities curve. The gain from trade is the extra output obtained from abroad—the imports obtained for a lower opportunity cost than if they were produced at home.

Political Considerations While a nation as a
whole gains from trade, trade may harm particular domestic industries and particular groups of resource suppliers. In our earlier comparative-advantage example, specialization and trade adversely affected the U.S. avocado industry and the Mexican soybean industry. Those industries might seek to preserve their economic positions by persuading their respective governments to protect them from imports—perhaps through tariffs or import quotas.

Those who directly benefit from import protection are few in number but have much at stake. Thus, they have a strong incentive to pursue political activity to achieve their aims. However, the overall cost of tariffs and quotas typically greatly exceeds the benefits. It is not uncommon to find that it costs the public $200,000 or more a year to protect a domestic job that pays less than one-fourth that amount. Moreover, because these costs are buried in the price of goods and spread out over millions of citizens, the cost borne by each individual citizen is quite small. In the political arena, the voice of the

CONSIDER THIS . . .

Buy American?

Will "buying American" make Americans better off? No, says Dallas Federal Reserve economist W. Michael Cox:

A common myth is that it is better for Americans to spend their money at home than abroad. The best way to expose the fallacy of this argument is to take it to its logical extreme. If it is better for me to spend my money here than abroad, then it is even better yet to buy in Texas than in New York, better yet to buy in Dallas than in Houston . . . in my own neighborhood . . . within my own family . . . to consume only what I can produce. Alone and poor.*

*"The Fruits of Free Trade," Federal Reserve Bank of Dallas, Annual Report 2002, p. 16.

relatively few producers demanding *protectionism* is loud and constant, whereas the voice of those footing the bill is soft or nonexistent.

Indeed, the public may be won over by the apparent plausibility ("Cut imports and prevent domestic unemployment") and the patriotic ring ("Buy American!") of the protectionist arguments. The alleged benefits of tariffs are immediate and clear-cut to the public, but the adverse effects cited by economists are obscure and dispersed over the entire economy. When political deal making is added in—"You back tariffs for the apparel industry in my state, and I'll back tariffs on the auto industry in your state"—the outcome can be a network of protective tariffs, import quotas, and export subsidies.

Costs to Society

Tariffs and quotas benefit domestic producers of the protected products, but they harm domestic consumers, who must pay higher-than-world prices for the protected goods. They also hurt domestic firms that use the protected goods as inputs in their production processes. For example, a tariff on imported steel would boost the price of steel girders, thus hurting firms that construct large buildings. Also, tariffs and quotas reduce competition in the protected industries. With less competition from foreign producers, domestic firms may be slow to design and implement cost-saving production methods and introduce new or improved products.

Multilateral Trade Agreements and Free-Trade Zones

When one nation enacts barriers against imports, the nations whose exports suffer may retaliate with trade barriers of their own. In such a *trade war*, escalating tariffs choke world trade and reduce everyone's economic well-being. The **Smoot-Hawley Tariff Act** of 1930 is a classic example. Although that act was meant to reduce imports and stimulate U.S. production, the high tariffs it authorized prompted adversely affected nations to retaliate with tariffs equally high. International trade fell, lowering the output and income of all nations. Economic historians generally agree that the Smoot-Hawley Tariff Act was a contributing cause of the Great Depression. Aware of that fact, nations have worked to lower tariffs worldwide. Their pursuit of free trade has been aided by powerful domestic interest groups: Exporters of goods and services, importers of foreign components used in "domestic" products, and domestic sellers of imported products all strongly support lower tariffs.

Figure 5.4 makes clear that while the United States was a high-tariff nation over much of its history, U.S. tariffs have generally declined during the past half-century. Today, U.S. tariffs average only 4.6 percent on the imports subject to tariff and a growing list of imports are no longer subject to any tariff at all.

Reciprocal Trade Agreements Act

The **Reciprocal Trade Agreements Act** of 1934 started the downward trend of tariffs. Aimed at reducing tariffs, this act had two main features:

- *Negotiating authority* It authorized the president to negotiate with foreign nations agreements that would reduce existing U.S. tariffs by up to 50 percent. Those reductions were contingent on the actions other nations took to lower tariffs on U.S. exports.

- *Generalized reductions* The specific tariff reductions negotiated between the United States and any particular nation were generalized through most-favored-nation clauses, which often accompany such agreements. These clauses stipulate that any subsequently reduced U.S. tariffs, resulting from negotiation with any other nation, would apply equally to any nation that signed the original agreement. So if the United States negotiates a reduction in tariffs on wristwatches with, say, France, the lower U.S. tariffs on imported French watches also apply to the imports of the other

FIGURE 5.4 U.S. tariff rates, 1860–2006. Historically, U.S. tariff rates have fluctuated. But beginning with the Reciprocal Trade Agreements Act of 1934, the trend has been downward.

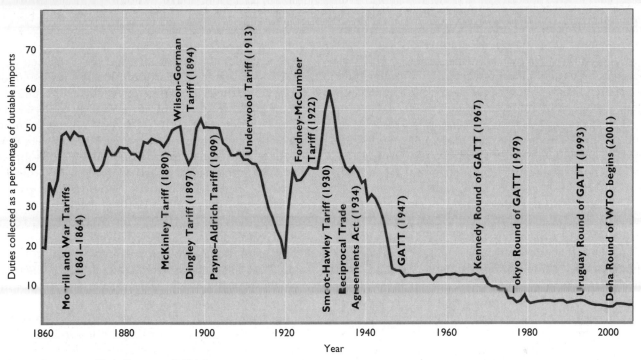

Source: U.S. International Trade Commission, FT-920 data.

nations having most-favored-nation status, say, Japan and Switzerland. This way, the reductions in U.S. tariffs automatically apply to many nations.

Today, most-favored-nations status is so common that the U.S. government has renamed it **normal-trade-relations (NTR) status.**

General Agreement on Tariffs and Trade

The Reciprocal Trade Agreements Act provided only bilateral (between two nations) negotiations. Its approach was broadened in 1947 when 23 nations, including the United States, signed the **General Agreement on Tariffs and Trade (GATT).** GATT was based on three principles: (1) equal, nondiscriminatory trade treatment for all member nations; (2) the reduction of tariffs by multilateral negotiation; and (3) the elimination of import quotas. Basically, GATT provided a forum for the negotiation of reduced trade barriers on a multilateral basis among nations.

Since the Second World War, member nations have completed eight "rounds" of GATT negotiations to reduce trade barriers. The eighth round of negotiations began in Uruguay in 1986. After seven years of complex discussions, in 1993 the 128 member nations reached a new agreement. The *Uruguay Round* agreement took effect on January 1, 1995, and its provisions were phased in through 2005.

Under this agreement, tariffs on thousands of products were eliminated or reduced, with overall tariffs dropping by 33 percent. The agreement also liberalized government rules that in the past impeded the global market for such services as advertising, legal services, tourist services, and financial services. Quotas on imported textiles and apparel were phased out and replaced with tariffs. Other provisions reduced agricultural subsidies paid to farmers and protected intellectual property (patents, trademarks, copyrights) against piracy.

World Trade Organization

The Uruguay Round agreement established the **World Trade Organization (WTO)** as GATT's successor. Some 153 nations belonged to the WTO in 2008. The WTO oversees trade agreements reached by the member nations and rules on trade disputes among them. It also provides forums for further rounds of trade negotiations. The ninth and latest round of negotiations—the **Doha Round**—was launched in Doha, Qatar, in late 2001. (The trade rounds occur over several years in several venues but are named after the city or country of origination.) The negotiations are aimed at further reducing tariffs and quotas, as well as agricultural subsidies that distort trade. One of this chapter's Web-based questions asks you to update the progress of the Doha Round.

GATT and the WTO have been positive forces in the trend toward liberalized world trade. The trade rules agreed upon by the member nations provide a strong and necessary bulwark against the protectionism called for by the special-interest groups in the various nations.

For that reason and others, the WTO is controversial. Critics are concerned that rules crafted to expand international trade and investment enable firms to circumvent national laws that protect workers and the environment. What good are minimum-wage laws, worker safety laws, collective bargaining rights, and environmental laws if firms can easily shift their production to nations that have weaker laws or consumers can buy goods produced in those countries?

Proponents of the WTO respond that labor and environmental protections should be pursued directly in nations that have low standards and via international organizations other than the WTO. These issues should not be linked to the process of trade liberalization, which confers widespread economic benefits across nations. Moreover, say proponents of the WTO, many environmental and labor concerns are greatly overblown. Most world trade is among advanced industrial countries, not between them and countries that have lower environmental and labor standards. Moreover, the free flow of goods and resources raises output and income in the developing nations. Historically, such increases in living standards have eventually resulted in stronger, not weaker, protections for the environment and for workers.

The European Union

Countries have also sought to reduce tariffs by creating regional *free-trade zones*—also called *trade blocs*. The most dramatic example is the **European Union (EU),** formerly called the European Economic Community. Initiated in 1958 as the Common Market, in 2003 the EU comprised 15 European nations—France, Germany, United Kingdom, Italy, Belgium, the Netherlands, Luxembourg, Denmark, Ireland, Greece, Spain, Portugal, Austria, Finland, and Sweden. In 2004, the EU expanded by 10 additional European countries—Poland, Hungary, Czech Republic, Slovakia, Lithuania, Latvia, Estonia, Slovenia, Malta, and Cyprus. In 2007, the addition of Bulgaria and Romania expanded the EU to 27 nations.

The EU Trade Bloc The EU has abolished tariffs and import quotas on nearly all products traded among the participating nations and established a common system of tariffs applicable to all goods received from nations outside the EU. It has also liberalized the movement of capital and labor within the EU and has created common policies in other economic matters of joint concern such as agriculture, transportation, and business practices. The EU is now a strong **trade bloc:** a group of countries having common identity, economic interests, and trade rules.

EU integration has achieved for Europe what the U.S. constitutional prohibition on tariffs by individual states has achieved for the United States: increased regional specialization, greater productivity, greater output, and faster economic growth. The free flow of goods and services has created large markets for EU industries. The resulting economies of large-scale production have enabled these industries to achieve much lower costs than they could have achieved in their small, single-nation markets.

The effects of EU success on nonmember nations such as the United States have been mixed. A peaceful and increasingly prosperous EU makes its members better customers for U.S. exports. But U.S. firms and other nonmember firms have been faced with tariffs and other barriers that make it difficult for them to compete against firms within the EU trade bloc. For example, autos produced in Germany and sold in Spain or France face no tariffs, whereas U.S. and Japanese autos exported to EU countries do. This puts U.S. and Japanese firms at a serious disadvantage.

By giving preferences to countries within their free-trade zone, trade blocs such as the EU tend to reduce their members' trade with non-bloc members. Thus, the world loses some of the benefits of a completely open global trading system. Eliminating that disadvantage has been one of the motivations for liberalizing global trade through the World Trade Organization. Those liberalizations apply equally to all nations that belong to the WTO.

The Euro One of the most significant accomplishments of the EU was the establishment of the so-called Euro Zone in the early 2000s. In 2008, 15 members of the EU used the **euro** as a common currency. Great Britain,

Denmark, and Sweden have opted out of the common currency, at least for now. But gone are French francs, German marks, Italian liras, and other national currencies within the Euro Zone.

Economists expect the adoption of the euro to raise the standard of living of the Euro Zone members over time. By ending the inconvenience and expense of exchanging currencies, the euro has enhanced the free flow of goods, services, and resources among the Euro Zone members. International trade among the member nations has increased by roughly 10 percent, with much of that increase happening because companies that previously sold products in only one or two European countries have now found it easier to market and sell their wares in all 15 Euro Zone countries. The euro has also allowed consumers and businesses to comparison shop for outputs and inputs, and this capability has increased competition, reduced prices, and lowered costs.

North American Free Trade Agreement

In 1993 Canada, Mexico, and the United States formed a major trade bloc. The **North American Free Trade Agreement (NAFTA)** established a free-trade zone that has about the same combined output as the EU but encompasses a much larger geographic area. NAFTA has eliminated tariffs and other trade barriers between Canada, Mexico, and the United States for most goods and services.

Critics of NAFTA feared that it would cause a massive loss of U.S. jobs as firms moved to Mexico to take advantage of lower wages and weaker regulations on pollution and workplace safety. Also, they were concerned that Japan and South Korea would build plants in Mexico and transport goods tariff-free to the United States, further hurting U.S. firms and workers.

In retrospect, critics were much too pessimistic. Since the passage of NAFTA in 1993, employment in the United States has increased by 22 million workers and the unemployment rate has declined from 6.9 to 4.7 percent. Increased trade among Canada, Mexico, and the United States has enhanced the standard of living in all three countries. **(Key Question 10)**

Trade-Related Issues

Although trade liberalization and increased international trade raise total output and income, they often disrupt existing patterns of production and resource allocations. Such disruptions can be highly painful to certain industries, firms, and workers in the countries affected. Little wonder, then, that international trade generates media and political controversy. The arguments for special trade protections are examined in a later chapter. Here, we examine two other trade-related issues that are in the news: trade adjustment assistance and offshoring of jobs. (In this chapter's Last Word, we examine another trade-related issue: fair-trade products.)

Trade Adjustment Assistance

A nation's comparative advantage in the production of a certain product is not fixed forever. As national economies evolve, the size and quality of their labor forces may change; the volume and composition of their capital stocks may shift; new technologies may emerge; and even the quality of land and the quantity of natural resources may be altered. As these changes take place, the relative efficiency with which a nation can produce specific goods will also change. Also, new trade agreements such as those we have discussed can suddenly leave formerly protected industries highly vulnerable to major disruption or even collapse.

Shifts in patterns of comparative advantage and removal of trade protection can hurt specific groups of workers. For example, the erosion of the United States' once strong comparative advantage in steel has caused production plant shutdowns and layoffs in the U.S. steel industry. The textile and apparel industries in the United States face similar difficulties. Clearly, not everyone wins from free trade (or freer trade). Some workers lose.

The **Trade Adjustment Assistance Act** of 2002 introduced some new, novel elements to help those hurt by shifts in international trade patterns. The law provides cash assistance (beyond unemployment insurance) for up to 78 weeks for workers displaced by imports or plant relocations abroad. To obtain the assistance, workers must participate in job searches, training programs, or remedial education. Also provided are relocation allowances to help displaced workers move geographically to new jobs within the United States. Refundable tax credits for health insurance serve as payments to help workers maintain their insurance coverage during the retraining and job search period. Workers who are 50 years of age or older are eligible for "wage insurance," which replaces some of the difference in pay (if any) between their old and new jobs. Many economists support trade adjustment assistance because it not only helps workers hurt by international trade but also helps create the political support necessary to reduce trade barriers and export subsidies.

As a College Student, You May Be Aware of Fair-Trade-Certified Products Such as Those Offered at Starbucks. On Some Campuses, Proponents of Fair-Trade Consumption Are Highly Active in Encouraging Fellow Students To Purchase Only Fair-Trade Goods. What Is Fair Trade All About? And How Effective Is it as an Economic Development Strategy?

Imports of goods by high-income nations from low-income nations increase the demand for labor in low-income nations. Other things equal, increases in labor demand raise wages and incomes. Some observers, however, conclude that the benefits that low-income countries derive from increased production—especially increased exports of agricultural commodities—accrue mainly to large corporations in those countries, some of which are owned by shareholders from high-income nations. Because workers in many low-income countries are highly immobile, have few employment options, and are not unionized, the large dominant sellers can supposedly keep an undeservedly large portion of the proceeds from added exports for themselves (in the form of profits) while simultaneously denying a fair share to their workers (by keeping wages low).

To counter this purported problem, consumer organizations in some of the high-income countries have tried to bypass the usual distribution channels and buy imported goods directly from producers or producer cooperatives that agree to *fair-trade standards*. Such standards guarantee the producers higher-than-market prices if they agree to pay their workers higher-than-market wages and to abide by rules regarding working conditions and workplace safety. Producers and products that meet the fair-trade standards are certified as fair-trade employers and fair-trade products. Fair-trade advocates in the rich nations then strongly urge consumers to purchase products—for example, coffee, wine, bananas, tea, fresh fruit, and cocoa—only from certified fair-trade producers. When pressure is sufficient, some corporate buyers of these products conclude that it may be more profitable to provide fair-trade products to customers than to risk being labeled an exploiter of third-world labor. Because of the higher-than-market prices and wages, fair-trade goods usually are more expensive than noncertified products.

In economic terms, the purpose of the fair-trade movement is to redistribute more of the total gains from international trade directly to low-income producers and workers by increasing the demand for fair-trade imports relative to otherwise identical imports.

Do these efforts succeed? Economists agree that some of the efforts of fair-trade advocates have succeeded in channeling sizable purchases away from otherwise identical substitutes and toward fair-trade goods. These increases in the demand for

But not all economists are keen on trade adjustment assistance. Loss of jobs from imports or plant relocations abroad is only a small fraction (about 4 percent in recent years) of total job losses in the economy each year. Many workers also lose their jobs because of changing patterns of demand, changing technology, bad management, and other dynamic aspects of a market economy. Some critics ask, "What makes losing one's job to international trade worthy of such special treatment, compared to losing one's job to, say, technological change or domestic competition?" Economists can find no totally satisfying answer.

Offshoring of Jobs

Not only are some U.S. jobs lost because of international trade, but some are lost because of globalization of resource markets. In recent years U.S. firms have found the outsourcing of work abroad increasingly profitable. Economists call this business activity **offshoring**: shifting work previously done by American workers to workers located in other nations. Offshoring is not a new practice but traditionally has involved components for U.S. manufacturing goods. For example, Boeing has long offshored the production of major airplane parts for its "American" aircraft.

Recent advances in computer and communications technology have enabled U.S. firms to offshore service jobs such as data entry, book composition, software coding, call-center operations, medical transcription, and claims processing to countries such as India. Where offshoring occurs, some of the value added in the production process accrues to foreign countries rather than the United States. So part of the income generated from the production of U.S. goods is paid to foreigners, not to American workers.

fair-trade goods, in turn, have increased the demand for the labor used to produce those goods. So, the fair-trade strategy "has worked" insofar as it has raised prices and wages for *some* sellers and *some* workers in low-wage countries—namely those involved with fair-trade programs.

Nevertheless, most economists question the overall effectiveness of the fair-trade approach as a broader economic development strategy. They say that price and wage setting by advocacy groups is based on highly subjective views of fairness that may be at odds with economic realities. Distortions of market prices and wages invite inefficiency and unintended consequences. For example, the higher fair-trade prices may encourage resources to remain producing the fair-trade products long after normal supply and demand circumstances would have encouraged them to move to more productive employment in other parts of agriculture or in manufacturing or services.

The consensus among economists is that fair-trade purchasing in the high-income nations has simply shifted labor demand within and among low-wage countries. Fair trade has not increased the *overall* labor demand nor the average pay of workers in low-wage nations. Sustainable increases in average pay require economywide gains in labor productivity—output per hour of work. Unfortunately, fair-trade purchasing does not accomplish that. Economywide gains in productivity and wages require improvements in the quantity and quality of education, more and improved capital goods, and the use of more efficient technology.

Some economists say that other action by people in high-income nations might benefit the low-income nations more effectively than fair-trade purchasing. For example, pressing for the removal of agricultural subsidies in high-income areas such as the United States and the European Union would reduce the overproduction of agricultural output that floods international markets and depresses international agricultural prices. Those low prices impoverish farmers in low-wage nations and encourage them to concentrate their efforts in producing agricultural commodities that are not produced in the wealthy countries and therefore are unsubsidized. In a sense, the low-wage countries get stuck overproducing low-profit agricultural commodities such as coffee, bananas, and cocoa—keeping those prices artificially low. Ironically, those very low prices (and the low agricultural wages that result) are precisely what the fair-trade movement tries to increase.

Offshoring is a wrenching experience for many Americans who lose their jobs, but it is not necessarily bad for the overall economy. Offshoring simply reflects a growing specialization and international trade in services, or, more descriptively, "tasks." That trade has been made possible by recent trade agreements and new information and communication technologies. As with trade in goods, trade in services reflects comparative advantage and is beneficial to both trading parties. Moreover, the United States has a sizable trade surplus with other nations in services. The United States gains by specializing in high-valued services such as transportation services, accounting services, legal services, and advertising services, where it still has a comparative advantage. It then "trades" to obtain lower-valued services such as call-center and data entry work, for which comparative advantage has gone abroad.

Offshoring also increases the demand for complementary jobs in the United States. Jobs that are close substitutes for existing U.S. jobs are lost, but complementary jobs in the United States are expanded. For example, the lower price of writing software code in India may mean a lower cost of software sold in the United States and abroad. That, in turn, may create more jobs for U.S.-based workers such as software designers, marketers, and distributors. Moreover, the offshoring may encourage domestic investment and expansion of firms in the United States by reducing their production costs and keeping them competitive worldwide. In some instances, "offshoring jobs" may equate to "importing competitiveness." Entire firms that might otherwise disappear abroad may remain profitable in the United States only because they can offshore some of their work.

- Governments curtail imports and promote exports through protective tariffs, import quotas, nontariff barriers, and export subsidies.
- The General Agreement on Tariffs and Trade (GATT) established multinational reductions in tariffs and import quotas. The Uruguay Round of GATT (1993) reduced tariffs worldwide, liberalized international trade in services, strengthened protections for intellectual property, and reduced agricultural subsidies.
- The World Trade Organization (WTO)—GATT's successor—rules on trade disputes and provides forums for negotiations on further rounds of trade liberalization. The current round is called the Doha Round.
- The European Union (EU) and the North American Free Trade Agreement (NAFTA) have reduced internal trade barriers among their members by establishing large free-trade zones. Of the 27 EU members (as of 2008), 15 now have a common currency—the euro.
- Increased international trade and offshoring of jobs have harmed some specific U.S. workers and have led to policies such as trade adjustment assistance to try to help them with their transitions to new lines of work.

Global Competition

Globalization—the integration of industry, commerce, communication, travel, and culture among the world's nations—is one of the major trends of our time. (See Global Perspective 5.3 for a list of the top 12 globalized nations, according to one set of criteria.) There is a lively debate internationally as to whether globalization is a positive or negative force. Those who support globalization focus on the improvements to general standards of living that it brings. Those who oppose it express concerns about its impacts on the environment, unionized workers, and the poor.

One thing about globalization is certain and relevant to our present discussion: It has brought intense competition both within the United States and across the globe. In the United States, imports have gained major shares of many markets, including those for cars, steel, lumber, car tires, clothing, sporting goods, electronics, and toys. Nevertheless, hundreds of U.S. firms have prospered in the global marketplace. Such firms as Boeing, McDonald's, Intel, Coca-Cola, Starbucks, Microsoft, Monsanto, Procter & Gamble, and Caterpillar have continued to retain high market shares at home and have dramatically expanded their sales abroad. Of course, not all firms have been successful. Some have not been able to compete, because their international competitors make higher-quality products, have lower production costs, or both.

The Top 12 Globalized Economies, 2007

Foreign Policy magazine publishes an annual list of the world's most globalized economies, based on 13 key indicators such as foreign trade, cross-border travel, Internet use, and international investment flows. Here is the magazine's list, in descending order, for 2007.

1. Singapore
2. Hong Kong
3. Netherlands
4. Switzerland
5. Ireland
6. Denmark
7. United States
8. Canada
9. Jordan
10. Estonia
11. Sweden
12. United Kingdom

Source: A. T. Kearney, *Foreign Policy*, **www.foreignpolicy.com.**

Is the heightened competition that accompanies the global economy a good thing? Although some domestic producers *do* get hurt and their workers must find employment elsewhere, foreign competition clearly benefits consumers and society in general. Imports break down the monopoly power of existing firms, thereby lowering product prices and providing consumers with a greater variety of goods. Foreign competition also forces domestic producers to become more efficient and to improve product quality; that has already happened in several U.S. industries, including steel and autos. Most U.S. firms can and do compete quite successfully in the global marketplace.

What about the U.S. firms that cannot compete successfully in open markets? The unfortunate reality is that they must sell off production facilities, scale back their operations, and try to develop new products. If they remain unprofitable despite their best efforts, they will need to go out of business. Persistent economic losses mean that scarce resources are not being used efficiently. Shifting those resources to alternative, profitable uses will increase total U.S. output. It will be far less expensive for the United States to provide training and, if necessary, relocation assistance to laid-off workers than to try to protect these jobs from foreign competition.

Summary

1. Goods and services flows, capital and labor flows, information and technology flows, and financial flows link the United States and other countries.

2. International trade is growing in importance globally and for the United States. World trade is significant to the United States in two respects: (a) The absolute volumes of U.S. imports and exports exceed those of any other single nation. (b) The United States is completely dependent on trade for certain commodities and materials that cannot be obtained domestically.

3. Principal U.S. exports include chemicals, agricultural products, consumer durables, semiconductors, and medical equipment. Principal imports include oil, automobiles, metals, household appliances, and consumer electronics. Quantitatively, Canada is the United States' most important trading partner.

4. Global trade has been greatly facilitated by (a) improvements in transportation technology, (b) improvements in communications technology, and (c) general declines in tariffs. The world's major trading nations by volume of trade are Germany, the United States, China, and Japan. Other major traders include other western European nations (France, the Netherlands, Italy, and the United Kingdom), along with Canada and the east and southeast Asian countries of South Korea, Taiwan, and Singapore.

5. Specialization based on comparative advantage enables nations to achieve higher standards of living through trade with other countries. A trading partner should specialize in products and services for which its domestic opportunity costs are lowest. The terms of trade must be such that both nations can obtain a product via trade at less opportunity costs than if they produced that product at home.

6. The foreign exchange market sets exchange rates between currencies. Each nation's imports create a supply of its own currency and a demand for foreign currencies. The resulting supply-demand equilibrium sets the exchange rate that links the currencies of all nations. Depreciation of a nation's currency reduces its imports and increases its exports; appreciation increases its imports and reduces its exports.

7. Governments influence trade flows through (a) protective tariffs, (b) quotas, (c) nontariff barriers, and (d) export subsidies. Such impediments to free trade result from misunderstandings about the advantages of free trade and from political considerations. By artificially increasing product prices, trade barriers cost U.S. consumers billions of dollars annually.

8. The Reciprocal Trade Agreements Act of 1934 marked the beginning of a trend toward lower U.S. tariffs. In 1947 the General Agreement on Tariffs and Trade (GATT) was formed to encourage nondiscriminatory treatment for all member nations, to reduce tariffs, and to eliminate import quotas. The Uruguay Round of GATT negotiations (1993) reduced tariffs and quotas, liberalized trade in services, reduced agricultural subsidies, reduced pirating of intellectual property, and phased out quotas on textiles.

9. GATT's successor, the World Trade Organization (WTO), has 153 member nations. It implements WTO agreements, rules on trade disputes between members, and provides forums for continued discussions on trade liberalization. The latest round of trade negotiations—the Doha Round—began in late 2001 and as of early 2008 was still in progress.

10. Free-trade zones (trade blocs) liberalize trade within regions but may at the same time impede trade with non-bloc members. Two examples of free-trade arrangements are the 27-member European Union (EU) and the North American Free Trade Agreement (NAFTA), comprising Canada, Mexico, and the United States. Fifteen of the EU nations have abandoned their national currencies for a common currency called the euro.

11. The Trade Adjustment Assistance Act of 2002 recognizes that trade liberalization and increased international trade can create job loss for many workers. The Act therefore provides cash assistance, education and training benefits, health care subsidies, and wage subsidies (for persons age 50 or older) to qualified workers displaced by imports or relocations of plants from the United States to abroad.

12. Offshoring is the practice of shifting work previously done by Americans in the United States to workers located in other nations. Although offshoring reduces some U.S. jobs, it lowers production costs, expands sales, and therefore may create other U.S. jobs. Less than 4 percent of all job losses in the United States each year are caused by imports, offshoring, and plant relocation abroad.

13. The global economy has created intense foreign competition in many U.S. product markets, but many U.S. firms are able to compete successfully abroad as well as at home.

Terms and Concepts

comparative advantage

terms of trade

foreign exchange market

exchange rates

depreciation

appreciation

protective tariffs

import quotas

nontariff barriers

export subsidies

Smoot-Hawley Tariff Act

Reciprocal Trade Agreements Act

normal-trade-relations (NTR) status

General Agreement on Tariffs and Trade (GATT)

World Trade Organization (WTO)

Doha Round

European Union (EU)

trade bloc

euro

North American Free Trade Agreement (NAFTA)

Trade Adjustment Assistance Act

offshoring

Study Questions

1. Describe the four major economic flows that link the United States with other nations. Provide a specific example to illustrate each flow. Explain the relationships between the top and bottom flows in Figure 5.1. **LO1**

2. How important is international trade to the U.S. economy? In terms of volume, does the United States trade more with the industrially advanced economies or with developing economies? What country is the United States' most important trading partner, quantitatively? **LO1**

3. What factors account for the rapid growth of world trade since the Second World War? Who are the major players in international trade today? Besides China and Japan, what other Asian nations play significant roles in international trade? **LO1**

4. **KEY QUESTION** The following are production possibilities tables for China and the United States. Assume that before specialization and trade the optimal product mix for China is alternative B and for the United States is alternative U. **LO2**

	China Production Possibilities					
Product	A	B	C	D	E	F
Apparel (in thousands)	30	24	18	12	6	0
Chemicals (in tons)	0	6	12	18	24	30

	U.S. Production Possibilities					
Product	R	S	T	U	V	W
Apparel (in thousands)	10	8	6	4	2	0
Chemicals (in tons)	0	4	8	12	16	20

a. Are comparative-cost conditions such that the two areas should specialize? If so, what product should each produce?

b. What is the total gain in apparel and chemical output that would result from such specialization?

c. What are the limits of the terms of trade? Suppose actual terms of trade are 1 unit of apparel for $1\frac{1}{2}$ units of chemicals and that 4 units of apparel are exchanged for 6 units of chemicals. What are the gains from specialization and trade for each nation?

d. Explain why this illustration allows you to conclude that specialization according to comparative advantage results in more efficient use of world resources.

5. Suppose that the comparative-cost ratios of two products—baby formula and tuna fish—are as follows in the hypothetical nations of Canswicki and Tunata:

Canswicki: 1 can baby formula ≡ 2 cans tuna fish

Tunata: 1 can baby formula ≡ 4 cans tuna fish

In what product should each nation specialize? Explain why terms of trade of 1 can baby formula ≡ $2\frac{1}{2}$ cans tuna fish would be acceptable to both nations. **LO2**

6. **KEY QUESTION** True or False? "U.S. exports create a demand for foreign currencies; foreign imports of U.S. goods create a supply of foreign currencies." Explain. Would a decline in U.S. consumer income or a weakening of U.S. preferences for foreign products cause the dollar to depreciate or to appreciate? Other things equal, what would be the effects of that depreciation or appreciation on U.S. exports and imports? **LO3**

7. If the European euro were to decline in value (depreciate) in the foreign exchange market, would it be easier or harder for the French to sell their wine in the United States? Suppose you were planning a trip to Paris. How would depreciation of the euro change the dollar cost of your trip? **LO3**

8. What measures do governments take to promote exports and restrict imports? Who benefits and who loses from protectionist policies? What is the net outcome for society? **LO4**

9. **KEY QUESTION** Identify and state the significance of each of the following: (a) WTO; (b) EU; (c) euro; (d) NAFTA. What commonality do they share? **LO5**

10. Explain: "Free-trade zones such as the EU and NAFTA lead a double life: They can promote free trade among members, but they pose serious trade obstacles for nonmembers." Do you think the net effects of trade blocs are good or bad for world trade? Why? How do the efforts of the WTO relate to these trade blocs? **LO5**

11. Speculate as to why some U.S. firms strongly support trade liberalization while other U.S. firms favor protectionism. Speculate as to why some U.S. labor unions strongly support trade liberalization while other U.S. labor unions strongly oppose it. **LO5**

12. What forms do trade adjustment assistance take in the United States? How does such assistance promote support for free trade agreements? Do you think workers who lose

their jobs because of changes in trade laws deserve special treatment relative to workers who lose their jobs because of other changes in the economy, say, changes in patterns of government spending? **LO5**

13. What is offshoring of white-collar service jobs and how does that practice relate to international trade? Why has it recently increased? Why do you think more than half of all the offshored jobs have gone to India? Give an example (other than that in the textbook) of how offshoring can eliminate some U.S. jobs while creating other U.S. jobs. **LO5**

14. **LAST WORD** How does a fair-trade product differ from an otherwise identical imported good? What is the purported benefit of fair-trade certification on purchases of goods such as chocolate, coffee, bananas, and tea? Do fair-trade goods improve average wage and level of income in low-income nations? Why or why not?

Web-Based Questions

1. **TRADE BALANCES WITH PARTNER COUNTRIES** The U.S. Census Bureau, at **www.census.gov/foreign-trade/ statistics/highlights/top/index.html,** lists the top trading partners of the United States (imports and exports added together) as well as the top 15 countries the United States exports to and imports from. Using the current year-to-date data, compare the top 15 countries to which the United States exports with the top 15 countries from which the United States imports. Are the countries the same? What percentage of U.S. imports and exports are accounted for by the top 15 trading partners? The top 5 trading partners represent what percent of U.S. imports and what percent of U.S. exports?

2. **FOREIGN EXCHANGE RATES—THE YEN FOR DOLLARS** The Federal Reserve System Web site, **www.federalreserve .gov/releases/H10/hist,** provides historical foreign-exchange-rate data for a wide variety of currencies. Look at the data

for the Japanese yen from 1995 to the present. Assume that you were in Tokyo every New Year's from January 1, 2000, to this year and bought a *bento* (box lunch) for 1000 yen each year. Convert this amount to dollars using the yen-dollar exchange rate for each January since 2000, and plot the dollar price of the *bento* over time. Has the dollar appreciated or depreciated against the yen? What was the least amount in dollars that your box lunch cost? The most?

3. **THE DOHA ROUND—WHAT IS THE CURRENT STATUS?** Determine and briefly summarize the current status of the Doha Round of trade negotiations (the Doha Development Agenda) by accessing the World Trade Organization site, **www.wto.org.** Is the round still in progress or has it been concluded with an agreement? If the former, when and where was the latest ministerial meeting? If the latter, what are the main features of the agreement?

FURTHER TEST YOUR KNOWLEDGE AT
www.mcconnell18e.com

PART TWO

Microeconomics of Product Markets

6

Elasticity, Consumer Surplus, and Producer Surplus

Today's market economies rely mainly on the activities of consumers, businesses, and resource suppliers to allocate resources efficiently. Those activities and their outcomes are the subject of microeconomics, to which we now turn.

In this chapter we extend Chapter 3's discussion of demand and supply by explaining significant ideas that help us answer such questions as: Why do buyers of some products (for example, ocean cruises) respond to price increases by substantially reducing their purchases while buyers of other products (say, gasoline) respond by only slightly cutting back their purchases? Why do higher market prices for some products (for example, chicken) cause producers to greatly increase their output while price rises for other products (say, gold) cause only limited increases in output? Why does the demand for some products (for example, books) rise a great deal when household income increases while the demand for other products (say, milk) rises just a little? How is it that most consumers obtain products at prices below the prices they actually would have been willing to pay? How is it that most producers obtain higher prices for their products than the prices they actually would have been willing to accept?

The ideas of *elasticity, consumer surplus*, and *producer surplus* help answer these questions. Let's begin by looking at elasticity.

Price Elasticity of Demand

The law of demand tells us that, other things equal, consumers will buy more of a product when its price declines and less when its price increases. But how much more or less will they buy? The amount varies from product to product and over different price ranges for the same product. It also may vary over time. And such variations matter. For example, a firm contemplating a price hike will want to know how consumers will respond. If they remain highly loyal and continue to buy, the firm's revenue will rise. But if consumers defect en masse to other sellers or other products, the firm's revenue will tumble.

The responsiveness (or sensitivity) of consumers to a price change is measured by a product's **price elasticity of demand.** For some products—for example, restaurant meals—consumers are highly responsive to price changes. Modest price changes cause very large changes in the quantity purchased. Economists say that the demand for such products is *relatively elastic* or simply *elastic.*

For other products—for example, toothpaste—consumers pay much less attention to price changes. Substantial price changes cause only small changes in the amount purchased. The demand for such products is *relatively inelastic* or simply *inelastic.*

The Price-Elasticity Coefficient and Formula

Economists measure the degree to which demand is price elastic or inelastic with the coefficient E_d, defined as

$$E_d = \frac{\text{percentage change in quantity demanded of product X}}{\text{percentage change in price of product X}}$$

The percentage changes in the equation are calculated by dividing the *change* in quantity demanded by the original

quantity demanded and by dividing the *change* in price by the original price. So we can restate the formula as

$$E_d = \frac{\text{change in quantity demanded of X}}{\text{original quantity demanded of X}} \div \frac{\text{change in price of X}}{\text{original price of X}}$$

Using Averages Unfortunately, an annoying problem arises in computing the price-elasticity coefficient. A price change from, say, $4 to $5 along a demand curve is a 25 percent (= $1/$4) increase, but the opposite price change from $5 to $4 along the same curve is a 20 percent (= $1/$5) decrease. Which percentage change in price should we use in the denominator to compute the price-elasticity coefficient? And when quantity changes, for example, from 10 to 20, it is a 100 percent (= 10/10) increase. But when quantity falls from 20 to 10 along the identical demand curve, it is a 50 percent (= 10/20) decrease. Should we use 100 percent or 50 percent in the numerator of the elasticity formula? Elasticity should be the same whether price rises or falls!

The simplest solution to the problem is to use the **midpoint formula** for calculating elasticity. This formula simply averages the two prices and the two quantities as the reference points for computing the percentages. That is,

$$E_d = \frac{\text{change in quantity}}{\text{sum of quantities}/2} \div \frac{\text{change in price}}{\text{sum of prices}/2}$$

For the same $5–$4 price range, the price reference is $4.50 [= ($5 + $4)/2], and for the same 10–20 quantity range, the quantity reference is 15 units [= (10 + 20)/2]. The percentage change in price is now $1/$4.50, or about 22 percent, and the percentage change in quantity is $\frac{10}{15}$, or about 67 percent. So E_d is about 3. This solution eliminates the "up versus down" problem. All the price-elasticity coefficients that follow are calculated using this midpoint formula.

Using Percentages Why use percentages rather than absolute amounts in measuring consumer responsiveness? There are two reasons.

First, if we use absolute changes, the choice of units will arbitrarily affect our impression of buyer responsiveness. To illustrate: If the price of a bag of popcorn at the local softball game is reduced from $3 to $2 and consumers increase their purchases from 60 to 100 bags, it will seem that consumers are quite sensitive to price changes and therefore that demand is elastic. After all, a price change of 1 unit has caused a change in the amount demanded of 40 units. But by changing the monetary unit from dollars to pennies (why not?), we find that a price change of 100 units (pennies) causes a quantity change of 40 units. This may falsely lead us to believe that demand is inelastic. We avoid this problem by using percentage changes. This particular price decline is the same whether we measure it in dollars or pennies.

Second, by using percentages, we can correctly compare consumer responsiveness to changes in the prices of different products. It makes little sense to compare the effects on quantity demanded of (1) a $1 increase in the price of a $10,000 used car with (2) a $1 increase in the price of a $1 soft drink. Here the price of the used car has increased by .01 percent while the price of the soft drink is up by 100 percent. We can more sensibly compare the consumer responsiveness to price increases by using some common percentage increase in price for both.

Elimination of Minus Sign We know from the downsloping demand curve that price and quantity demanded are inversely related. Thus, the price-elasticity coefficient of demand E_d will always be a negative number. As an example, if price declines, then quantity demanded will increase. This means that the numerator in our formula will be positive and the denominator negative, yielding a negative E_d. For an increase in price, the numerator will be negative but the denominator positive, again yielding a negative E_d.

Economists usually ignore the minus sign and simply present the absolute value of the elasticity coefficient to avoid an ambiguity that might otherwise arise. It can be confusing to say that an E_d of -4 is greater than one of -2. This possible confusion is avoided when we say an E_d of 4 reveals greater elasticity than one of 2. So, in what follows, we ignore the minus sign in the coefficient of price elasticity of demand and show only the absolute value. Incidentally, the ambiguity does not arise with supply because price and quantity supplied are positively related. All elasticity of supply coefficients therefore are positive numbers.

Interpretations of E_d

We can interpret the coefficient of price elasticity of demand as follows.

Elastic Demand Demand is **elastic** if a specific percentage change in price results in a larger percentage change in quantity demanded. Then E_d will be greater than 1. Example: Suppose that a 2 percent decline in the price of cut flowers results in a 4 percent increase in quantity demanded. Then demand for cut flowers is elastic and

$$E_d = \frac{.04}{.02} = 2$$

Inelastic Demand If a specific percentage change in price produces a smaller percentage change in quantity demanded, demand is **inelastic.** Then E_d will be less than 1. Example: Suppose that a 2 percent decline in the price of coffee leads to only a 1 percent increase in quantity demanded. Then demand is inelastic and

$$E_d = \frac{.01}{.02} = .5$$

Unit Elasticity The case separating elastic and inelastic demands occurs where a percentage change in price and the resulting percentage change in quantity demanded are the same. Example: Suppose that a 2 percent drop in the price of chocolate causes a 2 percent increase in quantity demanded. This special case is termed **unit elasticity** because E_d is exactly 1, or unity. In this example,

$$E_d = \frac{.02}{.02} = 1$$

Extreme Cases When we say demand is "inelastic," we do not mean that consumers are completely unresponsive to a price change. In that extreme situation, where a price change results in no change whatsoever in the quantity demanded, economists say that demand is **perfectly inelastic.** The price-elasticity coefficient is zero because there is no response to a change in price. Approximate examples include an acute diabetic's demand for insulin or an addict's demand for heroin. A line parallel to the vertical axis, such as D_1 in Figure 6.1a, shows perfectly inelastic demand graphically.

Conversely, when we say demand is "elastic," we do not mean that consumers are completely responsive to a price change. In that extreme situation, where a small price reduction causes buyers to increase their purchases from zero to all they can obtain, the elasticity coefficient is infinite ($= \infty$) and economists say demand is **perfectly elastic.** A line parallel to the horizontal axis, such as D_2 in

FIGURE 6.1 Perfectly inelastic and elastic demands.
Demand curve D_1 in (a) represents perfectly inelastic demand ($E_d = 0$). A
price increase will result in no change in quantity demanded. Demand curve
D_2 in (b) represents perfectly elastic demand. A price increase will cause
quantity demanded to decline from an infinite amount to zero ($E_d = \infty$).

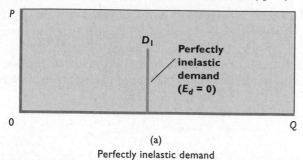

(a)
Perfectly inelastic demand

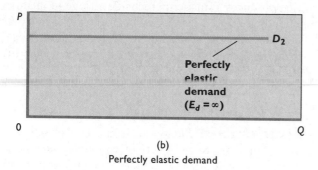

(b)
Perfectly elastic demand

A Bit of a Stretch

The following analogy might help you remember the distinction between "elastic" and "inelastic." Imagine two objects—one an Ace elastic bandage used to wrap injured joints and the other a relatively firm rubber tie-down (rubber strap) used for securing items for transport. The Ace bandage stretches a great deal when pulled with a particular force; the rubber tie-down stretches some, but not a lot.

Similar differences occur for the quantity demanded of various products when their prices change. For some products, a price change causes a substantial "stretch" of quantity demanded. When this stretch in percentage terms exceeds the percentage change in price, demand is elastic. For other products, quantity demanded stretches very little in response to the price change. When this stretch in percentage terms is less than the percentage change in price, demand is inelastic.

In summary:
* Elastic demand displays considerable "quantity stretch" (as with the Ace bandage).
* Inelastic demand displays relatively little "quantity stretch" (as with the rubber tie-down).

And through extension:
* Perfectly elastic demand has infinite quantity stretch.
* Perfectly inelastic demand has zero quantity stretch.

Figure 6.1b, shows perfectly elastic demand. You will see in Chapter 9 that such a demand applies to a firm—say, a mining firm that is selling its output in a purely competitive market.

The Total-Revenue Test

The importance of elasticity for firms relates to the effect of price changes on total revenue and thus on profits (= total revenue minus total costs).

Total revenue (TR) is the total amount the seller receives from the sale of a product in a particular time period; it is calculated by multiplying the product price (P) by the quantity sold (Q). In equation form:

$$\text{TR} = P \times Q$$

Graphically, total revenue is represented by the $P \times Q$ rectangle lying below a point on a demand curve. At point *a* in Figure 6.2a, for example, price is $2 and quantity demanded is 10 units. So total revenue is $20 (= $2 × 10), shown by the rectangle composed of the gold and orange areas under the demand curve. We know from basic geometry that the area of a rectangle is found by multiplying one side by the other. Here, one side is "price" ($2) and the other is "quantity demanded" (10 units).

Total revenue and the price elasticity of demand are related. In fact, the easiest way to infer whether demand is elastic or inelastic is to employ the **total-revenue test.** Here is the test: Note what happens to total revenue when price changes. If total revenue changes in the opposite direction from price, demand is elastic. If total revenue changes in the same direction as price, demand is inelastic. If total revenue does not change when price changes, demand is unit-elastic.

Elastic Demand If demand is elastic, a decrease in price will increase total revenue. Even though a lesser price is received per unit, enough additional units are sold to more than make up for the lower price. For an example,

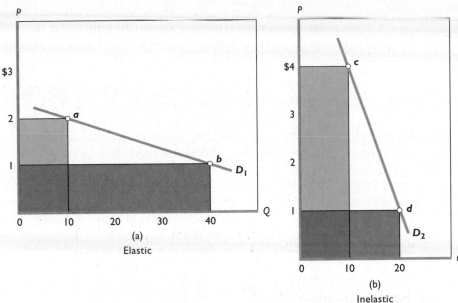

(a)
Elastic

(b)
Inelastic

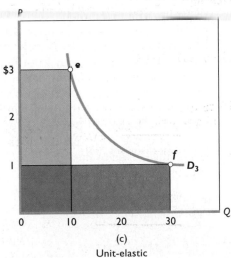

(c)
Unit-elastic

FIGURE 6.2 The total-revenue test for price elasticity. (a) Price declines from $2 to $1, and total revenue increases from $20 to $40. So demand is elastic. The gain in revenue (brown area) exceeds the loss of revenue (gold area). (b) Price declines from $4 to $1, and total revenue falls from $40 to $20. So, demand is inelastic. The gain in revenue (brown area) is less than the loss of revenue (gold area). (c) Price declines from $3 to $1, and total revenue does not change. Demand is unit-elastic. The gain in revenue (brown area) equals the loss of revenue (gold area).

look at demand curve D_1 in Figure 6.2a. We have already established that at point a, total revenue is $20 (= 2×10), shown as the gold plus orange area. If the price declines from $2 to $1 (point b), the quantity demanded becomes 40 units and total revenue is $40 (= 1×40). As a result of the price decline, total revenue has increased from $20 to $40. Total revenue has increased in this case because the $1 decline in price applies to 10 units, with a consequent revenue loss of $10 (the gold area). But 30 more units are sold at $1 each, resulting in a revenue gain of $30 (the brown area). Visually, the gain of the brown area clearly exceeds the loss of the gold area. As indicated, the overall result is a net increase in total revenue of $20 (= $30 − 10).

The analysis is reversible: If demand is elastic, a price increase will reduce total revenue. The revenue gained on the higher-priced units will be more than offset by the revenue lost from the lower quantity sold. Bottom line: Other things equal, when price and total revenue move in opposite directions, demand is elastic. E_d is greater than 1, meaning the percentage change in quantity demanded is greater than the percentage change in price.

Inelastic Demand If demand is inelastic, a price decrease will reduce total revenue. The increase in sales will not fully offset the decline in revenue per unit, and total revenue will decline. To see this, look at demand curve D_2 in Figure 6.2b. At point c on the curve, price is $4 and quantity demanded is 10. Thus total revenue is $40, shown by the combined gold and orange rectangle. If the price drops to $1 (point *d*), total revenue declines to $20, which obviously is less than $40. Total revenue has declined because the loss of revenue (the gold area) from the lower unit price is larger than the gain in revenue (the brown area) from the accompanying increase in sales. Price has fallen, and total revenue has also declined.

Our analysis is again reversible: If demand is inelastic, a price increase will increase total revenue. So, other things

> **WORKED PROBLEMS**
>
> **W 6.2**
>
> Total-revenue test

equal, when price and total revenue move in the same direction, demand is inelastic. E_d is less than 1, meaning the percentage change in quantity demanded is less than the percentage change in price.

Unit Elasticity In the special case of unit elasticity, an increase or a decrease in price leaves total revenue unchanged. The loss in revenue from a lower unit price is exactly offset by the gain in revenue from the accompanying increase in sales. Conversely, the gain in revenue from a higher unit price is exactly offset by the revenue loss associated with the accompanying decline in the amount demanded.

In Figure 6.2c (demand curve D_3) we find that at the price of $3, 10 units will be sold, yielding total revenue of $30. At the lower $1 price, a total of 30 units will be sold, again resulting in $30 of total revenue. The $2 price reduction causes the loss of revenue shown by the gold area, but this is exactly offset by the revenue gain shown by the brown area. Total revenue does not change. In fact, that would be true for all price changes along this particular curve.

Other things equal, when price changes and total revenue remains constant, demand is unit-elastic (or unitary). E_d is 1, meaning the percentage change in quantity equals the percentage change in price.

Price Elasticity along a Linear Demand Curve
Now a major confession! Although the demand curves depicted in Figure 6.2 nicely illustrate the total-revenue test for elasticity, two of the graphs involve specific movements along linear (straight-line) demand curves. That presents no problem for explaining the total-revenue test. However, you need to know that elasticity typically varies over the different price ranges of the same demand curve. (The exception is the curve in Figure 6.2c. Elasticity is 1 along the entire curve.)

Table 6.1 and Figure 6.3 demonstrate that elasticity typically varies over the different price ranges of the same demand schedule or curve. Plotting the hypothetical data for movie tickets shown in columns 1 and 2 of Table 6.1 yields demand curve *D* in Figure 6.3. Observe that the demand curve is linear. But we see from column 3 of the table that the price elasticity coefficient for this demand curve declines as we move from higher to lower prices. For all downsloping straight-line and most other demand curves, demand is more price-elastic toward the upper left (here, the $5−$8 price range of *D*) than toward the lower right (here, the $4−$1 price range of *D*).

This is the consequence of the arithmetic properties of the elasticity measure. Specifically, in the upper-left segment of the demand curve, the percentage change

> **INTERACTIVE GRAPHS**
>
> **G 6.1**
>
> Elasticity and revenue

in quantity is large because the original reference quantity is small. Similarly, the percentage change in price is

TABLE 6.1 Price Elasticity of Demand for Movie Tickets as Measured by the Elasticity Coefficient and the Total-Revenue Test

(1) Total Quantity of Tickets Demanded per Week, Thousands	(2) Price per Ticket	(3) Elasticity Coefficient (E_d)	(4) Total Revenue, (1) × (2)	(5) Total-Revenue Test
1	$8		$ 8000	
2	7	5.00	14,000	Elastic
3	6	2.60	18,000	Elastic
4	5	1.57	20,000	Elastic
5	4	1.00	20,000	Unit elastic
6	3	0.64	18,000	Inelastic
7	2	0.38	14,000	Inelastic
8	1	0.20	8000	Inelastic

FIGURE 6.3 The relation between price elasticity of Demand for movie tickets and total revenue. Demand curve D in (a) is based on Table 6.1 and is marked to show that the hypothetical weekly demand for movie tickets is elastic at higher price ranges and inelastic at lower price ranges. The total-revenue curve TR in (b) is derived from demand curve D. When price falls and TR increases, demand is elastic; when price falls and TR is unchanged, demand is unit-elastic; and when price falls and TR declines, demand is inelastic.

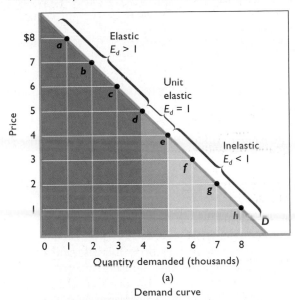

(a)
Demand curve

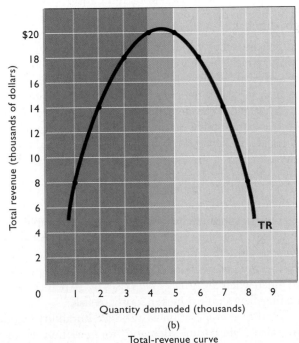

(b)
Total-revenue curve

small in that segment because the original reference price is large. The relatively large percentage change in quantity divided by the relatively small change in price yields a large E_d—an elastic demand.

The reverse holds true for the lower-right segment of the demand curve. Here the percentage change in quantity is small because the original reference quantity is large; similarly, the percentage change in price is large because the original reference price is small. The relatively small percentage change in quantity divided by the relatively large percentage change in price results in a small E_d—an inelastic demand.

The demand curve in Figure 6.3a also illustrates that the slope of a demand curve—its flatness or steepness—is not a sound basis for judging elasticity. The catch is that the slope of the curve is computed from *absolute* changes in price and quantity, while elasticity involves *relative* or *percentage* changes in price and quantity. The demand curve in Figure 6.3a is linear, which by definition means that the slope is constant throughout. But we have demonstrated that such a curve is elastic in its high-price ($8–$5) range and inelastic in its low-price ($4–$1) range. **(Key Question 2)**

Price Elasticity and the Total-Revenue Curve

In Figure 6.3b we graphed the total revenue per week to the theater owner that corresponds to each price-quantity combination indicated along demand curve D in Figure 6.3a. The price–quantity-demanded combination represented by point a on the demand curve yields total revenue of $8000 (= $8×1000 tickets). In Figure 6.3b, we graphed this $8000 amount vertically at 1 unit (1000 tickets) demanded. Similarly, the price–quantity-demanded combination represented by point b in the upper panel yields total revenue of $14,000 (= $7×2000 tickets). This amount is graphed vertically at 2 units (2000 tickets) demanded in the lower panel. The ultimate result of such graphing is total-revenue curve TR, which first slopes upward, then reaches a maximum, and finally turns downward.

Comparison of curves D and TR sharply focuses the relationship between elasticity and total revenue. Lowering the ticket price in the elastic range of demand—for example, from $8 to $5—increases total revenue. Conversely, increasing the ticket price in that range reduces total revenue. In both cases, price and total revenue change in opposite directions, confirming that demand is elastic.

The $5−$4 price range of demand curve D reflects unit elasticity. When price either decreases from $5 to $4 or increases from $4 to $5, total revenue remains $20,000. In both cases, price has changed and total revenue has remained constant, confirming that demand is unit-elastic when we consider these particular price changes.

TABLE 6.2 Price Elasticity of Demand: A Summary

Absolute Value of Elasticity Coefficient	Demand Is:	Description	Impact on Total Revenue of a:	
			Price Increase	Price Decrease
Greater than 1 ($E_d > 1$)	Elastic or relatively elastic	Quantity demanded changes by a larger percentage than does price	Total revenue decreases	Total revenue increases
Equal to 1 ($E_d = 1$)	Unit or unitary elastic	Quantity demanded changes by the same percentage as does price	Total revenue is unchanged	Total revenue is unchanged
Less than 1 ($E_d < 1$)	Inelastic or relatively inelastic	Quantity demanded changes by a smaller percentage than does price	Total revenue increases	Total revenue decreases

In the inelastic range of demand curve D, lowering the price—for example, from $4 to $1—decreases total revenue, as shown in Figure 6.3b. Raising the price boosts total revenue. In both cases, price and total revenue move in the same direction, confirming that demand is inelastic.

Table 6.2 summarizes the characteristics of price elasticity of demand. You should review it carefully. **(Key Questions 3 and 4)**

Determinants of Price Elasticity of Demand

We cannot say just what will determine the price elasticity of demand in each individual situation. However, the following generalizations are often helpful.

Substitutability Generally, the larger the number of substitute goods that are available, the greater the price elasticity of demand. Various brands of candy bars are generally substitutable for one another, making the demand for one brand of candy bar, say Snickers, highly elastic. Toward the other extreme, the demand for tooth repair (or tooth pulling) is quite inelastic because there simply are no close substitutes when those procedures are required.

The elasticity of demand for a product depends on how narrowly the product is defined. Demand for Reebok sneakers is more elastic than is the overall demand for shoes. Many other brands are readily substitutable for Reebok sneakers, but there are few, if any, good substitutes for shoes.

Proportion of Income Other things equal, the higher the price of a good relative to consumers' incomes, the greater the price elasticity of demand. A 10 percent increase in the price of low-priced pencils or chewing gum amounts to a few more pennies relative to one's income, and quantity demanded will probably decline only slightly. Thus, price elasticity for such low-priced items tends to be low. But a 10 percent increase in the price of relatively high-priced automobiles or housing means additional expenditures of perhaps $3000 or $20,000, respectively. These price increases are significant fractions of the annual incomes and budgets of most families, and quantities demanded will likely diminish significantly. Price elasticity for such items tends to be high.

Luxuries versus Necessities In general, the more that a good is considered to be a "luxury" rather than a "necessity," the greater is the price elasticity of demand. Electricity is generally regarded as a necessity; it is difficult to get along without it. A price increase will not significantly reduce the amount of lighting and power used in a household. (Note the very low price-elasticity coefficient of this good in Table 6.3.) An extreme case: A person does not decline an operation for acute appendicitis because the physician's fee has just gone up.

On the other hand, vacation travel and jewelry are luxuries, which, by definition, can easily be forgone. If the prices of vacation travel and jewelry rise, a consumer need not buy them and will suffer no great hardship without them.

What about the demand for a common product like salt? It is highly inelastic on three counts: Few good substitutes are available; salt is a negligible item in the family budget; and it is a "necessity" rather than a luxury.

Time Generally, product demand is more elastic the longer the time period under consideration. Consumers often need time to adjust to changes in prices. For example, when the price of a product rises, time is needed to find and experiment with other products to see if they are acceptable. Consumers may not immediately reduce their purchases very much when the price of beef rises by 10 percent, but in time they may shift to chicken, pork, or fish.

Another consideration is product durability. Studies show that "short-run" demand for gasoline is more inelastic ($E_d = .2$) than is "long-run" demand ($E_d = .7$). In the short run, people are "stuck" with their present cars and trucks, but with rising gasoline prices they eventually replace them with smaller, more fuel-efficient vehicles. They also switch to mass transit where it is available.

TABLE 6.3 Selected Price Elasticities of Demand

Product or Service	Coefficient of Price Elasticity of Demand (E_d)	Product or Service	Coefficient of Price Elasticity of Demand (E_d)
Newspapers	.10	Milk	.63
Electricity (household)	.13	Household appliances	.63
Bread	.15	Liquor	.70
Major League Baseball tickets	.23	Movies	.87
Telephone service	.26	Beer	.90
Cigarettes	.25	Shoes	.91
Sugar	.30	Motor vehicles	1.14
Medical care	.31	Beef	1.27
Eggs	.32	China, glassware, tableware	1.54
Legal services	.37	Residential land	1.60
Automobile repair	.40	Restaurant meals	2.27
Clothing	.49	Lamb and mutton	2.65
Gasoline	.60	Fresh peas	2.83

Source: Compiled from numerous studies and sources reporting price elasticity of demand.

Table 6.3 shows estimated price-elasticity coefficients for a number of products. Each reflects some combination of the elasticity determinants just discussed. **(Key Question 5)**

Applications of Price Elasticity of Demand

The concept of price elasticity of demand has great practical significance, as the following examples suggest.

Large Crop Yields The demand for most farm products is highly inelastic; E_d is perhaps .20 or .25. As a result, increases in the output of farm products arising from a good growing season or from increased productivity tend to depress both the prices of farm products and the total revenues (incomes) of farmers. For farmers as a group, the inelastic demand for their products means that large crop yields may be undesirable. For policymakers it means that achieving the goal of higher total farm income requires that farm output be restricted.

Excise Taxes The government pays attention to elasticity of demand when it selects goods and services on which to levy excise taxes. If a $1 tax is levied on a product and 10,000 units are sold, tax revenue will be $10,000 (= $1 × 10,000 units sold). If the government raises the tax to $1.50 but the higher price that results reduces sales to 4000 because of elastic demand, tax revenue will decline to $6000 (= $1.50 × 4000 units sold). Because

a higher tax on a product with elastic demand will bring in less tax revenue, legislatures tend to seek out products that have inelastic demand—such as liquor, gasoline, and cigarettes—when levying excises. In fact, the Federal government, in its effort to reduce the budget deficit, increased taxes on those very categories of goods in 1991.

Decriminalization of Illegal Drugs In recent years proposals to legalize drugs have been widely debated. Proponents contend that drugs should be treated like alcohol; they should be made legal for adults and regulated for purity and potency. The current war on drugs, it is argued, has been unsuccessful, and the associated costs—including enlarged police forces, the construction of more prisons, an overburdened court system, and untold human costs—have increased markedly. Legalization would allegedly reduce drug trafficking significantly by taking the profit out of it. Crack cocaine and heroin, for example, are cheap to produce and could be sold at low prices in legal markets. Because the demand of addicts is highly inelastic, the amounts consumed at the lower prices would increase only modestly. Addicts' total expenditures for cocaine and heroin would decline, and so would the street crime that finances those expenditures.

Opponents of legalization say that the overall demand for cocaine and heroin is far more elastic than proponents think. In addition to the inelastic demand of addicts, there is another market segment whose demand is relatively elastic. This segment consists of the occasional users or "dabblers," who use hard drugs when their prices are low but who abstain or substitute, say, alcohol when their prices are high. Thus, the lower prices associated with the legalization of hard drugs would increase consumption by dabblers. Also, removal of the legal prohibitions against using drugs might make drug use more socially acceptable, increasing the demand for cocaine and heroin.

Many economists predict that the legalization of cocaine and heroin would reduce street prices by up to 60 percent, depending on if and how much they were taxed. According to an important study, price declines of that size would increase the number of occasional users of heroin by 54 percent and the number of occasional users of cocaine by 33 percent. The total quantity of heroin demanded would rise by an estimated 100 percent, and the quantity of cocaine demanded would rise by 50 percent.[1] Moreover, many existing and first-time dabblers might in time become addicts. The overall result, say the opponents of legalization, would be higher social costs, possibly including an increase in street crime.

QUICK REVIEW 6.1

- The price elasticity of demand coefficient E_d is the ratio of the percentage change in quantity demanded to the percentage change in price. The *averages* of the two prices and two quantities are used as the base references in calculating the percentage changes.

- When E_d is greater than 1, demand is elastic; when E_d is less than 1, demand is inelastic; when E_d is equal to 1, demand is of unit elasticity.

- When price changes, total revenue will change in the opposite direction if demand is price-elastic, in the same direction if demand is price-inelastic, and not at all if demand is unit-elastic.

- Demand is typically elastic in the high-price (low-quantity) range of the demand curve and inelastic in the low-price (high-quantity) range of the curve.

- Price elasticity of demand is greater (a) the larger the number of substitutes available; (b) the higher the price of a product relative to one's budget; (c) the greater the extent to which the product is a luxury; and (d) the longer the time period involved.

Price Elasticity of Supply

ORIGIN OF THE IDEA

O 6.2
Price elasticity of supply

The concept of price elasticity also applies to supply. If the quantity supplied by producers is

relatively responsive to price changes, supply is elastic. If it is relatively insensitive to price changes, supply is inelastic.

We measure the degree of price elasticity or inelasticity of supply with the coefficient E_s, defined almost like E_d except that we substitute "percentage change in quantity supplied" for "percentage change in quantity demanded":

$$E_s = \frac{\text{percentage change in quantity supplied of product X}}{\text{percentage change in price of product X}}$$

For reasons explained earlier, the averages, or midpoints, of the before and after quantities supplied and the before and after prices are used as reference points for the percentage changes. Suppose an increase in the price of a good from \$4 to \$6 increases the quantity supplied from 10 units to 14 units. The percentage change in price would be $\frac{2}{5}$, or 40 percent, and the percentage change in quantity would be $\frac{4}{12}$, or 33 percent.

$$E_s = \frac{.33}{.40} = .83$$

In this case, supply is inelastic, since the price-elasticity coefficient is less than 1. If E_s is greater than 1, supply is elastic. If it is equal to 1, supply is unit-elastic. Also, E_s is never negative, since price and quantity supplied are directly related. Thus, there are no minus signs to drop, as was necessary with elasticity of demand.

The degree of **price elasticity of supply** depends on how easily—and therefore quickly—producers can shift resources between alternative uses. The easier and more rapidly producers can shift resources between alternative uses, the greater the price elasticity of supply. Take the case of Christmas trees. A firm's response to, say, an increase in the price of trees depends on its ability to shift resources from the production of other products (whose prices we assume remain constant) to the production of trees. And shifting resources takes time: The longer the time, the greater the resource "shiftability." So we can expect a greater response, and therefore greater elasticity of supply, the longer a firm has to adjust to a price change.

In analyzing the impact of time on elasticity, economists distinguish among the immediate market period, the short run, and the long run.

Price Elasticity of Supply: The Market Period

The **market period** is the period that occurs when the time immediately after a change in market price is too short for producers to respond with a change in quantity

---

[1] Henry Saffer and Frank Chaloupka, "The Demand for Illegal Drugs," *Economic Inquiry*, July 1999, pp. 401–411.

FIGURE 6.4 Time and the elasticity of supply. The greater the amount of time producers have to adjust to a change in demand, here from D_1 to D_2, the greater will be their output response. In the immediate market period (a) there is insufficient time to change output, and so supply is perfectly inelastic. In the short run (b) plant capacity is fixed, but changing the intensity of its use can alter output; supply is therefore more elastic. In the long run (c) all desired adjustments, including changes in plant capacity, can be made, and supply becomes still more elastic.

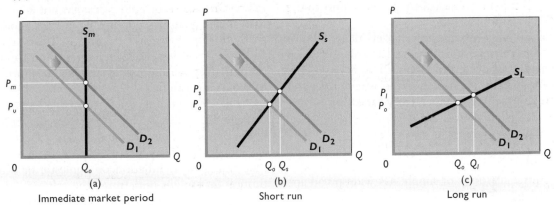

| (a) | (b) | (c) |
| Immediate market period | Short run | Long run |

supplied. Suppose the owner of a small farm brings to market one truckload of tomatoes that is the entire season's output. The supply curve for the tomatoes is perfectly inelastic (vertical); the farmer will sell the truckload whether the price is high or low. Why? Because the farmer can offer only one truckload of tomatoes even if the price of tomatoes is much higher than anticipated. He or she might like to offer more tomatoes, but tomatoes cannot be produced overnight. Another full growing season is needed to respond to a higher-than-expected price by producing more than one truckload. Similarly, because the product is perishable, the farmer cannot withhold it from the market. If the price is lower than anticipated, he or she will still sell the entire truckload.

The farmer's costs of production, incidentally, will not enter into this decision to sell. Though the price of tomatoes may fall far short of production costs, the farmer will nevertheless sell out to avoid a total loss through spoilage. During the market period, our farmer's supply of tomatoes is fixed: Only one truckload is offered no matter how high or low the price.

Figure 6.4a shows the farmer's vertical supply curve during the market period. Supply is perfectly inelastic because the farmer does not have time to respond to a change in demand, say, from D_1 to D_2. The resulting price increase from P_0 to P_m simply determines which buyers get the fixed quantity supplied; it elicits no increase in output.

However, not all supply curves need be perfectly inelastic immediately after a price change. If the product is not perishable and the price rises, producers may choose to increase quantity supplied by drawing down their inventories of unsold, stored goods. This will cause the market

supply curve to attain some positive slope. For our tomato farmer, the market period may be a full growing season; for producers of goods that can be inexpensively stored, there may be no market period at all.

Price Elasticity of Supply: The Short Run

The **short run** in microeconomics is a period of time too short to change plant capacity but long enough to use the fixed-sized plant more or less intensively. In the short run, our farmer's plant (land and farm machinery) is fixed. But he does have time in the short run to cultivate tomatoes more intensively by applying more labor and more fertilizer and pesticides to the crop. The result is a somewhat greater output in response to a presumed increase in demand; this greater output is reflected in a more elastic supply of tomatoes, as shown by S_s in Figure 6.4b. Note now that the increase in demand from D_1 to D_2 is met by an increase in quantity (from Q_0 to Q_s), so there is a smaller price adjustment (from P_0 to P_s) than would be the case in the market period. The equilibrium price is therefore lower in the short run than in the market period.

Price Elasticity of Supply: The Long Run

The **long run** in microeconomics is a time period long enough for firms to adjust their plant sizes and for new firms to enter (or existing firms to leave) the industry. In the "tomato industry," for example, our farmer has time to acquire additional land and buy more machinery and equipment. Furthermore, other farmers may, over time, be attracted to tomato farming by the increased demand and higher price. Such adjustments create a larger supply response, as represented by the more elastic supply curve S_L in Figure 6.4c. The outcome is a smaller price rise (P_0 to P_1) and a larger output increase (Q_0 to Q_l) in response to the increase in demand from D_1 to D_2.

There is no total-revenue test for elasticity of supply. Supply shows a positive or direct relationship between price and amount supplied; the supply curve is upsloping. Regardless of the degree of elasticity or inelasticity, price and total revenue always move together. **(Key Question 8)**

Applications of Price Elasticity of Supply

The idea of price elasticity of supply has widespread applicability, as suggested by the following examples.

Antiques and Reproductions

The *Antiques Road Show* is a popular PBS television program in which people bring antiques to a central location for appraisal by experts. Some people are pleased to learn that their old piece of furniture or funky folk art is worth a large amount, say, $30,000 or more.

The high price of an antique results from strong demand and limited, highly inelastic supply. Because a genuine antique can no longer be reproduced, its quantity supplied either does not rise or rises only slightly as its price goes up. The higher price might prompt the discovery of a few more of the remaining originals and thus add to the quantity available for sale, but this quantity response is usually quite small. So the supply of antiques and other collectibles tends to be inelastic. For one-of-a-kind antiques, the supply is perfectly inelastic.

Factors such as increased population, higher income, and greater enthusiasm for collecting antiques have increased the demand for antiques over time. Because the supply of antiques is limited and inelastic, those increases in demand have greatly boosted the prices of antiques.

Contrast the inelastic supply of original antiques with the elastic supply of modern "made-to-look-old" reproductions. Such faux antiques are quite popular and widely available at furniture stores and knickknack shops. When the demand for reproductions increases, the firms making them simply boost production. Because the supply of reproductions is highly elastic, increased demand raises their prices only slightly.

Volatile Gold Prices

The price of gold is quite volatile, sometimes shooting upward one period and plummeting downward the next. The main sources of these fluctuations are shifts in demand and highly inelastic supply. Gold production is a costly and time-consuming process of exploration, mining, and refining. Moreover, the physical availability of gold is highly limited. For both reasons, increases in gold prices do not elicit substantial increases in quantity supplied. Conversely, gold mining is costly to shut down and existing gold bars are expensive to store. Price decreases therefore do not produce large drops in the quantity of gold supplied. In short, the supply of gold is inelastic.

The demand for gold is partly derived from the demand for its uses, such as for jewelry, dental fillings, and coins. But people also demand gold as a speculative financial investment. They increase their demand for gold when they fear general inflation or domestic or international turmoil that might undermine the value of currency and more traditional investments. They reduce their demand when events settle down. Because of the inelastic supply of gold, even relatively small changes in demand produce relatively large changes in price. (Web-based question 1 at the end of the chapter provides an Internet source for finding current and past prices of gold.)

Cross Elasticity and Income Elasticity of Demand

Price elasticities measure the responsiveness of the quantity of a product demanded or supplied when its price changes. The consumption of a good also is affected by a change in the price of a related product or by a change in income.

Cross Elasticity of Demand

The **cross elasticity of demand** measures how sensitive consumer purchases of one product (say, X) are to a change in the price of some other product (say, Y). We calculate the coefficient of cross elasticity of demand E_{xy} just as we do the coefficient of simple price elasticity, except that we relate the percentage change in the consumption of X to the percentage change in the price of Y:

$$E_{xy} = \frac{\text{percentage change in quantity demanded of product X}}{\text{percentage change in price of product Y}}$$

This cross-elasticity (or cross-price-elasticity) concept allows us to quantify and more fully understand substitute and complementary goods, introduced in Chapter 3. *Unlike price elasticity, we allow the coefficient of cross elasticity of demand to be either positive or negative.*

Substitute Goods If cross elasticity of demand is positive, meaning that sales of X move in the same direction as a change in the price of Y, then X and Y are substitute goods. An example is Evian water (X) and Dasani (Y). An increase in the price of Evian causes consumers to buy more Dasani, resulting in a positive cross elasticity. The larger the positive cross-elasticity coefficient, the greater is the substitutability between the two products.

Complementary Goods When cross elasticity is negative, we know that X and Y "go together"; an increase in the price of one decreases the demand for the other. So the two are complementary goods. For example, a decrease in the price of digital cameras will increase the number of memory sticks purchased. The larger the negative cross-elasticity coefficient, the greater is the complementarity between the two goods.

Independent Goods A zero or near-zero cross elasticity suggests that the two products being considered are unrelated or independent goods. An example is walnuts and plums: We would not expect a change in the price of walnuts to have any effect on purchases of plums, and vice versa.

Application The degree of substitutability of products, measured by the cross-elasticity coefficient, is important to businesses and government. For example, suppose that Coca-Cola is considering whether or not to lower the price of its Sprite brand. Not only will it want to know something about the price elasticity of demand for Sprite (will the price cut increase or decrease total revenue?), but it will also be interested in knowing if the increased sales of Sprite will come at the expense of its Coke brand. How sensitive are the sales of one of its products (Coke) to a change in the price of another of its products (Sprite)? By how much will the increased sales of Sprite "cannibalize" the sales of Coke? A low cross elasticity would indicate that Coke and Sprite are weak substitutes for each other and that a lower price for Sprite would have little effect on Coke sales.

Government also implicitly uses the idea of cross elasticity of demand in assessing whether a proposed merger between two large firms will substantially reduce competition and therefore violate the antitrust laws. For example, the cross elasticity between Coke and Pepsi is high, making them strong substitutes for each other. Consequently, the government would likely block a merger between them because the merger would lessen competition. In contrast, the cross elasticity between cola and gasoline is low or zero. A merger between Coke and Shell would have a minimal effect on competition. So government would let that merger happen. (**Key Question 9**)

Income Elasticity of Demand

Income elasticity of demand measures the degree to which consumers respond to a change in their incomes by buying more or less of a particular good. The coefficient of income elasticity of demand E_i is determined with the formula

$$E_i = \frac{\text{percentage change in quantity demanded}}{\text{percentage change in income}}$$

Normal Goods For most goods, the income-elasticity coefficient E_i is positive, meaning that more of them are demanded as incomes rise. Such goods are called normal or superior goods, which we first described in Chapter 3. But the value of E_i varies greatly among normal goods. For example, income elasticity of demand for automobiles is about +3, while income elasticity for most farm products is only about +.20.

Inferior Goods A negative income-elasticity coefficient designates an inferior good. Retread tires, cabbage, long-distance bus tickets, used clothing, and muscatel wine are likely candidates. Consumers decrease their purchases of inferior goods as incomes rise.

Insights Coefficients of income elasticity of demand provide insights into the economy. For example, when recessions (business downturns) occur and incomes fall, income elasticity of demand helps predict which products will decline in demand more rapidly than others.

Products with relatively high income elasticity coefficients, such as automobiles (E_i = +3), housing (E_i = +1.5), and restaurant meals (E_i = +1.4), are generally hit hardest by recessions. Those with low or negative income elasticity coefficients are much less affected. For example, food products prepared at home (E_i = +.20) respond relatively little to income fluctuations. When incomes drop, purchases of food (and toothpaste and toilet paper) drop little compared to purchases of movie tickets, luxury vacations, and plasma screen TVs. Products we view as essential tend to have lower income elasticity coefficients than products we view as luxuries. When our incomes fall, we cannot easily eliminate or postpone the purchase of essential products. (**Key Question 10**)

TABLE 6.4 Cross and Income Elasticities of Demand

Value of Coefficient	Description	Type of Good(s)
Cross elasticity:		
Positive ($E_{wz} > 0$)	Quantity demanded of W changes in same direction as change in price of Z	Substitutes
Negative ($E_{xy} < 0$)	Quantity demanded of X changes in opposite direction from change in price of Y	Complements
Income elasticity:		
Positive ($E_i > 0$)	Quantity demanded of the product changes in same direction as change in income	Normal or superior
Negative ($E_i < 0$)	Quantity demanded of the product changes in opposite direction from change in income	Inferior

In Table 6.4 we provide a convenient synopsis of the cross-elasticity and income-elasticity concepts.

QUICK REVIEW 6.2

- Price elasticity of supply measures the sensitivity of suppliers to changes in the price of a product. The price-elasticity-of-supply coefficient E_s is the ratio of the percentage change in quantity supplied to the percentage change in price. The elasticity of supply varies directly with the amount of time producers have to respond to the price change.

- The cross-elasticity-of-demand coefficient E_{xy} is computed as the percentage change in the quantity demanded of product X divided by the percentage change in the price of product Y. If the cross-elasticity coefficient is positive, the two products are substitutes; if negative, they are complements.

- The income-elasticity coefficient E_i is computed as the percentage change in quantity demanded divided by the percentage change in income. A positive coefficient indicates a normal or superior good. The coefficient is negative for an inferior good.

Consumer and Producer Surplus

Our final goal for this chapter is to examine the following reality: Consumers and producers obtain "benefit surpluses" through market transactions. These surpluses vary in size among the various buyers and sellers.

Consumer Surplus

The benefit surplus received by a consumer or consumers in a market is called **consumer surplus**. It is defined as the difference between the maximum price a consumer is (or consumers are) willing to pay for a product and the actual price. In nearly all markets, consumers individually and collectively gain greater total utility in dollar terms (total satisfaction) from their purchases than the amount of their expenditures (= product price × quantity). This utility surplus arises because all consumers pay the equilibrium price even though many would be willing to pay more than that price to obtain the product.

Consider Figure 6.5, where the demand curve shows the buyers' maximum willingness to pay for each unit of the product and we assume that the equilibrium price, P_1, of oranges is $8 per bag. The portion of the demand curve D lying above the $8 equilibrium price shows that many consumers of oranges would be willing to pay more than $8 per bag rather than go without oranges.

See Table 6.5, for example, where column 2 reveals that Bob is willing to pay a maximum of $13 for a bag of oranges; Barb, $12; Bill, $11; Bart, $10; and Brent, $9. Betty,

FIGURE 6.5 Consumer surplus. Consumer surplus—shown as the green triangle—is the differences between the maximum prices consumers are willing to pay for a product and the lower equilibrium price, here assumed to be $8. For quantity Q_1, consumers are willing to pay the sum of the amounts represented by the green triangle and the tan rectangle. Because they need to pay only the amount shown as the tan rectangle, the green triangle shows consumer surplus.

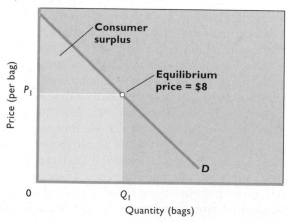

TABLE 6.5 **Consumer Surplus**

(1) Person	(2) Maximum Price Willing to Pay	(3) Actual Price (Equilibrium Price)	(4) Consumer Surplus
Bob	$13	$8	$5 (= $13 – $8)
Barb	12	8	4 (= $12 – $8)
Bill	11	8	3 (= $11 – $8)
Bart	10	8	2 (= $10 – $8)
Brent	9	8	1 (= $9 – $8)
Betty	8	8	0 (= $8 – $8)

in contrast, is willing to pay only the $8 equilibrium price. Because all six buyers listed obtain the oranges for the $8 equilibrium price (column 3), five of them obtain a consumer surplus. Column 4 shows that Bob receives a consumer surplus of $5 (= $13 – $8); Barb, $4 (= $12 – $8); Bill, $3 (= $11 – $8); Bart, $2 (= $10 – $8); and Brent, $1 (= $9 – $8). Only Betty receives no consumer surplus because her maximum willingness to pay $8 matches the $8 equilibrium price.

Obviously, most markets have more than six people. Suppose there are many other consumers besides Bob, Barb, Bill, Bart, Brent, and Betty in the market represented by Figure 6.5. It is reasonable to assume that many of these additional people are willing to pay more than $8 for a bag of oranges. By adding together the individual consumer surpluses obtained by our named and unnamed buyers, we obtain the collective consumer surplus in this specific market. To obtain the Q_1 bags of oranges represented, consumers collectively are willing to pay the total amount shown by the sum of the green triangle and tan rectangle under the demand curve and to the left of Q_1. But consumers need pay only the amount represented by the tan rectangle (= $P_1 \times Q_1$). So the green triangle is the consumer surplus in this market. It is the sum of the vertical distances between the demand curve and the $8 equilibrium price at each quantity up to Q_1. Alternatively, it is the sum of the gaps between maximum willingness to pay and actual price, such as those we calculated in Table 6.5.

Consumer surplus and price are inversely (negatively) related. Given the demand curve, higher prices reduce consumer surplus; lower prices increase it. To test this generalization, draw in an equilibrium price above $8 in Figure 6.5 and observe the reduced size of the triangle representing consumer surplus. When price goes up, the gap narrows between the maximum willingness to pay and the actual price. Next,

ORIGIN OF THE IDEA

O 6.3

Consumer surplus

draw in an equilibrium price below $8 and see that consumer surplus increases. When price declines, the gap widens between maximum willingness to pay and actual price.

Producer Surplus

Like consumers, producers also receive a benefit surplus in markets. This **producer surplus** is the difference between the actual price a producer receives (or producers receive) and the minimum acceptable price. The supply curve shows the seller's minimum acceptable price at each unit of the product. Sellers collectively receive a producer surplus in most markets because most sellers would be willing to accept a lower-than-equilibrium price if that were required to sell the product. Those lower acceptable prices for each of the units up to Q_1 are shown by the portion of the supply curve in Figure 6.6 lying to the left of and below the assumed $8 equilibrium price.

Suppose that Carlos, Courtney, Chuck, Cindy, Craig, and Chad are six of the many sellers of oranges in the market. Due to differences in production costs, suppose that Carlos' minimum acceptable payment for a bag of oranges is $3, as shown in column 2 of Table 6.6, whereas Courtney's minimum acceptable payment is $4, Chuck's is $5, Cindy's is $6, Craig's is $7, and Chad's is $8. But each seller receives as payment the equilibrium price of $8. As shown in column 4, Carlos thus obtains a producer surplus of $5 (= $8 – $3); Courtney, $4 (= $8 – $4); Chuck, $3 (= $8 – $5); Cindy, $2 (= $8 – $6); Craig, $1 (= $8 – $7); and Chad, zero (= $8 – $8).

FIGURE 6.6 Producer surplus. Producer surplus—shown as the orange triangle—is the differences between the actual price producers receive for a product (here $8) and the lower minimum payments they are willing to accept. For quantity Q_1, producers receive the sum of the amounts represented by the orange triangle plus the tan area. Because they need receive only the amount shown by the tan area to produce Q_1, the orange triangle represents producer surplus.

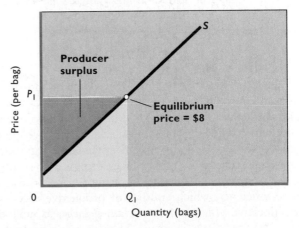

TABLE 6.6 Producer Surplus

(1) Person	(2) Minimum Acceptable Price	(3) Actual Price (Equilibrium Price)	(4) Producer Surplus
Carlos	$3	$8	$5 (= $8 − $3)
Courtney	4	8	4 (= $8 − $4)
Chuck	5	8	3 (= $8 − $5)
Cindy	6	8	2 (= $8 − $6)
Craig	7	8	1 (= $8 − $7)
Chad	8	8	0 (= $8 − $8)

By summing the producer surpluses of these sellers along with those of other sellers, we obtain the producer surplus for the entire market for oranges. In Figure 6.6, producers collect revenues of $P_1 \times Q_1$, which is the sum of the orange triangle and the tan area. As shown by the supply curve, however, revenues of only those illustrated by the tan area would be required to entice producers to offer Q_1 bags of oranges for sale. The sellers therefore receive a producer surplus shown by the orange triangle. That surplus is the sum of the vertical distances between the supply curve and the $8 equilibrium price at each of the quantities to the left of Q_1.

There is a direct (positive) relationship between equilibrium price and the amount of producer surplus. Given the supply curve, lower prices reduce producer surplus; higher prices increase it. If you pencil in a lower equilibrium price than $8, you will see that the producer surplus triangle gets smaller. The gaps between the minimum acceptable payments and the actual prices narrow when the price falls. If you pencil in an equilibrium price above $8, the size of the producer surplus triangle increases. The gaps between minimum acceptable payments and actual prices widen when the price increases.

> **WORKED PROBLEMS**
> **W 6.3**
> Consumer and producer surplus

Efficiency Revisited

In Figure 6.7 we bring together the demand and supply curves of Figures 6.5 and 6.6 to show the equilibrium price and quantity and the previously described regions of consumer and producer surplus. All markets that have downward-sloping demand curves and upward-sloping supply curves yield consumer and producer surplus.

The equilibrium quantity in Figure 6.7 reflects economic efficiency, which consists of productive efficiency and allocative efficiency. *Productive efficiency* is achieved

because competition forces producers to use the best techniques and combinations of resources in growing and selling oranges. Production costs of each level of output are minimized. *Allocative efficiency* is achieved because the correct quantity of output—Q_1—is produced relative to other goods and services. Points on the demand curve in Figure 6.7 measure the marginal benefit (MB) of oranges at each level of output. Points on the supply curve measure the marginal cost (MC) of oranges at each output level. The demand and supply curves intersect at the equilibrium output Q_1, indicating that MB = MC. (For the significance of the MB = MC equality for efficiency, review the discussion relating to Figure 1.3).

Our analysis of consumer and producer surplus provides another way of thinking about efficiency. Each point on a demand curve identifies not only the marginal benefit of the corresponding unit of output but also the *maximum willingness to pay* for it. Willingness to pay derives from the benefit that a product provides. Similarly, each point on the supply curve identifies not only the marginal cost of a good but also the *minimum acceptable price* for the good. To stay profitable, sellers must receive minimum prices that "cover" their marginal costs.

In Figure 6.7 the maximum willingness to pay for each bag of oranges up to Q_1 exceeds the corresponding minimum acceptable price. So each of these bags adds a positive amount (= maximum willingness to pay *minus* minimum acceptable price) to the *total* of consumer and producer surplus. Only at the equilibrium price Q_1, where maximum willingness to pay for the last unit equals minimum

FIGURE 6.7 Efficiency: maximum combined consumer and producer surplus. At quantity Q_1 the combined amount of consumer surplus, shown as the green triangle, and producer surplus, shown as the orange triangle, is maximized. Efficiency occurs because, at Q_1, maximum willingness to pay, indicated by the points on the demand curve, equals minimum acceptable price, shown by the points on the supply curve.

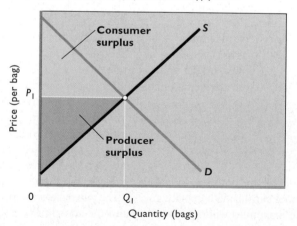

acceptable price for that unit, does society exhaust all the opportunities to add to combined consumer and producer surplus. So allocative efficiency occurs where the triangle representing "consumer surplus + producer surplus" is at its maximum size.

Other things equal, competitive markets produce equilibrium prices and quantities that maximize the sum of consumer and producer surplus. Allocative efficiency occurs at quantity levels where three conditions exist:

- MB = MC (Figure 1.3).
- Maximum willingness to pay = minimum acceptable price.
- Combined consumer and producer surplus is at a maximum.

Allocative efficiency and maximum benefit surpluses are the reasons that economists are so enamored of markets and why they usually think that markets are the best option for allocating resources in cases where they are possible.

Efficiency Losses (or Deadweight Losses)

Figure 6.8 demonstrates **efficiency losses**—reductions of combined consumer and producer surplus—associated with underproduction or overproduction of a product. Suppose that output is Q_2 rather than the efficient level Q_1. The sum of consumer and producer surplus, previously *abc*, falls to *adec*. So the combined consumer and producer surplus declines by the amount of the brown triangle to the left of Q_1. That triangle represents an efficiency loss to buyers and sellers. And since buyers and sellers are members of society, it represents an efficiency loss (or a so-called **deadweight loss**) to society.

For output levels from Q_2 to Q_1, the maximum willingness to pay by consumers (as reflected by points on the demand curve) exceeds the minimum acceptable price of sellers (as reflected by points on the supply curve). By failing to produce a product for which a consumer is willing to pay, say, $10, and for which a producer is willing to accept $6, society suffers a $4 loss of net benefits. The triangle *dbe* in Figure 6.8 shows the total loss of such net benefits due to the underproduction at Q_2.

In contrast, suppose that the number of oranges produced is Q_3 rather than the efficient level of Q_1. In Figure 6.8 the combined consumer and producer surplus therefore declines by *bfg*—the brown triangle to the right of Q_1. This triangle subtracts from the total consumer and producer surplus of *abc* that would occur if the quantity had been Q_1.

For all units beyond Q_1, the consumer's maximum willingness to pay is less than the producer's minimum acceptable price. Producing an item for which the maximum willingness to pay is, say, $7 and the minimum acceptable price is $10 subtracts $3 from society's net benefits. Such production is uneconomical and creates an efficiency loss (or deadweight loss) for society. The brown triangle *bfg* to the right of Q_1 in Figure 6.8 shows the total efficiency loss from overproduction at Q_3. We are again reminded that there can be too much as well as too little of a good thing. Under most conditions, however, a competitive market ensures that the "right amount" of a particular good gets produced. **(Key Question 15)**

FIGURE 6.8 Efficiency losses (or deadweight losses). Quantity levels less than or greater than the efficient quantity, Q_1, create efficiency losses. The triangle *dbe* shows the efficiency loss associated with underproduction Q_2, whereas the triangle *bfg* illustrates the efficiency loss associated with overproduction Q_3.

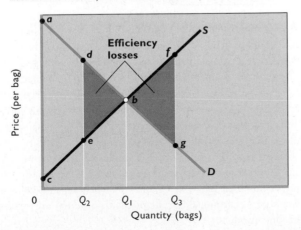

Elasticity and Pricing Power: Why Different Consumers Pay Different Prices

Firms and Nonprofit Institutions Often Recognize and Exploit Differences in Price Elasticity of Demand.

All buyers in a highly competitive market pay the same market price for the product, regardless of their individual price elasticities of demand. If the price rises, Jones may have an elastic demand and greatly reduce her purchases. Green may have a unit-elastic demand and reduce his purchases less than Jones. Lopez may have an inelastic demand and hardly curtail his purchases at all. But all three consumers will pay the single higher price regardless of their respective demand elasticities.

In later chapters we will find that not all sellers must passively accept a "one-for-all" price. Some firms have "market power" or "pricing power" that allows them to set their product prices in their best interests. For some goods and services, firms may find it advantageous to determine differences in price elasticity of demand and then charge different prices to different buyers.

It is extremely difficult to tailor prices for each customer on the basis of price elasticity of demand, but it is relatively easy to observe differences in group elasticities. Consider airline tickets. Business travelers generally have inelastic demand for air travel. Because their time is highly valuable, they do not see slower modes of transportation as realistic substitutes. Also, their employers pay for their tickets as part of their business expenses. In contrast, leisure travelers tend to have elastic demand. They have the option to drive rather than fly or to simply not travel at all. They also pay for their tickets out of their own pockets and thus are more sensitive to price.

Airlines recognize this group difference in price elasticity of demand and charge business travelers more than leisure travelers. To accomplish that, they have to dissuade business travelers from buying the less expensive round-trip tickets aimed at leisure travelers, so they try to place restrictions on the lower-priced tickets. For instance, they have at times made such tickets nonrefundable, required at least a 2-week advance purchase, and required Saturday-night stays. These restrictions chase off most business travelers who engage in last-minute travel and want to be home for the weekend. As a result, a business traveler often pays hundreds of dollars more for a ticket than a leisure traveler on the same plane.

Discounts for children are another example of pricing based on group differences in price elasticity of demand. For many products, children have more elastic demands than adults because children have low budgets, often financed by their parents. Sellers recognize the elasticity difference and price accordingly. The barber spends as much time cutting a child's hair as an adult's but charges the child much less. A child takes up a full seat at the baseball game but pays a lower price than an adult. A child snowboarder occupies the same space on a chairlift as an adult snowboarder but qualifies for a discounted lift ticket.

Finally, consider pricing by colleges and universities. Price elasticity of demand for higher education is greater for prospective students from low-income families than similar students from high-income families. This makes sense because tuition is a much larger proportion of household income for a low-income student or family than for his or her high-income counterpart. Desiring a diverse student body, colleges charge different *net* prices (= tuition *minus* financial aid) to the two groups on the basis of price elasticity of demand. High-income students pay full tuition, unless they receive merit-based scholarships. Low-income students receive considerable financial aid in addition to merit-based scholarships and, in effect, pay a lower *net* price.

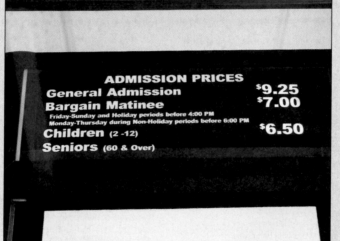

ADMISSION PRICES

General Admission	$9.25
Bargain Matinee	$7.00
Friday-Sunday and Holiday periods before 4:00 PM Monday-Thursday during Non-Holiday periods before 6:00 PM	
Children (2-12)	$6.50
Seniors (60 & Over)	

It is common for colleges to announce a large tuition increase and immediately cushion the news by emphasizing that they also are increasing financial aid. In effect, the college is increasing the tuition for students who have inelastic demand by the full amount and raising the *net* tuition of those with elastic demand by some lesser amount or not at all. Through this strategy, colleges boost revenue to cover rising costs while maintaining affordability for a wide range of students.

There are a number of other examples of dual or multiple pricing. All relate directly to price elasticity of demand. We will revisit this topic again in Chapter 10 when we analyze *price discrimination*—charging different prices to different customers for the same product.

Summary

1. Price elasticity of demand measures consumer response to price changes. If consumers are relatively sensitive to price changes, demand is elastic. If they are relatively unresponsive to price changes, demand is inelastic.

2. The price-elasticity coefficient E_d measures the degree of elasticity or inelasticity of demand. The coefficient is found by the formula

$$E_d = \frac{\text{percentage change in quantity demanded of X}}{\text{percentage change in price of X}}$$

Economists use the averages of prices and quantities under consideration as reference points in determining percentage changes in price and quantity. If E_d is greater than 1, demand is elastic. If E_d is less than 1, demand is inelastic. Unit elasticity is the special case in which E_d equals 1.

3. Perfectly inelastic demand is graphed as a line parallel to the vertical axis; perfectly elastic demand is shown by a line above and parallel to the horizontal axis.

4. Elasticity varies at different price ranges on a demand curve, tending to be elastic in the upper-left segment and inelastic in the lower-right segment. Elasticity cannot be judged by the steepness or flatness of a demand curve.

5. If total revenue changes in the opposite direction from prices, demand is elastic. If price and total revenue change in the same direction, demand is inelastic. Where demand is of unit elasticity, a change in price leaves total revenue unchanged.

6. The number of available substitutes, the size of an item's price relative to one's budget, whether the product is a luxury or a necessity, and length of time to adjust are all determinants of elasticity of demand.

7. The elasticity concept also applies to supply. The coefficient of price elasticity of supply is found by the formula

$$E_s = \frac{\text{percentage change in quantity supplied of X}}{\text{percentage change in price of X}}$$

The averages of the prices and quantities under consideration are used as reference points for computing percentage changes. Elasticity of supply depends on the ease of shifting resources between alternative uses, which varies directly with the time producers have to adjust to a price change.

8. Cross elasticity of demand indicates how sensitive the purchase of one product is to changes in the price of another product. The coefficient of cross elasticity of demand is found by the formula

$$E_{xy} = \frac{\text{percentage change in quantity demanded of X}}{\text{percentage change in price of Y}}$$

Positive cross elasticity of demand identifies substitute goods; negative cross elasticity identifies complementary goods.

9. Income elasticity of demand indicates the responsiveness of consumer purchases to a change in income. The coefficient of income elasticity of demand is found by the formula

$$E_i = \frac{\text{percentage change in quantity demanded of X}}{\text{percentage change in income}}$$

The coefficient is positive for normal goods and negative for inferior goods.

10. Consumer surplus is the difference between the maximum price that a consumer is willing to pay for a product and the lower price actually paid; producer surplus is the difference between the minimum price that a producer is willing to accept for a product and the higher price actually received. Collectively, consumer surplus is represented by the triangle under the demand curve and above the actual price, whereas producer surplus is shown by the triangle above the supply curve and below the actual price.

11. Graphically, the combined amount of producer and consumer surplus is represented by the triangle to the left of the intersection of the supply and demand curves that is below the demand curve and above the supply curve. At the equilibrium price and quantity in competitive markets, marginal benefit equals marginal cost, maximum willingness to pay equals minimum acceptable price, and the combined amount of consumer surplus and producer surplus is maximized.

12. Output levels that are either less than or greater than the equilibrium output create efficiency losses, also called deadweight losses. These losses are reductions in the combined amount of consumer surplus and producer surplus. Underproduction creates efficiency losses because output is not being produced for which maximum willingness to pay exceeds minimum acceptable price. Overproduction creates efficiency losses because output is being produced for which minimum acceptable price exceeds maximum willingness to pay.

Terms and Concepts

price elasticity of demand	inelastic demand	perfectly elastic demand
midpoint formula	unit elasticity	total revenue (TR)
elastic demand	perfectly inelastic demand	total-revenue test

price elasticity of supply

market period

short run

long run

cross elasticity of demand

income elasticity of demand

consumer surplus

producer surplus

efficiency losses (or deadweight losses)

Study Questions

1. Explain why the choice between 1, 2, 3, 4, 5, 6, 7, and 8 "units," or 1000, 2000, 3000, 4000, 5000, 6000, 7000, and 8000 movie tickets, makes no difference in determining elasticity in Table 6.1. **LO1**

2. **KEY QUESTION** Graph the accompanying demand data, and then use the midpoint formula for E_d to determine price elasticity of demand for each of the four possible $1 price changes. What can you conclude about the relationship between the slope of a curve and its elasticity? Explain in a nontechnical way why demand is elastic in the northwest segment of the demand curve and inelastic in the southeast segment. **LO1**

Product Price	Quantity Demanded
$5	1
4	2
3	3
2	4
1	5

3. **KEY QUESTION** Calculate total-revenue data from the demand schedule in question 2. Graph total revenue below your demand curve. Generalize about the relationship between price elasticity and total revenue. **LO2**

4. **KEY QUESTION** How would the following changes in price affect total revenue? That is, would total revenue increase, decline, or remain unchanged? **LO2**
   a. Price falls and demand is inelastic.
   b. Price rises and demand is elastic.
   c. Price rises and supply is elastic.
   d. Price rises and supply is inelastic.
   e. Price rises and demand is inelastic.
   f. Price falls and demand is elastic.
   g. Price falls and demand is of unit elasticity.

5. **KEY QUESTION** What are the major determinants of price elasticity of demand? Use those determinants and your own reasoning in judging whether demand for each of the following products is probably elastic or inelastic: (*a*) bottled water; (*b*) toothpaste; (*c*) Crest toothpaste; (*d*) ketchup; (*e*) diamond bracelets; (*f*) Microsoft Windows operating system. **LO1**

6. What effect would a rule stating that university students must live in university dormitories have on the price elasticity of demand for dormitory space? What impact might this in turn have on room rates? **LO1**

7. In November 1998 Vincent van Gogh's self-portrait sold at auction for $71.5 million. Portray this sale in a demand and supply diagram and comment on the elasticity of supply. Comedian George Carlin once mused, "If a painting can be forged well enough to fool some experts, why is the original so valuable?" Provide an answer. **LO3**

8. **KEY QUESTION** What is the formula for measuring the price elasticity of supply? Suppose the price of apples goes up from $20 to $22 a box. In direct response, Goldsboro Farms supplies 1200 boxes of apples instead of 1000 boxes. Compute the coefficient of price elasticity (midpoints approach) for Goldsboro's supply. Is its supply elastic, or is it inelastic? **LO3**

9. **KEY QUESTION** Suppose the cross elasticity of demand for products A and B is +3.6 and for products C and D is −5.4. What can you conclude about how products A and B are related? Products C and D? **LO4**

10. **KEY QUESTION** The income elasticities of demand for movies, dental services, and clothing have been estimated to be +3.4, +1, and +.5, respectively. Interpret these coefficients. What does it mean if an income elasticity coefficient is negative? **LO4**

11. Research has found that an increase in the price of beer would reduce the amount of marijuana consumed. Is cross elasticity of demand between the two products positive or negative? Are these products substitutes or complements? What might be the logic behind this relationship? **LO4**

12. Refer to Table 6.5. If the six people listed in the table are the only consumers in the market and the equilibrium price is $11 (not the $8 shown), how much consumer surplus will the market generate? **LO5**

13. Refer to Table 6.6. If the six people listed in the table are the only producers in the market and the equilibrium price is $6 (not the $8 shown), how much producer surplus will the market generate? **LO5**

14. Draw a supply and demand graph and identify the areas of consumer surplus and producer surplus. Given the demand curve, what impact will an increase in supply have on the amount of consumer surplus shown in your diagram? Explain why. **LO5**

15. **KEY QUESTION** Use the ideas of consumer surplus and producer surplus to explain why economists say competitive markets are efficient. Why are below- or above-equilibrium levels of output inefficient, according to these two sets of ideas? **LO5**

16. **LAST WORD** What is the purpose of charging different groups of customers different prices? Supplement the
three broad examples in the Last Word with two additional
examples of your own. Hint: Think of price discounts based
on group characteristic or time of purchase.

Web-Based Questions

1. **THE PRICE OF GOLD—TODAY, YESTERDAY, AND
THROUGHOUT THE YEAR** Visit **www.goldprices.com**
and use the chart to find the very latest price of gold. Compare that price to the price at the beginning of the day. Next,
select "1 year" at the bottom of the chart. What was the
highest price during the last 12 months? The lowest price?
Assume the price fluctuations observed resulted exclusively
from changes in demand. Would the observed price changes
have been greater or less if the gold supply had been elastic
rather than inelastic? Explain.

2. **PRICE, CROSS, AND INCOME ELASTICITIES—HOW
DO THEY RELATE TO ALCOHOL AND CIGARETTES?**
Go to the National Bureau of Economic Research (NBER)
Web site, **www.nber.org**, and select New Working Papers. In the Google search space, type "alcohol." Use the
titles and summaries of the papers to answer the following questions relating to elasticity: (*a*) Do the mentally ill
have perfectly inelastic demands for cigarettes and alcohol? (*b*) Does alcohol consumption increase in bad times?
(*c*) What is the effect of cigarette taxes (and smuggling)
on the consumption of alcohol? What does that imply
about the cross elasticity of demand between the two?
(*d*) Is binge drinking among college students sensitive to
the price of alcohol?

**FURTHER TEST YOUR KNOWLEDGE AT
www.mcconnell18e.com**

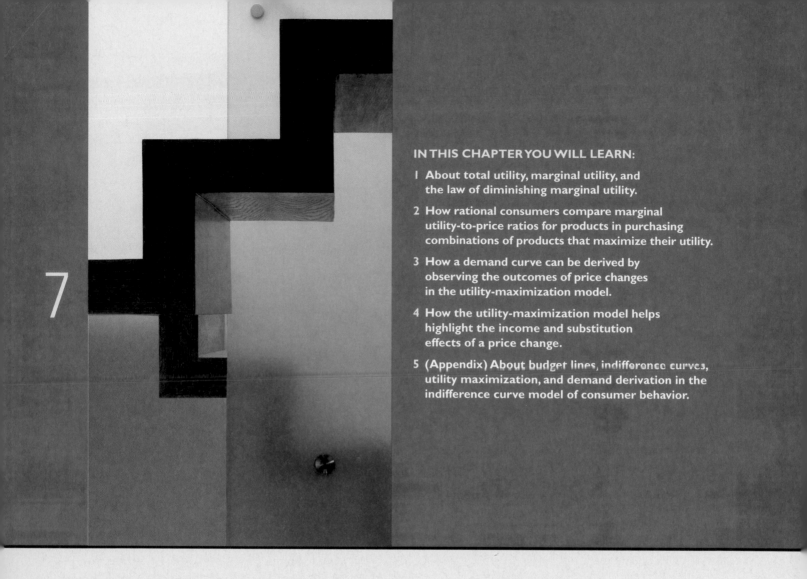

7

IN THIS CHAPTER YOU WILL LEARN:

1 About total utility, marginal utility, and the law of diminishing marginal utility.

2 How rational consumers compare marginal utility-to-price ratios for products in purchasing combinations of products that maximize their utility.

3 How a demand curve can be derived by observing the outcomes of price changes in the utility-maximization model.

4 How the utility-maximization model helps highlight the income and substitution effects of a price change.

5 (Appendix) About budget lines, indifference curves, utility maximization, and demand derivation in the indifference curve model of consumer behavior.

Consumer Behavior

If you were to compare the shopping carts of almost any two consumers, you would observe striking differences. Why does Paula have potatoes, peaches, and Pepsi in her cart while Sam has sugar, saltines, and 7-Up in his? Why didn't Paula also buy pasta and plums? Why didn't Sam have soup and spaghetti on his grocery list?

In this chapter, you will see how individual consumers allocate their incomes among the various goods and services available to them. Given a certain budget, how does a consumer decide which goods and services to buy? As we answer this question, you will also strengthen your understanding of the law of demand.

Law of Diminishing Marginal Utility

The simplest theory of consumer behavior rests squarely on the **law of diminishing marginal utility**. This principle, first discussed in Chapter 3, is that added satisfaction declines as a consumer acquires additional units of a given product. Although consumer wants in general may be insatiable, wants for particular items can be satisfied. In a specific span of time over which consumers' tastes remain unchanged, consumers can obtain as much of a particular good or service as they can afford. But the more of that product they obtain, the less they want still more of it.

Consider durable goods, for example. A consumer's desire for an automobile, when he or she has none, may be very strong. But the desire for a second car is less intense; and for a third or fourth, weaker and weaker. Unless they are collectors, even the wealthiest families rarely have more than a half-dozen cars, although their incomes would allow them to purchase a whole fleet of vehicles.

Terminology

Evidence indicates that consumers can fulfill specific wants with succeeding units of a product but that each added unit provides less utility than the last unit purchased. Recall that a consumer derives utility from a product if it can satisfy a want: **Utility** is want-satisfying power. The utility of a good or service is the satisfaction or pleasure one gets from consuming it. Keep in mind three characteristics of this concept:

- "Utility" and "usefulness" are not synonymous. Paintings by Picasso may offer great utility to art connoisseurs but are useless functionally (other than for hiding a crack on a wall).
- Utility is subjective. The utility of a specific product may vary widely from person to person. A lifted pickup truck may have great utility to someone who drives off-road but little utility to someone unable or unwilling to climb into the rig. Eyeglasses have tremendous utility to someone who has poor eyesight but no utility to a person with 20-20 vision.
- Utility is difficult to quantify. But for purposes of illustration we assume that people can measure satisfaction with units called *utils* (units of utility). For example, a particular consumer may get 100 utils of satisfaction from a smoothie, 10 utils of satisfaction from a candy bar, and 1 util of satisfaction from a stick of gum. These imaginary units of satisfaction are convenient for quantifying consumer behavior for explanatory purposes.

Total Utility and Marginal Utility

Total utility and marginal utility are related, but different, ideas. **Total utility** is the total amount of satisfaction or pleasure a person derives from consuming some specific quantity—for example, 10 units—of a good or service. **Marginal utility** is the *extra* satisfaction a consumer realizes from an additional unit of that product—for example, from the eleventh unit. Alternatively, marginal utility is the change in total utility that results from the consumption of 1 more unit of a product.

Figure 7.1 (Key Graph) and the accompanying table demonstrate the relation between total utility and marginal

CONSIDER THIS . . .

Vending Machines and Marginal Utility

Newspaper dispensing devices and soft-drink vending machines are similar in their basic operations. Both enable consumers to buy a product by inserting coins. But there is an important difference in the two devices. The newspaper dispenser opens to the full stack of papers and seemingly "trusts" the customer to take only a single copy, whereas the vending machine displays no such "trust," requiring the consumer to buy one can at a time. Why the difference?

The idea of diminishing marginal utility is key to solving this puzzle. Most consumers take only single copies from the newspaper box because the marginal utility of a second newspaper is nearly zero. They could grab a few extra papers and try to sell them on the street, but the revenue obtained would be small relative to their time and effort. So, in selling their product, newspaper publishers rely on "zero marginal utility of the second unit," not on "consumer honesty." Also, newspapers have little "shelf life"; they are obsolete the next day. In contrast, soft-drink sellers do not allow buyers to make a single payment and then take as many cans as they want. If they did, consumers would clean out the machine because the marginal utility of successive cans of soda diminishes slowly and buyers could take extra sodas and consume them later. Soft-drink firms thus vend their products on a pay-per-can basis.

In summary, newspaper publishers and soft-drink firms use alternative vending techniques because of the highly different rates of decline in marginal utility for their products. The newspaper seller uses inexpensive dispensers that open to the full stack of papers. The soft-drink seller uses expensive vending machines that limit the consumer to a single can at a time. Each vending technique is optimal under the particular economic circumstance.

keygraph

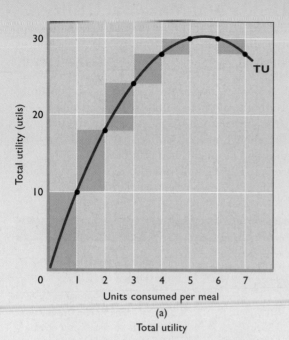

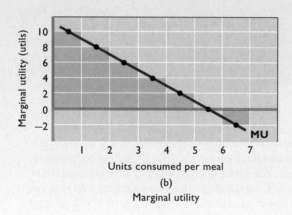

(a)
Total utility

(b)
Marginal utility

FIGURE 7.1 Total and marginal utility. Curves TU and MU are graphed from the data in the table. (a) As more of a product is consumed, total utility increases at a diminishing rate, reaches a maximum, and then declines. (b) Marginal utility, by definition, reflects the changes in total utility. Thus marginal utility diminishes with increased consumption, becomes zero when total utility is at a maximum, and is negative when total utility declines. As shown by the shaded rectangles in (a) and (b), marginal utility is the change in total utility associated with each additional taco. Or, alternatively, each new level of total utility is found by adding marginal utility to the preceding level of total utility.

(1) Tacos Consumed per Meal	(2) Total Utility, Utils	(3) Marginal Utility, Utils
0	0	
1	10	10
2	18	8
3	24	6
4	28	4
5	30	2
6	30	0
7	28	−2

QUICK QUIZ FOR FIGURE 7.1

1. Marginal utility:
   a. is the extra output a firm obtains when it adds another unit of labor.
   b. explains why product supply curves slope upward.
   c. typically rises as successive units of a good are consumed.
   d. is the extra satisfaction from the consumption of 1 more unit of some good or service.

2. Marginal utility in Figure 7.1b is positive, but declining, when total utility in Figure 7.1a is positive and:
   a. rising at an increasing rate.
   b. falling at an increasing rate.
   c. rising at a decreasing rate.
   d. falling at a decreasing rate.

3. When marginal utility is zero in graph (b), total utility in graph (a) is:
   a. also zero.
   b. neither rising nor falling.
   c. negative.
   d. rising, but at a declining rate.

4. Suppose the person represented by these graphs experienced a diminished taste for tacos. As a result the:
   a. TU curve would get steeper.
   b. MU curve would get flatter.
   c. TU and MU curves would shift downward.
   d. MU curve, but not the TU curve, would collapse to the horizontal axis.

Answers: 1. d; 2. c; 3. b; 4. c

136

utility. The curves reflect the data in the table. Column 2 shows the total utility associated with each level of consumption of tacos. Column 3 shows the marginal utility—the change in total utility—that results from the consumption of each successive taco. Starting at the origin

in Figure 7.1a, observe that each of the first five units increases total utility (TU), but by a diminishing amount. Total utility reaches a maximum with the addition of the sixth unit and then declines.

So in Figure 7.1b marginal utility (MU) remains positive but diminishes through the first five units (because total utility increases at a declining rate). Marginal utility is zero

for the sixth unit (because that unit doesn't change total utility). Marginal utility then becomes negative with the seventh

unit and beyond (because total utility is falling). Figure 7.1b and table column 3 reveal that each successive taco yields less extra utility, meaning fewer utils, than the preceding taco as the consumer's want for tacos comes closer and closer to fulfillment.[1] That is, the table and graph illustrate the law of diminishing marginal utility. **(Key Question 1)**

Marginal Utility and Demand

The law of diminishing marginal utility explains why the demand curve for a given product slopes downward. If successive units of a good yield smaller and smaller amounts of marginal, or extra, utility, then the consumer will buy additional units of a product only if its price falls. The consumer for whom Figure 7.1 is relevant may buy two tacos at a price of $1 each. But because he or she obtains less marginal utility from additional tacos, the consumer will choose not to buy more at that price. The consumer would rather spend additional dollars on products that provide more utility, not less utility. Therefore, additional tacos with less utility are not worth buying unless the price declines. (When marginal utility becomes negative, Taco Bell would have to pay you to consume another taco!) Thus, diminishing marginal utility supports the idea that price must decrease in order for quantity demanded to increase. In other words, consumers behave in ways that make demand curves downward-sloping.

---

[1]Technical footnote: In Figure 7.1b we graphed marginal utility at half-units. For example, we graphed the marginal utility of 4 utils at $3\frac{1}{2}$ units because "4 utils" refers neither to the third nor the fourth unit per se but to the *addition* or *subtraction* of the fourth unit.

Theory of Consumer Behavior

In addition to explaining the law of demand, the idea of diminishing marginal utility explains how consumers allocate their money incomes among the many goods and services available for purchase.

Consumer Choice and Budget Constraint

For simplicity, we will assume that the situation for the typical consumer has the following dimensions.

- *Rational behavior* The consumer is a rational person, who tries to use his or her money income to derive the greatest amount of satisfaction, or utility, from it. Consumers want to get "the most for their money" or, technically, to maximize their total utility. They engage in **rational behavior.**
- *Preferences* Each consumer has clear-cut preferences for certain of the goods and services that are available in the market. Buyers also have a good idea of how much marginal utility they will get from successive units of the various products they might purchase.
- *Budget constraint* At any point in time the consumer has a fixed, limited amount of money income. Since each consumer supplies a finite amount of human and property resources to society, he or she earns only limited income. Thus, as noted in Chapter 1, every consumer faces a **budget constraint,** even consumers who earn millions of dollars a year. Of course, this budget limitation is more severe for a consumer with an average income than for a consumer with an extraordinarily high income.
- *Prices* Goods are scarce relative to the demand for them, so every good carries a price tag. We assume that the price of each good is unaffected by the amount of it that is bought by any particular person. After all, each person's purchase is a tiny part of total demand. Also, because the consumer has a limited number of dollars, he or she cannot buy everything wanted. This point drives home the reality of scarcity to each consumer.

So the consumer must compromise; he or she must choose the most satisfying mix of goods and services. Different individuals will choose different mixes.

Utility-Maximizing Rule

Of all the different combinations of goods and services a consumer can obtain within his or her budget, which specific combination will yield the maximum utility or satisfaction? *To maximize satisfaction, the consumer should allocate his or her money income so that the last dollar spent on each product yields the same amount of extra (marginal) utility.* We call this the **utility-maximizing rule.** When the consumer has "balanced his or her margins" using this rule, he or she has achieved **consumer equilibrium** and has no incentive to alter his or her expenditure pattern. In fact, any person who has achieved consumer equilibrium would be worse off—total utility would decline—if there were any alteration in the bundle of goods purchased, providing there is no change in taste, income, products, or prices.

Numerical Example

An illustration will help explain the utility-maximizing rule. For simplicity we limit our example to two products, but the analysis also applies if there are more. Suppose consumer Holly is analyzing which combination of two products she should purchase with her fixed daily income of $10. Let's suppose these products are apples and oranges.

Holly's preferences for apples and oranges and their prices are the basic data determining the combination that will maximize her satisfaction. Table 7.1 summarizes those data, with column 2a showing the amount of marginal utility she will derive from each successive unit of A (apples) and with column 3a showing the same thing for product B (oranges). Both columns reflect the law of diminishing marginal utility, which, in this example, is assumed to begin with the second unit of each product purchased.

Marginal Utility per Dollar

To see how the utility-maximizing rule works, we must put the marginal-utility information in columns 2a and 3a on a per-dollar-spent basis. A consumer's choices are influenced not only by the extra utility that successive apples will yield but also by how many dollars (and therefore how many oranges) she must give up to obtain additional apples.

The rational consumer must compare the extra utility from each product with its added cost (that is, its price). Switching examples for a moment, suppose that you prefer a pizza whose marginal utility is, say, 36 utils to a movie whose marginal utility is 24 utils. But if the pizza's price is $12 and the movie costs only $6, you would choose the

TABLE 7.1 The Utility-Maximizing Combination of Apples and Oranges Obtainable with an Income of $10*

(1) Unit of Product	(2) Apple (Product A): Price = $1		(3) Orange (Product B): Price = $2	
	(a) Marginal Utility, Utils	(b) Marginal Utility per Dollar (MU/Price)	(a) Marginal Utility, Utils	(b) Marginal Utility per Dollar (MU/Price)
First	10	10	24	12
Second	8	8	20	10
Third	7	7	18	9
Fourth	6	6	16	8
Fifth	5	5	12	6
Sixth	4	4	6	3
Seventh	3	3	4	2

*It is assumed in this table that the amount of marginal utility received from additional units of each of the two products is independent of the quantity of the other product. For example, the marginal-utility schedule for apples is independent of the number of oranges obtained by the consumer.

movie rather than the pizza! Why? Because the marginal utility per dollar spent would be 4 utils for the movie (= 24 utils/$6) compared to only 3 utils for the pizza (= 36 utils/$12). You could see two movies for $12 and, assuming that the marginal utility of the second movie is, say, 16 utils, your total utility would be 40 utils. Clearly, 40 units of satisfaction (= 24 utils + 16 utils) from two movies are superior to 36 utils from the same $12 expenditure on one pizza.

To make the amounts of extra utility derived from differently priced goods comparable, marginal utilities must be put on a per-dollar-spent basis. We do this in columns 2b and 3b by dividing the marginal-utility data of columns 2a and 3a by the prices of apples and oranges—$1 and $2, respectively.

Decision-Making Process Table 7.1 shows Holly's preferences on a unit basis and a per-dollar basis as well as the price tags of apples and oranges. With $10 to spend, in what order should Holly allocate her dollars on units of apples and oranges to achieve the highest degree of utility within the $10 limit imposed by her income? And what specific combination of the two products will she have obtained at the time she uses up her $10?

Concentrating on columns 2b and 3b in Table 7.1, we find that Holly should first spend $2 on the first orange because its marginal utility per dollar of 12 utils is higher than the first apple's 10 utils. But now Holly finds herself indifferent about whether to buy a second orange or the first apple because the marginal utility per dollar of both is 10 utils. So she buys both of them. Holly now has 1 apple and 2 oranges. Also, the last dollar she spent on each good yielded the same marginal utility per dollar (10 utils). But this combination of apples and oranges does not represent the maximum amount of utility that Holly can obtain. It cost her only $5 [= (1 × $1) + (2 × $2)], so she has $5 remaining, which she can spend to achieve a still higher level of total utility.

Examining columns 2b and 3b again, we find that Holly should spend the next $2 on a third orange because marginal utility per dollar for the third orange is 9 compared with 8 for the second apple. But now, with 1 apple and 3 oranges, she is again indifferent between a second apple and a fourth orange because both provide 8 utils per dollar. So Holly purchases 1 more of each. Now the last dollar spent on each product provides the same marginal utility per dollar (8 utils), and Holly's money income of $10 is exhausted.

The utility-maximizing combination of goods attainable by Holly is 2 apples and 4 oranges. By summing marginal utility information from columns 2a and 3a, we find that Holly is obtaining 18 (= 10 + 8) utils of satisfaction from the 2 apples and 78 (= 24 + 20 + 18 + 16) utils of satisfaction from the 4 oranges. Her $10, optimally spent, yields 96 (= 18 + 78) utils of satisfaction.

Table 7.2 summarizes our step-by-step process for maximizing Holly's utility. Note that we have implicitly assumed that Holly spends her entire income. She neither borrows nor saves. However, saving can be regarded as a "commodity" that yields utility and can be incorporated into our analysis. In fact, we treat it that way in question 3 at the end of this chapter. **(Key Question 3)**

Inferior Options Holly can obtain other combinations of apples and oranges with $10, but none will yield as great a total utility as do 2 apples and 4 oranges. As an example, she can obtain 4 apples and 3 oranges for $10. But this combination yields only 93 utils, clearly inferior

WORKED PROBLEMS

W 7.1

Consumer choice

to the 96 utils provided by 2 apples and 4 oranges. True, there are other combinations apples and oranges (such as 4 apples and 5 oranges or 1 apple and 2 oranges) in which the marginal utility of the last dollar spent is the same for both goods. But all such combinations either are unobtainable with Holly's limited money income (as 4 apples and 5 oranges) or do not exhaust her money income (as 1 apple and 2 oranges) and therefore do not yield the maximum utility attainable.

Algebraic Generalization

Economists generalize the utility-maximizing rule by saying that a consumer will maximize her satisfaction when she allocates her money income so that the last dollar spent on product A, the last on product B, and so forth, yield equal amounts of additional, or marginal, utility. The marginal utility per dollar spent on A is indicated by the MU of product A divided by the price of A (column 2b in Table 7.1), and the marginal utility per dollar spent on B by the MU of product B divided by the price of B (column 3b in Table 7.1). Our utility-maximizing rule merely requires that these ratios be equal. Algebraically,

$$\frac{\text{MU of product A}}{\text{Price of A}} = \frac{\text{MU of product B}}{\text{Price of B}}$$

And, of course, the consumer must exhaust her available income. Table 7.1 shows us that the combination of 2 units of A (apples) and 4 of B (oranges) fulfills these conditions in that

$$\frac{8 \text{ utils}}{\$1} = \frac{16 \text{ utils}}{\$2}$$

and the consumer's $10 income is spent.

TABLE 7.2 **Sequence of Purchases to Achieve Consumer Equilibrium, Given the Data in Table 7.1**

Choice Number	Potential Choices	Marginal Utility per Dollar	Purchase Decision	Income Remaining
1	First apple	10	First orange for $2	$8 = $10 − $2
	First orange	12		
2	First apple	10	First apple for $1	$5 = $8 − $3
	Second orange	10	and second orange for $2	
3	Second apple	8	Third orange for $2	$3 = $5 − $2
	Third orange	9		
4	Second apple	8	Second apple for $1	$0 = $3 − $3
	Fourth orange	8	and fourth orange for $2	

If the equation is not fulfilled, then some reallocation of the consumer's expenditures between A and B (from the low to the high marginal-utility-per-dollar product) will increase the consumer's total utility. For example, if the consumer spent $10 on 4 of A (apples) and 3 of B (oranges), we would find that

$$\frac{\text{MU of A of 6 utils}}{\text{Price of A of }\$1} < \frac{\text{MU of B of 18 utils}}{\text{Price of B of }\$2}$$

Here the last dollar spent on A provides only 6 utils of satisfaction and the last dollar spent on B provides 9 (= 18/$2). So the consumer can increase total satisfaction by purchasing more of B and less of A. As dollars are reallocated from A to B, the marginal utility per dollar of A will increase while the marginal utility per dollar of B will decrease. At some new combination of A and B the two will be equal and consumer equilibrium will be achieved. Here that combination is 2 of A (apples) and 4 of B (oranges).

Utility Maximization and the Demand Curve

Once you understand the utility-maximizing rule, you can easily see why product price and quantity demanded are inversely related. Recall that the basic determinants of an individual's demand for a specific product are (1) preferences or tastes, (2) money income, and (3) the prices of other goods. The utility data in Table 7.1 reflect our consumer's preferences. We continue to suppose that her money income is $10. And, concentrating on the construction of an individual demand curve for oranges, we assume that the price of apples, now representing all "other goods," is still $1.

Deriving the Demand Schedule and Curve

We can derive a single consumer's demand schedule for oranges by considering alternative prices at which oranges might be sold and then determining the quantity the consumer will purchase. We already know one such price-quantity combination in the utility-maximizing example: Given tastes, income, and prices of other goods, Holly will purchase 4 oranges at $2.

Now let's assume the price of oranges falls to $1. The marginal-utility-per-dollar data of column 3b in Table 7.1 will double because the price of oranges has been halved; the new data for column 3b are in fact identical to those in column 3a. But the purchase of 2 apples and 4 oranges is no longer an equilibrium combination. By

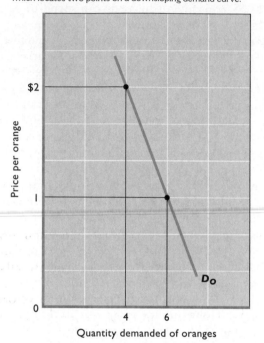

FIGURE 7.2 Deriving an individual demand curve At a price of $2 the consumer represented by the data in the table maximizes utility by purchasing 4 oranges. The decline in the price of oranges to $1 disrupts the consumer's initial utility-maximizing equilibrium. The consumer restores equilibrium by purchasing 6 rather than 4 oranges. Thus, a simple price-quantity schedule emerges, which locates two points on a downsloping demand curve.

Price per Orange	Quantity Demanded
$2	4
1	6

applying the same reasoning we used previously, we now find that Holly's utility-maximizing combination is 4 apples and 6 oranges. As summarized in the table in Figure 7.2, Holly will purchase 6 oranges when the price of oranges is $1. Using the data in this table, we can sketch the downward-sloping demand curve D_O shown in Figure 7.2. This exercise, then, clearly links the utility-maximizing behavior of a consumer and that person's downsloping demand curve for a particular product.

Income and Substitution Effects

Recall from Chapter 3 that the **income effect** is the impact that a change in the price of a product has on a consumer's real income and consequently on the quantity demanded of that good. In contrast, the **substitution effect** is the impact that a change in a product's price has on its relative expensiveness and consequently on the quantity demanded. Both effects help explain why a demand curve such as that in Figure 7.2 is downsloping.

Let's first look at the substitution effect. Recall that before the price of oranges declined, Holly was in equilibrium when purchasing 2 apples and 4 oranges because

$$\frac{\text{MU of apples of 8}}{\text{Price of apples of \$1}} = \frac{\text{MU of oranges of 16}}{\text{Price of oranges of \$2}}$$

But after the price of oranges declines from \$2 to \$1,

$$\frac{\text{MU of apples of 8}}{\text{Price of apples of \$1}} < \frac{\text{MU of oranges of 16}}{\text{Price of oranges of \$1}}$$

Clearly, the last dollar spent on oranges now yields greater utility (16 utils) than does the last dollar spent on apples (8 utils). This will lead Holly to switch, or substitute, purchases away from apples and towards oranges so as to restore consumer equilibrium. This substitution effect contributes to the inverse relationship between price and quantity that is found along her demand curve for oranges: When the price of oranges declines, the substitution effect causes Holly to buy more oranges.

What about the income effect? The decline in the price of oranges from \$2 to \$1 increases Holly's real income. Before the price decline, she maximized her utility and achieved consumer equilibrium by selecting 2 apples and 4 oranges. But at the lower \$1 price for oranges, Holly would have to spend only \$6 rather than \$10 to buy that particular combination of goods. That means that the lower price of oranges has freed up \$4 that can be spent on buying more apples, more oranges, or more of both. How many more of each fruit she ends up buying will be determined by applying the utility-maximizing rule to the new situation. But it is quite likely that the increase in real income caused by the reduction in the price of oranges will cause Holly to end up buying more oranges than before the price reduction. Any such increase in orange purchases is referred to as the income effect of the reduction in the price of oranges and it, too, helps to explain why demand curves are downward sloping: When the price of oranges falls, the income effect causes Holly to buy more oranges. **(Key Question 4)**

ORIGIN OF THE IDEA

O 7.2

Income and substitution effects

Applications and Extensions

Many real-world phenomena can be explained by applying the theory of consumer behavior.

iPods

Every so often a new product totally captures consumers' imagination. One such product is Apple's iPod, which debuted in November 2001. Less than six years later, Apple sold its 100 millionth unit. Furthermore, those units enabled Apple to sell more than 2.5 billion songs through its online iTunes Store.

The swift ascendancy of the iPod resulted mainly from a leapfrog in technology. Not only is the iPod much more compact than the portable digital CD player that it replaced, it can store and play back several thousand songs—whereas a single CD only has a 74-minute recording capacity. The improved portability and storage—the enhanced consumer satisfaction—caused a major shift in consumer demand away from the portable CD player and toward the iPod.

In the language of our analysis, Apple's introduction of the iPod severely disrupted consumer equilibrium. Consumers en masse concluded that iPods had a higher marginal-utility-to-price ratio ($= MU/P$) than the ratios for alternative products. They therefore shifted spending away from those other products and toward iPods as a way to increase total utility. Of course, for most people the marginal utility of a second or third iPod relative to price is quite low, so most consumers purchased only a single iPod. But Apple continued to enhance the iPod, enticing some of the buyers of older models to buy new models.

This example demonstrates a simple but important point: New products succeed by enhancing consumers' total utility. This "delivery of value" generates a revenue

M&M's, Final Exams, and Retirement Savings: Insights from Behavioral Economics

Over the Past 20 Years, Researchers Called Behavioral Economists Have Noted Behaviors That Differ from the Predictions of Standard Theory and Have Offered Interesting Explanations for Why They Occur.

We have just discussed how diminishing marginal utility underlies demand. The key insight is that even when we like a particular good or service, we like successive units of it less and less. Basically, we get fed up with it.

But consider this. Researchers offered moviegoers a mix of M&M's chocolate candies that only contained seven colors of M&M's and then counted how many of the candies they ate. Then, with a different group of moviegoers, they offered a mix of M&M's that had 10 different colors. In both cases, the candy was free and people could take as much or as little as they desired. The result? The moviegoers who were offered more colors ate 43 percent more candy even though every color tastes exactly the same.

So does this mean that people do not actually experience diminishing marginal utility, as economists assume? Not really. It just means that how quickly utility diminishes varies depending on context. And part of that context is *variety*.

To our ancient ancestors who were constantly struggling to have enough to eat, suddenly finding a rare type of food was such an unexpected blessing that it made sense to eat it immediately, regardless of whether they had just stuffed themselves with more ordinary foods. The vitamins and minerals of the rare and different food were simply too important to pass up. Hence, the modern human's instinct for variety—and for the fact that diminishing marginal utility sets in more slowly when people are offered a variety of products than just one or two.

The pressing needs of the present rather than the elusive possibilities of the future also appear to have produced human brains that have trouble making decisions involving events that will take place more than a few days or weeks in the future. For instance, suppose that at the beginning of a college semester researchers ask each student in a particular class if they would be willing to pay $20 to have the final exam delayed by one day. Typically only a handful of students are willing to pay the $20 fee for the one-day postponement. However, if you ask them the day before the exam, a large majority are suddenly willing to pay the $20 fee. Behavioral economists refer to this as "time inconsistency." Although people can correctly predict how

stream. If revenues exceed production costs, substantial profits can result—as they have for Apple.

The Diamond-Water Paradox

Early economists such as Adam Smith were puzzled by the fact that some "essential" goods had much lower prices than some "unimportant" goods. Why would water, essential to life, be priced below diamonds, which have much less usefulness? The paradox is resolved when we acknowledge that water is in great supply relative to demand and thus has a very low price per gallon. Diamonds, in contrast, are rare and are costly to mine, cut, and polish. Because their supply is small relative to demand, their price is very high per carat.

Moreover, the marginal utility of the last unit of water consumed is very low. The reason follows from our utility-maximizing rule. Consumers (and producers) respond to the very low price of water by using a great deal of it—for generating electricity, irrigating crops, heating buildings, watering lawns, quenching thirst, and so on. Consumption is expanded until marginal utility, which declines as more

water is consumed, equals its low price. On the other hand, relatively few diamonds are purchased because of their prohibitively high price, meaning that their marginal utility remains high. In equilibrium:

$$\frac{\text{MU of water (low)}}{\text{Price of water (low)}} = \frac{\text{MU of diamonds (high)}}{\text{Price of diamonds (high)}}$$

Although the marginal utility of the last unit of water consumed is low and the marginal utility of the last diamond purchased is high, the total utility of water is very high and the total utility of diamonds quite low. The total utility derived from the consumption of water is large because of the enormous amounts of water consumed. Total utility is the sum of the marginal utilities of all the gallons of water consumed, including the trillions of gallons that have far higher marginal utilities than the last unit consumed. In contrast, the total utility derived from diamonds is low since their high price means that

> **ORIGIN OF THE IDEA**
>
> **O 7.3**
>
> Diamond-water paradox

they will feel in the future—panicked a day before the upcoming exam!—those predicted feelings do not carry much weight when compared with their desire to spend the $20 today on current consumption.

This sort of behavior has important implications for retirement savings. If you ask 55-year-olds if it is important to save for retirement, they will not only say yes but will back it up by saving a lot. But if you ask 25-year-olds if it is important to save for retirement, they will also say yes, but usually will hardly save at all. Most will spend nearly all their income, and the vast majority will continue to behave this way until they are near retirement. Then, they will boost their saving considerably because they begin to realize that an impoverished retirement is a near-term possibility rather than a distant concern.

Recognizing the fact that young people do not take saving for retirement very seriously, governments have instituted public policies designed to counter this reality. For example, the Federal government recently passed legislation to encourage employers to change retirement savings programs from traditional plans where workers must "opt in" in order to participate to plans where workers are automatically enrolled and must "opt out" if they do not wish to participate. Studies indicate that this simple policy change causes enrollments to go up and stay up, boosting people's lifetime saving rates.

As another example, the Federal government requires nearly all workers to make Social Security contributions (which are used to pay benefits to currently eligible retirees). No "opt out" from the payroll taxes allowed! Because Social Security retirement benefits also will become available to workers when they age and retire, the system partially makes up for the fact that the human brain fails to put enough weight on distant possibilities, even very bad ones such as living in poverty in old age.

relatively few of them are bought. Thus the water-diamond "paradox" is solved: Water has much more total utility (roughly, usefulness) than diamonds even though the price of diamonds greatly exceeds the price of water. These relative prices relate to marginal utility, not total utility.

The Value of Time

The theory of consumer behavior has been generalized to account for the economic value of *time*. Both consumption and production take time. Time is a valuable economic commodity; by using an hour in productive work a person can earn $6, $10, $50, or more, depending on her or his education and skills. By using that hour for leisure or in consumption activities, the individual incurs the opportunity cost of forgone income; she or he sacrifices the $6, $10, or $50 that could have been earned by working.

Imagine a self-employed consumer named Linden who is considering buying a round of golf, on the one hand, and a concert, on the other. The market price of the golf game is $30 and that of the concert is $40. But the golf game takes more time than the concert. Suppose Linden spends 4 hours on the golf course but only 2 hours at the concert. If her time is worth $10 per hour, as evidenced by the $10 wage she can obtain by working, then the "full price" of the golf game is $70 (the $30 market price plus $40 worth of time). Similarly, the full price of the concert is $60 (the $40 market price plus $20 worth of time). We find that, contrary to what market prices alone indicate, the full price of the concert is really less than the full price of the golf game.

If we now assume that the marginal utilities derived from successive golf games and concerts are identical, traditional theory would indicate that Linden should consume more golf games than concerts because the market price of the former ($30) is lower than that of the latter ($40). But when time is taken into account, the situation is reversed and golf games ($70) are more expensive than concerts ($60). So it is rational for Linden to consume more concerts than golf games.

By accounting for time, we can explain certain observable phenomena that traditional theory does not explain. It may be rational for the unskilled worker or retiree whose time has little market value to ride a bus from Chicago to

Pittsburgh. But the corporate executive, whose time is very valuable, will find it cheaper to fly, even though bus fare is only a fraction of plane fare. It is sensible for the retiree, living on a modest company pension and a Social Security check, to spend many hours shopping for bargains at the mall or taking long trips in a motor home. It is equally intelligent for the highly paid physician, working 55 hours per week, to buy a new personal computer over the Internet and take short vacations at expensive resorts.

People in other nations often feel affluent Americans are "wasteful" of food and other material goods but "overly economical" in their use of time. Americans who visit developing countries find that time is used casually or "squandered," while material goods are very highly prized and carefully used. These differences are not a paradox or a case of radically different temperaments. The differences are primarily a rational reflection of the fact that the high productivity of labor in an industrially advanced society gives time a high market value, whereas the opposite is true in a low-income, developing country.

Medical Care Purchases

The method of payment for certain goods and services affects their prices at the time we buy them and significantly changes the amount purchased. Let's go back to Table 7.1. Suppose the $1 price for apples is its "true" value or opportunity cost. But now, for some reason, its price is only, say, $.20. A rational consumer clearly would buy more apples at $.20 than at the $1 price.

That is what happens with medical care. People in the United States who have health insurance pay a fixed premium once a month that covers, say, 80 percent of all incurred health care costs. This means that when they actually need health care, its price to them will be only 20 percent of the actual market price. How would you act in such a situation? When you are ill, you would likely purchase a great deal more medical care than you would if you were confronted with the full price. As a result, financing health care through insurance is an important factor in explaining today's high

expenditures on health care and the historical growth of such spending as a percentage of domestic output.

Similar reasoning applies to purchases of buffet meals. If you buy a meal at an all-you-can-eat buffet, you will tend to eat more than if you purchased it item by item. Why not eat that second dessert? Its marginal utility is positive and its "price" is zero!

Cash and Noncash Gifts

Marginal-utility analysis also helps us understand why people generally prefer cash gifts to noncash gifts costing the same amount. The reason is simply that the noncash gifts may not match the recipient's preferences and thus may not add as much as cash to total utility. Thought of differently, consumers know their own preferences better than the gift giver does, and the $100 cash gift provides more choices.

Look back at Table 7.1. Suppose Holly has zero earned income but is given the choice of a $2 cash gift or a noncash gift of 2 apples. Because 2 apples can be bought with $2, these two gifts are of equal monetary value. But by spending the $2 cash gift on the first orange, Holly could obtain 24 utils. The noncash gift of the first 2 apples would yield only 18 (= 10 + 8) units of utility. Conclusion: The noncash gift yields less utility to the beneficiary than does the cash gift.

Since giving noncash gifts is common, a considerable value of those gifts is potentially lost because they do not match their recipients' tastes. For example, Uncle Fred may have paid $15 for the Frank Sinatra CD he gave you for Christmas, but you would pay only $7.50 for it. Thus, a $7.50, or 50 percent, value loss is involved. Multiplied by billions spent on gifts each year, the potential loss of value is large.

But some of that loss is avoided by the creative ways individuals handle the problem. For example, newlyweds set up gift registries for their weddings to help match up their wants to the noncash gifts received. Also, people obtain cash refunds or exchanges for gifts so they can buy goods that provide more utility. And people have even been known to "recycle gifts" by giving them to someone else at a later time. All three actions support the proposition that individuals take actions to maximize their total utility.

Summary

1. The law of diminishing marginal utility states that beyond a certain quantity, additional units of a specific good will yield declining amounts of extra satisfaction to a consumer.

2. The utility-maximization model assumes that the typical consumer is rational and acts on the basis of well-defined preferences. Because income is limited and goods have prices,

the consumer cannot purchase all the goods and services he or she might want. The consumer therefore selects the attainable combination of goods that maximizes his or her utility or satisfaction.

3. A consumer's utility is maximized when income is allocated so that the last dollar spent on each product purchased yields

the same amount of extra satisfaction. Algebraically, the utility-maximizing rule is fulfilled when

$$\frac{\text{MU of product A}}{\text{Price of A}} = \frac{\text{MU of product B}}{\text{Price of B}}$$

and the consumer's total income is spent.

4. The utility-maximizing rule and the demand curve are logically consistent. Because marginal utility declines, a lower price is needed to induce the consumer to buy more of a particular product.

5. The utility-maximization model illuminates the income and substitution effects of a price change. The income effect implies that a decline in the price of a product increases the consumer's real income and enables the consumer to buy more of that product with a fixed money income. The substitution effect implies that a lower price makes a product relatively more attractive and therefore increases the consumer's willingness to substitute it for other products.

Terms and Concepts

law of diminishing marginal utility

utility

total utility

marginal utility

rational behavior

budget constraint

utility-maximizing rule

consumer equilibrium

income effect

substitution effect

Study Questions

1. **KEY QUESTION** Complete the following table and answer the questions below: **LO1**

Units Consumed	Total Utility	Marginal Utility
0	0	
1	10	10
2	—	8
3	25	—
4	30	—
5	—	3
6	34	—

a. At which rate is total utility increasing: a constant rate, a decreasing rate, or an increasing rate? How do you know?

b. "A rational consumer will purchase only 1 unit of the product represented by these data since that amount maximizes marginal utility." Do you agree? Explain why or why not.

c. "It is possible that a rational consumer will not purchase any units of the product represented by these data." Do you agree? Explain why or why not.

2. Mrs. Simpson buys loaves of bread and quarts of milk each week at prices of $1 and 80 cents, respectively. At present she is buying these products in amounts such that the marginal utilities from the last units purchased of the two products are 80 and 70 utils, respectively. Is she buying the utility-maximizing combination of bread and milk? If not, how should she reallocate her expenditures between the two goods? **LO2**

3. **KEY QUESTION** Columns 1 through 4 in the table below show the marginal utility, measured in utils, that Ricardo would get by purchasing various amounts of products A, B,

Column 1		Column 2		Column 3		Column 4		Column 5	
Units of A	MU	Units of B	MU	Units of C	MU	Units of D	MU	Number of Dollars Saved	MU
1	72	1	24	1	15	1	36	1	5
2	54	2	15	2	12	2	30	2	4
3	45	3	12	3	8	3	24	3	3
4	36	4	9	4	7	4	18	4	2
5	27	5	7	5	5	5	13	5	1
6	18	6	5	6	4	6	7	6	$\frac{1}{2}$
7	15	7	2	7	$3\frac{1}{2}$	7	4	7	$\frac{1}{4}$
8	12	8	1	8	3	8	2	8	$\frac{1}{8}$

C, and D. Column 5 shows the marginal utility Ricardo gets from saving. Assume that the prices of A, B, C, and D are $18, $6, $4, and $24, respectively, and that Ricardo has an income of $106. **LO2**

   a. What quantities of A, B, C, and D will Ricardo purchase in maximizing his utility?

   b. How many dollars will Ricardo choose to save?

   c. Check your answers by substituting them into the algebraic statement of the utility-maximizing rule.

4. **KEY QUESTION** You are choosing between two goods, X and Y, and your marginal utility from each is as shown in the table below. If your income is $9 and the prices of X and Y are $2 and $1, respectively, what quantities of each will you purchase to maximize utility? What total utility will you realize? Assume that, other things remaining unchanged, the price of X falls to $1. What quantities of X and Y will you now purchase? Using the two prices and quantities for X, derive a demand schedule (price–quantity-demanded table) for X. **LO3**

Units of X	MU$_x$	Units of Y	MU$_y$
1	10	1	0
2	8	2	7
3	6	3	6
4	4	4	5
5	3	5	4
6	2	6	3

5. How can time be incorporated into the theory of consumer behavior? Explain the following comment: "Want to make millions of dollars? Devise a product that saves Americans lots of time." **LO2**

6. Explain: **LO2**

   a. Before economic growth, there were too few goods; after growth, there is too little time.

   b. It is irrational for an individual to take the time to be completely rational in economic decision making.

   c. Telling Santa what you want for Christmas makes sense in terms of utility maximization.

7. In the last decade or so there has been a dramatic expansion of small retail convenience stores (such as Kwik Shops, 7 Elevens, Gas 'N Shops), although their prices are generally much higher than prices in large supermarkets. What explains the success of the convenience stores? **LO2**

8. Many apartment-complex owners are installing water meters for each apartment and billing the occupants according to the amount of water they use. This is in contrast to the former procedure of having a central meter for the entire complex and dividing up the water expense as part of the rent. Where individual meters have been installed, water usage has declined 10 to 40 percent. Explain that drop, referring to price and marginal utility. **LO3**

9. Using the utility-maximization rule as your point of reference, explain the income and substitution effects of an increase in the price of product B, with no change in the price of product A. **LO4**

10. **ADVANCED ANALYSIS** A mathematically "fair bet" is one in which a gambler bets, say, $100 for a 10 percent chance to win $1000 ($100 = 10 × $1000). Assuming diminishing marginal utility of dollars, explain why this is *not* a fair bet in terms of utility. Why is it even a less fair bet when the "house" takes a cut of each dollar bet? So is gambling irrational? **LO4**

11. **ADVANCED ANALYSIS** Let MU$_A$ = z = $10 - x$ and MU$_B$ = z = $21 - 2y$, where z is marginal utility per dollar measured in utils, x is the amount spent on product A, and y is the amount spent on product B. Assume that the consumer has $10 to spend on A and B—that is, $x + y = 10$. How is the $10 best allocated between A and B? How much utility will the marginal dollar yield? **LO3**

12. **LAST WORD** People at buffets put more on their plates and eat more the greater the variety of items they have to select from. How does this relate to the idea that diminishing marginal utility must be understood in context? Many people buy too much on their credit cards, even though they know they will be sorry when they get their credit card bill. Relate this fact to the idea of time inconsistency.

Web-Based Questions

1. **THE ESPN SPORTSZONE—TO FEE OR NOT TO FEE?** The ESPN cable TV network runs a major sports information site at **www.espn.com**. Most of the content is free, but ESPN has a premium membership (see its "Insider") available for a monthly or an annual fee. Similar, but fee-free, sports content can be found at the Web sites of CNN/Sports Illustrated, **www.cnnsi.com**, and CBS Sports Line, **cbs.sportsline.com**. Since ESPN has put a price tag on some of its sports content, it implies that the utility of a premium membership cannot be found at a no-fee site and is therefore worth the price. Is this the case?

Use the utility-maximization rule to justify your subscribing or not subscribing to the premium membership.

2. **HERE IS $500—GO SPEND IT AT WAL-MART** Assume that you and several classmates each receives a $500 credit voucher (good for today only) from Wal-Mart Online. Go to **www.wal-mart.com** and select $500 worth of merchandise. Use Add to Cart to keep a running total and use Review Cart to print your final selection. Compare your list with your classmates' lists. What explains the differences? Would you have purchased your items if you had received $500 in cash to be spent whenever and wherever you pleased?

Indifference Curve Analysis

The utility-maximization rule previously discussed requires individuals to measure and compare utility, much as a business would measure and compare costs or revenues. Such *cardinal utility* is measured in units such as 1, 2, 3, and 4 and can be added, subtracted, multiplied, and divided, just like the cardinal numbers in mathematics. More importantly, cardinal utility allows precise quantification of the marginal utilities upon which the utility-maximizing rule depends. In fact, the marginal-utility theory of consumer demand that we explained in the body of this chapter rests squarely on the assumption that economists be able to measure cardinal utility. The reality, however, is that measuring cardinal utility is highly difficult, at best. (Can you, for instance, state exactly how many utils you are getting from reading this book right now or how many utils you would get from watching a sunset?)

To avoid this measurement problem, economists have developed an alternative explanation of consumer behavior and equilibrium in which cardinal measurement is not required. In this more-advanced analysis, the consumer must simply *rank* various combinations of goods in terms of preference. For instance, Sally can simply report that she *prefers* 4 units of A to 6 units of B without having to put number values on how much she likes either option. The model of consumer behavior that is based upon such *ordinal utility* rankings is called indifference curve analysis. It has two main elements: budget lines and indifference curves.

The Budget Line: What Is Attainable

We know from Chapter 1 that a **budget line** (or, more technically, the *budget constraint*) is a schedule or curve showing various combinations of two products a consumer can purchase with a specific money income. If the price of product A is $1.50 and the price of product B is $1, a consumer could purchase all the combinations of A and B shown in the table in Figure 1 with $12 of money income. At one extreme, the consumer might spend all of his or her income on 8 units of A and have nothing left to spend on B. Or, by giving up 2 units of A and thereby "freeing" $3, the consumer could have 6 units of A and 3 of B. And so on to the other extreme, at which the consumer could buy 12 units of B at $1 each, spending his or her entire money income on B with nothing left to spend on A.

Figure 1 also shows the budget line graphically. Note that the graph is not restricted to whole units of A and B as is the table. Every point on the graph represents a possible combination of A and B, including fractional quantities. The slope of the graphed budget line measures the ratio of the price of B to the price of A; more precisely, the absolute value of the slope is $P_B/P_A = \$1.00/\$1.50 = \frac{2}{3}$. This is the mathematical way of saying that the consumer must forgo 2 units of A (measured on the vertical axis) to buy 3 units of B (measured on the horizontal axis). In moving

FIGURE 1 A consumer's budget line. The budget line shows all the combinations of any two products that can be purchased, given the prices of the products and the consumer's money income.

Units of A (Price = $1.50)	Units of B (Price = $1)	Total Expenditure
8	0	$12 (= $12 + $0)
6	3	$12 (= $9 + $3)
4	6	$12 (= $6 + $6)
2	9	$12 (= $3 + $9)
0	12	$12 (= $0 + $12)

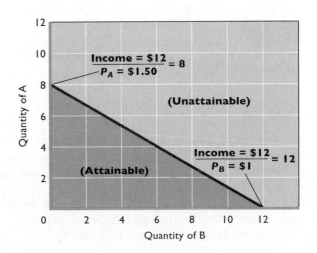

FIGURE 2 **A consumer's indifference curve.** Every point on indifference curve *I* represents some combination of products A and B, and all those combinations are equally satisfactory to the consumer. That is, each combination of A and B on the curve yields the same total utility.

Combination	Units of A	Units of B
j	12	2
k	6	4
l	4	6
m	3	8

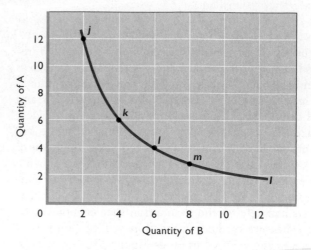

down the budget or price line, 2 units of A (at $1.50 each) must be given up to obtain 3 more units of B (at $1 each). This yields a slope of $\frac{2}{3}$.

The budget line has two other significant characteristics:

- *Income changes* The location of the budget line varies with money income. An increase in money income shifts the budget line to the right; a decrease in money income shifts it to the left. To verify this, recalculate the table in Figure 1, assuming that money income is (a) $24 and (b) $6, and plot the new budget lines in Figure 1.

- *Price changes* A change in product prices also shifts the budget line. A decline in the prices of both products—the equivalent of an increase in real income—shifts the curve to the right. (You can verify this by recalculating the table in Figure 1 and replotting Figure 1 assuming that $P_A = \$.75$ and $P_B = \$.50$.) Conversely, an increase in the prices of A and B shifts the curve to the left. (Assume $P_A = \$3$ and $P_B = \$2$, and rework the table and Figure 1 to substantiate this statement.)

Note what happens if P_B changes while P_A and money income remain constant. In particular, if P_B drops, say, from $1 to $.50, the lower end of the budget line fans outward to the right. Conversely, if P_B increases, say, from $1 to $1.50, the lower end of the line fans inward to the left. In both instances the line remains "anchored" at 8 units on the vertical axis because P_A has not changed.

Indifference Curves: What Is Preferred

Budget lines reflect "objective" market data, specifically income and prices. They reveal combinations of products A and B that can be purchased, given current money income and prices.

Indifference curves, on the other hand, reflect "subjective" information about consumer preferences for A

> **ORIGIN OF THE IDEA**
>
> **O 7.4**
>
> Indifference curves

and B. An **indifference curve** shows all the combinations of two products A and B that will yield the same total satisfaction or total utility to a consumer. The table and graph in Figure 2 present a hypothetical indifference curve for products A and B. The consumer's subjective preferences are such that he or she will realize the same total utility from each combination of A and B shown in the table or on the curve. So the consumer will be indifferent (will not care) as to which combination is actually obtained.

Indifference curves have several important characteristics.

Indifference Curves Are Downsloping An

indifference curve slopes downward because more of one product means less of the other if total utility is to remain unchanged. Suppose the consumer moves from one combination of A and B to another, say, from *j* to *k* in Figure 2. In so doing, the consumer obtains more of product B, increasing his or her total utility. But because total utility is the same everywhere on the curve, the consumer must give up some of the other product, A, to reduce total utility by a precisely offsetting amount. Thus "more of B" necessitates "less of A," and the quantities of A and B are inversely related. A curve that reflects inversely related variables is downward-sloping.

Indifference Curves Are Convex to the Origin Recall from the appendix to Chapter 1 that the slope of a curve at a particular point is measured by drawing a straight line that is tangent to that point and then measuring the "rise over run" of the straight line. If you drew such straight lines for several points on the curve in Figure 2, you would find that their slopes decline (in absolute terms) as you move down the curve. An indifference curve is therefore convex (bowed inward) to the origin of the graph. Its slope diminishes or becomes flatter as we move down the curve from *j* to *k* to *l*, and so on. Technically, the slope of an indifference curve at each point measures the **marginal rate of substitution (MRS)** of the combination of two goods represented by that point. The slope or MRS shows the rate at which the consumer who possesses the combination must substitute one good for the other (say, B for A) to remain equally satisfied. The diminishing slope of the indifference curve means that the willingness to substitute B for A diminishes as more of B is obtained.

The rationale for this convexity—that is, for a diminishing MRS—is that a consumer's subjective willingness to substitute B for A (or A for B) will depend on the amounts of B and A he or she has to begin with. Consider the table and graph in Figure 2 again, beginning at point *j*. Here, in relative terms, the consumer has a substantial amount of A and very little of B. Within this combination, a unit of B is very valuable (that is, its marginal utility is high), while a unit of A is less valuable (its marginal utility is low). The consumer will then be willing to give up a substantial amount of A to get, say, 2 more units of B. In this case, the consumer is willing to forgo 6 units of A to get 2 more units of B; the MRS is $\frac{6}{2}$, or 3, for the *jk* segment of the curve.

But at point *k* the consumer has less A and more B. Here A is somewhat more valuable, and B less valuable, "at the margin." In a move from point *k* to point *l*, the consumer is willing to give up only 2 units of A to get 2 more units of B, so the MRS is only $\frac{2}{2}$, or 1. Having still less of A and more of B at point *l*, the consumer is willing to give up

only 1 unit of A in return for 2 more units of B and the MRS falls to $\frac{1}{2}$ between *l* and *m*.[1]

In general, as the amount of B *increases*, the marginal utility of additional units of B *decreases*. Similarly, as the quantity of A *decreases*, its marginal utility *increases*. In Figure 2 we see that in moving down the curve, the consumer will be willing to give up smaller and smaller amounts of A to offset acquiring each additional unit of B. The result is a curve with a diminishing slope, a curve that is convex to the origin. The MRS declines as one moves southeast along the indifference curve.

The Indifference Map

The single indifference curve of Figure 2 reflects some constant (but unspecified) level of total utility or satisfaction. It is possible and useful to sketch a whole series of indifference curves or an **indifference map,** as shown in Figure 3. Each curve reflects a different level of total utility and therefore never crosses another indifference curve. Specifically, each curve to the right of our original curve (labeled I_3 in Figure 3) reflects combinations of A and B that yield more utility than I_3. Each curve to the left of I_3

FIGURE 3   An indifference map. An indifference map is a set of indifference curves. Curves farther from the origin indicate higher levels of total utility. Thus any combination of products A and B represented by a point on I_4 has greater total utility than any combination of A and B represented by a point on I_3, I_2, or I_1.

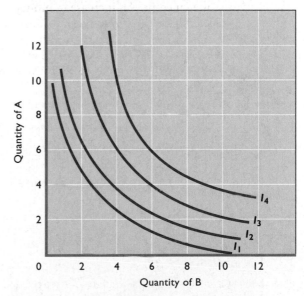

[1]MRS declines continuously between *j* and *k*, *k* and *l*, and *l* and *m*. Our numerical values for MRS relate to the curve segments between points and are not the actual values of the MRS at each point. For example, the MRS *at* point *l* is $\frac{2}{3}$.

reflects less total utility than I_3. As we move out from the origin, each successive indifference curve represents a higher level of utility. To demonstrate this fact, draw a line in a northeasterly direction from the origin; note that its points of intersection with successive curves entail larger amounts of both A and B and therefore higher levels of total utility.

Equilibrium at Tangency

Since the axes in Figures 1 and 3 are identical, we can superimpose a budget line on the consumer's indifference map, as shown in Figure 4. By definition, the budget line indicates all the combinations of A and B that the consumer can attain with his or her money income, given the prices of A and B. Of these attainable combinations, the consumer will prefer the combination that yields the greatest satisfaction or utility. Specifically, the utility-maximizing combination will be the combination lying on the highest attainable indifference curve. It is called the consumer's **equilibrium position**.

In Figure 4 the consumer's equilibrium position is at point X, where the budget line is *tangent* to I_3. Why not point Y? Because Y is on a lower indifference curve, I_2. By moving "down" the budget line—by shifting dollars from purchases of A to purchases of B—the consumer can attain an indifference curve farther from the origin and thereby increase the total utility derived from the same income. Why not point Z? For the same reason: Point Z is on a lower indifference

curve, I_1. By moving "up" the budget line—by reallocating dollars from B to A—the consumer can get on higher indifference curve I_3 and increase total utility.

How about point W on indifference curve I_4? While it is true that W would yield a greater total utility than X, point W is beyond (outside) the budget line and hence is *not* attainable by the consumer. Point X represents the optimal *attainable* combination of products A and B. Note that at the equilibrium position, X, the definition of tangency implies that the slope of the highest attainable indifference curve equals the slope of the budget line. Because the slope of the indifference curve reflects the MRS (marginal rate of substitution) and the slope of the budget line is P_B/P_A, the consumer's optimal or equilibrium position is the point where

$$\text{MRS} = \frac{P_B}{P_A}$$

(You may benefit by trying **Appendix Key Question 3** at this time.)

Equivalency at Equilibrium

As indicated at the beginning of this appendix, an important difference exists between the marginal-utility theory of consumer demand and the indifference curve theory. The marginal-utility theory assumes that utility is *numerically* measurable, that is, that the consumer can say how much extra utility he or she derives from each extra unit of A or B. The consumer needs that information to determine the utility-maximizing (equilibrium) position, which is defined by

$$\frac{\text{Marginal utility of A}}{\text{Price of A}} = \frac{\text{Marginal utility of B}}{\text{Price of B}}$$

The indifference curve approach imposes a less stringent requirement on the consumer. He or she need only specify whether a particular combination of A and B will yield more than, less than, or the same amount of utility as some other combination of A and B will yield. The consumer need only say, for example, that 6 of A and 7 of B will yield more (or less) satisfaction than will 4 of A and 9 of B. Indifference curve theory does not require that the consumer specify *how much* more (or less) satisfaction will be realized.

That being said, it is a remarkable mathematical fact that both models of consumer behavior will, in any given situation, point to exactly the same consumer equilibrium and, consequently, exactly the same demand behavior. This fact allows us to combine the separate pieces of information that each theory gives us about equilibrium in order to deduce an interesting property about marginal utilities that must also hold true in equilibrium. To see this, note that when we

FIGURE 4 **The consumer's equilibrium position.** The consumer's equilibrium position is represented by point X, where the black budget line is tangent to indifference curve I_3. The consumer buys 4 units of A at $1.50 per unit and 6 of B at $1 per unit with a $12 money income. Points Z and Y represent attainable combinations of A and B but yield less total utility, as is evidenced by the fact that they are on lower indifference curves. Point W would entail more utility than X, but it requires a greater income than the $12 represented by the budget line.

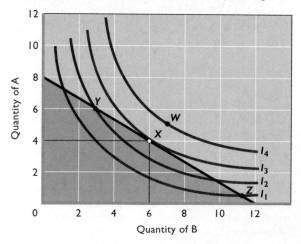

CONSIDER THIS . . .

Indifference Maps and Topographical Maps

The familiar topographical map may help you understand the idea of indifference curves and indifference curves and indifference maps. Each line on a topographical map represents a particular elevation above sea level, say, 4000 feet. Similarly, an indifference curve represents a particular level of total utility. When you move from one point on a specific elevation line to another, the elevation remains the same. So it is with an indifference curve. A move from one position to another on the curve leaves total utility unchanged. Neither elevation lines nor indifference curves can intersect. If they did, the meaning of each line or curve would be violated. An elevation line is "an equal-elevation line"; an indifference curve is "an equal-total-utility curve."

Like the topographical map, an indifference map contains not just one line but a series of lines. That is, the topographical map may have elevation lines representing successively higher elevations of 1000, 2000, 3000, 4000, and 5000 feet. Similarly, the indifference curves on the indifference map represent successively higher levels of total utility. The climber whose goal is to maximize elevation wants to get to the highest attainable elevation line; the consumer desiring to maximize total utility wants to get to the highest attainable indifference curve.

Finally, both topographical maps and indifference maps show only a few of the many such lines that could be drawn. The topographical map, for example, leaves out the elevation lines for 1001 feet, 1002, 1003, and so on. The indifference map leaves out all the indifference curves that could be drawn between those illustrated.

The Derivation of the Demand Curve

We noted earlier that with a fixed price for A, an increase in the price of B will cause the bottom of the budget line to fan inward to the left. We can use that fact to derive a demand curve for product B. In Figure 5a we reproduce the part of Figure 4 that shows our initial consumer equilibrium at point X. The budget line determining this

FIGURE 5 Deriving the demand curve. (a) When the price of product B is increased from $1 to $1.50, the equilibrium position moves from X to X', decreasing the quantity of product B demanded from 6 to 3 units. (b) The demand curve for product B is determined by plotting the $1–6-unit and the $1.50–3-unit price-quantity combinations for product B.

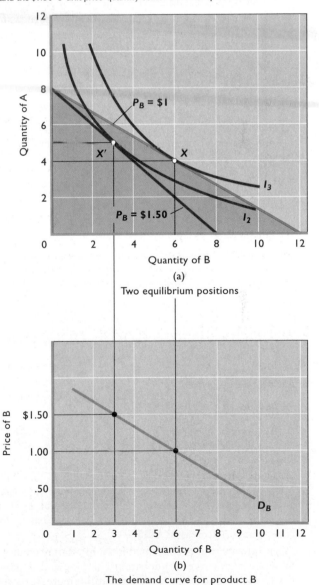

(a)
Two equilibrium positions

(b)
The demand curve for product B

compare the equilibrium situations in the two theories, we find that in the indifference curve analysis the MRS equals P_B/P_A at equilibrium; however, in the marginal-utility approach the ratio of marginal utilities equals P_B/P_A. We therefore deduce that at equilibrium the MRS is equivalent in the marginal-utility approach to the ratio of the marginal utilities of the last purchased units of the two products.[2]

---

[2]Technical footnote: If we begin with the utility-maximizing rule, $MU_A/P_A = MU_B/P_B$, and then multiply through by P_B and divide through by MU_A, we obtain $P_B/P_A = MU_B/MU_A$. In indifference curve analysis we know that at the equilibrium position MRS = P_B/P_A. Hence, at equilibrium, MRS also equals MU_B/MU_A.

equilibrium position assumes that money income is $12 and that $P_A = \$1.50$ and $P_B = \$1$. Let's see what happens to the equilibrium position when we increase P_B to $1.50 and hold both money income and the price of A constant. The result is shown in Figure 5a. The budget line fans to the left, yielding a new equilibrium point X' where it is tangent to lower indifference curve I_2. At X' the consumer buys 3 units of B and 5 of A, compared with 4 of A and 6 of B at X. Our interest is in B, and we now have sufficient information to locate two points on the demand curve for product B. We know that at equilibrium point X the price of B is $1 and 6 units are purchased; at equilibrium point X' the price of B is $1.50 and 3 units are purchased.

These data are shown graphically in Figure 5b as points on the consumer's demand curve for B. Note that the horizontal axes of Figure 5a and 5b are identical; both measure the quantity demanded of B. We can therefore drop vertical reference lines from Figure 5a down to the horizontal axis of Figure 5b. On the vertical axis of Figure 5b we locate the two chosen prices of B. Knowing that these prices yield the relevant quantities demanded, we locate two points on the demand curve for B. By simple manipulation of the price of B in an indifference curve–budget line context, we have obtained a downward-sloping demand curve for B. We have thus again derived the law of demand assuming "other things equal," since only the price of B was changed (the price of A and the consumer's money income and tastes remained constant). But, in this case, we have derived the demand curve without resorting to the questionable assumption that consumers can measure utility in units called "utils." In this indifference curve approach, consumers simply compare combinations of products A and B and determine which combination they prefer, given their incomes and the prices of the two products.

Appendix Summary

1. The indifference curve approach to consumer behavior is based on the consumer's budget line and indifference curves.

2. The budget line shows all combinations of two products that the consumer can purchase, given product prices and his or her money income.

3. A change in either product prices or money income moves the budget line.

4. An indifference curve shows all combinations of two products that will yield the same total utility to a consumer. Indifference curves are downward-sloping and convex to the origin.

5. An indifference map consists of a number of indifference curves; the farther from the origin, the higher the total utility associated with a curve.

6. The consumer is in equilibrium (utility is maximized) at the point on the budget line that lies on the highest attainable indifference curve. At that point the budget line and indifference curve are tangent.

7. Changing the price of one product shifts the budget line and determines a new equilibrium point. A downsloping demand curve can be determined by plotting the price-quantity combinations associated with two or more equilibrium points.

Appendix Terms and Concepts

budget line

indifference curve

marginal rate of
substitution (MRS)

indifference map

equilibrium position

Appendix Study Questions

1. What information is embodied in a budget line? What shifts occur in the budget line when money income (*a*) increases and (*b*) decreases? What shifts occur in the budget line when the price of the product shown on the vertical axis (*c*) increases and (*d*) decreases? **LO5**

2. What information is contained in an indifference curve? Why are such curves (*a*) downward-sloping and (*b*) convex to the origin? Why does total utility increase as the consumer moves to indifference curves farther from the origin? Why can't indifference curves intersect? **LO5**

3. **APPENDIX KEY QUESTION** Using Figure 4, explain why the point of tangency of the budget line with an indifference curve is the consumer's equilibrium position. Explain why any point where the budget line intersects an indifference curve is not equilibrium. Explain: "The consumer is in equilibrium where MRS $= P_B/P_A$." **LO5**

1. Assume that the data in the accompanying table give an indifference curve for Mr. Chen. Graph this curve, putting A on the vertical axis and B on the horizontal axis. Assuming that the prices of A and B are $1.50 and $1, respectively, and that Mr. Chen has $24 to spend, add his budget line to your graph. What combination of A and B will Mr. Chen purchase? Does your answer meet the MRS $= P_B/P_A$ rule for equilibrium? **LO5**

Units of A	Units of B
16	6
12	8
8	12
4	24

5. Explain graphically how indifference analysis can be used to derive a demand curve. **LO5**

6. **ADVANCED ANALYSIS** First, graphically illustrate a doubling of income without price changes in the indifference curve model. Next, on the same graph, show a situation in which the person whose indifference curves you are drawing buys considerably more of good B than good A after the income increase. What can you conclude about the relative coefficients of the income elasticity of demand for goods A and B (Chapter 6)? **LO5**

The Costs of Production

Our attention now turns from the behavior of consumers to the behavior of producers. In market economies, a wide variety of businesses produce an even wider variety of goods and services. Each of those businesses requires economic resources in order to produce its products. In obtaining and using resources, a firm makes monetary payments to resource owners (for example, workers) and incurs opportunity costs when using resources it already owns (for example, entrepreneurial talent). Those payments and opportunity costs together make up the firm's *costs of production,* which we discuss in this chapter.

Then, in the next several chapters, we bring product demand, product prices, and revenue back into the analysis and explain how firms compare revenues and costs in determining how much to produce. Our ultimate purpose is to show how those comparisons relate to economic efficiency.

Economic Costs

Costs exist because resources are scarce, are productive, and have alternative uses. When society uses a combination of resources to produce a particular product, it forgoes all alternative opportunities to use those resources for other purposes. The measure of the **economic cost,** or **opportunity cost,** of any resource used to produce a good is the value or worth the resource would have in its best alternative use.

We stressed this view of costs in our analysis of production possibilities in Chapter 1, where we found that the opportunity cost of producing more pizzas is the industrial robots that must be forgone. Similarly, the opportunity cost of the steel used in constructing office buildings is the value it would have in manufacturing automobiles or refrigerators. The paper used for printing economics textbooks is not available for printing encyclopedias or romance novels. And if an assembly-line worker is capable of assembling either personal computers or washing machines, then the cost to society of employing that worker in a computer plant is the contribution he or she would otherwise have made in producing washing machines.

Explicit and Implicit Costs

Now let's consider costs from the firm's viewpoint. Keeping opportunity costs in mind, we can say that economic costs are the payments a firm must make, or the incomes it must provide, to attract the resources it needs away from alternative production opportunities. Those payments to resource suppliers are explicit (revealed and expressed) or implicit (present but not obvious). So in producing products firms incur *explicit costs* and *implicit costs.*

- A firm's **explicit costs** are the monetary payments (or cash expenditures) it makes to those who supply labor services, materials, fuel, transportation services, and the like. Such money payments are for the use of resources owned by others.
- A firm's **implicit costs** are the opportunity costs of using its self-owned, self-employed resources. To the firm, implicit costs are the money payments that self-employed resources could have earned in their best alternative use.

  Example: Suppose you are earning $22,000 a year as a sales representative for a T-shirt manufacturer. At some point you decide to open a retail store of your own to sell T-shirts. You invest $20,000 of savings that have been earning you $1000 per year. And you decide that your new firm will occupy a small store that you own and have been renting out for $5000 per year. You hire one clerk to help you in the store, paying her $18,000 annually.

A year after you open the store, you total up your accounts and find the following:

Total sales revenue	$120,000
Cost of T-shirts	$40,000
Clerk's salary	18,000
Utilities	5000
Total (explicit) costs	63,000
Accounting profit	57,000

Looks good. You have an accounting profit of $57,000. A firm's accounting profit is what remains after it has paid individuals and other firms for the materials, capital, and labor they have supplied. But unfortunately your $57,000 accounting profit ignores your implicit costs and thus overstates the economic success of your venture. By providing your own financial capital, building, and labor, you incur implicit costs (forgone incomes) of $1000 of interest, $5000 of rent, and $22,000 of wages. If your entrepreneurial talent is worth, say, $5000 annually in other business endeavors of similar scope, you have also ignored that implicit cost. So:

Accounting profit	$57,000
Forgone interest	$ 1000
Forgone rent	5000
Forgone wages	22,000
Forgone entrepreneurial income	5000
Total implicit costs	33,000
Economic profit	24,000

Normal Profit as a Cost

The $5000 implicit cost of your entrepreneurial talent in the above example is a **normal profit.** As is true of the forgone rent and forgone wages, the payment you could otherwise receive for performing entrepreneurial functions is indeed an implicit cost. If you did not realize at least this minimum, or normal, payment for your effort, you could withdraw from this line of business and shift to a more attractive endeavor. So a normal profit is a cost of doing business.

The economist includes as costs of production all the costs—explicit and implicit, including a normal profit—required to attract and retain resources in a specific line of production. For economists, a firm's economic costs are the opportunity costs of the resources used, whether those resources are owned by others or by the firm. In our example, economic costs are $96,000 (= $63,000 of explicit costs + $33,000 of implicit costs).

Economic Profit (or Pure Profit)

Obviously, then, economists use the term "profit" differently from the way accountants use it. To the accountant, profit is the firm's total revenue less its explicit costs (or accounting costs). To the economist, **economic profit** is total revenue less economic costs (explicit and implicit costs, the latter including a normal profit to the entrepreneur). So when an economist says a certain firm is earning only enough revenue to cover its costs, this means it is meeting all explicit and implicit costs and the entrepreneur is receiving a payment just large enough to retain his or her talents in the present line of production.

If a firm's total revenue exceeds all its economic costs (explicit + implicit), any residual goes to the entrepreneur. That residual is called an *economic*, or *pure*, *profit*. In short:

$$\frac{\text{Economic}}{\text{profit}} = \frac{\text{total}}{\text{revenue}} - \frac{\text{economic}}{\text{cost}}$$

In our example, economic profit is $24,000, found by subtracting the $96,000 of economic cost from the $120,000 of revenue. An *economic* profit is not a cost because it is a return in excess of the normal profit that is required to retain the entrepreneur in this particular line of production. Even if the economic profit is zero, the entrepreneur is still covering all explicit and implicit costs, including a normal profit. In our example, as long as accounting profit is $33,000 or more (so economic profit is zero or more), you will be earning a $5000 normal profit and will therefore continue to operate your T-shirt store.

> **WORKED PROBLEMS**
> **W 8.1**
> Economic profit

Figure 8.1 shows the relationship among the various cost and profit concepts that we have just discussed. To

test yourself, you might want to enter cost data from our example in the appropriate blocks. **(Key Question 2)**

Short Run and Long Run

When the demand for a firm's product changes, the firm's profitability may depend on how quickly it can adjust the amounts of the various resources it employs. It can easily and quickly adjust the quantities employed of many resources such as hourly labor, raw materials, fuel, and power. It needs much more time, however, to adjust its *plant capacity*—the size of the factory building, the amount of machinery and equipment, and other capital resources. In some heavy industries such as aircraft manufacturing, a firm may need several years to alter plant capacity. Because of these differences in adjustment time, economists find it useful to distinguish between two conceptual periods: the short run and the long run. We will discover that costs differ in these two time periods.

Short Run: Fixed Plant The **short run** is a period too brief for a firm to alter its plant capacity, yet long enough to permit a change in the degree to which the fixed plant is used. The firm's plant capacity is fixed in the short run. However, the firm can vary its output by applying larger or smaller amounts of labor, materials, and other resources to that plant. It can use its existing plant capacity more or less intensively in the short run.

Long Run: Variable Plant From the viewpoint of an existing firm, the **long run** is a period long enough for it to adjust the quantities of all the resources that it employs, including plant capacity. From the industry's viewpoint, the long run also includes enough time for existing firms to dissolve and leave the industry or for new firms to be created and enter the industry. While the short run is a "fixed-plant" period, the long run is a "variable-plant" period.

Illustrations If Boeing hires 100 extra workers for one of its commercial airline plants or adds an entire shift of workers, we are speaking of the short run. If it adds a new production facility and installs more equipment, we are referring to the long run. The first situation is a *short-run adjustment;* the second is a *long-run adjustment.*

The short run and the long run are conceptual periods rather than calendar time periods. In light-manufacturing industries, changes in plant capacity may be accomplished almost overnight. A small T-shirt manufacturer can increase its plant capacity in a matter of days by ordering and installing two or three new cutting tables and several extra sewing machines. But for heavy industry the long run is a different matter. Shell Oil may require several years to construct a new gasoline refinery.

FIGURE 8.1 Economic profit versus accounting profit. Economic profit is equal to total revenue less economic costs. Economic costs are the sum of explicit and implicit costs and include a normal profit to the entrepreneur. Accounting profit is equal to total revenue less accounting (explicit) costs.

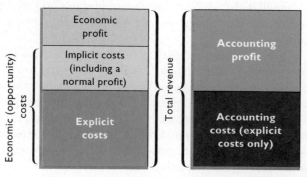

- Explicit costs are money payments a firm makes to outside suppliers of resources; implicit costs are the opportunity costs associated with a firm's use of resources it owns.
- Normal profit is the implicit cost of entrepreneurship. Economic profit is total revenue less all explicit and implicit costs, including normal profit.
- In the short run, a firm's plant capacity is fixed; in the long run, a firm can vary its plant size and firms can enter or leave the industry.

Short-Run Production Relationships

A firm's costs of producing a specific output depend on the prices of the needed resources and the quantities of resources (inputs) needed to produce that output. Resource supply and demand determine resource prices. The technological aspects of production, specifically the relationships between inputs and output, determine the quantities of resources needed. Our focus will be on the *labor*-output relationship, given a fixed plant capacity. But before examining that relationship, we need to define three terms:

- **Total product (TP)** is the total quantity, or total output, of a particular good or service produced.
- **Marginal product (MP)** is the extra output or added product associated with adding a unit of a variable resource, in this case labor, to the production process. Thus,

$$\text{Marginal product} = \frac{\text{change in total product}}{\text{change in labor input}}$$

- **Average product (AP)**, also called labor productivity, is output per unit of labor input:

$$\text{Average product} = \frac{\text{total product}}{\text{units of labor}}$$

In the short run, a firm can for a time increase its output by adding units of labor to its fixed plant. But by how much will output rise when it adds more labor? Why do we say "for a time"?

Law of Diminishing Returns

The answers are provided in general terms by the **law of diminishing returns.** This law assumes that technology is fixed and thus the techniques of production do not change. It states that as successive

Diminishing Returns from Study

Here is a noneconomic example of a relationship between "inputs" and "output" that may help you better understand the idea of diminishing returns. Suppose for an individual that

Total course learning = f (intelligence, quality of course materials, instructor effectiveness, class time, and study time)

where f means "function of" or "depends on." So this relationship supposes that total course learning depends on intelligence (however defined), quality of course materials such as the textbook, the effectiveness of the instructor, the amount of class time, and the amount of personal study time outside the class.

For analytical purposes, let's assume that one's intelligence, the quality of course materials, the effectiveness of the instructor, and the amount of class time are *fixed*—meaning they do not change over the length of the course. Now let's add units of study time per day over the length of the course to "produce" greater course learning. The first hour of study time per day increases total course learning. Will the second hour enhance course learning by as much as the first? By how much will the third, fourth, fifth, . . . fifteenth hour of study per day contribute to total course learning relative to the *immediate previous hour*?

We think you will agree that eventually diminishing returns to course learning will set in as successive hours of study are added each day. At some point the marginal product of an extra hour of study time will decline and, at some further point, become zero.

This is also true of production relationships within firms. As successive units of a variable input (say, labor) are added to a fixed input (say, capital), the marginal product of the variable input eventually declines. In short, diminishing returns will occur sooner or later. Total product eventually will rise at a diminishing rate, reach a maximum, and then decline.

units of a variable resource (say, labor) are added to a fixed resource (say, capital or land), beyond some point the extra, or marginal, product that can be attributed to each additional unit of the variable resource will decline. For example, if additional workers are hired to work with a constant amount of capital equipment, output will eventually rise by smaller and smaller amounts as more workers are hired.

Rationale Suppose a farmer has a fixed resource—80 acres of land—planted in corn. If the farmer does not cultivate the cornfields (clear the weeds) at all, the yield will be 40 bushels per acre. If he cultivates the land once, output may rise to 50 bushels per acre. A second cultivation may increase output to 57 bushels per acre, a third to 61, and a fourth to 63. Succeeding cultivations will add less and less to the land's yield. If this were not so, the world's needs for corn could be fulfilled by extremely intense cultivation of this single 80-acre plot of land. Indeed, if diminishing returns did not occur, the world could be fed out of a flowerpot. Why not? Just keep adding more seed, fertilizer, and harvesters!

The law of diminishing returns also holds true in nonagricultural industries. Assume a wood shop is manufacturing furniture frames. It has a specific amount of equipment such as lathes, planes, saws, and sanders. If this shop hired just one or two workers, total output and productivity (output per worker) would be very low. The workers would have to perform many different jobs, and the advantages of specialization would not be realized. Time would be lost in switching from one job to another, and machines would stand idle much of the time. In short, the plant would be understaffed, and production would be inefficient because there would be too much capital relative to the amount of labor.

The shop could eliminate those difficulties by hiring more workers. Then the equipment would be more fully used, and workers could specialize on doing a single job. Time would no longer be lost switching from job to job. As more workers were added, production would become more efficient and the marginal product of each succeeding worker would rise.

But the rise could not go on indefinitely. If still more workers were added, beyond a certain point, overcrowding would set in. Since workers would then have to wait in line to use the machinery, they would be underused. Total output would increase at a diminishing rate because, given the fixed size of the plant, each worker would have less capital equipment to work with as more and more labor was hired. The marginal product of additional workers would decline because there would be more labor in proportion to the fixed amount of capital. Eventually, adding still more workers would cause so much congestion that marginal product would become negative and total product would decline. At the extreme, the addition of more and more labor would exhaust all the standing room, and total product would fall to zero.

Note that the law of diminishing returns assumes that all units of labor are of equal quality. Each successive worker is presumed to have the same innate ability, motor coordination, education, training, and work experience. Marginal product ultimately diminishes, not because successive workers are less skilled or less energetic but because more workers are being used relative to the amount of plant and equipment available.

Tabular Example Table 8.1 is a numerical illustration of the law of diminishing returns. Column 2 shows the total product, or total output, resulting from combining each level of a variable input (labor) in column 1 with a fixed amount of capital.

TABLE 8.1 Total, Marginal, and Average Product: The Law of Diminishing Returns

(1) Units of the Variable Resource (Labor)	(2) Total Product (TP)	(3) Marginal Product (MP), Change in (2)/ Change in (1)		(4) Average Product (AP), (2)/(1)
0	0			—
1	10	10	Increasing marginal returns	10.00
2	25	15		12.50
3	45	20		15.00
4	60	15	Diminishing marginal returns	15.00
5	70	10		14.00
6	75	5		12.50
7	75	0	Negative marginal returns	10.71
8	70	−5		8.75

Column 3 shows the marginal product (MP), the change in total product associated with each additional unit of labor. Note that with no labor input, total product is zero; a plant with no workers will produce no output. The first three units of labor reflect increasing marginal returns, with marginal products of 10, 15, and 20 units, respectively. But beginning with the fourth unit of labor, marginal product diminishes continuously, becoming zero with the seventh unit of labor and negative with the eighth.

Average product, or output per labor unit, is shown in column 4. It is calculated by dividing total product (column 2) by the number of labor units needed to produce it (column 1). At 5 units of labor, for example, AP is 14 (= 70/5).

Graphical Portrayal Figure 8.2 (Key Graph)
shows the diminishing-returns data in Table 8.1 graphically and further clarifies the relationships between total, marginal, and average products. (Marginal product in Figure 8.2b is plotted halfway between the units of labor since it applies to the addition of each labor unit.)

Note first in Figure 8.2a that total product, TP, goes through three phases: It rises initially at an increasing rate; then it increases, but at a diminishing rate; finally, after reaching a maximum, it declines.

Geometrically, marginal product—shown by the MP curve in Figure 8.2b—is the slope of the total-product curve. Marginal product measures the change in total product associated with each succeeding unit of labor. Thus, the three phases of total product are also reflected in marginal product. Where total product is increasing at an increasing rate, marginal product is rising. Here, extra units of labor are adding larger and larger amounts to total product. Similarly, where total product is increasing but at a decreasing rate, marginal product is positive but falling. Each additional unit of labor adds less to total product than did the previous unit. When total product is at a maximum, marginal product is zero. When total product declines, marginal product becomes negative.

Average product, AP (Figure 8.2b), displays the same tendencies as marginal product. It increases, reaches a maximum, and then decreases as more and more units of labor are added to the fixed plant. But note the relationship between marginal product and average product: Where marginal product exceeds average product, average product rises. And where marginal product is less than average product, average product declines. It follows that

marginal product intersects average product where average product is at a maximum.

This relationship is a mathematical necessity. If you add a larger number to a total than the current average of that total, the average must rise. And if you add a smaller number to a total than the current average of that total, the average must fall. You raise your average examination grade only when your score on an additional (marginal) examination is greater than the average of all your past scores. You lower your average when your grade on an additional exam is below your current average. In our production example, when the amount an extra worker adds to total product exceeds the average product of all workers currently employed, average product will rise. Conversely, when an extra worker adds to total product an amount that is less than the current average product, then average product will decrease.

The law of diminishing returns is embodied in the shapes of all three curves. But, as our definition of the law of diminishing returns indicates, economists are most concerned with its effects on marginal product. The regions of increasing, diminishing, and negative marginal product (returns) are shown in Figure 8.2b. **(Key Question 4)**

Short-Run Production Costs
Production information such as that provided in Table 8.1 and Figure 8.2a and 8.2b must be coupled with resource prices to determine the total and per-unit costs of producing various levels of output. We know that in the short run some resources, those associated with the firm's plant, are fixed. Other resources, however, are variable. So short-run costs are either fixed or variable.

Fixed, Variable, and Total Costs
Let's see what distinguishes fixed costs, variable costs, and total costs from one another.

Fixed Costs **Fixed costs** are those costs that in total do not vary with changes in output. Fixed costs are associated with the very existence of a firm's plant and therefore must be paid even if its output is zero. Such costs as rental payments, interest on a firm's debts, a portion of depreciation on equipment and buildings, and insurance premiums are generally fixed costs; they do not increase even if a firm produces more. In column 2 of Table 8.2 we assume that the firm's total fixed cost is $100. By definition, this fixed cost is incurred at all levels of output, including zero. The firm cannot avoid paying fixed costs in the short run.

WORKED PROBLEMS

W 8.2

Total, marginal, and average product

ORIGIN OF THE IDEA

O 8.2

Production relationship

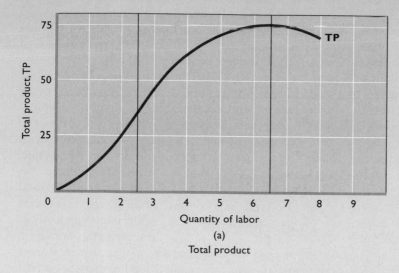

(a)
Total product

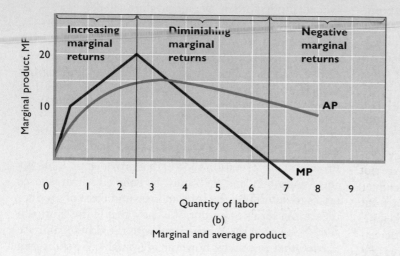

(b)
Marginal and average product

FIGURE 8.2 The law of diminishing returns. (a) As a variable resource (labor) is added to fixed amounts of other resources (land or capital), the total product that results will eventually increase by diminishing amounts, reach a maximum, and then decline.
(b) Marginal product is the change in total product associated with each new unit of labor. Average product is simply output per labor unit. Note that marginal product intersects average product at the maximum average product.

QUICK QUIZ FOR FIGURE 8.2

1. Which of the following is an assumption underlying these figures?
   a. Firms first hire "better" workers and then hire "poorer" workers.
   b. Capital and labor are both variable, but labor increases more rapidly than capital.
   c. Consumers will buy all the output (total product) produced.
   d. Workers are of equal quality.

2. Marginal product is:
   a. the change in total product divided by the change in the quantity of labor.
   b. total product divided by the quantity of labor.
   c. always positive.
   d. unrelated to total product.

3. Marginal product in graph (b) is zero when:
   a. average product in graph (b) stops rising.
   b. the slope of the marginal-product curve in graph (b) is zero.
   c. total product in graph (a) begins to rise at a diminishing rate.
   d. the slope of the total-product curve in graph (a) is zero.

4. Average product in graph (b):
   a. rises when it is less than marginal product.
   b. is the change in total product divided by the change in the quantity of labor.
   c. can never exceed marginal product.
   d. falls whenever total product in graph (a) rises at a diminishing rate.

Answers: 1. d; 2. a; 3. d; 4. a

TABLE 8.2 Total-, Average-, and Marginal-Cost Schedules for an Individual Firm in the Short Run

	Total-Cost Data			Average-Cost Data			Marginal Cost
(1) Total Product (Q)	(2) Total Fixed Cost (TFC)	(3) Total Variable Cost (TVC)	(4) Total Cost (TC) TC = TFC + TVC	(5) Average Fixed Cost (AFC) $AFC = \dfrac{TFC}{Q}$	(6) Average Variable Cost (AVC) $AVC = \dfrac{TVC}{Q}$	(7) Average Total Cost (ATC) $ATC = \dfrac{TC}{Q}$	(8) Marginal Cost (MC) $MC = \dfrac{\text{change in TC}}{\text{change in Q}}$
0	$100	$ 0	$ 100				
							$ 90
1	100	90	190	$100.00	$90.00	$190.00	
							80
2	100	170	270	50.00	85.00	135.00	
							70
3	100	240	340	33.33	80.00	113.33	
							60
4	100	300	400	25.00	75.00	100.00	
							70
5	100	370	470	20.00	74.00	94.00	
							80
6	100	450	550	16.67	75.00	91.67	
							90
7	100	540	640	14.29	77.14	91.43	
							110
8	100	650	750	12.50	81.25	93.75	
							130
9	100	780	880	11.11	86.67	97.78	
							150
10	100	930	1030	10.00	93.00	103.00	

Variable Costs

Variable costs are those costs that change with the level of output. They include payments for materials, fuel, power, transportation services, most labor, and similar variable resources. In column 3 of Table 8.2 we find that the total of variable costs changes directly with output. But note that the increases in variable cost associated with succeeding one-unit increases in output are not equal. As production begins, variable cost will for a time increase by a decreasing amount; this is true through the fourth unit of output in Table 8.2. Beyond the fourth unit, however, variable cost rises by increasing amounts for succeeding units of output.

The reason lies in the shape of the marginal-product curve. At first, as in Figure 8.2b, marginal product is increasing, so smaller and smaller increases in the amounts of variable resources are needed to produce successive units of output. Hence the variable cost of successive units of output decreases. But when, as diminishing returns are encountered, marginal product begins to decline, larger and larger additional amounts of variable resources are needed to produce successive units of output. Total variable cost therefore increases by increasing amounts.

Total Cost

Total cost is the sum of fixed cost and variable cost at each level of output:

$$TC = TFC + TVC$$

TC is shown in column 4 of Table 8.2. At zero units of output, total cost is equal to the firm's fixed cost. Then for each unit of the 10 units of production, total cost increases by the same amount as variable cost.

Figure 8.3 shows graphically the fixed-, variable-, and total-cost data given in Table 8.2. Observe that total variable cost, TVC, is measured vertically from the horizontal axis at each level of output. The amount of fixed cost,

FIGURE 8.3 Total cost is the sum of fixed cost and variable cost. Total variable cost (TVC) changes with output. Total fixed cost (TFC) is independent of the level of output. The total cost (TC) at any output is the vertical sum of the fixed cost and variable cost at that output.

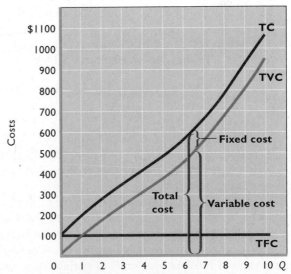

shown as TFC, is added vertically to the total-variable-cost curve to obtain the points on the total-cost curve TC.

The distinction between fixed and variable costs is significant to the business manager. Variable costs can be controlled or altered in the short run by changing production levels. Fixed costs are beyond the business manager's current control; they are incurred in the short run and must be paid regardless of output level.

Per-Unit, or Average, Costs

Producers are certainly interested in their total costs, but they are equally concerned with per-unit, or average, costs. In particular, average-cost data are more meaningful for making comparisons with product price, which is always stated on a per-unit basis. Average fixed cost, average variable cost, and average total cost are shown in columns 5 to 7, Table 8.2.

AFC Average fixed cost (AFC) for any output level is found by dividing total fixed cost (TFC) by that output (Q). That is,

$$AFC = \frac{TFC}{Q}$$

Because the total fixed cost is, by definition, the same regardless of output, AFC must decline as output increases. As output rises, the total fixed cost is spread over a larger and larger output. When output is just 1 unit in Table 8.2, TFC and AFC are the same at $100. But at 2 units of output, the total fixed cost of $100 becomes $50 of AFC or fixed cost per unit; then it becomes $33.33 per unit as $100 is spread over 3 units, and $25 per unit when spread over 4 units. This process is sometimes referred to as "spreading the overhead." Figure 8.4 shows that AFC graphs as a continuously declining curve as total output is increased.

AVC Average variable cost (AVC) for any output level is calculated by dividing total variable cost (TVC) by that output (Q):

$$AVC = \frac{TVC}{Q}$$

As added variable resources increase output, AVC declines initially, reaches a minimum, and then increases again. A graph of AVC is a U-shaped or saucer-shaped curve, as shown in Figure 8.4.

Because total variable cost reflects the law of diminishing returns, so must AVC, which is derived from total variable cost. Because marginal returns increase initially, fewer and fewer additional variable resources are needed to produce each of the first four units of output. As a result,

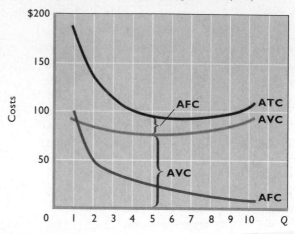

FIGURE 8.4 The average-cost curves. AFC falls as a given amount of fixed costs is apportioned over a larger and larger output. AVC initially falls because of increasing marginal returns but then rises because of diminishing marginal returns. Average total cost (ATC) is the vertical sum of average variable cost (AVC) and average fixed cost (AFC).

variable cost per unit declines. AVC hits a minimum with the fifth unit of output, and beyond that point AVC rises as diminishing returns require more and more variable resources to produce each additional unit of output.

Rephrased, at very low levels of output production is relatively inefficient and costly. Because the firm's fixed plant is understaffed, average variable cost is relatively high. As output expands, however, greater specialization and better use of the firm's capital equipment yield more efficiency, and variable cost per unit of output declines. As still more variable resources are added, a point is reached where diminishing returns are incurred. The firm's capital equipment is now staffed more intensively, and therefore each added input unit does not increase output by as much as preceding inputs. This means that AVC eventually increases.

You can verify the U or saucer shape of the AVC curve by returning to Table 8.1. Assume the price of labor is $10 per unit. By dividing average product (output per labor unit) into $10 (price per labor unit), we determine the labor cost per unit of output. Because we have assumed labor to be the only variable input, the labor cost per unit of output is the variable cost per unit of output, or AVC. When average product is initially low, AVC is high. As workers are added, average product rises and AVC falls. When average product is at its maximum, AVC is at its minimum. Then, as still more workers are added and average product declines, AVC rises. The "hump" of the average-product curve is reflected in the saucer or U shape of the AVC curve. As you will soon see, the two are mirror images of each other.

ATC

Average total cost (ATC) for any output level is found by dividing total cost (TC) by that output (Q) or by adding AFC and AVC at that output:

$$ATC = \frac{TC}{Q} = \frac{TFC}{Q} + \frac{TVC}{Q} = AFC + AVC$$

Graphically, ATC can be found by adding vertically the AFC and AVC curves, as in Figure 8.4. Thus the vertical distance between the ATC and AVC curves measures AFC at any level of output.

Marginal Cost

One final and very crucial cost concept remains: **Marginal cost (MC)** is the extra, or additional, cost of producing one more unit of output. MC can be determined for each added unit of output by noting the change in total cost that unit's production entails:

$$MC = \frac{\text{change in TC}}{\text{change in } Q}$$

Calculations In column 4, Table 8.2, production of the first unit of output increases total cost from \$100 to \$190. Therefore, the additional, or marginal, cost of that first unit is \$90 (column 8). The marginal cost of the second unit is \$80 (= \$270 − \$190); the MC of the third is \$70 (= \$340 − \$270); and so forth. The MC for each of the 10 units of output is shown in column 8.

MC can also be calculated from the total-variable-cost column because the only difference between total cost and total variable cost is the constant amount of fixed costs (\$100). Thus, the change in total cost and the change in total variable cost associated with each additional unit of output are always the same.

Marginal Decisions Marginal costs are costs the firm can control directly and immediately. Specifically,

WORKED PROBLEMS
W 8.3
Per-unit cost

MC designates all the cost incurred in producing the last unit of output. Thus, it also designates the cost that can be "saved" by not producing that last unit. Average-cost figures do not provide this information. For example, suppose the firm is undecided whether to produce 3 or 4 units of output. At 4 units Table 8.2 indicates that ATC is \$100. But the firm does not increase its total costs by \$100 by producing the fourth unit, nor does it save \$100 by not producing that unit. Rather, the change in

costs involved here is only \$60, as the MC column in Table 8.2 reveals.

A firm's decisions as to what output level to produce are typically marginal decisions, that is, decisions to produce a few more or a few less units. Marginal cost is the change in costs when one more or one less unit of output is produced. When coupled with marginal revenue (which, as you will see in Chapter 9, indicates the change in revenue from one more or one less unit of output), marginal cost allows a firm to determine if it is profitable to expand or contract its production. The analysis in the next three chapters focuses on those marginal calculations.

Graphical Portrayal Marginal cost is shown graphically in **Figure 8.5 (Key Graph)**. Marginal cost at first

INTERACTIVE GRAPHS
G 8.1
Production and costs

declines sharply, reaches a minimum, and then rises rather abruptly. This reflects the fact that variable costs, and therefore total cost, increase at first by decreasing amounts and then by increasing amounts (see columns 3 and 4, Table 8.2).

MC and Marginal Product The marginal-cost curve's shape is a consequence of the law of diminishing returns. Looking back at Table 8.1, we can see the relationship between marginal product and marginal cost. If all units of a variable resource (here labor) are hired at the same price, the marginal cost of each extra unit of output will fall as long as the marginal product of each additional worker is rising. This is true because marginal cost is the (constant) cost of an extra worker divided by his or her marginal product. Therefore, in Table 8.1, suppose that each worker can be hired for \$10. Because the first worker's marginal product is 10 units of output, and hiring this worker increases the firm's costs by \$10, the marginal cost of each of these 10 extra units of output is \$1 (= \$10/10 units). The second worker also increases costs by \$10, but the marginal product is 15, so the marginal cost of each of these 15 extra units of output is \$.67 (= \$10/15 units). Similarly, the MC of each of the 20 extra units of output contributed by the third worker is \$.50 (= \$10/20 units). To generalize, as long as marginal product is rising, marginal cost will fall.

But with the fourth worker diminishing returns set in and marginal cost begins to rise. For the fourth worker, marginal cost is \$.67 (= \$10/15 units); for the fifth worker, MC is \$1 (\$10/10 units); for the sixth, MC is \$2 (= \$10/5 units); and so on. If the price (cost) of the variable resource remains constant, increasing marginal returns will be reflected in a declining marginal cost, and diminishing

keygraph

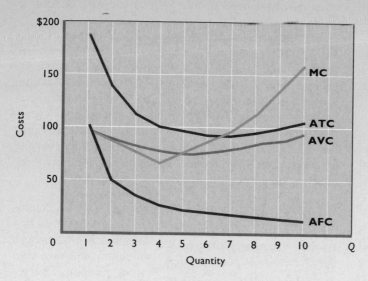

FIGURE 8.5 The relationship of the marginal-cost curve to the average-total-cost and average-variable-cost curves. The marginal-cost (MC) curve cuts through the average-total-cost (ATC) curve and the average-variable-cost (AVC) curve at their minimum points. When MC is below average total cost, ATC falls; when MC is above average total cost, ATC rises. Similarly, when MC is below average variable cost, AVC falls; when MC is above average variable cost, AVC rises.

QUICK QUIZ FOR FIGURE 8.5

1. The marginal-cost curve first declines and then increases because of:

  a. increasing, then diminishing, marginal utility.

  b. the decline in the gap between ATC and AVC as output expands.

  c. increasing, then diminishing, marginal returns.

  d. constant marginal revenue.

2. The vertical distance between ATC and AVC measures:

  a. marginal cost.

  b. total fixed cost.

  c. average fixed cost.

  d. economic profit per unit.

3. ATC is:

  a. AVC − AFC.

  b. MC + AVC.

  c. AFC + AVC.

  d. (AFC + AVC) × Q.

4. When the marginal-cost curve lies:

  a. above the ATC curve, ATC rises.

  b. above the AVC curve, ATC rises.

  c. below the AVC curve, total fixed cost increases.

  d. below the ATC curve, total fixed cost falls.

Answers: 1. c; 2. c; 3. c; 4. a

---

marginal returns in a rising marginal cost. The MC curve is a mirror reflection of the marginal-product curve. As you can see in Figure 8.6, when marginal product is rising, marginal cost is necessarily falling. When marginal product is at its maximum, marginal cost is at its minimum. And when marginal product is falling, marginal cost is rising.

Relation of MC to AVC and ATC Figure 8.5

shows that the marginal-cost curve MC intersects both the AVC and the ATC curves at their respective minimum points. As noted earlier, this marginal-average relationship

is a mathematical necessity, which a simple illustration will reveal. Suppose an NBA basketball player has scored an average of 20 points a game over the first three games of the season. Now, whether his average rises or falls as a result of playing a fourth (marginal) game will depend on whether the additional points he scores in that game are fewer or more than his current 20-point average. If in the fourth game he scores fewer than 20 points, his average will fall. For example, if he scores 16 points in the fourth game, his total points will rise from 60 to 76 and his average will fall from 20 to 19 (= 76/4). Conversely, if in the fourth (marginal) game he scores more than 20 points, say, 24, his total will increase from 60 to 84 and his average will rise from 20 to 21 (= 84/4).

So it is with costs. When the amount (the marginal cost) added to total cost is less than the current average total cost, ATC will fall. Conversely, when the marginal cost exceeds ATC, ATC will rise. This means in Figure 8.5 that as long as MC lies below ATC, ATC will fall, and whenever MC lies above ATC, ATC will rise. Therefore, at the point of intersection where MC equals ATC, ATC has just ceased to fall but has not yet begun to rise. This, by definition, is the minimum point on the ATC curve. The marginal-cost curve intersects the average-total-cost curve at the ATC curve's minimum point.

Marginal cost can be defined as the addition either to total cost or to total variable cost resulting from one more unit of output; thus this same rationale explains why the MC curve also crosses the AVC curve at the AVC curve's minimum point. No such relationship exists between the MC curve and the average-fixed-cost curve because the two are not related; marginal cost includes only those costs that change with output, and fixed costs by definition are those that are independent of output. **(Key Question 7)**

Shifts of the Cost Curves

Changes in either resource prices or technology will cause costs to change and cost curves to shift. If fixed costs double from $100 to $200, the AFC curve in Figure 8.5 would be shifted upward. At each level of output, fixed costs are higher. The ATC curve would also move upward because AFC is a component of ATC. But the positions of the AVC and MC curves would be unaltered because their locations are based on the prices of variable rather than fixed resources. However, if the price (wage) of labor or some other variable input rose, AVC, ATC, and MC would rise and those cost curves would all shift upward. The AFC curve would remain in place because fixed costs have not changed. And, of course, reductions in the prices of fixed or variable resources would reduce costs and produce shifts of the cost curves exactly opposite to those just described.

The discovery of a more efficient technology would increase the productivity of all inputs. The cost figures in Table 8.2 would all be lower. To illustrate, if labor is the only variable input, if wages are $10 per hour, and if average product is 10 units, then AVC would be $1. But if a technological improvement increases the average product of labor to 20 units, then AVC will decline to $.50. More generally, an upward shift in the productivity curves shown in Figure 8.6a means a downward shift in the cost curves portrayed in Figure 8.6b.

FIGURE 8.6 The relationship between productivity curves and cost curves. The marginal-cost (MC) curve and the average-variable-cost (AVC) curve in (b) are mirror images of the marginal-product (MP) and average-product (AP) curves in (a). Assuming that labor is the only variable input and that its price (the wage rate) is constant, then when MP is rising, MC is falling, and when MP is falling, MC is rising. Under the same assumptions, when AP is rising, AVC is falling, and when AP is falling, AVC is rising.

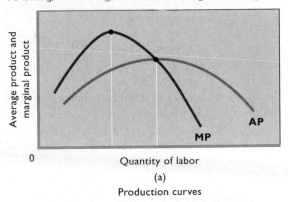

(a)
Production curves

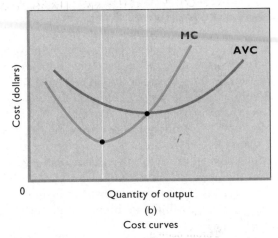

(b)
Cost curves

QUICK REVIEW 8.2

- The law of diminishing returns indicates that, beyond some point, output will increase by diminishing amounts as more units of a variable resource (labor) are added to a fixed resource (capital).

- In the short run, the total cost of any level of output is the sum of fixed and variable costs (TC = TFC + TVC).

- Average fixed, average variable, and average total costs are fixed, variable, and total costs per unit of output; marginal cost is the extra cost of producing one more unit of output.

- Average fixed cost declines continuously as output increases; average-variable-cost and average-total-cost curves are U-shaped, reflecting increasing and then diminishing returns; the marginal-cost curve falls but then rises, intersecting both the average-variable-cost curve and the average-total-cost curve at their minimum points.

Long-Run Production Costs

In the long run an industry and the individual firms it comprises can undertake all desired resource adjustments. That is, they can change the amount of all inputs used. The firm can alter its plant capacity; it can build a larger plant or revert to a smaller plant than that assumed in Table 8.2. The industry also can change its overall capacity; the long run allows sufficient time for new firms to enter or for existing firms to leave an industry. We will discuss the impact of the entry and exit of firms to and from an industry in the next chapter; here we are concerned only with changes in plant capacity made by a single firm. Let's couch our analysis in terms of average total cost (ATC), making no distinction between fixed and variable costs because all resources, and therefore all costs, are variable in the long run.

Firm Size and Costs

Suppose a manufacturer with a single plant begins on a small scale and, as the result of successful operations, expands to successively larger plant sizes with larger output capacities. What happens to average total cost as this occurs? For a time, successively larger plants will lower average total cost. However, eventually the building of a still larger plant may cause ATC to rise.

Figure 8.7 illustrates this situation for five possible plant sizes. ATC-1 is the short-run average-total-cost curve for the smallest of the five plants, and ATC-5, the curve for the largest. Constructing larger plants will lower the minimum average total costs through plant size 3. But then larger plants will mean higher minimum average total costs.

The Long-Run Cost Curve

The vertical lines perpendicular to the output axis in Figure 8.7 indicate the outputs at which the firm should change plant size to realize the lowest attainable average total costs of production. These are the outputs at which the per-unit costs for a larger plant drop below those for the current, smaller plant. For all outputs up to 20 units, the lowest average total costs are attainable with plant size 1. However, if the firm's volume of sales expands beyond 20 units but less than 30, it can achieve lower per-unit costs by constructing a larger plant, size 2. Although total cost will be higher at the expanded levels of production, the cost per unit of output will be less. For any output between 30 and 50 units, plant size 3 will yield the lowest average total costs. From 50 to 60 units of output, the firm must build the size-4 plant to achieve the lowest unit costs. Lowest average total costs for any output over 60 units require construction of the still larger plant, size 5.

Tracing these adjustments, we find that the long-run ATC curve for the enterprise is made up of segments of the short-run ATC curves for the various plant sizes that can be constructed. The long-run ATC curve shows the lowest average total cost at which *any output level* can be produced after the firm has had time to make all appropriate adjustments in its plant size. In Figure 8.7 the blue, bumpy curve is the firm's long-run ATC curve or, as it is often called, the firm's *planning curve*.

In most lines of production the choice of plant size is much wider than in our illustration. In many industries the number of possible plant sizes is virtually unlimited, and in time quite small changes in the volume of output will lead to changes in plant size. Graphically, this implies an unlimited number of short-run ATC curves, one for each output

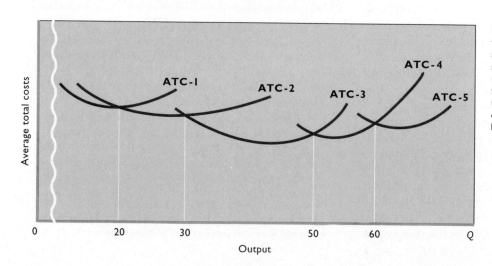

FIGURE 8.7 The long-run average-total-cost curve: five possible plant sizes. The long-run average-total-cost curve is made up of segments of the short-run cost curves (ATC-1, ATC-2, etc.) of the various-size plants from which the firm might choose. Each point on the bumpy planning curve shows the lowest unit cost attainable for any output when the firm has had time to make all desired changes in its plant size.

keygraph

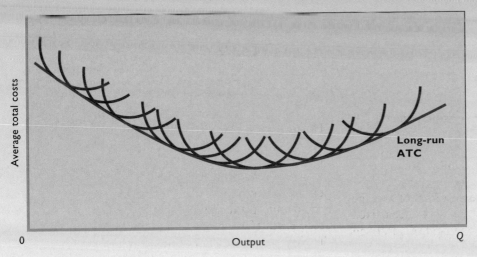

FIGURE 8.8 The long-run average-total-cost curve: unlimited number of plant sizes. If the number of possible plant sizes is very large, the long-run average-total-cost curve approximates a smooth curve. Economies of scale, followed by diseconomies of scale, cause the curve to be U-shaped.

QUICK QUIZ FOR FIGURE 8.8

1. The unlabeled red curves in this figure illustrate the:
   a. long-run average-total-cost curves of various firms constituting the industry.
   b. short-run average-total-cost curves of various firms constituting the industry.
   c. short-run average-total-cost curves of various plant sizes available to a particular firm.
   d. short-run marginal-cost curves of various plant sizes available to a particular firm.

2. The unlabeled red curves in this figure derive their shapes from:
   a. decreasing, then increasing, short-run returns.
   b. increasing, then decreasing, short-run returns.
   c. economies, then diseconomies, of scale.
   d. diseconomies, then economies, of scale.

3. The long-run ATC curve in this figure derives its shape from:
   a. decreasing, then increasing, short-run returns.
   b. increasing, then decreasing, short-run returns.
   c. economies, then diseconomies, of scale.
   d. diseconomies, then economies, of scale.

4. The long-run ATC curve is often called the firm's:
   a. planning curve.
   b. capital-expansion path.
   c. total-product curve.
   d. production possibilities curve.

Answers: 1. c; 2. b; 3. c; 4. a

level, as suggested by **Figure 8.8 (Key Graph).** Then, rather than being made up of segments of short-run ATC curves as in Figure 8.7, the long-run ATC curve is made up of all the points of tangency of the unlimited number of short-run ATC curves from which the long-run ATC curve is derived. Therefore, the planning curve is smooth rather than bumpy. Each point on it tells us the minimum ATC of producing the corresponding level of output.

Economies and Diseconomies of Scale

We have assumed that, for a time, larger and larger plant sizes will lead to lower unit costs but that, beyond some point, successively larger plants will mean higher average total costs. That is, we have assumed the long-run ATC curve is U-shaped. But why should this be? It turns out that the U shape is caused by economies and diseconomies of large-scale production, as we explain in a moment. But before we do, please understand that the U shape of the long-run average-total-cost curve *cannot* be the result of rising resource prices or the law of diminishing returns. First, our discussion assumes that resource prices are constant. Second, the law of diminishing returns does not apply to production in the long run. This is true because the law of diminishing returns only deals with situations in which a productive resource or input is held constant. Under our definition of "long run," all resources and inputs are variable.

167

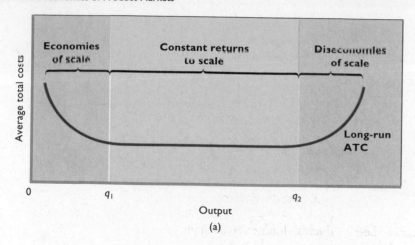

FIGURE 8.9 **Various possible long-run average-total-cost curves.** In (a), economies of scale are rather rapidly obtained as plant size rises, and diseconomies of scale are not encountered until a considerably large scale of output has been achieved. Thus, long-run average total cost is constant over a wide range of output. In (b), economies of scale are extensive, and diseconomies of scale occur only at very large outputs. Average total cost therefore declines over a broad range of output. In (c), economies of scale are exhausted quickly, followed immediately by diseconomies of scale. Minimum ATC thus occurs at a relatively low output.

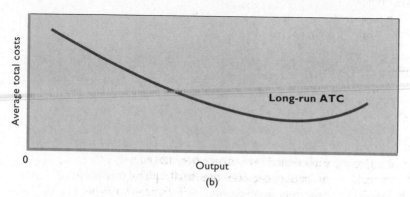

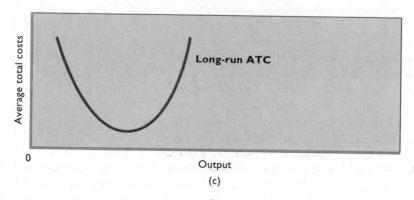

Economies of Scale **Economies of scale,** or economies of mass production, explain the downsloping part of the long-run ATC curve, as indicated in Figure 8.9, graphs (a), (b), and (c). As plant size increases, a number of factors will for a time lead to lower average costs of production.

Labor Specialization Increased specialization in the use of labor becomes more achievable as a plant increases in size. Hiring more workers means jobs can be divided and subdivided. Each worker may now have just one task to perform instead of five or six. Workers can work full-time on the tasks for which they have special skills. In a small plant, skilled machinists may spend half their time performing unskilled tasks, leading to higher production costs.

Further, by working at fewer tasks, workers become even more proficient at those tasks. The jack-of-all-trades doing five or six jobs is not likely to be efficient in any of them. Concentrating on one task, the same worker may become highly efficient.

Finally, greater labor specialization eliminates the loss of time that occurs whenever a worker shifts from one task to another.

Managerial Specialization

Large-scale production also means better use of, and greater specialization in, management. A supervisor who can handle 20 workers is underused in a small plant that employs only 10 people. The production staff could be doubled with no increase in supervisory costs.

Small firms cannot use management specialists to best advantage. For example, a marketing specialist working in a small plant may have to spend some of her time on functions outside of her area of expertise—for example, accounting, personnel, and finance. A larger scale of operations would allow her to supervise marketing full-time, while other specialists perform other managerial functions. Greater productivity and efficiency, along with lower unit costs, would be the net result.

Efficient Capital

Small firms often cannot afford the most efficient equipment. In many lines of production such machinery is available only in very large and extremely expensive units. Furthermore, effective use of the equipment demands a high volume of production, and that again requires large-scale producers.

In the automobile industry the most efficient fabrication method employs robotics and elaborate assembly-line equipment. Effective use of this equipment demands an annual output of several hundred thousand automobiles. Only very large-scale producers can afford to purchase and use this equipment efficiently. The small-scale producer is faced with a dilemma. To fabricate automobiles using other equipment is inefficient and therefore more costly per unit. But so, too, is buying and underutilizing the equipment used by the large manufacturers. Because it cannot spread the high equipment cost over very many units of output, the small-scale producer will be stuck with high costs per unit of output.

Other Factors

Many products entail design and development costs, as well as other "start-up" costs, which must be incurred regardless of projected sales. These costs decline per unit as output is increased. Similarly, advertising costs decline per auto, per computer, per stereo system, and per box of detergent as more units are produced and sold. Also, the firm's production and marketing expertise usually rises as it produces and sells more

output. This *learning by doing* is a further source of economies of scale.

All these factors contribute to lower average total costs for the firm that is able to expand its scale of operations. Where economies of scale are possible, an increase in all resources of, say, 10 percent will cause a more-than-proportionate increase in output of, say, 20 percent. The result will be a decline in ATC.

In many U.S. manufacturing industries, economies of scale have been of great significance. Firms that have expanded their scale of operations to obtain economies of mass production have survived and flourished. Those unable to expand have become relatively high-cost producers, doomed to struggle to survive.

Diseconomies of Scale

In time the expansion of a firm may lead to diseconomies and therefore higher average total costs.

The main factor causing **diseconomies of scale** is the difficulty of efficiently controlling and coordinating a firm's operations as it becomes a large-scale producer. In a small plant a single key executive may make all the basic decisions for the plant's operation. Because of the firm's small size, the executive is close to the production line, understands the firm's operations, and can make efficient decisions because the small plant size requires only a relatively small amount of information to be examined and understood in optimizing production.

This neat picture changes as a firm grows. One person cannot assemble, digest, and understand all the information essential to decision making on a large scale. Authority must be delegated to many vice presidents, second vice presidents, and so forth. This expansion of the management hierarchy leads to problems of communication and cooperation, bureaucratic red tape, and the possibility that decisions will not be coordinated. Similarly, decision making may be slowed down to the point that decisions fail to reflect changes in consumer tastes or technology quickly enough. The result is impaired efficiency and rising average total costs.

Also, in massive production facilities workers may feel alienated from their employers and care little about working efficiently. Opportunities to shirk, by avoiding work in favor of on-the-job leisure, may be greater in large plants than in small ones. Countering worker alienation and shirking may require additional worker supervision, which increases costs.

Where diseconomies of scale are operative, an increase in all inputs of, say, 10 percent will cause a less-than-proportionate increase in output of, say, 5 percent. As a consequence, ATC will increase. The rising portion of the long-run cost curves in Figure 8.9 illustrates diseconomies of scale.

Constant Returns to Scale In some industries a rather wide range of output may exist between the output at which economies of scale end and the output at which diseconomies of scale begin. That is, there may be a range of **constant returns to scale** over which long-run average cost does not change. The q_1q_2 output range of Figure 8.9a is an example. Here a given percentage increase in all inputs of, say, 10 percent will cause a proportionate 10 percent increase in output. Thus, in this range ATC is constant.

Minimum Efficient Scale and Industry Structure

Economies and diseconomies of scale are an important determinant of an industry's structure. Here we introduce the concept of **minimum efficient scale (MES),** which is the lowest level of output at which a firm can minimize long-run average costs. In Figure 8.9a that level occurs at q_1 units of output. Because of the extended range of constant returns to scale, firms producing substantially greater outputs could also realize the minimum attainable long-run average costs. Specifically, firms within the q_1 to q_2 range would be equally efficient. So we would not be surprised to find an industry with such cost conditions to be populated by firms of quite different sizes. The apparel, food processing, furniture, wood products, snowboard, banking, and small-appliance industries are examples. With an extended range of constant returns to scale, relatively large and relatively small firms can coexist in an industry and be equally successful.

Compare this with Figure 8.9b, where economies of scale continue over a wide range of outputs and diseconomies of scale appear only at very high levels of output. This pattern of declining long-run average total cost occurs in the automobile, aluminum, steel, and other heavy industries. The same pattern holds in several of the new industries related to information technology, for example, computer microchips, operating system software, and Internet service provision.

Given consumer demand, efficient production will be achieved with a few large-scale producers. Small firms cannot realize the minimum efficient scale and will not be able to compete. In the extreme, economies of scale might extend beyond the market's size, resulting in what is termed **natural monopoly,** a relatively rare market situation in which average total cost is minimized when only one firm produces the particular good or service.

Where economies of scale are few and diseconomies come into play quickly, the minimum efficient size occurs at a low level of output, as shown in Figure 8.9c. In such industries a particular level of consumer demand will support a large number of relatively small producers. Many retail trades and some types of farming fall into this category. So do certain kinds of light manufacturing such as the baking, clothing, and shoe industries. Fairly small firms are more efficient than larger-scale producers in such industries.

Our point here is that the shape of the long-run average-total-cost curve is determined by technology and the economies and diseconomies of scale that result. The shape of the long-run ATC curve, in turn, can be significant in determining whether an industry is populated by a relatively large number of small firms or is dominated by a few large producers, or lies somewhere in between.

But we must be cautious in our assessment because industry structure does not depend on cost conditions alone. Government policies, the geographic size of markets, managerial strategy and skill, and other factors must be considered in explaining the structure of a particular industry. **(Key Question 10)**

QUICK REVIEW 8.3

- Most firms have U-shaped long-run average-total-cost curves, reflecting economies and then diseconomies of scale.

- Economies of scale are the consequence of greater specialization of labor and management, more efficient capital equipment, and the spreading of start-up costs among more units of output.

- Diseconomies of scale are caused by the problems of coordination and communication that arise in large firms.

- Minimum efficient scale is the lowest level of output at which a firm's long-run average total cost is at a minimum.

Applications and Illustrations

The business world offers many examples relating to short-run costs, economies of scale, and minimum efficient scale (MES). Here are just a few.

The Doubling of the Price of Corn

In the appendix to Chapter 3, we explained that the price of corn has more than doubled in recent years due to a sharp increase in the production of ethanol, an alcohol-like substance that is refined from corn and can be blended with traditional gasoline, which is refined from oil. The increased production of ethanol has been the result of two factors. First, oil prices have increased rapidly, so that there is a much larger demand for ethanol as a substitute for oil-refined gasoline. Second, the government offered a large subsidy to ethanol producers, thereby encouraging them to convert more corn into ethanol.

The large increase in the price of corn has had a wide impact because corn is used as an important resource for a variety of products: For example, it is heavily used as live-stock feed for cattle, a sweetener (high-fructose corn syrup) for soft drinks, and the main ingredient in popular break-fast cereals. Corn is also used in tacos, tortillas, adhesives, candles, cardboard, and chewing gum.

Because of the higher price of corn, the firms producing these corn-based products experienced various degrees of increases in their short-run average variable costs, marginal costs, and average total costs. In terms of our analysis, their AVC, MC, and ATC curves all shifted upward. The extent of the upward shifts depended upon the relative importance of corn as a variable input in the various firms' individual production processes.

Successful Start-Up Firms

The U.S. economy has greatly benefited over the past several decades from the explosive growth of scores of highly successful start-up firms. These firms typically reduce their costs by moving from higher to lower points on their short-run cost curves and by downward and to-the-right shifts of their short-run cost curves via economies of scale. That has certainly been the case for such former start-up firms as Intel (microchips), Starbucks (coffee), Microsoft (software), Dell (personal computers), Google (Internet search engine), and Cisco Systems (Internet switching).

A major source of cost savings for rapidly growing firms is the ability to spread huge product development and advertising costs over a larger number of units of output. These firms also achieve economies of scale from learning by doing and through increased specialization of labor, management, and equipment. After starting up, such firms experience declining average total costs over the years or even decades it takes them to eventually reach their respective MESs.

The Verson Stamping Machine

In 1996 Verson (a U.S. firm located in Chicago) introduced a 49-foot-tall metal-stamping machine that is the size of a house and weighs as much as 12 locomotives. This $30 million machine, which cuts and sculpts raw sheets of steel into automobile hoods and fenders, enables automakers to make new parts in just 5 minutes, compared with 8 hours for older stamping presses. A single machine is designed to make 5 million auto parts per year. So, to achieve the cost saving from the machine, an auto manufacturer must have sufficient auto production to use all

these parts. By allowing the use of this cost-saving piece of equipment, large firm size achieves economies of scale.

The Daily Newspaper

The daily newspaper is undoubtedly one of the economy's great bargains. Think of all the resources that combine to produce it: reporters, delivery people, photographers, editors, management, printing presses, pulp mills, pulp mill workers, ink makers, loggers, logging truck drivers, and so on. Yet for 50 cents you can buy a high-quality newspaper in major cities.

The main reason for such low prices is the low average total costs that result from the spreading of fixed costs and the achieving of economies of scale. If only 100 or 200 people bought the paper each day, the average cost of each paper would be exceedingly high because the overhead costs would be spread over so few buyers. But when publishers sell thousands or hundreds of thousands of newspapers each day, they spread the overhead costs very widely. The large volume of sales also enables them to use specialized labor and large, highly efficient printing presses. Given sufficient scale and volume, the average total cost of a paper sinks to a few dimes. Moreover, the greater the number of readers, the greater is the amount of money that advertisers are willing to pay for advertising space. That added revenue helps keep the price of the newspaper low.

Aircraft and Concrete Plants

Why are there only two plants in the United States (both operated by Boeing) that produce large commercial aircraft and thousands of plants (owned by hundreds of firms) that produce ready-mixed concrete? The simple answer is that MES is radically different in the two industries. Why is that? First, while economies of scale are extensive in assembling large commercial aircraft, they are only very modest in mixing concrete. Manufacturing airplanes is a complex process that requires huge facilities, thousands of workers, and very expensive, specialized machinery. Economies of scale extend to huge plant sizes. But mixing Portland cement, sand, gravel, and water to produce concrete requires only a handful of workers and relatively inexpensive equipment. Economies of scale are exhausted at relatively small size.

The differing MESs also derive from the vastly different sizes of the geographic markets. The market for commercial airplanes is global, and aircraft manufacturers can deliver new airplanes anywhere in the world by flying them there. In contrast, the geographic market for a concrete plant is roughly the 50-mile radius within which the concrete can be delivered before it "sets up." So thousands of small concrete plants locate close to their customers in hundreds of small and large cities in the United States.

Sunk Costs Are Irrelevant in Decision Making.

There is an old saying: Don't cry over spilt milk. The message is that once you have spilled a glass of milk, there is nothing you can do to recover it, so you should forget about it and "move on from there." This saying has great relevance to what economists call sunk costs. Once these costs are incurred, they cannot be recovered.

Let's gain an understanding of this idea by applying it first to consumers and then to businesses. Suppose you buy an expensive ticket to an upcoming football game, but the morning of the game you wake up with a bad case of the flu. Feeling miserable, you step outside to find that the wind chill is about −10 degrees. You absolutely do not want to go to the game, but you remind yourself that you paid a steep price for the ticket. You call several people to try to sell the ticket, but you soon discover that no one is interested in it, even at a discounted price. You conclude that everyone who wants a ticket has one.

Should you go to the game? Economic analysis says that you should not take actions for which marginal cost exceeds marginal benefit. And, in this situation, the price you paid for the ticket is irrelevant to the decision. Both marginal or additional cost and marginal or additional benefit are forward-looking. If the marginal cost of going to the game is greater than the marginal benefit, the best decision is to go back to bed. This decision should be the same whether you paid $2, $20, or $200 for the game ticket because the price that you pay for something does not affect its marginal benefit. Once the ticket has been purchased and cannot be resold, its cost is irrelevant to the decision to attend the game. Since "you absolutely do not want to go," clearly the marginal cost exceeds the marginal benefit of the game.

Here is a second consumer example: Suppose a family is on vacation and stops at a roadside stand to buy some apples. The kids get back into the car and bite into their apples, immediately pronouncing them "totally mushy" and unworthy of another bite. Both parents agree that the apples are "terrible," but the father continues to eat his because, as he says, "We paid a premium price for them." One of the older children replies, "Dad, that is irrelevant." Although not stated very diplomatically, the child is exactly right. In making a new decision, you should ignore all costs that are not affected by the decision. The prior bad decision (in retrospect) to buy the apples should not dictate a second decision for which marginal benefit is less than marginal cost.

Now let's apply the idea of sunk costs to firms. Some of a firm's costs are not only fixed (recurring, but unrelated to the level of output) but sunk (unrecoverable). For example, a nonrefundable annual lease payment for the use of a store cannot be recouped once it has been paid. A firm's decision about whether to move from the store to a more profitable location does not depend on the amount of time remaining on the lease. If moving means greater profit, it makes sense to move whether there are 300 days, 30 days, or 3 days left on the lease.

Or, as another example, suppose a firm spends $1 million on R&D to bring out a new product, only to discover that the product sells very poorly. Should the firm continue to produce the product at a loss even when there is no realistic hope for future success? Obviously, it should not. In making this decision, the firm realizes that the amount it has spent in developing the product is irrelevant; it should stop production of the product and cut its losses. In fact, many firms have dropped products after spending millions of dollars on their development. A recent example is Pfizer's decision in 2007 to shelve its novel insulin inhaler because of poor sales and concerns about long-term side effects. The product withdrawal forced Pfizer to take a $2.8 billion pretax loss on this highly touted product.

In short, if a cost has been incurred and cannot be partly or fully recouped by some other choice, a rational consumer or firm should ignore it. Sunk costs are irrelevant. Don't cry over sunk costs.

Summary

1. Economic costs include all payments that must be received by resource owners to ensure a continued supply of needed resources to a particular line of production. Economic costs include explicit costs, which flow to resources owned and supplied by others, and implicit costs, which are payments for the use of self-owned and self-employed resources. One implicit cost is a normal profit to the entrepreneur. Economic profit occurs when total revenue exceeds total cost (= explicit costs + implicit costs, including a normal profit).

2. In the short run a firm's plant capacity is fixed. The firm can use its plant more or less intensively by adding or subtracting units of variable resources, but it does not have sufficient time in the short run to alter plant size.

3. The law of diminishing returns describes what happens to output as a fixed plant is used more intensively. As successive units of a variable resource such as labor are added to a fixed plant, beyond some point the marginal product associated with each additional unit of a resource declines.

4. Because some resources are variable and others are fixed, costs can be classified as variable or fixed in the short run. Fixed costs are independent of the level of output; variable costs vary with output. The total cost of any output is the sum of fixed and variable costs at that output.

5. Average fixed, average variable, and average total costs are fixed, variable, and total costs per unit of output. Average fixed cost declines continuously as output increases because a fixed sum is being spread over a larger and larger number of units of production. A graph of average variable cost is U-shaped, reflecting the law of diminishing returns. Average total cost is the sum of average fixed and average variable costs; its graph is also U-shaped.

6. Marginal cost is the extra, or additional, cost of producing one more unit of output. It is the amount by which total cost and total variable cost change when one more or one less unit of output is produced. Graphically, the marginal-cost curve intersects the ATC and AVC curves at their minimum points.

7. Lower resource prices shift cost curves downward, as does technological progress. Higher input prices shift cost curves upward.

8. The long run is a period of time sufficiently long for a firm to vary the amounts of all resources used, including plant size. In the long run all costs are variable. The long-run ATC, or planning, curve is composed of segments of the short-run ATC curves, and it represents the various plant sizes a firm can construct in the long run.

9. The long-run ATC curve is generally U-shaped. Economies of scale are first encountered as a small firm expands. Greater specialization in the use of labor and management, the ability to use the most efficient equipment, and the spreading of start-up costs among more units of output all contribute to economies of scale. As the firm continues to grow, it will encounter diseconomies of scale stemming from the managerial complexities that accompany large-scale production. The output ranges over which economies and diseconomies of scale occur in an industry are often an important determinant of the structure of that industry.

10. A firm's minimum efficient scale (MES) is the lowest level of output at which it can minimize its long-run average cost. In some industries, MES occurs at such low levels of output that numerous firms can populate the industry. In other industries, MES occurs at such high output levels that only a few firms can exist in the long run.

Terms and Concepts

economic (opportunity) cost

explicit costs

implicit costs

normal profit

economic profit

short run

long run

total product (TP)

marginal product (MP)

average product (AP)

law of diminishing returns

fixed costs

variable costs

total cost

average fixed cost (AFC)

average variable cost (AVC)

average total cost (ATC)

marginal cost (MC)

economies of scale

diseconomies of scale

constant returns to scale

minimum efficient scale (MES)

natural monopoly

Study Questions

1. Distinguish between explicit and implicit costs, giving examples of each. What are some explicit and implicit costs of attending college? Why does the economist classify normal profit as a cost? Is economic profit a cost of production? **LO1**

2. **KEY QUESTION** Gomez runs a small pottery firm. He hires one helper at $12,000 per year, pays annual rent of $5000 for his shop, and spends $20,000 per year on materials. He has $40,000 of his own funds invested in equipment (pottery wheels, kilns, and so forth) that could earn him $4000 per year if alternatively invested. He has been offered $15,000 per year to work as a potter for a competitor. He estimates his entrepreneurial talents are worth $3000 per year. Total annual revenue from pottery sales is $72,000. Calculate the accounting profit and the economic profit for Gomez's pottery firm. **LO1**

3. Which of the following are short-run and which are long-run adjustments? **LO1**
   a. Wendy's builds a new restaurant.
   b. Harley-Davidson Corporation hires 200 more production workers.
   c. A farmer increases the amount of fertilizer used on his corn crop.
   d. An Alcoa aluminum plant adds a third shift of workers.

4. **KEY QUESTION** Complete the table directly below by calculating marginal product and average product.

Plot the total, marginal, and average products and explain in detail the relationship between each pair of curves. Explain why marginal product first rises, then declines, and ultimately becomes negative. What bearing does the law of diminishing returns have on short-run costs? Be specific. "When marginal product is rising, marginal cost is falling. And when marginal product is diminishing, marginal cost is rising." Illustrate and explain graphically. **LO2**

5. Why can the distinction between fixed costs and variable costs be made in the short run? Classify the following as fixed or variable costs: advertising expenditures, fuel, interest on company-issued bonds, shipping charges, payments for raw materials, real estate taxes, executive salaries, insurance premiums, wage payments, depreciation and obsolescence charges, sales taxes, and rental payments on leased office machinery. "There are no fixed costs in the long run; all costs are variable." Explain. **LO3**

6. List several fixed and variable costs associated with owning and operating an automobile. Suppose you are considering whether to drive your car or fly 1000 miles to Florida for spring break. Which costs—fixed, variable, or both—would you take into account in making your decision? Would any implicit costs be relevant? Explain. **LO3**

7. **KEY QUESTION** A firm has fixed costs of $60 and variable costs as indicated in the table at the bottom of this page. Complete the table and check your calculations by referring to question 4 at the end of Chapter 9. **LO3**
   a. Graph total fixed cost, total variable cost, and total cost. Explain how the law of diminishing returns influences the shapes of the variable-cost and total-cost curves.
   b. Graph AFC, AVC, ATC, and MC. Explain the derivation and shape of each of these four curves and their relationships to one another. Specifically, explain in nontechnical terms why the MC curve intersects both the AVC and the ATC curves at their minimum points.

Inputs of Labor	Total Product	Marginal Product	Average Product
0	0		
1	15	_____	_____
2	34	_____	_____
3	51	_____	_____
4	65	_____	_____
5	74	_____	_____
6	80	_____	_____
7	83	_____	_____
8	82	_____	_____

Total Product	Total Fixed Cost	Total Variable Cost	Total Cost	Average Fixed Cost	Average Variable Cost	Average Total Cost	Marginal Cost
0	$_____	$ 0	$_____			$_____	
1	_____	45	_____	$_____	$_____	_____	$_____
2	_____	85	_____	_____	_____	_____	_____
3	_____	120	_____	_____	_____	_____	_____
4	_____	150	_____	_____	_____	_____	_____
5	_____	185	_____	_____	_____	_____	_____
6	_____	225	_____	_____	_____	_____	_____
7	_____	270	_____	_____	_____	_____	_____
8	_____	325	_____	_____	_____	_____	_____
9	_____	390	_____	_____	_____	_____	_____
10	_____	465	_____	_____	_____	_____	_____

c. Explain how the location of each curve graphed in question 7b would be altered if (1) total fixed cost had been $100 rather than $60 and (2) total variable cost had been $10 less at each level of output.

8. Indicate how each of the following would shift the (1) marginal-cost curve, (2) average-variable-cost curve, (3) average-fixed-cost curve, and (4) average-total-cost curve of a manufacturing firm. In each case specify the direction of the shift. **LO3**
   a. A reduction in business property taxes.
   b. An increase in the nominal wages of production workers.
   c. A decrease in the price of electricity.
   d. An increase in insurance rates on plant and equipment.
   e. An increase in transportation costs.

9. Suppose a firm has only three possible plant-size options, represented by the ATC curves shown in the accompanying figure. What plant size will the firm choose in producing (a) 50, (b) 130, (c) 160, and (d) 250 units of output? Draw the firm's long-run average-cost curve on the diagram and describe this curve. **LO4**

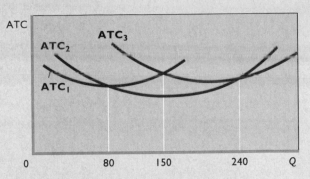

10. **KEY QUESTION** Use the concepts of economies and diseconomies of scale to explain the shape of a firm's long-run ATC curve. What is the concept of minimum efficient scale? What bearing can the shape of the long-run ATC curve have on the structure of an industry? **LO4**

11. **LAST WORD** What is a sunk cost? Provide an example of a sunk cost other than one from this book. Why are such costs irrelevant in making decisions about future actions?

Web-Based Questions

1. **THE WORLD'S 10 LARGEST FIRMS—WHAT ARE THEIR SOURCES OF ECONOMIES OF SCALE?** Find the Forbes 2000 list of the world's largest firms at **www.forbes.com/lists.** From the top 10 list, select three firms from three different industries and discuss the likely sources of the economies of scale that underlie their large size.

2. **CORPORATE ANNUAL REPORTS—IDENTIFY FIXED AND VARIABLE COSTS** Use the Google search engine at **www.google.com** to locate the home page of a company of your choice. Find and review the company's income statement in its annual report and classify the nonrevenue items as either fixed or variable costs. Are all costs clearly identifiable as either fixed or variable? What item would be considered accounting profit? Would economic profit be higher or lower than this accounting profit?

FURTHER TEST YOUR KNOWLEDGE AT
www.mcconnell18e.com

IN THIS CHAPTER YOU WILL LEARN:

1 The names and main characteristics of the four basic market models.

2 The conditions required for purely competitive markets.

3 How purely competitive firms maximize profits or minimize losses.

4 Why the marginal-cost curve and supply curve of competitive firms are identical.

5 How industry entry and exit produce economic efficiency.

6 The differences between constant-cost, increasing-cost, and decreasing-cost industries.

7 How long-run competitive equilibrium results in economic efficiency.

Pure Competition

In Chapter 7 we examined the relationship between product demand and total revenue, and in Chapter 8 we discussed costs of production. Now we want to connect revenues and costs to see how a business decides what price to charge and how much output to produce. But a firm's decisions concerning price and production depend greatly on the character of the industry in which it is operating. There is no "average" or "typical" industry. At one extreme is a single producer that dominates the market; at the other extreme are industries in which thousands of firms each produces a tiny fraction of market supply. Between these extremes are many other industries.

Since we cannot examine each industry individually, we will focus on four basic *models* of market structure. Together, these models will help you understand how price and output are determined in the many product markets in the economy. They also will help you evaluate the efficiency or inefficiency of those markets. Finally, these four models will provide a crucial background for assessing public policies (such as antitrust policy) relating to certain firms and industries.

TABLE 9.1 **Characteristics of the Four Basic Market Models**

	Market Model			
Characteristic	**Pure Competition**	**Monopolistic Competition**	**Oligopoly**	**Pure Monopoly**
Number of firms	A very large number	Many	Few	One
Type of product	Standardized	Differentiated	Standardized or differentiated	Unique; no close substitutes
Control over price	None	Some, but within rather narrow limits	Limited by mutual interdependence; considerable with collusion	Considerable
Conditions of entry	Very easy, no obstacles	Relatively easy	Significant obstacles	Blocked
Nonprice competition	None	Considerable emphasis on advertising, brand names, trademarks	Typically a great deal, particularly with product differentiation	Mostly public relations advertising
Examples	Agriculture	Retail trade, dresses, shoes	Steel, automobiles, farm implements, many household appliances	Local utilities

Four Market Models

Economists group industries into four distinct market structures: pure competition, pure monopoly, monopolistic competition, and oligopoly. These four market models differ in several respects: the number of firms in the industry, whether those firms produce a standardized product or try to differentiate their products from those of other firms, and how easy or how difficult it is for firms to enter the industry.

Very briefly the four models are as follows:

- **Pure competition** involves a very large number of firms producing a standardized product (that is, a product identical to that of other producers, such as cotton or cucumbers). New firms can enter or exit the industry very easily.
- **Pure monopoly** is a market structure in which one firm is the sole seller of a product or service (for example, a local electric utility). Since the entry of additional firms is blocked, one firm constitutes the entire industry. The pure monopolist produces a single unique product, so product differentiation is not an issue.
- **Monopolistic competition** is characterized by a relatively large number of sellers producing differentiated products (clothing, furniture, books). Present in this model is widespread *nonprice competition*, a selling strategy in which one firm tries to distinguish its product or service from all competing products on the basis of attributes like design and workmanship (an approach called *product differentiation*). Either entry to or exit from monopolistically competitive industries is quite easy.
- **Oligopoly** involves only a few sellers of a standardized or differentiated product, so each firm is affected by the decisions of its rivals and must take those decisions into account in determining its own price and output. Table 9.1 summarizes the characteristics of the four models for easy comparison and later reference. In discussing these market models, we will occasionally distinguish the characteristics of *pure competition* from those of the three other basic market structures, which together we will designate as **imperfect competition.**

Pure Competition: Characteristics and Occurrence

Although pure competition is relatively rare in the real world, this market model is highly relevant to several industries. In particular, we can learn much about markets for agricultural goods, fish products, foreign exchange, basic metals, and stock shares by studying the pure-competition model. Also, pure competition is a meaningful starting point for any discussion of price and output determination. Moreover, the operation of a purely competitive economy provides a standard, or norm, for evaluating the efficiency of the real-world economy.

Let's take a fuller look at pure competition, the focus of the remainder of this chapter:

- *Very large numbers* A basic feature of a purely competitive market is the presence of a large number of independently acting sellers, often offering their products in large national or international markets. Examples: markets for farm commodities, the stock market, and the foreign exchange market.
- *Standardized product* Purely competitive firms produce a standardized (identical or homogeneous)

product. As long as the price is the same, consumers will be indifferent about which seller to buy the product from. Buyers view the products of firms B, C, D, and E as perfect substitutes for the product of firm A. Because purely competitive firms sell standardized products, they make no attempt to differentiate their products and do not engage in other forms of nonprice competition.

- *"Price takers"* In a purely competitive market, individual firms do not exert control over product price. Each firm produces such a small fraction of total output that increasing or decreasing its output will not perceptibly influence total supply or, therefore, product price. In short, the competitive firm is a **price taker:** It cannot change market price; it can only adjust to it. That means that the individual competitive producer is at the mercy of the market. Asking a price higher than the market price would be futile. Consumers will not buy from firm A at $2.05 when its 9999 competitors are selling an identical product, and therefore a perfect substitute, at $2 per unit. Conversely, because firm A can sell as much as it chooses at $2 per unit, it has no reason to charge a lower price, say, $1.95. Doing that would shrink its profit.
- *Free entry and exit* New firms can freely enter and existing firms can freely leave purely competitive industries. No significant legal, technological, financial, or other obstacles prohibit new firms from selling their output in any competitive market.

Demand as Seen by a Purely Competitive Seller

We begin by examining demand from a competitive seller's viewpoint to see how it affects revenue. This seller might be a wheat farmer, a strawberry grower, a sheep rancher, a catfish raiser, or some other pure competitor. Because each purely competitive firm offers only a negligible fraction of total market supply, it must accept the price determined by the market; it is a price taker, not a price maker.

Perfectly Elastic Demand

The demand schedule faced by the *individual firm* in a purely competitive industry is perfectly elastic at the market price, as demonstrated in Figure 9.1. As shown in column 1 of the table in Figure 9.1, the market price is $131. The firm represented cannot obtain a higher price by restricting its output, nor does it need to lower its price to increase its sales volume. Columns 1 and 2 show

that the firm can produce as little or as much as it wants and sell all the units at $131 each.

We are *not* saying that *market* demand is perfectly elastic in a competitive market. Rather, market demand graphs as a downsloping curve. An entire industry (all firms producing a particular product) can affect price by changing industry output. For example, all firms, acting independently but simultaneously, can increase price by reducing output. But the individual competitive firm cannot do that. Its demand curve will plot as a straight, horizontal line such as *D* in Figure 9.1

Average, Total, and Marginal Revenue

The firm's demand schedule is also its average-revenue schedule. Price per unit to the purchaser is also revenue per unit, or average revenue, to the seller. To say that all buyers must pay $131 per unit is to say that the revenue per unit, or **average revenue** received by the seller, is $131. Price and average revenue are the same thing from different viewpoints.

The **total revenue** for each sales level is found by multiplying price by the corresponding quantity the firm can sell. (Column 1 multiplied by column 2 in the table in Figure 9.1 yields column 3.) In this case, total revenue increases by a constant amount, $131, for each additional unit of sales. Each unit sold adds exactly its constant price—no more or no less—to total revenue.

When a firm is pondering a change in its output, it will consider how its total revenue will change as a result. **Marginal revenue** is the change in total revenue (or the extra revenue) that results from selling one more unit of output. In column 3 of the table in Figure 9.1, total revenue is zero when zero units are sold. The first unit of output sold increases total revenue from zero to $131, so marginal revenue for that unit is $131. The second unit sold increases total revenue from $131 to $262, and marginal revenue is again $131. Note in column 4 that marginal revenue is a constant $131, as is price. *In pure competition, marginal revenue and price are equal.* **(Key Question 3)**

Figure 9.1 shows the purely competitive firm's total-revenue, demand, marginal-revenue, and average-revenue curves. Total revenue (TR) is a straight line that slopes upward to the right. Its slope is constant because each extra unit of sales increases TR by $131. The demand curve (*D*) is horizontal, indicating perfect price elasticity. The marginal-revenue (MR) curve coincides with the demand curve because the product price (and hence MR) is constant. The average revenue (AR) curve equals price and therefore also coincides with the demand curve.

FIGURE 9.1 A purely competitive firm's demand and revenue curves. The demand curve (*D*) of a purely competitive firm is a horizontal line (perfectly elastic) because the firm can sell as much output as it wants at the market price (here, $131). Because each additional unit sold increases total revenue by the amount of the price, the firm's total-revenue (TR) curve is a straight upward-sloping line and its marginal-revenue (MR) curve coincides with the firm's demand curve. The average-revenue (AR) curve also coincides with the demand curve.

Firm's Demand Schedule		Firm's Revenue Data	
(1) Product Price (P) (Average Revenue)	(2) Quantity Demanded (Q)	(3) Total Revenue (TR), (1) × (2)	(4) Marginal Revenue (MR)
$131	0	$ 0	
131	1	131	$131
131	2	262	131
131	3	393	131
131	4	524	131
131	5	655	131
131	6	786	131
131	7	917	131
131	8	1048	131
131	9	1179	131
131	10	1310	131

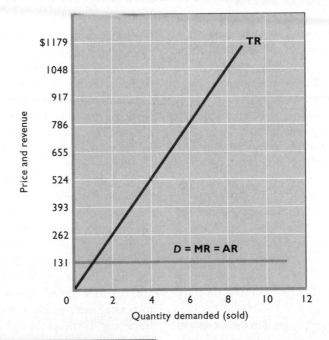

QUICK REVIEW 9.1

- In a purely competitive industry a large number of firms produce a standardized product and there are no significant barriers to entry.
- The demand seen by a purely competitive firm is perfectly elastic—horizontal on a graph—at the market price.
- Marginal revenue and average revenue for a purely competitive firm coincide with the firm's demand curve; total revenue rises by the product price for each additional unit sold.

Profit Maximization in the Short Run: Total-Revenue–Total-Cost Approach

Because the purely competitive firm is a price taker, it can maximize its economic profit (or minimize its loss) only by adjusting its *output*. And, in the short run, the firm has a fixed plant. Thus it can adjust its output only through changes in the amount of variable resources (materials, labor) it uses. It adjusts its variable

TABLE 9.2 The Profit-Maximizing Output for a Purely Competitive Firm: Total-Revenue–Total-Cost Approach (Price = $131)

(1) Total Product (Output) (Q)	(2) Total Fixed Cost (TFC)	(3) Total Variable Cost (TVC)	(4) Total Cost (TC)	PRICE: $131	
				(5) Total Revenue (TR)	(6) Profit (+) or Loss (−)
0	$100	$ 0	$ 100	$ 0	$−100
1	100	90	190	131	−59
2	100	170	270	262	−8
3	100	240	340	393	+53
4	100	300	400	524	+124
5	100	370	470	655	+185
6	100	450	550	786	+236
7	100	540	640	917	+277
8	100	650	750	1048	+298
9	100	780	*880*	*1179*	*+299*
10	100	930	1030	1310	+280

resources to achieve the output level that maximizes its profit.

There are two ways to determine the level of output at which a competitive firm will realize maximum profit or minimum loss. One method is to compare total revenue and total cost; the other is to compare marginal revenue and marginal cost. Both approaches apply to all firms, whether they are pure competitors, pure monopolists, monopolistic competitors, or oligopolists.[1]

We begin by examining profit maximization using the total-revenue–total-cost approach. Confronted with the market price of its product, the competitive producer will ask three questions: (1) Should we produce this product? (2) If so, in what amount? (3) What economic profit (or loss) will we realize?

Let's demonstrate how a pure competitor answers these questions, given certain cost data and a specific market price.

WORKED PROBLEMS

W 9.1

Profit maximization: TR−TC approach

Our cost data are already familiar because they are the fixed-cost, variable-cost, and total-cost data in Table 8.2, repeated in columns 1 to 4 in Table 9.2. (Recall that these data reflect explicit and implicit costs, including a normal profit.) Assuming that the market price is $131, the total revenue for each output level is found by multiplying output (total

product) by price. Total-revenue data are in column 5. Then in column 6 we find the profit or loss at each output level by subtracting total cost, TC (column 4), from total revenue, TR (column 5).

Should the firm produce? Definitely. It can obtain a profit by doing so. How much should it produce? Nine units. Column 6 tells us that this is the output at which total economic profit is at a maximum. What economic profit (or loss) will it realize? A $299 economic profit—the difference between total revenue ($1179) and total cost ($880).

Figure 9.2a compares total revenue and total cost graphically for this profit-maximizing case. Observe again that the total-revenue curve for a purely competitive firm is a straight line (Figure 9.1). Total cost increases with output because more production requires more resources. But the rate of increase in total cost varies with the relative efficiency of the firm. Specifically, the cost data reflect Chapter 8's law of diminishing marginal returns. From zero to four units of output, total cost increases at a decreasing rate as the firm uses its fixed resources more efficiently. With additional output, total cost begins to rise by ever-increasing amounts because of the diminishing returns accompanying more intensive use of the plant.

Total revenue and total cost are equal where the two curves in Figure 9.2a intersect (at roughly 2 units of output). Total revenue covers all costs (including a normal profit, which is included in the cost curve), but there is no economic profit. For this reason economists call this output a **break-even point**: an output at which a firm makes a *normal profit* but not an economic profit. If we extended the data beyond 10 units of output, another break-even point would occur where total cost catches up with total revenue, somewhere between 13 and 14 units of output in

---

[1]To make sure you understand these two approaches, we will apply both of them to output determination under pure competition. But since we want to emphasize the marginal approach, we will limit our graphical application of the total-revenue approach to a situation where the firm maximizes profits. We will then use the marginal approach to examine three cases: profit maximization, loss minimization, and shutdown.

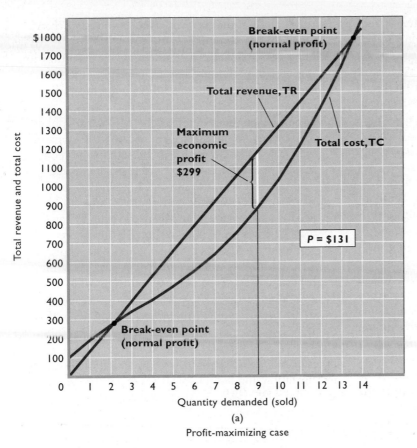

(a)
Profit-maximizing case

FIGURE 9.2 Total-revenue–total-cost approach to profit maximization for a purely competitive firm. (a) The firm's profit is maximized at that output (9 units) where total revenue, TR, exceeds total cost, TC, by the maximum amount. (b) The vertical distance between TR and TC in (a) is plotted as a total-economic-profit curve. Maximum economic profit is $299 at 9 units of output.

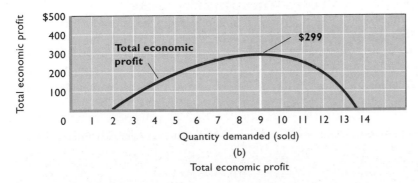

(b)
Total economic profit

Figure 9.2a. Any output within the two break-even points identified in the figure will yield an economic profit. The firm achieves maximum profit, however, where the vertical distance between the total-revenue and total-cost curves is greatest. For our particular data, this is at 9 units of output, where maximum profit is $299.

The profit-maximizing output is easier to see in Figure 9.2b, where total profit is graphed for each level of output. Where the total-revenue and total-cost curves intersect in Figure 9.2a, economic profit is zero, as shown by the total-profit line in Figure 9.2b. Where the vertical distance between TR and TC is greatest in the upper

graph, economic profit is at its peak ($299), as shown in the lower graph. This firm will choose to produce 9 units since that output maximizes its profit.

Profit Maximization in the Short Run: Marginal-Revenue– Marginal-Cost Approach

In the second approach, the firm compares the amounts that each *additional* unit of output would add to total revenue and to total cost. In other words, the firm compares the *marginal revenue* (MR) and the *marginal cost* (MC) of each successive unit of output. Assuming that producing is preferable to shutting down, the firm should produce any unit of output whose marginal revenue exceeds its marginal cost because the firm would gain more in revenue from selling that unit than it would add to its costs by producing it. Conversely, if the marginal cost of a unit of output exceeds its marginal revenue, the firm should not produce that unit. Producing it would add more to costs than to revenue, and profit would decline or loss would increase.

In the initial stages of production, where output is relatively low, marginal revenue will usually (but not always) exceed marginal cost. So it is profitable to produce through this range of output. But at later stages of production, where output is relatively high, rising marginal costs will exceed marginal revenue. Obviously, a profit-maximizing firm will want to avoid output levels in that range. Separating these two production ranges is a unique point at which marginal revenue equals marginal cost. This point is the key to the output-determining rule: *In the short run, the firm will maximize profit or minimize loss by producing the output at which marginal revenue equals marginal cost (as long as producing is preferable to shutting down).* This profit-maximizing guide is known as the **MR = MC rule.**

Keep in mind these features of the MR = MC rule:

- For most sets of MR and MC data, MR and MC will be precisely equal at a fractional level of output. In such instances the firm should produce the last complete unit of output for which MR exceeds MC.
- As noted, the rule applies only if producing is preferable to shutting down. We will show shortly that if marginal revenue does not equal or exceed average variable cost, the firm will shut down rather than produce the amount of output at which MR = MC.
- The rule is an accurate guide to profit maximization for all firms whether they are purely competitive, monopolistic, monopolistically competitive, or oligopolistic.
- The rule can be restated as $P = MC$ when applied to a purely competitive firm. Because the demand schedule faced by a competitive seller is perfectly elastic at the going market price, product price and marginal revenue are equal. So under pure competition (and only under pure competition) we may substitute P for MR in the rule: When producing is preferable to shutting down, the competitive firm that wants to maximize its profit or minimize its loss should produce at that point where price equals marginal cost ($P = MC$).

Now let's apply the MR = MC rule or, because we are considering pure competition, the $P = MC$ rule, first using the same price as used in our total-revenue–total-cost approach to profit maximization. Then, by considering other prices, we will demonstrate two additional cases: loss minimization and shutdown. It is crucial that you understand the MR = MC analysis that follows since it reappears in Chapters 10 and 11.

Profit-Maximizing Case

The first five columns in Table 9.3 reproduce the AFC, AVC, ATC, and MC data derived for our product in Table 8.2. It is the marginal-cost data of column 5 that we will compare with price (equals marginal revenue) for each unit of output. Suppose first that the market price, and

TABLE 9.3 The Profit-Maximizing Output for a Purely Competitive Firm: Marginal-Revenue–Marginal-Cost Approach (Price = $131)

(1) Total Product (Output)	(2) Average Fixed Cost (AFC)	(3) Average Variable Cost (AVC)	(4) Average Total Cost (ATC)	(5) Marginal Cost (MC)	(6) Price = Marginal Revenue (MR)	(7) Total Economic Profit (+) or Loss (−)
0						$−100
1	$100.00	$90.00	$190.00	$ 90	$131	−59
2	50.00	85.00	135.00	80	131	−8
3	33.33	80.00	113.33	70	131	+53
4	25.00	75.00	100.00	60	131	+124
5	20.00	74.00	94.00	70	131	+185
6	16.67	75.00	91.67	80	131	+236
7	14.29	77.14	91.43	90	131	+277
8	12.50	81.25	93.75	110	131	+298
9	*11.11*	*86.67*	*97.78*	*130*	*131*	*+299*
10	10.00	93.00	103.00	150	131	+280

TABLE 9.4 **The Loss-Minimizing Outputs for a Purely Competitive Firm: Marginal-Revenue–Marginal-Cost Approach** (Prices = $81 and $71)

(1) Total Product (Output)	(2) Average Fixed Cost (AFC)	(3) Average Variable Cost (AVC)	(4) Average Total Cost (ATC)	(5) Marginal Cost (MC)	(6) $81 Price = Marginal Revenue (MR)	(7) Profit (+) or Loss (−), $81 Price	(8) $71 Price = Marginal Revenue (MR)	(9) Profit (+) or Loss (−), $71 Price
0						$−100		$−100
				90	$81		$71	
1	$100.00	$90.00	$190.00		81	−109	71	−119
				80				
2	50.00	85.00	135.00		81	−108	71	−128
				70				
3	33.33	80.00	113.33		81	−97	71	−127
				60				
4	25.00	75.00	100.00		81	−76	71	−116
				70				
5	20.00	74.00	94.00		81	−65	71	−115
				80				
6	16.67	75.00	91.67		81	−64	71	−124
				90				
7	14.29	77.14	91.43		81	−73	71	−143
				110				
8	12.50	81.25	93.75		81	−102	71	−182
				130				
9	11.11	86.67	97.78		81	−151	71	−241
				150				
10	10.00	93.00	103.00		81	−220	71	−320

therefore marginal revenue, is $131, as shown in column 6 of Table 9.3 on the previous page.

What is the profit-maximizing output? Every unit of output up to and including the ninth unit represents greater marginal revenue than marginal cost of output. Each of the first 9 units therefore adds to the firm's profit and should be produced. The tenth unit, however, should not be produced. It would add more to cost ($150) than to revenue ($131). So 9 units is the profit-maximizing output.

The economic profit realized by producing 9 units can be calculated by subtracting total cost from total revenue. Multiplying price ($131) by output (9), we find that total revenue is $1179. From the average-total-cost data in Table 9.3, we see that ATC is $97.78 at 9 units of output. Multiplying $97.78 by 9 gives us total cost of $880.[2] The difference of $299 (= $1179 − $880) is the economic profit. Clearly, this firm will prefer to operate rather than shut down.

Perhaps an easier way to calculate the economic profit is to use this simple equation, in which A is average total cost:

$$\text{Profit} = (P - A) \times Q$$

So by subtracting the average total cost ($97.78) from the product price ($131), we obtain a per-unit profit of $33.22. Multiplying that amount by 9 units of output, we determine that the profit is $299. Take some time now to verify the numbers in column 7 in Table 9.3. You will find that

WORKED PROBLEMS

W 9.2

Profit maximization: MR = MC approach

INTERACTIVE GRAPHS

G 9.1

Short-run profit maximization

any output other than that which adheres to the MR = MC rule will mean either profits below $299 or losses.

Figure 9.3 (Key Graph) shows price (= MR) and marginal cost graphically. Price equals marginal cost at the profit-maximizing output of 9 units. There the per-unit economic profit is $P - A$, where P is the market price and A is the average total cost for an output of 9 units. The total economic profit is $9 \times (P - A)$, shown by the green rectangular area.

Note that the firm wants to maximize its total profit, not its per-unit profit. Per-unit profit is greatest at 7 units of output, where price exceeds average total cost by $39.57 (= $131 − $91.43). But by producing only 7 units, the firm would be forgoing the production of 2 additional units of output that would clearly contribute to total profit. The firm is happy to accept lower per-unit profits for additional units of output because they nonetheless add to total profit.

Loss-Minimizing Case

Now let's assume that the market price is $81 rather than $131. Should the firm still produce? If so, how much? And what will be the resulting profit or loss? The answers, respectively, are "Yes," "Six units," and "A loss of $64."

The first five columns in Table 9.4 are the same as those in Table 9.3. Column 6 shows the new price (equal

[2]Most of the unit-cost data are rounded figures. Therefore, economic profits calculated from them will typically vary by a few cents from the profits determined in the total-revenue–total-cost approach. Here we simply ignore the few-cents differentials to make our answers consistent with the results of the total-revenue–total-cost approach.

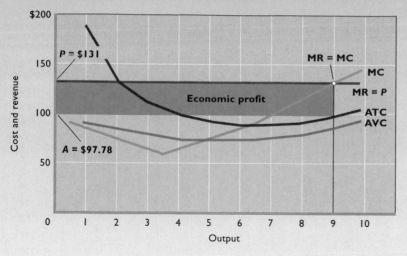

FIGURE 9.3 Short-run profit maximization for a purely competitive firm. The MR = MC output enables the purely competitive firm to maximize profits or to minimize losses. In this case MR (= P in pure competition) and MC are equal at an output Q of 9 units. There, P exceeds the average total cost A = $97.78, so the firm realizes an economic profit of P − A per unit. The total economic profit is represented by the green rectangle and is 9 × (P − A).

QUICK QUIZ FOR FIGURE 9.3

1. Curve MR is horizontal because:
   a. product price falls as output increases.
   b. the law of diminishing marginal utility is at work.
   c. the market demand for this product is perfectly elastic.
   d. the firm is a price taker.

2. At a price of $131 and 7 units of output:
   a. MR exceeds MC, and the firm should expand its output.
   b. total revenue is less than total cost.
   c. AVC exceeds ATC.
   d. the firm would earn only a normal profit.

3. In maximizing profits at 9 units of output, this firm is adhering to which of the following decision rules?

   a. Produce where MR exceeds MC by the greatest amount.
   b. Produce where P exceeds ATC by the greatest amount.
   c. Produce where total revenue exceeds total cost by the greatest amount.
   d. Produce where average fixed costs are zero.

4. Suppose price declined from $131 to $100. This firm's:
   a. marginal-cost curve would shift downward.
   b. economic profit would fall to zero.
   c. profit-maximizing output would decline.
   d. total cost would fall by more than its total revenue.

Answers: 1. d; 2. a; 3. c; 4. c

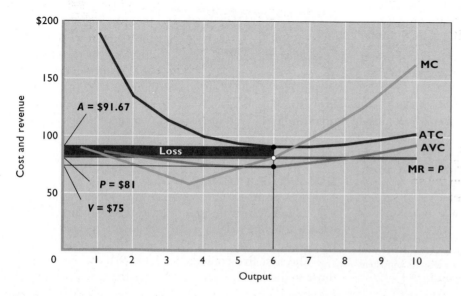

FIGURE 9.4 Short-run loss minimization for a purely competitive firm. If price P exceeds the minimum AVC (here $74 at Q = 5) but is less than ATC, the MR = MC output (here 6 units) will permit the firm to minimize its losses. In this instance the loss is A − P per unit, where A is the average total cost at 6 units of output. The total loss is shown by the red area and is equal to 6 × (A − P).

to MR), $81. Comparing columns 5 and 6, we find that the first unit of output adds $90 to total cost but only $81 to total revenue. One might conclude: "Don't produce—close down!" But that would be hasty. Remember that in the very early stages of production, marginal product is low, making marginal cost unusually high. The price–marginal cost relationship improves with increased production. For units 2 through 6, price exceeds marginal cost. Each of these 5 units adds more to revenue than to cost, and as shown in column 7, they decrease the total loss. Together they more than compensate for the "loss" taken on the first unit. Beyond 6 units, however, MC exceeds MR (= P). The firm should therefore produce 6 units. In general, the profit-seeking producer should always compare marginal revenue (or price under pure competition) with the rising portion of the marginal-cost schedule or curve.

Will production be profitable? No, because at 6 units of output the average total cost of $91.67 exceeds the price of $81 by $10.67 per unit. If we multiply that by the 6 units of output, we find the firm's total loss is $64. Alternatively, comparing the total revenue of $486 (= 6 × $81) with the total cost of $550 (= 6 × $91.67), we see again that the firm's loss is $64.

Then why produce? Because this loss is less than the firm's $100 of fixed costs, which is the $100 loss the firm would incur in the short run by closing down. The firm receives enough revenue per unit ($81) to cover its average variable costs of $75 and also provide $6 per unit, or a total of $36, to apply against fixed costs. Therefore, the firm's loss is only $64 (= $100 − $36), not $100.

This loss-minimizing case is shown graphically in Figure 9.4. Wherever price P exceeds average variable cost AVC but is less than ATC, the firm can pay part, but not all, of its fixed costs by producing. The loss is minimized by producing the output at which MC = MR (here, 6 units). At that output, each unit contributes $P − V$ to covering fixed cost, where V is the AVC at 6 units of output. The per-unit loss is $A − P = $10.67, and the total loss is $6 × (A − P)$, or $64, as shown by the red area.

Shutdown Case

Suppose now that the market yields a price of only $71. Should the firm produce? No, because at every output the firm's average variable cost is greater than the price (compare columns 3 and 8 in Table 9.4). The smallest loss it can incur by producing is greater than the $100 fixed cost it will lose by shutting down (as shown by column 9). The best action is to shut down.

You can see this shutdown situation in Figure 9.5. Price comes closest to covering average variable costs at

the MR (= P) = MC output of 5 units. But even here, price or revenue per unit would fall short of average variable cost by $3 (= $74 − $71). By producing at the MR (= P) = MC output, the firm would lose its $100 worth of fixed cost plus $15 ($3 of variable cost on each of the 5 units), for a total loss of $115. This compares

CONSIDER THIS . . .

The Still There Motel

Have you ever driven by a poorly maintained business facility and wondered why the owner does not either fix up the property or go out of business? The somewhat surprising reason is that it may be unprofitable to improve the facility yet profitable to continue to operate the business as it deteriorates. Seeing why will aid your understanding of the "stay open or shut down" decision facing firms experiencing declining demand.

Consider the story of the Still There Motel on Old Highway North, Anytown, USA. The owner built the motel on the basis of traffic patterns and competition existing several decades ago. But as interstate highways were built, the motel found itself located on a relatively untravelled stretch of road. Also, it faced severe competition from "chain" motels located much closer to the interstate highway.

As demand and revenue fell, Still There moved from profitability to loss ($P < $ ATC). But at first its room rates and annual revenue were sufficient to cover its total variable costs and contribute some to the payment of fixed costs such as insurance and property taxes ($P > $ AVC). By staying open, Still There lost less than it would have if it shut down. But since its total revenue did not cover its total costs (or $P < $ ATC), the owner realized that something must be done in the long run. The owner decided to lower total costs by reducing annual maintenance. In effect, the owner opted to allow the motel to deteriorate as a way of regaining temporary profitability.

This renewed profitability of Still There cannot last because in time no further reduction of maintenance costs will be possible. The deterioration of the motel structure will produce even lower room rates, and therefore even less total revenue. The owner of Still There knows that sooner or later total revenue will again fall below total cost (or P will again fall below ATC), even with an annual maintenance expense of zero. When that occurs, the owner will close down the business, tear down the structure, and sell the vacant property. But, in the meantime, the motel is still there—open, deteriorating, and profitable.

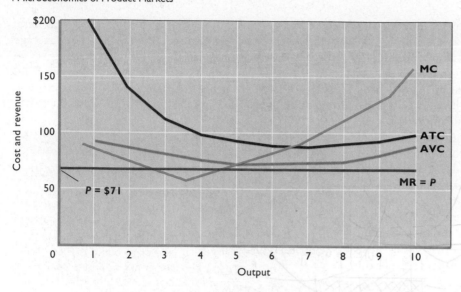

FIGURE 9.5 **The short-run shutdown case for a purely competitive firm.** If price P falls below the minimum AVC (here $74 at $Q = 5$), the competitive firm will minimize its losses in the short run by shutting down. There is no level of output at which the firm can produce and incur a loss smaller than its total fixed cost.

unfavorably with the $100 fixed-cost loss the firm would incur by shutting down and producing no output. So it will make sense for the firm to shut down rather than produce at a $71 price—or at any price less than the minimum average variable cost of $74.

The shutdown case reminds us of the qualifier to our MR $(= P) =$ MC rule. A competitive firm will maximize profit or minimize loss in the short run by producing that output at which MR $(= P) =$ MC, provided that market price exceeds minimum average variable cost.

Marginal Cost and Short-Run Supply

In the preceding section we simply selected three different prices and asked what quantity the profit-seeking competitive firm, faced with certain costs, would choose to offer in the market at each price. This set of product prices and corresponding quantities supplied constitutes part of the supply schedule for the competitive firm.

Table 9.5 summarizes the supply schedule data for those three prices ($131, $81, and $71) and four others. This table confirms the direct relationship between product price and quantity supplied that we identified in Chapter 3. Note first that the firm will not produce at price $61 or $71 because both are less than the $74 minimum AVC. Then note that quantity supplied increases as price increases. Observe finally that economic profit is higher at higher prices.

Generalized Depiction

Figure 9.6 (Key Graph) generalizes the MR = MC rule and the relationship between short-run production costs and the firm's supply behavior. The ATC, AVC, and MC curves are shown, along with several marginal-revenue lines drawn at possible market prices. Let's observe quantity supplied at each of these prices:

- Price P_1 is below the firm's minimum average variable cost, so at this price the firm won't operate at all. Quantity supplied will be zero, as it will be at all other prices below P_2.
- Price P_2 is just equal to the minimum average variable cost. The firm will supply Q_2 units of output (where $MR_2 =$ MC) and just cover its total variable cost. Its loss will equal its total fixed cost. (Actually, the firm would be indifferent as to shutting down or supplying Q_2 units of output, but we assume it produces.)

TABLE 9.5 **The Supply Schedule of a Competitive Firm Confronted with the Cost Data in Table 9.3**

Price	Quantity Supplied	Maximum Profit (+) or Minimum Loss (−)
$151	10	$+480
131	9	+299
111	8	+138
91	7	−3
81	6	−64
71	0	−100
61	0	−100

keygraph

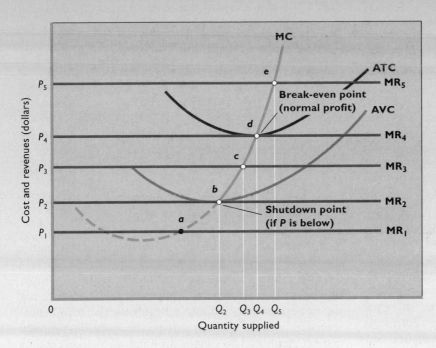

FIGURE 9.6 The P = MC rule and the competitive firm's short-run supply curve. Application of the P = MC rule, as modified by the shutdown case, reveals that the (solid) segment of the firm's MC curve that lies above AVC is the firm's short-run supply curve. More specifically, at price P_1, $P = MC$ at point a, but the firm will produce no output because P_1 is less than minimum AVC. At price P_2 the firm will operate at point b, where it produces Q_2 units and incurs a loss equal to its total fixed cost. At P_3 it operates at point c, where output is Q_3 and the loss is less than total fixed cost. With the price of P_4, the firm operates at point d; in this case the firm earns a normal profit because at output Q_4 price equals ATC. At price P_5 the firm operates at point e and maximizes its economic profit by producing Q_5 units.

QUICK QUIZ FOR FIGURE 9.6

1. Which of the following might increase product price from P_3 to P_5?
   a. An improvement in production technology.
   b. A decline in the price of a substitute good.
   c. An increase in the price of a complementary good.
   d. Rising incomes if the product is a normal good.

2. An increase in price from P_3 to P_5 would:
   a. shift this firm's MC curve to the right.
   b. mean that MR_5 exceeds MC at Q_3 units, inducing the firm to expand output to Q_5.
   c. decrease this firm's average variable costs.
   d. enable this firm to obtain a normal, but not an economic, profit.

3. At P_4:
   a. this firm has no economic profit.
   b. this firm will earn only a normal profit and thus will shut down.
   c. MR_4 will be less than MC at the profit-maximizing output.
   d. the profit-maximizing output will be Q_5.

4. Suppose P_4 is $10, P_5 is $15, Q_4 is 8 units, and Q_5 is 10 units. This firm's:
   a. supply curve is elastic over the Q_4–Q_5 range of output.
   b. supply curve is inelastic over the Q_4–Q_5 range of output.
   c. total revenue will decline if price rises from P_4 to P_5.
   d. marginal-cost curve will shift downward if price falls from P_5 to P_4.

Answers: 1. d; 2. b; 3. a; 4. b

- At price P_3 the firm will supply Q_3 units of output to minimize its short-run losses. At any other price between P_2 and P_4 the firm will minimize its losses by producing and supplying the quantity at which MR $(= P) = $ MC.
- The firm will just break even at price P_4. There it will supply Q_4 units of output (where $MR_4 = $ MC), earning a normal profit but not an economic profit. Total revenue will just cover total cost, including a normal profit, because the revenue per unit ($MR_4 = P_4$) and the total cost per unit (ATC) are the same.

- At price P_5 the firm will realize an economic profit by producing and supplying Q_5 units of output. In fact, at any price above P_4 the firm will obtain economic profit by producing to the point where MR $(= P) = $ MC.

Note that each of the MR $(= P) = $ MC intersection points labeled b, c, d and e in Figure 9.6 indicates a possible product price (on the vertical axis) and the corresponding quantity that the firm would supply at that price (on the horizontal axis). Thus, points such as these are on the upsloping supply curve of the competitive firm. Note too that quantity supplied would be zero at any price below the minimum average variable cost (AVC). *We can conclude that the portion of the firm's marginal-cost curve lying above its average-variable-cost curve is its short-run supply curve.* In Figure 9.6, the solid segment of the marginal-cost curve MC is this firm's **short-run supply curve.** It tells us the amount of output the firm will supply at each price in a series of prices.

Diminishing Returns, Production Costs, and Product Supply

We have now identified the links between the law of diminishing returns (Chapter 8), production costs, and product supply in the short run. Because of the law of diminishing returns, marginal costs eventually rise as more units of output are produced. And because marginal costs rise with output, a purely competitive firm must get successively higher prices to motivate it to produce additional units of output.

Viewed alternatively, higher product prices and marginal revenue encourage a purely competitive firm to expand output. As its output increases, the firm's marginal costs rise as a result of the law of diminishing returns. At some now greater output, the higher MC equals the new product price and MR. Profit once again is maximized, but at a greater total amount. Quantity supplied has increased in direct response to an increase in product price and the desire to maximize profit.

Changes in Supply

In Chapter 8 we saw that changes in such factors as the prices of variable inputs or in technology will alter costs and shift the marginal-cost or short-run supply curve to a new location. All else equal, for example, a wage increase would increase marginal cost and shift the supply curve in Figure 9.6 upward as viewed from the horizontal axis (leftward as viewed from the vertical axis). That is, supply would decrease. Similarly, technological progress that increases the productivity of labor would reduce marginal cost and shift the marginal-cost or supply curve downward as viewed from the horizontal axis (rightward as viewed from the vertical axis). This represents an increase in supply.

Firm and Industry: Equilibrium Price

In the preceding section we established the competitive firm's short-run supply curve by applying the MR (= P) = MC rule. But which of the various possible prices will actually be the market equilibrium price?

From Chapter 3 we know that the market equilibrium price will be the price at which the total quantity supplied of the product equals the total quantity demanded. So to

TABLE 9.6 Firm and Market Supply and Market Demand

(1) Quantity Supplied, Single Firm	(2) Total Quantity Supplied, 1000 Firms	(3) Product Price	(4) Total Quantity Demanded
10	10,000	$151	4000
9	9000	131	6000
8	*8000*	*111*	*8000*
7	7000	91	9000
6	6000	81	11,000
0	0	71	13,000
0	0	61	16,000

determine the equilibrium price, we first need to obtain a total supply schedule and a total demand schedule. We find the total supply schedule by assuming a particular number of firms in the industry and supposing that each firm has the same individual supply schedule as the firm represented in Figure 9.6. Then we sum the quantities supplied at each price level to obtain the total (or market) supply schedule. Columns 1 and 3 in Table 9.6 repeat the supply schedule for the individual competitive firm, as derived in Table 9.5. Suppose 1000 firms compete in this industry, all having the same total and unit costs as the single firm we discussed. This lets us calculate the market supply schedule (columns 2 and 3) by multiplying the quantity-supplied figures of the single firm (column 1) by 1000.

Market Price and Profits To determine the equilibrium price and output, these total-supply data must be compared with total-demand data. Let's assume that total demand is as shown in columns 3 and 4 in Table 9.6. By comparing the total quantity supplied and the total quantity demanded at the seven possible prices, we determine that the equilibrium price is $111 and the equilibrium quantity is 8000 units for the industry—8 units for each of the 1000 identical firms.

Will these conditions of market supply and demand make this a profitable or unprofitable industry? Multiplying product price ($111) by output (8 units), we find that the total revenue of each firm is $888. The total cost is $750, found by looking at column 4 in Table 9.2. The $138 difference is the economic profit of each firm. For the industry, total economic profit is $138,000. This, then, is a profitable industry.

Another way of calculating economic profit is to determine per-unit profit by subtracting average total cost ($93.75) from product price ($111) and multiplying the difference (per-unit profit of $17.25) by the firm's equilibrium

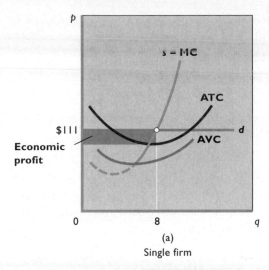

(a)
Single firm

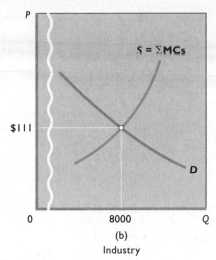

(b)
Industry

FIGURE 9.7 Short-run competitive equilibrium for (a) a firm and (b) the industry. The horizontal sum of the 1000 firms' individual supply curves (s) determines the industry supply curve (S). Given industry demand (D), the short-run equilibrium price and output for the industry are $111 and 8000 units. Taking the equilibrium price as given, the individual firm establishes its profit-maximizing output at 8 units and, in this case, realizes the economic profit represented by the green area.

level of output (8). Again we obtain an economic profit of $138 per firm and $138,000 for the industry.

Figure 9.7 shows this analysis graphically. The individual supply curves of each of the 1000 identical firms—one of which is shown as $s =$ MC in Figure 9.7a—are summed horizontally to get the total-supply curve $S =$ ΣMC of Figure 9.7b. With total-demand curve D, it yields the equilibrium price $111 and equilibrium quantity (for the industry) 8000 units. This equilibrium price is given and unalterable to the individual firm; that is, each firm's demand curve is perfectly elastic at the equilibrium price, as indicated by d in Figure 9.7a. Because the individual firm is a price taker, the marginal-revenue curve coincides with the firm's demand curve d. This $111 price exceeds the average total cost at the firm's equilibrium MR = MC output of 8 units, so the firm earns an economic profit represented by the green area in Figure 9.7a.

Assuming no changes in costs or market demand, these diagrams reveal a genuine equilibrium in the short run. No shortages or surpluses occur in the market to cause price or total quantity to change. Nor can any firm in the industry increase its profit by altering its output. Note, too, that higher unit and marginal costs, on the one hand, or weaker market demand, on the other, could change the situation so that Figure 9.7a resembles Figure 9.4 or Figure 9.5.

Firm versus Industry Figure 9.7 underscores a point made earlier: Product price is a given fact to the *individual* competitive firm,

but the supply plans of all competitive producers *as a group* are a basic determinant of product price.

If we recall the fallacy of composition (Last Word, Chapter 1), we find there is no inconsistency here. Although one firm, supplying a negligible fraction of total supply, cannot affect price, the sum of the supply curves of all the firms in the industry constitutes the industry supply curve, and that curve does have an important bearing on price. **(Key Question 4)**

QUICK REVIEW 9.2

- Profit is maximized, or loss minimized, at the output at which marginal revenue (or price in pure competition) equals marginal cost, provided that price exceeds average variable cost.
- If the market price is below the minimum average variable cost, the firm will minimize its losses by shutting down.
- The segment of the firm's marginal-cost curve that lies above the average-variable-cost curve is its short-run supply curve.
- Table 9.7 (on the next page) summarizes the MR = MC approach to determining the competitive firm's profit-maximizing output. It also shows the equivalent analysis in terms of total revenue and total cost.
- Under competition, equilibrium price is a given to the individual firm and simultaneously is the result of the production (supply) decisions of all firms as a group.

Profit Maximization in the Long Run

In the short run the industry is composed of a specific number of firms, each with a fixed, unalterable plant. Firms may shut down in the sense that they can produce

TABLE 9.7 **Output Determination in Pure Competition in the Short Run**

Question	Answer
Should this firm produce?	Yes, if price is equal to, or greater than, minimum average variable cost. This means that the firm is profitable or that its losses are less than its fixed cost.
What quantity should this firm produce?	Produce where MR (= P) = MC; there, profit is maximized (TR exceeds TC by a maximum amount) or loss is minimized.
Will production result in economic profit?	Yes, if price exceeds average total cost (TR will exceed TC). No, if average total cost exceeds price (TC will exceed TR).

zero units of output in the short run, but they do not have sufficient time to liquidate their assets and go out of business. By contrast, in the long run firms already in an industry have sufficient time either to expand or to contract their capacities. More important, the number of firms in the industry may either increase or decrease as new firms enter or existing firms leave. You need to know how these long-run adjustments affect price, quantity, and profits.

Assumptions

We make three simplifying assumptions, none of which alters our conclusions:

- *Entry and exit only* The only long-run adjustment is the entry or exit of firms. Moreover, we ignore all short-run adjustments in order to concentrate on the effects of the long-run adjustments.
- *Identical costs* All firms in the industry have identical cost curves. This assumption lets us discuss an "average," or "representative," firm, knowing that all other firms in the industry are similarly affected by any long-run adjustments that occur.
- *Constant-cost industry* The industry is a constant-cost industry. This means that the entry and exit of firms does not affect resource prices or, consequently, the locations of the average-total-cost curves of individual firms.

Goal of Our Analysis

The basic conclusion we seek to explain is this: After all long-run adjustments are completed, product price will be exactly equal to, and production will occur at, each firm's minimum average total cost.

This conclusion follows from two basic facts: (1) Firms seek profits and shun losses, and (2) under pure competition, firms are free to enter and leave an industry. If market price initially exceeds minimum average total costs, the resulting economic profits will attract new firms to the industry. But this industry expansion will increase supply until price is brought back down to equality with minimum average total cost. Conversely, if price is initially less

than minimum average total cost, resulting losses will cause firms to leave the industry. As they leave, total supply will decline, bringing the price back up to equality with minimum average total cost.

Long-Run Equilibrium

Consider the average firm in a purely competitive industry that is initially in long-run equilibrium. This firm is represented in Figure 9.8a, where MR = MC and price and minimum average total cost are equal at $50. Economic profit here is zero; the industry is in equilibrium or "at rest" because there is no tendency for firms to enter or to leave. The existing firms are earning normal profits, which, recall, are included in their cost curves. The $50 market price is determined in Figure 9.8b by market or industry demand D_1 and supply S_1. (S_1 is a short-run supply curve; we will develop the long-run industry supply curve in our discussion.)

As shown on the quantity axes of the two graphs, equilibrium output in the industry is 100,000 while equilibrium output for the single firm is 100. If all firms in the industry are identical, there must be 1000 firms (= 100,000/100).

Entry Eliminates Economic Profits Let's upset the long-run equilibrium in Figure 9.8 and see what happens. Suppose a change in consumer tastes increases product demand from D_1 to D_2. Price will rise to $60, as determined at the intersection of D_2 and S_1, and the firm's marginal-revenue curve will shift upward to $60. This $60 price exceeds the firm's average total cost of $50 at output 100, creating an economic profit of $10 per unit. This economic profit will lure new firms into the industry. Some entrants will be newly created firms; others will shift from less prosperous industries.

As firms enter, the market supply of the product increases, pushing the product price below $60. Economic profits persist, and entry continues until short-run supply increases to S_2. Market price falls to $50, as does marginal revenue for the firm. Price and minimum average total cost

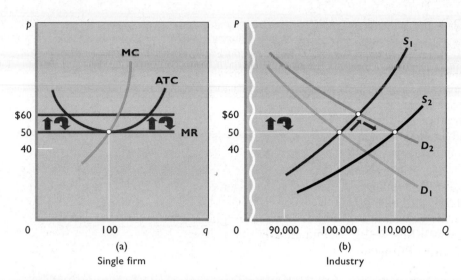

FIGURE 9.8 Temporary profits and the reestablishment of long-run equilibrium in (a) a representative firm and (b) the industry. A favorable shift in demand (D_1 to D_2) will upset the original industry equilibrium and produce economic profits. But those profits will entice new firms to enter the industry, increasing supply (S_1 to S_2) and lowering product price until economic profits are once again zero.

are again equal at $50. The economic profits caused by the boost in demand have been eliminated, and, as a result, the previous incentive for more firms to enter the industry has disappeared. Long-run equilibrium has been restored.

Observe in Figure 9.8a and 9.8b that total quantity supplied is now 110,000 units and each firm is producing 100 units. Now 1100 firms rather than the original 1000 populate the industry. Economic profits have attracted 100 more firms.

Exit Eliminates Losses
Now let's consider a shift in the opposite direction. We begin in Figure 9.9b with curves S_1 and D_1 setting the same initial long-run equilibrium situation as in our previous analysis, including the $50 price.

Suppose consumer demand declines from D_1 to D_3. This forces the market price and marginal revenue down to $40, making production unprofitable at the minimum ATC of $50. In time the resulting losses will induce firms to leave the industry. Their owners will seek a normal profit elsewhere rather than accept the below-normal profits (losses) now confronting them. As this exodus of firms proceeds, however, industry supply decreases, pushing the price up from $40 toward $50. Losses continue and more firms leave the industry until the supply curve shifts to S_3. Once this happens, price is again $50, just equal to the minimum average total cost. Losses have been eliminated and long-run equilibrium is restored.

In Figure 9.9a and 9.9b, total quantity supplied is now 90,000 units and each firm is producing 100 units. Only

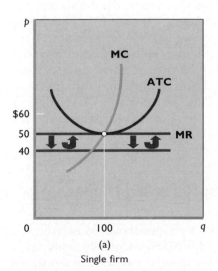

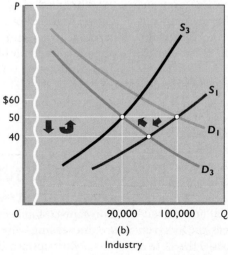

FIGURE 9.9 Temporary losses and the reestablishment of long-run equilibrium in (a) a representative firm and (b) the industry. An unfavorable shift in demand (D_1 to D_3) will upset the original industry equilibrium and produce losses. But those losses will cause firms to leave the industry, decreasing supply (S_1 to S_3) and increasing product price until all losses have disappeared.

900 firms, not the original 1000, populate the industry. Losses have forced 100 firms out.

You may have noted that we have sidestepped the question of which firms will leave the industry when losses occur by assuming that all firms have identical cost curves. In the "real world," of course, managerial talents differ. Even if resource prices and technology are the same for all firms, less skillfully managed firms tend to incur higher costs and therefore are the first to leave an industry when demand declines. Similarly, firms with less productive labor forces or higher transportation costs will be higher-cost producers and likely candidates to quit an industry when demand decreases.

We have now reached an intermediate goal: Our analysis verifies that competition, reflected in the entry and exit of firms, eliminates economic profits or losses by adjusting price to equal minimum long-run average total cost. In addition, this competition forces firms to select output levels at which average total cost is minimized.

Long-Run Supply for a Constant-Cost Industry

Although our analysis has dealt with the long run, we have noted that the market supply curves in Figures 9.8b and 9.9b are short-run curves. What then is the character of the **long-run supply curve** of a competitive industry? Our analysis points us toward an answer. The crucial factor here is the effect, if any, that changes in the number of firms in the industry will have on costs of the individual firms in the industry.

In our analysis of long-run competitive equilibrium we assumed that the industry under discussion was a **constant-cost industry.** This means that industry expansion or contraction will not affect resource prices and therefore production costs. Graphically, it means that the entry or exit of firms does not shift the long-run ATC curves of individual firms. This is the case when the industry's demand for resources is small in relation to the total demand for those resources. Then the industry can expand or contract without significantly affecting resource prices and costs.

What does the long-run supply curve of a constant-cost industry look like? The answer is contained in our previous analysis. There we saw that the entry and exit of firms changes industry output but always brings the product price back to its original level, where it is just equal to the constant minimum ATC. Specifically, we discovered that the industry would supply 90,000, 100,000, or 110,000 units of output, all at a price of $50 per unit. In other words, the long-run supply curve of a constant-cost industry is perfectly elastic.

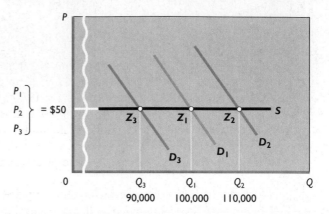

FIGURE 9.10 **The long-run supply curve for a constant-cost industry is horizontal.** Because the entry or exodus of firms does not affect resource prices or, therefore, unit costs, an increase in demand (D_1 to D_2) causes an expansion in industry output (Q_1 to Q_2) but no alteration in price ($50). Similarly, a decrease in demand (D_1 to D_3) causes a contraction of output (Q_1 to Q_3) but no change in price. This means that the long-run industry supply curve (S) is horizontal through points Z_1, Z_2 and Z_3.

This is demonstrated graphically in Figure 9.10, which uses data from Figures 9.8 and 9.9. Suppose industry demand is originally D_1, industry output is Q_1 (100,000 units), and product price is P_1 ($50). This situation, from Figure 9.8, is one of long-run equilibrium. We saw that when demand increases to D_2, upsetting this equilibrium, the resulting economic profits attract new firms. Because this is a constant-cost industry, entry continues and industry output expands until the price is driven back down to the level of the unchanged minimum ATC. This is at price P_2 ($50) and output Q_2 (110,000).

From Figure 9.9, we saw that a decline in market demand from D_1 to D_3 causes an exit of firms and ultimately restores equilibrium at price P_3 ($50) and output Q_3 (90,000 units). The points Z_1, Z_2, and Z_3 in Figure 9.10 represent these three price-quantity combinations. A line or curve connecting all such points shows the various price-quantity combinations that firms would produce if they had enough time to make all desired adjustments to changes in demand. This line or curve is the industry's long-run supply curve. In a constant-cost industry this curve (straight line) is horizontal, as in Figure 9.10, thus representing perfectly elastic supply.

Long-Run Supply for an Increasing-Cost Industry

Constant-cost industries are a special case. Most industries are **increasing-cost industries,** in which firms' ATC curves shift upward as the industry expands and downward as the industry contracts. Usually, the entry of new firms will increase resource prices, particularly in industries using specialized resources whose long-run supplies do not readily increase in response to increases in resource demand. Higher resource prices result in higher long-run average total costs for all firms in the industry. These higher costs cause upward shifts in each firm's long-run ATC curve.

Thus, when an increase in product demand results in economic profits and attracts new firms to an increasing-cost industry, a two-way squeeze works to eliminate those profits. As before, the entry of new firms increases market supply and lowers the market price. But now each firm's entire ATC curve also shifts upward. The overall result is a higher-than-original equilibrium price. The industry produces a larger output at a higher product price because the industry expansion has increased resource prices and the minimum average total cost.

Since greater output will be supplied at a higher price, the long-run industry supply curve is upsloping. Instead of supplying 90,000, 100,000, or 110,000 units at the same price of $50, an increasing-cost industry might supply 90,000 units at $45, 100,000 units at $50, and 110,000 units at $55. A higher price is required to induce more production, because costs per unit of output increase as production rises.

Figure 9.11 nicely illustrates the situation. Original market demand is D_1 and industry price and output are P_1 ($50) and Q_1 (100,000 units), respectively, at equilib-rium point Y_1. An increase in demand to D_2 upsets this equilibrium and leads to economic profits. New firms enter the industry, increasing both market supply and production costs of individual firms. A new price is established at point Y_2, where P_2 is $55 and Q_2 is 110,000 units.

Conversely, a decline in demand from D_1 to D_3 makes production unprofitable and causes firms to leave the industry. The resulting decline in resource prices reduces the minimum average total cost of production for firms that stay. A new equilibrium price is established at some level below the original price, say, at point Y_3, where P_3 is $45 and Q_3 is 90,000 units. Connecting these three equilibrium positions, we derive the upsloping long-run supply curve S in Figure 9.11.

Long-Run Supply for a Decreasing-Cost Industry

In **decreasing-cost industries,** firms experience lower costs as their industry expands. The personal computer industry is an example. As demand for personal comput-ers increased, new man-ufacturers of computers entered the industry and greatly increased the re-source demand for the components used to build them (for example, memory chips, hard drives, monitors, and operating software). The expanded production of the components enabled the producers of those items to achieve substantial econ-omies of scale. The decreased production costs of the components reduced their prices, which greatly lowered the computer manufacturers' average costs of produc-tion. The supply of personal computers increased by more than demand, and the price of personal computers declined.

You should rework the analysis underlying Figure 9.11 to show that the long-run supply curve of a decreasing-cost industry is *downsloping.* **(Key Question 6)**

INTERACTIVE GRAPHS

G 9.2

Long-run competitive supply

Pure Competition and Efficiency

Figure 9.12 (Key Graph) demonstrates the efficiency characteristics of the individual firms (Figure 9.12a) and the market (Figure 9.12b) after long-run adjustments in pure competition. Whether a purely competitive industry is a constant-cost industry or an increasing-cost industry,

FIGURE 9.11 The long-run supply curve for an increasing-cost industry is upsloping. In an increasing-cost industry the entry of new firms in response to an increase in demand (D_3 to D_1 to D_2) will bid up resource prices and thereby increase unit costs. As a result, an increased industry output (Q_3 to Q_1 to Q_2) will be forthcoming only at higher prices ($55 > $50 > $45). The long-run industry supply curve (S) therefore slopes upward through points Y_3, Y_1, and, Y_2.

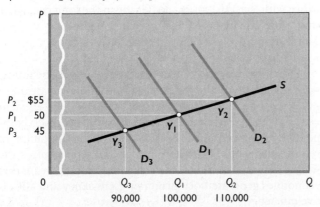

FIGURE 9.12 **Long-run equilibrium: a competitive firm and market.** (a) The equality of price (*P*), marginal cost (MC), and minimum average total cost (ATC) at output Q_f indicates that the firm is achieving productive efficiency and allocative efficiency. It is using the most efficient technology, charging the lowest price, and producing the greatest output consistent with its costs. It is receiving only a normal profit, which is incorporated into the ATC curve. The equality of price and marginal cost indicates that society allocated its scarce resources in accordance with consumer preferences. (b) In the purely competitive market, allocative efficiency occurs at the market equilibrium output Q_e. The sum of consumer surplus (green area) and producer surplus (orange area) is maximized.

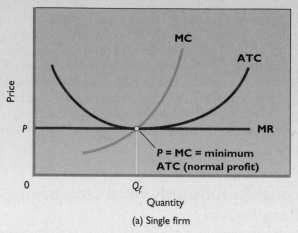

(a) Single firm

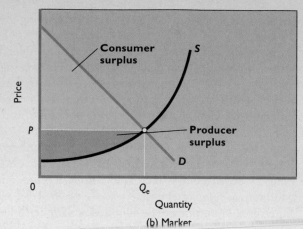

(b) Market

QUICK QUIZ FOR FIGURE 9.12

1. We know the firm is a price taker because:
   a. its MC curve slopes upward.
   b. its ATC curve is U-shaped.
   c. its MR curve is horizontal.
   d. MC and ATC are equal at the profit-maximizing output.

2. At this firm's profit-maximizing output:
   a. total revenue equals total cost.
   b. it is earning an economic profit.
   c. allocative, but not necessarily productive, efficiency is achieved.
   d. productive, but not necessarily allocative, efficiency is achieved.

3. The equality of *P*, MC, and minimum ATC:
   a. occurs only in constant-cost industries.
   b. encourages entry of new firms.
   c. means that the "right goods" are being produced in the "right ways."
   d. results in a zero accounting profit.

4. When *P* = MC = lowest ATC for individual firms, in the market:
   a. consumer surplus necessarily exceeds producer surplus.
   b. consumer surplus plus producer surplus is at a maximum.
   c. producer surplus necessarily exceeds consumer surplus.
   d. supply and demand are identical.

Answers: 1. c; 2. a; 3. c; 4. b

the final long-run equilibrium positions of all firms have the same basic efficiency characteristics. As shown in Figure 9.12a, price (and marginal revenue) will settle where it is equal to minimum average total cost: *P* (and MR) = minimum ATC. Moreover, since the marginal-cost curve intersects the average-total-cost curve at its minimum point, marginal cost and average total cost are equal: MC = minimum ATC. So in long-run equilibrium a triple equality occurs: *P* (and MR) = MC = minimum ATC. Output for each firm is Q_f.

This triple equality tells us that although a competitive firm may realize economic profit or loss in the short run, it will earn only a normal profit by producing in accor-

dance with the MR (= *P*) = MC rule in the long run. Also, this triple equality suggests certain conclusions of great social significance concerning the efficiency of a purely competitive economy.

Economists agree that, subject to Chapter 4's qualifications relating to public goods and externalities, an idealized purely competitive market economy leads to an efficient use of society's scarce resources. This is true because a competitive market economy uses the limited amounts of resources available to society in a way that maximizes the satisfaction of consumers. In particular, competitive market economies generate both productive efficiency and allocative efficiency.

Productive Efficiency:
$P =$ Minimum ATC

Productive efficiency requires that goods be produced in the least costly way. In the long run, pure competition forces firms to produce at the minimum average total cost of production and to charge a price that is just consistent with that cost. That is a highly favorable situation from the consumer's point of view. It means that unless firms use the best-available (least-cost) production methods and combinations of inputs, they will not survive. Stated differently, it means that the minimum amount of resources will be used to produce any particular output. Let's suppose that output in Figure 9.12a is cucumbers.

In the final equilibrium position shown in Figure 9.12a suppose each firm in the cucumber industry is producing 120 units (say, pickup truckloads) of output by using $5000 (equal to average total cost of $50 × 120 units) worth of resources. If one firm produced that same output at a total cost of, say, $7000, its resources would be used inefficiently. Society would be faced with a net loss of $2000 worth of alternative products. But this cannot happen in pure competition; this firm would incur a loss of $2000, requiring it either to reduce its costs or to go out of business.

Note, too, that consumers benefit from productive efficiency by paying the lowest product price possible under the prevailing technology and cost conditions. And the firm receives only a normal profit, which is part of its economic costs and thus incorporated in its ATC curve.

Allocative Efficiency: $P =$ MC

Allocative efficiency requires that resources be apportioned among firms and industries to yield the mix of products and services that is most wanted by society (least-cost production at each level of output assumed). Allocative efficiency is achieved when it is impossible to obtain any net gains for society by simply altering the combination of goods and services that are produced from society's limited supply of resources. Productive efficiency alone does not ensure the efficient allocation of resources. Least-cost production must be used to provide society with the "right goods"—the goods that consumers want most. Before we can show that the competitive market system does just that, we must discuss the social meaning of product prices. Two elements here are critical:

> ### ORIGIN OF THE IDEA
> ### O 9.1
> Allocative efficiency

- The money price of any product is society's measure of the relative worth of an additional unit of that product—for example, cucumbers. So the price of a unit of cucumbers is the marginal benefit derived from that unit of the product.

- Similarly, recalling the idea of opportunity cost, we see that the marginal cost of an additional unit of a product measures the value, or relative worth, of the other goods sacrificed to obtain it. In producing cucumbers, resources are drawn away from producing other goods. The marginal cost of producing a unit of cucumbers measures society's sacrifice of those other products.

In pure competition, when profit-motivated firms produce each good or service to the point where price (marginal benefit) and marginal cost are equal, society's resources are being allocated efficiently. Each item is being produced to the point at which the value of the last unit is equal to the value of the alternative goods sacrificed by its production. Altering the production of cucumbers would reduce consumer satisfaction. Producing cucumbers beyond the $P =$ MC point in Figure 9.12a would sacrifice alternative goods whose value to society exceeds that of the extra cucumbers. Producing cucumbers short of the $P =$ MC point would sacrifice cucumbers that society values more than the alternative goods its resources could produce. **(Key Question 7)**

Maximum Consumer and Producer Surplus

We confirm the existence of allocative efficiency in Figure 9.12b, where we see that pure competition maximizes the sum of the "benefit surpluses" to consumers and producers. Recall from Chapter 6 that **consumer surplus** is the difference between the maximum prices that consumers are willing to pay for a product (as shown by the demand curve) and the market price of that product. In Figure 9.12b, consumer surplus is the green triangle, which is the sum of the vertical distances between the demand curve and equilibrium price. In contrast, **producer surplus** is the difference between the minimum prices that producers are willing to accept for a product (as shown by the supply curve) and the market price of the product. Producer surplus is the sum of the vertical distances between the equilibrium price and the supply curve. Here producer surplus is the orange area.

At the equilibrium quantity Q_e, the combined amount of consumer surplus and producer surplus is maximized. Allocative efficiency occurs because, at Q_e, marginal benefit, reflected by points on the demand curve, equals marginal cost, reflected by the points on the supply curve. Alternatively, the maximum willingness of consumers to pay for unit Q_e equals the minimum acceptable price of that unit to producers. At any output less than Q_e, the sum of consumer and producer surplus—the combined size of the green and orange area—would be less than that shown.

Efficiency Gains from Entry: The Case of Generic Drugs

When a Generic Drug Becomes Available, the Price of the Drug Falls, Consumer Surplus Rises, and Society Experiences an Efficiency Gain.

The competitive model predicts that entry will lower price, expand output, and increase efficiency. A good actual-economy test of this prediction occurs where entry of new producers occurs in a formerly monopolized market. Such a situation occurs when prescription drugs lose their patent protection. A patent on a prescription drug gives the pharmaceutical company that developed it an exclusive right to produce and sell the medication for 20 years from the time of patent application. Because the FDA approval process averages 8 years, the exclusive right may last for as few as 12 years. The purpose of drug patents is to encourage research and development (R&D) leading to new medications and the increased well-being they enable. With patent protection, a firm can charge prices that exceed marginal cost and average total cost and thus earn economic profits on its popular brand-name medicines. Those economic profits provide a return on past development costs and help fund more R&D.

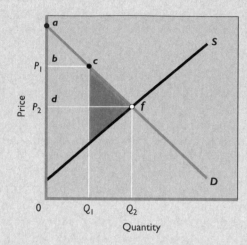

Although competitors can and often do develop similar drugs, they cannot copy and sell the patented medication. Such drugs as Lipitor (for high cholesterol), Singulair (for allergies), and Nexium (for gastrointestinal disorders) are examples of best-selling brand-name, patented drugs.

When a patent expires, any pharmaceutical company can produce and sell the drug under the generic name for the medication. An example of a generic is metroprolol (a substitute for the brand-name drug Lopressor), a beta-blocker used to treat high blood pressure. Because such generic drugs have the same chemical composition as the branded drug, they directly compete against it. The generic price is lower than the branded price, so the price of the drug (at least on average) drops as generics claim a share of the market. Studies indicate that price drop is typically 30–40 percent. Medical insurance plans either mandate that patients buy generics or provide financial incentives to encourage them do so when generics become available. Today, generics make up about 63 percent of all prescription drugs dispensed in the United States.

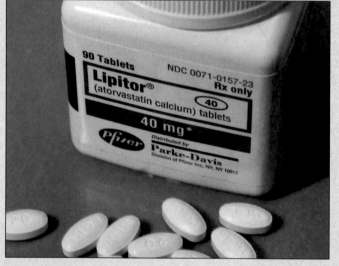

Seeing how patent expiration and the competition from generic drugs relate to consumer surplus and efficiency gains is useful. Consider the accompanying figure, which is similar to Figure 9.12b. The patent gives the firm monopoly power that allows it to charge a higher-than-competitive price. Suppose that the sole seller's profit-maximizing price is P_1. (We will examine how a monopolist would choose this price in the following chapter.)

The expiration of the patent creates competition from generics, which reduces the price of the medication from P_1 to, say, P_2. If you compare the consumer surplus triangles above the price lines, you can see that consumer surplus rises from *bac* to *daf* when the price falls. As the price of the medication drops from P_1 to P_2, output increases from Q_1 to Q_2. In this case, the efficiency gain from competition is shown by the addition of the gray triangle. At price P_2 and quantity Q_2, the combined amounts of consumer surplus and producer surplus are at a maximum. (In reality, the price might not drop all the way to P_2 because of continued loyalty to the branded drug by prescribing physicians.)

Patents aid consumers and society by encouraging the development of new medicines that might otherwise not be available. Entry of the generics at the time of patent expiration further helps consumers by lowering prices, increasing consumer surplus, and enhancing efficiency—just like the competitive model predicts.

At any output greater than Q_e, an efficiency loss (dead-weight loss) would subtract from the combined consumer and producer surplus shown by the green and orange area.

After long-run adjustments, pure competition produces both productive and allocative efficiency: A level of output at which P = MC = lowest ATC, marginal benefit = marginal cost, maximum willingness to pay for the last unit = minimum acceptable price for that unit, and combined consumer and producer surplus are maximized.

Dynamic Adjustments

A further attribute of purely competitive markets is their ability to restore the efficiency just described when disrupted by changes in the economy. A change in consumer tastes, resource supplies, or technology will automatically set in motion the appropriate realignments of resources. For example, suppose that cucumbers and pickles become dramatically more popular. First, the demand for cucumbers will increase in the market, increasing the price of cucumbers. So, at current output, the price of cucumbers will exceed their marginal cost. At this point efficiency will be lost, but the higher price will create economic profits in the cucumber industry and stimulate its expansion. The profitability of cucumbers will permit the industry to bid resources away from now less pressing uses, say, watermelons. Expansion of the industry will end only when the supply of cucumbers has expanded such that the price of cucumbers and their marginal cost are equal—that is, when allocative efficiency has been restored.

Similarly, a change in the supply of a particular resource—for example, the field laborers who pick cucumbers—or in a production technique will upset an existing price–marginal-cost equality by either raising or lowering marginal cost. The resulting inequality of MC and P will cause producers, in either pursuing profit or avoiding loss, to reallocate resources until product supply is such that price once again equals marginal cost. In so doing, they will correct any inefficiency in the allocation of resources that the original change may have temporarily imposed on the economy.

"Invisible Hand" Revisited

Finally, the highly efficient allocation of resources that a purely competitive economy promotes comes about because businesses and resource suppliers seek to further their self-interest. For private goods with no externalities (Chapter 4), the "invisible hand" (Chapter 2) is at work. The competitive system not only maximizes profits for individual producers but also, at the same time, creates a pattern of resource allocation that maximizes consumer satisfaction. The invisible hand thus organizes the private interests of producers in a way that is fully in sync with society's interest in using scarce resources efficiently. Striving for profit (and avoiding losses) produces highly desirable economic outcomes.

QUICK REVIEW 9.3

- In the long run, the entry of firms into an industry will compete away any economic profits, and the exit of firms will eliminate losses, so price and minimum average total cost are equal.
- The long-run supply curves of constant-, increasing-, and decreasing-cost industries are horizontal, upsloping, and downsloping, respectively.
- In purely competitive markets both productive efficiency (price equals minimum average total cost) and allocative efficiency (price equals marginal cost) are achieved in the long run.
- After long-run adjustments, purely competitive markets maximize the combined amounts of consumer surplus and producer surplus.

Summary

1. Economists group industries into four models based on their market structures: (a) pure competition, (b) pure monopoly, (c) monopolistic competition, and (d) oligopoly.

2. A purely competitive industry consists of a large number of independent firms producing a standardized product. Pure competition assumes that firms and resources are mobile among different industries.

3. In a competitive industry, no single firm can influence market price. This means that the firm's demand curve is perfectly elastic and price equals marginal revenue.

4. We can analyze short-run profit maximization by a competitive firm by comparing total revenue and total cost or by applying marginal analysis. A firm maximizes its short-run profit by producing the output at which total revenue exceeds total cost by the greatest amount.

5. Provided price exceeds minimum average variable cost, a competitive firm maximizes profit or minimizes loss in the short run by producing the output at which price or marginal revenue equals marginal cost. If price is less than average variable cost, the firm minimizes its loss by shutting down. If price is greater than average variable cost but is less than average total cost, the firm minimizes its loss by producing the P = MC output. If price also exceeds average total cost, the firm maximizes its economic profit at the P = MC output.

6. Applying the MR (= P) = MC rule at various possible market prices leads to the conclusion that the segment of the firm's short-run marginal-cost curve that lies above the firm's average-variable cost curve is its short-run supply curve.

7. In the long run, the market price of a product will equal the minimum average total cost of production. At a higher price, economic profits would cause firms to enter the industry until those profits had been competed away. At a lower price, losses would force the exit of firms from the industry until the product price rose to equal average total cost.

8. The long-run supply curve is horizontal for a constant-cost industry, upsloping for an increasing-cost industry, and downsloping for a decreasing-cost industry.

9. The long-run equality of price and minimum average total cost means that competitive firms will use the most efficient known technology and charge the lowest price consistent with their production costs. That is, the firms will achieve productive efficiency.

10. The long-run equality of price and marginal cost implies that resources will be allocated in accordance with consumer tastes. Allocative efficiency will occur. In the market, the combined amount of consumer surplus and producer surplus will be at a maximum.

11. The competitive price system will reallocate resources in response to a change in consumer tastes, in technology, or in resource supplies and will thereby maintain allocative efficiency over time.

Terms and Concepts

pure competition	total revenue	increasing-cost industry
pure monopoly	marginal revenue	decreasing-cost industry
monopolistic competition	break-even point	productive efficiency
oligopoly	MR = MC rule	allocative efficiency
imperfect competition	short-run supply curve	consumer surplus
price taker	long-run supply curve	producer surplus
average revenue	constant-cost industry	

Study Questions  | ECONOMICS

1. Briefly state the basic characteristics of pure competition, pure monopoly, monopolistic competition, and oligopoly. Under which of these market classifications does each of the following most accurately fit? (*a*) a supermarket in your hometown; (*b*) the steel industry; (*c*) a Kansas wheat farm; (*d*) the commercial bank in which you or your family has an account; (*e*) the automobile industry. In each case justify your classification. **LO1**

2. Strictly speaking, pure competition has never existed and probably never will. Then why study it? **LO2**

3. **KEY QUESTION** Use the following demand schedule to determine total revenue and marginal revenue for each possible level of sales: **LO2**

Product Price	Quantity Demanded	Total Revenue	Marginal Revenue
$2	0	$____	
2	1	____	$____
2	2	____	____
2	3	____	____
2	4	____	____
2	5	____	____

a. What can you conclude about the structure of the industry in which this firm is operating? Explain.

b. Graph the demand, total-revenue, and marginal-revenue curves for this firm.

c. Why do the demand and marginal-revenue curves coincide?

d. "Marginal revenue is the change in total revenue associated with additional units of output." Explain verbally and graphically, using the data in the table.

4. **KEY QUESTION** Assume the following cost data are for a purely competitive producer: **LO3**

Total Product	Average Fixed Cost	Average Variable Cost	Average Total Cost	Marginal Cost
0				
1	$60.00	$45.00	$105.00	$45
2	30.00	42.50	72.50	40
3	20.00	40.00	60.00	35
4	15.00	37.50	52.50	30
5	12.00	37.00	49.00	35
6	10.00	37.50	47.50	40
7	8.57	38.57	47.14	45
8	7.50	40.63	48.13	55
9	6.67	43.33	50.00	65
10	6.00	46.50	52.50	75

a. At a product price of $56, will this firm produce in the short run? Why or why not? If it is preferable to produce, what will be the profit maximizing or loss-minimizing output? Explain. What economic profit or loss will the firm realize per unit of output?

b. Answer the relevant questions of 4a assuming product price is $41.

c. Answer the relevant questions of 4a assuming product price is $32.

d. In the table below, complete the short-run supply schedule for the firm (columns 1 and 2) and indicate the profit or loss incurred at each output (column 3).

(1) Price	(2) Quantity Supplied, Single Firm	(3) Profit (+) or Loss (−)	(4) Quantity Supplied 1500 Firms
$26	_____	$_____	_____
32	_____	_____	_____
38	_____	_____	_____
41	_____	_____	_____
46	_____	_____	_____
56	_____	_____	_____
66	_____	_____	_____

e. Explain: "That segment of a competitive firm's marginal-cost curve that lies above its average-variable-cost curve constitutes the short-run supply curve for the firm." Illustrate graphically.

f. Now assume that there are 1500 identical firms in this competitive industry; that is, there are 1500 firms, each of which has the cost data shown in the table. Complete the industry supply schedule (column 4).

g. Suppose the market demand data for the product are as follows:

Price	Total Quantity Demanded
$26	17,000
32	15,000
38	13,500
41	12,000
46	10,500
56	9500
66	8000

What will be the equilibrium price? What will be the equilibrium output for the industry? For each firm? What will profit or loss be per unit? Per firm? Will this industry expand or contract in the long run?

5. Why is the equality of marginal revenue and marginal cost essential for profit maximization in all market structures? Explain why price can be substituted for marginal revenue in the MR = MC rule when an industry is purely competitive. **LO3**

6. KEY QUESTION Using diagrams for both the industry and a representative firm, illustrate competitive long-run equilibrium. Assuming constant costs, employ these diagrams to show how (*a*) an increase and (*b*) a decrease in market demand will upset that long-run equilibrium. Trace graphically and describe verbally the adjustment processes by which long-run equilibrium is restored. Now rework your analysis for increasing- and decreasing-cost industries and compare the three long-run supply curves. **LO6**

7. KEY QUESTION In long-run equilibrium, P = minimum ATC = MC. Of what significance for economic efficiency is the equality of P and minimum ATC? The equality of P and MC? Distinguish between productive efficiency and allocative efficiency in your answer. **LO7**

8. Suppose that purely competitive firms producing cashews discover that P exceeds MC. Will their combined output of cashews be too little, too much, or just right to achieve allocative efficiency? In the long run, what will happen to the supply of cashews and the price of cashews? Use a supply and demand diagram to show how that response will change the combined amount of consumer surplus and producer surplus in the market for cashews. **LO7**

9. LAST WORD How does a generic drug differ from its brand-name, previously patented equivalent? Explain why the price of a brand-name drug typically declines when an equivalent generic drug becomes available? Explain how that drop in price affects allocative efficiency.

Web-Based Questions

1. **YOU ARE A PURE COMPETITOR—WHAT WAS YOUR REVENUE YESTERDAY?** Suppose that you operate a purely competitive firm that buys and sells foreign currencies. Also suppose that yesterday your business activity consisted of buying 100,000 Swiss francs at the market exchange rate and selling them to U.S. travelers to Switzerland for a 3 percent commission. Go to the Federal Reserve Web site at **federalreserve.gov** and select, in order, Economic Research and Data, Statistics, and Foreign Exchange Rates. What was your total revenue in dollars yesterday (be sure to include your commission)? Why would your profit for the day be considerably less than this total revenue?

2. **ENTRY AND EXIT OF FIRMS—WHERE HAVE THEY OCCURRED?** Go to the Census Bureau Web site at **www.census.gov** and select Economic Census, then Comparative Statistics, and then Manufacturing (More data). Identify three manufacturing industries that experienced large percentage increases in the number of firms between 1997 and 2002. Identify three manufacturing industries that experienced large percentage decreases. What single factor is the most likely cause of the entry and exit differences between your two groups? Explain.

FURTHER TEST YOUR KNOWLEDGE AT
www.mcconnell18e.com

IN THIS CHAPTER YOU WILL LEARN:

1 The characteristics of pure monopoly.

2 How a pure monopoly sets its profit-maximizing output and price.

3 About the economic effects of monopoly.

4 Why a monopolist might prefer to charge different prices in different markets.

10

Pure Monopoly

We turn now from pure competition to pure monopoly, which is at the opposite end of the spectrum of industry structures listed in Table 9.1. You deal with monopolies more often than you might think. When you see the logo for Microsoft's Windows on your computer, you are dealing with a monopoly (or, at least, a near-monopoly). When you purchase certain prescription drugs, you are buying monopolized products. When you make a local telephone call, turn on your lights, or subscribe to cable TV, you may be patronizing a monopoly, depending on your location.

What precisely do we mean by pure monopoly, and what conditions enable it to arise and survive? How does a pure monopolist determine its profit-maximizing price and output quantity? Does a pure monopolist achieve the efficiency associated with pure competition? If not, what should the government do about it? A simplified model of pure monopoly will help us answer these questions. This will be the first of three models of imperfect competition.

An Introduction to Pure Monopoly

Pure monopoly exists when a single firm is the sole producer of a product for which there are no close substitutes. Here are the main characteristics of pure monopoly:

- *Single seller* A pure, or absolute, monopoly is an industry in which a single firm is the sole producer of a specific good or the sole supplier of a service; the firm and the industry are synonymous.

- *No close substitutes* A pure monopoly's product is unique in that there are no close substitutes. The consumer who chooses not to buy the monopolized product must do without it.

- *Price maker* The pure monopolist controls the total quantity supplied and thus has considerable control over price; it is a *price maker* (unlike a pure competitor, which has no such control and therefore is a *price taker*). The pure monopolist confronts the usual downward-sloping product demand curve. It can change its product price by changing the quantity of the product it produces. The monopolist will use this power whenever it is advantageous to do so.

- *Blocked entry* A pure monopolist has no immediate competitors because certain barriers keep potential competitors from entering the industry. Those barriers may be economic, technological, legal, or of some other type. But entry is totally blocked in pure monopoly.

- *Nonprice competition* The product produced by a pure monopolist may be either standardized (as with natural gas and electricity) or differentiated (as with Windows or Frisbees). Monopolists that have standardized products engage mainly in public relations advertising, whereas those with differentiated products sometimes advertise their products' attributes.

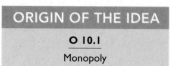

ORIGIN OF THE IDEA

O 10.1

Monopoly

Examples of Monopoly

Examples of *pure* monopoly are relatively rare, but there are many examples of less pure forms. In most cities, government-owned or government-regulated public utilities—natural gas and electric companies, the water company, the cable TV company, and the local telephone company—are all monopolies or virtually so.

There are also many "near-monopolies" in which a single firm has the bulk of sales in a specific market. Intel, for example, provides 80 percent of the central microprocessors used in personal computers. First Data Corporation, via its Western Union subsidiary, accounts for 80 percent of the market for money order transfers. Brannock Device Company has an 80 percent market share of the shoe sizing devices found in shoe stores. Wham-O, through its Frisbee brand, sells 90 percent of plastic throwing disks. The De Beers diamond syndicate effectively controls 55 percent of the world's supply of rough-cut diamonds (see this chapter's Last Word).

Professional sports teams are, in a sense, monopolies because they are the sole suppliers of specific services in large geographic areas. With a few exceptions, a single major-league team in each sport serves each large American city. If you want to see a live Major League Baseball game in St. Louis or Seattle, you must patronize the Cardinals or the Mariners, respectively. Other geographic monopolies exist. For example, a small town may be served by only one airline or railroad. In a small, isolated community, the local barber shop, dry cleaner, or grocery store may approximate a monopoly.

Of course, there is almost always some competition. Satellite television is a substitute for cable, and amateur softball is a substitute for professional baseball. The Linux operating system can substitute for Windows, and so on. But such substitutes are typically either more costly or in some way less appealing.

Dual Objectives of the Study of Monopoly

Monopoly is worth studying both for its own sake and because it provides insights about the more common market structures of monopolistic competition and oligopoly (Chapter 11). These two market structures combine, in differing degrees, characteristics of pure competition and pure monopoly.

Barriers to Entry

The factors that prohibit firms from entering an industry are called **barriers to entry.** In pure monopoly, strong barriers to entry effectively block all potential competition. Somewhat weaker barriers may permit oligopoly, a market structure dominated by a few firms. Still weaker barriers may permit the entry of a fairly large number of competing firms giving rise to monopolistic competition. And the absence of any effective entry barriers permits the entry of a very large number of firms, which provide the basis of pure competition. So barriers to entry are pertinent not only to the extreme case of pure monopoly but also to other market structures in which there is some degree of monopolistic conditions and behavior.

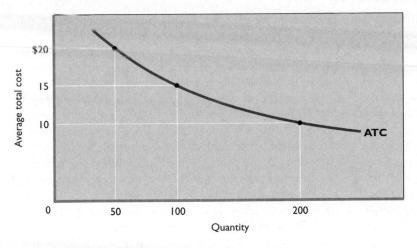

FIGURE 10.1 Economies of scale: the natural monopoly case. A declining long-run average-total-cost curve over a wide range of output quantities indicates extensive economies of scale. A single monopoly firm can produce, say, 200 units of output at lower cost ($10 each) than could two or more firms that had a combined output of 200 units.

Economies of Scale

Modern technology in some industries is such that economies of scale—declining average total cost with added firm size—are extensive. So a firm's long-run average-cost schedule will decline over a wide range of output. Given market demand, only a few large firms or, in the extreme, only a single large firm can achieve low average total costs.

Figure 10.1 indicates economies of scale over a wide range of outputs. If total consumer demand is within that output range, then only a single producer can satisfy demand at least cost. Note, for example, that a monopolist can produce 200 units at a per-unit cost of $10 and a total cost of $2000. If the industry has two firms and each produces 100 units, the unit cost is $15 and total cost rises to $3000 (= 200 units × $15). A still more competitive situation with four firms each producing 50 units would boost unit and total cost to $20 and $4000, respectively. Conclusion: When long-run ATC is declining, only a single producer, a monopolist, can produce any particular output at minimum total cost.

If a pure monopoly exists in such an industry, economies of scale will serve as an entry barrier and will protect the monopolist from competition. New firms that try to enter the industry as small-scale producers cannot realize the cost economies of the monopolist. They therefore will be undercut and forced out of business by the monopolist, which can sell at a much lower price and still make a profit because of its lower per-unit cost associated with its economies of scale. A new firm might try to start out big, that is, to enter the industry as a large-scale producer so as to achieve the necessary economies of scale. But the massive plant facilities required would necessitate huge amounts of financing, which a new and untried enterprise would find difficult to secure. In most cases the financial obstacles and

risks to "starting big" are prohibitive. This explains why efforts to enter such industries as computer operating software, commercial aircraft, and basic steel are so rare.

In the extreme circumstance, in which the market demand curve cuts the long-run ATC curve where average total costs are still declining, the single firm is called a *natural monopoly*. It might seem that a natural monopolist's lower unit cost would enable it to charge a lower price than if the industry were more competitive. But that won't necessarily happen. As with any monopolist, a natural monopolist may, instead, set its price far above ATC and obtain substantial economic profit. In that event, the lowest-unit-cost advantage of a natural monopolist would accrue to the monopolist as profit and not as lower prices to consumers. That is why the government regulates some natural monopolies, specifying the price they may charge. We will say more about that later.

ORIGIN OF THE IDEA
O 10.2
Minimum efficient scale

Legal Barriers to Entry: Patents and Licenses

Government also creates legal barriers to entry by awarding patents and licenses.

Patents A *patent* is the exclusive right of an inventor to use, or to allow another to use, her or his invention. Patents and patent laws aim to protect the inventor from rivals who would use the invention without having shared in the effort and expense of developing it. At the same time, patents provide the inventor with a monopoly position for the life of the patent. The world's nations have agreed on a uniform patent length of 20 years from the time of application. Patents have figured prominently in the growth of modern-day giants such as IBM, Pfizer, Intel, Xerox, General Electric, and DuPont.

Research and development (R&D) is what leads to most patentable inventions and products. Firms that gain monopoly power through their own research or by purchasing the patents of others can use patents to strengthen their market position. The profit from one patent can finance the research required to develop new patentable products. In the pharmaceutical industry, patents on prescription drugs have produced large monopoly profits that have helped finance the discovery of new patentable medicines. So monopoly power achieved through patents may well be self-sustaining, even though patents eventually expire and generic drugs then compete with the original brand.

Licenses Government may also limit entry into an industry or occupation through *licensing*. At the national level, the Federal Communications Commission licenses only so many radio and television stations in each geographic area. In many large cities one of a limited number of municipal licenses is required to drive a taxicab. The consequent restriction of the supply of cabs creates economic profit for cab owners and drivers. New cabs cannot enter the industry to drive down prices and profits. In a few instances the government might "license" itself to provide some product and thereby create a public monopoly. For example, in some states only state-owned retail outlets can sell liquor. Similarly, many states have "licensed" themselves to run lotteries.

Ownership or Control of Essential Resources

A monopolist can use private property as an obstacle to potential rivals. For example, a firm that owns or controls a resource essential to the production process can prohibit the entry of rival firms. At one time the International Nickel Company of Canada (now called Inco) controlled 90 percent of the world's known nickel reserves. A local firm may own all the nearby deposits of sand and gravel. And it is very difficult for new sports leagues to be created because existing professional sports leagues have contracts with the best players and have long-term leases on the major stadiums and arenas.

Pricing and Other Strategic Barriers to Entry

Even if a firm is not protected from entry by, say, extensive economies of scale or ownership of essential resources, entry may effectively be blocked by the way the monopolist responds to attempts by rivals to enter the industry. Confronted with a new entrant, the monopolist may "create an entry barrier" by slashing its price, stepping up its advertising, or taking other strategic actions to make it difficult for the entrant to succeed.

Examples of entry deterrence: In 2005 Dentsply, the dominant American maker of false teeth (70 percent market share) was found to have unlawfully precluded independent distributors of false teeth from carrying competing brands. The lack of access to the distributors deterred potential foreign competitors from entering the U.S. market. As another example, in 2001 a U.S. court of appeals upheld a lower court's finding that Microsoft used a series of illegal actions to maintain its monopoly in Intel-compatible PC operating systems (95 percent market share). One such action was charging higher prices for its Windows operating system to computer manufacturers that featured Netscape's Navigator rather than Microsoft's Internet Explorer.

Monopoly Demand

Now that we have explained the sources of monopoly, we want to build a model of pure monopoly so that we can analyze its price and output decisions. Let's start by making three assumptions:

- Patents, economies of scale, or resource ownership secures the firm's monopoly.
- No unit of government regulates the firm.
- The firm is a single-price monopolist; it charges the same price for all units of output.

The crucial difference between a pure monopolist and a purely competitive seller lies on the demand side of the market. The purely competitive seller faces a perfectly elastic demand at the price determined by market supply and demand. It is a price taker that can sell as much or as little as it wants at the going market price. Each additional unit sold will add the amount of the constant product price to the firm's total revenue. That means that marginal revenue for the competitive seller is constant and equal to product price. (Refer to Table 9.2 and Figure 9.1 for price, marginal-revenue, and total-revenue relationships for the purely competitive firm.)

The demand curve for the monopolist (and for any imperfectly competitive seller) is quite different from that of the pure competitor. Because the pure monopolist *is* the industry, its demand curve is *the market demand curve*. And because market demand is not perfectly elastic, the monopolist's demand curve is downsloping. Columns 1 and 2 in Table 10.1 illustrate this concept. Note that quantity demanded increases as price decreases.

TABLE 10.1 Revenue and Cost Data of a Pure Monopolist

	Revenue Data			Cost Data			
(1) Quantity of Output	(2) Price (Average Revenue)	(3) Total Revenue, (1) × (2)	(4) Marginal Revenue	(5) Average Total Cost	(6) Total Cost, (1) × (5)	(7) Marginal Cost	(8) Profit [+] or Loss [−]
0	$172	$ 0			$ 100		$−100
			$162			$ 90	
1	162	162		$190.00	190		−28
			142			80	
2	152	304		135.00	270		+34
			122			70	
3	142	426		113.33	340		+86
			102			60	
4	132	528		100.00	400		+128
			82			70	
5	122	610		94.00	470		+140
			62			80	
6	112	672		91.67	550		+122
			42			90	
7	102	714		91.43	640		+74
			22			110	
8	92	736		93.75	750		−14
			2			130	
9	82	738		97.78	880		−142
			−18			150	
10	72	720		103.00	1030		−310

In Chapter 9 we drew separate demand curves for the purely competitive industry and for a single firm in such an industry. But only a single demand curve is needed in pure monopoly because the firm and the industry are one and the same. We have graphed part of the demand data in Table 10.1 as demand curve *D* in Figure 10.2. This is the monopolist's demand curve *and* the market demand curve. The downward-sloping demand curve has three implications that are essential to understanding the monopoly model.

FIGURE 10.2 Price and marginal revenue in pure monopoly. A pure monopolist, or any other imperfect competitor with a downsloping demand curve such as *D*, must set a lower price in order to sell more output. Here, by charging $132 rather than $142, the monopolist sells an extra unit (the fourth unit) and gains $132 from that sale. But from this gain must be subtracted $30, which reflects the $10 less the monopolist charged for each of the first 3 units. Thus, the marginal revenue of the fourth unit is $102 (= $132 − $30), considerably less than its $132 price.

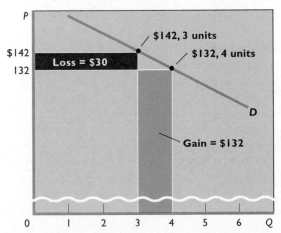

Marginal Revenue Is Less Than Price

With a fixed downsloping demand curve, the pure monopolist can increase sales only by charging a lower price. Consequently, marginal revenue—the change in total revenue associated with a one unit change in output—is less than price (average revenue) for every unit of output except the first. Why so? The reason is that the lower price of the extra unit of output also applies to all prior units of output. The monopolist could have sold these prior units at a higher price if it had not produced and sold the extra output. Each additional unit of output sold increases total revenue by an amount equal to its own price less the sum of the price cuts that apply to all prior units of output.

Figure 10.2 confirms this point. There, we have highlighted two price-quantity combinations from the monopolist's demand curve. The monopolist can sell 1 more unit at $132 than it can at $142 and that way obtain $132 (the blue area) of extra revenue. But to sell that fourth unit for $132, the monopolist must also sell the first 3 units at $132 rather than $142. The $10 reduction in revenue on 3 units results in a $30 revenue loss (the red area). The net difference in total revenue from selling a fourth unit is $102: the $132 gain from the fourth unit minus the $30 forgone on the first 3 units. This net gain (marginal revenue) of $102 from the fourth unit is clearly less than the $132 price of the fourth unit.

Column 4 in Table 10.1 shows that marginal revenue is always less than the corresponding product price in column 2, except for the first unit of output. Because marginal revenue is the change in total revenue associated with each additional unit of output, the declining amounts of marginal revenue in column 4 mean that total revenue increases at a diminishing rate (as shown in column 3).

We show the relationship between the monopolist's marginal-revenue curve and total-revenue curve in Figure 10.3. For this figure, we extended the demand and revenue data of columns 1 through 4 in Table 10.1, assuming that successive $10 price cuts each elicit 1 additional unit of sales. That is, the monopolist can sell 11 units at $62, 12 units at $52, and so on.

Note that the monopolist's MR curve lies below the demand curve, indicating that marginal revenue is less than price at every output quantity but the very first unit. Observe also the special relationship between total revenue (shown in the lower graph) and marginal revenue (shown in the top graph). Because marginal revenue is the change in total revenue, marginal revenue is positive while total revenue is increasing. When total revenue reaches its maximum, marginal revenue is zero. When total revenue is diminishing, marginal revenue is negative.

The Monopolist Is a Price Maker

All imperfect competitors, whether pure monopolists, oligopolists, or monopolistic competitors, face downward-sloping demand curves. So firms in those industries can to one degree or another influence total supply through their own output decisions. In changing market supply, they can also influence product price. Firms with downward-sloping demand curves are *price makers*.

This is most evident in pure monopoly, where one firm controls total output. The monopolist faces a downsloping demand curve in which each amount of output is associated with some unique price. Thus, in deciding on the quantity

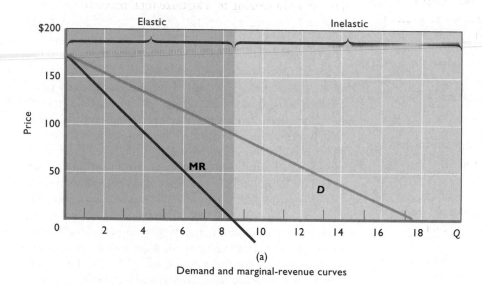

(a)
Demand and marginal-revenue curves

FIGURE 10.3 Demand, marginal revenue, and total revenue for a pure monopolist. (a) Because it must lower price on all units sold in order to increase its sales, an imperfectly competitive firm's marginal-revenue curve (MR) lies below its downsloping demand curve (D). The elastic and inelastic regions of demand are highlighted. (b) Total revenue (TR) increases at a decreasing rate, reaches a maximum, and then declines. Note that in the elastic region, TR is increasing and hence MR is positive. When TR reaches its maximum, MR is zero. In the inelastic region of demand, TR is declining, so MR is negative.

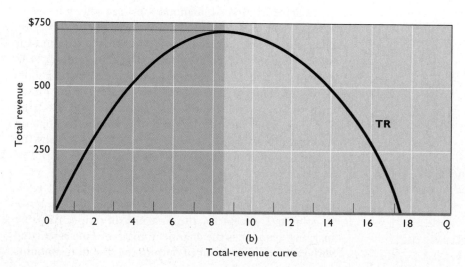

(b)
Total-revenue curve

of output to produce, the monopolist is also indirectly determining the price it will charge. Through control of output, it can "make the price." From columns 1 and 2 in Table 10.1 we find that the monopolist can charge a price of $72 if it produces and offers for sale 10 units, a price of $82 if it produces and offers for sale 9 units, and so forth.

The Monopolist Sets Prices in the Elastic Region of Demand

The total-revenue test for price elasticity of demand is the basis for our third implication. Recall from Chapter 6 that the total-revenue test reveals that when demand is elastic, a decline in price will increase total revenue. Similarly, when demand is inelastic, a decline in price will reduce total revenue. Beginning at the top of demand curve D in Figure 10.3a, observe that as the price declines from $172 to approximately $82, total revenue increases (and marginal revenue therefore is positive). This means that demand is elastic in this price range. Conversely, for price declines below $82, total revenue decreases (marginal revenue is negative), indicating that demand is inelastic there.

The implication is that a monopolist will never choose a price-quantity combination where price reductions cause total revenue to decrease (marginal revenue to be negative). The profit-maximizing monopolist will always want to avoid the inelastic segment of its demand curve in favor of some price-quantity combination in the elastic region. Here's why: To get into the inelastic region, the monopolist must lower price and increase output. In the inelastic region a lower price means less total revenue. And increased output always means increased total cost. Less total revenue and higher total cost yield lower profit. **(Key Question 4)**

QUICK REVIEW 10.1

- A pure monopolist is the sole supplier of a product or service for which there are no close substitutes.

- A monopoly survives because of entry barriers such as economies of scale, patents and licenses, the ownership of essential resources, and strategic actions to exclude rivals.

- The monopolist's demand curve is downsloping, and its marginal-revenue curve lies below its demand curve.

- The downsloping demand curve means that the monopolist is a price maker.

- The monopolist will operate in the elastic region of demand since in the inelastic region it can increase total revenue and reduce total cost by reducing output.

Output and Price Determination

At what specific price-quantity combination will a profit-maximizing monopolist choose to operate? To answer this question, we must add production costs to our analysis.

Cost Data

On the cost side, we will assume that although the firm is a monopolist in the product market, it hires resources competitively and employs the same technology as Chapter 9's competitive firm does. This lets us use the cost data we developed in Chapter 8 and applied in Chapter 9, so we can compare the price-output decisions of a pure monopoly with those of a pure competitor. Columns 5 through 7 in Table 10.1 restate the pertinent cost data from Table 8.2.

MR = MC Rule

A monopolist seeking to maximize total profit will employ the same rationale as a profit-seeking firm in a competitive industry. If producing is preferable to shutting down, it will produce up to the output at which marginal revenue equals marginal cost (MR = MC).

A comparison of columns 4 and 7 in Table 10.1 indicates that the profit-maximizing output is 5 units because the fifth unit is the last unit of output whose marginal revenue exceeds its marginal cost. What price will the monopolist charge? The demand schedule shown as columns 1 and 2 in Table 10.1 indicates there is only one price at which 5 units can be sold: $122.

This analysis is shown in **Figure 10.4 (Key Graph)**, where we have graphed the demand, marginal-revenue, average-total-cost, and marginal-cost data of Table 10.1. The profit-maximizing output occurs at 5 units of output (Q_m), where the marginal-revenue (MR) and marginal-cost (MC) curves intersect. There, MR = MC.

To find the price the monopolist will charge, we extend a vertical line from Q_m up to the demand curve D. The unique price P_m at which Q_m units can be sold is $122. In this case, it is the profit-maximizing price. The monopolist sets the quantity at Q_m to charge its profit-maximizing price of $122.

Columns 2 and 5 in Table 10.1 show that at 5 units of output, the product price ($122) exceeds the average total cost ($94). The monopolist thus obtains an economic profit of $28 per unit, and the total economic profit is $140 (= 5 units × $28). In Figure 10.4, per-unit profit is $P_m - A$, where A is the average total cost of producing Q_m units. Total economic profit is found by multiplying this per-unit profit by the profit-maximizing output Q_m.

INTERACTIVE GRAPHS

G 10.1

Monopoly

keygraph

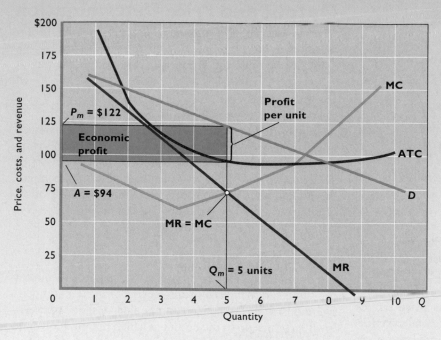

QUICK QUIZ FOR FIGURE 10.4

1. The MR curve lies below the demand curve in this figure because the:
   a. demand curve is linear (a straight line).
   b. demand curve is highly inelastic throughout its full length.
   c. demand curve is highly elastic throughout its full length.
   d. gain in revenue from an extra unit of output is less than the price charged for that unit of output.

2. The area labeled "Economic profit" can be found by multiplying the difference between P and ATC by quantity. It also can be found by:
   a. dividing profit per unit by quantity.
   b. subtracting total cost from total revenue.
   c. multiplying the coefficient of demand elasticity by quantity.
   d. multiplying the difference between P and MC by quantity.

3. This pure monopolist:
   a. charges the highest price that it could achieve.
   b. earns only a normal profit in the long run.
   c. restricts output to create an insurmountable entry barrier.
   d. restricts output to increase its price and total economic profit.

4. At this monopolist's profit-maximizing output:
   a. price equals marginal revenue.
   b. price equals marginal cost.
   c. price exceeds marginal cost.
   d. profit per unit is maximized.

Answers: 1. d; 2. b; 3. d; 4. c

Another way to determine the profit-maximizing output is by comparing total revenue and total cost at each possible level of production and choosing the output with the greatest positive difference. Use columns 3 and 6 in Table 10.1 to verify that 5 units is the profit-maximizing output. An accurate graphing of total revenue and total cost against output would also show the greatest difference (the maximum profit) at 5 units of output. Table 10.2 is a step-by-step summary

of the process for determining the profit-maximizing output, profit-maximizing price, and economic profit in pure monopoly. **(Key Question 5)**

No Monopoly Supply Curve

Recall that MR equals P in pure competition and that the supply curve of a purely competitive firm is determined by applying the MR ($= P$) = MC profit-maximizing rule. At any specific market-determined price, the purely competitive seller will maximize profit by supplying the quantity at which MC is equal to that price. When the market price

TABLE 10.2 Steps for Graphically Determining the Profit-Maximizing Output, Profit-Maximizing Price, and Economic Profit (if Any) in Pure Monopoly

Step 1.   Determine the profit-maximizing output by finding where MR = MC.

Step 2.   Determine the profit-maximizing price by extending a vertical line upward from the output determined in step 1 to the pure monopolist's demand curve.

Step 3.   Determine the pure monopolist's economic profit using one of two methods:

Method 1.   Find profit per unit by substracting the average total cost of the profit-maximizing output from the profit-maximizing price. Then multiply the difference by the profit-maximizing output to determine economic profit (if any).

Method 2.   Find total cost by multiplying the average total cost of the profit-maximizing output by that output. Find total revenue by multiplying the profit-maximizing output by the profit-maximizing price. Then subtract total cost from total revenue to determine economic profit (if any).

increases or decreases, the competitive firm produces more or less output. Each market price is thus associated with a specific output, and all such price-output pairs define the supply curve. This supply curve turns out to be the portion of the firm's MC curve that lies above the average-variable-cost curve (see Figure 9.6).

At first glance we would suspect that the pure monopolist's marginal-cost curve would also be its supply curve. But that is *not* the case. *The pure monopolist has no supply curve.* There is no unique relationship between price and quantity supplied for a monopolist. Like the competitive firm, the monopolist equates marginal revenue and marginal cost to determine output, but for the monopolist marginal revenue is less than price. Because the monopolist does not equate marginal cost to price, it is possible for different demand conditions to bring about different prices for the same output. To understand this point, refer to Figure 10.4 and pencil in a new, steeper marginal-revenue curve that intersects the marginal-cost curve at the same point as does the present marginal-revenue curve. Then draw in a new demand curve that is roughly consistent with your new marginal-revenue curve. With the new curves, the same MR = MC output of 5 units now means a higher profit-maximizing price. Conclusion: There is no single, unique price associated with each output level Q_m, and so there is no supply curve for the pure monopolist.

Misconceptions Concerning Monopoly Pricing

Our analysis exposes two fallacies concerning monopoly behavior.

Not Highest Price

Because a monopolist can manipulate output and price, people often believe it "will charge the highest price possible." That is incorrect. There are many prices above P_m in Figure 10.4, but the monopolist shuns them because they yield a smaller-than-maximum total profit. The monopolist seeks maximum total profit, not maximum price. Some high prices that could be charged would reduce sales and total revenue too severely to offset any decrease in total cost.

Total, Not Unit, Profit

The monopolist seeks maximum *total* profit, not maximum *unit* profit. In Figure 10.4 a careful comparison of the vertical distance between average total cost and price at various possible outputs indicates that per-unit profit is greater at a point slightly to the left of the profit-maximizing output Q_m. This is seen in Table 10.1, where unit profit at 4 units of output is $32 (= $132 − $100) compared with $28 (= $122 − $94) at the profit-maximizing output of 5 units. Here the monopolist accepts a lower-than-maximum per-unit profit because additional sales more than compensate for the lower unit profit. A profit-seeking monopolist would rather sell 5 units at a profit of $28 per unit (for a total profit of $140) than 4 units at a profit of $32 per unit (for a total profit of only $128).

Possibility of Losses by Monopolist

The likelihood of economic profit is greater for a pure monopolist than for a pure competitor. In the long run the pure competitor is destined to have only a normal profit, whereas barriers to entry mean that any economic profit realized by the monopolist can persist. In pure monopoly there are no new entrants to increase supply, drive down price, and eliminate economic profit.

But pure monopoly does not guarantee profit. The monopolist is not immune from changes in tastes that reduce the demand for its product. Nor is it immune from upward-shifting cost curves caused by escalating resource prices. If the demand and cost situation faced by the monopolist is far less favorable than that in Figure 10.4, the monopolist will incur losses in the short run. Despite its

FIGURE 10.5 **The loss-minimizing position of a pure monopolist.** If demand D is weak and costs are high, the pure monopolist may be unable to make a profit. Because P_m exceeds V, the average variable cost at the MR = MC output Q_m, the monopolist will minimize losses in the short run by producing at that output. The loss per unit is $A - P_m$, and the total loss is indicated by the red rectangle.

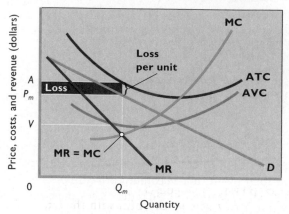

Like the pure competitor, the monopolist will not persist in operating at a loss. Faced with continuing losses, in the long run the firm's owners will move their resources to alternative industries that offer better profit opportunities. A monopolist such as the one depicted in Figure 10.5 must obtain a minimum of a normal profit in the long run or it will go out of business.

Economic Effects of Monopoly

Let's now evaluate pure monopoly from the standpoint of society as a whole. Our reference for this evaluation will be the outcome of long-run efficiency in a purely competitive market, identified by the triple equality $P = MC = $ minimum ATC.

Price, Output, and Efficiency

Figure 10.6 graphically contrasts the price, output, and efficiency outcomes of pure monopoly and a purely competitive *industry*. The $S = $ MC in Figure 10.6a, reminds us that the market supply curve S for a purely competitive industry is the horizontal sum of the marginal-cost curves of all the firms in the industry. Suppose there are 1000 such firms. Comparing their combined supply curves S with market demand D, we see that the purely competitive price and output are P_c and Q_c.

Recall that this price-output combination results in both productive efficiency and allocative efficiency.

dominance in the market (as, say, a seller of home sewing machines), the monopoly enterprise in Figure 10.5 suffers a loss, as shown, because of weak demand and relatively high costs. Yet it continues to operate for the time being because its total loss is less than its fixed cost. More precisely, at output Q_m the monopolist's price P_m exceeds its average variable cost V. Its loss per unit is $A - P_m$, and the total loss is shown by the red rectangle.

FIGURE 10.6 **Inefficiency of pure monopoly relative to a purely competitive industry.** (a) In a purely competitive industry, entry and exit of firms ensure that price (P_c) equals marginal cost (MC) and that the minimum average-total-cost output (Q_c) is produced. Both productive efficiency ($P = $ minimum ATC) and allocative efficiency ($P = $ MC) are obtained. (b) In pure monopoly, the MR curve lies below the demand curve. The monopolist maximizes profit at output Q_m, where MR = MC, and charges price P_m. Thus, output is lower (Q_m rather than Q_c) and price is higher (P_m rather than P_c) than they would be in a purely competitive industry. Monopoly is inefficient, since output is less than that required for achieving minimum ATC (here at Q_c) and because the monopolist's price exceeds MC. Monopoly creates an efficiency loss (here of area *abc*).

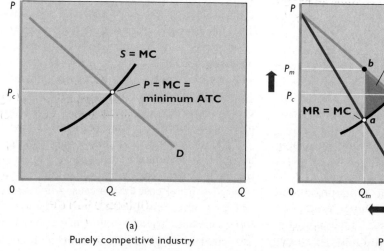
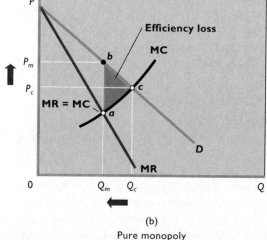

(a)
Purely competitive industry

(b)
Pure monopoly

Productive efficiency is achieved because free entry and exit force firms to operate where average total cost is at a minimum. The sum of the minimum-ATC outputs of the 1000 pure competitors is the industry output, here, Q_c. Product price is at the lowest level consistent with minimum average total cost. The *allocative efficiency* of pure competition results because production occurs up to that output at which price (the measure of a product's value or marginal benefit to society) equals marginal cost (the worth of the alternative products forgone by society in producing any given commodity). In short: $P = \text{MC} = \text{minimum ATC}$.

Now let's suppose that this industry becomes a pure monopoly (Figure 10.6b) as a result of one firm acquiring all its competitors. We also assume that no changes in costs or market demand result from this dramatic change in the industry structure. What formerly were 1000 competing firms is now a single pure monopolist consisting of 1000 noncompeting branches.

The competitive market supply curve S has become the marginal-cost curve (MC) of the monopolist, the summation of the MC curves of its many branch plants. (Since the monopolist does not have a supply curve, as such, we have removed the S label.) The important change, however, is on the demand side. From the viewpoint of each of the 1000 individual competitive firms, demand was perfectly elastic, and marginal revenue was therefore equal to price. Each firm equated MR (= price) and MC in maximizing profits. But market demand and individual demand are the same to the pure monopolist. The firm *is* the industry, and thus the monopolist sees the downsloping demand curve D shown in Figure 10.6b.

This means that marginal revenue is less than price, that graphically the MR curve lies below demand curve D. In using the MR = MC rule, the monopolist selects output Q_m and price P_m. A comparison of both graphs in Figure 10.6 reveals that the monopolist finds it profitable to sell a smaller output at a higher price than do the competitive producers.

Monopoly yields neither productive nor allocative efficiency. The monopolist's output is less than Q_c, the output at which average total cost is lowest. And price is higher than the competitive price P_c, which in long-run equilibrium in pure competition equals minimum average total cost. Thus the monopoly price *exceeds* minimum average total cost. Also, at the monopolist's Q_m output, product price is considerably higher than marginal cost, meaning that society values additional units of this monopolized product more highly than it values the alternative products the resources could otherwise produce. So the monopolist's profit-maximizing output results in an underallocation of resources. The monopolist finds it profitable to restrict output and therefore employ fewer resources than are justified from society's standpoint. So the monopolist does not achieve allocative efficiency.

As confirmed by the gray triangle labeled *abc* in Figure 10.6, monopoly creates an efficiency loss (or deadweight loss) for society. The sum of consumer surplus and producer surplus is not maximized. In monopoly, then:

- P exceeds MC.
- P exceeds lowest ATC.
- an efficiency loss occurs (the sum of consumer surplus + producer surplus is less than maximum).

Income Transfer

In general, monopoly transfers income from consumers to the stockholders who own the monopoly. Because of their market power, monopolists charge a higher price than would a purely competitive firm with the same costs. So monopolists in effect levy a "private tax" on consumers and often obtain substantial economic profits. These monopolistic profits are not equally distributed because corporate stock is largely owned by high-income groups. The owners of monopolistic enterprises thus tend to benefit at the expense of the consumers, who "overpay" for the product. Because, on average, these owners have more income than the buyers, monopoly increases income inequality.

Exception: If the buyers of a monopoly product are wealthier than the owners of the monopoly, the income transfer from consumers to owners may reduce income inequality. But, in general, this is not the case. In normal circumstances, monopoly contributes to income inequality.

Cost Complications

Our evaluation of pure monopoly has led us to conclude that, given identical costs, a purely monopolistic industry will charge a higher price, produce a smaller output, and allocate economic resources less efficiently than a purely competitive industry. These inferior results are rooted in the entry barriers characterizing monopoly.

Now we must recognize that costs may not be the same for purely competitive and monopolistic producers. The unit cost incurred by a monopolist may be either larger or smaller than that incurred by a purely competitive firm. There are four reasons why costs may differ: (1) economies of scale, (2) a factor called "X-inefficiency," (3) the need for monopoly-preserving expenditures, and (4) the "very long run" perspective, which allows for technological advance.

Economies of Scale Once Again Where economies of scale are extensive, market demand may not be sufficient to support a large number of competing firms, each producing at minimum efficient scale. In such cases, an industry of one or two firms would have a lower average total cost than would the same industry made up of numerous competitive firms. At the extreme, only a single firm—a natural monopoly—might be able to achieve the lowest long-run average total cost.

Some firms relating to new information technologies—for example, computer software, Internet service, and wireless communications—have displayed extensive economies of scale. As these firms have grown, their long-run average total costs have declined because of greater use of specialized inputs, the spreading of product development costs, and learning by doing. Also, *simultaneous consumption* and *network effects* have reduced costs.

A product's ability to satisfy a large number of consumers at the same time is called **simultaneous consumption** (or *nonrivalous consumption*). Dell Computers needs to produce a personal computer for each customer, but Microsoft needs to produce its Windows program only once. Then, at very low marginal cost, Microsoft delivers its program by disk or Internet to millions of consumers. Similar low cost of delivering product to additional customers is true for Internet service providers, music producers, and wireless communication firms. Because marginal costs are so low, the average total cost of output declines as more customers are added.

Network effects are present if the value of a product to each user, including existing users, increases as the total number of users rises. Good examples are computer software, cell phones, social networking software, palm computers, and other products related to the Internet. When other people have Internet service and devices to access it, a person can conveniently send e-mail messages to them. And when they have similar software, various documents, spreadsheets, and photos can be attached to the e-mail messages. The greater the number of persons connected to the system, the more the benefits of the product to each person are magnified.

Such network effects may drive a market toward monopoly because consumers tend to choose standard products that everyone else is using. The focused demand for these products permits their producers to grow rapidly and thus achieve economies of scale. Smaller firms, which either have higher-cost "right" products or "wrong" products, get acquired or go out of business.

Economists generally agree that some new information firms have not yet exhausted their economies of scale. But most economists question whether such firms are truly natural monopolies. Most firms eventually achieve their minimum efficient scale at less than the full size of the market. That means competition among firms is possible.

But even if natural monopoly develops, the monopolist is unlikely to pass cost reductions along to consumers as price reductions. So, with perhaps a handful of exceptions, economies of scale do not change the general conclusion that monopolies are inefficient relative to more competitive industries.

X-Inefficiency In constructing all the average-total-cost curves used in this book, we have assumed that the firm uses the most efficient existing technology. In other words, it uses the technology that permits it to achieve the lowest average total cost of whatever level of output it chooses to produce. **X-inefficiency** occurs when a firm produces output, whatever its level, at a higher cost than is necessary to produce it. In Figure 10.7 X-inefficiency is represented by operation at points X and X' above the lowest-cost ATC curve. At these points, per-unit costs are ATC_X (as opposed to ATC_1) for output Q_1 and $ATC_{X'}$ (as opposed to ATC_2) for

> **ORIGIN OF THE IDEA**
> **O 10.3**
> X-inefficiency

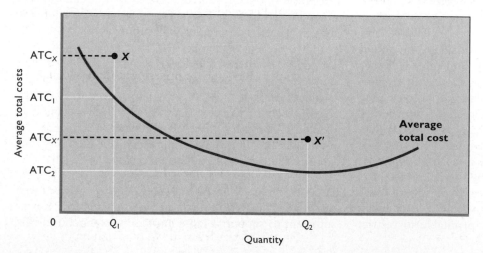

FIGURE 10.7 X-inefficiency. The average-total-cost curve (ATC) is assumed to reflect the minimum cost of producing each particular level of output. Any point above this "lowest-cost" ATC curve, such as X or X', implies X-inefficiency: operation at greater than lowest cost for a particular level of output.

output Q_2. Producing at any point above the average-total-cost curve in Figure 10.7 reflects inefficiency or "bad management" by the firm.

Why is X-inefficiency allowed to occur if it reduces profits? The answer is that managers may have goals, such as expanding power, an easier work life, avoiding business risk, or giving jobs to incompetent relatives, that conflict with cost minimization. Or X-inefficiency may arise because a firm's workers are poorly motivated or ineffectively supervised. Or a firm may simply become lethargic and inert, relying on rules of thumb in decision making as opposed to relevant calculations of costs and revenues.

For our purposes the relevant question is whether monopolistic firms tend more toward X-inefficiency than competitive producers do. Presumably they do. Firms in competitive industries are continually under pressure from rivals, forcing them to be internally efficient to survive. But monopolists are sheltered from such competitive forces by entry barriers, and that lack of pressure may lead to X-inefficiency.

Rent-Seeking Expenditures Rent-seeking behavior is any activity designed to transfer income or wealth to a particular firm or resource supplier at someone else's, or even society's, expense. We have seen that a monopolist can obtain an economic profit even in the long run. Therefore, it is no surprise that a firm may go to great expense to acquire or maintain a monopoly granted by government through legislation or an exclusive license. Such rent-seeking expenditures add nothing to the firm's output, but they clearly increase its costs. Taken alone, rent-seeking implies that monopoly involves higher costs and less efficiency than suggested in Figure 10.6b.

Technological Advance In the very long run, firms can reduce their costs through the discovery and implementation of new technology. If monopolists are more likely than competitive producers to develop more efficient production techniques over time, then the inefficiency of monopoly might be overstated. Since research and development (R&D) is the topic of optional Web Chapter 11W, we will provide only a brief assessment here.

The general view of economists is that a pure monopolist will not be technologically progressive. Although its economic profit provides ample means to finance research and development, it has little incentive to implement new techniques (or products). The absence of competitors means that there is no external pressure for technological advance in a monopolized market. Because of its sheltered market position, the pure monopolist can afford to be inefficient and lethargic; there simply is no major penalty for being so.

One caveat: Research and technological advance may be one of the monopolist's barriers to entry. Thus, the monopolist may continue to seek technological advance to avoid falling prey to new rivals. In this case technological advance is essential to the maintenance of monopoly. But then it is *potential* competition, not the monopoly market structure, that is driving the technological advance. By assumption, no such competition exists in the pure monopoly model; entry is completely blocked.

Assessment and Policy Options

Monopoly is a legitimate concern. Monopolists can charge higher-than-competitive prices that result in an underallocation of resources to the monopolized product. They can stifle innovation, engage in rent-seeking behavior, and foster X-inefficiency. Even when their costs are low because of economies of scale, there is no guarantee that the price they charge will reflect those low costs. The cost savings may simply accrue to the monopoly as greater economic profit.

Fortunately, however, monopoly is not widespread in the United States. Barriers to entry are seldom completely successful. Although research and technological advance may strengthen the market position of a monopoly, technology may also undermine monopoly power. Over time, the creation of new technologies may work to destroy monopoly positions. For example, the development of courier delivery, fax machines, and e-mail has eroded the monopoly power of the U.S. Postal Service. Cable television monopolies are now challenged by satellite TV and by new technologies that permit the transmission of audio and visual signals over the Internet.

Similarly, patents eventually expire; and even before they do, the development of new and distinct substitutable products often circumvents existing patent advantages. New sources of monopolized resources sometimes are found and competition from foreign firms may emerge. (See Global Perspective 10.1.) Finally, if a monopoly is sufficiently fearful of future competition from new products, it may keep its prices relatively low so as to discourage rivals from developing such products. If so, consumers may pay nearly competitive prices even though competition is currently lacking.

So what should government do about monopoly when it arises in the real world? Economists agree that government needs to look carefully at monopoly on a case-by-case basis. Three general policy options are available:

- If the monopoly is achieved and sustained through anticompetitive actions, creates substantial economic inefficiency, and appears to be long-lasting, the government can file charges against the monopoly under the antitrust laws. If found guilty of monopoly abuse, the firm can either be expressly prohibited from engaging in certain business activities or be broken into two or more competing firms. An example of the breakup approach was the dissolution of Standard Oil into several competing firms in 1911. In contrast, in 2001 an appeals court overruled a lower-court decision to divide Microsoft into two firms. Instead, Microsoft was prohibited from engaging in a number of specific anticompetitive business activities. (We discuss the antitrust laws and the Microsoft case in Chapter 18.)

- If the monopoly is a natural monopoly, society can allow it to continue to expand. If no competition emerges from new products, government may then decide to regulate its prices and operations. (We discuss this option later in this chapter and also in Chapter 18.)

- If the monopoly appears to be unsustainable over a long period of time, say, because of emerging new technology, society can simply choose to ignore it. (In Web Chapter 11W, we discuss the potential for real-world monopoly to collapse in the very long run.)

QUICK REVIEW 10.2

- The monopolist maximizes profit (or minimizes loss) at the output where $MR = MC$ and charges the price that corresponds to that output on its demand curve.

- The monopolist has no supply curve, since any of several prices can be associated with a specific quantity of output supplied.

- Assuming identical costs, a monopolist will be less efficient than a purely competitive industry because the monopolist produces less output and charges a higher price.

- The inefficiencies of monopoly may be offset or lessened by economies of scale and, less likely, by technological progress, but they may be intensified by the presence of X-inefficiency and rent-seeking expenditures.

Price Discrimination

We have assumed in this chapter that the monopolist charges a single price to all buyers. But under certain conditions the monopolist can increase its profit by charging different prices to different buyers. In so doing, the monopolist is engaging in **price discrimination,** the practice of selling a specific product at more than one price when the price differences are not justified by cost differences. Price discrimination can take three forms:

ORIGIN OF THE IDEA
O 10.4
Price discrimination

- Charging each customer in a single market the maximum price she or he is willing to pay.

- Charging each customer one price for the first set of units purchased and a lower price for subsequent units purchased.

- Charging some customers one price and other customers another price.

Conditions

The opportunity to engage in price discrimination is not readily available to all sellers. Price discrimination is possible when the following conditions are met:

- *Monopoly power* The seller must be a monopolist or, at least, must possess some degree of monopoly power, that is, some ability to control output and price.

- *Market segregation* At relatively low cost to itself, the seller must be able to segregate buyers into distinct classes, each of which has a different willingness or ability to pay for the product. This separation of buyers is usually based on different price elasticities of demand, as the examples below will make clear.

- *No resale* The original purchaser cannot resell the product or service. If buyers in the low-price segment of the market could easily resell in the high-price segment, the monopolist's price-discrimination strategy would create competition in the high-price segment. This competition would reduce the price in the high-price segment and undermine the monopolist's price-discrimination policy. This condition suggests that service industries such as the transportation industry or legal and medical services, where resale is impossible, are good candidates for price discrimination.

Examples of Price Discrimination

Price discrimination is widely practiced in the U.S. economy. For example, we noted in Chapter 6's Last Word that airlines charge high fares to business travelers, whose demand for travel is inelastic, and offer lower, highly restricted, nonrefundable fares to attract vacationers and others whose demands are more elastic.

Electric utilities frequently segment their markets by end uses, such as lighting and heating. The absence of reasonable lighting substitutes means that the demand for electricity for illumination is inelastic and that the price per kilowatt-hour for such use is high. But the availability of natural gas and petroleum for heating makes the demand for electricity for this purpose less inelastic and the price lower.

Movie theaters and golf courses vary their charges on the basis of time (for example, higher evening and weekend rates) and age (for example, lower rates for children, senior discounts). Railroads vary the rate charged per ton-mile of freight according to the market value of the product being shipped. The shipper of 10 tons of television sets or refrigerators is charged more than the shipper of 10 tons of gravel or coal.

The issuance of discount coupons, redeemable at purchase, is a form of price discrimination. It enables firms to give price discounts to their most price-sensitive customers who have elastic demand. Less price-sensitive consumers who have less elastic demand are not as likely to take the time to clip and redeem coupons. The firm thus makes a larger profit than if it had used a single-price, no-coupon strategy.

Finally, price discrimination often occurs in international trade. A Russian aluminum producer, for example, might sell aluminum for less in the United States than in Russia. In the United States, this seller faces an elastic demand because several substitute suppliers are available. But in Russia, where the manufacturer dominates the market and trade barriers impede imports, consumers have fewer choices and thus demand is less elastic.

Price Discrimination at the Ballpark

Take me out to the ball game . . .

Buy me some peanuts and Cracker Jack . . .

Professional baseball teams earn substantial revenues through ticket sales. To maximize profit, they offer significantly lower ticket prices for children (whose demand is elastic) than for adults (whose demand is inelastic). This discount may be as much as 50 percent.

If this type of price discrimination increases revenue and profit, why don't teams also price discriminate at the concession stands? Why don't they offer half-price hot dogs, soft drinks, peanuts, and Cracker Jack to children?

The answer involves the three requirements for successful price discrimination. All three requirements are met for game tickets: (1) The team has monopoly power; (2) it can segregate ticket buyers by age group, each group having a different elasticity of demand; and (3) children cannot resell their discounted tickets to adults.

It's a different situation at the concession stands. Specifically, the third condition is *not* met. If the team had dual prices, it could not prevent the exchange or "resale" of the concession goods from children to adults. Many adults would send children to buy food and soft drinks for them: "Here's some money, Billy. Go buy *six* hot dogs." In this case, price discrimination would reduce, not increase, team profit. Thus, children and adults are charged the same high prices at the concession stands. (These prices are high relative to those for the same goods at the local convenience store because the stadium sellers have a captive audience and thus considerable monopoly power.)

Graphical Analysis

Figure 10.8 demonstrates graphically the most frequently seen form of price discrimination—charging different prices to different classes of buyers. The two side-to-side graphs are for a single pure monopolist selling its product, say, software, in two segregated parts of the market. Figure 10.8a illustrates demand for software by small-business customers; Figure 10.8b, the demand for software by students. Student versions of the software are identical to the versions sold to businesses but are available (1 per person) only to customers with a student ID. Presumably, students have lower ability to pay for the software and are charged a discounted price.

FIGURE 10.8 **Price discrimination to different groups of buyers.** The price-discriminating monopolist represented here maximizes its total profit by dividing the market into two segments based on differences in elasticity of demand. It then produces and sells the MR = MC output in each market segment. (For visual clarity, average total cost (ATC) is assumed to be constant. Therefore MC equals ATC at all output levels.) (a) The firm charges a higher price (here, P_b) to customers who have a less elastic demand curve and (b) a lower price (here, P_s) to customers with a more elastic demand. The price discriminator's total profit is larger than it would be with no discrimination and therefore a single price.

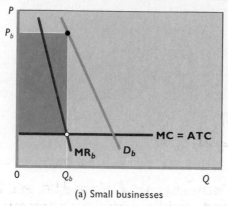

(a) Small businesses

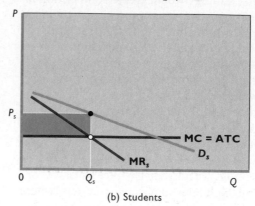

(b) Students

The demand curve D_b in the graph to the left indicates a relatively inelastic demand for the product on the part of business customers. The demand curve D_s in the righthand graph reflects the more elastic demand of students. The marginal revenue curves (MR_b and MR_s) lie below their respective demand curves, reflecting the demand–marginal revenue relationship previously described.

For visual clarity we have assumed that average total cost (ATC) is constant. Therefore marginal cost (MC) equals average total cost (ATC) at all quantities of output. These costs are the same for both versions of the software and therefore appear as the identical straight lines labeled "MC = ATC."

What price will the pure monopolist charge to each set of customers? Using the MR = MC rule for profit

WORKED PROBLEMS

W 10.2

Price discrimination

maximization, the firm will offer Q_b units of the software for sale to small businesses. It can sell that profit-maximizing output by charging price P_b. Again using the MR = MC rule, the monopolist will offer Q_s units of software to students. To sell those Q_s units, the firm will charge students the lower price P_s.

Firms engage in price discrimination because it enhances their profit. The numbers (not shown) behind the curves in Figure 10.8 would clearly reveal that the sum of the two profit rectangles shown in green exceeds the single profit rectangle the firm would obtain from a single monopoly price. How do consumers fare? In this case, students clearly benefit by paying a lower price than they would if the firm charged a single monopoly price; in contrast, the price discrimination results in a higher price for business customers. Therefore, compared to the single-price situation, students buy more of the software and small businesses buy less.

Such price discrimination is widespread in the economy and is illegal only when it is part of a firm's strategy to lessen or eliminate competition. We will discuss illegal price discrimination in Chapter 18, which covers antitrust policy. **(Key Question 6)**

Regulated Monopoly

Natural monopolies traditionally have been subject to *rate regulation* (price regulation), although the recent trend has been to deregulate wherever competition seems possible. For example, long-distance telephone calls, natural gas distribution, wireless communications, cable television, and long-distance electricity transmission have been, to one degree or another, deregulated over the past several decades. And regulators in some states are beginning to allow new entrants to compete with existing local telephone and electricity providers. Nevertheless, state and local regulatory commissions still regulate the prices that most local natural gas distributors, regional telephone companies, and local electricity suppliers can charge. These locally regulated monopolies are commonly called "public utilities."

Let's consider the regulation of a local natural monopoly, for example, a firm selling natural gas. Figure 10.9 shows the demand and the long-run cost curves facing our

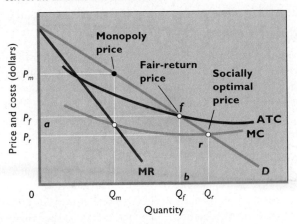

FIGURE 10.9 Regulated monopoly. The socially optimal price P_r, found where D and MC intersect, will result in an efficient allocation of resources but may entail losses to the monopoly. The fair-return price P_f will allow the monopolist to break even but will not fully correct the underallocation of resources.

Confronted with the legal price P_r, the monopolist will maximize profit or minimize loss by producing Q_r units of output because at this output MR $(- P_r) = $ MC. By making it illegal to charge more than P_r per unit, the regulatory agency has removed the monopolist's incentive to restrict output to Q_m to obtain a higher price and greater profit.

In short, the regulatory commission can simulate the allocative forces of pure competition by imposing the legal price P_r and letting the monopolist choose its profit-maximizing or loss-minimizing output. Production takes place where $P_r = $ MC, and this equality indicates an efficient allocation of resources to this product or service. The price that achieves allocative efficiency is called the **socially optimal price.**

Fair-Return Price: $P = $ ATC

But the socially optimal price P_r that equals marginal cost may be so low that average total costs are not covered, as is the case in Figure 10.9. The result is a loss for the firm. The reason lies in the basic character of our firm. Because it is required to meet the heaviest "peak" demands (both daily and seasonally) for natural gas, it has substantial excess production capacity when demand is relatively "normal." Its high level of investment in production facilities and economies of scale mean that its average total cost is likely to be greater than its marginal cost over a very wide range of outputs. In particular, as in Figure 10.9, average total cost is likely to be greater than the price P_r at the intersection of the demand curve and marginal-cost curve. Therefore, forcing the socially optimal price P_r on the regulated monopolist would result in short-run losses and long-run bankruptcy for the utility.

What to do? One option is to provide a public subsidy to cover the loss that marginal-cost pricing would entail. Another possibility is to condone price discrimination, allow the monopolist to charge some groups of customers prices above P_r, and hope that the additional revenue gained will permit the firm to cover costs.

In practice, regulatory commissions often have pursued a third option: They modify the objective of allocative efficiency and $P = $ MC pricing. Most regulatory agencies in the United States establish a **fair-return price.** They do so because the courts have ruled that a socially optimal price leading to losses and bankruptcy deprives the monopoly's owners of their private property without due process of law. The Supreme Court has held that regulatory agencies must permit a "fair return" to utility owners.

Remembering that total cost includes a normal or "fair" profit, we see in Figure 10.9 that a fair-return price should be on the average-total-cost curve. Because the demand

firm. Because of extensive economies of scale, the demand curve cuts the natural monopolist's long-run average-total-cost curve at a point where that curve is still falling. It would be inefficient to have several firms in this industry because each would produce a much smaller output, operating well to the left on the long-run average-total-cost curve. In short, each firm's lowest average total cost would be substantially higher than that of a single firm. So efficient, low-cost production requires a single seller.

We know by application of the MR = MC rule that Q_m and P_m are the profit-maximizing output and price that an unregulated monopolist would choose. Because price exceeds average total cost at output Q_m, the monopolist enjoys a substantial economic profit. Furthermore, price exceeds marginal cost, indicating an underallocation of resources to this product or service. Can government regulation bring about better results from society's point of view?

Socially Optimal Price: $P = $ MC

If the objective of a regulatory commission is to achieve allocative efficiency, it should attempt to establish a legal (ceiling) price for the monopolist that is equal to marginal cost. Remembering that each point on the market demand curve designates a price-quantity combination, and noting that the marginal-cost curve cuts the demand curve only at point r, we see that P_r is the only price on the demand curve equal to marginal cost. The maximum or ceiling price effectively causes the monopolist's demand curve to become horizontal (indicating perfectly elastic demand) from zero out to point r, where the regulated price ceases to be effective. Also, out to point r we have MR = P_r.

De Beers' Diamonds: Are Monopolies Forever?

De Beers Was One of the World's Strongest and Most Enduring Monopolies. But in Mid-2000 It Announced That It Could No Longer Control the Supply of Diamonds and Thus Would Abandon Its 66-Year Policy of Monopolizing the Diamond Trade.

De Beers, a Swiss-based company controlled by a South African corporation, produces about 45 percent of the world's rough-cut diamonds and purchases for resale a sizable number of the rough-cut diamonds produced by other mines worldwide. As a result, De Beers markets about 55 percent of the world's diamonds to a select group of diamond cutters and dealers. But that percentage has declined from 80 percent in the mid-1980s. Therein lies the company's problem.

Classic Monopoly Behavior

De Beers' past monopoly behavior and results are a classic example of the unregulated monopoly model illustrated in Figure 10.4. No matter how many diamonds it mined or purchased, it sold only the quantity of diamonds that would yield an "appropriate" (monopoly) price. That price was well above production costs, and De Beers and its partners earned monopoly profits.

When demand fell, De Beers reduced its sales to maintain price. The excess of production over sales was then reflected in growing diamond stockpiles held by De Beers. It also attempted to bolster demand through advertising ("Diamonds are forever"). When demand was strong, it increased sales by reducing its diamond inventories.

De Beers used several methods to control the production of many mines it did not own. First, it convinced a number of independent producers that "single-channel" or monopoly marketing through De Beers would maximize their profit. Second, mines that circumvented De Beers often found their market suddenly flooded with similar diamonds from De Beers' vast stockpiles. The resulting price decline and loss of profit often would encourage a "rogue" mine into the De Beers fold. Finally, De Beers simply purchased and stockpiled diamonds produced by independent mines so that their added supplies would not "undercut" the market.

An End of an Era? Several factors have come together to unravel the monopoly. New diamond discoveries resulted in a growing leakage of diamonds into world markets outside De Beers' control. For example, significant prospecting and trading in Angola occurred. Recent diamond discoveries in Canada's Northwest Territories pose another threat. Although De Beers is a participant in that region, a large uncontrolled supply of diamonds is expected to emerge. Similarly, Russia's diamond monopoly Alrosa recently agreed with European antitrust authorities to sell progressively larger quantities of diamonds directly to the international diamond market rather than continuing to market them through De Beers.

If that was not enough, Australian diamond producer Argyle opted to withdraw from the De Beers monopoly. Its annual production of mostly low-grade industrial diamonds accounts for about 6 percent of the global $8 billion diamond market. Moreover, the international media began to focus heavily on the role that diamonds play in financing the bloody civil wars in Africa. Fearing a consumer boycott of diamonds, De Beers pledged not to buy these "conflict" diamonds or do business with any firms that did. These diamonds, however, continue to find their way into the marketplace, eluding De Beers' control.

In mid-2000 De Beers abandoned its attempt to control the supply of diamonds. It announced that it planned to transform itself from a diamond cartel to a modern firm selling "premium" diamonds and other luxury goods under the De Beers label. It therefore would gradually reduce its $4 billion stockpile of diamonds and turn its efforts to increasing the overall demand for diamonds through advertising. De Beers proclaimed that it was changing its strategy to being "the diamond supplier of choice."

Diamonds may be forever, but the DeBeers diamond monopoly was not. Nevertheless, with its high market share and ability to control its own production levels, De Beers will continue to wield considerable influence over the price of rough-cut diamonds.

curve cuts average total cost only at point f, clearly P_f is the only price on the demand curve that permits a fair return. The corresponding output at regulated price P_f will be Q_f. Total revenue of $0afb$ will equal the utility's total cost of the same amount, and the firm will realize a normal profit.

Dilemma of Regulation

Comparing results of the socially optimal price ($P = MC$) and the fair-return price ($P = ATC$) suggests a policy dilemma, sometimes termed the *dilemma of regulation*. When its price is set to achieve the most efficient allocation of resources ($P = MC$), the regulated monopoly is likely to suffer losses. Survival of the firm would presumably depend on permanent public subsidies out of tax revenues. On the other hand, although a fair-return price ($P = ATC$) allows the monopolist to cover costs, it only partially resolves the underallocation of resources that the unregulated monopoly price would foster. That is, the fair-return price would increase output only from Q_m to Q_f in Figure 10.9, while the socially optimal output is Q_r. Despite this dilemma, regulation can improve on the results of monopoly from the social point of view. Price regulation (even at the fair-return price) can simultaneously reduce price, increase output, and reduce the economic profits of monopolies. **(Key Question 12)**

That said, we need to provide an important caution: "Fair-price" regulation of monopoly looks rather simple in theory but is amazingly complex in reality. In the actual economy, rate regulation is accompanied by large, expensive rate-setting bureaucracies and maze-like sets of procedures. Also, rate-decisions require extensive public input via letters and through public hearings. Rate decisions are subject to lengthy legal challenges. Further, because regulatory commissions must set prices sufficiently above costs to create fair returns, regulated monopolists have little incentive to minimize average total costs. When these costs creep up, the regulatory commissions must set higher prices.

Regulated firms therefore are noted for higher-than-competitive wages, more managers and staff than necessary, nicer-than-typical office buildings, and other forms of X-inefficiency. These inefficiencies help explain the trend of Federal, state, and local governments abandoning price regulation where the possibility of competition looks promising.

QUICK REVIEW 10.3

- Price discrimination occurs when a firm sells a product at different prices that are not based on cost differences.
- The conditions necessary for price discrimination are (a) monopoly power, (b) the ability to segregate buyers on the basis of demand elasticities, and (c) the inability of buyers to resell the product.
- Compared with single pricing by a monopolist, perfect price discrimination results in greater profit and greater output. Many consumers pay higher prices, but other buyers pay prices below the single price.
- Monopoly price can be reduced and output increased through government regulation.
- The socially optimal price ($P = MC$) achieves allocative efficiency but may result in losses; the fair-return price ($P = ATC$) yields a normal profit but fails to achieve allocative efficiency.

Summary

1. A pure monopolist is the sole producer of a commodity for which there are no close substitutes.

2. The existence of pure monopoly and other imperfectly competitive market structures is explained by barriers to entry in the form of (a) economies of scale, (b) patent ownership and research, (c) ownership or control of essential resources, and (d) pricing and other strategic behavior.

3. The pure monopolist's market situation differs from that of a competitive firm in that the monopolist's demand curve is downsloping, causing the marginal-revenue curve to lie below the demand curve. Like the competitive seller, the pure monopolist will maximize profit by equating marginal revenue and marginal cost. Barriers to entry may permit a monopolist to acquire economic profit even in the long run. However, (a) the monopolist does not charge "the highest price possible"; (b) the price that yields maximum total profit to the monopolist rarely coincides with the price that yields maximum unit profit; (c) high costs and a weak demand may prevent the monopolist from realizing any profit at all; and (d) the monopolist avoids the inelastic region of its demand curve.

4. With the same costs, the pure monopolist will find it profitable to restrict output and charge a higher price than would sellers in a purely competitive industry. This restriction of output causes resources to be misallocated, as is evidenced by the fact that price exceeds marginal cost in monopolized markets. Monopoly creates an efficiency loss (or deadweight loss) for society.

5. In general, monopoly transfers income from consumers to the owners of the monopoly. Because, on average, consumers of monopolized products have less income than the corporate owners, monopoly increases income inequality.

6. The costs monopolists and competitive producers face may not be the same. On the one hand, economies of scale may make lower unit costs available to monopolists but not to competitors. Also, pure monopoly may be more likely than pure competition to reduce costs via technological advance because of the monopolist's ability to realize economic profit, which can be used to finance research. On the other hand, X-inefficiency—the failure to produce with the least costly combination of inputs—is more common among monopolists than among competitive firms. Also, monopolists may make costly expenditures to maintain monopoly privileges that are conferred by government. Finally, the blocked entry

of rival firms weakens the monopolist's incentive to be technologically progressive.

7. A monopolist can increase its profit by practicing price discrimination, provided (a) it can segregate buyers on the basis of elasticities of demand and (b) its product or service cannot be readily transferred between the segregated markets.

8. Price regulation can be invoked to eliminate wholly or partially the tendency of monopolists to underallocate resources and to earn economic profits. The socially optimal price is determined where the demand and marginal-cost curves intersect; the fair-return price is determined where the demand and average-total-cost curves intersect.

Terms and Concepts

pure monopoly

barriers to entry

simultaneous consumption

network effects

X-inefficiency

rent-seeking behavior

price discrimination

socially optimal price

fair-return price

Study Questions

1. "No firm is completely sheltered from rivals; all firms compete for consumer dollars. If that is so, then pure monopoly does not exist." Do you agree? Explain. How might you use Chapter 6's concept of cross elasticity of demand to judge whether monopoly exists? **LO1**

2. Discuss the major barriers to entry into an industry. Explain how each barrier can foster either monopoly or oligopoly. Which barriers, if any, do you feel give rise to monopoly that is socially justifiable? **LO1**

3. How does the demand curve faced by a purely monopolistic seller differ from that confronting a purely competitive firm? Why does it differ? Of what significance is the difference? Why is the pure monopolist's demand curve not perfectly inelastic? **LO1**

4. **KEY QUESTION** Use the demand schedule to the upper right to calculate total revenue and marginal revenue at each quantity. Plot the demand, total-revenue, and marginal-revenue curves and explain the relationships between them. Explain why the marginal revenue of the fourth unit of output is $3.50, even though its price is $5. Use Chapter 6's total-revenue test for price elasticity to designate the elastic and inelastic segments of your graphed demand curve. What generalization can you make as to the relationship between marginal revenue and elasticity of demand? Suppose the marginal cost of successive units of output was zero. What output would the profit-seeking firm produce? Finally, use your analysis to explain why a monopolist would never produce in the inelastic region of demand. **LO1**

Price (P)	Quantity Demanded (Q)	Price (P)	Quantity Demanded (Q)
$7.00	0	$4.50	5
6.50	1	4.00	6
6.00	2	3.50	7
5.50	3	3.00	8
5.00	4	2.50	9

5. **KEY QUESTION** Suppose a pure monopolist is faced with the demand schedule shown below and the same cost data as the competitive producer discussed in question 4 at the end of Chapter 9. Calculate the missing total-revenue and marginal-revenue amounts, and determine the profit-maximizing price and profit-earning output for this monopolist. What is the monopolist's profit? Verify your answer graphically and by comparing total revenue and total cost. **LO2**

Price	Quantity Demanded	Total Revenue	Marginal Revenue
$115	0	$_____	
100	1	_____	$_____
83	2	_____	_____
71	3	_____	_____
63	4	_____	_____
55	5	_____	_____
48	6	_____	_____
42	7	_____	_____
37	8	_____	_____
33	9	_____	_____
29	10	_____	_____

6. **KEY QUESTION** Suppose that a price discriminating monopolist has segregated its market into two groups of buyers, the first group described by the demand and revenue data that you developed for question 5. The demand and revenue data for the second group of buyers is shown in the accompanying table. Assume that MC is $13 in both markets and MC = ATC at all output levels. What price will the firm charge in each market? Based solely on these two prices, what can you conclude about the relative elasticities of demand in the two markets? What will be this monopolist's total economic profit? **LO4**

Price	Quantity Demanded	Total Revenue	Marginal Revenue
$71	0	$ 0	
63	1	63	$63
55	2	110	47
48	3	144	34
42	4	168	24
37	5	185	17
33	6	198	13
29	7	203	5

7. Assume that a pure monopolist and a purely competitive firm have the same unit costs. Contrast the two with respect to (a) price, (b) output, (c) profits, (d) allocation of resources, and (e) impact on the distribution of income. Since both monopolists and competitive firms follow the MC = MR rule in maximizing profits, how do you account for the different results? Why might the costs of a purely competitive firm and those of a monopolist be different? What are the implications of such a cost difference? **LO3**

8. Critically evaluate and explain each statement: **LO3**
   a. Because they can control product price, monopolists are always assured of profitable production by simply charging the highest price consumers will pay.
   b. The pure monopolist seeks the output that will yield the greatest per-unit profit.

c. An excess of price over marginal cost is the market's way of signaling the need for more production of a good.
d. The more profitable a firm, the greater its monopoly power.
e. The monopolist has a pricing policy; the competitive producer does not.
f. With respect to resource allocation, the interests of the seller and of society coincide in a purely competitive market but conflict in a monopolized market.
g. In a sense the monopolist makes a profit for not producing; the monopolist produces profit more than it does goods.

9. Assume a monopolistic publisher has agreed to pay an author 15 percent of the total revenue from the sales of a text. Will the author and the publisher want to charge the same price for the text? Explain. **LO3**

10. U.S. pharmaceutical companies charge different prices for prescription drugs to buyers in different nations, depending on elasticity of demand and government-imposed price ceilings. Explain why these companies, for profit reasons, oppose laws allowing reimportation of drugs to the United States. **LO4**

11. Explain verbally and graphically how price (rate) regulation may improve the performance of monopolies. In your answer distinguish between (a) socially optimal (marginal-cost) pricing and (b) fair-return (average-total-cost) pricing. What is the "dilemma of regulation"? **LO2**

12. **KEY QUESTION** It has been proposed that natural monopolists should be allowed to determine their profit-maximizing outputs and prices and then government should tax their profits away and distribute them to consumers in proportion to their purchases from the monopoly. Is this proposal as socially desirable as requiring monopolists to equate price with marginal cost or average total cost? **LO3**

13. **LAST WORD** How was De Beers able to control the world price of diamonds over the past several decades even though it produced only 45 percent of the diamonds? What factors ended its monopoly? What is its new strategy for earning economic profit, rather than just normal profit?

Web-Based Questions

1. **IS MICROSOFT A MONOPOLY—WHAT DID THE COURTS CONCLUDE?** In 2002 a U.S. court of appeals imposed remedies relating to a lower court's findings that Microsoft had a monopoly in personal computer (PC) operating systems and had maintained its monopoly through illegal actions. At the U.S. Justice Department's Web site, **www.usdoj.gov,** use the DOJ Agencies listing to find Antitrust Division and then Antitrust Case Filings. Locate *U.S. v. Microsoft* and select District Court filings and then Court's Findings of Fact (11/5/99). On what basis did the court conclude that Microsoft was a monopoly (see Market Share)? What was Microsoft's market share of Intel-compatible PC operating systems? Of all operating systems, including those of Apple computers? What evidence did the court cite in claiming that Microsoft charged above-competitive prices (see Microsoft's Pricing Behavior)?

2. **GETTING TO KNOW YOUR STATE REGULATORY COMMISSION** Go to **www.yahoo.com** or some other standard search engine and type "public utility commissions" in the search box. Find the utilities commission for the state where you reside (or another state if you cannot find the Web site for your state commission). What industries does the state commission regulate? How many specific firms are registered or regulated? List the names of 10 such specific firms. Why are these and the other firms regulated?

FURTHER TEST YOUR KNOWLEDGE AT
www.mcconnell18e.com

11

Monopolistic Competition and Oligopoly

Most markets in the U.S. economy fall between the two poles of pure competition and pure monopoly. Real-world industries usually have fewer than the hundreds of producers required for pure competition and more than the single producer that defines pure monopoly. Most firms have distinguishable rather than standardized products and have some discretion over the prices they charge. Competition often occurs on the basis of price, quality, location, service, and advertising. Entry to most real-world industries ranges from easy to very difficult but is rarely completely blocked.

This chapter examines two models that more closely approximate these widespread markets. You will discover that *monopolistic competition* mixes a small amount of monopoly power with a large amount of competition. *Oligopoly,* in contrast, blends a large amount of monopoly power, a small amount of competition through entry, and considerable rivalry among industry firms. (You should quickly review Table 9.1, p. 177, at this point.)

Monopolistic Competition

Let's begin by examining **monopolistic competition,** which is characterized by (1) a relatively large number of sellers, (2) differentiated products (often promoted by heavy advertising), and (3) easy entry to, and exit from, the industry. The first and third characteristics provide the "competitive" aspect of monopolistic competition; the second characteristic provides the "monopolistic" aspect. In general, however, monopolistically competitive industries are much more competitive than they are monopolistic.

ORIGIN OF THE IDEA

O II.I

Monopolistic competition

Relatively Large Number of Sellers

Monopolistic competition is characterized by a fairly large number of firms, say, 25, 35, 60, or 70, not by the hundreds or thousands of firms in pure competition. Consequently, monopolistic competition involves:

- *Small market shares* Each firm has a comparatively small percentage of the total market and consequently has limited control over market price.
- *No collusion* The presence of a relatively large number of firms ensures that collusion by a group of firms to restrict output and set prices is unlikely.
- *Independent action* With numerous firms in an industry, there is no feeling of interdependence among them; each firm can determine its own pricing policy without considering the possible reactions of rival firms. A single firm may realize a modest increase in sales by cutting its price, but the effect of that action on competitors' sales will be nearly imperceptible and will probably trigger no response.

Differentiated Products

In contrast to pure competition, in which there is a standardized product, monopolistic competition is distinguished by **product differentiation.** Monopolistically competitive firms turn out variations of a particular product. They produce products with slightly different physical characteristics, offer varying degrees of customer service, provide varying amounts of locational convenience, or proclaim special qualities, real or imagined, for their products.

Let's examine these aspects of product differentiation in more detail.

Product Attributes

Product differentiation may entail physical or qualitative differences in the products themselves. Real differences in functional features, materials, design, and workmanship are vital aspects of product differentiation. Personal computers, for example, differ in terms of storage capacity, speed, graphic displays, and included software. There are dozens of competing principles of economics textbooks that differ in content, organization, presentation and readability, pedagogical aids, and graphics and design. Most cities have a variety of retail stores selling men's and women's clothes that differ greatly in styling, materials, and quality of work. Similarly, one pizza place may feature its thin-crust Neapolitan style pizza, while another may tout its thick-crust pizza.

Service

Service and the conditions surrounding the sale of a product are forms of product differentiation too. One shoe store may stress the fashion knowledge and helpfulness of its clerks. A competitor may leave trying on shoes and carrying them to the register to its customers but feature lower prices. Customers may prefer one-day over three-day dry cleaning of equal quality. The prestige appeal of a store, the courteousness and helpfulness of clerks, the firm's reputation for servicing or exchanging its products, and the credit it makes available are all service aspects of product differentiation.

Location

Products may also be differentiated through the location and accessibility of the stores that sell them. Small convenience stores manage to compete with large supermarkets, even though these minimarts have a more limited range of products and charge higher prices. They compete mainly on the basis of location—being close to customers and situated on busy streets. A motel's proximity to an interstate highway gives it a locational advantage that may enable it to charge a higher room rate than nearby motels in less convenient locations.

Brand Names and Packaging

Product differentiation may also be created through the use of brand names and trademarks, packaging, and celebrity connections. Most aspirin tablets are very much alike, but many headache sufferers believe that one brand—for example, Bayer, Anacin, or Bufferin—is superior and worth a higher price than a generic substitute. A celebrity's name associated with watches, perfume, or athletic shoes may enhance the appeal of those products for some buyers. Many customers prefer one style of ballpoint pen to another. Packaging that touts "natural spring" bottled water may attract additional customers.

Some Control over Price

Despite the relatively large number of firms, monopolistic competitors do have some control over their product prices because of product differentiation. If consumers prefer the products of specific sellers, then within limits they will pay more to satisfy their preferences. Sellers and buyers are not linked randomly, as in a purely competitive market. But the monopolistic competitor's control over price is quite limited since there are numerous potential substitutes for its product.

Easy Entry and Exit

Entry into monopolistically competitive industries is relatively easy compared to oligopoly or pure monopoly. Because monopolistic competitors are typically small firms, both absolutely and relatively, economies of scale are few and capital requirements are low. On the other hand, compared with pure competition, financial barriers may result from the need to develop and advertise a product that differs from rivals' products. Some firms have trade secrets relating to their products or hold trademarks on their brand names, making it difficult and costly for other firms to imitate them.

Exit from monopolistically competitive industries is relatively easy. Nothing prevents an unprofitable monopolistic competitor from holding a going-out-of-business sale and shutting down.

Advertising

The expense and effort involved in product differentiation would be wasted if consumers were not made aware of product differences. Thus, monopolistic competitors advertise their products, often heavily. The goal of product differentiation and advertising—so-called **nonprice competition**—is to make price less of a factor in consumer purchases and make product differences a greater factor. If successful, the firm's demand curve will shift to the right and will become less elastic.

Monopolistically Competitive Industries

Table 11.1 lists several manufacturing industries that approximate monopolistic competition. Economists measure the degree of industry concentration—the extent to which the largest firms account for the bulk of the industry's output—to identify monopolistically competitive (versus oligopolistic) industries. Two such measures are the four-firm concentration ratio and the Herfindahl index. They are listed in columns 2 and 3 of the table.

A **four-firm concentration ratio,** expressed as a percentage, is the ratio of the output (sales) of the four largest firms in an industry relative to total industry sales.

$$\text{Four-firm concentration ratio} = \frac{\text{Output of four largest firms}}{\text{Total output in the industry}}$$

Four-firm concentration ratios are very low in purely competitive industries in which there are hundreds or even thousands of firms each with a tiny market share. In contrast, four-firm ratios are high in oligopoly and pure monopoly. Industries in which the largest four firms account for 40 percent or more of the market are generally considered to be oligopolies. If the largest four firms account for less than 40 percent, they are likely to be monopolistically

TABLE 11.1 **Percentage of Output Produced by Firms in Selected Low-Concentration U.S. Manufacturing Industries**

(1) Industry	(2) Percentage of Industry Output* Produced by the Four Largest Firms	(3) Herfindahl Index for the Top 50 Firms	(1) Industry	(2) Percentage of Industry Output* Produced by the Four Largest Firms	(3) Herfindahl Index for the Top 50 Firms
Asphalt paving	25	207	Metal windows and doors	14	114
Plastic pipe	24	262	Women's dresses	13	84
Textile bags	24	263	Ready mix concrete	11	63
Bolts, nuts, and rivets	24	205	Wood trusses	10	50
Plastic bags	23	240	Stone products	10	59
Quick printing	22	319	Metal stamping	8	31
Textile machinery	20	206	Wood pallets	7	24
Sawmills	18	117	Sheet metal work	6	25
Jewelry	16	117	Signs	5	19
Curtains and draperies	16	111	Retail bakeries	4	7

*As measured by value of shipments. Data are for 2002. See **www.census.gov/epcd/www/concentration.html.**

Source: Bureau of Census, Census of Manufacturers, 2002.

competitive. Observe that the four-firm concentration ratios in Table 11.1 range from 4 percent to 25 percent.

Published concentration ratios such as those in Table 11.1 are helpful in categorizing industries but must be used cautiously because the market shares (percentage of total sales) are national in scope. Some markets with low national concentration ratios are highly localized. As shown in Table 11.1, the four-firm concentration ratio for ready-mix concrete is only 11 percent, suggesting a monopolistically competitive industry. But the sheer bulk of ready-mix concrete and the fact that it "sets up" as it dries limits the relevant market to a specific town, city, or metropolitan area. In such localized markets, only two or three ready-mix producers compete, not the numerous firms present in monopolistic competition.

Column 3 of Table 11.1 lists a second measure of concentration: the **Herfindahl index.** This index is the sum of the squared percentage market shares of all firms in the industry. In equation form:

$$\text{Herfindahl index} = (\%S_1)^2 + (\%S_2)^2 + (\%S_3)^2 + \cdots + (\%S_n)^2$$

where $\%S_1$ is the percentage market share of firm 1, $\%S_2$ is the percentage market share of firm 2, and so on for each of the n total firms in the industry. By squaring the percentage market shares of all firms in the industry, the Herfindahl index purposely gives much greater weight to larger, and thus more powerful, firms than to smaller ones. For a purely competitive industry, the index would approach zero since each firm's market share—$\%S$ in the equation—is extremely small. In the case of the single-firm industry, the index would be at its maximum of 10,000 (= 100^2), indicating an industry with complete monopoly power.

We will discover later in this chapter that the Herfindahl index is important for assessing oligopolistic industries. For purposes here, the relevant generalization is that the lower the Herfindahl index, the greater is the likelihood that an industry is monopolistically competitive rather than oligopolistic. Column 3 of Table 11.1 lists the Herfindahl index (computed for the top 50 firms, not all the industry firms) for several industries. Note that the index values are decidedly closer to the bottom limit of the Herfindahl index—0—than to its top limit—10,000.

The numbers in Table 11.1 are for manufacturing industries. In addition, many retail establishments in metropolitan areas are monopolistically competitive, including grocery stores, gasoline stations, hair salons, dry cleaners, clothing stores, and restaurants. Also, many providers of professional services such as medical care, legal assistance, real estate sales, and basic bookkeeping are monopolistic competitors.

Price and Output in Monopolistic Competition

How does a monopolistic competitor decide on its price and output? To explain, we initially assume that each firm in the industry is producing a specific differentiated product and engaging in a particular amount of advertising. Later we will see how changes in the product and in the amount of advertising modify our conclusions.

The Firm's Demand Curve

Our explanation is based on **Figure 11.1 (Key Graph).** The basic feature of that diagram is the elasticity of demand, as shown by the individual firm's demand curve. The demand curve faced by a monopolistically competitive seller is highly, but not perfectly, elastic. It is precisely this feature that distinguishes monopolistic competition from pure monopoly and pure competition. The monopolistic competitor's demand is more elastic than the demand faced by a pure monopolist because the monopolistically competitive seller has many competitors producing closely substitutable goods. The pure monopolist has no rivals at all. Yet, for two reasons, the monopolistic competitor's demand is not perfectly elastic like that of the pure competitor. First, the monopolistic competitor has fewer rivals; second, its products are differentiated, so they are not perfect substitutes.

The price elasticity of demand faced by the monopolistically competitive firm depends on the number of rivals and the degree of product differentiation. The larger the number of rivals and the weaker the product differentiation, the greater the price elasticity of each seller's demand, that is, the closer monopolistic competition will be to pure competition.

The Short Run: Profit or Loss

The monopolistically competitive firm maximizes its profit or minimizes its loss in the short run just as do the other firms we have discussed: by producing the output at which marginal revenue equals marginal cost (MR = MC). In Figure 11.1a the firm produces output Q_1, where MR = MC. As shown by demand curve D_1, it then can charge price P_1. It realizes an economic profit, shown by the green area [= $(P_1 - A_1) \times Q_1$].

But with less favorable demand or costs, the firm may incur a loss in the short run. We show this possibility in Figure 11.1b, where the firm's best strategy is to minimize its loss. It does so by producing output Q_2 (where MR = MC) and, as determined by demand curve D_2, by charging price P_2. Because price P_2 is less than average total cost A_2,

key graph

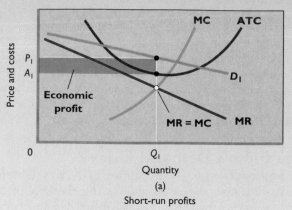

(a)

Quantity

Short-run profits

FIGURE 11.1 A monopolistically competitive firm: short run and long run. The monopolistic competitor maximizes profit or minimizes loss by producing the output at which MR = MC. The economic profit shown in (a) will induce new firms to enter, eventually eliminating economic profit. The loss shown in (b) will cause an exit of firms until normal profit is restored. After such entry and exit, the price will settle in (c) to where it just equals average total cost at the MR = MC output. At this price P_3 and output Q_3, the monopolistic competitor earns only a normal profit, and the industry is in long-run equilibrium.

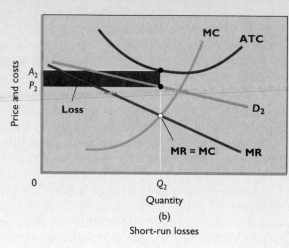

(b)

Short-run losses

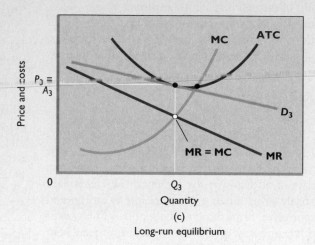

(c)

Long-run equilibrium

QUICK QUIZ FOR FIGURE 11.1

1. Price exceeds MC in:
   a. graph (a) only.
   b. graph (b) only.
   c. graphs (a) and (b) only.
   d. graphs (a), (b), and (c).
2. Price exceeds ATC in:
   a. graph (a) only.
   b. graph (b) only.
   c. graphs (a) and (b) only.
   d. graphs (a), (b), and (c).
3. The firm represented by Figure 11.1c is:
   a. making a normal profit.
   b. incurring a loss.

c. producing at the same level of output as a purely competitive firm.
d. producing a standardized product.

4. Which of the following pairs are both "competitionlike elements" in monopolistic competition?
   a. Price exceeds MR; standardized product.
   b. Entry is relatively easy; only a normal profit in the long run.
   c. Price equals MC at the profit-maximizing output; economic profits are likely in the long run.
   d. The firms' demand curve is downsloping; differentiated products.

Answers: 1. d; 2. a; 3. a; 4. b

the firm incurs a per-unit loss of $A_2 - P_2$ and a total loss represented as the red area [$= (A_2 - P_2) \times Q_2$].

The Long Run: Only a Normal Profit

In the long run, firms will enter a profitable monopolistically competitive industry and leave an unprofitable one. So a monopolistic competitor will earn only a normal profit in the long run or, in other words, will only break even. (Remember that the cost curves include both explicit and implicit costs, including a normal profit.)

Profits: Firms Enter
In the case of short-run profit (Figure 11.1a), economic profits attract new rivals because entry to the industry is relatively easy. As new firms enter, the demand curve faced by the typical firm shifts to the left (falls). Why? Because each firm has a smaller share of total demand and now faces a larger number of close-substitute products. This decline in the firm's demand reduces its economic profit. When entry of new firms has reduced demand to the extent that the demand curve is tangent to the average-total-cost curve at the profit-maximizing output, the firm is just making a normal profit. This situation is shown in Figure 11.1c, where demand is D_3 and the firm's long-run equilibrium output is Q_3. As Figure 11.1c indicates, any greater or lesser output will entail an average total cost that exceeds product price P_3, meaning a loss for the firm. At the tangency point between the demand curve and ATC, total revenue equals total costs. With the economic profit gone, there is no further incentive for additional firms to enter.

Losses: Firms Leave
When the industry suffers short-run losses, as in Figure 11.1b, some firms will exit in the long run. Faced with fewer substitute products and blessed with an expanded share of total demand, the surviving firms will see their demand curves shift to the right (rise), as to D_3. Their losses will disappear and give way to normal profits (Figure 11.1c). (For simplicity we have assumed constant costs; shifts in the cost curves as firms enter or leave would complicate our discussion slightly but would not alter our conclusions.)

Complications
The representative firm in the monopolistic competition model earns only a normal profit in the long run. That outcome may not always occur, however, in the real world of small firms as opposed to the theoretical model.

- Some firms may achieve sufficient product differentiation such that other firms cannot duplicate them, even over time. One hotel in a major city may have the best location relative to business and tourist activities. Or a firm may have developed a well known brand name that gives it a slight but very long-lasting advantage over imitators. Such firms may have sufficient monopoly power to realize modest economic profits even in the long run.

- Entry to some industries populated by small firms is not as free in reality as it is in theory. Because of product differentiation, financial barriers to entry are likely to be greater than they would be if the product were standardized. This suggests some monopoly power, with small economic profits continuing even in the long run.

INTERACTIVE GRAPHS
G 11.1
Monopolistic competition

With all things considered, however, the outcome that yields only a normal profit—the long-run equilibrium shown in Figure 11.1c—is a reasonable approximation of reality.

Monopolistic Competition and Efficiency

We know from Chapter 9 that economic efficiency requires the triple equality $P = MC = $ minimum ATC. The equality of price and minimum average total cost yields *productive efficiency*. The good is being produced in the least costly way, and the price is just sufficient to cover average total cost, including a normal profit. The equality of price and marginal cost yields *allocative efficiency*. The right amount of output is being produced, and thus the right amount of society's scarce resources is being devoted to this specific use.

How efficient is monopolistic competition, as measured against this triple equality?

Neither Productive nor Allocative Efficiency

In monopolistic competition, neither productive nor allocative efficiency occurs in long-run equilibrium. Figure 11.2 includes an enlargement of part of Figure 11.1c and clearly shows this. First note that the profit-maximizing price P_3 slightly exceeds the lowest average total cost, A_4. In producing the profit-maximizing output Q_3, the firm's average total cost therefore is slightly higher than optimal from society's perspective—productive efficiency is not achieved. Also note that the profit-maximizing price P_3 exceeds marginal cost (here M_3), meaning that monopolistic competition

FIGURE 11.2 The inefficiency of monopolistic competition. In long-run equilibrium a monopolistic competitor achieves neither productive nor allocative efficiency. Productive efficiency is not realized because production occurs where the average total cost A_3 exceeds the minimum average total cost A_4. Allocative efficiency is not achieved because the product price P_3 exceeds the marginal cost M_3. The result is an underallocation of resources and excess production capacity of $Q_4 - Q_3$.

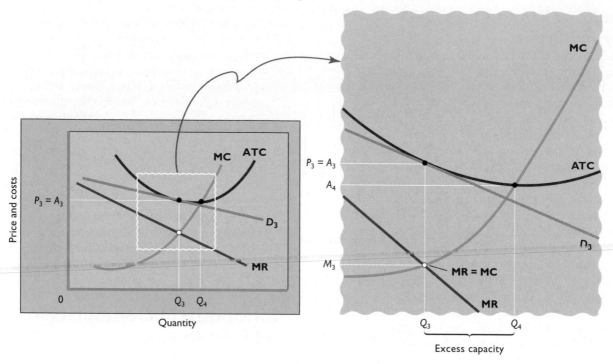

causes an underallocation of resources. Society values each unit of output between Q_3 and Q_4 more highly than the goods it would have to forgo to produce those units. Thus, to a modest extent, monopolistic competition also fails the allocative-efficiency test. Consumers pay a higher-than-competitive price and obtain a less-than-optimal output. Indeed, monopolistic competitors must charge a higher-than-competitive price in the long run in order to achieve a normal profit. The price–marginal cost gap experienced by each monopolistic firm creates an industrywide efficiency loss (or deadweight loss).

Excess Capacity

In monopolistic competition, the gap between the minimum-ATC output and the profit-maximizing output identifies **excess capacity:** plant and equipment that are underused because firms are producing less than the minimum-ATC output. This gap is shown as the distance between Q_4 and Q_3 in Figure 11.2. If each monopolistic competitor could profitably produce at the minimum-ATC output, fewer firms could produce the same total output, and the product could be sold at a lower price. Monopolistically competitive industries thus are overcrowded with firms, each

operating below its optimal capacity. This situation is typified by many kinds of retail establishments. For example, in most cities there is an abundance of small motels and restaurants that operate well below half capacity. **(Key Question 2)**

Product Variety

The situation portrayed in Figures 11.1c and 11.2 is not very satisfying to monopolistic competitors, since it foretells only a normal profit. But the profit-realizing firm of Figure 11.1a need not stand by and watch new competitors eliminate its profit by imitating its product, matching its customer service, and copying its advertising. Each firm has a product that is distinguishable in some way from those of the other producers. So the firm can attempt to stay ahead of competitors and sustain its profit through further product differentiation and better advertising. By developing or improving its product, it may be able to postpone, at least for a while, the outcome of Figure 11.1c.

Although product differentiation and advertising will add to the firm's costs, they can also increase the demand for its product. If demand increases by more than enough to compensate for the added costs, the firm will have improved its profit position. As Figure 11.2 suggests, the firm has little or no prospect of increasing profit by price cutting. So why not engage in nonprice competition?

Benefits of Product Variety

The product variety and product improvement that accompany the drive to maintain economic profit in monopolistic competition are a benefit for society—one that may offset the cost of the inefficiency associated with monopolistic competition. Consumers have a wide diversity of tastes: Some like regular fries, others like curly fries; some like contemporary furniture, others like traditional furniture. If a product is differentiated, then at any time the consumer will be offered a wide range of types, styles, brands, and quality gradations of that product. Compared with pure competition, this provides an advantage to the consumer. The range of choice is widened, and producers more fully meet the wide variation in consumer tastes.

The product improvement promoted by monopolistic competition further differentiates products and expands choices. And a successful product improvement by one firm obligates rivals to imitate or improve on that firm's temporary market advantage or else lose business. So society benefits from better products.

In fact, product differentiation creates a trade-off between consumer choice and productive efficiency. The stronger the product differentiation, the greater is the excess capacity and, therefore, the greater is the productive inefficiency. But the greater the product differentiation, the more likely the firms will satisfy the great diversity of consumer tastes. The greater is the excess-capacity problem, the wider the range of consumer choice.

Further Complexity

Finally, the ability to engage in nonprice competition makes the market situation of a monopolistic competitor more complex than Figure 11.1 indicates. That figure assumes a given (unchanging) product and a given level of advertising expenditures. But we know that, in practice, product attributes and advertising are not fixed. The monopolistically competitive firm juggles three factors—price, product, and advertising—in seeking maximum profit. It must determine what variety of product, selling at what price, and supplemented by what level of advertising will result in the greatest profit. This complex situation is not easily expressed in a simple, meaningful economic model. At best, we can say that each possible combination of price, product, and advertising poses a different demand and cost (production cost plus advertising cost) situation for the firm and that one combination yields the maximum profit. In practice, this optimal combination cannot be readily forecast but must be found by trial and error.

QUICK REVIEW 11.1

- Monopolistic competition involves a relatively large number of firms operating in a noncollusive way and producing differentiated products with easy industry entry and exit.

- In the short run, a monopolistic competitor will maximize profit or minimize loss by producing that output at which marginal revenue equals marginal cost.

- In the long run, easy entry and exit of firms cause monopolistic competitors to earn only a normal profit.

- A monopolistic competitor's long-run equilibrium output is such that price exceeds the minimum average total cost (implying that consumers do not get the product at the lowest price attainable) and price exceeds marginal cost (indicating that resources are underallocated to the product).

- The efficiency loss (or deadweight loss) associated with monopolistic competition is greatly muted by the benefits consumers receive from product variety.

Oligopoly

In terms of competitiveness, the spectrum of market structures reaches from pure competition, to monopolistic competition, to oligopoly, to pure monopoly (review Table 9.1). We now direct our attention to **oligopoly,** a market dominated by a few large producers of a homogeneous or differentiated product. Because of their "fewness," oligopolists have considerable control over their prices, but each must consider the possible reaction of rivals to its own pricing, output, and advertising decisions.

A Few Large Producers

The phrase "a few large producers" is necessarily vague because the market model of oligopoly covers much ground, ranging between pure monopoly, on the one hand, and monopolistic competition, on the other. Oligopoly encompasses the U.S. aluminum industry, in which three huge firms dominate an entire national market, and the situation in which four or five much smaller auto-parts stores enjoy roughly equal shares of the market in a medium-size town. Generally, however, when you hear a term such as "Big Three," "Big Four," or "Big Six," you can be sure it refers to an oligopolistic industry.

Homogeneous or Differentiated Products

An oligopoly may be either a **homogeneous oligopoly** or a **differentiated oligopoly,** depending on whether the firms in the oligopoly produce standardized (homogeneous) or differentiated products. Many industrial products (steel, zinc, copper, aluminum, lead, cement, industrial alcohol) are virtually standardized products that are produced in oligopolies. Alternatively, many consumer goods industries (automobiles, tires, household appliances, electronics equipment, breakfast cereals, cigarettes, and many sporting goods) are differentiated oligopolies. These differentiated oligopolies typically engage in considerable nonprice competition supported by heavy advertising.

Control over Price, but Mutual Interdependence

Because firms are few in oligopolistic industries, each firm is a "price maker"; like the monopolist, it can set its price and output levels to maximize its profit. But unlike the monopolist, which has no rivals, the oligopolist must consider how its rivals will react to any change in its price, output, product characteristics, or advertising. Oligopoly is thus characterized by *strategic behavior* and *mutual interdependence*. By **strategic behavior,** we simply mean self-interested behavior that takes into account the reactions of others. Firms develop and implement price, quality, location, service, and advertising strategies to "grow their business" and expand their profits. But because rivals are few, there is **mutual interdependence:** a situation in which each firm's profit depends not entirely on its own price and sales strategies but also on those of the other firms. So oligopolistic firms base their decisions on how they think rivals will react. Example: In deciding whether to increase the price of its cosmetics, L'Oreal will try to predict the response of the other major producers, such as Clinique. Second example: In deciding on its advertising strategy, Burger King will take into consideration how McDonald's might react.

Entry Barriers

The same barriers to entry that create pure monopoly also contribute to the creation of oligopoly. Economies of scale are important entry barriers in a number of oligopolistic industries, such as the aircraft, rubber, and copper industries. In those industries, three or four firms might each have sufficient sales to achieve economies of scale, but new firms would have such a small market share that they could not do so. They would then be high-cost producers, and as such they could not survive. A closely related barrier is the large expenditure for capital—the cost of obtaining necessary plant and equipment—required for entering certain industries. The jet engine, automobile, commercial aircraft, and petroleum-refining industries, for example, are all characterized by very high capital requirements.

The ownership and control of raw materials help explain why oligopoly exists in many mining industries, including gold, silver, and copper. In the computer, chemicals, consumer electronics, and pharmaceutical industries, patents have served as entry barriers. Moreover, oligopolists can preclude the entry of new competitors through preemptive and retaliatory pricing and advertising strategies.

Mergers

Some oligopolies have emerged mainly through the growth of the dominant firms in a given industry (examples: breakfast cereals, chewing gum, candy bars). But for other industries the route to oligopoly has been through mergers (examples: steel, in its early history, and, more recently, airlines, banking, and entertainment). The merging, or combining, of two or more competing firms may substantially increase their market share, and this in turn may allow the new firm to achieve greater economies of scale.

Another motive underlying the "urge to merge" is the desire for monopoly power. The larger firm that results from a merger has greater control over market supply and thus the price of its product. Also, since it is a larger buyer of inputs, it may be able to demand and obtain lower prices (costs) on its production inputs.

Oligopolistic Industries

Previously, we listed the four-firm concentration ratio—the percentage of total industry sales accounted for by the four largest firms—for a number of monopolistically competitive industries (see Table 11.1). Column 2 of Table 11.2 shows the four-firm concentration ratios for 21 oligopolistic industries. For example, the four largest U.S. producers of breakfast cereals make 78 percent of all breakfast cereals produced in the United States.

When the largest four firms in an industry control 40 percent or more of the market (as in Table 11.2), that industry is considered oligopolistic. Using this benchmark, about one-half of all U.S. manufacturing industries are oligopolies.

Although concentration ratios help identify oligopoly, they have four shortcomings.

Localized Markets We have already noted that concentration ratios apply to the nation as a whole, whereas the markets for some products are highly localized because

TABLE 11.2 **Percentage of Output Produced by Firms in Selected High-Concentration U.S. Manufacturing Industries**

(1) Industry	(2) Percentage of Industry Output* Produced by the Four Largest Firms	(3) Herfindahl Index for the Top 50 Firms	(1) Industry	(2) Percentage of Industry Output* Produced by the Four Largest Firms	(3) Herfindahl Index for the Top 50 Firms
Primary copper	99	ND[†]	Petrochemicals	85	2662
Cane sugar refining	99	ND	Electronic computers	85	2662
Cigarettes	95	ND	Small-arms ammunition	83	1901
Household laundry equipment	93	ND	Motor vehicles	81	2321
Beer	91	ND	Men's slacks and jeans	80	2515
Electric light bulbs	89	2582	Aircraft	81	ND
Glass containers	88	2582	Breakfast cereals	78	2521
Turbines and generators	88	ND	Household vacuum cleaners	78	2096
Household refrigerators and freezers	85	1986	Phosphate fertilizers	78	1853
			Tires	77	1807
Primary aluminum	85	ND	Electronic computers	76	2662

*As measured by value of shipments. Data are for 2002. See **www.census.gov/epcd/www/concentration.html.**
[†]ND = not disclosed.

Source: Bureau of Census, *Census of Manufacturers, 2002.*

of high transportation costs. Local oligopolies can exist even though national concentration ratios are low.

Interindustry Competition Concentration ratios are based on somewhat arbitrary definitions of industries. In some cases, they disguise significant **interindustry competition**—competition between two products associated with different industries. The high concentration ratio for the copper industry shown in Table 11.2 understates the competition in that industry because aluminum competes with copper in many applications (for example, in the market for electric transmission lines).

World Trade The data in Table 11.2 are only for products produced in the United States and may overstate concentration because they do not account for the **import competition** of foreign suppliers. The truck and auto tire industry is a good example. Although Table 11.2 shows that four U.S. firms produce 77 percent of the domestic output of tires, it ignores the fact that a very large portion of the truck and auto tires bought in the United States are imports. Many of the world's largest corporations are foreign, and many of them do business in the United States.

Dominant Firms The four-firm concentration ratio does not reveal the extent to which one or two firms dominate an industry. Suppose that in industry X one firm produces the entire industry output. In a second industry, Y,

four firms compete, each with 25 percent of the market. The concentration ratio is 100 percent for both these industries. But industry X is a pure monopoly, while industry Y is an oligopoly that may be experiencing significant economic rivalry. Most economists would agree that monopoly power (or market power) is substantially greater in industry X than in industry Y, a fact disguised by their identical 100 percent concentration ratios.

The Herfindahl index addresses this problem. Recall that this index is the sum of the squared percentage market shares of all firms in the industry. In equation form:

$$\text{Herfindahl index} = (\%S_1)^2 + (\%S_2)^2 + (\%S_3)^2 + \cdots + (\%S_n)^2$$

where $\%S_1$ is the percentage market share of firm 1, $\%S_2$ is the percentage market share of firm 2, and so on for each firm in the industry. Also remember that by squaring the percentage market shares of all firms in the industry, the Herfindahl index gives much greater weight to larger, and thus more powerful, firms than to smaller ones. In the case of the single-firm industry X, the index would be at its maximum of 100^2, or 10,000, indicating an industry with complete monopoly power. For our supposed four-firm industry Y, the index would be $25^2 + 25^2 + 25^2 + 25^2$, or 2500, indicating much less market power.

WORKED PROBLEMS

W 11.1

Measures of industry competition

The larger the Herfindahl index, the greater the market power within an industry. Note in Table 11.2 that the four-firm concentration ratios for the electronic computer industry and the tire industry are similar: 78 and 77 percent. But the Herfindahl index of 2662 for the electronic computer industry suggests greater market power than the 1807 index for the tire industry. Also, contrast the much larger Herfindahl indexes in Table 11.2 with those for the low-concentration industries in Table 11.1. **(Key Question 7)**

Oligopoly Behavior: A Game-Theory Overview

Oligopoly pricing behavior has the characteristics of certain games of strategy such as poker, chess, and bridge. The best way to play such a game depends on the way one's opponent plays. Players (and oligopolists) must pattern their actions according to the actions and expected reactions of rivals. The study of how people behave in strategic situations is called **game theory**. And we will use a simple game-theory model to analyze the pricing behavior of oligopolists. We assume that a duopoly, or two-firm oligopoly, is producing athletic shoes. Each of the two firms—let's call them RareAir and Uptown—has a choice of two pricing strategies: price high or price low. The profit each firm earns will depend on the strategy it chooses *and* the strategy its rival chooses.

> **ORIGIN OF THE IDEA**
> **O 11.2**
> Game theory

There are four possible combinations of strategies for the two firms, and a lettered cell in Figure 11.3 represents each combination. For example, cell C represents a low-price strategy for Uptown along with a high-price strategy for RareAir. Figure 11.3 is called a *payoff matrix* because each cell shows the payoff (profit) to each firm that would result from each combination of strategies. Cell C shows that if Uptown adopts a low-price strategy and RareAir a high-price strategy, then Uptown will earn $15 million (tan portion) and RareAir will earn $6 million (green portion).

Mutual Interdependence Revisited

The data in Figure 11.3 are hypothetical, but their relationships are typical of real situations. Recall that oligopolistic firms can increase their profits, and influence their rivals' profits, by changing their pricing strategies. Each firm's profit depends on its own pricing strategy and that of its rivals. This mutual interdependence of oligopolists is the most obvious point demonstrated by Figure 11.3. If Uptown adopts a high-price strategy, its profit will be $12 million provided that RareAir also employs a high-price

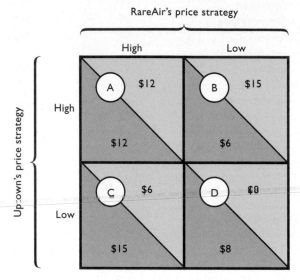

FIGURE 11.3 Profit payoff (in millions) for a two-firm oligopoly. Each firm has two possible pricing strategies. RareAir's strategies are shown in the top margin, and Uptown's in the left margin. Each lettered cell of this four-cell payoff matrix represents one combination of a RareAir strategy and an Uptown strategy and shows the profit that combination would earn for each. Assuming no collusion, the outcome of this game is Cell D, with both parties using low price strategies and earning $8 million of profits.

strategy (cell A). But if RareAir uses a low-price strategy against Uptown's high-price strategy (cell B), RareAir will increase its market share and boost its profit from $12 to $15 million. RareAir's higher profit will come at the expense of Uptown, whose profit will fall from $12 million to $6 million. Uptown's high-price strategy is a good strategy only if RareAir also employs a high-price strategy.

Collusion

Figure 11.3 also suggests that oligopolists often can benefit from **collusion**—that is, cooperation with rivals. To see the benefits of collusion, first suppose that both firms in Figure 11.3 are acting independently and following high-price strategies. Each realizes a $12 million profit (cell A).

Note that either RareAir or Uptown could increase its profit by switching to a low-price strategy (cell B or C). The low-price firm would increase its profit to $15 million and the high-price firm's profit would fall to $6 million. The high-price firm would be better off if it, too, adopted a low-price policy. Doing so would increase its profit from $6 million to $8 million (cell D). The effect of all this independent strategy shifting would be the reduction of both firms' profits from $12 million (cell A) to $8 million (cell D).

In real situations, too, independent action by oligopolists may lead to mutually "competitive" low-price strategies: Independent oligopolists compete with respect to

Creative Strategic Behavior

The following story, offered with tongue in cheek, illustrates a localized market that exhibits some characteristics of oligopoly, including strategic behavior.

Tracy Martinez's Native American Arts and Crafts store is located in the center of a small tourist town that borders on a national park. In its early days, Tracy had a minimonopoly. Business was brisk, and prices and profits were high.

To Tracy's annoyance, two "copycat" shops opened adjacent to her store, one on either side of her shop. Worse yet, the competitors named their shops to take advantage of Tracy's advertising. One was "Native Arts and Crafts"; the other, "Indian Arts and Crafts." These new sellers drew business away from Tracy's store, forcing her to lower her prices. The three side-by-side stores in the small, isolated town constituted a localized oligopoly for Native American arts and crafts.

Tracy began to think strategically about ways to boost profit. She decided to distinguish her shop from those on either side by offering a greater mix of high-quality, expensive products and a lesser mix of inexpensive souvenir items. The tactic worked for a while, but the other stores eventually imitated her product mix.

Then, one of the competitors next door escalated the rivalry by hanging up a large sign proclaiming "We Sell for Less!" Shortly thereafter, the other shop put up a large sign stating "We Won't Be Undersold!"

Not to be outdone, Tracy painted a colorful sign of her own and hung it above her door. It read "Main Entrance."

price policies, with each earning $12 million in profit (cell A). Both are tempted to cheat on this collusive pricing agreement because either firm can increase its profit to $15 million by lowering its price. If Uptown secretly cheats on the agreement by charging low prices, the payoff moves from cell A to cell C. Uptown's profit rises to $15 million, and RareAir's falls to $6 million.

If RareAir cheats, the payoff moves from cell A to cell B, and RareAir gets the $15 million. Fearful that each other will cheat, both firms will probably cheat and the game will settle back to cell D, with each firm using its low-price strategy. (The Consider This box on the prisoner's dilemma on the next page is highly relevant and we urge you to read it now. Also, the appendix to this chapter provides several additional applications of game theory.) **(Key Question 8)**

- An oligopoly is made up of relatively few firms producing either homogeneous or differentiated products; these firms are mutually interdependent.

- Barriers to entry such as scale economies, control of patents or strategic resources, or the ability to engage in retaliatory pricing characterize oligopolies. Oligopolies may result from internal growth of firms, mergers, or both.

- The four-firm concentration ratio shows the percentage of an industry's sales accounted for by its four largest firms; the Herfindahl index measures the degree of market power in an industry by summing the squares of the percentage market shares held by the individual firms in the industry.

- Game theory reveals that (a) oligopolies are mutually interdependent in their pricing policies; (b) collusion enhances oligopoly profits; and (c) there is a temptation for oligopolists to cheat on a collusive agreement.

price, and this leads to lower prices and lower profits. This outcome is clearly beneficial to consumers but not to the oligopolists, whose profits decrease.

How could oligopolists avoid the low-profit outcome of cell D? The answer is that they could collude, rather than establish prices competitively or independently. In our example, the two firms could agree to establish and maintain a high-price policy. So each firm will increase its profit from $8 million (cell D) to $12 million (cell A).

Incentive to Cheat

The payoff matrix also explains why an oligopolist might be strongly tempted to cheat on a collusive agreement. Suppose Uptown and RareAir agree to maintain high-

Three Oligopoly Models

To gain further insight into oligopolistic pricing and output behavior, we will examine three distinct pricing models: (1) the kinked-demand curve, (2) collusive pricing, and (3) price leadership.

Why not a single model, as in our discussions of the other market structures? There are two reasons:

- *Diversity of oligopolies* Oligopoly encompasses a greater range and diversity of market situations than do other market structures. It includes the *tight* oligopoly, in which two or three firms dominate an

CONSIDER THIS . . .

The Prisoner's Dilemma

In the game presented in Figure 11.3, both firms realize they would make higher profits if each used a high-price strategy. But each firm ends up choosing a low-price strategy because it fears that it will be worse off if the other firm uses a low-price strategy against it.

The game described is known as the *prisoner's dilemma game* because it is similar to a situation in which two people—let's call them Betty and Al—have committed a diamond heist and are being detained by the police as prime suspects. Unknown to the two, the evidence against them is weak, so that the best hope that the police have for getting a conviction is if one or both of the thieves confess to the crime. The police place Betty and Al in separate holding cells and offer each the same deal: Confess to the crime and receive a lighter prison sentence.

Each detainee therefore faces a dilemma. If Betty remains silent and Al confesses, Betty will end up with a long prison sentence. If Betty confesses and Al says nothing, Al will receive a long prison sentence. What happens? Fearful that the other person will confess, both confess, even though they each would be better off saying nothing. The "confess–confess outcome" is conceptually identical to the "low price–low price" outcome in Figure 11.3's pricing game.

entire market, and the *loose* oligopoly, in which six or seven firms share, say, 70 or 80 percent of a market while a "competitive fringe" of firms shares the remainder. It includes both differentiated and standardized products. It includes cases in which firms act in collusion and those in which they act independently. It embodies situations in which barriers to entry are very strong and situations in which they are not quite so strong. In short, the diversity of oligopoly does not allow us to explain all oligopolistic behaviors with a single market model.

- *Complications of interdependence* The mutual interdependence of oligopolistic firms complicates matters significantly. Because firms cannot predict the reactions of their rivals with certainty, they cannot estimate their own demand and marginal-revenue data. Without such data, firms cannot determine their profit-maximizing price and output, even in theory, as we will see.

Despite these analytical difficulties, two interrelated characteristics of oligopolistic pricing have been observed. First, if the macroeconomy is generally stable, oligopolistic prices are typically inflexible (or "rigid" or "sticky"). Prices change less frequently under oligopoly than under pure competition, monopolistic competition, and, in some instances, pure monopoly. Second, when oligopolistic prices do change, firms are likely to change their prices together, suggesting that there is a tendency to act in concert, or collusively, in setting and changing prices (as we mentioned in the preceding section). The diversity of oligopolies and the presence of mutual interdependence are reflected in the models that follow.

Kinked-Demand Theory: Noncollusive Oligopoly

Imagine an oligopolistic industry made up of three hypothetical firms (Arch, King, and Dave's), each having about one-third of the total market for a differentiated product. Assume that the firms are "independent," meaning that they do not engage in collusive price practices. Assume, too, that the going price for Arch's product is P_0 and its current sales are Q_0, as shown in **Figure 11.4a (Key Graph)**.

Now the question is, "What does the firm's demand curve look like?" Mutual interdependence and the uncertainty about rivals' reactions make this question hard to answer. The location and shape of an oligopolist's demand curve depend on how the firm's rivals will react to a price change introduced by Arch. There are two plausible assumptions about the reactions of Arch's rivals:

- *Match price changes* One possibility is that King and Dave's will exactly match any price change initiated by Arch. In this case, Arch's demand and marginal-revenue curves will look like the straight lines labeled D_1 and MR_1 in Figure 11.4a. Why are they so steep? Reason: If Arch cuts its price, its sales will increase only modestly because its two rivals will also cut their prices to prevent Arch from gaining an advantage over them. The small increase in sales that Arch (and its two rivals) will realize is at the expense of other industries; Arch will gain no sales from King and Dave's. If Arch raises its price, its sales will fall only modestly because King and Dave's will match its price increase. The industry will lose sales to other industries, but Arch will lose no customers to King and Dave's.

- *Ignore price changes* The other possibility is that King and Dave's will ignore any price change by Arch. In this case, the demand and marginal-revenue curves faced by Arch will resemble the straight lines D_2 and MR_2 in

key graph

FIGURE 11.4 The kinked-demand curve. (a) The slope of a noncollusive oligopolist's demand and marginal-revenue curves depends on whether its rivals match (straight lines D_1 and MR_1) or ignore (straight lines D_2 and MR_2) any price changes that it may initiate from the current price P_0. (b) In all likelihood an oligopolist's rivals will ignore a price increase but follow a price cut. This causes the oligopolist's demand curve to be kinked (D_2eD_1) and the marginal-revenue curve to have a vertical break, or gap (fg). Because any shift in marginal costs between MC_1 and MC_2 will cut the vertical (dashed) segment of the marginal-revenue curve, no change in either price P_0 or output Q_0 will result from such a shift.

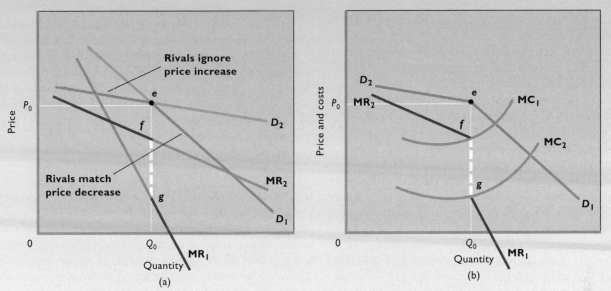

QUICK QUIZ FOR FIGURE 11.4

1. Suppose Q_0 in this figure represents annual sales of 5 million units for this firm. The other two firms in this three-firm industry sell 3 million and 2 million units, respectively. The Herfindahl index for this industry is:
   a. 100 percent.
   b. 400.
   c. 10.
   d. 3800.

2. The D_2e segment of the demand curve D_2eD_1 in graph (b) implies that:
   a. this firm's total revenue will fall if it increases its price above P_0.
   b. other firms will match a price increase above P_0.
   c. the firm's relevant marginal-revenue curve will be MR_1 for price increases above P_0.
   d. the product in this industry is necessarily standardized.

3. By matching a price cut, this firm's rivals can:
   a. increase their market shares.
   b. increase their marginal revenues.
   c. maintain their market shares.
   d. lower their total costs.

4. A shift of the marginal-cost curve from MC_2 to MC_1 in graph (b) would:
   a. increase the "going price" above P_0.
   b. leave price at P_0 but reduce this firm's total profit.
   c. leave price at P_0 but reduce this firm's total revenue.
   d. make this firm's demand curve more elastic.

Answers: 1. d; 2. a; 3. c; 4. b

Figure 11.4a. Demand in this case is considerably more elastic than it was under the previous assumption. The reasons are clear: If Arch lowers its price and its rivals do not, Arch will gain sales significantly at the expense of its two rivals because it will be underselling them. Conversely, if Arch raises its price and its rivals do not, Arch will lose many customers to King and Dave's, which will be underselling it. Because of product differentiation, however, Arch's sales will not fall to zero when it raises its price; some of Arch's customers will pay the higher price because they have a strong preference for Arch's product.

A Combined Strategy Now, which is the most logical assumption for Arch to make about how its rivals will react to any price change it might initiate? The answer is,

235

"It depends on the direction of the price change." Common sense and observation of oligopolistic industries suggest that a firm's rivals will match price declines below P_0 as they act to prevent the price cutter from taking their customers. But they will ignore price increases above P_0 because the rivals of the price-increasing firm stand to gain the business lost by the price booster. In other words, the dark-green left-hand segment of the "rivals ignore" demand curve D_2 seems relevant for price increases, and the dark-green right-hand segment of the "rivals match" demand curve D_1 seems relevant for price cuts. It is logical, then, or at least a reasonable assumption, that the noncollusive oligopolist faces the **kinked-demand curve** D_2eD_1, as shown in Figure 11.4b. Demand is highly elastic above the going price P_0 but much less elastic or even inelastic below that price.

Note also that if rivals match a price cut but ignore an increase, the marginal-revenue curve of the oligopolist will also have an odd shape. It, too, will be made up of two segments: the dark gray left-hand part of marginal-revenue curve MR_2 in Figure 11.4a and the dark gray right-hand part of marginal-revenue curve MR_1. Because of the sharp difference in elasticity of demand above and below the going price, there is a gap, or what we can simply treat as a vertical segment, in the marginal-revenue curve. We show this gap as the dashed segment in the combined marginal-revenue curve MR_2fgMR_1 in Figure 11.4b.

Price Inflexibility

This analysis helps explain why prices are generally stable in noncollusive oligopolistic industries. There are both demand and cost reasons.

On the demand side, the kinked-demand curve gives each oligopolist reason to believe that any change in price will be for the worse. If it raises its price, many of its customers will desert it. If it lowers its price, its sales at best will increase very modestly since rivals will match the lower price. Even if a price cut increases the oligopolist's total revenue somewhat, its costs may increase by a greater amount, depending on demand elasticity. For instance, if its demand is inelastic to the right of Q_0, as it may well be, then the firm's profit will surely fall. A price decrease in the inelastic region lowers the firm's total revenue, and the production of a larger output increases its total costs.

On the cost side, the broken marginal-revenue curve suggests that even if an oligopolist's costs change substantially, the firm may have no reason to change its price. In particular, all positions of the marginal-cost curve between MC_1 and MC_2 in Figure 11.4b will result in the firm's deciding on exactly the same price and output. For all those positions, MR equals MC at output Q_0; at that output, it will charge price P_0.

Criticisms of the Model

The kinked demand analysis has two shortcomings. First, it does not explain how the going price gets to be at P_0 in Figure 11.4 in the first place. It only helps explain why oligopolists tend to stick with an existing price. The kinked-demand curve explains price inflexibility but not price itself.

Second, when the macroeconomy is unstable, oligopoly prices are not as rigid as the kinked-demand theory implies. During inflationary periods, many oligopolists have raised their prices often and substantially. And during downturns (recessions), some oligopolists have cut prices. In some instances these price reductions have set off a **price war:** successive and continuous rounds of price cuts by rivals as they attempt to maintain their market shares. **(Key Question 9)**

Cartels and Other Collusion

Our game-theory model demonstrated that oligopolists might benefit from collusion. We can say that collusion occurs whenever firms in an industry reach an agreement to fix prices, divide up the market, or otherwise restrict competition among themselves. The disadvantages and uncertainties of noncollusive, kinked-demand oligopolies are obvious. There is always the danger of a price war breaking out, especially during a general business recession. Then each firm finds that, because of unsold goods and excess capacity, it can reduce per-unit costs by increasing market share. Then, too, a new firm may surmount entry barriers and initiate aggressive price cutting to gain a foothold in the market. In addition, the kinked-demand curve's tendency toward rigid prices may adversely affect profits if general inflationary pressures increase costs. However, by controlling price through collusion, oligopolists may be able to reduce uncertainty, increase profits, and perhaps even prohibit the entry of new rivals.

Price and Output

Assume once again that there are three hypothetical oligopolistic firms (Gypsum, Sheetrock, and GSR) producing, in this instance, gypsum drywall panels for finishing interior walls. All three firms produce a homogeneous product and have identical cost curves. Each firm's demand curve is indeterminate unless we know how its rivals will react to any price change. Therefore, we suppose each firm assumes that its two rivals will match either a price cut or a price increase. In other words, each firm has a demand curve like the straight line $D1$ in Figure 11.4a. And since they have identical cost data, and the same demand and thus marginal-revenue data, we can say that Figure 11.5 represents the position of each of our three oligopolistic firms.

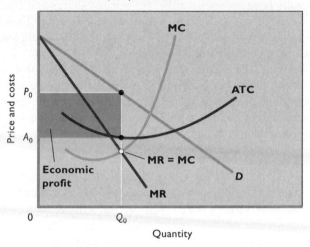

FIGURE 11.5 Collusion and the tendency toward joint-profit maximization. If oligopolistic firms face identical or highly similar demand and cost conditions, they may collude to limit their joint output and to set a single, common price. Thus each firm acts as if it were a pure monopolist, setting output at Q_0 and charging price P_0. This price and output combination maximizes each oligopolist's profit (green area) and thus the combined or joint profit of both.

What price and output combination should, say, Gypsum select? If Gypsum were a pure monopolist, the answer would be clear: Establish output at Q_0, where marginal revenue equals marginal cost, charge the corresponding price P_0, and enjoy the maximum profit attainable. However, Gypsum does have two rivals selling identical products, and if Gypsum's assumption that its rivals will match its price of P_0 proves to be incorrect, the consequences could be disastrous for Gypsum. Specifically, if Sheetrock and GSR actually charge prices below P_0, then Gypsum's demand curve D will shift sharply to the left as its potential customers turn to its rivals, which are now selling the same product at a lower price. Of course, Gypsum can retaliate by cutting its price too, but this will move all three firms down their demand curves, lowering their profits. It may even drive them to a point where average total cost exceeds price and losses are incurred.

So the question becomes, "Will Sheetrock and GSR want to charge a price below P_0?" Under our assumptions, and recognizing that Gypsum has little choice except to match any price they may set below P_0, the answer is no. Faced with the same demand and cost circumstances, Sheetrock and GSR will find it in their interest to produce Q_0 and charge P_0. This is a curious situation; each firm finds it most profitable to charge the same price, P_0, but only if its rivals actually do so! How can the three firms ensure the price P_0 and quantity Q_0 solution in which each is keenly interested? How can they avoid the less profitable outcomes associated with either higher or lower prices?

The answer is evident: They can collude. They can get together, talk it over, and agree to charge the same price, P_0. In addition to reducing the possibility of price wars, this will give each firm the maximum profit. (But it will also subject them to antitrust prosecution if they are caught!) For society, the result will be the same as would occur if the industry were a pure monopoly composed of three identical plants.

Overt Collusion: The OPEC Cartel
Collusion may assume a variety of forms. The most comprehensive form of collusion is the **cartel,** a group of producers that typically creates a formal written agreement specifying how much each member will produce and charge. Output must be controlled—the market must be divided up—in order to maintain the agreed-upon price. The collusion is overt, or open to view.

Undoubtedly the most significant international cartel is the Organization of Petroleum Exporting Countries (OPEC), comprising 13 oil-producing nations (see Global Perspective 11.1). OPEC produces 40 percent of the world's

GLOBAL PERSPECTIVE 11.1

The 13 OPEC Nations, Daily Oil Production, November 2007

The OPEC nations produce about 40 percent of the world's oil and 60 percent of the oil sold in world markets.

OPEC Country	Barrels of Oil
Saudi Arabia	8,904,000
Iran	3,843,000
Kuwait	2,538,000
Venezuela	2,368,000
Iraq	2,297,000
Nigeria	2,183,000
UAE	2,117,000
Angola	1,804,000
Libya	1,737,000
Algeria	1,417,000
Qatar	848,000
Indonesia	843,000
Ecuador	530,000

Source: OPEC, **www.opec.org.**

oil and supplies 60 percent of all oil traded internationally. In the late 1990s it reacted vigorously to very low oil prices by greatly restricting supply. Some non-OPEC producers supported the cutback in production, and within a 15-month period the price of oil shot up from $11 a barrel to $34 a barrel. Gasoline prices in the United States rose by as much as $1 a gallon in some markets. Fearing a global political and economic backlash from the major industrial nations, OPEC upped the production quotas for its members in mid-2000. The increases in oil supply that resulted reduced the price of oil to about $25, where it remained through 2002.

OPEC supply restrictions were less of a factor in the rising oil prices in the 2005–2008 period. In those years, rapidly rising demand for oil in China and supply uncertainties related to armed conflict in the middle East drove the price of oil to more than $130 a barrel. In fact, even the loosening of OPEC quotas was insufficient to prevent this price hike. Should circumstances change, however, OPEC clearly has the market power to hold the price of oil substantially above its marginal cost of production.

Covert Collusion: Examples
Cartels are illegal in the United States, and hence any collusion that exists is covert or secret. Yet there are numerous examples, as shown by evidence from antitrust (antimonopoly) cases. In 1993 the Borden, Pet, and Dean food companies, among others, either pleaded guilty to or were convicted of rigging bids on the prices of milk products sold to schools and military bases. By phone or at luncheons, company executives agreed in advance on which firm would submit the low bid for each school district or military base. In 1996 American agribusiness Archer Daniels Midland and three Japanese and South Korean firms were found to have conspired to fix the worldwide price and sales volume of a livestock feed additive. Executives for the firms secretly met in Hong Kong, Paris, Mexico City, Vancouver, and Zurich to discuss their plans.

In many other instances collusion is much subtler. Unwritten, informal understandings (historically called "gentlemen's agreements") are frequently made at cocktail parties, on golf courses, through phone calls, or at trade association meetings. In such agreements, executives reach verbal or even tacit (unspoken) understandings on product price, leaving market shares to be decided by nonprice competition. Although these agreements, too, violate antitrust laws—and can result in severe personal and corporate penalties—the elusive character of informal understandings makes them more difficult to detect.

Obstacles to Collusion
Normally, cartels and similar collusive arrangements are difficult to establish and maintain. Here are several barriers to collusion:

Demand and Cost Differences When oligopolists face different costs and demand curves, it is difficult for them to agree on a price. This is particularly the case in industries where products are differentiated and change frequently. Even with highly standardized products, firms usually have somewhat different market shares and operate with differing degrees of productive efficiency. Thus it is unlikely that even homogeneous oligopolists would have the same demand and cost curves.

In either case, differences in costs and demand mean that the profit-maximizing price will differ among firms; no single price will be readily acceptable to all, as we assumed was true in Figure 11.5. So price collusion depends on compromises and concessions that are not always easy to obtain and hence act as an obstacle to collusion.

Number of Firms Other things equal, the larger the number of firms, the more difficult it is to create a cartel or some other form of price collusion. Agreement on price by three or four producers that control an entire market may be relatively easy to accomplish. But such agreement is more difficult to achieve where there are, say, 10 firms, each with roughly 10 percent of the market, or where the Big Three have 70 percent of the market while a competitive fringe of 8 or 10 smaller firms battles for the remainder.

Cheating As the game-theory model makes clear, collusive oligopolists are tempted to engage in secret price cutting to increase sales and profit. The difficulty with such cheating is that buyers who are paying a high price for a product may become aware of the lower-priced sales and demand similar treatment. Or buyers receiving a price concession from one producer may use the concession as a wedge to get even larger price concessions from a rival producer. Buyers' attempts to play producers against one another may precipitate price wars among the producers. Although secret price concessions are potentially profitable, they threaten collusive oligopolies over time. Collusion is more likely to succeed when cheating is easy to detect and punish. Then the conspirators are less likely to cheat on the price agreement.

Recession Long-lasting recession usually serves as an enemy of collusion because slumping markets increase average total cost. In technical terms, as the oligopolists' demand and marginal-revenue curves shift to the left in Figure 11.5 in response to a recession, each firm moves leftward and upward to a higher operating point on its average-total-cost curve. Firms find they have substantial excess production capacity, sales are down, unit costs are up, and profits are being squeezed. Under such conditions, businesses may feel they can avoid serious profit reductions (or even losses) by cutting price and thus gaining sales at the expense of rivals.

Potential Entry The greater prices and profits that result from collusion may attract new entrants, including foreign firms. Since that would increase market supply and reduce prices and profits, successful collusion requires that colluding oligopolists block the entry of new producers.

Legal Obstacles: Antitrust Law U.S. antitrust laws prohibit cartels and price-fixing collusion. So less obvious means of price control have evolved in this country.

Price Leadership Model

Price leadership entails a type of implicit understanding by which oligopolists can coordinate prices without engaging in outright collusion based on formal agreements and secret meetings. Rather, a practice evolves whereby the "dominant firm"—usually the largest or most efficient in the industry—initiates price changes and all other firms more or less automatically follow the leader. Many industries, including farm machinery, cement, copper, newsprint, glass containers, steel, beer, fertilizer, cigarettes, and tin, are practicing, or have in the recent past practiced, price leadership.

Leadership Tactics An examination of price leadership in a variety of industries suggests that the price leader is likely to observe the following tactics.

Infrequent Price Changes Because price changes always carry the risk that rivals will not follow the lead, price adjustments are made only infrequently. The price leader does not respond to minuscule day-to-day changes in costs and demand. Price is changed only when cost and demand conditions have been altered significantly and on an industrywide basis as the result of, for example, industrywide wage increases, an increase in excise taxes, or an increase in the price of some basic input such as energy. In the automobile industry, price adjustments traditionally have been made when new models are introduced each fall.

Communications The price leader often communicates impending price adjustments to the industry through speeches by major executives, trade publication interviews, or press releases. By publicizing "the need to raise prices," the price leader seeks agreement among its competitors regarding the actual increase.

Limit Pricing The price leader does not always choose the price that maximizes short-run profits for the industry because the industry may want to discourage new firms from entering. If the cost advantages (economies of scale) of existing firms are a major barrier to entry, new entrants could

surmount that barrier if the price leader and the other firms set product price high enough. New firms that are relatively inefficient because of their small size might survive and grow if the industry sets price very high. So, in order to discourage new competitors and to maintain the current oligopolistic structure of the industry, the price leader may keep price below the short-run profit-maximizing level. The strategy of establishing a price that blocks the entry of new firms is called *limit pricing*.

Breakdowns in Price Leadership: Price Wars Price leadership in oligopoly occasionally breaks down, at least temporarily, and sometimes results in a price war. An example of disruption of price leadership occurred in the breakfast cereal industry, in which Kellogg traditionally had been the price leader. General Mills countered Kellogg's leadership in 1995 by reducing the prices of its cereals by 11 percent. In 1996 Post responded with a 20 percent price cut, which Kellogg then followed. Not to be outdone, Post reduced its prices by another 11 percent.

As another example, in late 2002 Burger King set off a price war by offering its bacon cheeseburger for 99¢. McDonald's countered by placing a price tag of $1 on its Big "N" Tasty burger, which competes directly against Burger King's popular Whopper. Burger King then offered a "limited-time special" of 99¢ for Whoppers.

Most price wars eventually run their course. When all firms recognize that low prices are severely reducing their profits, they again yield price leadership to one of the industry's leading firms. That firm then begins to raise prices, and the other firms willingly follow suit.

QUICK REVIEW 11.3

- In the kinked-demand theory of oligopoly, price is relatively inflexible because a firm contemplating a price change assumes that its rivals will follow a price cut and ignore a price increase.
- Cartels agree on production limits and set a common price to maximize the joint profit of their members as if each were a unit of a single pure monopoly.
- Collusion among oligopolists is difficult because of (a) demand and cost differences among sellers, (b) the complexity of output coordination among producers, (c) the potential for cheating, (d) a tendency for agreements to break down during recessions, (e) the potential entry of new firms, and (f) antitrust laws.
- Price leadership involves an informal understanding among oligopolists to match any price change initiated by a designated firm (often the industry's dominant firm).

Oligopoly and Advertising

We have noted that oligopolists would rather not compete on the basis of price and may become involved in price collusion. Nonetheless, each firm's share of the total market is typically determined through product development and advertising, for two reasons:

- Product development and advertising campaigns are less easily duplicated than price cuts. Price cuts can be quickly and easily matched by a firm's rivals to cancel any potential gain in sales derived from that strategy. Product improvements and successful advertising, however, can produce more permanent gains in market share because they cannot be duplicated as quickly and completely as price reductions.

- Oligopolists have sufficient financial resources to engage in product development and advertising. For most oligopolists, the economic profits earned in the past can help finance current advertising and product development.

Product development (or, more broadly, "research and development") is the subject of Web Chapter 11W, so we will confine our present discussion to advertising. In 2007, firms spent an estimated $285 billion on advertising in the United States and $630 billion worldwide. Advertising is prevalent in both monopolistic competition and oligopoly. Table 11.3 lists the 10 leading U.S. advertisers in 2006.

Advertising may affect prices, competition, and efficiency both positively and negatively, depending on the circumstances. While our focus here is on advertising by oligopolists, the analysis is equally applicable to advertising by monopolistic competitors.

Positive Effects of Advertising

In order to make rational (efficient) decisions, consumers need information about product characteristics and prices.

TABLE 11.3 **The Largest U.S. Advertisers, 2006**

Company	Advertising Spending Millions of $
Procter & Gamble	$4898
AT&T	3345
General Motors	3296
Time Warner	3089
Verizon	2822
Ford Motor	2577
GlaxoSmithKline	2444
Walt Disney	2320
Johnson & Johnson	2291
Unilever	2098

Source: Advertising Age, **www.adage.com.**

Media advertising may be a low-cost means for consumers to obtain that information. Suppose you are in the market for a high-quality camera that is not advertised or promoted in newspapers, in magazines, or on the Internet. To make a rational choice, you may have to spend several days visiting stores to determine the availability, prices, and features of various brands. This search entails both direct costs (gasoline, parking fees) and indirect costs (the value of your time). By providing information about the available options, advertising and Internet promotion reduce your search time and minimize these direct and indirect costs.

By providing information about the various competing goods that are available, advertising diminishes monopoly power. In fact, advertising is frequently associated with the introduction of new products designed to compete with existing brands. Could Toyota and Honda have so strongly challenged U.S. auto producers without advertising? Could FedEx have sliced market share away from UPS and the U.S. Postal Service without advertising?

Viewed this way, advertising is an efficiency-enhancing activity. It is a relatively inexpensive means of providing useful information to consumers and thus lowering their search costs. By enhancing competition, advertising results in greater economic efficiency. By facilitating the introduction of new products, advertising speeds up technological progress. By increasing sales and output, advertising can reduce long-run average total cost by enabling firms to obtain economies of scale.

Potential Negative Effects of Advertising

Not all the effects of advertising are positive, of course. Much advertising is designed simply to manipulate or persuade consumers—that is, to alter their preferences in favor of the advertiser's product. A television commercial that indicates that a popular personality drinks a particular brand of soft drink—and therefore that you should too— conveys little or no information to consumers about price or quality. In addition, advertising is sometimes based on misleading and extravagant claims that confuse consumers rather than enlighten them. Indeed, in some cases advertising may well persuade consumers to pay high prices for much-acclaimed but inferior products, forgoing better but unadvertised products selling at lower prices. Example: *Consumer Reports* has found that heavily advertised premium motor oils provide no better engine performance and longevity than do cheaper brands.

Firms often establish substantial brand-name loyalty and thus achieve monopoly power via their advertising (see Global Perspective 11.2). As a consequence, they are able to increase their sales, expand their market shares,

GLOBAL PERSPECTIVE 11.2

The World's Top 10 Brand Names, 2007

Here are the world's top 10 brands, based on four criteria: the brand's market share within its category, the brand's world appeal across age groups and nationalities, the loyalty of customers to the brand, and the ability of the brand to "stretch" to products beyond the original product.

World's Top 10 Brands

- Coca-Cola
- Microsoft
- IBM
- General Electric
- Nokia
- Toyota
- Intel
- McDonald's
- Disney
- Mercedes-Benz

Source: Interband, **www.interband.com.**

and enjoy greater profits. Larger profits permit still more advertising and further enlargement of the firm's market share and profit. In time, consumers may lose the advantages of competitive markets and face the disadvantages of monopolized markets. Moreover, new entrants to the industry need to incur large advertising costs in order to establish their products in the marketplace; thus, advertising costs may be a barrier to entry. **(Key Question 11)**

Advertising can also be self-canceling. The advertising campaign of one fast-food hamburger chain may be offset by equally costly campaigns waged by rivals, so each firm's demand actually remains unchanged. Few, if any, extra burgers will be purchased and each firm's market share will stay the same. But because of the advertising, all firms will experience higher costs and either their profits will fall or, through successful price leadership, their product prices will rise.

When advertising either leads to increased monopoly power or is self-canceling, economic inefficiency results.

Oligopoly and Efficiency

Is oligopoly, then, an efficient market structure from society's standpoint? How do the price and output decisions of the oligopolist measure up to the triple equality $P = MC =$ minimum ATC that occurs in pure competition?

Productive and Allocative Efficiency

Many economists believe that the outcome of some oligopolistic markets is approximately as shown in Figure 11.5. This view is bolstered by evidence that many oligopolists sustain sizable economic profits year after year. In that case, the oligopolist's production occurs where price exceeds marginal cost and average total cost. Moreover, production is below the output at which average total cost is minimized. In this view, neither productive efficiency (P = minimum ATC) nor allocative efficiency (P = MC) is likely to occur under oligopoly.

A few observers assert that oligopoly is actually less desirable than pure monopoly because government usually regulates pure monopoly in the United States to guard against abuses of monopoly power. Informal collusion among oligopolists may yield price and output results similar to those under pure monopoly yet give the outward appearance of competition involving independent firms.

Qualifications

We should note, however, three qualifications to this view:

- *Increased foreign competition* In recent decades foreign competition has increased rivalry in a number of oligopolistic industries—steel, automobiles, photographic film, electric shavers, outboard motors, and copy machines, for example. This has helped to break down such cozy arrangements as price leadership and to stimulate much more competitive pricing.

- *Limit pricing* Recall that some oligopolists may purposely keep prices below the short-run profit-maximizing level in order to bolster entry barriers. In essence, consumers and society may get some of the benefits of competition—prices closer to marginal cost and minimum average total cost—even without the competition that free entry would provide.

- *Technological advance* Over time, oligopolistic industries may foster more rapid product development and greater improvement of production techniques than would be possible if they were purely competitive. Oligopolists have large economic profits from which they can fund expensive research and development (R&D). Moreover, the existence of barriers to entry may give the oligopolist some assurance that it will reap the rewards of successful R&D. Thus, the short-run economic inefficiencies of oligopolists may be partly or wholly offset by the oligopolists' contributions to better products, lower prices, and lower costs over time. We say more about these dynamic aspects of rivalry in optional Web Chapter 11W.

The Beer Industry Was Once Populated by Hundreds of Firms and an Even Larger Number of Brands. But It Now Is an Oligopoly Dominated by a Handful of Producers.

Since the Second World War, profound changes have increased the level of concentration in the U.S. beer industry. In 1947 more than 400 independent brewing companies operated in the United States. By 1967, the number had declined to 124 and by 1980 it had dropped to just 33. In 1947 the largest five brewers sold only 19 percent of the nation's beer. In 2007, the Big Three brewers (Anheuser-Busch, SABMiller, and Molson/Coors) sold 76 percent. In 2007, Anheuser-Busch (48 percent) and SABMiller (18 percent) alone combined for 66 percent of industry sales. And, in late 2007, SABMiller acquired the U.S. operations of Molson/Coors, turning the Big Three into the Big Two. In 2008, Belgian brewer InBev purchased Anheuser-Busch. The U.S. beer industry clearly meets all the criteria of oligopoly.

Changes on the demand side of the market have contributed to the "shakeout" of small brewers from the industry. First, consumer tastes in the mass market have generally shifted from the stronger-flavored beers of the small brewers to the light products of the larger brewers. Second, there has been a shift from the consumption of beer in taverns to consumption of it in the home. The beer consumed in taverns was mainly "draft" or "tap" beer from kegs, supplied by local and regional brewers that could deliver the kegs in a timely fashion at relatively low transportation cost. But the large increase in the demand for beer consumed at home opened the door for large brewers that sold their beer in bottles and aluminum cans. The large brewers could ship their beer by truck or rail over long distances and compete directly with the local brewers.

Developments on the supply side of the market have been even more profound. Technological advances speeded up the bottling and canning lines. Today, large brewers can fill and close 2000 cans per line per minute. Large plants are also able to reduce labor costs through the automating of brewing and warehousing. Furthermore, plant construction costs per barrel of production capacity are about one-third less for a 4.5-million-barrel plant than for a 1.5-million-barrel plant. As a consequence of these and other factors, the minimum efficient scale in brewing is a plant size of about 4.5 million barrels. Additionally, studies indicate that further cost savings are available to brewing firms that have two or more separate large breweries in different regions of the country. Between the economies of scale from plant size and these cost savings from multiple plants, cost considerations deter entry to the mainline beer industry.

"Blindfold" taste tests confirm that most mass-produced American beers taste alike. So brewers greatly emphasize advertising. And here Anheuser-Busch and Miller-Coors, which sell national brands, enjoy major cost advantages over producers such as Pabst that have many regional brands (for example, Lonestar, Rainer, Schaefer, and Schmidts). The reason is that national television advertising is less costly *per viewer* than local TV advertising.

Up until the recent combination of Molson/Coors and SABMiller, mergers had not been the dominant factor in explaining the industry consolidation. Rather, that was largely caused by failing smaller breweries' (such as Heileman's) selling their assets and brands to competitors. Dominant firms have expanded by

Summary

1. The distinguishing features of monopolistic competition are (a) there are enough firms in the industry to ensure that each firm has only limited control over price, mutual interdependence is absent, and collusion is nearly impossible; (b) products are characterized by real or perceived differences so that economic rivalry entails both price and nonprice competition; and (c) entry to the industry is relatively easy. Many aspects of retailing, and some manufacturing industries in which economies of scale are few, approximate monopolistic competition.

2. The four-firm concentration ratio measures the percentage of total industry output accounted for by the largest four firms. The Herfindahl index sums the squares of the percent market shares of all firms in the industry.

3. Monopolistically competitive firms may earn economic profits or incur losses in the short run. The easy entry and exit of firms result in only normal profits in the long run.

4. The long-run equilibrium position of the monopolistically competitive producer is less efficient than that of the pure

heavily advertising their main brands and by creating new brands such as Lite, Bud Light, Genuine Draft, Keystone, and Icehouse rather than acquiring other brewers. This has sustained significant product differentiation, despite the declining number of major brewers.

The rise of the Miller Brewing Company from the seventh- to the second-largest producer in the 1970s was due in large measure to advertising and product differentiation. When the Philip Morris Company acquired Miller in 1970, the new management made two big changes. First, it "repositioned" Miller High Life beer into that segment of the market where potential sales were the greatest. Sold previously as the "champagne of beers," High Life had appealed heavily to upper-income consumers and to occasional women beer drinkers. Miller's new television ads featured young blue-collar workers, who were inclined to be greater beer consumers. Second, Miller then developed its low-calorie Lite beer, which was extensively promoted with Philip Morris advertising dollars. Lite proved to be the most popular new product in the history of the beer industry. Miller later introduced its Genuine Draft beer, which found its place within the top 10 brands.

But the story of the last three decades has been Anheuser-Busch InBev, (A-B), which has greatly expanded its market share. A-B now makes the nation's top two brands: Bud Light and Budweiser account for nearly half the beer sold in the United States. Part of A-B's success owes to the demise of regional competitors. But part also is the result of A-B's strategic prowess. It has constructed state-of-the-art breweries, created effective advertising campaigns, and forged strong relationships with regional distributors. Meanwhile, Miller's market share has declined slightly in recent years. In 2002 Philip Morris sold Miller to London-based SAB. SABMiller, as the firm is now called, has significantly redesigned Miller's labeling and marketing to enhance its appeal and to expand its presence overseas. Perhaps of greater importance, SABMiller's acquisition of Coors will immediately expand its U.S. market share from 18 percent to 29 percent.

Imported beers such as Heineken, Corona, and Guinness constitute about 15 percent of the market, with individual brands seeming to wax and wane in popularity. Some local or regional microbreweries such as Samuel Adams and Pyramid, which brew "craft" or specialty beers and charge super-premium prices, have whittled into the sales of the major brewers. Craft and speciality beers account for only 6 percent of beer consumed in the United States. But they are the fastest-growing segment of the U.S. industry. A-B, Miller, and Coors have taken notice, responding with specialty brands of their own (for example, Red Wolf, Red Dog, Killarney's, Icehouse, and Blue Moon) and by buying stakes in microbrewers Redhook Ale and Celis.

Sources: Based on Kenneth G. Elzinga, "Beer," in Walter Adams and James Brock (eds.), *The Structure of American Industry*, 10th ed. (Upper Saddle River, N.J.: Prentice Hall, 2001), pp. 85–113; and Douglas F. Greer, "Beer: Causes of Structural Change," in Larry Duetsch (ed.), *Industry Studies*, 2d ed. (New York: M. E. Sharpe, 1998), pp. 28–64. Updated data and information are mainly from *Beer Marketer's Insights*, **www.beerinsights.com**, and the Association of Brewers, **www.beertown.com**.

competitor. Under monopolistic competition, price exceeds marginal cost, indicating an underallocation of resources to the product, and price exceeds minimum average total cost, indicating that consumers do not get the product at the lowest price that cost conditions might allow.

5. Nonprice competition provides a way that monopolistically competitive firms can offset the long-run tendency for economic profit to fall to zero. Through product differentiation, product development, and advertising, a firm may strive to increase the demand for its product more than enough to cover the added cost of such nonprice competition. Consumers benefit from the wide diversity of product choice that monopolistic competition provides.

6. In practice, the monopolistic competitor seeks the specific combination of price, product, and advertising that will maximize profit.

7. Oligopolistic industries are characterized by the presence of few firms, each having a significant fraction of the market.

Firms thus situated engage in strategic behavior and are mutually interdependent: The behavior of any one firm directly affects, and is affected by, the actions of rivals. Products may be either virtually uniform or significantly differentiated. Various barriers to entry, including economies of scale, underlie and maintain oligopoly.

8. High concentration ratios are an indication of oligopoly (monopoly) power. By giving more weight to larger firms, the Herfindahl index is designed to measure market dominance in an industry.

9. Game theory (a) shows the interdependence of oligopolists' pricing policies, (b) reveals the tendency of oligopolists to collude, and (c) explains the temptation of oligopolists to cheat on collusive arrangements.

10. Noncollusive oligopolists may face a kinked-demand curve. This curve and the accompanying marginal-revenue curve help explain the price rigidity that often characterizes oligopolies; they do not, however, explain how the actual prices of products were first established.

11. The uncertainties inherent in oligopoly promote collusion. Collusive oligopolists such as cartels maximize joint profits—that is, they behave like pure monopolists. Demand and cost differences, a "large" number of firms, cheating through secret price concessions, recessions, and the antitrust laws are all obstacles to collusive oligopoly.

12. Price leadership is an informal means of collusion whereby one firm, usually the largest or most efficient, initiates price changes and the other firms in the industry follow the leader.

13. Market shares in oligopolistic industries are usually determined on the basis of product development and advertising. Oligopolists emphasize nonprice competition because (a) advertising and product variations are less easy for rivals to match and (b) oligopolists frequently have ample resources to finance nonprice competition.

14. Advertising may affect prices, competition, and efficiency either positively or negatively. Positive: It can provide consumers with low-cost information about competing products, help introduce new competing products into concentrated industries, and generally reduce monopoly power and its attendant inefficiencies. Negative: It can promote monopoly power via persuasion and the creation of entry barriers. Moreover, it can be self-canceling when engaged in by rivals; then it boosts costs and creates inefficiency while accomplishing little else.

15. Neither productive nor allocative efficiency is realized in oligopolistic markets, but oligopoly may be superior to pure competition in promoting research and development and technological progress.

16. Table 9.1, page 177, provides a concise review of the characteristics of monopolistic competition and oligopoly as they compare to those of pure competition and pure monopoly.

Terms and Concepts

monopolistic competition	homogeneous oligopoly	collusion
product differentiation	differentiated oligopoly	kinked-demand curve
nonprice competition	strategic behavior	price war
four-firm concentration ratio	mutual interdependence	cartel
Herfindahl index	interindustry competition	price leadership
excess capacity	import competition	
oligopoly	game theory	

Study Questions  | ECONOMICS

1. How does monopolistic competition differ from pure competition in its basic characteristics? From pure monopoly? Explain fully what product differentiation may involve. Explain how the entry of firms into its industry affects the demand curve facing a monopolistic competitor and how that, in turn, affects its economic profit. **LO1**

2. **KEY QUESTION** Compare the elasticity of the monopolistic competitor's demand with that of a pure competitor and a pure monopolist. Assuming identical long-run costs, compare graphically the prices and outputs that would result in the long run under pure competition and under monopolistic competition. Contrast the two market structures in terms of productive and allocative efficiency. Explain: "Monopolisti-

cally competitive industries are characterized by too many firms, each of which produces too little." **LO2**

3. "Monopolistic competition is monopolistic up to the point at which consumers become willing to buy close-substitute products and competitive beyond that point." Explain. **LO2**

4. "Competition in quality and service may be just as effective as price competition in giving buyers more for their money." Do you agree? Why? Explain why monopolistically competitive firms frequently prefer nonprice competition to price competition. **LO2**

5. Critically evaluate and explain: **LO2**
   a. In monopolistically competitive industries, economic profits are competed away in the long run; hence, there

is no valid reason to criticize the performance and efficiency of such industries.

b. In the long run, monopolistic competition leads to a monopolistic price but not to monopolistic profits.

6. Why do oligopolies exist? List five or six oligopolists whose products you own or regularly purchase. What distinguishes oligopoly from monopolistic competition? **LO3**

7. **KEY QUESTION** Answer the following questions, which relate to measures of concentration: **LO3**

   a. What is the meaning of a four-firm concentration ratio of 60 percent? 90 percent? What are the shortcomings of concentration ratios as measures of monopoly power?

   b. Suppose that the five firms in industry A have annual sales of 30, 30, 20, 10, and 10 percent of total industry sales. For the five firms in industry B, the figures are 60, 25, 5, 5, and 5 percent. Calculate the Herfindahl index for each industry and compare their likely competitiveness.

8. **KEY QUESTION** Explain the general meaning of the following profit payoff matrix for oligopolists C and D. All profit figures are in thousands. **LO4**

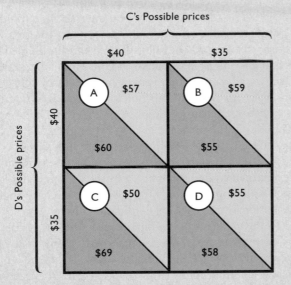

C's Possible prices

9. **KEY QUESTION** What assumptions about a rival's response to price changes underlie the kinked-demand curve for oligopolists? Why is there a gap in the oligopolist's marginal-revenue curve? How does the kinked-demand curve explain price rigidity in oligopoly? What are the shortcomings of the kinked-demand model? **LO5**

10. Why might price collusion occur in oligopolistic industries? Assess the economic desirability of collusive pricing. What are the main obstacles to collusion? Speculate as to why price leadership is legal in the United States, whereas price-fixing is not. **LO6**

11. **KEY QUESTION** Why is there so much advertising in monopolistic competition and oligopoly? How does such advertising help consumers and promote efficiency? Why might it be excessive at times? **LO7**

12. **ADVANCED ANALYSIS** Construct a game-theory matrix involving two firms and their decisions on high versus low advertising budgets and the effects of each on profits. Show a circumstance in which both firms select high advertising budgets even though both would be more profitable with low advertising budgets. Why won't they unilaterally cut their advertising budgets? **LO7**

13. **LAST WORD** What firm dominates the U.S. beer industry? What demand and supply factors have contributed to "fewness" in this industry?

a. Use the payoff matrix to explain the mutual interdependence that characterizes oligopolistic industries.

b. Assuming no collusion between C and D, what is the likely pricing outcome?

c. In view of your answer to 8b, explain why price collusion is mutually profitable. Why might there be a temptation to cheat on the collusive agreement?

Web-Based Questions:

1. **BOOKSELLING ON THE INTERNET—HOW DO SELLERS DIFFERENTIATE IDENTICAL BOOKS?** Use a search engine to find the current listings on the *New York Times* best-seller lists. Choose one hardbound book of fiction and one hardbound book of nonfiction from the top-five lists. Next, find the price, including shipping to your address, of your two books at both Amazon, **www.amazon.com,** and Barnes and Noble, **www.barnesandnoble.com.** Is one company less expensive? Identify the nonprice competition that might lead you to order from one company rather than the other.

2. **MARKET SHARES—TOP-10 LISTS** *Advertising Age,* at **www.adage.com,** compiles statistics on the market shares of some familiar products. Click on Data Center and then on Top Line Data. Download the Fact Pack for the latest year. Select the top-5, top-7, or top-10 lists for five separate nonmedia products. In general, do the very top sellers in your lists advertise more or less than the sellers toward the bottom of the lists? Are there exceptions? Do you think the top-10 lists would get turned upside down if the pattern of advertising were turned upside down? Why or why not?

Additional Game Theory Applications

We have seen that game theory is helpful in explaining mutual interdependence and strategic behavior by oligopolists. This appendix provides additional oligopoly-based applications of game theory.

A One-Time Game: Strategies and Equilibrium

Consider Figure 1, which lists strategies and outcomes for two fictitious producers of the computer memory chips referred to as DRAMs (Dynamic Random Access Memory circuits). Chipco is the single producer of these chips in the United States and Dramco is the only producer in China. Each firm has two alternative strategies: an international strategy, in which it competes directly against the other firm in both countries; and a national strategy, in which it sells only in its home country.

The game and payoff matrix shown in Figure 1 is a **one-time game** because the firms select their optimal strategies in a single time period without regard to possible interactions in subsequent time periods. The game is also a **simultaneous game** because the firms choose their

FIGURE 1 **A One-Time Game** In this single-period, positive-sum game, Chipco's international strategy is its dominant strategy—the alternative that is superior to any other strategy regardless of whatever Dramco does. Similarly, Dramco's international strategy is also its dominant strategy. With both firms choosing international strategies, the outcome of the game is Cell A, where each firm receives an $11 million profit. Cell A is a Nash equilibrium because neither firm will independently want to move away from it given the other firm's strategy.

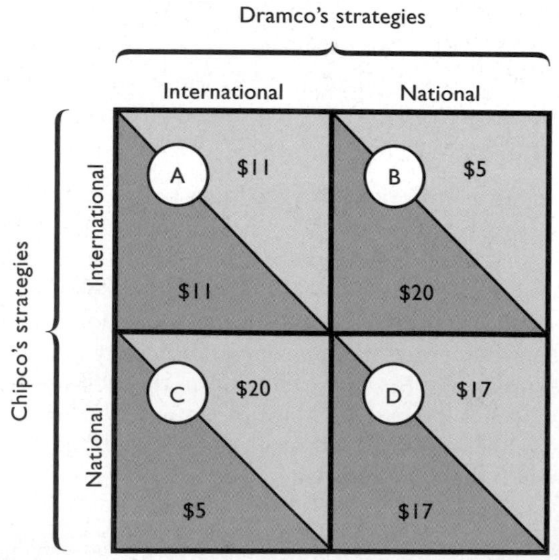

Dramco's strategies

strategies at the same time; and a **positive-sum game**, a game in which the sum of the two firms' outcomes (here, profits) is positive. In contrast, the net gain in a **zero-sum game** is zero because one firm's gain must equal the other firm's loss, and the net gain in a **negative-sum game** is negative. In some positive-sum games, both firms may have positive outcomes. That is the case in Figure 1.

To determine optimal strategies, Chipco looks across the two rows in the payoff matrix (tan portion of cells in millions of dollars) and Dramco looks down the two columns (green portion of cells). These payoffs indicate that both firms have a **dominant strategy**—an option that is better than any alternative option *regardless of what the other firm does*. To see this, notice that Chipco's international strategy will give it a higher profit than its national strategy—regardless of whether Dramco chooses to utilize an international or a national strategy. An international strategy will produce an $11 million profit for Chipco (tan portion of cell A) if Dramco also uses an international strategy while a national strategy will result in a $20 million profit for Chipco (tan portion of cell B) if Dramco uses a national strategy. Chipco's possible $11 million and $20 million outcomes are clearly better than the $5 million (cell C) and $17 million (cell D) outcomes it could receive if it chose to pursue a national strategy. Chipco's international strategy is, consequently, its dominant strategy. Using similar logic, Dramco also concludes that its international strategy is its dominant strategy.

In this particular case, the outcome (cell A) of the two dominant strategies is the game's **Nash equilibrium**—an outcome from which neither rival wants to deviate.[1] At the Nash equilibrium, both rivals see their current strategy as optimal *given the other firm's strategic choice*. The Nash equilibrium is the only outcome in the payoff matrix in Figure 1 that, once achieved, is stable and therefore will persist.[2]

Credible and Empty Threats

In looking for optimal strategies, Chipco and Dramco both note that they could increase their profit from $11 million to $17 million if they could agree to jointly pursue national strategies (cell D) instead of independently

---

[1]The Nash equilibrium is named for its discoverer, John F. Nash. Nash's life and Nobel Prize are the subject of the motion picture, A *Beautiful Mind*, directed by Ron Howard and starring Russell Crowe.

[2]Nash equilibriums can exist even in games that lack dominant strategies.

pursuing international strategies (cell A). Presumably the national strategies would leave the firms as pure monopolists in their domestic economies, with each able to set higher prices and obtain greater profits as a result. But if this territorial agreement were put in place, both firms would have an incentive to cheat on the agreement by secretly selling DRAMs in the other's country. That would temporarily move the game to either cell B or cell C. Once discovered, however, such cheating would undermine the territorial agreement and return the game to the Nash equilibrium (cell A).

Now let's add a new twist—a credible threat—to the game shown in Figure 1. A **credible threat** is a statement of coercion (a threat!) that is believable by the other firm. Suppose that Chipco is the lower-cost producer of DRAMs because of its superior technology. Also, suppose that Chipco approaches Dramco saying that Chipco intends to use its national strategy and expects Dramco to do the same. If Dramco decides against the national strategy or agrees to the strategy and then later cheats on the agreement, Chipco will immediately drop its price to an ultra-low level equal to its average total cost (ATC). Both firms know that Chipco's ATC price is below Dramco's ATC. Although Chipco will see its economic profit fall to zero, Dramco will suffer an economic loss and possibly go out of business.

If Chipco's threat is credible, the two firms represented in Figure 1 will abandon the Nash equilibrium (cell A) to deploy their national strategies and achieve highly profitable cell D. In game theory, credible threats such as this can help establish and maintain collusive agreements. A strong "enforcer" can help prevent cheating and maintain the group discipline needed for cartels, price-fixing conspiracies, and territorial understandings to successfully generate high profits.

But credible threats are difficult to achieve in the actual economy. For example, Dramco might rightly wonder why Chipco had not previously driven it out of business through an ultra-low price strategy. Is Chipco fearful of the U.S. antitrust authorities?

If Dramco does not wish to participate in the proposed scheme, it might counter Chipco's threat with its own: Forget that you ever talked to us and we will not take this illegal "offer" to the U.S. Justice Department. Dramco can make this threat because strict laws are in place against attempts to restrain trade through price-fixing and territorial agreements.

So Dramco may view Chipco's threat as simply an **empty threat**—a statement of coercion that is not believable by the threatened firm. If so, the Nash equilibrium will prevail, with both firms pursuing an international strategy.

Repeated Games and Reciprocity Strategies

The Chipco-Dramco game was a one-time game, but many strategic situations are repeated by the same oligopolists over and over again. For example, Coca Cola and Pepsi are mutually interdependent on pricing, advertising, and product development year after year, decade after decade. The same is true for Boeing and Airbus, Wal-Mart and Target, Toyota and General Motors, Budweiser and Miller, Nike and Adidas, and numerous other dominant pairs.

In a **repeated game**—a game that recurs more than once—the optimal strategy may be to cooperate and restrain oneself from competing as hard as possible so long as the other firm reciprocates by also not competing as hard as possible.[3] To see how this works, consider two hypothetical producers of soft drinks: 2Cool and ThirstQ. If 2Cool competes hard with ThirstQ in today's situation in which ThirstQ would like 2Cool to take things easy, ThirstQ will most likely retaliate against 2Cool in any subsequent situation where the circumstances are reversed. In contrast, if ThirstQ cooperates with 2Cool in game 1, ThirstQ can expect 2Cool to reciprocate in game 2 of their repeated interaction. Both firms know full well the negative long-run consequences of ever refusing to cooperate. So the cooperation continues, not only in game 2, but in games 3, 4, 5, and beyond. Figure 2 shows two side-by-side payoff matrixes for the two games. In Figure 2a, 2Cool and ThirstQ face a situation in which 2Cool is introducing a new cola called Cool Cola and has two advertising options: a high promotional budget to introduce the new product and a normal advertising budget. ThirstQ has the same two options: a high promotional budget to try to counter 2Cool's product introduction and a normal advertising budget.

The analysis is now familiar to you, and we will therefore greatly speed the pace. The dominant strategies for both firms are their large promotional advertising budgets and the Nash equilibrium is cell A. Both firms could do better at cell D if each agreed to use normal advertising budgets. But 2Cool could do better still. It could achieve the $16 million of profit in cell B, but only if ThirstQ holds its advertising budget to its normal level during the introduction of Cool Cola.

ThirstQ might voluntarily do just that! It knows that game 2 (Figure 2b) is forthcoming in which it will be

---

[3]We are assuming either an infinitely repeated game or a game of unknown time-horizon. Games with a known ending date undermine reciprocity strategies.

FIGURE 2 A Repeated Game with Reciprocity (a) in the payoff matrix to to the left, 2Cool introduces its new Cool Cola with a large promotional advertising budget, but its rival ThirstQ maintains its normal advertising budget even though it could counter 2Cool with a large advertising budget of its own and drive the outcome from Cell B to Cell A. ThirstQ forgoes this $2 million of extra profit because it knows that it will soon be introducing its own new product (Quench It). (b) In the payoff matrix to the right, ThirstQ introduces Quench It with a large promotional advertising budget. Cool2 reciprocates ThirstQ's earlier accommodation by not matching ThirstQ's promotional advertising budget and instead allowing the outcome of the repeated game to be Cell C. The profit of both 2Cool and ThirstQ therefore is larger over the two periods than if each firm had aggressively countered each other's single-period strategy.

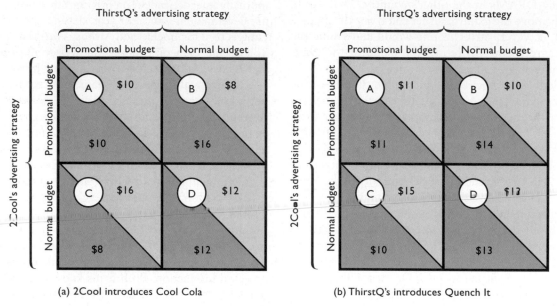

(a) 2Cool introduces Cool Cola

(b) ThirstQ's introduces Quench It

introducing its new product, Quench It. By leaving its advertising budget at its normal level during Cool2's introduction of Cool Cola, and thereby sacrificing profit of $2 million (= $10 million in cell A − $8 million in cell B), it can expect ThirstQ to reciprocate in the subsequent game in which it introduces Quench It. Without formally colluding—and risking antitrust penalties—game 1 ends at cell B and repeated game 2 ends at cell C. Using reciprocity, 2Cool's total profit of $26 million (= $16 million in game 1 + $10 million in game 2) exceeds the $21 million (= $10 million + $11 million) it would have earned without the reciprocity. ThirstQ similarly benefits. To check your understanding, confirm this fact using the numbers in the two matrixes.

First-Mover Advantages and Preemption of Entry

The games we have highlighted thus far have been games in which the two firms simultaneously select their optimal strategies. But in some actual economic circumstances, firms apply strategies sequentially: One firm moves first and commits to a strategy to which a rival firm must subsequently respond. In such a **sequential game,** the final outcome may depend critically upon which firm moves first since the first mover may have the opportunity to establish a Nash equilibrium that works in its favor.

Consider Figure 3, which identifies a game in which two large retailers—let's call them Big Box and Huge Box—are each considering building a large retail store in a small rural city. As indicated in the figure, each firm has two strategies: build or don't build. The payoff matrix reflects the fact that the city is not large enough to support two big box retailers profitably. If both retailers simultaneously build, the outcome will be cell A and each firm will lose $5 million. If neither firm builds, the outcome will be cell D with both firms securing zero profit. If only Big Box builds, the outcome will be cell B and Big Box will profit handsomely at $12 million. If Huge Box builds, but Big Box stays out, the outcome will be cell C and Huge Box will secure the $12 million profit. Either cell B or cell C is the possible Nash equilibrium. At either cell, both firms will have selected their best option in view of the strategy taken by the other firm.

FIGURE 3 **A First-Mover Advantage and the Preemption of Entry** In this game in which strategies are pursued sequentially, the firm that moves first can take advantage of the particular situation represented in which only a single firm can exist profitably in some geographical market. Here, we suppose that Big Box moves first with its "Build" strategy to achieve the $12 million profit outcome in Cell C. Huge Box then will find that it will lose money if it also builds because that will result in a $5 million loss, as shown in Cell A.

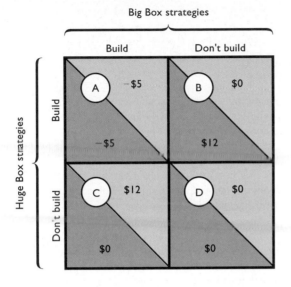

The payoff matrix in Figure 3 clearly reveals that whoever builds first will preempt the other retailer from entering the market. An extremely large **first-mover advantage** exists in this particular game. Suppose that a well-thought-out strategy and adequate financing leave Big Box better prepared than Huge Box to move quickly to build a large retail store in this city. By exploiting its first-mover advantage, Big Box drives the outcome to Cell C and preempts Huge Box's entry into this market.

Many firms in the actual economy have used variations of this first-mover strategy to a greater or lesser extent to preempt major rivals, or at least greatly slow their entry. Examples are Wal-Mart, Home Depot, Costco, Walgreens, Starbucks, and many more. The strategy, however, is highly risky because it requires the commitment of huge amounts of investment funds to saturate the market and preclude entry by other firms. Also, to be the first-mover in places that are being transformed from rural land into urban areas, firms may need to build their stores many months prior to the time when the area in question becomes developed enough to provide the store with significant business. That may mean losses until the market grows sufficiently for profitability. Some firms such as Wal-Mart have become huge, profitable international enterprises by using a first-mover strategy. Other firms, such as Krispy Creme Donuts, have lost millions of dollars because their extremely rapid expansion turned out to be unprofitable in many of their outlets because the expected customers never materialized.

Appendix Summary

1. Positive-sum games are games in which the payoffs to the firms sum to a positive number; zero-sum games are games in which the payoffs sum to zero; and negative-sum games are games in which the payoffs sum to less than zero. Positive-sum games allow for "win-win" opportunities, whereas zero-sum games always feature "I win/you lose" outcomes. Games can be either one-time games or repeated games. Decisions in games may be made either simultaneously or sequentially.

2. When two firms are playing a strategic game, a firm is said to have a dominant strategy if there is an option that leads to better outcomes than all other options regardless of what the other firm does. Not all games have dominant strategies. The Nash equilibrium is an outcome from which neither firm wants to deviate because both firms see their current strategy as optimal given the other firm's chosen strategy. The Nash equilibrium is stable and persistent. Attempts by the firms to rig games to achieve some other outcome are difficult to accomplish and maintain, although credible threats can sometimes work. In contrast, empty threats accomplish nothing and leave the outcome at the Nash equilibrium.

3. Reciprocity can improve outcomes for firms participating in repeated games. In such games, one firm avoids taking advantage of the other firm because it knows that the other firm can take advantage of it in subsequent games. This reciprocity increases firm profits relative to what they would have been without reciprocity.

4. Two possible Nash equilibriums can exist in sequential games with first-mover advantages. Which one occurs depends on which firm moves first since that firm can preempt the other firm, making it unprofitable for the other firm to match the move. Several real-world firms including Wal-Mart have successfully used first-mover advantages to saturate markets and preempt entry by rivals.

Appendix Terms and Concepts

one-time game	negative-sum game	empty threat
simultaneous game	dominant strategy	repeated game
positive-sum game	Nash equilibrium	sequential game
zero-sum game	credible threat	first-mover advantage

Appendix Study Questions

1. Is the game shown by Figure 11.3 in the chapter (not this appendix) a zero-sum game or is it a positive-sum game? How can you tell? Are there dominant strategies in this game? If so, what are they? What cell represents a Nash equilibrium and why? Explain why it is so difficult for Uptown and RareAir to achieve and maintain a more favorable cell than the Nash equilibrium in this single-period pricing game. **LO8**

2. Refer to the payoff matrix in question 8 at the end of this chapter. First, assume this is a one-time game. Explain how the $60/$57 outcome might be achieved through a credible threat. Next, assume this is a repeated game (rather than a one-time game) and that the interaction between the two firms occurs indefinitely. Why might collusion with a credible threat not be necessary to achieve the $60/$57 outcome? **LO8**

3. Refer to the payoff matrix below. **LO8**

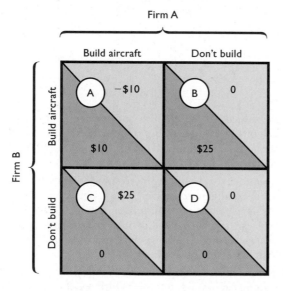

Assuming this is a sequential game with no collusion, what is the outcome if Firm A moves first to build a new type of commercial aircraft? Explain why first-mover strategies in the realworld are only as good as the profit projections on which they are based. How could a supposed "win" from moving first turn out to be a big loss, whereas the "loss" of being preempted turn out to be a blessing in disguise?

4. **ADVANCED** Suppose you are playing a game in which you and one other person each picks a number between 1 and 100, with the person closest to some randomly selected number between 1 and 100 winning the jackpot. (Ask your instructor to fund the jackpot.) Your opponent picks first. What number do you expect her to choose? Why? What number would you then pick? Why are the two numbers so close? How might this example relate to why Home Depot and Lowes, Walgreens and Rite-Aid, McDonald's and Burger King, Borders and Barnes & Noble, and other major pairs of rivals locate so close to each other in many well-defined geographical markets that are large enough for both firms to be profitable? **LO8**

IN THIS CHAPTER YOU WILL LEARN:

1 The differences between an invention, an innovation, and technological diffusion.

2 How entrepreneurs and other innovators further technological advance.

3 How a firm determines its optimal amount of research and development (R&D).

4 Why firms can benefit from their innovation even though rivals have an incentive to imitate it.

5 About the role of market structure in promoting technological advance.

6 How technological advance enhances productive efficiency and allocative efficiency.

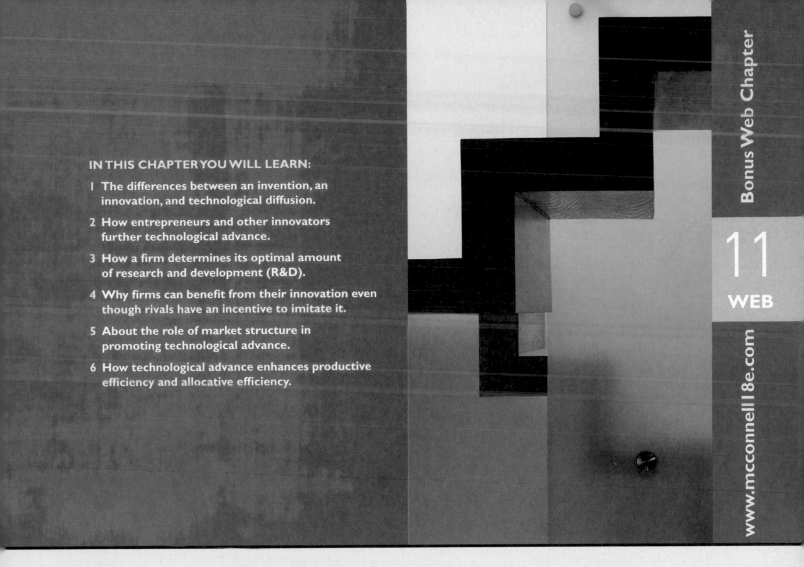

Technology, R&D, and Efficiency

Chapter 11 Web is a bonus chapter found at the book's Website, **www.mcconnell18e.com.** It extends the analysis of Part 2, "Microeconomics of Product Markets," by examining such topics as invention, innovation, R&D decision making, and creative destruction. Your instructor may (or may not) assign all or part of this chapter.

PART THREE

Microeconomics of Resource
Markets

The Demand for Resources

When you finish your education, you probably will be looking for a new job. But why would someone want to hire you? The answer, of course, is that you have a lot to offer. Employers have a demand for educated, productive workers like you.

We need to learn more about the demand for labor and other resources. So, we now turn from the pricing and production of *goods and services* to the pricing and employment of *resources*. Although firms come in various sizes and operate under highly different market conditions, each has a demand for productive resources. Firms obtain needed resources from households—the direct or indirect owners of land, labor, capital, and entrepreneurial resources. So, referring to the circular flow model (Figure 2.4, page 40), we shift our attention from the bottom loop of the diagram (where businesses supply products that households demand) to the top loop (where businesses demand resources that households supply).

This chapter looks at the *demand* for economic resources. Although the discussion is couched in terms of labor, the principles developed also apply to land, capital, and entrepreneurial ability. In Chapter 13 we will combine resource (labor) demand with labor *supply* to analyze wage rates. In Chapter 14 we will use resource demand and resource supply to examine the prices of, and returns to, other productive resources. Issues relating to the use of natural resources are the subject of Chapter 15.

Significance of Resource Pricing

Studying resource pricing is important for several reasons:

- *Money-income determination* Resource prices are a major factor in determining the income of households. The expenditures that firms make in acquiring economic resources flow as wage, rent, interest, and profit incomes to the households that supply those resources.

- *Cost minimization* To the firm, resource prices are costs. And to obtain the greatest profit, the firm must produce the profit-maximizing output with the most efficient (least costly) combination of resources. Resource prices play the main role in determining the quantities of land, labor, capital, and entrepreneurial ability that will be combined in producing each good or service (see Table 2.1, p. 36).

- *Resource allocation* Just as product prices allocate finished goods and services to consumers, resource prices allocate resources among industries and firms. In a dynamic economy, where technology and product demand often change, the efficient allocation of resources over time calls for the continuing shift of resources from one use to another. Resource pricing is a major factor in producing those shifts.

- *Policy issues* Many policy issues surround the resource market. Examples: To what extent should government redistribute income through taxes and transfers? Should government do anything to discourage "excess" pay to corporate executives? Should it increase the legal minimum wage? Is the provision of subsidies to farmers efficient? Should government encourage or restrict labor unions? The facts and debates relating to these policy questions are grounded on resource pricing.

Marginal Productivity Theory of Resource Demand

In discussing resource demand, we will first assume that a firm sells its output in a purely competitive product market and hires a certain resource in a purely competitive resource market. This assumption keeps things simple and is consistent with the model of a competitive labor market that we will develop in Chapter 13. In a competitive *product market*, the firm is a "price taker" and can dispose of as little or as much output as it chooses at the market price. The firm is selling such a negligible fraction of total output that its output decisions exert no influence on product price. Similarly, the firm also is a "price taker" (or "wage taker") in the competitive *resource market*. It purchases such a negligible fraction of the total supply of the resource that its buying (or hiring) decisions do not influence the resource price.

Resource Demand as a Derived Demand

Resource demand is the starting point for any discussion of resource prices. Other things equal, the demand for a resource is an inverse relationship between the price of the resource and the quantity of the resource demanded. This demand is a **derived demand**: It is derived from the products that the resources help produce. Resources usually do not directly satisfy customer wants but do so indirectly through their use in producing goods and services. Almost nobody wants to consume an acre of land, a John Deere tractor, or the labor services of a farmer, but millions of households do want to consume the food and fiber products that these resources help produce. Similarly, the demand for airplanes generates a demand for assemblers, and the demands for such services as income-tax preparation, haircuts, and child care create derived demands for accountants, barbers, and child care workers.

Marginal Revenue Product

Because resource demand is derived from product demand, the strength of the demand for any resource will depend on:

- The productivity of the resource in helping to create a good or service.
- The market value or price of the good or service it helps produce.

A resource that is highly productive in turning out a highly valued commodity will be in great demand. On the other hand, a relatively unproductive resource that is capable of producing only a minimally valued commodity will be in little demand. And no demand whatsoever will exist for a resource that is phenomenally efficient in producing something that no one wants to buy.

Productivity Table 12.1 shows the roles of resource productivity and product price in determining resource

TABLE 12.1 **The Demand for Labor: Pure Competition in the Sale of the Product**

(1) Units of Resource	(2) Total Product (Output)	(3) Marginal Product (MP)	(4) Product Price	(5) Total Revenue, (2) × (4)	(6) Marginal Revenue Product (MRP)
0	0		$2	$ 0	
		⌐——— 7			⌐——— $14
1	7		2	14	
		⌐——— 6			⌐——— 12
2	13		2	26	
		⌐——— 5			⌐——— 10
3	18		2	36	
		⌐——— 4			⌐——— 8
4	22		2	44	
		⌐——— 3			⌐——— 6
5	25		2	50	
		⌐——— 2			⌐——— 4
6	27		2	54	
		⌐——— 1			⌐——— 2
7	28		2	56	

demand. Here we assume that a firm adds one variable resource, labor, to its fixed plant. Columns 1 and 2 give the number of units of the resource applied to production and the resulting total product (output). Column 3 provides the **marginal product (MP)**, or additional output, resulting from using each additional unit of labor. Columns 1 through 3 remind us that the law of diminishing returns applies here, causing the marginal product of labor to fall beyond some point. For simplicity, we assume that these diminishing marginal returns—these declines in marginal product—begin with the first worker hired.

Product Price

But the derived demand for a resource depends also on the price of the product it produces. Column 4 in Table 12.1 adds this price information. Product price is constant, in this case at $2, because the product market is competitive. The firm is a price taker and will sell units of output only at this market price.

Multiplying column 2 by column 4 provides the total-revenue data of column 5. These are the amounts of revenue the firm realizes from the various levels of resource usage. From these total-revenue data we can compute **marginal revenue product (MRP)**—the change in total revenue resulting from the use of each additional unit of a resource (labor, in this case). In equation form,

$$\text{Marginal revenue product} = \frac{\text{change in total revenue}}{\text{unit change in resource quantity}}$$

The MRPs are listed in column 6 in Table 12.1.

Rule for Employing Resources: MRP = MRC

The MRP schedule, shown as columns 1 and 6, is the firm's demand schedule for labor. To understand why, you must first know the rule that guides a profit-seeking firm in hiring any resource:

To maximize profit, a firm should hire additional units of a specific resource as long as each successive unit adds more to the firm's total revenue than it adds to the firm's total cost.

Economists use special terms to designate what each additional unit of labor or other variable resource adds to total cost and what it adds to total revenue. We have seen that MRP measures how much each successive unit of a resource adds to total revenue. The amount that each additional unit of a resource adds to the firm's total (resource) cost is called its **marginal resource cost (MRC)**.

In equation form,

$$\text{Marginal resource cost} = \frac{\text{change in total (resource) cost}}{\text{unit change in resource quantity}}$$

So we can restate our rule for hiring resources as follows: It will be profitable for a firm to hire additional units of a resource up to the point at which that resource's MRP is equal to its MRC. For example, as the rule applies to labor, if the number of workers a firm is currently hiring is such that the MRP of the last worker exceeds his or her MRC, the firm can profit by hiring more workers. But if the number being hired is such that the MRC of the last worker exceeds his or her MRP, the firm is hiring workers who are not "paying their way" and it can increase its profit by discharging some workers. You may have recognized that this **MRP = MRC rule** is similar to the MR = MC profit-maximizing rule employed throughout our discussion of price and output determination. The rationale of the two rules is the same, but the point of reference is now *inputs* of a resource, not *outputs* of a product.

MRP as Resource Demand Schedule

Let's continue with our focus on labor, knowing that the analysis also applies to other resources. In a purely competitive labor market, market supply and market demand establish the wage rate. Because each firm hires such a small fraction of market supply, it cannot influence the market wage rate; it is a wage taker, not a wage maker. This means that for each additional unit of labor hired, total resource cost increases by exactly the amount of the constant market wage rate. The MRC of labor exactly equals the market wage rate. Thus, resource "price" (the market wage rate) and resource "cost" (marginal resource cost) are equal for a firm that hires a resource in a competitive labor market. Then the MRP = MRC rule tells us that, in pure competition, the firm will hire workers up to the point at which the market *wage rate* (its MRC) is equal to its MRP.

In terms of the data in columns 1 and 6 of Table 12.1, if the market wage rate is, say, $13.95, the firm will hire only one worker. This is so because the first worker adds $14 to total revenue and slightly less—$13.95—to total cost. In other words, because MRP exceeds MRC for the first worker, it is profitable to hire that worker. For each successive worker, however, MRC (= $13.95) exceeds MRP (= $12 or less), indicating that it will not be profitable to hire any of those workers. If the wage rate is $11.95, by the same reasoning we discover that it will pay the firm to hire both the first and second workers. Similarly, if the wage rate is $9.95, three workers will be hired. If it is $7.95, four. If it is $5.95, five. And so forth. So here is the key generalization: The MRP schedule constitutes the firm's demand for labor because each point on this schedule (or curve) indicates the number of workers the firm would hire at each possible wage rate.

In Figure 12.1, we show the D = MRP curve based on the data in Table 12.1.[1] The competitive firm's resource demand curve identifies an inverse relationship between the wage rate and the quantity of labor demanded, other things equal. The curve slopes downward because of diminishing marginal returns.

Resource Demand under Imperfect Product Market Competition

Our analysis of resource demand (here, labor demand) becomes more complex when the firm is selling its product in an imperfectly competitive market, one in which the firm is a price maker. Pure monopoly, oligopoly, and monopolistic competition in the product market all mean that

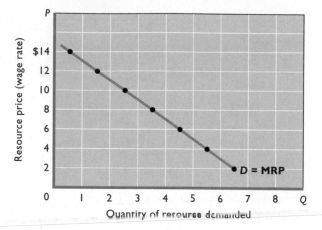

FIGURE 12.1 The purely competitive seller's demand for a resource. The MRP curve is the resource demand curve; each of its points relates a particular resource price (= MRP when profit is maximized) with a corresponding quantity of the resource demanded. Under pure competition, product price is constant; therefore, the downward slope of the D = MRP curve is due solely to the decline in the resource's marginal product (law of diminishing marginal returns).

the firm's product demand curve is downsloping; when the curve is fixed in place, the firm can increase its sales only by setting a lower price.

The productivity data in Table 12.1 are retained in columns 1 to 3 in Table 12.2. But here in Table 12.2 we show in column 4 that product price must be lowered to sell the marginal product of each successive worker. The MRP of the purely competitive seller of Table 12.1 falls for a single reason: Marginal product diminishes. But the MRP of the imperfectly competitive seller of Table 12.2 falls for two reasons: Marginal product diminishes *and* product price falls as output increases.

We emphasize that the lower price accompanying each increase in output (total product) applies not only to the marginal product of each successive worker but also to all prior output units that otherwise could have been sold at a higher price. Observe that the marginal product of the second worker is 6 units of output. These 6 units can be sold for $2.40 each, or, as a group, for $14.40. But $14.40 is not the MRP of the second worker. To sell these 6 units, the firm must take a 20-cent price cut on the 7 units produced by the first worker—units that otherwise could have been sold for $2.60 each. Thus, the MRP of the second worker is only $13 [= $14.40 − (7 × 20 cents)], as shown.

Similarly, the third worker adds 5 units to total product, and these units are worth $2.20 each, or $11 total. But to sell these 5 units, the firm must take a 20-cent price cut on the 13 units produced by the first two workers. So the third worker's MRP is only $8.40 [= $11 − (13 × 20 cents)]. The other figures in column 6 are derived similarly.

---

[1]Note that we plot the points in Figure 12.1 halfway between succeeding numbers of resource units because MRP is associated with the addition of 1 more unit. Thus in Figure 12.1, for example, we plot the MRP of the second unit ($12) not at 1 or 2 but at $1\frac{1}{2}$. This "smoothing" enables us to sketch a continuously downsloping curve rather than one that moves downward in discrete steps as each new unit of labor is hired.

TABLE 12.2 **The Demand for Labor: Imperfect Competition in the Sale of the Product**

(1) Units of Resource	(2) Total Product (Output)	(3) Marginal Product (MP)	(4) Product Price	(5) Total Revenue, (2) × (4)	(6) Marginal Revenue Product (MRP)
0	0		$2.80	$ 0	
		7			$18.20
1	7		2.60	18.20	
		6			13.00
2	13		2.40	31.20	
		5			8.40
3	18		2.20	39.60	
		4			4.40
4	22		2.00	44.00	
		3			2.25
5	25		1.85	46.25	
		2			1.00
6	27		1.75	47.25	
		1			−1.05
7	28		1.65	46.20	

In Figure 12.2 we graph the MRP data from Table 12.2 and label it "*D* = MRP (imperfect competition)." The broken-line resource demand curve, in contrast, is that of the purely competitive seller represented in Figure 12.1. A comparison of the two curves demonstrates that, other things equal, the resource demand curve of an imperfectly competitive seller is less elastic than that of a purely competitive seller. Consider the effects of an identical percentage decline in the wage rate (resource price) from $11 to $6 in Figure 12.2. Comparison of the two curves reveals that the imperfectly competitive seller (solid curve) does not expand the quantity of labor it employs by as large a percentage as does the purely competitive seller (broken curve).

FIGURE 12.2 **The imperfectly competitive seller's demand curve for a resource.** An imperfectly competitive seller's resource demand curve *D* (solid) slopes downward because both marginal product and product price fall as resource employment and output rise. This downward slope is greater than that for a purely competitive seller (dashed resource demand curve) because the pure competitor can sell the added output at a constant price.

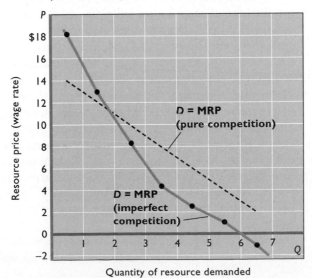

Quantity of resource demanded

It is not surprising that the imperfectly competitive producer is less responsive to resource price cuts than the purely competitive producer. The imperfect competitor's relative reluctance to employ more resources, and produce more output, when resource prices fall reflects its tendency to restrict output in the product market. Other things equal, the imperfectly competitive seller produces less of a product than a purely competitive seller. In producing that smaller output, it demands fewer resources. **(Key Question 2)**

WORKED PROBLEMS

W 12.1

Resource demand

Market Demand for a Resource

The total, or market, demand curve for a specific resource shows the various total amounts of the resource that firms will purchase or hire at various resource prices, other things equal. Recall that the total, or market, demand curve for a *product* is found by summing horizontally the demand curves of all individual buyers in the market. The market demand curve for a particular *resource* is derived in essentially the same way—by summing horizontally the individual demand or MRP curves for all firms hiring that resource.

QUICK REVIEW 12.1

- To maximize profit, a firm will purchase or hire a resource in an amount at which the resource's marginal revenue product equals its marginal resource cost (MRP = MRC).
- Application of the MRP = MRC rule to a firm's MRP curve demonstrates that the MRP curve is the firm's resource demand curve. In a purely competitive resource market, resource price (the wage rate) equals MRC.
- The resource demand curve of a purely competitive seller is downsloping solely because the marginal product of the resource diminishes; the resource demand curve of an imperfectly competitive seller is downsloping because marginal product diminishes *and* product price falls as output is increased.

CONSIDER THIS . . .

Superstars

In what economist Robert Frank calls "winner-take-all-markets," a few highly talented performers have huge earnings relative to the average performers in the market. Because consumers and firms seek out "top" performers, small differences in talent or popularity get magnified into huge differences in pay.

In these markets, consumer spending gets channeled toward a few performers. The media then "hypes" these individuals, which further increases the public's awareness of their talents. Many more consumers then buy the stars' products. Although it is not easy to stay on top, several superstars emerge.

The high earnings of superstars results from the high revenues they generate from their work. Consider Beyoncé Knowles. If she sold only a few thousand songs and attracted only a few hundred fans to each concert, the revenue she would produce—her marginal revenue product—would be quite modest. So, too, would be her earnings.

But consumers have anointed Beyoncé as queen of the R&B and hip-hop portion of pop culture. The demand for her music and concerts is extraordinarily high. She sells *millions* of songs, not thousands, and draws *thousands* to her concerts, not hundreds. Her extraordinarily high net earnings derive from her extraordinarily high MRP.

So it is for the other superstars in the "winner-take-all markets." Influenced by the media, but coerced by no one, consumers direct their spending toward a select few. The resulting strong demand for these stars' services reflects their high MRP. And because top talent (by definition) is very limited, superstars receive amazingly high earnings.

Determinants of Resource Demand

What will alter the demand for a resource—that is, shift the resource demand curve? The fact that resource demand is derived from *product demand* and depends on *resource productivity* suggests two "resource demand shifters." Also, our analysis of how changes in the prices of other products can shift a product's demand curve (Chapter 3) suggests another factor: changes in the *prices of other resources*.

Changes in Product Demand

Other things equal, an increase in the demand for a product will increase the demand for a resource used in its production, whereas a decrease in product demand will decrease the demand for that resource.

Let's see how this works. The first thing to recall is that a change in the demand for a product will change its price. In Table 12.1, let's assume that an increase in product demand boosts product price from $2 to $3. You should calculate the new resource demand schedule (columns 1 and 6) that would result and plot it in Figure 12.1 to verify that the new resource demand curve lies to the right of the old demand curve. Similarly, a decline in the product demand (and price) will shift the resource demand curve to the left. This effect—resource demand changing along with product demand—demonstrates that resource demand is derived from product demand.

Example: Assuming no offsetting change in supply, a decrease in the demand for new houses will drive down house prices. Those lower prices will decrease the MRP of construction workers, and therefore the demand for construction workers will fall. The resource demand curve such as in Figure 12.1 or Figure 12.2 will shift to the left.

Changes in Productivity

Other things equal, an increase in the productivity of a resource will increase the demand for the resource and a decrease in productivity will reduce the demand for the resource. If we doubled the MP data of column 3 in Table 12.1, the MRP data of column 6 would also double, indicating a rightward shift of the resource demand curve.

The productivity of any resource may be altered over the long run in several ways:

- ***Quantities of other resources*** The marginal productivity of any resource will vary with the quantities of the other resources used with it. The greater the amount of capital and land resources used with, say, labor, the greater will be labor's marginal productivity and, thus, labor demand.

- ***Technological advance*** Technological improvements that increase the quality of other resources, such as capital, have the same effect. The better the *quality* of capital, the greater the productivity of labor used with it. Dockworkers employed with a specific amount of real capital in the form of unloading cranes are more productive than dockworkers with the same amount of real capital embodied in older conveyor-belt systems.

- ***Quality of the variable resource*** Improvements in the quality of the variable resource, such as labor, will increase its marginal productivity and therefore its demand. In effect, there will be a new demand curve for a different, more skilled, kind of labor.

All these considerations help explain why the average level of (real) wages is higher in industrially advanced nations (for example, the United States, Germany, Japan, and France) than in developing nations (for example, Nicaragua, Ethiopia, Angola, and Cambodia). Workers in industrially advanced nations are generally healthier, better educated, and better trained than are workers in developing countries. Also, in most industries they work with a larger and more efficient stock of capital goods and more abundant natural resources. This creates a strong demand for labor. On the supply side of the market, labor is scarcer relative to capital in industrially advanced than in most developing nations. A strong demand and a relatively scarce supply of labor result in high wage rates in the industrially advanced nations.

Changes in the Prices of Other Resources

Changes in the prices of other resources may change the demand for a specific resource. For example, a change in the price of capital may change the demand for labor. The direction of the change in labor demand will depend on whether labor and capital are substitutes or complements in production.

Substitute Resources
Suppose the technology in a certain production process is such that labor and capital are substitutable. A firm can produce some specific amount of output using a relatively small amount of labor and a relatively large amount of capital, or vice versa. Now assume that the price of machinery (capital) falls. The effect on the demand for labor will be the net result of two opposed effects: the substitution effect and the output effect.

- *Substitution effect* The decline in the price of machinery prompts the firm to substitute machinery for labor. This allows the firm to produce its output at lower cost. So at the fixed wage rate, smaller quantities of labor are now employed. This **substitution effect** decreases the demand for labor. More generally, the substitution effect indicates that a firm will purchase more of an input whose relative price has declined and, conversely, use less of an input whose relative price has increased.

- *Output effect* Because the price of machinery has fallen, the costs of producing various outputs must also decline. With lower costs, the firm finds it profitable to produce and sell a greater output. The greater output increases the demand for all resources, including labor. So this **output effect** increases the demand for labor. More generally, the output effect means that the firm will purchase more of one particular input when the price of the other input falls and less of that particular input when the price of the other input rises.

- *Net effect* The substitution and output effects are both present when the price of an input changes, but they work in opposite directions. For a decline in the price of capital, the substitution effect decreases the demand for labor and the output effect increases it. The net change in labor demand depends on the relative sizes of the two effects: If the substitution effect outweighs the output effect, a decrease in the price of capital decreases the demand for labor. If the output effect exceeds the substitution effect, a decrease in the price of capital increases the demand for labor.

Complementary Resources Recall from Chapter 3 that certain products, such as computers and software, are complementary goods; they "go together" and are jointly demanded. Resources may also be complementary; an increase in the quantity of one of them used in the production process requires an increase in the amount used of the other as well, and vice versa. Suppose a small design firm does computer-assisted design (CAD) with relatively expensive personal computers as its basic piece of capital equipment. Each computer requires exactly one design engineer to operate it; the machine is not automated—it will not run itself—and a second engineer would have nothing to do.

Now assume that a technological advance in the production of these computers substantially reduces their price. There can be no substitution effect because labor and capital must be used in *fixed proportions*, one person for one machine. Capital cannot be substituted for labor. But there *is* an output effect. Other things equal, the reduction in the price of capital goods means lower production costs. Producing a larger output will therefore be profitable. In doing so, the firm will use both more capital and more labor. When labor and capital are complementary, a decline in the price of capital increases the demand for labor through the output effect.

We have cast our analysis of substitute resources and complementary resources mainly in terms of a decline in the price of capital. Table 12.3 summarizes the effects of an *increase* in the price of capital on the demand for labor. Please study it carefully.

Now that we have discussed the full list of the determinants of labor demand, let's again review their effects. Stated in terms of the labor resource, the demand for

TABLE 12.3 **The Effect of an Increase in the Price of Capital on the Demand for Labor, D_L**

(1) Relationship of Inputs	(2) Increase in the Price of Capital		
	(a) Substitution Effect	(b) Output Effect	(c) Combined Effect
Substitutes in production	Labor substituted for capital	Production costs up, output down, and less of both capital and labor used	D_L increases if the substitution effect exceeds the output effect; D_L decreases if the output effect exceeds the substitution effect
Complements in production	No substitution of labor for capital	Production costs up, output down, and less of both capital and labor used	D_L decreases

labor will increase (the labor demand curve will shift rightward) when:

- The demand for (and therefore the price of) the product produced by that labor *increases*.
- The productivity (MP) of labor *increases*.
- The price of a substitute input *decreases*, provided the output effect exceeds the substitution effect.
- The price of a substitute input *increases*, provided the substitution effect exceeds the output effect.
- The price of a complementary input *decreases*.

Be sure that you can "reverse" these effects to explain a *decrease* in labor demand.

Table 12.4 provides several illustrations of the determinants of labor demand, listed by the categories of determinants we have discussed. You will benefit by giving them a close look.

Occupational Employment Trends

Changes in labor demand have considerable significance since they affect wage rates and employment in specific occupations. Increases in labor demand for certain occupational groups result in increases in their employment; decreases in labor demand result in decreases in their employment. For illustration, let's first look at occupations for which labor demand is growing and then examine occupations for which it is declining. (Wage rates are the subject of the next chapter.)

The Fastest-Growing Occupations Table 12.5 lists the 10 fastest-growing U.S. occupations for 2006 to 2016, as measured by percentage changes and projected by the Bureau of Labor Statistics. It is no coincidence that the service occupations dominate the list. In general, the demand for service workers in the United States is rapidly outpacing the demand for manufacturing, construction, and mining workers.

Of the 10 fastest-growing occupations in percentage terms, three—personal and home care aides (people who provide home care for the elderly and disabled), home health care aides (people who provide short-term medical care after discharge from hospitals), and medical assistants—are related to health care. The rising demands for these

TABLE 12.4 **Determinants of Labor Demand: Factors That Shift the Labor Demand Curve**

Determinant	Examples
Change in product demand	Gambling increases in popularity, increasing the demand for workers at casinos. Consumers decrease their demand for leather coats, decreasing the demand for tanners. The Federal government increases spending on homeland security, increasing the demand for security personnel.
Change in productivity	An increase in the skill levels of physicians increases the demand for their services. Computer-assisted graphic design increases the productivity of, and demand for, graphic artists.
Change in the price of another resource	An increase in the price of electricity increases the cost of producing aluminum and reduces the demand for aluminum workers. The price of security equipment used by businesses to protect against illegal entry falls, decreasing the demand for night guards. The price of cell phone equipment decreases, reducing the cost of cell phone service; this in turn increases the demand for cell phone assemblers. Health-insurance premiums rise, and firms substitute part-time workers who are not covered by insurance for full-time workers who are.

TABLE 12.5 The 10 Fastest-Growing U.S. Occupations in Percentage Terms, 2006–2016

| Occupation | Employment, Thousands of Jobs | | Percentage Increase* |
	2006	2016	
Network systems and data communication analysts	262	402	53.4
Personal and home care aides	767	1156	50.6
Home health aides	787	1171	48.7
Software engineers, applications	507	733	44.6
Veterinary technicians	71	100	41.0
Personal financial advisors	176	248	41.0
Make-up artists	2	3	39.8
Medical assistants	417	565	35.4
Veterinarians	62	64	35.0
Substance abuse and behavioral disorder counselors	83	112	34.3

*Percentages and employment numbers may not reconcile due to rounding.

Source: Bureau of Labor Statistics, "Employment Projections," **www.bls.gov.**

TABLE 12.6 The 10 Most Rapidly Declining U.S. Occupations in Percentage Terms, 2006–2016

| Occupation | Employment, Thousands of Jobs | | Percentage Increase* |
	2006	2016	
Photographic processing machine operators	49	25	−49.8
File clerks	234	137	−41.3
Model makers and pattern makers, wood	4	2	−40.3
Telephone operators	27	16	−39.5
Shoe machine operators	4	3	−35.7
Forging machine operators	31	21	−30.4
Electrical coil winders, tapers, and finishers	23	16	−30.5
Fabric and apparel pattern makers	9	7	−28.6
Textile machine operators	122	88	−27.9
Sewing machine operators	233	170	−27.2

*Percentages and employment numbers may not reconcile due to rounding.

Source: Bureau of Labor Statistics, "Employment Projections," **www.bls.gov.**

types of labor are derived from the growing demand for health services, caused by several factors. The aging of the U.S. population has brought with it more medical problems, the rising standard of income has led to greater expenditures on health care, and the continued presence of private and public insurance has allowed people to buy more health care than most could afford individually.

Two of the fastest-growing occupations are directly related to computers. The increase in the demand for network systems and data communication analysts and computer software engineers arises from the rapid rise in the demand for computers, computer services, and Internet use. It also results from the rising marginal revenue productivity of these particular workers, given the vastly improved quality of the computer and communications equipment they work with. Moreover, price declines on such equipment have had stronger output effects than substitution effects, increasing the demand for these kinds of labor.

The Most Rapidly Declining Occupations

In contrast, Table 12.6 lists the 10 U.S. occupations with the greatest projected job loss (in percentage terms) between 2006 and 2016. Several of the occupations owe their declines mainly to "labor-saving" technological change. For example, automated or computerized equipment has greatly reduced the need for file clerks, model and pattern makers, and telephone operators. The advent of digital photography explains the projected decline in the employment of people operating photographic processing equipment.

Three of the occupations in the declining employment list are related to textiles and apparel. The U.S. demand for these goods is increasingly being filled through imports. Those jobs are therefore rapidly disappearing in the United States.

As we indicated, the "top-10" lists shown in Tables 12.5 and 12.6 are based on percentage changes. In terms of absolute job growth and loss, the greatest projected employment growth between 2006 and 2016 is for registered nurses (587,000 jobs) and retail sales persons (557,000 jobs). The greatest projected absolute decline in employment is for stock clerks (−131,000) and cashiers (−116,000 jobs).

Elasticity of Resource Demand

The employment changes we have just discussed have resulted from shifts in the locations of resource demand curves. Such changes in demand must be distinguished from changes in the quantity of a resource demanded caused by a change in the price of the specific resource under consideration. Such a change is caused not by a shift of the demand curve but, rather, by a movement from one point to another on a fixed resource demand curve. Example: In Figure 12.1 we note that an increase in the wage rate from $5 to $7 will reduce the quantity of labor demanded from 5 to 4 units. This is a change in the *quantity of labor demanded* as distinct from a *change in demand*.

The sensitivity of resource quantity to changes in resource prices is measured by the **elasticity of resource demand.** In coefficient form,

$$E_{rd} = \frac{\text{percentage change in resource quantity}}{\text{percentage change in resource price}}$$

When E_{rd} is greater than 1, resource demand is elastic; when E_{rd} is less than 1, resource demand is inelastic; and when E_{rd} equals 1, resource demand is unit-elastic. What determines the elasticity of resource demand? Several factors are at work.

Ease of Resource Substitutability

The degree to which resources are substitutable is a fundamental determinant of elasticity. The greater the substitutability of other resources, the more elastic is the demand for a particular resource. Because automated voice mail systems are highly substitutable for telephone receptionists, the demand for receptionists is quite elastic. In contrast, good substitutes for physicians are rare, so demand for them is less elastic or even inelastic. If a furniture manufacturer finds that several types of wood are equally satisfactory in making coffee tables, a rise in the price of any one type of wood may cause a sharp drop in the amount demanded as the producer substitutes some other type of wood for the type of wood whose price has gone up. At the other extreme, there may be no reasonable substitutes; bauxite is absolutely essential in the production of aluminum ingots. Thus, the demand for bauxite by aluminum producers is inelastic.

Time can play a role in the ease of input substitution. For example, a firm's truck drivers may obtain a substantial wage increase with little or no immediate decline in employment. But over time, as the firm's trucks wear out and are replaced, that wage increase may motivate the company to purchase larger trucks and in that way deliver the same total output with fewer drivers.

Elasticity of Product Demand

Because the demand for labor is a derived demand, the elasticity of the demand for the output that the labor is producing will influence the elasticity of the demand for labor. Other things equal, the greater the price elasticity of product demand, the greater the elasticity of resource demand. For example, suppose that the wage rate falls. This means a decline in the cost of producing the product and a drop in the product's price. If the elasticity of product demand is great, the resulting increase in the quantity of the product demanded will be large and thus necessitate a large increase in the quantity of labor to produce the additional output. This implies an elastic demand for labor. But if the demand for the product is inelastic, the increase in the amount of the product demanded will be small, as will be the increases in the quantity of labor demanded. This suggests an inelastic demand for labor.

Remember that the resource demand curve in Figure 12.1 is more elastic than the resource demand curve shown in Figure 12.2. The difference arises because in Figure 12.1 we assume a perfectly elastic product demand curve, whereas Figure 12.2 is based on a downsloping or less than perfectly elastic product demand curve.

Ratio of Resource Cost to Total Cost

The larger the proportion of total production costs accounted for by a resource, the greater the elasticity of demand for that resource. In the extreme, if labor cost is the only production cost, then a 20 percent increase in wage rates will shift all the firm's cost curves upward by 20 percent. If product demand is elastic, this substantial increase in costs will cause a relatively large decline in sales and a sharp decline in the amount of labor demanded. So labor demand is highly elastic. But if labor cost is only 50 percent of production cost, then a 20 percent increase in wage rates will increase costs by only 10 percent. With the same elasticity of product demand, this will cause a relatively small decline in sales and therefore in the amount of labor demanded. In this case the demand for labor is much less elastic. **(Key Question 5)**

QUICK REVIEW 12.2

- A resource demand curve will shift because of changes in product demand, changes in the productivity of the resource, and changes in the prices of other inputs.
- If resources A and B are substitutable, a decline in the price of A will decrease the demand for B provided the substitution effect exceeds the output effect. But if the output effect exceeds the substitution effect, the demand for B will increase.
- If resources C and D are complements, a decline in the price of C will increase the demand for D.
- Elasticity of resource demand measures the extent to which producers change the quantity of a resource they hire when its price changes.
- The elasticity of resource demand will be less the greater the difficulty of substituting other resources for the resource, the smaller the elasticity of product demand, and the smaller the proportion of total cost accounted for by the resource.

Optimal Combination of Resources*

So far, our main focus has been on one variable input, labor. But in the long run firms can vary the amounts of all the resources they use. That's why we need to consider what combination of resources a firm will choose when *all* its inputs are variable. While our analysis is based on two resources, it can be extended to any number of inputs.

We will consider two interrelated questions:

- What combination of resources will minimize costs at a specific level of output?
- What combination of resources will maximize profit?

The Least-Cost Rule

A firm is producing a specific output with the **least-cost combination of resources** when the last dollar spent on each resource yields the same marginal product. That is, the cost of any output is minimized when the ratios of marginal product to price of the last units of resources used are the same for each resource. In competitive resource markets, recall, marginal resource cost is the market resource price; the firm can hire as many or as few units of the resource as it wants at that price. Then, with just two resources, labor and capital, a competitive firm minimizes its total cost of a specific output when

$$\frac{\text{Marginal product of labor (MP}_L)}{\text{Price of labor }(P_L)} = \frac{\text{Marginal product of capital (MP}_C)}{\text{Price of capital }(P_C)} \quad (1)$$

Throughout, we will refer to the marginal products of labor and capital as MP_L and MP_C, respectively, and symbolize the price of labor by P_L and the price of capital by P_C.

A concrete example will show why fulfilling the condition in equation 1 leads to least-cost production. Assume that the price of both capital and labor is $1 per unit but that Siam Soups currently employs them in such amounts that the marginal product of labor is 10 and the marginal product of capital is 5. Our equation immediately tells us that this is not the least costly combination of resources:

$$\frac{MP_L = 10}{P_L = \$1} > \frac{MP_C = 5}{P_C = \$1}$$

Suppose Siam spends $1 less on capital and shifts that dollar to labor. It loses 5 units of output produced by the last dollar's worth of capital, but it gains 10 units of output from the extra dollar's worth of labor. Net output increases by

5 (= 10 − 5) units for the same total cost. More such shifting of dollars from capital to labor will push the firm *down* along its MP curve for labor and *up* along its MP curve for capital, increasing output and moving the firm toward a position of equilibrium where equation 1 is fulfilled. At that equilibrium position, the MP per dollar for the last unit of both labor and capital might be, for example, 7. And Siam will be producing a greater output for the same (original) cost.

Whenever the same total-resource cost can result in a greater total output, the cost per unit—and therefore the total cost of any specific level of output—can be reduced. Being able to produce a *larger* output with a *specific* total cost is the same as being able to produce a *specific* output with a *smaller* total cost. If Siam buys $1 less of capital, its output will fall by 5 units. If it spends only $.50 of that dollar on labor, the firm will increase its output by a compensating 5 units (= $\frac{1}{2}$ of the MP per dollar). Then the firm will realize the same total output at a $.50 lower total cost.

The cost of producing any specific output can be reduced as long as equation 1 does not hold. But when dollars have been shifted between capital and labor to the point where equation 1 holds, no additional changes in the use of capital and labor will reduce costs further. Siam will be producing that output using the least-cost combination of capital and labor.

All the long-run cost curves developed in Chapter 8 and used thereafter assume that the least-cost combination of inputs has been realized at each level of output. Any firm that combines resources in violation of the least-cost rule would have a higher-than-necessary average total cost at each level of output. That is, it would incur *X-inefficiency*, as discussed in Figure 10.7.

The producer's least-cost rule is analogous to the consumer's utility-maximizing rule described in Chapter 7. In achieving the utility-maximizing combination of goods, the consumer considers both his or her preferences as reflected in diminishing-marginal-utility data and the prices of the various products. Similarly, in achieving the cost-minimizing combination of resources, the producer considers both the marginal-product data and the price (costs) of the various resources.

The Profit-Maximizing Rule

Minimizing cost is not sufficient for maximizing profit. A firm can produce any level of output in the least costly way by applying equation 1. But only one unique level of output maximizes profit. Our earlier analysis of product markets showed that this profit-maximizing output occurs where marginal revenue equals marginal cost (MR = MC). Near the beginning of this chapter we determined that we could write this profit-maximizing condition as MRP = MRC as it relates to resource inputs.

---

*Note to Instructors: We consider this section to be optional. If desired, it can be skipped without loss of continuity. It can also be deferred until after the discussion of wage determination in the chapter that follows.

In a purely competitive resource market the marginal resource cost (MRC) is equal to the resource price P. Thus, for any competitive resource market, we have as our profit-maximizing equation

$$\text{MRP (resource)} = P \text{ (resource)}$$

This condition must hold for every variable resource, and in the long run all resources are variable. In competitive markets, a firm will therefore achieve its **profit-maximizing combination of resources** when each resource is employed to the point at which its marginal revenue product equals its resource price. For two resources, labor and capital, we need both

$$P_L = \text{MRP}_L \quad \text{and} \quad P_C = \text{MRP}_C$$

We can combine these conditions by dividing both sides of each equation by their respective prices and equating the results to get

$$\frac{\text{MRP}_L}{P_L} = \frac{\text{MRP}_C}{P_C} = 1 \qquad (2)$$

Note in equation 2 that it is not sufficient that the MRPs of the two resources be *proportionate* to their prices; the MRPs must be *equal* to their prices and the ratios therefore equal to 1. For example, if $\text{MRP}_L = \$15$, $P_L = \$5$, $\text{MRP}_C = \$9$, and $P_C = \$3$, Siam is underemploying both capital and labor even though the ratios of MRP to resource price are identical for both resources. The firm can expand its profit by hiring additional amounts of both capital and labor until it moves down their downsloping MRP curves to the points at which $\text{MRP}_L = \$5$ and $\text{MRP}_C = \$3$. The ratios will then be 5/5 and 3/3 and equal to 1.

The profit-maximizing position in equation 2 includes the cost-minimizing condition of equation 1. That is, if a

> **WORKED PROBLEMS**
> **W 12.2**
> Optimal combination of resources

firm is maximizing profit according to equation 2, then it must be using the least-cost combination of inputs to do so. However, the converse is not true: A firm operating at least cost according to equation 1 may not be operating at the output that maximizes its profit.

Numerical Illustration

A numerical illustration will help you understand the least-cost and profit-maximizing rules. In columns 2, 3, 2′, and 3′ in Table 12.7 we show the total products and marginal products for various amounts of labor and capital that are assumed to be the only inputs Siam needs in producing its soup. Both inputs are subject to diminishing returns.

We also assume that labor and capital are supplied in competitive resource markets at $8 and $12, respectively, and that Siam soup sells competitively at $2 per unit. For both labor and capital we can determine the total revenue associated with each input level by multiplying total product by the $2 product price. These data are shown in columns 4 and 4′. They enable us to calculate the marginal revenue product of each successive input of labor and capital as shown in columns 5 and 5′, respectively.

Producing at Least Cost What is the least-cost combination of labor and capital for Siam to use in producing, say, 50 units of output? The answer, which we can obtain by trial and error, is 3 units of labor and 2 units of capital. Columns 2 and 2′ indicate that this combination of labor and capital does, indeed, result in the required 50 (= 28 + 22) units of output. Now, note from columns 3 and 3′ that hiring 3 units of labor gives

TABLE 12.7 **Data for Finding the Least-Cost and Profit-Maximizing Combination of Labor and Capital, Siam Soups***

	Labor (Price = $8)					Capital (Price = $12)			
(1) Quantity	(2) Total Product (Output)	(3) Marginal Product	(4) Total Revenue	(5) Marginal Revenue Product	(1′) Quantity	(2′) Total Product (Output)	(3′) Marginal Product	(4′) Total Revenue	(5′) Marginal Revenue Product
0	0		$ 0		0	0		$ 0	
		12		$24			13		$26
1	12		24		1	13		26	
		10		20			9		18
2	22		44		2	22		44	
		6		12			6		12
3	28		56		3	28		56	
		5		10			4		8
4	33		66		4	32		64	
		4		8			3		6
5	37		74		5	35		70	
		3		6			2		4
6	40		80		6	37		74	
		2		4			1		2
7	42		84		7	38		76	

*To simplify, it is assumed in this table that the productivity of each resource is independent of the quantity of the other. For example, the total and marginal products of labor are assumed not to vary with the quantity of capital employed.

us $MP_L/P_L = \frac{6}{8} = \frac{3}{4}$ and hiring 2 units of capital gives us $MP_C/P_C = \frac{9}{12} = \frac{3}{4}$. So equation (1) is fulfilled. How can we verify that costs are actually minimized? First, we see that the total cost of employing 3 units of labor and 2 of capital is $48 [= (3 × $8) + (2 × $12)].

Other combinations of labor and capital will also yield 50 units of output, but at a higher cost than $48. For example, 5 units of labor and 1 unit of capital will produce 50 (= 37 + 13) units, but total cost is higher, at $52 [= (5 × $8) + (1 × $12)]. This comes as no surprise because 5 units of labor and 1 unit of capital violate the least-cost rule—$MP_L/P_L = \frac{4}{8}$, $MP_C/P_C = \frac{13}{12}$. Only the combination (3 units of labor and 2 units of capital) that minimizes total cost will satisfy equation 1. All other combinations capable of producing 50 units of output violate the cost-minimizing rule, and therefore cost more than $48.

Maximizing Profit
Will 50 units of output maximize Siam's profit? No, because the profit-maximizing terms of equation 2 are not satisfied when the firm employs 3 units of labor and 2 of capital. To maximize profit, each input should be employed until its price equals its marginal revenue product. But for 3 units of labor, labor's MRP in column 5 is $12 while its price is only $8. This means the firm could increase its profit by hiring more labor. Similarly, for 2 units of capital, we see in column 5' that capital's MRP is $18 and its price is only $12. This indicates that more capital should also be employed. By producing only 50 units of output (even though they are produced at least cost), labor and capital are being used in less-than-profit-maximizing amounts. The firm needs to expand its employment of labor and capital, thereby increasing its output.

Table 12.7 shows that the MRPs of labor and capital are equal to their prices, so equation 2 is fulfilled when Siam is employing 5 units of labor and 3 units of capital. So this is the profit-maximizing combination of inputs.[2] The firm's total cost will be $76, made up of $40 (= 5 × $8) of labor and $36 (= 3 × $12) of capital. Total revenue will be $130, found either by multiplying the total output of 65 (= 37 + 28) by the $2 product price or by summing the total revenues attributable to labor ($74) and to capital ($56). The difference between total revenue and total cost in this instance is $54 (= $130 − $76). Experiment with other combinations of labor and capital to demonstrate that they yield an economic profit of less than $54.

Note that the profit-maximizing combination of 5 units of labor and 3 units of capital is also a least-cost

---

[2]Because we are dealing with discrete (nonfractional) units of the two outputs here, the use of 4 units of labor and 2 units of capital is equally profitable. The fifth unit of labor's MRP and its price (cost) are equal at $8, so that the fifth labor unit neither adds to nor subtracts from the firm's profit; similarly, the third unit of capital has no effect on profit.

combination for this particular level of output. Using these resource amounts satisfies the least-cost requirement of equation 1 in that $MP_L/P_L = \frac{4}{8} - \frac{1}{2}$ and $MP_C/P_C = \frac{6}{12} = \frac{1}{2}$. (Key Questions 6 and 7)

Marginal Productivity Theory of Income Distribution

Our discussion of resource pricing is the cornerstone of the controversial view that fairness and economic justice are one of the outcomes of a competitive capitalist economy. Table 12.7 demonstrates, in effect, that workers receive income payments (wages) equal to the marginal contributions they make to their employers' outputs and revenues. In other words, workers are paid according to the value of the labor services that they contribute to production. Similarly, owners of the other resources receive income based on the value of the resources they supply in the production process.

In this **marginal productivity theory of income distribution,** income is distributed according to contribution to society's output.

ORIGIN OF THE IDEA

O 12.2

Marginal productivity theory of distribution

So, if you are willing to accept the proposition "To each according to the value of what he or she creates," income payments based on marginal revenue product provide a fair and equitable distribution of society's income.

This sounds reasonable, but you need to be aware of serious criticisms of this theory of income distribution:

- *Inequality* Critics argue that the distribution of income resulting from payment according to marginal productivity may be highly unequal because productive resources are very unequally distributed in the first place. Aside from their differences in mental and physical attributes, individuals encounter substantially different opportunities to enhance their productivity through education and training and the use of more and better equipment. Some people may not be able to participate in production at all because of mental or physical disabilities, and they would obtain no income under a system of distribution based solely on marginal productivity. Ownership of property resources is also highly unequal. Many owners of land and capital resources obtain their property by inheritance rather than through their own productive effort. Hence, income from inherited property resources conflicts with the "To each according to the value of what he or she creates" idea. Critics say that these inequalities call for progressive taxation and government spending

Input Substitution: The Case of ATMs

Banks Are Using More Automatic Teller Machines (ATMs) and Employing Fewer Human Tellers.

As you have learned from this chapter, a firm achieves its least-cost combination of inputs when the last dollar it spends on each input makes the same contribution to total output. This raises an interesting real-world question: What happens when technological advance makes available a new, highly productive capital good for which MP/P is greater than it is for other inputs, say, a particular type of labor? The answer is that the least-cost mix of resources abruptly changes, and the firm responds accordingly. If the new capital is a substitute for labor (rather than a complement), the firm replaces the particular type of labor with the new capital. That is exactly what is happening in the banking industry, in which ATMs are replacing human bank tellers.

ATMs made their debut about 37 years ago when U.S. firms Docutel and Diebold each introduced the product. Today, Diebold and NCR (also a U.S. firm) dominate global sales, with the Japanese firm Fujitsu being a distant third. The number of ATMs and their usage have exploded, and currently there are nearly 400,000 ATMs in the United States. In 1975, about 10 *million* ATM transactions occurred in the United States. Today there are about 11 *billion* U.S. ATM transactions each year.

ATMs are highly productive: A single machine can handle hundreds of transactions daily, thousands weekly, and millions over the course of several years. ATMs can not only handle cash withdrawals but also accept deposits and facilitate switches of funds between various accounts. Although ATMs are expensive for banks to buy and install, they are available 24 hours a day, and their cost per transaction is one-fourth the cost for human tellers. They rarely get "held up," and they do not quit their jobs (turnover among human tellers is nearly 50 percent per year). Moreover, ATMs are highly convenient; unlike human tellers, they are located not only at banks but also at busy street corners, workplaces, universities, and shopping malls. The same bank card that enables you to withdraw cash from your local ATM also enables you to withdraw pounds from an ATM in London, yen from an ATM in Tokyo, and even rubles from an ATM in Moscow. (All this, of course, assumes that you have money in your checking account!)

In the terminology of this chapter, the more productive, lower-priced ATMs have reduced the demand for a substitute in production—human tellers. Between 1990 and 2000, an estimated 80,000 human teller positions were eliminated, and more positions will disappear by 2010. Where will the people holding these jobs go? Most will eventually move to other occupations. Although the lives of individual tellers are disrupted, society clearly wins. Society obtains more convenient banking services as well as the other goods that these "freed-up" labor resources help produce.

Source: Based partly on Ben Craig, "Where Have All the Tellers Gone?" Federal Reserve Bank of Cleveland, *Economic Commentary*, Apr. 15, 1997; and statistics provided by the American Bankers Association.

---

programs aimed at creating an income distribution that will be more equitable than that which would occur if the income distribution were made strictly according to marginal productivity.

- *Market imperfections* The marginal productivity theory of income distribution rests on the assumptions of competitive markets. But, as we will see in Chapter 13, not all labor markets are highly competitive. In some labor markets employers exert their wage-setting power to pay less-than-competitive wages. And some workers, through labor unions, professional associations,

and occupational licensing laws, wield wage-setting power in selling their services. Even the process of collective bargaining over wages suggests a power struggle over the division of income. In wage setting through negotiations, market forces—and income shares based on marginal productivity—may get partially pushed into the background. In addition, discrimination in the labor market can distort earnings patterns. In short, because of real-world market imperfections, wage rates and other resource prices are not always based solely on contributions to output.

Summary

1. Resource prices help determine money incomes, and they simultaneously ration resources to various industries and firms.

2. The demand for any resource is derived from the product it helps produce. That means the demand for a resource will depend on its productivity and on the market value (price) of the good it is producing.

3. Marginal revenue product is the extra revenue a firm obtains when it employs 1 more unit of a resource. The marginal revenue product curve for any resource is the demand curve for that resource because the firm equates resource price and MRP in determining its profit-maximizing level of resource employment. Thus each point on the MRP curve indicates how many resource units the firm will hire at a specific resource price.

4. The firm's demand curve for a resource slopes downward because the marginal product of additional units declines in accordance with the law of diminishing returns. When a firm is selling in an imperfectly competitive market, the resource demand curve falls for a second reason: Product price must be reduced for the firm to sell a larger output. The market demand curve for a resource is derived by summing horizontally the demand curves of all the firms hiring that resource.

5. The demand curve for a resource will shift as the result of (a) a change in the demand for, and therefore the price of, the product the resource is producing; (b) changes in the productivity of the resource; and (c) changes in the prices of other resources.

6. If resources A and B are substitutable for each other, a decline in the price of A will decrease the demand for B provided the substitution effect is greater than the output effect. But if the output effect *exceeds* the substitution effect, a decline in the price of A will increase the demand for B.

7. If resources C and D are complementary or jointly demanded, there is only an output effect; a change in the price of C will change the demand for D in the opposite direction.

8. The majority of the 10 fastest-growing occupations in the United States—by percentage increase—relate to health care, computers, and veterinary care (review Table 12.5); the 10 most rapidly declining occupations by percentage decrease, however, are more mixed (review Table 12.6).

9. The elasticity of demand for a resource measures the responsiveness of producers to a change in the resource's price. The coefficient of the elasticity of resource demand is

$$E_{rd} = \frac{\text{percentage change in resource quantity}}{\text{percentage change in resource price}}$$

When E_{rd} is greater than 1, resource demand is elastic; when E_{rd} is less than 1, resource demand is inelastic; and when E_{rd} equals 1, resource demand is unit-elastic.

10. The elasticity of demand for a resource will be greater (a) the greater the ease of substituting other resources for labor, (b) the greater the elasticity of demand for the product, and (c) the larger the proportion of total production costs attributable to the resource.

11. Any specific level of output will be produced with the least costly combination of variable resources when the marginal product per dollar's worth of each input is the same—that is, when

$$\frac{\text{MP of labor}}{\text{Price of labor}} = \frac{\text{MP of capital}}{\text{Price of capital}}$$

12. A firm is employing the profit-maximizing combination of resources when each resource is used to the point where its marginal revenue product equals its price. In terms of labor and capital, that occurs when the MRP of labor equals the price of labor and the MRP of capital equals the price of capital—that is, when

$$\frac{\text{MRP of labor}}{\text{Price of labor}} = \frac{\text{MRP of capital}}{\text{Price of capital}} = 1$$

13. The marginal productivity theory of income distribution holds that all resources are paid according to their marginal contribution to output. Critics say that such an income distribution is too unequal and that real-world market imperfections result in pay above and below marginal contributions to output.

Terms and Concepts

derived demand

marginal product (MP)

marginal revenue product (MRP)

marginal resource cost (MRC)

MRP = MRC rule

substitution effect

output effect

elasticity of resource demand

least-cost combination of resources

profit-maximizing combination of resources

marginal productivity theory of income distribution

Study Questions

1. What is the significance of resource pricing? Explain how the factors determining resource demand differ from those determining product demand. Explain the meaning and significance of the fact that the demand for a resource is a derived demand. Why do resource demand curves slope downward? **LO1**

2. **KEY QUESTION** At the bottom of the page, complete the labor demand table for a firm that is hiring labor competitively and selling its product in a competitive market. **LO2**
   a. How many workers will the firm hire if the market wage rate is $27.95? $19.95? Explain why the firm will not hire a larger or smaller number of units of labor at each of these wage rates.
   b. Show in schedule form and graphically the labor demand curve of this firm.
   c. Now again determine the firm's demand curve for labor, assuming that it is selling in an imperfectly competitive market and that, although it can sell 17 units at $2.20 per unit, it must lower product price by 5 cents in order to sell the marginal product of each successive labor unit. Compare this demand curve with that derived in question 2b. Which curve is more elastic? Explain.

3. Suppose that marginal product tripled while product price fell by one-half in Table 12.1. What would be the new MRP values in Table 12.1? What would be the net impact on the location of the resource demand curve in Figure 12.1? **LO2**

4. In 2005 General Motors (GM) announced that it would reduce employment by 30,000 workers. What does this decision reveal about how it viewed its marginal revenue product (MRP) and marginal resource cost (MRC)? Why didn't GM reduce employment by more than 30,000 workers? By fewer than 30,000 workers? **LO3**

5. **KEY QUESTION** What factors determine the elasticity of resource demand? What effect will each of the following have on the elasticity or the location of the demand for resource C, which is being used to produce commodity X? Where there is any uncertainty as to the outcome, specify the causes of that uncertainty. **LO4**
   a. An increase in the demand for product X.
   b. An increase in the price of substitute resource D.

   c. An increase in the number of resources substitutable for C in producing X.
   d. A technological improvement in the capital equipment with which resource C is combined.
   e. A fall in the price of complementary resource E.
   f. A decline in the elasticity of demand for product X due to a decline in the competitiveness of product market X.

6. **KEY QUESTION** Suppose the productivity of capital and labor are as shown in the accompanying table. The output of these resources sells in a purely competitive market for $1 per unit. Both capital and labor are hired under purely competitive conditions at $3 and $1, respectively. **LO5**

Units of Capital	MP of Capital	Units of Labor	MP of Labor
0		0	
1	24	1	11
2	21	2	9
3	18	3	8
4	15	4	7
5	9	5	6
6	6	6	4
7	3	7	1
8	1	8	$\frac{1}{2}$

   a. What is the least-cost combination of labor and capital the firm should employ in producing 80 units of output? Explain.
   b. What is the profit-maximizing combination of labor and capital the firm should use? Explain. What is the resulting level of output? What is the economic profit? Is this the least costly way of producing the profit-maximizing output?

7. **KEY QUESTION** In each of the following four cases, MRP_L and MRP_C refer to the marginal revenue products of labor and capital, respectively, and P_L and P_C refer to their prices. Indicate in each case whether the conditions are consistent with maximum profits for the firm. If not, state which

Units of Labor	Total Product	Marginal Product	Product Price	Total Revenue	Marginal Revenue Product
0	0		$2	$_____	$_____
1	17	_____	2	_____	_____
2	31	_____	2	_____	_____
3	43	_____	2	_____	_____
4	53	_____	2	_____	_____
5	60	_____	2	_____	_____
6	65	_____	2	_____	_____

resource(s) should be used in larger amounts and which resource(s) should be used in smaller amounts. **LO5**

a. $MRP_L = \$8; P_L = \$4; MRP_C = \$8; P_C = \$4$
b. $MRP_L = \$10; P_L = \$12; MRP_C = \$14; P_C = \$9$
c. $MRP_L = \$6; P_L = \$6; MRP_C = \$12; P_C = \$12$
d. $MRP_L = \$22; P_L = \$26; MRP_C = \$16; P_C = \$19$

8. Florida citrus growers say that the recent crackdown on illegal immigration is increasing the market wage rates necessary to get their oranges picked. Some are turning to $100,000 to $300,000 mechanical harvesters known as "trunk, shake, and catch" pickers, which vigorously shake oranges from the trees. If widely adopted, what will be the effect on the demand for human orange pickers? What does that imply about the relative strengths of the substitution and output effects? **LO5**

9. **LAST WORD** Explain the economics of the substitution of ATMs for human tellers. Some banks are beginning to assess transaction fees when customers use human tellers rather than ATMs. What are these banks trying to accomplish?

Web-Based Questions

1. **SELECTED OCCUPATIONS—WHAT ARE THEIR EMPLOYMENT OUTLOOKS?** Use the A to Z index in the Bureau of Labor Statistics *Occupational Outlook*, at **www.bls.gov/oco/**, to determine the general and specific employment outlooks for (*a*) textile machinery operators, (*b*) financial managers, (*c*) computer operators, and (*d*) dental hygienists. Why do these job outlooks differ?

2. **THE OVERALL DEMAND FOR LABOR—IN WHICH COUNTRIES HAS IT INCREASED THE MOST?** In countries where real wages are steady or rising, increases in total employment reflect increases in labor demand. Go to the Bureau of Labor Statistics Web site, **www.bls.gov/fls**, and select Comparative Civilian Labor Force Statistics. Calculate the percentage increases in civilian employment for the United States, Japan, Germany, France, Great Britain, Italy, and Canada for the most recent 10-year period. Which three countries have had the greatest growth of labor demand, as measured by the percentage change in employment? Which three the smallest?

FURTHER TEST YOUR KNOWLEDGE AT
www.mcconnell18e.com

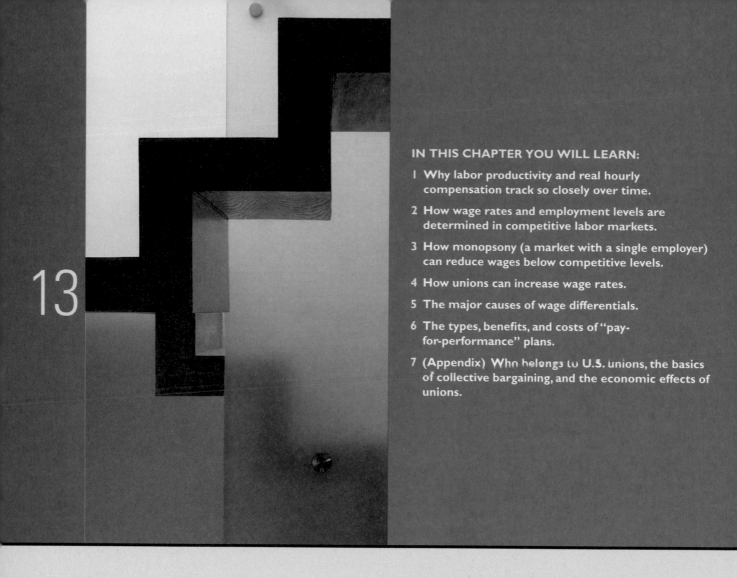

13

Wage Determination

Nearly 146 million Americans go to work each day. We work at an amazing variety of jobs for thousands of different firms and receive considerable differences in pay. What determines our hourly wage or annual salary? Why is the salary for, say, a topflight major-league baseball player $15 million or more a year, whereas the pay for a first-rate schoolteacher is $50,000? Why are starting salaries for college graduates who major in engineering and accounting so much higher than those for graduates majoring in journalism and sociology?

Having explored the major factors that underlie labor demand, we now bring *labor supply* into our analysis to help answer these questions. Generally speaking, labor supply and labor demand interact to determine the level of hourly wage rates or annual salaries in each occupation. Collectively, those wages and salaries make up about 70 percent of all income paid to American resource suppliers.

Labor, Wages, and Earnings

Economists use the term "labor" broadly to apply to (1) blue- and white-collar workers of all varieties, (2) professional people such as lawyers, physicians, dentists, and teachers; and (3) owners of small businesses, including barbers, plumbers, and a host of retailers who provide labor as they carry on their own businesses.

Wages are the price that employers pay for labor. Wages not only take the form of direct money payments such as hourly pay, annual salaries, bonuses, commissions, and royalties but also fringe benefits such as paid vacations, health insurance, and pensions. Unless stated otherwise, we will use the term "wages" to mean all such payments and benefits converted to an hourly basis. That will remind us that the wage rate is the price paid per unit of labor services, in this case an hour of work. It will also let us distinguish between the wage rate and labor earnings, the latter determined by multiplying the number of hours worked by the hourly wage rate.

We must also distinguish between nominal wages and real wages. A **nominal wage** is the amount of money received per hour, day, or year. A **real wage** is the quantity of goods and services a worker can obtain with nominal wages; real wages reveal the "purchasing power" of nominal wages.

Your real wage depends on your nominal wage and the prices of the goods and services you purchase. Suppose you receive a 5 percent increase in your nominal wage during a certain year but in that same year the price level increases by 3 percent. Then your real wage has increased by 2 percent (= 5 percent − 3 percent). Unless otherwise indicated, we will assume that the overall level of prices remains constant. In other words, we will discuss only *real* wages.

General Level of Wages

Wages differ among nations, regions, occupations, and individuals. Wage rates are much higher in the United States than in China or India. They are slightly higher in the north and east of the United States than in the south. Plumbers are paid less than NFL punters. And one physician may earn twice as much as another physician for the same number of hours of work. Wage rates also differ by gender, race, and ethnic background.

The general, or average, level of wages, like the general level of prices, includes a wide range of different wage rates. It includes the wages of bakers, barbers, brick masons, and brain surgeons. By averaging such wages, we can more easily compare wages among regions and among nations.

As Global Perspective 13.1 suggests, the general level of real wages in the United States is relatively high—although clearly not the highest in the world.

GLOBAL PERSPECTIVE 13.1

Hourly Wages of Production Workers, Selected Nations

Wage differences are pronounced worldwide. The data shown here indicate that hourly compensation in the United States is not as high as in some European nations. It is important to note, however, that the prices of goods and services vary greatly among nations and the process of converting foreign wages into dollars may not accurately reflect such variations.

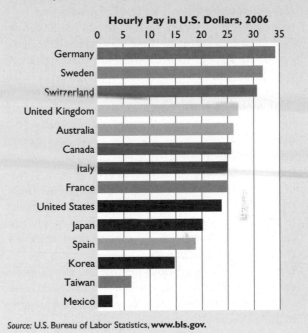

Hourly Pay in U.S. Dollars, 2006

Source: U.S. Bureau of Labor Statistics, **www.bls.gov.**

The simplest explanation for the high real wages in the United States and other industrially advanced economies (referred to hereafter as advanced economies) is that the demand for labor in those nations is relatively large compared to the supply of labor.

Role of Productivity

We know from the previous chapter that the demand for labor, or for any other resource, depends on its productivity. In general, the greater the productivity of labor, the greater is the demand for it. And if the total supply of labor is fixed, then the stronger the demand for labor, the higher is the average level of real wages. The demand for labor in the United States and the other major advanced economies is large because labor in those countries is highly productive. There are several reasons for that high productivity:

- *Plentiful capital* Workers in the advanced economies have access to large amounts of physical capital equipment (machinery and buildings). In the United States $90,000 of physical capital is available, on average, for each worker.

- *Access to abundant natural resources* In advanced economies, natural resources tend to be abundant in relation to the size of the labor force. Some of those resources are available domestically and others are imported from abroad. The United States, for example, is richly endowed with arable land, mineral resources, and sources of energy for industry.

- *Advanced technology* The level of production technology is generally high in advanced economies. Not only do workers in these economies have more capital equipment to work with, but that equipment is technologically superior to the equipment available to the vast majority of workers worldwide. Moreover, work methods in the advanced economies are steadily being improved through scientific study and research.

- *Labor quality* The health, vigor, education, and training of workers in advanced economies are generally superior to those in developing nations. This means that, even with the same quantity and quality of natural and capital resources, workers in advanced economies tend to be more efficient than many of their foreign counterparts.

- *Other factors* Less obvious factors also may underlie the high productivity in some of the advanced economies. In the United States, for example, such factors include (a) the efficiency and flexibility of management; (b) a business, social, and political environment that emphasizes production and productivity; (c) the vast size of the domestic market, which enables firms to engage in mass production; and (d) the increased specialization of production enabled by free-trade agreements with other nations.

Real Wages and Productivity

Figure 13.1 shows the close long-run relationship in the United States between output per hour of work and real hourly compensation (= wages and salaries + employers' contributions to social insurance and private benefit plans). Because real income and real output are two ways of viewing the same thing, real income (compensation) per worker can increase only at about the same rate as output per worker. When workers produce more real output per hour, more real income is available to distribute to them for each hour worked.

In the real world, however, suppliers of land, capital, and entrepreneurial talent also share in the income from production. Real wages therefore do not always rise in lockstep with gains in productivity over short spans of time. But over long periods, productivity and real wages tend to rise together.

Long-Run Trend of Real Wages

Basic supply and demand analysis helps explain the long-term trend of real-wage growth in the United States. The nation's labor force has grown significantly over the decades. But, as a result of the productivity-increasing

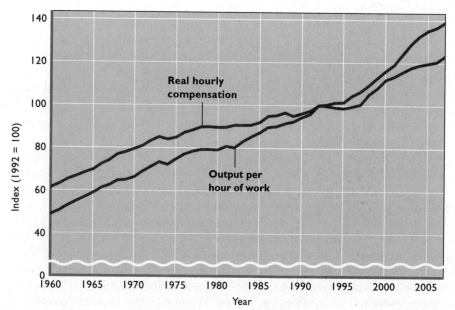

FIGURE 13.1 Output per hour and real hourly compensation in the United States. Over long periods of years, output per hour of work and real hourly compensation are closely related.

Source: Bureau of Labor Statistics, **stat.bls.gov.**

FIGURE 13.2 **The long-run trend of real wages in the United States.** The productivity of U.S. labor has increased substantially over the long run, causing the demand for labor D to shift rightward (that is, to increase) more rapidly than increases in the supply of labor S. The result has been increases in real wages.

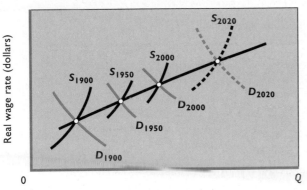

factors we have mentioned, increases in labor demand have outstripped increases in labor supply. Figure 13.2 shows several such increases in labor supply and labor demand. The result has been a long-run, or secular, increase in wage rates and employment. For example, real hourly compensation in the United States has roughly doubled since 1960. Over that same period, employment has increased by about 80 million workers.

A Purely Competitive Labor Market

Average levels of wages, however, disguise the great variation of wage rates among occupations and within occupations. What determines the wage rate paid for a specific type of labor? Demand and supply analysis again is revealing. Let's begin by examining labor demand and labor supply in a **purely competitive labor market.** In this type of market:

- Numerous firms compete with one another in hiring a specific type of labor.
- Each of many qualified workers with identical skills supplies that type of labor.
- Individual firms and individual workers are "wage takers" since neither can exert any control over the market wage rate.

Market Demand for Labor

Suppose 200 firms demand a particular type of labor, say, carpenters. These firms need not be in the same industry; industries are defined according to the products they produce and not the resources they employ. Thus, firms producing wood-framed furniture, wood windows and doors, houses and apartment buildings, and wood cabinets

will demand carpenters. To find the total, or market, labor demand curve for a particular labor service, we sum horizontally the labor demand curves (the marginal revenue product curves) of the individual firms, as indicated in **Figure 13.3 (Key Graph).** The horizontal summing of the 200 labor demand curves like d in Figure 13.3b yields the market labor demand curve D in Figure 13.3a.

Market Supply of Labor

On the supply side of a purely competitive labor market, we assume that no union is present and that workers individually compete for available jobs. The supply curve for each type of labor slopes upward, indicating that employers as a group must pay higher wage rates to obtain more workers. They must do this to bid workers away from other industries, occupations, and localities. Within limits, workers have alternative job opportunities. For example, they may work in other industries in the same locality, or they may work in their present occupations in different cities or states, or they may work in other occupations.

Firms that want to hire these workers (here, carpenters) must pay higher wage rates to attract them away from the alternative job opportunities available to them. They must also pay higher wages to induce people who are not currently in the labor force—who are perhaps doing household activities or enjoying leisure—to seek employment. In short, assuming that wages are constant in other labor markets, higher wages in a particular labor market entice more workers to offer their labor services in that market—a fact expressed graphically by the upward-sloping market supply-of-labor curve S in Figure 13.3a.

Labor Market Equilibrium

The intersection of the market labor demand curve and the market labor supply curve determines the equilibrium wage rate and level of employment in a purely competitive labor market. In Figure 13.3a the equilibrium wage rate is W_c ($10) and the number of workers hired is Q_c (1000). To the individual firm the market wage rate W_c is given. Each of the many firms employs such a small fraction of the total available supply of this type of labor that no single firm can influence the wage rate. As shown by the horizontal line s in Figure 13.3b, the supply of labor faced by an individual firm is perfectly elastic. It can hire as many or as few workers as it wants to at the market wage rate.

Each individual firm will maximize its profits (or minimize its losses) by hiring this type of labor up to the point at which marginal revenue product is equal to marginal resource cost. This is merely an application of the MRP = MRC rule we developed in Chapter 12.

FIGURE 13.3 Labor supply and labor demand in (a) a purely competitive labor market and (b) a single competitive firm. In a purely competitive labor market (a) the equilibrium wage rate W_c and the number of workers Q_c are determined by labor supply S and labor demand D. Because this market wage rate is given to the individual firm (b) hiring in this market, its labor supply curve $s = $ MRC is perfectly elastic. Its labor demand curve, d, is its MRP curve (here labeled mrp). The firm maximizes its profit by hiring workers up to where MRP = MRC. Area $0abc$ represents both the firm's total revenue and its total cost. The green area is its total wage cost; the brown area is its nonlabor costs, including a normal profit—that is, the firm's payments to the suppliers of land, capital, and entrepreneurship.

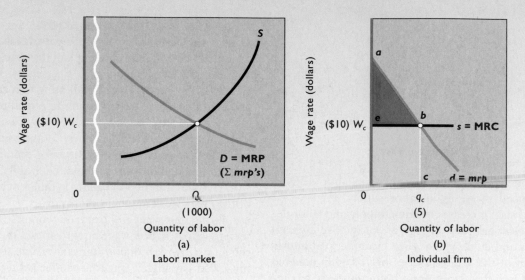

(a) Labor market

(b) Individual firm

QUICK QUIZ FOR FIGURE 13.3

1. The supply-of-labor curve S slopes upward in graph (a) because:
   a. the law of diminishing marginal utility applies.
   b. the law of diminishing returns applies.
   c. workers can afford to "buy" more leisure when their wage rates rise.
   d. higher wages are needed to attract workers away from other labor markets, household activities, and leisure.

2. This firm's labor demand curve d in graph (b) slopes downward because:
   a. the law of diminishing marginal utility applies.
   b. the law of diminishing returns applies.
   c. the firm must lower its price to sell additional units of its product.
   d. the firm is a competitive employer, not a monopsonist.

3. In employing five workers, the firm represented in graph (b):
   a. has a total wage cost of $6000.
   b. is adhering to the general principle of undertaking all actions for which the marginal benefit exceeds the marginal cost.
   c. uses less labor than would be ideal from society's perspective.
   d. experiences increasing marginal returns.

4. A rightward shift of the labor supply curve in graph (a) would shift curve:
   a. $d = mrp$ leftward in graph (b).
   b. $d = mrp$ rightward in graph (b).
   c. $s = $ MRC upward in graph (b).
   d. $s = $ MRC downward in graph (b).

Answers: 1. d; 2. b; 3. b; 4. d

As Table 13.1 indicates, when the price of a resource is imposed on the individual competitive firm, the marginal cost of that resource (MRC) is constant and is equal to the resource price. Note that MRC is constant at $10 and matches the $10 wage rate. Each additional worker hired adds precisely his or her own wage rate ($10 in this case) to the firm's total resource cost. So the firm in a purely competitive labor market maximizes its profit by hiring workers

to the point at which its wage rate equals MRP. In Figure 13.3b this firm will hire q_c (5) workers, paying each worker the market wage rate W_c ($10). The other 199 firms (not shown) that are hiring workers in this labor market will also each employ 5 workers and pay $10 per hour.

To determine a firm's total revenue from employing a particular number of labor units, we sum the MRPs of those units. For example, if a firm employs 3 labor units with

TABLE 13.1 The Supply of Labor: Pure Competition in the Hire of Labor

(1) Units of Labor	(2) Wage Rate	(3) Total Labor Cost (Wage Bill)	(4) Marginal Resource (Labor) Cost
0	$10	$ 0	
1	10	10	$10
2	10	20	10
3	10	30	10
4	10	40	10
5	10	50	10
6	10	60	10

marginal revenue products of $14, $13, and $12, respectively, then the firm's total revenue is $39 (= $14 + $13 + $12). In Figure 13.3b, where we are not restricted to whole units of labor, total revenue is represented by area $0abc$ under the MRP curve to the left of q_c. And what area represents the firm's total cost, including a normal profit? Answer: For q_c units, the same area—$0abc$. The green rectangle represents the firm's total wage cost ($0q_c \times 0W_c$). The brown triangle (total revenue minus total wage cost) represents the firm's nonlabor costs—its explicit and implicit payments to land, capital, and entrepreneurship. Thus, in this case, total cost (wages plus other income payments) equals total revenue. This firm and others like it are earning only a normal profit.

INTERACTIVE GRAPHS

G 13.1

Competitive labor market

So Figure 13.3b represents a long-run equilibrium for a firm that is selling its product in a purely competitive product market and hiring its labor in a purely competitive labor market. (Key Questions 3 and 4)

Monopsony Model

In the purely competitive labor market described in the preceding section, each employer hires too small an amount of labor to influence the wage rate. Each firm can hire as little or as much labor as it needs, but only at the market wage rate, as reflected in its horizontal labor supply curve. The situation is quite different in a **monopsony**, a market in which a single employer of labor has substantial buying (hiring) power. A labor market monopsony has the following characteristics:

- There is only a single buyer of a particular type of labor.
- This type of labor is relatively immobile, either geographically or because workers would have to acquire new skills.
- The firm is a "wage maker," because the wage rate it must pay varies directly with the number of workers it employs.

As is true of monopoly power, there are various degrees of monopsony power. In *pure* monopsony such power is at its maximum because only a single employer hires labor in the labor market. The best real-world examples are probably the labor markets in some towns that depend almost entirely on one major firm. For example, a silver-mining company may be almost the only source of employment in a remote Idaho town. A Colorado ski resort, a Wisconsin paper mill, or an Alaskan fish processor may provide most of the employment in its geographically isolated locale.

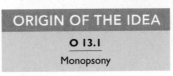

ORIGIN OF THE IDEA

O 13.1

Monopsony

In other cases three or four firms may each hire a large portion of the supply of labor in a certain market and therefore have some monopsony power. Moreover, if they tacitly or openly act in concert in hiring labor, they greatly enhance their monopsony power.

Upward-Sloping Labor Supply to Firm

When a firm hires most of the available supply of a certain type of labor, its decision to employ more or fewer workers affects the wage rate it pays to those workers. Specifically, if a firm is large in relation to the size of the labor market, it will have to pay a higher wage rate to attract labor away from other employment or from leisure. Suppose that only one employer hires a particular type of labor in a certain geographic area. In this pure monopsony situation, the labor supply curve for the *firm* and the total labor supply curve for the *labor market* are identical. The monopsonist's supply curve—represented by curve S in Figure 13.4—is upsloping because the firm must pay higher wage rates if it wants to attract and hire additional workers. This same curve is also the monopsonist's average-cost-of-labor curve. Each point on curve S indicates the wage rate (cost) per worker that must be paid to attract the corresponding number of workers.

MRC Higher Than the Wage Rate

When a monopsonist pays a higher wage to attract an additional worker, it must pay that higher wage not only to the additional worker, but to all the workers it is currently employing at a lower wage. If not, labor morale will deteriorate, and the employer will be plagued with labor unrest because of wage-rate differences existing for the same job. Paying a uniform wage to all workers means that the cost of an extra worker—the marginal resource (labor) cost (MRC)—is the sum of that worker's wage rate and the amount necessary to bring the wage rate of all current workers up to the new wage level.

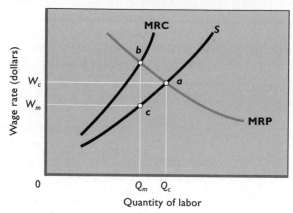

FIGURE 13.4 The wage rate and level of employment in a monopsonistic labor market. In a monopsonistic labor market the employer's marginal resource (labor) cost curve (MRC) lies above the labor supply curve *S*. Equating MRC with MRP at point *b*, the monopsonist hires Q_m workers (compared with Q_c under competition). As indicated by point *c* on *S*, it pays only wage rate W_m (compared with the competitive wage W_c).

Equilibrium Wage and Employment

How many units of labor will the monopsonist hire, and what wage rate will it pay? To maximize profit, the monopsonist will employ the quantity of labor Q_m in Figure 13.4, because at that quantity MRC and MRP are equal (point *b*).[1] The monopsonist next determines how much it must pay to attract these Q_m workers. From the supply curve *S*, specifically point *c*, it sees that it must pay wage rate W_m. Clearly, it need not pay a wage equal to MRP; it can attract and hire exactly the number of workers it wants (Q_m) with wage rate W_m. And that is the wage that it will pay.

> **INTERACTIVE GRAPHS**
> **G 13.2**
> Monopsony

> **WORKED PROBLEMS**
> **W 13.1**
> Labor markets: competition and monopsony

Contrast these results with those that would prevail in a competitive labor market. With competition in the hiring of labor, the level of employment would be greater (at Q_c) and the wage rate would be higher (at W_c). Other things equal, the monopsonist maximizes its profit by hiring a smaller number of workers and thereby paying a less-than-competitive wage rate. Society obtains a smaller output, and workers receive a wage rate that is less by *bc* than their marginal revenue product. Just as a monopolistic seller finds it profitable to restrict product output to realize an above-competitive price for its goods, the monopsonistic employer of resources finds it profitable to restrict employment in order to reduce wage rates below those that would occur under competitive conditions.

Table 13.2 illustrates this point. One worker can be hired at a wage rate of $6. But hiring a second worker forces the firm to pay a higher wage rate of $7. The marginal resource (labor) cost of the second worker is $8—the $7 paid to the second worker plus a $1 raise for the first worker. From another viewpoint, total labor cost is now $14 (= 2 × $7), up from $6. So the MRC of the second worker is $8 (= $14 − $6), not just the $7 wage rate paid to that worker. Similarly, the marginal labor cost of the third worker is $10—the $8 that must be paid to attract this worker from alternative employment plus $1 raises, from $7 to $8, for the first two workers.

Here is the key point: Because the monopsonist is the only employer in the labor market, its marginal resource (labor) cost exceeds the wage rate. Graphically, the monopsonist's MRC curve lies above the average-cost-of-labor curve, or labor supply curve *S*, as is clearly shown in Figure 13.4.

TABLE 13.2 The Supply of Labor: Monopsony in the Hire of Labor

(1) Units of Labor	(2) Wage Rate	(3) Total Labor Cost	(4) Marginal Resource (Labor) Cost
0	$ 5	$ 0	
1	6	6	$ 6
2	7	14	8
3	8	24	10
4	9	36	12
5	10	50	14
6	11	66	16

---

[1]The fact that MRC exceeds resource price when resources are hired or purchased under imperfectly competitive (monopsonistic) conditions calls for adjustments in Chapter 12's least-cost and profit-maximizing rules for hiring resources. (See equations 1 and 2 in the "Optimal Combination of Resources" section of Chapter 12.) Specifically, we must substitute MRC for resource price in the denominators of our two equations. That is, with imperfect competition in the hiring of both labor and capital, equation 1 becomes

$$\frac{MP_L}{MRC_L} = \frac{MP_C}{MRC_C} \qquad (1')$$

and equation 2 is restated as

$$\frac{MRP_L}{MRC_L} = \frac{MRP_C}{MRC_C} = 1 \qquad (2')$$

In fact, equations 1 and 2 can be regarded as special cases of 1' and 2' in which firms happen to be hiring under purely competitive conditions and resource price is therefore equal to, and can be substituted for, marginal resource cost.

Examples of Monopsony Power

Fortunately, monopsonistic labor markets are uncommon in the United States. In most labor markets, several potential employers compete for most workers, particularly for workers who are occupationally and geographically mobile. Also, where monopsony labor market outcomes might have otherwise occurred, unions have sprung up to counteract that power by forcing firms to negotiate wages. Nevertheless, economists have found some evidence of monopsony power in such diverse labor markets as the markets for nurses, professional athletes, public school teachers, newspaper employees, and some building-trade workers.

In the case of nurses, the major employers in most locales are a relatively small number of hospitals. Further, the highly specialized skills of nurses are not readily transferable to other occupations. It has been found, in accordance with the monopsony model, that, other things equal, the smaller the number of hospitals in a town or city (that is, the greater the degree of monopsony), the lower the beginning salaries of nurses.

Professional sports leagues also provide a good example of monopsony, particularly as it relates to the pay of first-year players. The National Football League, the National Basketball Association, and Major League Baseball assign first-year players to teams through "player drafts." That device prohibits other teams from competing for a player's services, at least for several years, until the player becomes a "free agent." In this way the league exercises monopsony power, which results in lower salaries than would occur under competitive conditions. **(Key Question 6)**

QUICK REVIEW 13.1

- Real wages have increased historically in the United States because labor demand has increased relative to labor supply.
- Over the long term, real wages per worker have increased at approximately the same rate as worker productivity.
- The competitive employer is a wage taker and employs workers at the point where the wage rate (= MRC) equals MRP.
- The labor supply curve to a monopsonist is upward-sloping, causing MRC to exceed the wage rate for each worker. Other things equal, the monopsonist, hiring where MRC = MRP, will employ fewer workers and pay a lower wage rate than would a purely competitive employer.

Three Union Models

Our assumption thus far has been that workers compete with one another in selling their labor services. But in some labor markets workers unionize and sell their labor services collectively. (We examine union membership, collective bargaining, and union impacts in detail in an appendix to this chapter. Here our focus is on three union wage models.)

When a union is formed in an otherwise competitive labor market, it usually bargains with a relatively large number of employers. It has many goals, the most important of which is to raise wage rates. It can pursue that objective in several ways.

Demand-Enhancement Model

Unions recognize that their ability to influence the demand for labor is limited. But, from the union's viewpoint, increasing the demand for union labor is highly desirable. As Figure 13.5 shows, an increase in labor demand will create a higher union wage along with more jobs.

Unions can increase the demand for their labor by increasing the demand for the goods or services they help produce. Political lobbying is the main tool for increasing the demand for union-produced goods or services. For example, construction unions have lobbied for new highways, mass-transit systems, and stadium projects. Teachers' unions and associations have pushed for increased public spending on education. Unions in the aerospace industry have lobbied to increase spending on the military and on space exploration. U.S. steel unions and forest-product workers have lobbied for tariffs and quotas on foreign imports of steel and lumber, respectively. Such trade restrictions shift the demand for labor away from foreign countries and toward unionized U.S. labor.

Unions can also increase the demand for union labor by altering the price of other inputs. For example, although union members are generally paid significantly more than the minimum wage, unions have strongly supported increases in the minimum wage. The purpose may be to

FIGURE 13.5 Unions and demand enhancement.
When unions can increase the demand for labor (say, from D_1 to D_2), they can realize higher wage rates (W_c to W_u) and more jobs (Q_c to Q_u).

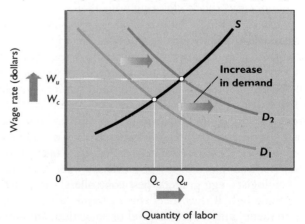

raise the price of low-wage, nonunion labor, which in some cases is substitutable for union labor. A higher minimum wage for nonunion workers will discourage employers from substituting such workers for union workers and will thereby bolster the demand for union members.

Similarly, unions have sometimes sought to increase the demand for their labor by supporting policies that will reduce or hold down the price of a complementary resource. For example, unions in industries that represent workers who transport fruits and vegetables may support legislation that allows low-wage foreign agricultural workers to temporarily work in the United States. Where union labor and another resource are complementary, a price decrease for the other resource will increase the demand for union labor through Chapter 12's output effect.

Exclusive or Craft Union Model

Unions can also boost wage rates by reducing the supply of labor, and over the years organized labor has favored policies to do just that. For example, labor unions have supported legislation that has (1) restricted permanent immigration, (2) reduced child labor, (3) encouraged compulsory retirement, and (4) enforced a shorter workweek.

Moreover, certain types of workers have adopted techniques designed to restrict the number of workers who can join their union. This is especially true of *craft unions*, whose members possess a particular skill, such as carpenters, brick masons, or plumbers. Craft unions have frequently forced employers to agree to hire only union members, thereby gaining virtually complete control of the labor supply. Then, by following restrictive membership policies—for example, long apprenticeships, very high initiation fees, and limits on the number of new members admitted—they have artificially restricted labor supply. As indicated in Figure 13.6, such practices result in higher wage rates and constitute what is called **exclusive unionism.** By excluding workers from unions and therefore from the labor supply, craft unions succeed in elevating wage rates.

This craft union model is also applicable to many professional organizations, such as the American Medical Association, the National Education Association, the American Bar Association, and hundreds of others. Such groups seek to limit competition for their services from less qualified labor suppliers. One way to accomplish that is through **occupational licensing.** Here a group of workers in a given occupation pressure Federal, state, or municipal government to pass a law that says that some occupational group (for example, barbers, physicians, lawyers, plumbers, cosmetologists, egg graders, pest controllers) can practice their trade only if they meet certain requirements. Those requirements might include level of education, amount of

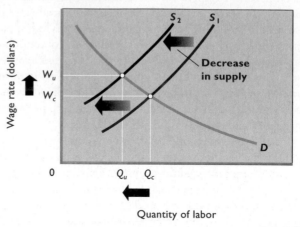

FIGURE 13.6 Exclusive or craft unionism. By reducing the supply of labor (say, from S_1 to S_2) through the use of restrictive membership policies, exclusive unions achieve higher wage rates (W_c to W_u). However, restriction of the labor supply also reduces the number of workers employed (Q_c to Q_u).

work experience, the passing of an examination, and personal characteristics ("the practitioner must be of good moral character"). Members of the licensed occupation typically dominate the licensing board that administers such laws. The result is self-regulation, which often leads to policies that serve only to restrict entry to the occupation and reduce labor supply.

The expressed purpose of licensing is to protect consumers from incompetent practitioners—surely a worthy goal. But such licensing, if abused, results in above-competitive wages and earnings for those in the licensed occupation (Figure 13.6). Moreover, licensing requirements often include a residency requirement, which inhibits the interstate movement of qualified workers. Some 600 occupations are now licensed in the United States.

Inclusive or Industrial Union Model

Instead of trying to limit their membership, however, most unions seek to organize all available workers. This is especially true of the *industrial unions*, such as those of the automobile workers and steelworkers. Such unions seek as members all available unskilled, semiskilled, and skilled workers in an industry. A union can afford to be exclusive when its members are skilled craftspersons for whom there are few substitutes. But for a union composed of unskilled and semiskilled workers, a policy of limited membership would make available to the employers numerous nonunion workers who are highly substitutable for the union workers.

An industrial union that includes virtually all available workers in its membership can put firms under great pressure

FIGURE 13.7 Inclusive or industrial unionism. By organizing virtually all available workers in order to control the supply of labor, inclusive industrial unions may impose a wage rate, such as W_u, which is above the competitive wage rate W_c. In effect, this changes the labor supply curve from S to aeS. At wage rate W_u, employers will cut employment from Q_c to Q_u.

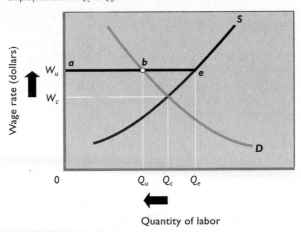

to agree to its wage demands. Because of its legal right to strike, such a union can threaten to deprive firms of their entire labor supply. And an actual strike can do just that.

We illustrate such **inclusive unionism** in Figure 13.7. Initially, the competitive equilibrium wage rate is W_c and the level of employment is Q_c. Now suppose an industrial union is formed that demands a higher, above-equilibrium wage rate of, say, W_u. That wage rate W_u would create a perfectly elastic labor supply over the range ae in Figure 13.7. If firms wanted to hire any workers in this range, they would have to pay the union-imposed wage rate. If they decide against meeting this wage demand, the union will supply no labor at all, and the firms will be faced with a strike. If firms decide it is better to pay the higher wage rate than to suffer a strike, they will cut back on employment from Q_c to Q_u.

By agreeing to the union's wage demand, individual employers become wage takers at the union wage rate W_u. Because labor supply is perfectly elastic over range ae, the marginal resource (labor) cost is equal to the wage rate W_u over this range. The Q_u level of employment is the result of employers' equating this MRC (now equal to the union wage rate) with MRP, according to our profit maximizing rule.

Note from point e on labor supply curve S that Q_e workers desire employment at wage W_u. But as indicated by point b on labor demand curve D, only Q_u workers are employed. The result is a surplus of labor of $Q_e - Q_u$ (also shown by distance eb). In a purely competitive labor market without the union, the effect of a surplus of unemployed workers would be lower wages. Specifically, the wage rate would fall to the equilibrium level W_c, where the quantity

of labor supplied equals the quantity of labor demanded (each Q_c). But this drop in wages does not happen, because workers are acting collectively through their union. Individual workers cannot offer to work for less than W_u; nor can employers pay less than that.

Wage Increases and Unemployment

Have U.S. unions been successful in raising the wages of their members? Evidence suggests that union members on average achieve a 15 percent wage advantage over non-union workers. But when unions are successful in raising wages, their efforts also have another major effect.

As Figures 13.6 and 13.7 suggest, the wage-raising actions achieved by both exclusive and inclusive unionism reduce employment in unionized firms. Simply put, a union's success in achieving above-equilibrium wage rates tends to be accompanied by a decline in the number of workers employed. That result acts as a restraining influence on union wage demands. A union cannot expect to maintain solidarity within its ranks if it seeks a wage rate so high that joblessness will result for, say, 20 or 30 percent of its members.

Bilateral Monopoly Model

Suppose a strong industrial union is formed in a monopsonist labor market rather that a competitive labor market, thereby creating a combination of the monopsony model and the inclusive unionism model. Economists call the result **bilateral monopoly** because in its pure form there is a single seller and a single buyer. The union is a monopolistic "seller" of labor that controls labor supply and can influence wage rates, but it faces a monopsonistic "buyer" of labor that can also affect wages by altering the amount of labor that it employs. This is not an uncommon case, particularly in less pure forms in which a single union confronts two, three, or four large employers. Examples: steel, automobiles, construction equipment, professional sports, and commercial aircraft.

Indeterminate Outcome of Bilateral Monopoly

We show this situation in Figure 13.8, where Figure 13.7 is superimposed onto Figure 13.4. The monopsonistic employer will seek the below-competitive-equilibrium wage rate W_m, and the union will press for some above-competitive-equilibrium wage rate such as W_u. Which will be the outcome? We cannot say with certainty. The outcome is "logically indeterminate" because the bilateral monopoly model does not explain what will happen at the

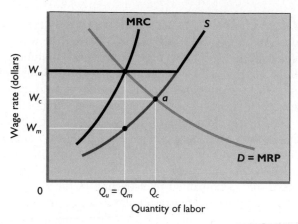

FIGURE 13.8 Bilateral monopoly in the labor market. A monopsonist seeks to hire Q_m workers (where MRC = MRP) and pay wage rate W_m corresponding to quantity Q_m on labor supply curve S. The inclusive union it faces seeks the above-equilibrium wage rate W_u. The actual outcome cannot be predicted by economic theory. It will result from bargaining between the two parties.

QUICK REVIEW 13.2

- In the demand enhancement union model, a union increases the wage rate by increasing labor demand through actions that increase product demand or alter the prices of related inputs.
- In the exclusive (craft) union model, a union increases wage rates by artificially restricting labor supply, through, say, long apprenticeships or occupational licensing.
- In the inclusive (industrial) union model, a union raises the wage rate by gaining control over a firm's labor supply and threatening to withhold labor via a strike unless a negotiated wage is obtained.
- Bilateral monopoly occurs in a labor market where a monopsonist bargains with an inclusive, or industrial, union. Wage and employment outcomes are determined by collective bargaining in this situation.

collective bargaining table. We can expect the wage outcome to lie somewhere between W_m and W_u. Beyond that, about all we can say is that the party with the greater bargaining power and the more effective bargaining strategy will probably get a wage closer to the one it seeks.

Desirability of Bilateral Monopoly

The wage and employment outcomes in this situation might be more economically desirable than the term "bilateral monopoly" implies. The monopoly on one side of the market might in effect cancel out the monopoly on the other side, yielding competitive or near-competitive results. If either the union or management prevailed in this market—that is, if the actual wage rate were either W_u or W_m—employment would be restricted to Q_m (where MRP = MRC), which is below the competitive level.

But now suppose the monopoly power of the union roughly offsets the monopsony power of management, and the union and management agree on wage rate W_c, which is the competitive wage. Once management accepts this wage rate, its incentive to restrict employment disappears; no longer can it depress wage rates by restricting employment. Instead, management hires at the most profitable resource quantity, where the bargained wage rate W_c (which is now the firm's MRC) is equal to the MRP. It hires Q_c workers. Thus, with monopoly on both sides of the labor market, the resulting wage rate and level of employment may be closer to competitive levels than would be the case if monopoly existed on only one side of the market. **(Key Question 7)**

The Minimum-Wage Controversy

Since the passage of the Fair Labor Standards Act in 1938, the United States has had a Federal **minimum wage.** That wage has ranged between 30 and 50 percent of the average wage paid to manufacturing workers and was $5.85 per hour in 2007, and is scheduled to rise to $6.55 in July 2008 and $7.25 in July 2009. Numerous states, however, have minimum wages that are higher than the Federal minimum wage. Some of these state minimum wages are considerably higher. For example, in 2008 the minimum wage in the state of Washington was $8.07 an hour. The purpose of the minimum wage is to provide a "wage floor" that will help less-skilled workers earn enough income to escape poverty.

Case against the Minimum Wage

Critics, reasoning in terms of Figure 13.7, contend that an above-equilibrium minimum wage (say, W_u) will simply cause employers to hire fewer workers. Downsloping labor demand curves are a reality. The higher labor costs may even force some firms out of business. Then some of the poor, low-wage workers whom the minimum wage was designed to help will find themselves out of work. Critics point out that a worker who is *unemployed* and desperate to find a job at a minimum wage of $6.55 per hour is clearly worse off than he or she would be if *employed* at a market wage rate of, say, $6.10 per hour.

A second criticism of the minimum wage is that it is "poorly targeted" to reduce household poverty. Critics point out that much of the benefit of the minimum wage accrues to workers, including many teenagers, who do not live in empoverished households.

Case for the Minimum Wage

Advocates of the minimum wage say that critics analyze its impact in an unrealistic context. Figure 13.7, advocates claim, assumes a competitive labor market. But in a less competitive, low-pay labor market where employers possess some monopsony power (Figure 13.8), the minimum wage can increase wage rates without causing significant unemployment. Indeed, a higher minimum wage may even produce more jobs by eliminating the motive that monopsonistic firms have for restricting employment. For example, a minimum-wage floor of W_c in Figure 13.8 would change the firm's labor supply curve to W_caS and prompt the firm to increase its employment from Q_m workers to Q_c workers.

Moreover, even if the labor market is competitive, the higher wage rate might prompt firms to find more productive tasks for low-paid workers, thereby raising their productivity. Alternatively, the minimum wage may reduce *labor turnover* (the rate at which workers voluntarily quit). With fewer low-productive trainees, the *average* productivity of the firm's workers would rise. In either case, the alleged negative employment effects of the minimum wage might not occur.

Evidence and Conclusions

Which view is correct? Unfortunately, there is no clear answer. All economists agree that firms will not hire workers who cost more per hour than the value of their hourly output. So there is some minimum wage sufficiently high that it would severely reduce employment. Consider $20 an hour, as an absurd example. But no current consensus exists on the employment effects of the present level of the minimum wage. Evidence in the 1980s suggested that minimum-wage hikes reduced employment of minimum-wage workers, particularly teenagers (16- to 19-year-olds). The consensus then was that a 10 percent increase in the minimum wage would reduce teenage employment by about 1 to 3 percent. But the minimum-wage hikes in 1991, 1996, and 1997 seemed to produce smaller employment declines among teenagers. It is possible that the more recent minimum wage increases merely matched the sort of wage increases that would have occurred in any event in competitive low-wage labor markets. Negative employment effects of minimum wages occur only when such minimums are above equilibrium wages.

The overall effect of the minimum wage is thus uncertain. On the one hand, the employment and unemployment effects of the minimum wage do not appear to be as great as many critics fear. On the other hand, because a large part of its effect is dissipated on nonpoverty families, the minimum wage is not as strong an antipoverty tool as many supporters contend.

Voting patterns and surveys make it clear, however, that the minimum wage has strong political support. Perhaps this stems from two realities: (1) More workers are believed to be helped than hurt by the minimum wage and (2) the minimum wage gives society some assurance that employers are not "taking undue advantage" of vulnerable, low-skilled workers.

Wage Differentials

Hourly wage rates and annual salaries differ greatly among occupations. In Table 13.3 we list average annual salaries for a number of occupations to illustrate such occupational **wage differentials.** For example, observe that surgeons on average earn eight times as much as retail salespersons. Not shown, there are also large wage differentials within some of the occupations listed. For example, some highly experienced surgeons earn several times as much income as surgeons just starting their careers. And, although average wages for retail salespersons are relatively low, some top salespersons selling on commission make several times the average wages listed for their occupation.

What explains wage differentials such as these? Once again, the forces of demand and supply are revealing. As we demonstrate in Figure 13.9, wage differentials can arise on either the supply or the demand side of labor markets. Figure 13.9a and 13.9b represent labor markets for two occupational groups that have identical *labor supply curves*. Labor market (a) has a relatively high equilibrium wage

TABLE 13.3 Average Annual Wages in Selected Occupations, 2007

Occupation	Average Annual Wages
1. Surgeons	$191,410
2. Aircraft pilots	148,810
3. Petroleum engineers	113,890
4. Financial managers	106,200
5. Law professors	95,510
6. Chemical engineers	84,240
7. Dental hygienists	64,910
8. Registered nurses	62,480
9. Police officers	50,670
10. Electricians	48,100
11. Travel agents	32,190
12. Barbers	25,860
13. Retail salespersons	24,530
14. Recreation workers	23,790
15. Teacher aides	22,820
16. Fast food cooks	16,860

Source: Bureau of Labor Statistics, **www.bls.gov.**

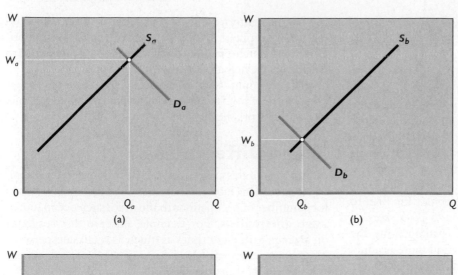

FIGURE 13.9 Labor demand, labor supply, and wage differentials. The wage differential between labor markets (a) and (b) results solely from differences in labor demand. In labor markets (c) and (d), differences in labor supply are the sole cause of the wage differential.

(W_a) because labor demand is very strong. In labor market (b) the equilibrium wage is relatively low (W_b) because labor demand is weak. Clearly, the wage differential between occupations (a) and (b) results solely from differences in the magnitude of labor demand.

Contrast that situation with Figure 13.9c and 13.9d, where the *labor demand curves* are identical. In labor market (c) the equilibrium wage is relatively high (W_c) because labor supply is highly restricted. In labor market (d) labor supply is highly abundant, so the equilibrium wage (W_d) is relatively low. The wage differential between (c) and (d) results solely from the differences in the magnitude of labor supply.

Although Figure 13.9 provides a good starting point for understanding wage differentials, we need to know *why* demand and supply conditions differ in various labor markets. There are several reasons.

Marginal Revenue Productivity

The strength of labor demand—how far rightward the labor demand curve is located—differs greatly among occupations

due to differences in how much various occupational groups contribute to the revenue of their respective employers. This revenue contribution, in turn, depends on the workers' productivity and the strength of the demand for the products they are helping to produce. Where labor is highly productive and product demand is strong, labor demand also is strong and, other things equal, pay is high. Top professional athletes, for example, are highly productive at producing sports entertainment, for which millions of people are willing to pay billions of dollars over the course of a season. So the **marginal revenue productivity** of these top players is exceptionally high, as are their salaries (as represented in Figure 13.9a). In contrast, in most occupations workers generate much more modest revenue for their employers, so their pay is lower (as in Figure 13.9b).

Noncompeting Groups

On the supply side of the labor market, workers are not homogeneous; they differ in their mental and physical capacities and in their education and training. At any given time the labor force is made up of many **noncompeting groups** of workers, each representing several occupations for which the members of a particular group qualify. In some groups qualified workers are relatively few, whereas in others they are plentiful. And workers in one group do not qualify for the occupations of other groups.

Ability Only a few workers have the ability or physical attributes to be brain surgeons, concert violinists, top fashion models, research chemists, or professional athletes. Because the supply of these particular types of labor is very small in relation to labor demand, their wages are high (as in Figure 13.9c). The members of these and similar groups do not compete with one another or with other skilled or semiskilled workers. The violinist does not compete with the surgeon, nor does the surgeon compete with the violinist or the fashion model.

The concept of noncompeting groups can be applied to various subgroups and even to specific individuals in a particular group. Some especially skilled violinists can command higher salaries than colleagues who play the same instrument. A handful of top corporate executives earn 10 to 20 times as much as the average chief executive officer. In each of these cases, the supply of top talent is highly limited since less-talented colleagues are only imperfect substitutes.

Education and Training Another source of wage differentials is differing amounts of **human capital,** which is the personal stock of knowledge, know-how, and skills that enables a person to be productive and thus to earn income. Such stocks result from investments in human capital. Like expenditures on machinery and equipment, productivity-enhancing expenditures on education or training are investments. In

ORIGIN OF THE IDEA

O 13.2

Human capital

both cases, people incur *present costs* with the intention that those expenditures will lead to a greater flow of *future earnings*.

Figure 13.10 indicates that workers who have made greater investments in education achieve higher incomes during their careers. The reason is twofold: (1) There are fewer such workers, so their supply is limited relative to less-educated workers, and (2) more-educated workers tend to be more productive and thus in greater demand. Figure 13.10 also indicates that the earnings of better-educated workers rise more rapidly than those of poorly educated workers. The primary reason is that employers provide more on-the-job training to the better-educated workers, boosting their marginal revenue productivity and therefore their earnings.

FIGURE 13.10 Education levels and individual annual earnings. Annual income by age is higher for workers with more education than less. Investment in education yields a return in the form of earnings differences enjoyed over one's work life.

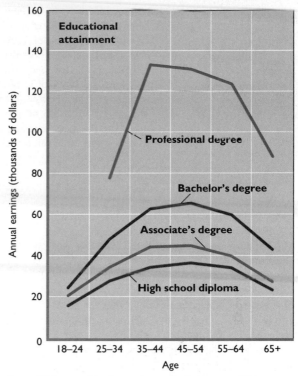

Source: U.S. Bureau of the Census. Data are for both sexes in 2006.

Although education yields higher incomes, it carries substantial costs. A college education involves not only direct costs (tuition, fees, books) but indirect or opportunity costs (forgone earnings) as well. Does the higher pay received by better-educated workers compensate for these costs? The answer is yes. Rates of return are estimated to be 10 to 13 percent for investments in secondary education and 8 to 12 percent for investments in college education. One generally accepted estimate is that each year of schooling raises a worker's wage by about 8 percent.

Compensating Differences

If the workers in a particular noncompeting group are equally capable of performing several different jobs, you might expect the wage rates to be identical for all these jobs. Not so. A group of high school graduates may be equally capable of becoming salesclerks or general construction workers. But these jobs pay different wages. In virtually all locales, construction laborers receive much higher wages than salesclerks. These wage differentials are called **compensating differences** because they must be paid to compensate for nonmonetary differences in various jobs.

CONSIDER THIS . . .

My Entire Life

Human capital is the accumulation of outcomes of prior investments in education, training, and other factors that increase productivity and earnings. It is the stock of knowledge, know-how, and skills that enables individuals to be productive and thus earn income. A valuable stock of human capital, together with a strong demand for one's services, can add up to a large capacity to earn income. For some people, high earnings have little to do with actual hours of work and much to do with their tremendous skill, which reflects their accumulated stock of human capital.

The point is demonstrated in the following story: It is said that a tourist once spotted the famous Spanish artist Pablo Picasso (1881–1973) in a Paris café. The tourist asked Picasso if he would do a sketch of his wife for pay. Picasso sketched the wife in a matter of minutes and said, "That will be 10,000 francs [roughly $2000]." Hearing the high price, the tourist became irritated, saying, "But that took you only a few minutes."

"No," replied Picasso, "it took me my entire life! "

The construction job involves dirty hands, a sore back, the hazard of accidents, and irregular employment, both seasonally and cyclically. The retail sales job means clean clothing, pleasant air-conditioned surroundings, and little fear of injury or layoff. Other things equal, it is easy to see why workers would rather pick up a credit card than a shovel. So the amount of labor that is supplied to construction firms (as in Figure 13.9c) is smaller than that which is supplied to retail shops (as in Figure 13.9d). Construction firms must pay higher wages than retailers to compensate for the unattractive nonmonetary aspects of construction jobs.

Such compensating differences spring up throughout the economy. Other things equal, jobs having high risk of injury or death pay more than comparable, safer jobs. Jobs lacking employer-paid health insurance, pensions, and vacation time pay more than comparable jobs that provide these "fringe benefits." Jobs with more flexible hours pay less than jobs with rigid work-hour requirements. Jobs with greater risk of unemployment pay more than comparable jobs with little unemployment risk. Entry-level jobs in occupations that provide very poor prospects for pay advancement pay more than entry-level jobs that have clearly defined "job ladders."

These and other compensating differences play an important role in allocating society's scarce labor resources. If very few workers want to be garbage collectors, then society must pay high wages to garbage collectors to get the garbage collected. If many more people want to be salesclerks, then society need not pay them as much as it pays garbage collectors to get those services performed.

Market Imperfections

Differences in marginal revenue productivity, amounts of human capital, and nonmonetary aspects of jobs explain most of the wage differentials in the economy. But some persistent differentials result from various market imperfections that impede workers from moving from lower-paying jobs to higher-paying jobs.

Lack of Job Information
Workers may simply be unaware of job opportunities and wage rates in other geographic areas and in other jobs for which they qualify. Consequently, the flow of qualified labor from lower-paying to higher-paying jobs—and thus the adjustments in labor supply—may not be sufficient to equalize wages within occupations.

Geographic Immobility
Workers take root geographically. Many are reluctant to move to new places. Doing so would involve leaving friends, relatives, and associates. It would mean forcing their children to change schools, having to sell their homes, and incurring the costs and inconveniences of adjusting to a new job and a new community. As Adam Smith noted over two centuries ago, "A [person] is of all sorts of luggage the most difficult to be transported." The reluctance or inability of workers to move enables geographic wage differentials within the same occupation to persist.

Unions and Government Restraints
Wage differentials may be reinforced by artificial restrictions on mobility imposed by unions and government. We have noted that craft unions find it to their advantage to restrict membership. After all, if carpenters and bricklayers become too plentiful, the wages they can command will decline. Thus the low-paid nonunion carpenter of Brush, Colorado, may be willing to move to Chicago in the pursuit of higher wages. But her chances for succeeding are slim. She may be unable to get a union card, and no card means no job. Similarly, an optometrist or lawyer qualified to practice in one state may not meet licensing requirements of other states, so his or her ability to move is limited. Other artificial barriers involve pension plans, health insurance benefits, and seniority rights that might be jeopardized by moving from one job to another.

Discrimination Despite legislation to the contrary, discrimination sometimes results in lower wages being paid to women and minority workers than to white males doing very similar or even identical work. Also, women and minorities may be crowded into certain low-paying occupations, driving down wages there and raising them elsewhere. If this *occupational segregation* keeps qualified women and minorities from taking higher-paying jobs, then differences in pay will persist. (We discuss discrimination in Chapter 20.)

All four considerations—differences in marginal revenue productivity, noncompeting groups, nonmonetary differences, and market imperfections—come into play in explaining actual wage differentials. For example, the differential between the wages of a physician and those of a construction worker can be explained on the basis of marginal revenue productivity and noncompeting groups. Physicians generate considerable revenue because of their high productivity and the strong willingness of consumers (via insurance) to pay for health care. Physicians also fall into a noncompeting group where, because of stringent training requirements, only relatively few persons qualify. So the supply of labor is small in relation to demand.

In construction work, where training requirements are much less significant, the supply of labor is great relative to demand. So wages are much lower for construction workers than for physicians. However, if not for the unpleasantness of the construction worker's job and the fact that his or her craft union observes restrictive membership policies, the differential would be even greater than it is.

Pay for Performance

The models of wage determination we have described in this chapter assume that worker pay is always a standard amount for each hour's work, for example, $15 per hour. But pay schemes are often more complex than that both in composition and in purpose. For instance, many workers receive annual salaries rather than hourly pay. And workers receive differing proportions of fringe benefits (health insurance, life insurance, paid vacations, paid sick-leave days, pension contributions, and so on) as part of their pay. Finally, some pay plans are designed to elicit a desired level of performance from workers. This last aspect of pay plans requires further elaboration.

The Principal-Agent Problem Revisited

In Chapter 4 we identified the *principal-agent problem* as it relates to possible differences in the interests of corporate stockholders (principals) and the executives (agents) they

hire. This problem extends to all paid employees. Firms hire workers because they are needed to help produce the goods and services the firms sell in their attempts to turn a profit. Workers are the firms' agents; they are hired to advance the interest (profit) of the firms. The principals are the firms; they hire agents to advance their goals. Firms and workers have one interest in common: They both want the firm to survive and thrive. That will ensure profit for the firm and continued employment and wages for the workers.

But the interests of firms and workers are not identical. As a result, a principal-agent problem arises. Workers may seek to increase their utility by shirking on the job, that is, by providing less than the agreed-upon effort or by taking unauthorized breaks. They may improve their well-being by increasing their leisure during paid work hours, without forfeiting income. The night security guard in a warehouse may leave work early or spend time reading a novel rather than making the assigned rounds. A salaried manager may spend time away from the office visiting with friends rather than attending to company business.

Firms (principals) have a profit incentive to reduce or eliminate shirking. One option is to monitor workers, but monitoring is difficult and costly. Hiring another worker to supervise or monitor the security guard might double the cost of maintaining a secure warehouse. Another way of resolving a principal-agent problem is through some sort of **incentive pay plan** that ties worker compensation more closely to worker output or performance. Such incentive pay schemes include piece rates; commissions and royalties; bonuses, stock options, and profit sharing; and efficiency wages.

Piece Rates Piece rates consist of compensation paid according to the number of units of output a worker produces. If a principal pays fruit pickers by the bushel or typists by the page, it need not be concerned with shirking or with monitoring costs.

Commissions or Royalties Unlike piece rates, commissions and royalties tie compensation to the value of sales. Employees who sell products or services—including real estate agents, insurance agents, stockbrokers, and retail salespersons—commonly receive *commissions* that are computed as a percentage of the monetary value of their sales. Recording artists and authors are paid *royalties*, computed as a certain percentage of sales revenues from their works. Such types of compensation link the financial interests of the salespeople, artists, and authors to the profit interest of the firms.

Bonuses, Stock Options, and Profit Sharing

Bonuses are payments in addition to one's annual salary that are based on some factor such as the performance of the individual worker, or of a group of workers, or of the firm itself. A professional baseball player may receive a bonus based on a high batting average, the number of home runs hit, or the number of runs batted in. A business manager may receive a bonus based on the profitability of her or his unit. *Stock options* allow workers to buy shares of their employer's stock at a fixed, lower price when the stock price rises. Such options are part of the compensation packages of top corporate officials, as well as many workers in relatively high-technology firms. *Profit-sharing plans* allocate a percentage of a firm's profit to its employees.

Efficiency Wages

The rationale behind *efficiency wages* is that employers will enjoy greater effort from their workers by paying them above-equilibrium wage rates. Glance back at Figure 13.3, which shows a competitive labor market in which the equilibrium wage rate is $10. What if an employer decides to pay an above-equilibrium wage of $12 per hour? Rather than putting the firm at a cost disadvantage compared with rival firms paying only $10, the higher wage might improve worker effort and productivity so that unit labor costs actually fall. For example, if each worker produces 10 units of output per hour at the $12 wage rate compared with only 6 units at the $10 wage rate, unit labor costs for the high-wage firm will be only $1.20 (= $12/10) compared to $1.67 (= $10/6) for firms paying the equilibrium wage.

An above-equilibrium wage may enhance worker efficiency in several ways. It enables the firm to attract higher-quality workers. It lifts worker morale. And it lowers turnover, resulting in a more experienced workforce, greater worker productivity, and lower recruitment and training costs. Because the opportunity cost of losing a higher-wage job is greater, workers are more likely to put forth their best efforts with less supervision and monitoring. In fact, efficiency wage payments have proved effective for many employers.

ORIGIN OF THE IDEA
O 13.4
Efficiency wages

Addenda: Negative Side Effects of Pay for Performance

Although pay for performance may help overcome the principal-agent problem and enhance worker productivity, such plans may have negative side effects and require careful design. Here are a few examples:

- The rapid production pace that piece rates encourage may result in poor product quality and may compromise the safety of workers. Such outcomes can be costly to the firm over the long run.
- Commissions may cause some salespeople to engage in questionable or even fraudulent sales practices, such as making exaggerated claims about products or recommending unneeded repairs. Such practices may lead to private lawsuits or government legal action.
- Bonuses based on personal performance may disrupt the close cooperation needed for maximum team production. A professional basketball player who receives a bonus for points scored may be reluctant to pass the ball to teammates.
- Since profit sharing is usually tied to the performance of the entire firm, less energetic workers can "free ride" by obtaining their profit share on the basis of the hard work by others.
- Stock options may prompt some unscrupulous executives to manipulate cost and revenue streams of their firms to create a false appearance of rapidly rising profit. When the firm's stock value rises, the executives exercise their stock options at inflated share prices and reap a personal fortune. In the early 2000s, some firms collapsed when the wrongdoings of their executives were exposed.
- There may be a downside to the reduced turnover resulting from above-market wages: Firms that pay efficiency wages have fewer opportunities to hire new workers and suffer the loss of the creative energy that they often bring to the workplace.

QUICK REVIEW 13.3

- Proponents of the minimum wage argue that it is needed to assist the working poor and to counter monopsony where it might exist; critics say that it is poorly targeted to reduce poverty and that it reduces employment.
- Wage differentials are attributable in general to the forces of supply and demand, influenced by differences in workers' marginal revenue productivity, education, and skills and by nonmonetary differences in jobs. But several labor market imperfections also play a role.
- As it applies to labor, the principal-agent problem is one of workers pursuing their own interests to the detriment of the employer's profit objective.
- Pay-for-performance plans (piece rates, commissions, royalties, bonuses, stock options, profit sharing, and efficiency wages) are designed to improve worker productivity by overcoming the principal-agent problem.

Are Chief Executive Officers (CEOs) Overpaid?

The Multimillion-Dollar Pay of Major Corporate CEOs Has Drawn Considerable Criticism.

Top executives of U.S. corporations typically receive total annual pay (salary, bonuses, and stock options) in the millions of dollars. As shown in Table 1, each of the top five paid U.S. executives earned $99 million or more in 2007.

CEO pay in the United States is not only exceptionally high relative to the average pay of U.S. managers and workers but also high compared to the CEO pay in other industrial countries. For example, in 2005 the CEO pay at firms with about $500 million in annual sales averaged $2.2 million in the United States, compared to $1.2 million in France and Germany and less than $600,000 in South Korea and Japan.*

Is high CEO pay simply the outcome of labor supply and labor demand, as is the pay for star athletes and entertainers? Does it reflect marginal revenue productivity—that is, the contributions by CEOs to their company's output and revenue?

Observers who answer affirmatively point out that decisions made by the CEOs of large corporations affect the productivity of every employee in the organization. Good decisions enhance productivity throughout the organization and increase revenue; bad decisions reduce productivity and revenue. Only executives who have consistently made good business decisions attain the top positions in large corporations. Because the supply of these people is highly limited and their marginal revenue productivity is enormous, they command huge salaries and performance bonuses.

Also, some economists note that CEO pay in the United States may be like the prizes professional golfers and tennis players receive for winning tournaments. These high prizes are designed to promote the productivity of all those who aspire to achieve them. In corporations the top prizes go to the winners of the "contests" among managers to attain, at least eventually, the CEO positions. Thus high CEO pay does not derive solely from the CEO's direct productivity. Instead, it may exist because the high pay creates incentives that raise the productivity of scores of other corporate executives who seek to achieve the top position. In this view, high CEO pay remains grounded on high productivity.

Critics of existing CEO pay acknowledge that CEOs deserve substantially higher salaries than ordinary workers or typical managers, but they question pay packages that run into the millions of dollars. They reject the "tournament pay" idea on the grounds that corporations require cooperative team effort by managers and executives, not the type of high-stakes competition promoted by "winner-take-most" pay. They believe that corporations, although owned by their shareholders, are controlled by corporate boards and professional executives. Because many board members are present or past CEOs of other corporations, they often exaggerate CEO importance and, consequently, overpay their own CEOs. These overpayments are at the expense of the firm's stockholders.

In summary, defenders of CEO pay say that high pay is justified by the direct or indirect marginal-revenue contribution of CEOs. Like it or not, CEO pay is market-determined pay. In contrast, critics say that multimillion-dollar CEO pay bears little relationship to marginal revenue productivity and is unfair to ordinary stockholders. It is clear from our discussion that this issue remains unsettled.

*Worldwide Total Remuneration, 2005–2006 (New York: Towers Perrin, Jan. 11, 2006, p. 20).

TABLE 1 The Five Highest-Paid U.S. CEOs, 2007

Name	Company	Total Pay, Millions
1. Lawrence J. Ellison	Oracle	$192
2. Frederic M. Poses	Trane	127
3. Aubrey K. McClendon	Chesapeake Energy	117
4. Angelo R. Mozilo	Countrywide	103
5. Howard D. Schultz	Starbucks	99

Source: Forbes, www.forbes.com.

Summary

1. The term "labor" encompasses all people who work for pay. The wage rate is the price paid per unit of time for labor. Labor earnings comprise total pay and are found by multiplying the number of hours worked by the hourly wage rate. The nominal wage rate is the amount of money received per unit of time; the real wage rate is the purchasing power of the nominal wage.

2. The long-run growth of real hourly compensation—the average real wage—roughly matches that of productivity, with both increasing over the long run.

3. Global comparisons suggest that real wages in the United States are relatively high, but not the highest, internationally. High real wages in the advanced industrial countries stem largely from high labor productivity.

4. Specific wage rates depend on the structure of the particular labor market. In a competitive labor market the equilibrium wage rate and level of employment are determined at the intersection of the labor supply curve and labor demand curve. For the individual firm, the market wage rate establishes a horizontal labor supply curve, meaning that the wage rate equals the firm's constant marginal resource cost. The firm hires workers to the point where its MRP equals its MRC.

5. Under monopsony the marginal resource cost curve lies above the resource supply curve because the monopsonist must bid up the wage rate to hire extra workers and must pay that higher wage rate to all workers. The monopsonist hires fewer workers than are hired under competitive conditions, pays less-than-competitive wage rates (has lower labor costs), and thus obtains greater profit.

6. A union may raise competitive wage rates by (a) increasing the derived demand for labor, (b) restricting the supply of labor through exclusive unionism, or (c) directly enforcing an above-equilibrium wage rate through inclusive unionism.

7. In many industries the labor market takes the form of bilateral monopoly, in which a strong union "sells" labor to a monopsonistic employer. The wage-rate outcome of this labor market model depends on union and employer bargaining power.

8. On average, unionized workers realize wage rates 15 percent higher than those of comparable nonunion workers.

9. Economists disagree about the desirability of the minimum wage as an antipoverty mechanism. While it causes unemployment for some low-income workers, it raises the incomes of those who retain their jobs.

10. Wage differentials are largely explainable in terms of (a) marginal revenue productivity of various groups of workers; (b) noncompeting groups arising from differences in the capacities and education of different groups of workers; (c) compensating wage differences, that is, wage differences that must be paid to offset nonmonetary differences in jobs; and (d) market imperfections in the form of lack of job information, geographic immobility, union and government restraints, and discrimination.

11. The principal-agent problem arises when workers provide less-than-expected effort. Firms may combat this by monitoring workers or by creating incentive pay schemes that link worker compensation to performance.

Terms and Concepts

wage rate

nominal wage

real wage

purely competitive labor market

monopsony

exclusive unionism

occupational licensing

inclusive unionism

bilateral monopoly

minimum wage

wage differentials

marginal revenue productivity

noncompeting groups

human capital

compensating differences

incentive pay plan

Study Questions  | ECONOMICS

1. Explain why the general level of wages is high in the United States and other industrially advanced countries. What is the single most important factor underlying the long-run increase in average real-wage rates in the United States? **LO1**

2. Why is a firm in a purely competitive labor market a *wage taker*? What would happen if it decided to pay less than the going market wage rate? **LO2**

3. **KEY QUESTION** Describe wage determination in a labor market in which workers are unorganized and many firms

actively compete for the services of labor. Show this situation graphically, using W_1 to indicate the equilibrium wage rate and Q_1 to show the number of workers hired by the firms as a group. Show the labor supply curve of the individual firm, and compare it with that of the total market. Why the differences? In the diagram representing the firm, identify total revenue, total wage cost, and revenue available for the payment of nonlabor resources. **LO2**

4. **KEY QUESTION** Complete the following labor supply table for a firm hiring labor competitively: **LO2**

Units of Labor	Wage Rate	Total Labor Cost (Wage Bill)	Marginal Resource (Labor) Cost
0	$14	$ _____	$ _____
1	14	_____	_____
2	14	_____	_____
3	14	_____	_____
4	14	_____	_____
5	14	_____	_____
6	14	_____	

a. Show graphically the labor supply and marginal resource (labor) cost curves for this firm. Explain the relationship of these curves to one another.
b. Plot the labor demand data of question 2 in Chapter 12 on the graph used in part *a* above. What are the equilibrium wage rate and level of employment? Explain.

5. Suppose the formerly competing firms in question 3 form an employers' association that hires labor as a monopsonist would. Describe verbally the effect on wage rates and employment. Adjust the graph you drew for question 3, showing the monopsonistic wage rate and employment level as W_2 and Q_2, respectively. Using this monopsony model, explain why hospital administrators sometimes complain about a "shortage" of nurses. How might such a shortage be corrected? **LO3**

6. **KEY QUESTION** Assume a firm is a monopsonist that can hire its first worker for $6 but must increase the wage rate by $3 to attract each successive worker. Draw the firm's labor supply and marginal resource cost curves and explain their relationships to one another. On the same graph, plot the labor demand data of question 2 in Chapter 12. What are the equilibrium wage rate and level of employment? Why do these differ from your answer to question 4? **LO3**

7. **KEY QUESTION** Assume a monopsonistic employer is paying a wage rate of W_m and hiring Q_m workers, as indicated in Figure 13.8. Now suppose an industrial union is formed that forces the employer to accept a wage rate of W_c. Explain verbally and graphically why in this instance the higher wage rate will be accompanied by an increase in the number of workers hired. **LO4**

8. Have you ever worked for the minimum wage? If so, for how long? Would you favor increasing the minimum wage by a dollar? By two dollars? By five dollars? Explain your reasoning. **LO5**

9. "Many of the lowest paid people in society—for example, short-order cooks—also have relatively poor working conditions. Hence, the notion of compensating wage differentials is disproved." Do you agree? Explain. **LO5**

10. What is meant by investment in human capital? Use this concept to explain (*a*) wage differentials and (*b*) the long-run rise of real wage rates in the United States. **LO5**

11. What is the principal-agent problem? Have you ever worked in a setting where this problem has arisen? If so, do you think increased monitoring would have eliminated the problem? Why don't firms simply hire more supervisors to eliminate shirking? **LO6**

12. **LAST WORD** Do you think exceptionally high pay to CEOs is economically justified? Why or why not?

Web-Based Questions

1. **REAL WAGES AND PRODUCTIVITY—ARE WORKERS' PAYCHECKS KEEPING UP?** Over the long run, real wages grow at about the same pace as labor productivity. Go to the Bureau of Labor Statistics Web site, **www.bls.gov/lpc,** and select Get Detailed Statistics (it is on the top row) and then scroll down to Major Sector Productivity and Costs Index. Select Most Requested Statistics to find current information on percentage changes in output per hour of all persons in the business sector (labor productivity) and percentage changes in real compensation per hour. Has real compensation per hour kept up with output per hour over the latest 3 years shown?

2. **MEN'S AND WOMEN'S EARNINGS IN PROFESSIONAL GOLF—WHY THE DIFFERENCES?** Go to **espn.com** and select Golf and then Money Leaders. What are the annual earnings to date of the top 10 men golfers on the PGA tour? What are the earnings of the top 10 women golfers on the LPGA tour? Why the general differences in earnings between the male and female golfers?

FURTHER TEST YOUR KNOWLEDGE AT
www.mcconnell18e.com

Labor Unions and Their Impacts

We have noted that unions can increase wage rates by augmenting the demand for labor (Figure 13.5) or by restricting or controlling the supply of labor (Figures 13.6 and 13.7). The purpose of this appendix is to provide some additional information about American unions, collective bargaining, and union impacts.

Union Membership

In 2007 about 15.7 million U.S. workers—12.1 percent of employed wage and salary workers—belonged to unions. Some 8 million of these U.S. union members belonged to one of many unions that are loosely and voluntarily affiliated with the **American Federation of Labor and the Congress of Industrial Organizations (AFL-CIO)** Examples of AFL-CIO unions are the United Autoworkers, Communications Workers, and United Steelworkers. Another 6 million union members belonged to one of the seven unions, including the Service Workers and Teamsters, loosely federated as **Change to Win.** The remaining union members belonged to other **independent unions** that were not affiliated with either federation.

The likelihood that any particular worker will be a union member depends mainly on the industry in which the worker is employed and his or her occupation. As shown in Figure 1a, the **unionization rate**—the percentage of workers unionized—is high in government, transportation, telecommunications, construction, and manufacturing. The unionization rate is very low in finance, agriculture, and retail trade. Figure 1b shows that unionism also varies greatly by occupation. Teachers, protective service workers, transportation workers, production workers, and social workers have high unionization rates; sales workers, food workers, and managers have very low rates.

Because disproportionately more men than women work in the industries and occupations with high unionization rates, men are more likely to be union members than women. Specifically, 13 percent of male wage and salary workers belong to unions compared with 11 percent of women. For the same reason, African-Americans have higher unionization rates than whites: 14 percent compared with 12 percent. The unionization rate for Asians is 11 percent; Hispanics, 10 percent. Unionism in the United States is largely an urban phenomenon. Six heavily urbanized, heavily industrialized states (New York, California, Pennsylvania, Illinois, Ohio, and Michigan) account for approximately half of all union members.

The Decline of Unionism

Since the mid-1950s, union membership has not kept pace with the growth of the labor force. While 25 percent of employed wage and salary workers belonged to unions in

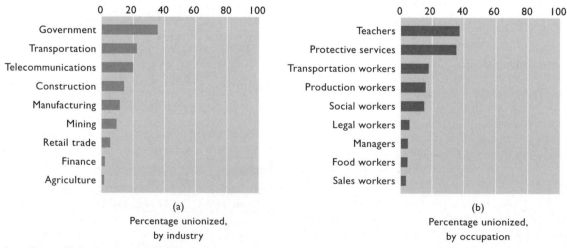

FIGURE 1 **Union membership as a percentage of employed wage and salary workers, selected industries and occupations, 2007.** In percentage terms, union membership varies greatly by (a) industry and (b) occupation.

(a) Percentage unionized, by industry

(b) Percentage unionized, by occupation

Source: Bureau of Labor Statistics, **www.bls.gov.**

the mid 1950s, today only 12.1 percent are union members. Over recent years, even the absolute number of union members has declined significantly. More than 22 million workers were unionized in 1980 but only 15.7 million in 2007.

Some of the major reasons for the decline of U.S. unionism involve structural changes in the economy. Employment has shifted away from manufactured goods (where unions have been stronger) and toward services (where unions have been weaker). Consumer demand has shifted toward foreign manufactured goods and away from goods produced by union labor in the United States. Industry has shifted from the northeast and midwest, where unionism is "a way of life," to "hard-to-organize" areas of the south and southwest. These and other factors have reduced the growth of union membership.

Also, management has greatly intensified its opposition to unions and has increasingly engaged in aggressive collective bargaining, including the use of strikebreakers. Within unionized firms, employers have substituted machinery for workers, subcontracted work to nonunion suppliers, and shifted production of components to low-wage nations. Nonunion firms have greatly improved their wage, fringe benefits, and working conditions. That has reduced the demand for unionism.

Collective Bargaining

Despite the overall decline of unionism, **collective bargaining** (the negotiation of labor contracts) remains an important feature of labor-management relations in several U.S. industries. The goal of collective bargaining is to establish a "work agreement" between the firm and the union.

Collective bargaining agreements (contracts) assume many forms, but typically cover several topics.

Union Status and Managerial Prerogatives

Union status is the degree of security afforded a union by the work agreement. The strongest form of union security is a **closed shop,** in which a worker must be (or must become) a member of the union before being hired. Under Federal labor law, such shops are illegal in industries other than transportation and construction.

In contrast, a **union shop** permits the employer to hire nonunion workers but provides that these workers must join the union within a specified period, say 30 days, or relinquish their jobs. An **agency shop** allows nonunion workers but requires nonunion workers to either pay union dues or donate an equivalent amount to charity. Union and agency shops are legal, except in the 22 states that expressly prohibit them through so-called **right-to-work laws.**

In an **open shop,** an employer may hire either union or nonunion workers. Those who are nonunion are not obligated to join the union or to pay union dues; they may continue on their jobs indefinitely as nonunion workers. Nevertheless, the wages, hours, and working conditions set forth in the work agreement apply to the nonunion workers as well as to the union workers.

The management side of the union-status issue is managerial prerogatives. Most work agreements contain clauses outlining certain decisions that are reserved solely for management. These prerogatives usually cover such matters as the size and location of plants, the products to be manufactured, and the types of equipment and materials to be used in production and in production scheduling.

Wages and Hours

The focal point of almost all bargaining agreements is wages (including fringe benefits) and hours. Both labor and management press for the advantage in wage bargaining. The arguments that unions use most frequently in demanding wage boosts are (1) "what others are getting"; (2) the employer's ability to pay, based on its profitability; (3) increases in the cost of living; and (4) increases in labor productivity.

Hours of work, voluntary versus mandatory overtime, holiday and vacation provisions, profit sharing, health plans, and pension benefits are other contract issues that must be addressed in the bargaining process.

Seniority and Job Protection

The uncertainty of employment in a market economy, along with the fear of antiunion discrimination on the part of employers, has made workers and their unions "job-conscious." The explicit and detailed provisions covering job opportunities that most agreements contain reflect this concern. Unions stress length of service, or *seniority,* as the basis for worker promotion and for layoff and recall. They want the worker with the longest continuous service to have the first chance at relevant promotions, to be the last one laid off, and to be the first one recalled from layoff.

In recent years, unions have become increasingly sensitive to losing jobs to nonunion subcontractors and to overseas workers. Unions sometimes seek limits on the firm's ability to subcontract out work or to relocate production facilities overseas.

Grievance Procedures

Even the most detailed and comprehensive work agreement cannot spell out all the specific issues and problems that might occur during its life. For example, suppose a particular worker gets reassigned to a less pleasant job. Was this reassignment for legitimate business reasons or, as the person suspects, because of a personality conflict with a particular manager? Labor contracts contain grievance procedures to resolve such matters.

The Bargaining Process

The date for the beginning of collective bargaining on a new contract is usually specified in the existing contract and is typically 60 days before the current one expires.

The union normally takes the initiative, presenting its demands in the form of specific wage, fringe-benefit, and other adjustments to the present union-management contract. The firm counters with an offer relating to these and other contract provisions. It is not unusual for the original union demand and the first offer by the firm to be far apart, not only because of the parties' conflicting goals but also because starting far apart leaves plenty of room for compromise and counter offers during the negotiations.

Hanging over the negotiations is the contract deadline, which occurs the moment the present contract expires. At that time there is a possibility of a **strike**—a work stoppage by the union—if it thinks its demands are not being satisfactorily met. But there is also the possibility that at the deadline the firm may engage in a **lockout,** in which it forbids the workers to return to work until a new contract is signed. In this setting of uncertainty prior to the deadline, both parties feel pressure to find mutually acceptable terms.

Although bluster and bickering often occur in collective bargaining, labor and management display a remarkable capacity for compromise and agreement. Typically they reach a compromise that is written into a new contract. Nevertheless, strikes and lockouts occasionally do occur. When they happen, workers lose income and firms lose profit. To stem their losses, both parties usually look for and eventually find ways to settle the labor dispute and get the workers back to work.

Bargaining, strikes, and lockouts occur within a framework of Federal labor law, specifically the **National Labor Relations Act (NLRA).** This act was first passed as the Wagner Act of 1935 and later amended by the Taft-Hartley Act of 1947 and the Landrum-Griffin Act of 1959. The act sets forth the *dos and don'ts* of union and management labor practices. For example, while union members can picket in front of a firm's business, they cannot block access to the business by customers, coworkers, or strikebreakers hired by the firm. Another example: Firms cannot refuse to meet and talk with the union's designated representatives.

Either unions or management can file charges of unfair labor practices under the labor law. The **National Labor Relations Board (NLRB)** has the authority to investigate such charges and to issue cease-and-desist orders in the event of a violation. The board also conducts worker elections to decide which specific union, if any, a group of workers might want to have represent them in collective bargaining.

Economic Effects of Unions

The most straightforward effect of unions is an increase in the wage rates for their members. The consensus estimate is that the overall union wage premium (wage advantage) averages about 15 percent. The effects of unions on output and efficiency, however, are slightly more complicated.

Featherbedding and Work Rules

Some unions diminish output and efficiency by engaging in "make-work" or "featherbedding" practices and resisting the introduction of output-increasing machinery and equipment. These productivity-reducing practices often arise in periods of technological change. For example, in 2002 the ILWU (dockworkers' union) obtained a contract provision guaranteeing 40-hour-per week jobs for all current ILWU clerical personnel for as long as they wish to continue working at their current jobs at West Coast ports. However, many of those workers will not be needed because the ports are rapidly moving toward labor-saving computerized systems for tracking cargo. Thus, many of the current clerical personnel will be paid for doing little or nothing. This will be very inefficient.

More generally, unions may reduce efficiency by establishing work rules and practices that impede putting the most productive workers in particular jobs. Under seniority rules, for example, workers may be promoted for their employment tenure rather than for their ability to perform the available job with the greatest efficiency. Also, unions might restrict the kinds of tasks workers may perform. Contract provisions may prohibit sheet-metal workers or bricklayers from doing the simple carpentry work often associated with their jobs. Observance of such rules means, in this instance, that firms must hire unneeded and underused carpenters.

Finally, critics of unions contend that union contracts often chip away at managerial prerogatives to establish work schedules, determine production targets, introduce new technology, and make other decisions contributing to productive efficiency.

Output Losses from Strikes

A second way unions can impair efficiency and output is through strikes. If union and management reach an impasse during their contract negotiations, a strike may result and the firm's production may cease for the strike's duration. If so, the firm will forgo sales and profit; workers will sacrifice income; and the economy might lose output. U.S. strike activity, however, has dwindled in the past few decades. In 2007 there were only 21 major work stoppages—strikes or lockouts involving 1000 or more employees. About 189,000 workers were idled by these work stoppages, with the average length of stoppages being 10.5 days. In 2007, the average amount of work time lost due to work stoppages was less than .005 percent of total estimated work time.

But the amount of work time lost is an imprecise indicator of the potential economic costs of strikes. These costs may be greater than indicated if strikes disrupt production in nonstruck firms that either supply inputs to struck firms or buy products from them. Example: An extended strike in the auto industry might reduce output and cause layoffs in firms producing, say, glass, tires, paints, and fabrics used in producing cars. It also may reduce sales and cause layoffs in auto dealerships.

On the other hand, the costs of strikes may be less than is implied by the work time lost by strikers if nonstruck firms increase their output to offset the loss of production by struck firms. While the output of General Motors declines when its workers strike, auto buyers may shift their demand to Ford, Toyota, or Honda, which will respond by increasing their employment and output.

Therefore, although GM and its employees are hurt by a strike, society as a whole may experience little or no decline in employment, real output, and income.

Efficiency Losses from Labor Misallocation

A third and more subtle way that unions might reduce efficiency and output is through the union wage advantage itself. Figure 2 splits the economy into two sectors, showing identical labor demand curves for the unionized sector and the nonunionized sector. If all markets are competitive and no union is initially present in either sector, the wage rate in both parts of the economy will be W_n and N_1 workers will be employed in each sector.

Now suppose workers form a union in sector 1 and succeed in increasing the wage rate from W_n to W_u. As a consequence, $N_1 N_2$ workers lose their jobs in the union sector. Assume that they all move to nonunion sector 2, where they are employed. This increase in labor supply (not shown) in the nonunion sector increases the quantity of labor supplied there from N_1 to N_3, reducing the wage rate from W_n to W_s.

Recall that the labor demand curves reflect the marginal revenue products (MRPs) of workers or, in other words, the contribution that each additional worker makes to domestic output. This means that area A + B + C in the union sector represents the sum of the MRPs—the

FIGURE 2 **The effects of the union wage advantage on the allocation of labor.** The higher wage W_u that the union receives in sector I causes the displacement of $N_1 N_2$ workers. The reemployment of these workers in sector 2 increases employment from N_1 to N_3 and reduces the wage rate there from W_n to W_s. The associated loss of output in the union sector is area A + B + C, while the gain in the nonunion sector is only D + E. The net loss of output is area B. This loss of output suggests that the union wage advantage has resulted in a misallocation of labor and a decline in economic efficiency.

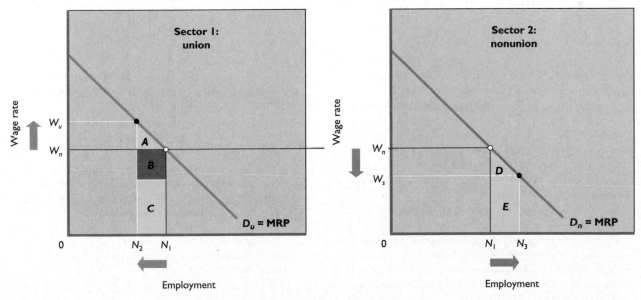

total contribution to domestic output—of the workers displaced by the wage increase achieved by the union. The reemployment of these workers in nonunion sector 2 produces an increase in domestic output shown by area D + E. Because area A + B + C exceeds area D + E, a net loss of domestic output is the result.

More precisely, because A = D and C = E, the efficiency loss attributable to the union wage advantage is represented by area B. Because the same amount of employed labor is now producing a smaller output, labor is being misallocated and used inefficiently. After the shift of $N_1 N_2$ workers to the nonunion sector has occurred, workers in both sectors will be paid wage rates according to their MRPs. But the workers who shifted sectors will be working at a lower MRP than before. An economy always obtains a larger domestic output when labor is reallocated from a low MRP use to a high-MRP use. But here the opposite has occurred. And assuming the union can maintain the W_u wage rate in its sector, a reallocation of labor from sector 2 to sector 1 will never occur.

Attempts to estimate the efficiency loss associated with union wage gains, however, suggest that it is very small: perhaps 0.2 to 0.4 percent (or one-fifth of 1 percent to two-fifths of 1 percent) of U.S. GDP. In 2007 this cost would be about $28 billion to $56 billion.

Offsetting Factors

Some long-run consequences of unionization may enhance productivity and reduce the efficiency loss from unions. One such impact is lower worker turnover within unionized firms. Compared with the rates at nonunion firms, the quit rates (resignation rates) for union workers are 31 to 65 percent lower, depending on the industry.

The union wage premium may reduce worker turnover by increasing the desirability of the union job relative to alternative employment. In economic terms, the higher opportunity cost of quitting reduces the frequency of quitting. Unions also may reduce turnover by using collective communication—the **voice mechanism**—to correct job dissatisfactions that otherwise would be "resolved" by workers quitting and taking other jobs—the **exit mechanism.** It might be risky for individual workers to express their dissatisfaction to employers because employers might retaliate by firing them as "troublemakers." But a union can provide workers with a collective voice to communicate problems and grievances to management and to press for satisfactory resolutions.

A lower quit rate may give a firm a more experienced, more productive workforce. Over time, that might offset a part of the higher costs and reduced profitability associated with the union premium. Also, having fewer resignations might reduce the firm's recruitment, screening, and hiring costs. Additionally, reduced turnover may encourage employers to invest more in the training (and therefore the productivity) of their workers. If a worker quits or "exits" at the end of, say, a year's training, the employer will get no return from providing that training. Lower turnover increases the likelihood that the employer will receive a return on the training it provides, thereby increasing its willingness to upgrade the skills of its workforce. All these factors may increase the long-run productivity of the unionized labor force and therefore reduce the efficiency loss caused by the union wage premium.

APPENDIX SUMMARY

1. About 8 million of the 15.7 million union members in 2007 belonged to unions affiliated with the AFL-CIO; another 6 million belonged to 7 unions loosely federated under the name Change to Win. The rest were members of other independent unions. About 12.1 percent of U.S. wage and salary workers in 2007 were union members, with government employees having the highest unionization rates. As an occupation, public school teachers have the highest rate of unionization—37 percent.

2. Union membership has declined as a percentage of the labor force and in absolute numbers in recent decades. Some of the key causes are structural changes such as the shift from manufacturing employment to service employment. Other causes include improved wages and working conditions in nonunion firms and increased managerial opposition to unions.

3. Collective bargaining determines the terms of union work agreements, which typically cover (a) union status and managerial prerogatives; (b) wages, hours, and working conditions; (c) control over job opportunities; and (d) grievance procedures. The bargaining process is governed by the National Labor Relations Act.

4. Union wages are on average about 15 percent higher than nonunion wages in comparable jobs. Restrictive union work rules, output losses from strikes, and labor misallocation from the union wage advantage are ways that unions may reduce efficiency, output, and productivity. The efficiency losses from unions may be partially offset in the long run by union productivity advances deriving from reduced labor turnover.

APPENDIX TERMS AND CONCEPTS

American Federation of Labor and the
Congress of Industrial Organizations
(AFL-CIO)

Change to Win

independent unions

unionization rate

collective bargaining

closed shop

union shop

agency shop

right-to-work laws

open shop

strike

lockout

National Labor Relations Act (NLRA)

National Labor Relations Board
(NLRB)

voice mechanism

exit mechanism

Appendix Study Questions

1. Which industries and occupations have the highest rates of unionization? Which the lowest? Speculate on the reasons for such large differences. **LO7**

2. What percentage of wage and salary workers are union members? Is this percentage higher, or is it lower, than in previous decades? Which of the factors explaining the trend do you think is most dominant? **LO7**

3. Suppose that you are president of a newly established local union about to bargain with an employer for the first time. List the basic areas you want covered in the work agreement. Why might you begin with a larger wage demand than you actually are willing to accept? What is the logic of a union threatening an employer with a strike during the collective bargaining process? Of an employer threatening the union with a lockout? What is the role of the deadline in encouraging agreement in collective bargaining? **LO7**

4. Explain how featherbedding and other restrictive work practices can reduce labor productivity. Why might strikes reduce the economy's output less than the loss of production by the struck firms? **LO7**

5. What is the estimated size of the union wage advantage? How might this advantage diminish the efficiency with which labor resources are allocated in the economy? Normally, labor resources of equal potential productivity flow from low-wage employment to high-wage employment. Why does that not happen to close the union wage advantage? **LO7**

6. Contrast the voice mechanism and the exit mechanism for communicating dissatisfaction. In what two ways do labor unions reduce labor turnover? How might such reductions increase productivity? **LO7**

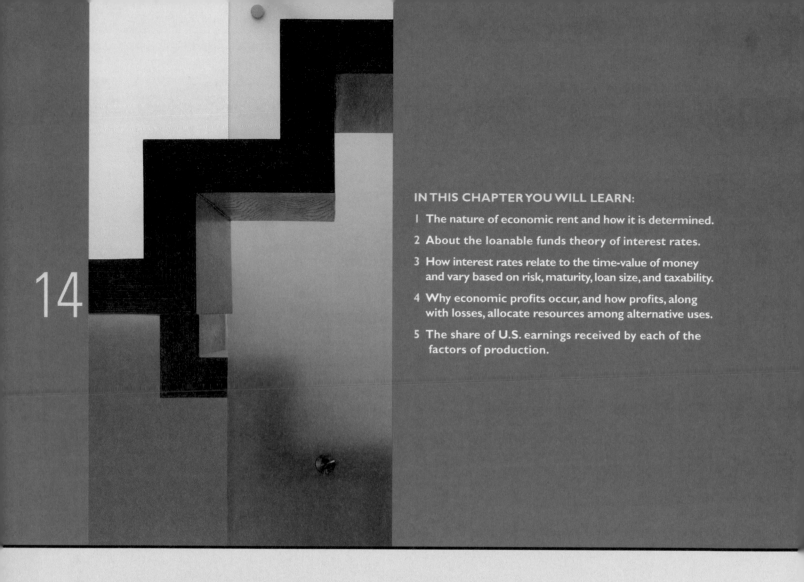

Rent, Interest, and Profit

How do land prices (and land rents) get established, and why do they differ? For example, why do 20 acres of land in the middle of the Nevada desert sell for $5000 while 20 prime acres along the Las Vegas strip command $500 million or more?

What determines interest rates and causes them to change? For instance, why were interest rates on 3-month bank certificates of deposit 6.7 percent in July 2000, 1.3 percent in January 2003, and 5.4 percent in June 2006? How does interest compound over time, and how does that compounding relate to the so-called *present value* and *future value* of a particular sum of money?

What are the sources of profits and losses and why do they vary? For example, why did Wal-Mart earn profits of $13 billion in 2007 whereas General Motors experienced losses of $39 billion?

In Chapter 13 we focused on resource payments in the forms of wages and salaries, which account for about 70 percent of all income paid to American resource suppliers. This chapter examines the other 30 percent of earnings, specifically rent, interest, and profit. We begin by looking at rent.

Economic Rent

To most people, "rent" means the money paid for the use of an apartment or a room in a residence hall. To the business executive, "rent" is a payment made for the use of a factory building, machine, or warehouse facility owned by others. Such definitions of rent can be confusing and ambiguous, however. Residence hall room rent, for example, may include other payments as well: interest on money the university borrowed to finance the dormitory, wages for custodial services, utility payments, and so on.

Economists use "rent" in a much narrower sense. **Economic rent** is the price paid for the use of land and other natural resources that are completely fixed in total supply. As you will see, this fixed overall supply distinguishes rental payments from wage, interest, and profit payments.

Let's examine this idea and some of its implications through supply and demand analysis. We first assume that all land has a single use, for example, growing wheat. We assume, too, that all land is of the same grade or quality, meaning that each arable (tillable) acre of land is as productive as every other acre. And we suppose that land is rented or leased in a competitive market in which many producers are demanding land and many landowners are offering land in the market.

In Figure 14.1, curve S represents the supply of arable land available in the economy as a whole, and curve D_2 represents the demand of producers for use of that land.

As with all economic resources, this demand is derived from the demand for the product being produced. Demand curves such as D_2 reflect the marginal revenue product (MRP = MP × P) of land. The curve slopes downward because of diminishing returns (MP declines) and because, for producers as a group, additional units of land result in greater output and thus lower output prices (P is less).

Perfectly Inelastic Supply

The unique feature of our analysis is on the supply side. For all practical purposes the supply of land is perfectly inelastic (in both the short run and the long run), as reflected in supply curve S. Land has no production cost; it is a "free and nonreproducible gift of nature." The economy has only so much land, and that's that. Of course, within limits any parcel of land can be made more usable by clearing, drainage, and irrigation. But these are capital improvements and not changes in the amount of land itself. Moreover, increases in the usability of land affect only a small fraction of the total amount of land and do not change the basic fact that land and other natural resources are fixed in supply.

Equilibrium Rent and Changes in Demand

Because the supply of land is fixed, demand is the only active determinant of land rent. In this case, supply is passive. And what determines the demand for land? The factors we discussed in Chapter 12: the price of the product produced on the land, the productivity of land (which depends in part on the quantity and quality of the resources with which land is combined), and the prices of the other resources that are combined with land.

If demand is D_2, as we have suggested, the equilibrium rent will be R_2. The quantity of land L_0 that producers wish to rent will equal the quantity of land available (also L_0). But if the demand for land in Figure 14.1 increased from D_2 to D_1, land rent would rise from R_2 to R_1. On the other hand, if the demand for land declined from D_2 to D_3, land rent would fall from R_2 to R_3. But, in either case, the amount of land supplied would remain the same at quantity L_0. Changes in economic rent have no effect on the amount of land available because the supply of land cannot be augmented. If the demand for land were only D_4, land rent would be zero. Land would be a *free good*—a good for which demand is so weak relative to supply that an excess supply of it occurs even if the market price is zero. In Figure 14.1, we show this excess supply as distance $b - a$ at rent of zero. This essentially was the situation in the free-land era of U.S. history.

The ideas underlying Figure 14.1 help answer one of our chapter-opening questions. Land prices and rents are so

FIGURE 14.1 The determination of land rent.
Because the supply S of land (and other natural resources) is perfectly inelastic, demand is the sole active determinant of land rent. An increase in demand from D_2 to D_1 or a decrease in demand from D_2 to D_3 will cause a considerable change in rent: from R_2 to R_1 in the first instance and from R_2 to R_3 in the second. But the amount of land supplied will remain at L_0. If demand is very weak (D_4) relative to supply, land will be a "free good," commanding no rent.

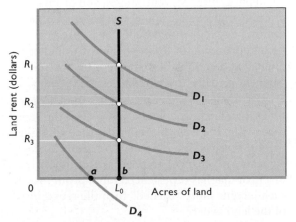

high along the Las Vegas strip because the demand for that land is tremendous. It is capable of producing exceptionally high revenue from gambling, lodging, and entertainment. In contrast, the demand for isolated land in the middle of the desert is highly limited because very little revenue can be generated from its use. (It is an entirely different matter, of course, if gold can be mined from the land, as is true of some isolated lands in Nevada!)

Land Rent: A Surplus Payment

The perfectly inelastic supply of land must be contrasted with the relatively elastic supply of capital, such as apartment buildings, machinery, and warehouses. In the long run, capital is *not* fixed in total supply. A higher price gives entrepreneurs the incentive to construct and offer larger quantities of property resources. Conversely, a decline in price induces suppliers to allow existing facilities to depreciate and not be replaced. The supply curves of these nonland resources are upward-sloping, meaning that the prices paid to such resources provide an **incentive function.** A high price provides an incentive to offer more of the resource, whereas a low price prompts resource suppliers to offer less.

Not so with unimproved land. Rent serves no incentive function because the total supply of land is fixed. Whether rent is $10,000, $500, $1, or $0 per acre, the same amount of land is available to society for use in production. This is why economists consider rent a *surplus payment* not necessary to ensure that land is available to the economy as a whole.

Application: A Single Tax on Land

If land is a gift of nature, costs nothing to produce, and would be available even without rental payments, why should rent be paid to those who by historical accident, by inheritance, or by misdeed happen to be landowners? Socialists have long argued that all land rents are unearned incomes. They urge that land should be nationalized (owned by the state) so that any payments for its use can be used by the government to further the well-being of the entire population rather than being used by a landowning minority.

Henry George's Proposal In the United States, criticism of rental payments took the form of a **single-tax movement,** which gained significant support in the late nineteenth century. Spearheaded by Henry George's provocative book *Progress and Poverty* (1879), supporters of this reform movement held that economic rent could be heavily taxed, or even taxed away, without diminishing the available supply of land or, therefore, the productive potential of the economy as a whole.

George observed that as population grew and the geographic frontier closed, landowners enjoyed larger and larger rents (or lease income) from their landholdings. That increase in rents was the result of a growing demand for a resource whose supply was perfectly inelastic. Some landlords were receiving fabulously high incomes, not through any productive effort but solely through their owning advantageously located land. George insisted that these increases in land rent belonged to the economy; he held that land rents should be heavily taxed and the revenue spent for public uses. In seeking popular support for his ideas on land taxation, George proposed that taxes on rental income be the *only* tax levied by government.

George's case for taxing land was based not only on equity or fairness but also on efficiency. That is, a tax on land is efficient because, unlike virtually every other tax, it does not alter the quantity supplied of the resource being taxed. A tax on wages reduces after-tax income and may weaken the incentive to work; an individual who decides to work for a $10 before-tax wage may decide to retire when an income tax reduces the wage to an after-tax $8. Similarly, a property tax on buildings lowers returns to investors in such property and might cause some to look for other investments. But no such reallocations of resources occur when land is taxed. The most profitable use of land before it is taxed remains the most profitable use after it is taxed. Of course, a landlord could withdraw land from production when a tax is imposed, but that would mean no rental income at all. And some rental income, no matter how small, is better than none.

Criticisms The single tax on land has very few remaining advocates. Critics of the idea have pointed out that:

- Current levels of government spending are such that a land tax alone would not bring in enough revenue; it is unrealistic to consider it as a single tax.
- Most income payments consist of a mixture of such elements as interest, rent, wages, and profits. Land is typically improved in some way, and economic rent cannot be readily disentangled from payments for such improvements. So in practice it would be difficult to determine how much of any specific income payment actually amounted to economic rent.
- So-called unearned income accrues to many people other than landowners, especially when the economy is growing. For example, consider the capital-gains income received by someone who, some 20 or 25 years ago, chanced to purchase (or inherit) stock in a firm that has experienced rapid profit growth. Is such income more "earned" than the rental income of the landowner?

- Historically, a piece of land is likely to have changed ownership many times. Former owners may have been the beneficiaries of past increases in the value of the land (and in land rent). It would hardly be fair to impose a heavy tax on recent buyers who paid a high price for their land and thus did not benefit from past increases in the price of the land that they now own.

Productivity Differences and Rent Differences

So far we have assumed that all units of land are of the same grade. That assumption is unrealistic. Different pieces of land vary greatly in productivity, depending on soil fertility and on such climatic factors as rainfall and temperature. Such factors explain, for example, why Kansas soil is excellently suited to wheat production, why the sagebrush plains of Wyoming are much less well suited, and why the desert of Arizona is nearly incapable of wheat production. Such productivity differences are reflected in resource demand and prices. Competitive bidding by producers will establish a high rent for highly productive Kansas land; less productive Wyoming land will command a much lower rent; and Arizona desert land may command no rent at all.

Location itself may be just as important in explaining differences in land rent. Other things equal, renters will pay more for a unit of land that is strategically located with respect to materials, transportation, labor, and customers than they will for a unit of land whose location is remote from these things. Examples include the enormously high land prices in major ski resorts and the high price of land that contains oil beneath it.

Figure 14.1, viewed from a slightly different perspective, reveals the rent differentials from quality differences in land. Assume, again, that only wheat can be produced on four grades of land, each of which is available in the fixed amount L_0. When combined with identical amounts of labor, capital, and entrepreneurial talent, the productivity or, more specifically, the marginal revenue product of each of the four grades of land is reflected in demand curves D_1, D_2, D_3, and D_4. Grade 1 land is the most productive, as shown by D_1, while grade 4 is the least productive, as shown by D_4. The resulting economic rents for grades 1, 2, and 3 land will be R_1, R_2, and R_3, respectively; the rent differential will mirror the differences in productivity of the three grades of land. Grade 4 land is so poor in quality that, given its supply S, farmers won't pay anything to use it. It will be a free good because it is not sufficiently scarce in relation to the demand for it to command a price or a rent.

Alternative Uses of Land

We have assumed that land has only one use. But the reality is that land normally has alternative uses. An acre of Kansas farmland may be useful for raising not only wheat but corn, oats, barley, and cattle; or it may be useful for building a house or a highway or as a factory site. In other words, any particular use of land involves an opportunity cost—the forgone production from the next best use of the resource. Where there are alternative uses, individual firms must pay rent to cover those opportunity costs in order to secure the use of land for their particular purposes. To the individual firm, rent is a cost of production, just as are wages and interest.

Recall that, as viewed by society, economic rent is not a cost. Society would have the same amount of land with or without the payment of economic rent. From society's perspective, economic rent is a surplus payment above that needed to gain the use of a resource. But individual firms do need to pay rent to attract land resources away from alternative uses. For firms, rental payments *are* a cost. **(Key Question 2)**

QUICK REVIEW 14.1

- Economic rent is the price paid for resources such as land whose supply is perfectly inelastic.
- Land rent is a surplus payment because land would be available to society even if this rent were not paid.
- The surplus nature of land rent served as the basis for Henry George's single-tax movement.
- Differential rents allocate land among alternative uses.

Interest

Interest is the price paid for the use of money. It is the price that borrowers need to pay lenders for transferring purchasing power from the present to the future. It can be thought of as the amount of money that must be paid for the use of $1 for 1 year.

- *Interest is stated as a percentage.* Interest is paid in kind, meaning that the borrower pays for the loan of money with money (interest). For that reason, interest is typically stated as a percentage of the amount of money borrowed rather than as a dollar amount. It is less clumsy to say that interest is "12 percent annually" than to say that interest is "$120 per year per $1000." Also, stating interest as a percentage makes comparison of the interest paid on loans of different amounts easier. By expressing interest as a percentage, we can immediately compare an interest payment of, say, $432 per year per $2880 with one of $1800 per year per $12,000. Both interest payments are 15 percent per year, which is not obvious from the actual dollar figures. This interest of 15 percent per year is referred to as a 15 percent interest rate.

- *Money is not a resource.* Money is *not* an economic resource. In the form of coins, paper currency, or checking accounts, money is not productive; it cannot produce goods and services. However, businesses "buy" the use of money because it can be used to acquire capital goods such as factories, machinery, warehouses, and so on. Such facilities clearly do contribute to production. Thus, in "hiring" the use of money capital, business executives are indirectly buying the use of real capital goods.

Loanable Funds Theory of Interest

In macroeconomics the interest rate is often viewed through the lens of the economy's total supply of and demand for money. But because our present focus is on microeconomics, it will be useful to consider a more micro-based theory of

<table>
<tr><td>**INTERACTIVE GRAPHS**</td></tr>
<tr><td>**G 14.1**</td></tr>
<tr><td>Loanable funds</td></tr>
</table>

interest here. Specifically, the **loanable funds theory of interest** explains the interest rate not in terms of the total

supply of and demand for *money* but, rather, in terms of the supply of and demand for *funds available for lending (and borrowing)*. As Figure 14.2 shows, the equilibrium interest rate (here, 8 percent) is the rate at which the quantities of loanable funds supplied and demanded are equal.

Let's first consider the loanable funds theory in simplified form. Specifically, assume households or consumers are the sole suppliers of loanable funds and businesses are the sole demanders. Also assume that lending occurs directly between households and businesses; no financial institutions are acting as intermediaries.

Supply of Loanable Funds
The supply of loanable funds is represented by curve S in Figure 14.2. Its upward slope indicates that households will make available a larger quantity of funds at high interest rates than at low interest rates. Most people prefer to use their incomes to purchase goods and services *today*, rather than delay purchases to sometime in the *future*. For people to delay consumption and increase their saving, they must be "bribed" or compensated by an interest payment. The larger the amount of that payment, the greater the deferral

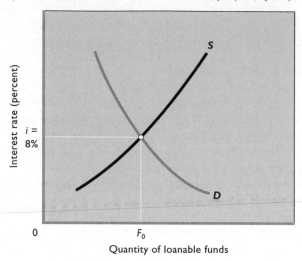

FIGURE 14.2 The market for loanable funds. The upsloping supply curve S for loanable funds reflects the idea that at higher interest rates, households will defer more of their present consumption (save more), making more funds available for lending. The downsloping demand curve D for loanable funds indicates that businesses will borrow more at lower interest rates than at higher interest rates. At the equilibrium interest rate (here, 8 percent), the quantities of loanable funds lent and borrowed are equal (here, F_0 each).

of household consumption and thus the greater the amount of money made available for loans.

There is disagreement among economists as to how much the quantity of loanable funds made available by suppliers changes in response to changes in the interest rate. Most economists view saving as being relatively insensitive to changes in the interest rate because people also save for reasons other than to secure interest payments. For example, they may save out of habit, or to have funds available for a "rainy day," or to accumulate funds for an expensive purchase. They also may save to have money available for retirement, make gifts to charitable organizations, or provide inheritances for children. The supply curve of loanable funds may therefore be more inelastic—displaying less quantity response to changes in i—than S in Figure 14.2 implies.

Demand for Loanable Funds
Businesses borrow loanable funds primarily to add to their stocks of capital goods, such as new plants or warehouses, machinery, and equipment. Assume that a firm wants to buy a machine that will increase output and sales such that the firm's total revenue will rise by $110 for the year. Also assume that the machine costs $100 and has a useful life of just 1 year. Comparing the $10 earned with the $100 cost of the machine, we find that the expected rate of return on this investment is 10 percent (= $10/$100) for the 1 year.

To determine whether the investment would be profitable and whether it should be made, the firm must compare the interest rate—the price of loanable funds—with the 10 percent expected rate of return. If funds can be borrowed at some rate less than the rate of return, say, at 8 percent, as in Figure 14.2, then the investment is profitable and should be made. But if funds can be borrowed only at an interest rate above the 10 percent rate of return, say, at 14 percent, the investment is unprofitable and should not be made.

Why is the demand for loanable funds downsloping, as in Figure 14.2? At higher interest rates fewer investment projects will be profitable and therefore a smaller quantity of loanable funds will be demanded. At lower interest rates, more investment projects will be profitable and therefore more loanable funds will be demanded. Indeed, as we have just seen, purchasing the $100 machine is profitable if funds can be borrowed at 8 percent but not if the firm must borrow at 14 percent.

ORIGIN OF THE IDEA

O 14.1

Interest rates

Extending the Model

We now make this simple model more realistic in several ways.

Financial Institutions Households rarely directly lend their savings to the businesses that are borrowing funds for investment. Instead, they place their savings in banks (and other financial institutions). The banks pay interest to savers in order to attract loanable funds and in turn lend those funds to businesses. Businesses borrow the funds from the banks, paying them interest for the use of the money. Financial institutions profit by charging borrowers higher interest rates than the interest rates they pay savers. Both interest rates, however, are based on the supply of and demand for loanable funds.

Changes in Supply Anything that causes households to be thriftier will prompt them to save more at each interest rate, shifting the supply curve rightward. For example, if interest earned on savings were to be suddenly exempted from taxation, we would expect the supply of loanable funds to increase and the equilibrium interest rate to decrease.

Conversely, a decline in thriftiness would shift the supply-of-loanable-funds curve leftward and increase the equilibrium interest rate. Illustration: If the government expanded social insurance to cover the costs of hospitalization, prescription drugs, and retirement living more fully, the incentive of households to save might diminish.

Changes in Demand On the demand side, anything that increases the rate of return on potential investments will increase the demand for loanable funds. Let's return to our earlier example, where a firm would receive additional revenue of $110 by purchasing a $100 machine and, therefore, would realize a 10 percent return on investment. What factors might increase or decrease the rate of return? Suppose a technological advance raised the productivity of the machine such that the firm's total revenue increased by $120 rather than $110. The rate of return would then be 20 percent, not 10 percent. Before the technological advance, the firm would have demanded zero loanable funds at, say, an interest rate of 14 percent. But now it will demand $100 of loanable funds at that interest rate, meaning that the demand curve for loanable funds has been shifted to the right.

Similarly, an increase in consumer demand for the firm's product will increase the price of its product. So even though the productivity of the machine is unchanged, its potential revenue will rise from $110 to perhaps $120, increasing the firm's rate of return from 10 to 20 percent. Again the firm will be willing to borrow more than previously at our presumed 8 or 14 percent interest rate, implying that the demand curve for loanable funds has shifted rightward. This shift in demand increases the equilibrium interest rate.

Conversely, a decline in productivity or in the price of the firm's product would shift the demand curve for loanable funds leftward, reducing the equilibrium interest rate.

Other Participants We must recognize that participation in the loanable funds market goes well beyond our simplification of households as suppliers of funds and businesses as demanders of funds. For example, while households are suppliers of loanable funds, many are also demanders of such funds. Households borrow to finance expensive purchases such as housing, automobiles, furniture, and household appliances. Governments also are on the demand side of the loanable funds market when they borrow to finance budgetary deficits. And businesses that have revenues in excess of their current expenditures may offer some of those revenues in the market for loanable funds. Thus, like households, businesses operate on both the supply and the demand sides of the market.

Finally, in addition to gathering and making available the savings of households, banks and other financial institutions also increase funds through the lending process and decrease funds when loans are paid back and not lent back out. The Federal Reserve (the nation's central bank) controls the amount of this bank activity and thus influences interest rates.

TABLE 14.1 Compound Interest, Future Value, and Present Value, 10 Percent Interest Rate

(1) Beginning Period Value	(2) Computation	(3) Total Interest	(4) End Period Value
$1000 (Year 1)	$1000 × 1.10 = $1100	$100	$1100 (= $1000 + $100)
$1100 (Year 2)	$1100 × 1.10 = $1210	$210 (= $100 + $110)	$1210 (= $1000 + $210)
$1210 (Year 3)	$1210 × 1.10 = $1331	$331 (= $100 + $110 + $121)	$1331 (= $1000 + $331)

This fact helps answer one of our chapter-opening questions: Why did the interest rate on 3-month certificates of deposit in the United States fall from 6.7 percent in 2000 to only 1.3 percent in early 2003? There are two reasons: (1) The demand for loanable funds sharply declined because businesses reduced their desire to purchase more capital goods and (2) the Federal Reserve, fighting recession and sluggish recovery, took monetary actions that greatly increased the supply of loanable funds. In contrast, between 2003 and 2006 the Federal Reserve restricted the growth of loanable funds. Because the demand for loanable funds increased more rapidly than the supply of loanable funds, interest rates such as those on 3-month certificates of deposit rose. As indicated in the chapter opening, that rate increased from 1.3 percent in January 2003 to 5.4 percent in June 2006. **(Key Question 6)**

Time-Value of Money

Interest is central to understanding the **time-value of money**—the idea that a specific amount of money is more valuable to a person the sooner it is obtained. A sum of money received today is equivalent to a larger amount of money in the future because today's sum can be placed in an interest-bearing account or a financial investment. The interest rate determines how fast the amount of money that is invested in the account will grow over time. It also determines a way in which a given amount of money today can be thought of as being equivalent to a larger amount of money in the future, and how a future amount of money can be thought of as being equivalent to a smaller amount of money today.

Compound Interest

Compound interest is the total interest that cumulates over time on money that is placed into an interest-bearing account. Table 14.1 helps us explain compound interest, as well as the related ideas of future value and present value. Suppose that Max places $1000 into an interest-bearing account at 10 percent interest with the intent to let the *principal* (the initial deposit) and interest compound for 3 years. The first row of each column shows the beginning period sum; the second column shows the yearly computation as to how that sum grows, given a particular interest rate. That growth is found by multiplying the dollar

amount at the beginning of each year by $1 + i$, where i is the interest rate expressed as a decimal.

In year 1 the 10 percent interest rate increases the money in the account from $1000 to $1100 (= $1000 × 1.10). So, as shown in Column 3, total interest is $100. Column 4 simply lists the $1100 again but reinforces that this amount consists of the original principal plus the total interest. Similarly, in year 2, the $1100 now in the account grows to $1210 (= $1100 × 1.10) because $110 of new interest accrues on the $1100. At the end of year 2, the principal remains $1000, but the total interest is $210 and the total amount in the account is $1210. Interest in year 3 is $121 and total interest rises to $331. After this $331 of total interest is added to the $1000 principle, the accumulation is $1331. As shown in Column 3, compound interest builds and builds over time.

Future Value and Present Value Now note from Table 14.1 that we can look at the time value of money in two distinct ways. **Future value** is the amount to which some current amount of money will grow as interest compounds over time. In our table, the future value (FV) of $1000 today at 10 percent interest is $1331 three years from now. Future value is always forward-looking.

But we can just as easily look backward from the end value of $1331 and ask how much that amount is worth today, given the 10 percent interest rate. **Present value** is today's value of some amount of money to be received in the future. In terms of the table, the present value (PV) of $1331 is $1000. Here, FV is "discounted" by three years at 10 percent to remove the $331 of compounded interest and therefore to obtain PV. (We will defer explaining the discounting procedure to our chapter on financial economics in the macro portion of *Economics*. But if you are interested in the mathematics, see the footnote below.)[1]

---

[1]The mathematics is as follows

$$FV = PV\,(1 + i)^t \quad \text{and} \quad PV = \frac{FV}{(1 + i)^t}$$

where i is the interest rate and t is time, here the number of years of compounding.

CONSIDER THIS . . .

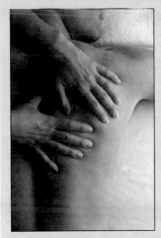

That Is Interest

The following story told by economist Irving Fisher (1867–1947) helps illustrate the time-value of money.

In the process of a massage, a masseur informed Fisher that he was a socialist who believed that "interest is the basis of capitalism and is robbery." Following the massage, Fisher asked, "How much do I owe you?"

The masseur replied, "Thirty dollars."

"Very well," said Fisher, "I will give you a note payable a hundred years hence. I suppose you have no objections to taking this note without any interest. At the end of that time, you, or perhaps your grandchildren, can redeem it."

"But I cannot afford to wait that long," said the masseur.

"I thought you said that interest was robbery. If interest is robbery, you ought to be willing to wait indefinitely for the money. If you are willing to wait ten years, how much would you require?"

"Well, I would have to get more than thirty dollars."

His point now made, Fisher replied, "That is interest."*

---

*Irving Fisher, as quoted in Irving Norton Fisher, *My Father Irving Fisher* (New York: Comet, 1956), p. 77.

With any positive interest rate (and assuming no inflation), a person would prefer to receive $1000 today rather than $1000 at some time in the future. The higher the interest rate, the greater is the *future value* of a specific amount of money today. To confirm, substitute a 20 percent interest rate for the 10 percent rate in Table 14.1 and rework the analysis. Finally, you should know that the analysis presented through the table is extendable to any number of years.

The time-value of money is an important concept. For example, it helps explain the optimal timing of natural resource extraction (Chapter 15). It also is critical to the entire field of financial economics (Chapter 34 of *Economics* or Chapter 17 of the macro-split version of *Economics*). In our present chapter, our goal is simply to stress that *money has time value because of the potential for compound interest.* **(Key Question 7)**

Range of Interest Rates

Although economists often speak in terms of a single interest rate, there are actually a number of interest rates. Table 14.2 lists several interest rates often referred to in the media. On January 15, 2008, these rates ranged from 3.17 to 13.74 percent. Why the differences?

- **Risk** Loans to different borrowers for different purposes carry varying degrees of risk. The greater the chance that the borrower will not repay the loan, the higher the interest rate the lender will charge to compensate for that risk.

- **Maturity** The time length of a loan or its *maturity* (when it needs to be paid back) also affects the interest rate. Other things equal, longer-term loans usually command higher interest rates than shorter-term loans. The long-term lender suffers the inconvenience and possible financial sacrifice of forgoing alternative uses of his or her money for a greater period.

- **Loan size** If there are two loans of equal maturity and risk, the interest rate on the smaller of the two loans usually will be higher. The costs of issuing a large loan and a small loan are about the same in dollars, but the cost is greater *as a percentage* of the smaller loan.

- **Taxability** Interest on certain state and municipal bonds is exempt from Federal income taxation. Because lenders are interested in their after-tax rate of

TABLE 14.2 Selected Interest Rates, January 15, 2008

Type of Interest Rate	Annual Percentage
20-year Treasury bond rate (interest rate on Federal government security used to finance the public debt)	4.30%
90-day Treasury Bill rate (interest rate on Federal government security used to finance the public debt)	3.17
Prime interest rate (interest rate used as a reference point for a wide range of bank loans)	7.25
30-year mortgage rate (fixed-interest rate on loans for houses)	5.69
4-year automobile loan rate (interest rate for new autos by automobile finance companies)	7.11
Tax-exempt state and municipal bond rate (interest rate paid on a low-risk bond issued by a state or local government)	4.15
Federal funds rate (interest rate on overnight loans between banks)	4.23
Consumer credit card rate (interest rate charged for credit card purchases)	13.74

Sources: Federal Reserve, **www.federalreserve.gov**, and Bankrate.com, **www.bankrate.com**.

interest, borrowing by states and local governments can attract lenders even though the borrowers pay low interest rates. Consider a high-income lender who pays a 35 percent Federal income tax (2008) on marginal income. He or she may prefer a 5 percent interest rate on a tax-exempt municipal bond to a 6 percent taxable interest rate on a corporate bond.

Pure Rate of Interest

Economists and financial specialists talk of "the" interest rate to simplify the cluster of rates (Table 14.2). When they do so, they usually have in mind the **pure rate of interest.** The pure rate is best approximated by the interest paid on long-term, virtually riskless securities such as long-term bonds of the U.S. government (20-year Treasury bonds). This interest payment can be thought of as being made solely for the use of money over an extended time period because risk and administrative costs are negligible and the interest rate on these bonds is not distorted by market imperfections. In January 2008, the pure rate of interest in the United States was 4.3 percent.

Role of the Interest Rate

The interest rate is a critical price that affects the *level* and *composition* of investment goods production, as well as the *amount* of R&D spending.

Interest and Total Output

A lower equilibrium interest rate encourages businesses to borrow more for investment. As a result, total spending in the economy rises, and if the economy has unused resources, so does total output. Conversely, a higher equilibrium interest rate discourages business from borrowing for investment, thereby reducing investment and total spending. Such a decrease in spending may be desirable if an economy is experiencing inflation.

The Federal Reserve often manages the interest rate to try to expand investment and output, on the one hand, or to reduce investment and inflation, on the other. It affects the interest rate by changing the supply of money. Increases in the money supply increase the supply of loanable funds, causing the equilibrium interest rate to fall. This boosts investment spending and expands the economy. In contrast, decreases in the money supply decrease the supply of loanable funds, boosting the equilibrium interest rate. As a result, investment is constrained and so is the economy.

Interest and the Allocation of Capital

Prices are rationing devices. The price of money—the interest rate—is certainly no exception. The interest rate rations the available supply of loanable funds to investment projects that have expected rates of return at or above the interest rate cost of the borrowed funds.

If, say, the computer industry expects to earn a return of 12 percent on the money it invests in physical capital and it can secure the required funds at an interest rate of 8 percent, it can borrow and expand its physical capital. If the expected rate of return on additional capital in the steel industry is only 6 percent, that industry will find it unprofitable to expand its capital at 8 percent interest. The interest rate allocates money, and ultimately physical capital, to the industries in which it will be most productive and therefore most profitable. Such an allocation of capital goods benefits society.

But the interest rate does not perfectly ration capital to its most productive uses. Large oligopolistic borrowers may be better able than competitive borrowers to pass interest costs on to consumers because they can change prices by controlling output. Also, the size, prestige, and monopsony power of large corporations may help them obtain funds on more favorable terms than can smaller firms, even when the smaller firms have similar rates of profitability.

Interest and R&D Spending

In Web Chapter 11W, we pointed out that, similar to an investment decision, a decision on how much to spend on R&D depends on the cost of borrowing funds in relationship to the expected rate of return. Other things equal, the lower the interest rate and thus the lower the cost of borrowing funds for R&D, the greater is the amount of R&D spending that is potentially profitable. Low interest rates encourage R&D spending; high interest rates discourage it.

Also, the interest rate allocates R&D funds to firms and industries for which the expected rate of return on R&D is the greatest. Ace Microcircuits may have an expected rate of return of 16 percent on an R&D project, while Glow Paints has only a 2 percent expected rate of return on its R&D project. With the interest rate at 8 percent, loanable funds will flow to Ace, not to Glow. Society will benefit by having R&D spending allocated to projects that have high enough expected rates of return to justify using scarce resources for R&D rather than for other purposes.

Nominal and Real Interest Rates

This discussion of the role of interest in investment decisions and in R&D decisions assumes that there is no inflation. If inflation exists, we must distinguish between nominal and real interest rates, just like we needed to distinguish between nominal and real wages in Chapter 13. The **nominal interest rate** is the rate of interest expressed in dollars of current value. The **real interest rate** is the rate of interest expressed in purchasing power—dollars of inflation-adjusted value. (For a comparison of nominal interest rates on bank loans in selected countries, see Global Perspective 14.1.)

Example: Suppose the nominal interest rate and the rate of inflation are both 10 percent. If you borrow $100, you must pay back $110 a year from now. However, because of 10 percent inflation, each of these 110 dollars will be worth 10 percent less. Thus, the real value or purchasing power of your $110 at the end of the year is only $100. In inflation-adjusted dollars you are borrowing $100 and at year's end you are paying back $100. While the nominal interest rate is 10 percent, the real interest rate is zero. We determine the real interest rate by subtracting the 10 percent inflation rate from the 10 percent nominal interest rate.

It is the real interest rate, not the nominal rate, that affects investment and R&D decisions. **(Key Question 10)**

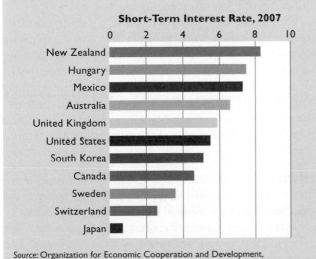

GLOBAL PERSPECTIVE 14.1

Short-Term Nominal Interest Rates, Selected Nations

These data show the short-term nominal interest rates (percentage rates on 3-month loans) in various countries in 2007. Because these are nominal rates, much of the variation reflects differences in rates of inflation. But differences in central bank monetary policies and in risk of default also explain the variations.

Short-Term Interest Rate, 2007

New Zealand	
Hungary	
Mexico	
Australia	
United Kingdom	
United States	
South Korea	
Canada	
Sweden	
Switzerland	
Japan	

Source: Organization for Economic Cooperation and Development, **www.oecd.org.**

Application: Usury Laws

A number of states have passed **usury laws**, which specify a maximum interest rate at which loans can be made.

Such rates are a special case of *price ceilings*, discussed in Chapter 3. The purpose of usury laws is to hold down the interest cost of borrowing, particularly for low-income borrowers. ("Usury" simply means exorbitant interest.)

Figure 14.2 helps us assess the impact of such legislation. The equilibrium interest rate there is 8 percent, but suppose a usury law specifies that lenders cannot charge more than 6 percent. The effects are as follows:

- **Nonmarket rationing** At 6 percent, the quantity of loanable funds demanded exceeds the quantity supplied: There is a shortage of loanable funds. Because the market interest rate no longer can ration the available loanable funds to borrowers, lenders (banks) have to do the rationing. We can expect them to make loans only to the most creditworthy borrowers (mainly wealthy, high-income people), thus defeating the goal of the usury law. Low-income, riskier borrowers are excluded from the market and may be forced to turn to loan sharks who charge illegally high interest rates.

- **Gainers and losers** Creditworthy borrowers gain from usury laws because they pay below-market interest rates. Lenders (ultimately bank shareholders) are losers because they receive 6 percent rather than 8 percent on each dollar lent.

- **Inefficiency** We have just seen how the equilibrium interest rate allocates money to the investments and the R&D projects whose expected rates of return are greatest. Under usury laws, funds are much less likely to be allocated by banks to the most productive projects. Suppose Mendez has a project so promising she would pay 10 percent for funds to finance it. Chen has a less-promising investment, and he would be willing to pay only 7 percent for financing. If the market were rationing funds, Mendez's highly productive project would be funded and Chen's would not. That allocation of funds would be in the interest of both Mendez and society. But with a 6 percent usury rate, Chen may get to the bank before Mendez and receive the loanable funds at 6 percent. So Mendez may not get funded. Legally controlled interest rates may thus inefficiently ration funds to less-productive investments or R&D projects.

Economic Profit

Recall from previous chapters that economists define profit narrowly. To accountants, "profit" is what remains of a firm's total revenue after it has paid individuals and other firms for the materials, capital, and labor they have supplied to the firm. To the economist, this definition overstates profit. The reason is that the accountant's view of profit considers only **explicit costs:** payments made by the firm to outsiders. It ignores **implicit costs:** the monetary income the firm sacrifices when it uses resources that it owns, rather than supplying those resources to the market. The economist considers implicit costs to be opportunity costs, and hence to be real costs that must be accounted for in determining profit. **Economic,** or **pure, profit** is what remains after all costs—both explicit and implicit costs, the latter including a normal profit—have been subtracted from a firm's total revenue. Economic profit may be either positive or negative (a loss).

Role of the Entrepreneur

The economist views profit as the return to a particular type of human resource: entrepreneurial ability. We know from earlier chapters that the entrepreneur (1) combines resources to produce a good or service; (2) makes basic, nonroutine policy decisions for the firm; (3) introduces innovations in the form of new products or new production processes; and (4) bears the economic risks associated with all those functions.

Part of the entrepreneur's return is a **normal profit.** This is the minimum payment necessary to retain the entrepreneur in his or her current line of production. We saw in Chapter 8 that normal profit is a cost—the cost of using entrepreneurial ability for a particular purpose. We saw also that a firm's total revenue may exceed its total cost; the excess revenue above all costs is its economic profit. This *residual profit* also goes to the entrepreneur. The entrepreneur is the *residual claimant:* the resource that receives what is left after all costs are paid.

Why should there be residual profit? There are three possible reasons, two relating to the risks involved in business and one based on monopoly power.

Sources of Economic Profit

Let's first construct an artificial economic environment in which economic profit would be zero. Then, by noting how the real world differs from such an environment, we will see where economic profit arises.

We begin with a purely competitive, static economy. A **static economy** is one in which the basic forces such as resource supplies, technological knowledge, and consumer tastes are constant and unchanging. As a result, all cost and supply data, on the one hand, and all demand and revenue data, on the other, are constant.

Given the unchanging nature of these data, the economic future is perfectly certain and foreseeable; there is no uncertainty. The outcome of any price or production policy can be accurately predicted. Furthermore, no product or production process is ever improved. Pure competition in this sort of static, risk-free, and purely predictable economy would mean that any economic profit or loss that might have existed in an industry will disappear with the entry or exit of firms in the long run. All costs, explicit and implicit, are just covered in the long run, so there is no economic profit in a static economy.

The idea of zero economic profit in a static competitive economy suggests that profit is linked to the dynamic nature of real-world capitalism and its accompanying uncertainty. Moreover, it indicates that economic profit may arise from a source other than the directing, innovating, and risk-bearing functions of the entrepreneur. That source is the presence of some amount of monopoly power. We therefore need to look at how risk, innovation, and monopoly relate to profit. Let's start with risk.

Risk and Profit In a real, dynamic economy the future is not certain and predictable; there is uncertainty. This means that the entrepreneur must assume risks. Some or all of economic profit may be a reward for assuming risks.

In linking economic profit with uncertainty and risk bearing, we must distinguish between risks that are insurable and risks that are not. Some types of risk such as fire, floods, theft, and accidents to employees are measurable; that is, their frequency of occurrence can be estimated accurately. Firms can avoid losses due to **insurable risks** by paying an annual fee (an insurance premium) to an insurance company. The entrepreneur need not bear such risks.

However, the entrepreneur must bear the uninsurable risks of business, and those risks are a potential source of economic profit. **Uninsurable risks** are mainly the uncontrollable and unpredictable changes in the demand and supply conditions facing the firm (and hence its revenues and costs). Uninsurable risks stem from three general sources:

- **Changes in the general economic environment** A downturn in business (a recession), for example, can lead to greatly reduced demand, sales, and revenues, and thus to business losses. An otherwise prosperous firm may experience such losses through no fault of its own.

- **Changes in the structure of the economy** Consumer tastes, technology, resource availability, and prices change constantly in the real world, bringing changes in production costs and revenues. For example, an airline earning economic profit one year may find its profit plunging the next year as the result of a significant increase in the price of jet fuel.

- **Changes in government policy** A newly instituted regulation, the removal of a tariff, or a change in national defense policy may significantly alter the cost and revenue data of the affected industry and firms.

Regardless of how such revenue and cost changes come about, they are risks that the firm and entrepreneur must take in order to stay in business. Some or all of the economic profit in a real, dynamic economy may be compensation for taking risks.

Innovations and Profit
Such uninsurable risks are beyond the control of the individual firm or industry and thus external to it. But one dynamic feature of capitalism—innovation—occurs at the initiative of the entrepreneur. Business firms deliberately introduce new methods of production to affect their costs favorably and new and improved products to affect their revenues favorably. The entrepreneur purposely undertakes to upset existing cost and revenue data in a way that promises to be profitable.

But again, uncertainty enters the picture. Despite exhaustive market surveys, new products or modifications of existing products may be economic failures. Similarly, of the many new novels, textbooks, movies, and video games that appear every year, only a handful garner large profits. Nor is it known with certainty whether new production machinery will actually yield projected cost economies.

Thus, innovations undertaken by entrepreneurs entail uncertainty and the possibility of losses, not just the potential for increased profit. Some of the economic profit in an innovative economy may be compensation for dealing with the uncertainty of innovation.

Monopoly and Profit
So far, we have linked economic profit with the uncertainties surrounding (1) the dynamic environment to which enterprises are exposed and (2) the dynamic business processes they initiate themselves. The existence of monopoly power is a final source of economic profit. Because a monopolist can restrict output and deter entry, it may persistently enjoy above-competitive prices and economic profit if demand is strong relative to cost.

Economic uncertainty and monopoly are closely intertwined as sources of economic profit. A firm with some monopoly power can reduce business risk, or at least manage it enough to reduce its adverse effects, and thus increase and prolong economic profit. Furthermore, a firm can use innovation as a source of monopoly power and a means of sustaining itself and its economic profit.

An important distinction between profit stemming from uncertainty and profit resulting from monopoly has to do with the social desirability of these two sources of profit. Bearing business risk and undertaking innovation in an uncertain economic environment are economically desirable functions. Obtaining monopoly profit is not economically desirable because it is typically founded on reduced output, above-competitive prices, and economic inefficiency. **(Key Question 12)**

Functions of Profit
Economic profit is the main energizer of the capitalistic economy. It influences both the level of economic output and the allocation of resources among alternative uses.

Profit and Total Output
The expectation of economic profit motivates firms to innovate. Innovation stimulates new investment, thereby increasing total output and employment. Thus, the pursuit of profit enhances economic growth by promoting innovation.

Profit and Resource Allocation
Profit also helps allocate resources among alternative lines of production, distribution, and sales. Entrepreneurs seek profit and shun losses. The occurrence of continuing profits in a firm or industry is a signal that society wants that particular firm or industry to expand. It attracts resources from firms and industries that are not profitable. But the rewards of profits are more than an inducement for a firm to expand; they also attract the financing needed

Determining the Price of Credit

A Variety of Lending Practices May Cause the Effective Interest Rate to Be Quite Different from What It Appears to Be.

Borrowing and lending—receiving and granting credit—are a way of life. Individuals receive credit when they negotiate a mortgage loan and when they use their credit cards. Individuals make loans when they open a savings account in a commercial bank or buy a government bond.

It is sometimes difficult to determine exactly how much interest we pay and receive when we borrow and lend. Let's suppose that you borrow $10,000 that you agree to repay plus $1000 of interest at the end of 1 year. In this instance, the interest rate is 10 percent per year. To determine the interest rate i, we compare the interest paid with the amount borrowed:

$$i = \frac{\$1000}{\$10,000} = 10\%$$

But in some cases a lender—say, a bank—will discount the interest payment at the time the loan is made. Thus, instead of giving the borrower $10,000, the bank discounts the $1000 interest payment in advance, giving the borrower only $9000. This increases the interest rate:

$$i = \frac{\$1000}{\$9000} = 11\%$$

While the absolute amount of interest paid is the same, in the second case the borrower has only $9000 available for the year.

An even more subtle point is that, to simplify their calculations, many financial institutions assume a 360-day year (twelve 30-day months). This means the borrower has the use of the lender's funds for 5 days less than the normal year. This use of a "short year" also increases the actual interest rate paid by the borrower.

The interest rate paid may change dramatically if a loan is repaid in installments. Suppose a bank lends you $10,000 and charges interest in the amount of $1000 to be paid at the end of the year. But the loan contract requires that you repay the $10,000 loan in 12 equal monthly installments. In effect, then, the average amount of the loan outstanding during the year is only $5000. Therefore:

$$i = \frac{\$1000}{\$5000} = 20\%$$

Here interest is paid on the total amount of the loan ($10,000) rather than on the outstanding balance (which averages $5000 for the year), making for a much higher interest rate.

Another factor that influences the effective interest rate is whether or not interest is compounded. Suppose you deposit $10,000 in a savings account that pays a 10 percent interest rate compounded semiannually. In other words, interest is paid

for expansion. In contrast, continuing losses penalize firms or industries that fail to adjust their productive efforts to match consumer wants. Such losses signal society's desire for the afflicted entities to contract.

So, in terms of our chapter-opening question, Wal-Mart garnered large profits because it was locating its stores close to customers and delivering the mix of products many consumers wanted at exceptionally low prices. These profits signaled that society wanted more of its scarce resources allocated to Wal-Mart stores. General Motors (GM), in contrast, was not delivering products equivalent in value to the costs of the resources used to provide them—so the firm suffered losses. The losses signaled that society would benefit from a reallocation of all or a part of those resources to some other use. Indeed, GM announced in early 2006 that it was closing five assembly plants, phasing out seven other facilities, eliminating 30,000 jobs, and restructuring its pension plans.

QUICK REVIEW 14.3

- Pure or economic profit is what remains after all explicit and implicit costs (including a normal profit) are subtracted from a firm's total revenue.

- Economic profit has three sources: the bearing of uninsurable risk, the uncertainty of innovation, and monopoly power.

- Profit and profit expectations affect the levels of investment, total spending, and domestic output; profit and loss also allocate resources among alternative uses.

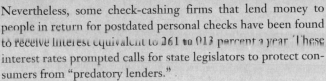

on your "loan" to the bank twice a year. At the end of the first 6 months, $500 of interest (10 percent of $10,000 for half a year) is added to your account. At the end of the year, interest is calculated on $10,500 so that the second interest payment is $525 (10 percent of $10,500 for half a year). Thus:

$$i = \frac{\$1025}{\$10,000} = 10.25\%$$

This means that a bank advertising a 10 percent interest rate compounded semiannually is actually paying more interest to its customers than is a competitor paying a simple (non-compounded) interest rate of 10.2 percent.

Two pieces of legislation have attempted to clarify interest charges and payments. The Truth in Lending Act of 1968 requires that lenders state the costs and terms of consumer credit in concise and uniform language, in particular, as an annual percentage rate (APR). More recently, the Truth in Savings Act of 1991 requires that all advertisements of deposit accounts by banks and other financial institutions disclose all fees connected with such accounts and the interest rate and annual percentage return on each account.

Nevertheless, some check-cashing firms that lend money to people in return for postdated personal checks have been found to receive interest equivalent to 261 to 913 percent a year. These interest rates prompted calls for state legislators to protect consumers from "predatory lenders."

More recently, many banks have established fee-based "bounce (overdraft) protection" for checking accounts. The bank agrees to pay each overdraft for a flat $35 o $37 fee. These fees are essentially interest on a loan for the amount of the overdraft. When the overdraft amount is small, the annual interest on the loan can easily exceed 1000 percent.

Similarly, late-payment fees on credit card accounts can boost the actual interest rate paid on credit card balances to extremely high levels. Furthermore, low "teaser" rates designed to attract new customers often contain "fine print" that raises the interest rate to 16 percent, or even 28 percent, if a payment on the account is late. Also, low initial rates on some variable rate mortgages eventually "reset" to higher rates, greatly increasing the monthly payments that are due. "Let the borrower (or depositor) beware" remains a fitting motto in the world of credit.

Income Shares

Our discussion in this and in the preceding chapter would not be complete without a brief reexamination of how U.S. income is distributed among wages, rent, interest, and profit.

It will be worth your while to look back at Figure 4.1, page 73. Although the income categories shown in that chart do not neatly fit the economic definitions of wages, rent, interest, and profits, they do provide insights about income shares in the United States. Note the dominant role of the labor resource and thus labor income in the U.S. economy. Even with labor income defined narrowly as "wages and salaries," labor receives about 70 percent of all income earned by Americans in a typical year. But some economists contend that the income of proprietors is largely composed of implicit wages and salaries and therefore should be added to the "wages and salaries" category to determine labor income. When we use this broad definition, labor's share rises to about 80 percent of national income, a percentage that has been remarkably stable in the United States since 1900. That leaves about 20 percent for capitalists in the form of rent, interest, and profit. Ironically, income from capital is a relatively small share of the U.S. economy, which we call a capitalist system.

Summary

1. Economic rent is the price paid for the use of land and other natural resources whose total supplies are fixed.

2. Rent is a surplus payment that is socially unnecessary because land would be available to the economy even without rental payments. The idea of land rent as a surplus payment gave rise to the single-tax movement of the late 1800s.

3. Differences in land rent result from differences in the fertility and climatic features of the land and differences in location.

4. Although land rent is a surplus payment rather than a cost to the economy as a whole, to individual firms and industries, rental payments are correctly regarded as costs. These payments must be made to gain the use of land, which has alternative uses.

5. Interest is the price paid for the use of money. In the loanable funds theory, the equilibrium interest rate is determined by the demand for and supply of loanable funds. Other things equal, an increase in the supply of loanable funds reduces the equilibrium interest rate, whereas a decrease in supply increases it; increases in the demand for loanable funds raise the equilibrium interest rate, whereas decreases in demand reduce it.

6. The time-value of money is the idea that $1 today has more value than $1 sometime in the future because the $1 today can be placed in an interest-bearing account and earn compound interest over time. Future value is the amount to which a current amount of money will grow through interest compounding. Present value is the current value of some money payment to be received in the future.

7. Interest rates vary in size because loans differ as to risk, maturity, amount, and taxability. Market imperfections cause additional variations. The pure rate of interest is the interest rate on long-term, virtually riskless, 20-year U.S. Treasury bonds.

8. The equilibrium interest rate influences the level of investment and helps ration financial and physical capital to specific firms and industries. Similarly, this rate influences the size and composition of R&D spending. The real interest rate, not the nominal rate, is critical to investment and R&D decisions.

9. Although designed to make funds available to low-income borrowers, usury laws tend to allocate credit to high-income persons, subsidize high-income borrowers at the expense of lenders, and lessen the efficiency with which loanable funds are allocated.

10. Economic, or pure, profit is the difference between a firm's total revenue and the sum of its explicit and implicit costs, the latter including a normal profit. Profit accrues to entrepreneurs for assuming the uninsurable risks associated with organizing and directing economic resources and for innovating. Profit also results from monopoly power.

11. Profit expectations influence innovating and investment activities and therefore the economy's levels of employment and economic growth. The basic function of profits and losses, however, is to allocate resources in accord with consumers' preferences.

12. The largest share of all income earned by Americans—about 70 percent—goes to labor, a share narrowly defined as "wages and salaries." When labor's share is more broadly defined to include "proprietors' income," it rises to about 80 percent of national income, leaving about 20 percent as capital's share.

Terms and Concepts

economic rent

incentive function

single-tax movement

loanable funds theory of interest

time-value of money

future value

present value

pure rate of interest

nominal interest rate

real interest rate

usury laws

explicit costs

implicit costs

economic or pure profit

normal profit

static economy

insurable risks

uninsurable risks

Study Questions  | ECONOMICS

1. How does the economist's use of the term "rent" differ from everyday usage? Explain: "Though rent need not be paid by society to make land available, rental payments are very useful in guiding land into the most productive uses." **LO1**

2. **KEY QUESTION** Explain why economic rent is a surplus payment when viewed by the economy as a whole but a cost of production from the standpoint of individual firms and industries. Explain: "Land rent performs no 'incentive function' for the overall economy." **LO1**

3. In the 1980s land prices in Japan surged upward in a "speculative bubble." Land prices then fell for 11 straight years between 1990 and 2001. What can we safely assume happened to *land rent* in Japan over those 11 years? Use graphical analysis to illustrate your answer. **LO1**

4. How does Henry George's proposal for a single tax on land relate to the elasticity of the supply of land? Why are there so few remaining advocates of George's proposal? **LO3**

5. If money is not an economic resource, why is interest paid and received for its use? What considerations account for the fact that interest rates differ greatly on various types of loans? Use those considerations to explain the relative sizes of the interest rates on the following: **LO2**
   a. A 10-year $1000 government bond.
   b. A $20 pawnshop loan.
   c. A 30-year mortgage loan on a $145,000 house.
   d. A 24-month $12,000 commercial bank loan to finance the purchase of an automobile.
   e. A 60-day $100 loan from a personal finance company.

6. **KEY QUESTION** Why is the supply of loanable funds upsloping? Why is the demand for loanable funds downsloping? Explain the equilibrium interest rate. List some factors that might cause it to change. **LO2**

7. **KEY QUESTION** Suppose that the interest rate is 4 percent. What is the future value of $100 four years from now? How much of the future value is total interest? By how much would total interest be greater at a 6 percent interest rate than at a 4 percent interest rate? **LO4**

8. Here is the deal: You can pay your college tuition at the beginning of the academic year or the same amount at the end of the academic year. You either already have the money in an interest-bearing account or will have to borrow it. Deal, or no deal? Explain your financial reasoning. Relate your answer to the time-value of money, present value, and future value. **LO4**

9. What are the major economic functions of the interest rate? How might the fact that many businesses finance their investment activities internally affect the efficiency with which the interest rate performs its functions? **LO3**

10. **KEY QUESTION** Distinguish between nominal and real interest rates. Which is more relevant in making investment and R&D decisions? If the nominal interest rate is 12 percent and the inflation rate is 8 percent, what is the real rate of interest? **LO3**

11. Historically, usury laws that put below-equilibrium ceilings on interest rates have been used by some states to make credit available to poor people who could not otherwise afford to borrow. Critics contend that poor people are those most likely to be hurt by such laws. Which view is correct? **LO3**

12. **KEY QUESTION** How do the concepts of accounting profit and economic profit differ? Why is economic profit smaller than accounting profit? What are the three basic sources of economic profit? Classify each of the following according to those sources: **LO4**
    a. A firm's profit from developing and patenting a new medication that greatly reduces cholesterol and thus diminishes the likelihood of heart disease and stroke.
    b. A restaurant's profit that results from the completion of a new highway past its door.
    c. The profit received by a firm due to an unanticipated change in consumer tastes.

13. Why is the distinction between insurable and uninsurable risks significant for the theory of profit? Carefully evaluate: "All economic profit can be traced to either uncertainty or the desire to avoid it." What are the major functions of economic profit? **LO4**

14. Explain the absence of economic profit in a purely competitive, static economy. Realizing that the major function of profit is to allocate resources according to consumer preferences, describe the allocation of resources in such an economy. **LO4**

15. What is the combined rent, interest, and profit share of the income earned by Americans in a typical year if proprietors' income is included within the labor (wage) share? **LO5**

16. **LAST WORD** Assume that you borrow $5000 and pay back the $5000 plus $250 in interest at the end of the year. Assuming no inflation, what is the real interest rate? What would the interest rate be if the $250 of interest had been discounted at the time the loan was made? What would the interest rate be if you were required to repay the loan in 12 equal monthly installments?

Web-Based Questions

1. **WHAT ARE THE CURRENT NOMINAL AND REAL INTEREST RATES?** Go to **www.federalreserve.gov** (Research and Data; Statistics: Releases and Historical Data; Selected Interest Rates) and **www.bankrate.com** to update the interest rates in Table 14.2 to their latest recorded values. In what direction, if any, have the interest rates changed? Find the current annual rate of inflation at **www.bls.gov/cpi** (Latest Numbers; CPI-U, U.S. City Average, All Items, 12-months ending with the last month). Subtract this annual rate of inflation from your updated interest rates in the table to determine the real interest rates in each category.

2. **CORPORATE PROFITS—WHICH INDUSTRIES ARE MAKING THE MOST?** The Bureau of Economic Analysis provides profit data for various industries in the United States.

Go to **www.bea.gov** and find National Income and Product Account Table 6.16D on Corporate Profits by Industry. Based on the most-recent figures, which of the following categories of industry classifications has the greatest profits: (*a*) financial or nonfinancial; (*b*) manufacturing, transportation, wholesale trade, or retail trade; (*c*) durable goods or nondurable goods? Compared to the same quarter a year earlier, which sectors had the largest and smallest percentage increases in profit? Which sectors, if any, experienced losses? What are the implications of the profit changes for expansion or contraction of the particular industries?

FURTHER TEST YOUR KNOWLEDGE AT
www.mcconnell18e.com

15

IN THIS CHAPTER YOU WILL LEARN:

1 Why falling birthrates mean that we are not likely to run out of natural resources.

2 Why using a mix of energy sources is efficient, even if some of them are quite costly.

3 Why running out of oil would not mean running out of energy.

4 How the profit motive can encourage resource conservation.

5 How to use property rights to prevent deforestation and fisheries extinctions.

Natural Resource and Energy Economics

People like to consume goods and services. But to produce those goods and services, natural resources must be used up. Some natural resources, such as solar energy, forests, and schools of fish, are renewable and can potentially be exploited indefinitely. Other resources, such as oil, iron ore, and coal, are in fixed supply and can be used only once. This chapter explores two issues in relation to our supplies of resources and energy. The first is whether we are likely to run out of resources in the near or even distant future and thereby face the possibility of either a drastic reduction in living standards or even, perhaps, the collapse of civilization as we know it. The second is how to best utilize and manage our resources so that we can maximize the benefits that we receive from them both now and in the future.

We begin the chapter by addressing the issue of whether we are about to run out of resources. We then turn to energy economics and natural resource economics, focusing on the incentive structures that help to promote conservation and sustainability.

Resource Supplies: Doom or Boom?

Since the beginning of the Industrial Revolution in the late 18th century, a historically unprecedented increase in both population and living standards has taken place. The world's population has increased from 1 billion people in 1800 to about 6.6 billion today, and the average person living in the United States enjoys a standard of living at least 12 times higher than that of the average American living in 1800. Stated slightly differently, many more people are alive today and levels of consumption per person are much higher. These two factors mean that human beings are now consuming vastly more resources than before the Industrial Revolution both in absolute terms and in per capita terms. This fact has led many observers to wonder if our current economic system and its high living standards are sustainable. In particular, will the availability of natural resources be sufficient to meet the growing demand for them?

A sensible response clearly involves looking at *both* resource demand and resource supply. We begin by examining human population growth because larger populations mean greater demand for resources.

Population Growth

We can trace the debate over the sustainability of resources back to 1798, when an Anglican minister in England named Thomas Malthus published *An Essay on the Principle of Population*. In that essay, Malthus argued that human living standards could only temporarily rise above subsistence levels. Any temporary increase in living standards would cause people to have more children and thereby increase the population. With so many more people to feed, per capita living standards would be driven back down to subsistence levels.

Unfortunately for Malthus' theory—but fortunately for society—higher living standards have *not* produced higher birthrates. In fact, just the opposite has happened. Higher standards of living are associated with *lower* birthrates. Birthrates are falling rapidly throughout the world and the majority of the world's population is now living in countries that have birthrates that are lower than the **replacement rate** necessary to keep their respective populations from falling over time.

Table 15.1 lists the total fertility rates for 12 selected nations including the United States. The **total fertility rate** is the average number of children that a woman is expected to have during her lifetime. Taking into account infant and child mortality, a total fertility rate of about 2.1 births per woman per lifetime is necessary to keep the population constant, since 2.1 children equals 1 child

TABLE 15.1 Total Fertility Rates for Selected Countries, 2007

Country	Total Fertility Rate
Australia	1.76
Canada	1.61
China	1.75
France	1.98
Germany	1.40
Hong Kong	0.98
Italy	1.29
Japan	1.23
Russia	1.39
South Korea	1.28
Sweden	1.66
United States	2.09

Source: The World Factbook, **www.cia.gov.** Data are 2007 estimates.

to replace the mother, 1 child to replace the father, and 0.1 extra child who can be expected to die before becoming old enough to reproduce.

As you can see from Table 15.1, total fertility rates in many nations are well below the 2.1 rate necessary to keep the population stable over time. As a result, populations are expected to fall rapidly in many countries over the next few decades, with, for instance, the population of Russia expected to fall by about one-third from its current level of 141 million people to fewer than 100 million in 2050. And Russia is not alone; 30 countries are expected to see their populations fall by at least 10 percent by 2050, and of these, 13 are expected to experience a decline of at least 20 percent by 2050.

Worldwide, the precipitous fall of birthrates means that many **demographers** (scientists who study human populations) now expect the world's population to reach a peak of 9 billion people or fewer sometime around the middle of this century before beginning to fall, perhaps quite rapidly. For instance, if the worldwide total fertility rate declines to 1 birth per woman per lifetime (which is higher than Hong Kong's current rate of 0.98 per woman per lifetime), then each generation will be only half as large as the previous one because there will be only one child on average for every two parents. And even a rate of 1.3 births per woman per lifetime will reduce a country's population by half in just under 45 years.

The world's population increased so rapidly from 1800 to the present day because the higher living standards that arrive when a country begins to modernize bring with them much lower death rates. Before modernization happens, death rates are typically so high that women have to give birth to more than six children per lifetime just to ensure that, on average, two will survive to adulthood. But once living standards begin to rise and modern medical care becomes available, death rates plummet so that nearly all children survive to adulthood. This causes a temporary population explosion because parents—initially unaware that such a revolutionary change in death rates has taken place—for a while keep having six or more children. The impression persists that they must have many children to ensure that at least two will survive to adulthood. The result is one or two generations of very rapid population growth until parents adjust to the new situation and reduce the number of children that they choose to have.

CONSIDER THIS . . .

Can Governments Raise Birthrates?

Low birthrates pose major problems for governments. The primary problem is that with very few children being born today, very few workers will be alive in a few decades to pay the large amounts of taxes that will be needed if governments are to keep their current promises regarding Social Security and other old-age pension programs. Too few young workers will be supporting too many elderly retirees. Another potential problem is a lack of soldiers. Consider Russia. With its population expected to fall by one-third by midcentury, defending its borders will be much harder.

As a response, Russian President Vladimir Putin announced a new policy in 2006 that would pay any Russian woman who chooses to have a second child a bounty worth 250,000 rubles ($9280). In addition, the Russian government promised to double monthly child benefits in an effort to make having children less financially burdensome for parents. Many other countries have experimented with similar policies. In 2004, France began offering its mothers a payment of €800 ($1040) for each child born and Italy began offering a €1000 ($1300) payment for second children.

As far as demographers can tell, however, these and other policies aimed at raising birthrates by offering maternity leave, free day care, or other subsidies to mothers or their children have not been able to generate any sustained increases in fertility levels in any country in which they have been attempted. Unless more effective policies are developed, fertility rates seem very likely to remain low and, as a result, the total demand placed on our limited supplies of natural resources may never again face the problem of a rapidly expanding population.

The overall world population is still increasing because many countries such as India and Indonesia began modernizing only relatively recently and are still in the transition phase where death rates have fallen but birthrates are still relatively high. Nevertheless, birthrates are falling rapidly nearly everywhere. This means that the end of rapid population growth is at hand. Furthermore, because fertility rates tend to fall below the replacement rate as countries modernize, we can also expect total world population to begin to decline during the twenty-first century. This is a critical fact to keep in mind when considering whether we are likely to ever face a resource crisis: Fewer people means fewer demands placed on society's scarce resources.

Demographers have been surprised, however, at just how low fertility rates have fallen and why they have fallen so far below the replacement rate in so many countries. The decline of fertility rates to such low levels is especially surprising given the fact that couples typically tell demographers that they would like to have *at least* two children. Because this implies that most couples would prefer higher total fertility rates than we actually observe, it seems probable that social or economic factors are constraining couples to have fewer children than they desire, thereby causing total fertility rates to fall so low. Demographers have not yet reached agreement on which factors are most important, but possible candidates include changing attitudes toward religion, the much wider career opportunities available to women in modern economies, and the expense of having children in modern societies. Indeed, children have been transformed from economic assets that could be put to work at an early age in agricultural societies into economic liabilities that are very costly to raise in modern societies where child labor is illegal and where children must attend school until adulthood. The nearby Consider This vignette discusses current government efforts to raise birthrates by offering financial incentives to parents.

Resource Consumption per Person

Thomas Malthus' tradition of predicting a collapse in living standards has been carried on to this day by various individuals and groups. One well-reported prediction was made by Stanford University butterfly expert Paul Ehrlich. In his 1968 book *The Population Bomb*, he made the Malthusian prediction that the population would soon outstrip resources so that "in the 1970s and 1980s hundreds of millions of people will starve to death in spite of any crash programs embarked upon now." Contrary to this prediction, no famines approaching these magnitudes materialized then and none appear likely today.

One reason that Ehrlich's pessimism was not borne out was because the population growth rate slowed dramatically

FIGURE 15.1 The Economist's commodity price index, 1850–2007. *The Economist* magazine's commodity price index attempts to keep track of the prices of the commodities most common in international trade. It is adjusted for inflation and scaled so that commodity prices in the years 1845–1850 are set to an index value of 100. The figure shows that real commodity prices are volatile (vary considerably from year to year) but are now 55 percent lower than they were in the mid-nineteenth century. This implies that commodity supplies have increased faster than commodity demands.

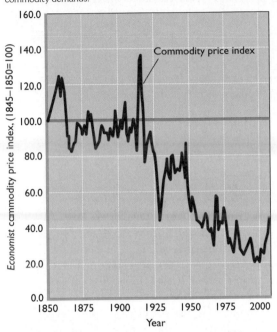

Source: The Economist, **www.economist.com.** Copyright 2008 by Economist Newspaper Group. Reproduced with permission of Economist Newspaper Group. Inflation adjustments made using the GDP deflator for the United States calculated by the Bureau of Economic Analysis, **www.bea.gov.**

as living standards around the world rose. Another reason is that the long-run evidence indicates that the supply of productive resources available to be made into goods and services has been increasing faster than the demand for those resources for at least 150 years. This is best seen by looking at Figure 15.1, which tracks *The Economist* magazine's commodity price index for the years 1850 to 2007. The index currently contains 25 important commodities including aluminum, copper, corn, rice, wheat, coffee, rubber, sugar, and soybeans. In earlier days, it included commodities such as candle wax, silk, and indigo, which were important at the time. The index also adjusts for inflation so that one can see how the real cost of commodities has evolved over time and it is standardized so that the real price of commodities during the years 1845 to 1850 is given a value of 100.

As Figure 15.1 demonstrates, a dramatic long-run decline in real commodity prices has occurred. With the current value of the index at about 45, the real cost of buying commodities today is roughly 55 percent lower than it was

in the initial 1845–1850 period. This means that commodity supplies have increased faster than commodity demands, since the only way that commodity prices could have fallen so much in the face of increasing demand is if the supply curve for commodities shifted to the right faster than the demand curve for commodities shifted to the right.

A key point is that the long-run fall of commodity prices implies that commodity supplies have grown faster than the sum total of the two pressures that have acted over this time to increase commodity demands. The first is the huge rise in the total number of people alive and therefore consuming resources (since 1850, the world's population has risen from 1.25 billion to 6.6 billion). The second is the huge rise in the amount of consumption *per person*. That is, more people are alive today than in 1850, and each person alive today is on average consuming several times more than the average person alive in 1850. Still, the long-run fall in commodity prices confirms that supplies have managed to grow fast enough to overcome both these demand-increasing pressures.

But will supplies be able to overcome these two pressures in the future? Prospects are hopeful. First, the rapid and continuing decline in birthrates means that the huge population increases that occurred during the nineteenth and twentieth centuries are not likely to continue in the future. Indeed, we have seen that population decline has begun in several countries and it now seems likely that overall world population will begin to decline within this century. This trend will moderate future increases in the total demand for goods and services. Second, resource consumption *per person* (as distinct from goods and services consumption per person) also has either leveled off or declined in the past decade or so in the richest countries, which currently consume the largest fraction of the world's resources.

This can best be seen by looking at Figures 15.2, 15.3, and 15.4, which show, respectively, how much water, energy, and other resources the United States has consumed on an annual basis both in total and per capita terms over the last few decades. The red lines in each figure show total annual use while the blue lines trace per capita annual use. To accommodate both sets of data, the units measuring total annual use are on the vertical scales on the left side of each figure while the units measuring per capita annual use are shown on the vertical scales on the right side of each figure.

The blue line in Figure 15.2 shows that per capita water use in the United States peaked in 1975 at 1941 gallons per person per day. It then fell by over 28 percent to just 1430 gallons per person per day in 2000. The blue line in Figure 15.3 shows that annual per capita energy use peaked at 360 million British thermal units per person in 1979 before settling down to around 340 million BTUs

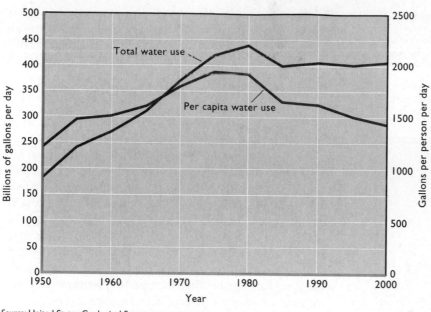

FIGURE 15.2 **Total and per capita water use in the United States, 1950–2000.** Average total water use in the United States peaked at 440 billion gallons per day in 1980 before declining to about 400 billion gallons per day in 1985, where it remained through 2000, the last year for which data were available. Average per capita water consumption fell 28 percent from a peak of 1941 gallons per person per day in 1975 to only 1430 gallons per person per day in 2000. These data are reported every 5 years. The 2005 data were not available at the time of publication, but they may be available when you read this. If interested, check the U.S. Geological Survey Web site.

Source: United States Geological Survey, **www.usgs.gov.**

per person after 1988. (A **British thermal unit,** or BTU, is the amount of energy required to raise the temperature of 1 pound of water by 1 degree Fahrenheit).

Finally, Figure 15.4 takes advantage of a fundamental principle of physics to show that the per capita use of other resources has also leveled off since 1990. This principle states that matter is neither created nor destroyed—only transformed—by the sorts of chemical reactions that take place as raw materials are turned into finished products and then consumed. As a result, we can measure how much use of solid objects like plastics, metals, and paper takes place by measuring how much solid waste (commonly called trash or garbage) is generated when they are thrown away.

Consequently, because Figure 15.4 shows that per capita trash generation has leveled off at about 4.5 pounds per person per day since 1990, we can conclude that per capita consumption of solids has also leveled off since that time.

These three figures give further cause for optimism on the availability of future resource supplies. We have already provided evidence that the number of people in the world is not likely to increase substantially. Figures 15.2, 15.3, and 15.4 show that per capita consumption levels are also likely to either level off or decline. Together, these two facts suggest that the total demand for resources is likely to reach a peak in the relatively near future before falling over time as populations decline.

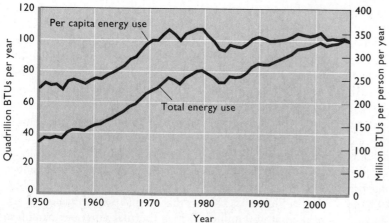

FIGURE 15.3 **Total and per capita energy consumption in the United States, 1950–2006.** Per capita energy consumption in the United States peaked at 360 million British thermal units (BTUs) per person per day in 1979. It then fell over the following decade before stabilizing in the late 1980s at a value of about 340 million BTUs per person per day. Total energy consumption between 1950 and 2006 nearly tripled, increasing from 34.6 quadrillion BTUs in 1950 to 99.9 quadrillion BTUs in 2006. Since 1990, total energy consumption has increased by an average of only 1.2 percent per year.

Source: United States Energy Information Administration, **www.eia.doe.gov.**

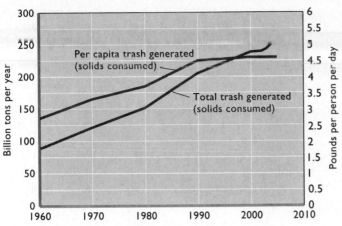

FIGURE 15.4 **Total and per capita trash generation in the United States, 1960–2005.** Although the total level of trash generated in the United States increased from 88.1 billion tons in 1960 to 251.3 billion tons in 2005, the amount of trash generated per person peaked in 1990 at 4.5 pounds per person per day, where it roughly remained through 2005. Because *trash generated is solids consumed*, we know that per capita consumption of solids has stayed relatively constant over the past 16 years.

Source: United States Environmental Protection Agency, **www.epa.gov.**

That being said, resource demand is likely to increase substantially for the next few decades as large parts of the world modernize and begin to consume as much per capita as the citizens of rich countries do today. For instance, per capita energy use in the United States in 2006 was 334 million BTUs per person. If every person in the world used that much energy, total annual energy demand would be 2204 quadrillion BTUs, or about 4.5 times the 2006 world production of 480 quadrillion BTUs. One of the world's great economic challenges over the coming decades will be to supply the resources that will be demanded as living standards in poorer countries rise to rich-country levels. But because population growth rates are slowing and because per capita resource uses in rich countries have leveled off, we can now foresee a maximum total demand for resources even if living standards all over the world rise to rich-country levels. Given the ongoing improvements in technology and productivity that characterize modern economies and that allow us to produce increasingly more from any given set of inputs, it consequently seems unlikely that we will run into a situation where the total demand for resources exhausts their overall supply.

Significant challenges, however, are still likely to appear in those places where local supplies of certain resources are extremely limited. Water, for instance, is a rare and precious commodity in many places, including the Middle East and the American Southwest. Governments will have to work hard to ensure that the limited supplies of water in such areas are used efficiently and that disputes over water rights are settled peacefully. Along the same lines, resources are often produced in certain areas but consumed in others with, for instance, one-quarter of the world's oil being produced in the Middle East but most of the demand for oil coming from Europe, North America, and East Asia. In such

cases, institutions must be developed that can move such resources from the areas in which they originate to the areas in which they are used. If not, local shortages may develop in the areas that cannot produce these resources despite the fact that the resources in question may at the same time be in very plentiful supply in the areas in which they are produced.

QUICK REVIEW 15.1

- Thomas Malthus and others have worried that increases in our demand for resources will outrun the supply of resources, but commodity prices have been falling for more than a century, indicating that supply has increased by more than demand.

- Because total fertility rates are very low and falling, population growth for the world will soon turn negative and thereby reduce the demand for natural resources.

- Per capita consumption of resources such as water, energy, and solids has either fallen or remained constant in the United States. If per capita consumption continues to stay the same or decrease while populations fall, total resource demand will fall—meaning that the demand for resources is unlikely to threaten to use up the available supply of resources.

Energy Economics

Energy economics studies how people deal with energy scarcity. This involves both demand and supply. In terms of energy supply, people are interested in attempting to find and exploit low-cost energy sources. But since energy is only one input into a production process, often the best energy source to use in a given situation is, paradoxically, actually rather expensive—yet still the best choice when other costs are taken into account. The economy therefore

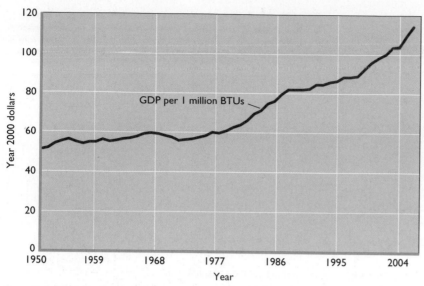

FIGURE 15.5 Inflation-adjusted GDP per million BTUs of energy consumption in the United States, 1950–2006. This figure shows the number of dollars' worth of real GDP the U.S. economy produced per million BTUs of energy consumed in each year from 1950 through 2006 when annual GDP figures are converted to year 2000 dollars to account for inflation. Energy efficiency has more than doubled during this period, with real output per energy input rising from $51.30 worth of GDP per million BTUs in 1950 to $114.29 worth of GDP per million BTUs in 2006.

Source: United States Energy Information Administration, **www.eia.doe.gov.**

develops and exploits many different energy sources, from fossil fuels to nuclear power.

In terms of energy demand, the most interesting fact is that per capita energy use has leveled off in recent years in developed countries, as we previously illustrated for the United States in Figure 15.3. This fact implies that our economy has become increasingly efficient at using energy to produce goods and services. This is best seen by noting that while per capita energy inputs remained fixed at roughly 340 million BTUs per person per year between 1988 and 2007, real GDP per person rose during that time period by 39 percent, so that people were able to make and consume nearly two-fifths more goods and services per person despite using no more energy per person.

This increase in energy efficiency has been part of a long historical trend, as Figure 15.5 makes quite clear. For the years 1950 through 2006, it shows the number of inflation-adjusted dollars of GDP that the U.S. economy has produced each year for every 1 million BTUs of energy consumed in the United States. The figure demonstrates that technological improvements greatly increased energy efficiency, so much so that although 1 million BTUs of energy yielded only $51.30 worth of goods and services in 1950, 1 million BTUs of energy yielded $114.29 worth of goods and services in 2006 (when the comparison is made using year 2000 dollars to account for inflation).

Keep this huge increase in energy efficiency in mind when considering the magnitude of future energy demands. Because better technology means that more output can be produced with the same amount of energy input, rising living standards in the future will not necessarily depend

on using more energy. The behavior of the U.S. economy since 1988 bears this out since, as we just pointed out, real GDP per person increased by nearly 40 percent between 1988 and 2006 while per capita energy inputs remained constant. Living standards can be raised without having to increase energy inputs.

Efficient Energy Use

We just saw that the United States has grown increasingly efficient at using energy. The same is true for other developed countries. An interesting fact about energy efficiency, however, is that it often involves using a mix of energy inputs, some of which are much more expensive than others. The best way to see why this is true is to examine electric power generation.

A typical electric plant has to serve tens of thousands of homes and businesses and is expected to deliver an uninterrupted supply of electricity 24 hours a day, 7 days a week. This task is not easy. The problem is that massive changes in energy demand occur over the course of a day. Demand is extremely low at night when people are sleeping, begins to rise rapidly in the morning as people wake up and turn on their lights, rises even more when they are at work, falls a bit as they commute home, rises back up a bit in the evening when they turn on their houselights to deal with the darkness and their televisions to deal with their boredom, and finally collapses as they turn out their lights and go to sleep.

The problem for electric companies as they try to minimize the cost of providing for such large variations in the demand for electricity is that the power plants that have the lowest operating costs also have the highest fixed costs in terms of construction. For instance, large coal-fired plants can produce energy at a cost of about 4 cents per kilowatt hour. But they can do this only if they are built large enough to exploit economies of scale and if they are then operated at full capacity. To see why this can be a problem, imagine that such a plant has a maximum generating capacity of 20 megawatts per hour but that its customers' peak afternoon demand for electricity is 25 megawatts per hour. One solution would be to build two 20-megawatt coal-fired plants. But that would be very wasteful because one would be operating at full capacity (and hence minimum cost), while the other would be producing only 5 megawatts of its 20-megawatt capacity. Given that such plants cost hundreds of millions of dollars to build, this would be very wasteful.

The solution that electric companies employ is to use a mix of different types of generation technology. This turns out to be optimal because even though some electricity generation plants have very high operating costs, they have low fixed costs (that is, they are very inexpensive to build). Thus, the power company in our example might build one large coal-fired plant to generate 20 of the required 25 megawatts of energy at 4 cents per kilowatt hour, but it would then build a small 5-megawatt natural gas generator to supply the rest. Such plants produce electricity at the much higher cost of 15 cents per kilowatt hour, but they are relatively inexpensive to build. As a result, this solution would save the electric company from having to build a second very expensive coal-fired plant that would wastefully operate well below its full capacity.

The result of this process of mixing generator technologies is that the United States currently generates electricity from a variety of energy sources, as we show in Figure 15.6. Half of it is generated at large, low-cost coal-fired plants with the rest coming from a variety of sources including hydroelectric power, natural gas, and renewable energy sources such as geothermal, wind, and solar.

Running Out of Energy?

Some observers worry that we may soon run out of the energy needed to power our economy. Their fears are based largely on the possibility that the world may run out of oil sometime in the next century. It is the case, however, that there is no likelihood of running out of energy. If anything, running out of oil would not mean running out of energy—just running out of *cheap* energy.

This is best seen by looking at Table 15.2, which compares oil prices with the prices at which other energy sources become economically viable. For instance, biodiesel, a type of diesel fuel made from decomposed plant wastes, is so expensive to produce that it becomes economically viable

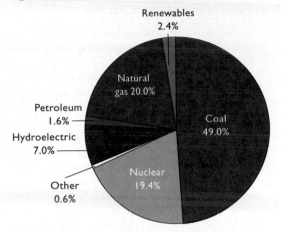

FIGURE 15.6 Percentages of U.S. electricity generated using various energy sources, 2006.
About 49 percent of U.S. electricity was generated by coal-fired plants in 2006, with natural gas and nuclear power accounting together for a further 39 percent of the total.

Source: United States Energy Information Administration, **www.eia.doe.gov.**

(that is, less costly to produce than oil) only if oil costs $80 or more per barrel. On the other hand, ethanol made from corn in the United States costs less to produce and would be an economically viable alternative to oil even if the price of oil were only $60 per barrel.

The key point to gather from this table, however, is that even if we were to run out of oil, alternatives would quickly become available. At a price of $40 per barrel, vast reserves of energy derived from tar sands, the conversion of natural gas and coal to liquid petroleum, and even ethanol derived from cheap Brazilian sugar cane become

TABLE 15.2 Oil Prices at Which Alternative Energy Sources Become Economically Viable

Oil Price per Barrel at Which Alternative Is Economically Viable	Alternative Fuel
$80	Biodiesel
60	U.S. corn-based ethanol*
50	Shale oil
40	Tar sands; Brazilian sugar-cane-based ethanol; gas to liquids;[†] coal-to-liquids[‡]
20	Conventional oil

*Excludes tax credits.

[†]Gas to liquid is economically viable at $40 if natural gas price is $2.50 or less per million BTUs.

[‡]Coal to liquid is economically viable at $40 if coal price is $15 per ton or less.

Sources: Cambridge Energy Research Associates, **www.cera.com;** *The Economist,* April 22, 2006, **www.economist.com.**

CONSIDER THIS . . .

Turning Entrails (and Nearly Anything Else) into Oil

Nature takes millions of years to apply the heat and pressure necessary to convert organic matter like dead plants and animals into oil. A company called Changing World Technologies can do the job in just 2 hours at a factory it opened in 2005 outside a turkey slaughterhouse in Carthage, Missouri.

Each day, 270 tons of discarded turkey parts (entrails, heads, feet, lungs, and so on) get converted into 500 barrels of fuel oil by means of a reaction tank that heats the debris to 500 degrees Fahrenheit while simultaneously pressurizing it to 600 pounds per square inch. The process replicates geologic pressures that normally take place in the earth's crust, pressures that break down the long chains of hydrocarbons found in plants and animals into the short chains of hydrocarbons that make up fossil fuels like methane, gasoline, and diesel. Even more amazing, the reaction tank can gulp down any sort of organic debris—used tires, Styrofoam cups, sewage water, plastic car parts—and turn it into a grade of fuel oil that can be immediately sold to utility companies for use in electric generators or that can be further refined into gasoline, diesel, and even hydrogen.

The factory produces its oil at a cost of $80 per barrel. At the time the factory opened in 2005, oil was selling for less than $50 per barrel. Thus, it was only thanks to a Federal biofuel subsidy of $42 per barrel that the factory was able to break even. With oil prices rising to well over $100 per barrel in 2008, however, the factory's oil is now extremely profitable—not only because the market price exceeds the firm's production cost, but because the firm also still receives the $42 per barrel biofuel subsidy on top of what it gets from selling its oil at the market price.

economically viable alternatives. At $50 per barrel, shale oil becomes a viable alternative. At $60 per barrel, corn-based ethanol becomes viable. And at $80 per barrel, so does biodiesel.

In fact, these prices can be thought of as a giant supply curve for energy, with rising energy prices leading to increased energy production. The result is that even if the supply of oil begins to dry up and oil prices consequently rise, other energy supplies will quickly be brought on line to fill the energy gap created by the decline in the amount of oil available. Also, the alternative prices listed in Table 15.2 are *current* alternative prices. As technologies improve, the costs of producing these alternatives are likely to fall and, as a result, the potential costs of replacing oil if it runs out will be even lower than suggested by the prices in the table. As a result, economists do not worry about running out of oil or, more generally, running out of energy. There is plenty of energy—the only question is price, and the impact of potentially increasing energy prices on the standard of living.

Finally, we need to acknowledge that energy sources differ not only in their prices but also with regard to the extent of negative externalities they may generate. Recall from Chapter 4 that negative externalities are costs—such as those associated with air pollution—that are transferred to society during the production process and therefore not reflected in product price. Such externalities need to be accounted for. Some energy sources are relatively "clean," creating little pollution or other externalities. Other sources currently are more problematic. For example, burning coal generates substantial particulate and carbon dioxide emissions that can contribute to health problems and global warming. But a caution is needed here: At sufficiently high prices of electricity, coal burning can be both economical and "clean." This is true because at sufficiently high electricity prices, the companies that burn coal to generate electricity are able to afford extensive expenditures on pollution reduction. Scrubbers can reduce soot from emissions and new technologies can capture and sequester carbon dioxide in underground storage. At sufficiently high energy prices, clean methods of producing energy are not confined to wind, solar, and other so-called alternative energy sources.

We will say much more about externalities and the policies designed to reduce them in the next chapter. (**Key Question 5**)

QUICK REVIEW 15.2

- Energy efficiency has consistently improved so that more output can be produced for every unit of energy used by the economy.

- After taking the very different fixed costs of different electricity-generating plants into account, utility companies find it efficient to use a variety of energy sources (coal, natural gas, nuclear) to deal with the large daily variations in energy demand with which they must cope.

- Even if we run out of oil, we will not run out of energy because many alternative sources of energy are available. These alternatives are, however, more costly than oil so that if we were to run out of oil, energy costs in the economy would most likely increase.

Natural Resource Economics

The major focus of natural resource economics is to design policies for extracting or harvesting a natural resource that will maximize the **net benefits** from doing so. The net benefits are simply the total dollar value of all benefits minus the total dollar value of all costs, so that a project's net benefit is equal to the dollar value of the gains or losses to be made. A key feature of such policies is that they take into account the fact that present and future decisions about how fast to extract or harvest a resource typically cannot be made independently. Taking more today means having less in the future and having more in the future is possible only by taking less today.

In applying this general rule, however, large differences between renewable natural resources and nonrenewable natural resources become apparent. **Renewable natural resources** include things like forests and wildlife, which are capable of growing back, or renewing themselves, if they are harvested at moderate rates. This leaves open the possibility of enjoying their benefits in perpetuity. Solar energy, the atmosphere, the oceans, and aquifers are also considered renewable natural resources either because they will continue providing us with their benefits no matter what we do (as is the case with solar energy) or because if we manage them well, we can continue to enjoy their benefits in perpetuity (as is the case with the atmosphere, the oceans, and aquifers). **Nonrenewable natural resources** include things like oil, coal, and metals, which either are in actual fixed supply (like the metals found in the earth's crust) or are renewed so slowly as to be in virtual fixed supply when viewed from a human time perspective (as is the case with fossil fuels like oil and coal, which take millions of years to form out of decaying plants and animals).

The key to optimally managing both renewable and nonrenewable resources is designing incentive structures that prompt decision makers to consider not only the net benefits to be made by using the resources under their control in the present but also the net benefits to be made by conserving the resources under their control in the present in order to be able to use more of them in the future. Once these incentive structures are in place, decision makers can weigh the costs and benefits of present use against the costs and benefits of future use in order to determine the optimal allocation of the resource between present and future uses. The key tool used in weighing these alternatives is present value, which allows decision makers to sensibly compare the net benefits of potential present uses with the net benefits of potential future uses.

Using Present Values to Evaluate Future Possibilities

Natural resource economics studies the optimal use of our limited supplies of resources. Decisions about optimal resource use typically involve choosing how resources will be exploited intertemporally, or over time. For instance, suppose that a poor country has just discovered that it possesses a small oil field. Should the country pump this oil today when it can make a profit of $50 per barrel, or should it wait 5 years to pump the oil given that it believes that in 5 years it will be able to make a profit of $60 per barrel due to lower production costs?

Answering this question requires consideration of the time-value of money, discussed in the previous chapter. We need to someway compare $60 worth of money in 5 years with $50 worth of money today. Economists make this comparision by converting the future quantity of money (in this case $60) into a present-day equivalent measured in present-day money. That way the two quantities of money can be compared using the same unit of measurement, present-day dollars.

The formula for calculating the present-day equivalent, or **present value,** for any future sum of money (in this case, $60 in 5 years) is described in our macroeconomic chapter on financial economics, but the intuition is simple. Suppose that the current market rate of interest is 5 percent per year. How much money would a person have to save and invest today at 5 percent interest in order to end up with exactly $60 in 5 years? The correct answer turns out to be $47.01 because if $47.01 is invested at an interest rate of 5 percent per year, it will grow into precisely $60 in 5 years. Stated slightly differently, $47.01 today can be thought of as being equivalent to $60 in 5 years because it is possible to transform $47.01 today into $60 in 5 years by simply investing it at the market rate of interest.

This fact is very important because it allows for a direct comparison of the benefits from the country's two possible courses of action. If it pumps its oil today, it will get $50 per barrel worth of present-day dollars. But if it pumps its oil in 5 years and gets $60 per barrel at that time, it will only get $47.01 per barrel worth of present-day dollars since the present value of $60 in 5 years is precisely $47.01 today. By measuring both possibilities in present-day dollars, the better choice of action becomes obvious: The country should pump its oil today, since $50 worth of present-day money is obviously greater than $47.01 worth of present-day money.

The ability to calculate present values also allows decision makers to use cost-benefit analysis in situations where the costs and benefits happen at different points in time. For instance, suppose that a forestry company is considering spending $1000 per acre to plant seedlings that it hopes will grow into trees that it will be able to harvest in 100 years. It expects that the wood from the trees will be worth $125,000 per acre in 100 years. Should it undertake this investment? The answer is *no* because at the current market interest rate of 5 percent per year, the present value of $125,000 in 100 years is only $950.56 today, which is less than the $1000 per acre that the firm would have to invest today to plant the seedlings. When both the benefits and costs of the project are measured in the same units (present-day dollars), it is clear that the project is a money loser and should be avoided.

More generally, the ability of policy makers to calculate present values and put present-day dollar values on future possibilities is vitally important because it helps to ensure that resources are allocated to their best possible uses over time. By enabling a decision maker to compare the costs and benefits of present use with the costs and benefits of future use, present value calculations help to ensure that a resource will be used at whatever point in time it will be most valuable.

This is especially important when it comes to conservation because there is always a temptation to use up a resource as fast as possible in the present rather than conserving some or all of it for future use. By putting a present-day dollar value on the net benefits to be gained by conservation and future use, present value calculations provide a financial incentive to make sure that resources will be conserved for future use whenever doing so will generate higher net benefits than using them in the present. Indeed, a large part of natural resource economics focuses on nothing more than ensuring that the net benefits that can be gained from conservation and future use are accounted for by governments, companies, and individuals that are in charge of deciding when and how to use our limited supply of resources. When these future net benefits are properly accounted for, resource use tends to be conservative and sustainable, whereas when they are not properly accounted for, environmental devastation tends to take place, including, as we will discuss in detail below, deforestation and fisheries collapse.

Nonrenewable Resources

Nonrenewable resources like oil, coal, and metals must be mined or pumped from the ground before they can be used. Oil companies and mining companies specialize in the extraction of nonrenewable resources and attempt to make a profit from extracting and then selling the resources that they mine or pump out of the ground. But because extraction is costly and because the price that they will get on the market for their products is uncertain, profits are not guaranteed and such companies must plan their operations carefully if they hope to realize a profit.

We must note, however, that because an oil field or a mineral deposit is typically very large and will take many years to fully extract, an extraction company's goal of "maximizing profits" actually involves attempting to choose an extraction strategy that will maximize a *stream* of profits—potential profits today as well as potential profits in the future. There is, of course, a trade-off. If the company extracts more today, its revenues will be larger today since it will have more product to sell today. On the other hand, more extraction today means that less of the resource will be left in the ground for future extraction and, consequently, future revenues will be smaller since future extraction will necessarily be reduced. Indeed, every bit of resource that is extracted and sold today comes at the cost of not being able to extract it and sell it in the future. Natural resource economists refer to this cost as the **user cost** of extraction because current extraction and use means lower future extraction and use.

Present Use versus Future Use

The concept of user cost is very helpful in showing how a resource extraction firm that is interested in maximizing its flow of profits over time will choose to behave in terms of how much it will choose to extract in the present as opposed to the future. To give a simple example, consider the case of a coal mining company called Black Rock whose mine will have to shut down in two years, when the company's lease expires. Because the mine will close in two years, the mine's production can be thought of as taking place either during the current year or next year. Black Rock's problem is to figure out how much to mine this year in order to maximize its stream of profits.

To see how Black Rock's managers might think about the problem, look at Figure 15.7, which shows the situation facing the company during the first year. Begin by noticing *P*, the market price at which Black Rock can sell each and every ton of coal that it extracts. The firm's managers will obviously want to take this price into consideration when deciding how much output to produce.

Next, consider the company's production costs, which we will refer to as **extraction costs,** or *EC*, since this is an extraction company. The extraction costs include all costs associated with running the mine, digging out the coal, and preparing the coal for sale. Notice that the *EC* curve that represents extraction costs in Figure 15.7 is upward sloping to reflect the fact that the company's marginal extraction costs increase the more the company extracts because

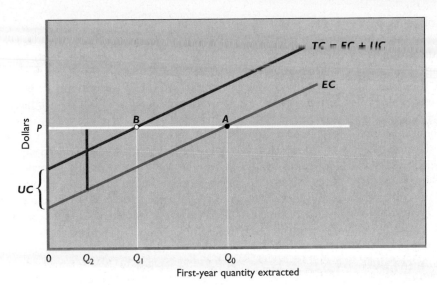

FIGURE 15.7 Choosing the optimal extraction level. A firm that takes account only of current extraction costs, EC, will produce Q_0 units of output in the current period—that is, all units for which the market price P exceeds extraction costs, EC. If it also takes account of user cost, UC, and the fact that current output reduces future output and profits, it will produce only Q_1 units of output—that is, only those units for which price exceeds the sum of extraction costs and user cost.

faster extraction involves having to rent or buy more equipment and having to either hire more workers or pay overtime to existing workers. Rapid extraction is costly, and the EC curve slopes upward to reflect this fact.

Next, consider how much output the firm's managers will choose to produce if they fail to take user cost into account. If the firm's managers ignore user cost, then they will choose to extract and sell Q_0 tons of coal (given by where the horizontal P line crosses the upward-sloping EC line at point A). They will do this because for each and every ton of coal that is extracted up to Q_0, the market price at which it can be sold exceeds its extraction cost—making each of those tons of coal profitable to produce.

But this analysis considers only potential first-year profits. None of those tons of coal *has* to be mined this year. Each of them could be left in the ground and mined during the second year. The question that Black Rock's managers have to ask is whether the company's total stream of profits would be increased by leaving some or all of those tons of coal in the ground this year in order to be mined and sold next year.

This question can be answered by taking account of user cost. Specifically, the company's managers can put a dollar amount on how much future profits are reduced by current extraction and then take that dollar amount into account when determining the optimal amount to extract this year. This process is best understood by looking once again at Figure 15.7. There, each ton of coal that is extracted this year is assumed to have a user cost of UC dollars per ton that is set equal to the present value of the profits that the firm would earn if the extraction and sale of each ton of coal were delayed until the second

year. Taking this user cost into account results in a total cost curve, or TC, that is exactly UC dollars higher than the extraction cost curve at every extraction level. This parallel upward shift reflects the fact that once the company takes user cost into account, its total costs must be equal to the sum of extraction costs and user cost. That is, $TC = EC + UC$.

If the firm's managers take user cost into account in this fashion, then they will choose to produce less output. In fact, they will choose to extract only Q_1 units of coal (shown by where the horizontal P line crosses the upward-sloping TC line at point B). They will produce exactly this much coal because for each and every ton of coal that is extracted up to Q_1, the market price at which it can be sold exceeds its total cost—including not only the current extraction cost but also the cost of forgone future profits, UC.

Another way to understand why Black Rock will limit its production to only Q_1 tons of coal is to realize that for every ton of coal up to Q_1, it is more profitable to extract during the current year than during the second year. This is best seen by looking at a particular ton of coal like Q_2. The profit that the firm can get by extracting Q_2 this year is equal to the difference between Q_2's extraction cost and the market price that it can fetch when it is sold. In terms of the figure, this first-year profit is equal to the length of the vertical red line that runs between the point on the EC curve above output level Q_2 and the horizontal P line.

Notice that the red line is longer than the vertical distance between the EC curve and the TC curve. This means that the first-year profit is greater than the present value of the second-year profit because the vertical distance between the EC curve and the TC curve is equal to UC, which is by definition the present value of the amount of profit that the company would get if it delayed producing Q_2 until the second year. It is therefore clear that if the firm wants to maximize its profit, it should produce Q_2 during the first year rather than during the second year since the profit to be made by current production exceeds the present value of the profit to be made by second-year production.

This is not true for the tons of coal between output levels Q_1 and Q_0. For these tons of coal, the first-year profit—which is, as before, equal to the vertical distance between the EC curve and the horizontal P line—is less than UC, the present value of the second-year profit that can be obtained by delaying production until the second year. Consequently, the extraction of these units should be delayed until the second year.

The model presented in Figure 15.7 demonstrates that the goal of profit-maximizing extraction firms is not to simply mine coal or pump oil as fast as possible. Instead, they are interested in extracting resources at whatever rate will maximize their streams of profit over time. This incentive structure is very useful to society because it means that our limited supplies of nonrenewable resources will be conserved for future extraction and use if extraction firms expect that demand (and hence profits) in the future will be higher than they are today. This can be seen in Figure 15.8, where user cost has increased in the current period from UC_0 to UC_1 to reflect an increase in expected future profits. This increase in user cost causes Black Rock's total cost curve to shift up from $TC_0 = EC + UC_0$ to $TC_1 = EC + UC_1$. This shift, in turn, reduces the optimal amount of current extraction from Q_0 tons of coal to only Q_1 tons of coal.

This reduction in the amount of coal currently extracted conserves coal for extraction and use in the future

when it will be in higher demand. Indeed, Black Rock's profit motive has caused it to reallocate extraction in a way that serves the interests of its customers and their desire to consume more in the future. Since the supply of this nonrenewable resource is limited, more consumption in the future implies less consumption today and Black Rock has accommodated this constraint by reducing extraction this year in order to increase it next year.

More generally speaking, Black Rock's behavior in this case demonstrates that under the right institutional structure, profit-maximizing firms will extract resources efficiently over time, meaning that each unit of the resource will tend to be extracted when the gains from doing so are the greatest. **(Key Question 7)**

Incomplete Property Rights Lead to Excessive Present Use

We just demonstrated that profit-maximizing extraction companies are very happy to decrease current extraction if they can benefit financially from doing so. In particular, they are willing to reduce current extraction if they have the ability to profit from the future extraction and sale of their product. Indeed, this type of a financial situation gives them the incentive to conserve any and all resources that would be more profitably extracted in the future.

This pleasant result breaks down completely if weak or uncertain property rights do not allow extraction companies to profit from conserving resources for future use. For instance, look back at Figure 15.7 and consider how much Black Rock would produce if it were suddenly told that its lease would expire at the end of this year rather than at the end of next year. This would be the equivalent of having a

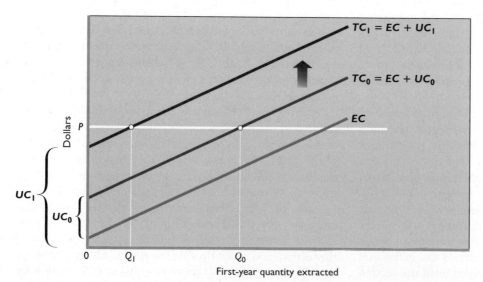

FIGURE 15.8 An increase in expected future profits leads to less current extraction. An increase in future profitability increases user cost from UC_0 to UC_1, thereby raising the total cost curve from TC_0 to TC_1. The firm responds by reducing current production from Q_0 to Q_1 in order to be able to extract more in the future and take advantage of the increase in future profitability.

user cost equal to zero because there would be no way for the company to profit in the future by reducing current extraction. As a result, the firm will take into account only current extraction costs, EC. The result will be that it will extract and sell Q_0 tons of coal, more than the Q_1 tons that it would extract if it could profit from conservation.

Applications

Resources tend to be extracted much too quickly if there is no way to profit from conservation. Let's examine two such situations.

Conflict Diamonds

The name **conflict diamonds** refers to diamonds that are mined by combatants in war zones in Africa in order to provide the hard currency that they need to finance their military activities. Most of these civil wars, however, are very unpredictable, so that control of the mines is tenuous, slipping from one army to another depending on the tide of war.

This fluidity has destroyed any incentive to conserve the resource since the only reason a person would reduce current extraction would be if he or she could benefit from that act of conservation by being able to extract more in the future. But because nobody can be sure of controlling a mine for more than a few months, extraction rates are always extremely high, with the only limit being extraction costs.

This behavior is very wasteful of the resource because once the war finally ends and money is needed to rebuild the country, whichever side wins will find precious few diamonds left to help pay for the reconstruction. Unfortunately, the incentive structures created by the uncertainty of war see to it that extraction takes place at far too rapid a pace, making no allowance for the possibility that future use would be better than present use.

Elephant Preservation

As with nonrenewable resources, renewable resources like wildlife also get used up much too fast if decision makers have no way of profiting from conservation—the only difference being that if a renewable wildlife resource is used too fast, it can become extinct. This was the situation facing elephants in Africa during the 1970s and 1980s when elephant populations in most parts of Africa declined drastically due to the illegal poaching of elephants for their ivory tusks. It was the case, however, that elephant populations in a few countries expanded considerably. The difference resulted from the fact that in certain countries like Botswana and Zimbabwe, property rights over elephants were given to local villagers, thereby giving them a strong financial incentive to preserve their local elephant populations. In particular, local villagers were allowed to keep the money that could

be earned by taking foreign tourists on safari to see the elephants in their area as well as the money that could be made by selling hunting rights to foreign sports hunters. This gave them a strong incentive to prevent poaching, and villagers quickly organized very effective patrols to protect and conserve their valuable resource.

By contrast, elephants belonged to the state in other countries, meaning that locals had no personal stake in the long-term survival of their local elephant populations since any elephant tourism money flowed to the state and other outsiders. This created the perverse incentive that the only way for a local to benefit financially from an elephant was by killing it to get its ivory. Indeed, most of the poaching in these countries was done by locals who had been given no way to benefit from the long-term survival of their local elephant populations. As with nonrenewable resources, the inability to benefit from conservation and future use causes people to increase their present use of renewable resources.

QUICK REVIEW 15.3

- Because nonrenewable resources are finite, it is very important to allocate their limited supply efficiently between present and future uses.
- If resource extraction companies can benefit from both present and future extraction, they will limit current extraction to only those units that are more profitable to extract in the present rather than in the future. This conserves resources for future use.
- If resource users have no way of benefiting from the conservation of a resource, they will use too much of it in the present and not save enough of it for future use—even if future use would be more beneficial than present use.

Renewable Resources

We just saw that under the right circumstances, extraction companies have a strong profit incentive to moderate their current extraction rates and conserve nonrenewable resources for future use. A similar incentive can also hold true for companies and individuals dealing with renewable resources like forests and wildlife. If property rights are structured properly, then decision makers will have an incentive to preserve resources and manage them on a sustainable basis, meaning that they will harvest the resources slowly enough that the resources can always replenish themselves.

On the other hand, if proper incentives are not in place, then high and nonsustainable harvest rates can quickly wipe out a renewable resource. Indeed, ecologists and natural resource economists can cite numerous examples of fish populations collapsing because of overfishing and of rainforests being wiped out because of overlogging. This section discusses the economics of renewable resources as well as policies that promote the sustainable use of renewable resources. To keep things concrete, we focus on forests and then fisheries.

Forest Management

Forests provide many benefits including wildlife habitat, erosion prevention, oxygen production, recreation, and, of course, wood. In 2005, just under 10 billion acres, or about 30 percent of the world's land area, was forested and about 555 million acres, or about 25 percent of the United States' land area, was forested. The amount of land covered by forests is, however, growing in some places but declining in others. This fact is apparent in Global Perspective 15.1, which gives the average annual percentage change over the years 1990 to 2000 in the amount of forest-covered land in 12 selected countries as well as in the entire world.

Economists believe that the large variation in growth rates seen in Global Perspective 15.1 is largely the result of differences in property rights. In certain areas, including the United States and western Europe, forests are either private property or strictly regulated government property. In either case, individuals or institutions have an incentive to harvest their forests on a sustainable basis because they can benefit not just from cutting down the trees currently alive but also from keeping their forests going in order to reap the benefits that they will give off in the future if they are managed on a sustainable basis.

By contrast, deforestation is proceeding rapidly in countries where property rights over forests are poorly enforced or nonexistent. To see why this is true, consider the situation facing competing loggers if nobody owns the property rights to a given forest. In such a situation, whoever chops down the forest first will be able to reap economic benefits because, while nobody can have ownership or control over a living tree, anybody can establish a property right to it by chopping it down and bringing it to market. In such a situation, everybody has an incentive to chop down as many trees as fast as they can in order to get to them before anyone else can. Sadly, nobody has an incentive to preserve trees for future use because—without enforceable property rights—person A has no way to prevent person B from chopping down the trees that person A would like to preserve.

To reduce and hopefully eliminate nonsustainable logging, governments and international agencies have been taking increasingly strong steps to define and enforce property rights over forest areas. One major result is that in areas such as the United States and Europe where strong property rights over forests have been established, virtually all

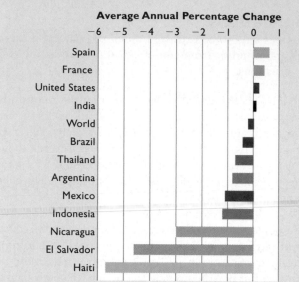

GLOBAL PERSPECTIVE 15.1

Average Annual Percentage Changes in the Amount of Land Covered by Forests, 1990–2000

Average annual percentage changes in the amount of land covered by forests vary greatly by nation, as indicated below.

Source: State of the World's Forests 2005, United Nations Food and Agriculture Organization, www.fao.org.

wood production is generated by commercially run forestry companies. These companies buy up large tracts of land on which they plant and harvest trees. Whenever a harvest takes place and the trees in a given area are chopped down, seedlings are planted to replace the felled trees, thereby replenishing the stock of trees. These companies are deeply concerned about the long-term sustainability of their operations and many often plant trees in the expectation that more than a century may pass before they are harvested.

Optimal Forest Harvesting

In cases where the property rights to a forest are clear and enforceable (as they are in the United States), forest owners have a strong incentive to manage their forests on a sustainable basis because they can reap the long-term benefits that derive from current acts of conservation. A key part of their long-term planning is deciding how often to harvest and then replant their trees.

This is an interesting problem because a commercial forestry company that grows trees for lumber or paper production must take into consideration the fact that trees grow at different rates over the course of their lifetimes.

FIGURE 15.9 A forest's growth rate depends on its age.

Because trees do not reach their most rapid growth rates until middle age, forestry companies have an incentive not to harvest them too early. But because growth then tapers off as the trees reach their maximum adult sizes, there is an incentive to chop them down before they are fully mature in order to replant the area with faster-growing young trees.

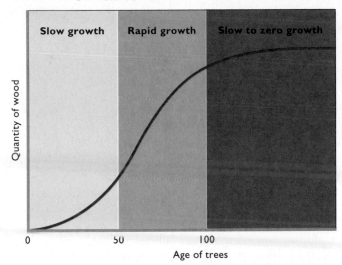

TABLE 15.3 Top 10 U.S. Fisheries in Dollar Terms, 2006

Fishery	Market Value of Catch
Lobster	$394,794,629
Sea scallop	385,958,874
Walleye pollock	329,878,840
White shrimp	220,239,520
Pacific halibut	201,904,348
Pacific cod	220,239,348
Brown shrimp	183,116,474
Sockeye salmon	159,474,734
Dungeness crab	148,932,266
Sablefish	132,154,995

Source: National Ocean Economics Program, **noep.mbari.org.** Information provided by Judith Kildow and the NOEP team at the Monterey Bay Aquarium Research Institute.

Indeed, Figure 15.9 shows that if the company plants an acre of land with seedlings and lets those seedlings grow into mature trees, the amount of wood contained in the trees at first grows rather slowly as the seedlings slowly grow into saplings, then grows quite quickly as the saplings mature into adult trees, and then tapers off as the trees reach their maximum adult sizes.

This growth pattern means that forestry companies have to think very carefully about when to harvest their trees. If they harvest and replant the acre of land when the trees are only 50 years old, they will miss out on the most rapid years of growth. On the other hand, there is not much point in letting the trees get much more than 100 years old before harvesting and replanting since at that age very little growth is left in them. The result is that the forestry company will choose to harvest the trees and replant the land when the trees reach an age of somewhere between 50 and 100 years old. The precise age will be chosen to maximize firm profits and will be affected not only by the growth rate of trees but also by other factors including the cost of harvesting the trees and, of course, the market price of wood and how it is expected to vary over time.

The key point to keep in mind, however, is that forestry companies that have secure property rights over their trees do not harvest them as soon as possible. Instead, they shepherd their resource and harvest their trees only when replacing older, slow-growing trees with younger, fast-growing trees finally becomes more profitable. And, of course, it must also be emphasized that forestry companies

replant. They do this because they know that they can benefit from the seedlings' eventual harvest, even if that is 50 or 100 years in the future. In countries where property rights are not secure, nobody replants after cutting down a forest because there is no way to prevent someone else from cutting down the new trees and stealing the harvest.

Optimal Fisheries Management

A **fishery** is a stock of fish or other marine animal that can be thought of as a logically distinct group. A fishery is typically identified by location and species—for example, Newfoundland cod, Pacific tuna, or Alaskan crab. Table 15.3 lists the top 10 U.S. fisheries in terms of how much their respective catches were worth in 2006.

The key difficulty with fishery management is that the only way to establish property rights over a fish swimming in the open ocean is to catch it and kill it. As long as the fish is alive and swimming in the open ocean, it belongs to nobody. But as soon as it is caught, it belongs to the person who catches it. This property rights system means that the only way to benefit economically from a fish is to catch it and thereby turn it into a private good.

This creates an incentive for fishers to be very aggressive and try to outfish each other, since the only way for them to benefit from a particular fish is to catch it before someone else does. The natural result of this perverse incentive has been tremendous overfishing, which has caused many fisheries to collapse and which threatens many others with collapse as well.

Two examples of fishery collapse are presented in Figure 15.10, which shows the number of metric tons per year of Maine red hake and Atlantic tuna that were caught between 1973 and 2004 by U.S. fishers. A **fishery collapse** happens when a fishery's population is sent into a rapid decline because fish are being harvested faster than they

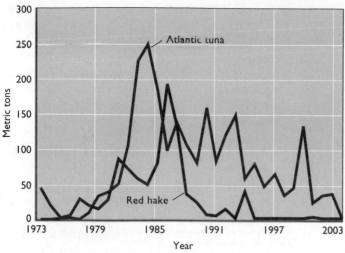

FIGURE 15.10 The collapse of two fisheries, 1973–2004. This figure shows how many metric tons of Atlantic tuna and Maine red hake were caught by U.S. fishing boats each year from 1973 to 2004. Overfishing has caused the population of both species to collapse, Maine red hake very abruptly and Atlantic tuna more slowly.

Source: National Marine Fisheries Service, National Oceanic and Atmospheric Administration, **www.nmfs.noaa.gov.**

can reproduce. The speed of the decline depends on how much faster harvesting is than reproduction. In the case of Maine red hake, the decline was very abrupt, with the annual catch falling from 190.3 million metric tons in 1986 down to only 4.1 million tons 5 years later. After making a minor resurgence in 1994, the fishery then totally collapsed, so that the catch has been less than 1 ton per year for most of the last decade despite the best efforts of fishers to catch more. The collapse of the Atlantic tuna fishery has been more gradual, presumably because the ratio of harvest to reproduction was not as extreme as it was for Maine red hake. But even when harvesting exceeds reproduction by only a small amount in a given year, the population declines. And if that pattern holds for many years, the population will be forced into collapse. This has been the case for Atlantic tuna. It's annual catch collapsed more gradually, from a peak of 248.9 million metric tons in 1984 down to only 4.1 million metric tons in 2004.

Overfishing and fishery collapse are now extremely common, so much so that worldwide stocks of large predatory fish like tuna, halibut, swordfish, and cod are believed to be 90 percent smaller than they were just 50 years ago. In addition, Table 15.4 shows that just 3 percent of world fisheries in 2003 were estimated to be underexploited, whereas 76 percent were categorized as fully exploited, overexploited, depleted, or (hopefully) recovering from depletion.

Policies to Limit Catch Sizes

Governments have tried several different polices to limit the number of fish that are caught each year in order to prevent fisheries from collapsing. They also hope to lower annual catch sizes down to sustainable levels, where the size of the catch does not exceed the fishery's ability to regenerate.

Unfortunately, many of these policies not only fail to reduce catch sizes but also create perverse incentives that raise fishing costs because they do not stop the free-for-all nature of fishing, whereby each fisher tries to catch as many fish as possible as fast as possible before anyone else can get to them.

For example, some policies attempt to reduce catch sizes by limiting the number of days per year that a certain species can be caught. For instance, the duration of the legal crabbing season in Alaska was once cut down from several months to just 4 days. Unfortunately, this policy failed to reduce catch sizes because crabbers compensated for the short legal crabbing season by buying massive boats that could harvest in 4 days the same amount of crab that they had previously needed months to gather.

Fishers bought the new, massive boats because while the new policy limited the number of days over which crabbers were allowed to compete, it did not lessen their incentive to try to catch as many crabs as possible before anyone else could get to them. Indeed, the massive new boats were a sort of arms race, with each fisher trying to buy a bigger,

TABLE 15.4 Status of World's Fisheries in 2003

Status	Percentage
Underexploited	3%
Moderately exploited	21
Fully exploited	52
Overexploited	16
Depleted	7
Recovering from depletion	1

Source: United Nations Food and Agriculture Organization, **www.fao.org.**

faster, more powerful boat than his competitors in order to be able to capture more of the available crabs during the limited 4-day season. The result, however, was a stalemate because if everybody is buying bigger, faster, more powerful boats, then nobody gains an advantage. Consequently, the policy actually made the situation worse. Not only did it fail to reduce catch size; it also drove up fishing costs. This was an especially pernicious result because the policy had been designed to help fishers by preserving the resource upon which their livelihoods depended.

Another failed policy attempted to limit catch size by limiting the number of fishing boats allowed to fish in a specific area. This policy failed because fishers compensated for the limit on the number of boats by operating bigger boats. That is, many small boats that could each catch only a few tons of fish were replaced by a few large boats that could each catch many tons of fish. Once again, catch sizes did not fall.

A policy that does work to reduce catch size goes by the acronym **TAC,** which stands for **total allowable catch.** Under this system, biologists determine the TAC for a given fishery, for instance, 100,000 tons per year. Fishers can then fish until a total of 100,000 tons have been brought to shore. At that point, fishing is halted for the year.

This policy has the benefit of actually limiting the size of the catch to sustainable levels. But it still encourages an arms race between the fishers because each fisher wants to try to catch as many fish as possible before the TAC limit is reached. The result is that even under a TAC, fishing costs rise because fishers buy bigger, faster boats as each one tries to fulfill as much of the overall TAC catch limit as possible.

The catch-limiting system that economists prefer not only limits the total catch size but also eliminates the arms race between fishers that drives up costs. The system is based on the issuance of **individual transferable quotas,** or **ITQs,** which are individual catch size limits that specify that the holder of an ITQ has the right to harvest a given quantity of a particular species during a given time period, for instance, 1000 tons of Alaskan king crab during the year 2009.

The individual catch sizes of all the ITQs that are issued for a given fishery during a specific year add up to the fishery's overall TAC for the year so that they put a sustainable limit on the overall catch size. This preserves the fishery from overexploitation. But the fact that the ITQ quotas are *individual* also eliminates the need for an arms race. Because each fisherman knows that he can take as long as he wants to catch his individual quota, he does not need a superexpensive, technologically sophisticated boat that is capable of hauling in massive amounts of fish in only a few days in order to beat his competitors to the punch. Instead, he can use smaller, less expensive, and simpler boats since he knows that he can fish slowly—perhaps year round if it suits him.

This move toward smaller boats and more leisurely fishing greatly reduces fishing costs. But ITQs offer one more cost-saving benefit. They encourage all of the fishing to be done by the lowest-cost, most-efficient fishing vessels. This is true because ITQs are *tradable* fishing quotas, meaning that they can be sold and thereby traded to other fishers. As we will explain, market pressures will cause them to be sold to the fishers who can catch fish most efficiently, at the lowest possible cost.

To see how this works, imagine a situation in which the market price of tuna is $10 per ton but in which a fisherman named Sven can barely make a profit because his old, slow boat is so expensive that it costs him $9 per ton to catch tuna. At that cost, if he does his own fishing and uses his ITQ quota of 1000 tons himself, he will make a profit of only $1000. At the same time, one of his neighbors, Tammy, has just bought a new, superefficient ship that can harvest fish at the very low cost of $6 per ton. This difference in costs means that Sven and Tammy will both find it advantageous to negotiate the sale of Sven's ITQ to Tammy. Sven, for his part, would be happy to accept any price higher than $1000 since $1000 is the most that he can make if he does his own fishing. Suppose that they agree on a price of $2 per ton, or $2000 total. In such a case, both are better off. Sven is happy because he gets $2000 rather than the $1000 that he would have earned if he had done his own fishing. And Tammy is happy because she is about to make a tidy profit. The 1000 tons of tuna that she can now catch will bring $10,000 in revenues when they are sold at the market price of $10 per ton, while her costs of bringing in that catch will be only $8000 since it costs $6000 in fishing costs at $6 per ton to bring in the catch plus the $2000 that she pays to Sven for the right to use his 1000-ton ITQ.

Notice, though, that society also benefits. If Sven had used his ITQ himself, he would have run up fishing costs of $9000 harvesting the 1000 tons of tuna that his quota allows. But because the permit was sold to Tammy, only $6000 in fishing costs are actually incurred. The tradable nature of ITQs promotes overall economic efficiency by creating an incentive structure that tends to move production toward the producers who have the lowest production costs.

It remains to be seen, however, if ITQs and other catch-reduction policies will be enough to save the world's fisheries. Since current international law allows countries to enforce ITQs and other conservation measures only within 200 miles of their shores, most of the world's oceans are a fishing free-for-all. Unless this changes and incentive structures are put in place to limit catch sizes in these areas, economic theory suggests that the fisheries there will continue to decline as fishers compete to catch as many fish as possible as fast as possible before anyone else can get to them. **(Key Question 11)**

Is Economic Growth Bad for the Environment?

Measures of Environmental Quality Are Higher in Richer Countries.

Many people are deeply concerned that environmental degradation is an inevitable consequence of economic growth. Their concern is lent credence by sensational media events like oil and chemical spills and by the indisputable fact that modern chemistry and industry have created and released into the environment many toxic chemicals and substances that human beings did not even know how to make a couple of centuries ago.

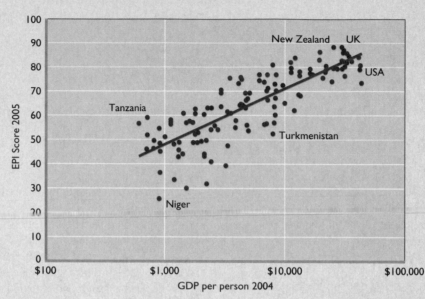

healthy than do poorer societies. Viewed from this perspective, economic growth and rising living standards are good for the environment because as societies get richer, they tend to spend more on things like reducing emissions from smokestacks, preventing the dumping of toxic chemicals, and insisting that sewage be purified before its water is returned to the environment. They also tend to institute better protections for sensitive ecosystems and engage in greater amounts of habitat preservation for endangered species.

But are these increasing expenditures

Economists, however, tend to be rather positive about economic growth and its consequences for the environment. They feel this way because significant evidence indicates that richer societies spend much more money on keeping their respective environments on environmentally beneficial goods and services enough to overcome the massive increases in environmental harm that seem likely to accompany the enormous amounts of production and consumption in which rich societies engage? The empirical record suggests

Summary

1. Per capita living standards in the United States are at least 12 times higher than they were in 1800. This increase in living standards has entailed using much larger amounts of resources to produce the much larger amounts of goods and services that are currently consumed. The increase in resource use can be attributed to two factors. First, there has been a large increase in resource use per person. Second, there are now many more people alive and consuming resources than at any previous time.

2. The large increase in total resource use has led to a spirited debate about whether our high and rising living standards are sustainable. In particular, will our demand for resources soon outstrip the supply of resources? A proper answer to this question involves examining the demand for resources as well as the supply of resources.

3. A good way to examine the demand for resources is to think of total resource demand as being the product of the amount of resources used per person times the number of people alive. Thomas Malthus famously predicted that higher living standards would tend to lead to higher birthrates. The opposite, however, has held true. Higher living standards have led to lower birthrates and the majority of the world's population now lives in countries where the total fertility rate is less than the replacement rate of 2.1 births per woman per lifetime necessary to keep a country's population stable over time.

4. The result is that world population growth is not only slowing but is actually turning negative in many countries. What is more, the effect of low birthrates is so strong that many demographers believe that the world's population will

that the answer is yes. The best evidence for this is given by the accompanying figure, in which each of 133 countries is represented by a point that indicates both its GDP per capita (measured on the horizontal axis using a logarithmic scale) and its year 2005 score on the Environmental Performance Index, or EPI.

This index, produced by researchers at Yale University, compares countries based on how well they are doing in terms of 16 environmental indicators, including atmospheric carbon emissions, measures of air and water quality, the degree of wilderness protection, energy efficiency, and measures of whether a country's fisheries and forests are being overexploited. Out of a maximum possible EPI score of 100, New Zealand and Sweden received the highest scores of, respectively, 88.0 and 87.8. The United States was ranked 28th with a score of 78.5 while the lowest-ranked country, Niger, received a score of 25.7.

When EPI scores are combined with measures of GDP per person in the figure, an extremely strong pattern emerges: Richer countries have higher EPI scores. In fact, the relationship between the two variables is so strong that 70 percent of the differences between countries in terms of EPI scores are explained by their differences in GDP per person. In addition, the logarithmic scale used on the horizontal axis allows us to look at the best-fit line drawn through the data and conclude that a 10-fold

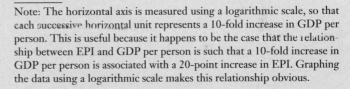

increase in GDP per capita (from, for instance, $1000 to $10,000) is associated with a 20-point increase in EPI. The figure is therefore clear confirmation that economic growth can not only go together with a healthy environment, but that economic growth actually promotes a healthy environment by making people rich enough to pay for pollution-reduction technologies that people living in poorer countries cannot afford.

Looking to the future, many economists are hopeful that economic growth and rising living standards will pay for the invention and implementation of new technologies that could make for an even cleaner environment. If the current pattern continues to hold, increased standards of living will lead to better environmental outcomes.

Note: The horizontal axis is measured using a logarithmic scale, so that each successive horizontal unit represents a 10-fold increase in GDP per person. This is useful because it happens to be the case that the relationship between EPI and GDP per person is such that a 10-fold increase in GDP per person is associated with a 20-point increase in EPI. Graphing the data using a logarithmic scale makes this relationship obvious.

Sources: The EPI data are from the Yale Center for Environmental Law and Policy, **www.yale.edu/epi.** The data on real GDP per person (at purchasing power parity) in 2004 are from *The World Factbook*, **www.cia.gov.**

reach a maximum of fewer than 9 billion people in the next 50 years before beginning to decline quite rapidly. That implies substantially reduced resource demand.

5. The evidence from the United States and other rich countries is that resource use per person has either fallen or leveled off during the past several decades. For instance, per capita water use in the United States fell 28 percent between 1975 and 2000. Per capita energy use has been stable since the late 1980s. And because the per capita generation of trash has been stable since 1990, we can infer that the per capita use of solid objects like metals, paper, and plastics has been stable since that time as well.

6. Combined with the expected decline in population levels, the fact that per capita resource use has either fallen or leveled off implies that the total demand for resources is likely to reach a peak in the relatively near future before falling over time as populations decline.

7. Natural resource economists predict that resource supplies are likely to grow faster than resource demands in the future. This confidence is based on the fact that since 1850 the real (inflation-adjusted) prices of resources have fallen by about 55 percent. Because this decline in prices happened at the same time that total resource use was increasing dramatically, it seems likely that resource supplies will continue to grow faster than resource demands since, going forward, resource use should grow less quickly than it has in the past because population growth has slowed (and is expected to turn negative) and because per capita resource use in recent decades has leveled off or turned negative.

8. Living standards can continue to rise without consuming more energy thanks to more efficient productive technologies, which can produce more output using the same amount of energy input. Indeed, real GDP per person in the United States increased by nearly 40 percent between

1988 and 2007 despite the fact that annual per capita energy consumption remained constant during those years.

9. Differences in fixed costs mean that a wide variety of energy sources are used in the economy despite the fact that some of these energy sources are much more costly than others. For instance, coal-fired electric generating plants use low-cost coal, but are extremely expensive to build so that they are used only in situations where very large generating capacities are required. By contrast, when smaller amounts of electricity are required, it often makes more sense to employ other generating technologies such as natural gas despite the fact that they use more expensive fuel.

10. We are not running out of energy. Even if we run out of oil, there are plenty of other energy sources including biodiesel, ethanol made from corn or sugar cane, and oil made from organic waste products. The only question is cost.

11. Renewable natural resources like forests and fisheries as well as nonrenewable natural resources like oil and coal tend to be overused in the present unless there are institutions created that provide resource users with a way to benefit from conservation. Governments can ensure this benefit by strictly defining and enforcing property rights so that users know that if they conserve a resource today, they will be able to use it in the future.

12. Encouraging conservation is especially difficult in the open ocean where it is impossible to either define or enforce property rights over fish because, by international law, nobody owns the open ocean and so anyone can fish there as much as they want. This lack of property rights leads to severe overfishing and an eventual collapse of the fishery.

13. Closer to shore, however, governments can define property rights within their sovereign waters and impose limits on fishing. The best system involves combining total allowable catch (TAC) limits for a given fishery with individual transferable quota (ITQ) limits for individual fishers.

Terms and Concepts

replacement rate	renewable natural resources	conflict diamonds
total fertility rate	nonrenewable natural resources	fishery
demographers	present value	fishery collapse
British thermal unit (BTU)	user cost	total allowable catch (TAC)
net benefits	extraction cost	individual transferable quota (ITQ)

Study Questions

1. Describe Thomas Malthus' theory of human reproduction. Does it make sense for some species—say bacteria or rabbits? What do you think makes humans different? **LO1**

2. Suppose that the current (first) generation consists of 1 million people, half of whom are women. If the total fertility rate is 1.3 and the only way people die is of old age, how big will the fourth generation (the great-grandchildren) be? How much smaller (in percentage terms) is each generation than the previous generation? How much smaller (in percentage terms) is the fourth generation than the first generation? Are you surprised by how quickly the population declines? **LO1**

3. Demographers have been very surprised that total fertility rates have fallen below 2.0, especially because most people in most countries tell pollsters that they would like to have at least two children. Can you think of any possible economic factors that may be causing women in so many countries to average fewer than two children per lifetime? What about other social or political changes? **LO1**

4. Resource consumption per person in the United States is either flat or falling, depending on the resource. Yet living standards are rising due to improvements in technology that allow more output to be produced for every unit of input used in production. What does this say about the likelihood of our running out of resources? Could we possibly maintain or improve our living standards even if the population were expected to rise in the future rather than fall? **LO1**

5. **KEY QUESTION** Suppose that you hear two people arguing about energy. One says that we are running out of energy. The other counters that we are running out of cheap energy. Explain which person is correct and why. **LO3**

6. A community has a nighttime energy demand of 50 megawatts but a peak daytime demand of 75 megawatts. It has the chance to build a 90-megawatt coal-fired plant that could easily supply all of its energy uses even at peak daytime demand. Should it necessarily proceed? Could there be lower-cost options? Explain. **LO2**

7. **KEY QUESTION** Recall the model of nonrenewable resource extraction presented in Figure 15.7. Suppose that a technological breakthrough means that extraction costs will fall in the future (but not in the present). What will this do to future profits and, therefore, to current user cost? Will current extraction increase or decrease? Compare this to a

situation where future extraction costs remain unchanged but current extraction costs fall. In this situation, does current extraction increase or decrease? Does the firm's behavior make sense in both situations? That is, does its response to the changes in production costs in each case maximize the firm's stream of profits over time? **LO4**

8. If the current market price rises, does current extraction increase or decrease? What if the future market price rises? Do these changes in current extraction help to ensure that the resource is extracted and used when it is most valuable? **LO4**

9. **ADVANCED ANALYSIS** Suppose that a government wants to reduce its economy's dependence on coal and decides as a result to tax coal mining companies $1 per ton for every ton of coal that they mine. Assuming that coal mining companies treat this tax as an increase in extraction costs this year, what effect will the tax have on current extraction in the model used in Figure 15.7? Now, think one step ahead. Suppose that the tax will be in place forever, so that it will also affect extraction costs in the future. Will the tax increase or decrease user cost? Does this effect increase or decrease the change in current extraction caused by the shift of the *EC* curve? Given your finding, should environmental taxes be temporary? **LO4**

10. **ADVANCED ANALYSIS** User cost is equal to the present value of future profits in the model presented in Figure 15.7. Will the optimal quantity to mine in the present year increase or decrease if the market rate of interest rises? Does your result make any intuitive sense? (Hint: If interest rates are up, would you want to have more or less money right now to invest at the market rate of interest?) **LO4**

11. **KEY QUESTION** Various cultures have come up with their own methods to limit catch size and prevent fishery collapse. In old Hawaii, certain fishing grounds near shore could be used only by certain individuals. And among lobstermen in Maine, strict territorial rights are handed out so that only certain people can harvest lobsters in certain waters. Discuss specifically how these systems provide incentives for conservation. Then think about the enforcement of these property rights. Do you think similar systems could be successfully enforced for deep sea fishing, far off shore? **LO5**

12. Aquaculture is the growing of fish, shrimp, and other seafood in enclosed cages or ponds. The cages and ponds not only keep the seafood from swimming away but also provide aquaculturalists with strong property rights over their animals. Does this provide a good incentive for low-cost production as compared with fishing in the open seas where there are few if any property rights? **LO5**

13. **LAST WORD** The figure in the Last Word section shows that a 10-fold increase in a country's GDP per person is associated with about a 20-point increase in EPI. Do you think that this pattern can be extrapolated out into the future? That is, could the United States (which currently has an EPI of 78.5) gain another 20 points if it increased its GDP per person by a factor of 10 from its current level? Explain. (Hint: Consider diminishing returns.)

Web-Based Questions

1. **U.S. ENERGY SOURCES AND USES** The Energy Information Agency (www.eia.doe.gov) of the United States government contains a treasure trove of data about both U.S. and international energy generation and consumption. Go to the Historical Data Overview page at www.eia.doe.gov/overview_hd.html and notice the Energy Flow diagram that appears at the upper right. Click on the diagram to expand it and then look it over. The diagram gives energy consumption and usage for the United States for the most recent year for which data is available. Is the United States totally dependent on oil imports? What fraction of its oil consumption does it have to import? Is it strange that even though the country is a net importer of petroleum, it exports some petroleum, too? What about the overall energy situation? What percentage of its overall energy consumption can it fulfill with domestically produced energy? What fraction of domestic production comes from renewable energy sources? Is this higher or lower than you were expecting?

2. **CARBON DIOXIDE EMISSIONS—RISING OR FALLING?** We presented evidence earlier that per capita consumption of water, energy, and solid objects like plastics and metals has been constant or falling in recent decades. The consumption of fossil fuels, however, is of special concern because of worries about global warming caused by the emission into the atmosphere of carbon dioxide and other so-called greenhouse gasses. Go to the Energy Information Agency's Environment page, www.eia.doe.gov/environment.html. Scan the International Emissions Data links and click on the one that says Per Capita Emissions in order to open up an Excel spreadsheet that contains per capita carbon dioxide emissions for almost all countries for each of the previous 20 years or so. Have per capita carbon dioxide emissions in the United States, Japan, and France grown, stayed about the same, or fallen over the past couple of decades? Does it surprise you to learn that over this time period France has moved to generate more than 80 percent of its electricity from nuclear power, which emits no carbon dioxide? What about emissions in China, Indonesia, and India? Why have emissions risen so much (in percentage terms) in these countries? (Hint: They are not as poor as they used to be.) If current trends in these countries continue, should we be worried? And could defining property rights over the atmosphere solve the problem?

PART FOUR

Microeconomics of Government

1 How public goods are distinguished from private goods.

2 The method for determining the optimal quantity of a public good.

3 The basics of cost-benefit analysis.

4 About externalities (spillover costs and benefits) and the methods to remedy them.

5 How information failures can justify government interventions in some markets.

IN THIS CHAPTER YOU WILL LEARN:

16

Public Goods, Externalities, and Information Asymmetries

The economic activities of government affect your well-being every day. If you drive to work or classes, you are using publicly provided highways and streets. If you attend a public college or university, taxpayers subsidize your education. When you receive a check from your part-time or summer job, you see deductions for income taxes and Social Security taxes. Government antipollution laws affect the air you breathe. Laws requiring seat belts, motorcycle helmets, and auto insurance are all government mandates.

This chapter examines government and *market failure*—a circumstance in which private markets do not bring about the allocation of resources that best satisfies society's wants. Where private markets fail, an economic role for government may arise. We want to examine that role as it relates to three kinds of market failure: public goods, externalities, and information asymmetries. Our discussion of externalities in turn facilitates a discussion of pollution, climate change, and related issues.

In the next chapter—Chapter 17—we continue our discussion of the microeconomics of government by first analyzing potential government inefficiencies—called *government failure*—and then considering the economics of taxation.

Public Goods

To understand public goods, we first need to revisit the characteristics of private goods.

Private Goods Characteristics

We have seen that a full range of **private goods** is produced through the competitive market system. These are the goods offered for sale in stores, in shops, and on the Internet. Examples include automobiles, clothing, personal computers, household appliances, and sporting goods. Private goods have two characteristics: rivalry and excludability:

- *Rivalry* (in consumption) means that when one person buys and consumes a product, it is not available for another person to buy and consume. When Adams purchases and drinks a bottle of mineral water, it is not available for Benson to purchase and consume.

- *Excludability* means that sellers can keep people who do not pay for a product from obtaining its benefits. Only people who are willing and able to pay the market price for bottles of water can obtain these drinks and the benefits they confer.

Consumers fully express their personal demands for private goods in the market. If Adams likes bottled mineral water, that fact will be known by her desire to purchase the product. Other things equal, the higher the price of bottled water, the fewer bottles she will buy. So Adams' demand for bottled water will reflect an inverse relationship between the price of bottled water and the quantity of it demanded. This is simply *individual* demand, as described in Chapter 3.

The *market* demand for a private good is the horizontal summation of the individual demand schedules (review Figure 3.2). Suppose just two consumers comprise the market for bottled water and the price is $1 per bottle. If Adams will purchase 3 bottles and Benson will buy 2, the market demand will reflect consumers' demand for 5 bottles at the $1 price. Similar summations of quantities demanded at other prices will generate the market demand schedule and curve.

Suppose the equilibrium price of bottled water is $1. Adams and Benson will buy a total of 5 bottles, and the sellers will obtain total revenue of $5 (= $1 × 5). If the sellers' cost per bottle is $.80, their total cost will be $4 (= $.80 × 5). So sellers charging $1 per bottle will obtain $5 of total revenue, incur $4 of total cost, and earn $1 of profits for the 5 bottles sold.

Because firms can profitably "tap market demand" for private goods, they will produce and offer them for sale. Consumers demand private goods, and profit-seeking suppliers produce goods that satisfy the demand. Consumers willing to pay the market price obtain the goods; nonpayers go without. A competitive market not only makes private goods available to consumers but also allocates society's resources efficiently to the particular product. There is neither underproduction nor overproduction of the product.

Public Goods Characteristics

Recall from Chapter 4 that certain other goods and services—**public goods**—have the opposite characteristics of private goods. Public goods are distinguished by nonrivalry and nonexcludability.

- *Nonrivalry* (in consumption) means that one person's consumption of a good does not preclude consumption of the good by others. Everyone can simultaneously obtain the benefit from a public good such as national defense, street lighting, a global positioning system, or environmental protection.

- *Nonexcludability* means there is no effective way of excluding individuals from the benefit of the good once it comes into existence. Once in place, you cannot exclude someone from benefiting from national defense, street lighting, a global positioning system, or environmental protection.

These two characteristics create a **free-rider problem.** Once a producer has provided a public good, everyone including nonpayers can obtain the benefit. Most people do not voluntarily pay for something they can obtain for free!

With only free riders, the demand for a public good does not get expressed in the market. With no market demand, firms have no potential to "tap the demand" for revenues and profits. The free-rider problem makes it impossible for firms to gather together resources and profitably provide the good. If society wants a public good, society will have to direct government to provide it. Government can finance the provision of such goods through taxation.

CONSIDER THIS . . .

Art for Art's Sake

Suppose an enterprising sculptor creates a piece of art costing $600 and, with permission, places it in the town square. Also suppose that Jack gets $300 of enjoyment from the art and Diane gets $400. Sensing this enjoyment and hoping to make a profit, the sculptor approaches Jack for a donation equal to his satisfaction. Jack falsely says that, unfortunately, he does not particularly like the piece. The sculptor then tries Diane, hoping to get $400 or so. Same deal: Diane professes not to like the piece either. Jack and Diane have become free riders. Although feeling a bit guilty, both reason that it makes no sense to pay for something when anyone can receive the benefits without paying for them. The artist is a quick learner; he vows never to try anything like that again.

Optimal Quantity of a Public Good

If consumers need not reveal their true demand for a public good in the marketplace, how can society determine the optimal amount of that good? The answer is that the government has to try to estimate the demand for a public good through surveys or public votes. It can then compare the marginal benefit (MB) of an added unit of the good against the government's marginal cost (MC) of providing it. Adhering to the MB = MC rule, government can provide the "right," meaning "efficient," amount of the public good.

Demand for Public Goods

The demand for a public good is somewhat unusual. Suppose Adams and Benson are the only two people in the society, and their marginal willingness to pay for a public good, national defense, is as shown in columns 1 and 2 and columns 1 and 3 in Table 16.1. Economists might have discovered these schedules through a survey asking hypothetical questions about how much each citizen was willing to pay for various types and amounts of public goods rather than go without them.

Notice that the schedules in Table 16.1 are price-quantity schedules, implying that they are demand schedules. Rather than depicting demand in the usual way—the

TABLE 16.1 Demand for a Public Good, Two Individuals

(1) Quantity of Public Good	(2) Adams' Willingness to Pay (Price)		(3) Benson's Willingness to Pay (Price)		(4) Collective Willingness to Pay (Price)
1	$4	+	$5	=	$9
2	3	+	4	=	7
3	2	+	3	=	5
4	1	+	2	=	3
5	0	+	1	=	1

quantity of a product someone is willing to buy at each possible price—these schedules show the price someone is willing to pay for the extra unit of each possible quantity. That is, Adams is willing to pay $4 for the first unit of the public good, $3 for the second, $2 for the third, and so on.

Suppose the government produces 1 unit of this public good. Because of nonrivalry, Adams' consumption of the good does not preclude Benson from also consuming it, and vice versa. So both consume the good, and neither volunteers to pay for it. But from Table 16.1 we can find the amount these two people would be willing to pay, together, rather than do without this 1 unit of the good. Columns 1 and 2 show that Adams would be willing to pay $4 for the first unit of the public good; columns 1 and 3 show that Benson would be willing to pay $5 for it. So the two people are jointly willing to pay $9 (= $4 + $5) for this first unit.

For the second unit of the public good, the collective price they are willing to pay is $7 (= $3 from Adams + $4 from Benson); for the third unit they will pay $5 (= $2 + $3); and so on. By finding the collective willingness to pay for each additional unit (column 4), we can construct a collective demand schedule (a willingness-to-pay schedule) for the public good. Here we are not adding the quantities demanded at each possible price, as we do when we determine the market demand for a private good. Instead, we are adding the prices that people are willing to pay for the last unit of the public good at each possible quantity demanded.

Figure 16.1 shows the same adding procedure graphically, using the data from Table 16.1. Note that we sum Adams' and Benson's willingness-to-pay curves *vertically* to derive the collective willingness-to-pay curve (demand curve). The summing procedure is upward from the lower graph to the middle graph to the top (total) graph. For example, the height of the collective demand curve D_c at 2 units of output in the top graph is $7, the sum of the amounts that Adams and Benson are each willing to pay for the second unit (= $3 + $4). Likewise, the height of the collective demand curve at 4 units of the public good is $3 (= $1 + $2).

FIGURE 16.1 The optimal amount of a public good.

The collective demand curve for a public good, as shown by D_c in (c), is found by summing vertically the individual willingness-to-pay curves D_1 in (a) and D_2 in (b) of Adams and Benson, the only two people in the economy. The supply curve of the public good represented in (c) slopes upward and to the right, reflecting rising marginal costs. The optimal amount of the public good is 3 units, determined by the intersection of D_c and S. At that output, marginal benefit (reflected in the collective demand curve D_c) equals marginal cost (reflected in the supply curve S).

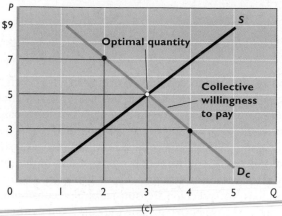

(c)
Collective demand and supply

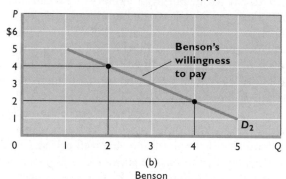

(b)
Benson

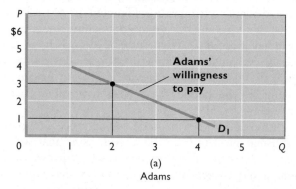

(a)
Adams

What does it mean in Figure 16.1a that, for example, Adams is willing to pay $3 for the second unit of the public good? It means that Adams expects to receive $3 of extra benefit or utility from that unit. And we know from the law of diminishing marginal utility that successive units of any good yield less and less added benefit. This is also true for public goods, explaining the downward slope of the willingness-to-pay curves of Adams, Benson, and society. These curves, in essence, are marginal-benefit (MB) curves. (**Key Question 1**)

Comparing MB and MC

The supply curve for any good, private or public, is its marginal-cost (MC) curve. Marginal cost rises as more of a good is produced. The reason is the law of diminishing returns, which applies whether a society is making missiles (a public good) or mufflers (a private good). In the short run, government has fixed resources (public capital) with which to "produce" public goods such as national defense. As it adds more units of a variable resource (labor) to these fixed resources, total product eventually rises at a diminishing rate. That means that marginal product falls and marginal cost rises, explaining why curve S in Figure 16.1c slopes upward.

We can now determine the optimal quantity of the public good. The collective demand curve D_c in Figure 16.1c measures society's marginal benefit of each unit of this par-

> **WORKED PROBLEMS**
> **W 16.1**
> Optimal amount of a public good

ticular good. The supply curve S in that figure measures society's marginal cost of each unit. The optimal quantity of this public good occurs where marginal benefit equals marginal cost, or where the two curves intersect. In Figure 16.1c that point is 3 units of the public good, where the collective willingness to pay for the last (third) unit—the marginal benefit—just matches that unit's marginal cost ($5 = $5). As we saw in Chapter 1, equating marginal benefit and marginal cost efficiently allocates society's scarce resources. (**Key Question 2**)

Cost-Benefit Analysis

The above example suggests a practical means, called **cost-benefit analysis,** for deciding whether to provide a particular public good and how much of it to provide. Like our example, cost-benefit analysis (or marginal-benefit–marginal-cost analysis) involves a comparison of marginal costs and marginal benefits.

Concept Suppose the Federal government is contemplating a highway construction plan. Because the economy's resources are limited, any decision to use more resources in the public sector will mean fewer resources for the private sector. There will be an opportunity cost, as well as a benefit. The cost is the loss of satisfaction resulting from the accompanying decline in the production of private goods; the benefit is the extra satisfaction resulting from the output of more

TABLE 16.2 Cost-Benefit Analysis for a National Highway Construction Project (in Billions)

(1) Plan	(2) Total Cost of Project	(3) Marginal Cost	(4) Total Benefit	(5) Marginal Benefit	(6) Net Benefit (4) − (2)
No new construction	$ 0		$ 0		$ 0
A: Widen existing highways	4	$ 4	5	$ 5	1
B: New 2-lane highways	10	6	13	8	3
C: New 4-lane highways	18	8	23	10	5
D: New 6-lane highways	28	10	26	3	−2

public goods. Should the needed resources be shifted from the private to the public sector? The answer is yes if the benefit from the extra public goods exceeds the cost that results from having fewer private goods. The answer is no if the cost of the forgone private goods is greater than the benefit associated with the extra public goods.

Cost-benefit analysis, however, can indicate more than whether a public program is worth doing. It can also help the government decide on the extent to which a project should be pursued. Real economic questions cannot usually be answered simply by "yes" or "no" but, rather, involve questions such as "how much" or "how little."

Illustration Although a few private toll roads exist, highways clearly have public goods characteristics because the benefits are widely diffused and highway use is difficult to price. Should the Federal government expand the Federal highway system? If so, what is the proper size or scope for the overall project?

Table 16.2 lists a series of increasingly ambitious and increasingly costly highway projects: widening existing two-lane highways; building new two-lane highways; building new four-lane highways; building new six-lane highways. The extent to which government should undertake highway construction depends on the costs and benefits. The costs are largely the costs of constructing and maintaining the highways; the benefits are improved flows of people and goods throughout the country.[1]

The table shows that total annual benefit (column 4) exceeds total annual cost (column 2) for plans A, B, and C, indicating that some highway construction is economically justifiable. We see this directly in column 6, where total costs (column 2) are subtracted from total annual benefits (column 4). Net benefits are positive for plans

A, B, and C. Plan D is not economically justifiable because net benefits are negative.

But the question of optimal size or scope for this project remains. Comparing the marginal cost (the change in total cost) and the marginal benefit (the change in total benefit) relating to each plan determines the answer. The guideline is well known to you from previous discussions: Increase an activity, project, or output as long as the marginal benefit (column 5) exceeds the marginal cost (column 3). Stop the activity at, or as close as possible to, the point at which the marginal benefit equals the marginal cost. Do not undertake a project for which marginal cost exceeds marginal benefit.

In this case plan C (building new four-lane highways) is the best plan. Plans A and B are too modest; the marginal benefits exceed the marginal costs, and there is a better option. Plan D's marginal cost ($10 billion) exceeds the marginal benefit ($3 billion) and therefore cannot be justified; it overallocates resources to the project. Plan C is closest to the theoretical optimum because its marginal benefit ($10 billion) still exceeds marginal cost ($8 billion) but approaches the MB = MC (or MC = MB) ideal.

This **marginal-cost–marginal-benefit rule** actually tells us which plan provides the maximum excess of total benefits over total costs or, in other words, the plan that provides society with the maximum net benefit. You can confirm directly in column 6 that the maximum net benefit (= $5 billion) is associated with plan C.

Cost-benefit analysis shatters the myth that "economy in government" and "reduced government spending" are synonymous. "Economy" is concerned with using scarce resources efficiently. If the marginal cost of a proposed government program exceeds its marginal benefit, then the proposed public program should not be undertaken. But if the marginal benefit exceeds the marginal cost, then it would be uneconomical or "wasteful" not to spend on that government program. Economy in government does not mean minimization of public spending. It means allocating resources between the private and public sectors

---

[1]Because the costs of public goods typically are immediate while the benefits often accrue over longer time periods, economists convert both costs and benefits to present values for comparison. Using present value properly accounts for the time-value of money, discussed in Chapters 14 and 15.

and among public goods to achieve maximum net benefit. **(Key Question 3)**

Externalities

In performing its allocation function, government not only produces public goods but also corrects for a market failure called **externalities,** or spillovers. Recall from Chapter 4 that an externality is a cost or a benefit accruing to an individual or group—a third party—that is *external* to a market transaction. An example of a negative externality is the cost of breathing polluted air; an example of a positive externality is the benefit of having everyone else inoculated against some disease. When there are negative externalities, an overproduction of the related product occurs and there is an overallocation of resources to this product. Conversely, underproduction and underallocation of resources result when positive externalities are present. We can demonstrate both graphically.

Negative Externalities

Figure 16.2a illustrates how negative externalities affect the allocation of resources. When producers shift some of their costs onto the community as external costs, producers' marginal costs are lower than otherwise. So their supply curves do not include or "capture" all the costs legitimately associated with the production of their goods. A polluting producer's supply curve such as S in Figure 16.2a therefore understates the total cost of production. The firm's supply curve lies to the right of (or below) the full-cost supply curve S_t, which would include the spillover cost. Through polluting and thus transferring costs to society, the firm enjoys lower production costs and has the supply curve S.

The outcome is shown in Figure 16.2a, where equilibrium output Q_e is larger than the optimal output Q_o. This means that resources are overallocated to the production of this commodity; too many units of it are produced.

INTERACTIVE GRAPHS
G 16.1
Externalities

Positive Externalities

Figure 16.2b shows the impact of positive externalities on resource allocation. When external benefits occur, the market demand curve D lies to the left of (or below) the full-benefits demand curve. That is, D does not include the external benefits of the product, whereas D_t does. Consider inoculations against a communicable disease. Watson and Weinberg benefit when they get vaccinated, but so do their associates Alvarez and Anderson, who are less likely to contract the disease from them. The market demand curve reflects only the direct, private benefits to Watson and Weinberg. It does not reflect the external benefits—the positive externalities—to Alvarez and Anderson, which are included in D_t.

The outcome is that the equilibrium output Q_e is less than the optimal output Q_o. The market fails to produce enough vaccinations, and resources are underallocated to this product.

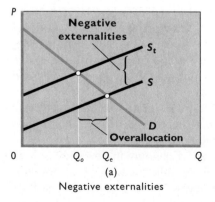

(a)

Negative externalities

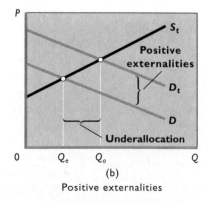

(b)

Positive externalities

FIGURE 16.2 Negative externalities and positive externalities. (a) With negative externalities borne by society, the producers' supply curve S is to the right of (below) the full-cost curve S_t. Consequently, the equilibrium output Q_e is greater than the optimal output Q_o. (b) When positive externalities accrue to society, the market demand curve D is to the left of (below) the full-benefit demand curve D_t. As a result, the equilibrium output Q_e is less than the optimal output Q_o.

Economists have explored several approaches to the problems of negative externalities and positive externalities. Let's first look at situations where government intervention is not needed and then at some possible government solutions.

Individual Bargaining: Coase Theorem

In the **Coase theorem,** conceived decades ago by economist Ronald Coase at the University of Chicago, government is not needed to remedy external costs or benefits where (1) property ownership is clearly defined, (2) the number of people involved is small, and (3) bargaining costs are negligible. Under these circumstances the government should confine its role to encouraging bargaining between affected individuals or groups. Property rights place a price tag on an externality, creating opportunity costs for all parties. Because the economic self-interests of the parties are at stake, bargaining will enable them to find a mutually acceptable solution to the externality problem.

Example of the Coase Theorem Suppose the owner of a large parcel of forestland is considering a plan to clear-cut (totally level) thousands of acres of mature fir trees. The complication is that the forest surrounds a lake with a popular resort on its shore. The resort is on land owned by the resort. The unspoiled beauty of the general area attracts vacationers from all over the nation to the resort, and the resort owner is against the clear-cutting. Should state or local government intervene to allow or prevent the tree cutting?

According to the Coase theorem, the forest owner and the resort owner can resolve this situation without government intervention. As long as one of the parties to the dispute has property rights to what is at issue, an incentive will exist for both parties to negotiate a solution acceptable to each. In our example, the owner of the timberland holds the property rights to the land to be logged and thus has the right to clear-cut it. The owner of the resort therefore has an economic incentive to negotiate with the forest owner to reduce the logging impact. Excessive logging of the forest surrounding the resort will reduce tourism and revenues to the resort owner.

But what is the economic incentive to the forest owner to negotiate with the resort owner? The answer draws directly on the idea of opportunity cost. One cost incurred in logging the forest is the forgone payment that the forest owner could obtain from the resort owner for agreeing not to clear-cut the fir trees. The resort owner might be willing to make a lump-sum or annual payment to the owner of the forest to avoid or minimize the negative externality. Or perhaps the resort owner might be willing to buy the forested land to prevent the logging. As viewed by the forest owner, a payment for not clear-cutting or a purchase price above the prior market value of the land is an opportunity cost of logging the land.

It is likely that both parties would regard a negotiated agreement as better than clear-cutting the firs.

Limitations Unfortunately, many externalities involve large numbers of affected parties, high bargaining costs, and community property such as air and water. In such situations private bargaining cannot be used as a remedy. As an example, the global-warming problem affects millions of people in many nations. The vast number of affected parties could not individually negotiate an agreement to remedy this problem. Instead, they must rely on their governments to represent the millions of affected parties and find an acceptable solution. We discuss some of these potential solutions later in this chapter.

Liability Rules and Lawsuits

Although private negotiation may not be a realistic solution to many externality problems, clearly established property rights may help in another way. The government has erected a framework of laws that define private property and protect it from damage done by other parties. Those laws, and the damage recovery system to which they give rise, permit parties suffering negative externalities to sue for compensation.

Suppose the Ajax Degreaser Company regularly dumps leaky barrels containing solvents into a nearby canyon owned by Bar Q Ranch. Bar Q eventually discovers this dump site and, after tracing the drums to Ajax, immediately contacts its lawyer. Soon after, Bar Q sues Ajax. If Ajax loses the case, it will have to pay for the cleanup, and may also have to pay Bar Q additional damages for ruining its property.

Clearly defined property rights and government liability laws thus help remedy some externality problems. They do so directly by forcing the perpetrator of the harmful externality to pay damages to those injured. They do so indirectly by discouraging firms and individuals from generating negative externalities for fear of being sued.

It is not surprising, then, that many externalities do not involve private property but rather property held in common by society. It is the public bodies of water, the public lands, and the public air, where ownership is less clear, that often bear the brunt of negative externalities.

Caveat: Like private negotiations, private lawsuits to resolve externalities have their own limitations. Large legal fees and major time delays in the court system are commonplace. Also, the uncertainty associated with the court outcome reduces the effectiveness of this approach. Will the court accept your claim that your emphysema has resulted from the smoke emitted by the factory next door, or will it conclude that your ailment is unrelated to the plant's pollution? Can you prove that a specific firm in the area is the source of the contamination of your well? What happens to Bar Q's suit if Ajax Degreaser goes out of business during the litigation?

Government Intervention

Government intervention may be needed to achieve economic efficiency when externalities affect large numbers of people or when community interests are at stake. Government can use direct controls and taxes to counter negative externalities; it may provide subsidies or public goods to deal with positive externalities.

Direct Controls The direct way to reduce negative externalities from a certain activity is to pass legislation limiting that activity. Such direct controls force the offending firms to incur the actual costs of the offending activity. Historically, direct controls in the form of uniform emission standards—limits on allowable pollution—have dominated American air pollution policy. For example, the Clean Air Act of 1990 (1) forced factories and businesses to install "maximum achievable control technology" to reduce emissions of 189 toxic chemicals by 90 percent between 1990 and 2000; (2) required a 30 to 60 percent reduction in tailpipe emissions from automobiles by 2000; (3) mandated a 50 percent reduction in the use of chlorofluorocarbons (CFCs), which deplete the ozone layer (CFCs are used widely as a coolant in refrigeration, a blowing agent for foam, and a solvent in the electronics industry); and (4) forced coal-burning utilities to cut their emissions of sulfur dioxide by about 50 percent to reduce the acid-rain destruction of lakes and forests. Clean-water legislation limits the amount of heavy metals, detergents, and other pollutants firms can discharge into rivers and bays. Toxic-waste laws dictate special procedures and dump sites for disposing of contaminated soil and solvents. Violating these laws means fines and, in some cases, imprisonment.

Direct controls raise the marginal cost of production because the firms must operate and maintain pollution control equipment. The supply curve S in Figure 16.3b, which does not reflect the external costs, shifts leftward to the full-cost supply curve, S_t. Product price increases, equilibrium output falls from Q_e to Q_o, and the initial overallocation of resources shown in Figure 16.3a is corrected.

Specific Taxes A second policy approach to negative externalities is for government to levy taxes or charges specifically on the related good. For example, the government has placed a manufacturing excise tax on CFCs, which deplete the stratospheric ozone layer protecting the earth from excessive solar ultraviolet radiation. Facing such an excise tax, manufacturers must decide whether to pay the tax or expend additional funds to purchase or develop substitute products. In either case, the tax raises

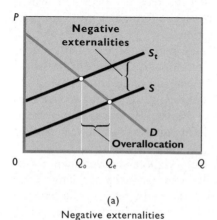

(a)
Negative externalities

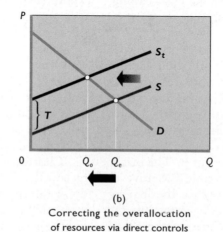

(b)
Correcting the overallocation
of resources via direct controls
or via a tax

FIGURE 16.3 Correcting for negative externalities. (a) Negative externalities result in an overallocation of resources. (b) Government can correct this overallocation in two ways: (1) using direct controls, which would shift the supply curve from S to S_t and reduce output from Q_e to Q_o, or (2) imposing a specific tax T, which would also shift the supply curve from S to S_t, eliminating the overallocation of resources.

the marginal cost of producing CFCs, shifting the private supply curve for this product leftward (or upward)

In Figure 16.3b, a tax equal to T per unit increases the firm's marginal cost, shifting the supply curve from S to S_t. The equilibrium price rises, and the equilibrium output declines from Q_e to the economically efficient level Q_o. The tax thus eliminates the initial overallocation of resources.

Subsidies and Government Provision

Where spillover benefits are large and diffuse, as in our earlier example of inoculations, government has three options for correcting the underallocation of resources:

- **Subsidies to buyers** Figure 16.4a again shows the supply-demand situation for positive externalities. Government could correct the underallocation of resources, for example, to inoculations, by subsidizing consumers of the product. It could give each new mother in the United States a discount coupon to be used to obtain a series of inoculations for her child. The coupon would reduce the "price" to the mother by, say, 50 percent. As shown in Figure 16.4b, this program would shift the demand curve for inoculations from too low D to the appropriate D_t. The number of inoculations would rise from Q_e to the economically optimal Q_o, eliminating the underallocation of resources shown in Figure 16.4a.

- **Subsidies to producers** A subsidy to producers is a specific tax in reverse. Taxes are payments *to* the government that increase producers' costs. Subsidies are payments *from* the government that decrease producers' costs. As shown in Figure 16.4c, a subsidy of U per inoculation to physicians and medical clinics would reduce their marginal costs and shift their supply curve rightward from S_t to S_t''. The output of inoculations would increase from Q_e to the optimal level Q_o, correcting the underallocation of resources shown in Figure 16.4a.

- **Government provision** Finally, where positive externalities are extremely large, the government may decide to provide the product as a public good. The U.S. government largely eradicated the crippling disease polio by administering free vaccines to all children. India ended smallpox by paying people in rural areas to come to public clinics to have their children vaccinated. **(Key Question 4)**

A Market-Based Approach to Negative Externalities

Another approach to negative externalities involves only limited government action. The idea is to create a market for externality rights. But before describing that approach, we first need to understand the idea called the **tragedy of the commons.**

The Tragedy of the Commons

The air, rivers, lakes, oceans, and public lands, such as parks and streets, are all objects for pollution because the rights to use those resources are held "in common" by society. No private

---

FIGURE 16.4 Correcting for positive externalities. (a) Positive externalities result in an underallocation of resources. (b) This underallocation can be corrected through a subsidy to consumers, which shifts market demand from D to D_t and increases output from Q_e to Q_o. (c) Alternatively, the underallocation can be eliminated by providing producers with a subsidy of U, which shifts their supply curve from S_t to S_t', increasing output from Q_e to Q_o.

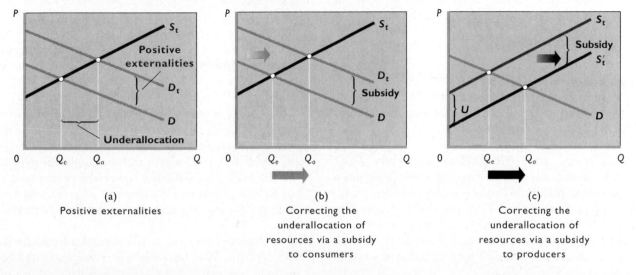

individual or institution has a monetary incentive to maintain the purity or quality of such resources.

We maintain the property we own—for example, we paint and repair our homes periodically—in part because we will recoup the value of these improvements at the time of sale. But as long as "rights" to air, water, and certain land resources are commonly held and are freely available, there is no incentive to maintain them or use them carefully. As a result, these natural resources are overused and thereby degraded or polluted.

For example, a common pasture in which anyone can graze cattle will quickly be overgrazed because each rancher has an incentive to graze as many cattle as possible. Similarly, commonly owned resources such as rivers, lakes, oceans, and the air get used beyond their capacity to absorb pollution. Manufacturers will choose the least-cost combination of inputs and bear only unavoidable costs. If they can dump waste chemicals into rivers and lakes rather than pay for proper disposal, some businesses will be inclined to do so. Firms will discharge smoke into the air if they can, rather than purchase expensive abatement facilities. Even Federal, state, and local governments sometimes discharge inadequately treated waste into rivers, lakes, or oceans to avoid the expense of constructing expensive treatment facilities. Many individuals avoid the costs of proper refuse pickup and disposal by burning their garbage or dumping it in the woods.

The problem is mainly one of incentives. There is no incentive to incur internal costs associated with reducing or eliminating pollution when those costs can be transferred externally to society. The fallacy of composition (Last Word, Chapter 1) also comes into play. Each person and firm reasons their individual contribution to pollution is so small that it is of little or no overall consequence. But their actions, multiplied by hundreds, thousands, or millions, overwhelm the absorptive capacity of the common resources. Society ends up with a degradation or pollution problem.

A Market for Externality Rights

This outcome gives rise to a market-based approach to correcting negative externalities. The idea is that the government can create a **market for externality rights.** We confine our discussion to pollution, although the same approach might be used with other externalities.

Operation of the Market

In this market-based approach—commonly called a **cap-and-trade program**— an appropriate pollution-control agency determines the amount of pollutants that firms can discharge into the water or air of a specific region annually while maintaining the water or air quality at some acceptable level. Suppose the agency ascertains that 500 tons of pollutants can be

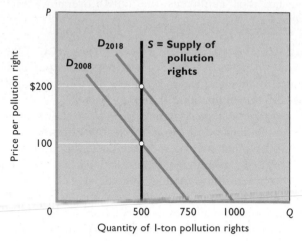

FIGURE 16.5 A market for pollution rights. The supply of pollution rights S is set by the government, which determines that a specific body of water can safely recycle 500 tons of waste. In 2008, the demand for pollution rights is D_{2008} and the 1-ton price is $100. The quantity of pollution is 500 tons, not the 750 tons it would have been without the pollution rights. Over time, the demand for pollution rights increases to D_{2018} and the 1-ton price rises to $200. But the amount of pollution stays at 500 tons, rather than rising to 1000 tons.

discharged into Metropolitan Lake and "recycled" by nature each year. Then 500 pollution rights, each entitling the owner to dump 1 ton of pollutants into the lake in 1 year, are made available for sale to producers each year. The quantity of these pollution rights is "capped," so supply is perfectly inelastic, as shown in Figure 16.5.

The demand for pollution rights, represented by D_{2008} in the figure, takes the same downsloping form as the demand for any other input. At higher prices, fewer pollution rights are demanded since firms substitute pollution abatement-equipment for pollution rights. An equilibrium market price for pollution rights, here $100, will be determined at which the environment-preserving quantity of pollution rights is rationed to polluters. Figure 16.5 shows that if the use of the lake as a dump site for pollutants were instead free, 750 tons of pollutants would be discharged into the lake; it would be "overconsumed," or polluted, in the amount of 250 tons.

Over time, as human and business populations expand, demand will increase, as from D_{2008} to D_{2018}. Without a market for pollution rights, pollution in 2018 would be 1000 tons, 500 tons beyond what can be assimilated by nature. With the market for pollution rights, the price would rise from $100 to $200, and the amount of pollutants would remain at 500 tons—the amount that the lake can recycle.

Advantages

This scheme has several advantages over direct controls. Most important, it reduces society's costs by allowing pollution rights to be bought and sold. This trading of pollution rights is the "trade" portion of the "cap-and-trade" terminology given to this type of scheme. Let's see how this cost reduction works. Assume that the present equilibrium price of pollution rights is $100, as shown by the intersection of the supply curve and demand curve (2008) in Figure 16.5. Next, suppose that the pollution in question is some specific noxious discharge into Metropolitan Lake. Suppose that it costs Acme Pulp Mill $20 a year to reduce this pollution by 1 ton while it costs Zemo Chemicals $800 a year to accomplish the same 1-ton reduction. Also assume that Zemo wants to expand production, but doing so will increase its pollution discharge by 1 ton.

Without a market for pollution rights, Zemo would have to use $800 of society's scarce resources to keep the 1-ton pollution discharge from occurring. But with a market for pollution rights, Zemo has a better option: It buys 1 ton of pollution rights for the $100 price shown in Figure 16.5. Acme is willing to sell Zemo 1 ton of pollution rights for $100 because that amount is more than Acme's $20 cost of reducing its pollution by 1 ton. Zemo increases its discharge by 1 ton; Acme reduces its discharge by 1 ton. Zemo benefits (by $800 − $100), Acme benefits (by $100 − $20), and society benefits (by $800 − $20). Rather than using $800 of its scarce resources to hold the discharge at the specified level, society uses only $20 of those resources. Cap-and-trade programs, with pollution rights, thus decrease the cost of reducing pollution.

Market-based plans have other advantages. Potential polluters have a monetary incentive not to pollute because they must pay for the right to discharge effluent. Conservation groups can fight pollution by buying up and withholding pollution rights, thereby reducing pollution below governmentally determined standards. As the demand for pollution rights increases over time, the growing revenue from the sale of a fixed quantity of pollution rights could be devoted to environmental improvement. At the same time, the rising price of pollution rights should stimulate the search for improved pollution-control techniques.

Real-World Examples Administrative and political problems have kept the government from replacing direct controls—such as uniform emission limits—with a full-scale market for pollution rights. But the Environmental Protection Agency (EPA) established a system of pollution rights, or "tradeable emission allowances," in the 1980s as part of a plan to reduce the sulfur dioxide emitted by coal-burning public utilities. Those emissions are the major source of acid rain. The market for such rights was greatly expanded by legislation in the 1990s.

The Clean Air Act of 1990 established a limited market for pollution rights, similar to that shown in Figure 16.5, by allowing utilities to trade emission credits provided by government. Utilities can obtain credits by reducing sulfur-dioxide emissions by more than the specified amount. They can then sell their emission credits to other utilities that find it less costly to buy the credits than to install additional pollution-control equipment.

This market for sulfur-dioxide-emission credits complements other air pollution policies that also permit the exchange of pollution rights. The EPA now allows firms to exchange pollution rights internally and externally. Polluters are allowed to transfer air pollution internally between individual sources within their plants. That is, as long as it meets the overall pollution standard assigned to it, a firm may increase one source of pollution by offsetting it with reduced pollution from another part of its operations.

The EPA also permits external trading of pollution rights. It has set targets for reducing air pollution in regions where the minimum standards are not being met. Previously, new pollution sources could not enter these regions unless existing polluters went out of business. But under the system of external trading rights, the EPA allows firms that reduce their pollution below set standards to sell their pollution rights to other firms. A new firm that wants to locate in the Los Angeles area, for example, might be able to buy rights to emit 20 tons of nitrous oxide annually from an existing firm that has reduced its emissions 20 tons below its allowable limit. The price of these emission rights will depend on their supply and demand.

Finally, in 2003 the EPA extended the market-based approach to the Clean Water Act. Industry, agriculture, and municipalities within a defined watershed can meet their EPA-approved maximum daily discharge limits through trading "water quality credits." Entities that find reducing water pollution extremely expensive can buy credits from entities that can reduce pollution relatively inexpensively. Therefore, society incurs less total cost in improving water quality.

Table 16.3 reviews the major methods for correcting externalities.

Society's Optimal Amount of Externality Reduction

Negative externalities such as pollution reduce the utility of those affected, rather than increase it. These spillovers are not economic goods but economic "bads." If something is bad, shouldn't society eliminate it? Why should society allow firms or municipalities to discharge *any* impure waste into public waterways or to emit *any* pollution into the air?

TABLE 16.3 **Methods for Dealing with Externalities**

Problem	Resource Allocation Outcome	Ways to Correct
Negative externalities (spillover costs)	Overproduction of output and therefore overallocation of resources	1. Individual bargaining 2. Liability rules and lawsuits 3. Tax on producers 4. Direct controls 5. Market for externality rights
Positive externalities (spillover benefits)	Underproduction of output and therefore underallocation of resources	1. Individual bargaining 2. Subsidy to consumers 3. Subsidy to producers 4. Government provision

Reducing a negative externality has a "price." Society must decide how much of a reduction it wants to "buy." Eliminating pollution might not be desirable, even if it were technologically feasible. Because of the law of diminishing returns, cleaning up the second 10 percent of pollutants from an industrial smokestack normally is more costly than cleaning up the first 10 percent. Eliminating the third 10 percent is more costly than cleaning up the second 10 percent, and so on. Therefore, cleaning up the last 10 percent of pollutants is the most costly reduction of all.

The marginal cost (MC) to the firm and hence to society—the opportunity cost of the extra resources used—rises as pollution is reduced more and more. At some point MC may rise so high that it exceeds society's marginal benefit (MB) of further pollution abatement (reduction). Additional actions to reduce pollution will therefore lower society's well-being; total cost will rise more than total benefit.

MC, MB, and Equilibrium Quantity Figure
16.6 shows both the rising marginal-cost curve, MC, for pollution reduction and the downsloping marginal-benefit curve, MB, for this outcome. MB slopes downward because of the law of diminishing marginal utility: The more pollution reduction society accomplishes, the lower the utility (and benefit) of the next unit of pollution reduction.

The **optimal reduction of an externality** occurs when society's marginal cost and marginal benefit of reducing that externality are equal (MC = MB). In Figure 16.6 this optimal amount of pollution abatement is Q_1 units. When MB exceeds MC, additional abatement moves society toward economic efficiency; the added benefit of cleaner air or water exceeds the benefit of any alternative use of the required resources. When MC exceeds MB, additional

abatement reduces economic efficiency; there would be greater benefits from using resources in some other way than to further reduce pollution.

In reality, it is difficult to measure the marginal costs and benefits of pollution control. Nevertheless, Figure 16.6 demonstrates that some pollution may be economically efficient. This is so not because pollution is desirable but because beyond some level of control, further abatement may reduce society's net well-being.

Shifts in Locations of the Curves The locations of the marginal-cost and marginal-benefit curves in

FIGURE 16.6 **Society's optimal amount of pollution abatement.** The optimal amount of externality reduction—in this case, pollution abatement—occurs at Q_1, where society's marginal cost MC and marginal benefit MB of reducing the spillover are equal.

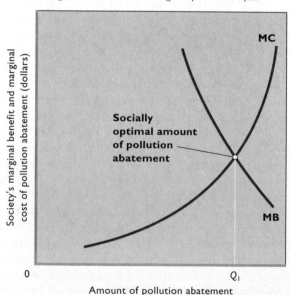

Figure 16.6 are not forever fixed. They can, and probably do, shift over time. For example, suppose that the technology of pollution-control equipment improved noticeably. We would expect the cost of pollution abatement to fall, society's MC curve to shift rightward, and the optimal level of abatement to rise. Or suppose that society were to decide that it wanted cleaner air and water because of new information about the adverse health effects of pollution. The MB curve in Figure 16.6 would shift rightward, and the optimal level of pollution control would increase beyond Q_1. Test your understanding of these statements by drawing the new MC and MB curves in Figure 16.6. **(Key Question 7)**

QUICK REVIEW 16.2

- Policies for coping with the overallocation of resources caused by negative externalities are (a) private bargaining, (b) liability rules and lawsuits, (c) direct controls, (d) specific taxes, and (e) markets for externality rights.

- Policies for correcting the underallocation of resources associated with positive externalities are (a) private bargaining, (b) subsidies to producers, (c) subsidies to consumers, and (d) government provision.

- The optimal amount of negative-externality reduction occurs where society's marginal cost and marginal benefit of reducing the externality are equal.

Climate Change

The United States has made significant progress in cleaning its air. According to the EPA, between 1990 and 2000 clean-air laws and antipollution efforts by businesses and local governments reduced concentrations of lead by 60 percent, carbon monoxide and sulfur dioxide by 36 percent each, particulate matter by 18 percent, nitrogen dioxide by 10 percent, and smog by 4 percent.

But significant air pollution problems remain, including the controversial **climate-change problem.** The earth's surface has warmed over the last century by about 1 degree Fahrenheit, with an acceleration of warming during the past two decades. Some of this surface warming may simply reflect natural fluctuations of the earth's warming and cooling, but the balance of scientific evidence suggests that human activity is a contributing factor. According to the EPA and international study groups, carbon dioxide and other gas emissions from factories, power plants, automobiles, and other human sources are cumulating in the earth's atmosphere and creating a greenhouse effect.

Because of the greenhouse effect, average temperatures are predicted to rise by 1 to 4.5 degrees Fahrenheit over the next 50 years and 2.2 to 10 degrees by 3000. Although there

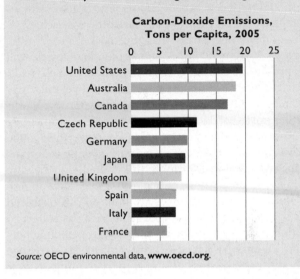

GLOBAL PERSPECTIVE 16.1

Carbon-Dioxide Emissions, Tons per Capita, Selected Nations

Carbon-dioxide emissions, the major type of greenhouse-gas emissions, vary per capita by nation primarily because of different degrees of industrialization and energy production from fossil fuels (coal, oil, and natural gas). The burning of such fuels is the major contributor to global warming.

Carbon-Dioxide Emissions, Tons per Capita, 2005

Source: OECD environmental data, **www.oecd.org**.

will be significant regional variation, scientists say many parts of the world will experience noticeable climatic changes. Rainfall will increase, rainfall patterns will change, and ocean levels will gradually rise by as much as 2 feet. Snow accumulations may decline in some regions and rise in others. More violent storms such as tornadoes and hurricanes may occur in some regions. (Global Perspective 16.1 lists per capita carbon-dioxide emissions for selected nations.)

The world's nations have responded to the climate-change threat collectively and individually. In the Kyoto Protocol of 1997, representatives of the industrially advanced nations agreed to cut their greenhouse-gas emissions by 6 to 8 percent below their 1990 levels by 2012. Since 1997 all signatory nations except the United States have ratified the Kyoto agreement although few are actually likely to meet the 2012 goals. In 2001 the United States opted out of the Kyoto agreement on a Senate vote of 95-0, concluding that the limitations on greenhouse gas would severely damage the U.S. economy. The United States also expressed great concern that the treaty excluded rapidly developing countries such as China, one of today's leading total emitters of carbon dioxide and other greenhouse gases. A year later the United States announced a "Global Climate Change" initiative designed to use clean-energy investments to reduce greenhouse gases per dollar of GDP by 18 percent by 2012.

Economists stress that climate-change policies that reduce greenhouse-gas emissions and thus slow or eliminate global warming create costs as well as benefits. Therefore it is imperative to consider the marginal costs and marginal benefits carefully in making policy decisions. Greenhouse-gas limits should not be so stringent that they end up costing society more than the value of the benefits they produce. But limits should not be so lenient that society forgoes substantial potential benefits that it would have otherwise achieved.

Economists also stress that the market mechanism, through its system of prices and profits and losses, will make appropriate adjustments based on new climatic realities. Air-conditioner sales may rise; snow shovel sales may fall. Some agricultural lands probably will be deserted; others farther north will be cultivated. The maple syrup industry in New England may shift to Canada. Nevertheless, the *transition costs*—the costs associated with making economic adjustments—of global warming will undoubtedly be very high unless some actions are taken to reduce greenhouse gases. But industrial economies are built on carbon-based energy sources, so the costs of reducing such gases are also quite high. The relevant question from the economic perspective becomes: Will it be less costly for society to reduce greenhouse-gas emissions or simply to try to mitigate their effects? No easy answer exists for this question. Some yet-unknown combination of "reduction" and "mitigation" may in fact turn out to be optimal.

If the Federal government decides to aggressively reduce carbon emissions, what general policies are available to it? Our prior discussion of externalities revealed two clear options:

- A carbon tax.
- A cap-and-trade program.

The Federal government could impose a carbon tax on each ton of carbon emitted. This tax would increase the marginal cost of production to all firms that emit carbon into the air through their production processes. Because of the added marginal cost, the supply curves within affected markets would shift to the left (as illustrated by the move from S to S_t in Figure 16.3). The reduced market supply would increase equilibrium price and reduce equilibrium quantity. With the lower output, carbon emissions in these industries would fall.

A carbon tax would require minimum government interference in the economy once the tax was in place. The Federal government could direct the revenues from the tax to research on cleaner production technologies or simply use the new revenues to reduce other taxes. But there would be no free lunch here: According to a 2007 study, a proposed $15 tax per ton of carbon emitted would add an estimated 14 cents to a gallon of gasoline, $1.63 to a kilowatt hour of electricity, $28.50 to a ton of coal, and $6.48 to a barrel of crude oil.

An alternative approach is a cap-and-trade program, based on the concepts embodied within Figure 16.5. The Federal government could place a cap or lid on total carbon emissions and then either hand out emission rights or auction them off. In ways previously discussed, the cap-and-trade program would reduce society's overall cost of lowering carbon emissions. In that regard, it would be more efficient than direct controls requiring each producer of greenhouse gas to reduce emissions by a fixed percentage amount. Existing cap-and-trade programs—including current European markets for carbon certificates—prove that this program can work. But such programs require considerable government oversight and enforcement of the rules.

QUICK REVIEW 16.3

- Society's pollution problem has largely resulted from increasing population, rising per capita consumption, certain changes in technology, and the so-called tragedy of the commons.
- The world's advanced industrial nations are struggling to reduce emissions of greenhouse gases, which most scientists conclude are contributing to global warming.
- Two alternative policies for reducing greenhouse gases are (a) a carbon tax and (b) a cap-and-trade system.

Information Failures

Thus far we have added new details and insights concerning two types of market failure: public goods and externalities. There is another, subtler, market failure. This one results when either buyers or sellers have incomplete or inaccurate information and their cost of obtaining better information is prohibitive. Technically stated, this market failure occurs because of **asymmetric information**—unequal knowledge possessed by the parties to a market transaction. Buyers and sellers do not have identical information about price, quality, or some other aspect of the good or service.

Sufficient market information normally is available to ensure that goods and services are produced and purchased efficiently. But in some cases inadequate information makes it difficult to distinguish trustworthy from untrustworthy

ORIGIN OF THE IDEA

O 16.3

Information failures

sellers or trustworthy from untrustworthy buyers. In these markets, society's scarce resources may not be used efficiently, thus implying that the government should intervene by increasing the information available to the market participants. Under rare circumstances the government may itself supply a good for which information problems have prohibited efficient production.

Inadequate Buyer Information about Sellers

Inadequate information among buyers about sellers and their products can cause market failure in the form of underallocation of resources. Two examples will help you understand this point.

Example: Gasoline Market

Assume an absurd situation: Suppose there is no system of weights and measures established by law, no government inspection of gasoline pumps, and no law against false advertising. Each gas station can use whatever measure it chooses; it can define a gallon of gas as it pleases. A station can advertise that its gas is 87 octane when in fact it is only 75. It can rig its pumps to indicate that it is providing more gas than the amount being delivered.

Obviously, the consumer's cost of obtaining reliable information under such chaotic conditions is exceptionally high, if not prohibitive. Customers or their representatives would have to buy samples of gas from various gas stations, have them tested for octane level, and test the accuracy of calibrations at the pump. And these activities would have to be repeated regularly, since a station owner could alter the product quality and the accuracy of the pump at will.

Because of the high costs of obtaining information about the seller, many consumers would opt out of this chaotic market. One tankful of a 50 percent mixture of gasoline and water would be enough to discourage most motorists from further driving. More realistically, the conditions in this market would encourage consumers to vote for political candidates who promise to provide a government solution. The oil companies and honest gasoline stations would most likely welcome government intervention. They would realize that accurate information, by enabling this market to work, would expand their total sales and profits.

The government has in fact intervened in the market for gasoline and other markets with similar potential information difficulties. It has established a system of weights and measures, employed inspectors to check the accuracy of gasoline pumps, and passed laws against fraudulent claims and misleading advertising. Clearly, these government activities have produced net benefits for society.

Example: Licensing of Surgeons

Suppose now that anyone could hang out a shingle and claim to be a surgeon, much as anyone can become a house painter. The market would eventually sort out the true surgeons from those who are "learning by doing" or are fly-by-night operators who move into and out of an area. As people died from unsuccessful surgeries, lawsuits for malpractice eventually would identify and eliminate most of the medical impostors. People needing surgery for themselves or their loved ones could obtain information from newspaper reports, Internet sites, or people who have undergone similar operations.

But this process of obtaining information for those needing surgery would take considerable time and would impose unacceptably high human and economic costs. There is a fundamental difference between getting an amateurish paint job on one's house and being on the receiving end of heart surgery by a bogus physician. The marginal cost of obtaining information about sellers in the surgery market would be excessively high. The risk of proceeding without good information would result in much less surgery than desirable—an underallocation of resources to surgery.

The government has remedied this market failure through a system of qualifying tests and licensing. The licensing provides consumers with inexpensive information about a service they only infrequently buy. The government has taken a similar role in several other areas of the economy. For example, it approves new medicines, regulates the securities industry, and requires warnings on containers of potentially hazardous substances. It also requires warning labels on cigarette packages and disseminates information about communicable diseases. And it issues warnings about unsafe toys and inspects restaurants for health-related violations.

Inadequate Seller Information about Buyers

Just as inadequate information about sellers can keep markets from achieving economic efficiency, so can inadequate information about buyers. The buyers may be consumers who buy products or firms that buy resources.

Moral Hazard Problem Private markets may underallocate resources to a particular good or service for which there is a severe **moral hazard problem.** The moral hazard problem is the tendency of one party to a contract or agreement to alter her or his behavior, after the contract is signed, in ways that could be costly to the other party.

Suppose a firm offers an insurance policy that pays a set amount of money per month to people who suffer divorces. The attractiveness of such insurance is that it would pool the economic risk of divorce among thousands of people and, in particular, would protect spouses and children from the economic hardship that divorce often brings. Unfortunately, the moral hazard problem reduces the likelihood that insurance companies can profitably provide this type of insurance.

After taking out such insurance, some people would alter their behavior in ways that impose heavy costs on the insurer. For example, married couples would have less of an incentive to get along and to iron out marital difficulties. At the extreme, some people might be motivated to obtain a divorce, collect the insurance, and then continue to live together. Such insurance could even promote more divorces, the very outcome it is intended to protect against. The moral hazard problem would force the insurer to charge such high premiums for this insurance that few policies would be bought. If the insurer could identify in advance those people most prone to alter their behavior, the firm could exclude them from buying it. But the firm's marginal cost of getting such information is too high compared with the marginal benefit. Thus, this market would fail.

Although divorce insurance is not available in the marketplace, society recognizes the benefits of insuring against the hardships of divorce. It has corrected for this underallocation of "hardship insurance" through child-support laws that dictate payments to the spouse who retains the children, when the economic circumstances warrant them. Alimony laws also play a role.

Since, unlike private firms, the government does not have to earn a profit when supplying services, it provides "divorce insurance" of sorts through the Temporary Assistance for Needy Families (TANF) program. If a divorce leaves a spouse with children destitute, she or he is eligible for TANF payments for a period of time. Government intervention does not eliminate the moral hazard problem, but it does offset the problem's adverse effects.

The moral hazard problem is also illustrated in the following statements:

- Drivers may be less cautious because they have car insurance.
- Medical malpractice insurance may increase the amount of malpractice.
- Guaranteed contracts for professional athletes may reduce the quality of their performance.

- Unemployment compensation insurance may lead some workers to shirk.
- Government insurance on bank deposits may encourage banks to make risky loans.

Adverse Selection Problem Another information problem resulting from inadequate information about buyers is the **adverse selection problem**. This problem arises when information known by the first party to a contract or agreement is not known by the second and, as a result, the second party incurs major costs. Unlike the moral hazard problem, which arises after a person signs a contract, the adverse selection problem arises at the time a person signs a contract.

In insurance, the adverse selection problem is that people who are most likely to need insurance payouts are those who buy insurance. For example, those in poorest health will seek to buy the most generous health insurance policies. Or, at the extreme, a person planning to hire an arsonist to "torch" his failing business has an incentive to buy fire insurance.

Our hypothetical divorce insurance sheds further light on the adverse selection problem. If the insurance firm sets the premiums on the basis of the average divorce rate, many married couples who are about to obtain a divorce will buy insurance. An insurance premium based on average probabilities will make a great buy for those about to get divorced. Meanwhile, those in highly stable marriages will not buy it.

The adverse selection problem thus tends to eliminate the pooling of low and high risks, which is the basis of profitable insurance. Insurance rates then must be so high that few people would want to (or be able to) buy such insurance.

Where private firms underprovide insurance because of information problems, the government often establishes some type of social insurance. It can require that everyone in a particular group take the insurance and thereby can overcome the adverse selection problem. Example: Although the Social Security system in the United States is partly insurance and partly an income transfer program, in its broadest sense it is insurance against poverty during old age. The Social Security program requires nearly universal participation: People who are most likely to need the minimum benefits that Social Security provides are automatically participants in the program. So, too, are those not likely to need the benefits. Consequently, no adverse selection problem emerges.

Workplace Safety The labor market also provides an example of how inadequate information about buyers (employers) can produce market failures.

CONSIDER THIS . . .

"Lemons"

Why does a new car lose substantial market value when it is purchased, even though the same car can sit on the dealer's lot for weeks, or even months, and still retain its market value? One plausible explanation for this paradox is based on the ideas of *asymmetric information* and *adverse selection.**

Used-car owners (potential sellers) have much better information about the mechanical condition of their cars than do potential buyers. Because of this asymmetric information, an *adverse selection problem* occurs. Owners of defective used cars—so-called lemons—have an incentive to sell their cars to unsuspecting buyers, whereas owners of perfectly operating used cars have an incentive to retain their used cars. Although a mix of both good and bad used cars is offered for sale, the mix is tilted toward the poorer-quality used cars. So the average quality of the used cars is lower than that of the same makes and models that are not for sale.

The typical consumer finds it difficult to identify the higher-quality used cars from the average- (lower-) quality used cars simply by looking at them or taking them for a test drive. Anticipating repair costs, the customer is willing to pay only a price that reflects the lower quality.†

So we have a solution to the paradox: When purchased, the market values of new cars drop quickly to the value of the average-quality used cars of the same year, make, and model offered for sale in the market. This is true even though many individual used cars may be in perfect operating condition. Adverse selection, asymmetric information, and the resulting risk of "buying someone else's problem" drop the value of used cars relative to new cars still on the lot.

---

*This explanation is based on the work of economist George Akerlof.

†Transferable warrantees reduce, but do not eliminate, the potential repair costs of used cars. Consumers lose time in arranging repairs and forgo the use of their cars when the repairs are being done.

For several reasons employers have an economic incentive to provide safe workplaces. A safe workplace reduces the amount of disruption of the production process created by job accidents and lowers the costs of recruiting, screening, training, and retaining new workers. It also reduces a firm's workers' compensation insurance premiums (legally required insurance against job injuries).

But a safe workplace is expensive: Safe equipment, protective gear, and a slower work pace all entail costs. The firm will decide how much safety to provide by comparing the marginal cost and marginal benefit of providing a safer workplace. Will this amount of job safety achieve economic efficiency, as well as maximize the firm's profit?

The answer is yes if the labor and product markets are competitive and if workers are fully aware of the job risks at various places of employment. With full information, workers will avoid employers having unsafe workplaces. The supply of labor to these establishments will be greatly restricted, forcing them to boost their wages to attract a workforce. The higher wages will then give these employers an incentive to provide increased workplace safety; safer workplaces will reduce wage expenses. Only firms that find it very costly to provide safer workplaces will choose to pay high compensating wage differentials rather than reduce workplace hazards.

But a serious problem arises when workers do not know that particular occupations or workplaces are unsafe. Because information involving the buyer—that is, about the employer and the workplace—is inadequate, the firm may not need to pay a wage premium to attract its workforce. Its incentive to remove safety hazards therefore will be diminished, and its profit-maximizing level of workplace safety will be less than economically desirable. In brief, the labor market will fail because of asymmetric information—in this case, sellers (workers) having less information than buyers (employers).

The government has several options for remedying this information problem:

- It can directly provide information to workers about the injury experience of various employers, much as it publishes the on-time performance of airlines.
- It can require that firms provide information to workers about known workplace hazards.
- It can establish standards of workplace safety and enforce them through inspections and penalties.

Although the Federal government has mainly employed the standards and enforcement approach to improve workplace safety, some critics contend that an information strategy might be less costly and more effective. (**Key Question 12**)

Qualification

Households and businesses have found many ingenious ways to overcome information difficulties without government intervention. For example, many firms offer product warranties to overcome the lack of information about themselves and their products. Franchising also helps

Lojack: A Case of Positive Externalities

Economists Ian Ayres and Steven Levitt Find That an Auto Antitheft Device Called *Lojack* Produces Large Spillover Benefits.

Private expenditures to reduce crime are estimated to be $300 billion annually and are growing at a faster rate than is spending on public crime prevention. Unfortunately, some forms of private crime prevention simply redistribute crime rather than reduce it. For example, car alarm systems that have red blinking warning lights may simply divert professional auto thieves to vehicles that do not have such lights and alarms. The owner of a car with such an alarm system benefits through reduced likelihood of theft but imposes a cost on other car owners who do not have such alarms. Their cars are more likely to be targeted for theft because other cars have visible security systems.

Some private crime prevention measures, however, actually reduce crime rather than simply redistribute it. One such measure is installation of a Lojack (or some similar) car retrieval system. Lojack is a tiny radio transmitter that is hidden in one of many possible places within the car. When an owner reports a stolen car, the police can remotely activate the transmitter. Police then can determine the car's precise location and track its subsequent movements.

The owner of the car benefits because the 95 percent retrieval rate on cars with the Lojack system is higher than the 60 percent retrieval rate for cars without the system. But, according to a study by Ayres and Levitt, the benefit to the car owner is only 10 percent of the total benefit. Ninety percent of the total benefit is external; it is a spillover benefit to other car owners in the community.

There are two sources of this positive externality. First, the presence of the Lojack device sometimes enables police to intercept the car while the thief is still driving it. For example, in California the arrest rate for cars with Lojack was three times greater than that for cars without it. The arrest puts the car thief out of commission for a time and thus reduces subsequent car thefts in the community. Second, and far more important, the device enables police to trace cars to "chop shops," where crooks disassemble cars for resale of the parts. When police raid the chop shop, they put the entire theft ring out of business. In Los Angeles alone, Lojack has eliminated 45 chop shops in just a few years. The purging of the chop shop and theft ring reduces auto theft in the community. So auto owners who do not have Lojack devices in their cars benefit from car owners who do. Ayres and Levitt estimate the *marginal social benefit* of Lojack—the marginal benefit to the Lojack car owner *plus* the spillover benefit to other car owners—is 15 times greater than the marginal cost of the device.

We saw in Figure 16.4a that the existence of positive externalities causes an insufficient quantity of a product and thus an underallocation of scarce resources to its production. The two general ways to correct the outcome are to subsidize the consumer, as shown in Figure 16.4b, or to subsidize the producer, as shown in Figure 16.4c. Currently, there is only one form of government intervention in place: state-mandated insurance discounts for people who install auto retrieval systems such as Lojack. In effect, those discounts on insurance premiums subsidize the consumer by lowering the "price" of the system to consumers. The lower price raises the number of systems installed. But, on the basis of their research, Ayres and Levitt contend that the current levels of insurance discounts are far too small to correct the underallocation that results from the positive externalities created by Lojack.

Source: Based on Ian Ayres and Steven D. Levitt, "Measuring Positive Externalities from Unobservable Victim Precaution: An Empirical Analysis of Lojack," *Quarterly Journal of Economics*, February 1998, pp. 43–77. The authors point out that Lojack did not fund their work in any way, nor do they have any financial stake in Lojack.

overcome this problem. When you visit a Wendy's or a Marriott, you know what you are going to get, as opposed to stopping at Slim's Hamburger Shop or the Triple Six Motel.

Also, some private firms and organizations specialize in providing information to buyers and sellers. *Consumer Reports*, *Mobil Travel Guide*, and numerous Internet sites provide product information; labor unions collect and disseminate information about job safety; and credit bureaus provide information about credit histories and past bankruptcies to lending institutions and insurance companies. Brokers, bonding agencies, and intermediaries also provide information to clients.

Economists agree, however, that the private sector cannot remedy all information problems. In some situations, government intervention is desirable to promote an efficient allocation of society's scarce resources.

QUICK REVIEW 16.4

- Asymmetric information is a source of potential market failure, causing society's scarce resources to be allocated inefficiently.

- Inadequate information about sellers and their products may lead to an underallocation of resources to those products.

- The moral hazard problem is the tendency of one party to a contract or agreement to alter its behavior in ways that are costly to the other party; for example, a person who buys insurance may willingly incur added risk.

- The adverse selection problem arises when one party to a contract or agreement has less information than the other party and incurs a cost because of that asymmetrical information. For example, an insurance company offering "no-medical-exam-required" life insurance policies may attract customers who have life-threatening diseases.

Summary

1. Public goods are distinguished from private goods. Private goods are characterized by rivalry (in consumption) and excludability. One person's purchase and consumption of a private good precludes others from also buying and consuming it. Producers can exclude nonpayers (free riders) from receiving the benefits. In contrast, public goods are characterized by nonrivalry (in consumption) and nonexcludability. Public goods are not profitable to private firms because nonpayers (free riders) can obtain and consume those goods. Only government is willing to provide desirable public goods, financing them through taxation.

2. The collective demand schedule for a particular public good is found by summing the prices that each individual is willing to pay for an additional unit. Graphically, that demand curve is therefore found by summing vertically the individual demand curves for that good. The resulting total demand curve indicates the collective willingness to pay for (or marginal benefit of) the last unit of any given amount of the public good.

3. The optimal quantity of a public good occurs where the society's willingness to pay for the last unit—the marginal benefit of the good—equals the marginal cost of the good.

4. Externalities, or spillovers, are costs or benefits that accrue to someone other than the immediate buyer or seller. Such costs or benefits are not captured in market demand or supply curves and therefore cause the output of certain goods to vary from society's optimal output. Negative externalities (or spillover costs or external costs) result in an overallocation of resources to a particular product. Positive externalities (or spillover benefits or external benefits) are accompanied by an underallocaton of resources to a particular product.

5. The Coase theorem suggests that private bargaining is capable of solving potential externality problems where (a) the property rights are clearly defined, (b) the number of people involved is small, and (c) bargaining costs are negligible.

6. Clearly established property rights and liability rules permit some negative externalities to be prevented or remedied through private lawsuits. Lawsuits, however, can be costly, time-consuming, and uncertain as to their results.

7. Direct controls and specific taxes can improve resource allocation in situations where negative externalities affect many people and community resources. Both direct controls (for example, smokestack emission standards) and specific taxes (for example, taxes on firms producing toxic chemicals) increase production costs and hence product price. As product price rises, the externality and overallocation of resources are reduced since less of the output is bought and sold.

8. Government can correct the underallocation of resources that results from positive externalities in a particular market either by subsidizing consumers (which increases market demand) or by subsidizing producers (which increases market supply). Such subsidies increase the equilibrium output, reducing or eliminating the positive externality and consequent underallocation of resources.

9. Markets for pollution rights, where firms can buy and sell the right to discharge a fixed amount of pollution, put a price on pollution and encourage firms to reduce or eliminate it.

10. The socially optimal amount of externality abatement occurs where society's marginal cost and marginal benefit of reducing the externality are equal. This optimal amount of pollution abatement is likely to be less than a 100 percent reduction. Changes in technology or changes in society's attitudes toward pollution can affect the optimal amount of pollution abatement.

11. A growing body of scientific evidence suggests that accumulation of carbon dioxide and other greenhouse gases in the earth's atmosphere may be contributing to a climate-change problem. In addressing the problem, society needs to assess the costs and benefits of reducing greenhouse gases as well as the costs and benefits of allowing the emission to rise and then mitigating the effects. Two distinct policies for reducing greenhouse gases are (a) a carbon tax on such emissions and (b) a cap-and-trade system that places a lid on the emissions and allows for trading of the pollution rights.

12. Asymmetric information between sellers and buyers can cause markets to fail. The moral hazard problem occurs when people alter their behavior after they sign a contract or reach an agreement, imposing costs on the other party. The adverse selection problem occurs when one party to a contract or agreement takes advantage of the other party's inadequate information, resulting in an unanticipated loss to the latter party.

Terms and Concepts

private goods	externalities	optimal reduction of an externality
public goods	Coase theorem	climate-change problem
free-rider problem	tragedy of the commons	asymmetric information
cost-benefit analysis	market for externality rights	moral hazard problem
marginal-cost–marginal-benefit rule	cap-and-trade program	adverse selection problem

Study Questions  |ECONOMICS

1. **KEY QUESTION** On the basis of the three individual demand schedules below, and assuming these three people are the only ones in the society, determine (a) the market demand schedule on the assumption that the good is a private good and (b) the collective demand schedule on the assumption that the good is a public good. Explain the differences, if any, in your schedules. **LO1**

schedule to ascertain the optimal quantity of this public good. Why is this the optimal quantity? **LO2**

P	Q_d
$19	10
16	8
13	6
10	4
7	2
4	1

3. **KEY QUESTION** The following table shows the total costs and total benefits in billions for four different antipollution programs of increasing scope. Which program should be undertaken? Why? **LO3**

Program	Total Cost	Total Benefit
A	$ 3	$ 7
B	7	12
C	12	16
D	18	19

Individual 1		Individual 2		Individual 3	
P	Q_d	P	Q_d	P	Q_d
$8	0	$8	1	$8	0
7	0	7	2	7	0
6	0	6	3	6	1
5	1	5	4	5	2
4	2	4	5	4	3
3	3	3	6	3	4
2	4	2	7	2	5
1	5	1	8	1	6

2. **KEY QUESTION** Use your demand schedule for a public good, determined in question 1, and the following supply

4. **KEY QUESTION** Why are spillover costs and spillover benefits also called negative and positive externalities?

Show graphically how a tax can correct for a negative externality and how a subsidy to producers can correct for a positive externality. How does a subsidy to consumers differ from a subsidy to producers in correcting for a positive externality? **LO4**

5. An apple grower's orchard provides nectar to a neighbor's bees, while the beekeeper's bees help the apple grower by pollinating the apple blossoms. Use Figure 16.2b to explain why this situation of dual positive externalities might lead to an underallocation of resources to apple growing and to beekeeping. How might this underallocation get resolved via the means suggested by the Coase theorem? **LO4**

6. Explain: "Without a market for pollution rights, dumping pollutants into the air or water is costless; in the presence of the right to buy and sell pollution rights, dumping pollutants creates an opportunity cost for the polluter." What is the significance of this opportunity cost to the search for better technology to reduce pollution? **LO4**

7. **KEY QUESTION** Explain the following statement, using the MB curve in Figure 16.6 to illustrate: "The optimal amount of pollution abatement for some substances, say, water from storm drains, is very low; the optimal amount of abatement for other substances, say, cyanide poison, is close to 100 percent." **LO4**

8. Explain the tragedy of the commons, as it relates to pollution. **LO4**

9. What is the climate-change problem? Using an example other than one in the text, explain how climate-change might hurt one industry, particular region, or country but help another. Distinguish between a carbon-tax and a cap-and-trade strategy for reducing greenhouse gases. Which of the two strategies do you think would have the most political support in an election in your home state? Explain your thinking. **LO4**

10. Explain how marketable emission credits add to overall economic efficiency, compared to across-the-board limitations on maximum discharges of air pollutants by firms. **LO4**

11. Why is it in the interest of new homebuyers and builders of new homes to have government building codes and building inspectors? **LO5**

12. **KEY QUESTION** Place an "M" beside the items in the following list that describe a moral hazard problem and an "A" beside those that describe an adverse selection problem: **LO5**
   a. A person with a terminal illness buys several life insurance policies through the mail.
   b. A person drives carelessly because he or she has automobile insurance.
   c. A person who intends to "torch" his warehouse takes out a large fire insurance policy.
   d. A professional athlete who has a guaranteed contract fails to stay in shape during the off-season.
   e. A woman who anticipates having a large family takes a job with a firm that offers exceptional child care benefits.

13. **LAST WORD** Explain how a global-positioning antitheft device installed by one car owner can produce a positive spillover to thousands of others in a city.

Web-Based Questions

1. **GLOBAL WARMING—THE EPA'S VIEW** Go to www.epa.gov and select Climate Change. What are the major greenhouse gases? How much greenhouse gas does the United States emit per person? What is the trend of emissions on a per-person basis? What is the trend of emissions per dollar of GDP in the United States? Use your own analysis to explain how total emissions can rise even though emissions per dollar of GDP substantially decline. Which of the two is more relevant for climate change?

2. **WORKPLACE SAFETY—OSHA'S ROLE** Visit www.osha.gov and first select Workers (under Audiences). How does a worker file a complaint or report a hazard? Where is the nearest OSHA office to you? Go back to the OSHA home page and select News Releases. In a sentence or two each, summarize three recent news releases that relate to fines or other penalties imposed by OSHA on employers for violations of workers' safety and health rules.

FURTHER TEST YOUR KNOWLEDGE AT
www.mcconnell18e.com

17

IN THIS CHAPTER YOU WILL LEARN:

1 The difficulties of conveying economic preferences through majority voting.

2 About "government failure" and why it occurs.

3 The different tax philosophies and ways to distribute a nation's tax burden.

4 The principles relating to tax shifting, tax incidence, and efficiency losses from taxes.

Public Choice Theory and the Economics of Taxation

In Chapter 16 we saw that private markets can occasionally produce *market failures,* which impede economic efficiency and justify government intervention in the economy. But the government's response to market failures is not without its own problems and pitfalls. Perhaps that is why government policies and decisions are the focus of hundreds of radio talk shows, television debates, and newspaper articles each day.

In this chapter, we explore a number of *government failures* that impede economic efficiency in the public sector. Our spotlight is first on selected aspects of **public choice theory**—the economic analysis of government decision making, politics, and elections — and then on the economics of taxation.

ORIGIN OF THE IDEA

O 17.1

Public choice theory

Revealing Preferences through Majority Voting

Through some process, society must decide which public goods and services it wants and in what amounts. It also must determine the extent to which it wants government to intervene in private markets to correct externalities. Decisions need to be made about the extent and type of regulation of business that is necessary, the amount of income redistribution that is desirable, and other such choices. Furthermore, society must determine the set of taxes it thinks is best for financing government. How should government apportion (divide) the total tax burden among the public?

Decisions such as these are made collectively in the United States through a democratic process that relies heavily on majority voting. Candidates for office offer alternative policy packages, and citizens elect people who they think will make the best decisions on their collective behalf. Voters "retire" officials who do not adequately represent their collective wishes and elect persons they think do. Also, citizens periodically have opportunities at the state and local levels to vote directly on public expenditures or new legislation.

Although the democratic process does a reasonably good job of revealing society's preferences, it is imperfect. Public choice theory demonstrates that majority voting can produce inefficiencies and inconsistencies.

Inefficient Voting Outcomes

Society's well-being is enhanced when government provides a public good whose total benefit exceeds its total cost. Unfortunately, majority voting does not always deliver that outcome.

Illustration: Inefficient "No" Vote Assume that the government can provide a public good, say, national defense, at a total expense of $900. Also assume that there are only three individuals—Adams, Benson, and Conrad—in the society and that they will share the $900 tax expense equally, each being taxed $300 if the proposed public good is provided. And assume, as Figure 17.1a illustrates, that Adams would receive $700 worth of benefits from having this public good; Benson, $250; and Conrad, $200.

What will be the result if a majority vote determines whether or not this public good is provided? Although people do not always vote strictly according to their own economic interest, it is likely Benson and Conrad will vote "no" because they will incur tax costs of $300 each while gaining benefits of only $250 and $200, respectively. Adams will vote "yes." So the majority vote will defeat the proposal even though the total benefit of $1150 (= $700 for Adams + $250 for Benson + $200 for Conrad) exceeds the total cost of $900. Resources should be devoted to this good, but they will not be. Too little of this public good will be produced.

Illustration: Inefficient "Yes" Vote Now consider a situation in which the majority favors a public good even though its total cost exceeds its total benefit. Figure 17.1b shows the details. Again, Adams, Benson, and Conrad will equally share the $900 cost of the public good; each will be taxed $300. But since Adams' benefit now is only $100 from the public good, she will vote against it. Meanwhile, Benson and Conrad will benefit by $350 each. They will vote for the public good because that benefit ($350) exceeds their tax payments ($300). The majority vote will provide a public good costing $900 that produces total benefits of only $800 (= $100 for Adams + $350 for Benson + $350

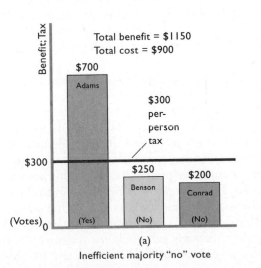

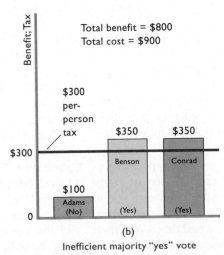

FIGURE 17.1 **Inefficient voting outcomes.** Majority voting can produce inefficient decisions. (a) Majority voting leads to rejection of a public good that would entail a greater total benefit than total cost. (b) Majority voting results in acceptance of a public good that has a higher total cost than total benefit.

(a)

Inefficient majority "no" vote

(b)

Inefficient majority "yes" vote

for Conrad). Society's resources will be inefficiently allocated to this public good. Too much of it will be produced.

Implications The point is that an inefficient outcome may occur as either an overproduction or an underproduction of a specific public good, and therefore as an overallocation or underallocation of resources for that particular use. In Chapter 16 we saw that government can improve economic efficiency by providing public goods that the market system will not make available. Now we have extended that analysis to reveal that government might fail to provide some public goods whose production is economically justifiable while providing other goods that are not economically warranted.

In our examples, each person has only a single vote, no matter how much he or she might gain or lose from a public good. In the first example (inefficient "no" vote), Adams would be willing to purchase a vote from either Benson or Conrad if buying votes were legal. That way Adams could be assured of obtaining the national defense she so highly values. But since buying votes is illegal, many people with strong preferences for certain public goods may have to go without them.

When individual consumers have a strong preference for a specific *private good*, they usually can find that good in the marketplace even though it may be unpopular with the majority of consumers. A consumer can buy beef tongue or liver and squid in some supermarkets, although it is doubtful that these products would be available if majority voting stocked the shelves. But a person cannot easily "buy" a *public good* such as national defense once the majority has decided against it.

Conversely, a consumer in the marketplace can decide against buying a particular product, even a popular one. But although you may not want national defense, you must "buy" it through your tax payments when the majority have decided they want it.

Conclusion: Because majority voting fails to incorporate the *strength* of the preferences of the individual voter, it may produce economically inefficient outcomes.

Interest Groups and Logrolling
Some, but not all, of the inefficiencies of majority voting get resolved through the political process. Two examples follow.

Interest Groups People who share strong preferences for a public good may band together into interest groups and use advertisements, mailings, and direct persuasion to convince others of the merits of that public good. Adams might try to persuade Benson and Conrad that it is in their best interest to vote for national defense—that national

defense is much more valuable to them than their $250 and $200 valuations. Such appeals are common in democratic politics. Sometimes they are successful; sometimes they are not.

Political Logrolling Perhaps surprisingly, **logrolling**—the trading of votes to secure favorable outcomes—can also turn an inefficient outcome into an efficient one. In our first example (Figure 17.1a), suppose that Benson has a strong preference for a different public good, for example, a new road, which Adams and Conrad do not think is worth the tax expense. That would provide an opportunity for Adams and Benson to trade votes to ensure provision of both national defense and the new road. That is, Adams and Benson would each vote "yes" on both measures. Adams would get the national defense and Benson would get the road. Without the logrolling, both public goods would have been rejected. This logrolling will add to society's well-being if, as was true for national defense, the road creates a greater overall benefit than cost.

But logrolling need not increase economic efficiency. Even if national defense and the road each costs more than the total benefit each produces, both might still be provided because of the vote trading. Adams and Benson might still engage in logrolling if each expects to secure a sufficient net gain from her or his favored public good, even though the gains would come at the clear expense of Conrad.

Logrolling is very common in state legislatures and Congress. It can either increase or diminish economic efficiency, depending on the circumstances.

Paradox of Voting

ORIGIN OF THE IDEA
O 17.1
Paradox of voting

Another difficulty with majority voting is the **paradox of voting**, a situation in which society may not be able to rank its preferences consistently through paired-choice majority voting.

Preferences Consider Table 17.1, in which we again assume a community of three voters: Adams, Benson, and Conrad. Suppose the community has three alternative public goods from which to choose: national defense, a road, and a weather warning system. We expect that each member of the community prefers the three alternatives in a certain order. For example, one person might prefer national defense to a road and a road to a weather warning system. We can attempt to determine the preferences of the community through paired-choice majority voting. Specifically, a vote can be held between any two of

TABLE 17.1 Paradox of Voting

Public Good	Preferences		
	Adams	**Benson**	**Conrad**
National defense	1st choice	3d choice	2d choice
Road	2d choice	1st choice	3d choice
Weather warning system	3d choice	2d choice	1st choice
Election	**Voting Outcomes: Winner**		
1. National defense vs. road	National defense (preferred by Adams and Conrad)		
2. Road vs. weather warning system	Road (preferred by Adams and Benson)		
3. National defense vs. weather warning system	Weather warning system (preferred by Benson and Conrad)		

the public goods, and the winner of that vote can then be matched against the third public good in another vote.

The three goods and the assumed individual preferences of the three voters are listed in the top part of Table 17.1. The data indicate that Adams prefers national defense to the road and the road to the weather warning system. This implies also that Adams prefers national defense to the weather warning system. Benson values the road more than the weather warning system and the warning system more than national defense. Conrad's order of preference is weather warning system, national defense, and road.

Voting Outcomes

The lower part of Table 17.1 shows the outcomes of three hypothetical elections decided through majority vote. In the first, national defense wins against the road because a majority of voters (Adams and Conrad) prefer national defense to the road. In the second election, to see whether this community wants a road or a weather warning system, a majority of voters (Adams and Benson) prefer the road.

We have determined that the majority of people in this community prefer national defense to a road and prefer a road to a weather warning system. It seems logical to conclude that the community prefers national defense to a weather warning system. But it does not!

To demonstrate this conclusion, we hold a direct election between national defense and the weather warning system. Row 3 shows that a majority of voters (Benson and Conrad) prefer the weather warning system to national defense. As listed in Table 17.1, then, the three paired-choice majority votes imply that this community is irrational: It seems to prefer national defense to a road and a

road to a weather warning system, but would rather have a weather warning system than national defense.

The problem is not irrational community preferences but rather a flawed procedure for determining those preferences. We see that the outcome from paired-choice majority voting may depend on the order in which the votes are taken up. Under some circumstances majority voting fails to make consistent choices that reflect the community's underlying preferences. As a consequence, government may find it difficult to provide the "correct" public goods by acting in accordance with majority voting. Important note: This critique is not meant to suggest that some better procedure exists. Majority voting is much more likely to reflect community preferences than decisions by, say, a dictator or a group of self-appointed leaders. **(Key Question 2)**

Median-Voter Model

One other aspect of majority voting reveals further insights into real-world phenomena. The **median-voter model** suggests that, under majority rule and consistent voting preferences, the median voter will in a sense determine the outcomes of elections. The median voter is the person holding the middle position on an issue: Half the other voters have stronger preferences for a public good, amount of taxation, or degree of government regulation, and half have weaker or negative preferences. The extreme voters on each side of an issue prefer the median choice rather than the other extreme position, so the median voter's choice predominates.

Example Suppose a society composed of Adams, Benson, and Conrad has reached agreement that as a society it needs a weather warning system. Each person independently is to submit a total dollar amount he or she thinks should be spent on the warning system, assuming each will be taxed one-third of that amount. An election will determine the size of the system. Because each person can be expected to vote for his or her own proposal, no majority will occur if all the proposals are placed on the ballot at the same time. Thus, the group decides on a paired-choice vote: They will first vote between two of the proposals and then match the winner of that vote against the remaining proposal.

The three proposals are as follows: Adams desires a $400 system; Benson wants an $800 system; Conrad opts for a $300 system. Which proposal will win? The median-voter model suggests it will be the $400 proposal submitted by the median voter, Adams. Half the other voters favor a more costly system; half favor a less costly system. To understand why the $400 system will be the outcome, let's conduct the two elections.

First, suppose that the $400 proposal is matched against the $800 proposal. Adams naturally votes for her $400 proposal, and Benson votes for his own $800 proposal. Conrad, who proposed the $300 expenditure for the warning system, votes for the $400 proposal because it is closer to his own. So Adams' $400 proposal is selected by a 2-to-1 majority vote.

Next, we match the $400 proposal against the $300 proposal. Again the $400 proposal wins. It gets a vote from Adams and one from Benson, who proposed the $800 expenditure and for that reason prefers a $400 expenditure to a $300 one. Adams, the median voter in this case, is in a sense the person who has decided the level of expenditure on a weather warning system for this society.

Real-World Applicability Although our illustration is simple, it explains a great deal. We do note a tendency for public choices to match most closely the median view. Political candidates, for example, take one set of positions to win the nomination of their political party; in so doing, they tend to appeal to the median voter within the party to get the nomination. They then shift their views more closely to the political center when they square off against opponents from the opposite political party. In effect, they redirect their appeal toward the median voter within the total population. They also try to label their opponents as being too liberal, or too conservative, and out of touch with "mainstream America." And they conduct polls and adjust their positions on issues accordingly.

Implications The median-voter model has two important implications:

- At any point in time, many people will be dissatisfied by the extent of government involvement in the economy. The size of government will largely be determined by the median preference, leaving many people desiring a much larger, or a much smaller, public sector. In the marketplace you can buy no zucchinis, 2 zucchinis, or 200 zucchinis, depending on how much you enjoy them. In the public sector you get the number of Stealth bombers and new highway projects the median voter prefers.

- Some people may "vote with their feet" by moving into political jurisdictions where the median voter's preferences are closer to their own. They may move from the city to a suburb where the level of government services, and therefore taxes, is lower. Or they may move into an area known for its excellent, but expensive, school system. Some may move to other states; a few may even move to other countries.

For these reasons, and because our personal preferences for publicly provided goods and services are not static, the median preference shifts over time. Moreover, information about people's preferences is imperfect, leaving much room for politicians to misjudge the true median position. When they do, they may have a difficult time getting elected or reelected. (**Key Question 3**)

Government Failure

As implied in our discussion of voting problems, government does not always perform its economic functions effectively and efficiently. In fact, public choice theory suggests that inherent shortcomings within the public sector can produce inefficient outcomes. Such shortcomings may result in **government failure**—inefficiency due to certain characteristics of the public sector. Let's consider some of these characteristics and outcomes.

Special Interests and Rent Seeking

Casual reflection suggests that "sound economics" and "good politics" are not always one and the same. Sound economics calls for the public sector to pursue various programs as long as marginal benefits exceed marginal costs. Good politics, however, suggests that politicians support programs and policies that will maximize their chance of getting elected and staying in office. The result may be that the government will promote the goals of groups of voters that have special interests to the detriment of the larger public. In the process, economic inefficiency may result.

Special-Interest Effect Efficient public decision making is often impaired by the **special-interest effect.** This is any outcome of the political process whereby a small number of people obtain a government program or policy that gives them large gains at the expense of a much greater number of persons who individually suffer small losses.

The small group of potential beneficiaries is well informed and highly vocal on the issue in question, and they press politicians for approval. The large number of people facing the very small individual losses, however, are generally uninformed on the issue. Politicians feel they will lose the campaign contributions and votes of the small special-interest group that backs the issue if they legislate against it but will lose very little support of the large group of uninformed voters, who are likely to evaluate the politicians on other issues of greater importance to them.

The special-interest effect is also evident in so-called *pork-barrel politics*, a means of securing a government project that yields benefits mainly to a single political district and its political representative. In this case, the special-interest group comprises local constituents, while the larger group consists of relatively uninformed taxpayers scattered across a much larger geographic area. Politicians clearly have a strong incentive to secure public goods ("pork") for their local constituents. Such goods win political favor because they are highly valued by constituents and the costs are borne mainly by taxpayers located elsewhere.

At the Federal level, pork-barrel politics often consists of congressional members inserting provisions in comprehensive legislation that authorize spending for specific home-state projects. Such narrow, specifically designated authorizations of expenditure are called **earmarks**. In 2007, legislation contained 11,700 such earmarks totalling $16.9 billion. These earmarks enable senators and representatives to provide benefits to in-state firms and organizations without subjecting the proposals to the usual evaluation and competitive bidding. Although some of the earmarked projects deliver benefits that exceed costs, many others are questionable, at best. These latter expenditures very likely reallocate some of society's scarce resources from higher-valued uses to lower-valued uses. Moreover, logrolling typically enters the picture. "Vote for my special local project and I will vote for yours" becomes part of the overall strategy for securing "pork" and remaining elected.

Finally, a politician's inclination to support the smaller group of special beneficiaries is enhanced because special-interest groups are often quite willing to help finance the campaigns of "right-minded" politicians and politicians who "bring home the pork." The result is that politicians may support special-interest programs and projects that cannot be justified on economic grounds.

Rent-Seeking Behavior The appeal to government for special benefits at taxpayers' or someone else's expense is called **rent seeking.** To economists, "rent" is a payment beyond the amount necessary to keep a resource supplied in its current use. Corporations, trade associations, labor unions, and professional organizations employ vast resources to secure favorable government policies that result in rent—higher profit or income than would occur under competitive market conditions. The government is able to dispense such rent directly or indirectly through laws, rules, hiring, and purchases. Elected officials are willing to provide such rent because they want to be responsive to key constituents, who in turn help them remain in office.

Here are some examples of "rent-providing" legislation or policies: tariffs on foreign products that limit competition and raise prices to consumers; tax breaks that benefit specific corporations; government construction projects that create union jobs but cost more than the benefits they yield; occupational licensing that goes beyond what is needed to protect consumers; and large subsidies to farmers by taxpayers. None of these is justified by economic efficiency.

Clear Benefits, Hidden Costs

Some critics say that vote-seeking politicians will not weigh objectively all the costs and benefits of various programs, as economic rationality demands in deciding which to support and which to reject. Because political officeholders must seek voter support every few years, they favor programs that have immediate and clear-cut benefits and vague or deferred costs. Conversely, politicians will reject programs with immediate and easily identifiable costs but with less measurable but very high long-term benefits.

Such biases may lead politicians to reject economically justifiable programs and to accept programs that are economically irrational. Example: A proposal to construct or expand mass-transit systems in large metropolitan areas may be economically rational on the basis of cost-benefit analysis. But if (1) the program is to be financed by immediate increases in highly visible income or sales taxes and (2) benefits will occur only years from now when the project is completed, then the vote-seeking politician may oppose the program.

Assume, on the other hand, that a program of Federal aid to municipal police forces is not justifiable on the basis of cost-benefit analysis. But if the cost is paid for from budget surpluses, the program's modest benefits may seem so large that it will gain approval.

Limited and Bundled Choice

Public choice theorists point out that the political process forces citizens and their elected representatives to be less selective in choosing public goods and services than they are in choosing private goods and services.

In the marketplace, the citizen as a consumer can exactly satisfy personal preferences by buying certain goods and not buying others. However, in the public sector the citizen as a voter is confronted with, say, only two or three candidates for an office, each representing a different "bundle" of programs (public goods and services). None of these bundles of public goods is likely to fit exactly the preferences of any particular voter. Yet the voter must choose one of them. The candidate who comes closest to voter Smith's preference may endorse national health insurance, increases in Social Security benefits, subsidies to tobacco farmers, and tariffs on imported goods. Smith is likely to vote for that candidate even though Smith strongly opposes tobacco subsidies.

In other words, the voter must take the bad with the good. In the public sector, people are forced to "buy" goods and services they do not want. It is as if, in going to a sporting-goods store, you were forced to buy an unwanted pool cue to get a wanted pair of running shoes. This is a situation where resources are not being used efficiently to satisfy consumer wants. In this sense, the provision of public goods and services is inherently inefficient.

Congress is confronted with a similar limited-choice, bundled-goods problem. Appropriations legislation combines hundreds, even thousands, of spending items into a single bill. Many of these spending items may be completely unrelated to the main purpose of the legislation. Yet congressional representatives must vote the entire package—yea or nay. Unlike consumers in the marketplace, they cannot be selective. **(Key Question 4)**

Bureaucracy and Inefficiency

Some economists contend that public agencies are generally less efficient than private businesses. The reason is not that lazy and incompetent workers somehow end up in the public sector while ambitious and capable people gravitate to the private sector. Rather, it is that the market system creates incentives and pressures for internal efficiency that are absent from the public sector. Private enterprises have a clear goal—profit. Whether a private firm is in a competitive or monopolistic market, efficient management means lower costs and higher profit. The higher profit not only benefits the firm's owners but enhances the promotion prospects of managers. Moreover, part of the managers' pay may be tied to profit via profit-sharing plans, bonuses, and stock options. There is no similar gain to government agencies and their managers—no counterpart to profit—to create a strong incentive to achieve efficiency.

The market system imposes a very obvious test of performance on private firms: the test of profit and loss. An efficient firm is profitable and therefore successful; it survives, prospers, and grows. An inefficient firm is unprofitable and unsuccessful; it declines and in time goes out of business. But there is no similar, clear-cut test with which to assess the efficiency or inefficiency of public agencies. How can anyone determine whether a public hydroelectricity provider, a state university, a local fire department, the Department of Agriculture, or the Bureau of Indian Affairs is operating efficiently?

Cynics even argue that a public agency that inefficiently uses its resources is likely to survive and grow! In the private sector, inefficiency and monetary loss lead to the abandonment of certain activities or products or even firms. But the government, they say, does not like to abandon activities in which it has failed. Some suggest that the typical response of the government to a program's failure is to increase its budget and staff. This means that public sector inefficiency just continues on a larger scale.

Furthermore, economists assert that government employees, together with the special-interest groups they serve, often gain sufficient political clout to block attempts to pare down or eliminate their agencies. Politicians who attempt to reduce the size of huge Federal bureaucracies such as those relating to agriculture, education, health and welfare, and national defense incur sizable political risk because bureaucrats and special-interest groups will team up to defeat them.

Finally, critics point out that government bureaucrats tend to justify their continued employment by looking for and eventually finding new problems to solve. It is not surprising that social "problems," as defined by government, persist or even expand.

The Last Word at the end of this chapter highlights several recent media-reported examples of the special-interest effect (including earmarks), the problem of limited and bundled choices, and problems of government bureaucracy.

Imperfect Institutions

It is possible to argue that such criticisms of public sector inefficiency are exaggerated and cynical. Perhaps they are. Nevertheless, they do tend to shatter the concept of a benevolent government that responds with precision and efficiency to the wants of its citizens. The market system of the private sector is far from perfectly efficient, and government's economic function is mainly to correct that system's shortcomings. But the public sector too is subject to deficiencies in fulfilling its economic function. "The relevant comparison is not between perfect markets and imperfect governments, nor between faulty markets and all-knowing, rational, benevolent governments, but between inevitably imperfect institutions."[1]

Because the market system and public agencies are both imperfect, it is sometimes difficult to determine whether a particular activity can be performed with greater success in the private sector or in the public sector. It is easy to reach agreement on opposite extremes: National defense must lie with the public sector, while automobile production can best be accomplished by the private sector. But what about health insurance? Parks and recreation areas? Fire protection? Garbage collection? Housing? Education? It is hard to assess every good or service and to say absolutely that it should

[1]Otto Eckstein, *Public Finance*, 3d ed. (Englewood Cliffs, N.J.: Prentice-Hall, 1973), p. 17.

be assigned to either the public sector or the private sector. Evidence: All the goods and services just mentioned are provided in part by *both* private enterprises and public agencies.

QUICK REVIEW 17.1

- Majority voting can produce voting outcomes that are inefficient; projects having greater total benefits than total costs may be defeated, and projects having greater total costs than total benefits may be approved.
- The paradox of voting occurs when voting by majority rule does not provide a consistent ranking of society's preferences for public goods and services.
- The median-voter model suggests that under majority rule and consistent voting preferences, the voter who has the middle preference will determine the outcome of an election.
- Government failure allegedly occurs as a result of rent seeking, pressure by special-interest groups, shortsighted political behavior, limited and bundled choices, and bureaucratic inefficiency.

Apportioning the Tax Burden

We now turn from the difficulties of making collective decisions about public goods to the difficulties of deciding how those goods should be financed.

It is difficult to measure precisely how the benefits of public goods are apportioned among individuals and institutions. We cannot accurately determine how much citizen Mildred Moore benefits from military installations, a network of highways, a public school system, the national weather bureau, and local police and fire protection.

The situation is different when it comes to paying for those benefits. Studies reveal with reasonable clarity how the overall tax burden is apportioned. (By "tax burden" we mean the total cost of taxes imposed on society.) This apportionment question affects each of us. The overall level of taxes is important, but the average citizen is much more concerned with his or her part of the overall tax burden.

Benefits Received versus Ability to Pay

Two basic philosophies coexist on how the economy's tax burden should be apportioned.

Benefits-Received Principle
The **benefits-received principle** of taxation asserts that households and businesses should purchase the goods and services of government in the same way they buy other commodities.

Those who benefit most from government-supplied goods or services should pay the taxes necessary to finance them. A few public goods are now financed on this basis. For example, money collected as gasoline taxes is typically used to finance highway construction and repairs. Thus people who benefit from good roads pay the cost of those roads. Difficulties immediately arise, however, when we consider widespread application of the benefits-received principle:

- How will the government determine the benefits that individual households and businesses receive from national defense, education, the court system, and police and fire protection? Recall that public goods are characterized by nonrivalry and nonexcludability. So benefits from public goods are especially widespread and diffuse. Even in the seemingly straightforward case of highway financing it is difficult to measure benefits. Good roads benefit owners of cars in different degrees. But others also benefit. For example, businesses benefit because good roads bring them workers and customers.
- The benefits-received principle cannot logically be applied to income redistribution programs. It would be absurd and self-defeating to ask poor families to pay the taxes needed to finance their welfare payments. It would be ridiculous to think of taxing only unemployed workers to finance the unemployment compensation payments they receive.

Ability-to-Pay Principle
The **ability-to-pay principle** of taxation asserts that the tax burden should be apportioned according to taxpayers' income and wealth. In the United States this means that individuals and businesses with larger incomes should pay more taxes in both absolute and relative terms than those with smaller incomes.

In justifying the ability-to-pay principle, proponents contend that each additional dollar of income received by a household yields a smaller amount of satisfaction or marginal utility when it is spent. Because consumers act rationally, the first dollars of income received in any time period will be spent on high-urgency goods that yield the greatest marginal utility. Successive dollars of income will go for less urgently needed goods and finally for trivial goods and services. This means that a dollar taken through taxes from a poor person who has few dollars represents a greater utility sacrifice than a dollar taken through taxes from a rich person who has many dollars. To balance the sacrifices that taxes impose on income receivers, taxes should be apportioned according to the amount of income a taxpayer receives.

This argument is appealing, but application problems arise here too. Although we might agree that the household earning $100,000 per year has a greater ability to pay taxes than a household receiving $10,000, we don't know exactly how much more ability to pay the first family has. Should the wealthier family pay the *same* percentage of its larger income, and hence a larger absolute amount, as taxes? Or should it be made to pay a *larger* fraction of its income as taxes? And how much larger should that fraction be? Who is to decide?

There is no scientific way of making utility comparisons among individuals and thus of measuring someone's relative ability to pay taxes. That is the main problem. In practice, the solution hinges on guesswork, the tax views of the political party in power, expediency, and how urgently the government needs revenue.

Progressive, Proportional, and Regressive Taxes

Any discussion of taxation leads ultimately to the question of tax rates. In Chapter 4 we noted that an *average tax rate* is the total tax paid divided by some base against which the tax is compared.

Definitions Taxes are classified as progressive, proportional, or regressive, depending on the relationship between average tax rates and taxpayer incomes. We focus on incomes because all taxes—whether on income, a product, a building, or a parcel of land—are ultimately paid out of someone's income.

- A tax is **progressive** if its average rate increases as income increases. Such a tax claims not only a larger absolute (dollar) amount but also a larger percentage of income as income increases.

- A tax is **regressive** if its average rate declines as income increases. Such a tax takes a smaller proportion of income as income increases. A regressive tax may or may not take a larger absolute amount of income as income increases. (You may want to derive an example to substantiate this conclusion.)

- A tax is **proportional** if its average rate *remains the same* regardless of the size of income.

We can illustrate these ideas with the personal income tax. Suppose tax rates are such that a household pays 10 percent of its income in taxes regardless of the size of its income. This is a *proportional* income tax. Now suppose the rate structure is such that a household with an annual taxable income of less than $10,000 pays 5 percent in income taxes; a household with an income of $10,000 to $20,000 pays 10 percent; one with a $20,000 to $30,000 income pays 15 percent; and so forth. This is a *progressive* income tax. Finally, suppose the rate declines as taxable income rises: You pay 15 percent if you earn less than $10,000; 10 percent if you earn $10,000 to $20,000; 5 percent if you earn $20,000 to $30,000; and so forth. This is a *regressive* income tax.

In general, progressive taxes are those that fall relatively more heavily on people with high incomes; regressive taxes are those that fall relatively more heavily on the poor. **(Key Question 7)**

Applications
Let's examine the progressivity, or regressivity, of several taxes.

Personal Income Tax We noted in Chapter 4 that the Federal personal income tax is progressive, with marginal tax rates (those assessed on additional income) ranging from 10 to 35 percent in 2008. Rules that allow individuals to deduct from income interest on home mortgages and property taxes and that exempt interest on state and local bonds from taxation tend to make the tax less progressive than these marginal rates suggest. Nevertheless, average tax rates rise with income.

Sales Taxes At first thought, a general sales tax with, for example, a 5 percent rate would seem to be proportional. But in fact it is regressive with respect to income. A larger portion of a low-income person's income is exposed to the tax than is the case for a high-income person; the rich pay no tax on the part of income that is saved, whereas the poor are unable to save. Example: "Low-income" Smith has an income of $15,000 and spends it all. "High-income" Jones has an income of $300,000 but spends only $200,000 and saves the rest. Assuming a 5 percent sales tax applies to all expenditures of each individual, we find that Smith pays $750 (5 percent of $15,000) in sales taxes and Jones pays $10,000 (5 percent of $200,000). But Smith pays $750/$15,000, or 5 percent of income, as sales taxes, while Jones pays $10,000/$300,000, or 3.3 percent of income. The general sales tax therefore is regressive.

Corporate Income Tax The Federal corporate income tax is essentially a proportional tax with a flat 35 percent tax rate. In the short run, the corporate owners (shareholders) bear the tax through lower dividends and share values. In the long run, workers may bear some of the tax since it reduces the return on investment and therefore slows capital accumulation. It also causes corporations to relocate to other countries that have lower tax rates. With less capital per worker, U.S. labor productivity may decline and wages may fall. To the extent this happens, the corporate income tax may be somewhat regressive.

Payroll Taxes Taxes levied on payrolls (Social Security and Medicare) are regressive because the Social Security tax applies to only a fixed amount of income. For example, in 2008 the Social Security tax rate was 6.2 percent, but only on the first $102,000 of a person's wage income. The Medicare tax was 1.45 percent of all wage income. Someone earning exactly $102,000 would pay $7803, or 7.65 percent (= 6.2 percent + 1.45 percent) of his or her income. Someone with twice that wage income, or $204,000, would pay $9282 (= $7803 on the first $102,000 + $1479 on the second $102,000), which is only 4.6 percent of his or her wage income. So the average payroll tax falls as income rises, confirming that the payroll tax is regressive.

Moreover, government does not collect payroll taxes on nonwage income (such as interest, dividends, or rents). High-income persons tend to derive a higher percentage of total income from nonwage sources than do people who have incomes below the $102,000 maximum on which social security taxes are paid. This makes payroll taxes even more regressive. If our individual with the $204,000 of wage income also received $204,000 of nonwage income, the $9282 of payroll tax would be only 2.3 percent of his or her total $408,000 income.

Property Taxes Most economists conclude that property taxes on buildings are regressive for the same reasons as are sales taxes. First, property owners add the tax to the rents that tenants are charged. Second, property taxes, as a percentage of income, are higher for low-income families than for high-income families because the poor must spend a larger proportion of their incomes for housing. This alleged regressivity of property taxes may be increased by differences in property-tax rates from locality to locality. In general, property-tax rates are higher in poorer areas, to make up for lower property values.

Tax Incidence and Efficiency Loss

Determining whether a particular tax is progressive, proportional, or regressive is complicated because those on whom taxes are levied do not always pay the taxes. We therefore need to try to locate the final resting place of a tax, or the **tax incidence.** The tools of elasticity of supply and demand will help. Let's focus on a hypothetical excise tax levied on wine producers. Do the producers really pay this tax, or do they shift it to wine consumers?

Elasticity and Tax Incidence

In Figure 17.2, S and D represent the pretax market for a certain domestic wine; the no-tax equilibrium price and quantity are $8 per bottle and 15 million bottles. Suppose that government levies an excise tax of $2 per bottle at the winery. Who will actually pay this tax?

FIGURE 17.2 The incidence of an excise tax. An excise tax of a specified amount, here $2 per unit, shifts the supply curve upward by the amount of the tax per unit: the vertical distance between S and S_t. This results in a higher price (here $9) to consumers and a lower after-tax price (here $7) to producers. Thus consumers and producers share the burden of the tax in some proportion (here equally at $1 per unit).

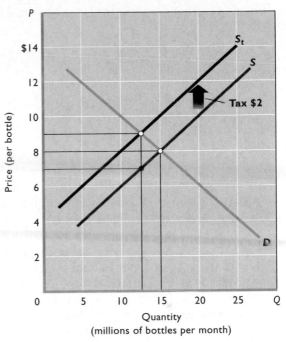

Quantity
(millions of bottles per month)

Division of Burden Since the government imposes the tax on the sellers (suppliers), we can view the tax as an addition to the marginal cost of the product. Now sellers must get $2 more for each bottle to receive the same per-unit profit they were getting before the tax. While sellers are willing to offer, for example, 5 million bottles of untaxed wine at $4 per bottle, they must now receive $6 per bottle (= $4 + $2 tax) to offer the same 5 million bottles. The tax shifts the supply curve upward (leftward) as shown in Figure 17.2, where S_t is the "after-tax" supply curve.

The after-tax equilibrium price is $9 per bottle, whereas the before-tax equilibrium price was $8. So, in this case, consumers pay half the $2 tax as a higher price; producers pay the other half in the form of a lower after-tax per-unit revenue. That is, after remitting the $2 tax per unit to government, producers receive $7, or $1 less than the $8 before-tax price. So, in this case, consumers and producers share the burden of the tax equally: Producers shift half the tax to consumers in the form of a higher price and bear the other half themselves.

INTERACTIVE GRAPHS

G 17.1

Tax incidence

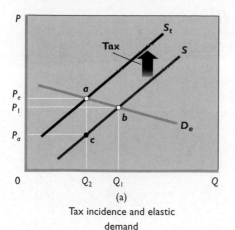

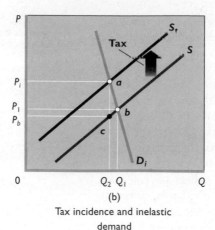

FIGURE 17.3 Demand elasticity and the incidence of an excise tax. (a) If demand is elastic in the relevant price range, price rises modestly (P_1 to P_e) when an excise tax is levied. Hence, the producers bear most of the tax burden. (b) If demand is inelastic, the price increases substantially (P_1 to P_i) and most of the tax is shifted to consumers.

(a) Tax incidence and elastic demand

(b) Tax incidence and inelastic demand

Note also that the equilibrium quantity declines because of the tax levy and the higher price that it imposes on consumers. In Figure 17.2 that decline in quantity is from 15 million bottles to 12.5 million bottles per month.

Elasticities If the elasticities of demand and supply were different from those shown in Figure 17.2, the incidence of tax would also be different. Two generalizations are relevant.

With a specific supply, the more inelastic the demand for the product, the larger is the portion of the tax shifted to consumers. To verify this, sketch graphically the extreme cases in which demand is perfectly elastic and perfectly inelastic. In the first case, the incidence of the tax is entirely on sellers; in the second, the tax is shifted entirely to consumers.

Figure 17.3 contrasts the more usual cases where demand is either relatively elastic or relatively inelastic in the relevant price range. With elastic demand (Figure 17.3a), a small portion of the tax ($P_e - P_1$) is shifted to consumers and

most of the tax ($P_1 - P_a$) is borne by the producers. With inelastic demand (Figure 17.3b), most of the tax ($P_i - P_1$) is shifted to consumers and only a small amount ($P_1 - P_b$) is paid by producers. In both graphs the per-unit tax is represented by the vertical distance between S_t and S.

Note also that the decline in equilibrium quantity ($Q_1 - Q_2$) is smaller when demand is more inelastic. This is the basis of our previous applications of the elasticity concept: Revenue-seeking legislatures place heavy excise taxes on liquor, cigarettes, automobile tires, telephone service, and other products whose demand is thought to be inelastic. Since demand for these products is relatively inelastic, the tax does not reduce sales by much, so the tax revenue stays high.

The second generalization is that, with a specific demand, the more inelastic the supply, the larger is the portion of the tax borne by producers. When supply is elastic (Figure 17.4a), the producers shift most of the tax ($P_e - P_1$) to consumers and bear only a small portion ($P_1 - P_a$)

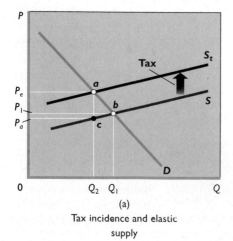

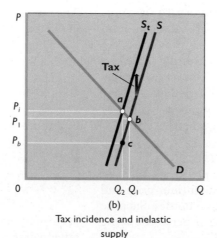

FIGURE 17.4 Supply elasticity and the incidence of an excise tax. (a) With elastic supply, an excise tax results in a large price increase (P_1 to P_e) and the tax is therefore paid mainly by consumers. (b) If supply is inelastic, the price rise is small (P_1 to P_i) and sellers bear most of the tax.

(a) Tax incidence and elastic supply

(b) Tax incidence and inelastic supply

themselves. But where supply is inelastic (Figure 17.4b), the reverse is true. The major portion of the tax $(P_1 - P_h)$ falls on sellers, and a relatively small amount $(P_i - P_1)$ is shifted to buyers. The equilibrium quantity also declines less with an inelastic supply than it does with an elastic supply.

Gold is an example of a product with an inelastic supply and therefore one where the burden of an excise tax (such as an extraction tax) would mainly fall on producers. On the other hand, because the supply of baseballs is relatively elastic, producers would pass on to consumers much of an excise tax on baseballs.

Efficiency Loss of a Tax

We just observed that producers and consumers typically each bear part of an excise tax levied on producers. Let's now look more closely at the overall economic effect of the excise tax. Consider Figure 17.5, which is identical to Figure 17.2 but contains the additional detail we need for our discussion.

Tax Revenues In our example, a $2 excise tax on wine increases its market price from $8 to $9 per bottle and reduces the equilibrium quantity from 15 million

bottles to 12.5 million. Government tax revenue is $25 million (= $2 × 12.5 million bottles), an amount shown as the rectangle *efac* in Figure 17.5. The elasticities of supply and demand in this case are such that consumers and producers each pay half this total amount, or $12.5 million apiece (= $1 + 12.5 million bottles). The government uses this $25 million of tax revenue to provide public goods and services. So this transfer of dollars from consumers and producers to government involves no loss of well-being to society.

Efficiency Loss The $2 tax on wine does more than require consumers and producers to pay $25 million of taxes; it also reduces the equilibrium amount of wine produced and consumed by 2.5 million bottles. The fact that consumers and producers demanded and supplied 2.5 million more bottles of wine before the tax means that those 2.5 million bottles provided benefits in excess of their production costs. This is clear from the following analysis.

Segment *ab* of demand curve *D* in Figure 17.5 indicates the willingness to pay—the marginal benefit—associated with each of the 2.5 million bottles consumed before (but not after) the tax. Segment *cb* of supply curve *S* reflects the marginal cost of each of the bottles of wine. For all but the very last one of these 2.5 million bottles, the marginal benefit (shown by a point on *ab*) exceeds the marginal cost (shown by a point on *cb*). Not producing these 2.5 million bottles of wine reduces well-being by an amount represented by the triangle *abc*. The area of this triangle identifies the **efficiency loss of the tax** (also called the *deadweight loss of the tax*). This loss is society's sacrifice of net benefit, because the tax reduces production and consumption of the product below their levels of economic efficiency, where marginal benefit and marginal cost are equal.

Role of Elasticities Most taxes create some degree of efficiency loss, but just how much depends on the supply and demand elasticities. Glancing back at Figure 17.3, we see that the efficiency loss area *abc* is greater in Figure 17.3a, where demand is relatively elastic, than in Figure 17.3b, where demand is relatively inelastic. Similarly, area *abc* is greater in Figure 17.4a than in Figure 17.4b, indicating a larger efficiency loss where supply is more elastic. Other things equal, the greater the elasticities of supply and demand, the greater the efficiency loss of a particular tax.

Two taxes yielding equal revenues do not necessarily impose equal costs on society. The government must keep this fact in mind in designing a tax system to finance

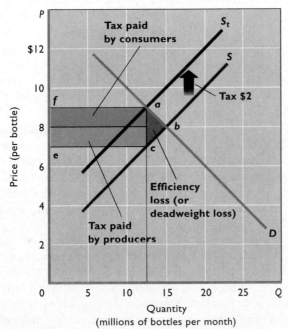

FIGURE 17.5 Efficiency loss (or deadweight loss) of a tax. The levy of a $2 tax per bottle of wine increases the price per bottle from $8 to $9 and reduces the equilibrium quantity from 15 million to 12.5 million. Tax revenue to the government is $25 million (area *efac*). The efficiency loss of the tax arises from the 2.5 million decline in output; the amount of that loss is shown as triangle *abc*.

beneficial public goods and services. In general, it should minimize the efficiency loss of the tax system in raising any specific dollar amount of tax revenue.

Qualifications

We must acknowledge, however, that other tax goals may be as important as, or even more important than, minimizing efficiency losses from taxes. Here are two examples:

- **Redistributive goals** Government may wish to impose progressive taxes as a way to redistribute income. The 10 percent excise tax the Federal government placed on selected luxuries in 1990 was an example. Because the demand for luxuries is elastic, substantial efficiency losses from this tax were to be expected. However, Congress apparently concluded that the benefits from the redistribution effects of the tax would exceed the efficiency losses.

  Ironically, in 1993 Congress repealed the luxury taxes on personal airplanes and yachts, mainly because the taxes had reduced quantity demanded so much that widespread layoffs of workers were occurring in those industries. But the 10 percent tax on luxury automobiles remained in place until it expired in 2003.

- **Reducing negative externalities** Our analysis of the efficiency loss of a tax assumes no negative externalities arising from either the production or consumption of the product in question. Where such spillover costs occur, the excise tax on the producers might actually improve allocative efficiency by reducing output and thus lessening the negative externality. For example, the $2 excise tax on wine in our example might be part of a broader set of excise taxes on alcoholic beverages. The government may have concluded that the consumption of these beverages produces certain negative externalities. Therefore, it might have purposely levied this $2 tax to shift the market supply curve such that the price of wine increased and the amount of resources allocated to wine declined (as in Figure 17.3b). **(Key Question 9)**

Probable Incidence of U.S. Taxes

Let's look now at the probable incidence of each of the major sources of tax revenue in the United States.

Personal Income Tax

The incidence of the personal income tax generally is on the individual because there is little chance for shifting it. For every dollar paid to the tax, individuals have one less dollar in their pocketbooks. The same ordinarily holds true for inheritance taxes.

Payroll Taxes

In 2008, employees and employers *each* paid 7.65 percent on the first $102,000 of a worker's annual earnings and 1.45 percent on all additional earnings. Workers bear the full burden of the Social Security payroll tax and Medicare tax levied on them. As is true for the income tax, they cannot shift these taxes to someone else.

What about the portion of payroll taxes levied on employers? Who pays that? The consensus view is that part of the employer portion of the tax gets shifted to workers in the form of lower before-tax wages. By making it more costly to hire workers, the payroll tax reduces the demand for labor relative to supply. That reduces the market wages that employers pay workers. In a sense, employers "collect" some of the payroll tax they owe from their workers.

Corporate Income Tax

In the short run, the incidence of the corporate income tax falls on the company's stockholders (owners), who bear the burden of the tax through lower dividends or smaller amounts of retained corporate earnings. Here is why. A firm currently charging the profit-maximizing price and producing the profit-maximizing output will have no reason to change product price, output, or wages when a tax on corporate income (profit) is imposed. The price and output combination yielding the greatest profit before the tax will still yield the greatest profit after a fixed percentage of the firm's profit is removed by a corporate income tax. So, the company's stockholders will not be able to shift the tax to consumers or workers.

As previously indicated, the situation may be different in the long run. Workers, in general, may bear a significant part of the corporate income tax in the form of lower wage growth. Because it reduces the return on investment, the corporate income tax may slow the accumulation of capital (plant and equipment). It also may prompt some U.S. firms to relocate abroad in countries that have lower corporate tax rates. In either case, the tax may slow the growth of U.S. labor productivity, which depends on American workers having access to more and better equipment. We know from Figure 13.1 that the growth of labor productivity is the main reason labor demand grows over time. If the corporate income tax reduces the growth of labor productivity, then labor demand and wages my rise less rapidly. In this indirect way—and over long periods of time—workers may bear part of the corporate income tax.

Sales and Excise Taxes

A *sales tax* is a general excise tax levied on a full range of consumer goods and services, whereas a *specific excise tax* is one levied only on a particular product. Sales taxes are usually transparent to the buyer, whereas excise taxes are often "hidden" in the price of the product. Sellers often shift both taxes partly or largely to consumers through higher product prices. Sales taxes and excise taxes may get shifted to different extents, however. Because a sales tax covers a much wider range of products than an excise tax, there is little chance for consumers to avoid the price boosts that sales taxes entail. They cannot reallocate their expenditures to untaxed, lower-priced products. Therefore, sales taxes tend to be shifted from producers in their entirety to consumers.

Excise taxes, however, fall on a select list of goods. Therefore, the possibility of consumers turning to substitute goods and services is greater. An excise tax on theater tickets that does not apply to other types of entertainment might be difficult to pass on to consumers via price increases. Why? The answer is provided in Figure 17.3a, where demand is elastic. A price boost to cover the excise tax on theater tickets might cause consumers to substitute alternative types of entertainment. The higher price would reduce sales so much that a seller would be better off to bear all, or a large portion of, the excise tax.

With other products, modest price increases to cover taxes may have smaller effects on sales. The excise taxes on gasoline, cigarettes, and alcoholic beverages provide examples. Here consumers have few good substitute products to which they can turn as prices rise. For these goods, the seller is better able to shift nearly all the excise tax to consumers. Example: Prices of cigarettes have gone up nearly in lockstep with the recent, substantial increases in excise taxes on cigarettes.

As indicated in Global Perspective 17.1, the United States depends less on sales and excise taxes for tax revenue than do several other nations.

Property Taxes
Many property taxes are borne by the property owner because there is no other party

to whom they can be shifted. This is typically true for taxes on land, personal property, and owner-occupied residences. Even when land is sold, the property tax is not likely to be shifted. The buyer will understand that

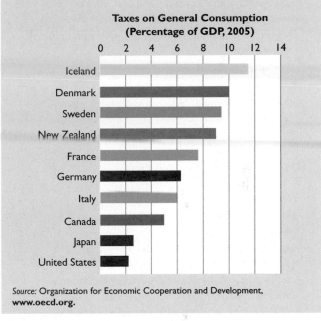

GLOBAL PERSPECTIVE 17.1

Taxes on General Consumption as a Percentage of GDP, Selected Nations

A number of advanced industrial nations rely much more heavily on consumption taxes—sales taxes, specific excise taxes, and value-added taxes—than does the United States. A value-added tax, which the United States does not have, applies only to the difference between the value of a firm's sales and the value of its purchases from other firms. As a percentage of GDP, the highest tax rates on consumption are in countries that have value-added taxes.

Source: Organization for Economic Cooperation and Development, **www.oecd.org.**

TABLE 17.2 The Probable Incidence of Taxes

Type of Tax	Probable Incidence
Personal income tax	The household or individual on which it is levied.
Payroll taxes	Workers pay the full tax levied on their earnings and part of the tax levied on their employers.
Corporate income tax	In the short run, the full tax falls on owners of the businesses. In the long run, some of the tax may be borne by workers through lower wages.
Sales tax	Consumers who buy the taxed products.
Specific excise taxes	Consumers, producers, or both, depending on elasticities of demand and supply.
Property taxes	Owners in the case of land and owner-occupied residences; tenants in the case of rented property; consumers in the case of business property.

"Government Failure" in the News

The Media Continually Report Government Actions That Illustrate Pork-Barrel Politics, Limited and Bundled Choices, or Bureaucratic Inefficiency.

Examples:

- In 2001, Congress appropriated $350,000 for the Chicago Wilderness Program, $273,000 for the Blue Springs (Missouri) Youth Outreach Unit for educational training in combating "Goth" culture, and $400,000 for the Montana Sheep Institute. (Citizens Against Government Waste, as reported in the *Lincoln Journal Star*)
- The 2001 Senate "economic stimulus" bill contained a $220 million subsidy for bison meat producers and eggplant, cauliflower, and pumpkin growers that experienced low prices during the 2000 and 2001 crop years. (*Los Angeles Times*)
- The disaster emergency relief section of the 2003 appropriations bill contained a provision to qualify catfish farmers for livestock compensation payments. Senator John McCain asked, "When did a catfish become analogous to a cow?" (Senator John McCain's Congressional "Pork" Web site, **www.mccain.senate.gov**)
- A 2003 spending bill contained 9300 earmarks for special projects. Included were $3 million for a Florida-based nonprofit program than provides golf instruction to children and teens around the country, $50 million to build an indoor rainforest in Iowa, and $225 million to repair a 61-year-old municipal swimming pool in Nevada. (Knight Ridder Newspapers and the Associated Press)

- A 2004 spending bill set aside $1 million for the Norwegian American Foundation; $443,000 to develop salmon-fortified baby food; $350,000 for music education programs at the Rock and Roll Hall of Fame in Cleveland; and $250,000 for sidewalks, street furniture, and façade improvements in Boca Raton, Florida. (Associated Press)
- The corporate tax relief bill of 2004 contained 633 pages, with 276 special provisions. Included were provisions that benefited "restaurant owners and Hollywood producers; makers of bows, arrows, tackle boxes, and sonar fish finders; NASCAR track owners; native Alaska whalers; and even importers of Chinese fans." (*Washington Post*)
- Government investigations determined that millions of dollars of disaster relief for victims of hurricane Katrina were squandered. For example, investigators discovered that the Federal Emergency Management Agency (FEMA) made payouts on as many as 900,000 claims for disaster relief that contained invalid Social Security numbers or false names and addresses. (*Seattle Times*)
- In 2007, the Government Accountability Office found that government employees used $146 million of unjustified premium-class airline travel. (Associated Press)
- The 2008 Labor, Health and Human Services and Education Act contained earmarks for everything from jazz at Lincoln Center in New York City to money for abstinence education programs in the state of Pennsylvania. The 2008 Defense Appropriate Act authorized $2.4 million for a California center for educational research previously named for the congressional representative sponsoring the provision. (Citizens Against Government Waste)

future taxes will have to be paid on it, and this expected taxation would be reflected in the price the buyer is willing to offer for the land.

Taxes on rented and business property are a different story. Taxes on rented property can be, and usually are, shifted wholly or in part from the owner to the tenant by the process of boosting the rent. Business property taxes are treated as a business cost and are taken into account in establishing product price; hence such taxes are ordinarily shifted to the firm's customers.

Table 17.2 (on the previous page) summarizes this discussion of the shifting and incidence of taxes.

The U.S. Tax Structure

Is the overall U.S. tax structure—Federal, state, and local taxes combined—progressive, proportional, or progressive? The question is difficult to answer. Estimates of the distribution of the total tax burden depend on the extent to which the various taxes are shifted to others, and who bears the burden is subject to dispute. But the majority view of economists who study taxes is as follows:

- *The Federal tax system is progressive.* Overall, higher-income groups pay larger percentages of their income as Federal taxes than do lower-income groups. Although Federal payroll taxes and excise taxes are regressive, the Federal income tax is sufficiently progressive to make the overall Federal tax system progressive. About one-third of the Federal income tax filers owe no tax at all. In fact, because of fully refundable tax credits designed to reduce poverty and promote work, millions of households receive tax rebates even though their income tax bill is zero. Most of the Federal income tax is paid by higher-income taxpayers. In 2005 (the latest year for which data have been compiled), the top 1 percent of income-tax filers paid 38.8 percent of the Federal income tax; the top 5 percent paid 60.7 percent of the tax.

    The overall progressivity of the Federal tax system is confirmed by comparing effective (average) tax rates, which are found by dividing the total of Federal income, payroll, and excise taxes paid at various income levels. In 2005, the 20 percent of the households with the lowest income paid an effective tax rate of 4.3 percent. The 20 percent of households with the highest income paid a 25.5 percent rate. The top 10 percent paid a 27.4 percent rate; the top 1 percent, a 31.2 percent rate.[2]

- *The state and local tax structures are largely regressive.* As a percentage of income, property taxes and sales taxes fall as income rises. Also, state income taxes are generally less progressive than the Federal income tax.

- *The overall U.S. tax system is slightly progressive.* Higher-income people carry a slightly larger tax burden, as a percentage of their income, than do lower-income people.

Caution: While the U.S. tax system *does not* substantially alter the distribution of income, the system of transfer payments *does* considerably reduce income inequality. Transfer payments to the poorest fifth of U.S. households almost quadruple their collective incomes. The combined tax-transfer system redistributes income by much more than does the tax system alone.

---

[2] *Historical Effective Federal Tax Rates, 1979–2005*, Congressional Budget Office, December 2007.

Summary

1. Public choice theory examines the economics of government decision making, politics, and elections.

2. Majority voting creates a possibility of (a) an underallocation or an overallocation of resources to a particular public good and (b) inconsistent voting outcomes. The median-voter model predicts that, under majority rule, the person holding the middle position on an issue will determine the outcome of an election involving that issue.

3. Public choice theorists cite reasons why government might be inefficient in providing public goods and services. (a) There are strong reasons for politicians to support special-interest legislation. (b) Politicians may be biased in favor of programs with immediate and clear-cut benefits and difficult-to-identify costs and against programs with immediate and easily identified costs and vague or deferred benefits. (c) Citizens as voters and congressional representatives face limited and bundled choices as to public goods and services, whereas consumers in the private sector can be highly selective in their choices. (d) Government bureaucracies have less incentive to operate efficiently than do private businesses.

4. The benefits-received principle of taxation states that those who receive the benefits of goods and services provided by government should pay the taxes required to finance them. The ability-to-pay principle states that those who have greater income should be taxed more, absolutely and relatively, than those who have less income.

5. The Federal personal income tax is progressive. The corporate income tax is roughly proportional. General sales, excise, payroll, and property taxes are regressive.

6. Excise taxes affect supply and therefore equilibrium price and quantity. The more inelastic the demand for a product, the greater is the portion of an excise tax that is shifted to consumers. The greater the inelasticity of supply, the larger is the portion of the tax that is borne by the seller.

7. Taxation involves the loss of some output whose marginal benefit exceeds its marginal cost. The more elastic the supply and demand curves, the greater is the efficiency loss (or deadweight loss) resulting from a particular tax.

8. Some taxes are borne by those taxed; other taxes are shifted to someone else. The income tax, the payroll tax levied on workers, and the corporate income tax (in the short run)

are borne by those taxed. In contrast, sales taxes are shifted to consumers, part of the payroll tax levied on employers is shifted to workers, and, in the long run, part of the corporate income tax is shifted to workers. Specific excise taxes may or may not be shifted to consumers, depending on the elasticities of demand and supply. Property taxes on owner-occupied property are borne by the owner; those on rental property are borne by tenants.

9. The Federal tax structure is progressive; the state and local tax structure is regressive; and the overall tax structure is slightly progressive.

Terms and Concepts

public choice theory	special-interest effect	progressive tax
logrolling	earmarks	regressive tax
paradox of voting	rent seeking	proportional tax
median-voter model	benefits-received principle	tax incidence
government failure	ability-to-pay principle	efficiency loss of a tax

Study Questions

1. Explain how affirmative and negative majority votes can sometimes lead to inefficient allocations of resources to public goods. Is this problem likely to be greater under a benefits-received or under an ability-to-pay tax system? Use the information in Figures 17.1a and 17.1b to show how society might be better off if Adams were allowed to buy votes. **LO1**

2. **KEY QUESTION** Explain the paradox of voting through reference to the accompanying table, which shows the ranking of three public goods by voters Jay, Dave, and Conan: **LO1**

Public Good	Rankings		
	Jay	Dave	Conan
Courthouse	2d choice	1st choice	3d choice
School	3d choice	2d choice	1st choice
Park	1st choice	3d choice	2d choice

3. **KEY QUESTION** Suppose there are only five people in a society and each favors one of the five highway construction options in Table 16.2 (include no highway construction as one of the options). Explain which of these highway options will be selected using a majority paired-choice vote. Will this option be the optimal size of the project from an economic perspective? **LO1**

4. **KEY QUESTION** How does the problem of limited and bundled choice in the public sector relate to economic efficiency? Why are public bureaucracies alleged to be less efficient than private enterprises? **LO2**

5. Explain: "Politicians would make more rational economic decisions if they weren't running for reelection every few years." **LO2**

6. Distinguish between the benefits-received and the ability-to-pay principles of taxation. Which philosophy is more evident in our present tax structure? Justify your answer. To which principle of taxation do you subscribe? Why? **LO3**

7. **KEY QUESTION** Suppose a tax is such that an individual with an income of $10,000 pays $2000 of tax, a person with an income of $20,000 pays $3000 of tax, a person with an income of $30,000 pays $4000 of tax, and so forth. What is each person's average tax rate? Is this tax regressive, proportional, or progressive? **LO3**

8. What is meant by a progressive tax? A regressive tax? A proportional tax? Comment on the progressivity or regressivity of each of the following taxes, indicating in each case where you think the tax incidence lies: (*a*) the Federal personal income tax; (*b*) a 4 percent state general sales tax; (*c*) a Federal excise tax on automobile tires; (*d*) a municipal property tax on real estate; (*e*) the Federal corporate income tax; (*f*) the portion of the payroll tax levied on employers. **LO3**

9. **KEY QUESTION** What is the incidence of an excise tax when demand is highly inelastic? Highly elastic? What effect does the elasticity of supply have on the incidence of an excise tax? What is the efficiency loss of a tax, and how does it relate to elasticity of demand and supply? **LO4**

10. **ADVANCED ANALYSIS** Suppose the equation for the demand curve for some product X is $P = 8 - .6Q$ and the supply curve is $P = 2 + .4Q$. What are the equilibrium price and quantity? Now suppose an excise tax is imposed on X such that the new supply equation is $P = 4 + .4Q$. How much tax revenue will this excise tax yield the government? Graph the curves, and label the area of the graph that represents the tax collection "TC" and the area that represents the efficiency loss of the tax "EL." Briefly explain why area EL is the efficiency loss of the tax but TC is not. **LO4**

11. **LAST WORD** How do the concepts of pork-barrel politics and logrolling relate to the items listed in the Last Word?

Web-Based Questions

1. **EARMARKS—EFFICIENT PUBLIC GOODS OR INEFFICIENT PUBLIC PORK?** The advocacy organization Citizens Against Government Waste (CAGW) identifies earmarks in current legislation that it concludes reflect government waste. Go to **www.cagw.org** and search through the CAGW Web site to find five recent examples of alleged wasteful expenditures. What kinds of additional information would you need before you accepted the group's assertion that each of the five projects is indeed wasteful? Explain how a Federally funded project might be wasteful from a national perspective, yet still be highly beneficial for a specific city or state.

2. **CALCULATING TAXES AND DETERMINING AVERAGE RATES** The Internal Revenue Service provides current tax-rate tables online at **www.irs.gov**. Enter Tax Tables in the search line and find 1040 Instructions (Tax Tables) for the latest tax year. Find the tax payment you would owe if you were a single taxpayer with a taxable income of (1) $23,360, (2) $46,200, and (3) $85,010 in the taxable year. Compare the average tax rates (taxable income/tax payment) for the three levels of income. Next, suppose that you live in a state with a 7 percent sales tax and that you spent 90 percent of your taxable income in the year. How much total sales tax would you pay at each income level? Add the total sales tax to the income tax for each income level and compute new average tax rates based on the combined income tax and sales tax as a percentage of taxable income. Compare the new percentages with the previous ones. What can you conclude from the comparison? (We are assuming that you take the standard deduction on your Federal income tax form and thus do not claim a sales tax deduction.)

FURTHER TEST YOUR KNOWLEDGE AT
www.mcconnell18e.com

PART FIVE

Microeconomic Issues
and Policies

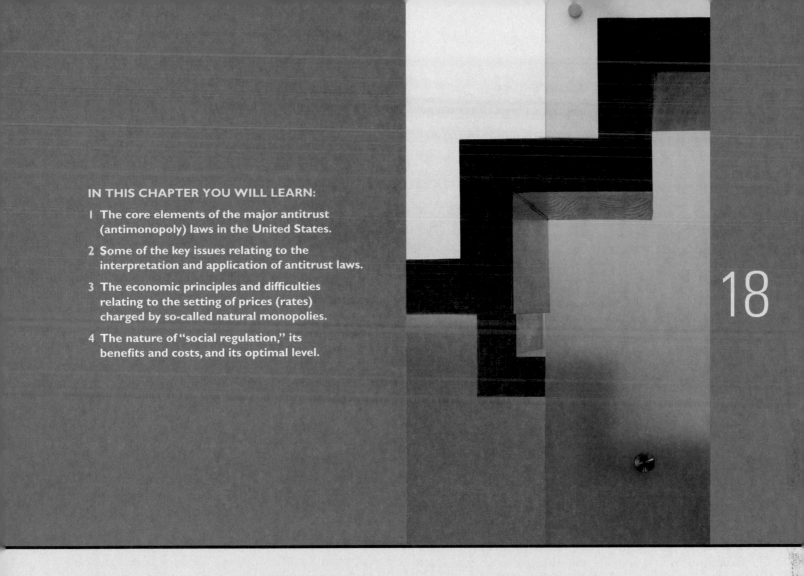

IN THIS CHAPTER YOU WILL LEARN:

1 The core elements of the major antitrust (antimonopoly) laws in the United States.

2 Some of the key issues relating to the interpretation and application of antitrust laws.

3 The economic principles and difficulties relating to the setting of prices (rates) charged by so-called natural monopolies.

4 The nature of "social regulation," its benefits and costs, and its optimal level.

18

Antitrust Policy and Regulation

We now can apply the economics of product markets (Part 2), resource markets (Part 3), and government (Part 4) to selected microeconomic issues and policies.

In this chapter we look at three sets of government policies toward business: antitrust policy, industrial regulation, and social regulation. **Antitrust policy** consists of the laws and government actions designed to prevent monopoly and promote competition. **Industrial regulation** pertains to government regulation of firms' prices (or "rates") within selected industries. **Social regulation** is government regulation of the conditions under which goods are produced, the physical characteristics of goods, and the impact of the production and consumption of goods on society.

Then, in the remaining four chapters of Part 5, we discuss issues and policies relating to agriculture, income inequality, health care, and immigration.

The Antitrust Laws

The underlying purpose of antitrust policy (antimonopoly policy) is to prevent monopolization, promote competition, and achieve allocative efficiency. Although all economists would agree that these are meritorious goals, there is sharp conflict of opinion about the appropriateness and effectiveness of U.S. antitrust policy. As we will see, antitrust policy over the years has been neither clear-cut nor consistent.

Historical Background

Just after the U.S. Civil War (1861–1865), local markets widened into national markets because of improved transportation facilities, mechanized production methods, and sophisticated corporate structures. In the 1870s and 1880s, dominant firms formed in several industries, including petroleum, meatpacking, railroads, sugar, lead, coal, whiskey, and tobacco. Some of these oligopolists, near-monopolists, or monopolists were known as *trusts*—business combinations that assign control to a single decision group ("trustees"). Because these trusts "monopolized" industries, the word "trust" became synonymous with "monopoly" in common usage. The public, government, and historians began to define a business monopoly as a large-scale dominant seller, even though that seller was not always "a sole seller" as specified in the model of pure monopoly.

These dominant firms often used questionable tactics in consolidating their industries and then charged high prices to customers and extracted price concessions from resource suppliers. Farmers and owners of small businesses were particularly vulnerable to the power of large corporate monopolies and were among the first to oppose them. Consumers, labor unions, and economists were not far behind in their opposition.

The main economic case against monopoly is familiar to you from Chapter 10. Monopolists tend to produce less output and charge higher prices than would be the case if their industries were competitive. With pure competition, production occurs where $P = \text{MC}$. This equality represents an efficient allocation of resources because P measures the marginal benefit to society of an extra unit of output while marginal cost MC reflects the cost of an extra unit. When $P = \text{MC}$, society cannot gain by producing 1 more or 1 less unit of the product. In contrast, a monopolist maximizes profit by equating marginal revenue (not price) with marginal cost. At this $\text{MR} = \text{MC}$ point, price exceeds marginal cost, meaning that society would obtain more benefit than it would incur cost by producing extra units. An underallocation of resources to the monopolized product occurs, and the economy suffers an efficiency loss. So society's economic well-being is less than it would be with greater competition.

In the late 1800s and early 1900s, government concluded that market forces in monopolized industries did not provide sufficient control to protect consumers, achieve fair competition, and achieve allocative efficiency. So it instituted two alternative means of control as substitutes for, or supplements to, market forces:

- *Regulatory agencies* In the few markets where the nature of the product or technology creates a *natural monopoly*, the government established public regulatory agencies to control economic behavior.
- *Antitrust laws* In most other markets, social control took the form of antitrust (antimonopoly) legislation designed to inhibit or prevent the growth of monopoly.

Four particular pieces of Federal legislation, as refined and extended by various amendments, constitute the basic law relating to monopoly structure and conduct.

Sherman Act of 1890

The public resentment of trusts that emerged in the 1870s and 1880s culminated in the **Sherman Act** of 1890. This cornerstone of antitrust legislation is surprisingly brief and, at first glance, directly to the point. The core of the act resides in two provisions:

- *Section 1* "Every contract, combination in the form of a trust or otherwise, or conspiracy, in restraint of trade or commerce among the several States, or with foreign nations is declared to be illegal."
- *Section 2* "Every person who shall monopolize, or attempt to monopolize, or combine or conspire with any person or persons, to monopolize any part of the trade or commerce among the several states, or with foreign nations, shall be deemed guilty of a felony" (as later amended from "misdemeanor").

The Sherman Act thus outlawed *restraints of trade* (for example, collusive price-fixing and dividing up markets) as well as *monopolization*. Today, the U.S. Department of Justice, the Federal Trade Commission, injured private parties, or state attorney generals can file antitrust suits against alleged violators of the act. The courts can issue injunctions to prohibit anticompetitive practices or, if necessary, break up monopolists into competing firms. Courts can also fine and imprison violators. Further, parties injured by illegal combinations and conspiracies can sue the perpetrators for *treble damages*—awards of three times the amount of the monetary injury done to them.

The Sherman Act seemed to provide a sound foundation for positive government action against business monopolies. However, early court interpretations limited the scope of the act and created ambiguities of law. It became clear that a more explicit statement of the government's antitrust sentiments was needed. The business community itself sought a clearer statement of what was legal and what was illegal.

Clayton Act of 1914

The **Clayton Act** of 1914 contained the desired elaboration of the Sherman Act. Four sections of the act, in particular, were designed to strengthen and make explicit the intent of the Sherman Act:

- Section 2 outlaws *price discrimination* when such discrimination is not justified on the basis of cost differences and when it reduces competition.
- Section 3 prohibits **tying contracts,** in which a producer requires that a buyer purchase another (or others) of its products as a condition for obtaining a desired product.
- Section 7 prohibits the acquisition of stocks of competing corporations when the outcome would be less competition.
- Section 8 prohibits the formation of **interlocking directorates**—situations where a director of one firm is also a board member of a competing firm—in large corporations where the effect would be reduced competition.

The Clayton Act simply sharpened and clarified the general provisions of the Sherman Act. It also sought to outlaw the techniques that firms might use to develop monopoly power and, in that sense, was a preventive measure. Section 2 of the Sherman Act, by contrast, was aimed more at breaking up existing monopolies.

Federal Trade Commission Act of 1914

The **Federal Trade Commission Act** created the five-member Federal Trade Commission (FTC), which has joint Federal responsibility with the U.S. Justice Department for enforcing the antitrust laws. The act gave the FTC the power to investigate unfair competitive practices on its own initiative or at the request of injured firms. It can hold public hearings on such complaints and, if necessary, issue **cease-and-desist orders** in cases where it discovers "unfair methods of competition in commerce."

The **Wheeler-Lea Act** of 1938 amended the Federal Trade Commission Act to give the FTC the additional responsibility of policing "deceptive acts or practices in commerce." In so doing, the FTC tries to protect the public against false or misleading advertising and the misrepresentation of products. So the Federal Trade Commission Act, as modified by the Wheeler-Lea Act, (1) established the FTC as an independent antitrust agency and (2) made unfair and deceptive sales practices illegal.

The FTC is highly active in enforcing the deceptive advertising statues. As one recent example, in 2007 the FTC fined four makers of over-the-counter diet pills a collective $25 million for claiming their products produced fast and permanent weight loss.

Celler-Kefauver Act of 1950

The **Celler-Kefauver Act** amended the Clayton Act, Section 7, which prohibits a firm from merging with a competing firm (and thereby lessening competition) by acquiring its stock. Firms could evade Section 7, however, by instead acquiring the physical assets (plant and equipment) of competing firms. The Celler-Kefauver Act closed that loophole by prohibiting one firm from obtaining the physical assets of another firm when the effect would be reduced competition. Section 7 of the Clayton Act now prohibits anticompetitive mergers no matter how they are undertaken. **(Key Question 2)**

Antitrust Policy: Issues and Impacts

The effectiveness of any law depends on how the courts interpret it and on the vigor of government enforcement. The courts have been inconsistent in interpreting the antitrust laws. At times, they have applied them vigorously, adhering closely to their spirit and objectives. At other times, their interpretations have rendered certain laws nearly powerless. The Federal government itself has varied considerably in its aggressiveness in enforcing the antitrust laws. Some administrations have made tough antitrust enforcement a high priority. Other administrations have taken a more laissez-faire approach, initiating few antitrust actions or even scaling back the budgets of the enforcement agencies.

Issues of Interpretation

Differences in judicial interpretations have led to vastly different applications of the antitrust laws. Two questions, in particular, have arisen: (1) Should the focus of antitrust policy be on monopoly behavior or on monopoly structure? (2) How broadly should markets be defined in antitrust cases?

Monopoly Behavior versus Monopoly Structure

A comparison of three landmark Supreme Court decisions reveals two distinct interpretations of Section 2 of the Sherman Act as it relates to monopoly behavior and structure.

In the 1911 **Standard Oil case,** the Supreme Court found Standard Oil guilty of monopolizing the petroleum industry through a series of abusive and anticompetitive actions. The Court's remedy was to divide Standard Oil into several competing firms. But the Standard Oil case left open an important question: Is every monopoly in violation of Section 2 of the Sherman Act or just those created or maintained by anticompetitive actions?

In the 1920 **U.S. Steel case,** the courts established a **rule of reason,** saying that not every monopoly is illegal. Only monopolies that "unreasonably" restrain trade violate Section 2 of the Sherman Act and are subject to antitrust action. Size alone was not an offense. Although U.S. Steel clearly possessed monopoly power, it was innocent of "monopolizing" because it had not resorted to illegal acts against competitors in obtaining that power nor had it unreasonably used its monopoly power. Unlike Standard Oil, which was a so-called bad trust, U.S. Steel was a "good trust" and therefore not in violation of the law.

In the **Alcoa case** of 1945 the courts touched off a 20-year turnabout. The Supreme Court sent the case to the U.S. court of appeals in New York because four of the Supreme Court justices had been involved with litigation of the case before their appointments. Led by Judge Hand the court of appeals held that, even though a firm's behavior might be legal, the mere possession of monopoly power (Alcoa held 90 percent of the aluminum ingot market) violated the antitrust laws. So Alcoa was found guilty of violating the Sherman Act.

These two cases point to a controversy in antitrust policy. Should a firm be judged by its behavior (as in the U.S. Steel case) or by its structure or market share (as in the Alcoa case)?

- "Structuralists" say that a firm with a very high market share will behave like a monopolist. Since the economic performance of such firms will be undesirable, they are legitimate targets for antitrust action. Changes in the structure of the industry, say, by splitting the monopolist into several smaller firms, will improve behavior and performance.

- "Behavioralists" assert that the relationship among structure, behavior, and performance is tenuous and unclear. They feel a monopolized or highly concentrated industry may be technologically progressive and have a good record of providing products of increasing quality at reasonable prices.

If a firm has served society well and has engaged in no anticompetitive practices, it should not be accused of antitrust violation just because it has an extraordinarily large market share. That share may be the product of superior technology, superior products, and economies of scale. "Why use antitrust laws to penalize efficient, technologically progressive, well-managed firms?" they ask.

Over the past 25 years, the courts have returned to the rule of reason first established in the 1920 U.S. Steel case, and most contemporary economists and antitrust enforcers reject strict structuralism. For instance, in 1982 the government dropped its 13-year-long monopolization case against IBM on the grounds that IBM had not unreasonably restrained trade. More recently, the government has made no attempt to break up Intel's monopoly in the sale of microcircuits for personal computers. And in prosecuting the Microsoft case (the subject of this chapter's Last Word), the Federal government made it clear that the behavior used by Microsoft to maintain and extend its monopoly, not the presence of its large market share, violated the Sherman Act. That is, the government in effect declared Microsoft "a bad monopoly."

The Relevant Market

Courts often decide whether or not market power exists by considering the share of the market held by the dominant firm. They have roughly adhered to a "90-60-30 rule" in defining monopoly: If a firm has a 90 percent market share, it is definitely a monopolist; if it has a 60 percent market share, it probably is a monopolist; if it has a 30 percent market share, it clearly is not a monopolist. The market share will depend on how the market is defined. If the market is defined broadly to include a wide range of somewhat similar products, the firm's market share will appear small. If the market is defined narrowly to exclude such products, the market share will seem large. The Supreme Court's task is to determine how broadly to define relevant markets, and it has not always been consistent.

In the Alcoa case, the Court used a narrow definition of the relevant market: the aluminum ingot market. But in the **DuPont cellophane case** of 1956 the Court defined the market very broadly. The government contended that DuPont, along with a licensee, controlled 100 percent of the cellophane market. But the Court accepted DuPont's contention that the relevant market included all "flexible packaging materials"—waxed paper, aluminum foil, and so forth, in addition to cellophane. Despite DuPont's monopoly in the "cellophane market," it controlled only 20 percent of the market for "flexible wrapping materials." The Court ruled that this did not constitute a monopoly.

Issues of Enforcement

Some U.S. presidential administrations have enforced the antitrust laws more strictly than others. The degree of Federal antitrust enforcement makes a difference in the overall degree of antitrust action in the economy. It is true that individual firms can sue other firms under the antitrust laws. For example, in 2005 AMD—a maker of microprocessors—filed an antitrust suit against Intel, claiming that Intel was a monopolist that used anticompetitive business practices to thwart the growth of AMD's market share. But major antitrust suits often last years and are highly expensive. Injured parties therefore often look to the Federal government to initiate and litigate such cases. Once the Federal government gains a conviction, the injured parties no longer need to prove guilt and can simply sue the violator to obtain treble damages. In many cases, lack of Federal antitrust action therefore means diminished legal action by firms.

Why might one administration enforce the antitrust laws more or less strictly than another? The main reason is differences in political philosophies about the market economy and the wisdom of intervention by government. There are two contrasting general perspectives on antitrust policy.

The *active antitrust perspective* is that competition is insufficient in some circumstances to achieve allocative efficiency and ensure fairness to consumers and competing firms. Firms occasionally use illegal tactics against competitors to dominate markets. In other instances, competitors collude to fix prices or merge to enhance their monopoly power. Active, strict enforcement of the antitrust laws is needed to stop illegal business practices, prevent anticompetitive mergers, and remedy monopoly. This type of government intervention maintains the viability and vibrancy of the market system and thus allows society to reap its full benefits. In this view, the antitrust authorities need to act much like the officials in a football game. They must observe the players, spot infractions, and enforce the rules.

In contrast, the *laissez-faire perspective* holds that antitrust intervention is largely unnecessary, particularly as it relates to monopoly. Economists holding this position view competition as a long-run dynamic process in which firms battle against each other for dominance of markets. In some markets, a firm successfully monopolizes the market, usually because of its superior innovativeness or business skill. But in exploiting its monopoly power to raise prices, these firms inadvertently create profit incentives and profit opportunities for other entrepreneurs and firms to develop alternative technologies and new products to better serve consumers. As discussed in Chapter 2 and expanded upon in Chapter 11Web, a process of *creative destruction* occurs in which today's monopolies are eroded and eventually destroyed by tomorrow's technologies

and products. The government therefore should not try to break up monopoly. It should stand aside and allow the long-run competitive process to work.

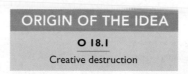

ORIGIN OF THE IDEA

O 18.1

Creative destruction

The extent to which a particular administration adheres to—or leans toward—one of these contrasting antitrust perspectives usually gets reflected in the appointments to the agencies overseeing antitrust policy. Those appointees help determine how strictly the laws are enforced.

Effectiveness of Antitrust Laws

Have the antitrust laws been effective? Although this question is difficult to answer, we can at least observe how the laws have been applied to monopoly, mergers, price-fixing, price discrimination, and tying contracts.

Monopoly On the basis of the rule of reason, the government has generally been lenient in applying antitrust laws to monopolies that have developed naturally. Generally, a firm will be sued by the Federal government only if it has a very high market share and there is evidence of abusive conduct in achieving, maintaining, or extending its market dominance.

Since the 1980s the issue of remedy arose in two particularly noteworthy monopoly cases. The first was the AT&T (American Telephone and Telegraph) case in which the government charged AT&T with violating the Sherman Act by engaging in anticompetitive practices designed to maintain its domestic telephone monopoly. As part of an out-of-court settlement between the government and AT&T, in 1982 AT&T agreed to divest itself of its 22 regional telephone-operating companies.

A second significant monopoly case was the **Microsoft case.** In 2000 Microsoft was found guilty of violating the Sherman Act by taking several unlawful actions designed to maintain its monopoly of operating systems for personal computers. A lower court ordered that Microsoft be split into two competing firms. A court of appeals upheld the lower-court finding of abusive monopoly but rescinded the breakup of Microsoft. Instead of the structural remedy, the eventual outcome was a behavioral remedy in which Microsoft was prohibited from engaging in a set of specific anticompetitive business practices.

The antitrust agency for the European Union (EU) has generally been more aggressive than the United States in prosecuting monopolists. For example, in 2004 the EU fined Microsoft $750,000 for monopolization and required it to share its computer coding with other firms

FIGURE 18.1 Types of mergers. Horizontal mergers (T + U) bring together firms selling the same product in the same geographic market; vertical mergers (F + Z) connect firms having a buyer-seller relationship; and conglomerate mergers (C + D) join firms in different industries or firms operating in different geographic areas.

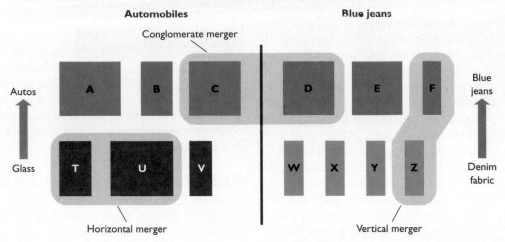

Mergers The treatment of mergers, or combinations of existing firms, varies with the type of merger and its effect on competition.

Merger Types There are three basic types of mergers, as represented in Figure 18.1. This figure shows two stages of production (the input stage and the output, or final-product, stage) for two distinct final-goods industries (autos and blue jeans). Each rectangle (A, B, C, . . . X, Y, Z) represents a particular firm.

A **horizontal merger** is a merger between two competitors that sell similar products in the same geographic market. In Figure 18.1 this type of merger is shown as a combination of glass producers T and U. Actual examples of such mergers include Chase Manhattan's merger with Chemical Bank, Boeing's merger with McDonnell Douglas, and Exxon's merger with Mobil.

A **vertical merger** is a merger between firms at different stages of the production process. In Figure 18.1, the merger between firm Z, a producer of denim fabric, and firm F, a producer of blue jeans, is a vertical merger. Vertical mergers are mergers between firms that have buyer-seller relationships. Actual examples of such mergers are PepsiCo's mergers with Pizza Hut, Taco Bell, and Kentucky Fried Chicken. PepsiCo supplies soft drinks to each of these fast-food outlets. (In 1997, PepsiCo spun off these entities into a separate company now called Yum! Brands.)

A **conglomerate merger** is officially defined as any merger that is not horizontal or vertical; in general, it is the combination of firms in different industries or firms operating in different geographic areas. Conglomerate mergers can extend the line of products sold, extend the territory in which products are sold, or combine totally unrelated companies. In Figure 18.1, the merger between firm C, an auto manufacturer, and firm D, a blue jeans producer, is a conglomerate merger. Real-world examples of conglomerate mergers include the merger between Walt Disney Company (movies) and the American Broadcasting Company (radio and television) and the merger between America Online (Internet service provider) and Time Warner (communications).

Merger Guidelines: The Herfindahl Index The Federal government has established very loose merger guidelines based on the Herfindahl index. Recall from Chapter 11 that this measure of concentration is the sum of the squared percentage market shares of the firms within an industry. An industry of only four firms, each with a 25 percent market share, has a Herfindahl index of 2500 $(= 25^2 + 25^2 + 25^2 + 25^2)$. In pure competition, where each firm's market share is minuscule, the index approaches $0 (= 0^2 + 0^2 + \cdots + 0^2)$. In pure monopoly, the index for that single firm is 10,000 $(= 100^2)$.

The U.S. government uses Section 7 of the Clayton Act to block horizontal mergers that will substantially lessen competition. It is likely to challenge a horizontal merger if the postmerger Herfindahl index would be high (above 1800) and if the merger has substantially increased the index (added 100 or more points). However, other factors, such as economies of scale, the degree of foreign competition, and the ease of entry of new firms, are also considered. Furthermore, horizontal mergers are usually allowed if one of the merging firms is suffering major and continuing losses. (This is one reason Boeing was allowed to acquire McDonnell Douglas in 1996: MD was losing money in producing its commercial airplanes.)

In recent years, the Federal government has blocked several proposed horizontal mergers. For example, it blocked the mergers between Staples and Office Depot, two major office-supply retailers; WorldCom and Sprint, two competing telecommunications firms; and Hughes (DirecTV) and Echostar (DISH), providers of direct broadcast satellite service.

Most *vertical mergers* escape antitrust prosecution because they do not substantially lessen competition in either of the two markets. (In Figure 18.1 neither the Herfindahl index in the industry producing denim fabric nor the index in the blue jeans industry changes when firms Z and F merge vertically.) However, a vertical merger between large firms in highly concentrated industries may be challenged. For example, in 1999 the threat of FTC action spurred Barnes & Noble to abandon its merger with Ingram Book group, the nation's largest book wholesaler. The merger would have enabled Barnes & Noble to set the wholesale price of books charged to its direct retail competitors such as Borders and Amazon.com.

Conglomerate mergers are generally permitted. If an auto manufacturer acquires a blue jeans producer, no antitrust action is likely since neither firm has increased its own market share as a result. That means the Herfindahl index remains unchanged in each industry. **(Key Question 5)**

Price-Fixing
Price-fixing among competitors is treated strictly. Evidence of price-fixing, even by small firms, will bring antitrust action, as will other collusive activities such as scheming to rig bids on government contracts or dividing up sales in a market. In antitrust law, these activities are known as **per se violations;** they are "in and of themselves" illegal, and therefore are *not* subject to the rule of reason. To gain a conviction, the government or other party making the charge need show only that there was a conspiracy to fix prices, rig bids, or divide up markets, not that the conspiracy succeeded or caused serious damage to other parties.

Price-fixing investigations and court actions are common. We list several relatively recent price-fixing cases in the Consider This box to the right.

Price Discrimination
Price discrimination is a common business practice that rarely reduces competition and therefore is rarely challenged by government. The exception occurs when a firm engages in price discrimination as part of a strategy to block entry or drive out competitors.

Tying Contracts
The Federal government strictly enforces the prohibition of tying contracts, particularly when practiced by dominant firms. For example, it stopped movie distributors from forcing theaters to buy the projection rights to a full package of films as a condition of showing a blockbuster movie. Also, it prevented Kodak—the dominant maker of photographic film—from requiring that consumers process their film only through Kodak.

CONSIDER THIS . . .

Of Catfish and Art (and Other Things in Common)

Examples of price-fixing are numerous. Here are just a few:

- In 1996 ConAgra and Hormel agreed to pay more than $21 million to settle their roles in a nationwide price-fixing case involving catfish.
- In 1996 Archer Daniels Midland (ADM) and other agribusinesses admitted fixing the prices of citric acid and an additive to livestock feed. In the early 2000s ADM, Cargill, and Corn Products admitted fixing the price of high-fructose syrup, a sweetener made from corn. In 2004 ADM paid $430 million to resolve the government's antitrust action.
- The U.S. Justice Department fined UCAR International $110 million in 1998 for scheming with competitors to fix prices and divide the world market for graphite electrodes used in steel mills.
- In 2001 a court found the auction houses Sotheby's and Christie's guilty of conspiring over a 6-year period to set the same commission rates for sellers at auctions.
- In the early 2000s, Samsung (South Korea), Hynix Semiconductor (South Korea), Infineon (Germany), and Micron (United States) were found to have fixed the price of dynamic random access memory chips (DRAMs), which are used in personal computers, printers, cell phones, and other electronic devices. In 2004 and 2005, the companies paid fines totaling $645 million.
- In 2007 British Airlines and Korean Air agreed to pay fines of $300 million each for conspiring to fix fuel surcharges on passenger tickets and cargo.

What then can we conclude about the overall effectiveness of antitrust laws? Antitrust policy has not been very effective in restricting the rise of or in breaking up monopolies or oligopolies resulting from legally undertaken internal expansions of firms. But most economists do not deem that to be a flaw. The antitrust laws have been used more effectively against predatory or abusive monopoly, but that effectiveness has been diminished by the slow legal process and consequently long time between the filing of charges and the implementation of remedies. In contrast, antitrust policy *has* been effective in blocking blatantly anticompetitive mergers and in identifying and prosecuting price-fixing and tying contracts.

Most economists conclude that, overall, U.S. antitrust policy has been moderately effective in achieving its goal of promoting competition and efficiency. Much of the success of antitrust policy arises from its deterrent effect on price-fixing and anticompetitive mergers. Some economists, however, think that enforcement of antitrust laws has been too weak. Others believe that parts of U.S. antitrust policy are anachronistic in an era of rapidly changing technology that continuously undermines existing monopoly power.

QUICK REVIEW 18.1

- The Sherman Act of 1890 outlaws restraints of trade and monopolization; the Clayton Act of 1914 as amended by the Celler-Kefauver Act of 1950 outlaws price discrimination (when anticompetitive), tying contracts, anticompetitive mergers, and interlocking directorates.

- The Federal Trade Commission Act of 1914 as bolstered by the Wheeler-Lea Act of 1938 created the Federal Trade Commission (FTC) and gave it authority to investigate unfair methods of competition and deceptive acts or practices in commerce.

- Currently, the courts judge monopoly using a "rule of reason," first established in the the U.S. Steel case of 1920. Under this rule, only monopolists that achieve or maintain their status abusively are in violation of the Sherman Act.

- "Structuralists" say highly concentrated industries will behave like monopolists; "behaviorists" hold that the relationship between industry structure and firm behavior is uncertain.

- The degree of strictness of enforcement of antitrust laws depends on the general antitrust philosophy of the U.S. administration and its appointees.

- Government treats existing monopoly relatively leniently, as long as it is not abusive; blocks most horizontal mergers between dominant, profitable firms in highly concentrated industries; and vigorously prosecutes price-fixing and tying contracts.

Industrial Regulation

Antitrust policy assumes that society will benefit if monopoly is prevented from evolving or if it is dissolved where it already exists. We now return to a special situation in which there is an economic reason for an industry to be organized monopolistically.

Natural Monopoly

A **natural monopoly** exists when economies of scale are so extensive that a single firm can supply the entire market at a lower unit cost than could a number of competing firms. Clear-cut circumstances of natural monopoly are relatively rare, but such conditions exist for many *public utilities*, such as local electricity, water, natural gas, and telephone providers. As we discussed in Chapter 10, large-scale operations in some cases are necessary to obtain low unit costs and a low product price. Where there is natural monopoly, competition is uneconomical. If the market were divided among many producers, economies of scale would not be achieved and unit costs and prices would be higher than necessary.

There are two possible alternatives for promoting better economic outcomes where natural monopoly exists. One is public ownership, and the other is public regulation.

Public ownership or some approximation of it has been established in a few instances. Examples: the Postal Service, the Tennessee Valley Authority, and Amtrak at the national level and mass transit, water supply systems, and garbage collection at the local level.

But *public regulation*, or what economists call *industrial regulation*, has been the preferred option in the United States. In this type of regulation, government commissions regulate the prices (usually called "rates") charged by natural monopolists. Table 18.1 lists the two major Federal regulatory commissions and their jurisdictions. It also notes that all 50 states have commissions that regulate the intrastate activities and "utility rates" of remaining natural monopolies.

TABLE 18.1 The Main Regulatory Commissions Providing Industrial Regulation

Commission (Year Established)	Jurisdiction
Federal Energy Regulatory Commission (1930)*	Electricity, gas, gas pipelines, oil pipelines, water-power sites
Federal Communications Commission (1934)	Telephones, television, cable television, radio, telegraph, CB radios, ham operators
State public utility commissions (50 states)	Electricity, gas, telephones

*Originally called the Federal Power Commission; renamed in 1977.

The economic objective of industrial regulation is embodied in the **public interest theory of regulation**. In that theory, industrial regulation is necessary to keep a natural monopoly from charging monopoly prices and thus harming consumers and society. The goal of such regulation is to garner for society at least part of the cost reductions associated with natural monopoly while avoiding the restrictions of output and high prices associated with unregulated monopoly. If competition is inappropriate or impractical, society should allow or even encourage a monopoly but regulate its prices. Regulation should then be structured so that ratepayers benefit from the economies of scale—the lower per-unit costs—that natural monopolists are able to achieve.

In practice, regulators seek to establish rates that will cover production costs and yield a "fair" return to the enterprise. The goal is to set price equal to average total cost so that the regulated firm receives a normal profit, as described in the "Regulated Monopoly" section of Chapter 10. In particular, you should carefully review Figure 10.9.

Problems with Industrial Regulation

There is considerable disagreement on the effectiveness of industrial regulation. Let's examine two criticisms.

Costs and Inefficiency

An unregulated firm has a strong incentive to reduce its costs at each level of output because that will increase its profit. The regulatory commission, however, confines the regulated firm to a normal profit or a "fair return" on the value of its assets. If a regulated firm lowers its operating costs, the rising profit eventually will lead the regulatory commission to require that the firm lower its rates in order to return its profits to normal. The regulated firm therefore has little or no incentive to reduce its operating costs.

Worse yet, higher costs do not result in lower profit. Because the regulatory commission must allow the public utility a fair return, the regulated monopolist can simply pass through higher production costs to consumers by charging higher rates. A regulated firm may reason that it might as well have high salaries for its workers, opulent working conditions for management, and the like, since the "return" is the same in percentage terms whether costs are minimized or not. So, although a natural monopoly reduces cost through economies of scale, industrial regulation fosters considerable X-inefficiency (Figure 10.7). Due to the absence of competition, the potential cost savings from natural monopoly may never actually materialize.

Perpetuating Monopoly A second general problem with industrial regulation is that it sometimes perpetuates monopoly long after the conditions of natural monopoly have ended.

Technological change often creates the potential for competition in some or even all portions of the regulated industry. Examples: Trucks began competing with railroads; transmission of voice and data by microwave and satellites began competing with transmission over telephone wires; satellite television began competing with cable television; and cell phones began competing with regular phones.

But spurred by the firms they regulate, commissions often protect the regulated firms from new competition by either blocking entry or extending regulation to competitors. Industrial regulation therefore may perpetuate a monopoly that is no longer a natural monopoly and would otherwise erode. Ordinary monopoly, protected by government, may supplant natural monopoly. If so, the regulated prices may exceed those that would occur with competition. The beneficiaries of outdated regulation are the regulated firms and their employees. The losers are consumers and the potential entrants.

Example: Regulation of the railroads by the Interstate Commerce Commission (ICC) was justified in the late 1800s and early 1900s. But by the 1930s, with the emergence of a network of highways, the trucking industry had seriously undermined the monopoly power of the railroads. That is, for the transport of many goods over many routes, railroad service was no longer a natural monopoly. At that time it would have been desirable to dismantle the ICC and let railroads and truckers, along with barges and airlines, compete with one another. Instead, in the 1930s the ICC extended regulation of rates to interstate truckers. The ICC remained in place until its elimination in 1996.

Second example: Until recently, unregulated long-distance telephone companies such as AT&T and MCI have been prohibited from offering local telephone services in competition with regulated local and regional telephone companies. But the very fact that these and other firms wanted to compete with regulated monopolies calls into question whether those local providers are in fact natural monopolies or, rather, are government-protected monopolies. **(Key Question 10)**

Legal Cartel Theory

The regulation of potentially competitive industries has produced the **legal cartel theory of regulation**. In place of having socially minded officials forcing regulation on natural monopolies to protect consumers, holders of this view see practical politicians "supplying" regulation to local, regional, and national firms that fear the impact of competition on their profits or even on their long-term survival. These firms desire regulation because it yields a legal monopoly that can virtually guarantee a profit. Specifically, the regulatory commission performs such functions as blocking entry (for example, in local telephone service). Or, where there are several firms, the commission divides up the market much like an illegal cartel (for example, prior to airline deregulation, the Civil Aeronautics Board assigned routes to specific airlines). The commission may also restrict potential competition by enlarging the "cartel" (for example, the ICC's addition of trucking to its regulatory domain).

While private cartels are illegal and unstable and often break down, the special attraction of a government-sponsored cartel under the guise of regulation is that it endures. The legal cartel theory of regulation suggests that regulation results from the rent-seeking activities of private firms and the desire of politicians to be responsive in order to win reelection (Chapter 17).

Proponents of the legal cartel theory of regulation note that the Interstate Commerce Commission was welcomed by the railroads and that the trucking and airline industries both supported the extension of ICC regulation to their industries, arguing that unregulated competition was severe and destructive.

Occupational licensing is a labor market application of the legal cartel theory. Certain occupational groups—barbers, dentists, hairstylists, interior designers, dietitians, lawyers—demand stringent licensing on the grounds that it protects the public from charlatans and quacks. But skeptics say the real reason may be to limit entry into the occupational group so that practitioners can receive monopoly incomes.

Deregulation

Beginning in the 1970s, evidence of inefficiency in regulated industries and the contention that the government was regulating potentially competitive industries contributed to a wave of deregulation. Since then, Congress and many state legislatures have passed legislation that has deregulated in varying degrees the airline, trucking, banking, railroad, natural gas, television, and electricity industries. Deregulation has also occurred in the telecommunications industry, where antitrust authorities dismantled the regulated monopoly known as the Bell System (AT&T).

Deregulation in the 1970s and 1980s was one of the most extensive experiments in economic policy to take place during the last 50 years.

The overwhelming consensus among economists is that deregulation has produced large net benefits for consumers and society. Most of the gains from deregulation have occurred in three industries: airlines, railroads, and trucking. Airfares (adjusted for inflation) have declined by about one-third, and airline safety has continued to improve. Trucking and railroad freight rates (again, adjusted for inflation) have dropped by about one-half.

Significant efficiency gains also have been realized in long-distance telecommunications, and there have been slight efficiency gains in cable television, stock brokerage services, and the natural gas industry. Moreover, deregulation has unleashed a wave of technological advances that have resulted in such new and improved products and services as fax machines, cellular phones, fiber-optic cable, microwave systems in communications, and the Internet.

The most recent and perhaps controversial industry to be deregulated is electricity. Deregulation is relatively advanced at the wholesale level, where firms can buy and sell electricity at market prices. They are also free to build generating facilities and sell electricity to local electricity providers at unregulated prices. In addition, several states have deregulated retail prices and encouraged households and businesses to choose among available electricity suppliers. This competition has generally lowered electricity rates for consumers and enhanced allocative efficiency.

But deregulation suffered a severe setback in California, where wholesale electricity prices, but not retail rates, were deregulated. Wholesale electricity prices surged in 2001 when California experienced electricity shortages. Because they could not pass on wholesale price increases to consumers, California electric utilities suffered large financial losses. California then filed lawsuits against several energy-trading companies that allegedly manipulated electricity supplies to boost the wholesale price of electricity during the California energy crisis. One multibillion-dollar energy trader—Enron—collapsed in 2002 when Federal investigators uncovered a pattern of questionable and fraudulent business and accounting practices.

The California deregulation debacle and the Enron collapse have muddied the overall assessment of electricity deregulation in the United States. It is simply much too soon to declare that deregulation of electricity is either a success or a failure.

- Natural monopoly occurs where economies of scale are so extensive that only a single firm can produce the product at minimum average total cost.
- The public interest theory of regulation says that government must regulate natural monopolies to prevent abuses arising from monopoly power. Regulated firms, however, have less incentive than competitive firms to reduce costs. That is, regulated firms tend to be X-inefficient.
- The legal cartel theory of regulation suggests that some firms seek government regulation to reduce price competition and ensure stable profits.
- Deregulation initiated by government in the past several decades has yielded large annual efficiency gains for society.

Social Regulation

The industrial regulation discussed in the preceding section has focused on the regulation of prices (or rates) in natural monopolies. But in the early 1960s a new type of regulation began to emerge. This *social regulation* is concerned with the conditions under which goods and services are produced, the impact of production on society, and the physical qualities of the goods themselves.

The Federal government carries out most of the social regulation, although states also play a role. In Table 18.2 we list the main Federal regulatory commissions engaged in social regulation.

Distinguishing Features

Social regulation differs from industrial regulation in several ways.

First, social regulation applies to far more firms than does industrial regulation. Social regulation is often applied "across the board" to all industries and directly

TABLE 18.2 **The Main Federal Regulatory Commissions Providing Social Regulation**

Commission (Year Established)	Jurisdiction
Food and Drug Administration (1906)	Safety and effectiveness of food, drugs, and cosmetics
Equal Employment Opportunity Commission (1964)	Hiring, promotion, and discharge of workers
Occupational Safety and Health Administration (1971)	Industrial health and safety
Environmental Protection Agency (1972)	Air, water, and noise pollution
Consumer Product Safety Commission (1972)	Safety of consumer products

affects more producers than does industrial regulation. For instance, while the industrial regulation of the Federal Energy Regulatory Commission (FERC) applies to a relatively small number of firms, Occupational Safety and Health Administration (OSHA) rules and regulations apply to firms in all industries.

Second, social regulation intrudes into the day-to-day production process to a greater extent than industrial regulation. While industrial regulation focuses on rates, costs, and profits, social regulation often dictates the design of products, the conditions of employment, and the nature of the production process. As examples, the Consumer Product Safety Commission (CPSC) regulates the design of potentially unsafe products, and the Environmental Protection Agency (EPA) regulates the amount of pollution allowed during production.

Finally, social regulation has expanded rapidly during the same period in which industrial regulation has waned. Between 1970 and 1980, the U.S. government created 20 new social regulatory agencies. More recently, Congress has established new social regulations to be enforced by existing regulatory agencies. For example, the Equal Employment Opportunity Commission, which is responsible for enforcing laws against workplace discrimination on the basis of race, gender, age, or religion, has been given the added duty of enforcing the Americans with Disabilities Act of 1990. Under this social regulation, firms must provide reasonable accommodations for qualified workers and job applicants with disabilities. Also, sellers must provide reasonable access for customers with disabilities.

The names of the regulatory agencies in Table 18.2 suggest the reasons for their creation and growth: As much of our society had achieved a fairly affluent standard of living by the 1960s, attention shifted to improvement in the nonmaterial quality of life. The new focus called for safer products, less pollution, improved working conditions, and greater equality of economic opportunity.

The Optimal Level of Social Regulation

While economists agree on the need for social regulation, they disagree on whether or not the current level of such regulation is optimal. Recall that an activity should be expanded as long as its marginal benefit (MB) exceeds its marginal cost (MC). If the MB of social regulation exceeds its MC, then there is too little social regulation. But if MC exceeds MB, there is too much (review Figure 16.6). Unfortunately, the marginal costs and benefits of social regulation are not always easy to measure and therefore may be illusory. So ideology about the proper size and role

The Microsoft Antitrust Case Is the Most Significant Monopoly Case since the Breakup of AT&T in the Early 1980s.

The Charges In May 1998 the U.S. Justice Department (under President Clinton), 19 individual states, and the District of Columbia (hereafter, "the government") filed antitrust charges against Microsoft under the Sherman Antitrust Act. The government charged that Microsoft had violated Section 2 of the act through a series of unlawful actions designed to maintain its "Windows" monopoly. It also charged that some of that conduct violated Section 1 of the Sherman Act.

Microsoft denied the charges, arguing it had achieved its success through product innovation and lawful business practices. Microsoft contended it should not be penalized for its superior foresight, business acumen, and technological prowess. It also pointed out that its monopoly was highly transitory because of rapid technological advance.

The District Court Findings In June 2000 the district court ruled that the relevant market was software used to operate Intel-compatible personal computers (PCs). Microsoft's 95 percent share of that market clearly gave it monopoly power. The court pointed out, however, that being a monopoly is not illegal. The

violation of the Sherman Act occurred because Microsoft used anticompetitive means to maintain its monopoly power.

According to the court, Microsoft feared that the success of Netscape's Navigator, which allowed people to browse the Internet, might allow Netscape to expand its software to include a competitive PC operating system—software that would threaten the Windows monopoly. It also feared that Sun's Internet applications of its Java programming language might eventually threaten Microsoft's Windows monopoly.

To counter these and similar threats, Microsoft illegally signed contracts with PC makers that required them to feature Internet Explorer on the PC desktop and penalized companies that promoted software products that competed with Microsoft products. Moreover, it gave friendly companies coding that linked Windows to software applications and withheld such coding from companies featuring Netscape. Finally, under license from Sun, Microsoft developed Windows-related Java software that made Sun's own software incompatible with Windows.

The District Court Remedy The district court ordered Microsoft to split into two competing companies, one initially selling the Windows operating system and the other initially selling Microsoft applications (such as Word, Hotmail, MSN, PowerPoint, and Internet Explorer). Both companies would be free to develop new

---

of government often drives the debate over social regulation as much as, or perhaps more than, economic cost-benefit analysis.

In Support of Social Regulation

Defenders of social regulation say that it has achieved notable successes and, overall, has greatly enhanced society's well-being. They point out that the problems that social regulation confronts are serious and substantial. According to the National Safety Council, about 5000 workers die annually in job-related accidents and 3.7 million workers suffer injuries that force them to miss a day or more of work. Air pollution continues to cloud major U.S. cities, imposing large costs in terms of reduced property values and increased health care expense. Numerous children and adults die each year because of poorly designed or manufactured products (for example, car tires) or tainted food (for example, *E. coli* in beef). Discrimination against some ethnic and racial minorities, persons with disabilities, and older workers reduces their earnings and imposes heavy costs on society.

Proponents of social regulation acknowledge that social regulation is costly. But they correctly point out that a high "price" for something does not necessarily mean that it should not be purchased. They say that the appropriate economic test should be not whether the costs of social regulation are high or low but, rather, whether the benefits of social regulation exceed the costs. After decades of neglect, they further assert, society cannot expect to cleanse the environment, enhance the safety of the workplace, and promote economic opportunity for all without incurring substantial costs. So statements about the huge costs of social regulation are irrelevant, say defenders, since the benefits are even greater. The public often underestimates those benefits since they are more difficult to measure than costs and often become apparent only after some time has passed (for example, the benefits of reducing global warming).

Proponents of social regulation point to its many specific benefits. Here are just a few examples: It is estimated that highway fatalities would be 40 percent greater annually in the absence of auto safety features mandated

products that compete with each other, and both could derive those products from the intellectual property embodied in the common products existing at the time of divestiture.

The Appeals Court Ruling In late 2000 Microsoft appealed the district court decision to a U.S. court of appeals. In 2001 the higher court affirmed that Microsoft illegally maintained its monopoly but tossed out the district court's decision to break up Microsoft. It agreed with Microsoft that the company was denied due process during the penalty phase of the trial and concluded that the district court judge had displayed an appearance of bias by holding extensive interviews with the press. The appeals court sent the remedial phase of the case to a new district court judge to determine appropriate remedies. The appeals court also raised issues relating to the wisdom of a structural remedy.

The Final Settlement At the urging of the new district court judge, the Federal government (then under President George W. Bush) and Microsoft negotiated a proposed settlement. With minor modification, the settlement became the final court order in 2002. The breakup was rescinded and replaced with a behavioral remedy. It (1) prevents Microsoft from retaliating against any firm that is developing, selling, or using software that competes with Microsoft Windows or Internet Explorer or is shipping a personal computer that includes both Windows and a non-Microsoft operating system; (2) requires Microsoft to establish uniform royalty and licensing terms for computer manufacturers wanting to include Windows on their PCs; (3) requires that manufacturers be allowed to remove Microsoft icons and replace them with other icons on the Windows desktop; and (4) calls for Microsoft to provide technical information to other companies so that they can develop programs that work as well with Windows as Microsoft's own products.

The Microsoft actions and conviction have indirectly resulted in billions of dollars of fines and payouts by Microsoft. Main examples: To AOL Time Warner (Netscape), $750 million; to the European Commission, $600 million; to Sun Microsystems, $1.6 billion; to Novell, $536 million; to Burst.com, $60 million; to Gateway, $150 million; to InterTrust, $440 million; to RealNetworks, $761 million; and to IBM, $850 million.

Source: United States v. Microsoft (District Court Conclusions of Law), April 2000; *United States v. Microsoft* (Court of Appeals), June 2001; *U.S. v. Microsoft* (Final Judgment), November 2002; and Reuters and Associated Press News Services.

through regulation. Compliance with child safety-seat and seat belt laws has significantly reduced the auto fatality rate for small children. The national air quality standards set by law have been reached in nearly all parts of the nation for sulfur dioxide, nitrogen dioxide, and lead. Moreover, recent studies clearly link cleaner air, other things equal, with increases in the values of homes. Affirmative action regulations have increased the labor demand for racial and ethnic minorities and females. The use of childproof lids has resulted in a 90 percent decline in child deaths caused by accidental swallowing of poisonous substances.

Some defenders of social regulation say there are many remaining areas in which greater regulation would generate net benefits to society. For instance, some call for greater regulation of the meat, poultry, and seafood industries to improve food safety. Others favor greater regulation of health care organizations and insurance companies to ensure "patients' rights" for consumers of health care services. Still others say that more regulation is needed to ensure that violent movies, CDs, and video games are not marketed to children.

Advocates of social regulation say that the benefits of such regulation are well worth the considerable costs. The costs are simply the price we must pay to create a hospitable, sustainable, and just society. **(Key Question 12)**

Criticisms of Social Regulation
Critics of social regulation contend that, in many instances, it has been expanded to the point where the marginal costs exceed the marginal benefits. In this view, society would achieve net benefits by cutting back on irritating social regulation. Critics say that many social regulation laws are poorly written, making regulatory objectives and standards difficult to understand. As a result, regulators pursue goals well beyond the original intent of the legislation. Businesses complain that regulators often press for additional increments of improvement, unmindful of costs.

Also, decisions must often be made and rules formed on the basis of inadequate information. Examples: Consumer Product Safety Commission (CPSC) officials may make decisions about certain cancer-causing ingredients in products on the basis of limited laboratory experiments with animals. Or government agencies may establish costly pollution standards to attack the global-warming problem without knowing for certain whether pollution is the main cause of the problem. These efforts, say critics, lead to excessive regulation of business.

Moreover, critics argue that social regulations produce many unintended and costly side effects. For instance, the Federal gas mileage standard for automobiles has been blamed for an estimated 2000 to 3900 traffic deaths a year because auto manufacturers have reduced the weight of vehicles to meet the higher miles-per-gallon standards. Other things equal, drivers of lighter cars have a higher fatality rate than drivers of heavier vehicles.

Finally, opponents of social regulation say that the regulatory agencies may attract overzealous workers who are hostile toward the market system and "believe" too fervently in regulation. For example, some staff members of government agencies may see large corporations as "bad guys" who regularly cause pollution, provide inadequate safety for workers, deceive their customers, and generally abuse their power in the community. Such biases can lead to seemingly never-ending calls for still more regulation, rather than objective assessments of the costs and benefits of added regulation.

Two Reminders

The debate over the proper amount of social regulation will surely continue. By helping determine costs and benefits, economic analysis can lead to more informed discussions and to better decisions. In this regard, we leave both ardent supporters and opponents of social regulation with pertinent reminders.

There Is No Free Lunch Fervent supporters of social regulation need to remember that "there is no free lunch." Social regulation can produce higher prices, stifle innovation, and reduce competition.

Social regulation raises product prices in two ways. It does so directly because compliance costs normally get passed on to consumers, and it does so indirectly by reducing labor productivity. Resources invested in making workplaces accessible to disabled workers, for example, are not available for investment in new machinery designed to increase output per worker. Where the wage rate is fixed, a drop in labor productivity increases the marginal and average total costs of production. In effect, the supply curve for the product shifts leftward, causing the price of the product to rise.

Social regulation may have a negative impact on the rate of innovation. Technological advance may be stifled by,

say, the fear that a new plant will not meet EPA guidelines or that a new medicine will require years of testing before being approved by the Food and Drug Administration (FDA).

Social regulation may weaken competition since it usually places a relatively greater burden on small firms than on large ones. The costs of complying with social regulation are, in effect, fixed costs. Because smaller firms produce less output over which to distribute those costs, their compliance costs per unit of output put them at a competitive disadvantage with their larger rivals. Social regulation is more likely to force smaller firms out of business, thus contributing to the increased concentration of industry.

Finally, social regulation may prompt some U.S. firms to move their operations to countries in which the rules are not as burdensome and therefore production costs are lower.

Less Government Is Not Always Better Than More On the opposite side of the issue, opponents of social regulation need to remember that less government is not always better than more government. While the market system is a powerful engine of producing goods and services and generating income, it has certain flaws and can camouflage certain abuses. Through appropriate amounts of social regulation government can clearly increase economic efficiency and thus society's well-being. Ironically, by "taking the rough edges off of capitalism," social regulation may be a strong pro capitalism force. Properly conceived and executed, social regulation helps maintain political support for the market system. Such support could quickly wane should there be a steady drumbeat of reports of unsafe workplaces, unsafe products, discriminatory hiring, choking pollution, deceived loan customers, and the like. Social regulation helps the market system deliver not only goods and services but also a "good society."

QUICK REVIEW 18.3

- Social regulation is concerned with the conditions under which goods and services are produced, the effects of production on society, and the physical characteristics of the goods themselves.

- Defenders of social regulation point to the benefits arising from policies that keep dangerous products from the marketplace, reduce workplace injuries and deaths, contribute to clean air and water, and reduce employment discrimination.

- Critics of social regulation say uneconomical policy goals, inadequate information, unintended side effects, and overzealous personnel create excessive regulation, for which regulatory costs exceed regulatory benefits.

Summary

1. The cornerstones of antitrust policy are the Sherman Act of 1890 and the Clayton Act of 1914. The Sherman Act specifies that "every contract, combination . . . or conspiracy in the restraint of interstate trade . . . is . . . illegal" and that any person who monopolizes or attempts to monopolize interstate trade is guilty of a felony.

2. If a company is found guilty of violating the antimonopoly provisions of the Sherman Act, the government can either break up the monopoly into competing firms (a structural remedy) or prohibit it from engaging in specific anticompetitive business practices (a behavioral remedy).

3. The Clayton Act was designed to bolster and make more explicit the provisions of the Sherman Act. It declares that price discrimination, tying contracts, intercorporate stock acquisitions, and interlocking directorates are illegal when their effect is to reduce competition.

4. The Federal Trade Commission Act of 1914 created the Federal Trade Commission to investigate antitrust violations and to prevent the use of "unfair methods of competition." The FTC Act was amended by the Wheeler-Lea Act of 1938 to outlaw false and deceptive representation of products to consumers. Empowered by cease-and-desist orders, the FTC serves as a watchdog agency over unfair, deceptive, or false claims made by firms about their own products or the products of their competitors.

5. The Celler-Kefauver Act of 1950 amended the Clayton Act of 1914 to prohibit one firm from acquiring the assets of another firm when the result will substantially reduce competition.

6. Issues in applying antitrust laws include (a) determining whether an industry should be judged by its structure or by its behavior; (b) defining the scope and size of the dominant firm's market; and (c) deciding how strictly to enforce the antitrust laws.

7. The courts treat price-fixing among competitors as a *per se violation*, meaning that the conduct is illegal independently of whether the conspiracy caused harm. In contrast, a *rule of reason* is used to assess monopoly. Only monopolies that unreasonably (abusively) achieve or maintain their status violate the law. Antitrust officials are more likely to challenge price-fixing, tying contracts, and horizontal mergers than to try to break up existing monopolies. Nevertheless, antitrust suits by the Federal government led to the breakup of the AT&T monopoly in the early 1980s.

8. The objective of industrial regulation is to protect the public from the market power of natural monopolies by regulating prices and quality of service.

9. Critics of industrial regulation contend that it can lead to inefficiency and rising costs and that in many instances it constitutes a legal cartel for the regulated firms. Legislation passed in the late 1970s and the 1980s has brought about varying degrees of deregulation in the airline, trucking, banking, railroad, and television broadcasting industries.

10. Studies indicate that deregulation of airlines, railroads, trucking, and telecommunications is producing sizable annual gains to society through lower prices, lower costs, and increased output. Less certain is the effect of the more recent deregulation of the electricity industry.

11. Social regulation is concerned with product safety, working conditions, and the effects of production on society. Whereas industrial regulation is on the wane, social regulation continues to expand. The optimal amount of social regulation occurs where $MB = MC$.

12. People who support social regulation point to its numerous specific successes and assert that it has greatly enhanced society's well-being. Critics of social regulation contend that businesses are excessively regulated to the point where marginal costs exceed marginal benefits. They also say that social regulation often produces unintended and costly side effects.

Terms and Concepts

antitrust policy	cease-and-desist order	Microsoft case
industrial regulation	Wheeler-Lea Act	horizontal merger
social regulation	Celler-Kefauver Act	vertical merger
Sherman Act	Standard Oil case	conglomerate merger
Clayton Act	U.S. Steel case	per se violations
tying contracts	rule of reason	natural monopoly
interlocking directorates	Alcoa case	public interest theory of regulation
Federal Trade Commission Act	DuPont cellophane case	legal cartel theory of regulation

Study Questions

1. Both antitrust policy and industrial regulation deal with monopoly. What distinguishes the two approaches? How does government decide to use one form of remedy rather than the other? **LO1, LO3**

2. **KEY QUESTION** Describe the major provisions of the Sherman and Clayton acts. What government entities are responsible for enforcing those laws? Are firms permitted to initiate antitrust suits on their own against other firms? **LO1**

3. Contrast the outcomes of the Standard Oil and U.S. Steel cases. What was the main antitrust issue in the DuPont cellophane case? In what major way do the Microsoft and Standard Oil cases differ? **LO2**

4. Why might one administration interpret and enforce the antitrust laws more strictly than another? How might a change of administrations affect a major monopoly case in progress? **LO2**

5. **KEY QUESTION** How would you expect antitrust authorities to react to: **LO2**
   a. A proposed merger of Ford and General Motors.
   b. Evidence of secret meetings by contractors to rig bids for highway construction projects.
   c. A proposed merger of a large shoe manufacturer and a chain of retail shoe stores.
   d. A proposed merger of a small life-insurance company and a regional candy manufacturer.
   e. An automobile rental firm that charges higher rates for last-minute rentals than for rentals reserved weeks in advance.

6. Suppose a proposed merger of firms would simultaneously lessen competition and reduce unit costs through economies of scale. Do you think such a merger should be allowed? **LO2**

7. In the 1980s, PepsiCo Inc., which then had 28 percent of the soft-drink market, proposed to acquire the Seven-Up Company. Shortly thereafter the Coca-Cola Company, with 39 percent of the market, indicated it wanted to acquire the Dr Pepper Company. Seven-Up and Dr Pepper each controlled about 7 percent of the market. In your judgment, was the government's decision to block these mergers appropriate? **LO2**

8. Why might a firm charged with violating the Clayton Act, Section 7, try arguing that the products sold by the merged firms are in separate markets? Why might a firm charged with violating Section 2 of the Sherman Act try convincing the court that none of its behavior in achieving and maintaining its monopoly was illegal? **LO2**

9. "The social desirability of any particular firm should be judged not on the basis of its market share but on the basis of its conduct and performance." Make a counterargument, referring to the monopoly model in your statement. **LO2**

10. **KEY QUESTION** What types of industries, if any, should be subjected to industrial regulation? What specific problems does industrial regulation entail? **LO3**

11. In view of the problems involved in regulating natural monopolies, compare socially optimal (marginal-cost) pricing and fair-return pricing by referring again to Figure 10.9. Assuming that a government subsidy might be used to cover any loss resulting from marginal-cost pricing, which pricing policy would you favor? Why? What problems might such a subsidy entail? **LO3**

12. **KEY QUESTION** How does social regulation differ from industrial regulation? What types of benefits and costs are associated with social regulation? **LO4**

13. Use economic analysis to explain why the optimal amount of product safety may be less than the amount that would totally eliminate risks of accidents and deaths. Use automobiles as an example. **LO4**

14. **LAST WORD** Under what law and on what basis did the Federal district court find Microsoft guilty of violating the antitrust laws? What was the initial district court's remedy? How did Microsoft fare with its appeal to the court of appeals? Was the final remedy in the case a structural remedy or a behavioral remedy?

Web-Based Questions

1. **THE FTC AND THE ANTITRUST DIVISION—RECENT LEGAL ACTIONS** Go to the FTC Web site, **www.ftc.gov**, to find press releases by selecting News. Briefly summarize two antitrust (not false advertising) actions taken by the FTC over the past 12 months. Next, go to the Web site of the U.S. Department of Justice's Antitrust Division, **www.usdoj.gov/atr/index.html**, and look under Recent Antitrust Case Filings. Briefly summarize two antitrust actions taken by the Antitrust Division during the past 12 months.

2. **THE CONSUMER PRODUCT SAFETY COMMISSION— WHAT IS IT AND WHAT DOES IT DO?** What are the major functions of the Consumer Product Safety Commission, **www.cpsc.gov**? Name two products from the current Most Wanted list (in the left column) and explain why they are dangerous. From Recalls and Product Safety News, identify two product categories of interest to you. List three specific product recalls for each of your two product categories and briefly explain the main reason for each recall.

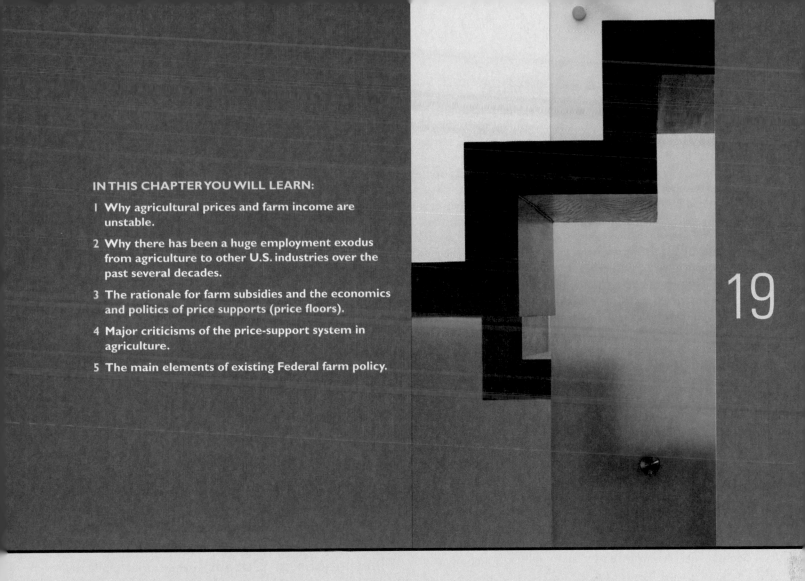

19

Agriculture: Economics and Policy

If you eat, you are part of agriculture! In the United States, agriculture is important for a number of reasons. It is one of the nation's largest industries and major segments of it provide real-world examples of the pure-competition model (Chapter 9). Also, agriculture clearly shows the effects of government policies that interfere with supply and demand. Further, the industry provides excellent illustrations of Chapter 17's special-interest effect and rent-seeking behavior. Finally, it demonstrates the globalization of markets for farm commodities.

This chapter examines the circumstances in agriculture that have resulted in government intervention, the types and outcomes of government intervention, and recent major changes in farm policy.

Economics of Agriculture

Although economists refer to "the agriculture industry," this segment of the economy is extremely diverse. Agriculture encompasses cattle ranches, fruit orchards, dairies, poultry plants, pig farms, grain farms, feed lots, vegetable plots, sugar-cane plantations, and much more. Some farm commodities (for example, soybeans and corn) are produced by thousands of individual farmers. Other farm commodities (such as poultry) are produced by just a handful of large firms. Some farm products (for example, wheat, milk, and sugar) are heavily subsidized through Federal government programs; other farm products (such as fruits, nuts, and potatoes) have much less government support.

Moreover, agriculture includes both farm products, or **farm commodities** (for example, wheat, soybeans, cattle, and rice), and also **food products** (items sold through restaurants or grocery stores). Generally, the number of competing firms in the market diminishes as farm products are refined into commercial food products. Although thousand of ranches and farms raise cattle, only four firms (Tyson, Excel, JBS, and Smithfield) account for 82 percent of red meat produced at cattle slaughtering/meat packing plants. And thousands of farms grow tomatoes, but only three companies (Heinz, Del-Monte, and Hunt) make the bulk of the ketchup sold in the United States.

Our focus in this chapter will be on farm commodities (or farm products) and the farms and ranches that produce them. Farm commodities usually are sold in highly competitive markets, whereas food products tend to be sold in markets characterized by monopolistic competition or oligopoly.

Partly because of large government subsidies, farming remains a generally profitable industry. U.S. consumers allocate 14 percent of their spending to food and farmers and ranchers receive about $285 billion of revenue annually from sales of crops and livestock. Over the years, however, American farmers have experienced severely fluctuating prices and periodically low incomes. Further, they have had to adjust to the reality that agriculture is a declining industry. The farm share of GDP has declined from about 7 percent in 1950 to 1 percent today.

Let's take a close look at both the short-run and long-run economics of U.S. agriculture.

The Short Run: Price and Income Instability

Price and income instability in agriculture results from (1) an inelastic demand for agricultural products, combined with (2) fluctuations in farm output and (3) shifts of the demand curve for farm products.

Inelastic Demand for Agricultural Products

In industrially advanced economies, the price elasticity of demand for agricultural products is low. For agricultural products in the aggregate, the elasticity coefficient is between .20 and .25. These figures suggest that the prices of farm products would have to fall by 40 to 50 percent for consumers to increase their purchases by a mere 10 percent. Consumers apparently put a low value on additional farm output compared with the value they put on additional units of alternative goods.

Why is this so? Recall that the basic determinant of elasticity of demand is substitutability. When the price of one product falls, the consumer tends to substitute that product for other products whose prices have not fallen. But in relatively wealthy societies this "substitution effect" is very modest for food. Although people may eat more, they do not switch from three meals a day to, say, five or six meals a day in response to a decline in the relative prices of farm products. Real biological factors constrain an individual's capacity to substitute food for other products.

The inelasticity of agricultural demand is also related to diminishing marginal utility. In a high-income economy, the population is generally well fed and well clothed; it is relatively saturated with the food and fiber of agriculture. Additional farm products therefore are subject to rapidly diminishing marginal utility. So very large price cuts are needed to induce small increases in food and fiber consumption.

Fluctuations in Output
Farm output tends to fluctuate from year to year, mainly because farmers have limited control over their output. Floods, droughts, unexpected frost, insect damage, and similar disasters can mean poor crops, while an excellent growing season means bumper crops (unusually large outputs). Such natural occurrences are beyond the control of farmers, yet they exert an important influence on output.

In addition to natural phenomena, the highly competitive nature of many parts of farming and ranching makes it difficult for those producers to form huge combinations to control production. If the thousands of widely scattered and independent producers happened to plant an unusually large or abnormally small portion of their land one year, an extra-large or a very small farm output would result even if the growing season were normal.

Curve D in Figure 19.1 suggests the inelastic demand for agricultural products. Combining that inelastic demand with the instability of farm production, we can see why agricultural prices and incomes are unstable. Even if the market demand for farm products remains fixed at D, its

FIGURE 19.1 **The effects of changes in farm output on agricultural prices and income.** Because of the inelasticity of demand for farm products, a relatively small change in farm output (from Q_n to Q_p or Q_b) will cause a relatively large change in agricultural prices (from P_n to P_p or P_b). Farm income will change from the orange area to the larger $0P_ppQ_p$ area or to the smaller $0P_bbQ_b$ area.

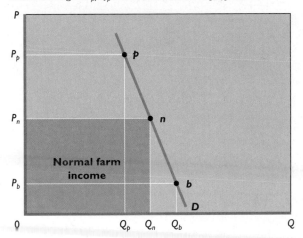

FIGURE 19.2 **The effect of a demand shift on agricultural prices and income.** Because of the highly inelastic demand for farm products, a small shift in demand (from D_1 to D_2) for farm products can drastically alter agricultural prices (P_1 to P_2) and farm income (area $0P_1aQ_n$ to area $0P_2bQ_n$), given a fixed level of production Q_n.

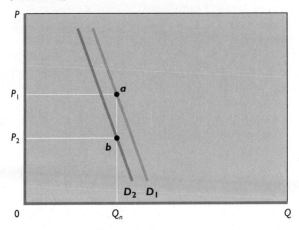

price inelasticity will magnify small changes in output into relatively large changes in agricultural prices and income. For example, suppose that a "normal" crop of Q_n results in a "normal" price of P_n and a "normal" farm income represented by the orange rectangle. A bumper crop or a poor crop will cause large deviations from these normal prices and incomes because of the inelasticity of demand.

If a good growing season occurs, the resulting large crop of Q_b will reduce farm income to that of area $0P_bbQ_b$. When demand is inelastic, an increase in the quantity sold will be accompanied by a more-than-proportionate decline in price. The net result is that total revenue, that is, total farm income, will decline disproportionately.

Similarly, a small crop caused by, say, drought will boost total farm income to that represented by area $0P_ppQ_p$. A decline in output will cause more-than-proportionate increases in price and income when demand is inelastic. Ironically, for farmers as a group, a poor crop may be a blessing and a bumper crop a hardship.

Conclusion: With a stable market demand for farm products, the inelasticity of that demand will turn relatively small changes in output into relatively larger changes in agricultural prices and income.

Fluctuations in Demand The third factor in the short-run instability of farm income results from shifts in the demand curve for agricultural products. Suppose that somehow farm output is stabilized at the "normal" level of Q_n in Figure 19.2. Now, because of the inelasticity of the demand for farm products, short-run changes in the

demand for those products will cause markedly different prices and incomes to be associated with this fixed level of output.

A slight decline in demand from D_1 to D_2 will reduce farm income from area $0P_1aQ_n$ to $0P_2bQ_n$. So a relatively small decline in demand gives farmers significantly less income for the same amount of farm output. Conversely, a slight increase in demand—as from D_2 to D_1—provides a sizable increase in farm income for the same volume of output. Again, large price and income changes occur because demand is inelastic.

It is tempting to argue that the sharp declines in agricultural prices that accompany a decrease in demand will cause many farmers to close down in the short run, reducing total output and alleviating the price and income declines. But farm production is relatively insensitive to price changes in the short run because farmers' fixed costs are high compared with their variable costs.

Interest, rent, tax, and mortgage payments on land, buildings, and equipment are the major costs faced by the farmer. These are all fixed charges. Furthermore, the labor supply of farmers and their families can also be regarded as a fixed cost. As long as they stay on their farms, farmers cannot reduce their costs by firing themselves. Their variable costs are the costs of the small amounts of extra help they may employ, as well as expenditures for seed, fertilizer, and fuel. As a result of their high proportion of fixed costs, farmers are usually better off working their land even when they are losing money since they would lose much more by shutting down their operations for the

FIGURE 19.3 U.S. farm exports as a percentage of farm output, 1950–2007. Exports of farm output have increased as a percentage of total farm output (the value of agricultural-sector production) in the United States. But this percentage has been quite variable, contributing to the instability of the demand for U.S. farm output.

Source: Derived by the authors from *Foreign Agricultural Trade of the United States,* **www.ers.usda.gov/Data/FATUS,** *and Agricultural Income and Finance Outlook,* **www.ers.usda.gov**.

year. Only in the long run will exiting the industry make sense for them.

But why is agricultural demand unstable? The major source of demand volatility in U.S. agriculture springs from its dependence on world markets. As we show in Figure 19.3, that dependency has increased since 1950. The yearly ups and downs of the line in the figure also reveal that, as a percentage of total U.S. farm output, farm exports are highly unstable.

The incomes of U.S. farmers are sensitive to changes in weather and crop production in other countries: Better crops abroad mean less foreign demand for U.S. farm products. Similarly, cyclical fluctuations in incomes in Europe or Southeast Asia, for example, may shift the demand for U.S. farm products. Changes in foreign economic policies may also change demand. For instance, if the nations of western Europe decide to provide their farmers with greater protection from foreign competition, U.S. farmers will have less access to those markets and demand for U.S. farm exports will fall.

International politics also add to demand instability. Changing political relations between the United States and China and the United States and Russia have boosted exports to those countries in some periods and reduced them in others. Changes in the international value of the dollar may also be critical. Depreciation of the dollar increases the demand for U.S. farm products (which become cheaper to foreigners), whereas appreciation of the dollar diminishes foreign demand for U.S. farm products.

Figure 19.4 shows inflation-adjusted U.S. prices for cattle, hogs, corn, and wheat during the second half of the twentieth century. The short-run economics of price volatility is evident. So too are the general decline of real (inflation-adjusted) agricultural prices.

The general price declines shown in Figure 19.4 continued through 2005. But agricultural prices jumped sharply in 2006 and 2007. For example, the inflation-adjusted price of corn increased from $1.72 a bushel in 2005 to $2.96 a bushel in 2007. The large price increases led some economists to wonder if the era of inflation-adjusted price decreases in agriculture had come to an end. They speculated that the rising demand for food in emerging economies such as China together with the growing demand for farm products to produce ethanol might reverse the long-run trend. But, as Figure 19.4 reveals, several previous spikes in agricultural prices have occurred. Each of these price spikes soon reverted to the general historical downward trend. Whether this pattern will again occur remains to be seen. **(Key Question 1)**

The Long Run: A Declining Industry

Two dynamic characteristics of agricultural markets explain why agriculture has been a declining industry:

- Over time, the supply of farm products has increased rapidly because of technological progress.
- The demand for farm products has increased slowly, because it is inelastic with respect to income.

Let's examine each of these supply and demand forces.

FIGURE 19.4 Inflation-adjusted U.S. agricultural prices, selected commodities, 1950–1998. Inflation-adjusted U.S. prices (in 1998 dollars) for cattle, hogs, corn, and wheat during the second half of the twentieth century reflected both volatility and general decline.

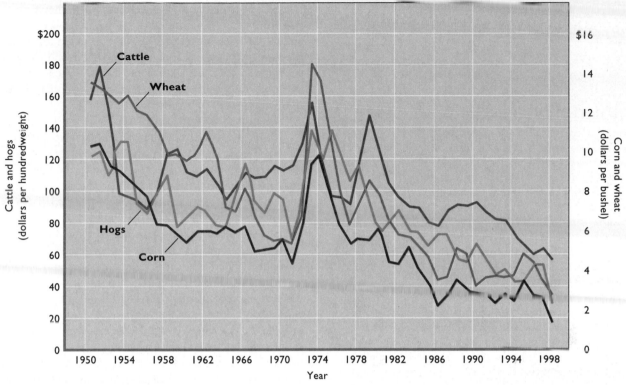

Source: Federal Reserve Bank of Minneapolis.

Technology and Supply Increases

A rapid rate of technological advance has significantly increased the supply of agricultural products. This technological progress has many roots: the mechanization of farms, improved techniques of land management, soil conservation, irrigation, development of hybrid crops, availability of improved fertilizers and insecticides, polymer-coated seeds, and improvements in the breeding and care of livestock. The amount of capital used per farmworker increased 15 times between 1930 and 1980, permitting a fivefold increase in the amount of land cultivated per farmer. The simplest measure of these advances is the U.S. Agriculture Department's index of farm output per unit of farm labor. In 1950 a single unit of farm labor could produce 13 units of farm output. This amount increased to 41 in 1970, 58 in 1980, 91 in 1990, 122 in 2000, and 144 in 2004. Over the last half-century, this physical productivity in agriculture has advanced twice as fast as that in the nonfarm economy.

Most of the technological advances in agriculture were not initiated by farmers. Rather, they are the result of government-sponsored programs of research and education and the initiative of the suppliers of farm inputs. Land-grant colleges, experiment stations, county agents of the Agricultural Extension Service, educational pamphlets issued by the United States Department of Agriculture (USDA), and the research departments of farm machinery, pesticide, and fertilizer producers have been the primary sources of technological advance in U.S. agriculture.

More recently, technological advance has been fueled by the incorporation of advanced information technologies into farming. Computers and the Internet give farmers instant access to information about soil conditions, estimated crop yields, farm-product prices, available land for purchase or lease, and much more. They also provide farmers with sophisticated business software to help track and manage their operations.

Lagging Demand

Increases in the demand for agricultural products have failed to keep pace with these technologically created increases in the supply of the products. The reason lies in the two major determinants of agricultural demand: income and population.

CONSIDER THIS . . .

Risky Business

The short-run instability of agricultural prices and farm income creates considerable risk in agriculture. Later in this chapter we will find that farm programs (direct payments, countercyclical payments, and "repay-or-default" loans) reduce the risk of farming for many farmers. But these programs are limited to certain crops, such as grains and oilseeds.

Fortunately, several private techniques for managing risk have become commonplace in agriculture. The purpose of these measures is to "smooth" income over time, "hedging" against short-run output and price fluctuations. Hedging is an action by a buyer or seller to protect against a change in future prices prior to an anticipated purchase or sale.

Farm risk-management techniques include.

- **Futures markets.** In the futures market, farmers can buy or sell farm products at prices fixed now, for delivery at a specified date in the future. If the price falls, farmers will still obtain revenue based on the higher price fixed in the futures market. If the price rises, the buyer will benefit by getting the farm commodity at the lower price fixed in the futures market.
- **Contracting with processors.** In advance of planting, farmers can directly contract with food processors (firms such as sugar beet refiners, ethanol plants, and feed lots) to assure themselves of a fixed price per unit of their farm or ranch output.
- **Crop revenue insurance.** Farmers can buy crop revenue insurance, which insures them against gross revenue losses resulting from storm damage and other natural occurrences.
- **Leasing land.** Farm operators can reduce their risk by leasing some of their land to other operators who pay them cash rent. The rent payment is stable, regardless of the quality of the crop and crop prices.
- **Nonfarm income.** Many farm households derive substantial parts of their total income from off-farm income, such as spousal work and agricultural investments. These more-stable elements of income cushion the instability of farm income.

Although farming remains a risky business, farm operators have found creative ways to manage the inherent risks of price and income instability.

In developing countries, consumers must devote most of their meager incomes to agricultural products—food and clothing—to sustain themselves. But as income expands beyond subsistence and the problem of hunger diminishes, consumers increase their outlays on food at ever-declining rates. Once consumers' stomachs are filled, they turn to the amenities of life that manufacturing and services, not agriculture, provide. Economic growth in the United States has boosted average per capita income far beyond the level of subsistence. As a result, increases in the incomes of U.S. consumers now produce less-than-proportionate increases in spending on farm products.

The demand for farm products in the United States is income-inelastic; it is quite insensitive to increases in income. Estimates indicate that a 10 percent increase in real per capita after-tax income produces about a 2 percent increase in consumption of farm products. That means a coefficient of income elasticity of .2 (= .02/.10). So as the incomes of Americans rise, the demand for farm products increases far less rapidly than the demand for goods and services in general.

The second reason for lagging demand relates to population growth. Once a certain income level has been reached, each consumer's intake of food and fiber becomes relatively fixed. Thus subsequent increases in demand depend directly on growth in the number of consumers. In most advanced nations, including the United States, the demand for farm products increases at a rate roughly equal to the rate of population growth. Because U.S. population growth has not been rapid, the increase in U.S. demand for farm products has not kept pace with the rapid growth of farm output.

Graphical Portrayal The combination of an inelastic and slowly increasing demand for agricultural products with a rapidly increasing supply puts strong downward pressure on agricultural prices and income. Figure 19.5 shows a large increase in agricultural supply accompanied by a very modest increase in demand. Because of the inelasticity of demand, those modest shifts result in a sharp decline in agricultural prices, accompanied by a relatively small increase in output. So farm income declines. On the graph, we see that farm income before the increases in demand and supply (measured by rectangle $0P_1aQ_1$) exceeds farm income after those increases ($0P_2bQ_2$). Because of an inelastic demand for farm products, an increase in supply of such products relative to demand creates persistent downward pressure on farm income.

Consequences The actual consequences of the demand and supply changes over time have been those predicted by the pure-competition model. The supply and demand conditions just outlined have increased the minimum efficient scale (MES) in agriculture and

FIGURE 19.5 The long-run decline of agricultural prices and farm income In the long run, increases in the demand for U.S. farm products (from D_1 to D_2) have not kept pace with the increases in supply (from S_1 to S_2) resulting from technological advances. Because agricultural demand is inelastic, these shifts have tended to depress agricultural prices (from P_1 to P_2) and reduce farm income (from $0P_1aQ_1$ to $0P_2bQ_2$) while increasing output only modestly (from Q_1 to Q_2).

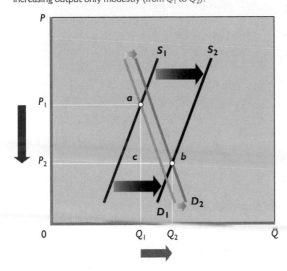

GLOBAL PERSPECTIVE 19.1

Percentage of Labor Force in Agriculture, Selected Nations, 2002–2004

High-income nations devote a much smaller percentage of their labor forces to agriculture than do low-income nations. Because their workforces are so heavily committed to producing the food and fiber needed for their populations, low-income nations have relatively less labor available to produce housing, schools, autos, and the other goods and services that contribute to a high standard of living.

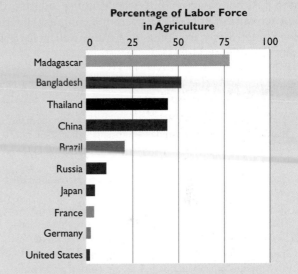

Source: World Bank, *World Development Report, 2008*, pp. 320–21. Copyright 2008 by World Bank. Reproduced with permission of World Bank.

reduced crop prices. Farms that are too small to realize productivity gains and take advantage of economies of scale have discovered that their average total costs exceed the (declining) prices for their crops. So they can no longer operate profitably. In the long run, financial losses in agriculture have triggered a massive exit of workers to other sectors of the economy, as shown by Table 19.1. They have also caused a major consolidation of smaller farms into larger ones. A person farming,

TABLE 19.1 U.S. Farm Employment and Number of Farms, 1950–2006

	Farm Employment*		
Year	**In Millions of People**	**As Percentage of Total Employment**	**Number of Farms, Thousands**
1950	9.3	15.8	5388
1960	6.2	9.4	3962
1970	4.0	5.0	2954
1980	3.5	3.5	2440
1990	2.5	2.1	2146
2000	2.2	1.6	2172
2006	1.9	1.3	2090

*Includes self-employed farmers, unpaid farmworkers, and hired farmworkers.

Sources: Derived by the authors from *Economic Report of the President, 2008*, Table B-100; U.S. Bureau of Labor Statistics, **www.bls.gov,** and Department of Agriculture, Economic Research Service, **www.ers.usda.gov.**

say, 240 acres of corn three decades ago is today likely to be farming two or three times that number of acres. Large corporate firms, collectively called **agribusiness,** have emerged in some areas of farming such as potatoes, beef, fruits, vegetables, and poultry. Today, there are about 2 million farms compared to 4 million in 1960, and farm labor constitutes about 1.3 percent of the U.S. labor force compared to 9.4 percent in 1960. (Global Perspective 19.1 compares the most recent labor-force percentages for several nations.)

Farm-Household Income

Traditionally, the income of farm households was well below that of nonfarm households. But even with the lower real crop prices, that imbalance has reversed. In 2006—a particularly good year for agriculture—the average income of farm households was $77,637 compared to $66,570 for all U.S. households. Outmigration, consolidation, rising farm productivity, and significant government subsidies have boosted farm income *per farm household* (of which there are fewer than before).

Also, members of farm households operating smaller farms have increasingly taken jobs in nearby towns and cities. On average, only 13 percent of the income of farm households derives from farming activities. This average, however, is pulled downward by the many households living in rural areas and operating small "residential farms." For households operating "commercial farms"—farms with annual sales of $250,000 or more—about 71 percent of the average $205,654 income in 2007 derived from farming. Although agriculture is a declining industry, the 8 percent of farm households operating commercial farms in the United States are doing remarkably well, at least as a group. **(Key Question 3)**

QUICK REVIEW 19.1

- Agricultural prices and incomes are volatile in the short run because an inelastic demand converts small changes in farm output and demand into relatively larger changes in prices and income.
- Technological progress has generated large increases in the supply of farm products over time.
- Increases in demand for farm products have been modest in the United States because demand is inelastic with respect to income and because population growth has been modest.
- The combination of large increases in supply and small increases in demand has made U.S. agriculture a declining industry (as measured by the value of agricultural output as a percentage of GDP).

Economics of Farm Policy

The U.S. government has subsidized agriculture since the 1930s with a "farm program" that includes (1) support for agricultural prices, income, and output; (2) soil and water conservation; (3) agricultural research; (4) farm credit; (5) crop insurance; and (6) subsidized sale of farm products in world markets.

We will focus on the main element of farm policy: the programs designed to prop up prices and income. This topic is particularly timely because in recent years (specifically, 1996, 2002, and 2008) Congress passed new farm laws replacing traditional forms of farm subsidies with new forms. To understand these new policies, we need to understand the policies they replaced and the purposes and outcomes of farm subsidies. Between 2000 and 2006, American farmers received an average of $18.3 billion of direct government subsidies each year. (As indicated

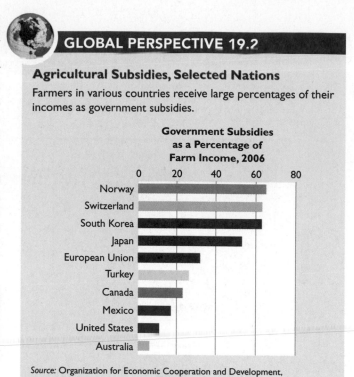

GLOBAL PERSPECTIVE 19.2

Agricultural Subsidies, Selected Nations

Farmers in various countries receive large percentages of their incomes as government subsidies.

Government Subsidies as a Percentage of Farm Income, 2006

Norway
Switzerland
South Korea
Japan
European Union
Turkey
Canada
Mexico
United States
Australia

Source: Organization for Economic Cooperation and Development, **www.oecd.org.**

in Global Perspective 19.2, farm subsidies are common in many nations.)

Rationale for Farm Subsidies

A variety of arguments have been made to justify farm subsidies over the decades:

- Although farm products are necessities of life, many farmers have relatively low incomes, so they should receive higher prices and incomes through public help.
- The "family farm" is a fundamental U.S. institution and should be nurtured as a way of life.
- Farmers are subject to extraordinary hazards—floods, droughts, and insects—that most other industries do not face. Without government help, farmers cannot fully insure themselves against these disasters.
- While many farmers face purely competitive markets for their outputs, they buy inputs of fertilizer, farm machinery, and gasoline from industries that have considerable market power. Whereas those resource-supplying industries are able to control their prices, farmers are at the "mercy of the market" in selling their output. The supporters of subsidies argue that agriculture warrants public aid to offset the disadvantageous market-power imbalances faced by farmers.

Background: The Parity Concept

The Agricultural Adjustment Act of 1933 established the **parity concept** as a cornerstone of agricultural policy. The rationale of the parity concept can be stated in both real and nominal terms. In real terms, parity says that year after year for a fixed output of farm products, a farmer should be able to acquire a specific total amount of other goods and services. A particular real output should always result in the same real income: "If a farmer could take a bushel of corn to town in 1912 and sell it for enough money to buy a shirt, he should be able to sell a bushel of corn today and buy a shirt." In nominal terms, the parity concept suggests that the relationship between the prices received by farmers for their output and the prices they must pay for goods and services should remain constant. The parity concept implies that if the price of shirts tripled over some time period, then the price of corn should have tripled too. Such a situation is said to represent 100 percent of parity.

The **parity ratio** is the ratio of prices received to prices paid, expressed as a percentage. That is:

$$\text{Parity ratio} = \frac{\text{prices received by farmers}}{\text{prices paid by farmers}}$$

Why farmers would benefit from having the prices of their products based on 100 percent of parity is obvious. By 2007 nominal prices paid by farmers had increased 16-fold since 1900–1914, whereas nominal prices received by farmers had increased only 7-fold. In 2007 the parity ratio stood at .42 (or 42 percent), indicating that prices received in 2007 could buy 42 percent as much as prices received in the 1910–1914 period. So farm policy calling for 100 percent of parity would require substantially higher prices for farm products.

Economics of Price Supports

The concept of parity provides the rationale for government price floors on farm products. In agriculture those minimum prices are called **price supports.** We have shown that, in the long run, the market prices received by farmers have not kept up with the prices paid by them. One way to achieve parity, or some percentage thereof, is to have the government establish above-equilibrium price supports for farm products.

Many different price-support programs have been tried, but they all tend to have similar effects, some of which are subtle and negative. Suppose in Figure 19.6 that the equilibrium price is P_e and the price support is P_s. Then the major effects would be as follows.

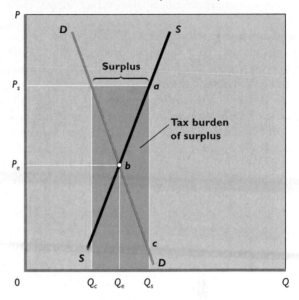

FIGURE 19.6 Price supports, agricultural surpluses, and transfers to farmers. The market demand D and supply S of a farm product yield equilibrium price P_e and quantity Q_e. An above-equilibrium price support P_s results in consumption of quantity Q_c, production of quantity Q_s, and a surplus of quantity Q_sQ_c. The orange rectangle represents a transfer of money from taxpayers to farmers. Area *bac* shows the efficiency loss to society.

Surplus Output The most obvious result is a product surplus. Consumers are willing to purchase only Q_c units at the supported price, while farmers supply Q_s units. What about the Q_sQ_c surplus that results? The government must buy it to make the above-equilibrium price support effective. As you will see, this surplus farm output means that agriculture receives an overallocation of resources.

Gain to Farmers Farmers benefit from price supports. In Figure 19.6, gross farm revenue rises from the free-market level represented by area $0P_ebQ_e$ to the larger, supported level shown by area $0P_saQ_s$.

Loss to Consumers Consumers lose; they pay a higher price (P_s rather than P_e) and consume less (Q_c rather than Q_e) of the product. In some instances differences between the market price and the supported price are substantial. For example, the U.S.-supported price of a pound of sugar is about two times the world market price, and a quart of fluid milk is estimated to cost consumers twice as much as it would without government programs. Moreover, the burden of higher food prices falls disproportionately on the poor because they spend a larger part of their incomes on food.

Efficiency Losses Society loses because price supports create allocative inefficiency by encouraging an overallocation of resources to agriculture. A price floor (P_s) attracts more resources to the agricultural sector than would the free-market price (P_e). Viewed through the pure-competition model, the market supply curve in Figure 19.6 represents the marginal costs of all farmers producing this product at the various output levels. An efficient allocation of resources occurs at point b, where the market price P_e is equal to marginal cost. So the output Q_e reflects that efficient allocation of resources.

In contrast, the output Q_s associated with the price support P_s represents an overallocation of resources; for all units of output between Q_e and Q_s, marginal costs (measured on curve S) exceed the prices people are willing to pay for those units (measured on curve D). Simply stated, the marginal cost of the extra production exceeds its marginal benefit to society. Society incurs an efficiency loss (or a deadweight loss) of area bac because of the price-support system.

Other Social Losses Society at large loses in other ways.

Taxpayers pay higher taxes to finance the government's purchase of the surplus. This added tax burden is equal to the surplus output Q_sQ_e multiplied by its price P_s, as shown by the orange area in Figure 19.6. Recall, too, that the mere collection of taxes imposes an efficiency loss (Figure 17.5). Also, the cost of storing surplus farm output adds to this tax burden.

Government's intervention in agriculture also entails administrative costs. Thousands of government workers are needed to administer U.S. price supports and other farm programs.

Finally, the rent-seeking activity involved—the pursuit of political support to maintain price supports—is costly and socially wasteful. Farm groups spend considerable sums to sustain political support for price floors and other programs that enhance farm incomes.

Environmental Costs We know from Figure 19.6 that price supports encourage additional production. Although some of that extra output may come from the use of additional land, much of it comes from heavier use of fertilizer and pesticides. Those pesticides and fertilizers may pollute the environment (for example, groundwater) and create residues in food that pose health risks to farmworkers and consumers. Research shows a positive relationship between the level of price-support subsidies and the use of agrochemicals.

Farm policy also may cause environmental problems in less obvious ways. Farmers benefit from price supports only when they use their land consistently for a specific crop such as corn or wheat. That creates a disincentive to practice crop rotation, which is a nonchemical technique for controlling pests. Farm policy thus encourages the substitution of chemicals for other forms of pest control.

Also, we know from the concept of derived demand that an increase in the price of a product will increase the demand for relevant inputs. In particular, price supports for farm products increase the demand for land. And the land that farmers bring into farm production is often environmentally sensitive "marginal" land, such as steeply sloped, erosion-prone land, or wetlands that provide wildlife habitat. Similarly, price supports result in the use of more water for irrigation, and the resulting runoff may contribute to soil erosion.

International Costs Actually, the costs of farm price supports go beyond those indicated by Figure 19.6. Price supports generate economic distortions that cross national boundaries. For example, price supports make the U.S. agricultural market attractive to foreign producers. But inflows of foreign agricultural products would serve to increase supplies in the United States, aggravating the problem of U.S. surpluses. To prevent that from happening, the United States is likely to impose import barriers in the form of tariffs or quotas. Those barriers tend to restrict the output of more-efficient foreign producers while encouraging more output from less-efficient U.S. producers. The result is a less-efficient use of world agricultural resources. This chapter's Last Word suggests that this is indeed the case for sugar.

Similarly, as the United States and other industrially advanced countries with similar agricultural programs dump surplus farm products on world markets, the prices of such products are depressed. Developing countries are often heavily dependent on world commodity markets for their incomes. So they are particularly hurt because their export earnings are reduced. Thus, U.S. subsidies for rice production have imposed significant costs on Thailand, a major rice exporter. Similarly, U.S. cotton programs have adversely affected Egypt, Mexico, and other cotton-exporting nations. **(Key Question 8)**

Reduction of Surpluses

Figure 19.6 suggests that programs designed to reduce market supply (shift S leftward) or increase market demand (shift D rightward) would help boost the market price toward the supported price P_s. Further, such programs would reduce or eliminate farm surpluses. The U.S. government has tried both supply and demand approaches to reduce or eliminate surpluses.

Restricting Supply

Until recently, public policy focused mainly on restricting farm output. In particular, **acreage allotments** accompanied price supports. In return for guaranteed prices for their crops, farmers had to agree to limit the number of acres they planted in that crop. The U.S. Department of Agriculture first set the price support and then estimated the amount of the product consumers would buy at the supported price. It then translated that amount into the total number of planted acres necessary to provide it. The total acreage was apportioned among states, counties, and ultimately individual farmers.

These supply-restricting programs were only partially successful. They did not eliminate surpluses, mainly because acreage reduction did not result in a proportionate decline in production. Some farmers retired their worst land and kept their best land in production. They also cultivated their tilled acres more intensively. Superior seed, more and better fertilizer and insecticides, and improved farm equipment were used to enhance output per acre. And nonparticipating farmers expanded their planted acreage in anticipation of overall higher prices. Nevertheless, the net effect of acreage allotment undoubtedly was a reduction of farm surpluses and their associated costs to taxpayers.

Bolstering Demand

Government has tried several ways to increase demand for U.S. agricultural products. For example, both government and private industry have spent large sums on research to create new uses for agricultural goods. The production of "gasohol," which is a blend of gasoline and alcohol (ethanol) made mainly from corn, is one such successful attempt to increase the demand for farm output. (See the nearby Consider This box for a fuller discussion of ethanol.) Recent attempts to promote "biodiesel," a fuel made from soybean oil and other natural vegetable oils, also fit the demand-enhancement approach.

The government has also created a variety of programs to stimulate consumption of farm products. For example, the objective of the food-stamp program is not only to reduce hunger but also to bolster the demand for food. Similarly, the Food for Peace program has enabled developing countries to buy U.S. surplus farm products with their own currencies, rather than having to use dollars. The Federal government spends millions of dollars each year to advertise and promote global sales of U.S. farm products. Furthermore, U.S. negotiators have pressed hard in international trade

negotiations to persuade foreign nations to reduce trade barriers to the importing of farm products.

During the era of price supports, the government's supply-restricting and demand-increasing efforts boosted agricultural prices and reduced surplus production, but they did not succeed in eliminating the sizable surpluses.

CONSIDER THIS . . .

Putting Corn in Your Gas Tank

Government's promotion of greater production and use of corn-based ethanol serves both as a good example of an attempt by government to bolster the demand for U.S. farm products and as an example of how price changes can ripple through markets and produce myriad secondary effects. Gasoline producers blend ethanol (an alcohol-like substance) with conventional gasoline refined from oil. The government's rationale for promoting ethanol is to reduce U.S. dependency on foreign oil, but the strongest proponents are from states in the Corn Belt.

The ethanol program has several facets, including tariffs on imported ethanol, subsidies to oil refineries that buy ethanol, and mandates to industry to increase their use of alternative fuels. The rising demand for ethanol that resulted contributed to a 50 percent rise in the inflation-adjusted price of a bushel of corn between 2005 and 2007.

But numerous secondary effects from the increased price of corn also occurred. Farmers shifted crops toward corn and away from soybeans, sorghum, and other crops. The decreases in the supply of these other crops raised their prices, too. Also, because corn is used as a major feedstock, the price of beef, pork, and chicken rose.

The ethanol subsidies had other secondary effects. The prices of seed, fertilizer, and farm land all increased. Because corn is a water-intensive crop, its expanded production resulted in faster withdrawals of irrigation water from underground aquifers. The refining of ethanol also depleted ground water or removed it from rivers. Moreover, the increased use of fertilizer in corn production increased the runoff of nitrogen from fertilizer into streams and rivers, causing environmental damage.

All these price increases, however, may moderate as farmers shift additional land to corn, increasing its supply and reducing its price. Nevertheless, these multiple impacts of public policy illustrate an important economic maxim: In the economy, it is difficult to do just *one* thing.

Criticisms and Politics

After decades of experience with government price-support programs, it became apparent in the 1990s that farm policy was not working well. Major criticisms of farm subsidies emerged, as did a more skeptical analysis of the politics of those subsidies.

Criticisms of the Parity Concept

Economists uniformly rejected the rationale of the parity concept. They found no economic logic in the proposition that if a bushel of wheat could buy a shirt in 1900, it should still be able to buy a shirt several decades later. The relative values of goods and services are established by supply and demand, and those relative values change over time as technology changes, resource prices change, tastes change, and substitute resources and new products emerge. A fully equipped personal computer, monitor, and printer cost as much as a cheap new automobile in 1985. That was not true just a decade later because the price of computer equipment had dropped so dramatically. Based on the parity concept, one could argue that price supports and subsidies were justified for computer manufacturers!

Criticisms of the Price-Support System

Criticisms of the price-support system were equally severe.

Symptoms, Not Causes The price-support strategy in agriculture was designed to treat the symptoms, not the causes of the farm problem. The root cause of the long-run farm problem was misallocation of resources between agriculture and the rest of the economy. Historically, the problem had been one of too many farmers. The effect of that misallocation was relatively low agricultural prices and low farm income. But the price and income supports encouraged people to stay in farming rather than move to nonfarm occupations. That is, the price and income orientation of the farm program slowed the reallocation of resources necessary to resolve the long-run farm problem.

Misguided Subsidies Because price supports were on a per-bushel basis, the subsidy system benefited those farmers who needed subsidies the least. If the goal of farm policy was to raise low farm incomes, it followed that any program of Federal aid should have been aimed at farmers with the lowest incomes. But the poor, low-output farmer did not produce and sell enough in the market to get much aid from price supports. Instead, the large, prosperous farmer reaped the benefits because of sizable output. On equity grounds, direct income payments to struggling farmers are highly preferable to indirect price-support subsidies that go primarily to large-scale, prosperous farmers. Better yet, say many economists, would be transition and retraining support for farmers willing to move out of farming and into other occupations and businesses in greater demand.

A related point concerns land values. The price and income benefits that the price-support system provided increased the value of farmland. By making crops more valuable, price supports made the land itself more valuable. That was helpful to farmers who owned the land they farmed but not to farmers who rented land. Farmers rented about 40 percent of their farmland, mostly from well-to-do nonfarm landlords. So, price supports became a subsidy to people who were not actively engaged in farming.

Policy Contradictions Because farm policy had many objectives, it often led to contradictions. Whereas most subsidized research was aimed at increasing farm productivity and the supply of farm products, acreage-allotment programs required that farmers take land out of production in order to reduce supply. Price supports for crops meant increased feed costs for ranchers and farmers and high consumer prices for animal products. Tobacco farmers were subsidized even though tobacco consumption was causing serious health problems. The U.S. sugar program raised prices for domestic producers by imposing import quotas that conflicted with free-trade policies. Conservation programs called for setting aside land for wildlife habitat, while price supports provided incentives to bring such acreage into production.

All these criticisms helped spawn policy reform. Nevertheless, as we will see, those reforms turned out to be less substantive than originally conceived. Nearly all these criticisms are as valid for current farm policy as they were for the price-support program.

The Politics of Farm Policy

In view of these criticisms, why did the United States continue its price-support program for 60 years and why does it still continue that program for sugar, milk, and tobacco? Why do farm subsidies in the billions of dollars still occur?

Public Choice Theory Revisited

Public choice theory (Chapter 17) helps answer these questions. Recall that rent-seeking behavior occurs when a group (a labor union, firms in a specific industry, or farmers producing a particular crop) uses political means to transfer income or wealth to itself at the expense of another group or of society as a whole. And recall that the special-interest effect involves a program or policy from which a small group receives large benefits at the expense of a much larger group whose members individually suffer small losses. Both rent-seeking behavior and the special interest effect help explain the politics of farm subsidies.

Suppose a certain group of farmers, say, peanut or sugar producers, organize and establish a well-financed political action committee (PAC). The PAC's job is to promote government programs that will transfer income to the group (this is rent-seeking behavior). The PAC vigorously lobbies U.S. senators and representatives to enact or to continue price supports, production quotas, or import quotas for peanuts or sugar. The PAC does this in part by making political contributions to sympathetic legislators. Although peanut production is heavily concentrated in a few states such as Georgia, Alabama, and Texas, the peanut PAC will also make contributions to legislators from other states in order to gain support.

But how can a small interest group like peanut or sugar growers successfully lobby to increase its own income at the expense of society as a whole? Because even though the total cost of the group's programs might be considerable, the cost imposed on each individual taxpayer is small (this is the special-interest effect). Taxpayers are likely to be uninformed about and indifferent to such programs since they have little at stake. Unless you grow sugar beets or peanuts, you probably have no idea how much these programs cost you as an individual taxpayer and consumer and therefore do not object when your legislator votes for, say, a sugar-support program. Thus, the PAC encounters little or no lobbying against its efforts.

Political logrolling—the trading of votes on policies and programs—also works to perpetuate certain programs: Senator Foghorn agrees to vote for a program that benefits Senator Moribund's constituents, and Moribund returns the favor. Example: Many members of Congress who represent low-income urban areas vote in favor of farm subsidies. In return, representatives of agricultural areas support such programs as food stamps, which subsidize food for the poor. The result is a rural-urban coalition through which representatives from both areas provide benefits for their constituents and enhance their reelection chances. Such coalitions help explain why farm subsidies persist and why the food-stamp program has been expanded over the years.

Large agribusinesses that supply inputs to agriculture also lend political support to farm subsidies because subsidies increase the amounts of agrochemicals and farm machinery that farmers are able to buy. And most of the thousands of government employees whose jobs depend on farm programs are highly supportive. So, too, are owners of farmland.

Public choice theory also tells us that politicians are likely to favor programs that have hidden costs. As we have seen, that is often true of farm programs. Our discussion of Figure 19.6 indicated that price supports involve not simply a transfer of money from taxpayer to farmer but costs that are hidden as higher food prices, storage costs for surplus output, costs of administering farm programs, and costs associated with both domestic and international misallocations of resources. Because those costs are largely indirect and hidden, farm programs are much more acceptable to politicians and the public than they would be if all costs were explicit.

Changing Politics

In spite of rent seeking, special interests, and logrolling, a combination of factors has somewhat altered the politics of farm subsidies.

Declining Political Support As the farm population declines, agriculture's political power weakens. The farm population was about 25 percent of the general population in the 1930s, when many U.S. farm programs were established; now it is less than 2 percent. Urban congressional representatives now constitute a 10-to-1 majority over their rural colleagues. An increasing number of legislators are critically examining farm programs for their effects on consumers' grocery bills as well as on farm incomes. Also, more farmers themselves are coming to resent the intrusion of the Federal government into their farming decisions. A few rural-state congressional members now support free-market agriculture.

World Trade Considerations The United States has taken the lead to reduce barriers to world trade in

The Sugar Program Is a Sweet Deal for Domestic Sugar Producers, but It Imposes Heavy Costs on Domestic Consumers, Domestic Candy Manufacturers, Foreign Producers, and the American Economy.

The continuing U.S. sugar program uses price supports and import quotas to guarantee a minimum price of sugar for domestic sugar producers. The program has significant effects, both domestically and internationally.

Domestic Costs Price supports and import quotas have boosted the domestic price of sugar to twice the world price (for 2007, \$.21 per pound compared to the international price of \$.12 per pound). The estimated aggregate cost to domestic consumers is between \$1.5 billion and \$1.9 billion per year. In contrast, each sugar producer receives from subsidies alone an amount estimated to be twice the nation's average family income. In one particular year, a single producer received an estimated \$30 million in benefits. Many sugar producers obtain more than \$1 million each year in benefits.

Import Quotas As a consequence of high U.S. domestic price supports, foreign sugar producers have a strong incentive to sell their output in the United States. But an influx of lower-priced foreign sugar into the U.S. domestic market would undermine U.S. price supports. The government therefore has imposed import quotas on foreign sugar. It decides how much sugar can be imported at a zero or very low tariff rate, and then it charges a prohibitively high tariff for any quantities above that amount. As the gap between U.S.-supported prices and world prices has widened, imports have declined as a percentage of sugar consumed in the United States. In 1975, about 30 percent of the sugar consumed in the United States was imported; currently about 20 percent comes from abroad. Domestic policy regarding the U.S. sugar industry largely dictates the nation's international trade policy with respect to sugar.

Developing Countries The loss of the U.S. market has had several harmful effects on sugar-exporting developing countries such as the Philippines, Brazil, and several Central American countries.

First, exclusion from the U.S. market has significantly reduced their export revenues—by an amount estimated to be many billions of dollars per year. That decline in export revenues is important because many of the sugar-producing countries depend on such revenues to pay interest and principal on large debts owed to the United States and other industrially advanced nations.

agricultural products. This has also contributed to the more critical attitude toward farm subsidies, particularly price supports. The nations of the European Union (EU) and many other nations support agricultural prices. And, to maintain their high domestic prices, they restrict imports of foreign farm products by imposing tariffs and quotas. They then try to rid themselves of their domestic surpluses by subsidizing exports into world markets. The effects on the United States are that (1) trade barriers hinder U.S. farmers from selling to EU nations and (2) subsidized exports from those nations depress world prices for agricultural products, making world markets less attractive to U.S. farmers.

Perhaps most important, farm programs such as those maintained by the EU and the United States distort both world agricultural trade and the international allocation of agricultural resources. Encouraged by artificially high prices, farmers in industrially advanced nations produce more food and fiber than they would otherwise. The resulting surpluses flow into world markets, where they depress prices. This means that farmers in countries with no farm programs—many of them developing countries—face artificially low prices for their exports, which signals them to produce less. Overall, the result is a shift in production away from what would occur on the basis of comparative advantage. As an example, price supports cause U.S. agricultural resources to be used for sugar production, even though sugar can be produced at perhaps half the cost in the Caribbean countries and Australia.

Recognizing these distortions, in 1994 the 128 nations then belonging to the World Trade Organization (WTO) agreed to reduce farm price-support programs by 20 percent by the year 2000 and to reduce tariffs and quotas on imported farm products by 15 percent. Larger, more significant, reductions of farm subsidies

Second, barred by quotas from sale in the U.S. market, the sugar produced by the developing countries has been added to world markets, where the increased supply has depressed the world price of sugar.

Third, domestic price supports have caused U.S. sugar production to expand to the extent that the United States may soon change from a sugar-importing to a sugar-exporting nation. That is, the U.S. sugar program may soon be a source of new competition for the sugar producers of the developing countries. Sugar price supports in the European Union have already turned that group of nations into sugar exporters.

U.S. Efficiency Loss The sugar program benefits sugar producers by about $1 billion annually but costs U.S. consumers about $1.5 billion to $1.9 billion each year. The excess of losses over gains is therefore $500 million to $900 million annually. This efficiency loss (or deadweight loss) results from the overallocation of U.S. resources to growing and processing sugar beets and sugar cane.

As a secondary effect, the higher domestic sugar prices have encouraged several U.S. confectionery firms (candy manufacturers) to relocate their operations to Canada or Mexico. According to the U.S. Commerce

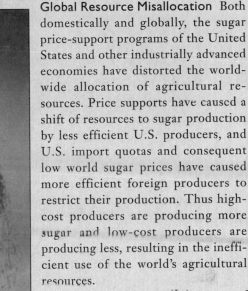

Department, for every American job that has been added by the price supports in the cane sugar and sugar beet industries, three American jobs have been lost in the industries buying sugar. The total job loss in the confectionery industry is estimated at 10,000 workers since 1997.

Global Resource Misallocation Both domestically and globally, the sugar price-support programs of the United States and other industrially advanced economies have distorted the worldwide allocation of agricultural resources. Price supports have caused a shift of resources to sugar production by less efficient U.S. producers, and U.S. import quotas and consequent low world sugar prices have caused more efficient foreign producers to restrict their production. Thus high-cost producers are producing more sugar and low-cost producers are producing less, resulting in the inefficient use of the world's agricultural resources.

Adding to the inefficient use of world resources, the relocation of candy manufacturers—to avoid artificially sweetened U.S. sugar prices—is moving capital and labor resources away from their place of comparative advantage.

and agricultural tariffs are part of the agenda of the most recent round of trade negotiations (the Doha Round). But reaching agreement on those reductions has proved difficult. As of the beginning of 2008, negotiations over these issues were completely stalled.

Recent Farm Policies

In the mid-1990s there was a common feeling among economists and political leaders that the goals and techniques of farm policy needed to be reexamined and revised. Moreover, crop prices were relatively high at the time and Congress wanted to reduce large Federal budget deficits.

Freedom to Farm Act of 1996

In 1996 Congress radically revamped 60 years of U.S. farm policy by passing the **Freedom to Farm Act.** The law ended price supports and acreage allotments for wheat, corn, barley, oats, sorghum, rye, cotton, and rice. Farmers were allowed to respond to changing crop prices by planting as much or as little of these crops as they chose. Also, they were free to plant crops of their choice. If the price of, say, oats increased, farmers could plant more oats and less barley. Markets, not government programs, were to determine the kinds and amounts of crops grown.

To ease the transition away from price supports, the Freedom to Farm Act granted declining annual transition payments through 2002. The $37 billion of total scheduled payments through 2002 was based on the production levels of the crops each farmer previously had grown under the price-support system. So a previous wheat farmer, for example, would receive cash payments for 7 years regardless of the current price of wheat or amount of wheat presently grown.

But this ambitious plan to wean American agriculture from subsidies unraveled in 1998 and 1999, when sharply reduced export demand and strong crop production in the United States depressed the prices of many farm products. Congress responded by supplementing the direct payments with large "emergency aid" payments to farmers. Agricultural subsidies for 1999–2002 averaged $20 billion annually—even more than they were before passage of the Freedom to Farm Act.

The Food, Conservation, and Energy Act of 2008

Since 2002, agricultural policy in the United States has substantially retreated from the free-market intent of the 1996 law. Current subsidy programs continue the "freedom to plant" and "direct payment" approaches to farm policy but make direct payments permanent and provide revenue protection for farmers. The revenue guarantees kick in automatically when crop prices (or total revenues) fall below targeted levels.

The **Food, Conservation and Energy Act of 2008** is the present law under which subsidies are provided. The law extends through 2012 and provides three main forms of cash commodity subsidies, with an option on one of them.

Direct Payments The **direct payments** under the 2008 law are similar to the transition payments paid under the Freedom to Farm Act. The cash payments are fixed for each crop based on a farmer's historical pattern of production and are unaffected by current crop prices or current production. Farmers are free to plant as much or as little of any particular crop as they want and still receive these payments. These direct payments do not decline from year to year. They are a permanent transfer payment from the Federal government (general taxpayers) to farmers.

Countercyclical Payments This component of farm policy ties a separate set of subsidies to the difference between market prices of specified farm products and a target price set for each crop. Like direct payments, these **countercyclical payments (CCPs)** are based on previous crops grown and are received regardless of the current crop planted. For example, the target price for corn in the years 2008–2012 is $2.63 per bushel. If corn is at or exceeds $2.63 in one of those years, the farmer who qualifies will receive no CCP. But if the price is below $2.63, the farmer will receive CCP payments geared to the size

of the price gap. The CCP system has returned a form of price supports to a prominent role in farm policy, but it bases those supports on past crops grown, not current crops planted.

Beginning in 2009, farmers will have the option of withdrawing from the CCP program and instead participating in the Average Crop Revenue Election (ACRE). This program will base farmers' counter cyclical payments on average crop yields per acre in their states over the past five years along with the average national price for the crop in the past two years.

Marketing Loans Finally, current law contains a **marketing loan program** under which farmers can receive a loan (on a per-unit-of-output basis) from a government lender. If the crop price at harvest is higher than the price specified in the loan (the loan price), farmers can repay their loans, with interest. If the crop price is lower than the loan price, farmers can forfeit their harvested crops to the lender and be free of their loans. In this second case, farmers receive a subsidy because the proceeds from the loan exceed the revenues from the sale of the crop in the market.

The 2008 farm law reduces the risk of price and revenue variable for farmers and increases farm income. But the law fails to address the problem of subsidies. However structured, subsides slow the exodus of resources from agriculture and maintain high production levels. This means lower crop prices and less market income for farmers. These lower prices and reduced market incomes, in turn, provide the rationale for continued government subsidies!

QUICK REVIEW 19.3

- Farm policy in the United States has been heavily criticized for delaying the shift of resources away from farming, directing most subsidies to wealthier farmers, and being fraught with policy contradictions.
- The persistence of farm subsidies can largely be explained in terms of rent-seeking behavior, the special-interest effect, political logrolling, and other aspects of public choice theory.
- The Freedom to Farm Act of 1996 eliminated price supports and acreage allotments for many of the nation's crops, while continuing direct subsidies to farmers.
- The Food, Conservation, and Energy Act of 2008 provides three major kinds of farm subsidies: direct payments, countercyclical payments, and marketing loans.

Summary

1. In the short run, the highly inelastic demand for farm products transforms small changes in output and small shifts in demand into large changes in prices and income.

2. Over the long run, rapid technological advance, together with a highly inelastic and relatively slow-growing demand for agricultural output, has made agriculture a declining industry in the United States and dictated that resources exit the industry.

3. Historically, farm policy has been centered on price and based on the parity concept, which suggests that the relationship between prices received and paid by farmers should be constant over time.

4. The use of price floors or price supports has a number of economic effects: It (a) causes surplus production; (b) increases the incomes of farmers; (c) causes higher consumer prices for farm products; (d) creates an overallocation of resources to agriculture; (e) obliges society to pay higher taxes to finance the purchase and storage of surplus output; (f) increases pollution because of the greater use of agrochemicals and vulnerable land; and (g) forces other nations to bear the costs associated with import barriers and depressed world agricultural prices.

5. With only limited success, the Federal government has pursued programs to reduce agricultural supply and increase agricultural demand as a way to reduce the surpluses associated with price supports.

6. Economists have criticized U.S. farm policy for (a) confusing symptoms (low farm incomes) with causes (excess capacity), (b) providing the largest subsidies to high-income farmers, and (c) creating contradictions among specific farm programs.

7. The persistence of agricultural subsidies can be explained by public choice theory and, in particular, as rent-seeking behavior, the special-interest effect; and political logrolling.

8. Political backing for price supports and acreage allotments has eroded for several reasons: (a) The number of U.S. farmers, and thus their political clout, has declined relative to the number of urban consumers of farm products; and (b) successful efforts by the United States to get other nations to reduce their farm subsidies have altered the domestic debate on the desirability of U.S. subsidies.

9. The Freedom to Farm Act of 1996 ended price supports and acreage allotments for wheat, corn, barley, oats, sorghum, rye, cotton, and rice. The law established declining annual transition payments through the year 2002, but those payments were no longer tied to crop prices or the current crop produced.

10. When crop prices plummeted in 1998 and 1999, Congress supplemented the transition payments of the Freedom to Farm Act with large amounts of emergency aid. Total subsidies to agriculture averaged $20 billion annually in the years 1999–2002.

11. Beginning in 2002, the Federal government retreated from the free-market principles of the Freedom to Farm Act, setting up a system of permanent direct payments to farmers along with countercyclical farm-revenue guarantees.

12. The Food, Conservation, and Energy Act of 2008 provides farmers with direct payments (based on previous crops planted), countercyclical payments (based on the differences between market prices and targeted prices), and marketing loans (based on a specified crop price and an option to either pay back the loan or forfeit the crop to the government lender).

Terms and Concepts

farm commodities	price supports	direct payments
food products	acreage allotments	countercyclical payments (CCPs)
agribusiness	Freedom to Farm Act	marketing loan program
parity concept	Food, Conservation, and Energy Act of 2008	
parity ratio		

Study Questions

1. **KEY QUESTION** Carefully evaluate: "The supply and demand for agricultural products are such that small changes in agricultural supply result in drastic changes in prices. However, large changes in agricultural prices have modest effects on agricultural output." (Hint: A brief review of the distinction between supply and quantity supplied may be helpful.) Do exports increase or reduce the instability of demand for farm products? Explain. **LO1**

2. What relationship, if any, can you detect between the facts that farmers' fixed costs of production are large and the supply of most agricultural products is generally inelastic? Be specific in your answer. **LO1**

3. **KEY QUESTION** Explain how each of the following contributes to the farm problem: **LO1, LO2**
   a. The inelasticity of demand for farm products.
   b. The rapid technological progress in farming.
   c. The modest long-run growth in demand for farm commodities.
   d. The volatility of export demand.

4. The key to efficient resource allocation is shifting resources from low-productivity to high-productivity uses. In view of the high and expanding physical productivity of agricultural resources, explain why many economists want to divert additional resources from farming to achieve allocative efficiency. **LO2**

5. Explain and evaluate: "Industry complains of the higher taxes it must pay to finance subsidies to agriculture. Yet the trend of agricultural prices has been downward while industrial prices have been moving upward, suggesting that on balance agriculture is actually subsidizing industry." **LO3**

6. "Because consumers as a group must ultimately pay the total income received by farmers, it makes no real difference whether the income is paid through free farm markets or through price supports supplemented by subsidies financed out of tax revenue." Do you agree? **LO3**

7. If in a given year the indexes of prices received and paid by farmers were 120 and 165, respectively, what would the parity ratio be? Explain the meaning of that ratio. **LO3**

8. **KEY QUESTION** Explain the economic effects of price supports. Explicitly include environmental and global impacts in your answer. On what grounds do economists contend that price supports cause a misallocation of resources? **LO3**

9. Use supply and demand curves to depict equilibrium price and output in a competitive market for some farm product. Then show how an above-equilibrium price floor (price support) would cause a surplus in this market. Demonstrate in your graph how government could reduce the surplus through a policy that (a) changes supply or (b) changes demand. Identify each of the following actual government

policies as primarily affecting the supply of or the demand for a particular farm product: acreage allotments; food-stamp program; Food for Peace program; a government buyout of dairy herds; export promotion. **LO3**

10. Do you agree with each of the following statements? Explain why or why not. **LO3, LO4**
    a. The problem with U.S. agriculture is that there are too many farmers. That is not the fault of farmers but the fault of government programs.
    b. The Federal government ought to buy up all U.S. farm surpluses and give them away to developing nations.
    c. All industries would like government price supports if they could get them; agriculture obtained price supports only because of its strong political clout.

11. What are the effects of farm subsidies such as those of the United States and the European Union on (a) domestic agricultural prices, (b) world agricultural prices, and (c) the international allocation of agricultural resources? **LO3**

12. Use public choice theory to explain the persistence of farm subsidies in the face of major criticisms of those subsidies. If the special-interest effect is so strong, what factors made it possible in 1996 for the government to end price supports and acreage allotments for several crops? **LO4**

13. What was the major intent of the Freedom to Farm Act of 1996? Do you agree with the intent? Why or why not? Did the law succeed in reducing overall farm subsidies? Why or why not? **LO5**

14. Distinguish the major features of direct subsidies, countercyclical payments, and marketing loan subsidies under the Food, Conservation, and Energy Act of 2008. In what way do countercyclical payments and marketing loans help reduce the volatility of farm income? In what way do direct subsidies perpetuate the long-run farm problem of too many resources in agriculture? **LO5**

15. **LAST WORD** What groups benefit and what groups lose from the U.S. sugar subsidy program?

Web-Based Questions

1. **AGRICULTURAL PRICES—WHAT'S UP, WHAT'S DOWN?** The USDA, at **www.nass.usda.gov**, provides up-to-date color charts of current data for agricultural prices received by farmers. Click on Charts and Maps on the left side. Then click on Agricultural Prices and then on Prices Received. Check the prices received for cattle, corn, cotton, hogs, milk, soybeans, and wheat and describe in general terms the price trend for each over the period shown in the chart. Why is knowing output levels, as well as prices, essential in evaluating how individual farmers have fared in the market over that period?

2. **FARM SIZE AND FARM SALES REVENUE** Go to **www.nass.usda.gov** and click on Charts and Maps. Then click on some of the links listed under Economics to find information on farm size and farm revenue. Which of these three states had the smallest and largest average farm sizes: California, Florida, or Texas? What was the national average size of farms with sales revenue of less than $10,000 in the latest year? More than $100,000? What percentage of farms had $100,000 or more of sales? What percentage of land was in farms earning $100,000 or more?

FURTHER TEST YOUR KNOWLEDGE AT
www.mcconnell18e.com

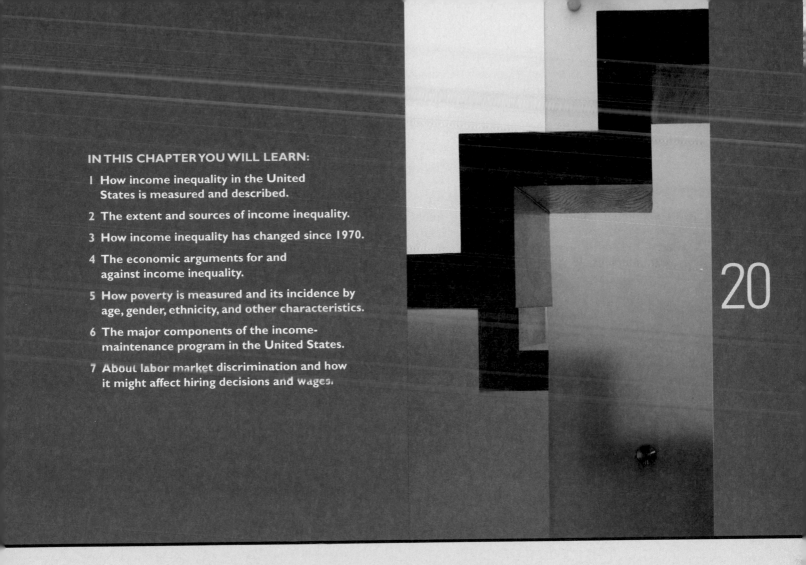

20

Income Inequality, Poverty, and Discrimination

Evidence that suggests wide income disparity in the United States is easy to find. In 2007 talk-show host Oprah Winfrey earned $260 million, golfer Tiger Woods earned $100 million, and rapper and music executive Jay-Z earned $83 million. In contrast, the salary of the president of the United States is $400,000, and the typical schoolteacher earns $45,000. A full-time minimum-wage worker at a fast-food restaurant makes about $11,000. Cash welfare payments to a mother with two children average $5000.

In 2006 about 36.5 million Americans—or 12.3 percent of the population—lived in poverty. An estimated 500,000 people were homeless in that year. The richest fifth of American households received about 50.5 percent of total income, while the poorest fifth received 3.4 percent.

What are the sources of income inequality? Is income inequality rising or falling? Is the United States making progress against poverty? What are the major income-maintenance programs in the United States? What role does discrimination play in reducing wages for some and increasing wages for others? These are some of the questions we will answer in this chapter.

Facts about Income Inequality

Average household income in the United States is among the highest in the world; in 2006, it was $66,570 per household (one or more persons occupying a housing unit). But that average tells us nothing about income inequality. To learn about that, we must examine how income is distributed around the average.

Distribution by Income Category

One way to measure **income inequality** is to look at the percentages of households in a series of income categories. Table 20.1 shows that 25.2 percent of all households had annual before-tax incomes of less than $25,000 in 2006, while another 19.1 percent had annual incomes of $100,000 or more. The data in the table suggest a wide dispersion of household income and considerable inequality of income in the United States.

Distribution by Quintiles (Fifths)

A second way to measure income inequality is to divide the total number of individuals, households, or families (two

TABLE 20.1 The Distribution of U.S. Income by Households, 2006

(1) Personal Income Category	(2) Percentage of All Households in This Category
Under $10,000	7.5
$10,000–$14,999	5.9
$15,000–$24,999	11.8
$25,000–$34,999	11.5
$35,000–$49,999	14.6
$50,000–$74,999	18.3
$75,000–$99,999	11.3
$100,000 and above	19.1
	100.0

Source: Bureau of the Census, **www.census.gov.**

or more persons related by birth, marriage, or adoption) into five numerically equal groups, or *quintiles*, and examine the percentage of total personal (before-tax) income received by each quintile. We do this for households in the table in Figure 20.1, where we also provide the upper income limit for each quintile. Any amount of income

FIGURE 20.1 **The Lorenz curve and Gini ratio.** The Lorenz curve is a convenient way to show the degree of income inequality (here, household income by quintile in 2006). The area between the diagonal (the line of perfect equality) and the Lorenz curve represents the degree of inequality in the distribution of total income. This inequality is measured numerically by the Gini ratio—area A (shown in brown) divided by area A + B (the brown + green area). The Gini ratio for the distribution shown is 0.470.

(1) Quintile (2006)	(2) Percentage of Total Income	(3) Upper Income Limit
Lowest 20 percent	3.4	$20,035
Second 20 percent	8.6	37,774
Third 20 percent	14.5	60,000
Fourth 20 percent	22.9	97,032
Highest 20 percent	50.5	No limit
Total	100.0	

Source: Bureau of the Census, **www.census.gov.** Numbers do not add to 100 percent due to rounding.

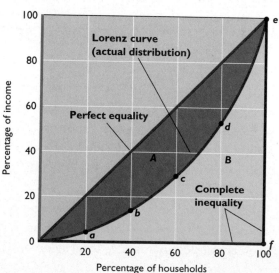

410

greater than that listed in each row of column 3 would place a household into the next higher quintile.

The Lorenz Curve and Gini Ratio

We can display the quintile distribution of personal income through a **Lorenz curve.** In Figure 20.1, we plot the cumulative percentage of households on the horizontal axis and the percentage of income they obtain on the vertical axis. The diagonal line 0e represents a *perfectly equal distribution of income* because each point along that line indicates that a particular percentage of households receive the same percentage of income. In other words, points representing 20 percent of all households receiving 20 percent of total income, 40 percent receiving 40 percent, 60 percent receiving 60 percent, and so on, all lie on the diagonal line.

By plotting the quintile data from the table in Figure 20.1, we obtain the Lorenz curve for 2006. The bottom 20 percent of all households received 3.4 percent of the income, as shown by

WORKED PROBLEMS

W 20.1

Lorenz curve

point *a*; the bottom 40 percent received 12 percent (= 3.4 + 8.6), as shown by point *b*; and so forth. The brown area between the diagonal line and the Lorenz curve is determined by the extent that the Lorenz curve sags away from the diagonal and indicates the degree of income inequality. If the actual income distribution were perfectly equal, the Lorenz curve and the diagonal would coincide and the brown area would disappear.

At the opposite extreme is complete inequality, where all households but one have zero income. In that case the Lorenz curve would coincide with the horizontal axis from 0 to point *f* (at 0 percent of income) and then would move immediately up from *f* to point *e* along the vertical axis (indicating that a single household has 100 percent of the total income). The entire area below the diagonal line (triangle 0ef) would indicate this extreme degree of inequality. So the farther the Lorenz curve sags away from the diagonal, the greater is the degree of income inequality.

The income inequality described by the Lorenz curve can be transformed into a **Gini ratio**—a numerical measure of the overall dispersion of income:

$$\text{Gini ratio} = \frac{\text{area between Lorenz curve and diagonal}}{\text{total area below the diagonal}}$$

$$= \frac{A \text{ (brown area)}}{A + B \text{ (brown + green area)}}$$

The Gini ratio is 0.470 for the distribution of household income shown in Figure 20.1. As the area between the Lorenz curve and the diagonal gets larger, the Gini ratio rises to reflect greater inequality. Lower Gini ratios denote less inequality; higher ratios indicate more inequality. The Gini coefficient for complete income equality is zero and for complete inequality is 1.

Because Gini ratios are numerical, they are easier to use than Lorenz curves for comparing the income distributions of different ethnic groups and countries. For example, in 2006 the Gini ratio of U.S. household income for Hispanics was 0.448; for whites, 0.462; for Asians, 0.476; and for African-Americans, 0.486.[1] Gini ratios for various nations range from 0.249 (Japan) to 0.743 (Namibia). Examples within this range include Sweden, 0.250; Italy, 0.350; Mexico, 0.481; and South Africa, 0.578.[2] **(Key Question 2)**

INTERACTIVE GRAPHS

G 20.1

Lorenz curve

Income Mobility: The Time Dimension

The income data used so far have a major limitation: The income accounting period of 1 year is too short to be very meaningful. Because the Census Bureau data portray the distribution of income in only a single year, they may conceal a more equal distribution over a few years, a decade, or even a lifetime. If Brad earns $1000 in year 1 and $100,000 in year 2, while Jenny earns $100,000 in year 1 and only $1000 in year 2, do we have income inequality? The answer depends on the period of measurement. Annual data would reveal great income inequality, but there would be complete equality over the 2-year period.

This point is important because evidence suggests considerable "churning around" in the distribution of income over time. Such movement of individuals or house-holds from one income quintile to another over time is called **income mobility.** For most income receivers, income starts at a relatively low level during youth, reaches a peak during middle age, and then declines. It follows that if all people receive exactly the same stream of income over their lifetimes, considerable income inequality would still exist in any specific year because of age differences. In any single year, the young and the old would receive low incomes while the middle-aged receive high incomes.

If we change from a "snapshot" view of income distribution in a single year to a "time exposure" portraying incomes over much longer periods, we find considerable

---

[1]U.S. Census Bureau, *Historical Income Tables*, **www.census.gov.**

[2]World Bank, *World Development Indicators, 2007*, **www.worldbank.org.**

FIGURE 20.2 The impact of taxes and transfers on U.S. income inequality. The distribution of household income is significantly more equal after taxes and transfers are taken into account than before. Transfers account for most of the lessening of inequality and provide most of the income received by the lowest quintile of households.

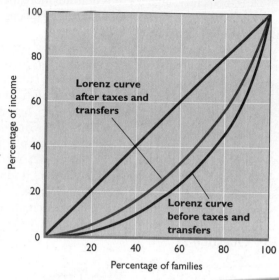

	Percentage of Total Income Received, 2005	
	(1)	(2)
Quintile	Before Taxes and Transfers	After Taxes and Transfers
Lowest 20 percent	1.5	4.4
Second 20 percent	7.3	9.9
Third 20 percent	14.0	15.3
Fourth 20 percent	23.4	23.1
Highest 20 percent	53.8	47.3

Source: Bureau of the Census, **www.census.gov.** The data include all money income from private sources, including realized capital gains and employer-provided health insurance. The "after taxes and transfers" data include the value of noncash transfers as well as cash transfers. Numbers do not add to 100 percent due to rounding. **www.census.gov.**

movement of income receivers among income classes. Between 1996 and 2005, half the individuals in the lowest quintile of the U.S. income distribution moved to a higher income quintile. Almost 25 percent made it to the middle fifth and 5 percent achieved the top quintile. The income mobility moved in both directions. About 57 percent of the top 1 percent of income receivers in 1996 had dropped out of that category by 2005. Overall, income mobility between 1996 and 2005 was the same as it was the previous 10 years. All this correctly suggests that income is more equally distributed over a 5-, 10-, or 20-year period than in any single year.[3]

In short, individual and family income mobility over time is significant; for many people, "low income" and "high income" are not permanent conditions. Also, the longer the time period considered, the more equal the distribution of income becomes.

Effect of Government Redistribution

The income data in Table 20.1 and Figure 20.1 include wages, salaries, dividends, and interest. They also include all cash transfer payments such as Social Security, unemployment compensation benefits, and welfare assistance to needy families. The data are before-tax data and therefore do not take into account the effects of personal income and payroll (Social Security) taxes that are levied directly

on income receivers. Nor do they include in-kind or **noncash transfers,** which provide specific goods or services rather than cash. Noncash transfers include such things as Medicare, Medicaid, housing subsidies, subsidized school lunches, and food stamps. Such transfers are "income-like," since they enable recipients to "purchase" goods and services.

One economic function of government is to redistribute income, if society so desires. Figure 20.2 and its table[4] reveal that government significantly redistributes income from higher- to lower-income households through taxes and transfers. Note that the U.S. distribution of household income before taxes and transfers are taken into account (dark red Lorenz curve) is substantially less equal than the distribution after taxes and transfers (light red Lorenz curve). Without government redistribution, the lowest 20 percent of households in 2005 would have received only 1.5 percent of total income. *With* redistribution, they received 4.4 percent, or three times as much.

Which contributes more to redistribution, government taxes or government transfers? The answer is transfers. Because the U.S. tax system is only modestly progressive, after-tax data would reveal only about 20 percent less inequality. Roughly 80 percent of the reduction in income inequality is attributable to transfer payments,

---

[3]U.S. Department of the Treasury, *Income Mobillity in the U.S. from 1996–2005,* November 13, 2007, pp. 1–22.

[4]The "before" data in this table differ from the data in the table in Figure 20.1 because the latter include cash transfers. Also, the data in Figure 20.2 are based on a broader concept of income than are the data in Figure 20.1.

which account for more than 75 percent of the income of the lowest quintile. Together with growth of job opportunities, transfer payments have been the most important means of alleviating poverty in the United States.

Causes of Income Inequality

There are several causes of income inequality in the United States. In general, the market system is permissive of a high degree of income inequality because it rewards individuals based on the contributions that they make, or the resources that they own, in producing society's output.

More specifically, the factors that contribute to income inequality are the following.

Ability

People have different mental, physical, and aesthetic talents. Some have inherited the exceptional mental qualities that are essential to such high-paying occupations as medicine, corporate leadership, and law. Others are blessed with the physical capacity and coordination to become highly paid professional athletes. A few have the talent to become great artists or musicians or have the beauty to become top fashion models. Others have very weak mental endowments and may work in low-paying occupations or may be incapable of earning any income at all. The intelligence and skills of most people fall somewhere in between.

Education and Training

Native ability alone rarely produces high income; people must develop and refine their capabilities through education and training. Individuals differ significantly in the amount of education and training they obtain and thus in their capacity to earn income. Such differences may be a matter of choice: Nguyen enters the labor force after graduating from high school, while Nyberg takes a job only after earning a college degree. Other differences may be involuntary: Nguyen and her parents may simply be unable to finance a college education.

People also receive varying degrees of on-the-job training, which contributes to income inequality. Some workers learn valuable new skills each year on the job and therefore experience significant income growth over time; others receive little or no on-the-job training and earn no more at age 50 than they did at age 30. Moreover, firms tend to select for advanced on-the-job training the workers who have the most formal education. That added training magnifies the education-based income differences between less-educated and better-educated individuals.

Discrimination

Discrimination in education, hiring, training, and promotion undoubtedly causes some income inequality. If discrimination confines certain racial, ethnic, or gender groups to lower-pay occupations, the supply of labor in those occupations will increase relative to demand, and hourly wages and income in those lower-pay jobs will decline. Conversely, labor supply will be artificially reduced in the higher-pay occupations populated by "preferred" workers, raising their wage rates and income. In this way, discrimination can add to income inequality. In fact, economists cannot account for all racial, ethnic, and gender differences in work earnings on the basis of differences in years of education, quality of education, occupations, and annual hours of work. Many economists attribute the unexplained residual to discrimination.

Economists, however, do not see discrimination by race, gender, and ethnicity as a dominant factor explaining income inequality. The income distributions *within* racial or ethnic groups that historically have been targets of discrimination—for example, African Americans—are similar to the income distribution for whites. Other factors besides discrimination are obviously at work.

Nevertheless, discrimination is an important concern since it harms individuals and reduces society's overall output and income. We will discuss it in more detail later in this chapter.

Preferences and Risks

Incomes also differ because of differences in preferences for market work relative to leisure, market work relative to work in the household, and types of occupations. People who choose to stay home with children, work part-time, or retire early usually have less income than those who make the opposite choices. Those who are willing to take arduous, unpleasant jobs (for example, underground mining or heavy construction), to work long hours with great intensity, or to "moonlight" will tend to earn more.

Individuals also differ in their willingness to assume risk. We refer here not only to the race-car driver or the professional boxer but also to the entrepreneur. Although many entrepreneurs fail, many of those who develop successful new products or services realize very substantial incomes. That contributes to income inequality.

Unequal Distribution of Wealth

Income is a *flow;* it represents a stream of wage and salary earnings, along with rent, interest, and profits, as depicted in Chapter 2's circular flow diagram. In contrast, wealth is a *stock,* reflecting at a particular moment the financial and real assets an individual has accumulated over time. A retired person may have very little income and yet own a home, mutual fund shares, and a pension plan that add up to considerable wealth. A new college graduate may be earning a substantial income as an accountant, middle manager, or engineer but has yet to accumulate significant wealth.

As you will discover in this chapter's Last Word, the ownership of wealth in the United States is more unequal than the distribution of income. This inequality of wealth leads to inequality in rent, interest, and dividends, which in turn contributes to income inequality. Those who own more machinery, real estate, farmland, stocks and bonds, and savings accounts obviously receive greater income from that ownership than people with less or no such wealth.

Market Power

The ability to "rig the market" on one's own behalf also contributes to income inequality. For example, in *resource* markets certain unions and professional groups have adopted policies that limit the supply of their services, thereby boosting the incomes of those "on the inside." Also, legislation that requires occupational licensing for, say, doctors, dentists, and lawyers can bestow market power that favors the licensed groups. In *product* markets, "rigging the market" means gaining or enhancing monopoly power, which results in greater profit and thus greater income to the firms' owners.

Luck, Connections, and Misfortune

Other forces also play a role in producing income inequality. Luck and "being in the right place at the right time" have helped individuals stumble into fortunes. Discovering oil on a ranch, owning land along a proposed freeway interchange, and hiring the right press agent have accounted for some high incomes. Personal contacts and political connections are other potential routes to attaining high income.

In contrast, economic misfortunes such as prolonged illness, serious accident, death of the family breadwinner, or unemployment may plunge a family into the low range of income. The burden of such misfortune is borne very unevenly by the population and thus contributes to income inequality. **(Key Question 5)**

Income inequality of the magnitude we have described is not exclusively an American phenomenon. Global Perspective 20.1 compares income inequality (here by individuals, not by households) in the United States with that in several other nations. Income inequality tends to be greatest in South American nations, where land and capital resources are highly concentrated in the hands of a relatively small number of wealthy families.

GLOBAL PERSPECTIVE 20.1

Percentage of Total Income Received by the Top One-Tenth of Income Receivers, Selected Nations

The share of income going to the highest 10 percent of income receivers varies among nations.

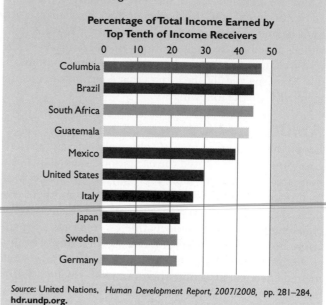

Percentage of Total Income Earned by Top Tenth of Income Receivers

Columbia
Brazil
South Africa
Guatemala
Mexico
United States
Italy
Japan
Sweden
Germany

Source: United Nations, *Human Development Report, 2007/2008*, pp. 281–284, **hdr.undp.org.**

QUICK REVIEW 20.1

- Data reveal considerable income inequality in the United States; in 2006 the richest fifth of all households received 50.5 percent of before-tax income, and the poorest fifth received 3.4 percent.

- The Lorenz curve depicts income inequality graphically by comparing percentages of total families and percentages of total income. The Gini ratio is a measure of the overall dispersion of income and is found by dividing the area between the diagonal and the Lorenz curve by the total area below the diagonal.

- The distribution of income is less unequal over longer time periods.

- Government taxes and transfers significantly reduce income inequality by redistributing income from higher-income groups to lower-income groups; the bulk of this redistribution results from transfer payments.

- Differences in ability, education and training, preferences for market work versus nonmarket activities, property ownership, and market power—along with discrimination and luck—help explain income inequality.

TABLE 20.2 **Percentage of Total Before-Tax Income Received by Each One-Fifth, and by the Top 5 Percent, of Households, Selected Years**

Quintile	1970	1975	1980	1985	1990	1995	2000	2006
Lowest 20 percent	4.1	4.4	4.3	4.0	3.9	3.7	3.6	3.4
Second 20 percent	10.8	10.5	10.3	9.7	9.6	9.1	8.9	8.6
Third 20 percent	17.4	17.1	16.9	16.3	15.9	15.2	14.8	14.5
Fourth 20 percent	24.5	24.8	24.9	24.6	24.0	23.3	23.0	22.9
Highest 20 percent	43.3	43.2	43.7	45.3	46.6	48.7	49.8	50.5
Total	100.0	100.0	100.0	100.0	100.0	100.0	100.0	100.0
Top 5 percent	16.6	15.9	15.8	17.0	18.6	21.0	22.1	22.3

Source: Bureau of the Census, **www.census.gov.** Numbers may not add to 100 percent due to rounding.

Income Inequality over Time

Over a period of years economic growth has raised incomes in the United States: In *absolute* dollar amounts, the entire distribution of income has been moving upward. But incomes may move up in *absolute* terms while leaving the *relative* distribution of income less equal, more equal, or unchanged. Table 20.2 shows how the distribution of household income has changed since 1970. This income is "before tax" and includes cash transfers but not noncash transfers.

Rising Income Inequality since 1970

It is clear from Table 20.2 that the distribution of income by quintiles has become more unequal since 1970. In 2006 the lowest 20 percent of households received 3.4 percent of total before-tax income, compared with 4.1 in 1970. Meanwhile, the income share received by the highest 20 percent rose from 43.3 in 1970 to 50.5 percent in 2006. Also, the percentage of income received by the top 5 percent of households rose significantly over the 1970–2006 period.

Causes of Growing Inequality

Economists suggest several major explanations for the growing U.S. income inequality since 1970.

Greater Demand for Highly Skilled Workers
Perhaps the most significant contributor to the growing income inequality has been an increasing demand by many firms for workers who are highly skilled and well-educated. Moreover, several industries requiring highly skilled workers have either recently emerged or expanded greatly, such as the computer software, business consulting, biotechnology, health care, and Internet industries. Because highly skilled workers remain relatively scarce, their wages have been bid up. Consequently, the wage differences between them and less-skilled workers have increased.

Between 1980 and 2005 the wage difference between college graduates and high school graduates rose from 28 percent to 47 percent for women and from 22 percent to 43 percent for men. And the so-called *90-10 ratio*—the hourly wage at the 90th percentile compared to the hourly wage at the 10th percentile—rose from 3.6 in 1980 to 4.5 in 2005.[5]

The rising demand for skill has also shown up in rapidly rising pay for chief executive officers (CEOs), sizable increases in income from stock options, substantial increases in income for professional athletes and entertainers, and huge fortunes for successful entrepreneurs. This growth of "superstar" pay has also contributed to rising income inequality.

Demographic Changes
The entrance of large numbers of less-experienced and less-skilled "baby boomers" into the labor force during the 1970s and 1980s may have contributed to greater income inequality in those two decades. Because younger workers tend to earn less income than older workers, their growing numbers contributed to income inequality. There has also been a growing tendency for men and women with high earnings potential to marry each other, thus increasing household income among the highest income quintiles. Finally, the number of households headed by single or divorced women has increased greatly. That trend has increased income inequality because such households lack a second major wage earner and also because the poverty rate for female-headed households is very high.

International Trade, Immigration, and Decline in Unionism
Other factors are probably at work as well. Stronger international competition from imports has reduced the demand for and employment of

---

[5]Economic Policy Institute, **www.epinet.org.** The college wage premiums are adjusted for differences in earnings based on race, ethnicity, marital status, and region.

CONSIDER THIS ...

Laughing at Shrek

Some economists say that the distribution of annual *consumption* is more meaningful for examining inequality of well-being than is the distribution of annual *income*. In a given year, people's consumption of goods and services may be above or below their income because they can save, draw down past savings, use credit cards, take out home mortgages, spend from inheritances, give money to charities, and so on. A recent study of the distribution of consumption finds that annual consumption inequality is less than income inequality. Moreover, consumption inequality has remained relatively constant over several decades, even though income inequality has increased.[*]

The Economist magazine extends the argument even further, pointing out that despite the recent increase in income inequality, the products consumed by the rich and the poor are far closer in functionality today than at any other time in history.

> More than 70 percent of Americans under the official poverty line own at least one car. And the distance between driving a used Hyundai Elantra and new Jaguar XJ is well nigh undetectable compared with the difference between motoring and hiking through the muck.... A wide screen plasma television is lovely, but you do not need one to laugh at "Shrek"....

> Those intrepid souls who make vast fortunes turning out ever higher-quality goods at ever lower prices widen the income gap while reducing the differences that really matter.[†]

Economists generally agree that products and experiences once reserved exclusively for the rich in the United States have, in fact, become more commonplace for nearly all income classes. But skeptics argue that *The Economist*'s argument is too simplistic. Even though both are water outings, there is a fundamental difference between yachting among the Greek isles on your private yacht and paddling on a local pond in your kayak.

---

[*]Dirk Krueger and Fabrizio Perri, "Does Income Inequality Lead to Consumption Inequality?" *Review of Economic Studies*, 2006, pp. 163–193.
[†]*The Economist*, "Economic Focus: The New (Improved) Gilded Age," December 22, 2007, p. 122.

less skilled (but highly paid) workers in such industries as the automobile and steel industries. The decline in such jobs has reduced the average wage for less-skilled workers. It also has swelled the ranks of workers in already low-paying industries, placing further downward pressure on wages there.

Similarly, the transfer of jobs to lower-wage workers in developing countries has exerted downward wage pressure on less-skilled workers in the United States. Also, an upsurge in the immigration of unskilled workers has increased the number of low-income households in the United States. Finally, the decline in unionism in the United States has undoubtedly contributed to wage inequality, since unions tend to equalize pay within firms and industries.

Two cautions: First, when we note growing income inequality, we are not saying that the "rich are getting richer and the poor are getting poorer" in terms of absolute income. Both the rich and the poor are experiencing rises in real income. Rather, what has happened is that, while incomes have risen in all quintiles, income growth has been fastest in the top quintile. Second, increased income inequality is not solely a U.S. phenomenon. The recent rise of inequality has also occurred in several other industrially advanced nations.

The Lorenz curve can be used to contrast the distribution of income at different points in time. If we plotted Table 20.2's data as Lorenz curves, we would find that the curves shifted farther away from the diagonal between 1970 and 2006. The Gini ratio rose from 0.394 in 1970 to 0.470 in 2006.

Equality versus Efficiency

The main policy issue concerning income inequality is how much is necessary and justified. While there is no general agreement on the justifiable amount, we can gain insight by exploring the cases for and against greater equality.

The Case for Equality: Maximizing Total Utility

The basic argument for an equal distribution of income is that income equality maximizes total consumer satisfaction (utility) from any particular level of output and income. The rationale for this argument is shown in Figure 20.3, in which we assume that the money incomes of two individuals, Anderson and Brooks, are subject to diminishing marginal utility. In any time period, income receivers spend the first dollars received on the products they value most—products whose marginal utility is high. As their most pressing wants become satisfied, consumers then spend additional dollars of income on less important, lower-marginal-utility goods. The identical diminishing-marginal-utility-from-income curves (MU_A and MU_B in the figure) reflect the assumption

FIGURE 20.3 The utility-maximizing distribution of income. With identical marginal-utility-of-income curves MU_A and MU_B, Anderson and Brooks will maximize their combined utility when any amount of income (say, $10,000) is equally distributed. If income is unequally distributed (say, $2500 to Anderson and $7500 to Brooks), the marginal utility derived from the last dollar will be greater for Anderson than for Brooks, and a redistribution of income toward equality will result in a net increase in total utility. The utility gained by equalizing income at $5000 each, shown by the blue area below curve MU_A in panel (a), exceeds the utility lost, indicated by the red area below curve MU_B in (b).

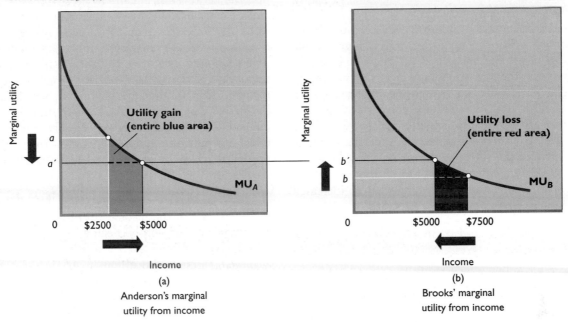

(a)
Anderson's marginal
utility from income

(b)
Brooks' marginal
utility from income

that Anderson and Brooks have the same capacity to derive utility from income.

Now suppose that there is $10,000 worth of income (output) to be distributed between Anderson and Brooks. According to proponents of income equality, the optimal distribution is an equal distribution, which causes the marginal utility of the last dollar spent to be the same for both persons. We can prove this by demonstrating that if the income distribution is initially unequal, then distributing income more equally can increase the combined utility of the two individuals.

Suppose that the $10,000 of income initially is distributed unequally, with Anderson getting $2500 and Brooks $7500. The marginal utility, a, from the last dollar received by Anderson is high, and the marginal utility, b, from Brooks' last dollar of income is low. If a single dollar of income is shifted from Brooks to Anderson—that is, toward greater equality—then Anderson's utility increases by a and Brooks' utility decreases by b. The combined utility then increases by a minus b (Anderson's large gain minus Brooks' small loss). The transfer of another dollar from Brooks to Anderson again increases their combined utility, this time by a slightly smaller amount. Continued transfer of dollars from Brooks to

Anderson increases their combined utility until the income is evenly distributed and both receive $5000. At that time their marginal utilities from the last dollar of income are equal (at a' and b'), and any further income redistribution beyond the $2500 already transferred would begin to create inequality and decrease their combined utility.

The area under the MU curve and to the left of the individual's particular level of income represents the total utility of that income. Therefore, as a result of the transfer of the $2500, Anderson has gained utility represented by the blue area below curve MU_A, and Brooks has lost utility represented by the red area below curve MU_B. The blue area is obviously greater than the red area, so income equality yields greater combined total utility than income inequality does.

The Case for Inequality: Incentives and Efficiency

Although the logic of the argument for equality is sound, critics attack its fundamental assumption that there is some fixed amount of output produced and therefore income to be distributed. Critics of income equality argue that the way in which income is distributed is an important determinant of the amount of output or income that is produced and is available for distribution.

Suppose once again in Figure 20.3 that Anderson earns $2500 and Brooks earns $7500. In moving toward equality, society (the government) must tax away some of Brooks' income and transfer it to Anderson. This tax and transfer process diminishes the income rewards of high-income Brooks and raises the income rewards of low-income Anderson; in so doing, it reduces the incentives of both to earn high incomes. Why should high-income Brooks work hard, save and invest, or undertake entrepreneurial risks when the rewards from such activities will be reduced by taxation? And why should low-income Anderson be motivated to increase his income through market activities when the government stands ready to transfer income to him? Taxes are a reduction in the rewards from increased productive effort; redistribution through transfers is a reward for diminished effort.

In the extreme, imagine a situation in which the government levies a 100 percent tax on income and distributes the tax revenue equally to its citizenry. Why would anyone work hard? Why would anyone work at all? Why would anyone assume business risk? Or why would anyone save (forgo current consumption) in order to invest? The economic incentives to "get ahead" will have been removed, greatly reducing society's total production and income. That is, the way income is distributed affects the size of that income. The basic argument for income inequality is that inequality is essential to maintain incentives to produce output and income—to get the output produced and income generated year after year.

The Equality-Efficiency Trade-off

At the essence of the income equality-inequality debate is a fundamental trade-off between equality and efficiency. In this **equality-efficiency trade-off**, greater income equality (achieved through redistribution of income) comes at the opportunity cost of reduced production and income. And greater production and income (through reduced redistribution) comes at the expense of less equality of income. The trade off obligates society to choose how much redistribution it wants, in view of the costs. If society decides it wants to redistribute income, it needs to determine methods that minimize the adverse effects on economic efficiency.

The Economics of Poverty

We now turn from the broader issue of income distribution to the more specific issue of very low income, or "poverty." A society with a high degree of income inequality can have a high, moderate, or low amount of poverty. We therefore need a separate examination of poverty.

Definition of Poverty

Poverty is a condition in which a person or a family does not have the means to satisfy basic needs for food, clothing, shelter, and transportation. The means include currently earned income, transfer payments, past savings, and property owned. The basic needs have many determinants, including family size and the health and age of its members.

The Federal government has established minimum income thresholds below which a person or a family is "in poverty." In 2006 an unattached individual receiving less than $9800 per year was said to be living in poverty. For a family of four, the poverty line was $20,000; for a family of six, it was $26,800. Based on these thresholds, in 2006

CONSIDER THIS . . .

Slicing the Pizza

The equality-efficiency trade-off might better be understood through an analogy. Assume that society's income is a huge pizza, baked year after year, *with the sizes of the pieces going to people on the basis of their contribution to making it.* Now suppose that for fairness reasons, society decides some people are getting pieces that are too large and others are getting pieces too small. But when society redistributes the pizza to make the sizes more equal, they discover the result is a smaller pizza than before. Why participate in making the pizza if you get a decent-size piece without contributing? The shrinkage of the pizza represents the efficiency loss—the loss of output and income—caused by the harmful effects of the redistribution on incentives to work, to save and invest, and to accept entrepreneurial risk. The shrinkage also reflects the resources that society must divert to the bureaucracies that administer the redistribution system.

How much pizza shrinkage will society accept while continuing to agree to the redistribution? If redistributing pizza to make it less unequal reduces the size of the pizza, what amount of pizza loss will society tolerate? Is a loss of 10 percent acceptable? 25 percent? 75 percent? This is the basic question in any debate over the ideal size of a nation's income redistribution program.

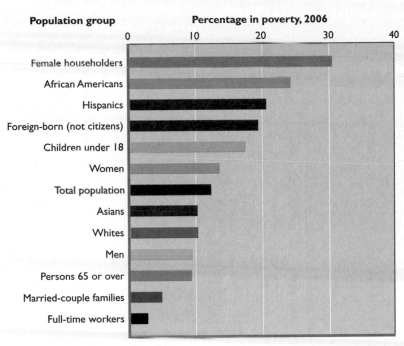

Population group | **Percentage in poverty, 2006**

Female householders
African Americans
Hispanics
Foreign-born (not citizens)
Children under 18
Women
Total population
Asians
Whites
Men
Persons 65 or over
Married-couple families
Full-time workers

FIGURE 20.4 Poverty rates among selected population groups, 2006. Poverty is disproportionately borne by African Americans, Hispanics, children, foreign-born residents who are not citizens, and families headed by women. People who are employed full-time, have a college degree, or are married tend to have low poverty rates.

Source: Bureau of the Census, **www.census.gov.**

about 36.5 million Americans lived in poverty. In 2006 the **poverty rate**—the percentage of the population living in poverty—was 12.3 percent.

Incidence of Poverty

The poor are heterogeneous: They can be found in all parts of the nation; they are of all races and ethnicities, rural and urban, young and old. But as Figure 20.4 indicates, poverty is far from randomly distributed. For example, the poverty rate for African Americans is above the national average, as is the rate for Hispanics, while the rate for whites and Asians is below the average. In 2006, the poverty rates for African Americans and Hispanics were 24.3 and 20.6 percent, respectively; the rate for whites and Asians, each was 10.3 percent.

Figure 20.4 shows that female-headed households (no husband present), foreign-born noncitizens, and children under 18 years of age have very high incidences of poverty. Marriage and full-time, year-round work are associated with low poverty rates, and, because of the Social Security system, the incidence of poverty among the elderly is less than that for the population as a whole.

The high poverty rate for children is especially disturbing because poverty tends to breed poverty. Poor children are at greater risk for a range of long-term problems, including poor health and inadequate education, crime, drug use, and teenage pregnancy. Many

of today's impoverished children will reach adulthood unhealthy and illiterate and unable to earn above-poverty incomes.

As many as half of people in poverty are poor for only 1 or 2 years before climbing out of poverty. But poverty is much more long-lasting among some groups than among others. In particular, African-American and Hispanic families, families headed by women, persons with little education and few labor market skills, and people who are dysfunctional because of drug use, alcoholism, or mental illness are more likely than others to remain in poverty. Also, long-lasting poverty is heavily present in depressed areas of cities, parts of the Deep South, and some Indian reservations. **(Key Question 10)**

Poverty Trends

As Figure 20.5 shows, the total poverty rate fell significantly between 1959 and 1969, stabilized at 11 to 13 percent over the next decade, and then rose in the early 1980s. In 1993 the rate was 15.1 percent, the highest since 1983. Between 1993 and 2000 the rate turned downward, falling to 11.3 percent in 2000. Because of recession, slow employment growth, and relatively slow wage growth, the poverty rate rose from 11.7 percent in 2001 to 12.7 percent in 2004. During the second half of the 1990s, poverty rates plunged for African Americans, Hispanics, and Asians, and they have remained historically low. Nevertheless, in 2006

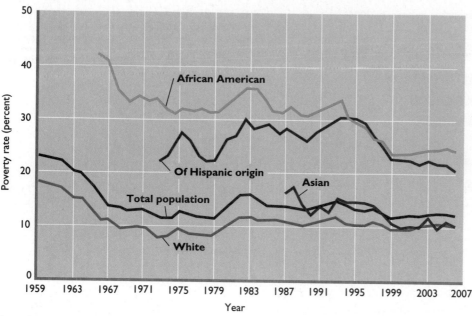

FIGURE 20.5 Poverty-rate trends, 1959–2006. Although the national poverty rate declined sharply between 1959 and 1969, it stabilized in the 1970s only to increase significantly in the early 1980s. Between 1993 and 2000 it substantially declined, before rising slightly again in the immediate years following the 2001 recession. Although poverty rates for African Americans and Hispanics are much higher than the average, they significantly declined during the 1990s.

Source: Bureau of the Census, **www.census.gov.**

African Americans and Hispanics still had poverty rates that were roughly double the rate for whites.

Measurement Issues

The poverty rates and trends in Figures 20.4 and 20.5 should be interpreted cautiously. The official income thresholds for defining poverty are necessarily arbitrary and therefore may inadequately measure the true extent of poverty in the United States.

Some observers say that the high cost of living in major metropolitan areas means that the official poverty thresholds exclude millions of families whose income is slightly above the poverty level but clearly inadequate to meet basic needs for food, housing, and medical care. These observers use city-by-city studies on "minimal income needs" to show that poverty in the United States is much more widespread than officially measured and reported.

In contrast, some economists point out that using income to measure poverty understates the standard of living of many of the people who are officially poor. When individual, household, or family *consumption* is considered rather than family *income*, some of the poverty in the United States disappears. Some low-income families maintain their consumption by drawing down past savings, borrowing against future income, or selling homes. Moreover, many poverty families receive substantial noncash benefits such as food stamps and rent subsidies that boost their living standards. Such "in-kind" benefits are not included in determining a family's official poverty status.

The U.S. Income-Maintenance System

Regardless of how poverty is measured, economists agree that considerable poverty exists in the United States. Helping those who have very low income is a widely accepted goal of public policy. A wide array of antipoverty programs, including education and training programs, subsidized employment, minimum-wage laws, and antidiscrimination policies, are designed to increase the earnings of the poor. In addition, a number of income-maintenance programs were devised to reduce poverty; the most important are listed in Table 20.3. These programs involve large expenditures and have numerous beneficiaries.

The U.S. income-maintenance system consists of two kinds of programs: (1) social insurance and (2) public assistance, or "welfare." Both are known as **entitlement programs,** because all eligible persons are ensured (entitled to) the benefits set forth in the programs.

Social Insurance Programs

Social insurance programs partially replace earnings that have been lost due to retirement, disability, or temporary unemployment; they also provide health insurance for the elderly. The main social insurance programs are Social Security, unemployment compensation, and Medicare. Benefits are viewed as earned rights and do not carry the stigma of public charity. These programs are financed primarily out of Federal payroll taxes. In these programs

TABLE 20.3 **Characteristics of Major Income-Maintenance Programs**

Program	Basis of Eligibility	Source of Funds	Form of Aid	Expenditures,* Billions	Beneficiaries, Millions
Social Insurance Programs					
Social Security	Age, disability, or death of parent or spouse; life-time work earnings	Federal payroll taxes on employers and employees	Cash	$594	50
Medicare	Age or disability	Federal payroll tax on employers and employees	Subsidized health insurance	$408	43
Unemployment compensation	Unemployment	State and Federal payroll taxes on employers	Cash	$34	8
Public Assistance Programs					
Supplemental Security Income (SSI)	Age or disability; income	Federal revenues	Cash	$37	7
Temporary Assistance for Needy Families (TANF)	Certain families with children; income	Federal-state-local revenues	Cash and services	$14	4
Food stamps	Income	Federal revenues	Vouchers	$33	26
Medicaid	Persons eligible for TANF or SSI and medically indigent	Federal-state-local revenues	Subsidized medical services	$276	58
Earned-income tax credit (EITC)	Low-wage working families	Federal revenues	Refundable tax credit, cash	$41	22

*Expenditures by Federal, state, and local governments; excludes administrative expenses.

Source: Social Security Administration, *Annual Statistical Supplement, 2007,* **www.socialsecurity.gov,** U.S. Department of Agriculture, **www.fns. usda.gov,** Internal Revenue Service, **www.irs.gov/taxstats,** and other government sources. Latest data.

the entire population shares the risk of an individual's losing income because of retirement, unemployment, disability, or illness. Workers (and employers) pay a part of wages into a government fund while they are working. The workers are then entitled to benefits when they retire or when a specified misfortune occurs.

Social Security and Medicare The major social insurance program is known as **Social Security.** It is a Federal pension program that replaces part of the earnings lost when workers retire, become disabled, or die. This gigantic program ($594 billion in 2007) is financed by compulsory payroll taxes levied on both employers and employees. Workers currently may retire at age 65 and receive full retirement benefits or retire early at age 62 with reduced benefits. When a worker dies, benefits accrue to his or her family survivors. Special provisions provide benefits for disabled workers.

Social Security covers over 90 percent of the workforce; some 50 million people receive Social Security benefits, with benefits for retirees averaging about $1082 per month. In 2008, those benefits were financed with a combined Social Security and Medicare payroll tax of 15.3 percent, with both the worker and the employer paying 7.65 percent on their first $102,000 of earnings.

The 7.65 percent tax comprises 6.2 percent for Social Security and 1.45 percent for Medicare. Self-employed workers pay a tax of 15.3 percent.

Medicare is a Federal insurance program that provides health insurance benefits to those 65 or older and people who are disabled. It is financed by payroll taxes on employers and employees. This overall 2.9 percent tax is paid on all work income, not just on the first $102,000. Medicare also makes available supplementary low-cost insurance programs that help pay for doctor visits and, beginning in 2006, prescription drug expenses. In 2007, some 43 million people received Medicare benefits. The benefits paid totaled $408 billion.

The number of retirees drawing Social Security and Medicare benefits is rapidly rising relative to the number of workers paying payroll taxes. As a result, Social Security and Medicare face serious long-term funding problems. These fiscal imbalances have spawned calls to reform the programs. (See Chapter 4's Last Word.)

Unemployment Compensation All 50 states sponsor unemployment insurance programs called **unemployment compensation,** a Federal–state social insurance program that makes income available to workers who are unemployed. This insurance is financed by a relatively

small payroll tax, paid by employers, which varies by state and by the size of the firm's payroll. Any insured worker who becomes unemployed can, after a short waiting period, become eligible for benefit payments. The program covers almost all wage and salary workers. The size of payments and the number of weeks they are made available vary considerably from state to state. Generally, benefits approximate 33 percent of a worker's wages up to a certain maximum payment. In 2007 benefits averaged about $277 weekly. The number of beneficiaries and the level of total disbursements vary with economic conditions.

Typically, unemployment compensation payments last for a maximum of 26 weeks. But during recessions—when unemployment rates soar—Congress extends the benefits for additional weeks.

Public Assistance Programs

Public assistance programs (welfare) provide benefits to people who are unable to earn income because of permanent disabling conditions or who have no or very low income and also have dependent children. These programs are financed out of general tax revenues and are regarded as public charity. They include "means tests" that require that individuals and families demonstrate low incomes in order to qualify for aid. The Federal government finances about two-thirds of the welfare program expenditures, and the rest is paid for by the states.

Many needy persons who do not qualify for social insurance programs are assisted through the Federal government's **Supplemental Security Income (SSI)** program. This is a Federal program (financed by general tax revenues) that provides a uniform nationwide minimum income for the aged, blind, and disabled who are unable to work and who do not qualify for Social Security aid. In 2007 the average monthly payment was $603 for individuals and $904 for couples with both people eligible. More than half the states provide additional income supplements to the aged, blind, and disabled.

The **Temporary Assistance for Needy Families (TANF)** is the basic welfare program for low-income families in the United States. The program is financed through general Federal tax revenues and consists of lump-sum payments of Federal money to states to operate their own welfare and work programs. These lump-sum payments are called TANF funds, and in 2007 about 3.9 million people (including children) received TANF assistance. TANF expenditures in 2007 were about $14 billion.

In 1996 TANF replaced the six-decade-old Aid for Families with Dependent Children (AFDC) program. Unlike that welfare program, TANF established work requirements and placed limits on the length of time a family can receive welfare payments. Specifically, the TANF program:

- Set a lifetime limit of 5 years on receiving TANF benefits and requires able-bodied adults to work after receiving assistance for 2 years.
- Ended food-stamp eligibility for able-bodied persons age 18 to 50 (with no dependent children) who are not working or engaged in job-training programs.
- Tightened the definition of "disabled children" as it applies for eligibility of low-income families for Supplemental Security Income (SSI) assistance.
- Established a 5-year waiting period on public assistance for new legal immigrants who have not become citizens.

In 1996 about 12.6 million people were welfare recipients, including children, or 4.8 percent of the U.S. population. By the middle of 2007 those totals had declined to 3.9 million and 1.3 percent of the population. The program has greatly increased the employment rate (= employment/population) for single mothers with children under age 6—a group particularly prone to welfare dependency. Today, that rate is about 13 percentage points higher than it was in 1996.

The **food-stamp program** is a Federal program (financed through general tax revenues) that permits eligible low-income persons to obtain vouchers that can be used to buy food. It is designed to provide all low-income Americans with a "nutritionally adequate diet." Under the program, eligible households receive monthly allotments of coupons that are redeemable for food. The amount of food stamps received varies inversely with a family's earned income.

Medicaid is a Federal program (financed by general tax revenues) that provides medical benefits to people covered by the SSI and TANF (basic welfare) programs. It helps finance the medical expenses of individuals participating in those programs.

The **earned-income tax credit (EITC)** is a refundable Federal tax credit provided to low-income wage earners to supplement their families' incomes and encourage work. It is available for low-income working families, with or without children. The credit reduces the Federal income taxes that such families owe or provides them with cash payments if the credit exceeds their tax liabilities. The purpose of the credit is to offset Social Security taxes paid by low-wage earners and thus keep the Federal government from "taxing families into poverty." In essence, EITC is a wage subsidy from the Federal government that works out to be as much as $2 per hour for the lowest-paid workers with families. Under the program many people owe no income tax and receive direct checks from the Federal government once a year. According to the Internal Revenue Service, 22 million taxpayers received $41 billion in payments from the EITC in 2006.

Several other welfare programs are not listed in Table 20.3. Some provide help in the form of noncash transfers. Head Start provides education, nutrition, and social services to economically disadvantaged 3- and 4-year-olds. Housing assistance in the form of rent subsidies and funds for construction is available to low-income families. Pell grants provide assistance to undergraduate students from low-income families. Low-income home energy assistance provides help with home heating bills. Other programs—such as veteran's assistance and black lung benefits—provide cash assistance to those eligible.

QUICK REVIEW 20.2

- The basic argument for income equality is that it maximizes total utility by equalizing the marginal utility of the last dollar of income received by all people.

- The basic argument for income inequality is that it is necessary as an economic incentive for production.

- By government standards, 36.5 million people in the United States, or 12.3 percent of the population, lived in poverty in 2006.

- The U.S. income-maintenance system includes both social insurance programs and public assistance (welfare) programs.

Discrimination

Although the majority of Americans who are in the lowest income quintile or in poverty are white, African Americans and Hispanics are in those two categories disproportionally to their total populations. For that reason, the percentages of all African Americans and Hispanics receiving public assistance from the TANF, SSI, and food stamp programs are also well above the average for the entire population. This fact raises the question of what role, if any, discrimination plays in reducing wages for some and increasing wages for others.

Discrimination is the practice of according people inferior treatment (for example, in hiring, occupational access, education and training, promotion, wage rate, or working conditions) on the basis of some factor such as race, gender, or ethnicity. People who practice discrimination are said to exhibit a prejudice or a bias against the groups they discriminate against.

Economic Analysis of Discrimination

Prejudice reflects complex, multifaceted, and deeply ingrained beliefs and attitudes. Thus, economics can contribute some insights into discrimination but no detailed explanations. With this caution in mind, let's look more deeply into the economics of discrimination.

Taste-for-Discrimination Model

The **taste-for-discrimination model** examines prejudice by using the emotion-free language of demand theory. It views discrimination as resulting from a preference or taste for which the discriminator is willing to pay. The model assumes that, for whatever reason, prejudiced people experience a subjective or psychic cost—a disutility—whenever they must interact with those they are biased against. Consequently, they are willing to pay a certain "price" to avoid interactions with the nonpreferred group. The size of this price depends directly on the degree of prejudice.

> **ORIGIN OF THE IDEA**
> **O 20.1**
> Taste-for-discrimination model

The taste-for-discrimination model is general, since it can be applied to race, gender, age, and religion. But our discussion focuses on employer discrimination, in which employers discriminate against nonpreferred workers. For concreteness, we will look at a white employer discriminating against African-American workers.

Discrimination Coefficient A prejudiced white employer behaves as if employing African-American workers would add a cost. The amount of this cost—this disutility—is reflected in a **discrimination coefficient**, d, measured in monetary units. Because the employer is not prejudiced against whites, the cost of employing a white worker is the white wage rate, W_w. However, the employer's perceived "cost" of employing an African-American worker is the African-American worker's wage rate, W_{aa}, plus the cost d involved in the employer's prejudice, or $W_{aa} + d$.

The prejudiced white employer will have no preference between African-American and white workers when the total cost per worker is the same, that is, when $W_w = W_{aa} + d$. Suppose the market wage rate for whites is $10 and the monetary value of the disutility the employer attaches to hiring African Americans is $2 (that is, $d = \$2$). This employer will be indifferent between hiring African Americans and whites only when the African-American wage rate is $8, since at this wage the perceived cost of hiring either a white or an African-American worker is $10:

$10 white wage = $8 African-American wage + $2 discrimination coefficient

It follows that our prejudiced white employer will hire African Americans only if their wage rate is sufficiently below that of whites. By "sufficiently" we mean at least the amount of the discrimination coefficient.

The greater a white employer's taste for discrimination as reflected in the value of d, the larger the difference between white wages and the lower wages at which African Americans will be hired. A "color-blind" employer whose d is $0 will hire equally productive African Americans and whites impartially if their wages are the same. A blatantly prejudiced white employer whose d is infinity would refuse to hire African Americans even if the African-American wage were zero.

Most prejudiced white employers will not refuse to hire African Americans under all conditions. They will, in fact, *prefer* to hire African Americans if the actual white-black wage difference in the market exceeds the value of d. In our example, if whites can be hired at $10 and equally productive African Americans at only $7.50, the biased white employer will hire African Americans. That employer is willing to pay a wage difference of up to $2 per hour for whites to satisfy his or her bias, but no more. At the $2.50 actual difference, the employer will hire African Americans.

Conversely, if whites can be hired at $10 and African Americans at $8.50, whites will be hired. Again, the biased employer is willing to pay a wage difference of up to $2 for whites; a $1.50 actual difference means that hiring whites is a "bargain" for this employer.

Prejudice and the Market African-American–White Wage Ratio

For a particular supply of African-American workers, the actual African-American–white wage ratio—the ratio determined in the labor market—will depend on the collective prejudice of white employers. To see why, consider Figure 20.6, which shows a labor market for *African-American* workers. Initially, suppose the relevant labor demand curve is D_1, so the equilibrium *African-American* wage is $8 and the equilibrium level of African-American employment is 16 million. If we assume that the *white* wage (not shown) is $10, then the initial African-American–white wage ratio is .80 (= $8/$10).

Now assume that prejudice against African-American workers increases—that is, the collective d of white employers rises. An increase in d means an increase in the perceived cost of African-American labor at each African-American wage rate, and that reduces the demand for African-American labor, say, from D_1 to D_2. The African-American wage rate falls from $8 to $6 in the market, and the level of African-American employment declines from 16 million to 12 million. The increase in white employer

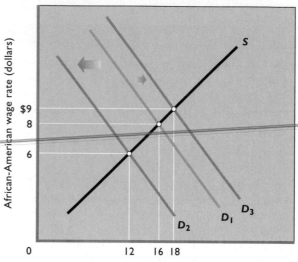

FIGURE 20.6 The African-American wage and employment level in the taste-for-discrimination model. An increase in prejudice by white employers as reflected in higher discrimination coefficients would decrease the demand for African-American workers, here from D_1 to D_2, and reduce the African-American wage rate and level of African-American employment. Not shown, this drop in the African-American wage rate would lower the African-American–white wage ratio. In contrast, if prejudice were reduced such that discrimination coefficients of employers declined, the demand for African-American labor would increase, as from D_1 to D_3, boosting the African-American wage rate and level of employment. The higher African-American wage rate would increase the African-American–white wage ratio.

prejudice reduces the African-American wage rate and thus the actual African-American–white wage ratio. If the white wage rate remains at $10, the new African-American–white ratio is .6 (= $6/$10).

Conversely, suppose social attitudes change such that white employers become less biased and their discrimination coefficient as a group declines. This decreases the perceived cost of African-American labor at each African-American wage rate, so the demand for African-American labor increases, as from D_1 to D_3. In this case, the African-American wage rate rises to $9, and employment of African-American workers increases to 18 million. The decrease in white employer prejudice increases the African-American wage rate and thus the actual African-American–white wage ratio. If the white wage remains at $10, the new African-American–white wage ratio is .9 (= $9/$10).

Competition and Discrimination

The taste-for-discrimination model suggests that competition will reduce discrimination in the very long run, as follows: The actual African-American–white wage difference for equally productive workers—say, $2—allows nondiscriminators to hire African Americans for less than whites. Firms that hire African-American workers will therefore have lower actual wage costs per unit of output and lower average total costs than will the firms that discriminate. These lower costs will allow nondiscriminators to underprice discriminating competitors, eventually driving them out of the market.

But critics of this implication of the taste-for-discrimination model say that it overlooks entry barriers to new firms and point out that progress in eliminating racial discrimination has been slow. Discrimination based on race has persisted in the United States and other market economies decade after decade. To explain why, economists have proposed alternative models. **(Key Question 12)**

Statistical Discrimination

A second theory of discrimination centers on the concept of **statistical discrimination,** in which people are judged on the basis of the average characteristics of the group to which they belong, rather than on their own personal characteristics or productivity. For example, insurance rates for teenage males are higher than those for teenage females. The difference is based on factual evidence indicating that, on average, young males are more likely than young females to be in accidents. But many young men are actually less accident-prone than the average young woman, and those men are discriminated against by having to pay higher insurance rates. The uniqueness of the theory of statistical discrimination is its suggestion that discriminatory outcomes are possible even where there is no prejudice.

Labor Market Example How does statistical discrimination show itself in labor markets? Employers with job openings want to hire the most productive workers available. They have their personnel department collect information concerning each job applicant, including age, education, and prior work experience. They may supplement that information with preemployment tests, which they feel are helpful indicators of potential job performance. But collecting detailed information about job applicants is very expensive, and predicting job performance on the basis of limited data is difficult. Consequently, some employers looking for inexpensive information may consider the *average* characteristics of women and minorities in determining whom to hire. They are in fact practicing statistical discrimination when they do so. They are using gender, race, or ethnic background as a crude indicator of production-related attributes.

Example: Suppose an employer who plans to invest heavily in training a worker knows that on average women are less likely to be career-oriented than men, more likely to quit work in order to care for young children, and more likely to refuse geographic transfers. Thus, on average, the return on the employer's investment in training is likely to be less when choosing a woman than when choosing a man. All else equal, when choosing between two job applicants, one a woman and the other a man, this employer is likely to hire the man.

Note what is happening here. Average characteristics for a *group* are being applied to *individual* members of that group. The employer is falsely assuming that *each and every* woman worker has the same employment tendencies as the *average* woman. Such stereotyping means that numerous women who are career-oriented, who plan to work after having children, and who are flexible as to geographic transfers will be discriminated against.

Profitable, Undesirable, but Not Malicious

The firm that practices statistical discrimination is not being malicious in its hiring behavior (although it may be violating antidiscrimination laws). The decisions it makes will be rational and profitable because *on average* its hiring decisions are likely to be correct. Nevertheless, many people suffer because of statistical discrimination, since it blocks the economic betterment of capable people. And since it is profitable, statistical discrimination tends to persist.

Occupational Segregation: The Crowding Model

The practice of **occupational segregation**—the crowding of women, African Americans, and certain ethnic groups into less desirable, lower-paying occupations—is still apparent in the U.S. economy. Statistics indicate that women are disproportionately concentrated in a limited number of occupations such as teaching, nursing, and secretarial and clerical jobs. African Americans and Hispanics are crowded into low-paying jobs such as those of laundry workers, cleaners and household aides, hospital orderlies, agricultural workers, and other manual laborers.

Let's look at a model of occupational segregation, using women and men as an example.

The Model The character and income consequences of occupational discrimination are revealed through a labor supply and demand model. We make the following assumptions:

- The labor force is equally divided between men and women workers. Let's say there are 6 million male and 6 million female workers.
- The economy comprises three occupations, X, Y, and Z, with identical labor demand curves, as shown in Figure 20.7.

FIGURE 20.7 The economics of occupational segregation. By crowding women into one occupation, men enjoy high wage rates of M in occupations X and Y, while women receive low wages of W in occupation Z. The elimination of discrimination will equalize wage rates at B and result in a net increase in the nation's output.

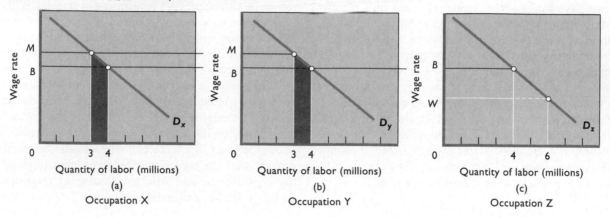

(a)	(b)	(c)
Occupation X	Occupation Y	Occupation Z

- Men and women have the same labor-force characteristics; each of the three occupations could be filled equally well by men or by women.

Effects of Crowding Suppose that, as a consequence of discrimination, the 6 million women are excluded from occupations X and Y and crowded into occupation Z, where they earn wage W. The men distribute themselves equally among occupations X and Y, meaning that 3 million male workers are in each occupation and have a common wage of M. (If we assume that there are no barriers to mobility between X and Y, any initially different distribution of males between X and Y would result in a wage differential between the two occupations. That would prompt labor shifts from the low- to the high-wage occupation until an equal distribution occurred.)

Because women are crowded into occupation Z, labor supply (not shown) is larger and their wage rate W is much lower than M. Because of the discrimination, this is an equilibrium situation that will persist as long as the crowding occurs. The occupational barrier means women cannot move into occupations X and Y in pursuit of a higher wage.

The result is a loss of output for society. To see why, recall again that labor demand reflects labor's marginal revenue product, which is labor's contribution to domestic output. Thus, the brown areas for occupations X and Y in Figure 20.7 show the decrease in domestic output—the market value of the marginal output—caused by subtracting 1 million women from each of these occupations. Similarly, the green area for occupation Z shows the increase in domestic output caused by moving 2 million women into occupation Z. Although society would gain the added output represented by the green area in occupation Z, it would lose the output represented by the

sum of the two brown areas in occupations X and Y. That output loss exceeds the output gain, producing a net output loss for society.

Eliminating Occupational Segregation Now assume that through legislation or sweeping changes in social attitudes, discrimination disappears. Women, attracted by higher wage rates, shift from occupation Z to X and Y; 1 million women move into X and another 1 million move into Y. Now there are 4 million workers in Z, and occupational segregation is eliminated. At that point there are 4 million workers in each occupation, and wage rates in all three occupations are equal, here at B. That wage equality eliminates the incentive for further reallocations of labor.

The new, nondiscriminatory equilibrium clearly benefits women, who now receive higher wages; it hurts men, who now receive lower wages. But women were initially harmed and men benefited through discrimination; removing discrimination corrects that situation.

Society also gains. The elimination of occupational segregation reverses the net output loss just discussed. Adding 1 million women to each of occupations X and Y in Figure 20.7 increases domestic output by the sum of the two brown areas. The decrease in domestic output caused by losing 2 million women from occupation Z is shown by the green area. The sum of the two increases in domestic output in X and Y exceeds the decrease in domestic output in Z. With the end of the discrimination, 2 million women workers have moved from occupation Z, where their contribution to domestic output (their MRP) is low, to higher-paying occupations X and Y, where their contribution to domestic output is high. Thus society gains a more efficient allocation of resources from the removal of occupational discrimination.

U.S. Family Wealth and Its Distribution

In 2006 the Federal Reserve Reported Its Latest Findings on Family Wealth (= Net Worth = Assets *Minus* Liabilities) in the United States. Between 1995 and 2004 Family Wealth Rose Rapidly and Became More Unequal.

The Federal Reserve conducts a Survey of Consumer Finances in the United States every 3 years, through which it determines median family wealth, average family wealth, and the distribution of wealth. *Median family wealth* is the wealth received by the family at the midpoint of the distribution; *average family wealth* is simply total wealth divided by the number of families. As shown in Table 1, median and average family wealth, adjusted for inflation, was considerably higher in 2004 than in 1995. That is, the value of family assets rose more rapidly than the value of liabilities, increasing net worth—or wealth. Between 1995 and 2004, median and average wealth rose by 31 percent and 72 percent, respectively. In general, American families are wealthier than they were before.

Table 2 looks at the distribution of family wealth for various percentile groups and reveals that the distribution of wealth is highly unequal. In 2004 the wealthiest 10 percent of families owned almost 70 percent of the total wealth and the top 1 percent owned 33 percent. The bottom 90 percent held only about 30 percent of the total wealth.

Moreover, the general trend is toward greater inequality of wealth. The lowest 90 percent of the families owned about 32 percent of total U.S. wealth in 1995, but that percentage fell to about 30 percent in 2004.

So from a normative standpoint, Tables 1 and 2 present a "mixed-news" combination. The welcome news is that median and average wealth in the United States rose substantially between 1995 and 2004. The discouraging news is that such wealth grew less rapidly for the typical American family than for the top 10 percent of American families over the entire period.

Tables 1 and 2 raise many interesting questions: Will the inequality of wealth continue to grow in the future? If so, what are the implications for the future character of the American society? Should government do more, or less, in the future to try to redistribute wealth? Would new government policies to redistribute wealth endanger or slow the creation of wealth and the growth of income for average Americans? The Federal estate tax is currently scheduled to phase out in 2010 and then return to very high levels. Should the phase-out be made permanent or replaced with a new estate tax at a lower rate?

Sources: Brian K. Bucks, Arthur B. Kennickell, and Kevin B. Moore, "Recent Changes in U.S. Family Finances: Evidence from the 2001 and 2004 Survey of Consumer Finances," *Federal Reserve Bulletin*, January 2006, p. 8; Arthur B. Kennickell, "Currents and Undercurrents: Changes in the Distribution of Wealth, 1989–2004," Survey of Consumer Finances working paper, January 2006, p. 11.

TABLE 1 Median and Average Family Wealth, Survey Years, 1995–2004 (in 2004 Dollars)

Year	Median	Average*
1995	$70,800	$260,800
1998	83,100	327,500
2001	91,700	421,500
2004	93,100	448,200

*The averages greatly exceed the medians because the averages are boosted by the multibillion-dollar wealth of a relatively few families.

TABLE 2 Percentage of Total Family Wealth Held by Different Percentile Groups, Survey Years, 1995–2004

Year	Percentile of Wealth Distribution		
	Bottom 90%	Top 10%	Top 1%
1995	32.2%	67.8%	34.6%
1998	31.4	68.6	33.9
2001	30.2	69.8	32.7
2004	30.5	69.5	33.4

Example: The easing of occupational barriers has led to a surge of women gaining advanced degrees in some high-paying professions. In recent years, for instance, the percentage of law degrees and medical degrees awarded to women has exceeded 40 percent, compared with less than 10 percent in 1970. **(Key Question 14)**

QUICK REVIEW 20.3

- Discrimination occurs when workers who have the same abilities, education, training, and experience as other workers receive inferior treatment with respect to hiring, occupational access, promotion, or wages.

- The taste-for-discrimination model sees discrimination as representing a preference or "taste" for which the discriminator is willing to pay.

- The theory of statistical discrimination says that employers often wrongly judge individuals on the basis of average group characteristics rather than on personal characteristics, thus harming those discriminated against.

- The crowding model of discrimination suggests that when women and minorities are systematically excluded from high-paying occupations and crowded into low-paying ones, their wages and society's domestic output are reduced.

Cost to Society as Well as to Individuals

It is obvious from all three models of discrimination that discrimination by race, ethnicity, gender, age, or other such factor imposes costs on those who are discriminated against. They have lower wages, less access to jobs, or both. Preferred workers in turn benefit from discrimination through less job competition, greater job access, and higher wages. But discrimination does more than simply transfer earnings from some people to others, thus contributing to income inequality and increasing poverty. Where it exists, discrimination also diminishes the economy's total output and income. In that regard, discrimination acts much like any other artificial barrier to free competition. By arbitrarily blocking qualified individuals from high-productivity (and thus high-wage) jobs, discrimination keeps those discriminated against from providing their maximum contribution to society's total output and total income. In terms of production possibilities analysis, discrimination locates society inside the production possibilities curve that would be available to it if there were no discrimination.

Discrimination redistributes a diminished amount of total income.

Summary

1. The distribution of income in the United States reflects considerable inequality. The richest 20 percent of households receive 50.5 percent of total income, while the poorest 20 percent receive 3.4 percent.

2. The Lorenz curve shows the percentage of total income received by each percentage of households. The extent of the gap between the Lorenz curve and a line of total equality illustrates the degree of income inequality.

3. The Gini ratio measures the overall dispersion of the income distribution and is found by dividing the area between the diagonal and the Lorenz curve by the entire area below the diagonal. The Gini ratio ranges from zero to 1, with higher ratios signifying greater degrees of income inequality.

4. Recognizing that the positions of individual families in the distribution of income change over time and incorporating the effects of noncash transfers and taxes would reveal less income inequality than do standard census data. Government transfers (cash and noncash) greatly lessen the degree of income inequality; taxes also reduce inequality, but not nearly as much as transfers.

5. Causes of income inequality include differences in abilities, in education and training, and in job tastes, along with

discrimination, inequality in the distribution of wealth, and an unequal distribution of market power.

6. Census data show that income inequality has increased since 1970. The major cause of the recent increases in income inequality is a rising demand for highly skilled workers, which has boosted their earnings significantly.

7. The basic argument for income equality is that it maximizes consumer satisfaction (total utility) from a particular level of total income. The main argument for income inequality is that it provides the incentives to work, invest, and assume risk and is necessary for the production of output, which, in turn, creates income that is then available for distribution.

8. Current statistics reveal that 12.3 percent of the U.S. population lives in poverty. Poverty rates are particularly high for female-headed families, young children, African Americans, and Hispanics.

9. The present income-maintenance program in the United States consists of social insurance programs (Social Security, Medicare, and unemployment compensation) and public assistance programs (SSI, TANF, food stamps, Medicaid, and earned-income tax credit).

10. Discrimination relating to the labor market occurs when women or minorities having the same abilities, education,

training, and experience as men or white workers are given inferior treatment with respect to hiring, occupational choice, education and training, promotion, and wage rates. Discrimination redistributes national income and, by creating inefficiencies, diminishes its size.

11. In the taste-for-discrimination model, some white employers have a preference for discrimination, measured by a discrimination coefficient *d*. Prejudiced white employers will hire African-American workers only if their wages are at least *d* dollars below those of whites. The model indicates that declines in the discrimination coefficients of white employers will increase the demand for African-American workers,

raising the African-American wage rate and the ratio of African-American wages to white wages. It also suggests that competition may eliminate discrimination in the long run.

12. Statistical discrimination occurs when employers base employment decisions about *individuals* on the average characteristics of *groups* of workers. That can lead to discrimination against individuals even in the absence of prejudice.

13. The crowding model of occupational segregation indicates how white males gain higher earnings at the expense of women and certain minorities who are confined to a limited number of occupations. The model shows that discrimination also causes a net loss of domestic output.

Terms and Concepts

income inequality	social insurance programs	food-stamp program
Lorenz curve	Social Security	Medicaid
Gini ratio	Medicare	earned-income tax credit (EITC)
income mobility	unemployment compensation	discrimination
noncash transfers	public assistance programs	taste for discrimination model
equality-efficiency trade-off	Supplemental Security Income (SSI)	discrimination coefficient
poverty rate	Temporary Assistance for Needy	statistical discrimination
entitlement programs	Families (TANF)	occupational segregation

Study Questions

1. Use quintiles to briefly summarize the degree of income inequality in the United States. How and to what extent does government reduce income inequality? **LO1**

2. **KEY QUESTION** Assume that Al, Beth, Carol, David, and Ed receive incomes of $500, $250, $125, $75, and $50, respectively. Construct and interpret a Lorenz curve for this five-person economy. What percentage of total income is received by the richest quintile and by the poorest quintile? **LO1**

3. How does the Gini ratio relate to the Lorenz curve? Why can't the Gini ratio exceed 1? What is implied about the direction of income inequality if the Gini ratio declines from 0.42 to 0.35? How would one show that change of inequality in the Lorenz diagram? **LO1**

4. Why is the lifetime distribution of income more equal than the distribution in any specific year? **LO1**

5. **KEY QUESTION** Briefly discuss the major causes of income inequality. With respect to income inequality, is there any difference between inheriting property and inheriting a high IQ? Explain. **LO2**

6. What factors have contributed to increased income inequality since 1970? **LO3**

7. Should a nation's income be distributed to its members according to their contributions to the production of that total income or according to the members' needs? Should society attempt to equalize income or economic

opportunities? Are the issues of equity and equality in the distribution of income synonymous? To what degree, if any, is income inequality equitable? **LO4**

8. Do you agree? Or disagree? Explain your reasoning. "There need be no trade-off between equality and efficiency. An 'efficient' economy that yields an income distribution that many regard as unfair may cause those with meager incomes to become discouraged and stop trying. So efficiency may be undermined. A fairer distribution of rewards may generate a higher average productive effort on the part of the population, thereby enhancing efficiency. If people think they are playing a fair economic game and this belief causes them to try harder, an economy with an equitable income distribution may be efficient as well."[6] **LO4**

9. Comment on or explain: **LO4**
   a. Endowing everyone with equal income will make for very unequal enjoyment and satisfaction.
   b. Equality is a "superior good"; the richer we become, the more of it we can afford.
   c. The mob goes in search of bread, and the means it employs is generally to wreck the bakeries.
   d. Some freedoms may be more important in the long run than freedom from want on the part of every individual.

---

[6]Paraphrased from Andrew Schotter, *Free Market Economics* (New York: St. Martin's Press, 1985), pp. 30–31.

e. Capitalism and democracy are really a most improbable mixture. Maybe that is why they need each other—to put some rationality into equality and some humanity into efficiency.

f. The incentives created by the attempt to bring about a more equal distribution of income are in conflict with the incentives needed to generate increased income.

10. **KEY QUESTION** How do government statisticians determine the poverty rate? How could the poverty rate fall while the number of people in poverty rises? Which group in each of the following pairs has the higher poverty rate: (*a*) children or people age 65 or over? (*b*) African Americans or foreign-born noncitizens? (*c*) Asians or Hispanics? **LO5**

11. What are the essential differences between social insurance and public assistance programs? Why is Medicare a social insurance program whereas Medicaid is a public assistance program? Why is the earned-income tax credit considered to be a public assistance program? **LO6**

12. **KEY QUESTION** The labor demand and supply data in the following table relate to a single occupation. Use them to answer the questions that follow. Base your answers on the taste-for-discrimination model. **LO7**

Quantity of Hispanic Labor Demanded, Thousands	Hispanic Wage Rate	Quantity of Hispanic Labor Supplied, Thousands
24	$16	52
30	14	44
35	12	35
42	10	28
48	8	20

a. Plot the labor demand and supply curves for Hispanic workers in this occupation.

b. What are the equilibrium Hispanic wage rate and quantity of Hispanic employment?

c. Suppose the white wage rate in this occupation is $16. What is the Hispanic-to-white wage ratio?

d. Suppose a particular employer has a discrimination coefficient *d* of $5 per hour. Will that employer hire Hispanic or white workers at the Hispanic-white wage ratio indicated in part *c?* Explain.

e. Suppose employers as a group become less prejudiced against Hispanics and demand 14 more units of Hispanic labor at each Hispanic wage rate in the table. What are the new equilibrium Hispanic wage rate and level of Hispanic employment? Does the Hispanic-white wage ratio rise or fall? Explain.

f. Suppose Hispanics as a group increase their labor services in that occupation, collectively offering 14 more units of labor at each Hispanic wage rate. Disregarding the changes indicated in part *e*, what are the new equilibrium Hispanic wage rate and level of Hispanic employment? Does the Hispanic-white wage ratio rise, or does it fall?

13. Males under the age of 25 must pay far higher auto insurance premiums than females in this age group. How does this fact relate to statistical discrimination? Statistical discrimination implies that discrimination can persist indefinitely, while the taste-for-discrimination model suggests that competition might reduce discrimination in the long run. Explain the difference. **LO7**

14. **KEY QUESTION** Use a demand and supply model to explain the impact of occupational segregation or "crowding" on the relative wage rates and earnings of men and women. Who gains and who loses from the elimination of occupational segregation? Is there a net gain or a net loss to society? Explain. **LO7**

15. **LAST WORD** Go to Table 1 in the Last Word and compute the ratio of average wealth to median wealth for each of the 4 years. What trend do you find? What is your explanation for the trend? The Federal estate tax redistributes wealth in two ways: by encouraging charitable giving, which reduces the taxable estate, and by heavily taxing extraordinarily large estates and using the proceeds to fund government programs. Do you favor repealing the estate tax? Explain.

Web-Based Questions

1. **HOW MUCH FAMILY INCOME DOES IT TAKE TO BE IN THE RICHEST 5 PERCENT?** Go to the U.S. Census Bureau Web site, **www.census.gov,** and select Income (under People), Historical Income Tables (CPS), and Income Inequality. What is the lower limit of household income for the richest 5 percent of families in the most recent year listed? Do the historical data in the table suggest the poor are getting poorer and the rich are getting richer in absolute terms? Return to the site's tables (under Househeolds) and determine what has happened to the relative income share of the richest 5 percent of households over the last 10 years listed.

2. **IS POVERTY ON THE RISE OR ON THE DECLINE?** Go to the U.S. Census Bureau Web site, **www.census.gov,** and

select Poverty (under People). Use the data provided to answer the following questions:

a. Is the number of people living below the official government poverty level higher or lower than it was in the preceding year? Than it was a decade earlier?

b. Is the poverty rate (in percent) higher or lower than it was in the preceding year for the general population, children under 18, blacks, Asians, Pacific Islanders, and whites?

c. How many states had increases in the poverty rate compared to the preceding year?

FURTHER TEST YOUR KNOWLEDGE AT
www.mcconnell18e.com

Health Care

Rarely can you read a newspaper or look at a television news program without encountering a story about the high costs of health care in the United States, seriously ill people who have no health insurance, or government health insurance programs that threaten to drain Federal and state budgets. Some news stories document disputes between employers and workers over sharing the cost of health insurance or cite instances of insurance companies dictating the medical care that doctors can provide. Competing plans for health care reform are often central issues in political campaigns. Moreover, difficult ethical questions concerning "extreme care" for the acutely or terminally ill arise from time to time.

Health care accounts for 16 percent of U.S. GDP and 10 percent of total employment, making it worthy of specific study. Further, the tools of microeconomic analysis are particularly helpful in understanding the U.S. health care system, major health care issues, and actual and proposed reforms.

The Health Care Industry

Because the boundaries of the health care industry are not precise, defining the industry is difficult. In general, it includes services provided in hospitals, nursing homes, laboratories, and physicians' and dentists' offices. It also includes prescription and nonprescription drugs, artificial limbs, and eyeglasses. Note, however, that many goods and services that may affect health are not included, for example, low-fat foods, vitamins, and health club services.

Health care is one of the largest U.S. industries, employing about 14 million people, including about 790,000 practicing physicians, or 266 doctors per 100,000 of population. There are about 5750 hospitals containing 947,000 beds. Americans make more than 1 billion visits to office-based physicians each year.

Twin Problems: Costs and Access

Two highly publicized problems are related to the U.S. health care system:

- The cost of health care has risen rapidly in response to higher prices and an increase in the quantity of services provided. (Spending on health care involves both "prices" and "quantities" and is often loosely referred to as "health care costs.") The price of medical care has increased faster than the overall price level. For example, the December-to-December index of medical care prices rose by 4.2 percent in 2004, 4.3 percent in 2005, 3.6 percent in 2006, and 5.2 percent in 2007. (The overall price index increased by an annual average of 3.3 percent for those four years.) Health care spending (price × quantity) grew by 8.0 percent in 2003, 6.9 percent in 2004, 6.5 percent in 2005, and 6.7 percent in 2006. It is projected to grow at an annual rate of 7.3 percent over the next 10 years.
- Some 45 million Americans do not have health insurance coverage, and many Americans have limited, or no, access to health care.

Efforts to reform health care have focused on controlling costs and making it accessible to everyone. Those two goals are related, since high and rising prices make health care services unaffordable to a significant portion of the U.S. population. In fact, a dual system of health care may be evolving in the United States. Those with insurance or other financial means receive the world's highest-quality medical treatment, but many people, because of their inability to pay, fail to seek out the most basic treatment. When they do seek treatment, they may receive poorer care than those who have insurance.

High and Rising Health Care Costs

We need to examine several aspects of health care spending and health care costs.

Health Care Spending

Health care spending in the United States is high and rising in both absolute terms and as a percentage of domestic output.

Total Spending on Health Care Figure 21.1a gives an overview of the major types of U.S. health care spending ($2.1 trillion in 2006). It shows that 31 cents of each health care dollar is spent on hospitals, while 21 cents goes to physicians and 23 cents for other health care services (dental, vision, and home care).

Figure 21.1b shows the sources of funds for health care spending. It reveals that four-fifths of health care spending is financed by insurance. Public insurance (Medicaid, Medicare, and insurance for veterans, current military personnel, and government employees) is the source of 47 cents of each dollar spent. Private insurance accounts for 34 cents. So public and private insurance combined provide 81 cents of each dollar spent. The remaining 19 cents comes directly out of the health care consumer's pocket. It is paid mainly as insurance **deductibles** (that is, the insured pays the first $250 or $500 of each year's health care costs before the insurer begins paying) or **copayments** (that is, the insured pays, say, 20 percent of all health care costs and the insurance company pays 80 percent).

Recall that Medicare is a nationwide Federal health care program available to Social Security beneficiaries and persons with disabilities. One part of Medicare is a hospital insurance program that, after a deductible of $1024 (in 2008), covers all reasonable costs for the first 60 days of inpatient care per "benefit period" and lesser amounts (on a cost-sharing basis) for additional days. Coverage is also provided for posthospital nursing services, home health care, and hospice care for the terminally ill. The second part of Medicare, a medical insurance program (for physicians' services, laboratory and other diagnostic tests, and outpatient hospital services), is voluntary but is heavily subsidized by government. The $96.40 monthly premiums (in 2008) that participants pay cover about one-fourth of the cost of the benefits provided.

Medicaid provides payment for medical benefits to certain low-income people, including the elderly, the blind, persons with disabilities, children, and adults with

FIGURE 21.1 **Health care expenditures and finance.** Total U.S. health care expenditures are extremely large ($2.1 trillion in 2006. (a) Most health care expenditures are for hospitals and the services of physicians and other skilled professionals. (b) Public and private insurance pay for four-fifths of health care.

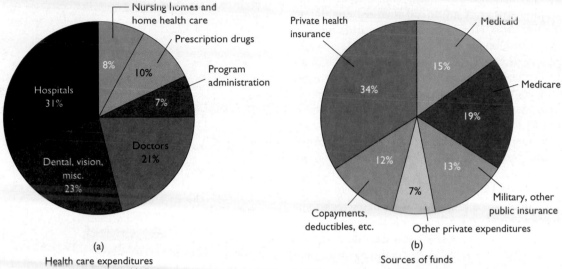

(a)
Health care expenditures

(b)
Sources of funds

Source: Centers for Medicare and Medicaid Services, **cms.hhs.gov**. Data are for 2006 and are compiled by the authors.

dependent children. Those who qualify for Temporary Aid for Needy Families (TANF) and the Supplemental Security Income (SSI) program are automatically eligible for Medicaid. Nevertheless, Medicaid covers less than half of those living in poverty. The Federal government and the states share the cost of Medicaid. On average, the states fund 43 percent and the Federal government 57 percent of each Medicaid dollar spent.

Overall, about 19 percent of each dollar spent on health care is financed by direct out-of-pocket payments by individuals. The fact that most U.S. health care is paid for by private insurance companies or the government is an important contributor to rising health care costs.

Percentage of GDP Figure 21.2 shows how U.S. health care spending has been increasing as a percentage of GDP. Health care spending absorbed 5.2 percent of GDP in 1960 but rose to 16 percent by 2006.

International Comparisons Global Perspective 21.1 reveals that among the industrialized nations, health care spending as a percentage of GDP is highest in the United States. It is reasonable to assume that health care spending varies positively with output and incomes, but that doesn't account for the higher U.S. health expenditures as a percentage of GDP. For whatever reason, the United States is "in a league of its own" as to its proportion of output devoted to health care.

Quality of Care: Are We Healthier?

To compare the quality of health care from country to country is difficult. Yet there is general agreement that medical care (although not health and not "preventive

FIGURE 21.2 **U.S. health care expenditures as a percentage of GDP.** U.S. health care spending as a percentage of GDP has greatly increased since 1960.

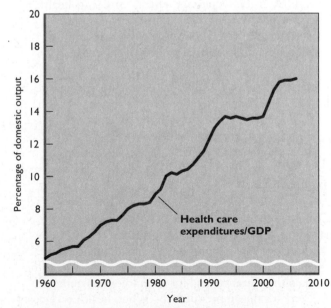

Source: Centers for Medicare and Medicaid Services, **cms.hhs.gov**.

treatment") in the United States is probably the best in the world. Average life expectancy in the United States has increased by 6 years since 1970, and U.S. physicians and hospitals employ the most advanced medical equipment and technologies. Also, more than half the world's medical research funding is done in the United States. As a result, the incidence of disease has been declining and the quality of treatment has been improving. Polio has been virtually eliminated, ulcers are successfully treated without surgery, angioplasty and coronary bypass surgery greatly benefit those with heart disease, sophisticated body scanners are increasingly available diagnostic tools, and organ transplants and prosthetic joint replacements are more and more common.

That is the good news. But there is other news as well. Despite new screening and treatment technologies, the breast cancer mortality rate has shown little change. Tuberculosis, a virtually forgotten disease, has reappeared. The AIDS epidemic has claimed more than 560,000 American lives. More generally, some experts say that high levels of health care spending have not produced significantly better health and well-being. U.S. health care expenditures are the highest in the world absolutely, as a proportion of GDP, and on a per capita basis. Yet many other nations rank higher than the United States in fixed life expectancy, maternal mortality, and infant mortality.

Economic Implications of Rising Costs

The most visible economic effects of rising health care costs are higher health insurance premiums to employers and higher out-of-pocket costs to workers. But rising health care costs have other economic effects as well.

Reduced Access to Care

Higher health care costs and insurance premiums reduce access to health care. Some employers reduce or eliminate health insurance as part of their pay packages and some uninsured workers go without private health insurance. Consequently, the number of uninsured grows. We will consider this issue in detail momentarily.

Labor Market Effects

Surging health care costs have three main effects on labor markets:

- *Slower wage growth* First, gains in workers' total compensation (wage plus fringe benefits, including health insurance paid for by employers) generally match gains in productivity. When health care costs (and thus insurance prices) rise more rapidly than

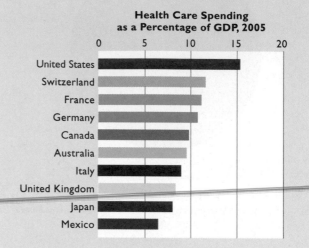

productivity, firms wanting to maintain the existing level of health care benefits for their workers must reduce the growth of the wage portion of the total compensation package. Thus, in the long run, workers bear the burden of rising health care costs in the form of slower-growing wages.

- *Use of part-time and temporary workers* The high cost of employer-provided health insurance has led some employers to restructure their workforces: Full-time workers with health insurance benefits are employed in smaller numbers, and uninsured part-time or temporary workers are employed in greater numbers. Similarly, a large, prosperous employer with a generous health care plan might reduce its health insurance expense by discharging its insured lower-wage workers—janitors, gardeners, and cafeteria staff—and replacing them with outside independent contractors who provide little or no health insurance for their employees.

- *Outsourcing (and Offshoring)* Burdened by rising insurance costs, some firms may find that shifting part of their work to domestic or international suppliers is profitable. This outsourcing may lower labor costs in situations where the outside suppliers provide lesser medical benefits to their workers. Offshoring (international outsourcing) has shifted jobs to developing economies such as Mexico, India, and China. Although labor productivity in these countries is considerably lower than that in the United States, lower wages and employer-provided medical benefits may be sufficient to make offshoring profitable. Rising domestic medical expenses therefore may join a host of other factors, including shifts in comparative advantage, in encouraging this practice.

Personal Bankruptcies Large, uninsured medical bills are one of the major causes of personal bankruptcy. Health care experts point out that medical bills are often the last to be paid because unlike other bills there is nothing to repossess, shut off, or foreclose. So medical bills sometimes build up beyond the point of a realistic means for full repayment. Even individuals who pay all bills in a timely fashion can find themselves in tremendous financial difficulty when they face large, uncompensated medical bills for major operations (such as open-heart surgery) and expensive medical procedures (such as cancer treatment).

Impact on Government Budgets The budgets of Federal, state, and local governments are negatively affected by spiraling and sometimes unpredictable health care expenditures. In the past two decades, spending for health care through Medicare and Medicaid has been by far the fastest-growing segment of the Federal budget. To cover those rising expenditures, the government must either raise taxes or reduce the portion of the budget used for national defense, education, environmental programs, scientific research, and other spending categories.

The states are also finding it difficult to cover their share of the Medicaid bill. Most of them have been forced to raise their tax rates and search for new sources of revenue, and many of them have had to reduce spending on nonhealth programs such as infrastructure maintenance, welfare, and education. Local governments face similar budget strains in trying to finance public health services, hospitals, and clinics.

Too Much Spending?
Increased spending on computers or houses would be a sign of prosperity, not a cause for alarm, because society is obtaining more of each. What is different about increased spending on health care? Maybe nothing, say some economists. William Nordhaus of Yale, for example, recently estimated that the economic value of increases in longevity over the last 100 years nearly equals the total value of the additional GDP during that period. According to Kevin Murphy and Robert Topel, economists at the University of Chicago, reduced mortality from heart disease alone contributes $1.5 trillion of benefits a year in the United States. That amount exceeds the entire annual GDP of Canada.

While all economists agree that improved health care has greatly contributed to society's GDP and well-being, many economists think that health care expenditures in the United States are inefficiently large. The production of health care requires scarce resources such as capital in the form of hospitals and diagnostic equipment and the highly skilled labor of physicians, technicians, and nurses. The total output of health care in the United States may be so large that health care, at the margin, is worth less than the alternative goods and services these resources could otherwise have produced. The United States therefore may be consuming health care beyond the $MB = MC$ point that defines efficiency.

If resources are overallocated to health care, society incurs an efficiency loss. Resources used excessively in health care could be used more productively to build new factories, support research and development, construct new bridges and roads, support education, improve the environment, or provide more consumer goods.

The suggested "too much of a good thing" results from peculiarities in the market for health care. We will see that the possibility of overspending arises from the way health care is financed, the asymmetry of information between consumers and providers, and the interaction of health insurance with technological progress in the industry.

Limited Access

The other health care problem is limited access. Even though there may be an overallocation of resources to health care, not all Americans can obtain the health care they need. In 2006 about 45 million Americans, or roughly 15 percent of the population, had no health insurance for the entire year. As health care costs (and therefore health care insurance premiums) continue to rise, the number of uninsured could grow.

Who are the medically uninsured? As incomes rise, so does the probability of being insured. So it is no surprise that the uninsured are concentrated among the poor. Medicaid is designed to provide health care for the poor who are on welfare. But many poor people work at low or minimum-wage jobs without health care benefits, earning "too much" to qualify for Medicaid yet not enough to afford private health insurance. About half of the uninsured have a family head who works full-time. Many single-parent families, African Americans, and Hispanics are uninsured simply because they are more likely to be poor.

Curiously, those with excellent health and those with the poorest health also tend to be uninsured. Many young people with excellent health simply choose not to buy health insurance. The chronically ill find it very difficult and too costly to obtain insurance because of the likelihood that they will incur substantial health care costs in the future. Because private health insurance is most frequently obtained through an employer, the unemployed are also likely to lack insurance.

Workers for smaller firms are also less likely to have health insurance. The main reason is that administrative expenses for a small firm may be 30 to 40 percent of insurance premiums, as opposed to only 10 percent for a large firm. Also, corporations can deduct health insurance premiums from income to obtain substantial tax savings. Small unincorporated businesses can deduct only part of their health insurance expenses.

Low-wage workers are also less likely to be insured. Earlier we noted that in the long run employers pass on the increasing expense of health care insurance to workers as lower wages. This option is not available to employers who are paying the minimum wage. Thus as health care insurance premiums rise, employers cut or eliminate this benefit from the compensation package for their minimum- and low-wage workers. As a result, these workers are typically uninsured.

Although many of the uninsured forgo health care, some do not. A few are able to pay for it out of pocket. Others may wait until their illness reaches a critical stage and then go to a hospital for admittance or to be treated in the emergency room. This form of treatment is more costly than if the patient had insurance and therefore had been treated earlier by a physician. It is estimated that hospitals provide $28 billion to $32 billion of uncompensated ("free") health care per year. The hospitals then try to shift these costs to those who have insurance or who can pay out of pocket. **(Key Question 2)**

QUICK REVIEW 21.1

- Health care spending in the United States has been increasing absolutely and as a percentage of gross domestic output.
- Rising health care costs have caused (a) more people to find health insurance unaffordable; (b) adverse labor market effects, including slower real-wage growth and increased use of part-time and temporary workers; and (c) restriction of nonhealth spending by governments.
- Rising health care spending may reflect an overallocation of resources to the health care industry.
- Approximately 15 percent of all Americans have no health insurance and, hence, no (or limited) access to health care.

Why the Rapid Rise in Costs?

The rising prices, quantities, and costs of health care services are the result of the demand for health care increasing much more rapidly than supply. We will examine the reasons for this in some detail. But first it will be helpful to understand certain characteristics of the health care market.

Peculiarities of the Health Care Market

We know that purely competitive markets achieve both allocative and productive efficiency: The most desired products are produced in the least costly way. We also have found that many imperfectly competitive markets, perhaps aided by regulation or the threat of antitrust action, provide outcomes generally accepted as efficient. What, then, are the special features of the health care market that have contributed to rising prices and thus escalating costs to buyers?

- **Ethical and equity considerations** Ethical questions inevitably intervene in markets when decisions involve the quality of life, or literally life or death. Although we might not consider it immoral or unfair if a person cannot buy a Mercedes or a personal computer, society regards it as unjust for people to be denied access to basic health care or even to the best available health care. In general, society regards health care as an "entitlement" or a "right" and is reluctant to ration it solely by price and income.

- **Asymmetric information** Health care buyers typically have little or no understanding of complex diagnostic and treatment procedures, while the physicians who are the health care sellers of those procedures possess detailed information. This creates the unusual situation in which the doctor (supplier) as the agent of the patient (consumer) tells the patient what health care services he or she should consume. We will say more about this shortly.

- **Positive externalities** The medical care market often generates positive externalities (spillover benefits). For example, an immunization against polio, smallpox, or measles benefits the immediate purchaser, but it also benefits society because it reduces the risk that other members of society will be infected with a highly contagious disease. Similarly, a healthy labor force is more productive, contributing to the general prosperity and well-being of society.

- **Third-party payments: insurance** Because four-fifths of all health care expenses are paid through public or private insurance, health care consumers pay much lower out-of-pocket "prices" than they would otherwise. Those lower prices are a distortion that results in "excess" consumption of health care services.

The Increasing Demand for Health Care

With these four features in mind, let's consider some factors that have increased the demand for health care over time.

Rising Incomes: The Role of Elasticities

Because health care is a normal good, increases in domestic income have caused increases in the demand for health care. While there is some disagreement as to the exact income elasticity of demand for health care, several studies for industrially advanced countries suggest that the income elasticity coefficient is about 1. This means that per capita health care spending rises approximately in proportion to increases in per capita income. For example, a 3 percent increase in income will generate a 3 percent increase in health care expenditures. There is some evidence that income elasticity may be higher in the United States, perhaps as high as 1.5.

Estimates of the price elasticity of demand for health care imply that it is quite inelastic, with this coefficient being as low as .2. This means that the quantity of health care consumed declines relatively little as price increases. For example, a 10 percent increase in price would reduce quantity demanded by only 2 percent. An important consequence is that total health care spending will increase as the price of health care rises.

The relative insensitivity of health care spending to price changes results from four factors. First, people consider health care a necessity, not a luxury. There are few, if any, good substitutes for medical care in treating injuries and infections and alleviating various ailments. Second, medical treatment is often provided in an emergency situation in which price considerations are secondary or irrelevant. Third, most consumers prefer a long-term relationship with their doctors and therefore do not "shop around" when health care prices rise. Fourth, most patients have insurance and are therefore not directly affected by the price of health care. If insured patients pay, for example, only 20 percent of their health care expenses, they are less concerned with price increases or price differences between hospitals and between doctors than they would be if they paid 100 percent themselves. **(Key Question 7)**

An Aging Population
The U.S. population is aging. People 65 years of age and older constituted approximately 9 percent of the population in 1960 but 12.4 percent in

2000. Projections for the year 2030 indicate 20 percent of the population will be 65 or over by that year.

This aging of the population affects the demand for health care because older people encounter more frequent and more prolonged spells of illness. Specifically, those 65 and older consume about three and one-half times as much health care as those between 19 and 64. In turn, people over 84 consume almost two and one-half times as much health care as those in the 65 to 69 age group. Health care expenditures are often extraordinarily high in the last year of one's life.

Looking ahead, in 2011 the 76 million people born between 1946 and 1964 will begin turning 65. We can expect that fact to create a substantial surge in the demand for health care.

Unhealthy Lifestyles
Substance abuse helps drive up health care costs. The abuse of alcohol, tobacco, and illicit drugs damages health and is therefore an important component of the demand for health care services. Alcohol is a major cause of injury-producing traffic accidents and liver disease. Tobacco use markedly increases the probability of cancer, heart disease, bronchitis, and emphysema. Illicit drugs are a major contributor to violent crime, health problems in infants, and the spread of AIDS. In addition, illicit-drug users make hundreds of thousands of costly visits to hospital emergency rooms each year. And overeating and lack of exercise contribute to heart disease, diabetes, and many other ailments. Obesity-related medical costs are estimated to be about $75 billion per year, with taxpayers picking up more than half the tab through Medicare and Medicaid.

The Role of Doctors
Physicians may increase the demand for health care in several ways.

Supplier-Induced Demand
As we mentioned before, doctors, the suppliers of medical services, have much more information about those services than consumers, who are the demanders. While a patient might be well informed about food products or more complex products such as cameras, he or she is not likely to be well informed about diagnostic tests such as magnetic resonance imaging or medical procedures such as joint replacements. Because of this asymmetric information (informational imbalance), a principal-agent problem emerges: The supplier, not the demander, decides what types and amounts of health care are to be consumed. This situation creates a possibility of "supplier-induced demand."

This possibility becomes especially relevant when doctors are paid on a **fee-for-service** basis, that is, paid separately for each service they perform. In light of the asymmetric information and fee-for-service arrangement, doctors have an opportunity and an incentive to suggest more health care services than are absolutely necessary (just as an auto repair shop has an opportunity and an incentive to recommend replacement of parts that are worn but still working).

More surgery is performed in the United States, where many doctors are paid a fee for each operation, than in foreign countries, where doctors are often paid annual salaries unrelated to the number of operations they perform. Furthermore, doctors who own X-ray or ultrasound machines do four times as many tests as doctors who refer their patients to radiologists. More generally, studies suggest that up to one-third of common medical tests and procedures are either inappropriate or of questionable value.

The seller's control over consumption decisions has another result: It eliminates much of the power buyers might have in controlling the growth of health care prices and spending.

Defensive Medicine "Become a doctor and support a lawyer," says a bumper sticker. The number of medical malpractice lawsuits admittedly is high. To a medical doctor, each patient represents not only a person in need but also a possible malpractice suit. As a result, physicians tend to practice **defensive medicine.** That is, they recommend more tests and procedures than are warranted medically or economically in order to protect themselves against malpractice suits.

Medical Ethics Medical ethics may drive up the demand for health care in two ways. First, doctors are ethically committed to use "best-practice" techniques in serving their patients. This often means the use of costly medical procedures that may be of only slight benefit to patients.

Second, public values seem to support the medical ethic that human life should be sustained as long as possible. This makes it difficult to confront the notion that health care is provided with scarce resources and therefore must be rationed like any other good. Can society afford to provide $5000-per-day intensive care to a comatose patient unlikely to be restored to reasonable health? Public priorities seem to indicate that such care should be provided, and those values again increase the demand for health care.

Role of Health Insurance

As we noted in Figure 21.1, 79 percent of health care spending is done not by health care consumers through direct out-of-pocket payments but by private health insurance companies or by the government through Medicare and Medicaid.

Individuals and families face potentially devastating monetary losses from a variety of hazards. Your house may burn down; you may be in an auto accident; or you may suffer a serious illness. An insurance program is a means of protection against the huge monetary losses that can result from such hazards. A number of people agree to pay certain amounts (premiums) periodically in return for the guarantee that they will be compensated if they should incur a particular misfortune. Insurance is a means of paying a relatively small known cost for protection against an uncertain and much larger cost. While health insurance is therefore highly beneficial, it also contributes to rising costs and possible overconsumption of health care.

The Moral Hazard Problem The moral hazard problem is the tendency of one party to an agreement to alter her or his behavior in a way that is costly to the other party. Health care insurance can change behavior in two ways. First, some insured people may be less careful about their health, taking fewer steps to prevent accident or illness. Second, insured individuals have greater incentives to use health care more intensively than they would if they did not have insurance. Let's consider both aspects of moral hazard.

Less Prevention Health insurance may increase the demand for health care by encouraging behaviors that require more health care. Although most people with health care insurance are probably as careful about their health as are those without insurance, some may be more inclined to smoke, avoid exercise, and eat unhealthful foods, knowing they have insurance. Similarly, some individuals may take up ski jumping or rodeo bull riding if they have insurance covering the costs of orthopedic surgeons. And if their insurance covers rehabilitation programs, some people may be more inclined to experiment with alcohol or drugs.

Overconsumption Insured people go to doctors more often and request more diagnostic tests and more complex treatments than they would if they were uninsured because, with health insurance, the price or opportunity cost of consuming health care is minimal. For example, many individuals with private insurance pay a fixed premium for coverage, and beyond that, aside from a modest deductible, their health care is "free." This situation differs from most markets, in which the price to the consumer reflects the full opportunity cost of each unit of the good or service. In all markets, price provides a direct economic incentive to restrict use of the product. The minimal direct price to the insured consumer of health care, in contrast, creates an incentive to overuse the health care system. Of course, the penalty for overuse will ultimately show up in higher insurance premiums, but all policyholders will share those premiums. The cost increase for the individual health consumer will be relatively small.

Also, the availability of insurance removes the consumer's budget constraint (spending limitation) when he or she decides to consume health care. Recall from Chapter 7 that budget constraints limit the purchases of most products. But insured patients face minimal or no out-of-pocket expenditures at the time they purchase health care. Because affordability is not the issue, health care may be overconsumed.

Government Tax Subsidy

Federal tax policy toward employer-financed health insurance works as a **tax subsidy** that strengthens the demand for health care services. Specifically, employees do not pay Federal income or payroll tax (Social Security) on the value of the health insurance they receive as an employee benefit. Employees thus request and receive more of their total compensation as nontaxed health care benefits and less in taxed wages and salaries.

The government rationale for this tax treatment is that positive spillover benefits are associated with having a healthy, productive workforce. So it is appropriate to encourage health insurance for workers. The tax break does enable more of the population to have health insurance, but it also contributes to greater consumption of health care. Combined with other factors, the tax break may result in an overconsumption of health care.

To illustrate: If the marginal tax rate is, say, 28 percent, $1 worth of health insurance is equivalent to 72 cents in after-tax pay. Because the worker can get more insurance for $1 than for 72 cents, the exclusion of health insurance from taxation increases purchases of health insurance, thus increasing the demand for health care. In essence, the 28-cent difference acts as a government subsidy to health care. A recent estimate suggests that this subsidy costs the Federal government $120 billion per year in forgone tax revenue and boosts private health insurance spending by about one-third. Actual health care spending may be 10 to 20 percent higher than otherwise because of the subsidy.

Graphical Portrayal

A simple demand and supply model illustrates the effect of health insurance on the health care market. Figure 21.3a depicts a competitive market for health care services; curve D shows the demand for health care services if all consumers are uninsured, and S represents the supply of health care. At market price P_a the equilibrium quantity of health care is Q_a.

Recall from our discussion of competitive markets that output Q_a results in allocative efficiency, which means there is no better alternative use for the resources allocated to producing that level of health care. To see what we mean by "no better use," recall that:

- As we move down along demand curve D, each succeeding point indicates, via the price it represents, the marginal benefit that consumers receive from that unit.
- The supply curve is the producers' marginal-cost curve. As we move up along the supply curve, each succeeding point indicates the marginal cost of that unit of health care.
- For each unit produced up to the equilibrium quantity Q_a, marginal benefit exceeds marginal cost (because points on D are above those on S). At Q_a marginal benefit equals marginal cost, designating allocative efficiency. No matter what else those resources could have produced, the greatest net benefit to society is obtained by using those resources to produce Q_a units of health care.

But allocative efficiency occurs only when consumers pay the full market price for a product, as is assumed in Figure 21.3a. What happens when we introduce health insurance that covers, say, two-thirds of all health care costs? In Figure 21.3b, with private or public health insurance in

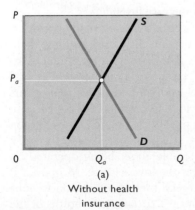

(a)
Without health
insurance

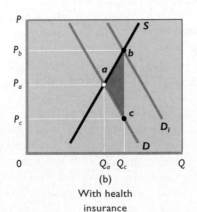

(b)
With health
insurance

FIGURE 21.3 Insurance and the overallocation of resources to health care. (a) Without health insurance, the optimal amount of health care consumed is Q_a, where the marginal benefit and marginal cost of health care are equal. (b) The availability of private and public insurance increases the demand for health care, as from D to D_i, and reduces the price to the consumer from P_a to P_c (here, equal to one-third of the full price P_b). This lower after-insurance price results in overconsumption (Q_c rather than Q_a). Area *abc* represents the efficiency loss from the overallocation of resources to health care.

place, consumers increase their demand for health care, as from D to D_i. At each possible price they desire more health care than before because insurance will pick up a large part of the bill. Given the supply curve of health care S, this increase in demand raises the price of health care to P_b. But with the insurance, consumers pay only one-third of the new higher price, and less than without the insurance. The new price facing them is only P_c ($= 1/3P_b$)—not the previous price P_a. So they increase their consumption of health care from Q_a to Q_c.

The added consumption (and production) of health care is inefficient. Between Q_a and Q_c each unit's marginal cost to society (measured on curve S) exceeds its marginal benefit (measured on before-insurance demand curve D). Each unit of health care between Q_a and Q_c is an overallocation of resources to health care. Triangle abc measures the efficiency loss from this overallocation.

Figure 21.3b implies that a trade-off exists between efficiency and equity. Standards of fairness or equity in the United States lead people to believe that all citizens should have access to basic health care, which is why government created social insurance in the form of Medicare and Medicaid. Also, it helps explain the Federal tax subsidy to private health insurance, which again makes health care more accessible. The problem, as Figure 21.3b shows, is that the greater the availability of insurance (and thus the more equitable society makes access to health care), the greater the overallocation of resources to the health care industry. This overallocation would be even greater if health care were provided completely "free" under a program of national health insurance. Consumers would purchase health care as long as the marginal benefit to themselves as individuals was positive, regardless of the true cost to society. **(Key Question 10)**

Supply Factors in Rising Health Care Prices

Supply factors have also played a role in rising health care prices. Specifically, the supply of health care services has increased, but more slowly than demand. A combination of factors has produced this relatively slow growth of supply.

Supply of Physicians The supply of physicians in the United States has increased over the years; in 1975 there were 169 physicians per 100,000 people; by 2006 there were 266. But this increase in supply has not kept up with the increase in the demand for physicians' services. As a result, physicians' fees and incomes have increased more rapidly than average prices and incomes for the economy as a whole.

Conventional wisdom has been that physician groups, for example, the American Medical Association, have purposely kept admissions to medical schools, and therefore the supply of doctors, artificially low. But that is too simplistic. A rapidly rising cost of medical education seems to be the main cause of the relatively slow growth of doctor supply. Medical training requires 4 years of college, 4 years of medical school, an internship, and perhaps 3 or 4 years of training in a medical specialty. The opportunity cost of this education has increased because the salaries of similarly capable people have soared in other professions. The direct expenses have also increased, largely due to the increasingly sophisticated levels of medical care and therefore of medical training.

High and rising education and training costs have necessitated high and rising doctors' fees to ensure an adequate return on this sort of investment in human capital. Physicians' incomes are indeed high, averaging in 2007 from about $160,000 for family care physicians up to $530,000 for neurosurgeons. But the costs of obtaining the skills necessary to become a physician are also very high. Data show that while doctors have high rates of return on their educational expenses, those returns are below the returns for lawyers and holders of masters of business administration degrees.

Slow Productivity Growth Productivity growth in an industry tends to reduce costs and increase supply. In the health care industry, such productivity growth has been modest. One reason is that health care is a service, and it is generally more difficult to increase productivity for services than for goods. It is relatively easy to increase productivity in manufacturing by mechanizing the production process. With more and better machinery, the same number of workers can produce greater output. But services often are a different matter. It is not easy, for example, to mechanize haircuts, child care, and pizza delivery. How do you significantly increase the productivity of physicians, nurses, and home care providers?

Also, competition for patients among many providers of health care has not been sufficiently brisk to force them to look for ways to reduce cost by increasing productivity. When buying most goods, customers typically shop around for the lowest price. This shopping requires that sellers keep their prices low and look to productivity increases to maintain or expand their profits. But patients rarely shop for the lowest prices when seeking medical care. In fact, a patient may feel uncomfortable about being operated on by a physician who charges the lowest price. Moreover, if insurance pays for the surgery, there is no reason to consider price at all. The point is that unusual features of the market for health care limit competitive pricing and thus reduce incentives to achieve cost saving via advances in productivity.

Changes in Medical Technology

Some technological advances in medicine have lowered costs. For example, the development of vaccines for polio, smallpox, and measles has greatly reduced health care expenditures for the treatment of those diseases. And reduced lengths of stays in hospitals have lowered the costs of medical care.

But many medical technologies developed since the Second World War have significantly increased the cost of medical care either by increasing prices or by extending procedures to a greater number of people. For example, because they give more accurate information, advanced body scanners costing up to $1000 per scan are often used in place of X rays that cost less than $100 for each scan. Desiring to offer the highest quality of service, hospitals want to use the very latest equipment and procedures. These newer, more expensive treatments are surely more effective than older ones. But doctors and hospital administrators both realize that the fixed high cost of such equipment means it must be used extensively to reduce the average cost per patient and recoup the investment at "fair return" charges per procedure.

As another example, organ transplants are extremely costly. Before the development of this technology, a person with a serious liver malfunction died. Now a liver transplant can cost $200,000 or more, with subsequent medical attention costing $10,000 to $20,000 per year for the rest of the patient's life.

Finally, consider new prescription medications. Pharmaceutical companies have developed very expensive drugs that often replace less expensive ones and are prescribed for a much wider range of physical and mental illnesses. Although these remarkable new medications greatly improve health care, they also contribute to rising health care costs.

The historical willingness of private and public insurance to pay for new treatments without regard to price and number of patients has contributed to the incentive to develop and use new technologies. Insurers, in effect, have encouraged research into and development of health care technologies, regardless of their cost. Recently, when insurance companies resisted paying for new expensive treatments such as bone marrow transplants, public outcries led them to change their minds. So expanding insurance coverage leads to new, often more expensive medical technologies, which in turn lead to a demand for a wider definition of what should be covered by insurance.

Relative Importance

According to most analysts, the demand and supply factors we have discussed vary in their impact on escalating health care costs. As we noted, the income elasticity of demand for health care is estimated to be +1 to +1.5, meaning that increased income brings with it proportionate or more-than-proportionate increases in health care spending. But rising income does not alone explain the rocketing increase in health care spending as a percentage of total domestic output (income). Furthermore, government studies estimate that the aging population accounts for less than 10 percent of the current increase in per capita health care spending.

Most experts attribute the relative rise in health care spending to (1) advances in medical technology, combined with (2) the medical ethic of providing the best treatment available, (3) private and public health insurance, and (4) fee-for-service physicians' payments by health insurance

CONSIDER THIS . . .

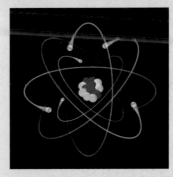

Cancer Fight Goes Nuclear*

Medical technology often improves health care but adds to health-care costs. *The New York Times* reports that several major medical centers are turning nuclear particle accelerators into medical devices to treat cancer. The machines, previously used only for physics research, accelerate protons to near the speed of light and direct them into cancerous tumors. Because the proton beams are more precise than are conventional radiation X-ray beams, the side effects are reduced and the treatment outcomes may be improved.

Each accelerator costs $100 million! The building housing the machine is the size of a football field and requires walls up to 18 feet thick. A concern has arisen that competition among medical centers will result in too many machines, each being underutilized. Also, once medical centers have invested in the machines, they will want to recoup their investment as soon as possible at the "fair-return" prices allowed by insurance companies. So physicians may feel pressure from the centers to use the devices on cancer patients even though less-costly alternatives might be equally effective. Patients, desiring the latest and best technology, will pressure physicians to use the proton therapies.

Welcome to the world of modern medicine—advanced technology, new and improved procedures, and rising medical costs!

Source: Based on Andrew Pollack, "Cancer Fight Goes Nuclear, with Heavy Price Tag," *New York Times*, December 26, 2007, **www.nytimes.com**.

firms. Through technological progress, great strides have been made in the diagnosis, treatment, and prevention of illness. But the third-party (insurance) payment system provides little incentive to limit the development or use of such technologies because it has no mechanism to force an equating of marginal costs and marginal benefits. And the "best treatment available" ethic, together with the fee-for-service payment system, ensures that any new technology with a positive marginal benefit will get used and be billed for, regardless of the marginal cost to society.

QUICK REVIEW 21.2

- Characteristics of the health care market are (a) the widespread view of health care as a "right," (b) asymmetric information between consumers and suppliers, (c) the presence of positive externalities, and (d) payment mostly by insurance.

- The demand for health care has increased for many reasons, including rising incomes, an aging population, unhealthy lifestyles, the role of doctors as advisers to patients, the practice of defensive medicine, and a fee-for-service payment system via health insurance.

- The supply of health care has grown slowly, primarily because of (a) relatively slow productivity growth in the health care industry, (b) rising costs of medical education and training, and (c) greater use of very-high-cost health care technologies.

Reform of the Health Care System

What, if anything, can be done to ensure access for more Americans to the health care system? And how might health care costs be contained? Reform of the health care system to achieve these two goals will be difficult. First, there is a trade-off between the two objectives: Greater access to the system will mean rising costs. Second, health care reform is complex because expectations (for example, access to the "best" medical care), tradition (the "right" to choose one's doctor), and the goals of self-interest groups (private insurers, health maintenance organizations, drug companies, physicians, and hospitals) all come into play.

This latter point is especially significant. The numerous affected interest groups will not passively accept rearrangement of costs and benefits in an industry that accounts for one-seventh of total U.S. spending. Physicians, hospitals, health insurers, health maintenance organizations, and drug companies seek to prevent price controls on their services and products. Older people—represented by AARP—want government to pay a larger portion of long-term (nursing-home) health care. Health insurance companies hope their business will not be curtailed by reforms. Labor unions advocate a generous basic-benefits package and oppose taxation of employer-financed health insurance. Drug companies want prescription drugs covered under Medicare. Psychiatrists, physical therapists, acupuncturists, and chiropractors want their services included in any new proposal. Trial lawyers want existing malpractice laws left alone. Small businesses strongly oppose any law requiring all companies to provide health insurance for their employees. The beer, liquor, and tobacco industries do not want additional "sin" taxes levied on them to help finance any reform proposal.

Universal Access

How can health care insurance, and thus health care, be made available to all U.S. citizens? Let's briefly consider three reform concepts.

"Play or Pay" Because much of the nation's health insurance is paid by employers, one way is to expand that coverage using a **play-or-pay** approach. All employers would be required to either provide a basic health insurance program for their workers and their dependents ("play") or pay a special payroll tax to finance health insurance for uninsured workers ("pay"). Some form of publicly sponsored health care plan would cover people who are not in the labor force and thus uninsured.

Such plans, however, probably would lead to lower real wages. Also, unemployment might increase in firms currently paying wages at or near the minimum wage.

Tax Credits and Vouchers Another approach, using tax credits and vouchers, would help the poor pay for health insurance. The Federal government would provide a tax credit, for example, of $1500 for a single person and $4000 for a family of four, to low-income individuals and families for use in purchasing health insurance. The size of the tax credit would diminish as the recipient's income rises. Those whose incomes are so low as to be exempt from the income tax would be issued a voucher for purchasing health insurance. This proposal is essentially a tax subsidy designed to make insurance more affordable to low-income people.

National Health Insurance The most far-reaching and controversial reform concept is to establish a system of **national health insurance (NHI)** along the lines of the present Canadian system. The Federal government would provide a basic package of health care to every U.S. resident at no direct charge or at a low cost-sharing level. The system would be financed out of tax revenues rather than out of insurance premiums.

NHI is not the same as socialized medicine. Under NHI the government would not own health care facilities such as hospitals, clinics, and nursing homes. Nor would health care practitioners such as doctors, nurses, and technicians be government employees. Under NHI the government would simply sponsor and finance basic health care for all citizens. Although the role of private health insurers would be reduced under NHI, they could provide health insurance for any medical procedures that were not covered in the basic NHI health care package.

Arguments for NHI Proponents say that NHI is the simplest and most direct way of providing universal access to health care:

- It allows patients to choose their own physicians.
- It would reduce administrative costs. The present system, it is argued, is administratively chaotic and expensive because hundreds of private health care insurers are involved, each with its own procedures and claim forms. Administration costs in the Canadian system are less than 5 percent of total health care costs compared with almost 17 percent in the United States.
- It would separate health care availability from employment and therefore would eliminate the hiring of part-time and temporary workers as a way to avoid providing health care insurance.
- It would allow the government to use its single-insurer market power to contain costs. The government could apply its buying power to mandate fees for various medical procedures and thus control physician and hospital costs. Hospitals would operate on budgets set by the government.

Arguments against NHI Opponents of NHI provide weighty counterarguments:

- Government-determined price ceilings on physicians' services are not likely to control costs. Doctors can protect their incomes from fixed fees by manipulating the amount of care they provide a patient. Suppose the maximum fee for an office visit is $50. Doctors might spread a given number of diagnostic tests over three or four office visits, although all the tests could be done in one visit. Or a doctor might require an office visit to explain test results instead of phoning the patient. Similar arguments apply to government regulation of hospital charges.
- In the Canadian system patients often have waits of weeks, months, or even years for certain diagnostic procedures and surgeries. This is the result of the Canadian government's effort to control expenditures by restricting hospitals' capital spending. To illustrate, there are only one-fifth as many magnetic resonance imaging machines per million people in Canada as in the United States. This results in a waiting list for use of MRIs in Canada. NHI might strongly conflict with U.S. expectations of medical care "on demand."
- Doctors can mount "strikes" against low payments from the government, as they have done is several areas of Canada. Such disruptions in medical care rarely happen in the United States.
- The Federal government has a very poor record of containing costs. Despite its considerable buying power, the Department of Defense, for example, has a long history of cost overruns and mismanagement. And, as you have seen, spending has spiraled upward under the government's Medicare and Medicaid programs. Also recall (Figure 21.3b) that insurance is a critical factor in the overconsumption of health care. Under NHI a completely "free" basic health care package would prompt consumers to "purchase" health care as long as marginal benefits were positive, regardless of the true cost to society.
- Subtle and perhaps undesirable redistribution effects would result under NHI. Under private health insurance, a particular health care insurance package costs the same regardless of the insured's income. This makes the cost of insurance resemble a regressive tax, since low-income workers pay a larger percentage of their incomes for the insurance than do high-income insurees. If NHI were financed out of personal income tax revenues, this financing would be progressive. Under NHI those with low incomes would receive health insurance and pay little or none of the cost. While some might view this as desirable, others believe that income redistribution in the United States has been overdone and that further redistribution through NHI would be unfair. Depending on the type of tax and its size, employers and workers in industries such as automobile and steel might receive windfalls in the form of higher profits and wages when NHI replaced their health insurance programs. Employers and workers in small retail establishments and fast-food restaurants, where health insurance is typically absent, might not realize such gains.

Cost Containment: Altering Incentives

Can the United States control the growth of health care costs, prices, and spending by reducing incentives to overconsume health care?

Deductibles and Copayments

Insurance companies have reacted to rising health care costs by imposing sizable deductibles and copayments on those they insure. Instead of covering all of an insuree's medical costs, a policy might now specify that the insuree pay the first $250 or $500 of each year's health care costs (the deductible) and 15 or 20 percent of all additional costs (the copayment). The deductible and copayment are intended to alleviate the overuse problem by creating a direct payment and therefore an opportunity cost to the health care consumer. The deductible has the added advantage of reducing the administrative costs of insurance companies in processing many small claims.

Managed Care

Managed-care organizations (or systems) are those in which medical services are controlled or coordinated by insurance companies or health care organizations in order to reduce health care expenditures. In 2005 about 88 percent of all U.S. workers received health care through such "managed care." These organizations are of two main types.

Some insurance companies have set up **preferred provider organizations (PPOs),** which require that hospitals and physicians accept discounted prices for their services as a condition for being included in the insurance plan. The policyholder receives a list of participating hospitals and doctors and is given, say, 80 to 100 percent reimbursement of health care costs when treated by PPO physicians and hospitals. If a patient chooses a doctor or hospital outside the PPO, the insurance company reimburses only 60 to 70 percent. In return for being included as a PPO provider, doctors and hospitals agree to rates set by the insurance company for each service. Because these fees are less than those usually charged, PPOs reduce health insurance premiums and health care expenditures.

Many Americans now receive their medical care from **health maintenance organizations (HMOs),** which provide health care services to a specific group of enrollees in exchange for a set annual fee per enrollee. HMOs employ their own physicians and contract for specialized services with outside providers and hospitals. They then contract with firms or government units to provide medical care for their workers, who thereby become HMO members. Because HMOs have fixed annual revenue, they may lose money if they provide "too much" care. So they have an incentive to hold down costs. They also have an incentive to provide preventive care in order to reduce the far larger expense of corrective care.

Both PPOs and HMOs are managed-care organizations because medical use and spending are "managed" by close monitoring of physicians' and hospitals' behavior; the purpose is to eliminate unnecessary diagnostic tests and remedial treatments. Doctors in managed-care organizations might not order an MRI scan or an ultrasound test or suggest surgery because their work is monitored and because they may have a fixed budget. In contrast, an independent fee-for-service physician may face little or no control and have a financial incentive to order the test or do the surgery. Doctors and hospitals in a managed-care organization often share in an "incentive pool" of funds when they meet their cost-control goals.

The advantages of managed-care plans are that they provide health care at lower prices than traditional insurance and emphasize preventive medicine. The disadvantages are that the patient usually is restricted to physicians employed by or under contract with the managed-care plan. Also, some say that the focus on reducing costs has gone too far, resulting in denial of highly expensive, but effective, treatment. This "too far" criticism was mainly leveled at HMOs, where incentives to reduce costs were the greatest. Perhaps because of a backlash against HMOs, firms have increasingly shifted managed care toward PPOs. In 2005, about 67 percent of workers obtained health care through PPOs, up from 42 percent in 2000. Less than one-fourth of workers now belong to HMOs.

Medicare and DRG

In 1983 the Federal government altered the way it makes payments for hospital services received by Medicare patients. Rather than automatically paying all costs related to a patient's treatment and length of hospital stay, Medicare submitted payments based on a **diagnosis-related-group (DRG) system.** Under DRG a hospital receives a fixed payment for treating each patient; that payment is an amount associated with one of several hundred carefully detailed diagnostic categories that best characterize the patient's condition and needs.

DRG-system payments obviously give hospitals the incentive to restrict the amount of resources used in treating patients. It is no surprise that under DRG the length of hospital stays has fallen sharply and more patients are treated on an outpatient basis. Critics, however, argue that this is evidence of diminished quality of medical care.

Recent Laws and Proposals

Although Congress has rejected major reforms of the health care system, it recently made some noteworthy changes.

Prescription Drug Coverage

Until recently, Medicare paid for doctor visits, hospitalization, and short-term nursing care, but not for prescription drugs. But these medications have become an integral part of modern health care, and their expense has claimed a growing part of the income of older Americans. Moreover, the number of older Americans and their adult children has greatly increased among the voting citizenry. Prompted by these medical, financial, and political realities, in late 2003 the Bush administration and Congress added prescription drug coverage to Medicare.

The Medicare Prescription Drug, Improvement, and Modernization Act of 2003 established **Medicare Part D,** beginning in 2006. Medicare enrollees can shop among private health insurance companies to buy highly subsidized insurance for prescription drugs. Under the standard plan, individual enrollees paid a monthly premium averaging about $35–$37 (in 2008), a $250 annual deductible, 25 percent of annual prescription costs up to $2250, then 100 percent of costs between $2250 and $3600, and 5 percent of costs above $3600. The gap in coverage between $2250 and $3600—the so-called donut hole—is designed to hold down program costs and thus enable the 95 percent coverage for annual prescription expenses above $3600 a year. Such high expenses are "catastrophic" for many retirees, and particularly for those receiving only Social Security income.

The law also bars the Federal government from establishing a formulary—a list of drugs that are covered by the insurance policies—although the private insurers may do so. Additionally, the law prohibits the Federal government from using its monopsony power (price-setting power as a large buyer) to negotiate prices with the pharmaceutical industry. Finally, it provides subsidies to large employers to encourage them to maintain existing prescription drug coverage in their retirees' health insurance plans.

In 2007, about 38 million Medicare beneficiaries had health insurance coverage for prescription drugs, with about 23 million of them covered through Medicare Part D. The remainder were covered through insurance from past employers, private insurance, or other government programs. The projected cost of the prescription drug coverage is $244 billion over its first 10 years. Proponents say prescription drug coverage will ease the burden of personal medical costs for millions of older Americans and greatly improve their health care. Critics point out that the huge added expense of Medicare Part D will exacerbate the gigantic underfunding problem facing Medicare in the coming decades. Other observers predict the new law will drive up already escalating drug prices by increasing the demand for prescription drugs without controlling their costs.

Health Savings Accounts The 2003 Medicare law also established **health savings accounts (HSAs).** These accounts are available to all workers who are covered by health insurance plans with annual deductibles of $1000 or more and do not have other first-dollar insurance coverage. Individuals can make tax-deductible contributions into their HSAs, even if they do not itemize deductions on their tax forms. Employers can also make tax-free contributions to workers' accounts if they choose. Earnings on the funds in HSAs are not taxable and the owners of these accounts can use them to pay for qualified medical expenses. Unused funds in HSAs accumulate and remain available for later out-of-pocket medical expenses. Account holders can place additional money into the accounts in each year between age 55 and the year they become eligible for Medicare.

HSAs are designed to promote personal saving out of which workers can pay routine health care expenses while working and can pay for Medicare copayments and deductibles later, during retirement. HSAs are also designed to reduce escalating medical expenses by interjecting an element of competition into health care delivery. Because individuals are using some of their own HSA money to pay for health care, they presumably will assess their personal marginal costs and marginal benefits in choosing how much and what type of health care to obtain. They will also have a strong incentive to inquire about and compare prices charged by various qualified medical providers. Holders of HSAs never lose their accumulated funds. The can remove money for nonmedical purchases but must pay income taxes and a 10 percent penalty on such withdrawals.

Limits on Malpractice Awards Congress has recently attempted to cap (at, say, $250,000 or $500,000) the "pain and suffering" awards on medical malpractice lawsuits against physicians. Those who support malpractice caps say that patients should receive full compensation for economic losses but not be made wealthy through huge jury awards. They contend that capping the awards will reduce medical malpractice premiums and therefore lower health care costs. Opponents of caps counter that large "pain and suffering" awards deter medical malpractice. If so, such awards improve the overall quality of the health care system. Opponents also point out that malpractice awards are a negligible percentage of total health care costs. Thirty-three states now (2008) have placed caps on the "pain and suffering" portion of malpractice awards.

The economic challenges facing health care will only get stronger. The combination of an aging population and advances in medical technology seem to be on a collision course with the reality of economic scarcity. Individuals and society will face increasingly difficult choices about how much health care to consume and how to pay for it.

In 2006 the State of Massachusetts Passed Legislation That will Require Everyone in the State to Have Health Care Insurance, Just as Many States Require All Car Owners to Have Auto Insurance. Is This Reform a Viable Model for the United States?

Recall from this chapter that one of the suggested options for health care reform in the United States is called "play or pay" because *employers* would have to provide basic health insurance ("play") or pay special payroll taxes to finance health insurance for the uninsured ("pay"). The state of Massachusetts has added a bold twist to "play or pay." This novel plan might be called "play to stay!"

Beginning on July 1, 2007, all *residents* of the state are required to have health insurance, much like owners of autos are required to have car insurance. In 2008, everyone will have to provide proof of health insurance on their state income tax forms. Those without insurance coverage will eventually face penalties ranging up to $1200 a year.

The purpose of the law is to create universal health insurance coverage for all state residents and eliminate free riders who do not have health insurance but use medical facilities for expensive "free" emergency care. That behavior simply transfers health care costs to other residents who must pay higher deductibles and coinsurance, larger insurance premiums (and thus receive less take-home pay), or greater state taxes to cover the costs.

The law is expected to reduce the cost of health insurance to those who are already insured by removing the current hidden surcharge for "uninsured patients." It also is expected to increase the demand for employer-provided health insurance by workers, even if the added benefits mean lower cash wages. If people must "play to stay," it will be important for them to seek out the least-expensive way to obtain health insurance coverage. Traditionally, that has been through group health insurance provided by employers as part of their compensation packages. Moreover, the law charges employers who do not offer health insurance $295 per worker per year to help subsidize those without employer-provided insurance. Employers can eliminate that expense by providing insurance.

But how will the poorest among the estimated 550,000 uninsured residents of Massachusetts obtain insurance? Here the subsidy and income redistribution side of the law comes into play. The state would spend as much as $1 billion annually to subsidize private insurance companies that provide new policies for basic health insurance. Because of the state subsidies, the price of these policies would range from about $250 per month to as little as nothing. Uninsured people who earn less than the Federal poverty line would pay no premiums but would pay small copayments when they obtain medical care. People above the poverty line but earning less than three times that amount would pay highly subsidized premiums based on their income levels.

Is this plan a potential model for the United States? Some observers think that it may be because it combines popular concepts such as personal responsibility and compassion for those in need. It also does not disrupt the current system of private health insurance, personal physicians, and established hospitals.

But critics point out that the health care problem is a problem not only of access but of high and rising costs. The cost-containment features of the plan are indirect and relatively weak. Universal coverage could simply drive up the demand for health care, placing additional upward pressure on the prices of medical services. Another problem for transferring the plan nationally is that the percentage of residents currently uninsured in Massachusetts is considerably lower than that of the nation as a whole. The overall cost of the plan to taxpayers at the Federal level might be prohibitive.

Will the Massachusetts plan create an adverse selection problem for nearby states? That is, will some low-income residents of Massachusetts move across the border to avoid paying for health insurance, no matter how small the premiums? If so, that problem could be overcome by a national plan, since the only escape from the mandate would be to move to another country!

Obviously, many questions about the Massachusetts law are still unanswered. In terms of health care reform, this is an experimental medicine. Economists will be very interested in assessing its costs, benefits, and side effects.

Summary

1. The U.S. health care industry comprises 9 million workers (including about 790,000 practicing physicians) and 5750 hospitals.

2. U.S. health care spending has increased both absolutely and as a percentage of GDP.

3. Rising health care costs and prices have (a) reduced access to the health care system, (b) contributed to slower real wage growth and expanded the employment of part-time and temporary workers, and (c) caused governments to restrict spending on nonhealth programs and to raise taxes.

4. The core of the health care problem is an alleged overallocation of resources to the health care industry.

5. About 45 million Americans, or 15 percent of the population, do not have health insurance. The uninsured are concentrated among the poor, the chronically ill, the unemployed, the young, those employed by small firms, and low-wage workers.

6. Special characteristics of the health care market include (a) the belief that health care is a "right," (b) an imbalance of information between consumers and suppliers, (c) the presence of positive externalities, and (d) the payment of most health care expenses by private or public insurance.

7. While rising incomes, an aging population, and substance abuse have all contributed to an increasing demand for health care, the role of doctors is also significant. Because of asymmetric information, physicians influence the demand for their own services. The fee-for-service payment system, combined with defensive medicine to protect against malpractice suits, also increases demand for health care.

8. The moral hazard problem arising from health insurance takes two forms: (a) People may be less careful of their health and (b) there is an incentive to overconsume health care.

9. The exemption of employer-paid health insurance from the Federal income tax subsidizes health care.

10. Slow productivity growth in the health care industry and, more important, cost-increasing advances in health care technology have restricted the expansion of the supply of medical care and have boosted prices.

11. Reforms designed to increase access to the health care system include (a) "play-or-pay" proposals designed to increase employer-sponsored health insurance, (b) tax credits and vouchers to help low-income families afford health care, and (c) national health insurance.

12. Insurance companies have introduced deductibles and copayments in an attempt to contain health care prices and spending.

13. Managed-care organizations—preferred provider organizations (PPOs) and health maintenance organizations (HMOs)—attempt to control their enrolled members' use of health care in order to contain health care costs.

14. The Medicare Prescription Drug, Improvement, and Modernization Act of 2003 added prescription drug benefits to the Medicare program for the first time. Under Medicare Part D, individuals pay small monthly premiums (about $35–$37 in 2008)) for subsidized private insurance coverage. The supplementary Medicare insurance requires a $250 annual deductible and pays 75 percent of the costs of prescription drugs up to $2250, zero from $2250 to $3600, and 95 percent above $3600.

15. The 2003 Medicare law also established health savings accounts (HSAs), which enable individuals who have high-deductible private insurance to place tax-free dollars into special accounts. Account holders can then withdraw funds to pay for routine medical expenses. Unused funds accumulate tax free and eventually become available to pay for the deductibles and copayments required under supplemental Medicare insurance plans. Funds withdrawn for nonmedical purposes require payment of income tax on the amount withdrawn, plus a 10 percent penalty.

Terms and Concepts

deductibles

copayments

fee for service

defensive medicine

tax subsidy

"play or pay"

national health insurance (NHI)

preferred provider organizations (PPOs)

health maintenance organizations (HMOs)

diagnosis-related-group (DRG) system

Medicare Part D

health savings accounts (HSAs)

Study Questions

1. Why would increased spending as a percentage of GDP on, say, household appliances or education in a particular economy be regarded as economically desirable? Why, then, is there so much concern about rising expenditures as a percentage of GDP on health care? **LO1**

2. **KEY QUESTION** What are the "twin problems" of the health care industry as viewed by society? How are they related? **LO1**

3. Briefly describe the main features of Medicare and Medicaid, indicating how each is financed. **LO1**

4. What are the implications of rapidly rising health care prices and spending for (*a*) the growth of real-wage rates, (*b*) government budgets, and (*c*) offshoring of U.S. jobs? Explain. **LO2**

5. Who are the main groups without health insurance?

6. List the special characteristics of the U.S. health care market and specify how each affects health care problems. **LO3**

7. **KEY QUESTION** What are the estimated income and price elasticities of demand for health care? How does each relate to rising health care costs? **LO4**

8. Briefly discuss the demand and supply factors that contribute to rising health costs. Specify how (*a*) asymmetric information, (*b*) fee-for-service payments, (*c*) defensive medicine, and (*d*) medical ethics might cause health care costs to rise. **LO4**

9. How do advances in medical technology and health insurance interact to drive up the costs of medical care? **LO4**

10. **KEY QUESTION** Using the concepts in Chapter 7's discussion of consumer behavior, explain how health care insurance results in an overallocation of resources to the health care industry. Use a demand and supply diagram to specify the resulting efficiency loss. **LO4**

11. How is the moral hazard problem relevant to the health care market? **LO4**

12. What is the rationale for exempting a firm's contribution to its workers' health insurance from taxation as worker income? What is the impact of this exemption on allocative efficiency in the health care industry? **LO4**

13. Comment on or explain: **LO5**
    a. Providing health insurance to achieve equity goals creates a trade-off with the efficient allocation of resources to the health care industry.
    b. If the government were to require employer-sponsored health insurance for all workers, the likely result would be an increase in the unemployment of low-wage workers.

14. Briefly describe (*a*) "play or pay," (*b*) tax credits and vouchers, and (*c*) national health insurance as means of increasing access to health care. What are the major criticisms of national health insurance? **LO5**

15. What are (*a*) preferred provider organizations and (*b*) health maintenance organizations? In your answer, explain how each is designed to alleviate the overconsumption of health care. **LO5**

16. What major factors led to the inclusion of prescription drug coverage under Medicare? Is the insurance purchased directly from the Federal government or from private insurers? What is the annual deductible under the coverage? In percentage terms, what is the copayment for prescription drug expenses below $2250 annually? What percentage of expenses is covered above $3600 annually? Why might the new coverage boost the price of prescription drugs? **LO6**

17. What are health savings accounts (HSAs)? How might they reduce the overconsumption of health care resulting from traditional insurance? How might they introduce an element of price competition into the health care system? **LO6**

18. **LAST WORD** Compare and contrast the general policy approach of the Massachusetts health care reform of 2006 and the Federal law that created health savings accounts. Are the two laws compatible with one another? Which of the two approaches do you think has the better chance of reducing the percentage of people without medical insurance? Which of the two approaches do you think has the better chance of reducing health care costs?

Web-Based Questions

1. **HEALTH EXPENDITURES PER CAPITA—GOING UP OR DOWN?** Go to the Web site of the Centers for Medicare and Medicaid, **www.cms.hhs.gov,** and use the search box to find information on *health expenditures per capita* for the United States. What was the level of such expenditures in 1990? In 2000? For the most recent year shown? Is the level of expenditures per capita projected to rise or to fall over the next 5 years? Find information on *health expenditures as a percentage of GDP.* Contrast the percentage for the latest year shown with the percentage projected for the most distant future year shown. Is the health care problem going away?

2. **THE UNINSURED—WHO ARE THEY?** Visit the U.S. Census Bureau Web site, **www.census.gov,** and select Health Insurance. Find information on people without health insurance coverage by selected characteristics. For the latest year shown, which region of the country had the largest number of uninsured people? What percentage of the total uninsured were Asian, black, Hispanic, and white? What percentage were under 35 years of age? What percentage worked full time?

FURTHER TEST YOUR KNOWLEDGE AT
www.mcconnell18e.com

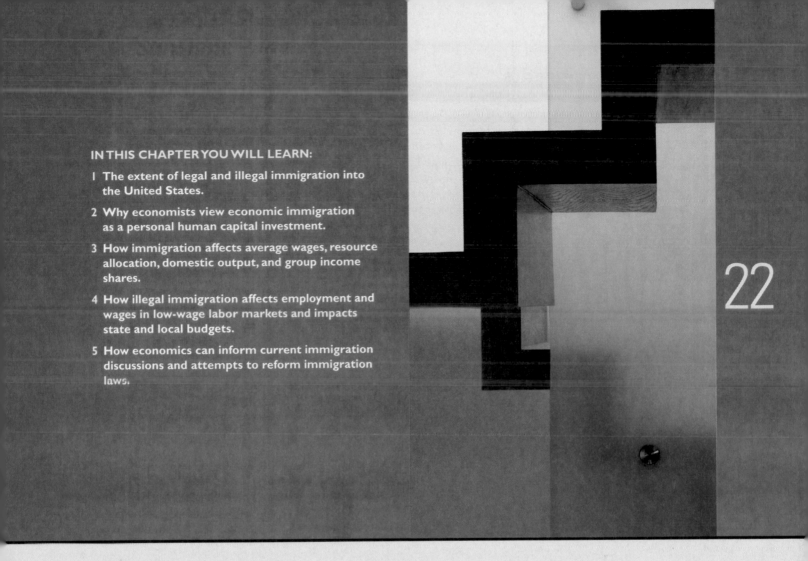

22

Immigration

The United States is a nation largely of immigrants and their descendents, yet immigration has long been a matter of heated controversy. Some immigration issues are political, social, and legal; others are economic. Our focus will be on economic issues and **economic immigrants**—international migrants motivated by economic gain. How many such immigrants come to the United States each year? What is their motivation and what economic impact do they make? Should more or fewer people be allowed to enter legally? What criteria, if any, should be used in allowing legal entry? How should the United States handle extensive illegal immigration?[1]

---

[1]Some of our discussion is drawn from our more advanced treatment of mobility and migration in our textbook on labor economics: Campbell R. McConnell, Stanley L. Brue, and David A. Macpherson, *Contemporary Labor Economics*, 8th ed. (New York: McGraw-Hill, 2008), pp. 275–304.

Number of Immigrants

U.S immigration consists of **legal immigrants**—immigrants who have permission to reside and work in the United States—and **illegal immigrants**—immigrants who arrive illegally or who enter legally on temporary visas but then fail to leave as stipulated. Legal immigrants include *permanent legal residents* ("green card" recipients) who have the right to stay in the country indefinitely and *temporary legal immigrants*, who have visas that allow them to stay until a specific date. Illegal immigrants are alternatively called unauthorized immigrants, illegal aliens, or, if working, undocumented workers.

Legal Immigrants

Figure 22.1 shows the annual levels of legal immigration into the United States since 1980. The spike in legal immigration from 1989 to 1991 resulted from an amnesty program through which many formerly illegal immigrants became legal residents. Between 2000 and 2007, legal immigration averaged 1 million a year. This number is higher than for earlier decades because beginning in 1990 the Federal government increased the annual immigration quota from 500,000 to 700,000. (We provide a historical overview of U.S. immigration policy in this chapter's Last Word.)

Augmenting quota immigrants in some years are thousands of legal immigrants who are refugees (people who flee their country for safety) or are entrants to the United States under special provisions of the immigration law. As an example of the latter, the current **H1-B provision** of the immigration law allows 65,000 high-skilled workers in "specialty occupations" to enter and work continuously in the United States for six years. Such high-skilled occupations include high-tech workers, scientists, and professors.

A total of 1,052,415 people became permanent legal residents of the United States in 2007. About 55 percent of them were women and 45 percent were men. Around 58 percent of all legal immigrants were married.

As shown in Figure 22.2, about 66 percent of the 1,052,415 legal immigrants in 2007 were family-sponsored. They were parents, children, siblings, or other qualified relatives of legal permanent U.S. residents. Another 15 percent were admitted based on employment-based preferences. Most of these immigrants were sponsored by employers. Refugees, "diversity immigrants," and others accounted for the remaining 19 percent. The 50,000 quota for diversity immigrants is filled with qualified immigrants who are from countries with low rates of immigration to the United States. Because applications by diversity immigrants exceed the 50,000 quota, the slots are filled through an annual lottery.

Although the percentage varies somewhat each year, current U.S. immigration law is heavily weighted toward family reunification. This weighting is much heavier than that in Canada, which gives considerably stronger preference to immigrants with high levels of education and work skill. Of course, immigration by family ties and immigration by employment preferences are not necessarily mutually exclusive since a portion of the immigrants admitted through family ties are highly educated and skilled.

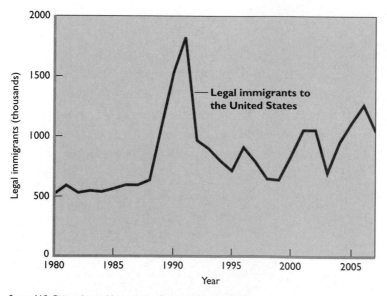

FIGURE 22.1 Legal immigration to the United States, 1980-2007. Legal immigration grew slowly between 1980 and 1988 and then spiked from 1989 to 1991 when previous illegal immigrants gained legal status as permanent residents under terms of an amnesty program. Since that spike, legal immigration has remained relatively high, partly because the immigration cap was raised from 500,000 to 700,000. Within the totals are thousands of refugees, grantees of political asylum, and entrants under special provisions of the immigration law.

Source: U.S. Citizenship and Immigration Services, **www.uscis.gov.**

FIGURE 22.2 Legal immigration by major category of admission, 2007. The large bulk of legal U.S. immigrants obtain their legal status via family ties to American residents.

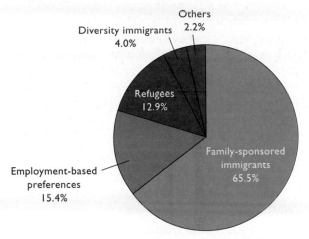

Source: Office of Immigration Statistics, Homeland Security, **www.dhs.gov.**

Table 22.1 shows the 10 leading countries of origin of U.S. legal permanent immigrants in 2007. Mexico topped the list with 148,640 immigrants, accounting for 15 percent of the total. China, the Philippines, and India were also heavy contributors to U.S. immigration in 2007. In recent years immigration has composed about one-third of the total growth of the U.S. population and one-half the growth of the U.S. labor force.

Illegal Immigrants

Our figures and tables do not include illegal immigrants. The U.S. Census Bureau estimates the number of illegal immigrants living in the United States through a residual approach. It finds the current total number of *all* immigrants

TABLE 22.1 U.S. Legal Immigrants by Top 10 Countries of Origin, 2007

Total	1,052,415
1. Mexico	148,640
2. China	76,655
3. Philippines	72,596
4. India	65,353
5. Colombia	33,187
6. Haiti	30,405
7. Cuba	29,104
8. Vietnam	28,691
9. Dominican Republic	28,024
10. El Salvador	21,127

through Census surveys and then subtracts the sum of the past annual inflows of *legal* immigrants. The residuals are large. In fact, the net annual inflow of illegal immigrants has averaged 350,000 per year over the last several years, with a high proportion of the inflow arriving from Mexico, the Caribbean, and Central America.

Some of these illegal immigrants move back and forth across the U.S.-Mexican border, but in 2007 as many as 12 million illegal immigrants were residing continuously in the United States. Increasingly, illegal immigrants are continuous residents, not temporary workers who follow the agricultural harvest (as was typical several decades ago). An estimated half the 12 million illegal immigrants originally came from Mexico, with many others arriving from nations spanning the globe. Illegal Mexican immigrants who work continuously in the United States work mainly outside of agriculture and, on average, have higher educational levels than Mexicans who do migrate to the United States. Women make up nearly 40 percent of the Mexican immigrants who illegally reside in the United States.

The Decision to Migrate

People immigrate into the United States (emigrate from their home countries) legally or illegally:

- To take advantage of superior economic opportunities.
- To escape political or religious oppression in their home countries.
- To reunite with family members or other loved ones, usually prior immigrants, who are already in the United States.

As previously stated, our interest is in economic immigration. Why do some workers uproot their lives to move from some other country to the United States? Why do other workers stay put?

Earnings Opportunities

The main driver of economic immigration is the opportunity to improve the immigrant's earnings and therefore standard of living. The chief attractor for economic immigrants is the availability of higher-paying jobs in the United States. In particular, immigrants can earn much higher wages in the United States than doing identical or nearly identical jobs in their home countries. Stated in terms of economic theory, immigrants reap larger financial rewards from their respective stocks of human capital when working in the United States rather than in their home countries.

Recall that **human capital** is the stock of knowledge, know-how, and skills that enables a person to be productive, and thus to earn income. Other things equal, greater stocks of human capital (for example, more education or better training) result in greater personal productivity and earnings. But whatever someone's stock of education and skill, the value of that human capital depends critically on the capacity for it to earn income. That is where economic migration comes in. By securing higher earnings, migrants can increase—often quickly and dramatically—the value of their human capital. Economic migrants move from one country to another for the same reason many internal migrants move from one city or state to another within their home country: to increase their pay and therefore achieve a higher standard of living.

Other things equal, larger wage differences between nations strengthen the incentive to migrate and therefore increase the flow of immigrants toward the country providing the greater wage opportunities. Today, major "magnet countries" that attract a lot of immigrants include Australia, Switzerland, the United States, and several Western European nations. Global Perspective 22.1 shows the percentage of labor forces composed of foreign-born workers in selected nations in 2004, the latest year for which data are available. Along with earnings opportunities, significant differences in educational opportunities, health care availability, and public pensions and welfare benefits play a role in international migration decisions.

Moving Costs

Immigration can be viewed as an investment decision. As with other investments, current sacrifices are necessary to achieve future benefits. In moving from one nation to another, workers incur personal costs. Some of these costs are explicit, out-of-pocket costs such as paying application fees (for example, $1010 for a green card) and a number of moving expenses. For illegal immigrants, a major explicit cost may be a payment to an expediter—a "coyote"—who charges as much as $2000 to smuggle someone into the United States and transport him or her to a major city such as Chicago, New York, Houston, or Los Angeles. Other costs of migrating are implicit. They are opportunity costs such as the income given up while the worker is moving and looking for a job in the new country. Still more subtle costs are incurred in leaving family and friends and adapting to a new culture, language, and climate. For illegal immigrants, there is the additional potential cost of being caught, jailed, and deported.

The prospective immigrant estimates and weighs all such costs against the expected benefits of the higher earnings in the new country. A person who estimates that the stream of future earnings exceeds the explicit and implicit

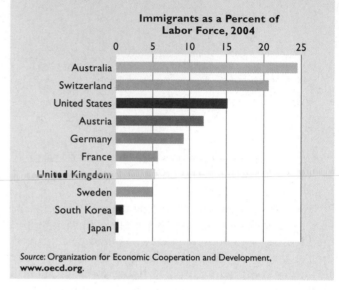

GLOBAL PERSPECTIVE 22.1

Immigrants as a Percent of the Labor Force, Selected Advanced Industrial Countries

Immigrants make up relatively large percentages of the labor forces in several advanced industrial countries, including Australia, Switzerland, and the United States, but not in other countries such as South Korea and Japan.

Immigrants as a Percent of Labor Force, 2004

Australia	
Switzerland	
United States	
Austria	
Germany	
France	
United Kingdom	
Sweden	
South Korea	
Japan	

Source: Organization for Economic Cooperation and Development, **www.oecd.org**.

costs of moving will migrate; a person who sees those costs as exceeding the future stream of earnings will stay put.[2]

Factors Affecting Costs and Benefits

Earnings differences provide the major incentive to migrate, but many nonwage factors also affect the cost-benefit evaluation of movement to another nation. Let's look at two key factors.

Distance Other things equal, greater distance reduces the likelihood of migration. Most obvious, transportation costs rise with distance. In addition, migration to more distant countries is often seen as riskier because information about job market conditions in distant countries is usually less certain than about job market conditions in nearby countries (although the Internet has greatly reduced this

[2]As with other investment decisions, the decision to move internationally requires a comparison of the *present value* of the stream of additional earnings and the *present value* of the costs of moving. Present value considerations (discussed in Chapters 14 and 15) complicate the decision to migrate but do not alter the basic analytical framework.

difference in recent years). Finally, the farther the move, the greater the possible costs of maintaining contact with friends and family. In terms of expense, a short trip back across a border by automobile is one thing; an airline flight to a different continent, quite another.

The majority of international migrants move to countries relatively close to their home countries. Most Mexican migrants move to the United States. The majority of Eastern European migrants move to Western Europe. Close proximity reduces the cost of the move relative to anticipated benefits.

Some migrants, of course, *do* move to far-away lands. They often reduce their costs of these long moves by following **beaten paths**—routes taken previously by family, relatives, and friends. They also tend to cluster, at least for awhile, in cities and neighborhoods populated by former and current immigrants. For example, thousands of Russian immigrants have located in Brooklyn, New York. Numerous Asian immigrants have located in San Francisco.

The earlier immigrants ease the transition for those who follow by providing job information, employment contacts, temporary living quarters, language help, and cultural continuity. That reduces the costs and increases the benefits of migration to those who follow. Eventually, some new immigrants exploit even better economic opportunities by moving from the original place of migration to other cities within the country to which they have migrated. New clusters of immigrants emerge and new migration networks result. For instance, these new clusters and networks help explain the rapid northward expansion of Latino immigrants during the past decade.

Age Younger workers are much more likely to migrate than older workers. Age affects both benefits and costs in the calculation to move or stay put. Particularly relevant, younger migrants have more years to recoup their costs of moving. Spread over decades, the higher wage in the new country builds to a large accumulation of additional earnings relative to the earnings that would have accrued if the person had not moved. In contrast, older people are closer to retirement and therefore may conclude that moving abroad simply is not worth the effort. Their added earnings over their remaining work years simply will not be sufficient to cover the costs of the disruption and move.

Younger migrants also tend to have lower moving costs than older workers. For example, they often have accumulated fewer personal possessions to transport. Younger workers generally have fewer roots and ties to the local community and so may find it easier to adapt to new customs and cultures. This greater flexibility reduces the perceived costs of moving and increases the likelihood that the younger person will move.

Younger workers are also more likely to be single or, if married, less likely to have started families than older workers. The potential costs of migrating multiply rapidly when spouses and families are present. Finding affordable housing large enough for families and enrolling children in new schools complicate the potential move. Also, when both spouses work, the secondary wage earner may face a period of unemployment before finding a new job in the new country.

In 2005 the median age for U.S. immigrants who had resided in the United States for less than a year was 25.

Other Factors Several other factors may affect the cost and benefit calculations of immigrants into the United States. Studies show that immigrants who lack English language skills do not, in general, fare as well in the U.S. workforce as immigrants who have those skills when they arrive. For some highly skilled immigrants, lower tax rates or opportunities to set up businesses in the United States may be the draw. Also, some immigrants to the United States may be willing to endure low or even negative personal returns on immigration simply so that their children have greater economic opportunities than at home. **(Key Question 2)**

QUICK REVIEW 22.1

- An average of 1 million legal immigrants and 350,000 illegal immigrants entered the United States each year between 2000 and 2007.
- In 2007 Mexico was the greatest single contributor (15 percent) to U.S. legal immigration. Hundreds of thousands of additional legal immigrants arrived from China, the Philippines, India, Columbia, and many other nations.
- Economists view economic migration as a personal investment; a worker will move internationally when the expected gain in earnings exceeds the explicit and implicit costs of moving.
- Other things equal, the greater the migration distance and the older the prospective migrant, the less likely the person will move.

Economic Effects of Immigration

Immigration creates personal gains for movers, and also affects wage rates, efficiency, output, and the division of income. Like international trade, migration produces large economic benefits but also creates short-term winners and losers. In particular, we will see that the wage-rate and division-of-income aspects of immigration are two main sources of controversy.

Personal Gains

The fact that economic immigration to the United States is sizeable and continuous affirms that in general the economic benefits of immigration to the immigrants exceed their costs. In economic terms, the inflows of legal and illegal immigration indicate that this investment has a positive return to movers. Studies confirm that the returns to immigrating to the United States are, on average, quite substantial. This should not be a surprise. For example, the real wages earned by recent Mexican male migrants to the United States are as much as six times higher than those earned by similarly educated men in Mexico.

Nevertheless, not all economic immigrants to the United States succeed. Migration decisions are based on expected benefits and are made under circumstances of uncertainty and imperfect information. High average rates of return do not guarantee that all migrants will benefit. In some cases the expected gain from immigration does not materialize—the anticipated job is not found in the new country, the living costs are higher than anticipated, the anticipated raises and promotions are not forthcoming, the costs of being away from family and friends are greater than expected. Major **backflows**—return migration to the home country—therefore occur in most international migration patterns, including those between the United States and other countries.

Although this return migration may be costly to those involved, it increases the availability of information about the United States to other potential migrants. These people are then able to better assess the benefits and costs of their own potential moves.

Also, although economic immigrants on average improve their standard of living, they may or may not achieve pay parity with similarly educated native-born workers. The skills that migrants possess are not always perfectly transferable between employers in different countries because of occupational licensing requirements, specific training, or differing languages. This lack of **skill transferability** may mean that migrants, although improving their own wage, may earn less than similarly employed native-born workers in the United States. Studies find that this is particularly true for immigrants who lack English-language skills.

On the other hand, a great deal of economic migration is characterized by **self-selection.** Because some migrants choose to move while others with similar skills do not, it is possible that those who move possess greater

CONSIDER THIS . . .

Stars and Stripes

Recent immigrants have contributed mightily to the vitality of the American economy. The Council of Economic Advisers reminds us that:

Skilled migrants, whether permanent or temporary, enrich our scientific and academic communities, boost the technical capabilities of U.S. firms (and the native-born workers employed there), augment the supply of health-care providers, and pay more in taxes than they absorb in government services. Many of these workers were educated in American universities and nearly all adjust easily to life in the United States in terms of language skills and employment. They make major innovative contributions in science, medicine, and engineering, and help keep the United States at the forefront of technological capability.[*]

Since 1990, U.S. immigrants have founded 1 of every 4 public companies backed by venture capital. Yahoo!, Intel, eBay, Google, and Sun Microsystems all have one or more immigrant founders. About half the engineers and people with computer science doctorates in the United States are foreign-born. One-fourth of U.S. major league baseball players were born abroad. Children of immigrants often dominate U.S. math and science competitions. And our list could go on.[†]

[*]*Economic Report of the President, 2007*, p. 201.
[†]National Foundation for American Policy, **www.nfap.net.**

motivation for personal economic gain and greater willingness to sacrifice current consumption for higher levels of later consumption. If so, these migrants may overcome the problem of imperfect skill transferability and eventually outdo domestic-born workers in wage and salary advancement. This possibility is particularly true of highly skilled immigrants such as scientists, engineers, physicians, and entrepreneurs.

Impacts on Wage Rates, Efficiency, and Output

Although the personal outcomes of immigration are relatively straightforward and easy to understand, the broader economic outcomes are somewhat complicated and obscure. A simple economic model of migration will help us sort through key cause-effect relationships and identify broader economic outcomes. In Figure 22.3a, D_u is the

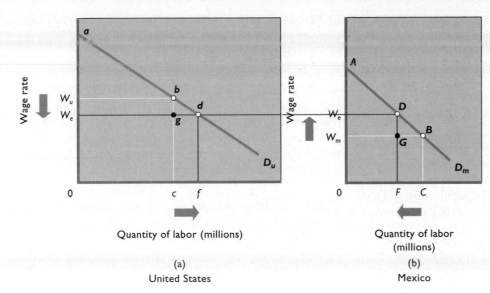

FIGURE 22.3 A simple immigration model. The migration of labor to high-wage United States (a) from low-wage Mexico (b) increases U.S. domestic output, reduces the average level of U.S. wages, and increases U.S. business income while having the opposite effects in Mexico. The U.S. gain in domestic output of *cbdf* exceeds Mexico's loss of domestic output of *FDBC*; thus the migration increases economic efficiency and produces a net gain in world output.

demand for labor in the United States; in Figure 22.3b, D_m is the demand for labor in Mexico. The demand for labor presumably is greater in the United States because it has more capital, advanced technology, and better infrastructure that enhance the productivity of labor. (Recall from Chapter 12 that the strength of labor demand is based on the marginal revenue productivity of labor.) Conversely, labor demand in Mexico is weaker since machinery and equipment are less abundant relative to labor, technology is less advanced, and infrastructure is less developed. We also assume that the before-migration labor forces of the United States and Mexico are c and C, respectively; that neither country is experiencing substantial long-term unemployment; and that labor quality in the two countries is the same.

If we further suppose that migration (1) has no cost, (2) occurs solely in response to wage differentials, and (3) is unimpeded by law in either country, then workers will migrate from Mexico to the United States until wage rates in the two countries are equal at W_e. At that level, CF (equals cf) workers will have migrated from Mexico to the United States. Although the U.S. wage level will fall from W_u to W_e, domestic output (the sum of the marginal revenue products of the entire workforce) will increase from $0abc$ to $0adf$. This domestic output is the total output produced within the borders of the United States and equals the domestic income earned within the U.S. borders.

In Mexico, the wage rate will rise from W_m to W_e, but domestic output will decline from $0ABC$ to $0ADF$. Observe that the gain in domestic output *cbdf* in the United States exceeds the loss of domestic output *FDBC* in Mexico. The

migration from Mexico to the United States has clearly increased the world's output and income.

The elimination of barriers to the international flow of labor tends to create worldwide **efficiency gains from migration.** The same number of workers—rearranged among countries—produces greater total output and income after migration than before migration. The world gains output (and income) because the freedom to migrate enables people to move to countries where they can contribute more to world production. Economic migration not only provides a positive investment return to the mover, it produces an overall efficiency gain. Migration enables the world to produce a larger output with its currently available resources. So labor mobility joins capital mobility and international trade in enhancing the world's standard of living.

Income Shares

With personal gains and overall productivity gains, why would anyone oppose immigration? Our graphical model helps answer that question. There are specific groups of gainers and losers from immigration in both nations.

In Figure 22.3, as workers move from Mexico to the United States in search of higher wages, U.S. output will increase while Mexican output will decrease. These gains partly explain why the United States encourages a relatively high level of immigration through high annual quotas. It also explains why some countries try to discourage outflows of labor from their countries. In particular, countries are rightfully concerned about the emigration of highly educated workers, particularly when those citizens received subsidized education at home. Such undesirable outflows are commonly called **brain drains.**

Figure 22.3 reveals a second consequence of immigration on income shares. The decline in the wage rate from W_u to W_e in the United States reduces the wage income of native-born U.S. workers from $0W_ubc$ to $0W_egc$. The opposite outcome occurs in Mexico, where the average wage for the native-born workers who do not migrate rises.

Although we can specify income gains and losses to domestic-born workers, we cannot say what will happen to the total wage income (= domestic-born wage income + immigrant wage income) in each country. That depends on the elasticities of labor demand. For example, if labor demand is elastic, the wage decrease in the United States will increase total wage income. In contrast, if labor demand is inelastic, the same wage decrease will cause total wage income to fall.

The immigration-caused decline in wage income for native-born U.S. workers is a major reason that many U.S. labor unions oppose increasing immigration quotas in the United States. Unions tend to resist policies that reduce the wages of their current membership or undercut their bargaining power by creating larger pools of potential workers for nonunion firms. In direct contrast, the increase in wages in the outflow country is a possible reason why labor groups in Mexico show little concern about the large-scale outflow of Mexican labor to the United States.

Finally, Figure 22.3 shows that the immigration enhances business income in the United States while reducing it in Mexico. The before-immigration domestic output and income in the United States is represented by area $0abc$. Total wage income is $0W_ubc$—the wage rate multiplied by the number of workers. The remaining triangular area W_uab shows business income before immigration. The same reasoning applies to Mexico, where the triangle W_mAB represents before-immigration business income.

Unimpeded immigration increases business income from W_uab to W_ead in the United States and reduces it from W_mAB to W_eAD in Mexico. Other things equal, owners of U.S. businesses benefit from immigration; owners of Mexican businesses are hurt by emigration. These outcomes are what we would expect intuitively; the United States is gaining "cheap" labor and Mexico is losing "cheap" labor. This conclusion is consistent with the historical fact that U.S. employers have often actively recruited immigrants and have generally supported

INTERACTIVE GRAPHS

G 22.1

Immigration

higher immigration quotas, liberal guest-worker programs, and expanded specialized work visas such as H1-Bs. **(Key Question 4)**

Complications and Modifications

Our model is a purposeful simplification of the much more complex actual reality. Not surprising, the model includes simplifying assumptions and overlooks some relevant factors. Relaxing some of the assumptions and introducing the omitted factors may affect our conclusions.

Costs of Migration Our model assumed that the movement of workers from Mexico to the United States is without personal cost, but we know that migrants incur explicit, out-of-pocket costs of physically moving and the implicit opportunity costs of forgone income during the move and transition.

In Figure 22.3, the presence of migration costs means that the flow of labor from Mexico to the United States will stop short of that required to close the wage differential entirely. Wage rates will remain somewhat higher in the United States than in Mexico, and that wage-rate difference will not encourage further migration to close up the wage gap. At some point, the remaining earnings gap between the two countries will not be sufficient to cover the marginal cost of migration. Migration will end, and the total output and income gain from migration will be less because wages have not equalized.

Remittances and Backflows Although most of the workers who acquire skills in the country of immigration do not return home, some migrants see their moves as temporary. They move to a more highly developed country; accumulate some wealth, training, or education through hard work and frugality; and return home to establish their own enterprises. During their time in the new country, these and other migrants frequently make sizable **remittances** to their families at home. These money transfers to the home country redistribute the net gain from migration between the countries involved.

In Figure 22.3, remittances by Mexican workers in the United States to their relatives in Mexico would cause the gain in U.S. income retained in the United States to be less than the domestic output and income gain shown. Similarly, the loss of income available in Mexico would be less than the domestic output and income loss shown. The World Bank estimates that $25 billion of remittances—an amount equal to 3 percent of Mexico's GDP—flowed to Mexico from other countries in 2007. Most of these remittances originate in the United States and are a major reason

GLOBAL PERSPECTIVE 22.2

Emigrant Remittances, Selected Developing Countries, 2007

Although both developing nations and advanced industrial nations receive remittances from their emigrants, most remittances flow toward developing nations. For some of these nations, the amount of remittances each year exceeds their direct foreign investment (economic investment by foreign individuals and firms).

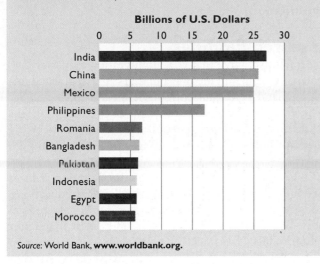

Billions of U.S. Dollars

Source: World Bank, **www.worldbank.org.**

Mexico favors liberal U.S. immigration laws and generally opposes U.S. policies to stem the flow of illegal immigrants across the U.S. border. (Global Perspective 22.2 shows selected developing countries receiving remittances by emigrants in 2007. For many developing countries, remittances exceed foreign direct investment—purchases of foreigners of lasting ownership interests in domestic firms—as a source of foreign currencies available to buy imported goods and services.)

Along with remittances, backflows of migrants to their home countries might also alter gains and losses through time. For example, if some Mexican workers who migrated to the United States acquired substantial labor market or managerial skills and then returned home, their enhanced human capital might contribute substantially to economic development in Mexico. Further, some of the more successful U.S. immigrants eventually may use their expertise and wealth to help build new businesses in Mexico. Both will eventually increase labor demand in Mexico and raise wage rates there.

Complementary versus Substitute Resources

Although the average wage rate of domestic-born workers may decline because of immigration, not all such workers will see their wages fall. Many immigrant workers and domestic-born workers are **complementary resources** rather than **substitute resources** (Chapter 12). When that is the case, the lower wage rate resulting from large-scale immigration reduces production costs, creating an output effect that raises labor demand for certain domestic-born workers. For example, the large number of immigrants working in the home building industry lowers construction wages and reduces the cost of home building. That in turn increases the number of houses built and sold, which increases the demand for domestic-born residents who help manufacture sheet rock, plumbing products, air conditioners, major appliances, and other home products.

Expansion of Capital

Long-run effects on capital are another reason native-born citizens may not be permanently harmed to the extent suggested by the simple immigration model. The stock of capital was implicitly constant in both countries in Figure 22.3, fixing the demand curves in place. But the rise in business income in the United States relative to the stock of capital produces a higher rate of return on capital. The higher rate of return stimulates overall investment, which in the long run adds to the size of the nation's stock of capital. Normally, the addition of new capital such as plant and equipment raises labor productivity, lowers production costs, and reduces product prices. As a result, wages and salaries rise because of increased demand for labor.

On the other hand, the inflow of illegal workers into certain low-wage occupations such as field harvesting may stifle R&D, technological advance, and investment in some industries. The easy availability of inexpensive legal or illegal immigrant labor provides little incentive to mechanize or otherwise economize on the use of labor. In this regard, economists note that the temporary slowing of the flow of illegal agricultural workers after the terrorist attacks of September 11, 2001, increased the purchase of mechanical harvesting equipment such as tree-trunk shakers used to harvest oranges.

Full Employment versus Unemployment

Our model conveniently assumes full employment in both countries. Mexican workers presumably leave low-paying jobs to take higher-paying jobs in the United States (more or less immediately). However, in many circumstances, the factor that pushes immigrants from their homelands is not simply low wages but chronic unemployment or underemployment. Many developing countries have large populations and surplus labor. A sizeable number of workers are either unemployed or so grossly underemployed that their contribution to domestic output is zero or near zero.

If we allow for this possibility, then Mexico would gain rather than lose by having such workers emigrate. Unemployed Mexicans are making no or little contribution to Mexico's domestic output and must be sustained by transfers from the rest of the labor force. The remaining Mexican labor force will be better off by the amount of the transfers after the unemployed workers have migrated to the United States.

The unemployed workers moving to the United States may reflect **negative self-selection**, in which movers are less capable and perhaps less motivated than similarly educated people who have jobs and stay in the origin nation. This possibility could conceivably join higher domestic wages and large remittances as an explanation of why Mexico generally opposes stronger border enforcement by the United States.

Conversely, if the Mexican immigrant workers are unable to find jobs in the United States and are sustained through transfers from employed U.S. workers, then the after-tax income of working Americans will decline. This fear is one reason many Americans oppose immigration of low-education, low-skilled workers to the United States.

Fiscal Impacts

What effects do immigrants have on tax revenues and government spending in the United States? Do they contribute to U.S. GDP, as our model suggests, or do they go on welfare and use "free" public goods, draining the government treasury?

Before the 1970s, the immigrant population was less likely to receive public assistance than people born in the United States. Migrants were typically young, single men with significant education and job training. They were readily employable in average-paying jobs and therefore were net contributors to the tax-expenditure system.

But the situation reversed between the 1970s and 1998, when immigrants began to use the welfare system proportionately more than natives. The changing mix of immigrants from relatively skilled workers toward unskilled workers explained the turnabout. Critics claimed that U.S. welfare programs were drawing unskilled (and often illegal) workers to the United States from some of the world's poorest nations. Immigrants made up more than 10 percent of Supplemental Security Income (SSI) rolls in 1998 compared to only 3.3 percent a decade before.

As a result of this trend, a major overhaul of the U.S. welfare system in 1996 denied welfare benefits to new legal immigrants for their first five years in the United States. Since 1996 cash welfare payments to immigrants have declined by 73 percent, food stamps by 39 percent, and SSI payments by 20 percent.

Nevertheless, low-income immigrants impose costs on state and local governments by enrolling children in public schools, using emergency health care facilities, and straining the criminal justice system. For low-income immigrants, these fiscal burdens substantially exceed taxes paid. We will say more about this later. (**Key Question 5**)

Research Findings

All economists agree that U.S. immigration increases U.S. domestic output and income and that highly educated immigrants and successful entrepreneurs add to the vitality of American enterprise. But in light of the complications just discussed, no single generalization is possible as to the impact of immigration on the wages of native-born U.S. workers.

The best evidence indicates that immigration reduces the wages of native-born workers who have low educations, and also may reduce the salaries of some highly trained native-born workers. For example, studies show that immigration reduces the wages of native-born Americans who do not have high school diplomas, native-born African-American men, and native-born holders of doctorate degrees.

The overall effect of immigration on the average American wage is much less clear. Scholarly estimates on that effect range from minus 3 percent to plus 2 percent.[3]

QUICK REVIEW 22.2

- Other things equal, immigration reduces the average wage rate, increases domestic output, lowers the total wage income of native-born workers, and bolsters business income in the destination nation; it has the opposite effects in the origin nation.

- Assessing the impacts of immigration is complicated by such factors as remittances and backflows, complementary versus substitute labor, investment impacts, unemployment, and fiscal effects.

---

[3]The research conclusions summarized in this section are based on very recent studies conducted individually or jointly by several prominent economists, including George Borjas, David Card, Richard Freeman, Jeffrey Grogger, Gordon Hanson, Lawrence Katz, Gianmarco Ottaviano, and Giovanni Peri.

The Illegal Immigration Debate

Much of the recent concern about immigration has focused on illegal immigration, not immigration per se. Economists point out that the strong inflow of undocumented workers to some extent reflects the increasing scarcity of domestic unskilled labor in the United States. Only about 12 percent of the native-born U.S. workforce has less than a high-school diploma today compared to about 50 percent in 1960. That scarcity has created significant employment opportunities for unskilled illegal immigrants. Illegal workers make up roughly 24 percent of all agricultural workers, 17 percent of all cleaning workers, 14 percent of construction workers, and 12 percent of food preparers.

Many Americans fear that illegal immigrants and their families depress wage rates in these and other already low-wage U.S. occupations and also burden American citizens through their use of public services such as emergency medical care and public schools. Are these concerns justified?

Employment Effects

Two extreme views on illegal immigration are often expressed. Some observers suggest that the employment of illegal workers decreases the employment of legal workers on a one-for-one basis. They erroneously suggest that the economy has only a fixed number of jobs at any time. Supposedly, every job taken by an illegal worker deprives a legal resident of that job. At the other extreme is the claim that illegal workers accept only work that legal residents will not perform. Viewed this way, illegal workers displace *no* legal residents from their jobs.

Both views are misleading. Consider Figure 22.4, which illustrates a market for unskilled field workers in agriculture. The downsloping curve D is a typical labor demand curve, here for field workers. The upsloping supply curve S_d is the labor supply of domestic-born workers, while curve S_t reflects the combined total supply of domestic-born workers and illegal immigrants. The horizontal distances between S_t and S_d at the various wage rates measure the number of illegal immigrants offering their labor services.

With illegal workers present, as implied by curve S_t, the equilibrium wage and level of employment in this labor market are W_t and Q_t. At the low wage of W_t, only *ab* domestic-born workers are willing to work as field hands; the other workers—*bd*—are illegal immigrants. The low employment of domestic-born workers presumably is caused by their better wage opportunities and working conditions in alternative occupations or by the availability of government transfer payments. Recall that illegal workers are not eligible for most welfare benefits.

FIGURE 22.4 The impacts of illegal workers in a low-wage labor market. Illegal workers in a low-wage labor market shift the labor supply curve, as from S_d to S_t, and reduce the market wage from W_d to W_t. At wage W_t, *ab* workers are domestic-born (or legal residents) and *bc* workers are illegal immigrants. If all the illegal workers were deported, however, Q_d American workers would be employed. To say that illegal workers do jobs that Americans are not willing to do (at any wage rate), therefore, is somewhat misleading. Similarly misleading is the conclusion that the deportation of illegal workers would boost the employment of American workers on a one-for-one basis.

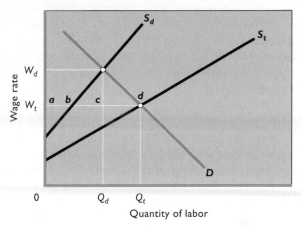

Can we therefore conclude from Figure 22.4 that illegal workers have filled field jobs that most U.S.-born workers do not want? The answer is "yes," but only with the proviso: "at wage rate W_t." With fewer illegal immigrants in this labor market, labor supply would be less than that shown by curve S_t. The wage rate would be higher than W_t, and more legal residents would offer their services as field hands. For example, if the United States cut off the full inflow of illegal workers to this market, the relevant supply curve would be S_d and the wage rate would rise to W_d. Then Q_d domestic-born workers as opposed to *ab* workers would work as field hands. The critical point is that the willingness of Americans to work at any particular job depends significantly on the wage rate being paid. A sufficiently high **compensating wage differential** (wage premium to compensate for undesirable work) will attract U.S. workers even to otherwise undesirable work.

The opposite argument, that illegal workers reduce the employment of Americans by an amount equal to the employment of illegal workers, is also misleading. Figure 22.4 reveals that the illegal workers increase the total number of jobs in the labor market. With illegal workers, the number of jobs is Q_t. Without those workers, it is only Q_d. The deportation of the illegal workers would not increase domestic employment on a one-for-one basis. Native-born employment would increase by the amount *bc* in this specific labor market, not by *bd*.

Generally, illegal immigration causes some substitution of illegal workers for domestic workers, but the amount of displacement is less than the total employment of the illegal workers. Illegal immigration—as with legal immigration—increases total employment in the United States.

Wage Effects

Large flows of illegal workers into specific low-wage labor markets reduce wage rates in those markets. Note in Figure 22.4 that the greater supply of field workers reduces their wage rate from W_d to W_t. Some U.S. wages—including those of field labors, food preparers, and house cleaners—are lower than otherwise because of illegal immigration.

As discussed previously, the overall effect of illegal immigration on the average wage rate in the economy is either a smaller decline or even positive. As with legal immigrants, some illegal workers are complementary inputs to domestic-born workers, not substitutes. An example of this complementarity would be illegal fruit pickers and the domestic-born truck drivers who deliver the fruit to grocery stores. The lower price of the fruit increases the amount of fruit demanded and thus the amount of it that needs to be delivered. That increases the labor demand for the complementary truck drivers, whose wage rates rise.

Only where illegal workers and legal workers are substitute resources will the increase in labor supply reduce the wages of other workers. Ironically, studies show that the largest negative impact of illegal immigrants is on the wages of previous immigrants, not on native-born workers.

Illegal immigration has very little effect on the average level of wages in the United States. That average wage level depends mainly on the nation's overall level of labor productivity, which illegal immigration does not appreciably affect. **(Key Question 9)**

Price Effects

Because illegal immigrants work at lower pay than would be necessary to attract native-born workers, the prices of goods and services that illegal workers produce are lower than they would be otherwise. The extent of such price reduction depends on several factors, including how much of the total cost of producing and delivering a product involves the services performed by illegal immigrants. In industries where illegal immigrants are heavily used—for example, construction, agriculture, landscaping, home cleaning, restaurant meals, and lodging—the presence of illegal workers may have a discernable downward price effect. Lower prices raise the standard of living of all Americans and their families.

Fiscal Impacts on Local and State Governments

One major and very legitimate concern about illegal immigration is the negative fiscal impact it has on local and state governments. Cities and states with high concentrations of illegal immigrants bear the main burden. The Federal government receives the payroll taxes and income taxes withheld from the earnings of some illegal immigrants, but the state and local governments bear most of the costs of their presence. Immigrants place their children in local schools, use local emergency medical care, and add to the cost of the criminal justice system, most of which is provided by state and local governments. Immigrants do, however, pay state sales taxes and taxes on gasoline, and indirectly pay property taxes built into rent.

The average fiscal burden (government benefits minus taxes paid) on state and local government for each low-skilled immigrant household may be as high as $9000 per person a year. In 2006 about 40 percent of the 4.5 million households falling into this low-skilled category were headed by illegal immigrants. One recent estimate of the fiscal burden for these households as a group is nearly $50 billion annually.

Other Concerns

Critics of illegal immigration point to other reasons to be concerned about illegal immigration. First, they say that allowing immigrants to enter the United States unlawfully undermines general respect for the law. If immigration laws can be broken, why can't other laws also be broken? The success of many immigrants in entering the United States and working for employers illegally rests on other criminal activity such as the creation of fake birth certificates, social security cards, and drivers' licenses. Also, some unauthorized immigrants engage in illegal activities such as drug smuggling, identity theft, and insurance fraud. Although U.S. immigrants (legal and illegal) have considerably lower prison rates than the native-born U.S. population, the crime rate for illegal immigrants is much higher than that of the native-born U.S. population.

Second, critics of ineffective border and employment law enforcement point out that illegal immigration is highly unfair to the thousands of people enduring the expense and long waits associated with the process for legally gaining the right to live and work in the United States.

Finally, some observers see national defense as the greatest long-term risk from porous borders. The flow of illegal entrants into the United States is clearly at

Immigration Reform: The Beaten Path to the Current Stalemate

In 2007 a Consensus Emerged That Comprehensive Immigration Reform was Needed to Stem the Tide of Illegal Immigration, Deal with the Reality of the 12 Million People Illegally in the United States, and Maintain the Desirable Flow of Temporary (Mainly Agricultural) Workers into the United States. What Happened?

At the heart of U.S. immigration law are immigration quotas. The Immigration Acts of 1921 and 1924 set annual quotas based on the number of foreign-born persons of various nationalities that had been living in the United States in specific census years. The law also allowed several categories of nonquota immigrants to enter the United States. Congress modified the law in 1952, but the basic quota system remained in place. Between 1921 and 1965, only 10 million people entered the United States. Half were nonquota immigrants and included 900,000 Canadians, 500,000 Mexicans, and thousands of spouses and children of U.S. citizens.

In 1965, Congress shifted the quota preferences away from northern and western European immigrants and toward a wider set of nationalities. Further amendments established a worldwide annual ceiling of 270,000 immigrants, set an annual limit of 20,000 immigrants from each nation, and developed a six-point preference system for giving priority to people who had specific job skills. Immediate relatives of U.S. citizens, refugees, and people seeking political asylum were exempt from these provisions and ceilings. Approximately 500,000 to 600,000 immigrants entered the United States legally each year between 1965 and 1986.

But illegal immigrants—mainly from Mexico—poured across the U.S.-Mexican border during this 21-year period. To deal with the large numbers of illegal immigrants residing continuously in the United States, the Immigration Reform and Control Act of 1986 created an amnesty program for those who had lived here since 1982. The act also tried to dampen the demand for illegal workers by prohibiting employers from knowingly hiring undocumented workers. That provision proved largely ineffective, however, because illegal workers simply obtained fraudulent documents.

Between 1965 and 1990, Congress increased the annual legal immigration limit from 270,000 to 500,000, not counting refugees. In late 1990 it further boosted the limit to 700,000. These increases in the legal limits did little to stop the flow of illegal immigrants, and the prior amnesty program most likely accelerated it.

In 2006, an estimated 12 million illegal residents were in the United States. In 2007 the Bush administration and several prominent congressional leaders from both parties tried to deal with the situation by proposing comprehensive reform of the U.S. immigration law. The main ingredients of the proposed reform were to:

- Boost funding for fencing, monitoring, and policing the U.S.-Mexican border.
- Increase fines on employers who hire illegal immigrants.
- Rebalance the current system of filling the immigration quota away from applicants with family ties and toward applicants with advanced education, high work skills, and greater English proficiency.
- Allow most of the 12 million illegal immigrants to apply for "Z visas" that would have allowed them to live and work in the United States legally.
- Create a guest-worker program allowing 200,000 foreign workers a year to obtain short-stay work visas.

After considerable debate and vociferous public response, the Senate rejected the proposed legislation. In particular, the new "amnesty" program for the 12 million illegal immigrants drew intense political fire. So did the tilt away from family reunification and toward immigration based on skills and education. Also, agricultural and other business interests expressed great concern about the relatively low annual limit (200,000) on guest workers.

After the defeat, an economic expert on illegal immigration stated, "Meanwhile, in Atlanta, Houston, Las Vegas, and many other cities, illegal immigrants woke up, said goodbye to their kids, and went off to work. The outcome could have been much worse."[*]

Other economists disagreed with that assessment, seeing a lost opportunity to achieve comprehensive immigration reform. Meanwhile, an effort to fence the U.S.-Mexican border is in progress and some states have passed stringent laws against hiring illegal workers. The political debate continues.

[*] Gordon H. Hanson, *The Wall Street Journal*, July 5, 2007, p. A15.

odds with the goal of homeland security. Ineffective border enforcement against illegal immigrants allows career criminals and even terrorists to enter the United States undetected.

Optimal Immigration

The immigration issues relating to quotas and illegal immigrants go well beyond simply economics. They are also political and cultural issues. Nevertheless, economics can help inform the debate. Economic analysis suggests that immigration can either benefit or harm a nation, depending on the number of immigrants; their education, skills, and work ethic; and the rate at which they can be absorbed into the economy without disruption.

From a strictly economic perspective, immigration should be expanded until its marginal benefits equal its marginal costs. The MB = MC conceptual framework explicitly recognizes that there can be too few immigrants, just as there can be too many. Moreover, it recognizes that from a strictly economic standpoint, not all immigrants are alike. Some immigrants generate more benefits to the U.S. economy than others; and some immigrants impose more costs on taxpayers than others. The immigration of, say, a highly educated scientist obviously has a different net economic impact than does the immigration of a long-term welfare recipient.

A nation sets the level of legal immigration through quotas and special provisions. In effect, it also sets the size of illegal immigration through how effectively it secures its borders and enforces its immigration laws. This chapter's Last Word examines immigration law and the latest (unsuccessful) attempt to reform it.

Summary

1. Legal immigrants may be either permanent immigrants (green card holders) or temporary immigrants who are legally in the country until a specific date. The United States admitted 1,052,415 legal permanent residents in 2007. About 55 percent of these immigrants were women; 45 percent were men. Roughly 58 percent of immigrants were married. The largest number of immigrants (148,640) was from Mexico, but Mexicans made up only 15 percent of the total legal immigration in 2007. The vast majority of legal immigrants gain that status because of family ties with U.S. citizens and other legal residents.

2. Illegal immigrants (also called unauthorized immigrants, illegal aliens, or undocumented workers) are people who enter the country unlawfully or overstay their prescribed exit dates. An estimated 350,000 illegal immigrants enter the United States each year, adding to the 12 million illegal immigrants already in the United States. The vast majority of illegal immigrants come from Mexico.

3. An economic migrant's decision to move to another country can be viewed as an investment, in which present sacrifices (explicit and implicit costs) are incurred to obtain larger lifetime gains (higher earnings). Other things equal, the shorter the distance of the move and the younger the potential economic migrant, the more likely the person will move to the destination country.

4. The simple immigration model suggests that, for a high-wage country, the movement of migrants from a low-wage country (a) increases domestic output (= domestic income), (b) reduces the average wage rate, (c) reduces total wage income of native-born workers, and (d) increases business income. The opposite effects occur in the low-wage country. Because the domestic output gains in the high-wage country exceed the domestic output losses in the low-wage country, labor resources are more efficiently allocated globally and world output rises.

5. The outcomes of immigration predicted by the simple immigration model become more complicated when considering (a) the costs of moving, (b) the possibility of remittances and backflows, (c) complementary rather than substitute labor, (d) impacts on investment, (e) the levels of unemployment in each country, and (f) the fiscal impact on the taxpayers of each country.

6. Legal U.S. residents who have less than a high school education seem to bear the brunt of the wage impact of immigration, although some high-educated workers are also affected. Immigration has little discernable effect on the overall average wage rate in the U.S. economy, with estimates ranging from a minus 3 percent to a plus 2 percent.

7. Illegal workers in the United States reduce wage rates in narrowly defined low-wage labor markets, but they do not reduce native-born employment by the full extent of the employment of the illegal workers. American workers who are complementary to illegal immigrant labor may experience an increase in the demand for their services and wages because of the illegal immigrants.

8. Illegal workers may increase the overall rate of return on capital, thus promoting greater national investment. However, large numbers of illegal workers in specific industries may reduce the incentive for those industries to mechanize. A very legitimate concern is that illegal workers and their families impose greater fiscal costs on state and local governments than they contribute to tax revenues.

Terms and Concepts

economic immigrants

legal immigrants

illegal immigrants

H1-B provision

human capital

beaten paths

backflows

skill transferability

self-selection

efficiency gains from migration

brain drains

remittances

complementary resources

substitute resources

negative self-selection

compensating wage differential

Study Questions

1. Which of the following statements are true? Which are false? Explain why the false statements are untrue. **LO1**
   a. More immigrants arrive to the United States each year illegally than legally.
   b. The majority of legal immigrants are men.
   c. Over half the new legal immigrants to the United States each year are from Mexico.
   d. Most legal immigrants to the United States gain their legal status through employment-based preferences.

2. **KEY QUESTION** In what respect is the economic decision to move across international borders an investment decision? Why do economic migrants move to some countries, but not to others? Cite an example of an explicit cost of moving; an implicit cost of moving. How do distance and age affect the migration decision? How does the presence of a large number of previous movers to a country affect the projected costs and benefits of subsequent movers? **LO2**

3. **ADVANCED ANALYSIS** Suppose that the projected lifetime earnings gains from migration exceed the costs of moving. Explain how the decision to move might be reversed when a person considers present value. **LO2**

4. **KEY QUESTION** Use the accompanying table for Neon and Zeon to answer the questions that follow. Assume that the wage rate shown equals hourly output and income and that the accumulated output and income are the sum of the marginal revenue products (MRPs) of each worker. **LO3**

Neon

Workers	Wage Rate = MRP	Domestic Output and Income
1	$21	$21
2	19	40 (= 21 + 19)
3	17	57 (= 21 + 19 + 17)
4	15	72
5	13	85
6	11	96
7	9	105

Zeon

Workers	Wage Rate = MRP	Domestic Output and Income
1	$15	$15
2	13	28 (= 15 + 13)
3	11	39 (= 15 + 13 + 11)
4	9	48
5	7	55
6	5	60
7	3	63

a. Which country has the greater stock of capital and technological prowess? How can you tell?

b. Suppose the equilibrium wage rate is $19 in Neon and $7 in Zeon. What is the domestic output (= domestic income) in the two countries?

c. Assuming zero migration costs and initial wage rates of $19 in Neon and $7 in Zeon, how many workers will move to Neon? Why will not more than that number of workers move to Neon?

d. After the move of workers, what will the equilibrium wage rate be in each country? What will the domestic output be after the migration? What is the amount of the combined gain in domestic output produced by the migration? Which country will gain output; which will lose output? How will the income of native-born workers be affected in each country?

5. **KEY QUESTION** How might the output and income gains from immigration shown by the simple immigration model be affected by (*a*) unemployment in the originating nation, (*b*) remittances by immigrants to the home country, and (*c*) backflows of migrants to the home country? **LO3**

6. Suppose initially that immigrant labor and native-born labor are complementary resources. Explain how a substantial immigration might change the demand for native-born workers, altering their wages. (Review the relevant portion of Chapter 12 if necessary to help answer this question.) Next, suppose that new immigrant labor and previous immigrant labor (not native-born) are substitute resources. Explain how a substantial immigration of new workers might affect the demand for previous immigrants, altering their wages. **LO3**

7. What is a "brain drain" as it relates to international migration? If emigrants are highly educated and received greatly subsidized education in the home country, is there any justification for that country to levy a "brain drain" tax on them? Do you see any problems with this idea? **LO3**

8. In July 2007 *The Wall Street Journal* (*WSJ*) reported that a growing shortage of skilled labor in Eastern European countries such as Slovakia was driving up wages in key industries and reducing business income. The reason for the shortages was a large migration of skilled Eastern European workers to Western European countries. Use the simple immigration model to demonstrate the key elements of the *WSJ* story as just described. **LO3**

9. **KEY QUESTION** Why is each of these statements somewhat misleading? (*a*) "Illegal immigrants take only jobs that no American wants." (*b*) "Deporting 100,000 illegal immigrants would create 100,000 job openings for Americans." **LO4**

10. Why are so many state and local governments greatly concerned about the Federal government's allegedly lax enforcement of the immigration laws and congressional proposals to grant legal status (amnesty) to the 12 million illegal immigrants in the United States? How might an amnesty program affect the flow of future border crossings? **LO5**

11. If someone favors the free movement of labor within the United States, is it inconsistent for that person also to favor restrictions on the international movement of labor? Why or why not? **LO5**

12. **LAST WORD** What were the five main features of the proposed immigration reform of 2007? Which of these features, as general principles, do you support? Which do you oppose? Explain your reasoning.

Web-Based Questions

1. **LEGAL IMMIGRANTS—WHO RECEIVED THE GREEN CARDS?** Go to the Web site of the U.S. Department of Homeland Security, **www.dhs.gov,** and select Immigration, then Immigration Statistics, and the Publications. Find the Annual Flow Report on U.S. Legal Permanent Residents for the latest year. How many people became legal U.S. permanent residents in that year? What percentage were family-sponsored immigrants? How many were married? What percentage of legal immigrants were 34 years or younger? What percentage, 65 or older? Which five countries supplied the most legal immigrants? What were the top five states of residence of new legal immigrants in that year and what percentage of the total immigration did they comprise?

2. **FOREIGN-BORN POPULATION—WHICH COUNTRIES HAVE THE MOST?** The United Nation's Department of Economic and Social Affairs, Population Division, tracks the total number of foreign-born people by nation. Find its Web site via a Google **www.google.com** search for "UN Population Division home page." Then select International Migration and Development and find the International Migration Wall Chart. Which five countries have the most foreign-born residents in absolute terms? Which five countries have the greatest percentage of foreign-born residents? Why do the two lists differ so substantially?

PART SIX

GDP, Growth, and Instability

IN THIS CHAPTER YOU WILL LEARN:

1 How macroeconomics studies both long-run economic growth and short-run fluctuations in output and unemployment.

2 Why economists focus on GDP, inflation, and unemployment when assessing the health of an entire economy.

3 That sustained increases in living standards are a historically recent phenomenon.

4 Why savings and investment are key factors in promoting rising living standards.

5 Why economists believe that "shocks" and "sticky prices" are responsible for short-run fluctuations in output and employment.

An Introduction to Macroeconomics

As you know from Chapter 1, macroeconomics studies the behavior of the economy as a whole. It is primarily concerned with two topics: long-run economic growth and the short-run fluctuations in output and employment that are often referred to as the **business cycle.** These phenomena are closely related because they happen simultaneously. Economies show a distinct growth trend that leads to higher output and higher standards of living in the long run, but in the short run there is a great deal of variability. Sometimes growth proceeds more rapidly and sometimes it proceeds more slowly. It may even turn negative for a while so that output and living standards actually decline, a situation referred to as a **recession.** This chapter provides an overview of the data that macroeconomists use to measure the status and growth of an entire economy as well as a preview of the models that they use to help explain both long-run growth and short-run fluctuations.

Performance and Policy

In order to understand how economies operate and how their performance might be improved, economists collect and analyze economic data. An almost infinite number of data items can be looked at, including the amount of new construction taking place each month, how many ships laden with cargo are arriving at our ports each year, and how many new inventions have been patented in the last few weeks. That being said, macroeconomists tend to focus on just a few statistics when trying to assess the health and development of an economy. Chief among these are real GDP, unemployment, and inflation.

- **Real GDP,** or **real gross domestic product,** measures the value of final goods and services produced within the borders of a given country during a given period of time, typically a year. This statistic is very useful because it can tell us whether an economy's output is growing. For instance, if the United States' real GDP in 2007 is larger than the United States' real GDP in 2006, then we know that U.S. output increased from 2006 to 2007. To get real GDP, government statisticians first calculate **nominal GDP,** which totals the dollar value of all goods and services produced within the borders of a given country using *their current prices during the year that they were produced.* But because nominal GDP uses current prices, it suffers from a major problem: It can increase from one year to the next even if there is no increase in output. To see how, consider a sculptor who produces 10 sculptures this year and 10 sculptures next year. Clearly, her output does not change. But if the price of sculptures rises from $10,000 this year to $20,000 next year, nominal GDP will rise from $100,000 (= 10 × $10,000) this year to $200,000 (= 10 × $20,000) next year because of the increase in prices. Real GDP corrects for price changes. As a result, we can compare real GDP numbers from one year to the next and really know if there is a change in output (rather than prices). Because more output means greater consumption possibilities—including not only the chance to consume more fun things like movies, vacations, and video games, but also more serious things like better health care and safer roads—economists and policymakers are deeply committed to encouraging a large and growing real GDP.
- **Unemployment** is the state a person is in if he or she cannot get a job despite being willing to work and actively seeking work. High rates of unemployment are undesirable because they indicate that a nation is not using a large fraction of its most important resource—the talents and skills of its people. Unemployment is a waste because we must count as a loss all the goods and services that unemployed workers could have produced if they had been working. Researchers have also drawn links between higher rates of unemployment and major social problems like higher crime rates and greater political unrest as well as higher rates of depression, heart disease, and other illnesses among unemployed individuals.
- **Inflation** is an increase in the overall level of prices. As an example, consider all the goods and services bought by a typical family over the course of one year. If the economy is experiencing inflation, it will cost the family more money to buy those goods and services this year than it cost to buy them last year. This can be problematic for several reasons. First, if the family's income does not rise as fast as the prices of the goods and services that it consumes, it won't be able to purchase as much as it used to and its standard of living will fall. Along the same lines, a surprise jump in inflation reduces the purchasing power of people's savings. Savings that they believed would be able to buy them a given amount of goods and services will turn out to buy them less than they expected due to the higher-than-expected prices.

Because these statistics are the standards by which economists keep track of long-run growth and short-run fluctuations, we will spend a substantial amount of time in the next few chapters examining how these statistics are computed, how well they are able to capture the well-being of actual people, and how they vary both across countries and over time. Once they are understood, we will build upon them in subsequent chapters by developing macroeconomic models of both long-run growth and short-run fluctuations. These will help us understand how policymakers attempt to maximize growth while minimizing unemployment and inflation.

Macroeconomic models also clarify many important questions about the powers and limits of government economic policy. These include:

- Can governments promote long-run economic growth?
- Can they reduce the severity of recessions by smoothing out short-run fluctuations?
- Are certain government policy tools like manipulating interest rates (monetary policy) more effective at mitigating short-run fluctuations than other government policy tools such as changes in tax rates or levels of government spending (fiscal policy)?

- Is there a trade-off between lower rates of unemployment and higher rates of inflation?
- Does government policy work best when it is announced in advance or when it is a surprise?

The answers to these questions are of crucial importance because of the vast differences in economic performance seen across various economies at different times. For instance, the amount of output generated by the U.S. economy grew at an average rate of 2.7 percent per year between 1995 and 2007 while the amount of output generated by the Japanese economy grew at an average rate of only 1.0 percent per year over the same time period. Could Japan have done as well as the United States if it had pursued different economic policies? Similarly, in 2007, unemployment in the United States was only 4.6 percent of the labor force, while it was 8.7 percent in Germany, 7.2 percent in India, 12.8 percent in Poland, and 80 percent in Zimbabwe. At the same time, the inflation rate in the United States was 2.7 percent, compared with 26,470 percent in Zimbabwe! Our models will help us understand why such large differences in rates of growth, unemployment, and inflation exist and how government policies influence them.

The Miracle of Modern Economic Growth

Rapid and sustained economic growth is a modern phenomenon. Before the Industrial Revolution began in the late 1700s in England, standards of living showed virtually no growth over hundreds or even thousands of years. For instance, the standard of living of the average Roman peasant was virtually the same at the start of the Roman Empire around the year 500 B.C. as it was at the end of the Roman Empire 1000 years later. Similarly, historians and archeologists have estimated that the standard of living enjoyed by the average Chinese peasant was essentially the same in the year A.D. 1800 as it was in the year A.D. 100.

That is not to say that the Roman and Chinese economies did not expand over time. They did. In fact, their total outputs of goods and services increased many times over. The problem was that as they did, their populations went up by similar proportions so that the amount of output *per person* remained virtually unchanged.

This historical pattern continued until the start of the Industrial Revolution, which ushered in not only factory production and automation but also massive increases in research and development so that new and better technologies were constantly being invented. The result was that output began to grow faster than the population. This meant that living standards began to rise as the amount of output *per person* increased.

Not all countries experienced this phenomenon, but those that did were said to be experiencing **modern economic growth** (in which output per person rises) as compared with earlier times in which output (but not output per person) increased. Under modern economic growth, the annual increase in output per person is often not large, perhaps 2 percent per year in countries such as England that were the first to industrialize. But when compounded over time, an annual growth rate of 2 percent adds up very rapidly. Indeed, it implies that the standard of living will double every 35 years. So if the average citizen of a country enjoying 2 percent growth begins this year with an income of $10,000, in 35 years that person will have an income of $20,000. And 35 years after that there will be another doubling so that her income in 70 years will be $40,000. And 35 years after that, the average citizen's income will double again to $80,000. Such high rates of growth are amazing when compared to the period before modern economic growth when standards of living remained unchanged century after century.

The vast differences in living standards seen today between rich and poor countries are almost entirely the result of the fact that only some countries have experienced modern economic growth. Indeed, before the start of the Industrial Revolution in the late 1700s, living standards around the world were very similar, so much so that the average standard of living in the richest parts of the world was at most only two or three times higher than the standard of living in the poorest parts of the world. By contrast, the citizens of the richest nations today have material standards of living that are on average more than 50 times higher than those experienced by citizens of the poorest nations, as can be seen by the GDP per person data for the year 2007 given in Global Perspective 23.1.

Global Perspective 23.1 facilitates international comparisons of living standards by making three adjustments to each country's GDP. First, it converts each country's GDP from its own currency into U.S. dollars so that there is no confusion about the values of different currencies. Second, it divides each country's GDP measured in dollars by the size of its population. The resulting number, *GDP per person*, is the average amount of output each person in each country could have if each country's total output were divided equally among its citizens. It is a measure of each country's average standard of living. Third, the table uses a method called *purchasing power parity* to adjust for the fact that prices are much lower in some countries than others. By making this adjustment, we can trust that $1 of GDP per person in the United States represents about the same quantity of goods and services as $1 of GDP per person in

GLOBAL PERSPECTIVE 23.1

GDP per Person, Selected Countries

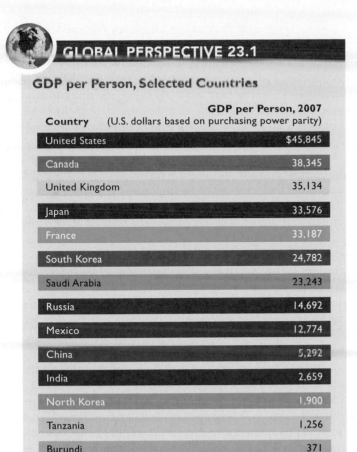

Country	GDP per Person, 2007 (U.S. dollars based on purchasing power parity)
United States	$45,845
Canada	38,345
United Kingdom	35,134
Japan	33,576
France	33,187
South Korea	24,782
Saudi Arabia	23,243
Russia	14,692
Mexico	12,774
China	5,292
India	2,659
North Korea	1,900
Tanzania	1,256
Burundi	371
Zimbabwe	188

Source: International Monetary Fund, **www.imf.org**, for all countries except for North Korea, the data for which comes from the *CIA World Factbook*, **www.cia.gov**.

any of the other countries. The resulting numbers—GDP per person adjusted for purchasing power parity—are presented in Global Perspective 23.1. **(Key Question 2)**

Savings, Investment, and Choosing between Present and Future Consumption

At the heart of economic growth is the principle that in order to raise living standards over time, an economy must devote at least some fraction of its current output to increasing future output. As implied in Chapter 1, this process requires both savings and investment, which we will define and discuss before returning to why they are so important for economic growth.

- **Savings** are generated when current consumption is less than current output (or when current spending is less than current income).

- **Investment** happens when resources are devoted to increasing future output—for instance by building a new research facility in which scientists invent the next generation of fuel-efficient automobiles or by constructing a modern, super-efficient factory.

Economics students are often confused about the way the word "investment" is used in economics. This is because only economists draw a distinction between "financial investment" and "economic investment."

Financial investment captures what ordinary people mean when they say investment, namely the purchase of assets like stocks, bonds, and real estate in the hope of reaping a financial gain. Anything of monetary value is an asset and, in everyday usage, people purchase—or "invest" in—assets hoping to receive a financial gain, either by eventually selling them at higher prices than they paid for them or by receiving a stream of payments as the owner of their assets (as is the case with landlords who rent the property they own to tenants). By contrast, when economists say "investment," they are referring to the much more specific concept of **economic investment,** which has to do with the creation and expansion of business enterprises. Specifically, economic investment only includes money spent purchasing *newly created* capital goods such as machinery, tools, factories, and warehouses.

Indeed, as defined and measured by economists, purely financial transactions such as swapping cash for a stock or a bond are not "investment." Neither is the purchase by a firm of a factory built several years ago and previously used by another company. Both types of transactions simply transfer the ownership of old assets from one party to another. They do not pay for *newly created* capital goods. As such, they are great examples of *financial investment*, but are not examples of the narrower idea of *economic investment.* So now that you know the difference, remember that purely financial transactions like buying Google stock or a five-year-old factory are indeed referred to as "investment"—except in economics!

When thinking about why savings and investment are so important for economic growth, the key point is that the amount of economic investment (hereafter, simply "investment") is ultimately limited by the amount of savings. The only way that more output can be directed at investment activities is if savings increase. But that, in turn, implies that individuals and society as a whole must make trade-offs between current and future consumption. This is true because the only way to pay for more investment—and the higher levels of future consumption that more investment can generate—is to increase savings in the present. But increased savings can only come at the price of reduced current consumption. Individuals and society as a whole must therefore wrestle with a choice between present consumption and future consumption, deciding how to balance the reductions in current consumption that are necessary to fund current investment against the higher levels of future consumption that can result from more current investment.

Banks and Other Financial Institutions

Households are the principal source of savings. But businesses are the main economic investors. So how do the savings generated by households when they spend less than they consume get transferred to businesses so that they can purchase newly created capital goods? The answer is through banks and other financial institutions such as mutual funds, pension plans, and insurance companies. These institutions collect the savings of households, rewarding savers with interest and dividends and sometimes capital gains (increases in asset values). The banks and other financial institutions then lend the funds to businesses, which invest in equipment, factories, and other capital goods.

Macroeconomics devotes considerable attention to money, banking, and financial institutions because a well-functioning financial system helps to promote economic growth and stability by encouraging savings and by properly directing that savings into the most productive possible investments.

Uncertainty, Expectations, and Shocks

Decisions about savings and investment are complicated by the fact that the future is uncertain. Investment projects sometimes produce disappointing results or even fail totally. As a result, firms spend considerable time trying to predict future trends so that they can, hopefully, invest only in projects that are likely to succeed. This implies that macroeconomics has to take into account **expectations** about the future.

Expectations are hugely important for two reasons. The more obvious reason involves the effect that changing expectations have on current behavior. If firms grow more pessimistic about the future returns that are likely to come from current investments, they are going to invest less today than they would if they were more optimistic. Expectations therefore have a large effect on economic growth since increased pessimism will lead to less current investment and, subsequently, less future consumption.

The less-obvious reason that expectations are so important has to do with what happens when expectations are unmet. Firms are often forced to cope with **shocks**—situations in which they were expecting one thing to happen but then something else happened. For instance, consider a situation in which a firm decides to build a high-speed railroad that will shuttle passengers between Washington, D.C., and New York. They do so expecting it to be very popular and make a handsome profit. But if it unexpectedly turns out to be unpopular and loses money, the railroad must figure out how to respond. Should the railroad go out of business completely? Should it attempt to see if it can turn a profit by hauling cargo instead of passengers? Is there a possibility that the venture might succeed if the firm borrows $30 million from a bank to pay for a massive advertising campaign? These sorts of decisions are necessitated by the shock and surprise of having to deal with an unexpected situation.

Economies are exposed to both demand shocks and supply shocks. **Demand shocks** are unexpected changes in the demand for goods and services. **Supply shocks** are unexpected changes in the supply of goods and services. Please note that the word *shock* only tells us that something unexpected has happened. It does not tell us whether what has happened is unexpectedly good or unexpectedly bad. To make things more clear, economists use more specific terms. For instance, a *positive demand shock* refers to a situation in which demand turns out to be higher than expected, while a *negative demand shock* refers to a situation in which demand turns out to be lower than expected.

Economists believe that most short-run fluctuations are the result of demand shocks. Supply shocks do happen in some cases and are very important when they do occur. But we will focus most of our attention in this chapter and subsequent chapters on demand shocks, how they affect the economy, and how government policy may be able to help the economy adjust to them. But why are demand shocks such a big problem? Why would we have to consider calling in the government to help deal with them? And why can't firms deal with demand shocks on their own?

The answer to these questions is that the prices of many goods and services are inflexible (slow to change, or "sticky") in the short run. As we will explain, this implies that price changes do not quickly equalize the quantities demanded of such goods and services with their respective quantities supplied. Instead, because prices are inflexible, the economy is forced to respond in the short run to demand shocks primarily through changes in output and employment rather than through changes in prices.

Although an economy as a whole is much more complex than a single firm, an analogy that uses a single car factory will be helpful in explaining why demand shocks and inflexible prices are so important to understanding most of the short-run fluctuations that affect the entire economy. Consider a car manufacturing company named Buzzer Auto. Like most companies, Buzzer Auto is in business to try to make a profit. Part of turning a profit involves trying to develop accurate expectations about future market conditions. Consequently, Buzzer constantly does market research to estimate future demand conditions so that it will, hopefully, only build cars that people are going to want to buy.

After extensive market research, Buzzer concludes that it could earn a modest profit if it builds and staffs an appropriately sized factory to build an environmentally friendly SUV, which it decides to call the Prion. Buzzer's marketing economists collaborate with Buzzer's engineers and conclude that expected profits will be maximized if the firm builds a factory that has an optimal output rate of 900 cars per week. If the factory operates at this rate, it can produce Prions for only $36,500 per vehicle. This is terrific because the firm's estimates for demand indicate that a supply of 900 vehicles per week can be sold at a price of $37,000 per vehicle—meaning that if everything goes according to plan, Buzzer Auto should make an accounting profit of $500 on each Prion that it produces and sells. Expecting these future conditions, Buzzer decides to build the factory, staff it with workers, and begin making the Prion.

Look at Figure 23.1a, which shows the market for Prions when the vertical supply curve for Prions is fixed at the factory's optimal output rate of 900 cars per week. Notice that we have drawn in three possible demand curves. D_L corresponds to low demand for the Prion; D_M corresponds to the medium level of demand that Buzzer's marketing economists are expecting to materialize; and D_H corresponds to high demand for the Prion. Figure 23.1a is consistent with the marketing economists' expectations: if all goes according to plan and the actual demand that materializes is D_M, the equilibrium price will in fact be $37,000 per Prion and the equilibrium quantity demanded will be 900 cars per week. Thus, if all goes according to expectations, the factory will have exactly the right capacity to meet the expected quantity demanded at the sales price of $37,000 per vehicle. In addition, the firm's books will show a profit of $500 per vehicle on each of the 900 vehicles that it builds and expects to sell each week at that price.

Here is the key point. If expectations are always fulfilled, Buzzer Auto will never contribute to any of the short-run fluctuations in output and unemployment that affect real-world economies. First, if everything always goes according to plan and Buzzer Auto's expectations

FIGURE 23.1 The effect of unexpected changes in demand under flexible and fixed prices. (a) If prices are flexible, then no matter what demand turns out to be, Buzzer Auto can continue to sell its optimal output of 900 cars per week since the equilibrium price will adjust to equalize the quantity demanded with the quantity supplied. (b) By contrast, if Buzzer Auto sticks with a fixed-price policy, then the quantity demanded will vary with the level of demand. At the fixed price of $37,000 per vehicle, the quantity demanded will be 700 cars per week if demand is D_L, 900 cars per week if demand is D_M, and 1150 cars per week if demand is D_H.

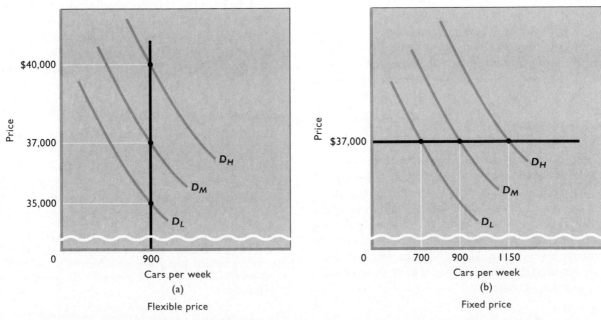

(a)

Flexible price

(b)

Fixed price

always come true, then the factory will always produce and sell at its optimal output rate of 900 cars per week. This would mean that it would never experience any fluctuations in output—either in the short run or in the long run. At the same time, since producing a constant output of 900 cars each week will always require the same number of workers, the factory's labor demand and employment should never vary. So if everything always goes according to plan, Buzzer Auto will never have any effect on unemployment because it will always hire a constant number of workers.

These facts imply that the short-run fluctuations in output and unemployment that we do see in the real world must be the result of shocks and things *not* going according to plan. In particular, business cycle fluctuations typically arise because the actual demand that materializes ends up being either lower or higher than what people were expecting. When this occurs, some adjustments will be necessary to bring the quantity demanded and the quantity supplied back into alignment. As we are about to explain, the nature of these adjustments varies hugely depending upon whether prices are flexible or inflexible.

Demand Shocks and Flexible Prices

Figure 23.1a illustrates the case of adjusting to unexpected changes in demand *when prices are flexible*. Here, if demand is unexpectedly low at D_L, the market price can adjust downward to $35,000 per vehicle so that the quantity demanded at that price will still be equal to the factory's optimal output rate of 900 cars per week. On the other hand, if demand is unexpectedly high at D_H, the market price can adjust upward to $40,000 per vehicle so that the quantity demanded will still be equal to the factory's optimal output rate of 900 cars per week. These adjustments imply that *if* the price of Prions is free to quickly adjust to new equilibrium levels in response to unexpected changes in demand, the factory could always operate at its optimal output rate of 900 cars per week. Only the amount of profit or loss will vary with demand.

Applying this logic to the economy as a whole, *if* the prices of goods and services could always adjust quickly to unexpected changes in demand, then the economy could always produce at its optimal capacity since prices would adjust to ensure that the quantity demanded of each good and service would always equal the quantity supplied. Simply put, if prices were fully flexible, there would be no short-run fluctuations: output would remain constant and unemployment levels would not change because firms would always need the same number of workers to produce the same amount of output.

Demand Shocks and Sticky Prices

In reality, many prices in the economy are inflexible and are not able to change rapidly when demand changes unexpectedly. Consider the extreme case shown in Figure 23.1b, in which the price of Prions is totally inflexible, fixed at $37,000 per Prion. Here, if demand unexpectedly falls from D_M to D_L, the quantity demanded at the fixed price of $37,000 will only be 700 cars per week, which is 200 cars fewer than the factory's optimal output of 900 cars per week. On the other hand, if demand is unexpectedly high at D_H, the quantity demanded at the fixed price of $37,000 will be 1150 cars per week, which is 250 cars more than the factory's optimal output of 900 cars per week.

One way for companies to deal with these unexpected shifts in quantity demanded would be to try to adjust the factory's output to match them. That is, during weeks of low demand, Buzzer Auto could attempt to produce only 700 Prions, while during weeks of high demand it could try to produce 1150 Prions. But this sort of flexible output strategy is very expensive because factories operate at their lowest costs when they are producing constantly at their optimal output levels; operating at either a higher or a lower production rate results in higher per-unit production costs.[1]

Knowing this, manufacturing firms typically attempt to deal with unexpected changes in demand by maintaining an inventory. An **inventory** is a store of output that has been produced but not yet sold. Inventories are useful because they can be allowed to grow or decline in periods when demand is unexpectedly low or high—thereby allowing production to proceed smoothly even when demand is variable. In our example, Buzzer Auto would maintain an inventory of unsold Prions. In weeks when demand is unexpectedly low, the inventory will increase by 200 Prions as the quantity demanded falls 200 vehicles short of the factory's optimal output. By contrast, during weeks when demand is unexpectedly high, the inventory will decrease as the quantity demanded exceeds the factory's optimal output by 250 cars. By allowing inventory levels to fluctuate with changes in demand, Buzzer Auto can respond to unexpected changes in demand by adjusting inventory levels rather than output levels. In addition, with any luck, the overall inventory level will stay roughly constant over time as unexpected increases and decreases roughly cancel each other out.

---

[1]If you have studied microeconomics, you will recognize that the firm's optimal output level of 900 cars per week is the level that minimizes the factory's average total cost (ATC) per vehicle of producing the Prion. Producing either more or fewer Prions will result in higher per-vehicle production costs.

But consider what will happen if the firm experiences many successive weeks of unexpectedly low demand. For each such week, the firm's inventory of unsold Prions will increase by 200 cars. The firm's managers will not mind if this happens for a few weeks, but if it continues for many weeks, then the managers will be forced to cut production because, among other things, there will simply be no place to park so many unsold vehicles. More importantly, holding large numbers of unsold cars in inventory is unprofitable because while costs must be incurred to build an unsold car, an unsold car obviously brings in no revenue. Constantly rising inventories hurt firm profits and the management will want to reduce output if it sees inventories rising week after week due to unexpectedly low demand.

This simplified story about a single car company explains why economists believe that a combination of unexpected changes in demand and inflexible prices are the key to understanding the short-run fluctuations that affect real-world economies. If prices were flexible, then the firm could always operate at the factory's optimal output level because prices would always adjust to ensure that it could sell its optimal output of 900 cars per week no matter what happens to demand. But if prices are inflexible, then an unexpected decline in demand that persists for any length of time will result in increasing inventories that will eventually force the firm's management to cut production to less than the optimal output level of 900 cars per week. When this happens, not only will output fall, but unemployment will also rise. The firm will lay off workers because fewer employees will be needed to produce fewer cars.

Generalizing this story to the economy as a whole, if demand falls off for many goods and services across the entire economy for an extended period of time, then the firms that make those goods and services will be forced to cut production. Manufacturing firms that maintain inventories will do so as they find inventories piling up due to sluggish sales. And services firms will do so as they encounter slow sales for their services. As both manufacturing and service output declines, the economy will go into recession, with GDP falling and unemployment rising.

On the other hand, if demand is unexpectedly high for a prolonged period of time, the economy will boom and unemployment will fall. In the case of our Prion example, for each week that demand is unexpectedly high, inventories will fall by 250 cars. If this keeps happening week after week, inventories will start to run out and the firm will have to react by increasing production

to more than the optimal output rate of 900 cars per week so that orders do not go unfilled. When this happens, GDP will increase as more cars per week are produced and unemployment will fall because the factory will have to hire more workers in order to produce the larger number of cars. (**Key Question 7**)

How Sticky Are Prices?

We have just shown that **inflexible prices**—or "**sticky prices**" as economists are fond of saying—help to explain how unexpected changes in demand lead to the fluctuations in GDP and employment that occur over the course of the business cycle. Of course, not all prices are sticky. Indeed, the markets for many commodities and raw materials such as corn, oil, and natural gas feature extremely **flexible prices** that react within seconds to changes in supply and demand. By contrast, the prices of most of the final goods and services that people consume are quite sticky, with the average good or service going 4.3 months between price changes. To get a better appreciation for the fact that price stickiness varies greatly by product or service, look at Table 23.1, which gives the average number of months between price changes for various common goods and services. The prices of some products like gasoline and airline tickets change very rapidly—about once a month or even less

TABLE 23.1 Average Number of Months between Price Changes for Selected Goods and Services

Item	Months
Coin-operated laundry machines	46.4
Newspapers	29.9
Haircuts	25.5
Taxi fare	19.7
Veterinary services	14.9
Magazines	11.2
Computer software	5.5
Beer	4.3
Microwave ovens	3.0
Milk	2.4
Electricity	1.8
Airline tickets	1.0
Gasoline	0.6

Source: Mark Bils and Peter J. Klenow, "Some Evidence on the Importance of Sticky Prices." *Journal of Political Economy,* October 2004, pp. 947–985.

Will Better Inventory Management Mean Fewer Recessions?

Computerized Inventory Tracking Has Greatly Accelerated How Quickly Companies Can Respond to Unexpected Changes in Demand

Before computers made it possible to track inventory changes in real time, firms could only react to unexpected shifts in demand very slowly. This was true because before computers, tracking inventory was a painful, slow process that basically involved having to hire people to physically count the items held in inventory—one at a time. Since this process was both costly and annoying, firms typically counted their inventories only a few times per year.

An unfortunate side effect of counting inventory so infrequently was that unexpected shifts in demand could cause large changes in inventory levels before anyone could find out about them. To see why this is true, consider a firm that counts its inventory just twice per year, for example, once in January and once in July. If the demand for its product suddenly falls in February and then remains low, the decline in demand will not be discovered until the July inventory count is taken. Only then will a high inventory level inform the firm's management that the demand for its product must have unexpectedly declined.

The long delay between when the shift in demand happens and when it is discovered means that the firm will very likely feel pressed to sharply reduce its production of new output since the fastest way to reduce its high inventory level will be to sharply reduce its output rate (so that new sales will exceed the reduced output rate). Following this policy, however, implies not only a large cut in output but also a substantial increase in unemployment since fewer workers will be needed to produce less output. As a result, infrequent inventory counting leads to strong fluctuations in output *and* employment because by the time an unexpected change in demand is discovered, it will have had plenty of time to cause a large change in inventory levels that will very likely be rectified by a large change in production levels.

By contrast, many economists believe that economic fluctuations may have become much less severe during the last 20 years because of the introduction of computerized inventory tracking systems that allow companies to track their inventory levels in real time. These systems keep continuous track of inventory levels by means of technologies like bar codes and laser scanners. This allows firms to tell almost immediately if demand has changed unexpectedly. As a result, the firms that have adopted these systems can make much more subtle changes to output and

than once a month. By contrast, haircuts and newspapers average more than two years between price changes. And coin-operated laundry machines average nearly four years between price changes!

In later chapters, we will discuss several factors that increase short-run price stickiness. But to keep the current discussion brief, let us focus on just two factors here. One factor is that companies selling final goods and services know that consumers prefer stable, predictable prices that do not fluctuate rapidly with changes in demand. Consumers would be annoyed if the same bottle of soda or shampoo cost one price one day, a different price the next day, and yet another price a week later. Volatile prices make planning more difficult, and, in addition, consumers who come in to buy the product on a day when the price happens to be high will likely feel that they are being taken advantage of. To avoid this, most firms try to maintain stable prices that do not change very often. Firms do have occasional sales where they lower prices, but on the whole they tend to try to keep prices stable and predictable—the result being price inflexibility.

Another factor that causes sticky prices has to do with the fact that in certain situations, a firm may be afraid that cutting its price may be counterproductive because its rivals might simply match the price cut—a situation often referred to as a "price war." This possibility is common among firms that only have one or two major rivals. Consider Coca-Cola and Pepsi. If Coca-Cola faces unexpectedly low demand for its product, it might be tempted to reduce its price in the hope that it can steal business away from Pepsi. But such a strategy would only work if Pepsi left its price alone when Coca-Cola cut its price. That, of course, is not likely. If Coca-Cola cuts its price, Pepsi will very likely cut its price in retaliation, doing its best to make sure that Coca-Cola doesn't steal away any of its customers. Thus, if Pepsi retaliates, Coca-Cola will only be made worse off by its decision to cut its price: It will not pick up much more business (because Pepsi also cut its price) and it will also be receiving less money for each bottle of Coke that it sells (because it lowered its own price.) Thus, firms that have to deal with the possibility of price wars often have sticky prices.

employment because they can discover the unexpected changes in demand before those unexpected changes have caused large shifts in inventory levels.

While it is not possible to "prove" that inventory management systems have led to smaller business cycle fluctuations, the behavior of the U.S. economy over the past 30 years is suggestive. The last severe recession happened in 1981–1982. Up to that point, recessions appeared to happen in the United States every five or so years and were often quite punishing, with high levels of unemployment and significant declines in output. But computerized inventory management systems began to be widely adopted during the 1980s and since that time the U.S. economy has only experienced two mild recessions, one in 1991–1992 and another in 2000–2001. Since these recessions were not only mild but about 10 years apart, some economists have taken this behavior as evidence that from now on recessions will be less frequent

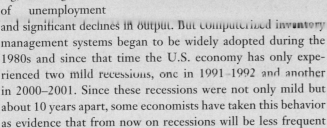

and less severe due to the recent improvements in inventory management.

Opinions vary, however, as to how much credit computerized inventory management should be given for the apparent reduction in the frequency and severity of the business cycle. Indeed, several other explanations have been put forward to explain why things seem to have improved. One hypothesis is that we may have just been lucky in recent years in that there have simply not been that many significant demand shocks. Another explanation is that governments may have learned from past mistakes and shifted to better economic policies. Taking the various competing explanations into account, it is safe to say that while no economist would give *all* the credit for the more moderate business cycle fluctuations of the past 25 years to computerized inventory management systems, nearly all would give at least some of the credit to these systems and the fact that they allow firms to rapidly react to unexpected changes in demand.

Categorizing Macroeconomic Models Using Price Stickiness

We have now demonstrated why price stickiness is believed to have such a large role in short-run economic fluctuations. It should be noted, however, that price stickiness moderates over time. This is true because firms that choose to use a fixed-price policy in the short run do not have to stick with that policy permanently. In particular, if unexpected changes in demand begin to look permanent, many firms will allow their prices to change so that price changes (in addition to quantity changes) can help to equalize quantities supplied with quantities demanded.

For this reason, economists speak of "sticky prices" rather than "stuck prices." Only in the very short run are prices totally inflexible. As time passes and prices are revised, the world looks much more like Figure 23.1a, in which prices are fully flexible, rather than Figure 23.1b, in which prices are totally inflexible. Indeed, the totally inflexible case shown in the right graph can be thought of

as the extremely short-run response to an unexpected change in demand, while the fully flexible case shown in the left graph can be thought of as a longer-run response to an unexpected change in demand. In terms of time durations, the extreme short run can be thought of as the first few weeks and months after a demand shock, while the long run can be thought of as extending from many months to several years after a demand shock happens.

This realization is very useful in categorizing and understanding the differences between the various macroeconomic models that we will be presenting in subsequent chapters. For instance, the aggregate expenditures model presented in Chapter 28 assumes perfectly inflexible prices (and wages) and thus is a model in which prices are not just sticky but completely stuck. By contrast, the aggregate demand–aggregate supply model presented in Chapter 29 allows for flexible prices (with or without flexible wages) and is therefore useful for understanding how the economy behaves over longer periods of time.

As you study these various models, keep in mind that we need different models precisely because the economy behaves so differently depending on how much time has passed after a demand shock. The differences in behavior result from the fact that prices go from stuck in the extreme short run to fully flexible in the long run. Using different models for different stages in this process gives us much better insights into not only how economies actually behave but also how various government and central bank policies may have different effects in the short run when prices are fixed versus the long run when prices are flexible.

Where will we go from here? In the remainder of Part 6, we examine how economists measure GDP and why GDP has expanded over time. Then, we discuss the terminology of business cycles and explore the measurement and types of unemployment and inflation. At that point you will be well-prepared to examine the economic models, monetary considerations, and stabilization policies that lie at the heart of macroeconomics.

Summary

1. Macroeconomics studies long-run economic growth and short-run economic fluctuations.

2. Macroeconomists focus their attention on three key economic statistics: real GDP, unemployment, and inflation. Real GDP measures the value of all final goods and services produced in a country during a given period of time. The unemployment rate measures the percentage of all workers who are not able to find paid employment despite being willing and able to work at currently available wages. The inflation rate measures the extent to which the overall level of prices is rising in the economy.

3. Before the Industrial Revolution, living standards did not show any sustained increases over time. Economies grew, but any increase in output tended to be offset by an equally large increase in the population, so that the amount of output per person did not rise. By contrast, since the Industrial Revolution began in the late 1700s, many nations have experienced modern economic growth in which output grows faster than population—so that standards of living rise over time.

4. Macroeconomists believe that one of the keys to modern economic growth is the promotion of savings and investment (for economists, the purchase of capital goods). Investment activities increase the economy's future potential output level. But investment must be funded by saving, which is only possible if people are willing to reduce current consumption. Consequently, individuals and society face a trade-off between current consumption and future consumption since the only way to fund the investment necessary to increase future consumption is by reducing current consumption in order to gather the savings necessary to fund that investment. Banks and other financial institutions help to convert saving into investment by taking the savings generated by households and lending it to businesses that wish to make investments.

5. Expectations have an important effect on the economy for two reasons. First, if people and businesses are more positive about the future, they will save and invest more. Second, individuals and firms must make adjustments to shocks—situations in which expectations are unmet and the future does not turn out the way people were expecting. In particular, shocks often imply situations where the quantity supplied of a given good or service does not equal the quantity demanded of that good or service.

6. If prices were always flexible and capable of rapid adjustment, then dealing with situations in which quantities demanded did not equal quantities supplied would always be easy since prices could simply adjust to the market equilibrium price at which quantities demanded equal quantities supplied. Unfortunately, real-world prices are often inflexible (or "sticky") in the short run so that the only way for the economy to adjust to such situations is through changes in output levels.

7. Sticky prices combine with shocks to drive short-run fluctuations in output and employment. Consider a negative demand shock in which demand is unexpectedly low. Because prices are fixed, the lower-than-expected demand will result in unexpectedly slow sales. This will cause inventories to increase. If demand remains low for an extended period of time, inventory levels will become too high and firms will have to cut output and lay off workers. Thus, when prices are inflexible, the economy adjusts to unexpectedly low demand through changes in output and employment rather than through changes in prices (which are not possible when prices are inflexible).

8. Prices are inflexible in the short run for various reasons, two of which are discussed in this chapter. First, firms often attempt to set and maintain stable prices in order to please customers who like predictable prices because they make for easy planning (and who might become upset if prices were volatile). Second, a firm with just a few competitors may be reluctant to cut its price due to the fear of starting a price war, a situation in which its competitors retaliate by cutting their prices as well—thereby leaving the firm worse off than it was to begin with.

Terms and Concepts

the business cycle	modern economic growth	shocks
recession	savings	demand shocks
real GDP (Gross Domestic Product)	investment	supply shocks
nominal GDP	financial investment	inventory
unemployment	economic investment	inflexible prices ("sticky prices")
inflation	expectations	flexible prices

Study Questions

1. Why do you think macroeconomists focus on just a few key statistics when trying to understand the health and trajectory of an economy? Would it be better to try to make use of all possible data? **LO2**

2. **KEY QUESTION** Consider a nation in which the volume of goods and services is growing by 5 percent per year. What is the likely impact of this high rate of growth on the power and influence of its government relative to other countries experiencing slower rates of growth? What about the effect of this 5 percent growth on the nation's living standards? Will these also necessarily grow by 5 percent per year, given population growth? Why or why not? **LO1**

3. A mathematical approximation called *the rule of 70* tells us that the number of years that it will take something that is growing to double in size is approximately equal to the number 70 divided by its percentage rate of growth. Thus, if Mexico's real GDP per person is growing at 7 percent per year, it will take about 10 years (= 70 ÷ 7) to double. Apply the rule of 70 to solve the following problem. Real GDP per person in Mexico in 2005 was about $11,000 per person, while it was about $44,000 per person in the United States. If real GDP per person in Mexico grows at the rate of 5 percent per year, about how long will it take Mexico's real GDP per person to reach the level that the United States was at in 2005? (Hint: How many times would Mexico's 2005 real GDP per person have to double to reach the United States' 2005 real GDP per person?) **LO3**

4. Why is there a trade-off between the amount of consumption that people can enjoy today and the amount of consumption that they can enjoy in the future? Why can't people enjoy more of both? How does saving relate to investment and thus to economic growth? What role do banks and other financial institutions play in aiding the growth process? **LO4**

5. How does investment as defined by economists differ from investment as defined by the general public? What would happen to the amount of investment made today if firms expected the future returns to such investment to be very low? What if firms expected future returns to be very high? **LO4**

6. Why, in general, do shocks force people to make changes? Give at least two examples from your own experience. **LO5**

7. **KEY QUESTION** Catalogue companies are the classic example of perfectly inflexible prices because once they print and ship out their catalogues, they are committed to selling at the prices printed in their catalogues. If a catalogue company finds its inventory of sweaters rising, what does that tell you about the demand for sweaters? Was it unexpectedly high, unexpectedly low, or as expected? If the company *could* change the price of sweaters, would it raise the price, lower the price, or keep the price the same? Given that the company cannot change the price of sweaters, consider the number of sweaters it orders each month from the company that makes its sweaters. If inventories become very high, will the catalogue company increase, decrease, or keep orders the same? Given what the catalogue company does with its orders, what is likely to happen to employment and output at the sweater manufacturer? **LO5**

8. Why are prices sticky? Explain the two reasons given in this chapter and then try to think of two more. **LO5**

9. **LAST WORD** Why do some economists believe that better inventory control software may help to reduce the frequency and severity of recessions? Could differences in technology explain why recessions appear to be more frequent and more severe in poorer countries?

Web-Based Questions

1. **DO ALL POOR COUNTRIES GROW FAST?** The *CIA World Factbook* is published annually and contains economic, political, and social data for nearly every country in the world. To pull up rankings of each country on each data item, go to **https://www.cia.gov/library/publications/the-world-factbook/docs/rankorderguide.html.** Scroll down to the Economy section and click on "GDP-real growth rate." Write down the growth rates of the countries with

the five highest real GDP growth rates and the five lowest real GDP growth rates. Go back to the Economy section and click on "GDP-per capita." (*Per capita* is Latin for *per person*.) Look up GDP per person for each of the countries whose growth rates you have just written down. Can we say that *all* poor countries grow fast? Should we assume that countries with lower levels of GDP per person will *automatically* be able to catch up with living standards in rich countries?

2. **IS REAL GDP PER PERSON A SUFFICIENT MEASURE OF WELL-BEING?** Economists tend to focus on real GDP per person as their primary way of comparing living standards among countries. But they are also aware that real GDP per person does not capture many factors that affect the quality of life. Go to the *CIA World Factbook's* rank-order page at **https://www.cia.gov/library/publications/the-world-factbook/docs/rankorderguide.html.** Under the People

section, click on "Infant mortality rate." Write down the rank and the infant mortality rate for the following four countries: the United States, France, Mexico, and China. Go back to the People section and click on "Life expectancy at birth-total." For each of the four countries, write down its rank and life expectancy at birth. Now compare the data you just wrote down for infant mortality and life expectancy at birth with the GDP per person data shown in Global Perspective 23.1. Does the country with the highest GDP per person have the lowest infant mortality or the highest life expectancy? Can poorer countries do well on these alternative measures of well-being? Could people be misled about differences in living standards if they only compared different countries' levels of GDP per person?

FURTHER TEST YOUR KNOWLEDGE AT
www.mcconnell18e.com

24

Measuring Domestic Output and National Income

"Disposable Income Flat." "Personal Consumption Surges." "Investment Spending Stagnates." "GDP Up 4 Percent." These headlines, typical of those found on Yahoo Finance or in *The Wall Street Journal*, give knowledgeable readers valuable information on the state of the economy. This chapter will help you interpret such headlines and understand the stories reported under them. Specifically, it will help you become familiar with the vocabulary and methods of national income accounting. In addition, the terms and ideas that you encounter in this chapter will provide a needed foundation for the macroeconomic analysis found in subsequent chapters.

Assessing the Economy's Performance

National income accounting measures the economy's overall performance. It does for the economy as a whole what private accounting does for the individual firm or for the individual household.

A business firm measures its flows of income and expenditures regularly—usually every 3 months or once a year. With that information in hand, the firm can gauge its economic health. If things are going well and profits are good, the accounting data can be used to explain that success. Were costs down? Was output up? Have market prices risen? If things are going badly and profits are poor, the firm may be able to identify the reason by studying the record over several accounting periods. All this information helps the firm's managers plot their future strategy.

National income accounting operates in much the same way for the economy as a whole. The Bureau of Economic Analysis (BEA, an agency of the Commerce Department) compiles the National Income and Product Accounts (NIPA) for the U.S. economy. This accounting enables economists and policymakers to:

- Assess the health of the economy by comparing levels of production at regular intervals.
- Track the long-run course of the economy to see whether it has grown, been constant, or declined.
- Formulate policies that will safeguard and improve the economy's health.

Gross Domestic Product

The primary measure of the economy's performance is its annual total output of goods and services or, as it is called, its *aggregate output*. There are several ways to measure aggregate output depending upon how one wishes to define "an economy." For instance, should the value of the cars produced at a Toyota plant in Ohio count as part of the output of the U.S. economy because they are made within the United States or as part of the Japanese economy because Toyota is a Japanese company? As mentioned in Chapter 23, **gross domestic product (GDP)** defines aggregate output as the dollar value of all final goods and services produced within the borders of a given country during a given period of time, typically a year. Under this definition, the value of the cars produced at the Toyota factory in Ohio clearly count as part of U.S. aggregate output rather than Japanese aggregate output because the cars are made within the borders of the United States.

TABLE 24.1 Comparing Heterogeneous Output by Using Money Prices

Year	Annual Output	Market Value
1	3 sofas and 2 computers	3 at $500 + 2 at $2000 = $5500
2	2 sofas and 3 computers	2 at $500 + 3 at $2000 = $7000

A Monetary Measure

If the economy produces three sofas and two computers in year 1 and two sofas and three computers in year 2, in which year is output greater? We can't answer that question until we attach a price tag to each of the two products to indicate how society evaluates their relative worth.

That's what GDP does. It is a *monetary measure*. Without such a measure we would have no way of comparing the relative values of the vast number of goods and services produced in different years. In Table 24.1 the price of sofas is $500 and the price of computers is $2000. GDP would gauge the output of year 2 ($7000) as greater than the output of year 1 ($5500) because society places a higher monetary value on the output of year 2. Society is willing to pay $1500 more for the combination of goods produced in year 2 than for the combination of goods produced in year 1.

Avoiding Multiple Counting

To measure aggregate output accurately, all goods and services produced in a particular year must be counted once and only once. Because most products go through a series of production stages before they reach the market, some of their components are bought and sold many times. To avoid counting those components each time, GDP includes only the market value of *final goods* and ignores *intermediate goods* altogether.

Intermediate goods are goods and services that are purchased for resale or for further processing or manufacturing. **Final goods** are consumption goods, capital goods, and services that are purchased by their final users, rather than for resale or for further processing or manufacturing.

Why is the value of final goods included in GDP but the value of intermediate goods excluded? Because the value of final goods already includes the value of all the intermediate goods that were used in producing them. Including the value of intermediate goods would amount to **multiple counting,** and that would distort the value of GDP.

To see why, suppose that five stages are needed to manufacture a wool suit and get it to the consumer—the final user. Table 24.2 shows that firm A, a sheep ranch, sells $120 worth of wool to firm B, a wool processor. Firm A pays out the $120 in wages, rent, interest, and profit. Firm B processes the wool and sells it to firm C, a suit manufacturer,

TABLE 24.2 **Value Added in a Five-Stage Production Process**

(1) Stage of Production	(2) Sales Value of Materials or Product	(3) Value Added
	$ 0	$120 (= $120 − $ 0)
Firm A, sheep ranch	120	60 (= 180 − 120)
Firm B, wool processor	180	40 (= 220 − 180)
Firm C, suit manufacturer	220	50 (= 270 − 220)
Firm D, clothing wholesaler	270	80 (= 350 − 270)
Firm E, retail clothier	350	
Total sales values	$1140	
Value added (total income)		$350

for $180. What does firm B do with the $180 it receives? It pays $120 to firm A for the wool and uses the remaining $60 to pay wages, rent, interest, and profit for the resources used in processing the wool. Firm C, the manufacturer, sells the suit to firm D, a wholesaler, which sells it to firm E, a retailer. Then at last a consumer, the final user, comes in and buys the suit for $350.

How much of these amounts should we include in GDP to account for the production of the suit? Just $350, the value of the final product. The $350 includes all the intermediate transactions leading up to the product's final sale. Including the sum of all the intermediate sales, $1140, in GDP would amount to multiple counting. The production and sale of the final suit generated just $350 of output, not $1140.

Alternatively, we could avoid multiple counting by measuring and cumulating only the *value added* at each stage. **Value added** is the market value of a firm's output *less* the value of the inputs the firm has bought from others. At each stage, the difference between what a firm pays for inputs and what it receives from selling the product made from those inputs is paid out as wages, rent, interest, and profit. Column 3 of Table 24.2 shows that the value added by firm B is $60, the difference between the $180 value of its output and the $120 it paid for the input from firm A. We find the total value of the suit by adding together all the values added by the five firms. Similarly, by calculating and summing the values added to all the goods and services produced by all firms in the economy, we can find the market value of the economy's total output—its GDP.

GDP Excludes Nonproduction Transactions

Although many monetary transactions in the economy involve final goods and services, many others do not. These nonproduction transactions must be excluded from GDP

because they have nothing to do with the generation of final goods. *Nonproduction transactions* are of two types: purely financial transactions and secondhand sales.

Financial Transactions Purely financial transactions include the following:

- *Public transfer payments* These are the social security payments, welfare payments, and veterans' payments that the government makes directly to households. Since the recipients contribute nothing to *current production* in return, to include such payments in GDP would be to overstate the year's output.
- *Private transfer payments* Such payments include, for example, the money that parents give children or the cash gifts given at Christmas time. They produce no output. They simply transfer funds from one private individual to another and consequently do not enter into GDP.
- *Stock market transactions* The buying and selling of stocks (and bonds) is just a matter of swapping bits of paper. Stock market transactions create nothing in the way of current production and are not included in GDP. Payments for the services provided by a stockbroker *are* included, however, because their services are currently provided and are thus a part of the economy's current output of goods and services.

Secondhand Sales Secondhand sales contribute nothing to current production and for that reason are excluded from GDP. Suppose you sell your 1965 Ford Mustang to a friend; that transaction would be ignored in reckoning this year's GDP because it generates no current production. The same would be true if you sold a brand-new Mustang to a neighbor a week after you purchased it. **(Key Question 3)**

Two Ways of Looking at GDP: Spending and Income

Let's look again at how the market value of total output—or of any single unit of total output—is measured. Given the data listed in Table 24.2, how can we measure the market value of a suit?

One way is to see how much the final user paid for it. That will tell us the market value of the final product. Or we can add up the entire wage, rental, interest, and profit incomes that were created in producing the suit. The second approach is the value-added technique used in Table 24.2.

The final-product approach and the value-added approach are two ways of looking at the same thing. What is spent on making a product is income to those who helped make it. If $350 is spent on manufacturing a suit, then $350 is the total income derived from its production.

We can look at GDP in the same two ways. We can view GDP as the sum of all the money spent in buying it. That is the *output approach*, or **expenditures approach.** Or we can view GDP in terms of the income derived or created from producing it. That is the *earnings* or *allocations approach*, or the **income approach.**

As illustrated in Figure 24.1, we can determine GDP for a particular year either by adding up all that was spent to buy total output or by adding up all the money that was derived as income from its production. Buying (spending money) and selling (receiving income) are two aspects of the same transaction. On the expenditures side of GDP, all final goods produced by the economy are bought either by three domestic sectors (households, businesses, and government) or by foreign buyers. On the income side (once certain statistical adjustments are made), the total receipts acquired from the sale of that total output are allocated to the suppliers of resources as wage, rent, interest, and profit.

The Expenditures Approach

To determine GDP using the expenditures approach, we add up all the spending on final goods and services that has taken place throughout the year. National income accountants use precise terms for the types of spending listed on the left side of Figure 24.1.

Personal Consumption Expenditures (C)

What we have called "consumption expenditures by households," the national income accountants call **personal consumption expenditures.** That term covers all expenditures by households on *durable consumer goods* (automobiles, refrigerators, video recorders), *nondurable consumer goods* (bread, milk, vitamins, pencils, toothpaste), and *consumer expenditures for services* (of lawyers, doctors, mechanics, barbers). The accountants use the symbol C to designate this component of GDP.

Gross Private Domestic Investment (I_g)

Under the heading **gross private domestic investment,** the accountants include the following items:

- All final purchases of machinery, equipment, and tools by business enterprises.
- All construction.
- Changes in inventories.

FIGURE 24.1 The expenditures and income approaches to GDP. There are two general approaches to measuring gross domestic product. We can determine GDP as the value of output by summing all expenditures on that output. Alternatively, with some modifications, we can determine GDP by adding up all the components of income arising from the production of that output.

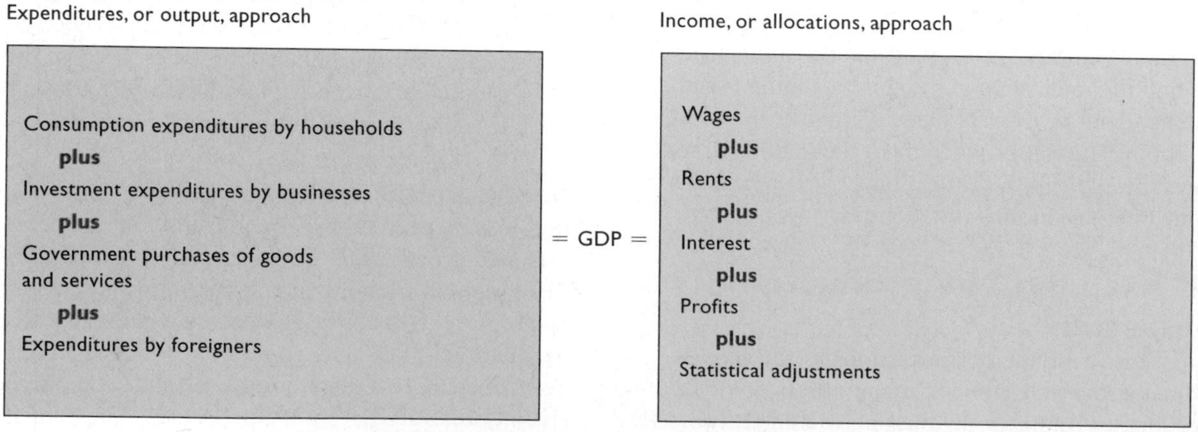

Expenditures, or output, approach

Consumption expenditures by households
plus
Investment expenditures by businesses
plus
Government purchases of goods and services
plus
Expenditures by foreigners

$= GDP =$

Income, or allocations, approach

Wages
plus
Rents
plus
Interest
plus
Profits
plus
Statistical adjustments

Notice that this list, except for the first item, includes more than we have meant by "investment" so far. The second item includes residential construction as well as the construction of new factories, warehouses, and stores. Why do the accountants regard residential construction as investment rather than consumption? Because apartment buildings and houses, like factories and stores, earn income when they are rented or leased. Owner-occupied houses are treated as investment goods because they *could be* rented to bring in an income return. So the national income accountants treat all residential construction as investment. Finally, increases in inventories (unsold goods) are considered to be investment because they represent, in effect, "unconsumed output." For economists, all new output that is not consumed is, by definition, capital. An increase in inventories is an addition (although perhaps temporary) to the stock of capital goods, and such additions are precisely how we define investment.

Positive and Negative Changes in Inventories

We need to look at changes in inventories more closely. Inventories can either increase or decrease over some period. Suppose they increased by $10 billion between December 31, 2006, and December 31, 2007. That means the economy produced $10 billion more output than was purchased in 2007. We need to count all output produced in 2007 as part of that year's GDP, even though some of it remained unsold at the end of the year. This is accomplished by including the $10 billion increase in inventories as investment in 2007. That way the expenditures in 2007 will correctly measure the output produced that year.

Alternatively, suppose that inventories decreased by $10 billion in 2007. This "drawing down of inventories" means that the economy sold $10 billion more of output in 2007 than it produced that year. It did this by selling goods produced in prior years—goods already counted as GDP in those years. Unless corrected, expenditures in 2007 will overstate GDP for 2007. So in 2007 we consider the $10 billion decline in inventories as "negative investment" and subtract it from total investment that year. Thus, expenditures in 2007 will correctly measure the output produced in 2007.

Noninvestment Transactions

So much for what investment *is*. You also need to know what it *isn't*. Investment does *not* include the transfer of paper assets (stocks, bonds) or the resale of tangible assets (houses, jewelry, boats). Such transactions merely transfer the ownership of existing assets. Investment has to do with the creation of *new* capital assets. The mere transfer (sale) of claims to existing capital goods does not create new capital.

Gross Investment versus Net Investment

As we have seen, the category gross private domestic investment includes (1) all final purchases of machinery, equipment, and tools; (2) all construction; and (3) changes in inventories. The words "private" and "domestic" mean that we are speaking of spending by private businesses, not by government (public) agencies, and that the investment is taking place inside the country, not abroad.

The word "gross" means that we are referring to *all* investment goods—both those that replace machinery, equipment, and buildings that were used up (worn out or made obsolete) in producing the current year's output and any net additions to the economy's stock of capital. Gross investment includes investment in replacement capital *and* in added capital.

In contrast, **net private domestic investment** includes *only* investment in the form of added capital. The amount of capital that is used up over the course of a year is called *depreciation*. So

Net investment = gross investment − depreciation

In typical years, gross investment exceeds depreciation. Thus net investment is positive and the nation's stock of capital rises by the amount of net investment. As illustrated in Figure 24.2, the stock of capital at the end of the year exceeds the stock of capital at the beginning of the year by the amount of net investment.

Gross investment need not always exceed depreciation, however. When gross investment and depreciation *are equal*, net investment is zero and there is no change in the size of the capital stock. When gross investment *is less than* depreciation, net investment is negative. The economy then is *disinvesting*—using up more capital than it is producing—and the nation's stock of capital shrinks. That happened in the Great Depression of the 1930s.

National income accountants use the symbol I for private domestic investment spending. To differentiate between gross investment and net investment, they add either the subscript g or the subscript n. But it is gross investment, I_g, that they use when tallying up GDP.

Government Purchases (*G*)

The third category of expenditures in the national income accounts is **government purchases,** officially labeled "government consumption expenditures and gross investment." These expenditures have two components: (1) expenditures for goods and services that government consumes in providing public services and (2) expenditures for *publicly owned capital* such as schools and highways, which have long lifetimes. Government purchases

Net
investment

Gross
investment

Depreciation

Consumption,
government
expenditures,
and net exports

Stock of
capital

January 1

Year's GDP

Stock
of
capital

December 31

FIGURE 24.2 Gross investment, depreciation, net investment, and the stock of capital. When gross investment exceeds depreciation during a year, net investment occurs. This net investment expands the stock of private capital from the beginning of the year to the end of the year by the amount of the net investment. Other things equal, the economy's production capacity expands.

(Federal, state, and local) include all government expenditures on final goods and all direct purchases of resources,

CONSIDER THIS . . .

Stock Answers about Flows

An analogy of a reservoir is helpful in thinking about a nation's capital stock, investment, and depreciation. Picture a reservoir that has water flowing in from a river and flowing out from an outlet after it passes through turbines. The volume of water in the reservoir *at any particular point in time* is a "stock." In contrast, the inflow from the river and outflow from the outlet are "flows."

The volume or stock of water in the reservoir will rise if the weekly inflow exceeds the weekly outflow. It will fall if the inflow is less than the outflow. And it will remain constant if the two flows are equal.

Now let's apply this analogy to the stock of capital, gross investment, and depreciation. The stock of capital is the total capital in place at any point in time and is analogous to the level of water in the reservoir. Changes in this capital stock over some period, for example, 1 year, depend on *gross investment* and *depreciation*. Gross investment (analogous to the reservoir inflow) is an addition of capital goods and therefore adds to the stock of capital, while depreciation (analogous to the reservoir outflow) is the using up of capital and thus subtracts from the capital stock. The capital stock increases when gross investment exceeds depreciation, declines when gross investment is less than depreciation, and remains the same when gross investment and depreciation are equal.

Alternatively, the stock of capital increases when *net investment* (gross investment *minus* depreciation) is positive. When net investment is negative, the stock of capital declines, and when net investment is zero, the stock of capital remains constant.

including labor. It does *not* include government transfer payments because, as we have seen, they merely transfer government receipts to certain households and generate no production of any sort. National income accountants use the symbol *G* to signify government purchases.

Net Exports (X_n)

International trade transactions are a significant item in national income accounting. But when calculating U.S. GDP, we must keep in mind that we want to total up only those expenditures that are used to purchase goods and services produced *within the borders of the United States*. Thus, we must add in the value of exports, *X*, since exports are by definition goods and services produced within the borders of the United States. Don't be confused by the fact that the expenditures made to buy up our exports are made by foreigners. The definition of GDP does not care about *who* is making expenditures on U.S.-made goods and services—only that the goods and services that they buy are made within the borders of the United States. Thus, foreign spending on our exports *must* be included in GDP.

At this point, you might incorrectly think that GDP should be equal to the sum of $C + I_g + G + X$. But this sum overstates GDP. The problem is that, once again, we must consider only expenditures made on *domestically produced* goods and services. As it stands, C, I_g, and G count up expenditures on consumption, investment, and government purchases *regardless* of where those goods and services are made. Crucially, not all of the C, I_g, or G expenditures are for domestically produced goods and services. Some of the expenditures are for imports—goods and services produced outside of the United States. Thus, since we wish to count *only* the part of C, I_g, and G that goes to purchasing domestically produced goods and services, we must subtract off the spending that goes to imports, M. Doing so yields the correct formula for calculating gross domestic product: $GDP = C + I_g + G + X - M$.

TABLE 24.3 Accounting Statement for the U.S. Economy, 2007 (in Billions)

Receipts: Expenditures Approach		Allocations: Income Approach*	
Sum of:		Sum of:	
Personal consumption expenditures (C)	$9734	Compensation of employees	$7874
Gross private domestic investment (I_g)	2125	Rents	65
Government purchases (G)	2690	Interest	603
Net exports (X_n)	−708	Proprietors' income	1043
		Corporate profits	1627
		Taxes on production and imports	1009
		Equals:	
		National income	**$12,221**
		National income	$12,221
		Less: Net foreign factor income	96
		Plus: Statistical discrepancy	29
		Plus: Consumption of fixed capital	1687
Equals:		*Equals:*	
Gross domestic product	**$13,841**	**Gross domestic product**	**$13,841**

*Some of the items in this column combine related categories that appear in the more detailed accounts.

Source: Bureau of Economic Analysis, **www.bea.gov**.

Accountants simplify this formula for GDP by defining **net exports**, X_n, to be equal to exports minus imports:

Net exports (X_n) = exports (X) − imports (M).

Using this definition of net exports, the formula for gross domestic product simplifies to,

$$GDP = C + I_g + G + X_n.$$

Table 24.3 shows that in 2007 Americans spent $708 billion more on imports than foreigners spent on U.S. exports. That is, net exports in 2007 were a *minus* $708 billion.

Putting It All Together: GDP = C + I_g + G + X_n

Taken together, the four categories of expenditures provide a measure of the market value of a given year's total output—its GDP. For the United States in 2007 (Table 24.3),

GDP = $9734 + 2125 + 2690 − 708 = $13,841 billion

Global Perspective 24.1 lists the GDPs of several countries. The values of GDP are converted to dollars using international exchange rates.

The Income Approach

Table 24.3 shows how 2007's expenditures of $13,841 billion were allocated as income to those responsible for producing the output. It would be simple if we could say that the entire amount of expenditures flowed back to them

GLOBAL PERSPECTIVE 24.1

Comparative GDPs in Trillions of Dollars, Selected Nations, 2007

The United States, Japan, and Germany have the world's highest GDPs. The GDP data charted below have been converted to U.S. dollars via international exchange rates.

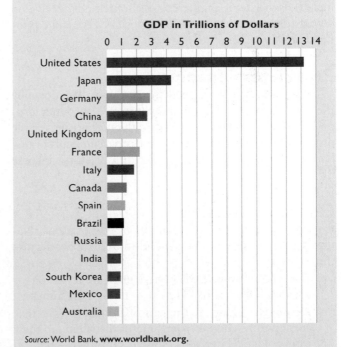

Source: World Bank, **www.worldbank.org**.

in the form of wages, rent, interest, and profit. But some expenditures flow to other recipients (such as the government) or to other uses (such as paying to replace the capital goods that have worn out while producing this year's GDP). These must be accounted for in order to balance the expenditures and income sides of the account. We will begin by looking at the items that make up *national income*.

Compensation of Employees

By far the largest share of national income—$7874 billion—was paid as wages and salaries by business and government to their employees. That figure also includes wage and salary supplements, in particular, payments by employers into social insurance and into a variety of private pension, health, and welfare funds for workers.

Rents

Rents consist of the income received by the households and businesses that supply property resources. They include the monthly payments tenants make to landlords and the lease payments corporations pay for the use of office space. The figure used in the national accounts is *net* rent—gross rental income minus depreciation of the rental property.

Interest

Interest consists of the money paid by private businesses to the suppliers of loans used to purchase capital. It also includes such items as the interest households receive on savings deposits, certificates of deposit (CDs), and corporate bonds.

Proprietors' Income

What we have loosely termed "profits" is broken down by the national income accountants into two accounts: proprietors' income, which consists of the net income of sole proprietorships, partnerships, and other unincorporated businesses; and corporate profits. Proprietors' income flows to the proprietors.

Corporate Profits

Corporate profits are the earnings of corporations. National income accountants subdivide corporate profits into three categories:

- *Corporate income taxes* These taxes are levied on corporations' profits. They flow to the government.
- *Dividends* These are the part of after-tax profits that corporations choose to pay out, or distribute, to their stockholders. They thus flow to households—the ultimate owners of all corporations.

- *Undistributed corporate profits* Any after-tax profits that are not distributed to shareholders are saved, or retained, by corporations to be invested later in new plants and equipment. Undistributed corporate profits are also called *retained earnings*.

Taxes on Production and Imports

The account called **taxes on production and imports** includes general sales taxes, excise taxes, business property taxes, license fees, and customs duties. Why do national income accountants add these indirect business taxes to wages, rent, interest, and profits in determining national income? The answer is, "to account for expenditures that are diverted to the government." Consider an item that would otherwise sell for $1 but costs $1.05 because the government has imposed a 5 percent sales tax. When this item is purchased, consumers will expend $1.05 to buy it. But only $1 will go to the seller (who will then distribute it as income in the form of wages, rent, interest, and profit in order to compensate resource providers). The remaining 5 cents will flow as revenue to the government. The GDP accountants handle the extra 5 cents by placing it into the category called "Taxes on Production and Imports" and loosely consider it to be "income" to government.

From National Income to GDP

We have just shown that expenditures on final goods and services flow either as income to private citizens or as "income" to government. As a result, **national income** is the total of all sources of private income (employee compensation, rents, interest, proprietors' income, and corporate profits) plus government revenue from taxes on production and imports. National income is all the income that flows to American-supplied resources, whether here or abroad, plus taxes on production and imports. But notice that the figure for national income shown in Table 24.3—$12,221 billion—is less than GDP as reckoned by the expenditures approach shown on the left side of the table. The two sides of the accounting statement are brought into balance by adding three items to national income.

Net Foreign Factor Income First, we need to make a slight adjustment in "national" income versus "domestic" income. National income includes the total income of Americans, whether it was earned in the United States or abroad. But GDP is a measure of *domestic* output—total output produced within the United States regardless of the nationality of those who provide the resources. So in moving from national income to GDP, we must consider the income Americans gain from supplying resources abroad and the income that foreigners gain by supplying resources in the United States. In 2007, American-owned resources earned $96 billion more abroad than foreign-owned resources earned in the United States. That difference is called *net foreign factor income*. Because it is earnings of Americans, it is included in U.S. national income. But this income is not part of domestic income because it reflects earnings from output produced in some other nation. Thus, we subtract net foreign factor income from U.S. national income to stay on the correct path to use the income approach to determine the value of U.S. *domestic* output (output produced within the U.S. borders).

Statistical Discrepancy

NIPA accountants add a statistical discrepancy to national income to make the income approach match the outcome of the expenditures approach. In 2007 that discrepancy was $29 billion.

Consumption of Fixed Capital

Finally, we must recognize that the useful lives of private capital equipment (such as bakery ovens or automobile assembly lines) extend far beyond the year in which they were produced. To avoid understating profit and income in the year of purchase and to avoid overstating profit and income in succeeding years, the cost of such capital must be allocated over its lifetime. The amount allocated is an estimate of how much of the capital is being used up each year. It is called *depreciation*. Accounting for depreciation results in a more accurate statement of profit and income for the economy each year. Publicly owned capital, such as court-houses and bridges, also requires a depreciation allowance in the national income accounts.

The huge depreciation charge made against private and publicly owned capital each year is called **consumption of fixed capital** because it is the allowance for capital that has been "consumed" in producing the year's GDP. It is the portion of GDP that is set aside to pay for the ultimate replacement of those capital goods.

The money allocated to consumption of fixed capital (the depreciation allowance) is a cost of production and thus included in the gross value of output. But this money is not available for other purposes, and, unlike other costs of production, it does not add to anyone's income. So it is not included in national income. We must therefore add it to national income to achieve balance with the economy's expenditures, as in Table 24.3.

Table 24.3 summarizes the expenditures approach and income approach to GDP. The left side shows what the U.S. economy produced in 2007 and what was spent to purchase it. The right side shows how those expenditures were allocated either as income to individuals, as revenue to the government, or to other uses such as paying for the replacement of depreciated capital.

> ### QUICK REVIEW 24.1
>
> - Gross domestic product (GDP) is a measure of the total market value of all final goods and services produced by the economy in a given year.
> - The expenditures approach to GDP sums the total spending on final goods and services: $GDP = C + I_g + G + X_n$.
> - The economy's stock of private capital expands when net investment is positive; stays constant when net investment is zero; and declines when net investment is negative.
> - The income approach to GDP sums compensation to employees, rent, interest, proprietors' income, corporate profits, and taxes on production and imports to obtain national income, and then subtracts net foreign factor income and adds a statistical discrepancy and consumption of fixed capital to obtain GDP.

Other National Accounts

Several other national accounts provide additional useful information about the economy's performance. We can derive these accounts by making various adjustments to GDP.

Net Domestic Product

As a measure of total output, GDP does not make allowances for replacing the capital goods used up in each year's production. As a result, it does not tell us how much new output was available for consumption and for additions to the stock of capital. To determine that, we must subtract from GDP the capital that was consumed in producing the GDP and that had to be replaced. That is, we need to subtract consumption of fixed capital (depreciation) from GDP. The result is a measure of **net domestic product (NDP):**

$$NDP = GDP - \text{consumption of fixed capital (depreciation)}$$

For the United States in 2007:

	Billions
Gross domestic product	$13,841
Less: Consumption of fixed capital	1687
Equals: Net domestic product	$12,154

NDP is simply GDP adjusted for depreciation. It measures the total annual output that the entire economy—households, businesses, government, and foreigners—can consume without impairing its capacity to produce in ensuing years.

National Income

Sometimes it is useful to know how much Americans earned for their contributions of land, labor, capital, and entrepreneurial talent. Recall that U.S. national income (NI) includes all income earned through the use of American owned resources, whether they are located at home or abroad. It also includes taxes on production and imports. To derive NI from NDP, we must subtract the aforementioned statistical discrepancy from NDP and add net foreign factor income, since the latter is income earned by Americans overseas minus income earned by foreigners in the United States.

For the United States in 2007:

	Billions
Net domestic product	$12,154
Less: Statistical discrepancy	29
Plus: Net foreign factor income	96
Equals: National income	$12,221

We know, too, that we can calculate national income through the income approach by simply adding up employee compensation, rent, interest, proprietors' income, corporate profit, and taxes on production and imports.

Personal Income

Personal income (PI) includes all income received, whether earned or unearned. It is likely to differ from national income (income earned) because some income earned—taxes on production and imports, Social Security taxes (payroll taxes), corporate income taxes, and undistributed corporate profits—is not received by households. Conversely, some income received—such as Social Security payments, unemployment compensation payments, welfare payments, disability and education payments to veterans, and private pension payments—is not earned. These transfer payments must be added to obtain PI.

In moving from national income to personal income, we must subtract the income that is earned but not received and add the income that is received but not earned. For the United States in 2007:

	Billions
National income	$12,221
Less: Taxes on production and imports	1009
Less: Social Security contributions	979
Less: Corporate income taxes	467
Less: Undistributed corporate profits	344
Plus: Transfer payments	2237*
Equals: Personal income	$11,659

*Includes statistical discrepancy

Disposable Income

Disposable income (DI) is personal income less personal taxes. Personal taxes include personal income taxes, personal property taxes, and inheritance taxes. Disposable income is the amount of income that households have left over after paying their personal taxes. They are free to divide that income between consumption (C) and saving (S):

$$DI = C + S$$

WORKED PROBLEMS
W 24.1
Measuring output and income

For the United States in 2007:

	Billions
Personal income	$11,659
Less: Personal taxes	1482
Equals: Disposable income	$10,177

Table 24.4 summarizes the relationships among GDP, NDP, NI, PI, and DI. **(Key Question 8)**

The Circular Flow Revisited

Figure 24.3 is an elaborate flow diagram that shows the economy's four main sectors along with the flows of

TABLE 24.4 The Relationship between GDP, NDP, NI, PI, and DI in the United States, 2007*

	Billions
Gross domestic product (GDP)	$13,841
Less: Consumption of fixed capital	1687
Equals: Net domestic product	$12,154
Net domestic product (NDP)	$12,154
Less: Statistical discrepancy	29
Plus: Net foreign factor income	96
Equals: National income (NI)	$12,221
National income (NI)	$12,221
Less: Taxes on production and imports	1009
Less: Social Security contributions	979
Less: Corporate income taxes	467
Less: Undistributed corporate profits	344
Plus: Transfer payments	2237
Equals: Personal income (PI)	$11,659
Personal income (PI)	$11,659
Less: Personal taxes	1482
Equals: Disposable income (DI)	$10,177

*Some of the items combine categories that appear in the more detailed accounts.
Source: Bureau of Economic Analysis, **www.bea.gov.**

FIGURE 24.3 U.S. domestic output and the flows of expenditure and income. This figure is an elaborate circular flow diagram that fits the expenditures and allocations sides of GDP to one another. The expenditures flows are shown in orange; the allocations or income flows are shown in green. You should trace through the income and expenditures flows, relating them to the five basic national income accounting measures.

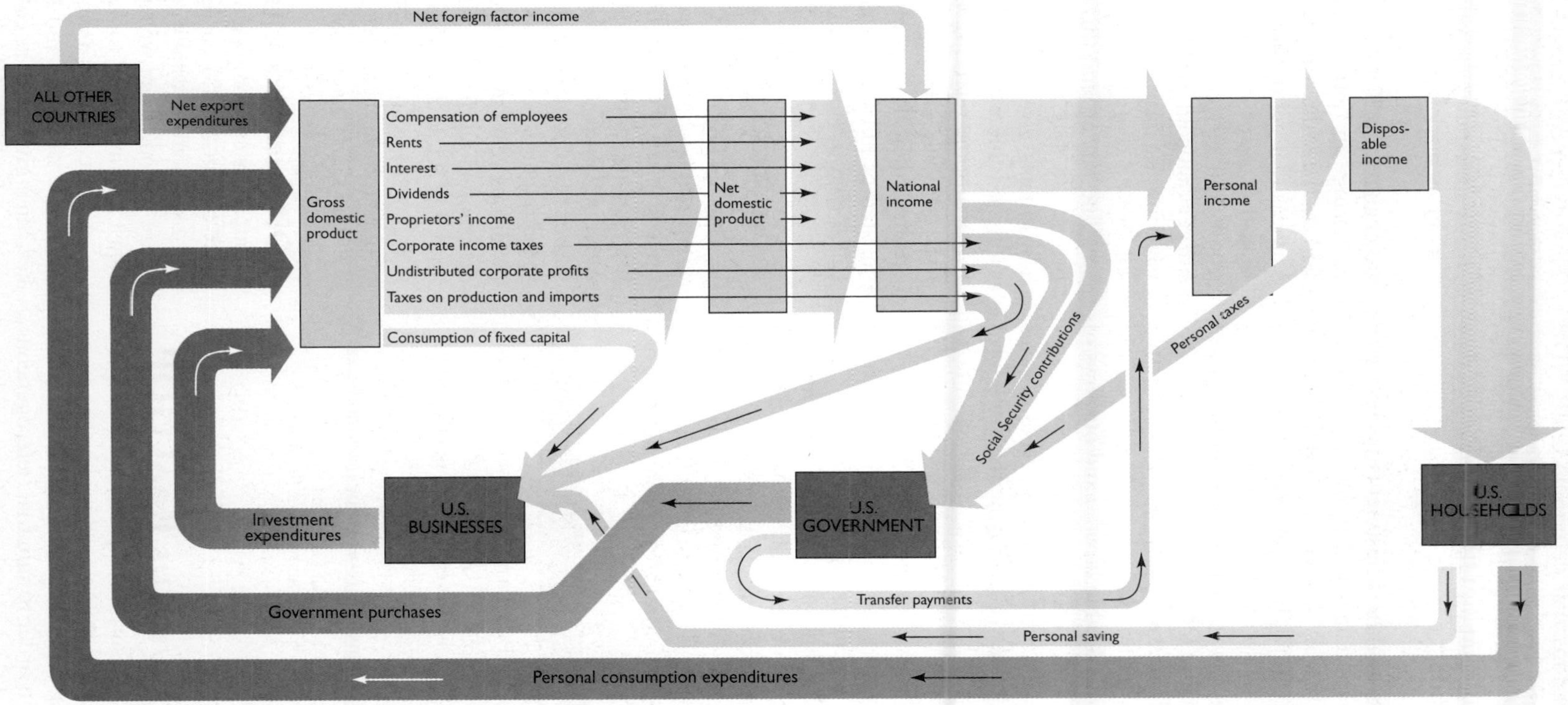

489

expenditures and allocations that determine GDP, NDP, NI, and PI. The orange arrows represent the spending flows—$C + I_g + G + X_n$—that together measure gross domestic product. To the right of the GDP rectangle are green arrows that show first the allocations of GDP and then the adjustments needed to derive NDP, NI, PI, and DI.

The diagram illustrates the adjustments necessary to determine each of the national income accounts. For example, net domestic product is smaller than GDP because consumption of fixed capital flows away from GDP in determining NDP. Also, disposable income is smaller than personal income because personal taxes flow away from PI (to government) in deriving DI.

Note the three domestic sectors of the economy: households, government, and businesses. The household sector has an inflow of disposable income and outflows of consumption spending and saving. The government sector has an inflow of revenue in the form of types of taxes and an outflow of government disbursements in the form of purchases and transfers. The business sector has inflows of three major sources of funds for business investment and an outflow of investment expenditures.

Finally, note the foreign sector (all other countries) in the flow diagram. Spending by foreigners on U.S. exports adds to U.S. GDP, but some of U.S. consumption, government, and investment expenditures buy imported products. The flow from foreign markets shows that we handle this complication by calculating net exports (U.S. exports minus U.S. imports). The net export flow may be a positive or negative amount, adding to or subtracting from U.S. GDP.

QUICK REVIEW 24.2

- Net domestic product (NDP) is the market value of GDP minus consumption of fixed capital (depreciation).
- National income (NI) is all income earned through the use of American-owned resources, whether located at home or abroad. NI also includes taxes on production and imports.
- Personal income (PI) is all income received by households, whether earned or not.
- Disposable income (DI) is all income received by households minus personal taxes.

Nominal GDP versus Real GDP

Recall that GDP is a measure of the market or money value of all final goods and services produced by the economy in a given year. We use money or nominal values as a common denominator in order to sum that heterogeneous output into a meaningful total. But that creates a problem:

How can we compare the market values of GDP from year to year if the value of money itself changes in response to inflation (rising prices) or deflation (falling prices)? After all, we determine the value of GDP by multiplying total output by market prices.

Whether there is a 5 percent increase in output with no change in prices or a 5 percent increase in prices with no change in output, the change in the value of GDP will be the same. And yet it is the *quantity* of goods and services that get produced and distributed to households that affects our standard of living, not the price of those goods and services. For instance, the McDonald's hamburger that sold for 89 cents in 2007 yields the same satisfaction as a nearly identical McDonald's hamburger that sold for 18 cents in 1967.

The way around this problem is to *deflate* GDP when prices rise and to *inflate* GDP when prices fall. These adjustments give us a measure of GDP for various years as if the value of the dollar had always been the same as it was in some reference year. A GDP based on the prices that prevailed when the output was produced is called unadjusted GDP, or **nominal GDP**. A GDP that has been deflated or inflated to reflect changes in the price level is called adjusted GDP, or **real GDP**.

Adjustment Process in a One-Product Economy

There are two ways we can adjust nominal GDP to reflect price changes. For simplicity, let's assume that the economy produces only one good, pizza, in the amounts indicated in Table 24.5 for years 1, 2, and 3. Suppose that we gather revenue data directly from the financial reports of the economy's pizza businesses to measure nominal GDP in various years. After completing our effort, we will have determined nominal GDP for each year, as shown in column 4 of Table 24.5. We will have no way of knowing to what extent changes in price and/or changes in quantity of output have accounted for the increases or decreases in nominal GDP that we observe.

GDP Price Index How can we determine real GDP in our pizza economy? One way is to assemble data on the price changes that occurred over various years (column 2) and use them to establish an overall price index for the entire period. Then we can use the index in each year to adjust nominal GDP to real GDP for that year.

A **price index** is a measure of the price of a specified collection of goods and services, called a "market basket," in a given year as compared to the price of an identical (or highly similar) collection of goods and services

TABLE 24.5 **Calculating Real GDP (Base Year = Year 1)**

Year	(1) Units of Output	(2) Price of Pizza per Unit	(3) Price Index (Year 1 = 100)	(4) Unadjusted, or Nominal, GDP, (1) × (2)	(5) Adjusted, or Real, GDP
1	5	$10	100	$ 50	$50
2	7	20	200	140	70
3	8	25	250	200	80
4	10	30	—	—	—
5	11	28	—	—	—

in a reference year. That point of reference, or benchmark, is known as the base period or base year. More formally,

$$\text{Price index in given year} = \frac{\text{price of market basket in specific year}}{\text{price of same market basket in base year}} \times 100 \quad (1)$$

By convention, the price ratio between a given year and the base year is multiplied by 100 to facilitate computation. For example, a price ratio of 2/1 (= 2) is expressed as a price index of 200. A price ratio of 1/3 (= .33) is expressed as a price index of 33.

In our pizza-only example, of course, our market basket consists of only one product. Column 2 of Table 24.5 reveals that the price of pizza was $10 in year 1, $20 in year 2, $25 in year 3, and so on. Let's select year 1 as our base year. Now we can express the successive prices of the contents of our market basket in, say, years 2 and 3 as compared to the price of the market basket in year 1:

$$\text{Price index, year 2} = \frac{\$20}{\$10} \times 100 = 200$$

$$\text{Price index, year 3} = \frac{\$25}{\$10} \times 100 = 250$$

For year 1 the index has to be 100, since that year and the base year are identical.

The index numbers tell us that the price of pizza rose from year 1 to year 2 by 100 percent {= [(200 − 100)/100] × 100} and from year 1 to year 3 by 150 percent {= [(250 − 100)/100] × 100}.

Dividing Nominal GDP by the Price Index

We can now use the index numbers shown in column 3 to deflate the nominal GDP figures in column 4. The simplest and most direct method of deflating is to express the index numbers as hundredths—in decimal form—and

then to divide them into corresponding nominal GDP. That gives us real GDP:

$$\text{Real GDP} = \frac{\text{nominal GDP}}{\text{price index (in hundredths)}} \quad (2)$$

Column 5 shows the results. These figures for real GDP measure the market value of the output of pizza in years 1, 2, and 3 as if the price of pizza had been a constant $10 throughout the 3-year period. In short, real GDP reveals the market value of each year's output measured in terms of dollars that have the same purchasing power as dollars had in the base year.

To test your understanding, extend Table 24.5 to years 4 and 5, using equations 1 and 2. Then run through the entire deflating procedure, using year 3 as the base period. This time you will have to inflate some of the nominal GDP data, using the same procedure as we used in the examples.

WORKED PROBLEMS

W 24.2

Real GDP and price indexes

ORIGIN OF THE IDEA

O 24.1

GDP price index

An Alternative Method

Another way to establish real GDP is to gather separate data on physical outputs (as in column 1) and their prices (as in column 2) of Table 24.5. We could then determine the market value of outputs in successive years *if the base-year price ($10) had prevailed*. In year 2, the 7 units of pizza would have a value of $70 (= 7 units × $10). As column 5 confirms, that $70 worth of output is year 2's real GDP. Similarly, we could determine the real GDP for year 3 by multiplying the 8 units of output that year by the $10 price in the base year.

Once we have determined real GDP through this method, we can identify the price index for a given year

TABLE 24.6 Steps for Deriving Real GDP from Nominal GDP

Method 1

1. Find nominal GDP for each year.
2. Compute a GDP price index.
3. Divide each year's nominal GDP by that year's price index (in hundredths) to determine real GDP.

Method 2

1. Break down nominal GDP into physical quantities of output and prices for each year.
2. Find real GDP for each year by determining the dollar amount that each year's physical output would have sold for if base-year prices had prevailed. (The GDP price index can then be found by dividing nominal GDP by real GDP.)

TABLE 24.7 Nominal GDP, Real GDP, and GDP Price Index, Selected Years

(1) Year	(2) Nominal GDP, Billions of $	(3) Real GDP, Billions of $	(4) GDP Price Index (2000 = 100)
1980	2789.5	5161.7	____
1985	4220.3	6053.7	69.7
1990	5803.1	____	81.6
2000	9817.0	9817.0	100.0
2003	10,960.8	____	106.4
2007	13,841.3	11,566.8	119.6

Source: Bureau of Economic Analysis, **www.bea.gov.**

simply by dividing the nominal GDP by the real GDP for that year:

$$\frac{\text{Price index}}{\text{(in hundredths)}} = \frac{\text{nominal GDP}}{\text{real GDP}} \quad (3)$$

Example: In year 2 we get a price index of 200—or, in hundredths, 2.00—which equals the nominal GDP of $140 divided by the real GDP of $70. Note that equation 3 is simply a rearrangement of equation 2. Table 24.6 summarizes the two methods of determining real GDP in our single-good economy. **(Key Question 11)**

Real-World Considerations and Data

In the real world of many goods and services, of course, determining GDP and constructing a reliable price index are far more complex matters than in our pizza-only economy. The government accountants must assign a "weight" to each of several categories of goods and services based on the relative proportion of each category in total output. They update the weights annually as expenditure patterns change and roll the base year forward year by year using a moving average of expenditure patterns. The GDP price index used in the United States is called the *chain-type annual-weights price index*—which hints at its complexity. We spare you the details.

Table 24.7 shows some of the real-world relationships between nominal GDP, real GDP, and the GDP price index. Here the reference year is 2000, where the value of the index is set at 100. Because the price level has been rising over the long run, the pre-2000 values of real GDP (column 3) are higher than the nominal values of GDP for those years (column 2). This upward adjustment acknowledges that prices were lower in the years before 2000, and thus nominal GDP understated the real output of those years in 2000 prices and must be inflated to show the correct relationship to other years.

Conversely, the rising price level of the post-2000 years caused nominal GDP figures for those years to overstate real output. So the statisticians deflate those figures to determine what real GDP would have been in other years if 2000 prices had prevailed. Doing so reveals that real GDP has been less than nominal GDP since 2000.

By inflating the nominal pre-2000 GDP data and deflating the post-2000 data, government accountants determine annual real GDP, which can then be compared with the real GDP of any other year in the series of years. So the real GDP values in column 3 are directly comparable with one another.

Once we have determined nominal GDP and real GDP, we can compute the price index. And once we have determined nominal GDP and the price index, we can calculate real GDP. Example: Nominal GDP in 2007 was $13,841.3 billion and real GDP was $11,566.8 billion. So the price level in 2007 was 119.6 (= $13,841.3/11,566.8 × 100), or 19.6 percent higher than in 2000. If we knew the nominal GDP and the price level only, we could find the real GDP for 2007 by dividing the nominal GDP of $13,841.3 by the 2007 price index, expressed in hundredths (1.1966).

To test your understanding of the relationships between nominal GDP, real GDP, and the price level, determine the values of the price index for 1980 in Table 24.7 and determine real GDP for 1990 and 2003. We have left those figures out on purpose. **(Key Question 12)**

QUICK REVIEW 24.3

- Nominal GDP is output valued at current prices. Real GDP is output valued at constant base-year prices.
- The GDP price index compares the price (market value) of all the goods and services included in GDP in a given year to the price of the same market basket in a reference year.
- Nominal GDP can be transformed into real GDP by dividing the nominal GDP by the GDP price index expressed in hundredths.

Shortcomings of GDP

GDP is a reasonably accurate and highly useful measure of how well or how poorly the economy is performing. But it has several shortcomings as a measure of both total output and well-being (total utility).

Nonmarket Activities

Certain productive activities do not take place in any market—the services of homemakers, for example, and the labor of carpenters who repair their own homes. Such activities never show up in GDP because the accountants who tally up GDP only get data on economic transactions involving *market activities*—that is, transactions in which output or resources are traded for money. Consequently, GDP understates a nation's total output because it does not count *unpaid work*. There is one exception: The portion of farmers' output that farmers consume themselves *is* estimated and included in GDP.

Leisure

The average workweek (excluding overtime) in the United States has declined since the beginning of the 1900s—from about 53 hours to about 35 hours. Moreover, the greater frequency of paid vacations, holidays, and leave time has shortened the work year itself. This increase in leisure time has clearly had a positive effect on overall well-being. But our system of national income accounting understates well-being by ignoring leisure's value. Nor does the system accommodate the satisfaction—the "psychic income"—that many people derive from their work.

Improved Product Quality

Because GDP is a quantitative measure rather than a qualitative measure, it fails to capture the full value of improvements in product quality. There is a very real difference in quality between a $200 cell phone purchased today and a cell phone that cost the same amount just a decade ago. Today's cell phone is digital and has greater memory capacity, a viewing screen, and quite likely a camera and an MP3 player.

Obviously quality improvement has a great effect on economic well-being, as does the quantity of goods produced. Although the BEA adjusts GDP for quality improvement for selected items, the vast majority of such improvement for the entire range of goods and services does not get reflected in GDP.

The Underground Economy

Embedded in our economy is a flourishing, productive underground sector. Some of the people who conduct business there are gamblers, smugglers, prostitutes, "fences" of stolen goods, drug growers, and drug dealers. They have good reason to conceal their incomes.

Most participants in the underground economy, however, engage in perfectly legal activities but choose illegally not to report their full incomes to the Internal Revenue Service (IRS). A barista at a coffee shop may report just a portion of the tips received from customers. Storekeepers may report only a portion of their sales receipts. Workers who want to hold on to their unemployment compensation benefits may take an "off-the-books" or "cash-only" job. A brick mason may agree to rebuild a neighbor's fireplace in exchange for the neighbor's repairing his boat engine. The value of none of these transactions shows up in GDP.

The value of underground transactions is estimated to be about 8 percent of the recorded GDP in the United States. That would mean that GDP in 2007 was understated by about $1.1 trillion. Global Perspective 24.2 shows estimates of the relative sizes of underground economies in selected nations.

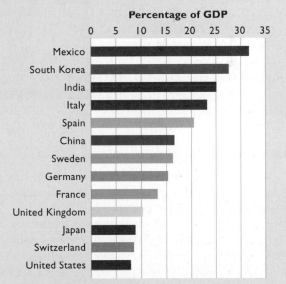

GLOBAL PERSPECTIVE 24.2

The Underground Economy as a Percentage of GDP, Selected Nations

Underground economies vary in size worldwide. Three factors that help explain the variation are (1) the extent and complexity of regulation, (2) the type and degree of taxation, and (3) the effectiveness of law enforcement.

Percentage of GDP

Mexico
South Korea
India
Italy
Spain
China
Sweden
Germany
France
United Kingdom
Japan
Switzerland
United States

Source: Friedrich Schneider and Dominik H. Enste, "Shadow Economies: Size, Causes, and Consequences," Journal of Economic Literature, March 2000, p. 104. Used by permission of Prof. Dr. Friedrich Schneider, Department of Economics, University of Linz and Dr. Dominik H. Enste.

The Bureau of Economic Analysis (BEA), an Agency of the Department of Commerce, Compiles the NIPA Tables. Where Does It Get the Actual Data?

Discussions of national income accounting often leave the impression that the data for the National Income and Product Accounts magically appear from some mysterious place. Let's take a tour to see where economists get their data.

Consumption The BEA derives the data for the consumption component of the GDP accounts from four main sources:

- The Census Bureau's *Retail Trade Survey,* which gains sales information from a sample of 22,000 firms.
- The Census Bureau's *Survey of Manufacturers,* which gathers information on shipments of consumer goods from 50,000 establishments.
- The Census Bureau's *Service Survey,* which collects sales data from 30,000 service businesses.
- Industry trade sources. For example, data on auto sales and aircraft are collected directly from auto and aircraft manufacturers.

Investment The sources of the data for the investment component of GDP include:

- All the sources above used to determine consumption. Purchases of capital goods are separated from purchases of consumer goods. For example, estimates of investment in equipment and software are based on manufacturers' shipments reported in the *Survey of Manufacturers,* the *Service Survey,* and industry sources.
- Census construction surveys. The Census Bureau's *Housing Starts Survey* and *Housing Sales Survey* produce the data used to measure the amount of housing construction, and

the *Construction Progress Reporting Survey* is the source of data on nonresidential construction. The BEA determines changes in business inventories through the *Retail Trade Survey,* the *Wholesale Trade Survey* (of 7100 wholesale firms), and the *Survey of Manufacturing.*

Government Purchases The data for government purchases (officially "government consumption and investment expenditures") are obtained through the following sources:

- The U.S. Office of Personnel Management, which collects data on wages and benefits, broken out by the private and public sector. Wages and benefits of government employees are the single largest "purchase" by Federal, state, and local government.
- The previously mentioned Census Bureau's construction surveys, which break out private and public sector construction expenditures.
- The Census Bureau's *Survey of Government Finance,* which provides data on government consumption and investment expenditures.

Net Exports The BEA determines net exports through two main sources:

- The U.S. Customs Service, which collects data on exports and imports of goods.
- BEA surveys of potential domestic exporters and importers of services, which collect data on exports and imports of services.

So there you have it. Not so magical after all!

Source: Based on Joseph A. Ritter, "Feeding the National Accounts," Federal Reserve Bank of St. Louis *Review,* March–April 2000, pp. 11–20. For those interested, this article also provides information on the sources of data for the income side of the national accounts.

GDP and the Environment

The growth of GDP is inevitably accompanied by "gross domestic by-products," including dirty air and polluted water, toxic waste, congestion, and noise. The social costs of the negative by-products reduce our economic well-being. And since those costs are not deducted from total output, GDP overstates our national well-being. Ironically, when money is spent to clean up pollution and reduce congestion, those expenses are added to the GDP!

Composition and Distribution of Output

The composition of output is undoubtedly important for well-being. But GDP does not tell us whether the currently produced mix of goods and services is enriching or potentially detrimental to society. GDP assigns equal weight to an assault rifle and a set of encyclopedias, as long as both sell for the same price. Moreover, GDP reveals nothing about the way output is distributed. Does 90 percent of the output go to 10 percent of the households, for example, or is the output more evenly distributed? The distribution of output may make a big difference for society's overall well-being.

Noneconomic Sources of Well-Being

Finally, the connection between GDP and well-being is problematic for another reason. Just as a household's income does not measure its total happiness, a nation's GDP does not measure its total well-being. Many things could make a society better off without necessarily raising GDP: a reduction of crime and violence, peaceful relations with other countries, people's greater civility toward one another, better understanding between parents and children, and a reduction of drug and alcohol abuse.

Summary

1. Gross domestic product (GDP), a basic measure of an economy's economic performance, is the market value of all final goods and services produced within the borders of a nation in a year.

2. Intermediate goods, nonproduction transactions, and secondhand sales are purposely excluded in calculating GDP.

3. GDP may be calculated by summing total expenditures on all final output or by summing the income derived from the production of that output.

4. By the expenditures approach, GDP is determined by adding consumer purchases of goods and services, gross investment spending by businesses, government purchases, and net exports: $GDP = C + I_g + G + X_n$.

5. Gross investment is divided into (a) replacement investment (required to maintain the nation's stock of capital at its existing level) and (b) net investment (the net increase in the stock of capital). In most years, net investment is positive and therefore the economy's stock of capital and production capacity increase.

6. By the income or allocations approach, GDP is calculated as the sum of compensation to employees, rents, interest, proprietors' income, corporate profits, taxes on production and imports *minus* net foreign factor income, *plus* a statistical discrepancy and consumption of fixed capital.

7. Other national accounts are derived from GDP. Net domestic product (NDP) is GDP less the consumption of fixed capital. National income (NI) is total income earned by a nation's resource suppliers plus taxes on production and imports; it is found by subtracting a statistical discrepancy from NDP and adding net foreign factor income to NDP. Personal income (PI) is the total income paid to households prior to any allowance for personal taxes. Disposable income (DI) is personal income after personal taxes have been paid. DI measures the amount of income available to households to consume or save.

8. Price indexes are computed by dividing the price of a specific collection or market basket of output in a particular period by the price of the same market basket in a base period and multiplying the result (the quotient) by 100. The GDP price index is used to adjust nominal GDP for inflation or deflation and thereby obtain real GDP.

9. Nominal (current-dollar) GDP measures each year's output valued in terms of the prices prevailing in that year. Real (constant-dollar) GDP measures each year's output in terms of the prices that prevailed in a selected base year. Because real GDP is adjusted for price-level changes, differences in real GDP are due only to differences in production activity.

10. GDP is a reasonably accurate and very useful indicator of a nation's economic performance, but it has its limitations. It fails to account for nonmarket and illegal transactions, changes in leisure and in product quality, the composition and distribution of output, and the environmental effects of production. GDP should not be interpreted as a complete measure of well-being.

Terms and Concepts

national income accounting

gross domestic product (GDP)

intermediate goods

final goods

multiple counting

value added

expenditures approach

income approach

personal consumption expenditures (C)

gross private domestic investment (I_g)

net private domestic investment

government purchases (G)

net exports (X_n)

taxes on production and imports

national income

consumption of fixed capital

net domestic product (NDP)

personal income (PI)

disposable income (DI)

nominal GDP

real GDP

price index

Study Questions  | ECONOMICS

1. In what ways are national income statistics useful? **LO1**

2. Explain why an economy's output, in essence, is also its income. **LO2**

3. **KEY QUESTION** Why do economists include only final goods and services in measuring GDP for a particular year? Why don't they include the value of the stocks and bonds bought and sold? Why don't they include the value of the used furniture bought and sold? **LO1**

4. What is the difference between gross private domestic investment and net private domestic investment? If you were to determine net domestic product (NDP) through the expenditures approach, which of these two measures of investment spending would be appropriate? Explain. **LO2**

5. Why are changes in inventories included as part of investment spending? Suppose inventories declined by $1 billion during 2008. How would this affect the size of gross private domestic investment and gross domestic product in 2008? Explain. **LO1**

6. Use the concepts of gross investment and net investment to distinguish between an economy that has a rising stock of capital and one that has a falling stock of capital. "In 1933 net private domestic investment was minus $6 billion. This means that in that particular year the economy produced no capital goods at all." Do you agree? Why or why not? Explain: "Though net investment can be positive, negative, or zero, it is quite impossible for gross investment to be less than zero." **LO2**

7. Define net exports. Explain how U.S. exports and imports each affect domestic production. Suppose foreigners spend $7 billion on U.S. exports in a specific year and Americans spend $5 billion on imports from abroad in the same year. What is the amount of the United States' net exports? Explain how net exports might be a negative amount. **LO2**

8. **KEY QUESTION** To the right is a list of domestic output and national income figures for a certain year. All figures are in billions. The questions that follow ask you to determine the major national income measures by both the expenditures and the income approaches. The results you obtain with the different methods should be the same. **LO2**

Personal consumption expenditures	$245
Net foreign factor income	4
Transfer payments	12
Rents	14
Statistical discrepancy	8
Consumption of fixed capital (depreciation)	27
Social Security contributions	20
Interest	13
Proprietors' income	33
Net exports	11
Dividends	16
Compensation of employees	223
Taxes on production and imports	18
Undistributed corporate profits	21
Personal taxes	26
Corporate income taxes	19
Corporate profits	56
Government purchases	72
Net private domestic investment	33
Personal saving	20

a. Using the above data, determine GDP by both the expenditures and the income approaches. Then determine NDP.

b. Now determine NI in two ways: first, by making the required additions or subtractions from NDP; and second, by adding up the types of income and taxes that make up NI.

c. Adjust NI (from part *b*) as required to obtain PI.

d. Adjust PI (from part *c*) as required to obtain DI.

9. Using the following national income accounting data, compute (*a*) GDP, (*b*) NDP, and (*c*) NI. All figures are in billions. **LO2**

Compensation of employees	$194.2
U.S. exports of goods and services	17.8
Consumption of fixed capital	11.8
Government purchases	59.4
Taxes on production and imports	14.4
Net private domestic investment	52.1
Transfer payments	13.9
U.S. imports of goods and services	16.5
Personal taxes	40.5
Net foreign factor income	2.2
Personal consumption expenditures	219.1
Statistical discrepancy	0

10. Why do national income accountants compare the market value of the total outputs in various years rather than actual physical volumes of production? What problem is posed by any comparison over time of the market values of various total outputs? How is this problem resolved? **LO4**

11. **KEY QUESTION** Suppose that in 1984 the total output in a single-good economy was 7000 buckets of chicken. Also suppose that in 1984 each bucket of chicken was priced at $10. Finally, assume that in 2000 the price per bucket of chicken was $16 and that 22,000 buckets were produced. Determine the GDP price index for 1984, using 2000 as the base year. By what percentage did the price level, as measured by this index, rise between 1984 and 2000? Use the two methods listed in Table 24.6 to determine real GDP for 1984 and 2000. **LO3**

12. **KEY QUESTION** The following table shows nominal GDP and an appropriate price index for a group of selected years. Compute real GDP. Indicate in each calculation whether you are inflating or deflating the nominal GDP data. **LO3**

Year	Nominal GDP, Billions	Price Index (2000 = 100)	Real GDP, Billions
1964	$ 663.6	22.13	$____
1974	1500.0	34.73	$____
1984	3933.2	67.66	$____
1994	7072.2	90.26	$____
2004	11,685.9	109.46	$____

13. Which of the following are included in this year's GDP? Explain your answer in each case. **LO5**
   a. Interest on an AT&T corporate bond.
   b. Social Security payments received by a retired factory worker.
   c. The unpaid services of a family member in painting the family home.
   d. The income of a dentist.
   e. The money received by Smith when she sells her economics textbook to a book buyer.
   f. The monthly allowance a college student receives from home.
   g. Rent received on a two-bedroom apartment.
   h. The money received by Josh when he resells his current-year-model Honda automobile to Kim.
   i. The publication of a college textbook.
   j. A 2-hour decrease in the length of the workweek.
   k. The purchase of an AT&T corporate bond.
   l. A $2 billion increase in business inventories.
   m. The purchase of 100 shares of GM common stock.
   n. The purchase of an insurance policy.

14. **LAST WORD** What government agency compiles the U.S. NIPA tables? In what U.S. department is it located? Of the several specific sources of information, name one source for each of the four components of GDP: consumption, investment, government purchases, and net exports.

Web-Based Questions

1. **UPDATE THE KEY NATIONAL INCOME AND PRODUCT ACCOUNT NUMBERS** Go to the Bureau of Economic Analysis Web site, **www.bea.gov,** and access the BEA interactively by selecting National Accounts and then National Income and Product Account Tables. Select Frequently Requested NIPA Tables, and find Table 1.1.5 on GDP. Update the data in the left column of the text's Table 24.3, using the latest available quarterly data. Search the full list of NIPA tables to find the latest reported data for national income (NI), personal income (PI), and disposable income (DI). Update the data in the text's Table 24.4 for these three items. By what percentages are GDP, NI, PI, and DI higher (or lower) than the numbers in the table?

2. **NOMINAL GDP AND REAL GDP—BOTH UP?** Visit the Bureau of Economic Analysis Web site, **www.bea.gov**, and access the BEA interactively by selecting National Accounts and then National Income and Product Account Tables. Select Frequently Requested NIPA Tables, and use Tables 1.1.5 and 1.1.6 to identify the GDP (nominal GDP) and real GDP for the past four quarters. Why was nominal GDP greater than real GDP in each of those quarters? What were the percentage changes in nominal GDP and real GDP for the most recent quarter? What accounts for the difference?

FURTHER TEST YOUR KNOWLEDGE AT
www.mcconnell18e.com

Economic Growth

People living in rich countries tend to take economic growth and rising standards of living for granted. Recessions—periods during which output declines—are normally infrequent and temporary, usually lasting less than a year. Once they pass, modern capitalistic economies return to growing, and living standards continue their seemingly inexorable rise.

But a look back at history or a look around the world today quickly dispels any confidence that economic growth and rising standards of living are automatic or routine. Historically, continually rising living standards are a recent phenomenon, seen only during the last century or two. Before that time, living standards barely rose—if at all—from one generation to the next. And a look around the world today reveals huge differences in standards of living resulting from the disturbing fact that, although some countries have enjoyed decades or even centuries of steadily rising per capita income levels, other countries have experienced hardly any economic growth at all.

This chapter investigates the causes of economic growth, what government policies appear to promote economic growth, and the controversies surrounding the benefits and costs of economic growth. As you will see, economic growth has been perhaps the most revolutionary and powerful force in history. Consequently, no study of economics is complete without a thorough understanding of the causes and consequences of economic growth.

Economic Growth

Economists define and measure **economic growth** as either:

- An increase in real GDP occurring over some time period.
- An increase in real GDP per capita occurring over some time period.

With either definition, economic growth is calculated as a percentage rate of growth per quarter (3-month period) or per year. For the first definition, for example, real GDP in the United States was $11,319.4 billion in 2006 and $11,566.8 billion in 2007. So the rate of economic growth in the United States for 2007 was 2.2 percent {= [($11,566.8 billion − $11,319.4 billion)/$11,319.4 billion] × 100}.

The second definition takes into consideration the size of the population. **Real GDP per capita** (or per capita output) is found by dividing real GDP by the size of the population. The resulting number is then compared in percentage terms with that of the previous period. For example, in the United States real GDP was $11,319.4 billion in 2006 and population was 299.8 million. So that year real U.S. GDP per capita was $37,757. In 2007, real per capita GDP rose to $38,301. So the rate of growth of GDP per capita for 2007 was 1.4 percent {= [($38,301 − $37,757)/$37,757] × 100}.

For measuring expansion of military potential or political preeminence, the growth of real GDP is more useful. Unless specified otherwise, growth rates reported in the news and by international agencies use this definition of economic growth. For comparing living standards, however, the second definition is superior. While China's GDP in 2006 was $2644 billion compared with Denmark's $275 billion, Denmark's real GDP per capita was $52,110 compared with China's meager $2000. And in some cases growth of real GDP can be misleading. Madagascar's real GDP grew at a rate of 1.7 percent per year from 1990–2004. But over the same period its annual population growth was 2.9 percent, resulting in a decline in real GDP per capita of roughly 1.2 percent per year. (**Key Question 2**)

Growth as a Goal

Growth is a widely held economic goal. The expansion of total output relative to population results in rising real wages and incomes and thus higher standards of living. An economy that is experiencing economic growth is better able to meet people's wants and resolve socioeconomic problems. Rising real wages and income provide richer opportunities to individuals and families—a vacation trip, a personal computer, a higher education—without sacrificing other opportunities and pleasures. A growing economy can undertake new programs to alleviate poverty, embrace diversity, cultivate the arts, and protect the environment without impairing existing levels of consumption, investment, and public goods production.

In short, *growth lessens the burden of scarcity*. A growing economy, unlike a static economy, can consume more today while increasing its capacity to produce more in the future. By easing the burden of scarcity—by relaxing society's constraints on production—economic growth enables a nation to attain its economic goals more readily and to undertake new endeavors that require the use of goods and services to be accomplished.

Arithmetic of Growth

Why do economists pay so much attention to small changes in the rate of economic growth? Because those changes really matter! For the United States, with a current GDP of about $13.8 trillion, the difference between a 3 percent and a 4 percent rate of growth is about $138 billion of output each year. For a poor country, a difference of one-half of a percentage point in the rate of growth may mean the difference between starvation and mere hunger.

The mathematical approximation called the **rule of 70** provides a quantitative grasp of the effect of economic growth. The rule of 70 tells us that we can find the number of years it will take for some measure to double, given its annual percentage increase, by dividing that percentage increase into the number 70. So

$$\begin{array}{c}\text{Approximate} \\ \text{number of years} \\ \text{required to double} \\ \text{real GDP}\end{array} = \frac{70}{\begin{array}{c}\text{annual percentage rate} \\ \text{of growth}\end{array}}$$

Examples: A 3 percent annual rate of growth will double real GDP in about 23 (= 70 ÷ 3) years. Growth of 8 percent per year will double real GDP in about 9 (= 70 ÷ 8) years. The rule of 70 is applicable generally. For example, it works for estimating how long it will take the price level or a savings account to double at various per-centage rates of infla-tion or interest. When compounded over many years, an apparently small difference in the rate of growth thus becomes highly significant. Suppose China and Italy start with identical GDPs, but then China grows at an 8 percent yearly rate, while Italy grows at 2 percent. China's GDP would double in about 9 years, while Italy's GDP would double in 35 years.

WORKED PROBLEMS

W 25.1

GDP growth

TABLE 25.1 Real GDP and per Capita Real GDP, Selected Years, 1950–2007

(1) Year	(2) Real GDP, Billions of 2000 $	(3) Population, Millions	(4) Real Per Capita GDP, 2000 $ (2) ÷ (3)
1950	$ 1773.3	152	$11,666
1960	2501.8	181	13,822
1970	3771.9	205	18,400
1980	5161.7	228	22,639
1990	7112.7	250	28,451
2000	9817.0	267	36,768
2007	11,566.8	303	38,174

Source: Data are from the Bureau of Economic Analysis, **www.bea.gov,** and the U.S. Census Bureau, **www.census.gov.**

Growth in the United States

Table 25.1 gives an overview of economic growth in the United States since 1950. Column 2 reveals strong growth as measured by increases in real GDP. Note that between 1950 and 2007 real GDP increased about sixfold. But the U.S. population also increased. Nevertheless, in column 4 we find that real GDP per capita rose more than threefold over these years.

What has been the *rate* of U.S. growth? Real GDP grew at an annual rate of about 3.5 percent between 1950 and 2007. Real GDP per capita increased 2.3 percent per year over that time. But we must qualify these raw numbers in several ways:

- *Improved products and services* Since the numbers in Table 25.1 do not fully account for the improve-ments in products and services, they understate the growth of economic well-being. Such purely quanti-tative data do not fully compare an era of vacuum tube computers and low-efficiency V8 hot rods with an era of digital cell phone networks and fuel-sipping, hybrid-drive vehicles.

- *Added leisure* The increases in real GDP and per capita GDP identified in Table 25.1 were accom-plished despite increases in leisure. The standard workweek, once 50 hours, is now about 35 hours (excluding overtime hours). Again the raw growth numbers understate the gain in economic well-being.

- *Other impacts* These measures of growth do not account for any effects growth may have had on the environment and the quality of life. If growth debases the physical environment and creates a stressful work environment, the bare growth

numbers will overstate the gains in well-being that result from growth. On the other hand, if growth leads to stronger environmental protections or a more secure and stress-free lifestyle, these numbers will understate the gains in well-being.

Two other points should be made about U.S. growth rates. First, they are not constant or smooth over time. Like those of other countries, U.S. growth rates vary quar-terly and annually depending on a variety of factors such as the introduction of major new inventions and the econ-omy's current position in the business cycle. Second, many countries share the U.S. experience of positive and ongo-ing economic growth. But, as previously noted, sustained growth is both a historically new occurrence and also one that is not shared equally by all countries.

QUICK REVIEW 25.1

- Economists measure economic growth as either (a) an increase in real GDP over time or (b) an increase in real GDP per capita over time.

- Real GDP in the United States has grown at an average annual rate of about 3.5 percent since 1950; real GDP per capita has grown at roughly a 2.3 percent annual rate over that same period.

Modern Economic Growth

We now live in an era of wireless high-speed Internet con-nections, genetic engineering, and space exploration. New inventions and new technologies drive continual econom-ic growth and ongoing increases in living standards. But it wasn't always like this. Economic growth and sustained increases in living standards are a historically recent phenomenon that started with the Industrial Revolution of the late 1700s. Before the Industrial Revolution, living standards were basically flat over long periods of time so that, for instance, Greek peasants living in the year 300 B.C. had about the same material standard of living as Greek peasants living in the year A.D. 1500. By contrast, our current era of **modern economic growth** is characterized by sustained and ongoing increases in living standards that can cause dramatic increases in the standard of living within less than a single human lifetime.

Economic historians informally date the start of the Industrial Revolution to the year 1776, when the Scottish inventor James Watt perfected a powerful and efficient steam engine. This steam engine inaugurated the modern era since the device could be used to drive industrial factory equipment, steamships, and steam locomotives.

The new industrial factories mass-produced goods for the first time. This meant that nearly all manufacturing shifted from items produced by hand by local craftsmen to items mass-produced in distant factories. The new steamships and steam locomotives meant that resources could easily flow to factories and that the products of factories could be shipped to distant consumers at low cost. The result was a huge increase in long-distance trade and a major population shift as people left farms to go work in the towns and cities where the new industrial factories were concentrated.

Steam power would later be largely replaced by electric power and many more inventions would follow the steam engine that started the Industrial Revolution. But the key point is that the last 200 or so years of history have been fundamentally different from anything that went before.

The biggest change has been change itself. Whereas in earlier times material standards of living and the goods and services that people produced and consumed changed very little even over the course of an entire human lifespan, nowadays people living in countries experiencing modern economic growth are constantly exposed to new technologies, new products, and new services.

What is more, modern economic growth has vastly affected cultural, social, and political arrangements.

- Culturally, the vast increases in wealth and living standards have allowed ordinary people for the first time in history to have significant time for leisure activities and the arts.
- Socially, countries experiencing modern economic growth have abolished feudalism, instituted universal public education, and largely eliminated ancient social norms and legal restrictions against women and minorities doing certain jobs or holding certain positions.

- Politically, countries experiencing modern economic growth have tended to move toward democracy, a form of government that was extremely rare before the start of the Industrial Revolution.

In addition, the average human lifespan has more than doubled, from an average of less than 30 years before modern economic growth began in the late 1700s to a worldwide average of over 67 years today. Thus, for the first time in world history, the average person can expect to live into old age. These and other changes speak to the truly revolutionary power of economic growth and naturally lead economists to consider the causes of economic growth and what policies could be pursued to sustain and promote it. Their desire is intensified by the reality that economic growth is distributed so unevenly around the world.

The Uneven Distribution of Growth

Modern economic growth has spread only slowly from its British birthplace. It first advanced to France, Germany, and other parts of western Europe in the early 1800s before spreading to the United States, Canada, and Australia by the mid 1800s. Japan began to industrialize in the 1870s, but the rest of Asia did not follow until the early to mid 1900s, at which time large parts of Central and South America as well as the Middle East also began to experience modern economic growth. Most recent has been Africa, which for the most part did not experience modern economic growth until the last few decades. Notably, some parts of the world have yet to experience modern economic growth at all.

The different starting dates for modern economic growth in various parts of the world are the main cause of the vast differences in per capita GDP levels seen today. The current huge gaps between rich countries like the United States and Japan and poor countries like North Korea and Burundi were shown previously in Global Perspective 23.1. But the huge divergence in living standards caused by the fact that different countries started modern economic growth at different times is best seen in Figure 25.1, which shows how GDP per capita has evolved since 1820 in the United States, western Europe, Latin America, Asia, and Africa.

To make the comparison of living standards easier, income levels in all places and at all times have been converted into 1990 U.S. dollars. Using this convention, it is clear that in 1820 per capita incomes in all areas were quite similar, with the richest area in the world in 1820, western Europe, having an average per capita income of $1232, while the poorest area of the world at that time, Africa, had an average per capita income of $418. Thus, in 1820, average incomes in the richest area were only about three times larger than those in the poorest area.

FIGURE 25.1 The great divergence. Income levels around the world were very similar in 1820. But they are now very different because certain areas, including the United States and western Europe, began experiencing modern economic growth much earlier than other areas.

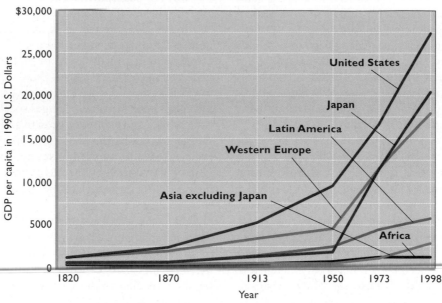

Source: Angus Maddison, *The World Economy: A Millenial Perspective*, (Paris: OECD, 2001), p. 264.

But because western Europe and the United States started experiencing modern economic growth earlier than other areas, they have now ended up vastly richer than other areas, despite the fact that per capita incomes in nearly all places have increased at least a bit. For instance, per capita GDP in the United States in 1998 was $27,331 while it was only $1368 in Africa. Thus, because modern economic growth has occurred for nearly two centuries in the United States compared to a few decades in Africa, average living standards in the United States in 1998 were nearly 20 times higher than those in Africa.

Catching Up Is Possible

Do not get the wrong impression looking at Figure 25.1. Countries that began modern economic growth more recently are *not* doomed to be permanently poorer than the countries that began modern economic growth at an earlier date. This is true because people can adopt technology more quickly than they can invent it. Broadly speaking, the richest countries today have achieved that status because they have the most advanced technology. But because they already have the most advanced technology, they must invent new technology to get even richer. Because inventing and implementing new technology is slow and costly, real GDP per capita in the richest **leader countries** typically grows by an average annual rate of just 2 or 3 percent per year.

By contrast, poorer **follower countries** can grow much faster because they can simply adopt existing technologies from rich leader countries. For instance, in many places in Africa today, the first telephones most people have ever been able to use are cell phones. That is, these countries have not even bothered to install the copper wires necessary for land-line telephones, which are basically a nineteenth-century technology. Instead, they have gone directly for Internet-capable mobile phone networks, a twenty-first-century technology. By doing so, they skip past many stages of technology and development that the United States and other currently rich countries had to pass through. In effect, they jump directly to the most modern, most highly productive technology. The result is that, under the right circumstances, it is possible for poorer countries to experience extremely rapid increases in living standards. This can continue until they have caught up with the leader countries and become leader countries themselves. Once that happens, their growth rates typically fall down to the 2 or 3 percent rate typical of leader countries. This happens because once they are also rich and using the latest technology, their growth rates are limited by the rate at which new technology can be invented and applied.

Table 25.2 shows both how the growth rates of leader countries are constrained by the rate of technological progress as well as how certain follower countries have been able to catch up by adopting more advanced technologies

TABLE 25.2 Real GDP per Capita in 1960 and 2004 Plus Average Annual Growth Rates of GDP per Capita from 1960–2004 for Eight Selected Countries. (Figures are in 1996 dollars.)

Country	Real GDP per Capita, 1960	Real GDP per Capita, 2004	Average Annual Growth Rate, 1960–2004
United States	$12,892	$36,098	2.3
United Kingdom	10,323	26,762	2.2
France	8,531	26,168	2.5
Ireland	5,294	28,957	3.9
Japan	4,509	24,661	3.9
Singapore	4,219	29,404	4.4
Hong Kong	3,322	29,642	5.0
South Korea	1,458	18,424	5.8

Note: GDP figures for all countries are measured in "international dollars" of equal value to U.S. dollars in 1996.

Source: Penn World Table version 6.2, **pwt.econ.upenn.edu.** Used by permission.

and growing rapidly. Table 25.2 shows real GDP per capita in 1960 and 2004 as well as the average annual growth rate of real GDP per capita between 1960 and 2004 for three countries—the United States, the United Kingdom, and France—that were already rich leader countries in 1960 as well as for five other nations that were relatively poor follower countries at that time. To make comparisons easy, the GDPs and GDPs per capita for all countries are expressed in terms of 1996 U.S. dollars. The countries are ordered by their respective GDPs per capita in 1960, so that the richest country in the world at the time, the United States, is listed first while the poorest of the eight selected countries at the time, South Korea, is listed last.

First, notice that the average annual growth rates of the three leader countries—the United States, the United Kingdom, and France—have all been between 2.2 and 2.5 percent per year because their growth rates are limited by the rate at which new technologies can be invented and applied. By contrast, the five countries that were follower countries in 1960 have been able to grow much faster, between 3.9 percent per year and 5.8 percent per year. This has had remarkable effects on their standards of living relative to the leader countries. For instance, Ireland's GDP per capita was only about half that of its neighbor, the United Kingdom, in 1960. But because Ireland grew at a 3.9 percent rate for the next 44 years while the United Kingdom grew at only a 2.2 percent rate over that time period, by 2004 Irish GDP per capita was actually higher than United Kingdom GDP per capita. Ireland had become a leader country, too.

The growth experiences of the other four nations that were poor in 1960 have been even more dramatic. Hong Kong, for instance, moved from a GDP per capita that was

less than one-third of that enjoyed by the United Kingdom in 1960 to a GDP per capita nearly 10 percent higher than that of the United Kingdom in 2004. The nearby Consider This box emphasizes how quickly small differences in growth rates can change both the level of real GDP per capita and how countries stand in relation to each other in terms of real GDP per capita. This chapter's Last Word on rapid economic growth in China also reinforces our point.

Finally, you may be puzzled as to why the GDP per capita of the United States in 2004 in Table 25.2 is so much higher than that of other rich leader countries. Why, for instance, is U.S. GDP per capita 40 percent higher than French GDP per capita? One important reason is that U.S. citizens put in substantially more labor time than do the citizens of most other leader countries. First, a much larger fraction of the U.S. population is employed than in other rich leader countries. Second, U.S. employees work many

CONSIDER THIS

Economic Growth Rates Matter!

When compounded over many decades, small absolute differences in rates of economic growth add up to substantial differences in real GDP and standards of living. Consider three hypothetical countries—Slogo, Sumgo, and Speedo. Suppose that in 2008 these countries have identical levels of real GDP ($6 trillion), population (200 million), and real GDP per capita ($30,000). Also, assume that annual real GDP growth is 2 percent in Slogo, 3 percent in Sumgo, and 4 percent in Speedo.

How will these alternative growth rates affect real GDP and real GDP per capita over a long period, say, a 70-year life span? By 2078 the 2, 3, and 4 percent growth rates would boost real GDP from $6 trillion to:

- $24 trilion in Slogo.
- $47 trillion in Sumgo.
- $93 trillion in Speedo.

For illustration, let's assume that each country experienced an average annual population growth of 1 percent over the 70 years. Then, in 2078 real GDP per capita would be about:

- $60,000 in Slogo.
- $118,000 in Sumgo.
- $233,000 in Speedo.

Even small differences in growth rates matter!

more hours per year than do employees in other rich leader countries. For example, 62.1 percent of the working-age population of the United States was employed in 2005 compared to 51.0 percent in France. That's a difference of about 20 percent. And American employees worked an average of 1804 total hours during 2005, compared to an average of 1505 total hours for French workers. That's also a difference of about 20 percent. Added together, these two differences between U.S. and French labor supply imply about a 40 percent difference in the total number of hours worked in the French and American economies. Thus, differences in labor supply can go a long way to explaining differences between rich leader countries in terms of their differing levels of GDP per person.

Buy why do Americans supply so much more labor than workers in France and other rich leader countries? Explanations put forth by economists include cultural differences regarding the proper balance between work and leisure, stronger unions in France and other rich leader countries, and more generous unemployment and welfare programs in France and other rich leader countries. France and other rich leader countries also tend to have higher tax rates than the United States—something that may significantly discourage employment. And, finally, the legal work-week is shorter in some countries than it is in the United States.

QUICK REVIEW 25.2

- Before the advent of modern economic growth starting in England in the late 1700s, living standards showed no sustained increases over time. Modern economic growth brings with it not only ongoing increases in GDP per capita but also profound cultural, social, and political changes.
- Large differences in standards of living exist today because certain areas like the United States have experienced nearly 200 years of modern economic growth while other areas have had only a few decades of economic growth.
- Poor follower countries can catch up with and even surpass the living standards of rich leader countries. The growth rates of rich country GDPs per capita are limited to about 2 percent per year because, in order to further increase their standards of living, rich countries must invent and apply new technologies. By contrast, poor follower countries can grow much faster because they can simply adopt the cutting-edge technologies and institutions already developed by rich leader countries.
- Substantial differences in living standards can be caused by differences in labor supply. This explains why U.S. GDP per capita is nearly a third higher than French GDP per capita despite both countries being technologically advanced leader countries.

Institutional Structures That Promote Growth

Table 25.2 demonstrates that poor follower countries can catch up and become rich leader countries by growing rapidly. But how does a country start that process and enter into modern economic growth? And once it has started modern economic growth, how does it keep the process going?

Economic historians have identified several institutional structures that promote and sustain modern economic growth. Some structures increase the savings and investment that are needed to fund the construction and maintenance of the huge amounts of infrastructure required to run modern economies. Other institutional structures promote the development of new technologies. And still others act to ensure that resources flow efficiently to their most productive uses. These growth-promoting institutional structures include

- *Strong property rights* These appear to be absolutely necessary for rapid and sustained economic growth. People will not invest if they believe that thieves, bandits, or a rapacious and tyrannical government will steal their investments or their expected returns.
- *Patents and copyrights* These are necessary if a society wants a constant flow of innovative new technologies and sophisticated new ideas. Before patents and copyrights were first issued and enforced, inventors and authors usually saw their ideas stolen before they could profit from them. By giving inventors and authors the exclusive right to market and sell their creations, patents and copyrights give a strong financial incentive to invent and create.
- *Efficient financial institutions* These are needed to channel the savings generated by households toward the businesses, entrepreneurs, and inventors that do most of society's investing and inventing. Banks as well as stock and bond markets appear to be institutions crucial to modern economic growth.
- *Literacy and widespread education* Without highly educated inventors, new technologies do not get developed. And without a highly educated work-force, it is impossible to implement those technologies and put them to productive use.
- *Free trade* Free trade promotes economic growth by allowing countries to specialize so that different types of output can be produced in the countries where they can be made most efficiently. In addition,

CONSIDER THIS . . .

Patents and Innovation

It costs U.S. and European drug companies about $1 billion to research, patent, and safety-test a new drug because literally thousands of candidate drugs fail for each drug that succeeds. The only way to cover these costs is by relying on patent protections that give a drug's developer the exclusive monopoly right to market and sell the new drug for 20 years after it is developed. The revenues over that time period will hopefully be enough to cover the drug's development costs and—if the drug is popular—generate a profit for the drug company. Once the 20 years are over, however, the drug will go "off patent" and anyone will be able to manufacture and sell it.

Leader and follower countries have gotten into heated disputes in recent years, however, because the follower countries have often refused to recognize the patents granted to pharmaceutical companies in rich countries. India, for instance, has allowed local drug companies to copy and sell drugs that were developed by U.S. companies and are still under patent protection in the United States.

This benefits Indian citizens because the local drug companies compete with each other and end up charging much less for a given drug than would the drug's patent holder if it could enforce its monopoly patent and act as the drug's only seller. On the other hand, the weak patent protections found in India also make it completely unprofitable for local drug companies to try to develop innovative new drugs because, without patent protections, they too will be unable to prevent rivals from copying their new drugs and selling them for extremely low prices. As a result, India has recently moved to strengthen its patent protections, realizing that unless it does so, it will never be able to provide the financial incentive that can transform its local drug companies from copycats into innovators. But note that the innovative new drugs that may result from the increased patent protections are not without a cost. As patent protections in India are improved, cheap copycat drugs will no longer be available to Indian consumers.

free trade promotes the rapid spread of new ideas so that innovations made in one country quickly spread to other countries.
- *A competitive market system* Under a market system, prices and profits serve as the signals that

tell firms what to make and how much of it to make. Rich leader countries vary substantially in terms of how much government regulation they impose on markets, but in all cases, firms have substantial autonomy to follow market signals in deciding on current production and in making investments to produce what they believe consumers will demand in the future.

Several other difficult-to-measure factors also influence a nation's capacity for economic growth. The overall social-cultural-political environment of the United States, for example, has encouraged economic growth. Beyond the market system that has prevailed in the United States, the United States also has had a stable political system characterized by democratic principles, internal order, the right of property ownership, the legal status of enterprise, and the enforcement of contracts. Economic freedom and political freedom have been "growth-friendly."

In addition, and unlike some nations, there are virtually no social or moral taboos on production and material progress in the United States. The nation's social philosophy has embraced wealth creation as an attainable and desirable goal and the inventor, the innovator, and the businessperson are accorded high degrees of prestige and respect in American society. Finally, Americans have a positive attitude toward work and risk taking, resulting in an ample supply of willing workers and innovative entrepreneurs. A flow of energetic immigrants has greatly augmented that supply.

The nearby Consider This box deals with how fast-growing follower countries such as India sometimes alter their growth-related institutional structures as they grow richer. Chapter 39W looks at the special problems of economic growth in developing nations.

Ingredients of Growth

Our discussion of modern economic growth and the institutional structures that promote it has purposely been general. We now want to focus our discussion on six factors that directly affect the *rate* of economic growth. These six "ingredients" of economic growth can be grouped into four supply factors, one demand factor, and one efficiency factor.

Supply Factors

Four of the ingredients of economic growth relate to the physical ability of the economy to expand. They are:
- Increases in the quantity and quality of natural resources.

- Increases in the quantity and quality of human resources.
- Increases in the supply (or stock) of capital goods.
- Improvements in technology.

These **supply factors**—changes in the physical and technical agents of production—enable an economy to expand its potential GDP.

Demand Factor

The fifth ingredient of economic growth is the **demand factor:**

- To achieve the higher production potential created by the supply factors, households, businesses, and government must *purchase* the economy's expanding output of goods and services.

When that occurs, there will be no unplanned increases in inventories and resources will remain fully employed. Economic growth requires increases in total spending to realize the output gains made available by increased production capacity.

Efficiency Factor

The sixth ingredient of economic growth is the **efficiency factor:**

- To reach its full production potential, an economy must achieve economic efficiency as well as full employment.

The economy must use its resources in the least costly way (productive efficiency) to produce the specific mix of goods and services that maximizes people's well-being (allocative efficiency). The ability to expand production, together with the full use of available resources, is not sufficient for achieving maximum possible growth. Also required is the efficient use of those resources.

The supply, demand, and efficiency factors in economic growth are related. Unemployment caused by insufficient total spending (the demand factor) may lower the rate of new capital accumulation (a supply factor) and delay expenditures on research (also a supply factor). Conversely, low spending on investment (a supply factor) may cause insufficient spending (the demand factor) and unemployment. Widespread inefficiency in the use of resources (the efficiency factor) may translate into higher costs of goods and services and thus lower profits, which in turn may slow innovation and reduce the accumulation of capital (supply factors).

ORIGIN OF THE IDEA

O 25.1
Growth theory

Economic growth is a dynamic process in which the supply, demand, and efficiency factors all interact.

Production Possibilities Analysis

To put the six factors affecting the rate of economic growth into better perspective, let's use the production possibilities analysis introduced in Chapter 1.

Growth and Production Possibilities

Recall that a curve like *AB* in Figure 25.2 is a production possibilities curve. It indicates the various *maximum* combinations of products an economy can produce with its fixed quantity and quality of natural, human, and capital resources and its stock of technological knowledge. An improvement in any of the supply factors will push the production possibilities curve outward, as from *AB* to *CD*.

But the demand factor reminds us that an increase in total spending is needed to move the economy from a point like *a* on curve *AB* to any of the points on the higher curve *CD*. And the efficiency factor reminds us that we need least-cost production and an optimal location on *CD* for the resources to make their maximum possible dollar contribution to total output. You will recall from Chapter 1 that this "best allocation" is determined by expanding production of each good until its marginal benefit equals its marginal cost. Here, we assume that this optimal combination of capital and consumer goods occurs at point *b*.

FIGURE 25.2 Economic growth and the production possibilities curve. Economic growth is made possible by the four supply factors that shift the production possibilities curve outward, as from *AB* to *CD*. Economic growth is realized when the demand factor and the efficiency factor move the economy from point *a* to point *b*.

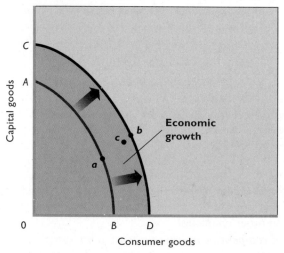

Example: The net increase in the size of the labor force in the United States in recent years has been 1.5 to 2 million workers per year. That increment raises the economy's production capacity. But obtaining the extra output that these added workers could produce depends on their success in finding jobs. It also depends on whether or not the jobs are in firms and industries where the workers' talents are fully and optimally used. Society does not want new labor-force entrants to be unemployed. Nor does it want pediatricians working as plumbers or pediatricians producing services for which marginal costs exceed marginal benefits.

Normally, increases in total spending match increases in production capacity, and the economy moves from a point on the previous production possibilities curve to a point on the expanded curve. Moreover, the competitive market system tends to drive the economy toward productive and allocative efficiency. Occasionally, however, the curve may shift outward but leave the economy behind at some level of operation such as c in Figure 25.2. Because c is inside the new production possibilities curve CD, the economy has not realized its potential for economic growth. **(Key Question 5)**

Labor and Productivity

Although the demand and efficiency factors are important, discussions of economic growth focus primarily on supply factors. Society can increase its real output and income in two fundamental ways: (1) by increasing its inputs of resources and (2) by raising the productivity of those inputs. Figure 25.3 concentrates on the input of *labor* and provides a useful framework for discussing the role of supply factors in growth. A nation's real GDP in any year depends on the input of labor (measured in hours of work) multiplied by **labor productivity** (measured as real output per hour of work):

$$\text{Real GDP} = \text{hours of work} \times \text{labor productivity}$$

Thought of this way, a nation's economic growth from one year to the next depends on its *increase* in labor inputs (if any) and its *increase* in labor productivity (if any).

Illustration: Assume that the hypothetical economy of Ziam has 10 workers in year 1, each working 2000 hours per year (50 weeks at 40 hours per week). The total input of labor therefore is 20,000 hours. If productivity (average real output per hour of work) is $10, then real GDP in Ziam will be $200,000 (= 20,000 × $10). If work hours rise to 20,200 and labor productivity rises to $10.40, Ziam's real

WORKED PROBLEMS

W 25.2

Productivity and economic growth

FIGURE 25.3 **The supply determinants of real output.**
Real GDP is usefully viewed as the product of the quantity of labor inputs (hours of work) multiplied by labor productivity.

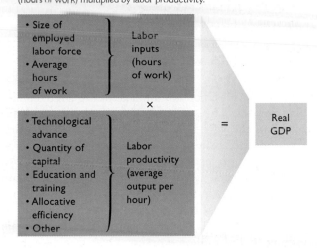

GDP will increase to $210,080 in year 2. Ziam's rate of economic growth will be about 5% [= ($210,080 − $200,000)/ $200,000] for the year.

Hours of Work What determines the number of hours worked each year? As shown in Figure 25.3, the hours of labor input depend on the size of the employed labor force and the length of the average workweek. Labor-force size depends on the size of the working-age population and the **labor-force participation rate**—the percentage of the working-age population actually in the labor force. The length of the average workweek is governed by legal and institutional considerations and by collective bargaining agreements negotiated between unions and employers.

Labor Productivity Figure 25.3 tells us that labor productivity is determined by technological progress, the quantity of capital goods available to workers, the quality of the labor itself, and the efficiency with which inputs are allocated, combined, and managed. Productivity rises when the health, training, education, and motivation of workers improve; when workers have more and better machinery and natural resources with which to work; when production is better organized and managed; and when labor is reallocated from less-efficient industries to more-efficient industries.

Accounting for Growth

The Council of Economic Advisers uses a system called **growth accounting** to assess the relative importance of the supply-side elements that contribute to changes in real

GDP. This system groups these elements into two main categories:

- Increases in hours of work.
- Increases in labor productivity.

Labor Inputs versus Labor Productivity

Table 25.3 provides the relevant data for the United States for five periods. The symbol "Q" in the table stands for "quarter" of the year. The beginning points for the first four periods are business-cycle peaks, and the last period includes future projections by the President's Council of Economic Advisers. It is clear from the table that both increases in the quantity of labor and increases in labor productivity are important sources of economic growth. Between 1953 and 2007, the labor force increased from 63 million to 154 million workers. Over that period the average length of the workweek remained relatively stable. Falling birthrates slowed the growth of the native population, but increased immigration partly offset that slowdown. As indicated in the Consider This box to the right, of particular significance was a surge of women's participation in the labor force. Partly as a result, U.S. labor-force growth averaged 1.7 million workers per year over the past 54 years.

The growth of labor productivity also has been important to economic growth. In fact, productivity growth has usually been the more significant factor, with the exception of 1973–1995 when productivity growth greatly slowed. For example, between 2001 and 2007, productivity growth was responsible for all of the 2.6 percent average annual economic growth. Between 2007 and 2013, productivity growth is projected to account for about 90 percent of the growth of real GDP.

Because increases in labor productivity are so important to economic growth, economists go to the trouble of investigating and assessing the relative importance of the factors that contribute to productivity growth. There are five factors that, together, appear to explain changes in productivity growth rates: technological advance, the amount of capital each worker has to work with, education and training, economies of scale, and resource allocation. We will examine each factor in turn, noting how much each factor contributes to productivity growth.

Technological Advance

The largest contributor to productivity growth is technological advance, which is thought to account for about 40 percent of productivity growth. As economist Paul Romer stated, "Human history teaches us that economic growth springs from better recipes, not just from more cooking."

Technological advance includes not only innovative production techniques but new managerial methods and new forms of business organization that improve the process of production. Generally, technological advance is generated by the discovery of new knowledge, which allows resources to be combined in improved ways that increase output. Once discovered and implemented, new knowledge soon becomes available to entrepreneurs and firms at relatively low cost. Technological advance therefore eventually spreads through the entire economy, boosting productivity and economic growth.

Technological advance and capital formation (investment) are closely related, since technological advance usually promotes investment in new machinery and equipment. In fact, technological advance is often *embodied* within new capital. For example, the purchase of new computers brings into industry speedier, more powerful computers that incorporate new technology.

Technological advance has been both rapid and profound. Gas and diesel engines, conveyor belts, and assembly lines are significant developments of the past. So, too, are fuel-efficient commercial aircraft, integrated microcircuits, personal computers, digital photography, and containerized shipping. More recently, technological

TABLE 25.3 **Accounting for Growth of U.S. Real GDP, 1953–2013 (Average Annual Percentage Changes)**

Item	1953 Q2 to 1973 Q4	1973 Q4 to 1995 Q2	1995 Q2 to 2001 Q1	2001 Q1 to 2007 Q3	2007 Q3 to 2013 Q4*
Increase in real GDP	3.6	2.8	3.8	2.6	2.8
Increase in quantity of labor	1.1	1.3	1.4	−0.1	0.3
Increase in labor productivity	2.5	1.5	2.4	2.7	2.5

*Rates beyond 2007 are projected rates.

Source: Derived from *Economic Report of the President, 2008*, p. 45.

Women, the Labor Force, and Economic Growth

The substantial rise in the number of women working in the paid workforce in the United States has been one of the major labor market trends of the past half-century. In 1965, some 40 percent of women worked full-time or part-time in paid jobs. Today, that number is 59 percent.

Women have greatly increased their productivity in the workplace, mostly by becoming better educated and professionally trained. Rising productivity has increased women's wage rates. Those higher wages have raised the opportunity costs—the forgone wage earnings—of staying at home. Women have therefore substituted employment in the labor market for traditional home activities. This substitution has been particularly pronounced among married women. (Single women have always had high labor-force participation rates.)

Furthermore, changing lifestyles and the widespread availability of birth control have freed up time for greater labor-force participation by women. Women not only have fewer children, but those children are spaced closer together in age. Thus women who leave their jobs during their children's early years return to the labor force sooner.

Greater access to jobs by women also has been a significant factor in the rising labor-force participation of women. Service industries—teaching, nursing, and office work, for instance—that traditionally have employed many women have expanded rapidly in the past several decades. Also, the population in general has shifted from farms and rural regions to urban areas, where jobs for women are more abundant and more geographically accessible. An increased availability of part-time jobs also has made it easier for women to combine labor market employment with child-rearing and household activities. Also, antidiscrimination laws and enforcement efforts have reduced barriers that previously discouraged or prevented women from taking traditional male jobs such as business managers, lawyers, professors, and physicians. More jobs are open to women today than a half-century ago.

In summary, women in the United States are better educated, more productive, and more efficiently employed than ever before. Their increased presence in the labor force has contributed greatly to U.S. economic growth.

advance has exploded, particularly in the areas of computers, photography, wireless communications, and the Internet. Other fertile areas of recent innovation are medicine and biotechnology.

Quantity of Capital

A second major contributor to productivity growth is increased capital, which explains roughly 30 percent of productivity growth. More and better plant and equipment make workers more productive. And a nation acquires more capital by saving some of its income and using that savings to invest in plant and equipment.

Although some capital substitutes for labor, most capital is complementary to labor—it makes labor more productive. A key determinant of labor productivity is the amount of capital goods available *per worker*. If both the aggregate stock of capital goods and the size of the labor force increase over a given period, the individual worker is not necessarily better equipped and productivity will not necessarily rise. But the quantity of capital equipment available per U.S. worker has increased greatly over time. (In 2006 it was about $97,140 per worker.)

Public investment in the U.S. **infrastructure** (highways and bridges, public transit systems, wastewater treatment facilities, water systems, airports, educational facilities, and so on) has also grown over the years. This publicly owned capital complements private capital. Investments in new highways promote private investment in new factories and retail stores along their routes. Industrial parks developed by local governments attract manufacturing and distribution firms.

Private investment in infrastructure also plays a large role in economic growth. One example is the tremendous growth of private capital relating to communications systems over the years.

Education and Training

Ben Franklin once said, "He that hath a trade hath an estate," meaning that education and training contribute to a worker's stock of **human capital**—the knowledge and skills that make a worker productive. Investment in human capital includes not only formal education but also on-the-job training. Like investment in physical capital, investment in human capital is an important means of increasing labor productivity and earnings. An estimated 15 percent of productivity growth derives from investments in people's education and skills.

One measure of a nation's quality of labor is its level of educational attainment. Figure 25.4 shows large gains in education attainment over the past several decades. In 1960 only 41 percent of the U.S. population age 25 or older had at least a high school education; and only 8 percent had a college or postcollege education. By 2007, those numbers had increased to 86 and 29 percent, respectively.

FIGURE 25.4 Changes in the educational attainment of the U.S. adult population. The percentage of the U.S. adult population, age 25 or older, completing high school and college has been rising over recent decades.

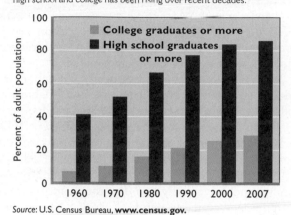

Source: U.S. Census Bureau, **www.census.gov.**

GLOBAL PERSPECTIVE 25.1

Average Test Scores of Eighth-Grade Students in Math and Science, Top 10 Countries and the United States

The test performance of U.S. eighth-grade students did not compare favorably with that of eighth-graders in several other nations in the Third International Math and Science Study (2003).

Mathematics

Rank		Score
1	Singapore	605
2	South Korea	589
3	Hong Kong	586
4	Taiwan	585
5	Japan	570
6	Belgium	537
7	Netherlands	536
8	Estonia	531
9	Hungary	529
10	Malaysia	508
15	United States	504

Science

Rank		Score
1	Singapore	578
2	Taiwan	571
3	South Korea	558
4	Hong Kong	556
5	Estonia	552
6	Japan	552
7	Hungary	543
8	Netherlands	536
9	United States	527
10	Australia	527

Clearly, more people are receiving more education than ever before.

But all is not upbeat with education in the United States. Many observers think that the quality of education in the United States has declined. For example, U.S. students perform poorly on science and math tests relative to students in many other nations (see Global Perspective 25.1). And the United States has been producing fewer engineers and scientists, a problem that may trace back to inadequate training in math and science in elementary and high schools. For these reasons, much recent public policy discussion and legislation has been directed toward improving the quality of the U.S. education and training system.

Economies of Scale and Resource Allocation

Economies of scale and improved resource allocation are a fourth and fifth source of productivity growth, and together they explain about 15 percent of productivity growth.

Economies of Scale Reductions in per-unit production costs that result from increases in output levels are called **economies of scale.** Markets have increased in size over time, allowing firms to increase output levels and thereby achieve production advantages associated with greater size. As firms expand their size and output, they are able to use larger, more productive equipment and employ methods of manufacturing and delivery that increase productivity. They also are better able to recoup substantial investments in developing new products and production methods. Examples: A large manufacturer of autos can use elaborate assembly lines with computerization and robotics, while smaller producers must settle for less-advanced technologies using more labor inputs. Large pharmaceutical firms greatly reduce the average amount of labor (researchers, production workers) needed to produce each pill as they increase the number of pills produced.

Accordingly, economies of scale result in greater real GDP and thus contribute to economic growth.

Improved Resource Allocation

Improved resource allocation means that workers over time have moved from low-productivity employment to high-productivity employment. Historically, many workers have shifted from agriculture, where labor productivity is low, to manufacturing, where it is quite high. More recently, labor has shifted away from some manufacturing industries to even higher-productivity industries such as computer software, business consulting, and pharmaceuticals. As a result of such shifts, the average productivity of U.S. workers has increased.

Also, discrimination in education and the labor market has historically deterred some women and minorities from entering high-productivity jobs. With the decline of such discrimination over time, many members of those groups have shifted from lower-productivity jobs to higher-productivity jobs. The result has been higher overall labor productivity and real GDP.

Finally, we know from discussions in Chapter 5 that tariffs, import quotas, and other barriers to international trade tend to relegate resources to relatively unproductive pursuits. The long-run movement toward liberalized international trade through international agreements has improved the allocation of resources, increased labor productivity, and expanded real output, both here and abroad. **(Key Question 8)**

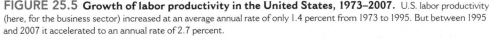

QUICK REVIEW 25.3

- Institutional structures that promote growth include strong property rights, patents, efficient financial institutions, education, and a competitive market system.
- The "ingredients" of economic growth to which we can attribute changes in growth rates include four supply factors (increases in the quantity and quality of natural resources, increases in the quantity and quality of human resources, increases in the stock of capital goods, and improvements in technology); one demand factor (increases in total spending); and one efficiency factor (achieving allocative and productive efficiency).
- Improvements in labor productivity accounted for about two-thirds of the increase in U.S. real GDP between 1990 and 2007; the use of more labor inputs accounted for the remainder.
- Improved technology, more capital, greater education and training, economies of scale, and better resource allocation have been the main contributors to U.S. productivity growth and thus to U.S. economic growth.

The Recent Productivity Acceleration

Figure 25.5 shows the growth of labor productivity (as measured by changes in the index of labor productivity) in the United States from 1973 to 2007, along with separate trend

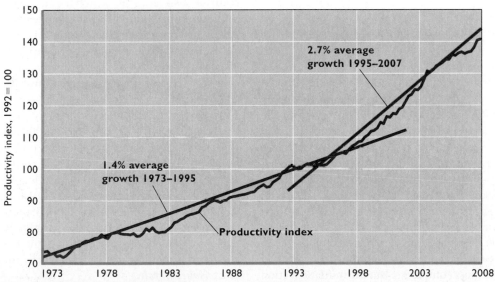

FIGURE 25.5 Growth of labor productivity in the United States, 1973–2007. U.S. labor productivity (here, for the business sector) increased at an average annual rate of only 1.4 percent from 1973 to 1995. But between 1995 and 2007 it accelerated to an annual rate of 2.7 percent.

Source: U.S. Bureau of Labor Statistics, **www.bls.gov.**

lines for 1973–1995 and 1995–2007. Labor productivity grew by an average of only 1.4 percent yearly over the 1973–1995 period. But productivity growth averaged 2.7 percent between 1995 and 2007. Many economists believe that this higher productivity growth resulted from a significant new wave of technological advance, coupled with global competition. Some economists are hopeful that the higher trend rates of productivity growth may be permanent.

This increase in productivity growth is important because real output, real income, and real wages are linked to labor productivity. To see why, suppose you are alone on an uninhabited island. The number of fish you can catch or coconuts you can pick per hour—your productivity—is your real wage (or real income) per hour. By *increasing* your productivity, you can improve your standard of living because you can gather more fish and more coconuts (goods) for each hour of work.

So it is for the economy as a whole: Over long periods, the economy's labor productivity determines its average real hourly wage. The economy's income per hour is equal to its output per hour. Productivity growth therefore is its main route for increasing its standard of living. It allows firms to pay higher wages without lowering their business profits. As we demonstrated in this chapter's first Consider This box, even a seemingly small percentage change in productivity growth, if sustained over several years, can make a substantial difference as to how fast a nation's standard of living rises. We know from the *rule of 70* that if a nation's productivity grows by 2.7 percent annually rather than 1.4 percent annually, its material standard of living will double in 26 years rather than 50 years.

Reasons for the Productivity Acceleration

Why has productivity growth increased relative to earlier periods?

The Microchip and Information Technology

The core element of the productivity speedup is an explosion of entrepreneurship and innovation based on the microprocessor, or *microchip*, which bundles transistors on a piece of silicon. Some observers liken the invention of the microchip to that of electricity, the automobile, air travel, the telephone, and television in importance and scope.

The microchip has found its way into thousands of applications. It has helped create a wide array of new products and services and new ways of doing business. Its immediate results were the pocket calculator, the bar-code scanner, the personal computer, the laptop computer, and more powerful business computers. But the miniaturization

of electronic circuits also advanced the development of many other products such as cell phones and pagers, computer-guided lasers, global positioning equipment, energy conservation systems, Doppler radar, digital cameras, and machines to decipher the human genome.

Perhaps of greatest significance, the widespread availability of personal and laptop computers stimulated the desire to tie them together. That desire promoted rapid development of the Internet and all its many manifestations, such as business-to-household and business-to-business electronic commerce (e-commerce). The combination of the computer, fiber-optic cable, wireless technology, and the Internet constitutes a spectacular advance in **information technology,** which has been used to connect all parts of the world.

New Firms and Increasing Returns

Hundreds of new **start-up firms** advanced various aspects of the new information technology. Many of these firms created more "hype" than goods and services and quickly fell by the wayside. But a number of firms flourished, eventually to take their places among the nation's largest firms. Examples of those firms include Intel (microchips); Apple and Dell (personal computers); Microsoft and Oracle (computer software); Cisco Systems (Internet switching systems); America Online (Internet service provision); Yahoo and Google (Internet search engines); and eBay and Amazon.com (electronic commerce). There are scores more! Most of these firms were either "not on the radar" or "a small blip on the radar" 30 years ago. Today each of them has large annual revenue and employs thousands of workers.

Successful new firms often experience **increasing returns,** a situation in which a given percentage increase in the amount of inputs a firm uses leads to an even larger percentage increase in the amount of output the firm produces. For example, suppose that a company called Techco decides to double the size of its operations to meet the growing demand for its services. After doubling its plant and equipment and doubling its workforce, say, from 100 workers to 200 workers, it finds that its total output has tripled from 8000 units to 24,000 units. Techco has experienced increasing returns; its output has increased by 200 percent, while its inputs have increased by only 100 percent. That is, its labor productivity has gone up from 80 units per worker (= 8000 units/100 workers) to 120 units per worker (= 24,000 units/200 workers). Increasing returns boost labor productivity and reduce per-unit production costs. Since these cost reductions result from increases in output levels, they are examples of *economies of scale.*

Both emerging firms as well as established firms can exploit several different sources of increasing returns and economies of scale.

- *More specialized inputs* Firms can use more specialized and thus more productive capital and workers as they expand their operations. A growing new e-commerce business, for example, can purchase highly specialized inventory management systems and hire specialized personnel such as accountants, marketing managers, and system maintenance experts.

- *Spreading of development costs* Firms can spread high product development costs over greater output. For example, suppose that a new software product costs $100,000 to develop and only $2 per unit to manufacture and sell. If the firm sells 1000 units of the software, its per-unit cost will be $102 [= ($100,000 + $2000)/1000], but if it sells 500,000 units, that cost will drop to only $2.20 [= ($100,000 + $1 million)/500,000].

- *Simultaneous consumption* Many recently developed products and services can satisfy large numbers of customers at the same time. Unlike a gallon of gas that needs to be produced for each buyer, a software program needs to be produced only once. It then becomes available at very low expense to thousands or even millions of buyers. The same is true of entertainment delivered on CDs, movies distributed on DVDs, and information disseminated through the Internet.

- *Network effects* Software and Internet service become more beneficial to a buyer the greater the number of households and businesses that also buy them. When others have Internet service, you can send e-mail messages to them. And when they also have software that allows display of documents and photos, you can attach those items to your e-mail messages. These interconnectivity advantages are called **network effects,** which are increases in the value of the product to each user, including existing users, as the total number of users rises. The domestic and global expansion of the Internet in particular has produced network effects, as have cell phones, pagers, palm computers, and other aspects of wireless communication. Network effects magnify the value of output well beyond the costs of inputs.

- *Learning by doing* Finally, firms that produce new products or pioneer new ways of doing business experience increasing returns through **learning by doing.** Tasks that initially may have taken firms hours may take them only minutes once the methods are perfected.

TABLE 25.4 Examples of Cost Reductions from Technology

- The cost of storing one megabit of information—enough for a 320-page book—fell from $5257 in 1975 to 17 cents in 1999.

- Prototyping each part of a car once took Ford weeks and cost $20,000 on average. Using an advanced 3-D object printer, Ford cut the time to just hours and the cost to less than $20.

- Studies show that telecommuting saves businesses about $20,000 annually for a worker earning $44,000—a saving in lost work time and employee retention costs, plus gains in worker productivity.

- Using scanners and computers, Weyerhaeuser increased the lumber yield and value from each log by 30 percent.

- Amoco used 3-D seismic exploration technology to cut the cost of finding oil from nearly $10 per barrel in 1991 to under $1 per barrel in 2000.

- Wal-Mart reduced the operating cost of its delivery trucks by 20 percent through installing computers, global positioning gear, and cell phones in 4300 vehicles.

- Banking transactions on the Internet cost 1 cent each, compared with $1.14 for face-to-face, pen-and-paper communication.

Source: Compiled and directly quoted from W. Michael Cox and Richard Alm, "The New Paradigm," Federal Reserve Bank of Dallas Annual Report, May 2000, various pages. Used by permission.

Whatever the particular source of increasing returns, the result is higher productivity, which tends to reduce the per-unit cost of producing and delivering products. Table 25.4 lists a number of specific examples of cost reduction from technology in recent years.

Global Competition The recent economy is characterized not only by information technology and increasing returns but also by heightened global competition. The collapse of the socialist economies in the late 1980s and early 1990s, together with the success of market systems, has led to a reawakening of capitalism throughout the world. The new information technologies have "shrunk the globe" and made it imperative for all firms to lower their costs and prices and to innovate in order to remain competitive. Free-trade zones such as NAFTA and the European Union (EU), along with trade liberalization through the World Trade Organization (WTO), have also heightened competition internationally by removing trade protection from domestic firms. The larger geographic markets, in turn, have enabled firms to expand beyond their national borders.

Implication: More Rapid Economic Growth

Other things equal, stronger productivity growth and heightened global competition allow the economy to achieve a higher rate of economic growth. A glance back at Figure 25.2 will help make this point. Suppose that the shift of the production possibilities curve from *AB* to *CD* reflects annual changes in potential output levels before the recent increase in growth rates. Then the higher growth rates of the more recent period of accelerated productivity growth would be depicted by a *larger* outward shift of the economy's production possibilities from *AB* to a curve beyond *CD*. When coupled with economic efficiency and increased total spending, the economy's real GDP would rise by even more than what is shown.

A caution: Economists who believe that the higher productivity growth rates experienced in recent years are likely to continue do not believe that the business cycle is dead. Their contention is limited to the belief that the *trend lines* of productivity growth and economic growth have become steeper. Real output may periodically deviate below and above the steeper trend—as it did when the economy slowed in the first two months of 2001 and receded over the following eight months of that year.

Skepticism about Permanence

Although most macroeconomists have revised their forecasts for long-term productivity growth upward, at least slightly, others are still skeptical and urge a "wait-and-see" approach. These macroeconomists acknowledge that the economy has experienced a rapid advance of new technology, some new firms have experienced increasing returns, and global competition has increased. But they wonder if these factors are sufficiently profound to produce a permanent new era of substantially higher rates of productivity growth and real GDP growth.

They also point out that productivity surged between 1975 and 1978 and between 1983 and 1986 but in each case soon reverted to its lower long-run trend. The higher trend line of productivity inferred from the short-run spurt of productivity could prove to be transient. Only by looking backward over long periods can economists distinguish the start of a new long-run trend from a shorter-term boost in productivity related to the business cycle and temporary factors.

What Can We Conclude?

Given the different views on the recent productivity acceleration, what should we conclude? Perhaps the safest conclusions are these:

- The prospects for a lasting increase in productivity growth are good (see Global Perspective 25.2).

GLOBAL PERSPECTIVE 25.2

Global Competitiveness Index

The Global Competitiveness Index published annually by the World Economic Forum measures each country's potential for economic growth. The index uses various factors—such as innovativeness, the capability to transfer technology among sectors, the efficiency of the financial system, rates of investment, and the degree of integration with the rest of the world—to measure a country's ability to achieve economic growth over time. Here is the top 10 list for 2007.

Country	Global Competitiveness Ranking, 2007
United States	1
Switzerland	2
Denmark	3
Sweden	4
Finland	5
Germany	6
Singapore	7
Japan	8
United Kingdom	9
Netherlands	10

Source: Copyright World Economic Forum, **www.weforum.org.**

Studies indicate that productivity increases related to information technology have spread to a wide range of industries, including services. Even in the recession year 2001 and then in 2002, when the economy was sluggish, productivity growth remained strong. Specifically, it averaged about 3.3 percent in the business sector over those two years. Productivity rose by 3.8 percent in 2003, 2.9 percent in 2004, and 2.0 percent in 2005, as the economy vigorously expanded.

- Time will tell. Productivity growth was just 1.0 percent in 2006 and 1.9 percent in 2007. Whether this is a temporary decline or not is uncertain. Thus, several more years must elapse before economists can declare the productivity acceleration seen after 1995 to be a long-run, sustainable trend. **(Key Question 11)**

- Over long time periods, labor productivity growth determines an economy's growth of real wages and its standard of living.
- Many economists believe that the United States has entered a period of faster productivity growth and higher rates of economic growth.
- The productivity acceleration is based on rapid technological change in the form of the microchip and information technology, increasing returns and lower per-unit costs, and heightened global competition that helps hold down prices.
- More-rapid U.S. productivity growth means that the U.S. economy can grow at higher annual rates than it could with less-rapid productivity growth. Nonetheless, many economists caution that it is still too early to determine whether the recent higher rates of productivity growth are a lasting long-run trend or a fortunate short-lived occurrence.

Is Growth Desirable and Sustainable?

Economists usually take for granted that economic growth is desirable and sustainable. But not everyone agrees.

The Antigrowth View

Critics of growth say industrialization and growth result in pollution, global warming, ozone depletion, and other environmental problems. These adverse negative externalities occur because inputs in the production process reenter the environment as some form of waste. The more rapid our growth and the higher our standard of living, the more waste the environment must absorb—or attempt to absorb. In an already wealthy society, further growth usually means satisfying increasingly trivial wants at the cost of mounting threats to the ecological system.

Critics of growth also argue that there is little compelling evidence that economic growth has solved sociological problems such as poverty, homelessness, and discrimination. Consider poverty: In the antigrowth view, American poverty is a problem of distribution, not production. The requisite for solving the problem is a firm commitment to redistribute wealth and income, not further increases in output.

Antigrowth sentiment also says that while growth may permit us to "make a better living," it does not give us "the good life." We may be producing more and enjoying it less. Growth means frantic paces on jobs, worker burnout, and alienated employees who have little or no control over

decisions affecting their lives. The changing technology at the core of growth poses new anxieties and new sources of insecurity for workers. Both high-level and low-level workers face the prospect of having their hard-earned skills and experience rendered obsolete by onrushing technology. High-growth economies are high-stress economies, which may impair our physical and mental health.

Finally, critics of high rates of growth doubt that they are sustainable. The planet Earth has finite amounts of natural resources available, and they are being consumed at alarming rates. Higher rates of economic growth simply speed up the degradation and exhaustion of the earth's resources. In this view, slower economic growth that is environmentally sustainable is preferable to faster growth.

In Defense of Economic Growth

The primary defense of growth is that it is the path to the greater material abundance and higher living standards desired by the vast majority of people. Rising output and incomes allow people to buy more education, recreation, and travel, more medical care, closer communications, more skilled personal and professional services, and better-designed as well as more numerous products. It also means more art, music, and poetry, theater, and drama. It can even mean more time and resources devoted to spiritual growth and human development.[1]

Growth also enables society to improve the nation's infrastructure, enhance the care of the sick and elderly, provide greater access for the disabled, and provide more police and fire protection. Economic growth may be the only realistic way to reduce poverty, since there is little political support for greater redistribution of income. The way to improve the economic position of the poor is to increase household incomes through higher productivity and economic growth. Also, a no-growth policy among industrial nations might severely limit growth in poor nations. Foreign investment and development assistance in those nations would fall, keeping the world's poor in poverty longer.

Economic growth has not made labor more unpleasant or hazardous, as critics suggest. New machinery is usually less taxing and less dangerous than the machinery it replaces. Air-conditioned workplaces are more pleasant than steamy workshops. Furthermore, why would an end to economic growth reduce materialism or alienation? The loudest protests against materialism are heard in those nations and

[1]Alice M. Rivlin, *Reviving the American Dream* (Washington, D.C.: Brookings Institution, 1992), p. 36.

China's Economic Growth Rate in the Past 25 Years Is Among the Highest Recorded for Any Country During Any Period of World History.

Propelled by capitalistic reforms, China has experienced nearly 9 percent annual growth rates over the past 25 years. Real output has more than quadrupled over that period. In 2006, China's growth rate was 10.7 percent and in 2007 it was 11.3 percent. Expanded output and income have boosted domestic saving and investment, and the growth of capital goods has further increased productivity, output, and income. The rising income, together with inexpensive labor, has attracted more foreign direct investment (a total of over $170 billion between 2005 and 2007).

China's real GDP and real income have grown much more rapidly than China's population. Per capita income has increased at a high annual rate of 8 percent since 1980. This is particularly noteworthy because China's population has expanded by 14 million a year (despite a policy that encourages one child per family). Based on exchange rates, China's per capita income is now about $2500 annually. But because the prices of many basic items in China are still low and are not totally reflected in exchange rates, Chinese per capita purchasing power is estimated to be equivalent to $5300 of income in the United States.

The growth of per capita income in China has resulted from increased use of capital, improved technology, and shifts of labor away from lower-productivity toward higher-productivity uses. One such shift of employment has been from agriculture toward rural and urban manufacturing. Another shift has been from state-owned enterprises toward private firms. Both shifts have raised the productivity of Chinese workers.

Chinese economic growth had been accompanied by a huge expansion of China's international trade. Chinese exports rose from $5 billion in 1978 to $1.2 trillion in 2007. These exports have provided the foreign currency needed to import consumer goods and capital goods. Imports of capital goods from industrially advanced countries have brought with them highly advanced technology that is embodied in, for example, factory design, industrial machinery, office equipment, and telecommunications systems.

China still faces some significant problems in its transition to the market system, however. At times, investment booms in China have resulted in too much spending relative to production

capacity. The result has been some periods of 15 to 25 percent annual rates of inflation. China confronted the inflation problem by giving its central bank more power so that, when appropriate, the bank can raise interest rates to damp down investment spending. This greater monetary control has reduced inflation significantly. China's inflation rate was a mild 1.2 percent in 2003, 4.1 percent in 2004, and 1.9 percent in 2005. More vigilance may be required, however, as inflation rebounded over the next two years, reaching 7.1 percent in 2007.

In addition, the overall financial system in China remains weak and inadequate. Many unprofitable state-owned enterprises owe colossal sums of money on loans made by the Chinese state-owned banks (an estimate is nearly $100 billion). Because most of these loans are not collectible, the government may need to bail out the banks to keep them in operation.

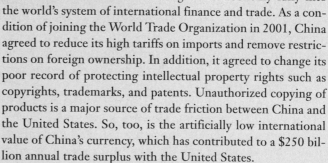

Unemployment is also a problem. Even though the transition from an agriculture-dominated economy to a more urban, industrial economy has been gradual, considerable displacement of labor has occurred. There is substantial unemployment and underemployment in the interior regions of China.

China still has much work to do to integrate its economy fully into the world's system of international finance and trade. As a condition of joining the World Trade Organization in 2001, China agreed to reduce its high tariffs on imports and remove restrictions on foreign ownership. In addition, it agreed to change its poor record of protecting intellectual property rights such as copyrights, trademarks, and patents. Unauthorized copying of products is a major source of trade friction between China and the United States. So, too, is the artificially low international value of China's currency, which has contributed to a $250 billion annual trade surplus with the United States.

China's economic development has been very uneven geographically. Hong Kong is a wealthy capitalist city with per capita income of about $29,000. The standard of living is also relatively high in China's southern provinces and coastal cities, although not nearly as high as it is in Hong Kong. In fact, people living in these special economic zones have been the major beneficiaries of China's rapid growth. In contrast, the majority of people living elsewhere in China have very low incomes. Despite its remarkable recent economic successes, China remains a relatively low-income nation. But that status is quickly changing.

groups that now enjoy the highest levels of material abundance! The high standard of living that growth provides has increased our leisure and given us more time for reflection and self-fulfillment.

Does growth threaten the environment? The connection between growth and environment is tenuous, say growth proponents. Increases in economic growth need not mean increases in pollution. Pollution is not so much a by-product of growth as it is a "problem of the commons." Much of the environment—streams, lakes, oceans, and the air—is treated as common property, with insufficient or no restrictions on its use. The commons have become our dumping grounds; we have overused and debased them. Environmental pollution is a case of negative externalities, and correcting this problem involves regulatory legislation, specific taxes ("effluent charges"), or market-based incentives to remedy misuse of the environment.

Those who support growth admit there are serious environmental problems. But they say that limiting growth is the wrong solution. Growth has allowed economies to reduce pollution, be more sensitive to environmental considerations, set aside wilderness, create national parks and monuments, and clean up hazardous waste, while still enabling rising household incomes. (See the Last Word in Chapter 15.)

Is growth sustainable? Yes, say the proponents of growth. If we were depleting natural resources faster than their discovery, we would see the prices of those resources rise. That has not been the case for most natural resources; in fact, the prices of most of them have declined (see Figure 15.1). And if one natural resource becomes too expensive, another resource will be substituted for it. Moreover, say economists, economic growth has to do with the expansion and application of human knowledge and information, not of extractable natural resources. In this view, economic growth is limited only by human imagination.

Summary

1. A nation's economic growth can be measured either as an increase in real GDP over time or as an increase in real GDP per capita over time. Real GDP in the United States has grown at an average annual rate of about 3.5 percent since 1950; real GDP per capita has grown at roughly a 2.3 percent annual rate over that same period.

2. Sustained increases in real GDP per capita did not happen until the past two centuries, when England and then other countries began to experience modern economic growth, which is characterized by institutional structures that encourage savings, investment, and the development of new technologies. Institutional structures that promote growth include strong property rights, patents, efficient financial institutions, education, and a competitive market system.

3. Because some nations have experienced nearly two centuries of modern economic growth while others have only recently begun to experience modern economic growth, some countries today are much richer than other countries.

4. It is possible, however, for countries that are currently poor to grow faster than countries that are currently rich because the growth rates of rich country GDPs per capita are limited to about 2 percent per year because, in order to continue growing, rich countries must invent and apply new technologies. By contrast, poor countries can grow much faster because they can simply adopt the institutions and cutting-edge technologies already developed by the rich countries.

5. The "ingredients" of economic growth to which we can attribute changes in growth rates include four supply factors (changes in the quantity and quality of natural resources, changes in the quantity and quality of human resources, changes in the stock of capital goods, and improvements in technology); one demand factor (changes in total spending); and one efficiency factor (changes in how well an economy achieves allocative and productive efficiency).

6. The growth of a nation's capacity to produce output can be illustrated graphically by an outward shift of its production possibilities curve.

7. Growth accounting attributes increases in real GDP either to increases in the amount of labor being employed or to increases in the productivity of the labor being employed. Increases in U.S. real GDP are mostly the result of increases in labor productivity. The increases in labor productivity can be attributed to technological progress, increases in the quantity of capital per worker, improvements in the education and training of workers, the exploitation of economies of scale, and improvements in the allocation of labor across different industries.

8. Over long time periods, the growth of labor productivity underlies an economy's growth of real wages and its standard of living. U.S. productivity rose by 2.7 percent annually between 1995 and 2007, compared to 1.4 percent annually between 1973 and 1995.

9. This recent productivity acceleration is based on (a) rapid technological change in the form of the microchip and information technology, (b) increasing returns and lower per-unit costs, and (c) heightened global competition that holds down prices.

10. The main sources of increasing returns in recent years are (a) use of more specialized inputs as firms grow, (b) the spreading of development costs, (c) simultaneous consumption by consumers, (d) network effects, and (e) learning by doing. Increasing returns mean higher productivity and lower per-unit production costs.

11. Skeptics wonder if the recent productivity acceleration is permanent, and suggest a wait-and-see approach. They point out that surges in productivity and real GDP growth have previously occurred during vigorous economic expansions but do not necessarily represent long-lived trends.

12. Critics of rapid growth say that it adds to environmental degradation, increases human stress, and exhausts the earth's finite supply of natural resources. Defenders of rapid growth say that it is the primary path to the rising living standards nearly universally desired by people, that it need not debase the environment, and that there are no indications that we are running out of resources. Growth is based on the expansion and application of human knowledge, which is limited only by human imagination.

Terms and Concepts

economic growth

real GDP per capita

rule of 70

modern economic growth

leader countries

follower countries

supply factors

demand factor

efficiency factor

labor productivity

labor-force participation rate

growth accounting

infrastructure

human capital

economies of scale

information technology

start-up firms

increasing returns

network effects

learning by doing

Study Questions

1. Why is economic growth important? Why could the difference between a 2.5 percent and a 3 percent annual growth rate be of great significance over several decades? **LO1**

2. **KEY QUESTION** Suppose an economy's real GDP is $30,000 in year 1 and $31,200 in year 2. What is the growth rate of its real GDP? Assume that population is 100 in year 1 and 102 in year 2. What is the growth rate of real GDP per capita? **LO2**

3. When and where did modern economic growth first happen? What are the major institutional factors that form the foundation for modern economic growth? What do they have in common? **LO1**

4. Why are some countries today much poorer than other countries? Are today's poor countries destined to always be poorer than today's rich countries? If so, explain why. If not, explain how today's poor countries can catch up or even pass today's rich countries. **LO1**

5. **KEY QUESTION** What are the four supply factors of economic growth? What is the demand factor? What is the efficiency factor? Illustrate these factors in terms of the production possibilities curve. **LO2**

6. Suppose that Alpha and Omega have identically sized working-age populations but that annual hours of work are much greater in Alpha than in Omega. Provide two possible explanations. **LO2**

7. Suppose that work hours in New Zombie are 200 in year 1 and productivity is $8 per hour worked. What is New Zombie's real GDP? If work hours increase to 210 in year 2 and productivity rises to $10 per hour, what is New Zombie's rate of economic growth? **LO2**

8. **KEY QUESTION** To what extent have increases in U.S. real GDP resulted from more labor inputs? From higher labor productivity? Rearrange the following contributors to the growth of productivity in order of their quantitative importance: economies of scale, quantity of capital, improved resource allocation, education and training, technological advance. **LO2**

9. True or false? If false, explain why. **LO1**
   a. Technological advance, which to date has played a relatively small role in U.S. economic growth, is destined to play a more important role in the future.
   b. Many public capital goods are complementary to private capital goods.
   c. Immigration has slowed economic growth in the United States.

10. Explain why there is such a close relationship between changes in a nation's rate of productivity growth and changes in its average real hourly wage. **LO2**

11. **KEY QUESTION** Relate each of the following to the recent productivity acceleration: **LO3**
    a. Information technology
    b. Increasing returns
    c. Network effects
    d. Global competition

12. Provide three examples of products or services that can be simultaneously consumed by many people. Explain why labor productivity greatly rises as the firm sells more units of the product or service. Explain why the higher level of sales greatly reduces the per-unit cost of the product. **LO3**

13. Productivity often rises during economic expansions and falls during economic recessions. Can you think of reasons why? Briefly explain. (Hint: Remember that the level of productivity involves both levels of output and levels of labor input.) **LO3**

14. **LAST WORD** Based on the information in this chapter, contrast the economic growth rates of the United States and China over the last 25 years. How does the real GDP per capita of China compare with that of the United States? Why is there such a huge disparity of per capita income between China's coastal cities and its interior regions?

Web-Based Questions

1. **U.S. ECONOMIC GROWTH—WHAT ARE THE LATEST RATES?** Go to the Bureau of Economic Analysis Web site, **www.bea.gov.** Click on Interactive Data Tables, then National Income and Product Accounts, and then Frequently Requested NIPA Tables to get to Table 1.1.1. What are the quarterly growth rates (annualized) for the U.S. economy for the last six quarters? Is the average of those rates above or below the long-run U.S. annual growth rate of 3.5 percent? Expand the range of years, if necessary, to find the last time real GDP declined in two or more successive quarters. What were those quarters?

2. **WHAT'S UP WITH PRODUCTIVITY?** Visit the Bureau of Labor Statistics Web site, **www.bls.gov.** In sequence, select Productivity and Costs, Get Detailed Productivity and Cost Statistics, and then Major Sector Productivity and Costs (which is listed under the heading Most Requested Statistics) to find quarterly growth rates (annualized) for business output per hour for the last six quarters. Is the average of those rates higher or lower than the 1.4 percent average annual growth rate of productivity during the 1973–1995 period?

3. **PRODUCTIVITY AND TECHNOLOGY—EXAMPLES OF INNOVATIONS** Recent innovations are increasing productivity. Go to the Timeline of Historic Inventions at **www.wikipedia.org/wiki/Timeline_of_invention.** Scroll down until you find the inventions made starting in the 1940s. Look at them and later inventions. Cite five technological "home runs" (for example, the transistor in 1947) and five technological "singles" (for example, the personal stereo in 1977). Which one innovation do you think has increased productivity the most? List two innovations since 1990. How might they have boosted productivity?

FURTHER TEST YOUR KNOWLEDGE AT
www.mcconnell18e.com

Business Cycles, Unemployment, and Inflation

Between 1996 and 2000, real GDP in the United States expanded briskly and the price level rose only slowly. The economy experienced neither significant unemployment nor inflation. Some observers felt that the United States had entered a "new era" in which the business cycle was dead. But that wishful thinking came to an end in March 2001, when the economy entered its ninth recession since 1950. Since 1970, real GDP has declined in the United States in five periods: 1973–1975, 1980, 1981–1982, 1990–1991, and 2001. The economy again stalled in 2008, producing talk of a possible recession.

Although the U.S. economy has experienced remarkable economic growth over time, high unemployment or inflation has sometimes been a problem. For example, between March 2001 and December 2001, unemployment rose by 2.2 million workers. The U.S. rate of inflation was 13.5 percent in 1980 and 5.4 percent in 1990. Further, other nations have suffered high unemployment rates or inflation rates in recent years. For example, the unemployment rate in Germany reached 10.7 percent in 2005. The inflation rate was 26,000 percent in Zimbabwe in 2007

In this chapter we provide an introductory look at macroeconomic instability. Our specific topics are the business cycle, unemployment, and inflation.

The Business Cycle

The long-run trend of the U.S. economy is one of economic growth. But growth has been interrupted by periods

ORIGIN OF THE IDEA

O 26.1

Business cycles

of economic instability usually associated with **business cycles.** Business cycles are alternating rises and declines in the level of economic activity, sometime over several years. Individual cycles (one "up" followed by one "down") vary substantially in duration and intensity.

Phases of the Business Cycle

Figure 26.1 shows the four phases of a generalized business cycle:

- At a **peak,** such as the middle peak shown in Figure 26.1, business activity has reached a temporary maximum. Here the economy is near or at full employment and the level of real output is at or very close to the economy's capacity. The price level is likely to rise during this phase.
- A **recession** is a period of decline in total output, income, and employment. This downturn, which lasts 6 months or more, is marked by the widespread

contraction of business activity in many sectors of the economy. Along with declines in real GDP, significant increases in unemployment occur. Table 26.1 documents the 9 recessions in the United States since 1950.

- In the **trough** of the recession or depression, output and employment "bottom out" at their lowest levels. The trough phase may be either short-lived or quite long.
- A recession is usually followed by a recovery and **expansion,** a period in which real GDP, income, and employment rise. At some point, the economy again approaches full employment. If spending then expands more rapidly than does production capacity, prices of nearly all goods and services will rise. In other words, inflation will occur.

Although business cycles all pass through the same phases, they vary greatly in duration and intensity. Many economists prefer to talk of business "fluctuations" rather than cycles because cycles imply regularity while fluctuations do not. The Great Depression of the 1930s resulted in a 27 percent decline in real GDP over a 3-year period in the United States and seriously impaired business activity for a decade. By comparison, the more recent U.S. recessions detailed in Table 26.1 were relatively mild in both intensity and duration.

FIGURE 26.1 The business cycle. Economists distinguish four phases of the business cycle; the duration and strength of each phase may vary.

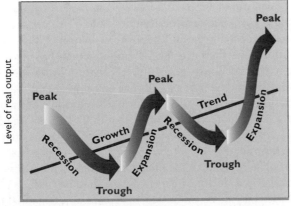

TABLE 26.1 U.S. Recessions since 1950

Period	Duration, Months	Depth (Decline in Real Output)
1953–54	10	−3.7%
1957–58	8	−3.9
1960–61	10	−1.6
1969–70	11	−1.0
1973–75	16	−4.9
1980	6	−2.3
1981–82	16	−3.3
1990–91	8	−1.8
2001	8	−0.5

Source: Economic Report of the President, 1993, p. 58. We have extended the 1993 table by appending 2001 data from the Council of Economic Advisers.

Recessions, of course, occur in other countries, too. At one time or another during the past 10 years, Argentina, Brazil, Colombia, Japan, Indonesia, Mexico, Germany, and South Korea experienced recessions.

Causation: A First Glance

The long-run trend of the U.S. economy is expansion and growth. That is why the business cycles in Figure 26.1 are drawn against a trend of economic growth. A key issue in macroeconomics is why the economy sees business cycle fluctuations rather than slow, smooth growth. In terms of Figure 26.1, why does output move up and down rather than just staying on the smooth growth trend line?

Economists have come up with several theories. But before turning to them, recall that in Chapter 23 we explained that these theories are founded on the idea that fluctuations are driven by shocks—unexpected events that individuals and firms may have trouble adjusting to. Also recall that short-run price stickiness is widely believed to be a major factor preventing the economy from rapidly adjusting to shocks. With prices sticky in the short run, price changes cannot quickly equalize the quantities demanded of goods and services with their respective quantities supplied after a shock has happened. Instead, the economy is forced to respond to shocks in the short run primarily through changes in output and employment rather than through changes in prices.

That being said, economists fall into several different camps when it comes to the types of shocks they believe to be responsible for business cycles. One group, for instance, stresses supply shocks caused by momentous innovations such as the railroad, the automobile, microchips, and the Internet. They believe that major inventions like these have a large impact on investment spending and consumption spending—and therefore on output, employment, and the price level. Because such major inventions occur irregularly and unexpectedly, they contribute to the variability of economic activity.

Another school of thought sees shocks to productivity as the major cause of business cycles. When productivity unexpectedly increases, the economy booms; when productivity unexpectedly falls, the economy goes into a recession. Others view the business cycle as a purely monetary phenomenon. They say that when a country's central bank shocks the economy by creating more money than people were expecting, an inflationary boom occurs. By contrast, printing less money than people were expecting triggers a decline in output and employment and, eventually, in the price level. Still others say that business cycles result from unexpected financial bubbles and bursts, which spill over through optimism or pessimism to affect the production of goods and services. And, finally, unexpected political events like wars or the 9/11 terrorist attacks also constitute major economic shocks to which the economy must adjust.

But whatever they see as the underlying forces driving economic shocks, most economists agree that the *immediate* cause of the large majority of cyclical changes in the levels of real output and employment is unexpected changes in the level of total spending. If total spending unexpectedly sinks and firms cannot lower prices, firms will find themselves selling fewer units of output (since with prices fixed, a decreased amount of spending implies fewer items purchased). Slower sales will cause firms to cut back on production. As they do, GDP will fall. And since fewer workers will be needed to produce less output, employment also will fall. The economy will contract and enter a recession.

By contrast, if the level of spending unexpectedly rises, output, employment, and incomes will rise. This is true because, with prices sticky, the increased spending will mean that consumers will be buying a larger volume of goods and services (since, with prices fixed, more spending means more items purchased). Firms will respond by increasing output. This will increase GDP. And because they will need to hire more workers to produce the larger volume of output, employment also will increase. The economy will boom and enjoy an expansion. Eventually, as time passes and prices become more flexible, prices are also likely to rise as a result of the increased spending.

Cyclical Impact: Durables and Nondurables

Although the business cycle is felt everywhere in the economy, it affects different segments in different ways and to different degrees.

Firms and industries producing *capital goods* (for example, housing, commercial buildings, heavy equipment, and farm implements) and *consumer durables* (for example, automobiles, personal computers, and refrigerators) are affected most by the business cycle. Within limits, firms can postpone the purchase of capital goods. For instance, when the economy goes into recession, producers frequently delay the purchase of new equipment and the construction of new plants. The business outlook simply does not warrant increases in the stock of capital goods. In good times, capital goods are usually replaced before they depreciate completely. But when recession strikes, firms patch up their old equipment and make do. As a result, investment in capital goods declines sharply. Firms that have excess plant capacity may not even bother to replace all the capital that is depreciating. For them, net investment may be negative.

The pattern is much the same for consumer durables such as automobiles and major appliances. When recession occurs and households must trim their budgets, purchases of these goods are often deferred. Families repair their old cars and appliances rather than buy new ones, and the firms producing these products suffer. (Of course, producers of capital goods and consumer durables also benefit most from expansions.)

In contrast, *service* industries and industries that produce *nondurable consumer goods* are somewhat insulated from the most severe effects of recession. People find it difficult to cut back on needed medical and legal services, for example. And a recession actually helps some service firms, such as pawnbrokers and law firms that specialize in bankruptcies. Nor are the purchases of many nondurable goods such as food and clothing easy to postpone. The quantity and quality of purchases of nondurables will decline, but not so much as will purchases of capital goods and consumer durables. (**Key Question 1**)

QUICK REVIEW 26.1

- The typical business cycle goes through four phases: peak, recession, trough, and expansion.

- Fluctuations in output and employment are caused by economic shocks combining with sticky prices.

- Sources of shocks include unexpected innovations, unexpected changes in productivity, unexpected changes in the money supply, unexpected changes in the level of total spending in the economy, and financial crises.

- During a recession, industries that produce capital goods and consumer durables normally suffer greater output and employment declines than do service and nondurable consumer goods industries.

Unemployment

Two problems that arise over the course of the business cycle are unemployment and inflation. Let's look at unemployment first.

Measurement of Unemployment

The U.S. Bureau of Labor Statistics (BLS) conducts a nationwide random survey of some 60,000 households each month to determine who is employed and who is not employed. In a series of questions, it asks which members of the household are working, unemployed and looking for work, not looking for work, and so on. From the answers, it determines an unemployment rate for the entire nation.

FIGURE 26.2 The labor force, employment, and unemployment, 2007. The labor force consists of persons 16 years of age or older who are not in institutions and who are (1) employed or (2) unemployed but seeking employment.

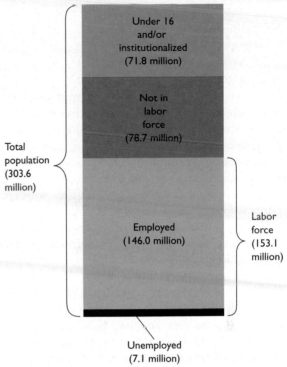

Source: Bureau of Labor Statistics, **www.bls.gov** (civilian labor force data, which excludes military employment).

Figure 26.2 helps explain the mathematics. The BLS divides the total U.S. population into three groups. One group is made up of people under 16 years of age and people who are institutionalized, for example, in mental hospitals or correctional institutions. Such people are not considered potential members of the labor force.

A second group, labeled "Not in labor force," is composed of adults who are potential workers but are not employed and are not seeking work. For example, they are homemakers, full-time students, or retirees.

The third group is the **labor force,** which constituted about 50 percent of the total population in 2007. The labor force consists of people who are able and willing to work. Both those who are employed and those who are unemployed but actively seeking work are counted as being in the labor force. The **unemployment rate** is the percentage of the labor force unemployed:

$$\text{Unemployment rate} = \frac{\text{unemployed}}{\text{labor force}} \times 100$$

The statistics included in Figure 26.2 show that in 2007 the unemployment rate averaged

$$\frac{7,078,000}{153,124,000} \times 100 = 4.6\%$$

WORKED PROBLEMS

W 26.1

Unemployment rate

Unemployment rates for selected years appear on the inside covers of this book.

Despite the use of scientific sampling and interviewing techniques, the data collected in this survey are subject to criticism:

- **Part-time employment** The BLS lists all part-time workers as fully employed. In 2007 about 20 million people worked part-time as a result of personal choice. But another 4.6 million part-time workers either wanted to work full-time and could not find suitable full-time work or worked fewer hours because of a temporary slack in consumer demand. These last two groups were, in effect, partially employed and partially unemployed. By counting them as fully employed, say critics, the official BLS data understate the unemployment rate.

- **Discouraged workers** You must be actively seeking work in order to be counted as unemployed. An unemployed individual who is not actively seeking employment is classified as "not in the labor force." The problem is that many workers, after unsuccessfully seeking employment for a time, become discouraged and drop out of the labor force. The number of such **discouraged workers** was 396,000 in 2007. By not counting discouraged workers as unemployed, say critics, the official BLS data understate the unemployment problem. **(Key Question 3)**

Types of Unemployment

There are three *types* of unemployment: frictional, structural, and cyclical.

Frictional Unemployment

At any given time some workers are "between jobs." Some of them will be moving voluntarily from one job to another. Others will have been fired and will be seeking reemployment. Still others will have been laid off temporarily because of seasonal demand. In addition to those between jobs, many young workers will be searching for their first jobs.

As these unemployed people find jobs or are called back from temporary layoffs, other job seekers and laid-off workers will replace them in the "unemployment pool." It is important to keep in mind that while the pool itself persists because there are always newly unemployed workers flowing into it, most workers do *not* stay in the unemployment pool for very long. Indeed, when the economy is strong, the majority of unemployed workers find new jobs within a couple of months. One should be careful not to make the mistake of confusing the permanence of the pool itself with the false idea that the pool's membership is permanent, too. On the other hand, there are workers who do remain unemployed and in the pool for very long periods of time—sometimes for many years. As we discuss the different types of unemployment below, notice that certain types tend to be transitory while others are associated with much longer spells of unemployment.

Economists use the term **frictional unemployment**—consisting of *search unemployment* and *wait unemployment*—for workers who are either searching for jobs or waiting to take jobs in the near future. The word "frictional" implies that the labor market does not operate perfectly and instantaneously (without friction) in matching workers and jobs.

Frictional unemployment is inevitable and, at least in part, desirable. Many workers who are voluntarily between jobs are moving from low-paying, low-productivity jobs to higher-paying, higher-productivity positions. That means greater income for the workers, a better allocation of labor resources, and a larger real GDP for the economy.

Structural Unemployment

Frictional unemployment blurs into a category called **structural unemployment.** Here, economists use "structural" in the sense of "compositional." Changes over time in consumer demand and in technology alter the "structure" of the total demand for labor, both occupationally and geographically.

Occupationally, the demand for certain skills (for example, sewing clothes or working on farms) may decline or even vanish. The demand for other skills (for example, designing software or maintaining computer systems) will intensify. Unemployment results because the composition of the labor force does not respond immediately or completely to the new structure of job opportunities. Workers who find that their skills and experience have become obsolete or unneeded thus find that they have no marketable talents. They are structurally unemployed until they adapt or develop skills that employers want.

Geographically, the demand for labor also changes over time. An example: the migration of industry and thus of employment opportunities from the Snow Belt to the Sun Belt over the past few decades. Another example is the movement of jobs from inner-city factories to suburban industrial parks. As job opportunities shift from one place to another, some workers become structurally unemployed.

The distinction between frictional and structural unemployment is hazy at best. The key difference is that *frictionally* unemployed workers have marketable skills and either live in areas where jobs exist or are able to move to areas where they do. *Structurally* unemployed workers find it hard to obtain new jobs without retraining, gaining additional education, or relocating. Frictional unemployment is short-term; structural unemployment is more likely to be long-term and consequently more serious.

Cyclical Unemployment

Unemployment that is caused by a decline in total spending is called **cyclical unemployment** and typically begins in the recession phase of the business cycle. As the demand for goods and services decreases, employment falls and unemployment rises. Cyclical unemployment results from insufficient demand for goods and services. The 25 percent unemployment rate in the depth of the Great Depression in 1933 reflected mainly cyclical unemployment, as did significant parts of the 9.7 percent unemployment rate in 1982, the 7.5 percent rate in 1992, and the 5.8 percent rate in 2002.

Cyclical unemployment is a very serious problem when it occurs. We will say more about its high costs later, but first we need to define "full employment."

Definition of Full Employment

Because frictional and structural unemployment is largely unavoidable in a dynamic economy, *full employment* is something less than 100 percent employment of the labor force. Economists say that the economy is "fully employed" when it is experiencing only frictional and structural unemployment. That is, full employment occurs when there is no cyclical unemployment.

Economists describe the unemployment rate that is consistent with full employment as the **full-employment rate of unemployment,** or the **natural rate of unemployment (NRU).** At the NRU, the economy is said to be producing its **potential output.** This is the real GDP that occurs when the economy is "fully employed."

Note that a fully employed economy does not mean zero unemployment. Even when the economy is fully employed, the NRU is some positive percentage because it takes time for frictionally unemployed job seekers to find open jobs they can fill. Also, it takes time for the structurally unemployed to achieve the skills and geographic relocation needed for reemployment.

"Natural" does not mean, however, that the economy will always operate at this rate and thus realize its potential output. When cyclical unemployment occurs, the economy has much more unemployment than that which would occur at the NRU. Moreover, the economy can operate for a while

at an unemployment rate *below* the NRU. At times, the demand for labor may be so great that firms take a stronger initiative to hire and train the structurally unemployed. Also, some homemakers, teenagers, college students, and retirees who were casually looking for just the right part-time or full-time jobs may quickly find them. Thus the unemployment rate temporarily falls below the natural rate.

Also, the NRU can vary over time. In the 1980s, the NRU was about 6 percent. Today, it is 4 to 5 percent. Why the decline?

- The proportion of younger workers in the labor force has declined as the baby-boom generation has aged. The labor force now has a larger proportion of middle-aged workers, who traditionally have lower unemployment rates.
- The growth of temporary-help agencies and the improved information resulting from the Internet have lowered the NRU by enabling workers to find jobs more quickly.
- The work requirements under the new welfare laws have moved many people from the ranks of the unemployed to the ranks of the employed.
- The doubling of the U.S. prison population since 1985 has removed relatively high unemployment individuals from the labor force and thus lowered the overall unemployment rate.

In the early to mid 1990s, a 4 to 5 percent rate of unemployment would have reflected excessive spending, an unbalanced labor market, and rising inflation; today, the same rate is consistent with a balanced labor market and a stable, low rate of inflation.

Economic Cost of Unemployment

Unemployment that is excessive involves great economic and social costs.

GDP Gap and Okun's Law

The basic economic cost of unemployment is forgone output. When the economy fails to create enough jobs for all who are able and willing to work, potential production of goods and services is irretrievably lost. In terms of Chapter 1's analysis, unemployment above the natural rate means that society is operating at some point inside its production possibilities curve. Economists call this sacrifice of output a **GDP gap**—the difference between actual and potential GDP. That is:

$$\text{GDP gap} = \text{actual GDP} - \text{potential GDP}$$

The GDP gap can be either negative (actual GDP < potential GDP) or positive (actual GDP > potential GDP). In the case of unemployment above the natural rate, it is negative because actual GDP falls short of potential GDP.

Potential GDP is determined by assuming that the natural rate of unemployment prevails. The growth of potential GDP is simply projected forward on the basis of the economy's "normal" growth rate of real GDP. Figure 26.3 shows the GDP gap for recent years in the United States. It also indicates the close correlation between the actual unemployment rate (Figure 26.3b) and the GDP gap (Figure 26.3a). The higher the unemployment rate, the larger is the GDP gap.

Macroeconomist Arthur Okun was the first to quantify the relationship between the unemployment rate and the GDP gap. On the basis of recent estimates, **Okun's law** indicates that for every 1 percentage point by which the actual unemployment rate exceeds the natural rate,

> **WORKED PROBLEMS**
>
> **W 26.2**
>
> Okun's law

a negative GDP gap of about 2 percent occurs. With this information, we can calculate the absolute loss of output associated with any above-natural unemployment rate. For example, in 1992 the unemployment rate was 7.4 percent, or 1.4 percentage points above that period's 6.0 percent natural rate of unemployment. Multiplying this 1.4 percent by Okun's 2 indicates that 1992's GDP gap was 2.8 percent of potential GDP (in real terms). By applying this 2.8 percent loss to 1992's potential GDP of $7337 billion, we find that the economy sacrificed $205 billion of real output because the natural rate of unemployment was not achieved. **(Key Question 5)**

As you can see in Figure 26.3, sometimes the economy's actual output will exceed its potential or full-employment output. Figure 26.3 reveals that an economic expansion in 1999 and 2000, for example, caused actual GDP to exceed potential GDP in those years. There was a positive GDP gap in 1999 and 2000. Actual GDP for a time can exceed potential GDP, but positive GDP gaps create inflationary pressures and cannot be sustained indefinitely.

Unequal Burdens

An increase in the unemployment rate from 5 to, say, 7 or 8 percent might be more tolerable to society if every worker's hours of work and wage income were reduced proportionally. But this is not the case. Part of the burden of unemployment is that its cost is unequally distributed.

Table 26.2 examines unemployment rates for various labor market groups for 2 years. The 2001 recession pushed the 2002 unemployment rate to 5.8 percent. In 2007, the economy achieved full employment, with a 4.6 percent unemployment rate. By observing the large variance in unemployment rates for the different groups within each

year and comparing the rates between the 2 years, we can generalize as follows:

- **Occupation** Workers in lower-skilled occupations (for example, laborers) have higher unemployment rates than workers in higher-skilled occupations (for example, professionals). Lower-skilled workers have more and longer spells of structural unemployment than higher-skilled workers. They also are less likely to be self-employed than are higher-skilled workers. Moreover, lower-skilled workers usually bear the brunt of recessions. Businesses generally retain most of their higher-skilled workers, in whom they have invested the expense of training.

- **Age** Teenagers have much higher unemployment rates than adults. Teenagers have lower skill levels, quit their jobs more frequently, are more frequently

TABLE 26.2 Unemployment Rates by Demographic Group: Recession (2002) and Full Employment (2007)*

Demographic Group	Unemployment Rate	
	2002	2007
Overall	5.8%	4.6%
Occupation:		
Managerial and professional	3.1	2.0
Operators, fabricators, and laborers	8.9	6.8
Age:		
16–19	16.5	13.9
African American, 16–19	29.8	29.0
White, 16–19	14.5	13.2
Male, 20+	5.3	4.1
Female, 20+	5.1	4.0
Race and ethnicity:		
African American	10.2	8.0
Hispanic	7.5	5.7
White	5.1	4.1
Gender:		
Women	5.6	4.5
Men	5.9	4.7
Education:†		
Less than high school diploma	8.4	6.9
High school diploma only	5.3	4.2
College degree or more	2.9	2.1
Duration:		
15 or more weeks	2.0	1.5

*Civilian labor-force data. In 2002 the economy was suffering the lingering unemployment effects of the 2001 recession. The 2007 data is from January 2007, when the economy was at full employment and before the economy began to slow in late 2007 due to the mortgage debt crisis.

†People age 25 or over.

Source: *Economic Report of the President; Employment and Earnings,* Census Bureau, **www.census.gov.**

FIGURE 26.3 Actual and potential GDP and the unemployment rate. (a) The difference between actual and potential GDP is the GDP gap. A negative GDP gap measures the output the economy sacrifices when actual GDP falls short of potential GDP. A positive GDP gap indicates that actual GDP is above potential GDP. (b) A high unemployment rate means a large GDP gap (negative), and a low unemployment rate means a small or even positive GDP gap.

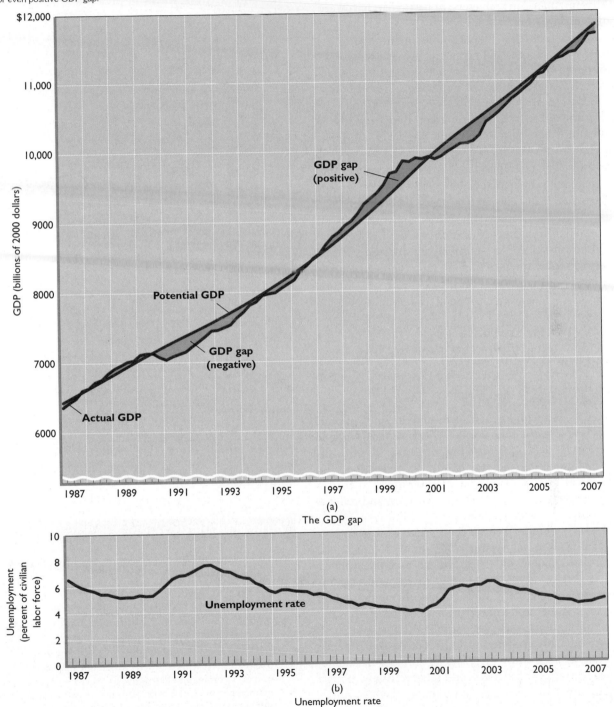

(a)
The GDP gap

(b)
Unemployment rate

Source: Data are from the Congressional Budget Office, **www.cbo.gov**, and Bureau of Economic Analysis, **www.bea.gov**.

"fired," and have less geographic mobility than adults. Many unemployed teenagers are new in the labor market, searching for their first jobs. Male African-American teenagers, in particular, have very high unemployment rates.

- *Race and ethnicity* The unemployment rate for African Americans and Hispanics is higher than that for whites. The causes of the higher rates include lower rates of educational attainment, greater concentration in lower-skilled occupations, and discrimination in the labor market. In general, the unemployment rate for African Americans is twice that of whites.
- *Gender* The unemployment rates for men and women are very similar.
- *Education* Less-educated workers, on average, have higher unemployment rates than workers with more education. Less education is usually associated with lower-skilled, less-permanent jobs; more time between jobs; and jobs that are more vulnerable to cyclical layoff.
- *Duration* The number of persons unemployed for long periods—15 weeks or more—as a percentage of the labor force is much lower than the overall unemployment rate. But that percentage rises significantly during recessions.

Noneconomic Costs

Severe cyclical unemployment is more than an economic malady; it is a social catastrophe. Unemployment means idleness. And idleness means loss of skills, loss of self-respect, plummeting morale, family disintegration, and sociopolitical unrest. Widespread joblessness increases poverty, heightens racial and ethnic tensions, and reduces hope for material advancement.

History demonstrates that severe unemployment can lead to rapid and sometimes violent social and political change. Witness Hitler's ascent to power against a background of unemployment in Germany. Furthermore, relatively high unemployment among some racial and ethnic minorities has contributed to the unrest and violence that has periodically plagued some cities in the United States and abroad. At the individual level, research links increases in suicide, homicide, fatal heart attacks and strokes, and mental illness to high unemployment.

International Comparisons

Unemployment rates differ greatly among nations at any given time. One reason is that nations have different natural rates of unemployment. Another is that nations may

GLOBAL PERSPECTIVE 26.1

Unemployment Rates in Five Industrial Nations, 1997–2007

Compared with Italy, France, and Germany, the United States had a relatively low unemployment rate in recent years.

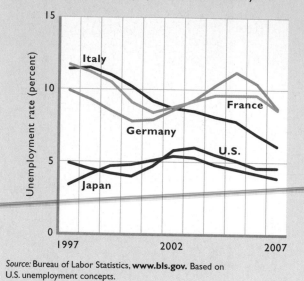

Source: Bureau of Labor Statistics, **www.bls.gov.** Based on U.S. unemployment concepts.

be in different phases of their business cycles. Global Perspective 26.1 shows unemployment rates for five industrialized nations in recent years. Between 1997 and 2007, the U.S. unemployment rate was considerably lower than the rates in Italy, France, and Germany. The nearby Consider This box explores why unemployment rates are so high in Europe.

QUICK REVIEW 26.2

- Unemployment is of three general types: frictional, structural, and cyclical.
- The natural unemployment rate (frictional plus structural) is presently 4 to 5 percent in the United States.
- A positive GDP gap occurs when actual GDP exceeds potential GDP; a negative GDP gap occurs when actual GDP falls short of potential GDP.
- Society loses real GDP when cyclical unemployment occurs; according to Okun's law, for each 1 percentage point of unemployment above the natural rate, the U.S. economy suffers a 2 percent decline in real GDP below its potential GDP.
- Lower-skilled workers, teenagers, African Americans and Hispanics, and less-educated workers bear a disproportionate burden of unemployment.

Why Is the Unemployment Rate in Europe So High?

Several European economies have had exceptionally high unemployment rates recently. For example, based on U.S. measurement concepts, the percentage unemployment rate in 2007 in France was 8.6 percent; in Germany, 8.7 percent; in Spain, 8.3 percent; and in Italy, 6.2 percent. Those numbers compare very unfavorably with the 4.6 percent in the United States that year. Furthermore, the high European unemployment rates do not appear to be cyclical. Even during business cycle peaks, the unemployment rates are higher than those in the United States. Unemployment rates are particularly high for European youth. For example, the unemployment rate for 20- to 24-year-olds in France was 18 percent in 2007 (compared to 8.2 percent in the United States).

The causes of high unemployment rates in these countries are complex, but European economists generally point to government policies and union contracts that have increased the business costs of hiring workers and have reduced the individual cost of being unemployed. Examples: High legal minimum wages have discouraged employers from hiring low-skilled workers. Generous welfare benefits and unemployment benefits have encouraged absenteeism, led to high job turnover, and weakened incentives for people to take available jobs.

Restrictions on firing of workers have made firms leery of adding workers during expansions. Short workweeks mandated by government or negotiated by unions have limited the ability of employers to spread their recruitment and training costs over a longer number of hours. Paid vacations and holidays of 30 to 40 days per year have boosted the cost of hiring workers. Also, high employer costs of pension and other benefits have discouraged hiring.

Attempts to make the labor market more flexible in France, Germany, Italy, and Spain have met with stiff political resistance—including large rallies and protests. The direction of future employment policy is unclear, but economists do not expect the high rates of unemployment in these nations to decline anytime soon.

Inflation

We now turn to inflation, another aspect of macroeconomic instability. The problems inflation poses are subtler than those posed by unemployment.

Meaning of Inflation

Inflation is a rise in the general level of prices. When inflation occurs, each dollar of income will buy fewer goods and services than before. Inflation reduces the "purchasing power" of money. But inflation does not mean that *all* prices are rising. Even during periods of rapid inflation, some prices may be relatively constant and others may even fall. For example, although the United States experienced high rates of inflation in the 1970s and early 1980s, the prices of video recorders, digital watches, and personal computers declined.

Measurement of Inflation

The main measure of inflation in the United States is the **Consumer Price Index (CPI),** compiled by the Bureau of Labor Statistics (BLS). The government uses this index to report inflation rates each month and each year. It also uses the CPI to adjust Social Security benefits and income tax brackets for inflation. The CPI reports the price of a "market basket" of some 300 consumer goods and services that are purchased by a typical urban consumer. (The GDP price index of Chapter 24 is a much broader measure of inflation since it includes not only consumer goods and services but also capital goods, goods and services purchased by government, and goods and services that enter world trade.)

The composition of the market basket for the CPI is based on spending patterns of urban consumers in a specific period, presently 2005–2006. The BLS updates the composition of the market basket every 2 years so that it reflects the most recent patterns of consumer purchases and captures the inflation that consumers are currently experiencing. The BLS arbitrarily sets the CPI equal to 100 for 1982–1984. So the CPI for any particular year is found as follows:

$$\text{CPI} = \frac{\text{price of the most recent market basket in the particular year}}{\text{price estimate of the market basket in 1982–1984}} \times 100$$

The rate of inflation is equal to the percentage growth of CPI from one year to the next. For example, the CPI was 207.3 in 2007, up from 201.6 in 2006. So the rate of inflation for 2007 is calculated as follows:

$$\text{Rate of inflation} = \frac{207.3 - 201.6}{201.6} \times 100 = 2.8\%$$

In Chapter 25, we discussed the mathematical approximation called *the rule of 70*, which tells us that we can find the number of years it will take for some measure to double, given its annual percentage increase, by dividing that percentage increase into the number 70. So a 3 percent annual rate of inflation will double the price level in about 23 (= 70 ÷ 3) years. Inflation of 8 percent per year will double the price level in about 9 (= 70 ÷ 8) years. **(Key Question 8)**

Facts of Inflation

Figure 26.4 shows the annual rates of inflation in the United States between 1960 and 2007. Observe that inflation reached double-digit rates in the 1970s and early 1980s but has since declined and has been relatively mild recently.

In recent years U.S. inflation has been neither unusually high nor low relative to inflation in several other industrial countries (see Global Perspective 26.2). Some nations (not shown) have had double-digit or even higher annual rates of inflation in recent years. In 2007, for example, the annual inflation rate in Burma was 40 percent; Venezuela, 20 percent; Iran, 17 percent; and in Mongolia, 15 percent. Recall from the chapter opener that inflation was 26,000 percent in Zimbabwe that year. For 2008, Zimbabwe's inflation rate was expected to exceed 100,000 percent!

Types of Inflation

Nearly all prices in the economy are set by supply and demand. Consequently, if the economy is experiencing inflation and the overall level of prices is rising, we need to look for an explanation in terms of supply and demand.

Demand-Pull Inflation Usually, increases in the price level are caused by an excess of total spending beyond

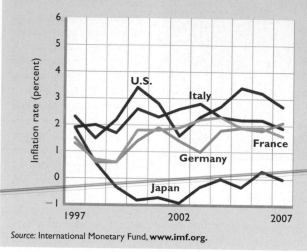

GLOBAL PERSPECTIVE 26.2

Inflation Rates in Five Industrial Nations, 1997–2007

Inflation rates in the United States in recent years were neither extraordinarily high nor extraordinarily low relative to rates in other industrial nations.

Source: International Monetary Fund, **www.imf.org.**

the economy's capacity to produce. Where inflation is rapid and sustained, the cause invariably is an overissuance of money by the central bank (the Federal Reserve in the United States). When resources are already fully employed, the business sector cannot respond to excess demand by expanding output. So the excess demand bids

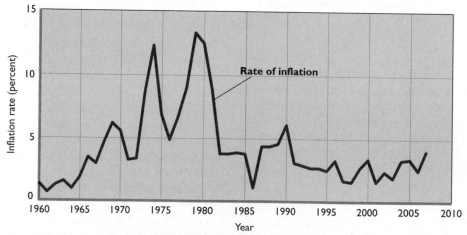

FIGURE 26.4 Annual inflation rates in the United States, 1960–2007. The major periods of inflation in the United States in the past 47 years were in the 1970s and 1980s.

Source: Bureau of Labor Statistics, **www.bls.gov.** Inflation rates reflect December-to-December changes in the Consumer Price Index.

up the prices of the limited output, producing **demand-pull inflation**. The essence of this type of inflation is "too much spending chasing too few goods."

Cost-Push Inflation

Inflation also may arise on the supply, or cost, side of the economy. During some periods in U.S. economic history, including the mid-1970s, the price level increased even though total spending was not excessive. These were periods when output and employment were both *declining* (evidence that total spending was not excessive) while the general price level was *rising*.

The theory of **cost-push inflation** explains rising prices in terms of factors that raise **per-unit production costs** at each level of spending. A per-unit production cost is the average cost of a particular level of output. This average cost is found by dividing the total cost of all resource inputs by the amount of output produced. That is,

$$\text{Per-unit production cost} = \frac{\text{total input cost}}{\text{units of output}}$$

Rising per-unit production costs squeeze profits and reduce the amount of output firms are willing to supply at the existing price level. As a result, the economy's supply of goods and services declines and the price level rises. In this scenario, costs are *pushing* the price level upward, whereas in demand-pull inflation demand is *pulling* it upward.

The major source of cost-push inflation has been so-called *supply shocks*. Specifically, abrupt increases in the costs of raw materials or energy inputs have on occasion driven up per-unit production costs and thus product prices. The rocketing prices of imported oil in 1973–1974 and again in 1979–1980 are good illustrations. As energy prices surged upward during these periods, the costs of producing and transporting virtually every product in the economy rose. Cost-push inflation ensued.

Complexities

The real world is more complex than the distinction between demand-pull and cost-push inflation suggests. It is difficult to distinguish between demand-pull inflation and cost-push inflation unless the original source of inflation is known. For example, suppose a significant increase in total spending occurs in a fully employed economy, causing demand-pull inflation. But as the demand-pull stimulus works its way through various product and resource markets, individual firms find their wage costs, material costs, and fuel prices rising. From their perspective they must raise their prices because production costs (someone else's prices) have risen. Although this inflation is clearly demand-pull in origin, it

CONSIDER THIS . . .

Clipping Coins

Some interesting early episodes of demand-pull inflation occurred in Europe during the ninth to the fifteenth centuries under feudalism.

In that economic system *lords* (or *princes*) ruled individual fiefdoms and their *vassals* (or *peasants*) worked the fields. The peasants initially paid parts of their harvest as taxes to the princes. Later, when the princes began issuing "coins of the realm," peasants began paying their taxes with gold coins.

Some princes soon discovered a way to transfer purchasing power from their vassals to themselves without explicitly increasing taxes. As coins came into the treasury, princes clipped off parts of the gold coins, making them slightly smaller. From the clippings they minted new coins and used them to buy more goods for themselves.

This practice of clipping coins was a subtle form of taxation. The quantity of goods being produced in the fiefdom remained the same, but the number of gold coins increased. With "too much money chasing too few goods," inflation occurred. Each gold coin earned by the peasants therefore had less purchasing power than previously because prices were higher. The increase of the money supply shifted purchasing power away from the peasants and toward the princes just as surely as if the princes had increased taxation of the peasants.

In more recent eras some dictators have simply printed money to buy more goods for themselves, their relatives, and their key loyalists. These dictators, too, have levied hidden taxes on their population by creating inflation.

The moral of the story is quite simple: A society that values price-level stability should not entrust the control of its money supply to people who benefit from inflation.

may mistakenly appear to be cost-push inflation to business firms and to government. Without proper identification of the source of the inflation, government and the Federal Reserve may be slow to undertake policies to reduce excessive total spending.

Another complexity is that cost-push inflation and demand-pull inflation differ in their sustainability. Demand-pull inflation will continue as long as there is excess total spending. Cost-push inflation is automatically self-limiting; it will die out by itself. Increased per-unit costs will reduce supply, and this means lower real output and employment. Those decreases will constrain further per-unit cost increases. In other words, cost-push inflation generates a recession. And in a recession, households and businesses concentrate on keeping their resources employed, not on pushing up the prices of those resources.

QUICK REVIEW 26.3

- Inflation is a rising general level of prices and is measured as a percentage change in a price index such as the CPI.

- For the past several years, the U.S. inflation rate has been within the general range of the rates of other advanced industrial nations and far below the rates experienced by some nations.

- Demand-pull inflation occurs when total spending exceeds the economy's ability to provide goods and services at the existing price level; total spending *pulls* the price level upward.

- Cost-push inflation occurs when factors such as rapid increases in the prices of imported raw materials drive up per-unit production costs at each level of output; higher costs *push* the price level upward.

Redistribution Effects of Inflation

Inflation redistributes real income. This redistribution helps some people and hurts some others while leaving many people largely unaffected. Who gets hurt? Who benefits? Before we can answer, we need some terminology.

Nominal and Real Income
There is a difference between money (or nominal) income and real income. **Nominal income** is the number of dollars received as wages, rent, interest, or profits. **Real income** is a measure of the amount of goods and services nominal income can buy; it is the purchasing power of nominal income, or income adjusted for inflation. That is,

$$\text{Real income} = \frac{\text{nominal income}}{\text{price index (in hundredths)}}$$

Inflation need not alter an economy's overall real income—its total purchasing power. It is evident from the above equation that real income will remain the same when nominal income rises at the same percentage rate as does the price index.

But when inflation occurs, not everyone's nominal income rises at the same pace as the price level. Therein lies the potential for redistribution of real income from some to others. If the change in the price level differs from the change in a person's nominal income, his or her real income will be affected. The following approximation (shown by the $\cong$ sign) tells us roughly how much real income will change:

Percentage change in real income	$\cong$	percentage change in nominal income	$-$	percentage change in price level

For example, suppose that the price level rises by 6 percent in some period. If Bob's nominal income rises by 6 percent, his real income will *remain unchanged*. But if his nominal income instead rises by 10 percent, his real income will *increase* by about 4 percent. And if Bob's nominal income rises by only 2 percent, his real income will *decline* by about 4 percent.[1]

WORKED PROBLEMS

W 26.3
Nominal and real income

Anticipations The redistribution effects of inflation depend upon whether or not it is expected. We will first discuss situations involving **unanticipated inflation.** As you will see, these cause real income and wealth to be redistributed, harming some and benefiting others. We will then discuss situations involving **anticipated inflation.** These are situations in which people see an inflation coming in advance. With the ability to plan ahead, people are able to avoid or lessen the redistribution effects associated with inflation.

Who Is Hurt by Inflation?
Unanticipated inflation hurts fixed-income recipients, savers, and creditors. It redistributes real income away from them and toward others.

Fixed-Income Receivers
People whose incomes are fixed see their real incomes fall when inflation occurs. The classic case is the elderly couple living on a private pension or annuity that provides a fixed amount of nominal income each month. They may have retired in, say, 1991 on what appeared to be an adequate pension. However, by 2007 they would have discovered that inflation had cut the purchasing power of that pension— their real income—one-third.

---

[1] A more precise calculation uses our equation for real income. In our first illustration above, if nominal income rises by 10 percent from $100 to $110 and the price level (index) rises by 6 percent from 100 to 106, then real income has increased as follows:

$$\frac{\$110}{1.06} = \$103.77$$

The 4 percent increase in real income shown by the simple formula in the text is a reasonable approximation of the 3.77 percent yielded by our more precise formula.

Similarly, landlords who receive lease payments of fixed dollar amounts will be hurt by inflation as they receive dollars of declining value over time. Likewise, public sector workers whose incomes are dictated by fixed pay schedules may suffer from inflation. The fixed "steps" (the upward yearly increases) in their pay schedules may not keep up with inflation. Minimum-wage workers and families living on fixed welfare incomes also will be hurt by inflation.

Savers Unanticipated inflation hurts savers. As prices rise, the real value, or purchasing power, of an accumulation of savings deteriorates. Paper assets such as savings accounts, insurance policies, and annuities that were once adequate to meet rainy-day contingencies or provide for a comfortable retirement decline in real value during inflation. The simplest case is the person who hoards money as a cash balance. A $1000 cash balance would have lost one-half its real value between 1984 and 2007. Of course, most forms of savings earn interest. But the value of savings will still decline if the rate of inflation exceeds the rate of interest.

Example: A household may save $1000 in a certificate of deposit (CD) in a commercial bank or savings and loan association at 6 percent annual interest. But if inflation is 13 percent (as it was in 1980), the real value or purchasing power of that $1000 will be cut to about $938 by the end of the year. Although the saver will receive $1060 (equal to $1000 plus $60 of interest), deflating that $1060 for 13 percent inflation means that its real value is only about $938 (= $1060 ÷ 1.13).

Creditors Unanticipated inflation harms creditors (lenders). Suppose Chase Bank lends Bob $1000, to be repaid in 2 years. If in that time the price level doubles, the $1000 that Bob repays will have only half the purchasing power of the $1000 he borrowed. True, if we ignore interest charges, the same number of dollars will be repaid as was borrowed. But because of inflation, each of those dollars will buy only half as much as it did when the loan was negotiated. As prices go up, the value of the dollar goes down. So the borrower pays back less valuable dollars than those received from the lender. The owners of Chase Bank suffer a loss of real income.

Who Is Unaffected or Helped by Inflation?

Some people are unaffected by inflation and others are actually helped by it. For the second group, inflation redistributes real income toward them and away from others.

Flexible-Income Receivers People who have flexible incomes may escape inflation's harm or even benefit from it. For example, individuals who derive their incomes solely from Social Security are largely unaffected by inflation because Social Security payments are *indexed* to the CPI. Benefits automatically increase when the CPI increases, preventing erosion of benefits from inflation. Some union workers also get automatic **cost-of-living adjustments (COLAs)** in their pay when the CPI rises, although such increases rarely equal the full percentage rise in inflation.

Some flexible-income receivers and all borrowers are helped by unanticipated inflation. The strong product demand and labor shortages implied by rapid demand-pull inflation may cause some nominal incomes to spurt ahead of the price level, thereby enhancing real incomes. For some, the 3 percent increase in nominal income that occurs when inflation is 2 percent may become a 7 percent increase when inflation is 5 percent. As an example, property owners faced with an inflation-induced real estate boom may be able to boost rents more rapidly than the rate of inflation. Also, some business owners may benefit from inflation. If product prices rise faster than resource prices, business revenues will increase more rapidly than costs. In those cases, the growth rate of profit incomes will outpace the rate of inflation.

Debtors Unanticipated inflation benefits debtors (borrowers). In our earlier example, Chase Bank's loss of real income from inflation is Bob's gain of real income. Debtor Bob borrows "dear" dollars but, because of inflation, pays back the principal and interest with "cheap" dollars whose purchasing power has been eroded by inflation. Real income is redistributed away from the owners of Chase Bank toward borrowers such as Bob.

The Federal government, which had amassed $9.0 trillion of public debt through 2007 has also benefited from inflation. Historically, the Federal government regularly paid off its loans by taking out new ones. Inflation permitted the Treasury to pay off its loans with dollars of less purchasing power than the dollars originally borrowed. Nominal national income and therefore tax collections rise with inflation; the amount of public debt owed does not. Thus, inflation reduces the real burden of the public debt to the Federal government.

Anticipated Inflation

The redistribution effects of inflation are less severe or are eliminated altogether if people anticipate inflation and can adjust their nominal incomes to reflect the expected price-level rises. The prolonged inflation that began in the late 1960s prompted many labor unions in the 1970s to insist on labor contracts with cost-of-living adjustment clauses.

Similarly, if inflation is anticipated, the redistribution of income from lender to borrower may be altered. Suppose a lender (perhaps a commercial bank or a savings and loan institution) and a borrower (a household) both agree that 5 percent is a fair rate of interest on a 1-year loan provided the price level is stable. But assume that inflation has been occurring and is expected to be 6 percent over the next year. If the bank lends the household $100 at 5 percent interest, the bank will be paid back $105 at the end of the year. But if 6 percent inflation does occur during that year, the purchasing power of the $105 will have been reduced to about $99. The lender will, in effect, have paid the borrower $1 for the use of the lender's money for a year.

The lender can avoid this subsidy by charging an *inflation premium*—that is, by raising the interest rate by 6 percent, the amount of the anticipated inflation. By charging 11 percent, the lender will receive back $111 at the end of the year. Adjusted for the 6 percent inflation, that amount will have roughly the purchasing power of $105 worth of today's money. The result then will be a mutually agreeable transfer of purchasing power from borrower to lender of $5, or 5 percent, for the use of $100 for 1 year. Financial institutions have also developed variable-interest-rate mortgages to protect themselves from the adverse effects of inflation. (Incidentally, this example points out that, rather than being a *cause* of inflation, high nominal interest rates are a *consequence* of inflation.)

Our example reveals the difference between the real rate of interest and the nominal rate of interest. The **real interest rate** is the percentage increase in *purchasing power* that the borrower pays the lender. In our example the real interest rate is 5 percent.

ORIGIN OF THE IDEA
O 26.2
Real interest rates

The **nominal interest rate** is the percentage increase in *money* that the borrower pays the lender, including that resulting from the built-in expectation of inflation, if any. In equation form:

$$\text{Nominal interest rate} = \text{real interest rate} + \text{inflation premium}$$
$$\text{(the expected rate of inflation)}$$

As illustrated in Figure 26.5, the nominal interest rate in our example is 11 percent.

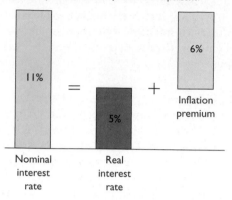

FIGURE 26.5 The inflation premium and nominal and real interest rates. The inflation premium—the expected rate of inflation—gets built into the nominal interest rate. Here, the nominal interest rate of 11 percent comprises the real interest rate of 5 percent plus the inflation premium of 6 percent.

Other Redistribution Issues

We end our discussion of the redistribution effects of inflation by making three final points:

- *Deflation* The effects of unanticipated **deflation**—declines in the price level—are the reverse of those of inflation. People with fixed nominal incomes will find their real incomes enhanced. Creditors will benefit at the expense of debtors. And savers will discover that the purchasing power of their savings has grown because of the falling prices.

- *Mixed effects* A person who is simultaneously an income earner, a holder of financial assets, and a debtor will probably find that the redistribution impact of unanticipated inflation is cushioned. If the person owns fixed-value monetary assets (savings accounts, bonds, and insurance policies), inflation will lessen their real value. But that same inflation may produce an increase in the person's nominal wage. Also, if the person holds a fixed-interest-rate mortgage, the real burden of that debt will decline. In short, many individuals are simultaneously hurt and helped by inflation. All these effects must be considered before we can conclude that any particular person's net position is better or worse because of inflation.

- *Arbitrariness* The redistribution effects of inflation occur regardless of society's goals and values. Inflation lacks a social conscience and takes from some and gives to others, whether they are rich, poor, young, old, healthy, or infirm.

Does Inflation Affect Output?

Thus far, our discussion has focused on how inflation redistributes a given level of total real income. But inflation also may affect an economy's level of real output (and thus its level of real income). The direction and significance of this effect on output depend on the type of inflation and its severity.

Cost-Push Inflation and Real Output

Recall that abrupt and unexpected rises in key resource prices such as oil can sufficiently drive up overall production costs to cause cost-push inflation. As prices rise, the quantity of goods and services demanded falls. So firms respond by producing less output, and unemployment goes up.

Economic events of the 1970s provide an example of how inflation can reduce real output. In late 1973 the Organization of Petroleum Exporting Countries (OPEC), by exerting its market power, managed to quadruple the price of oil. The cost-push inflationary effects generated rapid price-level increases in the 1973–1975 period. At the same time, the U.S. unemployment rate rose from slightly less than 5 percent in 1973 to 8.5 percent in 1975. Similar outcomes occurred in 1979–1980 in response to a second OPEC oil supply shock.

In short, cost-push inflation reduces real output. It redistributes a decreased level of real income.

Demand-Pull Inflation and Real Output

Economists do not fully agree on the effects of mild inflation (less than 3 percent) on real output. One perspective is that even low levels of inflation reduce real output because inflation diverts time and effort toward activities designed to hedge against inflation. Examples:

- Businesses must incur the cost of changing thousands of prices on their shelves and in their computers simply to reflect inflation.

- Households and businesses must spend considerable time and effort obtaining the information they need to distinguish between real and nominal values such as prices, wages, and interest rates.
- To limit the loss of purchasing power from inflation, people try to limit the amount of money they hold in their billfolds and checking accounts at any one time and instead put more money into interest-bearing accounts and stock and bond funds. But cash and checks are needed in even greater amounts to buy the higher-priced goods and services. So more frequent trips, phone calls, or Internet visits to financial institutions are required to transfer funds to checking accounts and billfolds, when needed.

Without inflation, these uses of resources, time, and effort would not be needed, and they could be diverted toward producing more valuable goods and services. Proponents of "zero inflation" bolster their case by pointing to cross-country studies that indicate that lower rates of inflation are associated with higher rates of economic growth. Even mild inflation, say these economists, is detrimental to economic growth.

In contrast, other economists point out that full employment and economic growth depend on strong levels of total spending. Such spending creates high profits, strong demand for labor, and a powerful incentive for firms to expand their plants and equipment. In this view, the mild inflation that is a by-product of strong spending is a small price to pay for full employment and continued economic growth. Moreover, a little inflation may have positive effects because it makes it easier for firms to adjust real wages downward when the demands for their products fall. With mild inflation, firms can reduce real wages by holding nominal wages steady. With zero inflation firms would need to cut nominal wages to reduce real wages. Such cuts in nominal wages are highly visible and may cause considerable worker resistance and labor strife.

Finally, defenders of mild inflation say that it is much better for an economy to err on the side of strong spending, full employment, economic growth, and mild inflation than on the side of weak spending, unemployment, recession, and deflation.

Hyperinflation

All economists agree that **hyperinflation,** which is extraordinarily rapid inflation, can have a devastating impact on real output and employment.

How, If at All, Do Changes in Stock Prices Relate to Macroeconomic Instability?

Every day, the individual stocks (ownership shares) of thousands of corporations are bought and sold in the stock market. The owners of the individual stocks receive dividends—a portion of the firm's profit. Supply and demand in the stock market determine the price of each firm's stock, with individual stock prices generally rising and falling in concert with the collective expectations for each firm's profits. Greater profits normally result in higher dividends to the stock owners, and, in anticipation of higher dividends, people are willing to pay a higher price for the stock.

The media closely monitor and report stock market averages such as the Dow Jones Industrial Average (DJIA)—the weighted-average price of the stocks of 30 major U.S. industrial firms. It is common for these price averages to change over time or even to rise or fall sharply during a single day. On "Black Monday," October 19, 1987, the DJIA fell by 20 percent. A sharp drop in stock prices also occurred in October 1997, mainly in response to rapid declines in stock prices in Hong Kong and other southeast Asia stock markets. In contrast, the stock market averages rose spectacularly in 1998 and 1999, with the DJIA rising 16 and 25 percent in those two years. In 2002, the DJIA fell 17 percent. In 2003, it rose by 25 percent.

The volatility of the stock market raises this question: Do changes in stock price averages and thus stock market wealth cause macroeconomic instability? Linkages between the stock market and the economy might lead us to answer "yes." Consider a sharp increase in stock prices. Feeling wealthier, stock owners respond by increasing their spending (the *wealth effect*). Firms react by increasing their purchases of new capital goods because they can finance such purchases through issuing new shares of high-valued stock (the *investment effect*). Of course, sharp declines in stock prices would produce the opposite results.

Studies find that changes in stock prices do affect consumption and investment but that these consumption and investment impacts are relatively weak. For example, a 10 percent sustained increase in stock market values in 1 year is associated with a 4 percent increase in consumption spending over the next 3 years. The investment response is even weaker. So typical day-to-day and year-to-year changes in stock market values have little impact on the macroeconomy.

In contrast, *stock market bubbles* can be detrimental to an economy. Such bubbles are huge run-ups of overall stock prices, caused by excessive optimism and frenzied buying. The rising stock values are unsupported by realistic prospects of the future strength of the economy and the firms operating in it. Rather than slowly decompress, such bubbles may burst and cause harm to the economy. The free fall of stock values, if long-lasting, causes reverse wealth effects. The stock market crash also may create an overall pessimism about the economy that undermines consumption and investment spending even further. Indeed, many economists believe that the stock market crash of 1929 helped to contribute to the onset of the Great Depression during the 1930s by creating a tremendous amount of pessimism regarding the future.

A related question: Even though typical changes in stock prices do not cause recession or inflation, might they predict such maladies? That is, since stock market values are based on expected profits, wouldn't we expect rapid changes in stock price averages to forecast changes in future business conditions? Indeed, stock prices often do fall prior to recessions and rise prior to expansions. For this reason stock prices are among a group of 10 variables that constitute an index of leading indicators (Last Word, Chapter 30). Such an index may provide a useful clue to the future direction of the economy. But taken alone, stock market prices are not a reliable predictor of changes in GDP. Stock prices have fallen rapidly in some instances with no recession following. Black Monday itself did not produce a recession during the following 2 years. In other instances, recessions have occurred with no prior decline in stock market prices.

As prices shoot up sharply and unevenly during hyperinflation, people begin to anticipate even more rapid inflation and normal economic relationships are disrupted. Business owners do not know what to charge for their products. Consumers do not know what to pay. Resource suppliers want to be paid with actual output, rather than with rapidly depreciating money. Money eventually becomes almost worthless and ceases to do its job as a medium of exchange. Businesses, anticipating further price increases, may find that hoarding both materials and finished products is profitable. Individual savers may decide to buy nonproductive wealth—jewels, gold, and other precious metals, real estate, and so forth—rather than providing funds that can be borrowed to purchase capital equipment. The economy may be thrown into a state of barter, and production and exchange drop further. The net result is economic collapse and, often, political chaos.

Examples of hyperinflation are Germany after the First World War and Japan after the Second World War. In Germany, "prices increased so rapidly that waiters changed the prices on the menu several times during the course of a lunch. Sometimes customers had to pay double the price listed on the menu when they ordered."[2] In postwar Japan, in 1947 "fisherman and farmers . . . used scales to weigh currency and change, rather than bothering to count it."[3]

There are also more recent examples: Between June 1986 and March 1991 the cumulative inflation in Nicaragua was 11,895,866,143 percent. From November 1993 to December 1994 the cumulative inflation rate in the Democratic Republic of Congo was 69,502 percent. From February 1993 to January 1994 the cumulative inflation rate in Serbia was 156,312,790 percent.[4]

Such dramatic hyperinflations are always the consequence of highly imprudent expansions of the money supply by government. The rocketing money supply produces frenzied total spending and severe demand-pull inflation. Zimbabwe's 26,000 percent inflation in 2007 is just the latest example.

---

[2]Theodore Morgan, *Income and Employment*, 2nd ed. (Englewood Cliffs, N.J.: Prentice Hall, 1952), p. 361.
[3]Raburn M. Williams, *Inflation! Money, Jobs, and Politicians* (Arlington Heights, Ill.: AHM Publishing, 1980), p. 2.
[4]Stanley Fischer, Ratna Sahay, and Carlos Végh, "Modern Hyper- and High Inflations," *Journal of Economic Literature*, September 2002, p. 840.

Summary

1. The United States and other industrial economies have gone through periods of fluctuations in real GDP, employment, and the price level. Although they have certain phases in common—peak, recession, trough, expansion—business cycles vary greatly in duration and intensity.

2. Although economists explain the business cycle in terms of underlying causal factors such as major innovations, productivity shocks, money creation, and financial crises, they generally agree that changes in the level of total spending are the immediate causes of fluctuating real output and employment.

3. The business cycle affects all sectors of the economy, though in varying ways and degrees. The cycle has greater effects on output and employment in the capital goods and durable consumer goods industries than in the services and nondurable goods industries.

4. Economists distinguish between frictional, structural, and cyclical unemployment. The full employment or natural rate of unemployment, which is made up of frictional and structural unemployment, is currently between 4 and 5 percent. The presence of part-time and discouraged workers makes it difficult to measure unemployment accurately.

5. The GDP gap, which can be either a positive or a negative value, is found by subtracting potential GDP from actual GDP. The economic cost of unemployment, as measured by the GDP gap, consists of the goods and services forgone by society when its resources are involuntarily idle. Okun's law suggests that every 1-percentage-point increase in unemployment above the natural rate causes an additional 2 percent negative GDP gap.

6. Inflation is a rise in the general price level and is measured in the United States by the Consumer Price Index (CPI). When inflation occurs, each dollar of income will buy fewer goods and services than before. That is, inflation reduces the purchasing power of money.

7. Unemployment rates and inflation rates vary widely globally. Unemployment rates differ because nations have different natural rates of unemployment and often are in different phases of their business cycles. Inflation and unemployment rates in the United States recently have been in the middle to low range compared with rates in other industrial nations.

8. Economists discern both demand-pull and cost-push (supply-side) inflation. Demand-pull inflation results from an excess of total spending relative to the economy's capacity to produce. The main source of cost-push inflation is abrupt and rapid increases in the prices of key resources. These supply shocks push up per-unit production costs and ultimately raise the prices of consumer goods.

9. Unanticipated inflation arbitrarily redistributes real income at the expense of fixed-income receivers, creditors, and

savers. If inflation is anticipated, individuals and businesses may be able to take steps to lessen or eliminate adverse redistribution effects.

10. When inflation is anticipated, lenders add an inflation premium to the interest rate charged on loans. The nominal interest rate thus reflects the real interest rate plus the inflation premium (the expected rate of inflation).

11. Cost-push inflation reduces real output and employment. Proponents of zero inflation argue that even mild demand-pull inflation (1 to 3 percent) reduces the economy's real output. Other economists say that mild inflation may be a necessary by-product of the high and growing spending that produces high levels of output, full employment, and economic growth.

12. Hyperinflation, caused by highly imprudent expansions of the money supply, may undermine the monetary system and cause severe declines in real output.

Terms and Concepts

business cycles

peak

recession

trough

expansion

labor force

unemployment rate

discouraged workers

frictional unemployment

structural unemployment

cyclical unemployment

full-employment rate of unemployment

natural rate of unemployment (NRU)

potential output

GDP gap

Okun's law

inflation

Consumer Price Index (CPI)

demand-pull inflation

cost-push inflation

per-unit production costs

nominal income

real income

unanticipated inflation

anticipated inflation

cost-of-living adjustments (COLAs)

real interest rate

nominal interest rate

deflation

hyperinflation

Study Questions

1. **KEY QUESTION** What are the four phases of the business cycle? How long do business cycles last? How do seasonal variations and long-run trends complicate measurement of the business cycle? Why does the business cycle affect output and employment in capital goods industries and consumer durable goods industries more severely than in industries producing consumer nondurables? **LO1**

2. What factors make it difficult to determine the unemployment rate? Why is it difficult to distinguish between frictional, structural, and cyclical unemployment? Why is unemployment an economic problem? What are the consequences of a negative GDP gap? What are the noneconomic effects of unemployment? **LO2**

3. **KEY QUESTION** Use the following data to calculate (*a*) the size of the labor force and (*b*) the official unemployment rate: total population, 500; population under 16 years of age or institutionalized, 120; not in labor force, 150; unemployed, 23; part-time workers looking for full-time jobs, 10. **LO2**

4. Since the United States has an unemployment compensation program that provides income for those out of work, why should we worry about unemployment? **LO2**

5. **KEY QUESTION** Assume that in a particular year the natural rate of unemployment is 5 percent and the actual rate of unemployment is 9 percent. Use Okun's law to determine the size of the GDP gap in percentage-point terms. If the potential GDP is $500 billion in that year, how much output is being forgone because of cyclical unemployment? **LO1**

6. Explain how an increase in your nominal income and a decrease in your real income might occur simultaneously. Who loses from inflation? Who loses from unemployment? If you had to choose between (*a*) full employment with a 6 percent annual rate of inflation and (*b*) price stability with an 8 percent unemployment rate, which would you choose? Why? **LO3**

7. What is the Consumer Price Index (CPI) and how is it determined each month? How does the Bureau of Labor Statistics calculate the rate of inflation from one year to the next? What effect does inflation have on the purchasing power of a dollar? How does it explain differences between nominal and real interest rates? How does deflation differ from inflation? **LO2**

8. **KEY QUESTION** If the CPI was 110 last year and is 121 this year, what is this year's rate of inflation? What is the "rule of 70"? How long would it take for the price level to double if inflation persisted at (*a*) 2, (*b*) 5, and (*c*) 10 percent per year? **LO2**

9. Distinguish between demand-pull inflation and cost-push inflation. Which of the two types is most likely to be associated with a negative GDP gap? Which with a positive GDP gap, in which actual GDP exceeds potential GDP? **LO3**

10. Explain how hyperinflation might lead to a severe decline in total output. **LO3**

11. Evaluate as accurately as you can how each of the following individuals would be affected by unanticipated inflation of 10 percent per year: **LO3**

   a. A pensioned railroad worker.

   b. A department-store clerk.

   c. A unionized automobile assembly-line worker.

   d. A heavily indebted farmer.

   e. A retired business executive whose current income comes entirely from interest on government bonds.

   f. The owner of an independent small-town department store.

12. **LAST WORD** Suppose that stock prices were to fall by 10 percent in the stock market. All else equal, would the lower stock prices be likely to cause a decrease in real GDP? How might they predict a decline in real GDP?

Web-Based Questions

1. **WHAT IS THE CURRENT U.S. UNEMPLOYMENT RATE?** Visit the Bureau of Labor Statistics Web Site, **www.bls.gov/news.release/empsit.toc.htm,** and select Employment Situation Summary. What month (and year) is summarized? What was the unemployment rate for that month? How does that rate compare with the rate in the previous month? What were the unemployment rates for adult men, adult women, teenagers, blacks, Hispanics, and whites? How did these rates compare with those a month earlier?

2. **WHAT IS THE CURRENT U.S. INFLATION RATE?** Visit the Bureau of Labor Statistics Web Site, **www.bls.gov/news.release/cpi.toc.htm,** and select Consumer Price Index Summary. What month (and year) is summarized? What was the CPI-U for the month? What was the rate of inflation (change in the CPI-U) for the month? How does that rate of inflation compare with the rate for the previous month? Which two categories of goods or services had the greatest price increases for the month? Which two had the lowest price increases (or greatest price decreases) for the month?

FURTHER TEST YOUR KNOWLEDGE AT
www.mcconnell18e.com

PART SEVEN

Macroeconomic Models and Fiscal Policy

IN THIS CHAPTER YOU WILL LEARN:

1 **How changes in income affect consumption (and saving).**

2 **About factors other than income that can affect consumption.**

3 **How changes in real interest rates affect investment.**

4 **About factors other than the real interest rate that can affect investment.**

5 **Why changes in investment increase or decrease real GDP by a multiple amount.**

27

Basic Macroeconomic Relationships*

In Chapter 26 we discussed the business cycle, unemployment, and inflation. Our eventual goal is to build economic models that can explain these phenomena. This chapter begins that process by examining the basic relationships that exist between three different pairs of economic aggregates. (Recall that to economists "aggregate" means "total" or "combined.") Specifically, this chapter looks at the relationships between:

- income and consumption (and income and saving).
- the interest rate and investment.
- changes in spending and changes in output.

---

*Note to the Instructor: If you wish to bypass the aggregate expenditures model (Keynesian cross model) covered in full in Chapter 28, assigning the present chapter will provide a seamless transition to the AD-AS model of Chapter 29 and the chapters beyond. If you want to cover the aggregate expenditure model, this present chapter provides the necessary building blocks.

What explains the trends in consumption (consumer spending) and saving reported in the news? How do changes in interest rates affect investment? How can initial changes in spending ultimately produce multiplied changes in GDP? The basic macroeconomic relationships discussed in this chapter answer these questions.

The Income-Consumption and Income-Saving Relationships

The other-things-equal relationship between income and consumption is one of the best-established relationships in macroeconomics. In examining that relationship, we are also exploring the relationship between income and saving. Recall that economists define *personal saving* as "not spending" or as "that part of disposable (after-tax) income not consumed." Saving (*S*) equals disposable income (DI) *minus* consumption (*C*).

Many factors determine a nation's levels of consumption and saving, but the most significant is disposable income. Consider some recent historical data for the United States. In Figure 27.1 each dot represents consumption and disposable income for 1 year since 1985. The line *C* that is loosely fitted to these points shows that consumption is directly (positively) related to disposable income; moreover, households spend most of their income.

But we can say more. The **45° (degree) line** is a reference line. Because it bisects the 90° angle formed by the two axes of the graph, each point on it is equidistant from the two axes. At each point on the 45° line, consumption would equal disposable income, or *C* = DI. Therefore, the vertical distance between the 45° line and any point on the horizontal axis measures either consumption or disposable income. If we let it measure disposable income, the vertical distance between it and the consumption line labeled *C* represents

FIGURE 27.1 Consumption and disposable income, 1985–2007. Each dot in this figure shows consumption and disposable income in a specific year. The line *C*, which generalizes the relationship between consumption and disposable income, indicates a direct relationship and shows that households consume most of their after-tax incomes.

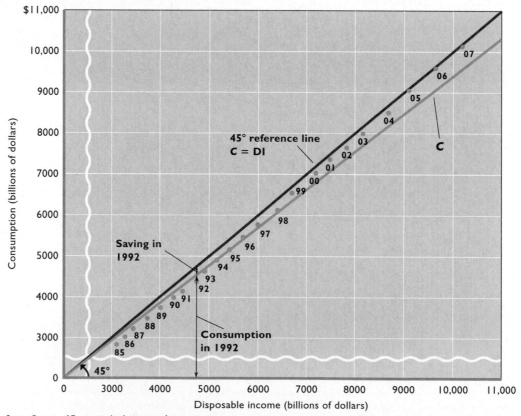

Source: Bureau of Economic Analysis, **www.bea.gov.**

542

the amount of saving (*S*) in that year. Saving is the amount by which actual consumption in any year falls short of the 45° line—($S = DI - C$). For example, in 1992 disposable income was $4751 billion and consumption was $4385 billion, so saving was $366 billion. Observe that the vertical distance between the 45° line and line *C* increases as we move rightward along the horizontal axis and decreases as we move leftward. Like consumption, saving typically varies directly with the level of disposable income. That historical pattern, however, has temporarily broken down in recent years.

The Consumption Schedule

The dots in Figure 27.1 represent historical data—the actual amounts of DI, *C*, and *S* in the United States over a period of years. But, because we want to understand how

ORIGIN OF THE IDEA
O 27.1
Income-consumption relationship

the economy would behave under different possible scenarios, we need a schedule showing the various amounts that households would *plan* to

consume at each of the various levels of disposable income that might prevail at some specific time. Columns 1 and 2 of Table 27.1, represented in **Figure 27.2a (Key Graph),** show the hypothetical consumption schedule that we require. This **consumption schedule** (or "consumption function") reflects the direct consumption–disposable income relationship suggested by the data in Figure 27.1, and it is consistent with many household budget studies. In the aggregate, households increase their spending as their disposable income rises and spend a larger proportion

of a small disposable income than of a large disposable income.

The Saving Schedule

It is relatively easy to derive a **saving schedule** (or "saving function"). Because saving equals disposable income less consumption ($S = DI - C$), we need only subtract consumption (Table 27.1, column 2) from disposable income (column 1) to find the amount saved (column 3) at each DI. Thus, columns 1 and 3 in Table 27.1 are the saving schedule, represented in Figure 27.2b. The graph shows that there is a direct relationship between saving and DI but that saving is a smaller proportion of a small DI than of a large DI. If households consume a smaller and smaller proportion of DI as DI increases, then they must be saving a larger and larger proportion.

Remembering that at each point on the 45° line consumption equals DI, we see that *dissaving* (consuming in excess of after-tax income) will occur at relatively low DIs. For example, at $370 billion (row 1, Table 27.1), consumption is $375 billion. Households can consume more than their current incomes by liquidating (selling for cash) accumulated wealth or by borrowing. Graphically, dissaving is shown as the vertical distance of the consumption schedule above the 45° line or as the vertical distance of the saving schedule below the horizontal axis. We have marked the dissaving at the $370 billion level of income in Figure 27.2a and 27.2b. Both vertical distances measure the $5 billion of dissaving that occurs at $370 billion of income.

In our example, the **break-even income** is $390 billion (row 2, Table 27.1). This is the income level at which

TABLE 27.1 Consumption and Saving Schedules (in Billions) and Propensities to Consume and Save

(1) Level of Output and Income (GDP = DI)	(2) Consumption (C)	(3) Saving (S), (1) − (2)	(4) Average Propensity to Consume (APC), (2)/(1)	(5) Average Propensity to Save (APS), (3)/(1)	(6) Marginal Propensity to Consume (MPC), Δ(2)/Δ(1)*	(7) Marginal Propensity to Save (MPS), Δ(3)/Δ(1)*
(1) $370	$375	$−5	1.01	−.01		
(2) 390	390	0	1.00	.00	.75	.25
(3) 410	405	5	.99	.01	.75	.25
(4) 430	420	10	.98	.02	.75	.25
(5) 450	435	15	.97	.03	.75	.25
(6) 470	450	20	.96	.04	.75	.25
(7) 490	465	25	.95	.05	.75	.25
(8) 510	480	30	.94	.06	.75	.25
(9) 530	495	35	.93	.07	.75	.25
(10) 550	510	40	.93	.07	.75	.25

*The Greek letter Δ, delta, means "the change in."

keygraph

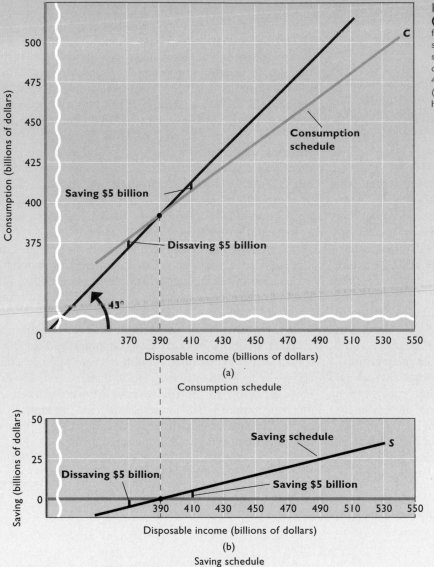

FIGURE 27.2 **(a) Consumption and (b) saving schedules.** The two parts of this figure show the income-consumption and income-saving relationships in Table 27.1 graphically. The saving schedule in (b) is found by subtracting the consumption schedule in (a) vertically from the 45° line. Consumption equals disposable income (and saving thus equals zero) at $390 billion for these hypothetical data.

QUICK QUIZ FOR FIGURE 27.2

1. The slope of the consumption schedule in this figure is .75. Thus, the:
    a. slope of the saving schedule is 1.33.
    b. marginal propensity to consume is .75.
    c. average propensity to consume is .25.
    d. slope of the saving schedule is also .75.

2. In this figure, when consumption is a positive amount, saving:
    a. must be a negative amount.
    b. must also be a positive amount.
    c. can be either a positive or a negative amount.
    d. is zero.

3. In this figure:
    a. the marginal propensity to consume is constant at all levels of income.
    b. the marginal propensity to save rises as disposable income rises.
    c. consumption is inversely (negatively) related to disposable income.
    d. saving is inversely (negatively) related to disposable income.

4. When consumption equals disposable income:
    a. the marginal propensity to consume is zero.
    b. the average propensity to consume is zero.
    c. consumption and saving must be equal.
    d. saving must be zero.

Answers: 1. b; 2. c; 3. a; 4. d

544

households plan to consume their entire incomes ($C = DI$). Graphically, the consumption schedule cuts the 45° line, and the saving schedule cuts the horizontal axis (saving is zero) at the break-even income level.

At all higher incomes, households plan to save part of their incomes. Graphically, the vertical distance between the consumption schedule and the 45° line measures this saving (see Figure 27.2a), as does the vertical distance between the saving schedule and the horizontal axis (see Figure 27.2b). For example, at the $410 billion level of income (row 3, Table 27.1), both these distances indicate $5 billion of saving.

Average and Marginal Propensities

Columns 4 to 7 in Table 27.1 show additional characteristics of the consumption and saving schedules.

APC and APS The fraction, or percentage, of total income that is consumed is the **average propensity to consume (APC)**. The fraction of total income that is saved is the **average propensity to save (APS).** That is,

$$APC = \frac{consumption}{income}$$

and

$$APS = \frac{saving}{income}$$

For example, at $470 billion of income (row 6 in Table 27.1), the APC is $\frac{450}{470} = \frac{45}{47}$, or about 96 percent, while the APS is $\frac{20}{470} = \frac{2}{47}$, or about 4 percent. Columns 4 and 5 in Table 27.1 show the APC and APS at each of the 10 levels of DI; note in the table that the APC falls and the APS rises as DI increases, as was implied in our previous comments.

Because disposable income is either consumed or saved, the fraction of any DI consumed plus the fraction saved (not consumed) must exhaust that income. Mathematically, $APC + APS = 1$ at any level of disposable income, as columns 4 and 5 in Table 27.1 illustrate.

Global Perspective 27.1 shows APCs for several countries.

MPC and MPS The fact that households consume a certain proportion of a particular total income, for example, $\frac{45}{47}$ of a $470 billion disposable income, does not guarantee they will consume the same proportion of any *change* in income they might receive. The proportion, or fraction, of any change in income consumed is called the **marginal propensity to consume (MPC)**, "marginal" meaning "extra" or "a change in." Equivalently, the MPC is the ratio of a change in consumption to a change in the

Average Propensities to Consume, Selected Nations

There are surprisingly large differences in average propensities to consume (APCs) among nations. The United States, Canada, and the United Kingdom in particular have substantially higher APCs, and thus lower APSs, than other advanced economies.

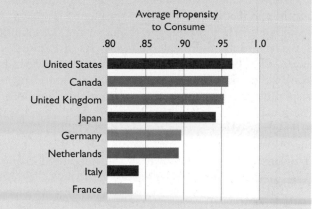

Source: Statistical Abstract of the United States 2006, p. 875, and authors' calculations. Latest data.

income that caused the consumption change:

$$MPC = \frac{change\ in\ consumption}{change\ in\ income}$$

Similarly, the fraction of any change in income saved is the **marginal propensity to save (MPS)**. The MPS is the ratio of a change in saving to the change in income that brought it about:

$$MPS = \frac{change\ in\ saving}{change\ in\ income}$$

If disposable income is $470 billion (row 6 horizontally in Table 27.1) and household income rises by $20 billion to $490 billion (row 7), households will consume $\frac{15}{20}$, or $\frac{3}{4}$, and save $\frac{5}{20}$, or $\frac{1}{4}$, of that increase in income. In other words, the MPC is $\frac{3}{4}$ or .75, and the MPS is $\frac{1}{4}$ or .25, as shown in columns 6 and 7.

The sum of the MPC and the MPS for any change in disposable income must always be 1. Consuming or saving out of extra income is an either-or proposition; the fraction of any change in income not consumed is, by definition, saved. Therefore, the fraction consumed (MPC) plus the fraction saved (MPS) must exhaust the whole change in income:

$$MPC + MPS = 1$$

In our example, .75 plus .25 equals 1.

MPC and MPS as Slopes

The MPC is the numerical value of the slope of the consumption schedule, and the MPS is the numerical value of the slope of the saving

WORKED PROBLEMS

W 27.1

Consumption and saving

schedule. We know from the appendix to Chapter 1 that the slope of any line is the ratio of the vertical change to the horizontal change occasioned in moving from one point to another on that line.

Figure 27.3 measures the slopes of the consumption and saving lines, using enlarged portions of Figure 27.2a and 27.2b. Observe that consumption changes by $15 billion (the vertical change) for each $20 billion change in disposable income (the horizontal change). The slope of the consumption line is thus .75 (= $15/$20), which is the value of the MPC. Saving changes by $5 billion (shown as the vertical change) for every $20 billion change in disposable income (shown as the horizontal change).

FIGURE 27.3 The marginal propensity to consume and the marginal propensity to save. The MPC is the slope ($\Delta C/\Delta DI$) of the consumption schedule, and the MPS is the slope ($\Delta S/\Delta DI$) of the saving schedule. The Greek letter delta (Δ) means "the change in."

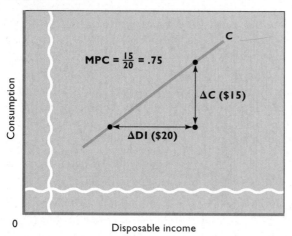

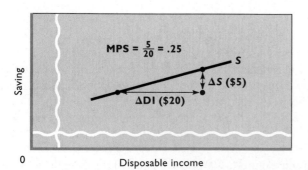

The slope of the saving line therefore is .25 (= $5/$20), which is the value of the MPS. **(Key Question 5)**

Nonincome Determinants of Consumption and Saving

The amount of disposable income is the basic determinant of the amounts households will consume and save. But certain determinants other than income might prompt households to consume more or less at each possible level of income and thereby change the locations of the consumption and saving schedules. Those other determinants are wealth, borrowing, expectations, and interest rates.

Wealth A household's wealth is the dollar amount of all the assets that it owns minus the dollar amount of its liabilities (all the debt that it owes). Households build wealth by saving money out of current income. The point of building wealth is to increase consumption possibilities. The larger the stock of wealth that a household can build up, the larger will be its present and future consumption possibilities.

Events sometimes suddenly boost the value of existing wealth. When this happens, households tend to increase their spending and reduce their saving. This so-called **wealth effect** shifts the consumption schedule upward and the saving schedule downward. They move in response to households taking advantage of the increased consumption possibilities afforded by the sudden increase in wealth. Examples: In the late 1990s, skyrocketing U.S. stock values expanded the value of household wealth by increasing the value of household assets. Predictably, households spent more and saved less. In contrast, a modest "reverse wealth effect" occurred in 2000 and 2001, when stock prices sharply fell.

Borrowing Household borrowing also affects consumption. When a household borrows, it can increase current consumption beyond what would be possible if its spending were limited to its disposable income. By allowing households to spend more, borrowing shifts the current consumption schedule upward.

But note that there is "no free lunch." While borrowing in the present allows for higher consumption in the present, it necessitates lower consumption in the future when the debts that are incurred due to the borrowing must be repaid. Stated a bit differently, increased borrowing increases debt (liabilities), which in turn reduces household wealth (since *wealth = assets − liabilities*). This reduction in wealth reduces future consumption possibilities in much the same way that a decline in asset values would. But note that the term "reverse wealth effect" is reserved for situations in which wealth unexpectedly changes because asset values unexpectedly change. It is not used to refer to situations such as the one being discussed here where wealth is intentionally reduced by households through borrowing and piling up debt in order to increase current consumption.

Expectations Household expectations about future prices and income may affect current spending and saving. For example, expectations of rising prices tomorrow may trigger more spending and less saving today. Thus, the current consumption schedule shifts up and the current saving schedule shifts down. Or expectations of a recession and thus lower income in the future may lead households to reduce consumption and save more today. If so, the consumption schedule will shift down and the saving schedule will shift up.

Real Interest Rates When real interest rates (those adjusted for inflation) fall, households tend to borrow more, consume more, and save less. A lower interest rate, for example, induces consumers to purchase automobiles and other goods bought on credit. A lower interest rate also diminishes the incentive to save because of the reduced interest "payment" to the saver. These effects on consumption and saving, however, are very modest. They mainly shift consumption toward some products (those bought on credit) and away from others. At best, lower interest rates shift the consumption schedule slightly upward and the saving schedule slightly downward. Higher interest rates do the opposite.

Other Important Considerations

There are several additional important points regarding the consumption and saving schedules:

- *Switching to real GDP* When developing macroeconomic models, economists change their focus from the relationship between consumption (and saving) and *disposable income* to the relationship between consumption (and saving) and *real domestic output (real GDP)*. This modification is reflected in Figure 27.4a and 27.4b, where the horizontal axes measure real GDP.
- *Changes along schedules* The movement from one point to another on a consumption schedule (for example, from *a* to *b* on C_0 in Figure 27.4a) is a *change in the amount consumed* and is solely caused by a change in real GDP. On the other hand, an upward or downward shift of the entire schedule,

FIGURE 27.4 Shifts of the (a) consumption and (b) saving schedules. Normally, if households consume more at each level of real GDP, they are necessarily saving less. Graphically this means that an upward shift of the consumption schedule (C_0 to C_1) entails a downward shift of the saving schedule (S_0 to S_1). If households consume less at each level of real GDP, they are saving more. A downward shift of the consumption schedule (C_0 to C_2) is reflected in an upward shift of the saving schedule (S_0 to S_2). This pattern breaks down, however, when taxes change; then the consumption and saving schedules move in the *same* direction—opposite to the direction of the tax change.

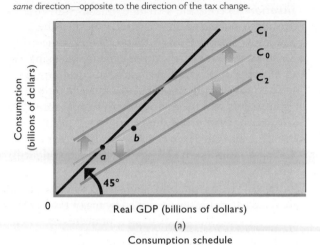

(a)
Consumption schedule

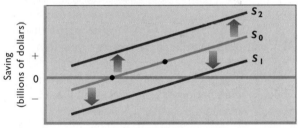

Real GDP (billions of dollars)

(b)
Saving schedule

for example, a shift from C_0 to C_1 or C_2 in Figure 27.4a, is a *shift of the consumption schedule* and is caused by changes in any one or more of the *nonincome* determinants of consumption just discussed.

A similar distinction in terminology applies to the saving schedule in Figure 27.4b.

- *Schedule shifts* Changes in wealth, expectations, interest rates, and household debt will shift the consumption schedule in one direction and the saving schedule in the opposite direction. If households decide to consume more at each possible level of real GDP, they must save less, and vice versa. (Even when they spend more by borrowing, they are, in effect, reducing their current saving by the amount borrowed since borrowing is, effectively, "negative saving.") Graphically, if the consumption schedule shifts upward from C_0 to C_1 in Figure 27.4a, the saving schedule shifts downward, from S_0 to S_1 in Figure 27.4b. Similarly, a downward shift of the consumption schedule from C_0 to C_2 means an upward shift of the saving schedule from S_0 to S_2.

- **Taxation** In contrast, a change in taxes shifts the consumption and saving schedules in the same direction. Taxes are paid partly at the expense of consumption and partly at the expense of saving. So an increase in taxes will reduce both consumption and saving, shifting the consumption schedule in Figure 27.4a and the saving schedule in Figure 27.4b downward. Conversely, households will partly consume and partly save any decrease in taxes. Both the consumption schedule and saving schedule will shift upward.

- **Stability** The consumption and saving schedules usually are relatively stable unless altered by major tax increases or decreases. Their stability may be because consumption-saving decisions are strongly influenced by long-term considerations such as saving to meet emergencies or saving for retirement. It may also be because changes in the nonincome determinants frequently work in opposite directions and therefore may be self-canceling.

> **INTERACTIVE GRAPHS**
>
> **G 27.1**
>
> Consumption and saving schedules

QUICK REVIEW 27.1

- Both consumption spending and saving rise when disposable income increases; both fall when disposable income decreases.

- The average propensity to consume (APC) is the fraction of any specific level of disposable income that is spent on consumer goods; the average propensity to save (APS) is the fraction of any specific level of disposable income that is saved. The APC falls and the APS rises as disposable income increases.

- The marginal propensity to consume (MPC) is the fraction of a change in disposable income that is consumed and it is the slope of the consumption schedule; the marginal propensity to save (MPS) is the fraction of a change in disposable income that is saved and it is the slope of the saving schedule.

- Changes in consumer wealth, consumer expectations, interest rates, household debt, and taxes can shift the consumption and saving schedules (as they relate to real GDP).

What Wealth Effect?

The consumption schedule is relatively stable even during rather extraordinary times. Between March 2000 and July 2002, the U.S. stock market lost a staggering $3.7 trillion of value (yes, trillion). Yet consumption spending was greater at the end of that period than at the beginning. How can that be? Why didn't a "reverse wealth effect" reduce consumption?

There are a number of reasons. Of greatest importance, the amount of consumption spending in the economy depends mainly on the *flow* of income, not the *stock* of wealth. Disposable income (DI) in the United States is about $10 trillion annually and consumers spend a large portion of it. Even though there was a mild recession in 2001, DI and consumption spending were both greater in July 2002 than in March 2000. Second, the Federal government cut personal income tax rates during this period and that bolstered consumption spending. Third, household wealth did not fall by the full amount of the $3.7 trillion stock market loss because the market value of houses increased dramatically over this period. Finally, lower interest rates during this period enabled many households to refinance their mortgages, reduce monthly loan payments, and increase their current consumption.

For all these offsetting reasons, the general consumption-income relationship of Figure 27.2 held steady in the face of the extraordinary loss of stock market value.

The Interest-Rate–Investment Relationship

In our consideration of major macro relationships, we next turn to the relationship between the real interest rate and investment. Recall that investment consists of expenditures on new plants, capital equipment, machinery, inventories, and so on. The investment decision is a marginal-benefit–marginal-cost decision: The marginal benefit from investment is the expected rate of return businesses hope to realize. The marginal cost is the interest rate that must be paid for borrowed funds. Businesses will invest in all projects for which the expected rate of return exceeds the interest rate. Expected returns (profits) and the interest rate therefore are the two basic determinants of investment spending.

Expected Rate of Return

Investment spending is guided by the profit motive; businesses buy capital goods only when they think such purchases will be profitable. Suppose the owner of a small cabinetmaking shop is considering whether to invest in a new sanding machine that costs $1000 and has a useful life of only 1 year. (Extending the life of the machine beyond 1 year complicates the economic decision but does not change the fundamental analysis. We discuss the valuation of returns beyond 1 year in Chapter 34.) The new machine will increase the firm's output and sales revenue. Suppose the net expected revenue from the machine (that is, after such operating costs as power, lumber, labor, and certain taxes have been subtracted) is $1100. Then, after the $1000 cost of the machine is subtracted from the net expected revenue of $1100, the firm will have an expected profit of $100. Dividing this $100 profit by the $1000 cost of the machine, we find that the **expected rate of return**, r, on the machine is 10 percent (= $100/$1000). It is important to note that this is an *expected* rate of return, not a *guaranteed* rate of return. The investment may or may not generate as much revenue or as much profit as anticipated. Investment involves risk.

The Real Interest Rate

One important cost associated with investing that our example has ignored is interest, which is the financial cost of borrowing the $1000 of *money* "capital" to purchase the $1000 of *real* capital (the sanding machine).

The interest cost of the investment is computed by multiplying the interest rate, i, by the $1000 borrowed to buy the machine. If the interest rate is, say, 7 percent, the total interest cost will be $70. This compares favorably with the net expected return of $100, which produced the 10 percent expected rate of return. If the investment works out as expected, it will add $30 to the firm's profit. We can generalize as follows: If the expected rate of return (10 percent) exceeds the interest rate (here, 7 percent), the investment should be undertaken. The firm expects the investment to be profitable. But if the interest rate (say, 12 percent) exceeds the expected rate of return (10 percent), the investment should not be undertaken. The firm expects the investment to be unprofitable. The firm should undertake all investment projects it thinks will be profitable. That means it should invest up to the point where $r = i$ because then it has undertaken all investment for which r exceeds i.

This guideline applies even if a firm finances the investment internally out of funds saved from past profit rather than borrowing the funds. The role of the interest rate in the investment decision does not change. When the firm uses money from savings to invest in the sander, it incurs an opportunity cost because it forgoes the interest income it could have earned by lending the funds to someone else. That interest cost, converted to percentage terms, needs to be weighed against the expected rate of return.

The *real* rate of interest, rather than the *nominal* rate, is crucial in making investment decisions. Recall from Chapter 26 that the nominal interest rate is expressed in dollars of current value, while the real interest rate is stated in dollars of constant or inflation-adjusted value. Recall that the real interest rate is the nominal rate less the rate of inflation. In our sanding machine illustration, our implicit assumption of a constant price level ensures that all our data, including the interest rate, are in real terms.

But what if inflation *is* occurring? Suppose a $1000 investment is expected to yield a real (inflation-adjusted) rate of return of 10 percent and the nominal interest rate is 15 percent. At first, we would say the investment would be unprofitable. But assume there is ongoing inflation of 10 percent per year. This means the investing firm will pay back dollars with approximately 10 percent less in purchasing power. While the nominal interest rate is 15 percent, the real rate is only 5 percent (= 15 percent − 10 percent). By comparing this 5 percent real interest rate with the 10 percent expected real rate of return, we find that the investment is potentially profitable and should be undertaken. **(Key Question 7)**

Investment Demand Curve

We now move from a single firm's investment decision to total demand for investment goods by the entire business sector. Assume that every firm has estimated the expected rates of return from all investment projects and has recorded those data. We can cumulate (successively sum) these data by asking: How many dollars' worth of investment projects have an expected rate of return of, say, 16 percent or more? How many have 14 percent or more? How many have 12 percent or more? And so on.

Suppose no prospective investments yield an expected return of 16 percent or more. But suppose there are $5 billion of investment opportunities with expected rates of return between 14 and 16 percent; an additional $5 billion yielding between 12 and 14 percent; still an additional $5 billion yielding between 10 and 12 percent; and an additional $5 billion in each successive 2 percent range of yield down to and including the 0 to 2 percent range.

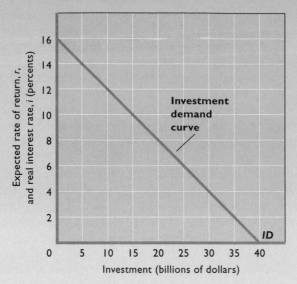

FIGURE 27.5 **The investment demand curve.** The investment demand curve is constructed by arraying all potential investment projects in descending order of their expected rates of return. The curve slopes downward, reflecting an inverse relationship between the real interest rate (the financial "price" of each dollar of investing) and the quantity of investment demanded.

QUICK QUIZ FOR FIGURE 27.5

1. The investment demand curve:
   a. reflects a direct (positive) relationship between the real interest rate and investment.
   b. reflects an inverse (negative) relationship between the real interest rate and investment.
   c. shifts to the right when the real interest rate rises.
   d. shifts to the left when the real interest rate rises.

2. In this figure:
   a. greater cumulative amounts of investment are associated with lower expected rates of return on investment.
   b. lesser cumulative amounts of investment are associated with lower expected rates of return on investment.
   c. higher interest rates are associated with higher expected rates of return on investment, and therefore greater amounts of investment.
   d. interest rates and investment move in the same direction.

3. In this figure, if the real interest rate falls from 6 to 4 percent:
   a. investment will increase from 0 to $30 billion.
   b. investment will decrease by $5 billion.
   c. the expected rate of return will rise by $5 billion.
   d. investment will increase from $25 billion to $30 billion.

4. In this figure, investment will be:
   a. zero if the real interest rate is zero.
   b. $40 billion if the real interest rate is 16 percent.
   c. $30 billion if the real interest rate is 4 percent.
   d. $20 billion if the real interest rate is 12 percent.

Answers: 1. b; 2. a; 3. d; 4. c

To cumulate these figures for each rate of return, r, we add the amounts of investment that will yield each particular rate of return r or higher. This provides the data in Table 27.2, shown graphically in **Figure 27.5 (Key Graph)**. In Table 27.2 the number opposite 12 percent, for example, means there are $10 billion of investment opportunities that will yield an expected rate of return of 12 percent or more. The $10 billion includes the $5 billion of investment expected to yield a return of 14 percent or more plus the $5 billion expected to yield between 12 and 14 percent.

We know from our example of the sanding machine that an investment project will be undertaken if its expected rate of return, r, exceeds the real interest rate, i. Let's first suppose i is 12 percent. Businesses will undertake all investments for which r exceeds 12 percent. That is, they will invest until the 12 percent rate of return equals the 12 percent interest rate. Figure 27.5 reveals that $10 billion of investment spending will be undertaken at a 12 percent interest rate; that means $10 billion of investment projects have an expected rate of return of 12 percent or more.

TABLE 27.2 Expected Rate of Return and Investment

Expected Rate of Return (r)	Cumulative Amount of Investment Having This Rate of Return or Higher, Billions per Year
16%	$ 0
14	5
12	10
10	15
8	20
6	25
4	30
2	35
0	40

Put another way: At a financial "price" of 12 percent, $10 billion of investment goods will be demanded. If the interest rate is lower, say, 8 percent, the amount of investment for which r equals or exceeds i is $20 billion. Thus, firms will demand $20 billion of investment goods at an 8 percent real interest rate. At 6 percent, they will demand $25 billion of investment goods.

By applying the marginal-benefit–marginal-cost rule that investment projects should be undertaken up to the point where $r = i$, we see that we can add the real interest rate to the vertical axis in Figure 27.5. The curve in Figure 27.5 not only shows rates of return; it shows the quantity of investment demanded at each "price" i (interest rate) of investment. The vertical axis in Figure 27.5 shows the various possible real interest rates, and the horizontal axis shows the corresponding quantities of investment demanded. The inverse (downsloping) relationship between the interest rate (price) and dollar quantity of investment demanded conforms to the law of demand discussed in Chapter 3. The curve ID in Figure 27.5 is the economy's **investment demand curve.** It shows the amount of investment forthcoming at each real interest rate. The level of investment depends on the expected rate of return and the real interest rate. **(Key Question 8)**

Shifts of the Investment Demand Curve

Figure 27.5 shows the relationship between the interest rate and the amount of investment demanded, other things

equal. When other things change, the investment demand curve shifts. In general, any factor that leads businesses collectively to expect greater rates of return on their investments increases investment demand. That factor shifts the investment demand curve to the right, as from ID_0 to ID_1 in Figure 27.6. Any factor that leads businesses collectively to expect lower rates of return on their investments shifts the curve to the left, as from ID_0 to ID_2. What are those non-interest-rate determinants of investment demand?

Acquisition, Maintenance, and Operating Costs
The initial costs of capital goods, and the estimated costs of operating and maintaining those goods, affect the expected rate of return on investment. When these costs rise, the expected rate of return from prospective investment projects falls and the investment demand curve shifts to the left. Example: Higher electricity costs associated with operating tools and machinery shifts the investment demand curve to the left. Lower costs, in contrast, shift it to the right.

Business Taxes
When government is considered, firms look to expected returns *after taxes* in making their investment decisions. An increase in business taxes lowers the expected profitability of investments and shifts the investment demand curve to the left; a reduction of business taxes shifts it to the right.

Technological Change
Technological progress—the development of new products, improvements in existing

FIGURE 27.6 Shifts of the investment demand curve. Increases in investment demand are shown as rightward shifts of the investment demand curve; decreases in investment demand are shown as leftward shifts of the investment demand curve.

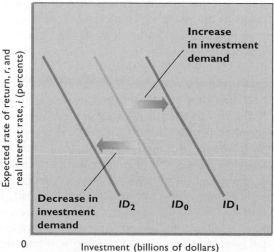

products, and the creation of new machinery and production processes—stimulates investment. The development of a more efficient machine, for example, lowers production costs or improves product quality and increases the expected rate of return from investing in the machine. Profitable new products (cholesterol medications, Internet services, high-definition televisions, cellular phones, and so on) induce a flurry of investment as businesses tool up for expanded production. A rapid rate of technological progress shifts the investment demand curve to the right.

Stock of Capital Goods on Hand
The stock of capital goods on hand, relative to output and sales, influences investment decisions by firms. When the economy is overstocked with production facilities and when firms have excessive inventories of finished goods, the expected rate of return on new investment declines. Firms with excess production capacity have little incentive to invest in new capital. Therefore, less investment is forthcoming at each real interest rate; the investment demand curve shifts leftward.

When the economy is understocked with production facilities and when firms are selling their output as fast as they can produce it, the expected rate of return on new investment increases and the investment demand curve shifts rightward.

Planned Inventory Changes
Recall from Chapter 24 that the definition of investment includes changes in inventories of unsold goods. An increase in inventories is counted as positive investment while a decrease in inventories is counted as negative investment. It is important to remember that some inventory changes are planned, while others are unplanned. Since the investment demand curve deals only with *planned* investment, it is only affected by *planned* changes that firms desire to make to their inventory levels. If firms are planning to increase their inventories, the investment demand curve shifts to the right. If firms are planning on decreasing their inventories, the investment demand curve shifts to the left.

Firms make planned changes to their inventory levels mostly because they are expecting either faster or slower sales. A firm that expects its sales to double in the next year will want to keep more inventory in stock, thereby increasing its investment demand. By contrast, a firm that is expecting slower sales will plan on reducing its inventory, thereby reducing its overall investment demand. But because life often does not turn out as expected, firms often find that the actual amount of inventory investment that they end up making is either greater or less than what they had planned. The size of the gap is, naturally, the dollar amount of their *unplanned* inventory changes. These

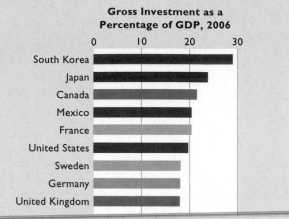

GLOBAL PERSPECTIVE 27.2

Gross Investment Expenditures as a Percentage of GDP, Selected Nations

As a percentage of GDP, investment varies widely by nation. These differences, of course, can change from year to year.

Gross Investment as a Percentage of GDP, 2006

South Korea, Japan, Canada, Mexico, France, United States, Sweden, Germany, United Kingdom

Source: International Financial Statistics, International Monetary Fund, **www.imf.org.** Used by permission.

unplanned inventory adjustments will play a large role in the aggregate expenditures model studied in Chapter 28.

Expectations
We noted that business investment is based on expected returns (expected additions to profit). Most capital goods are durable, with a life expectancy of 10 or 20 years. Thus, the expected rate of return on capital investment depends on the firm's expectations of future sales, future operating costs, and future profitability of the product that the capital helps produce. These expectations are based on forecasts of future business conditions as well as on such elusive and difficult-to-predict factors as changes in the domestic political climate, international relations, population growth, and consumer tastes. If executives become more optimistic about future sales, costs, and profits, the investment demand curve will shift to the right; a pessimistic outlook will shift the curve to the left.

Global Perspective 27.2 compares investment spending relative to GDP for several nations in a recent year. Domestic real interest rates and investment demand determine the levels of investment relative to GDP.

Instability of Investment
In contrast to consumption, investment is unstable; it rises and falls quite often. Investment, in fact, is the most volatile component of total spending—so much so that most of the fluctuations in output and employment that happen over

FIGURE 27.7 **The volatility of investment.** Annual percentage changes in investment spending are often several times greater than the percentage changes in GDP. (Data are in real terms.)

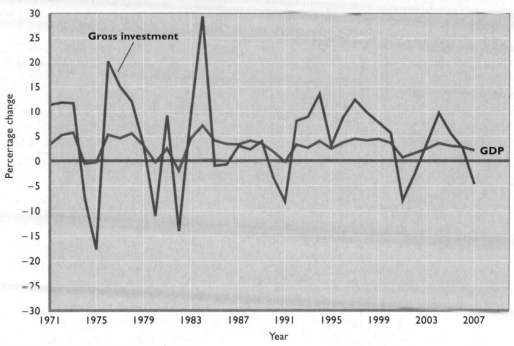

Source: Bureau of Economic Analysis, **www.bea.gov.**

the course of the business cycle can be attributed to increases and decreases in investment. Figure 27.7 shows just how volatile investment in the United States has been. Note that its swings are much greater than those of GDP.

Several factors explain the variability of investment.

Durability
Because of their durability, capital goods have indefinite useful lifespans. Within limits, purchases of capital goods are discretionary and therefore can be postponed. Firms can scrap or replace older equipment and buildings, or they can patch them up and use them for a few more years. Optimism about the future may prompt firms to replace their older facilities and such modernizing will call for a high level of investment. A less optimistic view, however, may lead to smaller amounts of investment as firms repair older facilities and keep them in use.

Irregularity of Innovation
We know that technological progress is a major determinant of investment. New products and processes stimulate investment. But history suggests that major innovations such as railroads, electricity, automobiles, fiber optics, and computers occur quite irregularly. When they do happen, they induce a vast upsurge or "wave" of investment spending that in time recedes.

A contemporary example is the tremendous popularity of the personal computer and Internet, which has caused a

wave of investment in those industries and in many related industries such as computer software and electronic commerce. Some time in the future, this particular surge of investment undoubtedly will level off.

Variability of Profits
When evaluating whether or not to undertake a given investment, a firm's expectations about the potential profitability of that potential investment are influenced to some degree by the size of the profits currently being earned by other firms that have made similar investments. Current profits, however, are themselves highly variable. Thus, the variability of profits contributes to the volatile nature of the incentive to invest.

The instability of profits may cause investment fluctuations in a second way. Profits are a major source of funds for business investment. U.S. businesses sometimes prefer this internal source of financing to increases in external debt or stock issue.

In short, expanding profits give firms both greater incentives and greater means to invest; declining profits have the reverse effects. The fact that actual profits are variable thus adds doubly to the instability of investment.

Variability of Expectations
Firms tend to project current business conditions into the future. But their expectations can change quickly when some event suggests a significant possible change in future business conditions.

Changes in exchange rates, changes in the outlook for international peace, court decisions in key labor or antitrust cases, legislative actions, changes in trade barriers, changes in governmental economic policies, and a host of similar considerations may cause substantial shifts in business expectations.

The stock market also can influence business expectations because firms look to it as one of several indicators of society's overall confidence in future business conditions. Rising stock prices tend to signify public confidence in the business future, while falling stock prices may imply a lack of confidence. The stock market, however, is often driven by "herd behavior" in which financial investors follow the lead of others rather than think independently. When stock prices rise because others are buying, they also buy; when stock prices are falling because others are selling, they also sell. This behavior can greatly magnify the volatility of stock prices that otherwise would be much more stable. Business can easily confuse these large swings in stock prices for real changes in society's optimism or pessimism about future business conditions. If they do, businesses are likely to respond by overadjusting their investment plans in one direction or the other. In this way, stock market volatility can add to the instability of investment spending.

For all these reasons, changes in investment cause most of the fluctuations in output and employment that occur over the course of the business cycle. In terms of Figures 27.5 and 27.6, we would represent volatility of investment as occasional and substantial shifts in the investment demand curve.

QUICK REVIEW 27.2

- A specific investment will be undertaken if the expected rate of return, r, equals or exceeds the real interest rate, i.
- The investment demand curve shows the total monetary amounts that will be invested by an economy at various possible real interest rates.
- The investment demand curve shifts when changes occur in (a) the costs of acquiring, operating, and maintaining capital goods, (b) business taxes, (c) technology, (d) the stock of capital goods on hand, and (e) business expectations.

The Multiplier Effect*

A final basic relationship that requires discussion is the relationship between changes in spending and changes in real GDP. Assuming that the economy has room to

---

*Instructors who cover the full aggregate expenditures (AE) model (Chapter 28) rather than moving directly to aggregate demand and aggregate supply (Chapter 29) may choose to defer this discussion until after the analysis of equilibrium real GDP.

expand—so that increases in spending do not lead to increases in prices—there is a direct relationship between these two aggregates. More spending results in a higher GDP; less spending results in a lower GDP. But there is much more to this relationship. A change in spending, say, investment, ultimately changes output and income by more than the initial change in investment spending. That surprising result is called the *multiplier effect*: a change in a component of total spending leads to a larger change in GDP. The **multiplier** determines how much larger that change will be; it is the ratio of a change in GDP to the initial change in spending (in this case, investment). Stated generally,

$$\text{Multiplier} = \frac{\text{change in real GDP}}{\text{initial change in spending}}$$

By rearranging this equation, we can also say that

$$\text{Change in GDP} = \text{multiplier} \times \text{initial change in spending}$$

So if investment in an economy rises by $30 billion and GDP increases by $90 billion as a result, we then know from our first equation that the multiplier is 3 (= $90/$30).

Note these three points about the multiplier:

- The "initial change in spending" is usually associated with investment spending because of investment's volatility. But changes in consumption (unrelated to changes in income), net exports, and government purchases also lead to the multiplier effect.
- The "initial change in spending" associated with investment spending results from a change in the real interest rate and/or a shift of the investment demand curve.
- Implicit in the preceding point is that the multiplier works in both directions. An increase in initial spending will create a multiple increase in GDP, while a decrease in spending will create a multiple decrease in GDP.

Rationale

The multiplier effect follows from two facts. First, the economy supports repetitive, continuous flows of expenditures and income through which dollars spent by Smith are received as income by Chin and then spent by Chin and received as income by Gonzales, and so on. (This chapter's Last Word presents this idea in a humorous way.) Second, any change in income will change both consumption and saving in the same direction as, and by a fraction of, the change in income.

It follows that an initial change in spending will set off a spending chain throughout the economy. That chain of spending, although of diminishing importance at each successive step, will cumulate to a multiple change in GDP. Initial changes in spending produce magnified changes in output and income.

Table 27.3 illustrates the rationale underlying the multiplier effect. Suppose that a $5 billion increase in investment spending occurs. We assume that the MPC is .75, the MPS is .25, and prices remain constant. That is, neither the initial increase in spending nor any of the subsequent increases in spending will cause prices to rise.

The initial $5 billion increase in investment generates an equal amount of wage, rent, interest, and profit income because spending and receiving income are two sides of the same transaction. How much consumption will be induced by this $5 billion increase in the incomes of households? We find the answer by applying the marginal propensity to consume of .75 to this change in income. Thus, the $5 billion increase in income initially raises consumption by $3.75 (= .75 × $5) billion and saving by $1.25 (= .25 × $5) billion, as shown in columns 2 and 3 in Table 27.3.

Other households receive as income (second round) the $3.75 billion of consumption spending. Those households consume .75 of this $3.75 billion, or $2.81 billion, and save .25 of it, or $.94 billion. The $2.81 billion that is consumed flows to still other households as income to be spent or saved (third round). And the process continues, with the added consumption and income becoming less in each round. The process ends when there is no more additional income to spend.

Figure 27.8 shows several rounds of the multiplier process of Table 27.3 graphically. As shown by rounds 1 to 5, each round adds a smaller and smaller violet block to national income and GDP. The process, of course, continues beyond the five rounds shown (for convenience we have simply cumulated the subsequent declining blocks

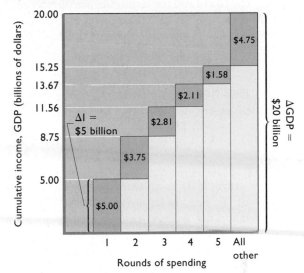

FIGURE 27.8 The multiplier process (MPC = .75). An initial change in investment spending of $5 billion creates an equal $5 billion of new income in round 1. Households spend $3.75 (= .75 × $5) billion of this new income, creating $3.75 of added income in round 2. Of this $3.75 of new income, households spend $2.81 (= .75 × $3.75) billion, and income rises by that amount in round 3. Such income increments over the entire process get successively smaller but eventually produce a total change of income and GDP of $20 billion. The multiplier therefore is 4 (= $20 billion/$5 billion).

into a single block labeled "All other"). The accumulation of the additional income in each round—the sum of the violet blocks—is the total change in income or GDP resulting from the initial $5 billion change in spending. Because the spending and respending effects of the increase in investment diminish with each successive round of spending, the cumulative increase in output and income eventually ends. In this case, the ending occurs when $20 billion of additional income accumulates. Thus, the multiplier is 4 (= $20 billion/$5 billion).

TABLE 27.3 The Multiplier: A Tabular Illustration (in Billions)

	(1) Change in Income	(2) Change in Consumption (MPC = .75)	(3) Change in Saving (MPS = .25)
Increase in investment of **$5.00**	$5.00	$ 3.75	$1.25
Second round	3.75	2.81	.94
Third round	2.81	2.11	.70
Fourth round	2.11	1.58	.53
Fifth round	1.58	1.19	.39
All other rounds	4.75	3.56	1.19
Total	**$20.00**	$15.00	$5.00

The Multiplier and the Marginal Propensities

You may have sensed from Table 27.3 that the fractions of an increase in income consumed (MPC) and saved (MPS) determine the cumulative respending effects of any initial change in spending and therefore determine the size of the multiplier. The MPC and the multiplier are directly related and the MPS and the multiplier are inversely related. The precise formulas are as shown in the next two equations:

$$\text{Multiplier} = \frac{1}{1 - \text{MPC}}$$

Recall, too, that MPC + MPS = 1. Therefore MPS = 1 − MPC, which means we can also write the multiplier formula as

$$\text{Multiplier} = \frac{1}{\text{MPS}}$$

This latter formula is a quick way to determine the multiplier. All you need to know is the MPS.

The smaller the fraction of any change in income saved, the greater the respending at each round and, therefore, the greater the multiplier. When the MPS is .25, as in our example, the multiplier is 4. If the MPS were .2, the multiplier would be 5. If the MPS were .33, the multiplier would be 3. Let's see why.

Suppose the MPS is .2 and businesses increase investment by $5 billion. In the first round of Table 27.3, consumption will rise by $4 billion (= MPC of .8 × $5 billion) rather than by $3.75 billion because saving will increase by $1 billion (= MPS of .2 × $5 billion) rather than $1.25 billion. The greater rise in consumption in round 1 will produce a greater increase in income in round 2. The same will be true for all successive rounds. If we worked through all rounds of the multiplier, we would find that the process ends when income has cumulatively increased by $25 billion, not the $20 billion shown in the table. When the MPS is .2 rather than .25, the multiplier is 5 (= $25 billion/$5 billion) as opposed to 4 (= $20 billion/$5 billion.)

If the MPS were .33 rather than .25, the successive increases in consumption and income would be less than those in Table 27.3. We would discover that the process ended with a $15 billion increase in income rather than the $20 billion shown. When the MPS is .33, the multiplier is 3 (= $15 billion/$5 billion). The mathematics works such that the multiplier is equal to the reciprocal of the MPS. The reciprocal of any number is the quotient you obtain by dividing 1 by that number.

A large MPC (small MPS) means the succeeding rounds of consumption spending shown in Figure 27.8

diminish slowly and thereby cumulate to a large change in income. Conversely, a small MPC (a large MPS) causes the increases in consumption to decline quickly, so the cumulative change in income is small. The relationship between the MPC (and thus the MPS) and the multiplier is summarized in Figure 27.9.

FIGURE 27.9 **The MPC and the multiplier.** The larger the MPC (the smaller the MPS), the greater the size of the multiplier.

MPC	Multiplier
.9	10
.8	5
.75	4
.67	3
.5	2

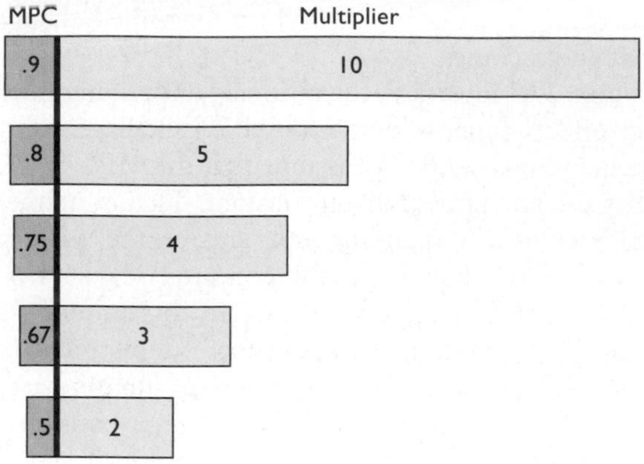

WORKED PROBLEMS

W 27.2

Multiplier effect

QUICK REVIEW 27.3

- The multiplier effect reveals that an initial change in spending can cause a larger change in domestic income and output. The multiplier is the factor by which the initial change is magnified: multiplier = change in real GDP/initial change in spending.

- The higher the marginal propensity to consume (the lower the marginal propensity to save), the larger the multiplier: multiplier = 1/(1 − MPC) or 1/MPS.

How Large Is the Actual Multiplier Effect?

The multiplier we have just described is based on simplifying assumptions. Consumption of domestic output rises by the increases in income minus the increases in saving. But in reality, consumption of domestic output increases in each round by a lesser amount than implied by the MPS alone. In addition to saving, households use some of the extra income in each round to purchase additional goods from abroad (imports) and pay additional taxes. Buying imports and paying taxes drains off some of the additional

Humorist Art Buchwald Examines the Multiplier

WASHINGTON—The recession hit so fast that nobody knows exactly how it happened. One day we were the land of milk and honey and the next day we were the land of sour cream and food stamps.

This is one explanation.

Hofberger, the Ford sales-man in Tomcat, Va., a suburb of Washington, called up Little-ton, of Littleton Menswear & Haberdashery, and said, "Good news, the new Fords have just come in and I've put one aside for you and your wife."

Littleton said, "I can't, Hofberger, my wife and I are getting a divorce."

"I'm sorry," Littleton said, "but I can't afford a new car this year. After I settle with my wife, I'll be lucky to buy a bicycle."

Hofberger hung up. His phone rang a few minutes later.

"This is Bedcheck the painter," the voice on the other end said. "When do you want us to start painting your house?"

"I changed my mind," said Hofberger, "I'm not going to paint the house."

"But I ordered the paint," Bedcheck said. "Why did you change your mind?"

"Because Littleton is getting a divorce and he can't afford a new car."

That evening when Bedcheck came home his wife said, "The new color television set arrived from Gladstone's TV Shop."

"Take it back," Bedcheck told his wife.

"Why?" she demanded.

"Because Hofberger isn't going to have his house painted now that the Littletons are getting a divorce."

The next day Mrs. Bedcheck dragged the TV set in its car-ton back to Gladstone. "We don't want it."

Gladstone's face dropped. He immediately called his travel agent, Sandstorm. "You know that trip you had scheduled for me to the Virgin Islands?"

"Right, the tickets are all written up."

"Cancel it. I can't go. Bedcheck just sent back the color TV set because Hofberger didn't sell a car to Littleton because they're going to get a divorce and she wants all his money."

Sandstorm tore up the airline tickets and went over to see his banker, Gripsholm. "I can't pay back the loan this month because Gladstone isn't going to the Virgin Islands."

Gripsholm was furious. When Rudemaker came in to borrow money for a new kitchen he needed for his res-taurant, Gripsholm turned him down cold. "How can I loan you money when Sand-storm hasn't repaid the money he borrowed?"

Rudemaker called up the contractor, Eagleton, and said he couldn't put in a new kitchen. Eagleton laid off eight men.

Meanwhile, Ford announced it was giving a rebate on its new models. Hofberger called up Littleton immediately. "Good news," he said, "even if you are getting a divorce, you can afford a new car."

"I'm not getting a divorce," Littleton said. "It was all a mis-understanding and we've made up."

"That's great," Hofberger said. "Now you can buy the Ford."

"No way," said Littleton. "My business has been so lousy I don't know why I keep the doors open."

"I didn't realize that," Hofberger said.

"Do you realize I haven't seen Bedcheck, Gladstone, Sand-storm, Gripsholm, Rudemaker or Eagleton for more than a month? How can I stay in business if they don't patronize my store?"

Source: Art Buchwald, "Squaring the Economic Circle," *Cleveland Plain Dealer*, Feb. 22, 1975. Reprinted by permission.

consumption spending (on domestic output) created by the increases in income. So the multiplier effect is reduced and the 1/MPS formula for the multiplier overstates the actual outcome. To correct that problem, we would need to change the multiplier equation to read "1 divided by the fraction of the change in income that is not spent on domestic output." Also, we will find in later chapters that an increase in spending may be partly dissipated as inflation rather than realized fully as an increase in real GDP. This happens when increases in spending drive up prices. The multiplier process still happens, but it induces a much smaller change in real output because, at higher prices, any given amount of spending buys less real output. The Council of Economic Advisers, which advises the U.S. president on economic matters, has estimated that the actual multiplier effect for the United States is about 2. So keep in mind throughout later discussions that the actual multiplier is less than the multipliers in our simple examples. **(Key Question 9)**

Summary

1. Other things equal, there is a direct (positive) relationship between income and consumption and income and saving. The consumption and saving schedules show the various amounts that households intend to consume and save at the various income and output levels, assuming a fixed price level.

2. The *average* propensities to consume and save show the fractions of any total income that are consumed and saved; APC + APS = 1. The *marginal* propensities to consume and save show the fractions of any change in total income that are consumed and saved; MPC + MPS = 1.

3. The locations of the consumption and saving schedules (as they relate to real GDP) are determined by (a) the amount of wealth owned by households, (b) expectations of future prices and incomes, (c) real interest rates, (d) household debt, and (e) tax levels. The consumption and saving schedules are relatively stable.

4. The immediate determinants of investment are (a) the expected rate of return and (b) the real rate of interest. The economy's investment demand curve is found by cumulating investment projects, arraying them in descending order according to their expected rates of return, graphing the result, and applying the rule that investment should be undertaken up to the point at which the real interest rate, i, equals the expected rate of return, r. The investment demand curve reveals an inverse (negative) relationship between the interest rate and the level of aggregate investment.

5. Shifts of the investment demand curve can occur as the result of changes in (a) the acquisition, maintenance, and operating costs of capital goods; (b) business taxes; (c) technology; (d) the stocks of capital goods on hand; and (e) expectations.

6. Either changes in interest rates or shifts of the investment demand curve can change the level of investment.

7. The durability of capital goods, the irregular occurrence of major innovations, profit volatility, and the variability of expectations all contribute to the instability of investment spending.

8. Through the multiplier effect, an increase in investment spending (or consumption spending, government purchases, or net export spending) ripples through the economy, ultimately creating a magnified increase in real GDP. The multiplier is the ultimate change in GDP divided by the initiating change in investment or some other component of spending.

9. The multiplier is equal to the reciprocal of the marginal propensity to save: The greater is the marginal propensity to save, the smaller is the multiplier. Also, the greater is the marginal propensity to consume, the larger is the multiplier.

10. Economists estimate that the actual multiplier effect in the U.S. economy is about 2, which is less than the multiplier in the text examples.

Terms and Concepts

45° (degree) line	average propensity to consume (APC)	wealth effect
consumption schedule	average propensity to save (APS)	expected rate of return
saving schedule	marginal propensity to consume (MPC)	investment demand curve
break-even income	marginal propensity to save (MPS)	multiplier

Study Questions  |ECONOMICS

1. Very briefly summarize the relationships shown by (*a*) the consumption schedule, (*b*) the saving schedule, (*c*) the investment demand curve, and (*d*) the multiplier effect. Which of these relationships are direct (positive) relationships and which are inverse (negative) relationships? Why are consumption and saving in the United States greater today than they were a decade ago? **LO1, LO3**

2. Precisely how do the APC and the MPC differ? Why must the sum of the MPC and the MPS equal 1? What are the basic determinants of the consumption and saving schedules? Of your personal level of consumption? **LO1**

3. Explain how each of the following will affect the consumption and saving schedules (as they relate to GDP) or the investment schedule, other things equal: **LO1, LO3**
   a. A large increase in the value of real estate, including private houses.
   b. A decline in the real interest rate.
   c. A sharp, sustained decline in stock prices.
   d. An increase in the rate of population growth.
   e. The development of a cheaper method of manufacturing computer chips.
   f. A sizable increase in the retirement age for collecting Social Security benefits.
   g. An increase in the Federal personal income tax.

4. Explain why an upward shift of the consumption schedule typically involves an equal downshift of the saving schedule. What is the exception to this relationship? **LO1**

5. **KEY QUESTION** Complete the following table: **LO1**
   a. Show the consumption and saving schedules graphically.
   b. Find the break-even level of income. Explain how it is possible for households to dissave at very low income levels.
   c. If the proportion of total income consumed (APC) decreases and the proportion saved (APS) increases as income rises, explain both verbally and graphically how the MPC and MPS can be constant at various levels of income.

6. What are the basic determinants of investment? Explain the relationship between the real interest rate and the level of investment. Why is investment spending unstable? How is it possible for investment spending to increase even in a period in which the real interest rate rises? **LO3, LO4**

7. **KEY QUESTION** Suppose a handbill publisher can buy a new duplicating machine for $500 and the duplicator has a 1-year life. The machine is expected to contribute $550 to the year's net revenue. What is the expected rate of return? If the real interest rate at which funds can be borrowed to purchase the machine is 8 percent, will the publisher choose to invest in the machine? Explain. **LO3**

8. **KEY QUESTION** Assume there are no investment projects in the economy that yield an expected rate of return of 25 percent or more. But suppose there are $10 billion of investment projects yielding expected returns of between 20 and 25 percent; another $10 billion yielding between 15 and 20 percent; another $10 billion between 10 and 15 percent; and so forth. Cumulate these data and present them graphically, putting the expected rate of return on the vertical axis and the amount of investment on the horizontal axis. What will be the equilibrium level of aggregate investment if the real interest rate is (*a*) 15 percent, (*b*) 10 percent, and (*c*) 5 percent? Explain why this curve is the investment demand curve. **LO3, LO4**

9. **KEY QUESTION** What is the multiplier effect? What relationship does the MPC bear to the size of the multiplier? The MPS? What will the multiplier be when the MPS is 0, .4, .6, and 1? What will it be when the MPC is 1, .90, .67, .50, and 0? How much of a change in GDP will result if firms increase their level of investment by $8 billion and the MPC is .80? If the MPC is .67? **LO5**

10. Why is the actual multiplier for the U.S. economy less than the multiplier in this chapter's simple examples? **LO5**

11. **ADVANCED ANALYSIS** Linear equations for the consumption and saving schedules take the general form $C = a + bY$

Level of Output and Income (GDP = DI)	Consumption	Saving	APC	APS	MPC	MPS
$240	$_____	$−4	___	___		
260	_____	0	___	___	___	___
280	_____	4	___	___	___	___
300	_____	8	___	___	___	___
320	_____	12	___	___	___	___
340	_____	16	___	___	___	___
360	_____	20	___	___	___	___
380	_____	24	___	___	___	___
400	_____	28	___	___	___	___

and $S = -a + (1 - b)Y$, where C, S, and Y are consumption, saving, and national income, respectively. The constant a represents the vertical intercept, and b represents the slope of the consumption schedule. **LO1**

a. Use the following data to substitute numerical values for a and b in the consumption and saving equations.

b. What is the economic meaning of b? Of $(1 - b)$?

National Income (Y)	Consumption (C)
$ 0	$ 80
100	140
200	200
300	260
400	320

c. Suppose that the amount of saving that occurs at each level of national income falls by $20 but that the values of b and $(1 - b)$ remain unchanged. Restate the saving and consumption equations for the new numerical values, and cite a factor that might have caused the change.

12. **ADVANCED ANALYSIS** Suppose that the linear equation for consumption in a hypothetical economy is $C = 40 + .8Y$. Also suppose that income (Y) is $400. Determine ($a$) the marginal propensity to consume, (b) the marginal propensity to save, (c) the level of consumption, (d) the average propensity to consume, (e) the level of saving, and (f) the average propensity to save. **LO1**

13. **LAST WORD** What is the central economic idea humorously illustrated in Art Buchwald's piece, "Squaring the Economic Circle"? How does the central idea relate to recessions, on the one hand, and vigorous expansions, on the other?

Web-Based Questions

1. **THE BEIGE BOOK AND CURRENT CONSUMER SPENDING** Go to the Federal Reserve Web site, **www.federalreserve.gov,** and select About the Fed, then The Federal Reserve System, and then Districts and Banks. Find your Federal Reserve District. Next, return to the Fed home page and select Monetary Policy, then Reports, and then Beige Book. What is the Beige Book? Locate the current Beige Book report and compare consumer spending for the entire U.S. economy with consumer spending in your Federal Reserve District. What are the economic strengths and weaknesses in both? Are retailers reporting that recent sales have met their expectations? What are their expectations for the future?

2. **INVESTMENT INSTABILITY—CHANGES IN REAL PRIVATE NONRESIDENTIAL FIXED INVESTMENT** The Bureau of Economic Analysis provides data for real private nonresidential

fixed investment in table form at **www.bea.gov.** Access the BEA interactively by first clicking on National, then Interactive Tables: National Income and Product Accounts Tables, and then "Choose a table from a list of All NIPA Tables." Scroll down until you find Table 5.3.5, "Private Fixed Investment by Type (A) (Q)." Has recent real private nonresidential fixed investment been volatile (as measured by percentage change from previous quarters)? Which is the largest component of this type of investment, (a) structures or (b) equipment and software? Which of these two components has been more volatile? How do recent quarterly percentage changes compare with the previous years' changes? Looking at the investment data, what investment forecast would you make for the upcoming year?

FURTHER TEST YOUR KNOWLEDGE AT
www.mcconnell18e.com

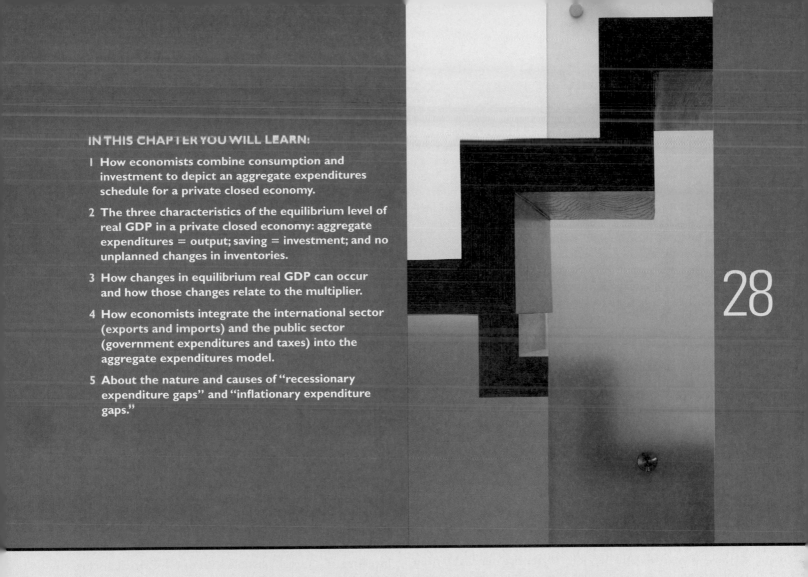

28

IN THIS CHAPTER YOU WILL LEARN:

1 How economists combine consumption and investment to depict an aggregate expenditures schedule for a private closed economy.

2 The three characteristics of the equilibrium level of real GDP in a private closed economy: aggregate expenditures = output; saving = investment; and no unplanned changes in inventories.

3 How changes in equilibrium real GDP can occur and how those changes relate to the multiplier.

4 How economists integrate the international sector (exports and imports) and the public sector (government expenditures and taxes) into the aggregate expenditures model.

5 About the nature and causes of "recessionary expenditure gaps" and "inflationary expenditure gaps."

The Aggregate Expenditures Model

Two of the most critical questions in macroeconomics are: (1) What determines the level of GDP, given a nation's production capacity? (2) What causes real GDP to rise in one period and to fall in another? To answer these questions we construct the aggregate expenditures model, which has its origins in 1936 in the writings of British economist John Maynard Keynes (pronounced "Caines"). The basic premise of the aggregate expenditures model—also known as the "Keynesian cross" model—is that the amount

ORIGIN OF THE IDEA

O 28.1

Aggregate expenditures model

of goods and services produced and therefore the level of employment depend directly on the level of aggregate expenditures (total spending). Businesses will produce only a level of output that they think they can profitably sell. They will idle their workers and machinery when there are no markets for their goods and services. When aggregate expenditures fall, total output and employment decrease; when aggregate expenditures rise, total output and employment increase.

Assumptions and Simplifications

The simplifying assumptions underpinning the aggregate expenditures model reflect the economic conditions that were prevalent during the Great Depression. As discussed in this chapter's Last Word, Keynes created the model during the middle of the Great Depression in the hopes of understanding both why the Great Depression had happened as well as how it might be ended.

The most fundamental assumption behind the aggregate expenditures model is that prices in the economy are fixed. In the terminology of Chapter 23, the aggregate expenditures model is an extreme version of a sticky price model. In fact, it is a stuck-price model since prices cannot change at all.

Keynes made this assumption because the economy during the Great Depression was operating far below its potential output. Real GDP in the United States declined by 27 percent from 1929 to 1933 and the unemployment rate rose to 25 percent. Thousands of factories sat idle, gathering dust and producing nothing because nobody wanted to buy their output. To Keynes, this massive unemployment of labor and capital meant that even if a sudden increase in demand occurred, prices were unlikely to rise at all because the massive oversupply of productive resources would keep prices low. Consequently, he focused his attention on how the economy might reach an equilibrium in a situation in which prices were likely to be stuck for a while.

His solution involves realizing that even if prices are stuck, firms will still be able to receive feedback from the markets about how much they should produce. With prices stuck, this feedback obviously cannot come in the form of changing prices. Instead, it comes in the form of unplanned changes in firm inventory levels. As we will explain, these changes can guide firms to an equilibrium level of GDP. Crucially, this equilibrium level of GDP can be well below a nation's potential output—meaning that the aggregate expenditures model can explain the situation of massive unemployment that the economy found itself in during the Great Depression.

But the aggregate expenditures model is not just of historical interest. It can be used fruitfully even today because, as we explained in Chapter 23, prices in the modern economy are very sticky and sometimes nearly stuck in the short run. As a result, the aggregate expenditures model can help us understand how the modern economy is likely to initially adjust to various economic shocks, including changes in things such as tax rates, government spending, consumption expenditures, and investment spending.

We will build up the aggregate expenditures model in simple stages. Let's first look at aggregate expenditures and equilibrium GDP in a *private closed economy*—one without international trade or government. Then we will "open" the "closed" economy to exports and imports and also convert our "private" economy to a more realistic "mixed" economy that includes government purchases (or, more loosely, "government spending") and taxes.

In addition, until we introduce taxes into the model, we will assume that real GDP equals disposable income (DI). For instance, if $500 billion of output is produced as GDP, households will receive exactly $500 billion of disposable income that they can then consume or save. And finally, unless specified otherwise, we will assume (as Keynes did) that the economy has excess production capacity and unemployed labor so that an increase in aggregate expenditures will increase real output and employment but not raise the price level.

Consumption and Investment Schedules

In the private closed economy, the two components of aggregate expenditures are consumption, C, and gross investment, I_g. Because we examined the *consumption schedule* (Figure 27.2a) in the previous chapter, there is no need to repeat that analysis here. But to add the investment decisions of businesses to the consumption plans of households, we need to construct an investment schedule showing the amounts business firms collectively intend to invest—their **planned investment**—at each possible level of GDP. Such a schedule represents the investment plans of businesses in the same way the consumption schedule represents the consumption plans of households. In developing the investment schedule, we will assume that this planned investment is independent of the level of current disposable income or real output.

Suppose the investment demand curve is as shown in Figure 28.1a and the current real interest rate is 8 percent. This means that firms will spend $20 billion on investment goods. Our assumption tells us that this $20 billion of investment will occur at both low and high levels of GDP. The line I_g in Figure 28.1b shows this graphically; it is the economy's **investment schedule.** You should not confuse this investment schedule I_g with the investment demand curve *ID* in Figure 28.1a. The investment schedule shows the amount of investment forthcoming at each level of GDP. As indicated in Figure 28.1b, the interest rate and investment demand curve together determine this amount ($20 billion). Table 28.1 shows the investment schedule in tabular form. Note that investment (I_g) in column 2 is $20 billion at all levels of real GDP.

FIGURE 28.1 **(a) The investment demand curve and (b) the investment schedule.** (a) The level of investment spending (here, $20 billion) is determined by the real interest rate (here, 8 percent) together with the investment demand curve *ID*. (b) The investment schedule I_g relates the amount of investment ($20 billion) determined in (a) to the various levels of GDP.

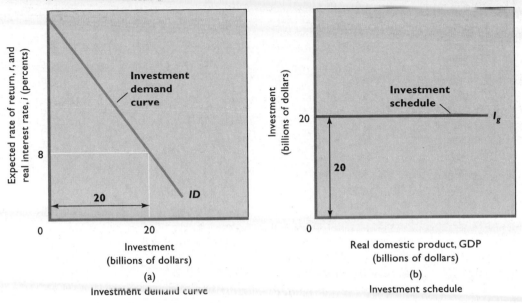

(a)
Investment demand curve

(b)
Investment schedule

TABLE 28.1 **The Investment Schedule (in Billions)**

(1) Level of Real Output and Income	(2) Investment (I_g)
$370	$20
390	20
410	20
430	20
450	20
470	20
490	20
510	20
530	20
550	20

Equilibrium GDP: $C + I_g = GDP$

Now let's combine the consumption schedule of Chapter 27 and the investment schedule here to explain the equilibrium levels of output, income, and employment in the private closed economy.

Tabular Analysis

Columns 2 through 5 in Table 28.2 repeat the consumption and saving schedules of Table 27.1 and the investment schedule of Table 28.1.

Real Domestic Output Column 2 in Table 28.2 lists the various possible levels of total output—of real GDP—that the private sector might produce. Producers are willing to offer any of these 10 levels of output if they can expect to receive an identical level of income from the sale of that output. For example, firms will produce $370 billion of output, incurring $370 billion of costs (wages, rents, interest, and normal profit costs) only if they believe they can sell that output for $370 billion. Firms will offer $390 billion of output if they think they can sell that output for $390 billion. And so it is for all the other possible levels of output.

Aggregate Expenditures In the private closed economy of Table 28.2, aggregate expenditures consist of consumption (column 3) plus investment (column 5). Their sum is shown in column 6, which along with column 2 makes up the **aggregate expenditures schedule** for the private closed economy. This schedule shows the amount $(C + I_g)$ that will be spent at each possible output or income level.

At this point we are working with *planned investment*—the data in column 5, Table 28.2. These data show the amounts firms plan or intend to invest, not the amounts they actually will invest if there are unplanned changes in inventories. More about that shortly.

TABLE 28.2 Determination of the Equilibrium Levels of Employment, Output, and Income: A Closed Private Economy

(1) Possible Levels of Employment, Millions	(2) Real Domestic Output (and Income) (GDP = DI),* Billions	(3) Consumption (C), Billions	(4) Saving (S), Billions	(5) Investment (I_g), Billions	(6) Aggregate Expenditures (C + I_g), Billions	(7) Unplanned Changes in Inventories, (+ or −)	(8) Tendency of Employment, Output, and Income
(1) 40	$370	$375	$−5	$20	$395	$−25	Increase
(2) 45	390	390	0	20	410	−20	Increase
(3) 50	410	405	5	20	425	−15	Increase
(4) 55	430	420	10	20	440	−10	Increase
(5) 60	450	435	15	20	455	−5	Increase
(6) 65	470	450	20	20	470	0	Equilibrium
(7) 70	490	465	25	20	485	+5	Decrease
(8) 75	510	480	30	20	500	+10	Decrease
(9) 80	530	495	35	20	515	+15	Decrease
(10) 85	550	510	40	20	530	+20	Decrease

*If depreciation and net foreign factor income are zero, government is ignored and it is assumed that all saving occurs in the household sector of the economy, then GDP as a measure of domestic output is equal to NI, PI, and DI. This means that households receive a DI equal to the value of total output.

Equilibrium GDP

Of the 10 possible levels of GDP in Table 28.2, which is the equilibrium level? Which total output is the economy capable of sustaining?

The equilibrium output is that output whose production creates total spending just sufficient to purchase that output. So the equilibrium level of GDP is the level at which the total quantity of goods produced (GDP) equals the total quantity of goods purchased ($C + I_g$). If you look at the domestic output levels in column 2 and the aggregate expenditures levels in column 6, you will see that this equality exists only at $470 billion of GDP (row 6). That is the only output at which economy-wide spending is precisely equal to the amount needed to move that output off the shelves. At $470 billion of GDP, the annual rates of production and spending are in balance. There is no overproduction, which would result in a piling up of unsold goods and consequently cutbacks in the production rate. Nor is there an excess of total spending, which would draw down inventories of goods and prompt increases in the rate of production. In short, there is no reason for businesses to alter this rate of production; $470 billion is the **equilibrium GDP.**

Disequilibrium

No level of GDP other than the equilibrium level of GDP can be sustained. At levels of GDP *less than* equilibrium, spending always exceeds GDP. If, for example, firms produced $410 billion of GDP (row 3 in Table 28.2), they would find it would yield $405 billion in consumer spending. Supplemented by $20 billion of planned investment, aggregate expenditures ($C + I_g$) would be $425 billion, as shown in column 6. The economy would provide an annual rate of spending more than sufficient to purchase the $410 billion of annual production. Because buyers would be taking goods off the shelves faster than firms could produce them, an unplanned decline in business inventories of $15 billion would occur (column 7) if this situation continued. But businesses can adjust to such an imbalance between aggregate expenditures and real output by stepping up production. Greater output will increase employment and total income. This process will continue until the equilibrium level of GDP is reached ($470 billion).

The reverse is true at all levels of GDP *greater than* the $470 billion equilibrium level. Businesses will find that these total outputs fail to generate the spending needed to clear the shelves of goods. Being unable to recover their costs, businesses will cut back on production. To illustrate: At the $510 billion output (row 8), business managers would find spending is insufficient to permit the sale of all that output. Of the $510 billion of income that this output creates, $480 billion would be received back by businesses as consumption spending. Though supplemented by $20 billion of planned investment spending, total expenditures ($500 billion) would still be $10 billion below the $510 billion quantity produced. If this imbalance persisted, $10 billion of inventories would pile up (column 7). But businesses can adjust to this unintended accumulation of unsold goods by cutting back on the rate of production. The resulting decline in output would mean fewer jobs and a decline in total income.

WORKED PROBLEMS

W 28.1

Equilibrium GDP

key graph

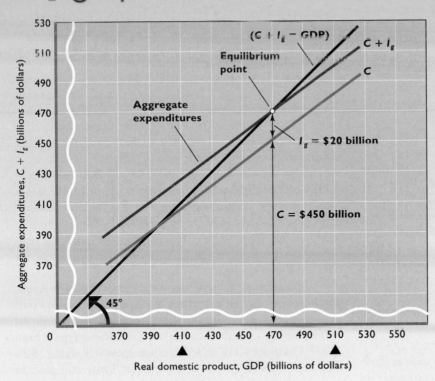

FIGURE 28.2 **Equilibrium GDP.** The aggregate expenditures schedule $C + I_g$ is determined by adding the investment schedule I_g to the upsloping consumption schedule C. Since investment is assumed to be the same at each level of GDP, the vertical distances between C and $C + I_g$ do not change. Equilibrium GDP is determined where the aggregate expenditures schedule intersects the 45° line, in this case at $470 billion.

QUICK QUIZ FOR FIGURE 28.2

1. In this figure, the slope of the aggregate expenditures schedule $C + I_g$:
   a. increases as real GDP increases.
   b. falls as real GDP increases.
   c. is constant and equals the MPC.
   d. is constant and equals the MPS.

2. At all points on the 45° line:
   a. equilibrium GDP is possible.
   b. aggregate expenditures exceed real GDP.
   c. consumption exceeds investment.
   d. aggregate expenditures are less than real GDP.

3. The $490 billion level of real GDP is not at equilibrium because:
   a. investment exceeds consumption.
   b. consumption exceeds investment.
   c. planned $C + I_g$ exceeds real GDP.
   d. planned $C + I_g$ is less than real GDP.

4. The $430 billion level of real GDP is not at equilibrium because:
   a. investment exceeds consumption.
   b. consumption exceeds investment.
   c. planned $C + I_g$ exceeds real GDP.
   d. planned $C + I_g$ is less than real GDP.

Graphical Analysis

We can demonstrate the same analysis graphically. In **Figure 28.2 (Key Graph)** the 45° line developed in Chapter 27 now takes on increased significance. Recall that at any point on this line, the value of what is being measured on the horizontal axis (here, GDP) is equal to the value of what is being measured on the vertical axis (here, aggregate expenditures, or $C + I_g$). Having discovered in our tabular analysis that the equilibrium level of domestic output is determined where $C + I_g$ equals GDP, we can say

that the 45° line in Figure 28.2 is a graphical statement of that equilibrium condition.

Now we must graph the aggregate expenditures schedule onto Figure 28.2. To do this, we duplicate the consumption schedule C in Figure 27.2a and add to it vertically the constant $20 billion amount of investment I_g from Figure 28.1b. This $20 billion is the amount we assumed firms plan to invest at all levels of GDP. Or, more directly, we can plot the $C + I_g$ data in column 6, Table 28.2.

Observe in Figure 28.2 that the aggregate expenditures line $C + I_g$ shows that total spending rises with income and output (GDP), but not as much as income rises. That is true because the marginal propensity to consume—the slope of line C—is less than 1. A part of any increase in income will be saved rather than spent. And because the aggregate expenditures line $C + I_g$ is parallel to the consumption line C, the slope of the aggregate expenditures line also equals the MPC for the economy and is less than 1. For our particular data, aggregate expenditures rise by $15 billion for every $20 billion increase in real output and income because $5 billion of each $20 billion increment is saved. Therefore, the slope of the aggregate expenditures line is .75 (= $\Delta\$15/\Delta\$20$).

The equilibrium level of GDP is determined by the intersection of the aggregate expenditures schedule and the 45° line. This intersection locates the only point at which aggregate expenditures (on the vertical axis) are equal to GDP (on the horizontal axis). Because Figure 28.2 is based on the data in Table 28.2, we once again find that equilibrium output is $470 billion. Observe that consumption at this output is $450 billion and investment is $20 billion.

It is evident from Figure 28.2 that no levels of GDP *above* the equilibrium level are sustainable because at those levels $C + I_g$ falls short of GDP. Graphically, the aggregate expenditures schedule lies below the 45° line in those situations. At the $510 billion GDP level, for example, $C + I_g$ is only $500 billion. This underspending causes inventories to rise, prompting firms to readjust production downward, in the direction of the $470 billion output level.

Conversely, at levels of GDP *below* $470 billion, the economy wants to spend in excess of what businesses are producing. Then $C + I_g$ exceeds total output. Graphically, the aggregate expenditures schedule lies above the 45° line. At the $410 billion GDP level, for example, $C + I_g$ totals

---

INTERACTIVE GRAPHS

G 28.1

Equilibrium GDP

$425 billion. This excess spending causes inventories to fall below their planned level, prompting firms to adjust production upward, in the direction of the $470 billion output level. Once production reaches that level, it will be sustained there indefinitely unless there is some change in the location of the aggregate expenditures line.

Other Features of Equilibrium GDP

We have seen that $C + I_g$ = GDP at equilibrium in the private closed economy. A closer look at Table 28.2 reveals two more characteristics of equilibrium GDP:

- Saving and *planned* investment are equal.
- There are no *unplanned* changes in inventories.

Saving Equals Planned Investment

As shown by row 6 in Table 28.2, saving and planned investment are both $20 billion at the $470 billion equilibrium level of GDP.

Saving is a **leakage** or withdrawal of spending from the economy's circular flow of income and expenditures. Saving is what causes consumption to be less than total output or GDP. Because of saving, consumption by itself is insufficient to remove domestic output from the shelves, apparently setting the stage for a decline in total output.

However, firms do not intend to sell their entire output to consumers. Some of that output will be capital goods sold to other businesses. Investment—the purchases of capital goods—is therefore an **injection** of spending into the income-expenditures stream. As an adjunct to consumption, investment is thus a potential replacement for the leakage of saving.

If the leakage of saving at a certain level of GDP exceeds the injection of investment, then $C + I_g$ will be less than GDP and that level of GDP cannot be sustained. Any GDP for which saving exceeds investment is an above-equilibrium GDP. Consider GDP of $510 billion (row 8 in Table 28.2). Households will save $30 billion, but firms will plan to invest only $20 billion. This $10 billion excess of saving over planned investment will reduce total spending to $10 billion below the value of total output. Specifically, aggregate expenditures will be $500 billion while real GDP is $510 billion. This spending deficiency will reduce real GDP.

Conversely, if the injection of investment exceeds the leakage of saving, then $C + I_g$ will be greater than GDP and drive GDP upward. Any GDP for which investment exceeds saving is a below-equilibrium GDP. For example, at a GDP of $410 billion (row 3 in Table 28.2), households will save only $5 billion, but firms will invest $20 billion. So investment exceeds saving by $15 billion. The small leakage of saving at this relatively low GDP level is more than compensated for by the larger injection of investment spending. That causes $C + I_g$ to exceed GDP and drives GDP higher.

Only where $S = I_g$—where the leakage of saving of $20 billion is exactly offset by the injection of planned investment of $20 billion—will aggregate expenditures ($C + I_g$) equal real output (GDP). That $C + I_g$ = GDP equality is what defines the equilibrium GDP. **(Key Question 2)**

No Unplanned Changes in Inventories

As part of their investment plans, firms may decide to increase or decrease their inventories. But, as confirmed in line 6 of Table 28.2, there are no **unplanned changes in inventories** at equilibrium GDP. This fact, along with

$C + I_g$ = GDP, and $S = I_g$ is a characteristic of equilibrium GDP in the private closed economy.

Unplanned changes in inventories play a major role in achieving equilibrium GDP. Consider, as an example, the $490 billion *above-equilibrium* GDP shown in row 7 of Table 28.2. What happens if firms produce that output, thinking they can sell it? Households save $25 billion of their $490 billion DI, so consumption is only $465 billion. Planned investment—which includes *planned* changes in inventories—is $20 billion (column 5). So aggregate expenditures $(C + I_g)$ are $485 billion and sales fall short of production by $5 billion. Firms retain that extra $5 billion of goods as an *unplanned* increase in inventories (column 7). It results from the failure of total spending to remove total output from the shelves.

Because changes in inventories are a part of investment, we note that *actual investment* is $25 billion. It consists of $20 billion of planned investment *plus* the $5 billion unplanned increase in inventories. Actual investment equals the saving of $25 billion, even though saving exceeds planned investment by $5 billion. Because firms cannot earn profits by accumulating unwanted inventories, the $5 billion unplanned increase in inventories will prompt them to cut back employment and production. GDP will fall to its equilibrium level of $470 billion, at which unplanned changes in inventories are zero.

Now look at the *below-equilibrium* $450 billion output (row 5, Table 28.2). Because households save only $15 billion of their $450 billion DI, consumption is $435 billion. Planned investment by firms is $20 billion, so aggregate expenditures are $455 billion. Sales exceed production by $5 billion. This is so only because a $5 billion unplanned decrease in business inventories has occurred. Firms must *disinvest* $5 billion in inventories (column 7). Note again that actual investment is $15 billion ($20 billion planned *minus* the $5 billion decline in inventory investment) and is equal to saving of $15 billion, even though planned investment exceeds saving by $5 billion. The unplanned decline in inventories, resulting from the excess of sales over production, will encourage firms to expand production. GDP will rise to $470 billion, at which unplanned changes in inventories are zero.

When economists say differences between investment and saving can occur and bring about changes in equilibrium GDP, they are referring to planned investment and saving. Equilibrium occurs only when planned investment and saving are equal. But when unplanned changes in inventories are considered, investment and saving are always equal, regardless of the level of GDP. That is true because actual investment consists of planned investment and unplanned investment (unplanned changes in inventories). Unplanned changes in inventories act as a balancing item that equates the actual amounts saved and invested in any period.

Changes in Equilibrium GDP and the Multiplier

In the private closed economy, the equilibrium GDP will change in response to changes in either the investment schedule or the consumption schedule. Because changes in the investment schedule usually are the main source of instability, we will direct our attention toward them.

Figure 28.3 shows the effect of changes in investment spending on the equilibrium real GDP. Suppose that the expected rate of return on investment rises or that the real interest rate falls such that investment spending increases by $5 billion. That would be shown as an upward shift of the investment schedule in Figure 28.1b. In Figure 28.3, the $5 billion increase of investment spending will increase aggregate expenditures from $(C + I_g)_0$ to $(C + I_g)_1$ and raise equilibrium real GDP from $470 billion to $490 billion.

If the expected rate of return on investment decreases or if the real interest rate rises, investment spending will decline by, say, $5 billion. That would be shown as a downward shift of the investment schedule in Figure 28.1b and a downward shift of the aggregate expenditures schedule from $(C + I_g)_0$ to $(C + I_g)_2$ in Figure 28.3. Equilibrium GDP will fall from $470 billion to $450 billion.

In our examples, a $5 billion change in investment spending leads to a $20 billion change in output and income. So the *multiplier* is 4 (= $20/$5). The MPS is .25, meaning that for every $1 billion of new income, $.25 billion of new saving occurs. Therefore, $20 billion of new income is needed to generate $5 billion of new saving. Once that increase in income and saving occurs, the economy is back in equilibrium—$C + I_g$ = GDP; saving and investment are equal; and there are no unplanned changes in inventories. You can see, then, why the multiplier is equal to 1/MPS and that the multiplier process is an integral part of the aggregate expenditures model. (A brief review of Table 27.3 and Figure 27.8 will be helpful at this point.)

QUICK REVIEW 28.1

- In a private closed economy, equilibrium GDP occurs where aggregate expenditures equal real domestic output $(C + I_g = \text{GDP})$.
- At equilibrium GDP, saving equals planned investment $(S = I_g)$ and unplanned changes in inventories are zero.
- Actual investment consists of planned investment plus unplanned changes in inventories (+ or −) and is always equal to saving in a private closed economy.
- Through the multiplier effect, an initial change in investment spending can cause a magnified change in domestic output and income.

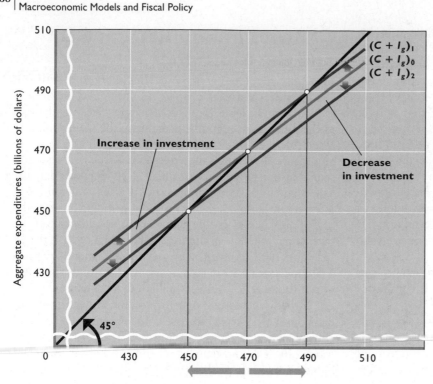

FIGURE 28.3 **Changes in the equilibrium GDP caused by shifts in the aggregate expenditures schedule and the investment schedule.** An upward shift of the aggregate expenditures schedule from $(C + I_g)_0$ to $(C + I_g)_1$ will increase the equilibrium GDP. Conversely, a downward shift from $(C + I_g)_0$ to $(C + I_g)_2$ will lower the equilibrium GDP. The extent of the changes in equilibrium GDP will depend on the size of the multiplier, which in this case is 4 (=20/5). The multiplier is equal to 1/MPS (here, 4 = 1/.25).

Adding International Trade

We next move from a closed economy to an open economy that incorporates exports (X) and imports (M). Our focus will be on **net exports** (exports minus imports), which may be either positive or negative.

Net Exports and Aggregate Expenditures

Like consumption and investment, exports create domestic production, income, and employment for a nation. Although U.S. goods and services produced for export are sent abroad, foreign spending on those goods and services increases production and creates jobs and incomes in the United States. We must therefore include exports as a component of U.S. aggregate expenditures.

Conversely, when an economy is open to international trade, it will spend part of its income on imports—goods and services produced abroad. To avoid overstating the value of domestic production, we must subtract the amount spent on imported goods because such spending generates production and income abroad rather than at home. So, to correctly measure aggregate expenditures for domestic goods and services, we must subtract expenditures on imports from total spending.

In short, for a private closed economy, aggregate expenditures are $C + I_g$. But for an open economy, aggregate expenditures are $C + I_g + (X - M)$. Or, recalling that net exports (X_n) equal ($X - M$), we can say that aggregate expenditures for a private open economy are $C + I_g + X_n$.

The Net Export Schedule

A net export schedule lists the amount of net exports that will occur at each level of GDP. Table 28.3 shows two possible net export schedules for the hypothetical economy represented in Table 28.2. In net export schedule X_{n1} (columns 1 and 2), exports exceed imports by \$5 billion at each level of GDP. Perhaps exports are \$15 billion while imports are \$10 billion. In schedule X_{n2} (columns 1 and 3), imports are \$5 billion higher than exports. Perhaps imports are \$20 billion while exports are \$15 billion. To simplify our discussion, we assume in both schedules that net exports are independent of GDP.[1]

_____

[1] In reality, although our exports depend on foreign incomes and are thus independent of U.S. GDP, our imports do vary directly with our own domestic national income. Just as our domestic consumption varies directly with our GDP, so do our purchases of foreign goods. As our GDP rises, U.S. households buy not only more Pontiacs and more Pepsi but also more Porsches and more Perrier. However, for now we will ignore the complications of the positive relationship between imports and U.S. GDP.

TABLE 28.3 Two Net Export Schedules (in Billions)

(1) Level of GDP	(2) Net Exports, X_{n1} (X > M)	(3) Net Exports, X_{n2} (X < M)
$370	$+5	$-5
390	+5	-5
410	+5	-5
430	+5	-5
450	+5	-5
470	+5	-5
490	+5	-5
510	+5	-5
530	+5	-5
550	+5	-5

Figure 28.4b represents the two net export schedules in Table 28.3. Schedule X_{n1} is above the horizontal axis and depicts positive net exports of $5 billion at all levels of GDP. Schedule X_{n2}, which is below the horizontal axis, shows negative net exports of $5 billion at all levels of GDP.

Net Exports and Equilibrium GDP

The aggregate expenditures schedule labeled $C + I_g$ in Figure 28.4a reflects the private closed economy. It shows the combined consumption and gross investment expenditures occurring at each level of GDP. With no foreign sector, the equilibrium GDP is $470 billion.

But in the private open economy, net exports can be either positive or negative. Let's see how each of the net export schedules in Figure 28.4b affects equilibrium GDP.

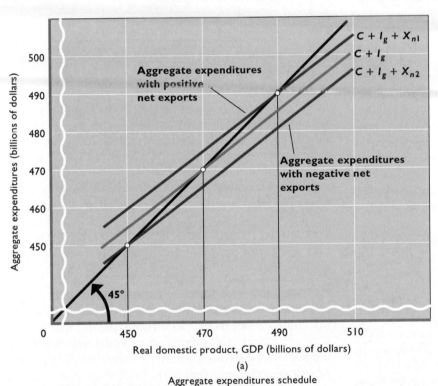

(a)
Aggregate expenditures schedule

(b)
Net export schedule, X_n

FIGURE 28.4 Net exports and equilibrium GDP. Positive net exports such as shown by the net export schedule X_{n1} in (b) elevate the aggregate expenditures schedule in (a) from the closed-economy level of $C + I_g$ to the open-economy level of $C + I_g + X_{n1}$. Negative net exports such as depicted by the net export schedule X_{n2} in (b) lower the aggregate expenditures schedule in (a) from the closed-economy level of $C + I_g$ to the open-economy level of $C + I_g + X_{n2}$.

Positive Net Exports Suppose the net export schedule is X_{n1}. The \$5 billion of additional net export expenditures by the rest of the world is accounted for by adding that \$5 billion to the $C + I_g$ schedule in Figure 28.4a. Aggregate expenditures at each level of GDP are then \$5 billion higher than $C + I_g$ alone. The aggregate expenditures schedule for the open economy thus becomes $C + I_g + X_{n1}$. In this case, international trade increases equilibrium GDP from \$470 billion in the private closed economy to \$490 billion in the private open economy. Adding net exports of \$5 billion has increased GDP by \$20 billion, in this case implying a multiplier of 4.

Generalization: Other things equal, positive net exports increase aggregate expenditures and GDP beyond what they would be in a closed economy. Be careful to notice that this increase is the result of exports being larger than imports. This is true because exports and imports have opposite effects on the measurement of domestically produced output. Exports increase real GDP by increasing expenditures on domestically produced output. Imports, by contrast, must be subtracted when calculating real GDP because they are expenditures directed toward output produced abroad. It is only because net exports are positive in this example—so that the expansionary effect of exports outweighs the reductions caused by imports—that we get the overall increase in real GDP. As the next section shows, if net exports are negative, then the reductions caused by imports will outweigh the expansionary effect of exports so that domestic real GDP will decrease.

Negative Net Exports Suppose that net exports are a negative \$5 billion as shown by X_{n2} in Figure 28.4b. This means that our hypothetical economy is importing \$5 billion more of goods than it is exporting. The aggregate expenditures schedule shown as $C + I_g$ in Figure 28.4a therefore overstates the expenditures on domestic output at each level of GDP. We must reduce the sum of expenditures by the \$5 billion net amount spent on imported goods. We do that by subtracting the \$5 billion of net imports from $C + I_g$.

The relevant aggregate expenditures schedule in Figure 28.4a becomes $C + I_g + X_{n2}$ and equilibrium GDP falls from \$470 billion to \$450 billion. Again, a change in net exports of \$5 billion has produced a fourfold change in GDP, reminding us that the multiplier in this example is 4.

This gives us a corollary to our first generalization: Other things equal, negative net exports reduce aggregate expenditures and GDP below what they would be in a closed economy. When imports exceed exports, the contractionary effect of the larger amount of imports outweighs the expansionary effect of the smaller amount of exports, and equilibrium real GDP decreases.

Our generalizations of the effects of net exports on GDP mean that a decline in X_n—a decrease in exports or an increase

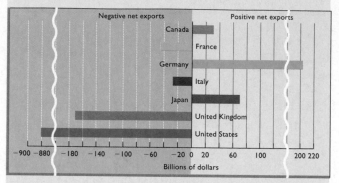

GLOBAL PERSPECTIVE 28.1

Net Exports of Goods, Selected Nations, 2006

Some nations, such as Germany and Japan, have positive net exports; other countries, such as the United States and the United Kingdom, have negative net exports.

Source: World Trade Organization. WTO Publications, **www.wto.org**. Used by permission.

in imports—reduces aggregate expenditures and contracts a nation's GDP. Conversely, an increase in X_n—the result of either an increase in exports or a decrease in imports—increases aggregate expenditures and expands GDP.

As is shown in Global Perspective 28.1, net exports vary greatly among the major industrial nations. **(Key Question 9)**

International Economic Linkages

Our analysis of net exports and real GDP suggests how circumstances or policies abroad can affect U.S. GDP.

Prosperity Abroad A rising level of real output and income among U.S. foreign trading partners enables the United States to sell more goods abroad, thus raising U.S. net exports and increasing its real GDP (assuming initially there is excess capacity). There is good reason for Americans to be interested in the prosperity of our trading partners. Their good fortune enables them to buy more of our exports, increasing our income and enabling us in turn to buy more foreign imports. These imported goods are the ultimate benefit of international trade. Prosperity abroad transfers some of that prosperity to Americans.

Tariffs Suppose foreign trading partners impose high tariffs on U.S. goods to reduce their imports from the United States and thus increase production in their economies. Their imports, however, are U.S. exports. So when they restrict their imports to stimulate *their* economies, they are reducing U.S. exports and depressing *our* economy. We are likely to retaliate by imposing tariffs on their products. If so, their exports to us will decline and their net exports may fall. It is not clear, then, whether tariffs increase or decrease a nation's net exports. In the Great Depression of the 1930s various nations, including the United States, imposed trade barriers as a way of reducing domestic unemployment. But rounds of retaliation simply throttled world trade, worsened the Depression, and increased unemployment.

Exchange Rates Depreciation of the dollar relative to other currencies (discussed in Chapter 5) enables people abroad to obtain more dollars with each unit of their own currencies. The price of U.S. goods in terms of those currencies will fall, stimulating purchases of U.S. exports. Also, U.S. customers will find they need more dollars to buy foreign goods and, consequently, will reduce their spending on imports. The increased exports and decreased imports will increase U.S. net exports and thus expand the nation's GDP.

Whether depreciation of the dollar will actually raise real GDP or produce inflation depends on the initial position of the economy relative to its full-employment output. If the economy is operating below its full-employment level, prices are likely to be sticky or even stuck due to a large oversupply of unemployed labor and capital. In such a situation, depreciation of the dollar and the resulting rise in net exports will increase aggregate expenditures and expand real GDP without increasing prices. But if the economy is already fully employed, then there will not be a huge oversupply of unemployed labor and capital keeping prices sticky. In such a situation, prices will be flexible and the increase in net exports and aggregate expenditures will cause demand-pull inflation. Because resources are already fully employed, the increased spending cannot expand real output; but it can and does increase the prices of the existing output. Having said this, however, we need to caution you that evidence from the actual economy suggests that, even at full employment, the inflationary consequences of dollar depreciation are very small.

This last example has been cast only in terms of depreciation of the dollar. You should think through the impact that appreciation of the dollar would have on net exports and equilibrium GDP.

QUICK REVIEW 28.2

- Positive net exports increase aggregate expenditures relative to the closed economy and, other things equal, increase equilibrium GDP.

- Negative net exports decrease aggregate expenditures relative to the closed economy and, other things equal, reduce equilibrium GDP.

- In the open economy changes in (a) prosperity abroad, (b) tariffs, and (c) exchange rates can affect U.S. net exports and therefore U.S. aggregate expenditures and equilibrium GDP.

Adding the Public Sector

Our final step in constructing the full aggregate expenditures model is to move the analysis from a private (no-government) open economy to an economy with a public sector (sometimes called a "mixed economy"). This means adding government purchases and taxes to the model.

For simplicity, we will assume that government purchases are independent of the level of GDP and do not alter the consumption and investment schedules. Also, government's net tax revenues—total tax revenues less "negative taxes" in the form of transfer payments—are derived entirely from personal taxes. Finally, a fixed amount of taxes is collected regardless of the level of GDP.

Government Purchases and Equilibrium GDP

Suppose the government decides to purchase $20 billion of goods and services regardless of the level of GDP and tax collections.

Tabular Example Table 28.4 shows the impact of this purchase on the equilibrium GDP. Columns 1 through 4 are carried over from Table 28.2 for the private closed economy, in which the equilibrium GDP was $470 billion. The only new items are exports and imports in column 5 and government purchases in column 6. (Observe in column 5 that net exports are zero.) As shown in column 7, the addition of government purchases to private spending $(C + I_g + X_n)$ yields a new, higher level of aggregate expenditures $(C + I_g + X_n + G)$. Comparing columns 1 and 7, we find that aggregate expenditures and real output are equal at a higher level of GDP. Without government purchases, equilibrium GDP was $470 billion (row 6); *with* government purchases, aggregate expenditures and real output are equal at $550 billion (row 10). Increases in public spending, like increases in private spending, shift the aggregate expenditures schedule upward and produce a higher equilibrium GDP.

Note, too, that government spending is subject to the multiplier. A $20 billion increase in government purchases has increased equilibrium GDP by $80 billion (from $470 billion to $550 billion). The multiplier in this example is 4.

This $20 billion increase in government spending is *not* financed by increased taxes. Shortly, we will demonstrate that increased taxes *reduce* equilibrium GDP.

Graphical Analysis In Figure 28.5, we vertically add $20 billion of government purchases, G, to the level of private spending, $C + I_g + X_n$. That added $20 billion raises the aggregate expenditures schedule (private plus

TABLE 28.4 The Impact of Government Purchases on Equilibrium GDP

(1) Real Domestic Output and Income (GDP = DI), Billions	(2) Consumption (C), Billions	(3) Savings (S), Billions	(4) Investment (I_g), Billions	(5) Net Exports (X_n), Billions		(6) Government Purchases (G), Billions	(7) Aggregate Expenditures ($C + I_g + X_n + G$), Billions (2) + (4) + (5) + (6)
				Exports (X)	Imports (M)		
(1) $370	$375	$−5	$20	$10	$10	$20	$415
(2) 390	390	0	20	10	10	20	430
(3) 410	405	5	20	10	10	20	445
(4) 430	420	10	20	10	10	20	460
(5) 450	435	15	20	10	10	20	475
(6) 470	450	20	20	10	10	20	490
(7) 490	465	25	20	10	10	20	505
(8) 510	480	30	20	10	10	20	520
(9) 530	495	35	20	10	10	20	535
(10) **550**	**510**	**40**	**20**	**10**	**10**	**20**	**550**

public) to $C + I_g + X_n + G$, resulting in an $80 billion increase in equilibrium GDP, from $470 to $550 billion.

A decline in government purchases G will lower the aggregate expenditures schedule in Figure 28.5 and result in a multiplied decline in the equilibrium GDP. Verify in Table 28.4 that if government purchases were to decline from $20 billion to $10 billion, the equilibrium GDP would fall by $40 billion.

Taxation and Equilibrium GDP

The government not only spends but also collects taxes. Suppose it imposes a **lump-sum tax,** which is a tax of a constant amount or, more precisely, a tax yielding the same amount of tax revenue at each level of GDP. Let's assume this tax is $20 billion, so that the government obtains $20 billion of tax revenue at each level of GDP regardless of the level of government purchases.

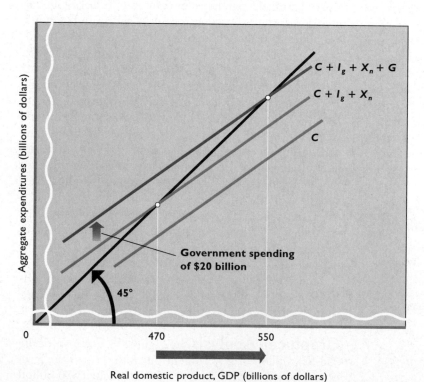

FIGURE 28.5 Government spending and equilibrium GDP. The addition of government expenditures of G to our analysis raises the aggregate expenditures ($C + I_g + X_n + G$) schedule and increases the equilibrium level of GDP, as would an increase in C, I_g, or X_n.

TABLE 28.5 Determination of the Equilibrium Levels of Employment, Output, and Income: Private and Public Sectors

(1) Real Domestic Output and Income (GDP = NI = PI), Billions	(2) Taxes (T), Billions	(3) Disposable Income (DI), Billions, (1) − (2)	(4) Consumption (Cₐ), Billions	(5) Saving (Sₐ), Billions (3)−(4)	(6) Investment (Iₘ), Billions	(7) Net Exports (Xₙ), Billions Exports (X)	Imports (M)	(8) Government Purchases (G), Billions	(9) Aggregate Expenditures (Cₐ + Iₘ + Xₙ + G), Billions, (4) + (6) + (7) + (8)
(1) $370	$20	$350	$360	$−10	$20	$10	$10	$20	$400
(2) 390	20	370	375	−5	20	10	10	20	415
(3) 410	20	390	390	0	20	10	10	20	430
(4) 430	20	410	405	5	20	10	10	20	445
(5) 450	20	430	420	10	20	10	10	20	460
(6) 470	20	450	435	15	20	10	10	20	475
(7) *490*	*20*	*470*	*450*	*20*	*20*	*10*	*10*	*20*	*490*
(8) 510	20	490	465	25	20	10	10	20	505
(9) 530	20	510	480	30	20	10	10	20	520
(10) 550	20	530	495	35	20	10	10	20	535

Tabular Example In Table 28.5, which continues our example, we find taxes in column 2, and we see in column 3 that disposable (after-tax) income is lower than GDP (column 1) by the $20 billion amount of the tax. Because households use disposable income both to consume and to save, the tax lowers both consumption and saving. The MPC and MPS tell us how much consumption and saving will decline as a result of the $20 billion in taxes. Because the MPC is .75, the government tax collection of $20 billion will reduce consumption by $15 billion (= .75 × $20 billion). Since the MPS is .25, saving will drop by $5 billion (= .25 × $20 billion).

Columns 4 and 5 in Table 28.5 list the amounts of consumption and saving *at each level of GDP*. Note they are $15 billion and $5 billion smaller than those in Table 28.4. Taxes reduce disposable income relative to GDP by the amount of the taxes. This decline in DI reduces both consumption and saving at each level of GDP. The MPC and the MPS determine the declines in C and S.

To find the effect of taxes on equilibrium GDP, we calculate aggregate expenditures again, as shown in column 9, Table 28.5. Aggregate spending is $15 billion less at each level of GDP than it was in Table 28.4. The reason is that after-tax consumption, designated by Cₐ, is $15 billion less at each level of GDP. A comparison of real output and aggregate expenditures in columns 1 and 9 shows that the aggregate amounts produced and purchased are equal only at $490 billion of GDP (row 7). The $20 billion lump-sum tax has reduced equilibrium GDP by $60 billion, from $550 billion (row 10, Table 28.3) to $490 billion (row 7, Table 28.4).

Graphical Analysis In Figure 28.6 the $20 billion increase in taxes shows up as a $15 (not $20) billion decline in the aggregate expenditures (Cₐ + Iₘ + Xₙ + G) schedule. This decline in the schedule results solely from a decline in the consumption C component of aggregate expenditures. The equilibrium GDP falls from $550 billion to $490 billion because of this tax-caused drop in consumption. With no change in government expenditures, tax increases lower the aggregate expenditures schedule relative to the 45° line and reduce the equilibrium GDP.

In contrast to our previous case, a *decrease* in existing taxes will raise the aggregate expenditures schedule in Figure 28.6 as a result of an increase in consumption at all GDP levels. You should confirm that a tax reduction of $10 billion (from the present $20 billion to $10 billion) would increase the equilibrium GDP from $490 billion to $520 billion. **(Key Question 12)**

Differential Impacts You may have noted that equal changes in G and T do not have equivalent impacts on GDP. The $20 billion increase in G in our illustration, subject to the multiplier of 4, produced an $80 billion increase in real GDP. But the $20 billion increase in taxes reduced GDP by only $60 billion. Given an MPC of .75, the tax increase of $20 billion reduced consumption by only $15 billion (not $20 billion) because saving also fell by $5 billion. Subjecting the $15 billion decline in consumption to the multiplier of

WORKED PROBLEMS

W 28.2

Complete aggregate expenditures model

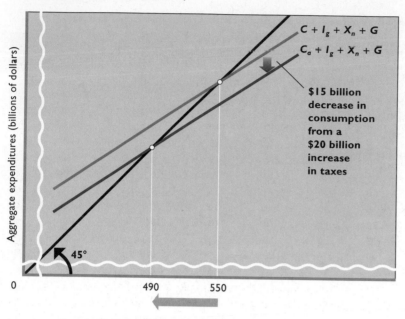

FIGURE 28.6 **Taxes and equilibrium GDP.** If the MPC is .75, the $20 billion of taxes will lower the consumption schedule by $15 billion and cause a $60 billion decline in the equilibrium GDP. In the open economy with government, equilibrium GDP occurs where C_a (after-tax income) + I_g + X_n + G = GDP. Here that equilibrium is $490 billion.

4, we find the tax increase of $20 billion reduced GDP by $60 billion (not $80 billion).

Table 28.5 and Figure 28.6 constitute the complete aggregate expenditures model for an open economy with government. When total spending equals total production, the economy's output is in equilibrium. In the open mixed economy, equilibrium GDP occurs where

$$C_a + I_g + X_n + G = \text{GDP.}$$

Injections, Leakages, and Unplanned Changes in Inventories

The related characteristics of equilibrium noted for the private closed economy also apply to the full model. In particular, it is still the case that injections into the income-expenditures stream equal leakages from the income stream. For the private closed economy, $S = I_g$. For the expanded economy, imports and taxes are added leakages. Saving, importing, and paying taxes are all uses of income that subtract from potential consumption. Consumption will now be less than GDP—creating a potential spending gap—in the amount of after-tax saving (S_a), imports (M), and taxes (T). But exports (X) and government purchases (G), along with investment (I_g), are injections into the income-expenditures stream. At the equilibrium GDP, the sum of the leakages equals the sum of injections. In symbols:

$$S_a + M + T = I_g + X + G$$

You should use the data in Table 28.5 to confirm this equality between leakages and injections at the equilibrium GDP of $490 billion. Also, substantiate that a lack of such equality exists at all other possible levels of GDP.

Although not directly shown in Table 28.5, the equilibrium characteristic of "no unplanned changes in inventories" will also be fulfilled at the $490 billion GDP. Because aggregate expenditures equal GDP, all the goods and services produced will be purchased. There will be no unplanned increase in inventories, so firms will have no incentive to reduce their employment and production. Nor will they experience an unplanned decline in their inventories, which would prompt them to expand their employment and output in order to replenish their inventories.

INTERACTIVE GRAPHS

G 28.2

Changes in GDP

Equilibrium versus Full-Employment GDP

A key point about the equilibrium GDP of the aggregate expenditures model is that it need not equal the economy's full-employment GDP. In fact, Keynes specifically designed the model so that it could explain situations like the Great Depression, during which the economy was seemingly stuck at a bad equilibrium in which real GDP was far below potential output. As we will show you in a moment, Keynes also used the model to suggest policy recommendations for moving the economy back toward potential output and full employment.

The fact that equilibrium and potential GDP in the aggregate expenditure model need not match also reveals critical insights about the causes of demand-pull inflation. We will first examine the "expenditure gaps" that give rise to differences between equilibrium and potential GDP and then see how the model helps to explain the recession of 2001 and the recent period in which the United States achieved potential output even while experiencing massive net export deficits.

Recessionary Expenditure Gap

Suppose in **Figure 28.7 (Key Graph),** panel (a), that the full-employment level of GDP is $510 billion and the aggregate expenditures schedule is AE_1. (For simplicity, we will now dispense with the $C_a + I_g + X_n + G$ labeling.) This schedule intersects the $45°$ line to the left of the economy's full-employment output, so the economy's equilibrium GDP of $490 billion is $20 billion short of its full-employment output of $510 billion. According to column 1 in Table 28.2, total employment at the full-employment GDP is 75 million workers. But the economy depicted in Figure 28.7a is employing only 70 million workers; 5 million available workers are not employed. For that reason, the economy is sacrificing $20 billion of output.

A **recessionary expenditure gap** is the amount by which aggregate expenditures *at the full-employment GDP* fall short of those required to achieve the full-employment GDP. Insufficient total spending contracts or depresses the economy. Table 28.5 shows that at the full-employment level of $510 billion (column 1), the corresponding level of aggregate expenditures is only $505 billion (column 9). The recessionary expenditure gap is thus $5 billion, the amount by which the aggregate expenditures curve would have to shift upward to realize equilibrium at the full-employment GDP. Graphically, the recessionary expenditure gap is the *vertical* distance (measured at the full-employment GDP) by which the actual aggregate expenditures schedule AE_1 lies below the hypothetical full-employment aggregate expenditures schedule AE_0. In Figure 28.7a, this recessionary expenditure gap is $5 billion. Because the multiplier is 4, there is a $20 billion differential (the recessionary expenditure gap of $5 billion times the multiplier of 4) between the equilibrium GDP and the full-employment GDP. This $20 billion difference is a negative *GDP gap*—an idea we

first developed when discussing cyclical unemployment in Chapter 26.

Keynes' Solution to a Recessionary Expenditure Gap Keynes pointed to two different policies that a government might pursue to close a recessionary expenditure gap and achieve full employment. The first is to increase government spending. The second is to lower taxes. Both work by increasing aggregate expenditures.

Look back at Figure 28.5. There we showed how an increase in government expenditures G will increase overall aggregate expenditures and, consequently, the equilibrium real GDP. Applying this strategy to the situation in Figure 28.7a, government could completely close the $20 billion negative GDP gap between the initial equilibrium of $490 billion and the economy's potential output of $510 billion if it increased spending by the $5 billion amount of the recessionary expenditure gap. Given the economy's multiplier of 4, the $5 billion increase in G would create a $20 billion increase in equilibrium real GDP, thereby bringing the economy to full employment.

Government also could lower taxes to close the recessionary expenditure gap and thus eliminate the negative GDP gap. Look back at Figure 28.6 in which an increase in taxes resulted in lower after-tax consumption spending and a smaller equilibrium real GDP. Keynes simply suggested a reversal of this process: Since an increase in taxes lowers equilibrium real GDP, a decrease in taxes will raise equilibrium GDP. The decrease in taxes will leave consumers with higher after-tax income. That will lead to higher consumption expenditures and an increase in equilibrium real GDP.

But by how much should the government cut taxes? By exactly $6.67 billion. That is because the MPC is .75. The tax cut of $6.67 billion will increase consumers' after-tax income by $6.67 billion. They will then increase consumption spending by .75 of that amount, or $5 billion. This will increase aggregate expenditures by the $5 billion needed to close the recessionary expenditure gap. The economy's equilibrium real GDP will rise to its potential output of $510 billion.

But a big warning is needed here: As the economy moves closer to its potential output, it becomes harder to justify Keynes' assumption that prices are stuck. As the economy closes its negative GDP gap, nearly all workers are employed and nearly all factories are operating at or near full capacity. In such a situation, there is no massive oversupply of productive resources to keep prices from rising. In fact, economists know from real-world experience that in such situations prices are not fully stuck. Instead, they become increasingly flexible as the economy moves nearer to potential output.

FIGURE 28.7 **Recessionary and inflationary expenditure gaps.** The equilibrium and full-employment GDPs may not coincide. (a) A recessionary expenditure gap is the amount by which aggregate expenditures at the full-employment GDP fall short of those needed to achieve the full-employment GDP. Here, the $5 billion recessionary expenditure gap causes a $20 billion negative GDP gap. (b) An inflationary expenditure gap is the amount by which aggregate expenditures at the full-employment GDP exceed those just sufficient to achieve the full-employment GDP. Here, the inflationary expenditure gap is $5 billion; this overspending produces demand-pull inflation.

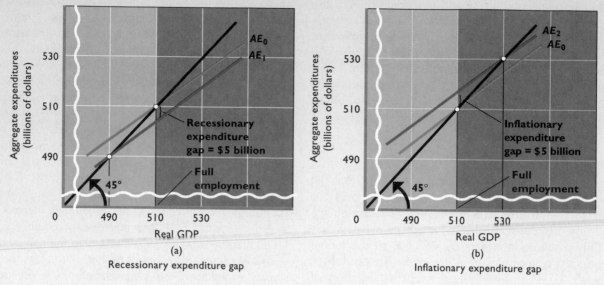

(a)
Recessionary expenditure gap

(b)
Inflationary expenditure gap

This fact is one of the major limitations of the aggregate expenditures model and is the reason why we will develop a different model that can handle inflation in the next chapter. That being said, it is nevertheless true that

the aggregate expenditures model is still very useful despite its inability to handle flexible prices. For instance, as we explained in Chapter 23, even an economy operating near full employment will show sticky or even stuck prices in the

short run. In such situations, the intuitions of the aggregate expenditures model will still hold true. The benefit of the aggregate demand–aggregate supply model that we develop in the next chapter is that it also can show us what happens over longer periods, as prices (and wages) become more flexible and are increasingly able to adjust.

Inflationary Expenditure Gap

Economists use the term **inflationary expenditure gap** to describe the amount by which an economy's aggregate expenditures *at the full-employment GDP* exceed those just necessary to achieve the full-employment level of GDP. In Figure 28.7b, there is a $5 billion inflationary expenditure gap at the $510 billion full-employment GDP. This is shown by the vertical distance between the actual aggregate expenditures schedule AE_2 and the hypothetical schedule AE_0, which would be just sufficient to achieve the $510 billion full-employment GDP. Thus, the inflationary expenditure gap is the amount by which the aggregate expenditures schedule would have to shift downward to realize equilibrium at the full-employment GDP.

But why does the name "inflationary expenditure gap" contain the word *inflationary*? In particular, what does the situation depicted in Figure 28.7b have to do with inflation? The answer lies in the answer to a different question: *Could the economy actually achieve and maintain an equilibrium real GDP that is substantially above the full-employment output level?*

The unfortunate answer is no. It is unfortunate because if such a thing were possible, then the government could make real GDP as high as it wanted by simply increasing G to an arbitrarily high number. Graphically, it could raise the AE_2 curve in Figure 28.7b as far up as it wanted, thereby raising equilibrium real GDP up as high as it wanted. Living standards would skyrocket! But this is not possible because, by definition, all the workers in the economy are fully employed at the full-employment output level. Producing a bit more than the full-employment output level for a few months might be possible if you could convince all the workers to work overtime day after day. But there simply isn't enough labor to have the economy produce at much more than potential output for any extended period of time.

So what *does* happen in situations in which aggregate expenditures are so high that the model predicts an equilibrium level of GDP beyond potential output? The answer is twofold. First, the economy ends up producing either at potential output or just above potential output due to the limited supply of labor. Second, the economy experiences demand-pull inflation. With the supply of output limited by the supply of labor, high levels of aggregate expenditures simply act to drive up prices. Nominal GDP will increase because of the higher price level, but real GDP will not. **(Key Question 13)**

Application: The U.S. Recession of 2001

The U.S. economy grew briskly in the last half of the 1990s, with real GDP expanding at about 4 percent annually and the unemployment rate averaging roughly 4.5 percent. The economic boom and low rates of unemployment,

however, did not spark inflation, as had been the case in prior business cycles. Exceptionally strong productivity growth in the late 1990s increased the economy's production capacity and enabled aggregate expenditures to expand without causing inflation. In terms of Figure 28.7b, it was as if the full-employment level of real GDP expanded from $510 billion to $530 billion at the same time the aggregate expenditures curve rose from AE_0 to AE_2. So the inflationary expenditure gap of $5 billion never materialized. Between 1995 and 1999, inflation averaged less than 2.5 percent annually.

But the booming economy of the second half of the 1990s produced notable excesses. A large number of ill-conceived Internet-related firms were born, attracting billions of investment dollars. Investment spending surged throughout the economy and eventually added too much production capacity. A stock market "bubble" developed as stock market investing became a national pastime. Consumers increased their household debt to expand their consumption. Some unscrupulous executives engaged in fraudulent business practices to further their own personal interests.

The boom ended in the early 2000s. Hundreds of Internet-related start-up firms folded. Many firms, particularly those in telecommunications and aircraft manufacturing, began to experience severe overcapacity. The stock market bubble burst, erasing billions of dollars of "paper" wealth. Firms significantly reduced their investment spending because of lower estimates of rates of return. In March 2001 aggregate expenditures declined sufficiently to push the economy into its ninth recession since 1950. The unemployment rate rose from 4.2 percent in February 2001 to 5.8 percent in December 2001. In terms of Figure 28.7a, a recessionary expenditure gap emerged. The terrorist attacks of September 11, 2001, damaged consumer confidence and prolonged the recession through 2001. In 2002 the economy resumed economic growth, but the unemployment rate remained a stubbornly high 6 percent at the end of 2002. Even so, the recession of 2001 was relatively mild by historical standards and in view of the unusual set of circumstances.

Application: Full-Employment Output, with Large Negative Net Exports

In 2007 the United States had negative net exports of $560 billion in real (2000) dollar terms, yet its actual (real) GDP of $11,567 billion roughly matched its potential (real) GDP of $11,687. The economy experienced neither a recessionary expenditure gap nor an inflationary expenditure

Say's Law, the Great Depression, and Keynes

The Aggregate Expenditure Theory Emerged as a Critique of Classical Economics and as a Response to the Great Depression.

Until the Great Depression of the 1930s, many prominent economists, including David Ricardo (1772–1823) and John Stuart Mill (1806–1873), believed that the market system would ensure full employment of an economy's resources. These so-called *classical economists* acknowledged that now and then abnormal circumstances such as wars, political upheavals, droughts, speculative crises, and gold rushes would occur, deflecting the economy from full-employment status. But when such deviations occurred, the economy would automatically adjust and soon return to full-employment output. For example, a slump in output and employment would result in lower prices, wages, and interest rates, which in turn would increase consumer spending, employment, and investment spending. Any excess supply of goods and workers would soon be eliminated.

Classical macroeconomists denied that the level of spending in an economy could be too low to bring about the purchase of the entire full-employment output. They based their denial of inadequate spending in part on *Say's law*, attributed to the nineteenth-century French economist J. B. Say (1767–1832). This law is the disarmingly simple idea that the very act of producing goods generates income equal to the value of the goods produced. The production of any output automatically provides the income needed to buy that output. More succinctly stated, *supply creates its own demand*.

Say's law can best be understood in terms of a barter economy. A woodworker, for example, produces or supplies furniture as a means of buying or demanding the food and clothing produced by other workers. The woodworker's supply of furniture is the income that he will "spend" to satisfy his demand for other goods. The goods he buys (demands) will have a total value exactly equal to the goods he produces (supplies). And

so it is for other producers and for the entire economy. Demand must be the same as supply!

ORIGIN OF THE IDEA

O 28.2
Say's law

Assuming that the composition of output is in accord with consumer preferences, all markets would be cleared of their outputs. It would seem that all firms need to do to sell a full-employment output is to produce that level of output. Say's law guarantees there will be sufficient spending to purchase it all.

The Great Depression of the 1930s called into question the theory that supply creates its own demand (Say's law). In the United States, real GDP declined by 27 percent and the unemployment rate rocketed to nearly 25 percent. Other nations experienced similar impacts. And cyclical unemployment lingered for a decade. An obvious inconsistency exists between a theory that says that unemployment is virtually impossible and the actual occurrence of a 10-year siege of substantial unemployment.

In 1936 British economist John Maynard Keynes (1883–1946) explained why cyclical unemployment could occur in a market economy. In his *General Theory of Employment, Interest, and Money*, Keynes attacked the foundations of classical theory and developed the ideas underlying the aggregate expenditures model. Keynes disputed Say's law, pointing out that not all income need be spent in the same period that it is produced. Investment spending, in particular, is volatile, said Keynes. A substantial decline in investment will lead to insufficient total spending. Unsold goods will accumulate in producers' warehouses, and producers will respond by reducing their output and discharging workers. A recession or depression will result, and widespread cyclical unemployment will occur. Moreover, said Keynes, recessions or depressions are not likely to correct themselves. In contrast to the more laissez-faire view of the classical economists, Keynes argued that government should play an active role in stabilizing the economy.

gap. It was fully employed, with an unemployment rate of 4.6 percent.

How could this outcome be? Doesn't the aggregate expenditure model suggest that large negative net exports reduce aggregate expenditures and therefore decrease equilibrium GDP, presumably to below its potential level? That undesirable outcome is possible, *other things equal*. But in 2007 large domestic consumption, investment, and government expenditures fully made up for the $560 billion of negative net exports. In 2007, U.S. consumers spent (in real terms) $8267 billion. Businesses invested $1831 billion, even though total U.S. saving was negative. The Federal government spent $2022 billion, financing more than one-fourth of that amount through borrowing.

Negative net exports—even large ones—do not preclude achieving full-employment output. Aggregate expenditures in total were sufficient in 2007 to purchase the potential output, with no unplanned changes in inventories. The $C_a + I_g + G$ expenditures were financed, in part, by foreigners whose large trade surpluses with the United States left them with equally large quantities of U.S. dollars. People and business abroad willingly lent many of those dollars to the United States in anticipation of high returns. That foreign lending in turn helped finance the high U.S. domestic spending.

QUICK REVIEW 28.3

- Government purchases shift the aggregate expenditures schedule upward and raise the equilibrium GDP.
- Taxes reduce disposable income, lower consumption spending and saving, shift the aggregate expenditures schedule downward, and reduce the equilibrium GDP.
- A recessionary expenditure gap is the amount by which an economy's aggregate expenditures schedule must shift upward to achieve the full-employment GDP; an inflationary expenditure gap is the amount by which the economy's aggregate expenditures schedule must shift downward to achieve full-employment GDP and eliminate demand-pull inflation.

Summary

1. The aggregate expenditures model views the total amount of spending in the economy as the primary factor determining the level of real GDP that the economy will produce. The model assumes that prices are fixed. Keynes made this assumption to reflect the general circumstances of the Great Depression and the fact that there existed such huge over-supplies of labor and other productive resources that increases in spending were unlikely to drive up prices.

2. For a private closed economy the equilibrium level of GDP occurs when aggregate expenditures and real output are equal or, graphically, where the $C + I_g$ line intersects the 45° line. At any GDP greater than equilibrium GDP, real output will exceed aggregate spending, resulting in unplanned investment in inventories and eventual declines in output and income (GDP). At any below-equilibrium GDP, aggregate expenditures will exceed real output, resulting in unplanned disinvestment in inventories and eventual increases in GDP.

3. At equilibrium GDP, the amount households save (leakages) and the amount businesses plan to invest (injections) are equal. Any excess of saving over planned investment will cause a shortage of total spending, forcing GDP to fall. Any excess of planned investment over saving will cause an excess of total spending, inducing GDP to rise. The change

in GDP will in both cases correct the discrepancy between saving and planned investment.

4. At equilibrium GDP, there are no unplanned changes in inventories. When aggregate expenditures diverge from real GDP, an unplanned change in inventories occurs. Unplanned increases in inventories are followed by a cutback in production and a decline of real GDP. Unplanned decreases in inventories result in an increase in production and a rise of GDP.

5. Actual investment consists of planned investment plus unplanned changes in inventories and is always equal to saving.

6. A shift in the investment schedule (caused by changes in expected rates of return or changes in interest rates) shifts the aggregate expenditures curve and causes a new equilibrium level of real GDP. Real GDP changes by more than the amount of the initial change in investment. This multiplier effect ($\Delta GDP/\Delta I_g$) accompanies both increases and decreases in aggregate expenditures and also applies to changes in net exports (X_n) and government purchases (G).

7. The net export schedule in the model of the open economy relates net exports (exports minus imports) to levels of real GDP. For simplicity, we assume that the level of net exports is the same at all levels of real GDP.

8. Positive net exports increase aggregate expenditures to a higher level than they would if the economy were "closed" to international trade. Negative net exports decrease aggregate expenditures relative to those in a closed economy, decreasing equilibrium real GDP by a multiple of their amount. Increases in exports or decreases in imports have an expansionary effect on real GDP, while decreases in exports or increases in imports have a contractionary effect.

9. Government purchases in the model of the mixed economy shift the aggregate expenditures schedule upward and raise GDP.

10. Taxation reduces disposable income, lowers consumption and saving, shifts the aggregate expenditures curve downward, and reduces equilibrium GDP.

11. In the complete aggregate expenditures model, equilibrium GDP occurs where $C_a + I_g + X_n + G = $ GDP. At the equilibrium GDP, *leakages* of after-tax saving (S_a), imports (M), and taxes (T) equal *injections* of investment (I_g), exports (X), and government purchases (G): $S_a + M + T = I_g + X_n + G$. Also, there are no unplanned changes in inventories.

12. The equilibrium GDP and the full-employment GDP may differ. A recessionary expenditure gap is the amount by which aggregate expenditures at the full-employment GDP fall short of those needed to achieve the full-employment GDP. This gap produces a negative GDP gap (actual GDP minus potential GDP). An inflationary expenditure gap is the amount by which aggregate expenditures at the full-employment GDP exceed those just sufficient to achieve the full-employment GDP. This gap causes demand-pull inflation.

13. Keynes believed that prices during the Great Depression were relatively inflexible at low levels due to high unemployment. In such a situation, the government could increase real GDP (by increasing government expenditures or lowering taxes) without having to worry about inflation. By contrast, if an economy's GDP gap is more moderate so that there are not such high rates of unemployment, then it is less likely that prices will be sticky. The closer an economy is to its full-employment output level, the more likely it is that any increase in aggregate expenditures will lead to inflation along with any increase in real GDP.

Terms and Concepts

planned investment	leakage	lump-sum tax
investment schedule	injection	recessionary expenditure gap
aggregate expenditures schedule	unplanned changes in inventories	inflationary expenditure gap
equilibrium GDP	net exports	

Study Questions

1. What is an investment schedule and how does it differ from an investment demand curve? **LO1**

2. **KEY QUESTION** Assuming the level of investment is $16 billion and independent of the level of total output, complete the accompanying table and determine the equilibrium levels of output and employment in this private closed economy. What are the sizes of the MPC and MPS? **LO1**

Possible Levels of Employment, Millions	Real Domestic Output (GDP = DI), Billions	Consumption, Billions	Saving, Billions
40	$240	$244	$ _____
45	260	260	_____
50	280	276	_____
55	300	292	_____
60	320	308	_____
65	340	324	_____
70	360	340	_____
75	380	356	_____
80	400	372	_____

3. Using the consumption and saving data in question 2 and assuming investment is $16 billion, what are saving and planned investment at the $380 billion level of domestic output? What are saving and actual investment at that level? What are saving and planned investment at the $300 billion level of domestic output? What are the levels of saving and actual investment? Use the concept of unplanned investment to explain adjustments toward equilibrium from both the $380 billion and the $300 billion levels of domestic output. **LO1**

4. Why is saving called a *leakage*? Why is planned investment called an *injection*? Why must saving equal planned investment at equilibrium GDP in the private closed economy? Are unplanned changes in inventories rising, falling, or constant at equilibrium GDP? Explain. **LO2**

5. What effect will each of the changes listed in Study Question 3 of Chapter 27 have on the equilibrium level of GDP in the private closed economy? Explain your answers. **LO3**

6. By how much will GDP change if firms increase their investment by $8 billion and the MPC is .80? If the MPC is .67? **LO3**

7. Depict graphically the aggregate expenditures model for a private closed economy. Now show a decrease in the aggregate

expenditures schedule and explain why the decline in real GDP in your diagram is greater than the initial decline in aggregate expenditures. What would be the ratio of a decline in real GDP to the initial drop in aggregate expenditures if the slope of your aggregate expenditures schedule was .8? **LO3**

8. Suppose that a certain country has an MPC of .9 and a real GDP of $400 billion. If its investment spending decreases by $4 billion, what will be its new level of real GDP? **LO3**

9. **KEY QUESTION** The data in columns 1 and 2 in the accompanying table are for a private closed economy: **LO4**

   a. Use columns 1 and 2 to determine the equilibrium GDP for this hypothetical economy.

   b. Now open up this economy to international trade by including the export and import figures of columns 3 and 4. Fill in columns 5 and 6 and determine the equilibrium GDP for the open economy. Explain why this equilibrium GDP differs from that of the closed economy.

   c. Given the original $20 billion level of exports, what would be net exports and the equilibrium GDP if imports were $10 billion greater at each level of GDP?

   d. What is the multiplier in this example?

(1) Real Domestic Output (GDP = DI), Billions	(2) Aggregate Expenditures, Private Closed Economy, Billions	(3) Exports, Billions	(4) Imports, Billions	(5) Net Exports, Billions	(6) Aggregate Expenditures, Private Open Economy, Billions
$200	$240	$20	$30	$_____	$_____
250	280	20	30	_____	_____
300	320	20	30	_____	_____
350	360	20	30	_____	_____
400	400	20	30	_____	_____
450	440	20	30	_____	_____
500	480	20	30	_____	_____
550	520	20	30	_____	_____

10. Assume that, without taxes, the consumption schedule of an economy is as follows: **LO4**

GDP, Billions	Consumption, Billions
$100	$120
200	200
300	280
400	360
500	440
600	520
700	600

   a. Graph this consumption schedule and determine the MPC.

   b. Assume now that a lump-sum tax is imposed such that the government collects $10 billion in taxes at all levels of GDP. Graph the resulting consumption schedule and compare the MPC and the multiplier with those of the pretax consumption schedule.

11. Explain graphically the determination of equilibrium GDP for a private economy through the aggregate expenditures model. Now add government purchases (any amount you choose) to your graph, showing its impact on equilibrium GDP. Finally, add taxation (any amount of lump-sum tax that you choose) to your graph and show its effect on equilibrium GDP. Looking at your graph, determine whether equilibrium GDP has increased, decreased, or stayed the same given the sizes of the government purchases and taxes that you selected. **LO4**

12. **KEY QUESTION** Refer to columns 1 and 6 in the table for question 9. Incorporate government into the table by assuming that it plans to tax and spend $20 billion at each possible level of GDP. Also assume that the tax is a personal tax and that government spending does not induce a shift in the private aggregate expenditures schedule. Compute and explain the change in equilibrium GDP caused by the addition of government. **LO4**

13. **KEY QUESTION** Refer to the table on the next page in answering the questions that follow: **LO5**

   a. If full employment in this economy is 130 million, will there be an inflationary expenditure gap or a recessionary expenditure gap? What will be the consequence of this gap? By how much would aggregate expenditures in column 3 have to change at each level of GDP to eliminate the inflationary expenditure gap or the recessionary expenditure gap? Explain. What is the multiplier in this example?

   b. Will there be an inflationary expenditure gap or a recessionary expenditure gap if the full-employment level of output is $500 billion? Explain the consequences. By how much would aggregate expenditures in column 3 have to change at each level of GDP to eliminate the gap? What is the multiplier in this example?

c. Assuming that investment, net exports, and government expenditures do not change with changes in real GDP, what are the sizes of the MPC, the MPS, and the multiplier?

(1) Possible Levels of Employment, Millions	(2) Real Domestic Output, Billions	(3) Aggregate Expenditures $(C_a + I_g + X_n + G)$, Billions
90	$500	$520
100	550	560
110	600	600
120	650	640
130	700	680

14. **ADVANCED ANALYSIS** Assume that the consumption schedule for a private open economy is such that consumption $C = 50 + 0.8Y$. Assume further that planned investment I_g and net exports X_n are independent of the level of real GDP and constant at $I_g = 30$ and $X_n = 10$. Recall also that, in equilibrium, the real output produced (Y) is equal to aggregate expenditures: $Y = C + I_g + X_n$. **LO4**

a. Calculate the equilibrium level of income or real GDP for this economy.

b. What happens to equilibrium Y if I_g changes to 10? What does this outcome reveal about the size of the multiplier?

15. Answer the following questions, which relate to the aggregate expenditures model: **LO4, LO5**

a. If C_a is $100, I_g is $50, X_n is $-$10, and G is $30, what is the economy's equilibrium GDP?

b. If real GDP in an economy is currently $200, C_a is $100, I_g is $50, X_n is $-$10, and G is $30, will the economy's real GDP rise, fall, or stay the same?

c. Suppose that full-employment (and full-capacity) output in an economy is $200. If C_a is $150, I_g is $50, X_n is $-$10, and G is $30, what will be the macroeconomic result?

16. **LAST WORD** What is Say's law? How does it relate to the view held by classical economists that the economy generally will operate at a position on its production possibilities curve (Chapter 1)? Use production possibilities analysis to demonstrate Keynes' view on this matter.

Web-Based Questions

1. **THE MULTIPLIER—CALCULATING HYPOTHETICAL CHANGES IN GDP** Go to the Bureau of Economic Analysis at **www.bea.gov,** and select Interactive Data Tables, which is listed under Publications. On that page, select National Income and Product Accounts. Go to the List of All NIPA Tables and then find Table 1.1.5, which contains the most recent values for nominal GDP $= C_a + I_g + G + (X - M)$. Assume that the MPC is .75 and that, for each of the following, the values of the initial variables are those you just discovered. Determine the new value of GDP if, other things equal, (*a*) investment increased by 5 percent, (*b*) imports increased by 5 percent while exports increased by 5 percent, (*c*) consumption increased by 5 percent, and (*d*) government spending increased by 5 percent. Which of the changes, (*a*) through (*d*), caused the greatest change in GDP in absolute dollars?

2. **GDP GAP AND EXPENDITURE GAP** The St. Louis Federal Reserve Bank at **www.research.stlouisfed.org/fred2** provides data on both real GDP (chained 2000 dollars) and real potential GDP for the United States. To get to the data, first click on Gross Domestic Product (GDP) and Components. Then click on GDP/GNP. What was potential GDP for the third quarter of 2001? What was the actual level of real GDP for that quarter? What was the size difference between the two—the negative GDP gap? If the multiplier was 2 in that period, what was the size of the economy's recessionary expenditure gap?

FURTHER TEST YOUR KNOWLEDGE AT
www.mcconnell18e.com

IN THIS CHAPTER YOU WILL LEARN:

1 About aggregate demand (AD) and the factors that cause it to change.

2 About aggregate supply (AS) and the factors that cause it to change.

3 How AD and AS determine an economy's equilibrium price level and level of real GDP.

4 How the AD-AS model explains periods of demand-pull inflation, cost-push inflation, and recession.

5 (Appendix) How the aggregate demand curve relates to the aggregate expenditures model.

29

Aggregate Demand and Aggregate Supply

In early 2000, Alan Greenspan, then chair of the Federal Reserve, made the following statement:

> Through the so-called wealth effect, [recent stock market gains] have tended to foster increases in aggregate demand beyond the increases in supply. It is this imbalance . . . that contains the potential seeds of rising inflationary . . . pressures that could undermine the current expansion. Our goal [at the Federal Reserve] is to extend the expansion by containing its imbalances and avoiding the very recession that would complete the business cycle.[1]

Although the Federal Reserve held inflation in check, it did not accomplish its goal of extending the decade-long economic expansion. In March 2001 the U.S. economy experienced a recession and the

---

[1]Alan Greenspan, speech to the New York Economics Club, Jan. 13, 2000.

expansionary phase of the business cycle ended. Recovery and economic expansion resumed in 2002 and picked up considerable strength over the next couple of years so that the economy was again operating at full employment by late 2004. Full employment continued through 2007.

We will say more about recession and expansion later. Our immediate focus is the terminology in the Greenspan quotation, which is precisely the language of the **aggregate demand–aggregate supply model (AD-AS model).** The AD-AS model—the subject of this chapter—enables us to analyze changes in real GDP and the price level simultaneously. The AD-AS model thus provides keen insights on inflation, recession, and unemployment. In later chapters, we will see that it also nicely depicts macroeconomic stabilization policies, such as those used in 2008 to try to prevent recession.

Aggregate Demand

Aggregate demand is a schedule or curve that shows the amounts of real output (real GDP) that buyers collectively desire to purchase at each possible price level. The relationship between the price level (as measured by the GDP price index) and the amount of real GDP demanded is inverse or negative. When the price level rises, the quantity of real GDP demanded decreases; when the price level falls, the quantity of real GDP demanded increases.

Aggregate Demand Curve

The inverse relationship between the price level and real GDP is shown in Figure 29.1, where the aggregate demand curve AD slopes downward, as does the demand curve for an individual product.

Why the downward slope? The explanation is *not* the same as that for why the demand for a single product slopes

FIGURE 29.1 **The aggregate demand curve.** The downsloping aggregate demand curve AD indicates an inverse (or negative) relationship between the price level and the amount of real output purchased.

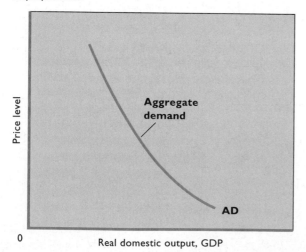

downward. That explanation centered on the income effect and the substitution effect. When the price of an *individual* product falls, the consumer's (constant) nominal income allows a larger purchase of the product (the income effect). And, as price falls, the consumer wants to buy more of the product because it becomes relatively less expensive than other goods (the substitution effect).

But these explanations do not work for aggregates. In Figure 29.1, when the economy moves down its aggregate demand curve, it moves to a lower general price level. But our circular flow model tells us that when consumers pay lower prices for goods and services, less nominal income flows to resource suppliers in the form of wages, rents, interest, and profits. As a result, a decline in the price level does not necessarily mean an increase in the nominal income of the economy as a whole. Thus, a decline in the price level need not produce an income effect, where more output is purchased because lower nominal prices leave buyers with greater real income.

Similarly, in Figure 29.1, prices in general are falling as we move down the aggregate demand curve, so the rationale for the substitution effect (where more of a specific product is purchased because it becomes cheaper relative to all other products) is not applicable. There is no *overall* substitution effect among domestically produced goods when the price level falls.

If the conventional substitution and income effects do not explain the downward slope of the aggregate demand curve, what does? The explanation rests on three effects of a price-level change.

Real-Balances Effect A change in the price level produces a **real-balances effect.** Here is how it works: A higher price level reduces the real value or purchasing power of the public's accumulated savings balances. In particular, the real value of assets with fixed money values, such as savings accounts or bonds, diminishes. Because a higher price level erodes the purchasing power of such assets, the public is poorer in real terms and will reduce its spending. A household might buy a new car or a plasma TV if the purchasing power of its financial asset balances is, say, $50,000. But if inflation erodes the purchasing power of its asset balances to $30,000, the household may defer its purchase. So a higher price level means less consumption spending.

Interest-Rate Effect The aggregate demand curve also slopes downward because of the **interest-rate effect.** When we draw an aggregate demand curve, we assume that the supply of money in the economy is fixed. But when the price level rises, consumers need more money for purchases and businesses need more money to meet their payrolls and to buy other resources. A $10 bill will do when the price of an item is $10, but a $10 bill plus a $1 bill is needed when the item costs $11. In short, a higher price level increases the demand for money. So, given a fixed supply of money, an increase in money demand will drive up the price paid for its use. That price is the interest rate.

Higher interest rates curtail investment spending and interest-sensitive consumption spending. Firms that expect a 6 percent rate of return on a potential purchase of capital will find that investment potentially profitable when the interest rate is, say, 5 percent. But the investment will be unprofitable and will not be made when the interest rate has risen to 7 percent. Similarly, consumers may decide not to purchase a new house or new automobile when the interest rate on loans goes up. So, by increasing the demand for money and consequently the interest rate, a higher price level reduces the amount of real output demanded.

Foreign Purchases Effect The final reason why the aggregate demand curve slopes downward is the **foreign purchases effect.** When the U.S. price level rises relative to foreign price levels (and exchange rates do not respond quickly or completely), foreigners buy fewer U.S. goods and Americans buy more foreign goods. Therefore, U.S. exports fall and U.S. imports rise. In short, the rise in the price level reduces the quantity of U.S. goods demanded as net exports.

These three effects, of course, work in the opposite direction for a decline in the price level. A decline in the price level increases consumption through the real-balances effect and interest-rate effect; increases investment through the interest-rate effect; and raises net exports by increasing exports and decreasing imports through the foreign purchases effect.

Changes in Aggregate Demand

Other things equal, a change in the price level will change the amount of aggregate spending and therefore change the amount of real GDP demanded by the economy. Movements along a fixed aggregate demand curve represent these changes in real GDP. However, if one or more of those "other things" change, the entire aggregate demand curve will shift. We call these other things **determinants of aggregate demand** or, less formally, *aggregate demand shifters.* They are listed in Figure 29.2.

Changes in aggregate demand involve two components:
- A change in one of the determinants of aggregate demand that directly changes the amount of real GDP demanded.
- A multiplier effect that produces a greater ultimate change in aggregate demand than the initiating change in spending.

In Figure 29.2, the full rightward shift of the curve from AD_1 to AD_2 shows an increase in aggregate demand, separated into these two components. The horizontal distance between AD_1 and the broken curve to its right illustrates an initial increase in spending, say, $5 billion of added investment. If the economy's MPC is .75, for example, then the simple multiplier is 4. So the aggregate demand curve shifts rightward from AD_1 to AD_2—four times the distance between AD_1 and the broken line. The multiplier process magnifies the initial change in spending into successive rounds of new consumption spending. After the shift, $20 billion (= $5 × 4) of additional real goods and services are demanded at each price level.

Similarly, the leftward shift of the curve from AD_1 to AD_3 shows a decrease in aggregate demand, the lesser amount of real GDP demanded at each price level. It also involves the initial decline in spending (shown as the horizontal distance between AD_1 and the dashed line to its left), followed by multiplied declines in consumption spending and the ultimate leftward shift to AD_3.

Let's examine each of the determinants of aggregate demand listed in Figure 29.2.

Consumer Spending

Even when the U.S. price level is constant, domestic consumers may alter their purchases of U.S.-produced real output. If those consumers decide to buy more output at each price level, the aggregate demand curve will shift to the right, as from AD_1 to AD_2 in Figure 29.2. If they decide to buy less output, the aggregate demand curve will shift to the left, as from AD_1 to AD_3.

Several factors other than a change in the price level may change consumer spending and therefore shift the

FIGURE 29.2 Changes in aggregate demand. A change in one or more of the listed determinants of aggregate demand will shift the aggregate demand curve. The rightward shift from AD₁ to AD₂ represents an increase in aggregate demand; the leftward shift from AD₁ to AD₃ shows a decrease in aggregate demand. The vertical distances between AD₁ and the dashed lines represent the initial changes in spending. Through the multiplier effect, that spending produces the full shifts of the curves.

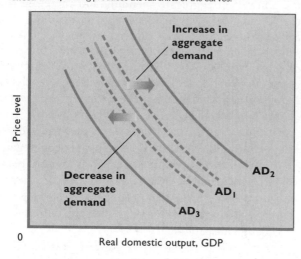

Determinants of Aggregate Demand: Factors That Shift the Aggregate Demand Curve

1. Change in consumer spending
   a. Consumer wealth
   b. Consumer expectations
   c. Household borrowing
   d. Taxes
2. Change in investment spending
   a. Interest rates
   b. Expected returns
      • Expected future business conditions
      • Technology
      • Degree of excess capacity
      • Business taxes
3. Change in government spending
4. Change in net export spending
   a. National income abroad
   b. Exchange rates

aggregate demand curve. As Figure 29.2 shows, those factors are real consumer wealth, consumer expectations, household debt, and taxes. Because our discussion here parallels that of Chapter 27, we will be brief.

Consumer Wealth
Consumer wealth is the total dollar value of all assets owned by consumers in the economy less the dollar value of their liabilities (debts). Assets include stocks, bonds, and real estate. Liabilities include mortgages, car loans, and credit card balances.

Consumer wealth sometimes changes suddenly and unexpectedly due to surprising changes in asset values. An unforeseen increase in the stock market is a good example. The increase in wealth prompts pleasantly surprised consumers to save less and buy more out of their current incomes than they had previously been planning. The resulting increase in consumer spending—the so-called *wealth effect*—shifts the aggregate demand curve to the right. In contrast, an unexpected decline in asset values will cause an unanticipated reduction in consumer wealth at each price level. As consumers tighten their belts in response to the bad news, a "reverse wealth effect" sets in. Unpleasantly surprised consumers increase savings and reduce consumption, thereby shifting the aggregate demand curve to the left.

Household Borrowing
Consumers can increase their consumption spending by borrowing. Doing so shifts

the aggregate demand curve to the right. By contrast, a decrease in borrowing for consumption purposes shifts the aggregate demand curve to the left. The aggregate demand curve will also shift to the left if consumers increase their savings rates in order to pay off their debts. With more money flowing to debt repayment, consumption expenditures decline and the AD curve shifts left.

Consumer Expectations
Changes in expectations about the future may alter consumer spending. When people expect their future real incomes to rise, they tend to spend more of their current incomes. Thus, current consumption spending increases (current saving falls) and the aggregate demand curve shifts to the right. Similarly, a widely held expectation of surging inflation in the near future may increase aggregate demand today because consumers will want to buy products before their prices escalate. Conversely, expectations of lower future income or lower future prices may reduce current consumption and shift the aggregate demand curve to the left.

Personal Taxes
A reduction in personal income tax rates raises take-home income and increases consumer purchases at each possible price level. Tax cuts shift the aggregate demand curve to the right. Tax increases reduce consumption spending and shift the curve to the left.

Investment Spending

Investment spending (the purchase of capital goods) is a second major determinant of aggregate demand. A decline in investment spending at each price level will shift the aggregate demand curve to the left. An increase in investment spending will shift it to the right. In Chapter 27 we saw that investment spending depends on the real interest rate and the expected return from investment.

Real Interest Rates

Other things equal, an increase in real interest rates will lower investment spending and reduce aggregate demand. We are not referring here to the "interest-rate effect" that results from a change in the price level. Instead, we are identifying a change in the real interest rate resulting from, say, a change in a nation's money supply. An increase in the money supply lowers the interest rate, thereby increasing investment and aggregate demand. A decrease in the money supply raises the interest rate, reducing investment and decreasing aggregate demand.

Expected Returns

Higher expected returns on investment projects will increase the demand for capital goods and shift the aggregate demand curve to the right. Alternatively, declines in expected returns will decrease investment and shift the curve to the left. Expected returns, in turn, are influenced by several factors:

- **Expectations about future business conditions** If firms are optimistic about future business conditions, they are more likely to forecast high rates of return on current investment and therefore may invest more today. On the other hand, if they think the economy will deteriorate in the future, they will forecast low rates of return and perhaps will invest less today.
- **Technology** New and improved technologies enhance expected returns on investment and thus increase aggregate demand. For example, recent advances in microbiology have motivated pharmaceutical companies to establish new labs and production facilities.
- **Degree of excess capacity** A rise in excess capacity—unused capital—will reduce the expected return on new investment and hence decrease aggregate demand. Other things equal, firms operating factories at well below capacity have little incentive to build new factories. But when firms discover that their excess capacity is dwindling or has completely disappeared, their expected returns on new investment in factories and capital equipment rise. Thus, they increase their investment spending, and the aggregate demand curve shifts to the right.

- **Business taxes** An increase in business taxes will reduce after-tax profits from capital investment and lower expected returns. So investment and aggregate demand will decline. A decrease in business taxes will have the opposite effects.

The variability of interest rates and expected returns makes investment highly volatile. In contrast to consumption, investment spending rises and falls often, independent of changes in total income. Investment, in fact, is the least stable component of aggregate demand.

Government Spending

Government purchases are the third determinant of aggregate demand. An increase in government purchases (for example, more military equipment) will shift the aggregate demand curve to the right, as long as tax collections and interest rates do not change as a result. In contrast, a reduction in government spending (for example, fewer transportation projects) will shift the curve to the left.

Net Export Spending

The final determinant of aggregate demand is net export spending. Other things equal, higher U.S. *exports* mean an increased foreign demand for U.S. goods. So a rise in net exports (higher exports relative to imports) shifts the aggregate demand curve to the right. In contrast, a decrease in U.S. net exports shifts the aggregate demand curve leftward. (These changes in net exports are *not* those prompted by a change in the U.S. price level—those associated with the foreign purchases effect. The changes here are shifts of the AD curve, not movements along the AD curve.)

What might cause net exports to change, other than the price level? Two possibilities are changes in national income abroad and changes in exchange rates.

National Income Abroad

Rising national income abroad encourages foreigners to buy more products, some of which are made in the United States. U.S. net exports thus rise, and the U.S. aggregate demand curve shifts to the right. Declines in national income abroad do the opposite: They reduce U.S. net exports and shift the U.S. aggregate demand curve to the left.

Exchange Rates

Changes in the dollar's exchange rate—the price of foreign currencies in terms of the U.S. dollar—may affect U.S. exports and therefore aggregate demand. Suppose the dollar depreciates in terms of the euro (meaning the euro appreciates in terms of the dollar). The new, relatively lower value of dollars and higher value of euros enables European consumers to obtain more dollars with each euro. From their perspective, U.S. goods are now less expensive; it takes fewer euros to obtain them. So European consumers buy more U.S. goods, and U.S. exports rise. But American consumers can now obtain fewer euros for each dollar. Because they must pay more dollars to buy European goods, Americans reduce their imports. U.S. exports rise and U.S. imports fall. Conclusion: Dollar depreciation increases net exports (imports go down; exports go up) and therefore increases aggregate demand.

Dollar appreciation has the opposite effects: Net exports fall (imports go up; exports go down) and aggregate demand declines.

QUICK REVIEW 29.1

- Aggregate demand reflects an inverse relationship between the price level and the amount of real output demanded.

- Changes in the price level create real-balances, interest-rate, and foreign purchases effects that explain the downward slope of the aggregate demand curve.

- Changes in one or more of the determinants of aggregate demand (Figure 29.2) alter the amounts of real GDP demanded at each price level; they shift the aggregate demand curve. The multiplier effect magnifies initial changes in spending into larger changes in aggregate demand.

- An increase in aggregate demand is shown as a rightward shift of the aggregate demand curve; a decrease, as a leftward shift of the curve.

Aggregate Supply

Aggregate supply is a schedule or curve showing the relationship between the price level and the amount of real domestic output that firms in the economy produce. This relationship varies depending on the time horizon and how quickly output prices and input prices can change. We will define three time horizons:

- In the *immediate short run*, both input prices as well as output prices are fixed.
- In the *short run*, input prices are fixed, but output prices can vary.
- In the *long run*, input prices as well as output prices can vary.

In Chapter 23, we discussed both the immediate short run and the long run in terms of how an automobile maker named Buzzer Auto responds to changes in the demand for its new car, the Prion. Here we extend the logic of that chapter to the economy as a whole in order to discuss how total output varies with the price level in the immediate

short run, the short run, and the long run. As you will see, the relationship between the price level and total output is different in each of the three time horizons because input prices are stickier than output prices. While both become more flexible as time passes, output prices usually adjust more rapidly.

Aggregate Supply in the Immediate Short Run

Depending on the type of firm, the immediate short run can last anywhere from a few days to a few months. It lasts as long as *both* input prices and output prices stay fixed. Input prices are fixed in both the immediate short run and the short run by contractual agreements. In particular, 75 percent of the average firm's costs are wages and salaries—and these are almost always fixed by labor contracts for months or years at a time. As a result, they are usually fixed for a much longer duration than output prices, which can begin to change within a few days or a few months depending upon the type of firm.

That being said, output prices are also typically fixed in the immediate short run. This is most often caused by firms setting fixed prices for their customers and then agreeing to supply whatever quantity demanded results at those fixed prices. For instance, once an appliance manufacturer sets its annual list prices for refrigerators, stoves, ovens, and microwaves, it is obligated to supply however many or few appliances customers want to buy at those prices. Similarly, a catalogue company is obliged to sell however much customers want to buy of its products at the prices listed in its current catalogue. And it is obligated to supply those quantities demanded until it sends out its next catalogue.

With output prices fixed and firms selling however much customers want to purchase at those fixed prices, the **immediate-short-run aggregate supply curve** AS_{ISR} is a horizontal line, as shown in Figure 29.3. The AS_{ISR} curve is horizontal at the overall price level P_1, which is calculated from all of the individual prices set by the various firms in the economy. Its horizontal shape implies that the total amount of output supplied in the economy depends directly on the volume of spending that results at price level P_1. If total spending is low at price level P_1, firms will supply a small amount to match the low level of spending. If total spending is high at price level P_1, they will supply a high level of output to match the high level of spending. The amount of output that results may be higher than or lower than the economy's full-employment output level Q_f.

Notice, however, that firms will respond in this manner to changes in total spending only as long as output

FIGURE 29.3 Aggregate supply in the immediate short run. In the immediate short run, the aggregate supply curve AS_{ISR} is horizontal at the economy's current price level, P_1. With output prices fixed, firms collectively supply the level of output that is demanded at those prices.

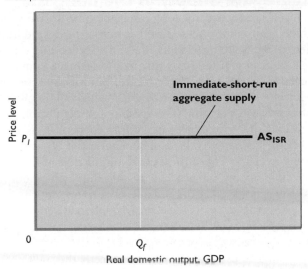

prices remain fixed. As soon as firms are able to change their product prices, they can respond to changes in aggregate spending not only by increasing or decreasing output but also by raising or lowering prices. This is the situation that leads to the upward-sloping short-run aggregate supply curve that we discuss next.

Aggregate Supply in the Short Run

The short run begins after the immediate short run ends. As it relates to macroeconomics, the short run is a period of time during which output prices are flexible, but input prices are either totally fixed or highly inflexible.

These assumptions about output prices and input prices are general—they relate to the economy in the aggregate. Naturally, some input prices are more flexible than others. Since gasoline prices are quite flexible, a package delivery firm like UPS that uses gasoline as an input will have at least one very flexible input price. On the other hand, wages at UPS are set by five-year labor contracts negotiated with its drivers' union, the Teamsters. Because wages are the firm's largest and most important input cost, it is the case that, overall, UPS faces input prices that are inflexible for several years at a time. Thus, its "short run"—during which it can change the shipping prices that it charges its customers but during which it must deal with substantially fixed input prices—is actually quite long. Keep this in mind as we derive the short-run aggregate supply for the entire economy. Its applicability does not

depend on some arbitrary definition of how long the "short run" should be. Instead, the short-run for which the model is relevant is any period of time during which output prices are flexible, but input prices are fixed or nearly fixed.

As illustrated in Figure 29.4, the **short-run aggregate supply curve** AS slopes upward because, with input prices fixed, changes in the price level will raise or lower real firm profits. To see how this works, consider an economy that has only a single multiproduct firm called Mega Buzzer and in which the firm's owners must receive a real profit of $20 in order to produce the full-employment output of 100 units. Assume the owner's only input (aside from entrepreneurial talent) is 10 units of hired labor at $8 per worker, for a total wage cost of $80. Also, assume that the 100 units of output sell for $1 per unit, so total revenue is $100. Mega Buzzer's nominal profit is $20 (= $100 − $80), and using the $1 price to designate the base-price index of 100, its real profit is also $20 (= $20/1.00). Well and good; the full-employment output is produced.

Next consider what will happen if the price of Mega Buzzer's output doubles. The doubling of the price level will boost total revenue from $100 to $200, but since we are discussing the short run during which input prices are fixed, the $8 nominal wage for each of the 10 workers will remain unchanged so that total costs stay at $80. Nominal profit will rise from $20 (= $100 − $80) to

FIGURE 29.4 The aggregate supply curve (short run). The upsloping aggregate supply curve AS indicates a direct (or positive) relationship between the price level and the amount of real output that firms will offer for sale. The AS curve is relatively flat below the full-employment output because unemployed resources and unused capacity allow firms to respond to price-level rises with large increases in real output. It is relatively steep beyond the full-employment output because resource shortages and capacity limitations make it difficult to expand real output as the price level rises.

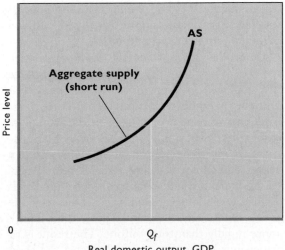

$120 (= $200 − $80). Dividing that $120 profit by the new price index of 200 (= 2.0 in hundredths), we find that Mega Buzzer's real profit is now $60. The rise in the real reward from $20 to $60 prompts the firm (economy) to produce more output. Conversely, price-level declines reduce real profits and cause the firm (economy) to reduce its output. So, in the short run, there is a direct, or positive, relationship between the price level and real output. When the price level rises, real output rises and when the price level falls, real output falls. The result is an upward-sloping short-run aggregate supply curve.

Notice, however, that the slope of the short-run aggregate supply curve is not constant. It is relatively flat at outputs below the full-employment output level Q_f and relatively steep at outputs above it. This has to do with the fact that per-unit production costs underlie the short-run aggregate supply curve. Recall from Chapter 26 that

$$\text{Per-unit production cost} = \frac{\text{total input cost}}{\text{units of output}}$$

The per-unit production cost of any specific level of output establishes that output's price level because the associated price level must cover all the costs of production, including profit "costs."

As the economy expands in the short run, per-unit production costs generally rise because of reduced efficiency. But the extent of that rise depends on where the economy is operating relative to its capacity. When the economy is operating below its full-employment output, it has large amounts of unused machinery and equipment and large numbers of unemployed workers. Firms can put these idle human and property resources back to work with little upward pressure on per-unit production costs. And as output expands, few if any shortages of inputs or production bottlenecks will arise to raise per-unit production costs. That is why the slope of the short-run aggregate supply curve increases only slowly at output levels below the full-employment output level Q_f.

On the other hand, when the economy is operating beyond Q_f, the vast majority of its available resources are already employed. Adding more workers to a relatively fixed number of highly used capital resources such as plant and equipment creates congestion in the workplace and reduces the efficiency (on average) of workers. Adding more capital, given the limited number of available workers, leaves equipment idle and reduces the efficiency of capital. Adding more land resources when capital and labor are highly constrained reduces the efficiency of land resources. Under these circumstances, total input costs rise more rapidly than total output. The result is rapidly rising per-unit production costs that give the short-run

aggregate supply curve its rapidly increasing slope at output levels beyond Q_f.

Aggregate Supply in the Long Run

In macroeconomics, the long run is the time horizon over which both input prices as well as output prices are flexible. It begins after the short run ends. Depending on the type of firm and industry, this may be from a couple of weeks to several years in the future. But for the economy as a whole, it is the time horizon over which all output and input prices—including wage rates—are fully flexible.

The **long-run aggregate supply curve** AS_{LR} is vertical at the economy's full-employment output Q_f as shown in Figure 29.5. The vertical curve means that in the long run the economy will produce the full-employment output level no matter what the price level is. How can this be? Shouldn't higher prices cause firms to increase output? The explanation lies in the fact that in the long run when both input prices as well as output prices are flexible, profit levels will always adjust so as to give firms exactly the right profit incentive to produce exactly the full-employment output level, Q_f.

To see why this is true, look back at the short-run aggregate supply curve AS shown in Figure 29.4. Suppose that the economy starts out producing at the full-employment output level Q_f and that the price level at that moment has an index value of 100. Now suppose that output prices double, so that the price index goes to 200. We

FIGURE 29.5 Aggregate supply in the long run. The long-run aggregate supply curve AS_{LR} is vertical at the full-employment level of real GDP (Q_f) because in the long run wages and other input prices rise and fall to match changes in the price level. So price-level changes do not affect firms' profits and thus they create no incentive for firms to alter their output.

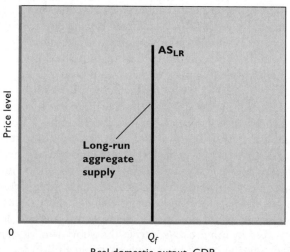

previously demonstrated for our single-firm economy that this doubling of the price level would cause profits to rise in the short run and that the higher profits would motivate the firm to increase output.

This outcome, however, is totally dependent upon the fact that input prices are fixed in the short run. Consider what will happen in the long run when they are free to change. Firms can only produce beyond the full-employment output level by running factories and businesses at extremely high rates. This creates a great deal of demand for the economy's limited supply of productive resources. In particular, labor is in great demand because the only way to produce beyond full employment is if workers are working overtime.

As time passes and input prices are free to change, the high demand will start to raise input prices. In particular, overworked employees will demand and receive raises as employers scramble to deal with the labor shortages that arise when the economy is producing at above its full-employment output level. As input prices increase, firm profits will begin to fall. And as they decline, so does the motive firms have to produce more than the full-employment output level. This process of rising input prices and falling profits continues until the rise in input prices exactly matches the initial change in output prices (in our example, they both double). When that happens, firm profits in real terms return to their original level so that firms are once again motivated to produce at exactly the full-employment output level. This adjustment process means that in the long run the economy will produce at full employment regardless of the price level (in our example, at either $P = 100$ or $P = 200$). That is why the long-run aggregate supply curve AS_{LR} is vertical above the full-employment output level. Every possible price level on the vertical axis is associated with the economy producing at the full-employment output level in the long run once input prices adjust to exactly match changes in output prices.

Focusing on the Short Run

The immediate-short-run aggregate supply curve, the short-run aggregate supply curve, and the long-run aggregate supply curve are all important. Each curve is appropriate to situations that match their respective assumptions about the flexibility of input and output prices. In the remainder of the book, we will have several different opportunities to refer to each curve. But our focus in the rest of this chapter and the several chapters that immediately follow will be on short-run aggregate supply curves, such as the AS curve shown in Figure 29.4. Indeed, unless explicitly stated otherwise, all references to "aggregate supply" are to the AS curve and to aggregate supply in the short run.

Our emphasis on the short-run aggregate supply curve AS stems from out interest in understanding the business cycle in the simplest possible way. It is a fact that real-world economies typically manifest simultaneous changes in both their price levels and their levels of real output. The upward-sloping short-run AS curve is the only version of aggregate supply that can handle simultaneous movements in both of these variables. By contrast, the price level is assumed fixed in the immediate-short-run version of aggregate supply illustrated in Figure 29.3 and the economy's output is always equal to the full-employment output level in the long-run version of aggregate supply shown in Figure 29.5. This renders these versions of the aggregate supply curve less useful as part of a core model for analyzing business cycles and demonstrating the short-run government policies designed to deal with them. In our current discussion, we will reserve use of the immediate short run and long run for specific, clearly identified situations. Later in the book we will explore how the short-run and long-run AS curves are linked, and how that linkage adds several additional insights about business cycles and policy.

Changes in Aggregate Supply

An existing aggregate supply curve identifies the relationship between the price level and real output, other things equal. But when one or more of these other things change, the curve itself shifts. The rightward shift of the curve from AS_1 to AS_2 in Figure 29.6 represents an increase in aggregate supply, indicating that firms are willing to produce and sell more real output at each price level. The leftward shift of the curve from AS_1 to AS_3 represents a decrease in aggregate supply. At each price level, firms produce less output than before.

Figure 29.6 lists the other things that cause a shift of the aggregate supply curve. Called the **determinants of aggregate supply** or *aggregate supply shifters*, they collectively position the aggregate supply curve and shift the curve when they change. Changes in these determinants raise or lower per-unit production costs *at each price level (or each level of output)*. These changes in per-unit production cost affect profits, thereby leading firms to alter the amount of output they are willing to produce *at each price level*. For example, firms may collectively offer $9 trillion of real output at a price level of 1.0 (100 in index value), rather than $8.8 trillion. Or they may offer $7.5 trillion rather than $8 trillion. The point is that when one of the determinants listed in Figure 29.6 changes, the aggregate supply curve shifts to the right or left. Changes that reduce per-unit production costs shift the aggregate supply curve to the right, as from AS_1 to AS_2; changes that increase per-unit production costs shift it

FIGURE 29.6 **Changes in aggregate supply.** A change in one or more of the listed determinants of aggregate supply will shift the aggregate supply curve. The rightward shift of the aggregate supply curve from AS_1 to AS_2 represents an increase in aggregate supply; the leftward shift of the curve from AS_1 to AS_3 shows a decrease in aggregate supply.

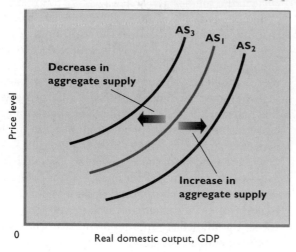

Determinants of Aggregate Supply: Factors That Shift the Aggregate Supply Curve

1. Change in input prices
   a. Domestic resource prices
   b. Prices of imported resources
2. Change in productivity
3. Change in legal-institutional environment
   a. Business taxes and subsidies
   b. Government regulations

to the left, as from AS_1 to AS_3. When per-unit production costs change for reasons other than changes in real output, the aggregate supply curve shifts.

The three aggregate supply determinants listed in Figure 29.6 require more discussion.

Input Prices

Input or resource prices—to be distinguished from the output prices that make up the price level—are a major ingredient of per-unit production costs and therefore a key determinant of aggregate supply. These resources can either be domestic or imported.

Domestic Resource Prices
As stated earlier, wages and salaries make up about 75 percent of all business costs. Other things equal, decreases in wages reduce per-unit production costs. So the aggregate supply curve shifts to the right. Increases in wages shift the curve to the left. Examples:

- Labor supply increases because of substantial immigration. Wages and per-unit production costs fall, shifting the AS curve to the right.
- Labor supply decreases because a rapid increase in pension income causes many older workers to opt for early retirement. Wage rates and per-unit production costs rise, shifting the AS curve to the left.

Similarly, the aggregate supply curve shifts when the prices of land and capital inputs change. Examples:

- The price of machinery and equipment falls because of declines in the prices of steel and electronic

components. Per-unit production costs decline, and the AS curve shifts to the right.
- The supply of available land resources expands through discoveries of mineral deposits, irrigation of land, or technical innovations that transform "nonresources" (say, vast desert lands) into valuable resources (productive lands). The price of land declines, per-unit production costs fall, and the AS curve shifts to the right.

Prices of Imported Resources
Just as foreign demand for U.S. goods contributes to U.S. aggregate demand, resources imported from abroad (such as oil, tin, and copper) add to U.S. aggregate supply. Added supplies of resources—whether domestic or imported—typically reduce per-unit production costs. A decrease in the price of imported resources increases U.S. aggregate supply, while an increase in their price reduces U.S. aggregate supply.

A good example of the major effect that changing resource prices can have on aggregate supply is the oil price hikes of the 1970s. At that time, a group of oil-producing nations called the Organization of Petroleum Exporting Countries (OPEC) worked in concert to decrease oil production in order to raise the price of oil. The 10-fold increase in the price of oil that OPEC achieved during the 1970s drove up per-unit production costs and jolted the U.S. aggregate supply curve leftward. By contrast, a sharp decline in oil prices in the mid-1980s resulted in a rightward shift of the U.S. aggregate supply curve. In 1999 OPEC again reasserted itself, raising oil prices and therefore per-unit production costs for some U.S. producers including airlines and shipping companies like FedEx and UPS. More recent increases in the price of oil have been mostly due to increases in demand rather than changes in supply caused by OPEC. But keep in mind that no matter what their cause, increases in the price of oil and other resources raise production costs and decrease aggregate supply.

Exchange-rate fluctuations are one factor that may alter the price of imported resources. Suppose that the dollar appreciates, enabling U.S. firms to obtain more foreign currency with each dollar. This means that domestic producers face a lower *dollar* price of imported resources. U.S. firms will respond by increasing their imports of foreign resources, thereby lowering their per-unit production costs at each level of output. Falling per-unit production costs will shift the U.S. aggregate supply curve to the right.

A depreciation of the dollar will have the opposite set of effects and will shift the aggregate supply curve to the left.

Productivity

The second major determinant of aggregate supply is **productivity,** which is a measure of the relationship between a nation's level of real output and the amount of resources used to produce that output. Productivity is a measure of average real output, or of real output per unit of input:

$$\text{Productivity} = \frac{\text{total output}}{\text{total inputs}}$$

An increase in productivity enables the economy to obtain more real output from its limited resources. It does this by reducing the per-unit cost of output (per-unit production cost). Suppose, for example, that real output is 10 units, that 5 units of input are needed to produce that quantity, and that the price of each input unit is $2. Then

$$\text{Productivity} = \frac{\text{total output}}{\text{total inputs}} = \frac{10}{5} = 2$$

and

$$\text{Per-unit production cost} = \frac{\text{total input cost}}{\text{total output}}$$

$$= \frac{\$2 \times 5}{10} = \$1$$

Note that we obtain the total input cost by multiplying the unit input cost by the number of inputs used.

Now suppose productivity increases so that real output doubles to 20 units, while the price and quantity of the input remain constant at $2 and 5 units. Using the above equations, we see that productivity rises from 2 to 4 and that the

WORKED PROBLEMS

W 29.1

Productivity and costs

per-unit production cost of the output falls from $1 to $.50. The doubled productivity has reduced the per-unit production cost by half.

By reducing the per-unit production cost, an increase in productivity shifts the aggregate supply curve to the right. The main source of productivity advance is improved production technology, often embodied within new plant and equipment that replaces old plant and equipment. Other sources of productivity increases are a better-educated and better-trained workforce, improved forms of business enterprises, and the reallocation of labor resources from lower-productivity to higher-productivity uses.

Much rarer, decreases in productivity increase per-unit production costs and therefore reduce aggregate supply (shift the curve to the left).

Legal-Institutional Environment

Changes in the legal-institutional setting in which businesses operate are the final determinant of aggregate supply. Such changes may alter the per-unit costs of output and, if so, shift the aggregate supply curve. Two changes of this type are (1) changes in taxes and subsidies and (2) changes in the extent of regulation.

Business Taxes and Subsidies Higher business taxes, such as sales, excise, and payroll taxes, increase per-unit costs and reduce short-run aggregate supply in much the same way as a wage increase does. An increase in such taxes paid by businesses will increase per-unit production costs and shift aggregate supply to the left.

Similarly, a business subsidy—a payment or tax break by government to producers—lowers production costs and increases short-run aggregate supply. For example, the Federal government subsidizes firms that blend ethanol (derived from corn) with gasoline to increase the U.S. gasoline supply. This reduces the per-unit production cost of making blended gasoline. To the extent that this and other subsidies are successful, the aggregate supply curve shifts rightward.

Government Regulation It is usually costly for businesses to comply with government regulations. More regulation therefore tends to increase per-unit production costs and shift the aggregate supply curve to the left. "Supply-side" proponents of deregulation of the economy have argued forcefully that, by increasing efficiency and reducing the paperwork associated with complex regulations, deregulation will reduce per-unit costs and shift the aggregate supply curve to the right. Other economists are less certain. Deregulation that results in accounting manipulations, monopolization, and business failures is likely to shift the AS curve to the left rather than to the right.

QUICK REVIEW 29.2

- The immediate-short-run aggregate supply curve is horizontal at the economy's current price level to reflect the fact that in the immediate short run input and output prices are fixed so that producers will supply whatever quantity of real output is demanded at the current output prices.

- The short-run aggregate supply curve (or simply the "aggregate supply curve") is upward-sloping because it reflects the fact that in the short run wages and other input prices remain fixed while output prices vary. Given fixed resource costs, higher output prices raise firm profits and encourage them to increase their output levels. The curve's upward slope reflects rising per-unit production costs as output expands.

- The long-run aggregate supply curve is vertical because, given sufficient time, wages and other input prices rise and fall to match price-level changes; because price-level changes do not change real rewards, they do not change production decisions.

- By altering per-unit production costs independent of changes in the level of output, changes in one or more of the determinants of aggregate supply (Figure 29.6) shift the aggregate supply curve.

- An increase in short-run aggregate supply is shown as a rightward shift of the aggregate supply curve; a decrease is shown as a leftward shift of the curve.

Equilibrium and Changes in Equilibrium

Of all the possible combinations of price levels and levels of real GDP, which combination will the economy gravitate toward, at least in the short run? **Figure 29.7 (Key Graph)** and its accompanying table provide the answer. Equilibrium occurs at the price level that equalizes the amounts of real output demanded and supplied. The intersection of the aggregate demand curve AD and the aggregate supply curve AS establishes the economy's **equilibrium price level** and **equilibrium real output.** So aggregate demand and aggregate supply *jointly* establish the price level and level of real GDP.

In Figure 29.7 the equilibrium price level and level of real output are 100 and $510 billion, respectively. To illustrate why, suppose the price level is 92 rather than 100. We see from the table that the lower price level will encourage

businesses to produce real output of $502 billion. This is shown by point *a* on the AS curve in the graph. But, as revealed by the table and point *b* on the aggregate demand curve, buyers will want to purchase $514 billion of real output at price level 92. Competition among buyers to purchase the lesser available real output of $502 billion will eliminate the $12 billion (= $514 billion − $502 billion) shortage and pull up the price level to 100.

As the table and graph show, the rise in the price level from 92 to 100 encourages producers to increase their real output from $502 billion to $510 billion and causes buyers

---

INTERACTIVE GRAPHS

G 29.1

Aggregate demand–aggregate supply

---

to scale back their purchases from $514 billion to $510 billion. When equality occurs between the amounts of real output produced and purchased, as it does at price level 100, the economy has achieved equilibrium (here, at $510 billion of real GDP).

Now let's apply the AD-AS model to various situations that can confront the economy. For simplicity we will use *P* and *Q* symbols, rather than actual numbers. Remember that these symbols represent, respectively, price index values and amounts of real GDP.

Increases in AD: Demand-Pull Inflation

Suppose the economy is operating at its full-employment output and businesses and government decide to increase their spending—actions that shift the aggregate demand curve to the right. Our list of determinants of aggregate demand (Figure 29.2) provides several reasons why this shift might occur. Perhaps firms boost their investment spending because they anticipate higher future profits from investments in new capital. Those profits are predicated on having new equipment and facilities that incorporate a number of new technologies. And perhaps government increases spending to expand national defense.

As shown by the rise in the price level from P_1 to P_2 in Figure 29.8, the increase in aggregate demand beyond the full-employment level of output causes inflation. This is *demand-pull inflation* because the price level is being pulled up by the increase in aggregate demand. Also, observe that the increase in demand expands real output from the full-employment level Q_f to Q_1. The distance between Q_1 and Q_f is a positive, or "inflationary," GDP gap. Actual GDP exceeds potential GDP.

The classic American example of demand-pull inflation occurred in the late 1960s. The escalation of the war in Vietnam resulted in a 40 percent increase in defense

FIGURE 29.7 The equilibrium price level and equilibrium real GDP. The intersection of the aggregate demand curve and the aggregate supply curve determines the economy's equilibrium price level. At the equilibrium price level of 100 (in index-value terms), the $510 billion of real output demanded matches the $510 billion of real output supplied. So the equilibrium GDP is $510 billion.

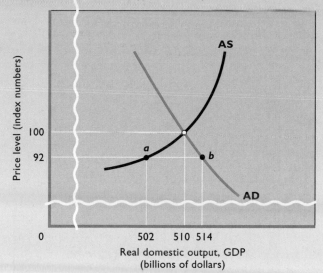

Real Output Demanded (Billions)	Price Level (Index Number)	Real Output Supplied (Billions)
$506	108	$513
508	104	512
510	*100*	*510*
512	96	507
514	92	502

QUICK QUIZ FOR FIGURE 29.7

1. The AD curve slopes downward because:
   a. per-unit production costs fall as real GDP increases.
   b. the income and substitution effects are at work.
   c. changes in the determinants of AD alter the amounts of real GDP demanded at each price level.
   d. decreases in the price level give rise to real-balances effects, interest-rate effects, and foreign purchases effects that increase the amounts of real GDP demanded.

2. The AS curve slopes upward because:
   a. per-unit production costs rise as real GDP expands toward and beyond its full-employment level.
   b. the income and substitution effects are at work.
   c. changes in the determinants of AS alter the amounts of real GDP supplied at each price level.
   d. increases in the price level give rise to real-balances effects, interest-rate effects, and foreign purchases effects that increase the amounts of real GDP supplied.

3. At price level 92:
   a. a GDP surplus of $12 billion occurs that drives the price level up to 100.
   b. a GDP shortage of $12 billion occurs that drives the price level up to 100.
   c. the aggregate amount of real GDP demanded is less than the aggregate amount of GDP supplied.
   d. the economy is operating beyond its capacity to produce.

4. Suppose real output demanded rises by $4 billion at each price level. The new equilibrium price level will be:
   a. 108.
   b. 104.
   c. 96.
   d. 92.

Answers: 1. d; 2. a; 3. b; 4. b

spending between 1965 and 1967 and another 15 percent increase in 1968. The rise in government spending, imposed on an already growing economy, shifted the economy's aggregate demand curve to the right, producing the worst inflation in two decades. Actual GDP exceeded potential GDP, thereby creating an inflationary GDP gap.

Inflation jumped from 1.6 percent in 1965 to 5.7 percent by 1970. **(Key Question 4)**

A careful examination of Figure 29.8 reveals an interesting point concerning the multiplier effect. The increase in aggregate demand from AD_1 to AD_2 increases real output only to Q_1, not to Q_2, because part of the

FIGURE 29.8 An increase in aggregate demand that causes demand-pull inflation. The increase of aggregate demand from AD_1 to AD_2 causes demand-pull inflation, shown as the rise in the price level from P_1 to P_2. It also causes an inflationary GDP gap of Q_1 minus Q_f. The rise of the price level reduces the size of the multiplier effect. If the price level had remained at P_1, the increase in aggregate demand from AD_1 to AD_2 would increase output from Q_f to Q_2 and the multiplier would have been at full strength. But because of the increase in the price level, real output increases only from Q_f to Q_1 and the multiplier effect is reduced.

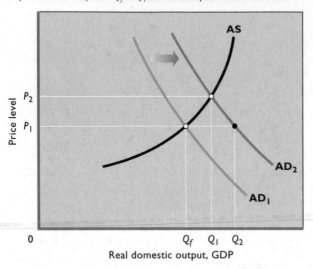

FIGURE 29.9 A decrease in aggregate demand that causes a recession. If the price level is downwardly inflexible at P_1, a decline of aggregate demand from AD_1 to AD_2 will move the economy leftward from a to b along the horizontal broken-line segment (similar to an immediate-short-run aggregate supply curve) and reduce real GDP from Q_f to Q_1. Idle production capacity, cyclical unemployment, and a recessionary GDP gap (of Q_1 minus Q_f) will result. If the price level were flexible downward, the decline in aggregate demand would move the economy depicted from a to c instead of from a to b.

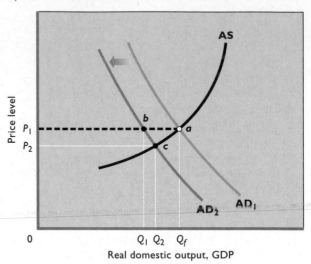

increase in aggregate demand is absorbed as inflation as the price level rises from P_1 to P_2. Had the price level remained at P_1, the shift of aggregate demand from AD_1 to AD_2 would have increased real output to Q_2. The full-strength multiplier effect of Chapters 27 and 28 would have occurred. But in Figure 29.8 inflation reduced the increase in real output—and thus the multiplier effect—by about one-half. For any initial increase in aggregate demand, the resulting increase in real output will be smaller the greater is the increase in the price level. Price-level flexibility weakens the realized multiplier effect.

Decreases in AD: Recession and Cyclical Unemployment

Decreases in aggregate demand describe the opposite end of the business cycle: recession and cyclical unemployment (rather than above-full employment and demand-pull inflation). For example, in 2000 investment spending substantially declined in the wake of an overexpansion of capital during the second half of the 1990s. In Figure 29.9 we show the resulting decline in aggregate demand as a leftward shift from AD_1 to AD_2.

But now we add an important twist to the analysis—a twist that makes use of the fact that fixed prices lead to horizontal aggregate supply curves (a fact explained earlier in

this chapter in the section on the immediate-short-run aggregate supply curve). What goes up—the price level—does not always go down. *Deflation*—a decline in the price level—is a rarity in the American economy. Suppose, for example, that the economy represented by Figure 29.9 moves from a to b, rather than from a to c. The outcome is a decline of real output from Q_f to Q_1, with *no* change in the price level. In this case, it is as if the aggregate supply curve in Figure 29.9 is horizontal at P_1, to the left of Q_f, as indicated by the dashed line. This decline of real output from Q_f to Q_1 constitutes a *recession*, and since fewer workers are needed to produce the lower output, *cyclical unemployment* arises. The distance between Q_1 and Q_f is a negative, or "recessionary," GDP gap—the amount by which actual output falls short of potential output.

Close inspection of Figure 29.9 also reveals that without a fall in the price level, the multiplier is at full strength. With the price level stuck at P_1, real GDP decreases by $Q_f - Q_1$, which matches the full leftward shift of the AD curve. The multiplier of Chapters 27 and 28 is at full strength when changes in aggregate demand occur along what, in effect, is a horizontal segment of the AS curve. This full-strength multiplier would also exist for an increase in aggregate demand from AD_2 to AD_1 along this broken line, since none of the increase in output would be dissipated as inflation. We will say more about that in Chapter 30.

All recent recessions in the United States have mimicked the "GDP gap but no deflation" scenario shown in Figure 29.9. Consider the recession of 2001, which resulted from a significant decline in investment spending. Because of the resulting decline in aggregate demand, GDP fell short of potential GDP by an average $67 billion for each of the last three quarters of the year. Between February 2001 and December 2001, unemployment increased by 1.8 million workers, and the nation's unemployment rate rose from 4.2 percent to 5.8 percent. Although the rate of inflation fell—an outcome called *disinflation*—the price level did not decline. That is, deflation did not occur.

Real output takes the brunt of declines in aggregate demand in the U.S. economy because the price level tends to be inflexible in a downward direction. There are numerous reasons for this.

- *Fear of price wars* Some large firms may be concerned that if they reduce their prices, rivals not only will match their price cuts but may retaliate by making even deeper cuts. An initial price cut may touch off an unwanted *price war*: successively deeper and deeper rounds of price cuts. In such a situation, each firm eventually ends up with far less profit or higher losses than would be the case if each had simply maintained its prices. For this reason, each firm may resist making the initial price cut, choosing instead to reduce production and lay off workers.

- *Menu costs* Firms that think a recession will be relatively short-lived may be reluctant to cut their prices. One reason is what economists metaphorically call **menu costs,** named after their most obvious example: the cost of printing new menus when a restaurant decides to reduce its prices. But lowering prices also creates other costs. Additional costs derive from (1) estimating the magnitude and duration of the shift in demand to determine whether prices should be lowered, (2) repricing items held in inventory, (3) printing and mailing new catalogs, and (4) communicating new prices to customers, perhaps through advertising. When menu costs are present, firms may choose to avoid them by retaining current prices. That is, they may wait to see if the decline in aggregate demand is permanent.

- *Wage contracts* Firms rarely profit from cutting their product prices if they cannot also cut their wage rates. Wages are usually inflexible downward because large parts of the labor force work under contracts prohibiting wage cuts for the duration of the contract. (Collective bargaining agreements in major industries frequently run for 3 years.) Similarly, the wages and salaries of nonunion workers are usually adjusted once a year, rather than quarterly or monthly.

- *Morale, effort, and productivity* Wage inflexibility downward is reinforced by the reluctance of many employers to reduce wage rates. Some current wages may be so-called **efficiency wages**—wages that elicit maximum work effort and thus minimize labor costs per unit of output. If worker productivity (output per hour of work) remains constant, lower wages *do* reduce labor costs per unit of output. But lower wages might impair worker morale and work effort, thereby reducing productivity. Considered alone, lower productivity raises labor costs per unit of output because less output is produced. If the higher labor costs resulting from reduced productivity exceed the cost savings from the lower wage, then wage cuts will increase rather than reduce labor costs per unit of output. In such situations, firms will resist lowering wages when they are faced with a decline in aggregate demand.

- *Minimum wage* The minimum wage imposes a legal floor under the wages of the least-skilled workers. Firms paying those wages cannot reduce that wage rate when aggregate demand declines.

ORIGIN OF THE IDEA
O 29.2
Efficiency wage

But a major "caution" is needed here: Although most economists agree that prices and wages tend to be inflexible downward in the short run, prices and wages are more flexible than in the past. Intense foreign competition and the declining power of unions in the United States have undermined the ability of workers and firms to resist price and wage cuts when faced with falling aggregate demand. This increased flexibility may be one reason the recession of 2001 was relatively mild. The U.S. auto manufacturers, for example, maintained output in the face of falling demand by offering zero-interest loans on auto purchases. This, in effect, was a disguised price cut. But our description in Figure 29.9 remains valid. In the 2001 recession, the overall price level did not decline although output fell by .5 percent and unemployment rose by 1.8 million workers.

Decreases in AS: Cost-Push Inflation

Suppose that a major terrorist attack on oil facilities severely disrupts world oil supplies and drives up oil prices by, say, 300 percent. Higher energy prices would spread through the economy, driving up production and distribution costs on a wide variety of goods. The U.S. aggregate supply curve would shift to the left, say, from AS_1 to AS_2 in Figure 29.10. The resulting increase in the price level would be *cost-push inflation*.

The effects of a leftward shift in aggregate supply are doubly bad. When aggregate supply shifts from AS_1 to AS_2, the economy moves from *a* to *b*. The price level rises from

FIGURE 29.10 A decrease in aggregate supply that causes cost-push inflation. A leftward shift of aggregate supply from AS_1 to AS_2 raises the price level from P_1 to P_2 and produces cost-push inflation. Real output declines and a recessionary GDP gap (of Q_1 minus Q_f) occurs.

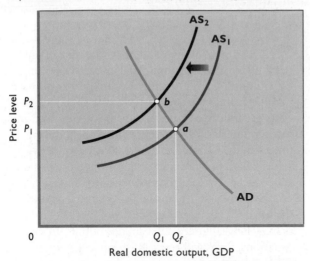

P_1 to P_2 and real output declines from Q_f to Q_1. Along with the cost-push inflation, a recession (and negative GDP gap) occurs. That is exactly what happened in the United States in the mid-1970s when the price of oil rocketed upward. Then, oil expenditures were about 10 percent of U.S. GDP, compared to only 3 percent today. So, as indicated in this chapter's Last Word, the U.S. economy is now less vulnerable to cost-push inflation arising from such "aggregate supply shocks." That said, it is not *immune* from such shocks.

Increases in AS: Full Employment with Price-Level Stability

Between 1996 and 2000, the United States experienced a combination of full employment, strong economic growth, and very low inflation. Specifically, the unemployment rate fell to 4 percent and real GDP grew nearly 4 percent annually, *without igniting inflation*. At first thought, this "macroeconomic bliss" seems to be incompatible with the AD-AS model. The aggregate supply curve suggests that increases in aggregate demand that are sufficient for over-full employment will raise the price level (see Figure 29.8). Higher inflation, so it would seem, is the inevitable price paid for expanding output beyond the full-employment level.

But inflation remained very mild in the late 1990s. Figure 29.11 helps explain why. Let's first suppose that aggregate demand increased from AD_1 to AD_2 along

CONSIDER THIS . . .

Ratchet Effect

A *ratchet analogy* is a good way to think about the effects of changes in aggregate demand on the price level. A ratchet is a tool or mechanism such as a winch, car jack, or socket wrench that cranks a wheel forward but does not allow it to go backward. Properly set, each allows the operator to move an object (boat, car, or nut) in one direction while preventing it from moving in the opposite direction.

Product prices, wage rates, and per-unit production costs are highly flexible upward when aggregate demand increases along the aggregate supply curve. In the United States, the price level has increased in 57 of the 58 years since 1950.

But when aggregate demand decreases, product prices, wage rates, and per-unit production costs are inflexible downward. The U.S. price level has declined in only a single year (1955) since 1950, even though aggregate demand and real output have declined in a number of years.

In terms of our analogy, increases in aggregate demand ratchet the U.S. price level upward. Once in place, the higher price level remains until it is ratcheted up again. The higher price level tends to remain even with declines in aggregate demand.

FIGURE 29.11 Growth, full employment, and relative price stability. Normally, an increase in aggregate demand from AD_1 to AD_2 would move the economy from *a* to *b* along AS_1. Real output would expand to Q_2, and inflation would result (P_1 to P_3). But in the late 1990s, significant increases in productivity shifted the aggregate supply curve, as from AS_1 to AS_2. The economy moved from *a* to *c* rather than from *a* to *b*. It experienced strong economic growth (Q_1 to Q_3), full employment, and only very mild inflation (P_1 to P_2) before receding in March 2001.

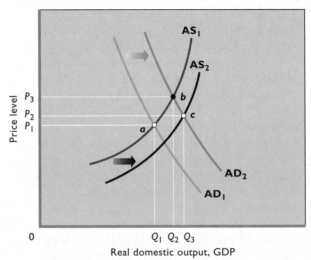

Has the Impact of Oil Prices Diminished?

Significant Changes in Oil Prices Historically Have Shifted the Aggregate Supply Curve and Greatly Affected the U.S. Economy. Have the Effects of Such Changes Weakened?

The United States has experienced several aggregate supply shocks—abrupt shifts of the aggregate supply curve—caused by significant changes in oil prices. In the mid-1970s the price of oil rose from $4 to $12 per barrel, and then again in the late 1970s it increased to $24 per barrel and eventually to $35. These oil price increases shifted the aggregate supply curve leftward, causing rapid cost-push inflation and ultimately rising unemployment and a negative GDP gap.

In the late 1980s and through most of the 1990s, oil prices fell, sinking to a low of $11 per barrel in late 1998. This decline created a positive aggregate supply shock beneficial to the U.S. economy. But in response to those low oil prices, in late 1999 OPEC teamed with Mexico, Norway, and Russia to restrict oil output and thus boost prices. That action, along with a rapidly growing international demand for oil, sent oil prices upward once again. By March 2000 the price of a barrel of oil reached $34, before settling back to about $25 to $28 in 2001 and 2002.

Some economists feared that the rising price of oil would increase energy prices by so much that the U.S. aggregate supply curve would shift to the left, creating cost-push inflation. But inflation in the United States remained modest.

Then came a greater test: A "perfect storm"—continuing conflict in Iraq, the rising demand for oil in India and China, a pickup of economic growth in several industrial nations, disruption of oil production by hurricanes, and concern about political developments in Venezuela—pushed the price of oil to over $60 a barrel in 2005. (You can find the current daily price of oil at OPEC's Web site, **www.opec.org.**) The U.S. inflation rate rose in 2005, but *core inflation* (the inflation rate after subtracting changes in the prices of food and energy) remained steady. Why have rises in oil prices lost their inflationary punch?

In the early 2000s, other determinants of aggregate supply swamped the potential inflationary impacts of the oil price increases. Lower production costs resulting from rapid productivity advance and lower input prices from global competition more than compensated for the rise in oil prices. Put simply, aggregate supply did not decline as it had in earlier periods.

Perhaps of greater importance, oil prices are a less significant factor in the U.S. economy than they were in the 1970s. Prior to 1980, changes in oil prices greatly affected core inflation in the United States. But since 1980 they have had very little effect on core inflation.* The main reason has been a significant decline in the amount of oil and gas used in producing each dollar of U.S. output. In 2005 producing a dollar of real GDP required about 7000 Btus of oil and gas, compared to 14,000 Btus in 1970. (A Btu, or British thermal unit, is the amount of energy required to heat one pound of water by one degree Fahrenheit.) Part of this decline resulted from new production techniques spawned by the higher oil and energy prices. But equally important has been the changing relative composition of GDP, away from larger, heavier items (such as earth-moving equipment) that are energy-intensive to make and transport and toward smaller, lighter items (such as microchips and software). Experts on energy economics estimate that the U.S. economy is about 33 percent less sensitive to oil price fluctuations than it was in the early 1980s and 50 percent less sensitive than in the mid-1970s.†

A final reason why changes in oil prices seem to have lost their inflationary punch is that the Federal Reserve has become more vigilant and adept at maintaining price stability through monetary policy. The Fed did not let the oil price increases of 1999–2000 become generalized as core inflation. The same turned out to be true with the dramatic rise in oil prices that resulted from the "perfect storm" of 2005. It remains to be seen whether the Fed can do the same with the dramatic demand-driven rise in oil prices that happened in 2007–2008, when the price of oil rose from just over $50 per barrel in January 2007 to over $140 per barrel in July 2008. (We will discuss monetary policy in depth in Chapter 33.)

---

*Mark A. Hooker, "Are Oil Shocks Inflationary? Asymmetric and Nonlinear Specifications versus Changes in Regimes," *Journal of Money, Credit and Banking*, May 2002, pp. 540–561.

†Stephen P. A. Brown and Mine K. Yücel, "Oil Prices and the Economy," Federal Reserve Bank of Dallas *Southwest Economy*, July–August 2000, pp. 1–6.

aggregate supply curve AS_1. Taken alone, that increase in aggregate demand would move the economy from a to b. Real output would rise from full-employment output Q_1 to beyond-full-employment output Q_2. The economy would experience inflation, as shown by the increase in the price level from P_1 to P_3. Such inflation had occurred at the end of previous vigorous expansions of aggregate demand, including the expansion of the late 1980s.

Between 1990 and 2000, however, larger-than-usual increases in productivity occurred because of a burst of new technology relating to computers, the Internet, inventory management systems, electronic commerce, and so on. We represent this higher-than-usual productivity growth as the rightward shift from AS_1 to AS_2 in Figure 29.11. The relevant aggregate demand and aggregate supply curves thus became AD_2 and AS_2, not AD_2 and AS_1. Instead of moving from a to b, the economy moved from a to c. Real output increased from Q_1 to Q_3, and the price level rose only modestly (from P_1 to P_2). The shift of the aggregate supply curve from AS_1 to AS_2 accommodated the rapid increase in aggregate demand and kept inflation mild. This remarkable combination of rapid productivity growth, rapid real GDP growth, full employment, and relative price-level stability led some observers to proclaim that the United States was experiencing a "new era" or a New Economy.

But in 2001 the New Economy came face-to-face with the old economic principles. Aggregate demand declined because of a substantial fall in investment spending, and in March 2001 the economy experienced a recession. The terrorist attacks of September 11, 2001, further dampened private spending and prolonged the recession throughout 2001. The unemployment rate rose from 4.2 percent in January 2001 to 6 percent in December 2002.

Throughout 2001 the Federal Reserve lowered interest rates to try to halt the recession and promote recovery. Those Fed actions, along with Federal tax cuts, increased military spending, and strong demand for new housing, helped spur recovery. The economy haltingly resumed its economic growth in 2002 and 2003 and then expanded rapidly in 2004 and 2005. Robust growth continued in 2006 and the first three quarters of 2007. But the economy greatly slowed in late 2007 and early 2008, leading many economists to predict a 2008 recession.

We will examine stabilization policies, such as those carried out by the Federal government and the Federal Reserve, in chapters that follow. **(Key Questions 5, 6, and 7)**

QUICK REVIEW 29.3

- The equilibrium price level and amount of real output are determined at the intersection of the aggregate demand curve and the aggregate supply curve.
- Increases in aggregate demand beyond the full-employment level of real GDP cause demand-pull inflation.
- Decreases in aggregate demand cause recessions and cyclical unemployment, partly because the price level and wages tend to be inflexible in a downward direction.
- Decreases in aggregate supply cause cost-push inflation.
- Full employment, high economic growth, and price stability are compatible with one another if productivity-driven increases in aggregate supply are sufficient to balance growing aggregate demand.

Summary

1. The aggregate demand–aggregate supply model (AD-AS model) is a variable-price model that enables analysis of simultaneous changes of real GDP and the price level.

2. The aggregate demand curve shows the level of real output that the economy will purchase at each price level.

3. The aggregate demand curve is downsloping because of the real-balances effect, the interest-rate effect, and the foreign purchases effect. The real-balances effect indicates that inflation reduces the real value or purchasing power of fixed-value financial assets held by households, causing cutbacks in consumer spending. The interest-rate effect means that, with a specific supply of money, a higher price level increases the demand for money, thereby raising the interest rate and reducing investment purchases. The foreign purchases effect suggests that an increase in one

country's price level relative to the price levels in other countries reduces the net export component of that nation's aggregate demand.

4. The determinants of aggregate demand consist of spending by domestic consumers, by businesses, by government, and by foreign buyers. Changes in the factors listed in Figure 29.2 alter the spending by these groups and shift the aggregate demand curve. The extent of the shift is determined by the size of the initial change in spending and the strength of the economy's multiplier.

5. The aggregate supply curve shows the levels of real output that businesses will produce at various possible price levels. The slope of the aggregate supply curve depends upon the flexibility of input and output prices. Since these vary over time, aggregate supply curves are categorized into three time horizons,

each having different underlying assumptions about the flexibility of input and output prices.

6. The *immediate-short-run aggregate supply curve* assumes that both input prices and output prices are fixed. With output prices fixed, the aggregate supply curve is a horizontal line at the current price level. The *short-run aggregate supply curve* assumes nominal wages and other input prices remain fixed while output prices vary. The aggregate supply curve is generally upsloping because per-unit production costs, and hence the prices that firms must receive, rise as real output expands. The aggregate supply curve is relatively steep to the right of the full-employment output level and relatively flat to the left of it. The *long-run aggregate supply curve* assumes that nominal wages and other input prices fully match any change in the price level. The curve is vertical at the full-employment output level.

7. Because the short-run aggregate supply curve is the only version of aggregate supply that can handle simultaneous changes in the price level and real output, it serves well as the core aggregate supply curve for analyzing the business cycle and economic policy. Unless stated otherwise, all references to "aggregate supply" refer to short-run aggregate supply and the short-run aggregate supply curve.

8. Figure 29.6 lists the determinants of aggregate supply: input prices, productivity, and the legal-institutional environment. A change in any one of these factors will change per-unit production costs at each level of output and therefore will shift the aggregate supply curve.

9. The intersection of the aggregate demand and aggregate supply curves determines an economy's equilibrium price level and real GDP. At the intersection, the quantity of real GDP demanded equals the quantity of real GDP supplied.

10. Increases in aggregate demand to the right of the full-employment output cause inflation and positive GDP gaps (actual GDP exceeds potential GDP). An upsloping aggregate supply curve weakens the multiplier effect of an increase in aggregate demand because a portion of the increase in aggregate demand is dissipated in inflation.

11. Shifts of the aggregate demand curve to the left of the full-employment output cause recession, negative GDP gaps, and cyclical unemployment. The price level may not fall during recessions because of downwardly inflexible prices and wages. This inflexibility results from fear of price wars, menu costs, wage contracts, efficiency wages, and minimum wages. When the price level is fixed, full multiplier effects occur along what, in essence, is an immediate-short-run aggregate supply curve.

12. Leftward shifts of the aggregate supply curve reflect increases in per-unit production costs and cause cost-push inflation, with accompanying negative GDP gaps.

13. Rightward shifts of the aggregate supply curve, caused by large improvements in productivity, help explain the simultaneous achievement of full employment, economic growth, and price stability that occurred in the United States between 1996 and 2000. The recession of 2001, however, ended the expansionary phase of the business cycle. Expansion resumed in the 2002–2007 period, before stalling in late 2007 and early 2008.

Terms and Concepts

aggregate demand–aggregate supply (AD-AS) model

aggregate demand

real-balances effect

interest-rate effect

foreign purchases effect

determinants of aggregate demand

aggregate supply

immediate-short-run aggregate supply curve

short-run aggregate supply curve

long-run aggregate supply curve

determinants of aggregate supply

productivity

equilibrium price level

equilibrium real output

menu costs

efficiency wages

Study Questions

1. Why is the aggregate demand curve downsloping? Specify how your explanation differs from the explanation for the downsloping demand curve for a single product. What role does the multiplier play in shifts of the aggregate demand curve? **LO1**

2. Distinguish between "real-balances effect" and "wealth effect," as the terms are used in this chapter. How does each relate to the aggregate demand curve? **LO1**

3. What assumptions cause the immediate-short-run aggregate supply curve to be horizontal? Why is the long-run aggregate supply curve vertical? Explain the shape of the short-run aggregate supply curve. Why is the short-run curve relatively flat to the left of the full-employment output and relatively steep to the right? **LO2**

4. **KEY QUESTION** Suppose that the aggregate demand and aggregate supply schedules for a hypothetical economy are as shown below: **LO3**

Amount of Real GDP Demanded, Billions	Price Level (Price Index)	Amount of Real GDP Supplied, Billions
$100	300	$450
200	250	400
300	200	300
400	150	200
500	100	100

a. Use these sets of data to graph the aggregate demand and aggregate supply curves. What is the equilibrium price level and the equilibrium level of real output in this hypothetical economy? Is the equilibrium real output also necessarily the full-employment real output? Explain.

b. Why will a price level of 150 not be an equilibrium price level in this economy? Why not 250?

c. Suppose that buyers desire to purchase $200 billion of extra real output at each price level. Sketch in the new aggregate demand curve as AD_1. What factors might cause this change in aggregate demand? What is the new equilibrium price level and level of real output?

5. **KEY QUESTION** Suppose that a hypothetical economy has the following relationship between its real output and the input quantities necessary for producing that output: **LO3**

Input Quantity	Real GDP
150.0	$400
112.5	300
75.0	200

a. What is productivity in this economy?

b. What is the per-unit cost of production if the price of each input unit is $2?

c. Assume that the input price increases from $2 to $3 with no accompanying change in productivity. What is the new per-unit cost of production? In what direction would the $1 increase in input price push the economy's aggregate supply curve? What effect would this shift of aggregate supply have on the price level and the level of real output?

d. Suppose that the increase in input price does not occur but, instead, that productivity increases by 100 percent. What would be the new per-unit cost of production? What effect would this change in per-unit production cost have on the economy's aggregate supply curve? What effect would this shift of aggregate supply have on the price level and the level of real output?

6. **KEY QUESTION** What effects would each of the following have on aggregate demand or aggregate supply? In each case use a diagram to show the expected effects on the equilibrium price level and the level of real output. Assume all other things remain constant. **LO3**

a. A widespread fear of depression on the part of consumers.

b. A $2 increase in the excise tax on a pack of cigarettes.

c. A reduction in interest rates at each price level.

d. A major increase in Federal spending for health care.

e. The expectation of rapid inflation.

f. The complete disintegration of OPEC, causing oil prices to fall by one-half.

g. A 10 percent reduction in personal income tax rates.

h. A sizable increase in labor productivity (with no change in nominal wages).

i. A 12 percent increase in nominal wages (with no change in productivity).

j. Depreciation in the international value of the dollar.

7. **KEY QUESTION** Assume that (a) the price level is flexible upward but not downward and (b) the economy is currently operating at its full-employment output. Other things equal, how will each of the following affect the equilibrium price level and equilibrium level of real output in the short run? **LO3**

a. An increase in aggregate demand.

b. A decrease in aggregate supply, with no change in aggregate demand.

c. Equal increases in aggregate demand and aggregate supply.

d. A decrease in aggregate demand.

e. An increase in aggregate demand that exceeds an increase in aggregate supply.

8. Explain how an upsloping aggregate supply curve weakens the realized multiplier effect. **LO3**

9. Why does a reduction in aggregate demand reduce real output, rather than the price level? Why might a full-strength multiplier apply to a decrease in aggregate demand? **LO3**

10. Explain: "Unemployment can be caused by a decrease of aggregate demand or a decrease of aggregate supply." In each case, specify the price-level outcomes. **LO4**

11. Use shifts of the AD and AS curves to explain (a) the U.S. experience of strong economic growth, full employment, and price stability in the late 1990s and early 2000s and (b) how a strong negative wealth effect from, say, a precipitous drop in the stock market could cause a recession even though productivity is surging. **LO4**

12. In early 2001 investment spending sharply declined in the United States. In the 2 months following the September 11, 2001, attacks on the United States, consumption also declined. Use AD-AS analysis to show the two impacts on real GDP. **LO4**

13. **LAST WORD** Go to the OPEC Web site, **www.opec.org**, and find the current "OPEC basket price" of oil. By clicking on that amount, you will find the annual prices of oil for the past 5 years. By what percentage is the current price higher

or lower than 5 years ago? Next, go to the Bureau of Economic Analysis Web site, **www.bea.gov,** and use the interactive feature to find U.S. real GDP for the past years. By what percentage is real GDP higher or lower than it was

5 years ago? What if, anything, can you conclude about the relationship between the price of oil and the level of real GDP in the United States?

Web-Based Questions

1. **FEELING WEALTHIER; SPENDING MORE?** Access the Bureau of Economic Analysis Web site, **www.bea.gov,** interactively. Select Interactive Data Tables, which is listed under Publications. On that page, select National Income and Product Accounts. Go to the List of All NIPA Tables and then find Table 1.1.6, which will give you access to real GDP figures for the U.S. economy. Find the annual levels of real GDP and real consumption for 1996 and 1999. Did consumption increase more rapidly or less rapidly in percentage terms than real GDP? At **www.dowjones.com** in sequence select DJIA, Index Data, and Historical Values to find the level of the Dow Jones Industrial Average (DJIA) stock market index on June 1, 1996, and June 1, 1999. What was the percentage change in the DJIA over that period? How might that change help explain your findings about the growth of consumption versus real GDP between 1996 and 1999?

2. **THE RECESSION OF 2001—WHICH COMPONENT OF AD DECLINED THE MOST?** Use the interactive feature of the Bureau of Economic Analysis Web site, **www.bea.gov,** to access the National Income and Product Account Tables. Select Interactive Data Tables, which is listed under Publications. On that page, select National Income and Product Accounts. Go to the List of All NIPA Tables and then find Table 1.1.6, which will give you access to real GDP figures for the U.S. economy. From Table 1.1.6 find the levels of real GDP, personal consumption expenditures (C), gross private investment (I_g), net exports (X_n), and government consumption expenditures and gross investment (G) in the first and third quarters of 2001. By what percentage did real GDP decline over this period? Which of the four broad components of aggregate demand decreased by the largest percentage amount?

FURTHER TEST YOUR KNOWLEDGE AT
www.mcconnell18e.com

The Relationship of the Aggregate Demand Curve to the Aggregate Expenditures Model*

The aggregate demand curve of this chapter and the aggregate expenditures model of Chapter 28 are intricately related.

Derivation of the Aggregate Demand Curve from the Aggregate Expenditures Model

We can directly connect the downward-sloping aggregate demand curve to the aggregate expenditures model by relating various possible price levels to corresponding equilibrium GDPs. In Figure 1 we have stacked the aggregate expenditures model (Figure 1a) and the aggregate demand curve (Figure 1b) vertically. This is possible because the horizontal axes of both models measure real GDP. Now let's derive the AD curve in three distinct steps. (Throughout this discussion, keep in mind that price level P_1 is lower than price level P_2, which is lower than price level P_3.)

- First suppose that the economy's price level is P_1 and its aggregate expenditures schedule is AE_1, the top schedule in Figure 1a. The equilibrium GDP is then Q_1 at point 1. So in Figure 1b we can plot the equilibrium real output Q_1 and the corresponding price level P_1. This gives us one point 1' in Figure 1b.

- Now assume the price level rises from P_1 to P_2. Other things equal, this higher price level will (1) decrease the value of real balances (wealth), decreasing consumption expenditures; (2) increase the interest rate, reducing investment and interest-sensitive consumption expenditures; and (3) increase imports and decrease exports, reducing net export expenditures. The aggregate expenditures schedule will fall from AE_1 to, say, AE_2 in Figure 1a, giving us

equilibrium Q_2 at point 2. In Figure 1b we plot this new price-level–real-output combination, P_2 and Q_2, as point 2'.

FIGURE 1 **Deriving the aggregate demand curve from the aggregate expenditures model.** (a) Rising price levels from P_1 to P_2 to P_3 shift the aggregate expenditures curve downward from AE_1 to AE_2 to AE_3 and reduce real GDP from Q_1 to Q_2 to Q_3. (b) The aggregate demand curve AD is derived by plotting the successively lower real GDPs from the upper graph against the P_1, P_2, and P_3 price levels.

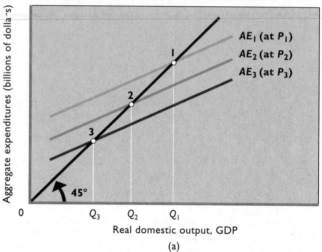

(a)
Aggregate expenditures model

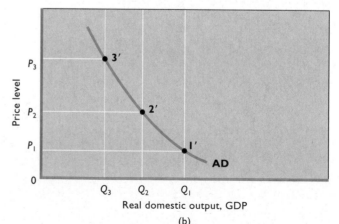

(b)
Aggregate demand–aggregate supply model

---

*This appendix presumes knowledge of the aggregate expenditures model discussed in Chapter 28 and should be skipped if Chapter 28 was not assigned.

- Finally, suppose the price level rises from P_2 to P_3. The value of real balances falls, the interest rate rises, exports fall, and imports rise. Consequently, the consumption, investment, and net export schedules fall, shifting the aggregate expenditures schedule downward from AE_2 to AE_3, which gives us equilibrium Q_3 at point 3. In Figure 1b, this enables us to locate point 3', where the price level is P_3 and real output is Q_3.

In summary, increases in the economy's price level will successively shift its aggregate expenditures schedule downward and will reduce real GDP. The resulting price-level–real-GDP combinations will yield various points such as 1', 2', and 3' in Figure 1b. Together, such points locate the downward-sloping aggregate demand curve for the economy.

Aggregate Demand Shifts and the Aggregate Expenditures Model

The determinants of aggregate demand listed in Figure 29.2 are the components of the aggregate expenditures model discussed in Chapter 28. When there is a change in one of the determinants of aggregate demand, the aggregate expenditures schedule shifts upward or downward. We can easily link such shifts of the aggregate expenditures schedule to shifts of the aggregate demand curve.

Let's suppose that the price level is constant. In Figure 2 we begin with the aggregate expenditures schedule at AE_1 in the top diagram, yielding real output of Q_1. Assume now that investment increases in response to more optimistic business expectations, so the aggregate expenditures schedule rises from AE_1 to AE_2. (The notation "at P_1" reminds us that the price level is assumed constant.) The result will be a multiplied increase in real output from Q_1 to Q_2.

In Figure 2b the increase in investment spending is reflected in the horizontal distance between AD_1 and the broken curve to its right. The immediate effect of the increase in investment is an increase in aggregate demand by the exact amount of the new spending. But then the multiplier process magnifies the initial increase in investment into successive rounds of consumption spending and an ultimate multiplied increase in aggregate demand from AD_1 to AD_2. Equilibrium real output rises from Q_1 to Q_2, the same multiplied increase in real GDP as that in the top graph. The initial increase in investment in the top graph has shifted the AD curve in the lower graph by a horizontal

FIGURE 2 Shifts in the aggregate expenditures schedule and in the aggregate demand curve. (a) A change in some determinant of consumption, investment, or net exports (other than the price level) shifts the aggregate expenditures schedule upward from AE_1 to AE_2. The multiplier increases real output from Q_1 to Q_2. (b) The counterpart of this change is an initial rightward shift of the aggregate demand curve by the amount of initial new spending (from AD_1 to the broken curve). This leads to a multiplied rightward shift of the curve to AD_2, which is just sufficient to show the same increase of real output as that in the aggregate expenditures model.

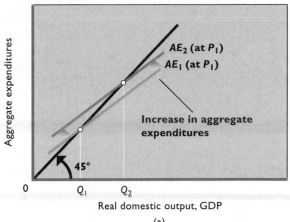

Real domestic output, GDP

(a)

Aggregate expenditures model

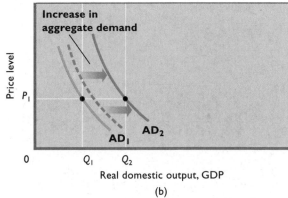

Real domestic output, GDP

(b)

Aggregate demand–aggregate supply model

distance equal to the change in investment times the multiplier. This particular change in real GDP is still associated with the constant price level P_1. To generalize,

$$\text{Shift of AD curve} = \text{initial change in spending} \times \text{multiplier}$$

Appendix Summary

1. A change in the price level alters the location of the aggregate expenditures schedule through the real-balances, interest-rate, and foreign purchases effects. The aggregate demand curve is derived from the aggregate expenditures model by allowing the price level to change and observing the effect on the aggregate expenditures schedule and thus on equilibrium GDP.

2. With the price level held constant, increases in consumption, investment, government, and net export expenditures shift the aggregate expenditures schedule upward and the aggregate demand curve to the right. Decreases in these spending components produce the opposite effects.

Appendix Study Questions

1. Explain carefully: "A change in the price level shifts the aggregate expenditures curve but not the aggregate demand curve." **LO5**

2. Suppose that the price level is constant and that investment decreases sharply. How would you show this decrease in the aggregate expenditures model? What would be the outcome for real GDP? How would you show this fall in investment in the aggregate demand–aggregate supply model, assuming the economy is operating in what, in effect, is a horizontal section of the aggregate supply curve? **LO5**

Fiscal Policy, Deficits, and Debt

In the previous chapter we saw that an excessive increase in aggregate demand can cause demand-pull inflation and that a significant decline in aggregate demand can cause recession and cyclical unemployment. For these reasons, the Federal government sometimes uses budgetary actions to try to "stimulate the economy" or "rein in inflation." Such countercyclical **fiscal policy** consists of deliberate changes in government spending and tax collections designed to achieve full employment, control inflation, and encourage economic growth. (The adjective "fiscal" simply means "financial.")

ORIGIN OF THE IDEA

O 30.1

Fiscal policy

We begin this chapter by examining the logic behind fiscal policy, its current status, and its limitations. Then we examine a closely related topic: the U.S. public debt.

Fiscal Policy and the AD-AS Model

The fiscal policy defined above is *discretionary* (or "active"). It is often initiated on the advice of the president's **Council of Economic Advisers (CEA),** a group of three economists appointed by the president to provide expertise and assistance on economic matters. Discretionary changes in government spending and taxes are *at the option* of the Federal government. They do not occur automatically. Changes that occur without congressional action are *nondiscretionary* (or "passive" or "automatic"), and we will examine them later in this chapter.

Expansionary Fiscal Policy

When recession occurs, an **expansionary fiscal policy** may be in order. Consider Figure 30.1, where we suppose that a sharp decline in investment spending has shifted the economy's aggregate demand curve to the left from AD_1 to AD_2. (Disregard the arrows and dashed downsloping line for now.) The cause of the recession may be that profit expectations on investment projects have dimmed, curtailing investment spending and reducing aggregate demand.

Suppose the economy's potential or full-employment output is $510 billion in Figure 30.1. If the price level is inflexible downward at P_1, the broken horizontal line in effect becomes the relevant aggregate supply curve. The aggregate demand curve moves leftward and reduces real GDP from $510 billion to $490 billion. A negative GDP gap of $20 billion (= $490 billion − $510 billion) arises. An increase in unemployment accompanies this negative GDP gap because fewer workers are needed to produce the

reduced output. In short, the economy depicted is suffering both recession and cyclical unemployment.

What fiscal policy should the Federal government adopt to try to stimulate the economy? It has three main options: (1) increase government spending, (2) reduce taxes, or (3) use some combination of the two. If the Federal budget is balanced at the outset, expansionary fiscal policy will create a government **budget deficit**—government spending in excess of tax revenues.

Increased Government Spending Other things equal, a sufficient increase in government spending will shift an economy's aggregate demand curve to the right, from AD_2 to AD_1 in Figure 30.1. To see why, suppose that the recession prompts the government to initiate $5 billion of new spending on highways, education, and health care. We represent this new $5 billion of government spending as the horizontal distance between AD_2 and the dashed line immediately to its right. At each price level, the amount of real output that is demanded is now $5 billion greater than that demanded before the expansion of government spending.

But the initial increase in aggregate demand is not the end of the story. Through the multiplier effect, the aggregate demand curve shifts to AD_1, a distance that exceeds that represented by the originating $5 billion increase in government purchases. This greater shift occurs because the multiplier process magnifies the initial change in spending into successive rounds of new consumption spending. If the economy's MPC is .75, then the simple multiplier is 4. So the aggregate demand curve shifts rightward by four times the distance between AD_2 and the broken line.

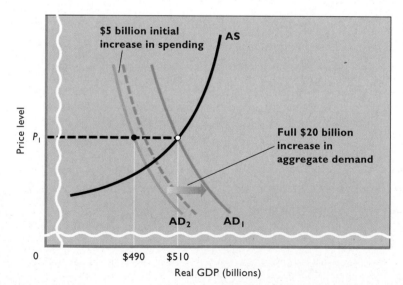

FIGURE 30.1 Expansionary fiscal policy. Expansionary fiscal policy uses increases in government spending or tax cuts to push the economy out of recession. In an economy with an MPC of .75, a $5 billion increase in government spending or a $6.67 billion decrease in personal taxes (producing a $5 billion initial increase in consumption) expands aggregate demand from AD_2 to the downsloping dashed curve. The multiplier then magnifies this initial increase in spending to AD_1. So real GDP rises along the broken horizontal aggregate supply line by $20 billion.

Because this *particular* increase in aggregate demand occurs along the horizontal broken-line segment of aggregate supply, real output rises by the full extent of the multiplier. Observe that real output rises to $510 billion, up $20 billion from its recessionary level of $490 billion. Concurrently, unemployment falls as firms increase their employment to the full-employment level that existed before the recession.

Tax Reductions

Alternatively, the government could reduce taxes to shift the aggregate demand curve rightward, as from AD₂ to AD₁. Suppose the government cuts personal income taxes by $6.67 billion, which increases disposable income by the same amount. Consumption will rise by $5 billion (= MPC of .75 × $6.67 billion) and saving will go up by $1.67 billion (= MPS of .25 × $6.67 billion). In this case the horizontal distance between AD₂ and the dashed downsloping line in Figure 30.1 represents only the $5 billion initial increase in consumption spending. Again, we call it "initial" consumption spending because the multiplier process yields successive rounds of increased consumption spending. The aggregate demand curve eventually shifts rightward by four times the $5 billion initial increase in consumption produced by the tax cut. Real GDP rises by $20 billion, from $490 billion to $510 billion, implying a multiplier of 4. Employment increases accordingly.

You may have noted that a tax cut must be somewhat larger than the proposed increase in government spending if it is to achieve the same amount of rightward shift in the aggregate demand curve. This is because part of a tax reduction increases saving, rather than consumption. To increase initial consumption by a specific amount, the government must reduce taxes by more than that amount.

With an MPC of .75, taxes must fall by $6.67 billion for $5 billion of new consumption to be forthcoming because $1.67 billion is saved (not consumed). If the MPC had instead been, say, .6, an $8.33 billion reduction in tax collections would have been necessary to increase initial consumption by $5 billion. The smaller the MPC, the greater the tax cut needed to accomplish a specific initial increase in consumption and a specific shift in the aggregate demand curve.

Combined Government Spending Increases and Tax Reductions

The government may combine spending increases and tax cuts to produce the desired initial increase in spending and the eventual increase in aggregate demand and real GDP. In the economy depicted in Figure 30.1, the government might increase its spending by $1.25 billion while reducing taxes by $5 billion. As an exercise, you should explain why this combination will produce the targeted $5 billion initial increase in new spending.

If you were assigned Chapter 28, think through these three fiscal policy options in terms of the recessionary-expenditure-gap analysis associated with the aggregate expenditures model (Figure 28.7). And recall from the appendix to Chapter 29 that rightward shifts of the aggregate demand curve relate directly to upward shifts of the aggregate expenditures schedule. **(Key Question 2)**

Contractionary Fiscal Policy

When demand-pull inflation occurs, a restrictive or **contractionary fiscal policy** may help control it. Look at Figure 30.2, where the full-employment level of real GDP is $510 billion. The economy starts at equilibrium at point *a*, where the initial aggregate demand curve AD₃ intersects

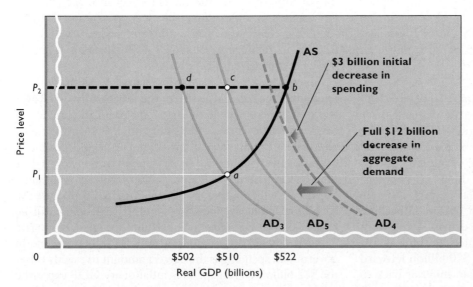

FIGURE 30.2 Contractionary fiscal policy under the ratchet effect.
Contractionary fiscal policy uses decreases in government spending or increases in taxes to reduce demand-pull inflation. Contractionary fiscal policy must take the ratchet effect into account. Here, an increase in aggregate demand from AD₃ to AD₄ has driven the economy to equilibrium *b* and ratcheted the price level up to P_2. To return the economy to producing at full employment, $510 billion, the government can either reduce government spending by $3 billion or increase taxes by $4 billion (which will produce a $3 billion decrease in consumption since the MPC is .75). Either policy will shift aggregate demand leftward by $3 billion, from AD₄ to the dashed line. The multiplier effect then shifts the curve farther left, to AD₅. With the price level fixed at P_2, the economy's new equilibrium is established at point *c*, where the horizontal dashed segment of aggregate supply intersects AD₅. The inflationary GDP gap is eliminated while the price level remains at P_2.

$3 billion initial decrease in spending

Full $12 billion decrease in aggregate demand

Price level — P_2, P_1

Real GDP (billions) — $502 — $510 — $522

AD₃   AD₅   AD₄

AS

aggregate supply curve AS. Suppose that after going through the multiplier process, a $5 billion initial increase in investment and net export spending shifts the aggregate demand curve to the right by $20 billion, from AD_3 to AD_4. (Ignore the downsloping dashed line for now.) Given the upward-sloping AS curve, however, the equilibrium GDP does not rise by the full $20 billion. It only rises by $12 billion, to $522 billion, thereby creating an inflationary GDP gap of $12 billion ($522 billion – $510 billion). The upward slope of the AS curve means that some of the rightward movement of the AD curve ends up causing demand-pull inflation rather than increased output. As a result, the price level rises from P_1 to P_2 and the equilibrium moves to point b.

Without a government response, the inflationary GDP gap will cause further inflation (as input prices rise in the long run to meet the increase in output prices). If the government looks to fiscal policy to eliminate the inflationary GDP gap, its options are the opposite of those used to combat recession. It can (1) decrease government spending, (2) raise taxes, or (3) use some combination of those two policies. When the economy faces demand-pull inflation, fiscal policy should move toward a government **budget surplus**—tax revenues in excess of government spending.

But before discussing how the government can either decrease government spending or increase taxes to move toward a government budget surplus and control inflation, we have to keep in mind that the price level is like a ratchet. While increases in aggregate demand that expand real output beyond the full-employment level tend to ratchet the price level upward, declines in aggregate demand do not seem to push the price level downward. This means that stopping inflation is a matter of halting the rise of the price level, not trying to lower it to the previous level. It also means that the government must take the ratchet effect into account when deciding how big a cut in spending or an increase in taxes it should undertake.

Decreased Government Spending

Reduced government spending shifts the aggregate demand curve leftward to control demand-pull inflation. To see why the ratchet effect matters so much, look at Figure 30.2 and consider what would happen if the government ignored the ratchet effect and attempted to design a spending-reduction policy to eliminate the inflationary GDP gap. Since the $12 billion gap was caused by the $20 billion rightward movement of the aggregate demand curve from AD_3 to AD_4, the government might naively think that it could solve the problem by causing a $20 billion leftward shift of the aggregate demand curve to move it back to

where it originally was. It could attempt to do so by reducing government spending by $5 billion and then allowing the multiplier effect to expand that initial decrease into a $20 billion decline in aggregate demand. That would shift the aggregate demand curve leftward by $20 billion, putting it back at AD_3.

This policy would work fine if there were no ratchet effect and if prices were flexible. The economy's equilibrium would move back from point b to point a, with equilibrium GDP returning to the full-employment level of $510 billion and the price level falling from P_2 back to P_1.

But because there *is* a ratchet effect, this scenario is not what will actually happen. Instead, the ratchet effect implies that the price level is stuck at P_2, so that the broken horizontal line at price level P_2 becomes the relevant aggregate supply curve. This means that when the government reduces spending by $5 billion in order to shift the aggregate demand curve back to AD_3, it will actually cause a recession! The new equilibrium will not be at point a. It will be at point d, where aggregate demand curve AD_3 crosses the broken horizontal line. At point d, real GDP is only $502 billion, $8 billion below the full-employment level of $510 billion.

The problem is that with what in essence is an immediate-short-run AS curve, the multiplier is at full effect. With the price level fixed and the aggregate supply curve horizontal, the $20 billion leftward shift of the aggregate demand curve causes a full $20 billion decline in real GDP. None of the change in aggregate demand can be dissipated as a change in the price level (as it can be when aggregate supply is upward-sloping). As a result, equilibrium GDP declines by the full $20 billion, falling from $522 billion to $502 billion and putting it $8 billion below potential output. By not taking the ratchet effect into account, the government has overdone the decrease in government spending, replacing a $12 billion inflationary GDP gap with an $8 billion recessionary GDP gap. This is clearly not what it had in mind.

Here's how it can avoid this scenario. First, the government takes account of the size of the inflationary GDP gap. It is $12 billion. Second, it knows that with the price level fixed, aggregate supply will be horizontal so that the multiplier will be in full effect. Thus, it knows that any decline in government spending will be multiplied by a factor of 4. It then reasons that government spending will have to decline by only $3 billion rather than $5 billion. Why? Because the $3 billion initial decline in government spending will be multiplied by 4, creating a $12 billion decline in aggregate demand. Under the circumstances, a $3 billion decline in government spending is the correct amount to exactly offset the $12 billion GDP gap. This inflationary GDP gap is the problem that government wants to eliminate. To succeed, it need not undo the full increase in aggregate demand that caused the inflation in the first place.

Graphically, the horizontal distance between AD_4 and the dashed line to its left represents the $3 billion decrease in government spending. Once the multiplier process is complete, this spending cut will shift the aggregate demand curve leftward from AD_4 to AD_5. With the price level fixed at P_2 and aggregate supply in this area represented by the horizontal dashed line, the economy will come to equilibrium at point c. The economy will operate at its potential output of $510 billion. The inflationary GDP gap will be eliminated. And because the government took the ratchet effect correctly into account, the government will not accidentally push the economy into a recession by making an overly large initial decrease in government spending.

Increased Taxes Just as government can use tax cuts to increase consumption spending, it can use tax *increases to reduce consumption* spending. If the economy in Figure 30.2 has an MPC of .75, the government must raise taxes by $4 billion. The $4 billion tax increase reduces saving by $1 billion (= the MPS of .25 × $4 billion). This $1 billion reduction in saving, by definition, is not a reduction in spending. But the $4 billion tax increase also reduces consumption spending by $3 billion (= the MPC of .75 × $4 billion), as shown by the distance between AD_4 and the dashed line to its left in Figure 30.2. After the multiplier process is complete, this initial $3 billion decline in consumption will cause aggregate demand to shift leftward by $12 billion at each price level (multiplier of 4 × $3 billion). With the economy moving to point c, the inflationary GDP gap will be closed and the inflation will be halted.

Combined Government Spending Decreases and Tax Increases

The government may choose to combine spending decreases and tax increases in order to reduce aggregate demand and check inflation. To check your understanding, determine why a $1.5 billion decline in government spending combined with a $2 billion increase in taxes would shift the aggregate demand curve from AD_4 to AD_5. Also, if you were assigned Chapter 28, explain the three fiscal policy options for fighting inflation by referring to the inflationary-expenditure-gap concept developed with the aggregate expenditures model (Figure 28.7). And recall from the appendix to Chapter 29 that leftward shifts of the aggregate demand curve are associated with downshifts of the aggregate expenditures schedule.

INTERACTIVE GRAPHS

G 30.1

Fiscal policy

Policy Options: *G* or *T*?

Which is preferable as a means of eliminating recession and inflation? The use of government spending or the use of taxes? The answer depends largely on one's view as to whether the government is too large or too small.

Economists who believe there are many unmet social and infrastructure needs usually recommend that government spending be increased during recessions. In times of demand-pull inflation, they usually recommend tax increases. Both actions either expand or preserve the size of government.

Economists who think that the government is too large and inefficient usually advocate tax cuts during recessions and cuts in government spending during times of demand-pull inflation. Both actions either restrain the growth of government or reduce its size.

The point is that discretionary fiscal policy designed to stabilize the economy can be associated with either an expanding government or a contracting government. **(Key Question 3)**

QUICK REVIEW 30.1

- Discretionary fiscal policy is the purposeful change of government expenditures and tax collections by government to promote full employment, price stability, and economic growth.

- The government uses expansionary fiscal policy to shift the aggregate demand curve rightward in order to expand real output. This policy entails increases in government spending, reductions in taxes, or some combination of the two.

- The government uses contractionary fiscal policy to shift the aggregate demand curve leftward in an effort to halt demand-pull inflation. This policy entails reductions in government spending, tax increases, or some combination of the two.

- To be implemented correctly, contractionary fiscal policy must properly account for the ratchet effect and the fact that prices will not fall as the government shifts the aggregate demand curve leftward.

Built-In Stability

To some degree, government tax revenues change automatically over the course of the business cycle and in ways that stabilize the economy. This automatic response, or built-in stability, constitutes nondiscretionary (or "passive" or "automatic") budgetary policy and results from the makeup of most tax systems. We did not include this built-in stability in our discussion of fiscal policy because we implicitly assumed that the same amount of tax revenue was being collected at each level of GDP. But the actual U.S. tax system is such that *net tax revenues* vary directly with GDP. (Net taxes are tax revenues less transfers and subsidies. From here on, we will use the simpler "taxes" to mean "net taxes.")

Virtually any tax will yield more tax revenue as GDP rises. In particular, personal income taxes have progressive rates and thus generate more-than-proportionate increases in tax revenues as GDP expands. Furthermore, as GDP rises and more goods and services are purchased, revenues from corporate income taxes and from sales taxes and excise taxes also increase. And, similarly, revenues from payroll taxes rise as economic expansion creates more jobs. Conversely, when GDP declines, tax receipts from all these sources also decline.

Transfer payments (or "negative taxes") behave in the opposite way from tax revenues. Unemployment compensation payments and welfare payments decrease during economic expansion and increase during economic contraction.

Automatic or Built-In Stabilizers

A **built-in stabilizer** is anything that increases the government's budget deficit (or reduces its budget surplus) during a recession and increases its budget surplus (or reduces its budget deficit) during an expansion without requiring explicit action by policymakers. As Figure 30.3 reveals, this is precisely what the U.S. tax system does. Government expenditures G are fixed and assumed to be independent of the level of GDP. Congress decides on a

particular level of spending, but it does not determine the magnitude of tax revenues. Instead, it establishes tax rates, and the tax revenues then vary directly with the level of GDP that the economy achieves. Line T represents that direct relationship between tax revenues and GDP.

Economic Importance The economic importance of the direct relationship between tax receipts and GDP becomes apparent when we consider that:

- Taxes reduce spending and aggregate demand.
- Reductions in spending are desirable when the economy is moving toward inflation, whereas increases in spending are desirable when the economy is slumping.

As shown in Figure 30.3, tax revenues automatically increase as GDP rises during prosperity, and since taxes reduce household and business spending, they restrain the economic expansion. That is, as the economy moves toward a higher GDP, tax revenues automatically rise and move the budget from deficit toward surplus. In Figure 30.3, observe that the high and perhaps inflationary income level GDP_3 automatically generates a contractionary budget surplus.

Conversely, as GDP falls during recession, tax revenues automatically decline, increasing spending and cushioning the economic contraction. With a falling GDP, tax receipts decline and move the government's budget from surplus toward deficit. In Figure 30.3, the low level of income GDP_1 will automatically yield an expansionary budget deficit.

Tax Progressivity Figure 30.3 reveals that the size of the automatic budget deficits or surpluses—and therefore built-in stability—depends on the responsiveness of tax revenues to changes in GDP. If tax revenues change sharply as GDP changes, the slope of line T in the figure will be steep and the vertical distances between T and G (the deficits or surpluses) will be large. If tax revenues change very little when GDP changes, the slope will be gentle and built-in stability will be low.

The steepness of T in Figure 30.3 depends on the tax system itself. In a **progressive tax system,** the average tax rate (= tax revenue/GDP) rises with GDP. In a **proportional tax system,** the average tax rate remains constant as GDP rises. In a **regressive tax system,** the average tax rate falls as GDP rises. The progressive tax system has the steepest tax line T of the three. However, tax revenues will rise with GDP under both the progressive and the proportional tax systems, and they may rise, fall, or stay the same under a regressive tax system. The main point is this: The more progressive the tax system, the greater the economy's built-in stability.

FIGURE 30.3 Built-in stability. Tax revenues T vary directly with GDP, and government spending G is assumed to be independent of GDP. As GDP falls in a recession, deficits occur automatically and help alleviate the recession. As GDP rises during expansion, surpluses occur automatically and help offset possible inflation.

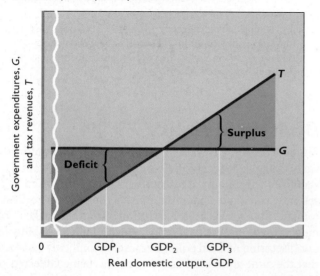

The built-in stability provided by the U.S. tax system has reduced the severity of business fluctuations, perhaps by as much as 8 to 10 percent of the change in GDP that otherwise would have occurred.[1] But built-in stabilizers can only diminish, not eliminate, swings in real GDP. Discretionary fiscal policy (changes in tax rates and expenditures) or monetary policy (central bank–caused changes in interest rates) will be needed to correct a recession or inflation of any appreciable magnitude.

Evaluating Fiscal Policy

How can we determine whether a government's discretionary fiscal policy is expansionary, neutral, or contractionary? We cannot simply examine the actual budget deficits or surpluses that take place under the current policy because they will necessarily include the automatic changes in tax revenues that accompany every change in GDP. In addition, the expansionary or contractionary strength of any change in discretionary fiscal policy depends not on its absolute size but on how large it is relative to the size of the economy. So, in evaluating the status of fiscal policy, we must adjust deficits and surpluses to eliminate automatic changes in tax revenues and also compare the sizes of the adjusted budget deficits and surpluses to the level of potential GDP.

Standardized Budget

Economists use the **standardized budget** (also called the *full-employment budget*) to adjust actual Federal budget deficits and surpluses to account for the changes in tax revenues that happen automatically whenever GDP changes. The standardized budget measures what the Federal budget deficit or surplus would have been under existing tax rates and government spending levels if the economy had achieved its full-employment level of GDP (its potential output). The idea essentially is to compare *actual* government expenditures with the tax revenues *that would have occurred* if the economy had achieved full-employment GDP. That procedure removes budget deficits or surpluses that arise simply because of changes in GDP and thus tell us nothing about whether the government's current discretionary fiscal policy is fundamentally expansionary, contractionary, or neutral.

Consider Figure 30.4a, where line *G* represents government expenditures and line *T* represents tax revenues. In full-employment year 1, government expenditures of $500 billion equal tax revenues of $500 billion, as indicated

by the intersection of lines *G* and *T* at point *a*. The standardized budget deficit in year 1 is zero—government expenditures equal the tax revenues forthcoming at the full-employment output GDP₁. Obviously, the full-employment deficit *as a percentage of potential GDP* is also zero. The government's fiscal policy is neutral.

Now suppose that a recession occurs and GDP falls from GDP₁ to GDP₂, as shown in Figure 30.4a. Let's also assume that the government takes no discretionary action, so lines *G* and *T* remain as shown in the figure. Tax revenues automatically fall to $450 billion (point *c*) at GDP₂, while government spending remains unaltered at $500 billion (point *b*). A $50 billion budget deficit (represented by distance *bc*) arises. But this **cyclical deficit** is simply a by-product of the economy's slide into recession, not the result of discretionary fiscal actions by the government. We would be wrong to conclude from this deficit that the government is engaging in an expansionary fiscal policy. The government's fiscal policy has not changed. It is still neutral.

That fact is highlighted when we consider the standardized budget deficit for year 2 in Figure 30.4a. The $500 billion of government expenditures in year 2 is shown by *b* on line *G*. And, as shown by *a* on line *T*, $500 billion of tax revenues would have occurred if the economy had achieved its full-employment GDP. Because both *b* and *a* represent $500 billion, the standardized budget deficit in year 2 is zero, as is this deficit as a percentage of potential GDP. Since the standardized deficits are zero in both years, we know that government did not change its discretionary fiscal policy, even though a recession occurred and an actual deficit of $50 billion resulted.

Next, consider Figure 30.4b. Suppose that real output declined from full-employment GDP₃ to GDP₄. But also suppose that the Federal government responded to the recession by reducing tax rates in year 4, as represented by the downward shift of the tax line from *T*₁ to *T*₂. What has happened to the size of the standardized deficit? Government expenditures in year 4 are $500 billion, as shown by *e*. We compare that amount with the $475 billion of tax revenues that would occur if the economy achieved its full-employment GDP. That is, we compare position *e* on line *G* with position *h* on line *T*₂. The $25 billion of tax revenues by which *e* exceeds *h* is the standardized budget deficit for year 4. As a percentage of potential GDP, the standardized budget deficit has increased from zero in year 3 (before the tax-rate cut) to some positive percent [= ($25 billion/GDP₃) × 100] in year 4. This increase in the relative size of the full-employment deficit between the two years reveals that the new fiscal policy is *expansionary*.

In contrast, if we observed a standardized deficit (as a percentage of potential GDP) of zero in one year, followed

[1]Alan J. Auerbach and Daniel Feenberg, "The Significance of Federal Taxes as Automatic Stabilizers," *Journal of Economic Perspectives*, Summer 2000, p. 54.

FIGURE 30.4 Standardized deficits. (a) In the left-hand graph, the standardized deficit is zero at the full-employment output GDP_1. But it is also zero at the recessionary output GDP_2 because the $500 billion of government expenditures at GDP_2 equals the $500 billion of tax revenues that would be forthcoming at the full-employment GDP_1. There has been no change in fiscal policy. (b) In the right-hand graph, discretionary fiscal policy, as reflected in the downward shift of the tax line from T_1 to T_2, has increased the standardized budget deficit from zero in year 3 to $25 billion in year 4. This is found by comparing the $500 billion of government spending in year 4 with the $475 billion of taxes that would accrue at the full-employment GDP_3. Such a rise in the standardized deficit (as a percentage of potential GDP) identifies an expansionary fiscal policy.

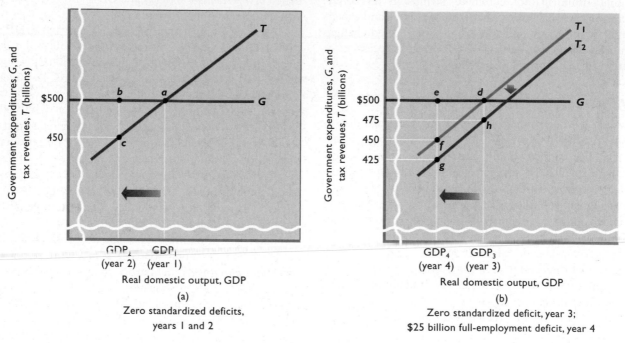

(a)
Zero standardized deficits,
years 1 and 2

(b)
Zero standardized deficit, year 3;
$25 billion full-employment deficit, year 4

by a standardized budget surplus in the next, we could conclude that fiscal policy has changed from being neutral to being contractionary. Because the standardized budget adjusts for automatic changes in tax revenues, the increase in the standardized budget surplus reveals that government either decreased its spending (G) or increased tax rates such that tax revenues (T) increased. These changes in G and T are precisely the discretionary actions that we have identified as elements of a *contractionary* fiscal policy.

Recent U.S. Fiscal Policy

Table 30.1 lists the actual Federal budget deficits and surpluses (column 2) and the standardized deficits and surpluses (column 3), as percentages of actual and potential GDP, respectively, for recent years. Observe that the standardized deficits are generally smaller than the actual deficits. This is because the actual deficits include cyclical deficits, whereas the standardized deficits do not. The latter deficits provide the information needed to assess discretionary fiscal policy and determine whether it is expansionary, contractionary, or neutral.

Column 3 shows that fiscal policy was expansionary in the early 1990s. Consider 1992, for example. From the table we see that the actual budget deficit was 4.5 percent

TABLE 30.1 Federal Deficits (−) and Surpluses (+) as Percentages of GDP, 1992–2007

(1) Year	(2) Actual Deficit − or Surplus +	(3) Standardized Deficit − or Surplus +[*]
1992	−4.5	−2.9
1993	−3.8	−2.9
1994	−2.9	−2.1
1995	−2.2	−2.0
1996	−1.4	−1.2
1997	−0.3	−1.0
1998	+0.8	−0.4
1999	+1.4	+0.1
2000	+2.5	+1.1
2001	+1.3	+1.0
2002	−1.5	−1.2
2003	−3.4	−2.5
2004	−3.5	−2.4
2005	−2.6	−1.9
2006	−1.9	−1.8
2007	−1.3	−1.4

[*]As a percentage of potential GDP.

Source: Congressional Budget Office, **www.cbo.gov.**

of GDP and the standardized budget deficit was 2.9 percent of potential GDP. The economy was recovering from the 1990–1991 recession, so tax revenues were relatively low. But even if the economy had been at full employment in 1992, with the greater tax revenues that would have implied, the Federal budget would have been in deficit by 2.9 percent. And that percentage was greater than the deficits in the prior 2 years. So the standardized budget deficit in 1992 clearly reflected expansionary fiscal policy.

But the large standardized budget deficits were projected to continue even when the economy fully recovered from the 1990–1991 recession. The concern was that the large actual and standardized deficits were inappropriate for a full-employment economy. In 1993 the Clinton administration and Congress increased personal income and corporate income tax rates to prevent these potential outcomes. Observe from column 3 of Table 30.1 that the standardized budget deficits shrank each year and eventually gave way to surpluses in 1999, 2000, and 2001.

U.S. stock markets crashed in 2000 and the economy began to slow later that year, with the economy slipping into recession by March 2001. The Congress and the Bush administration responded by passing tax cuts of $44 billion in 2001 and $52 billion in 2002. This fiscal policy action helped to simulate the economy and offset the recession as well as the second economic blow that arrived with the September 11, 2001, terrorist attacks. Further tax cuts totaling $122 billion over two years as well as an extension of unemployment benefits were passed in March 2002.

As seen in Table 30.1, the standardized budget moved from a *surplus* of 1.1 percent of potential GDP in 2000 to a *deficit* of 1.2 percent in 2002. Clearly, fiscal policy had turned expansionary. Nevertheless, the economy remained very sluggish through 2002 and into 2003. In June of that year, Congress again cut taxes, this time by an enormous $350 billion over several years. Specifically, the tax legislation accelerated the reduction of marginal tax rates already scheduled for future years and slashed tax rates on income from dividends and capital gains. It also increased tax breaks for families and small businesses. This tax package increased the standardized budget deficit as a percentage of potential GDP to –2.5 percent in 2003. The economy strengthened and real output grew between 2003 and 2007. Full employment was restored. But starting in the summer of 2007, a crisis in the market for mortgage loans occurred and spread quickly to other financial markets. (We discuss this crisis in detail in Chapter 33.) Households in particular retrenched on their spending and in the last quarter of 2007 the economy slowed. With economists

GLOBAL PERSPECTIVE 30.1

Standardized Budget Deficits or Surpluses as a Percentage of Potential GDP, Selected Nations

In 2007 some nations had standardized budget surpluses, while others had standardized budget deficits. These surpluses and deficits varied as a percentage of each nation's potential GDP. Generally, the surpluses represented contractionary fiscal policy and the deficits expansionary fiscal policy.

Standardized Budget Surplus or Deficit as a Percentage of Potential GDP, 2007

Source: Organization for Economic Cooperation and Development, *OECD Economic Outlook,* **www.oecd.org.**

projecting a 50-50 prospect of a recession in 2008, Congress acted quickly to enact expansionary fiscal policy in the form of the Economic Stimulus Act of 2008. This law provided a total of $152 billion in stimulus. Some of it came in the form of tax breaks for businesses, but most of it arrived in the form of checks of up to $600 each that were mailed to taxpayers, veterans, and Social Security recipients in May of 2008. It was hoped that those receiving checks would spend the money, thereby boosting consumption and aggregate demand. We urge you to track the economy to see if it receded in 2008 by going to the Bureau of Economic Analysis Web site, **www.bea.gov,** and checking changes in real GDP from quarter to quarter. **(Key Question 6)**

Global Perspective 30.1 shows the magnitudes of the standardized deficits or surpluses of a number of countries in a recent year.

Budget Deficits and Projections

Figure 30.5 shows the absolute magnitudes of recent U.S. budget surpluses and deficits. It also shows the projected

FIGURE 30.5 Federal budget deficits and surpluses, actual and projected, fiscal years 1994–2014 (in billions of nominal dollars). The annual budget deficits of 1992 through 1997 gave way to budget surpluses from 1998 through 2001. Deficits reappeared in 2002 and are projected to continue through 2011.

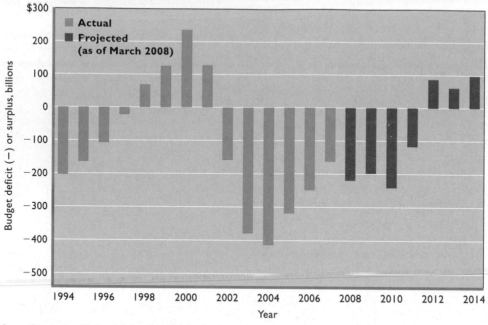

Source: Congressional Budget Office, **www.cbo.gov.**

future deficits or surpluses as published by the Congressional Budget Office (CBO). The United States has been experiencing large budget deficits that are expected to continue for several years. But projected deficits and surpluses are subject to large and frequent changes, as government alters its fiscal policy and GDP growth accelerates or slows. So we suggest that you update this figure by going to the Congressional Budget Office Web site, **www.cbo.gov**, and selecting Budget Projections, which are listed under Budget and Economic Information. On that page, click on the "pdf" hyperlink to open an Adobe Acrobat file containing the CBO's Baseline Budget Projections. The relevant numbers are in the row Deficit (−) or Surplus.

Social Security Considerations

The surpluses and deficits in Figure 30.5 include all tax revenues, even those obligated for future Social Security payments. Recall from the Last Word in Chapter 4 that Social Security is basically a "pay-as-you-go plan" in which the mandated benefits paid out each year are financed by the payroll tax revenues received each year. But current tax rates now bring in more revenue than current payouts, in

partial preparation for the massive increase in payouts that the system will begin having to make as the baby boom generation enters retirement over the next two decades. The Federal government saves the excess revenues by purchasing U.S. securities and holding them in the Social Security trust fund.

Some economists argue that these present Social Security surpluses ($288 billion in 2007) should be subtracted from Federal government revenue when calculating present Federal deficits. Because these surpluses represent future government obligations on a dollar-for-dollar basis, they should not be considered revenue offsets to current government spending. Without the Social Security surpluses, the total budget deficit in 2007 would have been $450 billion rather than the $162 billion shown.

Problems, Criticisms, and Complications

Economists recognize that governments may encounter a number of significant problems in enacting and applying fiscal policy.

Problems of Timing

Several problems of timing may arise in connection with fiscal policy.

- *Recognition lag* The recognition lag is the time between the beginning of recession or inflation and the certain awareness that it is actually happening. This lag arises because the economy does not move smoothly through the business cycle. Even during good times, the economy has slow months interspersed with months of rapid growth and expansion. This makes recognizing a recession difficult since several slow months will have to happen in succession before people can conclude with any confidence that the good times are over and a recession has begun. The same is true with inflation. Even periods of moderate inflation have months of high inflation—so that several high-inflation months must come in sequence before people can confidently conclude that inflation has moved to a higher level. Attempts to get a jump on the recognition lag by attempting to predict the future course of the economy also have proven to be largely futile (see this chapter's Last Word on the index of leading indicators). As a result, the economy is often 4 to 6 months into a recession or inflation before the situation is clearly discernible in the relevant statistics. Due to this recognition lag, the economic downslide or the inflation may become more serious than it would have if the situation had been identified and acted on sooner.

- *Administrative lag* The wheels of democratic government turn slowly. There will typically be a significant lag between the time the need for fiscal action is recognized and the time action is taken. Following the terrorist attacks of September 11, 2001, the U.S. Congress was stalemated for 5 months before passing a compromise economic stimulus law in March 2002. (In contrast, the Federal Reserve began lowering interest rates the week after the attacks.)

- *Operational lag* A lag also occurs between the time fiscal action is taken and the time that action affects output, employment, or the price level. Although changes in tax rates can be put into effect relatively quickly once new laws are passed, government spending on public works—new dams, interstate highways, and so on—requires long planning periods and even longer periods of construction. Such spending is of questionable use in offsetting short (for example, 6- to 12-month) periods of recession. Consequently, discretionary fiscal policy has increasingly relied on tax changes rather than on changes in spending as its main tool.

Political Considerations

Fiscal policy is conducted in a political arena. That reality not only may slow the enactment of fiscal policy but also may create the potential for political considerations swamping economic considerations in its formulation. It is a human trait to rationalize actions and policies that are in one's self-interest. Politicians are very human—they want to get reelected. A strong economy at election time will certainly help them. So they may favor large tax cuts under the guise of expansionary fiscal policy even though that policy is economically inappropriate. Similarly, they may rationalize increased government spending on popular items such as farm subsidies, health care, highways, education, and homeland security.

At the extreme, elected officials and political parties might collectively "hijack" fiscal policy for political purposes, cause inappropriate changes in aggregate demand, and thereby cause (rather than avert) economic fluctuations. For instance, before an election, they may try to stimulate the economy to improve their reelection hopes. And then after the election, they may try to use contractionary fiscal policy to dampen the excessive aggregate demand that they caused with their preelection stimulus. In short, elected officials may cause so-called **political business cycles.** Such scenarios are difficult to document and prove, but there is little doubt that political considerations weigh heavily in the formulation of fiscal policy. The question is how often those political considerations run counter to "sound economics."

Future Policy Reversals

Fiscal policy may fail to achieve its intended objectives if households expect future reversals of policy. Consider a tax cut, for example. If taxpayers believe the tax reduction is temporary, they may save a large portion of their tax cut, reasoning that rates will return to their previous level in the future. They save more now so that they will be able draw on this extra savings to maintain their future consumption levels if taxes do indeed rise again in the future. So a tax reduction thought to be temporary may not increase present consumption spending and aggregate demand by as much as our simple model (Figure 30.1) suggests.

The opposite may be true for a tax increase. If taxpayers think it is temporary, they may reduce their saving to pay the tax while maintaining their present consumption. They may reason they can restore their saving when the tax rate again falls. So the tax increase may not reduce current consumption and aggregate demand by as much as policymakers intended.

To the extent that this so-called *consumption smoothing* occurs over time, fiscal policy will lose some of its strength. The lesson is that tax-rate changes that households view as permanent are more likely to alter consumption and aggregate demand than tax changes they view as temporary.

Offsetting State and Local Finance

The fiscal policies of state and local governments are frequently *pro-cyclical*, meaning that they worsen rather than correct recession or inflation. Unlike the Federal government, most state and local governments face constitutional or other legal requirements to balance their budgets. Like households and private businesses, state and local governments increase their expenditures during prosperity and cut them during recession. During the Great Depression of the 1930s, most of the increase in Federal spending was offset by decreases in state and local spending. During and immediately following the recession of 2001, many state and local governments had to offset lower tax revenues resulting from the reduced personal income and spending of their citizens. They offset the decline in revenues by raising tax rates, imposing new taxes, and reducing spending.

Crowding-Out Effect

Another potential flaw of fiscal policy is the so-called **crowding-out effect:** An expansionary fiscal policy (deficit spending) may increase the interest rate and reduce investment spending, thereby weakening or canceling the stimulus of the expansionary policy. The rising interest rate might also potentially crowd out interest-sensitive consumption spending (such as purchasing automobiles on credit). But since investment is the most volatile component of GDP, the crowding-out effect focuses its attention on investment and whether the stimulus provided by deficit spending may be partly or even fully neutralized by an offsetting reduction in investment spending.

To see the potential problem, realize that whenever the government borrows money (as it must if it is deficit spending), it increases the overall demand for money. If the monetary authorities are holding the money supply constant, this increase in demand will raise the price paid for borrowing money: the interest rate. Because investment spending varies inversely with the interest rate, some investment will be choked off or "crowded out."

ORIGIN OF THE IDEA

O 30.2

Crowding out

Economists vary in their opinions about the strength of the crowding-out effect. An important thing to keep in mind is that crowding out is likely to be less of a problem when the economy is in recession. This is true because investment demand tends to be low during recessions. Why? Because sales are slow during recessions, so that most businesses end up with substantial amounts of excess capacity. As a result, they do not have much incentive to add new machinery or build new factories. After all, why should they add capacity when some of the capacity they already have is lying idle?

With investment demand low during a recession, the crowding-out effect is likely to be very small. Simply put, with investment demand at such a low level due to the recession, there is not as much investment for the government to crowd out. Even if deficit spending does increase the interest rate, the effect on investment may be fully offset by the improved investment prospects that businesses expect from the fiscal stimulus.

By contrast, when the economy is operating at or near full capacity, investment demand is likely to be quite high so that crowding out is likely to be a much more serious problem. When the economy is booming, factories will be running at or near full capacity and firms will have high investment demand for two reasons. First, equipment running at full capacity wears out fast, so firms will be doing a lot of investment just to replace machinery and equipment that wears out and depreciates. Second, the economy is likely to be growing overall so that firms will be investing not just to replace worn-out equipment in order to keep their productive capacity from deteriorating, but also so that they can make *additions* to their productive capacity.

Current Thinking on Fiscal Policy

Where do these complications leave us as to the advisability and effectiveness of discretionary fiscal policy? In view of the complications and uncertain outcomes of fiscal policy, some economists argue that it is better not to engage in it at all. Those holding that view point to the superiority of monetary policy (changes in interest rates engineered by the Federal Reserve) as a stabilizing device or believe that most economic fluctuations tend to be mild and self-correcting.

But most economists believe that fiscal policy remains an important, useful policy lever in the government's macroeconomic toolkit. The current popular view is that fiscal policy can help push the economy in a particular direction but cannot fine-tune it to a precise macroeconomic outcome. Mainstream economists generally agree that monetary policy is the best month-to-month stabilization tool for the U.S. economy. If monetary policy is doing its job, the government should maintain a relatively neutral fiscal policy, with a standardized budget deficit or surplus of no more than 2 percent of potential GDP. It should hold major discretionary fiscal policy in reserve to help counter situations where recession threatens to be deep and long-lasting or where a substantial reduction in aggregate demand might help to eliminate a large inflationary gap and aid the Federal Reserve in its efforts to quell the major bout of inflation caused by that large inflationary gap.

Finally, economists agree that proposed fiscal policy should be evaluated for its potential positive and negative impacts on long-run productivity growth. The short-run policy tools used for conducting active fiscal policy often have long-run impacts. Countercyclical fiscal policy should be shaped to strengthen, or at least not impede, the growth of long-run aggregate supply (shown as a rightward shift of the long-run aggregate supply curve in Figure 29.5). For example, a tax cut might be structured to enhance work effort, strengthen investment, and encourage innovation. Alternatively, an increase in government spending might center on preplanned projects for public capital (highways, mass transit, ports, airports), which are complementary to private investment and thus support long-term economic growth. **(Key Question 8)**

QUICK REVIEW 30.2

- Automatic changes in net taxes (taxes minus transfers) add a degree of built-in stability to the economy.

- The standardized budget compares government spending to the tax revenues that would accrue if there were full employment; changes in standardized budget deficits or surpluses (as percentages of potential GDP) reveal whether fiscal policy is expansionary, neutral, or contractionary.

- Standardized budget deficits are distinct from cyclical deficits, which simply reflect declines in tax revenues resulting from reduced GDP.

- Time lags, political problems, expectations, and state and local finances complicate fiscal policy.

- The crowding-out effect indicates that an expansionary fiscal policy may increase the interest rate and reduce investment spending.

The Public Debt

The national or **public debt** is essentially the total accumulation of the deficits (minus the surpluses) the Federal government has incurred through time. These deficits have emerged mainly because of war financing, recessions, and fiscal policy. In 2007 the total public debt was $9.01 trillion—$4.27 trillion held by the public and $4.73 trillion held by Federal agencies and the Federal

Reserve. (You can find the size of the public debt, to the penny, at the Web site of the Department of Treasury, Bureau of the Public Debt, at **www.treasurydirect.gov/ NP/BPDLogin?application=np**).

Ownership

The total public debt of $9.01 trillion represents the total amount of money owed by the Federal government to the holders of **U.S. securities:** financial instruments issued by the Federal government to borrow money to finance expenditures that exceed tax revenues. These U.S. securities (loan instruments) are of four types: Treasury bills (short-term securities), Treasury notes (medium-term securities), Treasury bonds (long-term securities), and U.S. saving bonds (long-term, nonmarketable bonds).

Figure 30.6 shows that the public held 47 percent of the Federal debt in 2007 and that Federal government agencies and the Federal Reserve (the U.S. central bank) held the other 53 percent. In this case the "public" consists of individuals here and abroad, state and local governments, and U.S. financial institutions. Foreigners held

FIGURE 30.6 Ownership of the total public debt, 2007.
The total public debt can be divided into the proportion held by the public (47 percent) and the proportion held by Federal agencies and the Federal Reserve System (53 percent). Of the total debt, 25 percent is foreign-owned.

Debt held outside the Federal government and Federal Reserve (47%)

Debt held by the Federal government and Federal Reserve (53%)

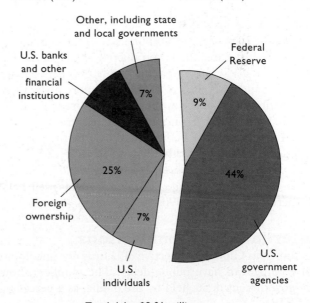

Other, including state and local governments

U.S. banks and other financial institutions

Federal Reserve

7%

9%

25%

44%

Foreign ownership

7%

U.S. individuals

U.S. government agencies

Total debt: $9.01 trillion

Source: U.S. Treasury, **www.fms.treas.gov/bulletin.**

FIGURE 30.7 **Federal debt held by the public as a percentage of GDP, 1970–2007.** As a percentage of GDP, the Federal debt held by the public (held outside the Federal Reserve and Federal government agencies) increased sharply over the 1980–1995 period and declined significantly between 1995 and 2001. Since 2001, the percentage has gone up again, but remains lower than it was in the 1990s.

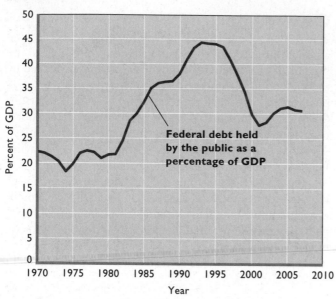

Source: Economic Report of the President, **www.gpoaccess.gov/eop/index.html.**

GLOBAL PERSPECTIVE 30.2

Publicly Held Debt: International Comparisons

Although the United States has the world's largest public debt, a number of other nations have larger debts as percentages of their GDPs.

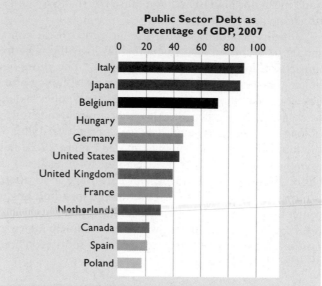

Source: Organization for Economic Cooperation and Development, *OECD Economic Outlook,* **www.oecd.org.** These debt calculations included Federal, state, and local debt (not just Federal debt as in Figure 30.7).

about 25 percent of the total debt in 2007. So, most of the debt is held internally, not externally. Americans owe three-fourths of the debt to Americans.

Debt and GDP

A simple statement of the absolute size of the debt ignores the fact that the wealth and productive ability of the U.S. economy is also vast. A wealthy, highly productive nation can incur and carry a large public debt more easily than a poor nation can. A more meaningful measure of the public debt relates it to an economy's GDP. Figure 30.7 shows the relative size of the Federal debt held by the public (as opposed to that held by the Federal Reserve and Federal agencies) over time. This percentage—30.6 percent in 2007—has increased since 2001 but remains well below the percentages in the 1990s.

International Comparisons

As shown in Global Perspective 30.2, it is not uncommon for countries to have public debts. The numbers shown are government debts held by the public, as a percentage of GDP.

Interest Charges

Many economists conclude that the primary burden of the debt is the annual interest charge accruing on the bonds sold to finance the debt. In 2007 interest on the total public debt was $237 billion, which is now the fourth-largest item in the Federal budget (behind income security, national defense, and health).

Interest payments were 1.7 percent of GDP in 2007. That percentage reflects the level of taxation (the average tax rate) required to pay the interest on the public debt. That is, in 2007 the Federal government had to collect taxes equal to 1.7 percent of GDP to service the total public debt. This percentage was down from 3.2 percent in 1990 and 2.3 percent in 2000 thanks to relatively low interest costs of borrowing and a smaller debt-to-GDP ratio.

False Concerns

You may wonder if the large public debt might bankrupt the United States or at least place a tremendous burden on your children and grandchildren. Fortunately, these are false concerns. People were wondering the same things 50 years ago!

Bankruptcy

The large U.S. public debt does not threaten to bankrupt the Federal government, leaving it unable to meet its financial obligations. There are two main reasons: refinancing and taxation.

Refinancing
The public debt is easily refinanced. As portions of the debt come due on maturing Treasury bills, notes, and bonds each month, the government does not cut expenditures or raise taxes to provide the funds required. Rather, it refinances the debt by selling new bonds and using the proceeds to pay holders of the maturing bonds. The new bonds are in strong demand because lenders can obtain a relatively good interest return with no risk of default by the Federal government.

Taxation
The Federal government has the constitutional authority to levy and collect taxes. A tax increase is a government option for gaining sufficient revenue to pay interest and principal on the public debt. Financially distressed private households and corporations cannot extract themselves from their financial difficulties by taxing the public. If their incomes or sales revenues fall short of their expenses, they can indeed go bankrupt. But the Federal government does have the option to impose new taxes or increase existing tax rates if necessary to finance its debt.

Burdening Future Generations

In 2007 public debt per capita was $29,987. Was each child born in 2007 handed a $29,987 bill from the Federal government? Not really. The public debt does not impose as much of a burden on future generations as commonly thought.

The United States owes a substantial portion of the public debt to itself. U.S. citizens and institutions (banks, businesses, insurance companies, governmental agencies, and trust funds) own about 75 percent of the U.S. government securities. Although that part of the public debt is a liability to Americans (as taxpayers), it is simultaneously an asset to Americans (as holders of Treasury bills, Treasury notes, Treasury bonds, and U.S. savings bonds).

To eliminate the American-owned part of the public debt would require a gigantic transfer payment from Americans to Americans. Taxpayers would pay higher taxes, and holders of the debt would receive an equal amount for

their U.S. securities. Purchasing power in the United States would not change. Only the repayment of the 25 percent of the public debt owned by foreigners would negatively impact U.S. purchasing power.

The public debt increased sharply during the Second World War. But the decision to finance military purchases through the sale of government bonds did not shift the economic burden of the war to future generations. The economic cost of the Second World War consisted of the civilian goods society had to forgo in shifting scarce resources to war goods production (recall production possibilities analysis). Regardless of whether society financed this reallocation through higher taxes or through borrowing, the real economic burden of the war would have been the same. That burden was borne almost entirely by those who lived during the war. They were the ones who did without a multitude of consumer goods to enable the United States to arm itself and its allies. The next generation inherited the debt from the war but also an equal amount of government bonds. It also inherited the enormous benefits from the victory—namely, preserved political and economic systems at home and the "export" of those systems to Germany, Italy, and Japan. Those outcomes enhanced postwar U.S. economic growth and helped raise the standard of living of future generations of Americans.

Substantive Issues

Although the preceding issues relating to the public debt are false concerns, a number of substantive issues are not. Economists, however, attach varying degrees of importance to them.

Income Distribution
The distribution of ownership of government securities is highly uneven. Some people own much more than the $29,987-per-person portion of government securities; other people own less or none at all. In general, the ownership of the public debt is concentrated among wealthier groups, who own a large percentage of all stocks and bonds. Because the overall Federal tax system is only slightly progressive, payment of interest on the public debt mildly increases income inequality. Income is transferred from people who, on average, have lower incomes to the higher-income bondholders. If greater income equality is one of society's goals, then this redistribution is undesirable.

Incentives
The current public debt necessitates annual interest payments of $237 billion. With no increase in the size of the

debt, that interest charge must be paid out of tax revenues. Higher taxes may dampen incentives to bear risk, to innovate, to invest, and to work. So, in this indirect way, a large public debt may impair economic growth.

Foreign-Owned Public Debt

The 25 percent of the U.S. debt held by citizens and institutions of foreign countries *is* an economic burden to Americans. Because we do not owe that portion of the debt "to ourselves," the payment of interest and principal on this **external public debt** enables foreigners to buy some of our output. In return for the benefits derived from the borrowed funds, the United States transfers goods and services to foreign lenders. Of course, Americans also own debt issued by foreign governments, so payment of principal and interest by those governments transfers some of their goods and services to Americans. **(Key Question 10)**

Crowding-Out Effect Revisited

A potentially more serious problem is the financing (and continual refinancing) of the large public debt, which can transfer a real economic burden to future generations by passing on to them a smaller stock of capital goods. This possibility involves the previously discussed crowding-out effect: the idea that public borrowing drives up real interest rates, which reduces private investment spending. As we mentioned earlier, if public borrowing only happened during recessions, crowding out would not likely be much of a problem. Because private investment demand tends to be low during recessions, any increase in interest rates caused by public borrowing will at most cause a small reduction in investment spending. By contrast, a large public debt may cause crowding-out problems because the need to continuously refinance the debt will entail large amounts of borrowing not just during recessions but also during times when the economy is at full employment and investment demand tends to be very high. In such situations, any increase in interest rates caused by the borrowing necessary to refinance the debt may result in a substantial decline in investment spending. If the amount of current investment crowded out is extensive, future generations will inherit an economy with a smaller production capacity and, other things equal, a lower standard of living.

A Graphical Look at Crowding Out

We know from Chapter 27 that the real interest rate is inversely related to the amount of investment spending. When graphed, that relationship is shown as a downward-sloping investment demand curve, such as either

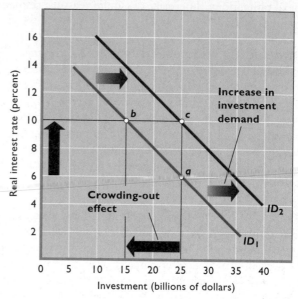

FIGURE 30.8 The investment demand curve and the crowding-out effect. If the investment demand curve (ID_1) is fixed, the increase in the interest rate from 6 percent to 10 percent caused by financing a large public debt will move the economy from a to b and crowd out $10 billion of private investment and decrease the size of the capital stock inherited by future generations. However, if the public goods enabled by the debt improve the investment prospects of businesses, the private investment demand curve will shift rightward, as from ID_1 to ID_2. That shift may offset the crowding-out effect wholly or in part. In this case, it moves the economy from a to c.

ID_1 or ID_2 in Figure 30.8. Let's first consider curve ID_1. (Ignore curve ID_2 for now.) Suppose that government borrowing increases the real interest rate from 6 percent to 10 percent. Investment spending will then fall from $25 billion to $15 billion, as shown by the economy's move from a to b. That is, the financing of the debt will compete with the financing of private investment projects and crowd out $10 billion of private investment. So the stock of private capital handed down to future generations will be $10 billion less than it would have been without the need to finance the public debt.

Public Investments and Public-Private Complementarities

But even with crowding out, two factors could partly or fully offset the net economic burden shifted to future generations. First, just as private expenditures may involve either consumption or investment, so it is with public goods. Part of the government spending enabled by the public debt is for public investment outlays (for example, highways, mass transit systems, and electric power facilities) and "human capital" (for example, investments in education, job training, and health). Like private expenditures on machinery and equipment,

One of Several Tools Policymakers Use to Develop Forecasts about the Future Direction of Real GDP Is a Monthly Index of 10 Variables That in the Past Have Sometimes Provided Correct Advance Notice of Changes in GDP.

The Conference Board's *index of leading indicators* has often (but not always!) reached a peak or a trough in advance of corresponding turns in the business cycle.* Thus, changes in this composite index of 10 economic variables provide a rough guide to the future direction of the economy. Such advance warning helps policymakers formulate appropriate macroeconomic policy.

Here is how each of the 10 components of the index would change if it were predicting a decline in real GDP. The opposite changes would forecast a rise in real GDP.

1. *Average workweek* Decreases in the length of the average workweek of production workers in manufacturing foretell declines in future manufacturing output and possible declines in real GDP.

2. *Initial claims for unemployment insurance* Higher first-time claims for unemployment insurance are associated with falling employment and subsequently sagging real GDP.

3. *New orders for consumer goods* Decreases in the number of orders received by manufacturers for consumer goods portend reduced future production—a decline in real GDP.

4. *Vendor performance* Somewhat ironically, better on-time delivery by sellers of inputs indicates slackening business demand for final output and potentially falling real GDP.

5. *New orders for capital goods* A drop in orders for capital equipment and other investment goods implies reduced future spending by businesses and thus reduced aggregate demand and lower real GDP.

6. *Building permits for houses* Decreases in the number of building permits issued for new homes imply future declines in investment and therefore the possibility that real GDP will fall.

7. *Stock prices* Declines in stock prices often are reflections of expected declines in corporate sales and profits. Also, lower stock prices diminish consumer wealth, leading to possible cutbacks in consumer spending. Lower stock prices also make it less attractive for firms to issue new shares of stock as a way of raising funds for investment. Thus, declines in stock prices can mean declines in future aggregate demand and real GDP.

8. *Money supply* Decreases in the nation's money supply are associated with falling real GDP.

9. *Interest-rate spread* Increases in short-term nominal interest rates typically reflect monetary policies designed to slow the economy. Such policies have much less effect on long-term interest rates, which usually are higher than short-term rates. So a smaller difference between short-term interest rates and long-term interest rates suggests restrictive monetary policies and potentially a future decline in GDP.

10. *Consumer expectations* Less favorable consumer attitudes about future economic conditions, measured by an index of consumer expectations, foreshadow lower consumption spending and potential future declines in GDP.

None of these factors alone consistently predicts the future course of the economy. It is not unusual in any month, for example, for one or two of the indicators to be decreasing while the other indicators are increasing. Rather, changes in the composite of the 10 components are what in the past have provided advance notice of a change in the direction of GDP. To the extent that the index has been successful, the rule of thumb is that three successive monthly declines or increases in the index indicate the economy will soon turn in that same direction.

But while that rule of thumb has correctly signaled business fluctuations on many occasions, it leaves a lot to be desired. At times the index has provided false warnings of recessions that never happened. In other instances, recessions have so closely followed the downturn in the index that policymakers have not had sufficient time to make use of the "early" warning. Moreover, changing structural features of the economy have, on occasion, rendered the existing index obsolete and necessitated its revision.

Given these caveats, the index of leading indicators can best be thought of as a helpful but rather unreliable signaling device that authorities must employ with considerable caution when formulating macroeconomic policy.

---

*The Conference Board is a private, nonprofit research and business membership group, with more than 2700 corporate and other members in 60 nations. See **www.conferenceboard.org**.

those **public investments** increase the economy's future production capacity. Because of the financing through debt, the stock of public capital passed on to future generations may be higher than otherwise. That greater stock of public capital may offset the diminished stock of private capital resulting from the crowding-out effect, leaving overall production capacity unimpaired.

So-called public-private complementarities are a second factor that could reduce the crowding out effect. Some public and private investments are complementary. Thus, the public investment financed through the debt could spur some private-sector investment by increasing its expected rate of return. For example, a Federal building in a city may encourage private investment in the form of nearby office buildings, shops, and restaurants. Through its complementary effect, the spending on public capital may shift the private investment demand curve to the right, as from ID_1 to ID_2 in Figure 30.8. Even though the government borrowing boosts the interest rate from 6 percent to 10 percent, total private investment need not fall. In the case shown as the move from a to c in Figure 30.8, it remains at $25 billion. Of course, the increase in investment demand might be smaller than that shown. If it were smaller, the crowding-out effect

would not be fully offset. But the point is that an increase in investment demand may counter the decline in investment that would otherwise result from the higher interest rate. **(Key Question 13)**

QUICK REVIEW 30.3

- The U.S. public debt—$9.01 trillion in 2007—is essentially the total accumulation of Federal budget deficits minus surpluses over time; about 25 percent of the public debt is held by foreigners.
- As a percentage of GDP, the portion of the debt held by the public is lower today than it was in the mid-1990s and is in the middle range of such debts among major industrial nations.
- The Federal government is in no danger of going bankrupt because it needs only to refinance (not retire) the public debt and it can raise revenues, if needed, through higher taxes.
- The borrowing and interest payments associated with the public debt may (a) increase income inequality; (b) require higher taxes, which may dampen incentives; and (c) impede the growth of the nation's stock of capital through crowding out of private investment.

Summary

1. Fiscal policy consists of deliberate changes in government spending, taxes, or some combination of both to promote full employment, price-level stability, and economic growth. Fiscal policy requires increases in government spending, decreases in taxes, or both—a budget deficit—to increase aggregate demand and push an economy from a recession. Decreases in government spending, increases in taxes, or both—a budget surplus—are appropriate fiscal policy for dealing with demand-pull inflation.

2. Built-in stability arises from net tax revenues, which vary directly with the level of GDP. During recession, the Federal budget automatically moves toward a stabilizing deficit; during expansion, the budget automatically moves toward an anti-inflationary surplus. Built-in stability lessens, but does not fully correct, undesired changes in the real GDP.

3. The standardized budget measures the Federal budget deficit or surplus that would occur if the economy operated at full employment throughout the year. Cyclical deficits or surpluses are those that result from changes in GDP. Changes in the standardized deficit or surplus provide meaningful information as to whether the government's fiscal policy is expansionary, neutral, or contractionary. Changes in the

actual budget deficit or surplus do not, since such deficits or surpluses can include cyclical deficits or surpluses.

4. Certain problems complicate the enactment and implementation of fiscal policy. They include (a) timing problems associated with recognition, administrative, and operational lags; (b) the potential for misuse of fiscal policy for political rather than economic purposes; (c) the fact that state and local finances tend to be pro-cyclical; (d) potential ineffectiveness if households expect future policy reversals; and (e) the possibility of fiscal policy crowding out private investment.

5. Most economists believe that fiscal policy can help move the economy in a desired direction but cannot reliably be used to fine-tune the economy to a position of price stability and full employment. Nevertheless, fiscal policy is a valuable backup tool for aiding monetary policy in fighting significant recession or inflation.

6. The large Federal budget deficits of the 1980s and early 1990s prompted Congress in 1993 to increase tax rates and limit government spending. As a result of these policies, along with a very rapid and prolonged economic expansion, the deficits dwindled to $22 billion in 1997. Large budget surpluses occurred from 1998 through 2001. In 2001 the

Congressional Budget Office projected that $5 trillion of annual budget surpluses would accumulate between 2000 and 2010.

7. In 2001 the Bush administration and Congress chose to reduce marginal tax rates and phase out the Federal estate tax. A recession occurred in 2001, the stock market crashed, and Federal spending for the war on terrorism rocketed. The Federal budget swung from a surplus of $128 billion in 2001 to a deficit of $158 billion in 2002. In 2003 the Bush administration and Congress accelerated the tax reductions scheduled under the 2001 tax law and cut tax rates on capital gains and dividends. The purposes were to stimulate a sluggish economy. In 2007 the budget deficit was $162 billion and deficits are projected to continue through 2011 before surpluses again reemerge.

8. The public debt is the total accumulation of the government's deficits (minus surpluses) over time and consists of Treasury bills, Treasury notes, Treasury bonds, and U.S. savings bonds. In 2007 the U.S. public debt was $9.01 trillion, or $29,987 per person. The public (which here includes banks and state and local governments) holds 47 percent of that Federal debt; the Federal Reserve and Federal agencies hold the other 53 percent. Foreigners hold 25 percent of the Federal debt. Interest payments as a percentage of GDP were about 1.7 percent in 2007. This is down from 3.2 percent in 1990.

9. The concern that a large public debt may bankrupt the government is a false worry because (a) the debt needs only to be refinanced rather than refunded and (b) the Federal government has the power to increase taxes to make interest payments on the debt.

10. In general, the public debt is not a vehicle for shifting economic burdens to future generations. Americans inherit not only most of the public debt (a liability) but also most of the U.S. securities (an asset) that finance the debt.

11. More substantive problems associated with public debt include the following: (a) Payment of interest on the debt may increase income inequality. (b) Interest payments on the debt require higher taxes, which may impair incentives. (c) Paying interest or principal on the portion of the debt held by foreigners means a transfer of real output abroad. (d) Government borrowing to refinance or pay interest on the debt may increase interest rates and crowd out private investment spending, leaving future generations with a smaller stock of capital than they would have otherwise.

12. The increase in investment in public capital that may result from debt financing may partly or wholly offset the crowding-out effect of the public debt on private investment. Also, the added public investment may stimulate private investment, where the two are complements.

Terms and Concepts

fiscal policy	built-in stabilizer	political business cycle
Council of Economic Advisers (CEA)	progressive tax system	crowding-out effect
expansionary fiscal policy	proportional tax system	public debt
budget deficit	regressive tax system	U.S. securities
contractionary fiscal policy	standardized budget	external public debt
budget surplus	cyclical deficit	public investments

Study Questions

1. What is the role of the Council of Economic Advisers (CEA) as it relates to fiscal policy? Class assignment: Determine the names and educational backgrounds of the present members of the CEA. **LO1**

2. **KEY QUESTION** Assume that a hypothetical economy with an MPC of .8 is experiencing severe recession. By how much would government spending have to increase to shift the aggregate demand curve rightward by $25 billion? How large a tax cut would be needed to achieve the same increase in aggregate demand? Why the difference? Determine one possible combination of government spending increases and tax decreases that would accomplish the same goal. **LO1**

3. **KEY QUESTION** What are government's fiscal policy options for ending severe demand-pull inflation? Which of these fiscal options do you think might be favored by a person who wants to preserve the size of government? A person who thinks the public sector is too large? How does the "ratchet effect" affect anti-inflationary fiscal policy? **LO1**

4. (For students who were assigned Chapter 28) Use the aggregate expenditures model to show how government fiscal policy could eliminate either a recessionary expenditure gap or an inflationary expenditure gap (Figure 28.7). Explain how equal-size increases in *G* and *T* could eliminate a recessionary gap and how equal-size decreases in *G* and *T* could eliminate an inflationary gap. **LO1**

5. Explain how built-in (or automatic) stabilizers work. What are the differences between proportional, progressive, and regressive tax systems as they relate to an economy's built-in stability? **LO2**

6. **KEY QUESTION** Define the standardized budget, explain its significance, and state why it may differ from the actual budget. Suppose the full-employment, noninflationary level of real output is GDP_3 (not GDP_2) in the economy depicted in Figure 30.3. If the economy is operating at GDP_2, instead of GDP_3, what is the status of its standardized budget? The status of its current fiscal policy? What change in fiscal policy would you recommend? How would you accomplish that in terms of the G and T lines in the figure? **LO3**

7. Some politicians have suggested that the United States enact a constitutional amendment requiring that the Federal government balance its budget annually. Explain why such an amendment, if strictly enforced, would force the government to enact a contractionary fiscal policy whenever the economy experienced a severe recession. **LO1**

8. **KEY QUESTION** Briefly state and evaluate the problem of time lags in enacting and applying fiscal policy. Explain the idea of a political business cycle. How might expectations of a near-term policy reversal weaken fiscal policy based on changes in tax rates? What is the crowding-out effect, and why might it be relevant to fiscal policy? In view of your answers, explain the following statement: "Although fiscal policy clearly is useful in combating the extremes of severe recession and demand-pull inflation, it is impossible to use fiscal policy to fine-tune the economy to the full-employment, noninflationary level of real GDP and keep the economy there indefinitely." **LO1**

9. **ADVANCED ANALYSIS** (For students who were assigned Chapter 28) Assume that, without taxes, the consumption schedule for an economy is as shown below: **LO2**

GDP, Billions	Consumption, Billions
$100	$120
200	200
300	280
400	360
500	440
600	520
700	600

a. Graph this consumption schedule and determine the size of the MPC.

b. Assume that a lump-sum (regressive) tax of $10 billion is imposed at all levels of GDP. Calculate the tax rate at each level of GDP. Graph the resulting consumption schedule and compare the MPC and the multiplier with those of the pretax consumption schedule.

c. Now suppose a proportional tax with a 10 percent tax rate is imposed instead of the regressive tax. Calculate and graph the new consumption schedule and note the MPC and the multiplier.

d. Finally, impose a progressive tax such that the tax rate is 0 percent when GDP is $100, 5 percent at $200, 10 percent at $300, 15 percent at $400, and so forth. Determine and graph the new consumption schedule, noting the effect of this tax system on the MPC and the multiplier.

e. Explain why proportional and progressive taxes contribute to greater economic stability, while a regressive tax does not. Demonstrate, using a graph similar to Figure 30.3.

10. **KEY QUESTION** How do economists distinguish between the absolute and relative sizes of the public debt? Why is the distinction important? Distinguish between refinancing the debt and retiring the debt. How does an internally held public debt differ from an externally held public debt? Contrast the effects of retiring an internally held debt and retiring an externally held debt. **LO4**

11. True or false? If false, explain why. **LO4**
   a. The total public debt is more relevant to an economy than the public debt as a percentage of GDP.
   b. An internally held public debt is like a debt of the left hand owed to the right hand.
   c. The Federal Reserve and Federal government agencies hold more than three-fourths of the public debt.
   d. The portion of the U.S. debt held by the public (and not by government entities) was larger as a percentage of GDP in 2007 than it was in 1995.
   e. In recent years, Social Security payments to retirees have exceeded Social Security tax revenues from workers and their employers.

12. Why might economists be quite concerned if the annual interest payments on the debt sharply increased as a percentage of GDP? **LO4**

13. **KEY QUESTION** Trace the cause-and-effect chain through which financing and refinancing of the public debt might affect real interest rates, private investment, the stock of capital, and economic growth. How might investment in public capital and complementarities between public capital and private capital alter the outcome of the cause-effect chain? **LO4**

14. What would happen to the stated sizes of Federal budget deficits or surpluses if the current annual additions or subtractions from the Social Security trust fund were excluded? **LO4**

15. **LAST WORD** What is the index of leading economic indicators, and how does it relate to discretionary fiscal policy?

Web-Based Questions

1. **LEADING ECONOMIC INDICATORS—HOW GOES THE ECONOMY?** The Conference Board, at **www.conference-board.org**, tracks the leading economic indicators. Check the summary of the index of leading indicators and its individual components for the latest month. Is the index up or down? Which specific components are up, and which are down? What has been the trend of the composite index over the past 3 months?

2. **TABLE 30.1—WHAT ARE THE LATEST NUMBERS?** Go to the Congressional Budget Office Web site, **www.cbo.gov**, and select Historical Budget Data. On that page, click on the "pdf" hyperlink to open up an Adobe Acrobat file containing the necessary data. Find the historical data for the actual budget deficit or surplus (total). Update column 2 of Table 30.1. Next, find the historical data for the standardized (full-employment) budget deficit or surplus as a percentage of potential GDP. Update column 3 of Table 30.1. Is fiscal policy more expansionary or less expansionary than it was in 2005?

FURTHER TEST YOUR KNOWLEDGE AT
www.mcconnell18e.com

PART EIGHT

Money, Banking, and
Monetary Policy

31

IN THIS CHAPTER YOU WILL LEARN:

1 About the functions of money and the components of the U.S. money supply.

2 What "backs" the money supply, making us willing to accept it as payment.

3 The makeup of the Federal Reserve and the U.S. banking system.

4 The functions and responsibilities of the Federal Reserve.

Money and Banking

Money is a fascinating aspect of the economy:

> Money bewitches people. They fret for it, and they sweat for it. They devise most ingenious ways to get it, and most ingenuous ways to get rid of it. Money is the only commodity that is good for nothing but to be gotten rid of. It will not feed you, clothe you, shelter you, or amuse you unless you spend it or invest it. It imparts value only in parting. People will do almost anything for money, and money will do almost anything for people. Money is a captivating, circulating, masquerading puzzle.[1]

In this chapter and the two chapters that follow, we want to unmask the critical role of money and the monetary system in the economy. When the monetary system is working properly, it provides the

---

[1]Federal Reserve Bank of Philadelphia, "Creeping Inflation," *Business Review*, August 1957, p. 3.

lifeblood of the circular flows of income and expenditure. A well-operating monetary system helps the economy achieve both full employment and the efficient use of resources. A malfunctioning monetary system distorts the allocation of resources and creates severe fluctuations in the economy's levels of output, employment, and prices.

The Functions of Money

Just what is money? There is an old saying that "money *is* what money *does*." In a general sense, anything that performs the functions of money *is* money. Here are those functions:

- *Medium of exchange* First and foremost, money is a **medium of exchange** that is usable for buying and selling goods and services. A bakery worker does not want to be paid 200 bagels per week. Nor does the bakery owner want to receive, say, halibut in exchange for bagels. Money, however, is readily acceptable as payment. As we saw in Chapter 2, money is a social invention with which resource suppliers and producers can be paid and that can be used to buy any of the full range of items available in the marketplace. As a medium of exchange, money allows society to escape the complications of barter. And because it provides a convenient way of exchanging goods, money enables society to gain the advantages of geographic and human specialization.

- *Unit of account* Money is also a **unit of account.** Society uses monetary units—dollars, in the United States—as a yardstick for measuring the relative worth of a wide variety of goods, services, and resources. Just as we measure distance in miles or kilometers, we gauge the value of goods in dollars.

  With money as an acceptable unit of account, the price of each item need be stated only in terms of the monetary unit. We need not state the price of cows in terms of corn, crayons, and cranberries. Money aids rational decision making by enabling buyers and sellers to easily compare the prices of various goods, services, and resources. It also permits us to define debt obligations, determine taxes owed, and calculate the nation's GDP.

- *Store of value* Money also serves as a **store of value** that enables people to transfer purchasing power from the present to the future. People normally do not spend all their incomes on the day they receive them. In order to buy things later, they store some of their wealth as money. The money you place in a safe or a checking account will still be available to you a few weeks or months from now. When inflation is nonexistent or mild, holding money is a reltively risk-free way to store your wealth for later use.

People can, of course, choose to hold some or all of their wealth in a wide variety of assets besides money. These include real estate, stocks, bonds, precious metals such as gold, and even collectible items like fine art or comic books. But a key advantage that money has over all other assets is that it has the most *liquidity*, or spendability.

An asset's **liquidity** is the ease with which it can be converted quickly into the most widely accepted and easily spent form of money, cash, with little or no loss of purchasing power. The more liquid an asset is, the more quickly it can be converted into cash and used for either purchases of goods and services or purchases of other assets.

Levels of liquidity vary radically. By definition, cash is perfectly liquid. By contrast, a house is highly illiquid for two reasons. First, it may take several months before a willing buyer can be found and a sale negotiated so that its value can be converted into cash. Second, there is a loss of purchasing power when the house is sold because numerous fees have to be paid to real estate agents and other individuals in order to complete the sale.

As we are about to discuss, our economy uses several different types of money including cash, coins, checking account deposits, savings account deposits, and even more exotic things like deposits in money market mutual funds. As we describe the various forms of money in detail, take the time to compare their relative levels of liquidity—both with each other and as compared to other assets like stocks, bonds, and real estate. Cash is perfectly liquid. Other forms of money are highly liquid, but less liquid than cash.

The Components of the Money Supply

Money is a "stock" of some item or group of items (unlike income, for example, which is a "flow"). Societies have used many items as money, including whales' teeth, circular stones, elephant-tail bristles, gold coins, furs, and pieces of paper. Anything that is widely accepted as a medium of exchange can serve as money. In the United States,

FIGURE 31.1 Components of money supply _M1_ and money supply _M2_, in the United States.
(a) _M1_ is a narrow definition of the money supply that includes currency (in circulation) and checkable deposits. (b) _M2_ is a broader definition that includes _M1_ along with several other relatively liquid account balances.

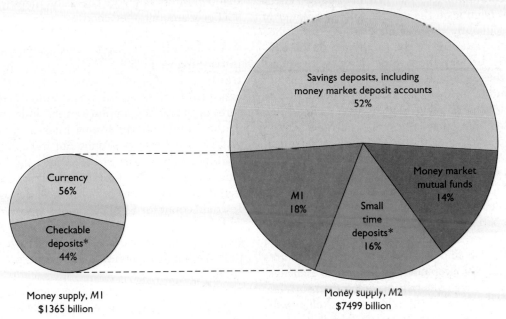

Money supply, _M1_
$1365 billion

Money supply, _M2_
$7499 billion

*These categories include other, quantitatively smaller components such as traveler's checks.

Source: Federal Reserve System, **www.federalreserve.gov.** Data are for January 2008.

currency is not the only form of money. As you will see, certain debts of government and financial institutions also are used as money.

Money Definition _M1_

The narrowest definition of the U.S. money supply is called **_M1_.** It consists of:

- Currency (coins and paper money) in the hands of the public.
- All checkable deposits (all deposits in commercial banks and "thrift" or savings institutions on which checks of any size can be drawn).[2]

Government and government agencies supply coins and paper money. Commercial banks ("banks") and savings institutions ("thrifts") provide checkable deposits. Figure 31.1a shows the amounts of each category of money in the _M1_ money supply.

Currency: Coins + Paper Money The currency of the United States consists of metal coins and paper

money. The coins are issued by the U.S. Treasury while the paper money consists of **Federal Reserve Notes** issued by the Federal Reserve System (the U.S. central bank). The coins are minted by the U.S. Mint while the paper money is printed by the Bureau of Engraving and Printing. Both the U.S. Mint and the Bureau of Engraving and Printing are part of the U.S. Department of the Treasury.

As with the currencies of other countries, the currency of the United States is **token money.** This means that the face value of any piece of currency is unrelated to its _intrinsic value_—the value of the physical material (metal or paper and ink) out of which that piece of currency is constructed. Governments make sure that face values exceed intrinsic values in order to discourage people from destroying coins and bills in order to resell the material that they are made out of. For instance, if 50-cent pieces each contained 75 cents' worth of metal, then it would be profitable to melt them down and sell the metal. Fifty-cent pieces would disappear from circulation very quickly!

Figure 31.1a shows that currency (coins and paper money) constitutes 56 percent of the _M1_ money supply in the United States.

Checkable Deposits The safety and convenience of checks has made **checkable deposits** a large component of the _M1_ money supply. You would not think of

[2]In the ensuing discussion, we do not discuss several of the quantitatively less significant components of the definitions of money in order to avoid a maze of details. For example, traveler's checks are included in the _M1_ money supply. The statistical appendix of any recent _Federal Reserve Bulletin_ provides more comprehensive definitions.

stuffing $4896 in bills in an envelope and dropping it in a mailbox to pay a debt. But writing and mailing a check for a large sum is commonplace. The person cashing a check must endorse it (sign it on the reverse side); the writer of the check subsequently receives a record of the cashed check as a receipt attesting to the fulfillment of the obligation. Similarly, because the writing of a check requires endorsement, the theft or loss of your checkbook is not nearly as calamitous as losing an identical amount of currency. Finally, it is more convenient to write a check than to transport and count out a large sum of currency. For all these reasons, checkable deposits (checkbook money) are a large component of the stock of money in the United States. About 44 percent of $M1$ is in the form of checkable deposits, on which checks can be drawn.

It might seem strange that checking account balances are regarded as part of the money supply. But the reason is clear: Checks are nothing more than a way to transfer the ownership of deposits in banks and other financial institutions and are generally acceptable as a medium of exchange. Although checks are less generally accepted than currency for small purchases, for major purchases most sellers willingly accept checks as payment. Moreover, people can convert checkable deposits into paper money and coins on demand; checks drawn on those deposits are thus the equivalent of currency.

To summarize:

Money, $M1$ = currency + checkable deposits

Institutions That Offer Checkable Deposits

In the United States, a variety of financial institutions allow customers to write checks in any amount on the funds they have deposited. **Commercial banks** are the primary depository institutions. They accept the deposits of households and businesses, keep the money safe until it is demanded via checks, and in the meantime use it to make available a wide variety of loans. Commercial bank loans provide short-term financial capital to businesses, and they finance consumer purchases of automobiles and other durable goods.

Savings and loan associations (S&Ls), mutual savings banks, and credit unions supplement the commercial banks and are known collectively as savings or **thrift institutions,** or simply "thrifts." *Savings and loan associations* and *mutual savings banks* accept the deposits of households and businesses and then use the funds to finance housing mortgages and to provide other loans. *Credit unions* accept deposits from and lend to "members," who usually are a group of people who work for the same company.

The checkable deposits of banks and thrifts are known variously as demand deposits, NOW (negotiable order of withdrawal) accounts, ATS (automatic transfer service) accounts, and share draft accounts. Their commonality is that depositors can write checks on them whenever, and in whatever amount, they choose.

Two Qualifications We must qualify our discussion in two important ways. First, currency held by the U.S. treasury, the Federal Reserve banks, commercial banks, and thrift institutions is *excluded* from $M1$ and other measures of the money supply. A paper dollar or four quarters in the billfold of, say, Emma Buck obviously constitutes just $1 of the money supply. But if we counted currency held by banks as part of the money supply, the same $1 would count for $2 of money supply when Emma deposited the currency into her checkable deposit in her bank. It would count for $1 of checkable deposit owned by Buck and also $1 of currency in the bank's cash drawer or vault. By excluding currency held by banks when determining the total supply of money, we avoid this problem of double counting.

Also *excluded* from the money supply are any checkable deposits of the government (specifically, the U.S. Treasury) or the Federal Reserve that are held by commercial banks or thrift institutions. This exclusion is designed to enable a better assessment of the amount of money available *to the private sector* for potential spending. The amount of money available to households and businesses is of keen interest to the Federal Reserve in conducting its monetary policy (a topic we cover in detail in Chapter 33).

Money Definition M2

A second and broader definition of money includes $M1$ plus several near-monies. **Near-monies** are certain highly liquid financial assets that do not function directly or fully as a medium of exchange but can be readily converted into currency or checkable deposits. There are three categories of near-monies included in the *M2* definition of money:

- *Savings deposits, including money market deposit accounts* A depositor can easily withdraw funds from a **savings account** at a bank or thrift or simply request that the funds be transferred from a savings account to a checkable account. A person can also withdraw funds from a **money market deposit account (MMDA),** which is an interest-bearing account containing a variety of interest-bearing short-term securities. MMDAs, however, have a minimum-balance requirement and a limit on how often a person can withdraw funds.

- *Small (less than $100,000) time deposits* Funds from **time deposits** become available at their maturity. For example, a person can convert a 6-month time deposit ("certificate of deposit," or "CD") to currency without penalty 6 months or more after it has been deposited. In return for this withdrawal limitation, the financial institution pays a higher interest rate on such deposits than it does on its MMDAs. Also, a person can "cash in" a CD at any time but must pay a severe penalty.

- *Money market mutual funds held by individuals* By making a telephone call, using the Internet, or writing a check for $500 or more, a depositor can redeem shares in a **money market mutual fund (MMMF)** offered by a mutual fund company. Such companies use the combined funds of individual shareholders to buy interest-bearing short-term credit instruments such as certificates of deposit and U.S. government securities. Then they can offer interest on the MMMF accounts of the shareholders (depositors) who jointly own those financial assets. The MMMFs in $M2$ include only the MMMF accounts held by individuals; those held by businesses and other institutions are excluded.

All three categories of near-monies imply substantial liquidity. Thus, in equation form,

$$\text{Money, } M2 = \begin{array}{l} M1 + \text{savings deposits,} \\ \text{including MMDAs} + \text{small} \\ \text{(less than \$100,000) time deposits} \\ + \text{MMMFs held by individuals} \end{array}$$

In summary, $M2$ includes the immediate medium-of-exchange items (currency and checkable deposits) that constitute $M1$ plus certain near-monies that can be easily converted into currency and checkable deposits. In Figure 31.1b we see that the addition of all these items yields an $M2$ money supply that is about five times larger than the narrower $M1$ money supply. **(Key Question 4)**

QUICK REVIEW 31.1

- Money serves as a medium of exchange, a unit of account, and a store of value.
- The narrow $M1$ definition of money includes currency held by the public plus checkable deposits in commercial banks and thrift institutions.
- Thrift institutions as well as commercial banks offer accounts on which checks can be written.
- The $M2$ definition of money includes $M1$ plus savings deposits, including money market deposit accounts, small (less than $100,000) time deposits, and money market mutual fund balances held by individuals.

CONSIDER THIS . . .

Are Credit Cards Money?

You may wonder why we have ignored credit cards such as Visa and MasterCard in our discussion of how the money supply is defined. After all, credit cards are a convenient way to buy things and account for about 25% of the dollar value of all transactions in the United States. The answer is that a credit card is not money. Rather, it is a convenient means of obtaining a short-term loan from the financial institution that issued the card.

What happens when you purchase an item with a credit card? The bank that issued the card will reimburse the store, charging it a transaction fee, and later you will reimburse the bank. Rather than reduce your cash or checking account with each purchase, you bunch your payments once a month. You may have to pay an annual fee for the services provided, and if you pay the bank in installments, you will pay a sizable interest charge on the loan. Credit cards are merely a means of deferring or postponing payment for a short period. Your checking account balance that you use to pay your credit card bill *is* money; the credit card is *not* money.*

Although credit cards are not money, they allow individuals and businesses to "economize" in the use of money. Credit cards enable people to hold less currency in their billfolds and, prior to payment due dates, fewer checkable deposits in their bank accounts. Credit cards also help people coordinate the timing of their expenditures with their receipt of income.

*A bank debit card, however, is very similar to a check in your checkbook. Unlike a purchase with a credit card, a purchase with a debit card creates a direct "debit" (a subtraction) from your checking account balance. That checking account balance is money—it is part of $M1$.

What "Backs" the Money Supply?

The money supply in the United States essentially is "backed" (guaranteed) by government's ability to keep the value of money relatively stable. Nothing more!

Money as Debt

The major components of the money supply—paper money and checkable deposits—are debts, or promises to pay. In the United States, paper money is the circulating debt of the Federal Reserve Banks. Checkable deposits are the debts of commercial banks and thrift institutions.

Paper currency and checkable deposits have no intrinsic value. A $5 bill is just an inscribed piece of paper. A checkable deposit is merely a bookkeeping entry. And coins, we know, have less intrinsic value than their face value. Nor will government redeem the paper money you hold for anything tangible, such as gold. To many people, the fact that the government does not back the currency with anything tangible seems implausible and insecure. But the decision not to back the currency with anything tangible was made for a very good reason. If the government backed the currency with something tangible like gold, then the supply of money would vary with how much gold was available. By not backing the currency, the government avoids this constraint and indeed receives a key freedom—the ability to provide as much or as little money as needed to maintain the value of money and to best suit the economic needs of the country. In effect, by choosing not to back the currency, the government has chosen to give itself the ability to freely "manage" the nation's money supply. Its monetary authorities attempt to provide the amount of money needed for the particular volume of business activity that will promote full employment, price-level stability, and economic growth.

Nearly all today's economists agree that managing the money supply is more sensible than linking it to gold or to some other commodity whose supply might change arbitrarily and capriciously. For instance, if we used gold to back the money supply so that gold was redeemable for money and vice versa, then a large increase in the nation's gold stock as the result of a new gold discovery might increase the money supply too rapidly and thereby trigger rapid inflation. Or a long-lasting decline in gold production might reduce the money supply to the point where recession and unemployment resulted.

In short, people cannot convert paper money into a fixed amount of gold or any other precious commodity. Money is exchangeable only for paper money. If you ask the government to redeem $5 of your paper money, it will swap one paper $5 bill for another bearing a different serial number. That is all you can get. Similarly, checkable deposits can be redeemed not for gold but only for paper money, which, as we have just seen, the government will not redeem for anything tangible.

Value of Money

So why are currency and checkable deposits money, whereas, say, Monopoly (the game) money is not? What gives a $20 bill or a $100 checking account entry its value? The answer to these questions has three parts.

Acceptability Currency and checkable deposits are money because people accept them as money. By virtue of long-standing business practice, currency and checkable deposits perform the basic function of money: They are acceptable as a medium of exchange. We accept paper money in exchange because we are confident it will be exchangeable for real goods, services, and resources when we spend it.

Legal Tender Our confidence in the acceptability of paper money is strengthened because government has designated currency as **legal tender**. Specifically, each bill contains the statement "This note is legal tender for all debts, public and private." That means paper money is a valid and legal means of payment of any debt that was contracted in dollars. (But private firms and government are not mandated to accept cash. It is not illegal for them to specify payment in noncash forms such as checks, cashier's checks, money orders, or credit cards.)

The general acceptance of paper currency in exchange is more important than the government's decree that money is legal tender, however. The government has never decreed checks to be legal tender, and yet they serve as such in many of the economy's exchanges of goods, services, and resources. But it is true that government agencies—the Federal Deposit Insurance Corporation (FDIC) and the National Credit Union Administration (NCUA)—insure individual deposits of up to $100,000 at commercial banks and thrifts. That fact enhances our willingness to use checkable deposits as a medium of exchange.

Relative Scarcity The value of money, like the economic value of anything else, depends on its supply and demand. Money derives its value from its scarcity relative to its utility (its want-satisfying power). The utility of money lies in its capacity to be exchanged for goods and services, now or in the future. The economy's demand for money thus depends on the total dollar volume of transactions in any period plus the amount of money individuals and businesses want to hold for future transactions. With a reasonably constant demand for money, the supply of money provided by the monetary authorities will determine the domestic value or "purchasing power" of the monetary unit (dollar, yen, peso, or whatever).

Money and Prices

The purchasing power of money is the amount of goods and services a unit of money will buy. When money rapidly loses its purchasing power, it loses its role as money.

The Purchasing Power of the Dollar The amount a dollar will buy varies inversely with the price level; that is, a reciprocal relationship exists between the general price level and the purchasing power of the dollar. When the consumer price index or "cost-of-living" index goes up, the value of the dollar goes down, and vice versa. Higher prices lower the value of the dollar because more dollars are needed to buy a particular amount of goods, services, or resources. For example, if the price level doubles, the value of the dollar declines by one-half, or 50 percent.

Conversely, lower prices increase the purchasing power of the dollar because fewer dollars are needed to obtain a specific quantity of goods and services. If the price level falls by, say, one-half, or 50 percent, the purchasing power of the dollar doubles.

In equation form, the relationship looks like this:

$$\$V = 1/P$$

To find the value of the dollar $\$V$, divide 1 by the price level P expressed as an index number (in hundredths). If the price level is 1, then the value of the dollar is 1. If the price level rises to, say, 1.20, $\$V$ falls to .833; a 20 percent increase in the price level reduces the value of the dollar by 16.67 percent. Check your understanding of this reciprocal relationship by determining the value of $\$V$ and its percentage rise when P falls by 20 percent from $1 to .80. **(Key Question 6)**

Inflation and Acceptability In Chapter 26 we noted situations in which a nation's currency became worthless and unacceptable in exchange. These instances of runaway inflation, or *hyperinflation*, happened when the government issued so many pieces of paper currency that the purchasing power of each of those units of money was almost totally undermined. The infamous post–World War I hyperinflation in Germany is an example. In December 1919 there were about 50 billion marks in circulation. Four years later there were 496,585,345,900 billion marks in circulation! The result? The German mark in 1923 was worth an infinitesimal fraction of its 1919 value.[3]

Runaway inflation may significantly depreciate the value of money between the time it is received and the time it is spent. Rapid declines in the value of a currency may cause it to cease being used as a medium of exchange. Businesses and households may refuse to accept paper money in exchange because they do not want to bear the loss in its value that will occur while it is in their possession. (All this despite the fact that the government says that paper currency is legal tender!) Without an acceptable domestic medium of exchange, the economy may simply revert to barter. Alternatively, more stable currencies such as the U.S. dollar or European euro may come into widespread use. At the extreme, a country may adopt a foreign currency as its own official currency as a way to counter hyperinflation.

Similarly, people will use money as a store of value only as long as there is no sizable deterioration in the value of that money because of inflation. And an economy can effectively employ money as a unit of account only when its purchasing power is relatively stable. A monetary yardstick that no longer measures a yard (in terms of purchasing power) does not permit buyers and sellers to establish the terms of trade clearly. When the value of the dollar is declining rapidly, sellers do not know what to charge and buyers do not know what to pay.

Stabilizing Money's Purchasing Power

Rapidly rising price levels (rapid inflation) and the consequent erosion of the purchasing power of money typically result from imprudent economic policies. Since the purchasing power of money and the price level vary inversely, stabilization of the purchasing power of a nation's money requires stabilization of the nation's price level. Such price-level stability (2–3 percent annual inflation) mainly necessitates intelligent management or regulation of the nation's money supply and interest rates (*monetary policy*). It also requires appropriate *fiscal policy* supportive of the efforts of the nation's monetary authorities to hold down inflation. In the United States, a combination of legislation, government policy, and social practice inhibits imprudent expansion of the money supply that might jeopardize money's purchasing power. The critical role of the U.S. monetary authorities (the Federal Reserve) in maintaining the purchasing power of the dollar is the subject of Chapter 33. For now, simply note that they make available a particular quantity of money, such as *M2* in Figure 31.1, and can change that amount through their policy tools.

QUICK REVIEW 31.2

- In the United States, all money consists essentially of the debts of government, commercial banks, and thrift institutions.
- These debts efficiently perform the functions of money as long as their value, or purchasing power, is relatively stable.
- The value of money is rooted not in specified quantities of precious metals but in the amount of goods, services, and resources that money will purchase.
- The value of the dollar (its domestic purchasing power) is inversely related to the price level.
- Government's responsibility in stabilizing the purchasing power of the monetary unit calls for (a) effective control over the supply of money by the monetary authorities and (b) the application of appropriate fiscal policies by the president and Congress.

---

[3]Frank G. Graham, *Exchange, Prices and Production in Hyperinflation Germany, 1920-1923* (Princeton, N.J.: Princeton University Press, 1930), p. 13.

The Federal Reserve and the Banking System

In the United States, the "monetary authorities" we have been referring to are the members of the Board of Governors of the **Federal Reserve System** (the "Fed"). As shown in Figure 31.2, the Board directs the activities of the 12 Federal Reserve Banks, which in turn control the lending activity of the nation's banks and thrift institutions. The Fed's major goal is to control the money supply. But since checkable deposits in banks are such a large part of the money supply, an important part of its duties involves assuring the stability of the banking system.

Historical Background

Early in the twentieth century, Congress decided that centralization and public control were essential for an efficient banking system. Decentralized, unregulated banking had fostered the inconvenience and confusion of numerous private bank notes being used as currency. It also had resulted in occasional episodes of monetary mismanagement such that the money supply was inappropriate to the needs of the economy. Sometimes "too much" money precipitated rapid inflation; other times "too little money" stunted the economy's growth by hindering the production and exchange of goods and services. No single entity was charged with creating and implementing nationally consistent banking policies.

Furthermore, acute problems in the banking system occasionally erupted when banks either closed down or insisted on immediate repayment of loans to prevent their own failure.

At such times, a banking crisis could emerge, with individuals and businesses who had lost confidence in their banks attempting to simultaneously withdraw all of their money—thereby further crippling the already weakened banks.

An unusually acute banking crisis in 1907 motivated Congress to appoint the National Monetary Commission to study the monetary and banking problems of the economy and to outline a course of action for Congress. The result was the Federal Reserve Act of 1913.

Let's examine the various parts of the Federal Reserve System and their relationship to one another.

Board of Governors

The central authority of the U.S. money and banking system is the **Board of Governors** of the Federal Reserve System. The U.S. president, with the confirmation of the Senate, appoints the seven Board members. Terms are 14 years and staggered so that one member is replaced every 2 years. In addition, new members are appointed when resignations occur. The president selects the chairperson and vice-chairperson of the Board from among the members. Those officers serve 4-year terms and can be reappointed to new 4-year terms by the president. The long-term appointments provide the Board with continuity, experienced membership, and independence from political pressures that could result in inflation.

The 12 Federal Reserve Banks

The 12 **Federal Reserve Banks,** which blend private and public control, collectively serve as the nation's "central bank." These banks also serve as bankers' banks.

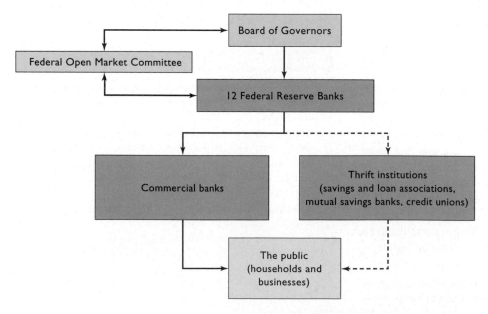

FIGURE 31.2 Framework of the Federal Reserve System and its relationship to the public. With the aid of the Federal Open Market Committee, the Board of Governors makes the basic policy decisions that provide monetary control of the U.S. money and banking systems. The 12 Federal Reserve Banks implement these decisions.

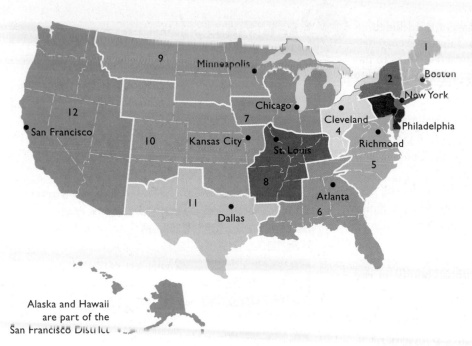

FIGURE 31.3 **The 12 Federal Reserve Districts.** The Federal Reserve System divides the United States into 12 districts, each having one central bank and in some instances one or more branches of the central bank.

Source: Federal Reserve Bulletin, **www.federalreserve.gov/pubs/bulletin.**

Central Bank Most nations have a single central bank—for example, Britain's Bank of England or Japan's Bank of Japan. The United States' central bank consists of 12 banks whose policies are coordinated by the Fed's Board of Governors. The 12 Federal Reserve Banks accommodate the geographic size and economic diversity of the United States and the nation's large number of commercial banks and thrifts.

Figure 31.3 locates the 12 Federal Reserve Banks and indicates the district that each serves. These banks implement the basic policy of the Board of Governors.

Quasi-Public Banks The 12 Federal Reserve Banks are quasi-public banks, which blend private ownership and public control. Each Federal Reserve Bank is owned by the private commercial banks in its district. (Federally chartered banks are required to purchase shares of stock in the Federal Reserve Bank in their district.) But the Board of Governors, a government body, sets the basic policies that the Federal Reserve Banks pursue.

Despite their private ownership, the Federal Reserve Banks are in practice public institutions. Unlike private firms, they are not motivated by profit. The policies they follow are designed by the Board of Governors to promote the well-being of the economy as a whole. Thus, the activities of the Federal Reserve Banks are frequently at odds with the profit motive.[4] Also, the Federal Reserve Banks do not compete with commercial banks. In general, they do not deal with the public; rather, they interact with the government and commercial banks and thrifts.

Bankers' Banks The Federal Reserve Banks are "bankers' banks." They perform essentially the same functions for banks and thrifts as those institutions perform for the public. Just as banks and thrifts accept the deposits of and make loans to the public, so the central banks accept the deposits of and make loans to banks and thrifts. Normally, these loans average only about $150 million a day. But in emergency circumstances the Federal Reserve Banks become the "lender of last resort" to the banking system and can lend out as much as needed to ensure that banks and thrifts can meet their cash obligations. On the day after terrorists attacked the United States on September 11, 2001, the Fed lent $45 *billion* to U.S. banks and thrifts. The Fed wanted to make sure that the destruction and disruption in New York City and the Washington, D.C., area did not precipitate a nationwide banking crisis.

[4]Although it is not their goal, the Federal Reserve Banks have actually operated profitably, largely as a result of the Treasury debts they hold. Part of the profit is used to pay 6 percent annual dividends to the commercial banks that hold stock in the Federal Reserve Banks; the remaining profit is usually turned over to the U.S. Treasury.

But the Federal Reserve Banks have a third function, which banks and thrifts do not perform: They issue currency. Congress has authorized the Federal Reserve Banks to put into circulation Federal Reserve Notes, which constitute the economy's paper money supply. **(Key Question 8)**

FOMC

The **Federal Open Market Committee (FOMC)** aids the Board of Governors in conducting monetary policy. The FOMC is made up of 12 individuals:

* The seven members of the Board of Governors.
* The president of the New York Federal Reserve Bank.
* Four of the remaining presidents of Federal Reserve Banks on a 1-year rotating basis.

The FOMC meets regularly to direct the purchase and sale of government securities (bills, notes, bonds) in the open market in which such securities are bought and sold on a daily basis. We will find in Chapter 33 that the purpose of these aptly named *open-market operations* is to control the nation's money supply and influence interest rates. The Federal Reserve Bank in New York City conducts most of the Fed's open-market operations.

Commercial Banks and Thrifts

There are about 7300 commercial banks. Roughly three-fourths are state banks. These are private banks chartered (authorized) by the individual states to operate within those states. One-fourth are private banks chartered by the Federal government to operate nationally; these are national banks. Some of the U.S. national banks are very large, ranking among the world's largest financial institutions (see Global Perspective 31.1).

The 11,000 thrift institutions—most of which are credit unions—are regulated by agencies separate and apart from the Board of Governors and the Federal Reserve Banks. For example, the operations of savings and loan associations are regulated and monitored by the Treasury Department's Office of Thrift Supervision. But the thrifts *are* subject to monetary control by the Federal Reserve System. In particular, like the banks, thrifts are required to keep a certain percentage of their checkable deposits as "reserves." In Figure 31.2 we use dashed arrows to indicate that the thrift institutions are partially subject to the control of the Board of Governors and the central banks. Decisions concerning monetary policy affect the thrifts along with the commercial banks.

Fed Functions and the Money Supply

The Fed performs several functions, some of which we have already identified but they are worth repeating:

GLOBAL PERSPECTIVE 31.1

The World's 12 Largest Financial Institutions

The world's 12 largest private sector financial institutions are headquartered in Europe, Japan, and the United States (2007 data).

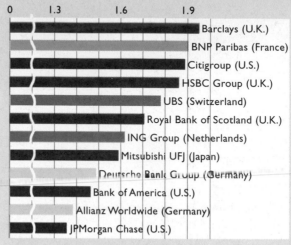

Source: Forbes Global 2000, **www.forbes.com.**

* ***Issuing currency*** The Federal Reserve Banks issue Federal Reserve Notes, the paper currency used in the U.S. monetary system. (The Federal Reserve Bank that issued a particular bill is identified in black in the upper left of the front of the newly designed bills. "A1," for example, identifies the Boston bank, "B2" the New York bank, and so on.)
* ***Setting reserve requirements and holding reserves*** The Fed sets reserve requirements, which are the fractions of checking account balances that banks must maintain as currency reserves. The central banks accept as deposits from the banks and thrifts any portion of their mandated reserves not held as vault cash.
* ***Lending money*** From time to time the Fed lends money to banks and thrifts and charges them an interest rate called the *discount rate*. In times of financial emergencies, the Fed serves as a lender of last resort to critical parts of the U.S. financial industry.
* ***Providing for check collection*** The Fed provides the banking system with a means for collecting checks. If Sue writes a check on her Miami bank or thrift to Joe, who deposits it in his Dallas bank or thrift, how does the Dallas bank collect the money represented by the check drawn against the Miami bank?

Answer: The Fed handles it by adjusting the reserves (deposits) of the two banks.

- *Acting as fiscal agent* The Fed acts as the fiscal agent (provider of financial services) for the Federal government. The government collects huge sums through taxation, spends equally large amounts, and sells and redeems bonds. To carry out these activities, the government uses the Fed's facilities.

- *Supervising banks* The Fed supervises the operations of banks. It makes periodic examinations to assess bank profitability, to ascertain that banks perform in accordance with the many regulations to which they are subject, and to uncover questionable practices or fraud.[5]

- *Controlling the money supply* Finally, and most important, the Fed has ultimate responsibility for regulating the supply of money, and this in turn enables it to influence interest rates. The major task of the Fed is to manage the money supply (and thus interest rates) according to the needs of the economy. This involves making an amount of money available that is consistent with high and rising levels of output and employment *and* a relatively constant price level. While all the other functions of the Fed are routine activities or have a service nature, managing the nation's money supply requires making basic, but unique, policy decisions. (We discuss those decisions in detail in Chapter 33.)

Federal Reserve Independence

Congress purposely established the Fed as an independent agency of government. The objective was to protect the Fed from political pressures so that it could effectively control the money supply and maintain price stability. Political pressures on Congress and the executive branch may at times result in inflationary fiscal policies, including tax cuts and special-interest spending. If Congress and the executive branch also controlled the nation's monetary policy, citizens and lobbying groups undoubtedly would pressure elected officials to keep interest rates low even though at times high interest rates are necessary to reduce aggregate demand and thus control inflation. An independent monetary authority (the Fed) can take actions to increase interest rates when higher rates are needed to stem inflation. Studies show that countries that have independent central banks like the Fed have lower rates of inflation, on average, than countries that have little or no central bank independence.

---

[5]The Fed is not alone in this task of supervision. The individual states supervise all banks that they charter. The Comptroller of the Currency supervises all national banks, and the Office of Thrift Supervision supervises all thrifts. Also, the Federal Deposit Insurance Corporation supervises all banks and thrifts whose deposits it insures.

Recent Developments in Money and Banking

The banking industry is undergoing a series of sweeping changes, spurred by competition from other financial institutions, the globalization of banking, and advances in information technology.

The Relative Decline of Banks and Thrifts

Banks and thrifts are just two of several types of firms that offer financial services. Table 31.1 lists the major categories of firms within the U.S. **financial services industry** and gives examples of firms in each category. Although banks and thrifts remain the only institutions that offer checkable deposits that have no restrictions on either the number or size of checks, their share of total financial assets (value of things owned) is declining. In 1980 banks and thrifts together held nearly 60 percent of financial assets in the United States. By 2007 that percentage had declined to about 22 percent.

Where did the declining shares of the banks and thrifts go? Pension funds, insurance firms, and particularly securities firms and mutual fund companies expanded their shares of financial assets. (Mutual fund companies offer shares of a wide array of stock and bond funds, as well as the previously mentioned money market funds.) Clearly, between 1980 and 2007, U.S. households and businesses channeled relatively more saving away from banks and thrifts and toward other financial institutions. Those other institutions generally offered higher rates of return on funds than did banks and thrifts, largely because they could participate more fully in national and international stock and bond markets.

Consolidation among Banks and Thrifts

During the past two decades, many banks have purchased bankrupt thrifts or have merged with other banks. Two examples of mergers of major banks are the mergers of J.P. Morgan Chase and Bank One in 2004 and the purchase of LaSalle Bank by Bank of America in 2007. Major savings and loans also have merged. The purpose of such mergers is to create large regional or national banks or thrifts that can compete more effectively in the financial services industry. Consolidation of traditional banking is expected to continue; there are 5200 fewer banks today than there were in 1990. Today, the seven largest U.S. banks and thrifts hold roughly one-third of total bank deposits.

TABLE 31.1 **Major U.S. Financial Institutions (as of August 2008)**

Institution	Description	Examples
Commercial banks	State and national banks that provide checking and savings accounts, sell certificates of deposit, and make loans. The Federal Deposit Insurance Corporation (FDIC) insures checking and savings accounts up to $100,000.	J.P. Morgan Chase, Bank of America, Citibank, Wells Fargo, Wachovia
Thrifts	Savings and loan associations (S&Ls), mutual saving banks, and credit unions that offer checking and savings accounts and make loans. Historically, S&Ls made mortgage loans for houses while mutual savings banks and credit unions made small personal loans, such as automobile loans. Today, major thrifts offer the same range of banking services as commercial banks. The Federal Deposit Insurance Corporation and the National Credit Union Administration insure checking and savings deposits up to $100,000.	Washington Mutual, Golden State (owned by Citigroup), Golden West (owned by Wachovia), Charter One
Insurance companies	Firms that offer policies (contracts) through which individuals pay premiums to insure against some loss, say, disability or death. In some life insurance policies and annuities, the funds are invested for the client in stocks and bonds and paid back after a specified number of years. Thus, insurance sometimes has a saving or financial-investment element.	Prudential, New York Life, Massachusetts Mutual
Mutual fund companies	Firms that pool deposits by customers to purchase stocks or bonds (or both). Customers thus indirectly own a part of a particular set of stocks or bonds, say stocks in companies expected to grow rapidly (a growth fund) or bonds issued by state governments (a municipal bond fund).	Fidelity, Vanguard, Putnam, Dreyfus, Kemper
Pension funds	For-profit or nonprofit institutions that collect savings from workers (or from employers on their behalf) throughout their working years and then buy stocks and bonds with the proceeds and make monthly retirement payments.	TIAA-CREF, Teamsters' Union
Securities firms	Firms that offer security advice and buy and sell stocks and bonds for clients. More generally known as *stock brokerage firms*.	Merrill Lynch, Smith Barney, Lehman Brothers, Charles Schwab
Investment banks	Firms that help corporations and governments raise money by selling stocks and bonds. They also typically offer advisory services for corporate mergers and acquisitions as well as brokerage services and advice.	Goldman Sachs, Bain Capital, Morgan Stanley, Deutsche Bank, Nomura Securities

Convergence of Services Provided by Financial Institutions

In 1996 Congress greatly loosened the Depression-era prohibition against banks selling stocks, bonds, and mutual funds, and it ended the prohibition altogether in the Financial Services Modernization Act of 1999. Banks, thrifts, pension companies, insurance companies, and securities firms can now merge with one another and sell each other's products. Thus, the lines between the subsets of the financial industry are beginning to blur. Many banks have acquired stock brokerage firms and, in a few cases, insurance companies. For example, Citigroup now owns Smith Barney, a large securities firm. Many large banks (for example, Wells Fargo) and pension funds (for example, TIAA-CREF) now provide mutual funds, including money market funds that pay relatively high interest and on which checks of $500 or more can be written.

The lifting of restraints against banks and thrifts should work to their advantage because they can now provide their customers with "one-stop shopping" for financial services. In general, the reform will likely intensify competition and encourage financial innovation. The downside is that financial losses in securities subsidiaries—such as could occur during a major recession—could increase the number of bank failures. Such failures might undermine confidence in the entire banking system and complicate the Fed's task of maintaining an appropriate money supply.

Globalization of Financial Markets

Another significant banking development is the increasing integration of world financial markets. Major foreign financial institutions now have operations in the United States, and U.S. financial institutions do business abroad. For example, Visa, MasterCard, and American Express offer worldwide credit card services. Moreover, U.S. mutual fund companies now offer a variety of international stock and bond funds. Globally, financial capital increasingly flows in search of the highest risk-adjusted returns. As a result, U.S. banks increasingly compete with foreign banks for both deposits and loan customers.

Recent advances in computer and communications technology are likely to speed up the trend toward international financial integration. Yet the bulk of investment in the major nations is still financed through domestic saving within each nation.

Electronic Payments

Finally, the rapid advance of new payment forms and Internet "banking" is of great significance to financial institutions and central banks. Households and businesses increasingly use **electronic payments,** not currency and checks, to buy products, pay bills, pay income taxes, transfer bank funds, and handle recurring mortgage and utility payments.

Several electronic-based means of making payments and transferring funds have pushed currency and checks aside. *Credit cards* enable us to make immediate purchases using credit established in advance with the card provider. In most cases, a swipe of the credit card makes the transaction electronically. Credit card balances can be paid via the Internet, rather than by sending a check to the card provider. *Debit cards* work much like credit cards but, since no loan is involved, more closely resemble checks. The swipe of the card authorizes an electronic payment directly to the seller from the buyer's bank account.

Other electronic payments include *Fedwire* transfers. This system, maintained by the Federal Reserve, enables banks to transfer funds to other banks. Individuals and businesses can also "wire" funds between financial institutions, domestically or internationally. Households can "send" funds or payments to businesses using *automated clearinghouse transactions* (ACHs). For example, they can make recurring utility and mortgage payments and transfer funds among financial institutions. The ACH system also allows sellers to scan checks at point of sale, convert them to ACH payments, and move the funds immediately from the buyer's checking account to the seller's checking account. Then the seller immediately hands the check back to the customer.

Some experts believe the next step will be greater use of *electronic money,* which is simply an entry in an electronic file stored in a computer. Electronic money will be deposited, or "loaded," into an account through electronic deposits of paychecks, retirement benefits, stock dividends, and other sources of income. The owner of the account will withdraw, or "unload," the money from his or her account through Internet payments to others for a wide variety of goods and services. PayPal—used by 164 million account holders in 190 countries—roughly fits this description, and is familiar to eBay users. Buyers and sellers establish accounts based on funds in checking accounts or funds available via credit cards. Customers then can securely make electronic payments or transfer funds to other holders of PayPal accounts.

In the future, the public may be able to insert so-called *smart cards* into card readers connected to their computers and load electronic money onto the card. These plastic cards contain computer chips that store information, including the amount of electronic money the consumer has loaded. When purchases or payments are made, their amounts are automatically deducted from the balance in the card's memory. Consumers will be able to transfer traditional money to their smart cards through computers or cell phones or at automatic teller machines. Thus, it will be possible for nearly all payments to be made through the Internet or a smart card.

A few general-use smart cards with embedded programmable computer chips are available in the United States, including cards issued by Visa, MasterCard, and American Express ("Blue Cards"). More common are *stored-value cards*, which facilitate purchases at the establishments that issued them. Examples are prepaid phone cards, copy-machine cards, mass-transit cards, single-store gift cards, and university meal-service cards. Like the broader smart cards, these cards are "reloadable," meaning the amounts stored on them can be increased. A number of retailers—including FedEx stores, Sears, Starbucks, Walgreens, and Wal-Mart—make stored-value cards available to their customers.

Electronic money also appears poised to make a big impact in developing countries where bank branches are few and far between. Companies like M-PESA in Kenya, Wizzit in South Africa, and G-Cash in the Philippines are now taking advantage of the fact that while those countries have few banks, they have extensive cellular phone networks. Cell phone subscribers can deposit cash at cell phone stores and then freely send each other electronic payments using their phones. Customers receiving payments can use the electronic money that they receive to make further electronic payments or, if they like, withdraw the money for cash at their local cell phone store. The safety and convenience of these systems is expected to be a substantial boost to local consumers and businesspeople.

QUICK REVIEW 31.3

- The Federal Reserve System consists of the Board of Governors and 12 Federal Reserve Banks.
- The 12 Federal Reserve Banks are publicly controlled central banks that deal with banks and thrifts rather than with the public.
- The Federal Reserve's major role is to regulate the supply of money in the economy.
- Recent developments in banking are the (a) relative decline in traditional banking; (b) consolidation within the banking industry; (c) convergence of services offered by banks, thrifts, insurance companies, pension funds, and mutual funds; (d) globalization of banking; and (e) widespread emergence of electronic transactions.

A Large Amount of U.S. Currency Is Circulating Abroad.

Like commercial aircraft, computer software, and movies, American currency has become a major U.S. "export." Russians hold about $80 billion of U.S. currency and Argentinians hold $50 billion. The Turkish government estimates that $10 billion of U.S. dollars is circulating in Turkey. In all, an estimated $450 billion of U.S. currency is circulating abroad. That amounts to about 60 percent of the total U.S. currency held by the public.

Dollars leave the United States when Americans buy imports, travel in other countries, or send dollars to relatives living abroad. The United States profits when the dollars stay in other countries. It costs the government about 4 cents to print a dollar. For someone abroad to obtain that new dollar, $1 worth of resources, goods, or services must be sold to Americans. These commodities are U.S. gains. The dollar goes abroad and, assuming it stays there, presents no claim on U.S. resources or goods or services. Americans in effect make 96 cents on the dollar (= $1 gain in resources, goods, or services − the 4-cent printing cost). It's like American Express selling traveler's checks that never get cashed.

Black markets and other illegal activity undoubtedly fuel some of the demand for U.S. cash abroad. The dollar is king in covert trading in diamonds, weapons, and pirated software. Billions of cash dollars are involved in the narcotics trade. But the illegal use of dollars is only a small part of the story. The massive volume of dollars in other nations reflects a global search for monetary stability. On the basis of past experience, foreign citizens are confident that the dollar's purchasing power will remain relatively steady.

Following the collapse of the Soviet Union in the early 1990s, high rates of inflation led many Russians to abandon rubles for U.S. dollars. While the dollar retained its purchasing power in Russia, the purchasing power of the ruble plummeted. As a result, many Russians still hold large parts of their savings in

dollars today. Recently, however, some Russians have transferred part or all of their holdings of dollars to euros.

In Brazil, where inflation rates above 1000% annually were once common, people have long sought the stability of dollars. In the shopping districts of Beijing and Shanghai, Chinese consumers trade their domestic currency for dollars. In Bolivia half of all bank accounts are denominated in dollars. There is a thriving "dollar economy" in Vietnam, and even Cuba has partially legalized the use of U.S. dollars. The U.S. dollar is the official currency in Panama and Liberia. Immediately after the invasion of Iraq in 2003, the purchasing power of the Iraqi dinar fell dramatically because the looting of banks placed many more dinars into circulation. The United States and British forces began paying Iraqi workers in U.S. dollars, and dollars in effect became the transition currency in the country.

Is there any financial risk for people who hold dollars in foreign countries? While the dollar is likely to hold its purchasing power internally in those nations, holders of dollars do face *exchange-rate risk*. If the international value of the dollar depreciates, as it did from 2005 to 2007, more dollars are needed to buy goods imported from countries other than the United States. Those goods, priced in, say, euros, Swiss francs, or yen, become more expensive to holders of dollars. Offsetting that "downside risk," of course, is the "upside opportunity" of the dollar's appreciating.

There is little risk for the United States in satisfying the world's demand for dollars. If all the dollars came rushing back to the United States at once, the nation's money supply would surge, possibly causing demand-pull inflation. But there is not much chance of that happening. Overall, the global greenback is a positive economic force. It is a reliable medium of exchange, unit of account, and store of value that facilitates transactions that might not otherwise occur. Dollar holdings have helped buyers and sellers abroad overcome special monetary problems. The result has been increased output in those countries and thus greater output and income globally.

Summary

1. Anything that is accepted as (a) a medium of exchange, (b) a unit of monetary account, and (c) a store of value can be used as money.

2. There are two major definitions of the money supply. *M*1 consists of currency and checkable deposits; *M*2 consists of *M*1 plus savings deposits, including money market deposit accounts, small (less than $100,000) time deposits, and money market mutual fund balances held by individuals.

3. Money represents the debts of government and institutions offering checkable deposits (commercial banks and thrift institutions) and has value because of the goods, services, and resources it will command in the market. Maintaining the purchasing power of money depends largely on the government's effectiveness in managing the money supply.

4. The U.S. banking system consists of (a) the Board of Governors of the Federal Reserve System, (b) the 12 Federal Reserve Banks, and (c) some 7300 commercial banks and 11,000 thrift institutions (mainly credit unions). The Board of Governors is the basic policymaking body for the entire banking system. The directives of the Board and the Federal Open Market Committee (FOMC) are made effective through the 12 Federal Reserve Banks, which are simultaneously (a) central banks, (b) quasi-public banks, and (c) bankers' banks.

5. The major functions of the Fed are to (a) issue Federal Reserve Notes, (b) set reserve requirements and hold reserves deposited by banks and thrifts, (c) lend money to banks and thrifts, (d) provide for the rapid collection of checks, (e) act as the fiscal agent for the Federal government, (f) supervise the operations of the banks, and (g) regulate the supply of money in the best interests of the economy.

6. The Fed is essentially an independent institution, controlled neither by the president of the United States nor by Congress. This independence shields the Fed from political pressure and allows it to raise and lower interest rates (via changes in the money supply) as needed to promote full employment, price stability, and economic growth.

7. Between 1980 and 2007, banks and thrifts lost considerable market share in the financial services industry to pension funds, insurance companies, mutual funds, and securities firms. Other recent banking developments of significance include the consolidation of the banking and thrift industry; the convergence of services offered by banks, thrifts, mutual funds, investment banks, securities firms, and pension companies; the globalization of banking services; and the emergence of the Internet and electronic payments.

Terms and Concepts

medium of exchange	commercial banks	legal tender
unit of account	thrift institutions	Federal Reserve System
store of value	near-monies	Board of Governors
liquidity	*M*2	Federal Reserve Banks
*M*1	savings account	Federal Open Market Committee (FOMC)
Federal Reserve Notes	money market deposit account (MMDA)	
token money	time deposits	financial services industry
checkable deposits	money market mutual fund (MMMF)	electronic payments

Study Questions

1. What are the three basic functions of money? Describe how rapid inflation can undermine money's ability to perform each of the three functions. **LO1**

2. Which two of the following financial institutions offer checkable deposits included within the *M*1 money supply: mutual fund companies; insurance companies; commercial banks; securities firms; thrift institutions? Which of the following is not included in either *M*1 or *M*2: currency held by the public; checkable deposits; money market mutual fund

balances; small (less than $100,000) time deposits; currency held by banks; savings deposits. **LO1**

3. Explain and evaluate the following statements: **LO2**
   a. The invention of money is one of the great achievements of humankind, for without it the enrichment that comes from broadening trade would have been impossible.
   b. Money is whatever society says it is.
   c. In most economies of the world, the debts of government and commercial banks are used as money.

d. People often say they would like to have more money, but what they usually mean is that they would like to have more goods and services.

e. When the price of everything goes up, it is not because everything is worth more but because the currency is worth less.

f. Any central bank can create money; the trick is to create enough, but not too much, of it.

4. **KEY QUESTION** What are the components of the *M*1 money supply? What is the largest component? Which of the components of *M*1 is *legal tender?* Why is the face value of a coin greater than its intrinsic value? What near-monies are included in the *M*2 money supply? **LO1, LO2**

5. What "backs" the money supply in the United States? What determines the value (domestic purchasing power) of money? How does the purchasing power of money relate to the price level? Who in the United States is responsible for maintaining money's purchasing power? **LO2**

6. **KEY QUESTION** Suppose the price level and value of the dollar in year 1 are 1 and $1, respectively. If the price level rises to 1.25 in year 2, what is the new value of the dollar? If, instead, the price level falls to .50, what is the value of the dollar? What generalization can you draw from your answers? **LO2**

7. How is the chairperson of the Federal Reserve System selected? Describe the relationship between the Board of Governors of the Federal Reserve System and the 12 Federal Reserve Banks. What are the composition and purpose of the Federal Open Market Committee (FOMC)? **LO3**

8. **KEY QUESTION** What is meant when economists say that the Federal Reserve Banks are central banks, quasi-public banks, and bankers' banks? What are the seven basic functions of the Federal Reserve System? **LO4**

9. Following are two hypothetical ways in which the Federal Reserve Board might be appointed. Would you favor either of these two methods over the present method? Why or why not? **LO3**

a. Upon taking office, the U.S. president appoints seven people to the Federal Reserve Board, including a chair. Each appointee must be confirmed by a majority vote of the Senate, and each serves the same 4-year term as the president.

b. Congress selects seven members from its ranks (four from the House of Representatives and three from the Senate) to serve at its pleasure as the Board of Governors of the Federal Reserve System.

10. What are the major categories of firms that make up the U.S. financial services industry? Did the bank and thrift share of the financial services market rise, fall, or stay the same between 1980 and 2007? Are there more or fewer banks today than a decade ago? Why are the lines between the categories of financial firms becoming more blurred than in the past? **LO3**

11. How does a debit card differ from a credit card? How does a stored-value card differ from both? Suppose that a person has a credit card, debit card, and stored-value card. Create a fictional scenario in which the person uses all three cards in the same day. Explain the person's logic for using one card rather than one of the others for each transaction. How do Fedwire and ACH transactions differ from credit card, debit card, and stored-value card transactions? **LO1**

12. **LAST WORD** Over the years, the Federal Reserve Banks have printed many billions of dollars more in currency than U.S. households, businesses, and financial institutions now hold. Where is this "missing" money? Why is it there?

Web-Based Questions

1. **WHO ARE THE MEMBERS OF THE FEDERAL RESERVE BOARD?** The Federal Reserve Board Web site, **www.federalreserve.gov/BIOS,** provides detailed biographies of the seven members of the Board of Governors. What is the composition of the Board with regard to age, gender, education, previous employment, and ethnic background? Which Board members are near the ends of their terms?

2. **CURRENCY TRIVIA** Visit the Publications page of the Federal Reserve Bank of Atlanta, **www.frbatlanta.org/ publica/pubs_index.cfm.** Scroll down the page and click on the link that reads *Dollars and Cents: Fundamental Facts about U.S. Money.* Use the information you find to answer the following questions: What are the denominations of Federal Reserve Notes now being printed? What was the largest-denomination Federal Reserve Note ever printed and circulated, and when was it last printed? What are some tips for spotting counterfeit currency? When was the last silver dollar minted? What have been the largest and smallest U.S. coin denominations since the Coinage Act of 1792?

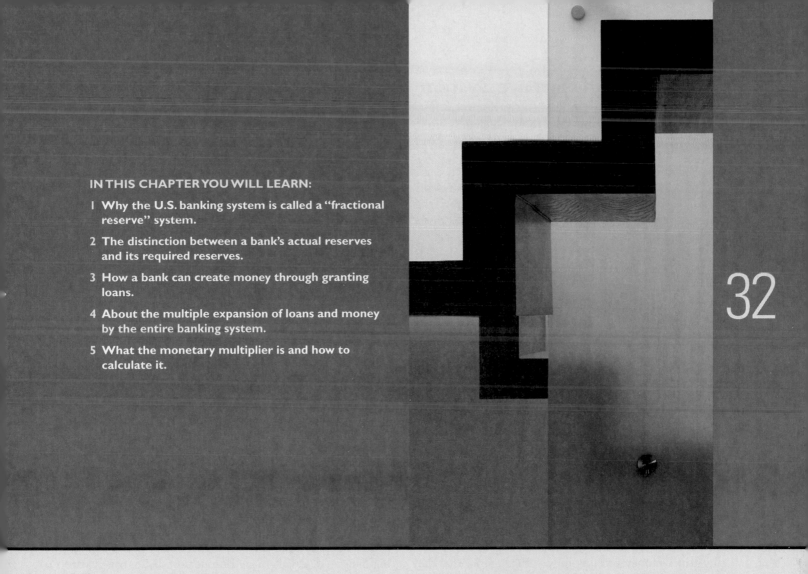

IN THIS CHAPTER YOU WILL LEARN:

1 Why the U.S. banking system is called a "fractional reserve" system.

2 The distinction between a bank's actual reserves and its required reserves.

3 How a bank can create money through granting loans.

4 About the multiple expansion of loans and money by the entire banking system.

5 What the monetary multiplier is and how to calculate it.

32

Money Creation

We have seen that the *M*1 money supply consists of currency (coins and Federal Reserve Notes) and checkable deposits and that *M*1 is a base component of *M*2, a broader measure of the money supply that also includes savings deposits, small time deposits, and deposits to money market mutual funds. The U.S. Mint produces the coins and the U.S. Bureau of Engraving and Printing creates the Federal Reserve Notes. So who creates the checkable deposits? Surprisingly, it is loan officers! Although that may sound like something a congressional committee should investigate, the monetary authorities are well aware that banks and thrifts create checkable deposits. In fact, the Federal Reserve relies on these institutions to create this vital component of the nation's money supply.

The Fractional Reserve System

The United States, like most other countries today, has a **fractional reserve banking system** in which only a portion (fraction) of checkable deposits are backed up by cash in bank vaults or deposits at the central bank. Our goal is to explain this system and show how commercial banks can create checkable deposits by issuing loans. Our examples will involve commercial banks, but remember that thrift institutions also provide checkable deposits. So the analysis applies to banks and thrifts alike.

Illustrating the Idea: The Goldsmiths

Here is the history behind the idea of the fractional reserve system.

When early traders began to use gold in making transactions, they soon realized that it was both unsafe and inconvenient to carry gold and to have it weighed and assayed (judged for purity) every time they negotiated a transaction. So by the sixteenth century they had begun to deposit their gold with goldsmiths, who would store it in vaults for a fee. On receiving a gold deposit, the goldsmith would issue a receipt to the depositor. Soon people were paying for goods with goldsmiths' receipts, which served as one of the first types of paper money.

At this point the goldsmiths—embryonic bankers—used a 100 percent reserve system; they backed their circulating paper money receipts fully with the gold that they held "in reserve" in their vaults. But because of the public's acceptance of the goldsmiths' receipts as paper money, the goldsmiths soon realized that owners rarely redeemed the gold they had in storage. In fact, the goldsmiths observed that the amount of gold being deposited with them in any week or month was likely to exceed the amount that was being withdrawn.

Then some clever goldsmith hit on the idea that paper "receipts" could be issued in excess of the amount of gold held. Goldsmiths would put these receipts, which were redeemable in gold, into circulation by making interest-earning loans to merchants, producers, and consumers. A borrower might, for instance, borrow $10,000 worth of gold receipts today with the promise to repay $10,500 worth of gold receipts in one year (a 5 percent interest rate). Borrowers were willing to accept loans in the form of gold receipts because the receipts were accepted as a medium of exchange in the marketplace.

This was the beginning of the fractional reserve system of banking, in which reserves in bank vaults are a fraction of the total money supply. If, for example, the goldsmith issued $1 million in receipts for actual gold in storage and another $1 million in receipts as loans, then the total value of paper money in circulation would be $2 million—twice the value of the gold. Gold reserves would be a fraction (one-half) of outstanding paper money.

Significant Characteristics of Fractional Reserve Banking

The goldsmith story highlights two significant characteristics of fractional reserve banking. First, banks can create money through lending. In fact, goldsmiths created money when they made loans by giving borrowers paper money that was not fully backed by gold reserves. The quantity of such money goldsmiths could create depended on the amount of reserves they deemed prudent to have available. The smaller the amount of reserves thought necessary, the larger the amount of paper money the goldsmiths could create. Today, gold is no longer used as bank reserves. Instead, currency itself serves as bank reserves so that the creation of checkable deposit money by banks (via their lending) is limited by the amount of *currency reserves* that the banks feel obligated, or are required by law, to keep.

A second reality is that banks operating on the basis of fractional reserves are vulnerable to "panics" or "runs." A goldsmith who issued paper money equal to twice the value of his gold reserves would be unable to convert all that paper money into gold in the event that all the holders of that money appeared at his door at the same time demanding their gold. In fact, many European and U.S. banks were once ruined by this unfortunate circumstance. However, a bank panic is highly unlikely if the banker's reserve and lending policies are prudent. Indeed, one reason why banking systems are highly regulated industries is to prevent runs on banks.

This is also why the United States has the system of deposit insurance that we discussed in the last chapter. By guaranteeing deposits, deposit insurance helps to prevent the sort of bank runs that used to happen so often before deposit insurance was available. In these situations, rumors would spread that a bank was about to go bankrupt and that it only had a small amount of reserves left in its vaults. Bank runs are called "bank runs" because depositors would run to the bank trying to be one of the lucky few to withdraw their money while the bank had any reserves left. The rumors were usually totally unfounded. But, unfortunately, the bank would still go bankrupt even if it began the day with its normal amount of reserves. With so many customers withdrawing money simultaneously, it would run out of reserves and be forced to default on its obligations to its remaining depositors. By guaranteeing depositors that they will always get their money, deposit insurance removes the incentive to try to withdraw one's deposit before anyone else can. It thus stops most bank runs.

A Single Commercial Bank

To illustrate the workings of the modern fractional reserve banking system, we need to examine a commercial bank's balance sheet.

The **balance sheet** of a commercial bank (or thrift) is a statement of assets and claims on assets that summarizes the financial position of the bank at a certain time. Every balance sheet must balance; this means that the value of *assets* must equal the amount of claims against those assets. The claims shown on a balance sheet are divided into two groups: the claims of nonowners against the firm's assets, called *liabilities*, and the claims of the owners of the firm against the firm's assets, called *net worth*. A balance sheet is balanced because

$$Assets = liabilities + net\ worth$$

Every $1 change in assets must be offset by a $1 change in liabilities + net worth. Every $1 change in liabilities + net worth must be offset by a $1 change in assets.

Now let's work through a series of bank transactions involving balance sheets to establish how individual banks can create money.

Transaction 1: Creating a Bank

Suppose some far-sighted citizens of the town of Wahoo, Nebraska (yes, there is such a place), decide their town needs a new commercial bank to provide banking services for that growing community. Once they have secured a state or national charter for their bank, they turn to the task of selling, say, $250,000 worth of stock (equity shares) to buyers, both in and out of the community. Their efforts meet with success and the Bank of Wahoo comes into existence—at least on paper. What does its balance sheet look like at this stage?

The founders of the bank have sold $250,000 worth of shares of stock in the bank—some to themselves, some to other people. As a result, the bank now has $250,000 in cash on hand and $250,000 worth of stock shares outstanding. The cash is an asset to the bank. Cash held by a bank is sometimes called **vault cash** or till money. The shares of stock outstanding constitute an equal amount of claims that the owners have against the bank's assets. Those shares of stock constitute the net worth of the bank. The bank's balance sheet reads:

Creating a Bank Balance Sheet 1: Wahoo Bank			
Assets		Liabilities and net worth	
Cash	$250,000	Stock shares	$250,000

Each item listed in a balance sheet such as this is called an *account*.

Transaction 2: Acquiring Property and Equipment

The board of directors (who represent the bank's owners) must now get the new bank off the drawing board and make it a reality. First, property and equipment must be acquired. Suppose the directors, confident of the success of their venture, purchase a building for $220,000 and pay $20,000 for office equipment. This simple transaction changes the composition of the bank's assets. The bank now has $240,000 less in cash and $240,000 of new property assets. Using blue to denote accounts affected by each transaction, we find that the bank's balance sheet at the end of transaction 2 appears as follows:

Acquiring Property and Equipment Balance Sheet 2: Wahoo Bank			
Assets		Liabilities and net worth	
Cash	$ 10,000	Stock shares	$250,000
Property	240,000		

Note that the balance sheet still balances, as it must.

Transaction 3: Accepting Deposits

Commercial banks have two basic functions: to accept deposits of money and to make loans. Now that the bank is operating, suppose that the citizens and businesses of Wahoo decide to deposit $100,000 in the Wahoo bank. What happens to the bank's balance sheet?

The bank receives cash, which is an asset to the bank. Suppose this money is deposited in the bank as checkable deposits (checking account entries), rather than as savings accounts or time deposits. These newly created *checkable deposits* constitute claims that the depositors have against the assets of the Wahoo bank and thus are a new liability account. The bank's balance sheet now looks like this:

Accepting Deposits Balance Sheet 3: Wahoo Bank			
Assets		Liabilities and net worth	
Cash	$110,000	Checkable deposits	$100,000
Property	240,000		
		Stock shares	250,000

There has been no change in the economy's total supply of money as a result of transaction 3, but a change has occurred in the composition of the money supply. Bank money, or checkable deposits, has increased by $100,000, and currency held by the public has decreased by $100,000. Currency held by a bank, you will recall, is not part of the economy's money supply.

A withdrawal of cash will reduce the bank's checkable-deposit liabilities and its holdings of cash by the amount of the withdrawal. This, too, changes the composition, but not the total supply, of money in the economy.

Transaction 4: Depositing Reserves in a Federal Reserve Bank

All commercial banks and thrift institutions that provide checkable deposits must by law keep **required reserves.** Required reserves are an amount of funds equal to a specified percentage of the bank's own deposit liabilities. A bank must keep these reserves on deposit with the Federal Reserve Bank in its district or as cash in the bank's vault. To simplify, we suppose the Bank of Wahoo keeps its required reserves entirely as deposits in the Federal Reserve Bank of its district. But remember that vault cash is counted as reserves and real-world banks keep a significant portion of their own reserves in their vaults.

The "specified percentage" of checkable-deposit liabilities that a commercial bank must keep as reserves is known as the **reserve ratio**—the ratio of the required reserves the commercial bank must keep to the bank's own outstanding checkable-deposit liabilities:

$$\text{Reserve ratio} = \frac{\text{commercial bank's required reserves}}{\text{commercial bank's checkable-deposit liabilities}}$$

If the reserve ratio is $\frac{1}{10}$, or 10 percent, the Wahoo bank, having accepted $100,000 in deposits from the public, would have to keep $10,000 as reserves. If the ratio is $\frac{1}{5}$, or 20 percent, $20,000 of reserves would be required. If $\frac{1}{2}$, or 50 percent, $50,000 would be required.

The Fed has the authority to establish and vary the reserve ratio within limits legislated by Congress. The limits now prevailing are shown in Table 32.1. The first $9.3 million of checkable deposits held by a commercial bank or thrift is exempt from reserve requirements. A 3 percent reserve is required on checkable deposits of between $9.3 million and $43.9 million. A 10 percent reserve is required on checkable deposits over $43.9 million, although the Fed can vary that percentage between 8 and 14 percent. Currently, no reserves are

TABLE 32.1 Reserve Requirements (Reserve Ratios) for Banks and Thrifts, 2008

Type of Deposit	Current Requirement	Statutory Limits
Checkable deposits:		
$0–$9.3 million	0%	3%
$9.3–$43.9 million	3	3
Over $43.9 million	10	8–14
Noncheckable nonpersonal savings and time deposits	0	0–9

Source: Federal Reserve, Regulation D, **www.federalreserve.gov.** Data are for 2008.

required against noncheckable nonpersonal (business) savings or time deposits, although up to 9 percent can be required. Also, after consultation with appropriate congressional committees, the Fed for 180 days may impose reserve requirements outside the 8–14 percent range specified in Table 32.1.

In order to simplify, we will suppose that the reserve ratio for checkable deposits in commercial banks is $\frac{1}{5}$, or 20 percent. Although 20 percent obviously is higher than the requirement really is, the figure is convenient for calculations. Because we are concerned only with checkable (spendable) deposits, we ignore reserves on noncheckable savings and time deposits. The main point is that reserve requirements are fractional, meaning that they are less than 100 percent. This point is critical in our analysis of the lending ability of the banking system.

By depositing $20,000 in the Federal Reserve Bank, the Wahoo bank will just be meeting the required 20 percent ratio between its reserves and its own deposit liabilities. We will use "reserves" to mean the funds commercial banks deposit in the Federal Reserve Banks, to distinguish those funds from the public's deposits in commercial banks.

But suppose the Wahoo bank anticipates that its holdings of checkable deposits will grow in the future. Then, instead of sending just the minimum amount, $20,000, it sends an extra $90,000, for a total of $110,000. In so doing, the bank will avoid the inconvenience of sending additional reserves to the Federal Reserve Bank each time its own checkable-deposit liabilities increase. And, as you will see, it is these extra reserves that enable banks to lend money and earn interest income.

Actually, a real-world bank would not deposit *all* its cash in the Federal Reserve Bank. However, because (1) banks as a rule hold vault cash only in the amount of $1\frac{1}{2}$ or 2 percent of their total assets and (2) vault cash can be counted as reserves, we will assume for simplicity that all of Wahoo's cash is deposited in the Federal Reserve Bank and therefore constitutes the commercial bank's actual reserves. By making this simplifying assumption, we do not need to bother adding two assets—"cash" and "deposits in the Federal Reserve Bank"—to determine "reserves."

After the Wahoo bank deposits $110,000 of reserves at the Fed, its balance sheet becomes:

Depositing Reserves at the Fed Balance Sheet 4: Wahoo Bank			
Assets		Liabilities and net worth	
Cash	$ 0	Checkable deposits	$100,000
Reserves	110,000		
Property	240,000	Stock shares	250,000

There are three things to note about this latest transaction.

Excess Reserves A bank's **excess reserves** are found by subtracting its *required reserves* from its **actual reserves:**

Excess reserves = actual reserves − required reserves

In this case,

Actual reserves	$110,000
Required reserves	−20,000
Excess reserves	$ 90,000

The only reliable way of computing excess reserves is to multiply the bank's checkable-deposit liabilities by the reserve ratio to obtain required reserves ($100,000 × 20 percent = $20,000) and then to subtract the required reserves from the actual reserves listed on the asset side of the bank's balance sheet.

To test your understanding, compute the bank's excess reserves from balance sheet 4, assuming that the reserve ratio is (1) 10 percent, (2) $33\frac{1}{3}$ percent, and (3) 50 percent.

We will soon demonstrate that the ability of a commercial bank to make loans depends on the existence of excess reserves. Understanding this concept is crucial in seeing how the banking system creates money.

Control You might think the basic purpose of reserves is to enhance the liquidity of a bank and protect commercial bank depositors from losses. Reserves would constitute a ready source of funds from which commercial banks could meet large, unexpected cash withdrawals by depositors.

But this reasoning breaks down under scrutiny. Although historically reserves have been seen as a source of liquidity and therefore as protection for depositors, a bank's required reserves are not great enough to meet sudden, massive cash withdrawals. If the banker's nightmare should materialize—everyone with checkable deposits appearing at once to demand those deposits in cash—the actual reserves held as vault cash or at the Federal Reserve Bank would be insufficient. The banker simply could not meet this "bank panic." Because reserves are fractional, checkable deposits may be much greater than a bank's required reserves.

So commercial bank deposits must be protected by other means. Periodic bank examinations are one way of promoting prudent commercial banking practices. Furthermore, insurance funds administered by the Federal Deposit Insurance Corporation (FDIC) and the National Credit Union Administration (NCUA) insure individual deposits in banks and thrifts up to $100,000.

If it is not the purpose of reserves to provide for commercial bank liquidity, then what is their function? *Control* is the answer. Required reserves help the Fed control the lending ability of commercial banks. The Fed can take certain actions that either increase or decrease commercial bank reserves and affect the ability of banks to grant credit. The objective is to prevent banks from overextending or underextending bank credit. To the degree that these policies successfully influence the volume of commercial bank credit, the Fed can help the economy avoid business fluctuations. Another function of reserves is to facilitate the collection or "clearing" of checks. **(Key Question 2)**

Asset and Liability Transaction 4 brings up another matter. Specifically, the reserves created in transaction 4 are an asset to the depositing commercial bank because they are a claim this bank has against the assets of another institution—the Federal Reserve Bank. The checkable deposit you get by depositing money in a commercial bank is an asset to you and a liability to the bank (since the bank is liable for repaying you whenever you choose to withdraw your deposit). In the same way, the reserves that a commercial bank establishes by depositing money in a bankers' bank are an asset to the commercial bank and a liability to the Federal Reserve Bank.

Transaction 5: Clearing a Check Drawn against the Bank

Assume that Fred Bradshaw, a Wahoo farmer, deposited a substantial portion of the $100,000 in checkable deposits that the Wahoo bank received in transaction 3. Now suppose that Fred buys $50,000 of farm machinery from the Ajax Farm Implement Company of Surprise, Nebraska. Bradshaw pays for this machinery by writing a $50,000 check against his deposit in the Wahoo bank. He gives the check to the Ajax Company. What are the results?

Ajax deposits the check in its account with the Surprise bank. The Surprise bank increases Ajax's checkable deposits by $50,000 when Ajax deposits the check. Ajax is now paid in full. Bradshaw is pleased with his new machinery.

Now the Surprise bank has Bradshaw's check. This check is simply a claim against the assets of the Wahoo bank. The Surprise bank will collect this claim by sending the check (along with checks drawn on other banks) to the regional Federal Reserve Bank. Here a bank employee will clear, or collect, the check for the Surprise bank by increasing Surprise's reserve in the Federal Reserve Bank by $50,000 and decreasing the Wahoo bank's reserve by that same amount. The check is "collected" merely by making bookkeeping notations to the effect that Wahoo's claim against the Federal Reserve Bank is reduced by $50,000 and Surprise's claim is increased by $50,000.

Finally, the Federal Reserve Bank sends the cleared check back to the Wahoo bank, and for the first time the Wahoo bank discovers that one of its depositors has drawn a check for $50,000 against his checkable deposit. Accordingly, the Wahoo bank reduces Bradshaw's checkable deposit by $50,000 and notes that the collection of this check has caused a $50,000 decline in its reserves at the Federal Reserve Bank. All the balance sheets balance: The Wahoo bank has reduced both its assets (reserves) and its liabilities (checkable deposits) by $50,000. The Surprise bank has $50,000 more in both assets (reserves) and liabilities (checkable deposits). Ownership of reserves at the Federal Reserve Bank has changed—with Wahoo owning $50,000 less and Surprise owning $50,000 more—but total reserves stay the same.

Whenever a check is drawn against one bank and deposited in another bank, collection of that check will reduce both the reserves and the checkable deposits of the bank on which the check is drawn. Conversely, if a bank receives a check drawn on another bank, the bank receiving the check will, in the process of collecting it, have its reserves and deposits increased by the amount of the check. In our example, the Wahoo bank loses $50,000 in both reserves and deposits to the Surprise bank. But there is no loss of reserves or deposits for the banking system as a whole. What one bank loses, another bank gains.

If we bring all the other assets and liabilities back into the picture, the Wahoo bank's balance sheet looks like this at the end of transaction 5:

Clearing a Check
Balance Sheet 5: Wahoo Bank

Assets		Liabilities and net worth	
Reserves	$ 60,000	Checkable deposits	$ 50,000
Property	240,000	Stock shares	250,000

Verify that with a 20 percent reserve requirement, the bank's excess reserves now stand at $50,000.

> **QUICK REVIEW 32.1**
>
> - When a bank accepts deposits of cash, the composition of the money supply is changed, but the total supply of money is not directly altered.
> - Commercial banks and thrifts are obliged to keep required reserves equal to a specified percentage of their own checkable-deposit liabilities as cash or on deposit with the Federal Reserve Bank of their district.
> - The amount by which a bank's actual reserves exceed its required reserves is called excess reserves.
> - A bank that has a check drawn and collected against it will lose to the recipient bank both reserves and deposits equal to the value of the check.

Money-Creating Transactions of a Commercial Bank

The next two transactions are crucial because they explain (1) how a commercial bank can literally create money by making loans and (2) how banks create money by purchasing government bonds from the public.

Transaction 6: Granting a Loan

In addition to accepting deposits, commercial banks grant loans to borrowers. What effect does lending by a commercial bank have on its balance sheet?

Suppose the Gristly Meat Packing Company of Wahoo decides it is time to expand its facilities. Suppose, too, that the company needs exactly $50,000—which just happens to be equal to the Wahoo bank's excess reserves—to finance this project.

Gristly goes to the Wahoo bank and requests a loan for this amount. The Wahoo bank knows the Gristly Company's fine reputation and financial soundness and is convinced of its ability to repay the loan. So the loan is granted. In return, the president of Gristly hands a promissory note—a fancy IOU—to the Wahoo bank. Gristly wants the convenience and safety of paying its obligations by check. So, instead of receiving a bushel basket full of currency from the bank, Gristly gets a $50,000 increase in its checkable-deposit account in the Wahoo bank.

The Wahoo bank has acquired an interest-earning asset (the promissory note, which it files under "Loans") and has created checkable deposits (a liability) to "pay" for this asset. Gristly has swapped an IOU for the right to draw an additional $50,000 worth of checks against its checkable deposit in the Wahoo bank. Both parties are pleased.

At the moment the loan is completed, the Wahoo bank's position is shown by balance sheet 6a:

When a Loan Is Negotiated Balance Sheet 6a: Wahoo Bank			
Assets		Liabilities and net worth	
Reserves	$ 60,000	Checkable	
Loans	50,000	deposits	$100,000
Property	240,000	Stock shares	250,000

All this looks simple enough. But a close examination of the Wahoo bank's balance statement reveals a startling fact: When a bank makes loans, it creates money. The president of Gristly went to the bank with something that is *not* money—her IOU—and walked out with something that *is* money—a checkable deposit.

Contrast transaction 6a with transaction 3, in which checkable deposits were created but only as a result of currency having been taken out of circulation. There was a change in the *composition* of the money supply in that situation but no change in the *total supply* of money. But when banks lend, they create checkable deposits that *are* money. By extending credit, the Wahoo bank has "monetized" an IOU. Gristly and the Wahoo bank have created and then swapped claims. The claim created by Gristly and given to the bank is not money; an individual's IOU is not acceptable as a medium of exchange. But the claim created by the bank and given to Gristly *is* money; checks drawn against a checkable deposit are acceptable as a medium of exchange.

Much of the money we use in our economy is created through the extension of credit by commercial banks. This checkable-deposit money may be thought of as "debts" of commercial banks and thrift institutions. Checkable deposits are bank debts in the sense that they are claims that banks and thrifts promise to pay "on demand."

But certain factors limit the ability of a commercial bank to create checkable deposits ("bank money") by lending. The Wahoo bank can expect the newly created checkable deposit of $50,000 to be a very active account. Gristly would not borrow $50,000 at, say, 7, 10, or 12 percent interest for the sheer joy of knowing that funds were available if needed.

Assume that Gristly awards a $50,000 building contract to the Quickbuck Construction Company of Omaha. Quickbuck, true to its name, completes the expansion promptly and is paid with a check for $50,000 drawn by Gristly against its checkable deposit in the Wahoo bank. Quickbuck, with headquarters in Omaha, does not deposit this check in the Wahoo bank but instead deposits it in the Fourth National Bank of Omaha. Fourth National now has a $50,000 claim against the Wahoo bank. The check is collected in the manner described in transaction 5. As a result, the Wahoo bank loses both reserves and deposits equal to the amount of the check; Fourth National acquires $50,000 of reserves and deposits.

In summary, assuming a check is drawn by the borrower for the entire amount of the loan ($50,000) and is given to a firm that deposits it in some other bank, the Wahoo bank's balance sheet will read as follows after the check has been cleared against it:

After a Check Is Drawn on the Loan Balance Sheet 6b: Wahoo Bank			
Assets		Liabilities and net worth	
Reserves	$ 10,000	Checkable	
Loans	50,000	deposits	$ 50,000
Property	240,000	Stock shares	250,000

After the check has been collected, the Wahoo bank just meets the required reserve ratio of 20 percent (= $10,000/$50,000). The bank has *no* excess reserves. This poses a question: Could the Wahoo bank have lent more than $50,000— an amount greater than its excess reserves— and still have met the 20 percent reserve requirement when a check for the full amount of the loan was cleared against it? The answer is no; the bank is "fully loaned up."

Here is why: Suppose the Wahoo bank had lent $55,000 to the Gristly company and that the Gristly company had spent all of that money by writing a $55,000 check to Quickbuck Construction. Collection of the check against the Wahoo bank would have lowered its reserves to $5,000 (= $60,000 − $55,000), and checkable deposits would once again stand at $50,000 (= $105,000 − $55,000). The ratio of actual reserves to checkable deposits would then be $5,000/$50,000, or only 10 percent. Because the reserve requirement is 20 percent, the Wahoo bank could not have lent $55,000.

> **WORKED PROBLEMS**
>
> **W 32.1**
>
> Single bank accounting

By experimenting with other amounts over $50,000, you will find that the maximum amount the Wahoo bank could lend at the outset of transaction 6 is $50,000. This amount is identical to the amount of excess reserves the bank had available when the loan was negotiated.

A single commercial bank in a multibank banking system can lend only an amount equal to its initial preloan excess reserves. When it lends, the lending bank faces the possibility that checks for the entire amount of the loan will be drawn and cleared against it. If that happens, it will lose (to other banks) reserves equal to the amount it lends. So, to be safe, it limits its lending to the amount of its excess reserves.

Bank creation of money raises an interesting question: If banks create checkable-deposit money when they lend their excess reserves, is money destroyed when borrowers pay off their loans? The answer is yes. When loans are paid off, the process just described works in reverse. Checkable deposits decline by the amount of the loan repayment.

Transaction 7: Buying Government Securities

When a commercial bank buys government bonds from the public, the effect is substantially the same as lending. New money is created.

Assume that the Wahoo bank's balance sheet initially stands as it did at the end of transaction 5. Now suppose that instead of making a $50,000 loan, the bank buys $50,000 of government securities from a securities dealer. The bank receives the interest-bearing bonds, which appear on its balance statement as the asset "Securities," and gives the dealer an increase in its checkable-deposit account. The Wahoo bank's balance sheet appears as follows:

Buying Government Securities			
Balance Sheet 7: Wahoo Bank			
Assets		Liabilities and net worth	
Reserves	$ 60,000	Checkable deposits	$100,000
Securities	50,000		
Property	240,000	Stock shares	250,000

Checkable deposits, that is, the supply of money, have been increased by $50,000, as in transaction 6. Bond purchases from the public by commercial banks increase the supply of money in the same way as lending to the public does. The bank accepts government bonds (which are not money) and gives the securities dealer an increase in its checkable deposits (which *are* money).

Of course, when the securities dealer draws and clears a check for $50,000 against the Wahoo bank, the bank loses both reserves and deposits in that amount and then just meets the legal reserve requirement. Its balance sheet now reads precisely as in 6b except that "Securities" is substituted for "Loans" on the asset side.

Finally, the *selling* of government bonds to the public by a commercial bank—like the repayment of a loan—reduces the supply of money. The securities buyer pays by check, and both "Securities" and "Checkable deposits" (the latter being money) decline by the amount of the sale.

Profits, Liquidity, and the Federal Funds Market

The asset items on a commercial bank's balance sheet reflect the banker's pursuit of two conflicting goals:

- *Profit* One goal is profit. Commercial banks, like any other businesses, seek profits, which is why the bank makes loans and buys securities—the two major earning assets of commercial banks.

- *Liquidity* The other goal is safety. For a bank, safety lies in liquidity, specifically such liquid assets as cash and excess reserves. A bank must be on guard for depositors who want to transform their checkable deposits into cash. Similarly, it must guard against more checks clearing against it than are cleared in its favor, causing a net outflow of reserves. Bankers thus seek a balance between prudence and profit. The compromise is between assets that earn higher returns and highly liquid assets that earn no returns.

An interesting way in which banks can partly reconcile the goals of profit and liquidity is to lend temporary excess reserves held at the Federal Reserve Banks to other commercial banks. Normal day-to-day flows of funds to banks rarely leave all banks with their exact levels of required reserves. Also, funds held at the Federal Reserve Banks are highly liquid, but they do not draw interest. Banks therefore lend these excess reserves to other banks on an overnight basis as a way of earning additional interest without sacrificing long-term liquidity. Banks that borrow in this Federal funds market—the market for immediately available reserve balances at the Federal Reserve—do so because they are temporarily short of required reserves. The interest rate paid on these overnight loans is called the **Federal funds rate.**

We would show an overnight loan of reserves from the Surprise bank to the Wahoo bank as a decrease in reserves at the Surprise bank and an increase in reserves at the Wahoo bank. Ownership of reserves at the Federal Reserve Bank of Kansas City would change, but total reserves would not be affected. Exercise: Determine what other changes would be required on the Wahoo and Surprise banks' balance sheets as a result of the overnight loan. **(Key Questions 4 and 8)**

QUICK REVIEW 32.2

- Banks create money when they make loans; money vanishes when bank loans are repaid.

- New money is created when banks buy government bonds from the public; money disappears when banks sell government bonds to the public.

- Banks balance profitability and safety in determining their mix of earning assets and highly liquid assets.

- Banks borrow and lend temporary excess reserves on an overnight basis in the Federal funds market; the interest rate on these loans is the Federal funds rate.

The Banking System: Multiple-Deposit Expansion

Thus far we have seen that a single bank in a banking system can lend one dollar for each dollar of its excess reserves. The situation is different for all commercial banks as a group. We will find that the commercial banking system can lend—that is, can create money—by a multiple of its excess reserves. This multiple lending is accomplished even though each bank in the system can lend only "dollar for dollar" with its excess reserves.

How do these seemingly paradoxical results come about? To answer this question succinctly, we will make three simplifying assumptions:

- The reserve ratio for all commercial banks is 20 percent.
- Initially all banks are meeting this 20 percent reserve requirement exactly. No excess reserves exist; or, in the parlance of banking, they are "loaned up" (or "loaned out") fully in terms of the reserve requirement.
- If any bank can increase its loans as a result of acquiring excess reserves, an amount equal to those excess reserves will be lent to one borrower, who will write a check for the entire amount of the loan and give it to someone else, who will deposit the check in another bank. This third assumption means that the worst thing possible happens to every lending bank—a check for the entire amount of the loan is drawn and cleared against it in favor of another bank.

The Banking System's Lending Potential

Suppose a junkyard owner finds a $100 bill while dismantling a car that has been on the lot for years. He deposits the $100 in bank A, which adds the $100 to its reserves. We will record only changes in the balance sheets of the various commercial banks. The deposit changes bank A's balance sheet as shown by entries (a_1):

Multiple-Deposit Expansion Process
Balance Sheet: Commercial Bank A

Assets		Liabilities and net worth	
Reserves	$+100 ($a_1$)	Checkable deposits	$+100 ($a_1$)
	−80 (a_3)		+80 (a_2)
Loans	+80 (a_2)		−80 (a_3)

Recall from transaction 3 that this $100 deposit of currency does not alter the money supply. While $100 of checkable-deposit money comes into being, it is offset by the $100 of currency no longer in the hands of the public (the junkyard owner). But bank A *has* acquired excess reserves of $80. Of the newly acquired $100 in currency, 20 percent, or $20, must be earmarked for the required reserves on the new $100 checkable deposit, and the remaining $80 goes to excess reserves. Remembering that a single commercial bank can lend only an amount equal to its excess reserves, we conclude that bank A can lend a maximum of $80. When a loan for this amount is made, bank A's loans increase by $80 and the borrower gets an $80 checkable deposit. We add these figures—entries (a_2)—to bank A's balance sheet.

But now we make our third assumption: The borrower draws a check ($80) for the entire amount of the loan, and gives it to someone who deposits it in bank B, a different bank. As we saw in transaction 6, bank A loses both reserves and deposits equal to the amount of the loan, as indicated in entries (a_3). The net result of these transactions is that bank A's reserves now stand at +$20 (= $100 − $80), loans at +$80, and checkable deposits at +$100 (= $100 + $80 − $80). When the dust has settled, bank A is just meeting the 20 percent reserve ratio.

Recalling our previous discussion, we know that bank B acquires both the reserves and the deposits that bank A has lost. Bank B's balance sheet is changed as in entries (b_1):

Multiple-Deposit Expansion Process
Balance Sheet: Commercial Bank B

Assets		Liabilities and net worth	
Reserves	$+80 ($b_1$)	Checkable deposits	$+80 ($b_1$)
	−64 (b_3)		+64 (b_2)
Loans	+64 (b_2)		−64 (b_3)

When the borrower's check is drawn and cleared, bank A loses $80 in reserves and deposits and bank B gains $80 in reserves and deposits. But 20 percent, or $16, of bank B's new reserves must be kept as required reserves against the new $80 in checkable deposits. This means that bank B has $64 (= $80 − $16) in excess reserves. It can therefore lend $64 [entries ($b_2$)]. When the new borrower draws a check for the entire amount and deposits it in bank C, the reserves and deposits of bank B both fall by $64 [entries ($b_3$)]. As a result of these transactions, bank B's reserves now stand at +$16 (= $80 − $64), loans at +$64, and checkable deposits at +$80 (= $80 + $64 − $64). After all this, bank B is just meeting the 20 percent reserve requirement.

We are off and running again. Bank C acquires the $64 in reserves and deposits lost by bank B. Its balance sheet changes as in entries (c_1):

Multiple-Deposit Expansion Process Balance Sheet: Commercial Bank C		
Assets	Liabilities and net worth	
Reserves	$+64.00 (c_1)	Checkable deposits	$+64.00 (c_1)
	$-51.20 (c_3)		$+51.20 (c_2)
Loans	$+51.20 (c_2)		$-51.20 (c_3)

Exactly 20 percent, or $12.80, of these new reserves will be required reserves, the remaining $51.20 being excess reserves. Hence, bank C can safely lend a maximum of $51.20. Suppose it does [entries (c_2)]. And suppose the borrower draws a check for the entire amount and gives it to someone who deposits it in another bank [entries (c_3)].

We could go ahead with this procedure by bringing banks D, E, F, G, . . . , N, and so on into the picture. In fact, the process will go on almost indefinitely, just as long as banks further down the line receive at least one penny in new reserves that they can use to back another round of lending and money creation. But we suggest that you work

through the computations for banks D, E, and F to be sure you understand the procedure.

The entire analysis is summarized in Table 32.2. Data for banks D through N are supplied on their own rows so that you may check your computations. The last row of the table consolidates into one row everything that happens for all banks down the line after bank N. Our conclusion is startling: On the basis of only $80 in excess reserves (acquired by the banking system when someone deposited $100 of currency in bank A), the entire commercial banking system is able to lend $400, the sum of the amounts in column 4. The banking system can lend excess reserves by a multiple of 5 (= $400/$80) when the reserve ratio is 20 percent. Yet each single bank in the banking system is lending only an amount equal to its own excess reserves. How do we explain this? How can the banking system as a whole lend by a multiple of its excess reserves, when each individual bank can lend only dollar for dollar with its excess reserves?

The answer is that reserves lost by a single bank are not lost to the banking system as a whole. The reserves lost by bank A are acquired by bank B. Those lost by B are gained by C. C loses to D, D to E, E to F, and so forth. Although reserves can be, and are, lost by individual banks in the banking system, there is no loss of reserves for the banking system as a whole.

TABLE 32.2 Expansion of the Money Supply by the Commercial Banking System

Bank	(1) Acquired Reserves and Deposits	(2) Required Reserves (Reserve Ratio = .2)	(3) Excess Reserves, (1) − (2)	(4) Amount Bank Can Lend; New Money Created = (3)
Bank A	$100.00 (a_1)	$20.00	**$80.00**	$ 80.00 (a_2)
Bank B	80.00 (a_3, b_1)	16.00	64.00	64.00 (b_2)
Bank C	64.00 (b_3, c_1)	12.80	51.20	51.20 (c_2)
Bank D	51.20	10.24	40.96	40.96
Bank E	40.96	8.19	32.77	32.77
Bank F	32.77	6.55	26.21	26.21
Bank G	26.21	5.24	20.97	20.97
Bank H	20.97	4.20	16.78	16.78
Bank I	16.78	3.36	13.42	13.42
Bank J	13.42	2.68	10.74	10.74
Bank K	10.74	2.15	8.59	8.59
Bank L	8.59	1.72	6.87	6.87
Bank M	6.87	1.37	5.50	5.50
Bank N	5.50	1.10	4.40	4.40
Other banks	21.99	4.40	17.59	17.59
Total amount of money created (sum of the amounts in column 4)				**$400.00**

An individual bank can safely lend only an amount equal to its excess reserves, *but the commercial banking system can lend by a multiple of its collective excess reserves*. This contrast, incidentally, is an illustration of why it is imperative that we keep the fallacy of composition (Last Word, Chapter 1) firmly in mind. Commercial banks as a group can create money by lending in a manner much different from that of the individual banks in the group.

The Monetary Multiplier

The banking system magnifies any original excess reserves into a larger amount of newly created checkable-deposit money. The *checkable-deposit multiplier*, or **monetary multiplier,** is similar in concept to the spending-income multiplier in Chapter 27. That multiplier exists because the expenditures of one household become some other household's income; the multiplier magnifies a change in initial spending into a larger change in GDP. The spending-income multiplier is the reciprocal of the MPS (the leakage into saving that occurs at each round of spending).

Similarly, the monetary multiplier exists because the reserves and deposits lost by one bank become reserves of another bank. It magnifies excess reserves into a larger creation of checkable-deposit money. The monetary multiplier m is the reciprocal of the required reserve ratio R (the leakage into required reserves that occurs at each step in the lending process). In short,

$$\text{Monetary multiplier} = \frac{1}{\text{required reserve ratio}}$$

or, in symbols,

$$m = \frac{1}{R}$$

In this formula, m represents the maximum amount of new checkable-deposit money that can be created by a single dollar of excess reserves, given the value of R. By multiplying the excess reserves E by m, we can find the maximum amount of new checkable-deposit money, D, that can be created by the banking system. That is,

$$\text{Maximum checkable-deposit creation} = \text{excess reserves} \times \text{monetary multiplier}$$

or, more simply,

$$D = E \times m$$

In our example in Table 32.2, R is .20, so m is 5 (= 1/.20). This implies that

$$D = \$80 \times 5 = \$400$$

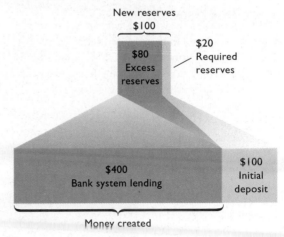

FIGURE 32.1 The outcome of the money expansion process. A deposit of $100 of currency into a checking account creates an initial checkable deposit of $100. If the reserve ratio is 20 percent, only $20 of reserves is legally required to support the $100 checkable deposit. The $80 of excess reserves allows the banking system to create $400 of checkable deposits through making loans. The $100 of reserves supports a total of $500 of money ($100 + $400).

New reserves
$100

$80 Excess reserves

$20 Required reserves

$400 Bank system lending

$100 Initial deposit

Money created

Figure 32.1 depicts the final outcome of our example of a multiple-deposit expansion of the money supply. The initial deposit of $100 of currency into the bank (lower right-hand box) creates new reserves of an equal amount (upper box). With a 20 percent reserve ratio, however, only $20 of reserves are needed to "back up" this $100 checkable deposit. The excess reserves of $80 permit the creation of $400 of new checkable deposits via the making of loans, confirming a monetary multiplier of 5. The $100 of new reserves supports a total supply of money of $500, consisting of the $100 initial checkable deposit plus $400 of checkable deposits created through lending.

WORKED PROBLEMS

W 32.2

Money creation

Higher reserve ratios mean lower monetary multipliers and therefore less creation of new checkable-deposit money via loans; smaller reserve ratios mean higher monetary multipliers and thus more creation of new checkable-deposit money via loans. With a high reserve ratio, say, 50 percent, the monetary multiplier would be 2 (= 1/.5), and in our example the banking system could create only $100 (= $50 of excess reserves × 2) of new checkable deposits. With a low reserve ratio, say, 5 percent, the monetary multiplier would be 20 (= 1/.05), and the banking system could create $1900 (= $95 of excess reserves × 20) of new checkable deposits.

The Bank Panics of 1930 to 1933

A Series of Bank Panics in the Early 1930s Resulted in a Multiple Contraction of the Money Supply.

In the early months of the Great Depression, before there was deposit insurance, several financially weak banks went out of business. As word spread that customers of those banks had lost their deposits, a general concern arose that something similar could happen at other banks. Depositors became frightened that their banks did not, in fact, still have all the money they had deposited. And, of course, in a fractional reserve banking system, that is the reality. Acting on their fears, people en masse tried to withdraw currency—that is, to "cash out" their accounts from their banks. They wanted to get their money before it was all gone. Economists liken this sort of collective response to "herd" or "flock" behavior. The sudden "run on the banks" caused many previously financially sound banks to declare bankruptcy. More than 9000 banks failed within 3 years.

The massive conversion of checkable deposits to currency during 1930 to 1933 reduced the nation's money supply. This might seem strange, since a check written for "cash" reduces checkable-deposit money and increases currency in the hands of the public by the same amount. So how does the money supply decline? Our discussion of the money-creation process provides the answer, but now the story becomes one of money destruction.

Suppose that people collectively cash out $10 billion from their checking accounts. As an immediate result, checkable-deposit money declines by $10 billion, while currency held by the public increases by $10 billion. But here is the catch: Assuming a reserve ratio of 20 percent, the $10 billion of currency in the banks had been supporting $50 billion of deposit money, the $10 billion of deposits plus $40 billion created through loans. The $10 billion withdrawal of currency forces banks to reduce loans (and thus checkable-deposit money) by $40 billion to continue to meet their reserve requirement. In short, a $40 billion destruction of deposit money occurs. This is the scenario that occurred in the early years of the 1930s.

Accompanying this multiple contraction of checkable deposits was the banks' "scramble for liquidity" to try to meet further withdrawals of currency. To obtain more currency, they sold many of their holdings of government securities to the public. You know from this chapter that a bank's sale of government securities to the public, like a reduction in loans, reduces the money supply. People write checks for the securities, reducing their checkable deposits, and the bank uses the currency it obtains to meet the ongoing bank run. In short, the loss of reserves from the banking system, in conjunction with the scramble for security, reduced the amount of checkable-deposit money by far more than the increase in currency in the hands of the public. Thus, the money supply collapsed.

In 1933, President Franklin Roosevelt ended the bank panic by declaring a "national bank holiday." This closed all national banks for 1 week so that government inspectors could have time to go over each bank's accounting records. Only healthy banks with plenty of reserves were allowed to reopen. This meant that when the holiday was over, people could trust in any bank that had been allowed to reopen. This policy, along with the initiation of the federal deposit insurance program, reassured depositors and ended the bank panics.

But before these policies could begin to turn things around, the nation's money supply had plummeted by 25 to 33 percent, depending on how narrowly or broadly the money supply is defined. This was the largest drop in the money supply in U.S. history. This decline contributed substantially to the nation's deepest and longest depression. Simply put, less money meant less spending on goods and services as well as fewer loans for businesses. Both effects exacerbated the Great Depression.

Today, a multiple contraction of the money supply of the 1930–1933 magnitude is unthinkable. FDIC insurance has kept individual bank failures from becoming general panics. Also, while the Fed stood idly by during the bank panics of 1930 to 1933, today it would take immediate and dramatic actions to maintain the banking system's reserves and the nation's money supply. Those actions are the subject of Chapter 33.

You might experiment with the following two brainteasers to test your understanding of multiple credit expansion by the banking system.

- Rework the analysis in Table 32.2 (at least three or four steps of it) assuming the reserve ratio is 10 percent. What is the maximum amount of money the banking system can create upon acquiring $100 in new reserves and deposits? (The answer is not $800!)

- Suppose the banking system is loaned up and faces a 20 percent reserve ratio. Explain how it might have to reduce its outstanding loans by $400 when a $100 cash withdrawal from a checkable-deposit account forces one bank to draw down its reserves by $100. **(Key Question 13)**

Reversibility: The Multiple Destruction of Money

The process we have described is reversible. Just as checkable-deposit money is created when banks make loans, checkable-deposit money is destroyed when loans are paid off. Loan repayment, in effect, sets off a process of multiple destruction of money the opposite of the multiple creation process. Because loans are both made and paid off in any period, the direction of the loans, checkable deposits, and money supply in a given period will depend on the net effect of the two processes. If the dollar amount of loans made in some period exceeds the dollar amount of loans paid off, checkable deposits will expand and the money supply will increase. But if the dollar amount of loans is less than the dollar amount of loans paid off, checkable deposits will contract and the money supply will decline.

QUICK REVIEW 32.3

- A single bank in a multibank system can safely lend (create money) by an amount equal to its excess reserves; the banking system can lend (create money) by a multiple of its excess reserves.

- The monetary multiplier is the reciprocal of the required reserve ratio; it is the multiple by which the banking system can expand the money supply for each dollar of excess reserves.

- The monetary multiplier works in both directions, it applies to money destruction from the payback of loans as well as the money creation from the making of loans.

Summary

1. Modern banking systems are fractional reserve systems: Only a fraction of checkable deposits is backed by currency.

2. The operation of a commercial bank can be understood through its balance sheet, where assets equal liabilities plus net worth.

3. Commercial banks keep required reserves on deposit in a Federal Reserve Bank or as vault cash. These required reserves are equal to a specified percentage of the commercial bank's checkable-deposit liabilities. Excess reserves are equal to actual reserves minus required reserves.

4. Banks lose both reserves and checkable deposits when checks are drawn against them.

5. Commercial banks create money—checkable deposits, or checkable-deposit money—when they make loans. The creation of checkable deposits by bank lending is the most important source of money in the U.S. economy. Money is destroyed when lenders repay bank loans.

6. The ability of a single commercial bank to create money by lending depends on the size of its excess reserves. Generally speaking, a commercial bank can lend only an amount equal to its excess reserves. Money creation is thus limited because, in all likelihood, checks drawn by borrowers will be deposited in other banks, causing a loss of reserves and deposits to the lending bank equal to the amount of money that it has lent.

7. Rather than making loans, banks may decide to use excess reserves to buy bonds from the public. In doing so, banks merely credit the checkable-deposit accounts of the bond sellers, thus creating checkable-deposit money. Money vanishes when banks sell bonds to the public because bond buyers must draw down their checkable-deposit balances to pay for the bonds.

8. Banks earn interest by making loans and by purchasing bonds; they maintain liquidity by holding cash and excess reserves. Banks having temporary excess reserves often lend them overnight to banks that are short of required reserves. The interest rate paid on loans in this Federal funds market is called the Federal funds rate.

9. The commercial banking system as a whole can lend by a multiple of its excess reserves because the system as a whole cannot lose reserves. Individual banks, however, can lose reserves to other banks in the system.

10. The multiple by which the banking system can lend on the basis of each dollar of excess reserves is the reciprocal of the reserve ratio. This multiple credit expansion process is reversible.

Terms and Concepts

fractional reserve banking system	required reserves	actual reserves
balance sheet	reserve ratio	Federal funds rate
vault cash	excess reserves	monetary multiplier

Study Questions  | ECONOMICS

1. Why must a balance sheet always balance? What are the major assets and claims on a commercial bank's balance sheet? **LO1**

2. **KEY QUESTION** Why does the Federal Reserve require commercial banks to have reserves? Explain why reserves are an asset to commercial banks but a liability to the Federal Reserve Banks. What are excess reserves? How do you calculate the amount of excess reserves held by a bank? What is the significance of excess reserves? **LO2**

3. "Whenever currency is deposited in a commercial bank, cash goes out of circulation and, as a result, the supply of money is reduced." Do you agree? Explain why or why not. **LO3**

4. **KEY QUESTION** "When a commercial bank makes loans, it creates money; when loans are repaid, money is destroyed." Explain. **LO3**

5. Explain why a single commercial bank can safely lend only an amount equal to its excess reserves but the commercial banking system as a whole can lend by a multiple of its excess reserves. What is the monetary multiplier, and how does it relate to the reserve ratio? **LO4**

6. Assume that Jones deposits $500 in currency into her checkable-deposit account in First National Bank. A half-hour later Smith obtains a loan for $750 at this bank. By how much and in what direction has the money supply changed? Explain. **LO3**

7. Suppose the National Bank of Commerce has excess reserves of $8000 and outstanding checkable deposits of $150,000. If the reserve ratio is 20 percent, what is the size of the bank's actual reserves? **LO4**

8. **KEY QUESTION** Suppose that Continental Bank has the simplified balance sheet shown below and that the reserve ratio is 20 percent: **LO5**
   a. What is the maximum amount of new loans that this bank can make? Show in column 1 how the bank's balance sheet will appear after the bank has lent this additional amount.

   b. By how much has the supply of money changed? Explain.
   c. How will the bank's balance sheet appear after checks drawn for the entire amount of the new loans have been cleared against the bank? Show the new balance sheet in column 2.
   d. Answer questions *a*, *b*, and *c* on the assumption that the reserve ratio is 15 percent.

9. The Third National Bank has reserves of $20,000 and checkable deposits of $100,000. The reserve ratio is 20 percent. Households deposit $5000 in currency into the bank that is added to reserves. What level of excess reserves does the bank now have? **LO4**

10. Suppose again that the Third National Bank has reserves of $20,000 and checkable deposits of $100,000. The reserve ratio is 20 percent. The bank now sells $5000 in securities to the Federal Reserve Bank in its district, receiving a $5000 increase in reserves in return. What level of excess reserves does the bank now have? Why does your answer differ (yes, it does!) from the answer to question 9? **LO4**

11. Suppose a bank discovers that its reserves will temporarily fall slightly short of those legally required. How might it remedy this situation through the Federal funds market? Now assume the bank finds that its reserves will be substantially and permanently deficient. What remedy is available to this bank? (Hint: Recall your answer to question 4.) **LO4**

12. Suppose that Bob withdraws $100 of cash from his checking account at Security Bank and uses it to buy a camera from Joe, who deposits the $100 in his checking account in Serenity Bank. Assuming a reserve ratio of 10 percent and no initial excess reserves, determine the extent to which (*a*) Security Bank finds itself short of required reserves, (*b*) Serenity Bank finds it has excess reserves, and (*c*) loans, checkable deposits, and the money supply change as a result of the transactions. **LO4**

Assets		(1)	(2)	Liabilities and net worth		(1)	(2)
Reserves	$22,000	——	——	Checkable deposits	$100,000	——	——
Securities	38,000	——	——				
Loans	40,000	——	——				

13. **KEY QUESTION** Suppose the simplified consolidated balance sheet shown below is for the entire commercial banking system. All figures are in billions. The reserve ratio is 25 percent. **LO5**

Assets		(1)	Liabilities and net worth		(1)
Reserves	$ 52	___	Checkable deposits	$200	___
Securities	48	___			
Loans	100	___			

a. What amount of excess reserves does the commercial banking system have? What is the maximum amount the banking system might lend? Show in column 1 how the consolidated balance sheet would look after this amount has been lent. What is the monetary multiplier?

b. Answer the questions in part *a* assuming the reserve ratio is 20 percent. Explain the resulting difference in the lending ability of the commercial banking system.

14. **LAST WORD** Explain how the bank panics of 1930 to 1933 produced a decline in the nation's money supply. Why are such panics highly unlikely today?

Web-Based Questions

1. **ASSETS AND LIABILITIES OF ALL COMMERCIAL BANKS IN THE UNITED STATES** The Federal Reserve, at **www.federalreserve.gov/releases/h8/Current,** provides an aggregate balance sheet for commercial banks in the United States. Check the current release, and look in the asset column for "Loans and leases." Rank the following components of loans and leases in terms of size: commercial and industrial, real estate, consumer, security, and other. Over the past 12 months, which component has increased by the largest percentage? By the largest absolute amount? Has the net worth (assets less liabilities) of all commercial banks in the United States increased, decreased, or remained constant during the past year?

2. **RESERVE REQUIREMENTS—ANY CHANGES TO TABLE 32.1?** Go to the Fed's Web site, **www.federalreserve.gov,** and select Monetary Policy. Click on Policy Tools, then Reserve Requirements. On that page, scroll down and read the table labeled Reserve Requirements. Does any part of Table 32.1 need updating? If so, prepare a new, updated table. Scroll down further and look at the table labeled Low Reserve Tranche Amounts and Exemption Amounts since 1982. Does Fed policy regarding reserve requirements change fairly often?.

33

IN THIS CHAPTER YOU WILL LEARN:

1 How the equilibrium interest rate is determined in the market for money.

2 The goals and tools of monetary policy.

3 About the Federal funds rate and how the Fed controls it.

4 The mechanisms by which monetary policy affects GDP and the price level.

5 The effectiveness of monetary policy and its shortcomings.

Interest Rates and Monetary Policy

Some newspaper commentators have stated that the chairman of the Federal Reserve Board (previously Alan Greenspan and now Ben Bernanke) is the second most powerful person in the United States, after the U.S. president. That is undoubtedly an exaggeration because the chair has only a single vote on the 7-person Federal Reserve Board and 12-person Federal Open Market Committee. But there can be no doubt about the chair's influence, the overall importance of the Federal Reserve, and the **monetary policy** that it conducts. Such policy consists of deliberate changes in the money supply to influence interest rates and thus the total level of spending in the economy. The goal is to achieve and maintain price-level stability, full employment, and economic growth.

Interest Rates

The Fed's primary influence is on the money supply and interest rates. Interest rates can be thought of in several ways. Most basically, **interest** is the price paid for the use of money. It is also the price that borrowers need to pay lenders for transferring purchasing power to the future. And it can be thought of as the amount of money that must be paid for the use of $1 for 1 year. Although there are many different interest rates that vary by purpose, size, risk, maturity, and taxability, we will simply speak of "*the* interest rate" unless stated otherwise.

Let's see how the interest rate is determined. Because it is a "price," we again turn to demand and supply analysis for the answer.

The Demand for Money

Why does the public want to hold some of its wealth as *money?* There are two main reasons: to make purchases with it and to hold it as an asset.

Transactions Demand, D_t People hold money because it is convenient for purchasing goods and services. Households usually are paid once a week, every 2 weeks, or monthly, whereas their expenditures are less predictable and typically more frequent. So households must have enough money on hand to buy groceries and pay mortgage and utility bills. Nor are business revenues and expenditures simultaneous. Businesses need to have money available to pay for labor, materials, power, and other inputs. The demand for money as a medium of exchange is called the **transactions demand** for money.

The level of nominal GDP is the main determinant of the amount of money demanded for transactions. The larger the total money value of all goods and services exchanged in the economy, the larger the amount of money needed to negotiate those transactions. The transactions demand for money varies directly with nominal GDP. We specify *nominal* GDP because households and firms will want more money for transactions if prices rise or if real output increases. In both instances a larger dollar volume will be needed to accomplish the desired transactions.

In **Figure 33.1a (Key Graph)** we graph the quantity of money demanded for transactions against the interest rate. For simplicity, let's assume that the amount demanded depends exclusively on the level of nominal GDP and is independent of the interest rate. (In reality, higher interest rates are associated with slightly lower volumes of money demanded for transactions.) Our simplifying assumption allows us to graph the transactions demand, D_t, as a vertical line. This demand curve is positioned at $100 billion, on the assumption that each dollar held for transactions purposes is spent on an average of three times per year and that nominal GDP is $300 billion. Thus the public needs $100 billion (= $300 billion/3) to purchase that GDP.

Asset Demand, D_a The second reason for holding money derives from money's function as a store of value. People may hold their financial assets in many forms, including corporate stocks, corporate or government bonds, or money. To the extent they want to hold money as an asset, there is an **asset demand** for money.

People like to hold some of their financial assets as money (apart from using it to buy goods and services) because money is the most liquid of all financial assets; it is immediately usable for purchasing other assets when opportunities arise. Money is also an attractive asset to hold when the prices of other assets such as bonds are expected to decline. For example, when the price of a bond falls, the bondholder who sells the bond prior to the payback date of the full principal will suffer a loss (called a *capital loss*). That loss will partially or fully offset the interest received on the bond. There is no such risk of capital loss in holding money.

The disadvantage of holding money as an asset is that it earns no or very little interest. Checkable deposits pay either no interest or lower interest rates than bonds. Currency itself earns no interest at all.

Knowing these advantages and disadvantages, the public must decide how much of its financial assets to hold as money, rather than other assets such as bonds. The answer depends primarily on the rate of interest. A household or a business incurs an opportunity cost when it holds money; in both cases, interest income is forgone or sacrificed. If a bond pays 6 percent interest, for example, holding $100 as cash or in a noninterest checkable account costs $6 per year of forgone income.

The amount of money demanded as an asset therefore varies inversely with the rate of interest (which is the opportunity cost of holding money as an asset). When the interest rate rises, being liquid and avoiding capital losses becomes more costly. The public reacts by reducing its holdings of money as an asset. When the interest rate falls, the cost of being liquid and avoiding capital losses also declines. The public therefore increases the amount of financial assets that it wants to hold as money. This inverse relationship just described is shown by D_a in Figure 33.1b.

> **ORIGIN OF THE IDEA**
>
> **O 33.1**
>
> Liquidity preference

Total Money Demand, D_m As shown in Figure 33.1, we find the **total demand for money**, D_m, by

keygraph

FIGURE 33.1 The demand for money, the supply of money, and the equilibrium interest rate. The total demand
for money D_m is determined by horizontally adding the asset demand for money D_a to the transactions demand D_t. The transactions demand is
vertical because it is assumed to depend on nominal GDP rather than on the interest rate. The asset demand varies inversely with the interest
rate because of the opportunity cost involved in holding currency and checkable deposits that pay no interest or very low interest. Combining the
money supply (stock) S_m with the total money demand D_m portrays the market for money and determines the equilibrium interest rate i_e.

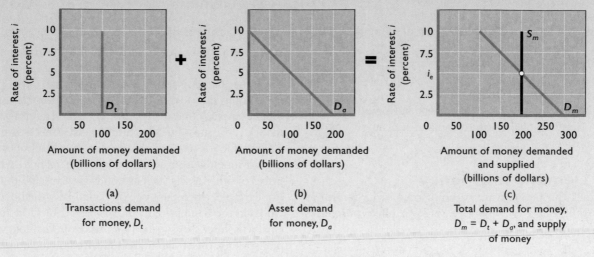

QUICK QUIZ FOR FIGURE 33.1

1. In this graph, at the interest rate i_e (5 percent):
   a. the amount of money demanded as an asset is $50 billion.
   b. the amount of money demanded for transactions is $200 billion.
   c. bond prices will decline.
   d. $100 billion is demanded for transactions, $100 billion is demanded as an asset, and the money supply is $200 billion.

2. In this graph, at an interest rate of 10 percent:
   a. no money will be demanded as an asset.
   b. total money demanded will be $200 billion.
   c. the Federal Reserve will supply $100 billion of money.
   d. there will be a $100 billion shortage of money.

3. Curve D_a slopes downward because:
   a. lower interest rates increase the opportunity cost of holding money.
   b. lower interest rates reduce the opportunity cost of holding money.

   c. the asset demand for money varies directly (positively) with the interest rate.
   d. the transactions-demand-for-money curve is perfectly vertical.

4. Suppose the supply of money declines to $100 billion. The equilibrium interest rate would:
   a. fall, the amount of money demanded for transactions would rise, and the amount of money demanded as an asset would decline.
   b. rise, and the amounts of money demanded both for transactions and as an asset would fall.
   c. fall, and the amounts of money demanded both for transactions and as an asset would increase.
   d. rise, the amount of money demanded for transactions would be unchanged, and the amount of money demanded as an asset would decline.

Answers: 1. d; 2. a; 3. b; 4. d

---

horizontally adding the asset demand to the transactions demand. The resulting downward-sloping line in Figure 33.1c represents the total amount of money the public wants to hold, both for transactions and as an asset, at each possible interest rate.

Recall that the transactions demand for money depends on the nominal GDP. A change in the nominal GDP—working through the transactions demand for money—will shift the total money demand curve. Specifically, an increase

WORKED PROBLEMS

W 33.1

Demand for money

in nominal GDP means that the public wants to hold a larger amount of money for transactions, and that extra demand will shift the total money demand curve to the right. In contrast, a decline in the nominal GDP will shift the total money demand curve to the left. As an example, suppose nominal GDP increases from $300 billion to $450 billion

662

and the average dollar held for transactions is still spent three times per year. Then the transactions demand curve will shift from $100 billion (= $300 billion/3) to $150 billion ($450 billion/3). The total money demand curve will then lie $50 billion farther to the right at each possible interest rate.

The Equilibrium Interest Rate

We can combine the demand for money with the supply of money to determine the equilibrium rate of interest. In Figure 33.1c, the vertical line, S_m, represents the money supply. It is a vertical line because the monetary authorities and financial institutions have provided the economy with some particular stock of money. Here it is $200 billion.

Just as in a product market or a resource market, the intersection of demand and supply determines the equilibrium price in the market for money. Here, the equilibrium "price" is the interest rate (i_e)—the price that is paid for the use of money over some time period.

Changes in the demand for money, the supply of money, or both can change the equilibrium interest rate. For reasons that will soon become apparent, we are most interested in changes in the supply of money. The impor-

> **INTERACTIVE GRAPHS**
> **G 33.1**
> Equilibrium interest rate

tant generalization is this: An increase in the supply of money will lower the equilibrium interest rate; a decrease in the supply of money will raise the equilibrium interest rate. **(Key Questions 1 and 2)**

Interest Rates and Bond Prices

Interest rates and bond prices are inversely related. When the interest rate increases, bond prices fall; when the interest rate falls, bond prices rise. Why so? First understand that bonds are bought and sold in financial markets and that the price of bonds is determined by bond demand and bond supply.

Suppose that a bond with no expiration date pays a fixed $50 annual interest payment and is selling for its face value of $1000. The interest yield on this bond is 5 percent:

$$\frac{\$50}{\$1000} = 5\% \text{ interest yield}$$

Now suppose the interest rate in the economy rises to $7\frac{1}{2}$ percent from 5 percent. Newly issued bonds will pay $75 per $1000 lent. Older bonds paying only $50 will not be salable at their $1000 face value. To compete with the $7\frac{1}{2}$ percent bond, the price of this bond will need to fall to $667 to remain competitive. The $50 fixed annual

interest payment will then yield $7\frac{1}{2}$ percent to whoever buys the bond:

$$\frac{\$50}{\$667} = 7\frac{1}{2}\%$$

Next suppose that the interest rate falls to $2\frac{1}{2}$ percent from the original 5 percent. Newly issued bonds will pay $25 on $1000 loaned. A bond paying $50 will be highly attractive. Bond buyers will bid up its price to $2000, at which price the yield will equal $2\frac{1}{2}$ percent:

$$\frac{\$50}{\$2000} = 2\frac{1}{2}\%$$

The point is that bond prices fall when the interest rate rises and rise when the interest rate falls. There is an inverse relationship between the interest rate and bond prices. **(Key Question 3)**

> **WORKED PROBLEMS**
> **W 33.2**
> Bond prices and interest rates

QUICK REVIEW 33.1

- People demand money for transaction and asset purposes.
- The total demand for money is the sum of the transactions and asset demands; it is graphed as an inverse relationship (downward-sloping line) between the interest rate and the quantity of money demanded.
- The equilibrium interest rate is determined by money demand and supply; it occurs when people are willing to hold the exact amount of money being supplied by the monetary authorities.
- Interest rates and bond prices are inversely related.

The Consolidated Balance Sheet of the Federal Reserve Banks

With this basic understanding of interest rates, we can turn to monetary policy, which relies on changes in interest rates to be effective. The 12 Federal Reserve Banks together constitute the U.S. "central bank," nicknamed the "Fed." (Global Perspective 33.1 also lists some of the other central banks in the world, along with their nicknames.)

The Fed's balance sheet helps us consider how the Fed conducts monetary policy. Table 33.1 consolidates the pertinent assets and liabilities of the 12 Federal Reserve Banks as of February 14, 2008. You will see that some of the Fed's assets and liabilities differ from those found on the balance sheet of a commercial bank.

TABLE 33.1 Consolidated Balance Sheet of the 12 Federal Reserve Banks, February 14, 2008 (in Millions)

Assets		Liabilities and Net Worth	
Securities	$713,369	Reserves of commercial banks	$ 11,312
Loans to commercial banks	60,039	Treasury deposits	4,979
All other assets	111,689	Federal Reserve Notes (outstanding)	778,937
		All other liabilities and net worth	89,869
Total	885,097	Total	885,097

Source: Federal Reserve Statistical Release, H.4.1, February 14, 2008, **www.federalreserve.gov.**

GLOBAL PERSPECTIVE 33.1

Central Banks, Selected Nations

The monetary policies of the world's major central banks are often in the international news. Here are some of their official names, along with a few of their popular nicknames.

Australia: Reserve Bank of Australia (RBA)
Canada: Bank of Canada
Euro Zone: European Central Bank (ECB)
Japan: The Bank of Japan (BOJ)
Mexico: Banco de Mexico (Mex Bank)
Russia: Central Bank of Russia
Sweden: Sveriges Riksbank
United Kingdom: Bank of England
United States: Federal Reserve System (the "Fed") (12 regional Federal Reserve Banks)

Assets

The two main assets of the Federal Reserve Banks are securities and loans to commercial banks. (Again, we will simplify by referring only to *commercial banks*, even though the analysis also applies to *thrifts*—savings and loans, mutual savings banks, and credit unions.)

Securities The securities shown in Table 33.1 are government bonds that have been purchased by the Federal Reserve Banks. They consist largely of Treasury bills (short-term securities), Treasury notes (mid-term securities), and Treasury bonds (long-term securities) issued by the U.S. government to finance past budget deficits. These securities are part of the public debt—the money borrowed by the Federal government. The Federal Reserve Banks bought these securities from commercial banks and the public through open-market operations. Although they

are an important source of interest income to the Federal Reserve Banks, they are mainly bought and sold to influence the size of commercial bank reserves and, therefore, the ability of those banks to create money by lending.

Loans to Commercial Banks For reasons that will soon become clear, commercial banks occasionally borrow from Federal Reserve Banks. The IOUs that commercial banks give these "bankers' banks" in return for loans are listed on the Federal Reserve balance sheet as "Loans to commercial banks." They are assets to the Fed because they are claims against the commercial banks. To commercial banks, of course, these loans are liabilities in that they must be repaid. Through borrowing in this way, commercial banks can increase their reserves.

Liabilities

On the "liabilities and net worth" side of the Fed's consolidated balance sheet, three entries are noteworthy: reserves, Treasury deposits, and Federal Reserve Notes.

Reserves of Commercial Banks The Fed requires that the commercial banks hold reserves against their checkable deposits. When held in the Federal Reserve Banks, these reserves are listed as a liability on the Fed's balance sheet. They are assets on the books of the commercial banks, which still own them even though they are deposited at the Federal Reserve Banks.

Treasury Deposits The U.S. Treasury keeps deposits in the Federal Reserve Banks and draws checks on them to pay its obligations. To the Treasury these deposits are assets; to the Federal Reserve Banks they are liabilities. The Treasury creates and replenishes these deposits by depositing tax receipts and money borrowed from the public or from the commercial banks through the sale of bonds.

Federal Reserve Notes Outstanding As we have seen, the supply of paper money in the United States consists of Federal Reserve Notes issued by the Federal

Reserve Banks. When this money is circulating outside the Federal Reserve Banks, it constitutes claims against the assets of the Federal Reserve Banks. The Fed thus treats these notes as a liability.

Tools of Monetary Policy

With this look at the Federal Reserve Banks' consolidated balance sheet, we can now explore how the Fed can influence the money-creating abilities of the commercial banking system. The Fed has four tools of monetary control it can use to alter the reserves of commercial banks:

- Open-market operations
- The reserve ratio
- The discount rate
- The term auction facility

Open-Market Operations

Bond markets are "open" to all buyers and sellers of corporate and government bonds (securities). The Federal Reserve is the largest single holder of U.S. government securities. The U.S. government, not the Fed, issued these Treasury bills, Treasury notes, and Treasury bonds to finance past budget deficits. Over the decades, the Fed has purchased these securities from major financial institutions that buy and sell government and corporate securities for themselves or their customers.

The Fed's **open-market operations** consist of the buying of government bonds from, or the selling of government bonds to, commercial banks and the general public. (The Fed actually buys and sells the government bonds to commercial banks and the public through two dozen or so large financial firms, called "primary dealers.") Open-market operations are the Fed's most important day-to-day instrument for influencing the money supply.

Buying Securities Suppose that the Fed decides to have the Federal Reserve Banks buy government bonds. They can purchase these bonds either from commercial banks or from the public. In both cases the reserves of the commercial banks will increase.

From Commercial Banks When Federal Reserve Banks buy government bonds *from commercial banks,*

(*a*) The commercial banks give up part of their holdings of securities (the government bonds) to the Federal Reserve Banks.

(*b*) The Federal Reserve Banks, in paying for these securities, place newly created reserves in the accounts of the commercial banks at the Fed. (These reserves are created "out of thin air," so to speak!) The reserves of the commercial banks go up by the amount of the purchase of the securities.

We show these outcomes as (*a*) and (*b*) on the following consolidated balance sheets of the commercial banks and the Federal Reserve Banks:

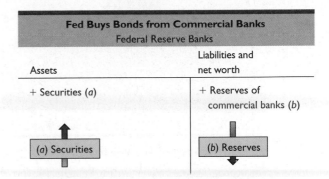

The upward arrow shows that securities have moved from the commercial banks to the Federal Reserve Banks. So we enter " − Securities" (minus securities) in the asset column of the balance sheet of the commercial banks. For the same reason, we enter " + Securities" in the asset column of the balance sheet of the Federal Reserve Banks.

The downward arrow indicates that the Federal Reserve Banks have provided reserves to the commercial banks. So we enter " + Reserves" in the asset column of the balance sheet for the commercial banks. In the liability column of the balance sheet of the Federal Reserve Banks, the plus sign indicates that although commercial bank reserves have increased, they are a liability to the Federal Reserve Banks because the reserves are owned by the commercial banks.

What is most important about this transaction is that when Federal Reserve Banks purchase securities from commercial banks, they increase the reserves in the banking system, which then increases the lending ability of the commercial banks.

From the Public The effect on commercial bank reserves is much the same when Federal Reserve Banks purchase securities from the general public. Suppose the

FIGURE 33.2 **The Federal Reserve's purchase of bonds and the expansion of the money supply.** Assuming all banks are loaded up initially, a Federal Reserve purchase of a $1000 bond from either a commercial bank or the public can increase the money supply by $5000 when the reserve ratio is 20 percent. In the left panel of the diagram, the purchase of a $1000 bond from a commercial bank creates $1000 of excess reserves that support a $5000 expansion of checkable deposits through loans. In the right panel, the purchase of a $1000 bond from the public creates a $1000 checkable deposit but only $800 of excess reserves because $200 of reserves is required to "back up" the $1000 new checkable deposit. The commercial banks can therefore expand the money supply by only $4000 by making loans. This $4000 of checkable-deposit money plus the new checkable deposit of $1000 equals $5000 of new money.

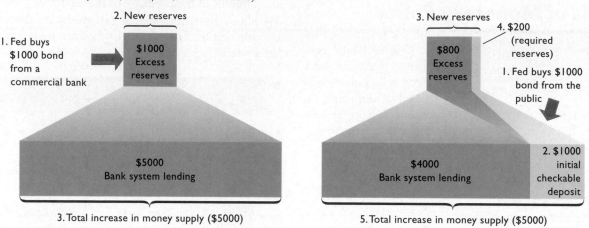

Gristly Meat Packing Company has government bonds that it sells in the open market to the Federal Reserve Banks. The transaction has several elements:

(a) Gristly gives up securities to the Federal Reserve Banks and gets in payment a check drawn by the Federal Reserve Banks on themselves.

(b) Gristly promptly deposits the check in its account with the Wahoo bank.

(c) The Wahoo bank sends this check against the Federal Reserve Banks to a Federal Reserve Bank for collection. As a result, the Wahoo bank enjoys an increase in its reserves.

To keep things simple, we will dispense with showing the balance sheet changes resulting from the Fed's sale or purchase of bonds from the public. But two aspects of this transaction are particularly important. First, as with Federal Reserve purchases of securities directly from commercial banks, the purchases of securities from the public increase the lending ability of the commercial banking system. Second, the supply of money is directly increased by the Federal Reserve Banks' purchase of government bonds (aside from any expansion of the money supply that may occur from the increase in commercial bank reserves). This direct increase in the money supply has taken the form of an increased amount of checkable deposits in the economy as a result of Gristly's deposit.

The Federal Reserve Banks' purchases of securities from the commercial banking system differ slightly from their purchases of securities from the public. If we assume that all commercial banks are loaned up initially, Federal Reserve bond purchases *from commercial banks* increase the actual reserves and excess reserves of commercial banks by the entire amount of the bond purchases. As shown in the left panel in Figure 33.2, a $1000 bond purchase from a commercial bank increases both the actual and the excess reserves of the commercial bank by $1000.

In contrast, Federal Reserve Bank purchases of bonds from the public increase actual reserves but also increase checkable deposits when the sellers place the Fed's check into their personal checking accounts. Thus, a $1000 bond purchase from the public would increase checkable deposits by $1000 and hence the actual reserves of the loaned-up banking system by the same amount. But with a 20 percent reserve ratio applied to the $1000 checkable deposit, the excess reserves of the banking system would be only $800 since $200 of the $1000 would have to be held as reserves.

However, in both transactions the end result is the same: When Federal Reserve Banks buy securities in the open market, commercial banks' reserves are increased. When the banks lend out an amount equal to their excess reserves, the nation's money supply will rise. Observe in Figure 33.2 that a $1000 purchase of bonds by the Federal Reserve results in a potential of $5000 of additional money, regardless of whether the purchase was made from commercial banks or from the general public.

> **WORKED PROBLEMS**
>
> **W 33.3**
> Open-market operations

Selling Securities As you may suspect, when the Federal Reserve Banks sell government bonds, commercial banks' reserves are reduced. Let's see why.

To Commercial Banks When the Federal Reserve Banks sell securities in the open market to commercial banks,

(*a*) The Federal Reserve Banks give up securities that the commercial banks acquire.

(*b*) The commercial banks pay for those securities by drawing checks against their deposits—that is, against their reserves—in Federal Reserve Banks. The Fed collects on those checks by reducing the commercial banks' reserves accordingly.

The balance-sheet changes—again identified by (*a*) and (*b*)—appear as shown below. The reduction in commercial bank reserves is indicated by the minus signs before the appropriate entries.

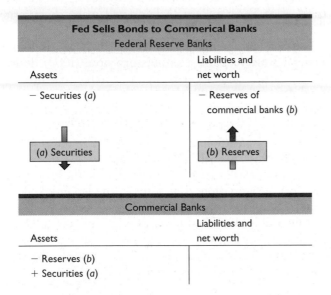

Fed Sells Bonds to Commercial Banks

Federal Reserve Banks

Assets	Liabilities and net worth
− Securities (*a*)	− Reserves of commercial banks (*b*)

(*a*) Securities

(*b*) Reserves

Commercial Banks

Assets	Liabilities and net worth
− Reserves (*b*)	
+ Securities (*a*)	

To the Public When the Federal Reserve Banks sell securities to the public, the outcome is much the same. Let's put the Gristly Company on the buying end of government bonds that the Federal Reserve Banks are selling:

(*a*) The Federal Reserve Banks sell government bonds to Gristly, which pays with a check drawn on the Wahoo bank.

(*b*) The Federal Reserve Banks clear this check against the Wahoo bank by reducing Wahoo's reserves.

(*c*) The Wahoo bank returns the canceled check to Gristly, reducing Gristly's checkable deposit accordingly.

Federal Reserve bond sales of $1000 to the commercial banking system reduce the system's actual and excess reserves by $1000. But a $1000 bond sale to the public reduces excess reserves by $800 because the public's checkable-deposit money is also reduced by $1000 by the sale. Since the commercial banking system's outstanding checkable deposits are reduced by $1000, banks need keep $200 less in reserves.

Whether the Fed sells bonds to the public or to commercial banks, the result is the same: When Federal Reserve Banks sell securities in the open market, commercial bank reserves are reduced. If all excess reserves are already lent out, this decline in commercial bank reserves produces a decline in the nation's money supply. In our example, a $1000 sale of government securities results in a $5000 decline in the money supply whether the sale is made to commercial banks or to the general public. You can verify this by reexamining Figure 33.2 and tracing the effects of a *sale* of a $1000 bond by the Fed either to commercial banks or to the public.

What makes commercial banks and the public willing to sell government securities to, or buy them from, Federal Reserve Banks? The answer lies in the price of bonds and their interest yields. We know that bond prices and interest rates are inversely related. When the Fed buys government bonds, the demand for them increases. Government bond prices rise, and their interest yields decline. The higher bond prices and their lower interest yields prompt banks, securities firms, and individual holders of government bonds to sell them to the Federal Reserve Banks.

When the Fed sells government bonds, the additional supply of bonds in the bond market lowers bond prices and raises their interest yields, making government bonds attractive purchases for banks and the public.

The Reserve Ratio

The Fed also can manipulate the **reserve ratio** in order to influence the ability of commercial banks to lend. Suppose a commercial bank's balance sheet shows that reserves are $5000 and checkable deposits are $20,000. If the legal reserve ratio is 20 percent (row 2, Table 33.2), the bank's required reserves are $4000. Since actual reserves are $5000, the excess reserves of this bank are $1000. On the basis of $1000 of excess reserves, this one bank can lend $1000; however, the banking system as a whole can create a maximum of $5000 of new checkable-deposit money by lending (column 7).

Raising the Reserve Ratio Now, what if the Fed raised the reserve ratio from 20 to 25 percent? (See row 3.) Required reserves would jump from $4000 to $5000, shrinking excess reserves from $1000 to zero. Raising the reserve ratio increases the amount of required reserves banks must keep. As a consequence, either banks lose excess reserves, diminishing their ability to create money by lending, or they find their reserves deficient and are forced to contract checkable deposits and therefore the money supply. In the

TABLE 33.2 The Effects of Changes in the Reserve Ratio on the Lending Ability of Commercial Banks

(1) Reserve Ratio, %	(2) Checkable Deposits	(3) Actual Reserves	(4) Required Reserves	(5) Excess Reserves, (3) − (4)	(6) Money-Creating Potential of Single Bank, = (5)	(7) Money-Creating Potential of Banking System
(1) 10	$20,000	$5000	$2000	$ 3000	$ 3000	$30,000
(2) 20	20,000	5000	4000	1000	1000	5000
(3) 25	20,000	5000	5000	0	0	0
(4) 30	20,000	5000	6000	−1000	−1000	−3333

example in Table 33.2, excess reserves are transformed into required reserves, and the money-creating potential of our single bank is reduced from $1000 to zero (column 6). Moreover, the banking system's money-creating capacity declines from $5000 to zero (column 7).

What if the Fed increases the reserve requirement to 30 percent? (See row 4.) The commercial bank, to protect itself against the prospect of failing to meet this requirement, would be forced to lower its checkable deposits and at the same time increase its reserves. To reduce its checkable deposits, the bank could let outstanding loans mature and be repaid without extending new credit. To increase reserves, the bank might sell some of its bonds, adding the proceeds to its reserves. Both actions would reduce the supply of money.

Lowering the Reserve Ratio

What would happen if the Fed lowered the reserve ratio from the original 20 percent to 10 percent? (See row 1.) In this case, required reserves would decline from $4000 to $2000, and excess reserves would jump from $1000 to $3000. The single bank's lending (money-creating) ability would increase from $1000 to $3000 (column 6), and the banking system's money-creating potential would expand from $5000 to $30,000 (column 7). Lowering the reserve ratio transforms required reserves into excess reserves and enhances the ability of banks to create new money by lending.

The examples in Table 33.2 show that a change in the reserve ratio affects the money-creating ability of the *banking system* in two ways:

- It changes the amount of excess reserves.
- It changes the size of the monetary multiplier.

For example, when the legal reserve ratio is raised from 10 to 20 percent, excess reserves are reduced from $3000 to $1000 and the checkable-deposit multiplier is reduced from 10 to 5. The money-creating potential of the banking system declines from $30,000 (= $3000 × 10) to $5000 (= $1000 × 5). Raising the reserve ratio forces banks to reduce the amount of checkable deposits they create through lending.

The Discount Rate

One of the functions of a central bank is to be a "lender of last resort." Occasionally, commercial banks have unexpected and immediate needs for additional funds. In such cases, each Federal Reserve Bank will make short-term loans to commercial banks in its district.

When a commercial bank borrows, it gives the Federal Reserve Bank a promissory note (IOU) drawn against itself and secured by acceptable collateral—typically U.S. government securities. Just as commercial banks charge interest on the loans they make to their clients, so too Federal Reserve Banks charge interest on loans they grant to commercial banks. The interest rate they charge is called the **discount rate.**

As a claim against the commercial bank, the borrowing bank's promissory note is an asset to the lending Federal Reserve Bank and appears on its balance sheet as "Loans to commercial banks." To the commercial bank the IOU is a liability, appearing as "Loans from the Federal Reserve Banks" on the commercial bank's balance sheet. [See the two (*a*) entries on the balance sheets below.]

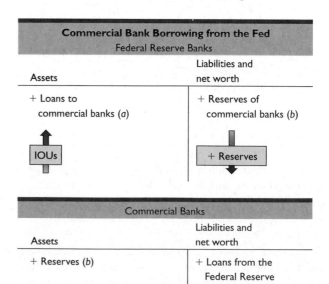

Commercial Bank Borrowing from the Fed

In providing the loan, the Federal Reserve Bank increases the reserves of the borrowing commercial bank. Since no required reserves need be kept against loans from Federal Reserve Banks, all new reserves acquired by borrowing from Federal Reserve Banks are excess reserves. [These changes are reflected in the two (*b*) entries on the balance sheets.]

In short, borrowing from the Federal Reserve Banks by commercial banks increases the reserves of the commercial banks and enhances their ability to extend credit.

The Fed has the power to set the discount rate at which commercial banks borrow from Federal Reserve Banks. From the commercial banks' point of view, the discount rate is a cost of acquiring reserves. A lowering of the discount rate encourages commercial banks to obtain additional reserves by borrowing from Federal Reserve Banks. When the commercial banks lend new reserves, the money supply increases.

An increase in the discount rate discourages commercial banks from obtaining additional reserves through borrowing from the Federal Reserve Banks. So the Fed may raise the discount rate when it wants to restrict the money supply. **(Key Question 5)**

Term Auction Facility

The fourth Fed tool for altering bank reserves is its **term auction facility.** This tool was introduced in December 2007 in response to the mortgage debt crisis, in which tens of thousands of homeowners defaulted on mortgage loans when they experienced higher mortgage interest rates and falling home prices. (We discuss this financial mess in detail in this chapter's Last Word.) Under the term auction facility, the Fed holds two auctions each month at which banks bid for the right to borrow reserves for 28-day periods. For instance, the Fed might auction off $20 billion in reserves. Banks that want to participate in the auction submit bids that include two pieces of information: how much they wish to borrow and the interest rate that they would be willing to pay. As an example, Wahoo bank might want to borrow $1 billion and offer to pay an annual interest rate of 4.35 percent.

These bids are submitted secretly. Once they are received, Fed officials arrange them from highest to lowest by interest rate. The limited pool of $20 billion goes to those banks that offer to pay the highest interest rates for the money that they desire to borrow. But the rate that all the auction winners actually pay is the same—it is the rate offered by the lowest bidder whose bid is accepted. For instance, suppose that 56 banks submit bids that total $36 billion. The Fed sorts these from highest to lowest based upon interest rates and then goes down the list to see

how many banks can get their desired loan amounts before exhausting the $20 billion. Suppose that the top 23 banks together wish to borrow $18 billion and that the 24th bank wishes to borrow the remaining $2 billion. Since its request would exhaust the $20 billion that is being auctioned off, its interest rate is the one that all 24 of the auction-winning banks will have to pay.

Lending through the term auction facility guarantees that the amount of reserves that the Fed wishes to lend will be borrowed. This is true because the auction procedure for determining the interest rate on the loans serves to produce an equilibrium price (interest rate) at which the quantity demanded of loans exactly equals the quantity supplied of loans (the amount of reserves that the Fed is auctioning off). The Fed finds this to be very helpful when it wants to increase reserves by a specific amount because it can be sure that those reserves will, in fact, be borrowed, thereby increasing the overall level of reserves in the banking system. In contrast, lowering the discount rate may or may not produce the exact level of borrowing the Fed desires.

It was this very positive aspect of the term auction facility that caused the Fed to start using it in late 2007 when it wished to increase bank reserves during the mortgage debt crisis. Reserves fell dramatically during that crisis and the Fed wanted to be sure to increase reserves so that banks would have excess reserves and therefore the ability to keep making loans.

In terms of balance sheets, however, loans of reserves borrowed by auction-winning banks under the term auction facility work exactly the same as loans of reserves taken out by banks when they are borrowing at the discount rate. Commercial banks send IOUs to the Fed and the Fed sends reserves to the commercial banks. As a result, the Fed can modulate the money supply by increasing or decreasing the amount of reserves that it auctions off every two weeks under the term auction facility.

Relative Importance

All four of the Fed's instruments of monetary control are useful in particular economic circumstances, but open-market operations are clearly the most important of the four tools over the course of the business cycle. The buying and selling of securities in the open market has the advantage of flexibility—government securities can be purchased or sold daily in large or small amounts—and the impact on bank reserves is prompt. And, compared with reserve-requirement changes, open-market operations work subtly and less directly. Furthermore, the ability of the Federal Reserve Banks to affect commercial bank reserves through the purchase and sale of bonds is virtually unquestionable.

The Federal Reserve Banks have very large holdings of government securities ($730 billion in early 2008 for example). The sale of those securities could theoretically reduce commercial bank reserves to zero.

Changing the reserve requirement is a potentially powerful instrument of monetary control, but the Fed has used this technique only sparingly. Normally, it can accomplish its monetary goals more easily through open-market operations. The limited use of changes in the reserve ratio undoubtedly relates to the fact that reserves earn no interest. Indeed, when the Fed raises or lowers the reserve ratio, it has a substantial effect on bank profits because it implicitly changes the amount of money on which banks are forced to earn a zero percent rate of return. The last change in the reserve requirement was in 1992, when the Fed reduced the requirement from 12 percent to 10 percent. The main purpose was to shore up the profitability of banks and thrifts in the aftermath of the 1990–1991 recession rather than to reduce interest rates by increasing reserves and expanding the money supply.

Until recently, the discount rate was mainly a passive tool of monetary control, with the Fed raising and lowering the rate simply to keep it in line with other interest rates. However, during the mortgage debt crisis, the Fed aggressively lowered the discount rate independently of other interest rates in order to provide a cheap and plentiful source of reserves to banks whose reserves were being sharply reduced by unexpectedly high default rates on home mortgage loans. Banks borrowed billions at the lower discount rate. This allowed them to meet reserve ratio requirements and thereby preserved their ability to keep extending loans.

As the mortgage debt crisis grew more severe, however, the Fed found that banks became increasingly reluctant to borrow at the discount rate for fear that such borrowing would be interpreted by their own lenders and stockholders as a sign of being in deep financial trouble. This prompted the Fed to create the term auction facility and, perhaps more importantly, to make it anonymous. When the Fed holds an auction of reserves using the term auction facility, banks submit their bids anonymously and auction winners are given their loans anonymously. This anonymity ensures that banks will participate in the auctions since they do not have to worry about being suspected of being in a financially weak condition.

The success of the term auction facility has led the Fed to adopt the auction of reserves as a fourth permanent tool of monetary policy. That being said, most economists believe that it will probably only be used during times of crisis when the Fed believes that the banking system can be helped by a large, quick injection of reserves.

QUICK REVIEW 33.2

- The Fed has four main tools of monetary control, each of which works by changing the amount of reserves in the banking system: (a) conducting open-market operations (the Fed's buying and selling of government bonds to the banks and the public); (b) changing the reserve ratio (the percentage of commercial bank deposit liabilities required as reserves); (c) changing the discount rate (the interest rate the Federal Reserve Banks charge on loans to banks and thrifts); and (d) auctioning off reserves to banks using the term auction facility.

- Open-market operations are the Fed's monetary control mechanism of choice for routine increases or decreases in bank reserves over the business cycle; in contrast, changes in reserve requirements, aggressive changes in discount rates, and auctions of reserves are used only in special situations.

Targeting the Federal Funds Rate

The Federal Reserve focuses monetary policy on the interest rate that it can best control: the **Federal funds rate.** From the previous chapter, you know that this is the rate of interest that banks charge one another on overnight loans made from temporary excess reserves. Recall that the Federal Reserve requires banks (and thrifts) to deposit in their regional Federal Reserve Bank a certain percentage of their checkable deposits as reserves. At the end of any business day, some banks temporarily have excess reserves (more actual reserves than required) and other banks have reserve deficiencies (fewer reserves than required). Because reserves held at the Federal Reserve Banks do not earn interest, banks with excess reserves desire to lend out their temporary excess reserves overnight to other banks that temporarily need them to meet their reserve requirements. The funds being lent and borrowed overnight are called "Federal funds" because they are reserves (funds) that are required by the Federal Reserve to meet reserve requirements. An equilibrium interest rate—the Federal funds rate—arises in this market for bank reserves.

The Federal Reserve targets the Federal funds rate by manipulating the supply of reserves that are offered in the Federal funds market. As previously explained, by buying and selling government bonds, the Fed can increase or decrease the reserves in the banking system. These changes in total reserves in turn affect the amount of *excess reserves* that are available for supply to the Federal funds market by whichever banks end up with them on a given day. For instance, suppose that the level of loans and checkable deposits at Wahoo bank are constant on a certain day. If the Fed then engages in open-market operations such that Wahoo's total reserves increase, Wahoo will find that it has excess reserves. It will want to loan out these excess reserves to bank customers as soon as possible. But in the meanwhile it will supply these funds overnight in the Federal funds market.

The Federal Open Market Committee (FOMC) meets regularly to choose a desired Federal funds rate. It then directs the Federal Reserve Bank of New York to undertake whatever open-market operations may be necessary to achieve and maintain the targeted rate. We demonstrate how this works in Figure 33.3, where we initially assume the Fed desires a 4 percent interest rate. The demand curve for Federal funds, D_f, is downsloping because lower interest rates give the banks with reserve deficiencies a greater incentive to borrow Federal funds rather than reduce loans as a way to meet their reserve requirements. The supply curve for Federal funds, S_{f1}, is somewhat unusual. Specifically, it is horizontal at the targeted Federal funds rate, here 4 percent. (Disregard supply curves S_{f2} and S_{f3} for now.) It is horizontal because the Fed uses open-market operations to manipulate the supply of Federal funds so that the quantity supplied of Federal funds will exactly

equal the quantity demanded of Federal funds at the targeted interest rate.

In this case, the Fed seeks to achieve an equilibrium Federal funds rate of 4 percent. In Figure 33.3 it is successful. Note that at the 4 percent Federal funds rate, the quantity of Federal funds supplied (Q_{f1}) equals the quantity of funds demanded (also Q_{f1}). This 4 percent Federal funds rate will remain, as long as the supply curve of Federal funds is horizontal at 4 percent. If the demand for Federal funds increases (D_f shifts to the right along S_{f1}), the Fed will use its open-market operations to increase the availability of reserves such that the 4 percent Federal funds rate is retained. If the demand for Federal funds declines (D_f shifts to the left along S_{f1}), the Fed will withdraw reserves to keep the Federal funds rate at 4 percent.

Expansionary Monetary Policy

Suppose that the economy faces recession and unemployment. How will the Fed respond? It will initiate an **expansionary monetary policy** (or "easy money policy"). This policy will lower the interest rate to bolster borrowing and spending, which will increase aggregate demand and expand real output. The Fed's immediate step will be to announce a lower target for the Federal funds rate, say 3.5 percent instead of 4 percent. To achieve that lower rate, the Fed will use open-market operations to buy bonds from banks and the public. We know from previous discussion that the purchase of bonds increases the reserves in the banking system. Alternatively, the Fed could expand reserves by lowering the reserve requirement, lowering the discount rate, or auctioning off more reserves, but these alternative tools are less frequently used than open-market operations.

The greater reserves in the banking system produce two critical results:

- The supply of Federal funds increases, lowering the Federal funds rate to the new targeted rate. We show this in Figure 33.3 as a downward shift to the horizontal supply curve from S_{f1} to S_{f2}. The equilibrium Federal funds rate falls to 3.5 percent, just as the FOMC wanted. The equilibrium quantity of reserves in the overnight market for reserves rises from Q_{f1} to Q_{f2}.
- A multiple expansion of the nation's money supply occurs (as we demonstrated in Chapter 32). Given the demand for money, the larger money supply places a downward pressure on other interest rates.

One such rate is the **prime interest rate**—the benchmark interest rate used by banks as a reference point for a wide range of interest rates charged on loans to businesses and individuals. The prime interest rate is higher than the

FIGURE 33.3 Targeting the Federal funds rate In implementing monetary policy, the Federal Reserve determines a desired Federal funds rate and then uses open-market operations (buying and selling of U.S. securities) to add or subtract bank reserves to achieve and maintain that targeted rate. In an expansionary monetary policy, the Fed increases the supply of reserves, for example, from S_{f1} to S_{f2} in this case, to move the Federal funds rate from 4 percent to 3.5 percent. In a restrictive monetary policy, it decreases the supply of reserves, say, from S_{f1} to S_{f3}. Here, the Federal funds rate rises from 4 percent to 4.5 percent.

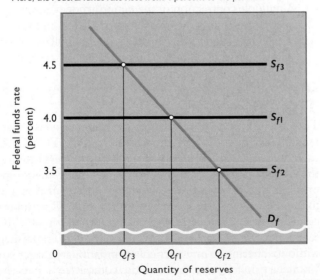

FIGURE 33.4 The prime interest rate and the Federal funds rate in the United States, 1998–2008. The prime interest rate rises and falls with changes in the Federal funds rate.

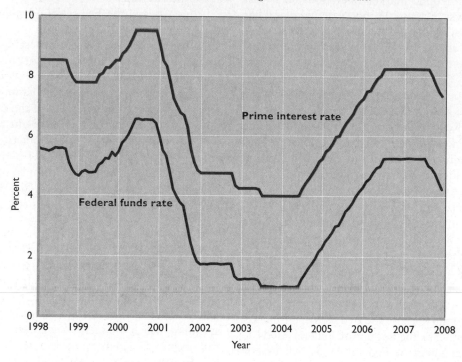

Federal funds rate because the prime rate involves longer, more risky loans than overnight loans between banks. But the Federal funds rate and the prime interest rate closely track one another, as evident in Figure 33.4.

Restrictive Monetary Policy

The opposite monetary policy is in order for periods of rising inflation. The Fed will then undertake a **restrictive monetary policy** (or "tight money policy"). This policy will increase the interest rate in order to reduce borrowing and spending, which will curtail the expansion of aggregate demand and hold down price-level increases. The Fed's immediate step will be to announce a higher target for the Federal funds rate, say 4.5 percent instead of 4 percent. Through open-market operations, the Fed will sell bonds to the banks and the public and the sale of those bonds will absorb reserves in the banking system. Alternatively, the Fed could absorb reserves by raising the reserve requirement, raising the discount rate, or reducing the amount of reserves that it auctions off. But, open-market operations are usually sufficient to accomplish the goal.

The smaller reserves in the banking system produce two results opposite those discussed for an expansionary monetary policy:

- The supply of Federal funds decreases, raising the Federal funds rate to the new targeted rate. We show this in Figure 33.3 as an upward shift of the horizonal supply curve from S_{f1} to S_{f3}. The equilibrium Federal funds rate rises to 4.5 percent, just as the FOMC wanted, and the equilibrium quantity of funds in this market falls to Q_{f3}.
- A multiple contraction of the nation's money supply occurs (as demonstrated in Chapter 32). Given the demand for money, the smaller money supply places an upward pressure on other interest rates. For example, the prime interest rate rises.

The Taylor Rule

The proper Federal funds rate for a certain period is a matter of policy discretion by the members of the FOMC. At each of their meetings, committee members assess whether the current target for the Federal funds rate remains appropriate for achieving the twin goals of low inflation and full employment. If the majority of the FOMC members conclude that a change in the rate is needed, the FOMC sets a new targeted rate. This new target is established without adhering to any particular "inflationary target" or "monetary policy rule." Instead, the committee targets the

CONSIDER THIS . . .

The Fed as a Sponge

A good way to remember the role of the Fed in setting the Federal funds rate might be to imagine a bowl of water, with the amount of water in the bowl representing the stock of reserves in the banking system. Then think of the FOMC as having a large sponge, labeled open-market operations. When it wants to decrease the Federal funds rate, it uses the sponge—soaked with water (reserves) created by the Fed—to squeeze new reserves into the banking system bowl. It continues this process until the higher supply of reserves reduces the Federal funds rate to the Fed's desired level. If the Fed wants to increase the Federal funds rate, it uses the sponge to absorb reserves from the bowl (banking system). As the supply of reserves falls, the Federal funds rate rises to the Fed's desired level.

Federal funds rate at the level most appropriate for the current underlying economic conditions.

A rule of thumb suggested by economist John Taylor of Stanford roughly tracks the actual policy of the Fed. This rule of thumb builds on the belief held by many economists that central banks are willing to tolerate a small positive rate of inflation if doing so will help the economy to produce at potential output. The **Taylor rule** assumes that the Fed has a 2 percent "target rate of inflation" that it is willing to tolerate and that the FOMC follows three rules when setting its target for the Federal funds rate:

- When real GDP equals potential GDP and inflation is at its target rate of 2 percent, the Federal funds target rate should be 4 percent, implying a real Federal funds rate of 2 percent (= 4 percent nominal Federal funds rate – 2 percent inflation rate).
- For each 1 percent increase of real GDP above potential GDP, the Fed should raise the *real* Federal funds rate by ½ percentage point.
- For each 1 percent increase in the inflation rate above its 2 percent target rate, the Fed should raise the *real* Federal funds rate by ½ percentage point. (Note, though, that in this case each ½ percentage point increase in the real rate will require a

1.5 percentage point increase in the nominal rate in order to account for the underlying 1 percent increase in the inflation rate.)

The last two rules are applied independently of each other so that if real GDP is above potential output and at the same time inflation is above the 2 percent target rate, the Fed will apply both rules and raise real interest rates in response to both factors. For instance, if real GDP is 1 percent above potential output and inflation is simultaneously 1 percent above the 2 percent target rate, then the Fed will raise the *real* Federal funds rate by 1 percentage point (= ½ percentage point for the excessive GDP + ½ percentage point for the excessive inflation).

Also notice that the last two rules are reversed for situations in which real GDP falls below potential GDP or inflation falls below 2 percent. Each 1 percent decline in real GDP below potential GDP or fall in inflation below 2 percent calls for a decline of the *real* Federal funds rate by ½ percentage point.

We reemphasize that the Fed has no official allegiance to the Taylor rule. It changes the Federal funds rate to any level that it deems appropriate.

ORIGIN OF THE IDEA

O 33.4

Taylor rule

QUICK REVIEW 33.3

- The Fed conducts its monetary policy by establishing a targeted Federal funds interest rate—the rate that commercial banks charge one another for overnight loans of reserves.
- An expansionary monetary policy (loose money policy) lowers the Federal funds rate, increases the money supply, and lowers other interest rates.
- A restrictive monetary policy (tight money policy) increases the Federal funds rate, reduces the money supply, and increases other interest rates.
- The Fed uses it discretion in setting the Federal funds target rate, but its decisions regarding monetary policy and the target rate appear to be broadly consistent with the Taylor rule.

Monetary Policy, Real GDP, and the Price Level

We have identified and explained the tools of expansionary and contractionary monetary policy. We now want to emphasize how monetary policy affects the economy's levels of investment, aggregate demand, real GDP, and prices.

INTERACTIVE GRAPHS

G 33.2

Monetary policy

FIGURE 33.5 **Monetary policy and equilibrium GDP.** An expansionary monetary policy that shifts the money supply curve rightward from S_{m1} to S_{m2} in (a) lowers the interest rate from 10 to 8 percent in (b). As a result, investment spending increases from $15 billion to $20 billion, shifting the aggregate demand curve rightward from AD_1 to AD_2 in (c) so that real output rises from the recessionary level of $880 billion to the fullemployment level $Q_f = \$900$ billion along the horizontal dashed segment of aggregate supply. In (d), the economy at point a has an inflationary output gap of $10 billion because it is producing at $910 billion, $10 billion above potential output. A restrictive monetary policy that shifts the money supply curve leftward from $Sm_3 = \$175$ billion to just $162.5 billion in (a) will increase the interest rate from 6 to 7 percent. Investment spending thus falls by $2.5 billion from $25 billion to $22.5 billion in (b). This initial decline is multiplied by 4 by the multiplier process so that the aggregate demand curve shifts leftward in (d) by $10 billion from AD_3 to AD_4, moving the economy along the horizontal dashed segment of aggregate supply to equilibrium b. This returns the economy to full employment and eliminates the inflationary output gap.

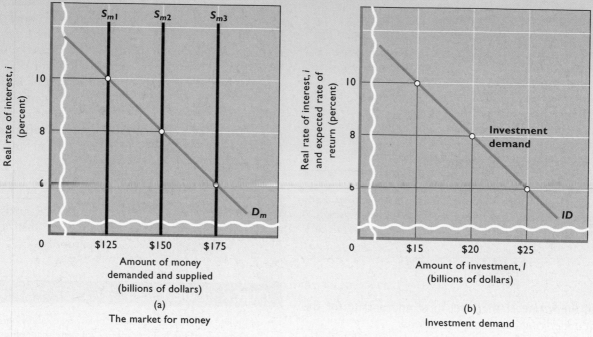

(a)
The market for money

(b)
Investment demand

QUICK QUIZ FOR FIGURE 33.5

1. The ultimate objective of an expansionary monetary policy is depicted by:
   a. a decrease in the money supply from S_{m3} to S_{m2}.

   b. a reduction of the interest rate from 8 to 6 percent.
   c. an increase in investment from $20 billion to $25 billion.
   d. an increase in real GDP from Q_1 to Q_f.

Cause-Effect Chain

The four diagrams in **Figure 33.5 (Key Graph)** will help you understand how monetary policy works toward achieving its goals.

Market for Money Figure 33.5a represents the market for money, in which the demand curve for money and the supply curve of money are brought together. Recall that the total demand for money is made up of the transactions and asset demands.

This figure also shows three potential money supply curves, S_{m1}, S_{m2}, and S_{m3}. In each case, the money supply is shown as a vertical line representing some fixed amount of money determined by the Fed.

The equilibrium interest rate is the rate at which the amount of money demanded and the amount supplied are equal. With money demand D_m in Figure 33.5a, if the supply of money is $125 billion ($S_{m1}$), the equilibrium interest rate is 10 percent. With a money supply of $150 billion ($S_{m2}$), the equilibrium interest rate is 8 percent; with a money supply of $175 billion ($S_{m3}$), it is 6 percent.

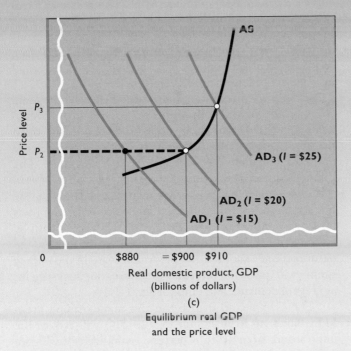

(c)

Equilibrium real GDP
and the price level

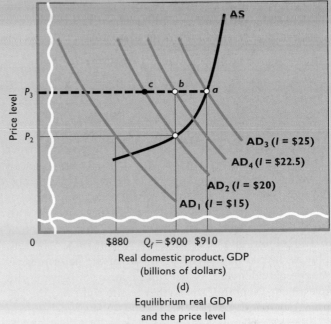

(d)

Equilibrium real GDP
and the price level

2. A successful restrictive monetary policy is evidenced by a shift in the money supply curve from:
   a. S_{m3} to a point half way between S_{m2} and S_{m3}, a decrease in investment from $25 billion to $22.5 billion, and a decline in aggregate demand from AD_3 to AD_4.
   b. S_{m1} to S_{m2}, an increase in investment from $20 billion to $25 billion, and an increase in real GDP from Q_1 to Q_f.
   c. S_{m3} to S_{m2}, a decrease in investment from $25 billion to $20 billion, and a decline in the price level from P_3 to P_2.
   d. S_{m3} to S_{m2}, a decrease in investment from $25 billion to $20 billion, and an increase in aggregate demand from AD_2 to AD_3.

3. The Federal Reserve could increase the money supply from S_{m1} to S_{m2} by:
   a. increasing the discount rate.
   b. reducing taxes.
   c. buying government securities in the open market.
   d. increasing the reserve requirement.

4. If the spending-income multiplier is 4 in the economy depicted, an increase in the money supply from $125 billion to $150 billion will:
   a. shift the aggregate demand curve rightward by $20 billion.
   b. increase real GDP by $25 billion.
   c. increase real GDP by $100 billion.
   d. shift the aggregate demand curve leftward by $5 billion.

Answers: 1. d; 2. c; 3. c; 4. a

You know from Chapter 27 that the real, not the nominal, rate of interest is critical for investment decisions. So here we assume that Figure 33.5a portrays real interest rates.

Investment These 10, 8, and 6 percent real interest rates are carried rightward to the investment demand curve in Figure 33.5b. This curve shows the inverse relationship between the interest rate—the cost of borrowing to invest—and the amount of investment spending. At the 10 percent interest rate, it will be profitable for

the nation's businesses to invest $15 billion; at 8 percent, $20 billion; at 6 percent, $25 billion.

Changes in the interest rate mainly affect the investment component of total spending, although they also affect spending on durable consumer goods (such as autos) that are purchased on credit. The impact of changing interest rates on investment spending is great because of the large cost and long-term nature of capital purchases. Capital equipment, factory buildings, and warehouses are tremendously expensive. In absolute terms, interest charges on funds borrowed for these purchases are considerable.

Similarly, the interest cost on a house purchased on a long-term contract is very large: A $\frac{1}{2}$-percentage-point change in the interest rate could amount to thousands of dollars in the total cost of buying a home.

In brief, the impact of changing interest rates is mainly on investment (and, through that, on aggregate demand, output, employment, and the price level). Moreover, as Figure 33.5b shows, investment spending varies inversely with the real interest rate.

Equilibrium GDP

Figure 33.5c shows the impact of our three real interest rates and corresponding levels of investment spending on aggregate demand. (Ignore Figure 33.5d for the time being. We will return to it shortly.) As noted, aggregate demand curve AD_1 is associated with the $15 billion level of investment, AD_2 with investment of $20 billion, and AD_3 with investment of $25 billion. That is, investment spending is one of the determinants of aggregate demand. Other things equal, the greater the investment spending, the farther to the right lies the aggregate demand curve.

Suppose the money supply in Figure 33.5a is $150 billion ($S_{m2}$), producing an equilibrium interest rate of 8 percent. In Figure 33.5b we see that this 8 percent interest rate will bring forth $20 billion of investment spending. This $20 billion of investment spending joins with consumption spending, net exports, and government spending to yield aggregate demand curve AD_2 in Figure 33.5c. The equilibrium levels of real output and prices are $Q_f = $900 billion and P_2, as determined by the intersection of AD_2 and the aggregate supply curve AS.

To test your understanding of these relationships, explain why each of the other two levels of money supply in Figure 33.5a results in a different interest rate, level of investment, aggregate demand curve, and equilibrium real output.

Effects of an Expansionary Monetary Policy

Recall that the inflationary ratchet effect discussed in Chapter 29 describes the fact that real-world price levels tend to be downwardly inflexible. Thus, with our economy starting from the initial equilibrium where AD_2 intersects AS, the price level will be downwardly inflexible at P_2 so that aggregate supply will be horizontal to the left of Q_f. This means that if aggregate demand decreases, the economy's equilibrium will move leftward along the dashed horizontal line shown in Figure 33.5c.

Just such a decline would happen if the money supply fell to $125 billion ($S_{m1}$), shifting the aggregate demand curve leftward to AD_1 in Figure 33.5c. This results in a real output of $880 billion, $20 billion less than the economy's full-employment output level of $900 billion. The economy will be experiencing recession, a negative GDP gap, and substantial unemployment. The Fed therefore should institute an expansionary monetary policy.

To increase the money supply, the Fed will take some combination of the following actions: (1) buy government securities from banks and the public in the open market, (2) lower the legal reserve ratio, (3) lower the discount rate, and (4) increase reserve auctions. The intended outcome will be an increase in excess reserves in the commercial banking system and a decline in the Federal funds rate. Because excess reserves are the basis on which commercial banks and thrifts can earn profit by lending and thus creating checkable-deposit money, the nation's money supply will rise. An increase in the money supply will lower the interest rate, increasing investment, aggregate demand, and equilibrium GDP.

For example, an increase in the money supply from $125 billion to $150 billion ($S_{m1}$ to S_{m2}) will reduce the interest rate from 10 to 8 percent, as indicated in Figure 33.5a, and will boost investment from $15 billion to $20 billion, as shown in Figure 33.5b. This $5 billion increase in investment will shift the aggregate demand curve rightward by more than the increase in investment because of the multiplier effect. If the economy's MPC is .75, the multiplier will be 4, meaning that the $5 billion increase in investment will shift the AD curve rightward by $20 billion (= 4 × $5 billion) at each price level. Specifically, aggregate demand will shift from AD_1 to AD_2, as shown in Figure 33.5c. This rightward shift in the aggregate demand curve along the dashed horizontal part of aggregate supply will eliminate the negative GDP gap by increasing GDP from $880 billion to the full-employment GDP of $Q_f = $900 billion.[1]

Column 1 in Table 33.3 summarizes the chain of events associated with an expansionary monetary policy.

Effects of a Restrictive Monetary Policy

To prevent Figure 33.5c from getting too crowded as we consider restrictive monetary policy, we will combine the money market in Figure 33.5a and the investment demand

---

[1]To keep things simple, we assume that the increase in real GDP does not increase the demand for money. In reality, the transactions demand for money would rise, slightly dampening the decline in the interest rate shown in Figure 33.5a.

TABLE 33.3 Monetary Policies for Recession and Inflation

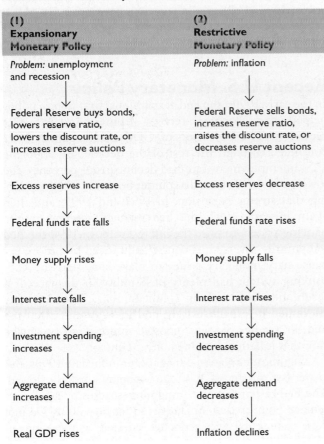

(1) Expansionary Monetary Policy	(2) Restrictive Monetary Policy
Problem: unemployment and recession	*Problem:* inflation
↓	↓
Federal Reserve buys bonds, lowers reserve ratio, lowers the discount rate, or increases reserve auctions	Federal Reserve sells bonds, increases reserve ratio, raises the discount rate, or decreases reserve auctions
↓	↓
Excess reserves increase	Excess reserves decrease
↓	↓
Federal funds rate falls	Federal funds rate rises
↓	↓
Money supply rises	Money supply falls
↓	↓
Interest rate falls	Interest rate rises
↓	↓
Investment spending increases	Investment spending decreases
↓	↓
Aggregate demand increases	Aggregate demand decreases
↓	↓
Real GDP rises	Inflation declines

curve of Figure 33.5b that we have already been using with the aggregate demand and aggregate supply curves shown in Figure 33.5d. Figure 33.5d represents exactly the same economy as Figure 33.5c but adds some extra curves that relate only to our explanation of restrictive monetary policy.

To see how restrictive monetary policy works, let us first consider a situation in which the economy moves from a full-employment equilibrium to operating at more than full employment so that inflation is a problem and restrictive monetary policy would be appropriate. Assume that the economy begins at the full-employment equilibrium where AD_2 and AS intersect. At this equilibrium, $Q_f = \$900$ billion and the price level is P_2.

Next, assume that the money supply grows to $175 billion ($S_{m3}$) in Figure 33.5a. This results in an interest rate of 6 percent, investment spending of $25 billion, and aggregate demand AD_3. As the AD curve shifts to the right

from AD_2 to AD_3 in Figure 33.5d, the economy will move along the upwardsloping AS curve until it comes to an equilibrium at point *a*, where AD_3 intersects AS. At the new equilibrium, the price level has risen to P_3 and the equilibrium level of real GDP has risen to $910 billion, indicating an inflationary GDP gap of $10 billion (= $910 billion − $900 billion). Aggregate demand AD_3 is excessive relative to the economy's full-employment level of real output $Q_f = \$900$ billion. To rein in spending, the Fed will institute a restrictive monetary policy.

The Federal Reserve Board will direct Federal Reserve Banks to undertake some combination of the following actions: (1) sell government securities to banks and the public in the open market, (2) increase the legal reserve ratio, (3) increase the discount rate, and (4) decrease the amount of reserves auctioned off under the term auction facility. Banks then will discover that their reserves are below those required and that the Federal funds rate has increased. So they will need to reduce their checkable deposits by refraining from issuing new loans as old loans are paid back. This will shrink the money supply and increase the interest rate. The higher interest rate will discourage investment, lowering aggregate demand and restraining demand-pull inflation.

But the Fed must be careful about just how much to decrease the money supply. The problem is that the inflation ratchet will take effect at the new equilibrium point *a*, such that prices will be inflexible at price level P_3. As a result, aggregate supply to the left of point *a* will be the horizontal dashed line shown in Figure 33.5d. This means that the Fed cannot simply lower the money supply to S_{m2} in Figure 33.5a. If it were to do that, investment demand would fall to $20 billion in Figure 33.5b and the AD curve would shift to the left from AD_3 back to AD_2. But because of inflexible prices, the economy's equilibrium would move to point *c*, where AD_2 intersects the horizontal dashed line that represents aggregate supply to the left of point *a*. This would put the economy into a recession, with equilibrium output below the full-employment output level of $Q_f = \$900$ billion.

What the Fed needs to do to achieve full employment is to move the AD curve back only from AD_2 to AD_4, so that the economy will come to equilibrium at point *b*. This will require a $10 billion decrease in aggregate demand, so that equilibrium output falls from $910 billion at point a to $Q_f = \$900$ billion at point *b*. The Fed can achieve this shift by setting the supply of money in Figure 33.5a at $162.5 billion. To see how this works, draw in a vertical money supply curve in Figure 33.5a at $162.5 billion and label it as S_{m4}. It will be exactly halfway between money supply curves S_{m2} and S_{m3}. Notice that the intersection of S_{m4} with the money demand curve D_m will result in an interest rate of 7 percent. In Figure 33.5b, this interest rate of 7 percent will result in investment spending of $22.5 billion (halfway between $20 billion and $25 billion). Thus, by setting the money supply at $162.5 billion, the Fed can reduce investment spending by $2.5 billion, lowering it from the $25 billion associated with AD_3 down to only $22.5 billion. This decline in investment spending will initially shift the AD curve only $2.5 billion to the left of AD_3. But then the multiplier process will work its magic. Since the multiplier is 4 in our model, the AD curve will end up moving by a full $10 billion ($= 4 \times \$2.5$ billion) to the left, to AD_4. This shift will move the economy to equilibrium b, returning output to the full employment level and eliminating the inflationary GDP gap.[2]

Column 2 in Table 33.3 summarizes the cause-effect chain of a tight money policy.

Monetary Policy: Evaluation and Issues

Monetary policy has become the dominant component of U.S. national stabilization policy. It has two key advantages over fiscal policy:

- Speed and flexibility.
- Isolation from political pressure.

Compared with fiscal policy, monetary policy can be quickly altered. Recall that congressional deliberations may delay the application of fiscal policy for months. In contrast, the Fed can buy or sell securities from day to day and thus affect the money supply and interest rates almost immediately.

Also, because members of the Fed's Board of Governors are appointed and serve 14-year terms, they are relatively isolated from lobbying and need not worry about retaining their popularity with voters. Thus, the Board, more readily than Congress, can engage in politically unpopular policies (higher interest rates) that may be necessary for the long-term health of the economy. Moreover, monetary policy is a subtler and more politically conservative measure than fiscal policy. Changes

---

[2]Again, we assume for simplicity that the decrease in nominal GDP does not feed back to reduce the demand for money and thus the interest rate. In reality, this would occur, slightly dampening the increase in the interest rate show in Figure 33.5a.

in government spending directly affect the allocation of resources, and changes in taxes can have extensive political ramifications. Because monetary policy works more subtly, it is more politically palatable.

Recent U.S. Monetary Policy

In the early 1990s, the Fed's expansionary monetary policy helped the economy recover from the 1990–1991 recession. The expansion of GDP that began in 1992 continued through the rest of the decade. By 2000 the U.S. unemployment rate had declined to 4 percent—the lowest rate in 30 years. To counter potential inflation during that strong expansion, in 1994 and 1995, and then again in early 1997, the Fed reduced reserves in the banking system to raise the interest rate. In 1998 the Fed temporarily reversed its course and moved to a more expansionary monetary policy to make sure that the U.S. banking system had plenty of liquidity in the face of a severe financial crisis in southeast Asia. The economy continued to expand briskly, and in 1999 and 2000 the Fed, in a series of steps, boosted interest rates to make sure that inflation remained under control.

Significant inflation did not occur in the late 1990s. But in the last quarter of 2000 the economy abruptly slowed. The Fed responded by cutting interest rates by a full percentage point in two increments in January 2001. Despite these rate cuts, the economy entered a recession in March 2001. Between March 20, 2001, and August 21, 2001, the Fed cut the Federal funds rate from 5 percent to 3.5 percent in a series of steps. In the 3 months following the terrorist attacks of September 11, 2001, it lowered the Federal funds rate from 3.5 percent to 1.75 percent, and it left the rate there until it lowered it to 1.25 percent in November 2002. Partly because of the Fed's actions, the prime interest rate dropped from 9.5 percent at the end of 2000 to 4.25 percent in December 2002.

Economists generally credit the Fed's adroit use of monetary policy as one of a number of factors that helped the U.S. economy achieve and maintain the rare combination of full employment, price-level stability, and strong economic growth that occurred between 1996 and 2000. The Fed also deserves high marks for helping to keep the recession of 2001 relatively mild, particularly in view of the adverse economic impacts of the terrorist attacks of September 11, 2001, and the steep stock market drop in 2001–2002.

In 2003 the Fed left the Federal funds rate at historic lows. But as the economy began to expand robustly in 2004, the Fed engineered a gradual series of rate hikes designed to boost the prime interest rate and other interest rates to make sure that aggregate demand continued to grow at a pace consistent with low inflation. By the summer of 2006, the target for the Federal funds rate had risen to 5.25 per cent and the prime rate was 8.25 percent. With the economy enjoying robust, noninflationary growth, the Fed left the Federal funds rate at 5.25 percent for over a year until the mortgage debt crisis threatened the economy during the late summer of 2007 (see this chapter's Last Word). In response to the crisis, the Fed took several actions. In August it lowered the discount rate by half a percentage point. Then, between September 2007 and April 2008, it lowered the target for the Federal funds rate from 5.25 per cent to 2 percent. The Fed also initiated the term auction facility in December 2007 and took a series of extraordinary actions to prevent the failure of key financial firms. All these monetary actions and "lender-of-last resort" functions helped to stabilize the banking sector and stimulate the economy—thereby offsetting at least some of the damage done by the mortgage debt crisis. The Federal Reserve was lauded by many observers.

Problems and Complications

Despite its recent successes in the United States, monetary policy has certain limitations and faces real-world complications.

Lags Recall that fiscal policy is hindered by three delays, or lags—a recognition lag, an administrative lag, and an operational lag. Monetary policy also faces a recognition lag and an operational lag, but because the Fed can decide and implement policy changes within days, it avoids the long administrative lag that hinders fiscal policy.

A recognition lag affects monetary policy because normal monthly variations in economic activity and the price level mean that the Fed may not be able to quickly recognize when the economy is truly starting to recede or when inflation is really starting to rise. Once the Fed acts, an operation lag of 3 to 6 months affects monetary policy because that much time is typically required for interest-rate changes to have their full impacts on investment, aggregate demand, real GDP, and the price level. These two lags complicate the timing of monetary policy.

Cyclical Asymmetry Monetary policy may be highly effective in slowing expansions and controlling inflation but less reliable in pushing the economy from a severe recession. Economists say that monetary policy may suffer from **cyclical asymmetry.**

If pursued vigorously, a restrictive monetary policy could deplete commercial banking reserves to the point where banks would be forced to reduce the volume of loans. That would mean a contraction of the money supply, higher interest rates, and reduced aggregate demand. The Fed can absorb reserves and eventually achieve its goal.

But it cannot be certain of achieving its goal when it adds reserves to the banking system. An expansionary

---

CONSIDER THIS . . .

Pushing on a String

In the late 1990s and early 2000s, the central bank of Japan used an expansionary monetary policy to reduce real interest rates to zero. Even with "interest-free" loans available, most consumers and businesses did not borrow and spend more. Japan's economy continued to sputter in and out of recession.

The Japanese circumstance illustrates the possible *asymmetry* of monetary policy, which economists have likened to "pulling versus pushing on a string." A string may be effective at pulling something back to a desirable spot, but it is ineffective at pushing it toward a desired location.

So it is with monetary policy, say some economists. Monetary policy can readily *pull* the aggregate demand curve to the left, reducing demand-pull inflation. There is no limit on how much a central bank can restrict a nation's money supply and hike interest rates. Eventually, a sufficiently restrictive monetary policy will reduce aggregate demand and inflation.

But during severe recession, participants in the economy may be highly pessimistic about the future. If so, an expansionary monetary policy may not be able to push the aggregate demand curve to the right, increasing real GDP. The central bank can produce excess reserves in the banking system by reducing the reserve ratio, lowering the discount rate, purchasing government securities, and increasing reserve auctions. But commercial banks may not be able to find willing borrowers for those excess reserves, no matter how low interest rates fall. Instead of borrowing and spending, consumers and businesses may be more intent on reducing debt and increasing saving in preparation for expected worse times ahead. If so, monetary policy will be ineffective. Using it under those circumstances will be much like pushing on a string.

key graph

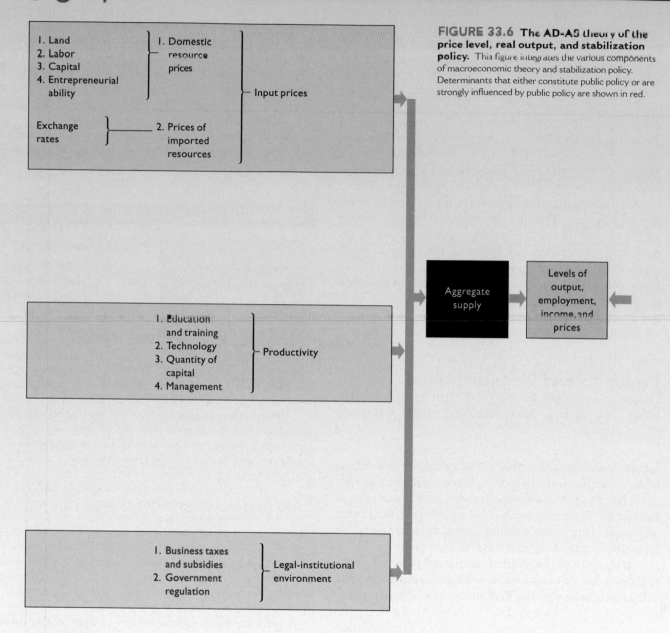

FIGURE 33.6 The AD-AS theory of the price level, real output, and stabilization policy. This figure integrates the various components of macroeconomic theory and stabilization policy. Determinants that either constitute public policy or are strongly influenced by public policy are shown in red.

QUICK QUIZ FOR FIGURE 33.6

1. All else equal, an increase in domestic resource availability will:
   a. increase input prices, reduce aggregate supply, and increase real output.
   b. raise labor productivity, reduce interest rates, and lower the international value of the dollar.
   c. increase net exports, increase investment, and reduce aggregate demand.
   d. reduce input prices, increase aggregate supply, and increase real output.

2. All else equal, an expansionary monetary policy during a recession will:
   a. lower the interest rate, increase investment, and reduce net exports.
   b. lower the interest rate, increase investment, and increase aggregate demand.
   c. increase the interest rate, increase investment, and reduce net exports.
   d. reduce productivity, aggregate supply, and real output.

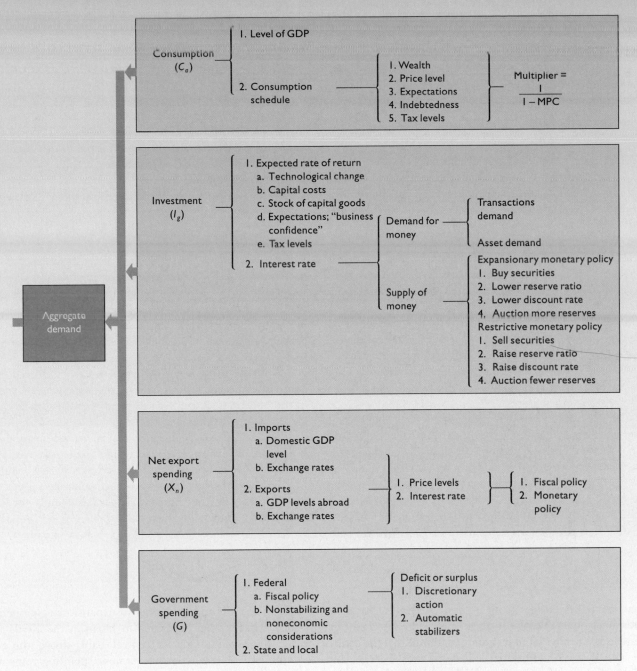

3. A personal income tax cut, combined with a reduction in corporate income and excise taxes, would:
  a. increase consumption, investment, aggregate demand, and aggregate supply.
  b. reduce productivity, raise input prices, and reduce aggregate supply.
  c. increase government spending, reduce net exports, and increase aggregate demand.
  d. increase the supply of money, reduce interest rates, increase investment, and expand real output.

4. An appreciation of the dollar would:
  a. reduce the price of imported resources, lower input prices, and increase aggregate supply.
  b. increase net exports and aggregate demand.
  c. increase aggregate supply and aggregate demand.
  d. reduce consumption, investment, net export spending, and government spending.

Answers: 1. d; 2. b; 3. a; 4. a

The Mortgage Debt Crisis: The Fed Responds

In 2007, Massive Defaults on Home Mortgages Threatened to Bring the Credit Markets to a Halt. The Fed Acted Quickly to Restore Confidence and Keep Loans Flowing.

In 2007, a major wave of defaults on home mortgages threatened the health of any financial institution that had invested in home mortgages either directly or indirectly. A majority of these mortgage defaults were on *subprime mortgage loans*—high-interest rate loans to home buyers with higher-than-average credit risk. Crucially, several of the biggest indirect investors in these subprime loans had been banks. The banks had lent money to investment companies that had invested in mortgages. When the mortgages started to go bad, many investment funds "blew up" and couldn't repay the loans they had taken out from the banks. The banks had to "write off" (declare unrecoverable) the loans they had made to the investment funds. Doing so meant reducing the banks' reserves, which in turn limited their ability to generate new loans. This was a major threat to the economy since both consumers and businesses rely on loans to finance consumption and investment expenditures.

In the second half of 2007 and into early 2008, the Federal Reserve took several important steps to increase bank reserves and avert a financial crisis. In August 2007, it fulfilled its important (but thankfully rarely needed) role as a "lender of last resort" by lowering the discount rate and encouraging banks to borrow reserves directly from the Fed. When many banks proved reluctant to borrow reserves at the discount rate (because they thought that doing so might make them appear to be in bad financial condition and in need of a quick loan from the Fed), the Fed introduced the anonymous term auction facility in December as an innovative new way of encouraging banks to borrow reserves and thereby preserve their ability to keep extending loans. Most importantly, the FOMC lowered the target for the Federal funds rate first from 5.25 percent to 4.75 percent in September, then to 4.50 percent in October, down to 4.25 percent in December, and then down to 2 percent in April 2008. To accomplish these rate cuts, it bought bonds in the open market and auctioned off reserves. The greater reserves expanded bank lending.

The lower Federal funds rate also resulted in lower interest rates in general, thereby bolstering aggregate demand. Many observers had been worried that the **mortgage debt crisis** might lead nervous consumers and businesses to cut back on spending out of fear that the crisis might increase the likelihood of a recession. By increasing aggregate demand, the Fed decreased this possibility and reassured both consumers and businesses about the economy's prospects going forward.

A strange thing about the crisis was that before it happened, banks had mistakenly believed that an innovation known as the "mortgage-backed security" had eliminated their exposure to mortgage defaults. Mortgage-backed securities are a type of bond backed by mortgage payments. To create them, banks and other mortgage lenders would first make mortgage loans. But then instead of holding those loans as assets on their balance sheets and collecting the monthly mortgage payments, the banks and other mortgage lenders would bundle hundreds or thousands of them together and sell them off as a bond—in

monetary policy suffers from a "You can lead a horse to water, but you can't make it drink" problem. The Fed can create excess reserves, but it cannot guarantee that the banks will actually make additional loans and thus increase the supply of money. If commercial banks seek liquidity and are unwilling to lend, the efforts of the Fed will be of little avail. Similarly, businesses can frustrate the intentions of the Fed by not borrowing excess reserves. And the public may use money paid to them through Fed sales of U.S. securities to pay off existing bank loans, rather than on increased spending on goods and services.

Furthermore, a severe recession may so undermine business confidence that the investment demand curve shifts to the left and frustrates an expansionary monetary policy. That is what happened in Japan in the 1990s and early 2000s. Although its central bank drove the real interest rate to 0 percent, investment spending remained low and the Japanese economy stayed mired in recession. In fact, deflation—a fall in the price level—occurred. The Japanese experience reminds us that monetary policy is not a certain cure for the business cycle.

In March 2003 some members of the Fed's Open Market Committee expressed concern about potential deflation in the United States if the economy remained weak. But the economy soon began to vigorously expand, and deflation did not occur. **(Key Question 8)**

essence selling the right to collect all of the future mortgage payments. The banks would get a cash payment for the bond and the bond buyer would start to collect the mortgage payments.

From the banks' perspective, this seemed like a smart business decision because it transferred any future default risk on those mortgages to the buyer of the bond. The banks thought that they were off the hook. Unfortunately for them, however, they lent a substantial portion of the money they got selling the bonds to investment funds that invested in mortgage-backed bonds. So while the banks were no longer directly exposed to mortgage default risk, they were still indirectly exposed to it. And so when many homebuyers started to default on their mortgages, the banks still lost money.

But what had caused the skyrocketing mortgage default rates in the first place? There were many causes, including declining real-estate values. But an important factor was the bad incentives provided by the bonds. Since the banks and other mortgage lenders thought that they were no longer exposed to mortgage default risk, they became very sloppy in their lending practices—so much so that people were granted subprime mortgage loans that they were very unlikely to be able to repay. Some mortgage companies were so eager to sign up new homebuyers (in order to bundle their loans together to sell bonds) that they stopped running credit checks and even allowed applicants to claim higher incomes than they were actually earning in order to qualify for big loans. The natural result was that many of these people took on "too much mortgage" and were soon failing to make their monthly payments.

Politicians and financial regulators are now examining whether tighter lending rules would help to offset the "pass the buck" incentives created by mortgage-backed securities and prevent loans from being issued to people who are very unlikely to be able to make the required monthly payments. They also are considering ways to help homeowners who took on too much debt to remain in their homes since defaults on these loans would increase the supply of homes for sale in the real estate market and reduce house prices, which in turn could produce further defaults and reduce confidence in the overall economy.

QUICK REVIEW 33.4

- The Fed is engaging in an expansionary monetary policy when it increases the money supply to reduce interest rates and increase investment spending and real GDP; it is engaging in a restrictive monetary policy when it reduces the money supply to increase interest rates and reduce investment spending and inflation.
- The Fed managed low inflation and strong growth during the 1990s. The crises of 9/11 and the 2001 recession caused the Fed to lower rates aggressively, which it did again during the mortgage debt crisis that started in 2007.
- The main strengths of monetary policy are (a) speed and flexibility and (b) political acceptability; its main weaknesses are (a) time lags and (b) potential ineffectiveness during severe recession.

The "Big Picture"

Figure 33.6 (Key Graph) on pages 680 and 681 brings together the analytical and policy aspects of macroeconomics discussed in this and the eight preceding chapters. This "big picture" shows how the many concepts and principles discussed relate to one another and how they constitute a coherent theory of the price level and real output in a market economy.

Study this diagram and you will see that the levels of output, employment, income, and prices all result from the interaction of aggregate supply and aggregate demand. The items shown in red relate to public policy.

Summary

1. The goal of monetary policy is to help the economy achieve price stability, full employment, and economic growth.

2. The total demand for money consists of the transactions demand and asset demand for money. The amount of money demanded for transactions varies directly with the nominal GDP; the amount of money demanded as an asset varies directly with the interest rate. The market for money combines the total demand for money with the money supply to determine equilibrium interest rates.

3. Interest rates and bond prices are inversely related.

4. The four available instruments of monetary policy are (a) open-marsket operations, (b) the reserve ratio, (c) the discount rate, and (d) the term auction facility.

5. The Federal funds rate is the interest rate that banks charge one another for overnight loans of reserves. The prime interest rate is the benchmark rate that banks use as a reference rate for a wide range of interest rates on short-term loans to businesses and individuals.

6. The Fed adjusts the Federal funds rate to a level appropriate for economic conditions. In an expansionary monetary policy, it purchases securities from commercial banks and the general public to inject reserves into the banking system. This lowers the Federal funds rate to the targeted level and also reduces other interest rates (such as the prime rate). In a restrictive monetary policy, the Fed sells securities to commercial banks and the general public via open-market operations. Consequently, reserves are removed from the banking system, and the Federal funds rate and other interest rates rise.

7. Monetary policy affects the economy through a complex cause-effect chain: (a) Policy decisions affect commercial bank reserves; (b) changes in reserves affect the money supply; (c) changes in the money supply alter the interest rate; (d) changes in the interest rate affect investment; (e) changes in investment affect aggregate demand; (f) changes in aggregate demand affect the equilibrium real GDP and the price level. Table 33.3 draws together all the basic ideas relevant to the use of monetary policy.

8. The advantages of monetary policy include its flexibility and political acceptability. In recent years, the Fed has used monetary policy to keep inflation low while helping limit the depth of the recession of 2001, to boost the economy as it recovered from that recession, and to help stabilize the banking sector in the wake of the mortgage debt crisis. Today, nearly all economists view monetary policy as a significant stabilization tool.

9. Monetary policy has two major limitations and potential problems: (a) Recognition and operation lags complicate the timing of monetary policy. (b) In a severe recession, the reluctance of firms to borrow and spend on capital goods may limit the effectiveness of an expansionary monetary policy.

Terms and Concepts

monetary policy	reserve ratio	prime interest rate
interest	discount rate	restrictive monetary policy
transactions demand	term auction facility	Taylor rule
asset demand	Federal funds rate	cyclical asymmetry
total demand for money	expansionary monetary policy	mortgage debt crisis
open-market operations		

Study Questions

1. **KEY QUESTION** What is the basic determinant of (*a*) the transactions demand and (*b*) the asset demand for money? Explain how these two demands can be combined graphically to determine total money demand. How is the equilibrium interest rate in the money market determined? Use a graph to show the impact of an increase in the total demand for money on the equilibrium interest rate (no change in money supply). Use your general knowledge of equilibrium prices to explain why the previous interest rate is no longer sustainable. **LO1**

2. **KEY QUESTION** Assume that the following data characterize a hypothetical economy: money supply = $200 billion; quantity of money demanded for transactions = $150 billion; quantity of money demanded as an asset = $10 billion at 12 percent interest, increasing by $10 billion for each 2-percentage-point fall in the interest rate. **LO1**

   a. What is the equilibrium interest rate? Explain.

   b. At the equilibrium interest rate, what are the quantity of money supplied, the total quantity of money demanded, the amount of money demanded for transactions, and the amount of money demanded as an asset?

3. **KEY QUESTION** Suppose a bond with no expiration date has a face value of $10,000 and annually pays a fixed amount of interest

of interest of $800. Compute and enter in the spaces provided in the accompanying table either the interest rate that the bond would yield to a bond buyer at each of the bond prices listed or the bond price at each of the interest yields shown. What generalization can be drawn from the completed table? **LO1**

Bond Price	Interest Yield, %
$ 8,000	_____
_____	8.9
$10,000	_____
$11,000	_____
_____	6.2

4. Use commercial bank and Federal Reserve Bank balance sheets to demonstrate the impact of each of the following transactions on commercial bank reserves: **LO2**
   a. Federal Reserve Banks purchase securities from banks.
   b. Commercial banks borrow from Federal Reserve Banks at the discount rate.
   c. The Fed reduces the reserve ratio.
   d. Commercial banks borrow from Federal Reserve Banks after winning an auction held as part of the term auction facility.

5. **KEY QUESTION** In the accompanying tables you will find consolidated balance sheets for the commercial banking system and the 12 Federal Reserve Banks. Use columns 1 through 3 to indicate how the balance sheets would read after each of transactions *a* to *c* is completed. Do not cumulate your answers; that is, analyze each transaction separately, starting in each case from the figures provided. All accounts are in billions of dollars. **LO2**
   a. A decline in the discount rate prompts commercial banks to borrow an additional $1 billion from the Federal Reserve Banks. Show the new balance-sheet figures in column 1 of each table.
   b. The Federal Reserve Banks sell $3 billion in securities to members of the public, who pay for the bonds with checks. Show the new balance-sheet figures in column 2 of each table.
   c. The Federal Reserve Banks buy $2 billion of securities from commercial banks. Show the new balance-sheet figures in column 3 of each table.
   d. Now review each of the above three transactions, asking yourself these three questions: (1) What change, if any, took place in the money supply as a direct and immediate result of each transaction? (2) What increase or decrease in the commercial banks' reserves took place in each transaction? (3) Assuming a reserve ratio of

	Consolidated Balance Sheet: All Commercial Banks		
	(1)	(2)	(3)
Assets:			
Reserves	$ 33	___	___	___
Securities	60	___	___	___
Loans	60	___	___	___
Liabilities and net worth:			
Checkable deposits	$150	___	___	___
Loans from the Federal Reserve Banks	3	___	___	___

	Consolidated Balance Sheet: The 12 Federal Reserve Banks		
	(1)	(2)	(3)
Assets:			
Securities	$60	___	___	___
Loans to commercial banks	3	___	___	___
Liabilities and net worth:			
Reserves of commercial banks	$33	___	___	___
Treasury deposits	3	___	___	___
Federal Reserve Notes	27	___	___	___

20 percent, what change in the money-creating potential of the commercial banking system occurred as a result of each transaction?

6. What is the basic objective of monetary policy? What are the major strengths of monetary policy? Why is monetary policy easier to conduct than fiscal policy in a highly divided national political environment? **LO2**

7. Distinguish between the Federal funds rate and the prime interest rate. Why is one higher than the other? Why do changes in the two rates closely track one another? **LO3**

8. **KEY QUESTION** Suppose that you are a member of the Board of Governors of the Federal Reserve System. The economy is experiencing a sharp rise in the inflation rate. What change in the Federal funds rate would you recommend? How would your recommended change get accomplished? What impact would the actions have on the lending ability of the banking system, the real interest rate, investment spending, aggregate demand, and inflation? **LO4**

9. Suppose that inflation is 2 percent, the Federal funds rate is 4 percent, and real GDP falls 2 percent below potential GDP. Acording to the Taylor rule, in what direction and by how much should the Fed change the real Federal funds rate? **LO4**

10. Explain the links between changes in the nation's money supply, the interest rate, investment spending, aggregate demand, and real GDP (and the price level). **LO4**

11. What do economists mean when they say that monetary policy can exhibit cyclical asymmetry? Why is this possibility significant to policymakers? **LO5**

12. **LAST WORD** How do mortgage backed securities work? Why did banks think that selling mortgage backed securities would relieve them of the risks involved with mortgage lending? How did the banks indirectly come to once again be exposed to mortgage lending risks? What happened to bank reserves during the mortgage debt crisis? How did the Fed respond?

Web-Based Questions

1. **CURRENT U.S. INTEREST RATES** Visit the Federal Reserve's Web site at **www.federalreserve.gov**, and select Economic Research and Data, then Statistical Releases and Historical Data, Selected Interest Rates (weekly), and Historical Data to find the most recent values for the following interest rates: the Federal funds rate, the discount rate, and the prime interest rate. Are these rates higher or lower than they were 3 years ago? Have they increased, decreased, or remained constant over the past year?

2. **THE FEDERAL RESERVE ANNUAL REPORT** Visit the Federal Reserve's Web site at **www.federalreserve.gov**, and select Monetary Policy. Then click on Reports and then Monetary Policy Report to the Congress to retrieve the current annual report (Sections 1 and 2). Summarize the policy actions of the Board of Governors during the most recent period. In the Fed's opinion, how did the U.S. economy perform?

FURTHER TEST YOUR KNOWLEDGE AT
www.mcconnell18e.com

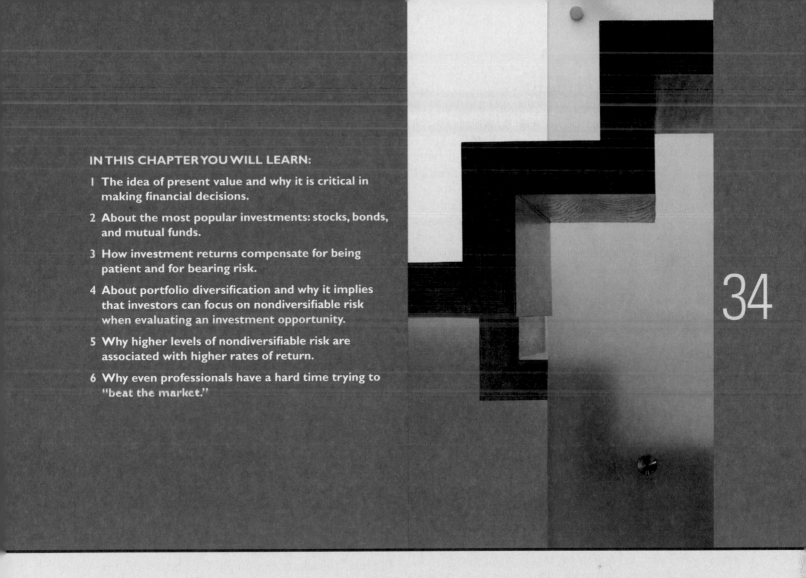

34

Financial Economics

Financial economics studies investor preferences and how they affect the trading and pricing of financial assets like stocks, bonds, and real estate. The two most important investor preferences are a desire for high rates of return and a dislike of risk and uncertainty. This chapter will explain how these preferences interact to produce a strong positive relationship between risk and return: the riskier an investment, the higher its rate of return. This positive relationship compensates investors for bearing risk. And it is enforced by a powerful set of buying and selling pressures known as arbitrage, which ensures consistency across investments so that assets with identical levels of risk generate identical rates of return. As we will demonstrate, this consistency makes it extremely difficult for anyone to "beat the market" by finding a set of investments that can generate high rates of return at low levels of risk. Instead, investors are stuck with a trade-off: If they want higher rates of return, they must accept higher levels of risk. On average, higher risk results in higher returns. But it can also result in large losses, as it did for investors in subprime mortgage loans in late 2007 and in 2008.

Financial Investment

Financial economics focuses its attention on the investments that individuals and firms make in the wide variety of assets available to them in our modern economy. But before proceeding, it is important for you to recall the difference between economic investment and financial investment.

Economic investment refers either to paying for *new* additions to the capital stock or *new* replacements for capital stock that has worn out. Thus, *new* factories, houses, retail stores, construction equipment, and wireless networks are all good examples of economic investments. And so are purchases of office computers to replace computers that have become obsolete as well as purchases of new commercial airplanes to replace planes that have served out their useful lives.

In contrast, financial investment is a far broader, much more inclusive concept. It includes economic investment and a whole lot more. **Financial investment** refers to either buying an asset or building an asset in the expectation of financial gain. It does not distinguish between *new* assets and *old* assets. Purchasing an old house or an old factory is just as much a financial investment as purchasing a new house or a new factory. For financial investment, it does not matter if the purchase of an asset adds to the capital stock, replaces the capital stock, or does neither. Investing in old comic books is just as much a financial investment as building a new refinery. Finally, unlike economic investment, financial investment can involve either *financial assets* (such as stocks, bonds, and futures contracts) or *real assets* (such as land, factories, and retail stores).

When bankers, entrepreneurs, corporate executives, retirement planners, and ordinary people use the word "investment," they almost always mean financial investment. In fact, the ordinary meaning of the word investment *is* financial investment. So for this chapter, we will use the word investment in its ordinary sense of "financial investment" rather than in the far narrower sense of "economic investment," which is used throughout the rest of this book.

Present Value

One of the fundamental ideas in financial economics is **present value**—the present-day value, or worth, of returns or costs that are expected to arrive in the future. The ability to calculate present values is especially useful when investors wish to determine the proper current price to pay for an asset. In fact, the proper current price for any risk-free investment *is* the present value of its expected future returns. And while some adjustments have to be made when determining the proper price of a risky investment, the process is entirely based upon the logic of present value. So we begin

TABLE 34.1 Compounding: $100 at 8 Percent Interest

(1) Years of Compounding	(2) Compounding Computation	(3) Value at Year's End
1	$100 (1.08)	$108.00
2	100 $(1.08)^2$	116.64
3	100 $(1.08)^3$	125.97
4	100 $(1.08)^4$	136.05
5	100 $(1.08)^5$	146.93
17	100 $(1.08)^{17}$	370.00

our study of finance by explaining present value and how it can be used to price risk-free assets. Once that is accomplished, we will turn our attention to risk and how the financial markets determine the prices of risky assets by taking into account investor preferences regarding the trade-off between potential return and potential risks.

Compound Interest

The best way to understand present value is by first understanding compound interest. **Compound interest** describes how quickly an investment increases in value when interest is paid, or compounded, not only on the original amount invested but also on all interest payments that have been previously made.

As an example of compound interest in action, consider Table 34.1, which shows the amount of money that $100 invested today becomes if it increases, or compounds, at an 8 percent annual interest rate, i, for various numbers of years. To make things simple, let's express the 8 percent annual interest rate as a decimal so that it becomes $i = .08$. The key to understanding compound interest is to realize that 1 year's worth of growth at interest rate i will always result in $(1 + i)$ times as much money at the end of a year as there was at the beginning of the year. Consequently, if the first year begins with $100 and if $i = .08$, then $(1 + .08)$ or 1.08 times as much money—$108—will be available at the end of the year. We show the computation for the first year in column 2 of Table 34.1 and display the $108 outcome in column 3. The same logic would also apply with other initial amounts. If a year begins with $500, there will be 1.08 times more money after 1 year, or $540. Algebraically, for any given number of dollars X at the beginning of a particular year, there will be $(1 + i) X$ dollars, or, alternatively, $X(1 + i)$ dollars, after 1 year's worth of growth.

We can use this formula to consider what happens if the initial investment of $100 that grew into $108 after 1 year continues to grow at 8 percent interest for a second year. The $108 available at the beginning of the second year will grow into an amount of money that is 1.08 times larger by the end of the second year. That amount, as shown in Table 34.1, is $116.64. Notice that the computation in the table is made by multiplying the initial $100 by $(1.08)^2$. That is because the original $100 is compounded by 1.08 into $108 and then the $108 is again compounded by 1.08. More generally, since the second year begins with $(1 + i)X$ dollars, it will grow to $(1 + i)(1 + i)X = (1 + i)^2X$ dollars by the end of the second year.

Similar reasoning shows that the amount of money at the end of 3 years has to be $(1 + i)^3X$ since the amount of money at the beginning of the third year, $(1 + i)^2X$, gets multiplied by $(1 + i)$ to convert it into the amount of money at the end of the third year. In terms of Table 34.1, that amount is $125.97, which is $(1.08)^3\$100$.

As you can see, we now have a fixed pattern. The $100 that is invested at the beginning of the first year becomes $(1 + i)\$100$ after 1 year, $(1 + i)^2\$100$ after 2 years, $(1 + i)^3\$100$ after 3 years, and so on. It therefore is clear that the amount of money after t years will be $(1 + i)^t\$100$. This pattern always holds true, regardless of the size of the initial investment. Thus, investors know that if X dollars is invested today and earns compound interest at the rate i, it will grow into exactly $(1 + i)^tX$ dollars after t years. Economists express this fact by writing

$$X \text{ dollars today} = (1 + i)^tX \text{ dollars in } t \text{ years} \qquad (1)$$

Equation 1 captures the idea that if investors have the opportunity to invest X dollars today at interest rate i, then they have the ability to transform X dollars today into $(1 + i)^tX$ dollars in t years.

But notice that the logic of the equality also works in reverse, so that it can also be thought of as showing that $(1 + i)^tX$ dollars in t years can be transformed into X dollars today. That may seem very odd, but it is exactly what happens when people take out loans. For instance, consider a situation where an investor named Roberto takes out a loan for $100 dollars today, a loan that will accumulate interest at 8 percent per year for 5 years. Under such an arrangement, the amount Roberto owes will grow with compound interest into $(1.08)^5\$100 = \$146.93$ dollars in 5 years. This means that Roberto can convert $146.93 dollars in 5 years (the amount required to pay off the loan) into $100 dollars today (the amount he borrows.)

Consequently, the compound interest formula given in equation 1 defines not only the rate at which present amounts of money can be converted to future amounts of money but also the rate at which future amounts of money can be converted into present amounts of money. It allows us to measure the so-called *time-value of money*. In the model that follows, we exploit the ability of equation 1 to convert future dollars into present dollars.

The Present Value Model

The present value model simply rearranges equation 1 to make it easier to transform future amounts of money into present amounts of money. To derive the formula used to calculate the present value of a future amount of money, we divide both sides of equation 1 by $(1 + i)^t$ to obtain

$$\frac{X}{(1 + i)^t} \text{ dollars today} = X \text{ dollars in } t \text{ years} \qquad (2)$$

The logic of equation 2 is identical to that of equation 1. Both allow investors to convert present amounts of money into future amounts of money and vice versa. However, equation 2 makes it much more intuitive to convert a given number of dollars in the future into their present-day equivalent. In fact, it says that X dollars in t years converts into exactly $X/(1 + i)^t$ dollars today. This may not seem important, but it is actually very powerful because it allows investors to easily calculate how much they should pay for any given asset.

WORKED PROBLEMS

W 34.1

Present value

To see why this is true, understand that an asset's owner obtains the right to receive one or more future payments. If an investor is considering buying an asset, her problem is to try to determine how much she should pay today to buy the asset and receive those future payments. Equation 2 makes this task very easy. If she knows how large any given payment will be (X dollars), when it will arrive (in t years), and what the interest rate (i) is, then she can apply equation 2 to determine the payment's present value: its value in present-day dollars. If she does this for each of the future payments that the asset in question is expected to make, she will be able to calculate the overall present value of all the asset's future payments by simply summing together the present values of each of the individual payments. This will allow her to determine the price she should pay for the asset. In particular, *the asset's price should exactly equal the total present value of all of the asset's future payments.*

As a simple example, suppose that Cecilia has the chance to buy an asset that is guaranteed to return a single payment of exactly $370.00 in 17 years. Again let's assume the interest rate is 8 percent per year. Then the present value of that future payment can be determined using equation 2 to equal precisely $370.00/(1 + 0.08)^{17} = \$370.00/(1.08)^{17} = \$100$ today. This is confirmed in the row for year 17 in Table 34.1.

To see why Cecilia should be willing to pay a price that is *exactly* equal to the $100 present value of the asset's single future payment of $370.00 in 17 years, consider the following thought experiment. What would happen if she were to invest $100 today in an alternative investment that is guaranteed to compound her money for 17 years at 8 percent per year? How large would her investment in this alternative become? Equation 1 and Table 34.1 tell us that the answer is exactly $370.00 in 17 years.

This is very important because it shows that Cecelia and other investors have two different possible ways of purchasing the right to receive $370.00 in 17 years. They can either:

- Purchase the asset in question for $100.
- Invest $100 in the alternative asset that pays 8 percent per year.

Because either investment will deliver the same future benefit, both investments are in fact identical. Consequently, they should have identical prices—meaning that each will cost precisely $100 today.

A good way to see why this must be the case is by considering how the presence of the alternative investment affects the behavior of both the potential buyers and the potential sellers of the asset in question. First, notice that Cecelia and other potential buyers would never pay more than $100 for the asset in question because they know that they could get the same future return of $370.00 in 17 years by investing $100 in the alternative investment. At the same time, people selling the asset in question would not sell it to Cecelia or other potential buyers for anything less than $100 since they know that the only other way for Cecelia and other potential buyers to get a future return of $370.00 in 17 years is by paying $100 for the alternative investment. Since Cecelia and the other potential buyers will not pay more than $100 for the asset in question and its sellers will not accept less than $100 for the asset in question, the result will be that the asset in question and the alternative investment will have the exact same price of $100 today.

QUICK REVIEW 34.1

- Financial investment refers to buying an asset with the hope of financial gain.
- Compound interest is the payment of interest not only on the original amount invested but also on any interest payments previously made; X dollars today growing at interest rate i will become $(1 + i)^t X$ dollars in t years.
- The present value formula facilitates transforming future amounts of money into present-day amounts of money; X dollars in t years converts into exactly $X/(1 + i)^t$ dollars today.
- An investment's proper current price is equal to the sum of the present values of all the future payments that it is expected to make.

Applications

Present value is not only an important idea for understanding investment, but it has many everyday applications. Let's examine two of them.

Take the Money and Run?
The winners of state lotteries are typically paid their winnings in equal installments spread out over 20 years. For instance, suppose that Zoe gets lucky one week and wins a $100 million jackpot. She will not be paid $100 million all at once. Rather, she will receive $5 million per year for 20 years, for a total of $100 million.

Zoe may object to this installment payment system for a variety of reasons. For one thing, she may be very old, so that she is not likely to live long enough to collect all of the payments. Alternatively, she might prefer to receive her winnings immediately so that she could make large immediate donations to her favorite charities or large immediate investments in a business project that she would like to get started. And, of course, she may just be impatient and want to buy a lot of really expensive consumption goods sooner rather than later.

Fortunately for Zoe, if she does have a desire to receive her winnings sooner rather than later, several private financial companies are ready and willing to help her. They do this by arranging swaps. Lottery winners sell the right to receive their installment payments in exchange for a single lump sum that they get immediately. The people who hand over the lump sum receive the right to collect the installment payments.

Present value is crucial to arranging these swaps since it is used to determine the value of the lump sum that lottery winners like Zoe will receive in exchange for giving up their installment payments. The lump sum in any case is simply equal to the sum of the present values of each of the future payments. Assuming an interest rate of 5 percent per year, the sum of the present values of each of Zoe's 20 installment payments of $5 million is $62,311,051.71. So, depending on her preferences, Zoe can either receive that amount immediately or $100 million spread out over 20 years.

Salary Caps and Deferred Compensation
Another example of present value comes directly from the sporting news. Many professional sports leagues worry that richer teams, if not held in check, would outbid poorer teams for the best players. The result would be a situation in which only the richer teams have any real chance of doing well and winning championships.

To prevent this from happening, many leagues have instituted salary caps. These are upper limits on the total amount of money that each team can spend on salaries during a given season. For instance, one popular basketball league has a salary cap of about $50 million per season, so that the combined value of the salaries that each team pays its players can be no more than $50 million.

Typically, however, the salary contracts that are negotiated between individual players and their teams are for multiple seasons. This means that during negotiations, players are often asked to help their team stay under the current season's salary cap by agreeing to receive more compensation in later years. For instance, suppose that a team's current payroll is $45 million but that it would like to sign a superstar nicknamed HiTop to a two-year contract. HiTop, however, is used to earning $10 million per year. This is a major problem for the team because the $50 million salary cap means that the most that the team can pay HiTop for the current season is $5 million.

A common solution is for HiTop to agree to receive only $5 million the first season in order to help the team stay under the salary cap. In exchange for this concession, the team agrees to pay HiTop more than the $10 million he would normally demand for the second season. The present value formula is used to figure out how large his second-season salary should be. In particular, the player can use the present value formula to figure out that if the interest rate is 8 percent per year, he should be paid a total of $15,400,000 during his second season, since this amount will equal the $10 million he wants for the second season plus $5.4 million to make up for the $5 million reduction in his salary during the first season. That is, the present value of the $5.4 million that he will receive during the second season precisely equals the $5 million that he agrees to give up during the first season.

Some Popular Investments

The number and types of financial "instruments" in which one can invest are very numerous, amazingly creative, and highly varied. Most are much more complicated than the investments we used to explain compounding and present value. But, fortunately, all investments share three features:

- They require that investors pay some price— determined in the market—to acquire them.
- They give their owners the chance to receive future payments.
- The future payments are typically risky.

These features allow us to treat all assets in a unified way. Three of the more popular investments are stocks, bonds, and mutual funds. In 2004, the median value of stock holdings for U.S. families that held stocks was $15,000; the median value for bonds, $65,000; and the median value for "pooled funds" (mainly mutual funds) was $40,400.[1]

---

[1]Federal Reserve, "Recent Changes in U.S. Family Finances: Evidence from the 2001 and 2004 Survey of Consumer Finances," p. A14.

Stocks

Recall that **stocks** are ownership shares in a corporation. If an investor owns 1 percent of a corporation's shares, she gets 1 percent of the votes at the shareholder meetings that select the company's managers and she is also entitled to 1 percent of any future profit distributions. There is no guarantee, however, that a company will be profitable.

Firms often lose money and sometimes even go **bankrupt,** meaning that they are unable to make timely payments on their debts. In the event of a bankruptcy, control of a corporation's assets is given to a bankruptcy judge, whose job is to enforce the legal rights of the people who lent the company money by doing what he can to see that they are repaid. Typically, this involves selling off the corporation's assets (factories, real estate patents, etc.) to raise the money necessary to pay off the company's debts. The money raised by selling the assets may be greater than or less than what is needed to fully pay off the firm's debts. If it is more than what is necessary, any remaining money is divided equally among shareholders. If it is less than what is necessary, then the lenders do not get repaid in full and have to suffer a loss.

A key point, however, is that the maximum amount of money that shareholders can lose is what they pay for their shares. If the company goes bankrupt owing more than the value of the firm's assets, shareholders do not have to make up the difference. This **limited liability rule** limits the risks involved in investing in corporations and encourages investors to invest in stocks by capping their potential losses at the amount that they paid for their shares.

When firms are profitable, however, investors can look forward to gaining financially in either or both of two possible ways. The first is through **capital gains,** meaning that they sell their shares in the corporation for more money than they paid for them. The second is by receiving **dividends,** which are equal shares of the corporation's profits. As we will soon explain, a corporation's current share price is determined by the size of the capital gains and dividends that investors expect the corporation to generate in the future.

Bonds

Bonds are debt contracts that are issued most frequently by governments and corporations. They typically work as follows: An initial investor lends the government or the corporation a certain amount of money, say $1000, for a certain period of time, say 10 years. In exchange, the government or corporation promises to make a series of semiannual payments in addition to returning the $1000 at the end of the 10 years. The semiannual payments constitute interest on the loan. For instance, the bond agreement may specify that the borrower will pay $30 every six months. This means that the bond will pay $60 per year in payments, which is equivalent to a 6 percent rate of interest on the initial $1000 loan.

The initial investor is free, however, to sell the bond at any time to other investors, who then gain the right to receive any of the remaining semiannual payments as well as the final $1000 payment when the bond expires after 10 years. As we will soon demonstrate, the price at which the bond will sell if it is indeed sold to another investor will depend on the current rates of return available on other investments offering a similar stream of future payments and facing a similar level of risk.

The primary risk a bondholder faces is the possibility that the corporation or government that issues his bond will **default** on, or fail to make, the bond's promised payments. This risk is much greater for corporations, but it also faces local and state governments in situations where they cannot raise enough tax revenue to make their bond payments or where defaulting on bond payments is politically easier than reducing spending on other items in the government's budget to raise the money needed to keep making bond payments. The U.S. Federal government, however, has never defaulted on its bond payments and is very unlikely to ever default for the simple reason that it has the right to print money and can therefore just print whatever money it needs to make its bond payments on time.

A key difference between bonds and stocks is that bonds are much more predictable. Unless a bond goes into default, its owner knows both how big its future payments will be and exactly when they will arrive. By contrast, stock prices and dividends are highly volatile because they depend on profits, which vary greatly depending on the overall business cycle and on factors specific to individual firms and industries—things such as changing consumer preferences, variations in the costs of inputs, and changes in the tax code. As we will demonstrate later, the fact that bonds are typically more predictable (thus less risky) than stocks explains why they generate lower average rates of return than stocks. Indeed, this difference in rates of return has been very large historically. From 1926 to 2007, stocks on average returned just over 11 percent per year worldwide while bonds on average returned only a bit over 6 percent per year worldwide.

Mutual Funds

A **mutual fund** is a company that maintains a professionally managed **portfolio,** or collection, of either stocks or bonds. The portfolio is purchased by pooling the money of many investors. Since these investors provide the money to purchase the portfolio, they own it and any gains or losses generated by the portfolio flow directly to them. Table 34.2 lists the 10 largest U.S. mutual funds based on their assets.

TABLE 34.2 The 10 Largest Mutual Funds, February 2008

Fund Name	Assets under Management, Billions
American Funds Growth Fund of America A	$96.7
American Funds Capital World Growth and Income A	85.4
American Funds Capital Income Builder A	83.5
Fidelity Contrafund	80.3
American Funds Investment Company of America A	78.1
American Funds Washington Mutual A	70.9
American Funds Fund of America A	69.8
PIMCO Total Returns Institutional	69.4
American Funds Euro Pacific Growth A	67.4
Dodge & Cox Stock Fund	65.7

Source: Morningstar, **www.morningstar.com.**

Most of the more than 8000 mutual funds currently operating in the United States choose to maintain portfolios that invest in specific categories of bonds or stocks. For instance, some fill their portfolios exclusively with the stocks of small tech companies, while others buy only bonds issued by certain state or local governments. In addition, there are **index funds,** whose portfolios are selected to exactly match a stock or bond index. Indexes follow the performance of a particular group of stocks or bonds in order to gauge how well a particular category of investments is doing. For instance, the Standard & Poor's 500 Index contains the 500 largest stocks trading in the United States in order to capture how the stocks of large corporations vary over time, while the Lehman 10-Year Corporate Bond Index follows a representative collection of 10-year corporate bonds to see how well corporate bonds do over time.

An important distinction must be drawn between actively managed and passively managed mutual funds. **Actively managed funds** have portfolio managers who constantly buy and sell assets in an attempt to generate high returns. By contrast, index funds are **passively managed funds** because the assets in their portfolios are chosen to exactly match whatever stocks or bonds are contained in their respective underlying indexes.

Later in the chapter, we will discuss the relative merits of actively managed funds and index funds, but for now we merely point out that both types are very popular and that, overall, investors had placed about $12 trillion into mutual funds by the end of 2007. By way of comparison, U.S. GDP in 2007 was $13.8 trillion and the estimated value of all the financial assets held by households in 2007 (including everything from real estate to checking account deposits) was about $46 trillion.

Calculating Investment Returns

Investors buy assets in order to obtain one or more future payments. The simplest case is purchasing an asset for resale. For instance, an investor may buy a house for $300,000 with the hope of selling it for $360,000 in one year. On the other hand, he could also rent out the house for $3000 per month and thereby receive a stream of future payments. And he, of course, could do a little of both, paying $300,000 for the house now in order to rent it out for five years and then sell it. In that case, he is expecting a stream of smaller payments followed by a large one.

Economists have developed a common framework for evaluating the gains or losses of assets that only make one future payment as well as those that make many future payments. They state the gain or loss as a **percentage rate of return,** by which they mean the percentage gain or loss (relative to the buying price) over a given period of time, typically a year. For instance, if a person buys a rare comic book today for $100 and sells it in 1 year for $125, she is said to make a 25 percent per year rate of return because she would divide the gain of $25 by the purchase price of $100. By contrast, if she were only able to sell it for $92, then she would be said to have made a loss of 8 percent per year since she would divide the $8 loss by the purchase price of $100.

A similar calculation is made for assets that deliver a series of payments. For instance, an investor who buys a house for $300,000 and expects to rent it out for $3000 per month would be expecting to make a 12 percent per year rate of return because he would divide his $36,000 per year in rent by the $300,000 purchase price of the house.

Asset Prices and Rates of Return

A very fundamental concept in financial economics is that *an investment's rate of return is inversely related to its price.* That is, the higher the price, the lower the rate of return.

To see why this is true, consider a house that is rented out for $2000 per month. If an investor pays $100,000 for the house, he will earn a 24 percent per year rate of return because the $24,000 in annual rent payments will be divided by the $100,000 purchase price of the house. But suppose that the purchase price of the house rises to $200,000. In that case, he would earn only a 12 percent per year rate of return since the $24,000 in annual rent payments would be divided by the much larger purchase price of $200,000. Consequently, as the price of the house goes up, the rate of return from renting it goes down.

The underlying cause of this inverse relationship is the fact that the rent payments are fixed in value so that there is an upper limit to the financial rewards of owning the house. As a result, the more an investor pays for the house, the lower his rate of return will be.

Arbitrage

Arbitrage happens when investors try to take advantage and profit from situations where two identical or nearly identical assets have different rates of return. They do so by simultaneously selling the asset with the lower rate of return and buying the asset with the higher rate of return. For instance, consider what would happen in a case where two very similar T-shirt companies start with different rates of return despite the fact that they are equally profitable and have equally good future prospects. To make things concrete, suppose that a company called T4me starts out with a rate of return of 10 percent per year while TSTG (T-Shirts to Go) starts out with a rate of return of 15 percent per year.

Since both companies are basically identical and have equally good prospects, investors in T4me will want to shift over to TSTG, which offers higher rates of return for the same amount of risk. As they begin to shift over, however, the prices of the two companies will change—and with them, the rates of return on the two companies. In particular, since so many investors will be selling the shares of the lower-return company, T4me, the supply of its shares trading on the stock market will rise so that its share price will fall. But since asset prices and rates of return are inversely related, this will cause its rate of return to rise.

At the same time, however, the rate of return on the higher-return company, TSTG, will begin to fall. This has to be the case because, as investors switch from T4me to TSTG, the increased demand for TSTG's shares will drive up their price. And as the price of TSTG goes up, its rate of return must fall.

The interesting thing is that this arbitrage process will continue—with the rate of return on the higher-return company falling and the rate of return on the lower-return company rising—until both companies have the same rate of return. This convergence must happen because as long as the rates of return on the two companies are not identical, there will always be some investors who will want to sell the shares of the lower-return company in order to buy the shares of the higher-return company. As a result, arbitrage will continue until the rates of return are equal.

What is even more impressive, however, is that generally only a very short while is needed for prices to equalize. In fact, for highly traded assets like stocks and bonds, arbitrage will often force the rates of return on identical or nearly identical investments to converge within a matter of minutes or sometimes even within a matter of seconds. This is very helpful to small investors who do not have a large amount of time to study the thousands of potential investment opportunities available in the financial markets. Thanks to arbitrage, they can invest with the confidence that assets with similar characteristics will have similar rates of return. As we discuss in the next section, this is especially important when it comes to risk—a characteristic that financial economists believe investors care about very deeply. **(Key Question 6)**

QUICK REVIEW 34.2

- Three popular forms of financial investments are stocks (ownership shares in corporations that give their owners a share in any future profits), bonds (debt contracts that promise to pay a fixed series of payments in the future), and mutual funds (pools of investor money used to buy a portfolio of stocks or bonds).

- Investment gains or losses are typically expressed as a percentage rate of return: the percentage gain or loss (relative to the investment's purchase price) over a given period of time, typically a year.

- Asset prices and percentage rates of return are inversely related.

- Arbitrage refers to the buying and selling that takes place to equalize the rates of return on identical or nearly identical assets.

Risk

Investors purchase assets in order to obtain one or more future payments. As used by financial economists, the word **risk** refers to the fact that investors never know with total certainty what those future payments will turn out to be.

The underlying problem is that the future is uncertain. Many factors affect an investment's future payments, and each of these may turn out better or worse than expected. As a simple example, consider buying a farm. Suppose that in an average year, the farm will generate a profit of $100,000. But if a freak hailstorm damages the crops, the profit will fall to only $60,000. On the other hand, if weather conditions turn out to be perfect, the profit will rise to $120,000. Since there is no way to tell in advance what will happen, investing in the farm is risky.

Also notice that when financial economists use the word *risk*, they do not use it in the normal way in which people think of risk as meaning that something bad may potentially happen (as in, "There is a risk that this experimental medicine may kill you"). Instead, the way the word risk is used in financial economics, it only means that an outcome (good or bad) lacks certainty. For instance, suppose that you are gifted a raffle ticket that will pay you either $100 or $200 when a drawing is made in one month. There are no bad outcomes in this situation, only good ones. But because you do not know with certainty which outcome you will receive, the situation is, by definition, risky.

Diversification

Investors have many options regarding their portfolios, or collections of investments. Among other things, they can choose to concentrate their wealth in just one or two investments or spread it out over a large number of investments. **Diversification** is the name given to the strategy of investing in a large number of investments in order to reduce the overall risk to the entire portfolio.

The underlying reason that diversification generally succeeds in reducing risk is best summarized by the old saying, "Don't put all your eggs in one basket." If an investor's portfolio consists of only one investment, say one stock, then if anything awful happens to that stock, the investor's entire portfolio will suffer greatly. By contrast, if the investor spreads his wealth over many stocks, then a bad outcome for any one particular stock will cause only a small amount of damage to the overall portfolio. In addition, it will typically be the case that if something bad is happening to one part of the portfolio, something good will be happening to another part of the portfolio and the two effects will tend to offset each other. Thus, the risk to the overall portfolio is reduced by diversification.

It must be stressed, however, that while diversification can reduce a portfolio's risks, it cannot eliminate them entirely. The problem is that even if an investor has placed each of his eggs into a different basket, all of the eggs may still end up broken if all of the different baskets somehow happen to get dropped simultaneously. That is, even if an investor has created a well-diversified portfolio, all of the investments still have a chance to do badly simultaneously. As an example, consider recession: With economic activity declining and consumer spending falling, nearly all companies face reduced sales and lowered profits, a fact that will cause their stock prices to decline simultaneously. Consequently, even if an investor has diversified his portfolio across many different stocks, his overall wealth is likely to decline because nearly all of his many investments will do badly simultaneously.

Financial economists build on the intuition behind the benefits and limits to diversification to divide an individual investment's overall risk into two components, diversifiable risk and nondiversifiable risk. **Diversifiable risk** (or "idiosyncratic risk") is the risk that is specific to a given investment and that can be eliminated by diversification. For instance, a soda pop maker faces the risk that the demand for its product may suddenly decline because people will want to drink mineral water instead of soda pop. But this risk does not matter if an investor has a diversified portfolio

---

ORIGIN OF THE IDEA

O 34.1

Portfolio diversification

that contains stock in the soda pop maker as well as stock in a mineral water maker. This is true because when the stock price of the soda pop maker falls due to the change in consumer preferences, the stock price of the mineral water maker will go up—so that, as far as the overall portfolio is concerned, the two effects will offset each other.

By contrast, **nondiversifiable risk** (or "systemic risk") pushes all investments in the same direction at the same time so that there is no possibility of using good effects to offset bad effects. The best example of a nondiversifiable risk is the business cycle. If the economy does well, then corporate profits rise and nearly every stock does well. But if the economy does badly, then corporate profits fall and nearly every stock does badly. As a result, even if one were to build a well-diversified portfolio, it would still be affected by the business cycle because nearly every asset contained in the portfolio would move in the same direction at the same time whenever the economy improved or worsened.

That being said, creating a diversified portfolio is still an investor's best strategy because doing so at least eliminates diversifiable risk. Indeed, it should be emphasized that for investors who have created diversified portfolios, all diversifiable risks will be eliminated, so that the only remaining source of risk will be nondiversifiable risk.

An extremely important implication of this fact is that when an investor considers whether to add any particular investment to a portfolio that is already diversified, she can ignore the investment's diversifiable risk. She can ignore it because, as part of a diversified portfolio, the investment's diversifiable risk will be "diversified away." Indeed, the only risk left will be the amount of nondiversifiable risk that the investment carries with it. This is very important because it means that she can base her decision about whether to add a potential new investment to her portfolio on a comparison between the potential investment's level of nondiversifiable risk and its potential returns. If she finds this trade-off attractive, she will add the investment, whereas if it seems unattractive, she will not.

The next section shows how investors can measure each asset's level of nondiversifiable risk as well as its potential returns to facilitate such comparisons. **(Key Question 8)**

Comparing Risky Investments

Economists believe that the two most important factors affecting investment decisions are returns and risk—specifically nondiversifiable risk. But for investors to properly compare different investments on the basis of returns and risk, they need ways to measure returns and risk. The two standard measures are, respectively, the average expected rate of return and the beta statistic.

Average Expected Rate of Return Each investment's **average expected rate of return** is the probability weighted average of the investment's possible future rates of return. The term **probability weighted average** simply means that each of the possible future rates of return is multiplied by its probability expressed as a decimal (so that a 50 percent probability is .5 and a 23 percent probability is .23) before being added together to obtain the average. For instance, if an investment has a 75 percent probability of generating 11 percent per year and a 25 percent probability of generating 15 percent per year, then its average expected rate of return will be 12 percent = (.75 × 11 percent) + (.25 × 15 percent). By weighting each possible outcome by its probability, this process ensures that the resulting average gives more weight to those outcomes that are more likely to happen (unlike the normal averaging process that would treat every outcome the same).

Once investors have calculated the average expected rates of return for all the assets they are interested in, there will naturally be some impulse to simply invest in those assets having the highest average expected rates of return. But while this might satisfy investor cravings for higher rates of return, it would not take proper account of the fact that investors dislike risk and uncertainty. To quantify their dislike, investors require a statistic that can measure each investment's risk level.

Beta One popular statistic that measures risk is called beta. **Beta** is a *relative* measure of nondiversifiable risk. It measures how the nondiversifiable risk of a given asset or portfolio of assets compares with that of the **market portfolio**, which is the name given to a portfolio that contains every asset available in the financial markets. The market portfolio is a useful standard of comparison because it is as diversified as possible. In fact, since it contains every possible asset, every possible diversifiable risk will be diversified away—meaning that it will be exposed *only* to nondiversifiable risk. Consequently, it can serve as a useful benchmark against which to measure the levels of nondiversifiable risk to which individual assets are exposed.

Such comparisons are very simple because the beta statistic is standardized such that the market portfolio's level of nondiversifiable risk is set equal to 1.0. Consequently, an asset with beta = .5 has a level of nondiversifiable risk that is one-half of that possessed by the market portfolio, while an asset with beta = 2.0 has twice as much nondiversifiable risk as the market portfolio. In addition, the beta numbers of various assets also can be used to compare them with each other. For instance, an asset with beta = 2.0 has four times as much exposure to nondiversifiable risk as does an asset with beta = .5.

Another useful feature of beta is that it can be calculated not only for individual assets but also for portfolios. Indeed, it can be calculated for portfolios no matter how many or how few assets they contain and no matter what those assets happen to be. This fact is very convenient for mutual fund investors because it means that they can use beta to quickly see how the nondiversifiable risk of any given fund's portfolio compares with that of other potential investments that they may be considering.

The beta statistic is used along with average expected rates of return to give investors standard measures of risk and return that can be used to sensibly compare different investment opportunities. As we will discuss in the next section, this leads to one of the most fundamental relationships in financial economics: riskier assets have higher rates of return.

Relationship of Risk and Average Expected Rates of Return

The fact that investors dislike risk has a profound effect on asset prices and average expected rates of return. In particular, their dislike of risk and uncertainty causes investors to pay higher prices for less-risky assets and lower prices for more-risky assets. But since asset prices and average expected rates of return are inversely related, this implies that less risky assets will have lower average expected rates of return than more risky assets.

Stated a bit more clearly: *Risk levels and average expected rates of return are positively related.* The more risky an investment is, the higher its average expected rate of return will be. A great way to understand this relationship is to think of higher average expected rates of return as being a form of compensation. Since investors dislike risk, they demand higher levels of compensation the more risky an asset is. The higher levels of compensation come in the form of higher average expected rates of return.

Be sure to note that this phenomenon affects all assets. Regardless of whether the assets are stocks or bonds or real estate or anything else, assets with higher levels of risk always end up with higher average expected rates of return to compensate investors for the higher levels of risk involved. No matter what the investment opportunity is, investors examine its possible future payments, determine how risky they are, and then select a price that reflects those risks. Since less-risky investments get higher prices, they end up with lower rates of return, whereas more-risky investments end up with lower prices and, consequently, higher rates of return. (**Key Question 9**)

The Risk-Free Rate of Return

We have just shown that there is a positive relationship between risk and returns, with higher returns serving to compensate investors for higher levels of risk. One investment, however, is considered to be risk-free for all intents and purposes. That investment is short-term U.S. government bonds.

These bonds are short-term loans to the U.S. government, with the duration of the loans ranging from 4 weeks to 26 weeks. They are considered to be essentially risk-free because there is almost no chance that the U.S. government will not be able to repay these loans on time and in

GLOBAL PERSPECTIVE 34.1

Investment Risks Vary across Different Countries

The International Country Risk Guide is a monthly publication that attempts to distill the political, economic, and financial risks facing 140 countries into a single "composite risk rating" number for each country, with higher numbers indicating less risk and more safety. The table below presents the January 2008 ranks and rating numbers for 15 countries including the three least risky (ranked 1 through 3) and the three most risky (ranked 138 through 140.) Ratings numbers above 80 are considered *very low risk;* 70–80 are considered *low risk;* 60–70 *moderate risk;* 50–60 *high risk;* and below 50 *very high risk.*

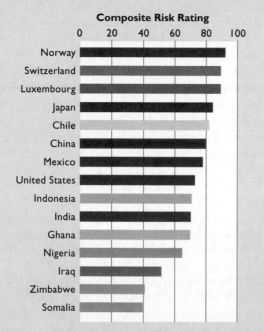

Composite Risk Rating

Norway, Switzerland, Luxembourg, Japan, Chile, China, Mexico, United States, Indonesia, India, Ghana, Nigeria, Iraq, Zimbabwe, Somalia

Source: *The International Country Risk Guide,* January 2008. Published by the PRS (Political Risk Survey) Group, Inc. **www.prsgroup.com/icrg/icrg.html.** Used by permission of the PRS Group, Inc.

full. Although it is true that the U.S. government may eventually be destroyed or disabled to such an extent that it will not be able to repay some of its loans, the chances of such a calamity happening within 4 or even 26 weeks are essentially zero. Consequently, because it is a near certainty that the bonds will be repaid in full and on time, they are considered by investors to be risk-free.

Since higher levels of risk lead to higher rates of return, a person might be tempted to assume—incorrectly—that since government bonds are risk-free, they should earn a zero percent rate of return. The problem with this line of thinking is that it mistakenly assumes that risk is the *only* thing that rates of return compensate for. The truth is that rates of return compensate not only for risk but also for something that economists call time preference.

Time preference refers to the fact that because people tend to be impatient, they typically prefer to consume things in the present rather than in the future. Stated more concretely, most people, if given the choice between a serving of their favorite dessert immediately or a serving of their favorite dessert in five years, will choose to consume their favorite dessert immediately.

This time preference for consuming sooner rather than later affects the financial markets because people want to be compensated for delayed consumption. In particular, if Dave asks Oprah to lend him $1 million for one year, he is implicitly asking Oprah to delay consumption for a year because if she lends Dave the $1 million, she will not be able to spend that money herself for at least a year. If Oprah is like most people and has a preference for spending her $1 million sooner rather than later, the only way Dave will be able to convince Oprah to let him borrow $1 million is to offer her some form of compensation. The compensation comes in the form of an interest payment that will allow Oprah to consume more in the future than she can now. For instance, Dave can offer to pay Oprah $1.1 million in one year in exchange for $1 million today. That is, Oprah will get back the $1 million she lends to Dave today as well as an extra $100,000 to compensate her for being patient.

Notice the very important fact that this type of interest payment has nothing to do with risk. It is purely compensation for being patient and must be paid even if there is no risk involved and 100 percent certainty that Dave will fulfill his promise to repay.

Since short-term U.S. government bonds are for all intents and purposes completely risk-free and 100 percent likely to repay as promised, their rates of return are *purely* compensation for time preference and the fact that people must be compensated for delaying their own consumption

opportunities when they lend money to the government. One consequence of this fact is that the rate of return earned by short-term U.S. government bonds is often referred to as the **risk-free interest rate**, or i^f, to clearly indicate that the rate of return that they generate is not in any way a compensation for risk.

It should be kept in mind, however, that the Federal Reserve has the power to change the risk-free interest rate generated by short-term U.S. government bonds. As discussed in Chapter 33, the Federal Reserve can raise or lower the interest rate earned by government bonds by making large purchases or sales of bonds in the bond markets—an activity referred to as open-market operations. This means that the Federal Reserve determines the risk-free interest rate and, consequently, the compensation that investors receive for being patient. As we will soon demonstrate, this fact is very important because by manipulating the reward for being patient, the Federal Reserve can affect the rate of return and prices of not only government bonds but all assets.

The Security Market Line

Investors must be compensated for time preference as well as for the amount of nondiversifiable risk that an investment carries with it. This section introduces a simple model called the **Security Market Line,** which indicates how this compensation is determined for all assets no matter what their respective risk levels happen to be.

The underlying logic of the model is this: Any investment's average expected rate of return has to be the sum of two parts—one that compensates for time preference and another that compensates for risk. That is,

$$\begin{aligned} \text{Average expected} &= \text{rate that compensates for} \\ \text{rate of return} &\quad \text{time preference} \\ &\quad + \text{rate that compensates for risk} \end{aligned}$$

As we explained, the compensation for time preference is equal to the risk-free interest rate, i^f, that is paid on government bonds. As a result, this equation can be simplified to

$$\begin{aligned} \text{Average expected} &= i^f + \text{rate that compensates} \\ \text{rate of return} &\quad \text{for risk} \end{aligned}$$

Finally, because economists typically refer to the rate that compensates for risk as the **risk premium,** this equation can be simplified even further to

$$\text{Average expected rate of return} = i^f + \text{risk premium}$$

Naturally, the size of the risk premium that compensates for risk will vary depending on how risky an investment happens to be. In particular, it will depend on how

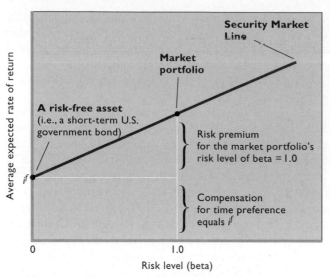

FIGURE 34.1 The Security Market Line. The Security Market Line shows the relationship between average expected rates of return and risk levels that must hold for every asset or portfolio trading in the financial markets. Each investment's average expected rate of return is the sum of the risk-free interest rate that compensates for time preference as well as a risk premium that compensates for the investment's level of risk. The Security Market Line's upward slope reflects the fact that investors must be compensated for higher levels of risk with higher average expected rates of return.

big or small the investment's beta is. Investments with large betas and lots of nondiversifiable risk will obviously require larger risk premiums than investments that have small betas and low levels of nondiversifiable risk. And, in the most extreme case, risk-free assets that have betas equal to zero will require no compensation for risk at all since they obviously have no risk to compensate for.

This logic is translated into the graph presented in Figure 34.1. The horizontal axis of Figure 34.1 measures risk levels using beta; the vertical axis measures average expected rates of return. As a result, any investment can be plotted on Figure 34.1 just as long as we know its beta and its average expected rate of return. We have plotted two investments in Figure 34.1. The first is a risk-free short-term U.S. government bond, which is indicated by the lower-left dot in the figure. The second is the market portfolio, which is indicated by the upper-right dot in the figure.

The lower dot marking the position of the risk-free bond is located where it is because it is a risk-free asset having a beta = 0 and because its average expected rate of return is given by i^f. These values place the lower dot i^f percentage points up the vertical axis, as shown in Figure 34.1. Note that this location conveys the logic that because this asset has no risk, its average expected rate of return only has to compensate investors for time preference—which is why its average expected rate of return is equal to precisely i^f and no more.

The market portfolio, by contrast, is risky so that its average expected rate of return must compensate investors not only for time preference but also for the level of risk to which the market portfolio is exposed, which by definition is beta = 1.0. This implies that the vertical distance from the horizontal axis to the upper dot is equal to the sum of i^f and the market portfolio's risk premium.

The straight line connecting the risk-free asset's lower dot and the market portfolio's upper dot is called the Security Market Line, or SML. The SML is extremely important because it defines the relationship between average expected rates of return and risk levels that must hold for all assets and all portfolios trading in the financial markets. The SML illustrates the idea that every asset's average expected rate of return is the sum of a rate of return that compensates for time preference and a rate of return that compensates for risk. More specifically, the SML has a vertical intercept equal to the rate of interest earned by short-term U.S. government bonds and a positive slope that compensates investors for risk.

As we explained earlier, the precise location of the intercept at any given time is determined by the Federal Reserve's monetary policy and how it affects the rate of return on short-term U.S. government bonds. The slope of the SML, however, is determined by investors' feelings about risk and how much compensation they require for dealing with it. If investors greatly dislike risk, then the SML will have to be very steep, so that any given increase in risk on the horizontal axis will result in a very large increase in compensation as measured by average expected rates of return on the vertical axis. On the other hand, if investors dislike risk only moderately, then the SML will be relatively flat since any given increase in risk on the horizontal axis would require only a moderate increase in compensation as measured by average expected rates of return on the vertical axis.

It is important to realize that once investor preferences about risk have determined the slope of the SML

FIGURE 34.2 Risk levels determine average expected rates of return.

The Security Market Line can be used to determine an investment's average expected rate of return based on its risk level. In this figure, investments having a risk level of beta = X will have an average expected rate of return of Y percent per year. This average expected rate of return will compensate investors for time preference in addition to providing them exactly the right sized risk premium to compensate them for dealing with a risk level of beta = X.

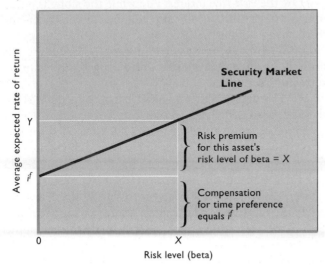

FIGURE 34.3 Arbitrage and the Security Market Line.

Arbitrage pressures will tend to move any asset or portfolio that lies off of the Security Market Line back onto the Security Market Line. For instance, asset A has an average expected rate of return that exceeds the average expected rate of return Y that the Security Market Line tells us is necessary to compensate investors for time preference and for dealing with risk level beta = X. As a result, asset A will become very popular and many investors will rush to buy it. This will drive its price up and (because prices and average expected rates of return are inversely related) drive its average expected rate of return down. Arbitrage will continue to happen until point A moves vertically down onto the SML. Arbitrage also will cause asset C, whose average expected rate of return is too low, to move up vertically onto the Security Market Line because as investors begin to sell asset C (because its average expected rate of return is too low), its price will fall, thereby raising its average expected rate of return.

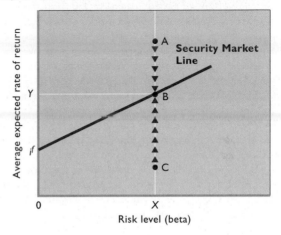

and monetary policy has determined its vertical intercept, the SML plots out the precise relationship between risk levels and average expected rates of return *that should hold for every asset*. For instance, consider Figure 34.2, where there is an asset whose risk level on the horizontal axis is beta = X. The SML tells us that every asset with that risk level should have an average expected rate of return equal to Y on the vertical axis. This average expected rate of return exactly compensates for both time preference and the fact that the asset in question is exposed to a risk level of beta = X.

Finally, it should be pointed out that arbitrage will ensure that all investments having an identical level of risk also will have an identical rate of return—the return given by the SML. This is illustrated in Figure 34.3, where the three assets A, B, and C all share the same risk level of beta = X but initially have three different average expected rates of return. Since asset B lies on the SML, it has the average expected rate of return Y that precisely compensates investors for time preference and risk level X. Asset A, however, has a higher average expected rate of return that overcompensates investors while asset C has a lower average expected rate of return that undercompensates investors.

Arbitrage pressures will quickly eliminate these over- and undercompensations. For instance, consider what will happen to asset A. Investors will be hugely attracted to its

overly high rate of return and will rush to buy it. That will drive up its price. But because average expected rates of return and prices are inversely related, the increase in price will cause its average expected rate of return to fall. Graphically, this means that asset A will move vertically downward as illustrated in Figure 34.3. And it will continue to move vertically downward until it reaches the SML since only then will it have the average expected rate of return Y that properly compensates investors for time preference and risk level X.

A similar process also will move asset C back to the SML. Investors will dislike the fact that its average expected rate of return is so low. This will cause them to sell it, driving down its price. Since average expected rates of return and prices are inversely related, this will cause its average expected rate of return to rise, thereby causing C to rise vertically as illustrated in Figure 34.3. And as with point A, point C will continue to rise until it reaches the SML, since only then will it have the average expected rate of return Y that properly compensates investors for time preference and risk level X. **(Key Question 11)**

CONSIDER THIS . . .

Does Ethical Investing Increase Returns?

In the last 10 years, ethical investment funds have become very popular. These mutual funds invest only in companies and projects that are consistent with the social and moral preferences of their investors. For instance, some of them avoid investing in tobacco companies or oil companies, while others seek to invest all of their money into companies seeking alternative energy sources or companies that promise not to employ child labor in their factories. Some ethical investment funds deliver average rates of return that are better than those generated by ordinary funds that do not select their investments on the basis of ethical or moral criteria. This has led some people to conclude that "doing good leads to doing well."

However, this analysis fails to take into account the fact that riskier investments generate higher rates of return. Indeed, a closer analysis shows that the higher returns generated by many ethical funds appear to be the result of their investing in riskier companies. So while there may be excellent moral reasons for investing in ethical funds, ethical investing, by itself, does not appear to generate higher returns.

In fact, it is even possible to imagine a situation in which ethical investing could generate *lower* rates of return. Because of the inverse relationship between asset prices and average expected rates of return, if investors preferred ethical companies, they would drive up their prices and thereby lower their rates of return relative to other companies. If that were to happen, then ethical investors might just have to seek solace in the proverb that states that "doing good is its own reward."

An Increase in the Risk-Free Rate

We have just explained how the position of the Security Market Line is fixed by two factors. The vertical intercept is set by the risk-free interest rate while the slope is determined by the amount of compensation investors demand for bearing nondiversifiable risk. As a result, changes in either one of these factors can shift the SML and thereby cause large changes in both average expected rates of return and asset prices.

As an example, consider what happens to the SML if the Federal Reserve changes policy and uses open-market operations (described in Chapter 33) to raise the interest rates of short-term U.S. government bonds. Since the risk-free interest rate earned by these bonds is also the SML's vertical intercept, an increase in their interest rate will cause the SML's vertical intercept to shift upward, as illustrated in Figure 34.4. This, in turn, causes a parallel upward shift of the SML from SML_1 to SML_2. (The shift is parallel because nothing has happened that would affect the SML's slope, which is determined by the amount of compensation that investors demand for bearing risk.)

Notice what this upward shift implies. Not only does the rate of return on short-term U.S. government bonds increase when the Federal Reserve changes policy, but the rate of return on risky assets increases as well. For instance, consider asset A, which originally has rate of return Y_1. After the SML shifts upward, asset A ends up with the higher rate of return Y_2. There is a simple intuition behind this increase. Risky assets must compete with risk-free assets for investor money. When the Federal Reserve increases the rate of return on risk-free short-term U.S. government bonds, they become more attractive to investors. But to get the money to

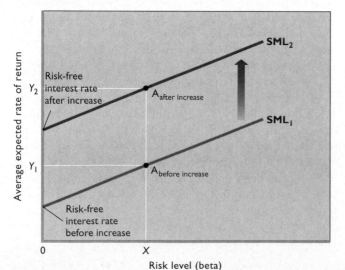

FIGURE 34.4 An increase in risk-free interest rates causes the SML to shift up vertically. The risk-free interest rate set by the Federal Reserve is the Security Market Line's vertical intercept. Consequently, if the Federal Reserve increases the risk-free interest rate, the Security Market Line's vertical intercept will move up. This rise in the risk-free interest rate will result in a decline in all asset prices and thus an increase in the average expected rate of return on all assets. So the Security Market Line will shift up parallel from SML_1 to SML_2. Here, asset A with risk level beta = X sees its average expected rate of return rise from Y_1 to Y_2.

Why Do Index Funds Beat Actively Managed Funds?

Mutual fund investors have a choice between putting their money into actively managed mutual funds or into passively managed index funds. Actively managed funds constantly buy and sell assets in an attempt to build portfolios that will generate average expected rates of return that are higher than those of other portfolios possessing a similar level of risk. In terms of Figure 34.3, they try to construct portfolios similar to point A, which has the same level of risk as portfolio B but a much higher average expected rate of return. By contrast, the portfolios of index funds simply mimic the assets that are included in their underlying indexes and make no attempt whatsoever to generate higher returns than other portfolios having similar levels of risk.

As a result, expecting actively managed funds to generate higher rates of return than index funds would seem only natural. Surprisingly, however, the exact opposite actually holds true. Once costs are taken into account, the average returns generated by index funds trounce those generated by actively managed funds by well over 1 percent per year. Now, 1 percent per year may not sound like a lot, but the compound interest formula of equation 1 shows that $10,000 growing for 30 years at 10 percent per year becomes $170,449.40, whereas that same amount of money growing at 11 percent for 30 years becomes $220,892.30. For anyone saving for retirement, an extra 1 percent per year is a very big deal.

Why do actively managed funds do so much worse than index funds? The answer is twofold. First, arbitrage makes it virtually impossible for actively managed funds to select portfolios that will do any better than index funds that have similar levels of risk. As a result, *before taking costs into account*, actively managed funds and index funds produce very similar returns. Second, actively managed funds charge their investors much higher fees than do passively managed funds, so that, *after taking costs into account*, actively managed funds do worse by about 1 percent per year.

Let us discuss each of these factors in more detail. The reason that actively managed funds cannot do better than index funds before taking costs into account has to do with the power of arbitrage to ensure that investments having equal levels of risk also have equal average expected rates of return. As we explained above with respect to Figure 34.3, assets and portfolios that deviate from the SML are very quickly forced back onto the SML by arbitrage, so that assets and portfolios with equal levels of risk have equal average expected rates of return. This implies that index funds and actively managed funds with equal levels of risk will end up with identical average expected rates of return despite the best efforts of actively managed funds to produce superior returns.

The reason actively managed funds charge much higher fees than index funds is because they run up much higher costs while trying to produce superior returns. Not only do they have to pay large salaries to professional fund managers; they also have to pay for the massive amounts of trading that those managers engage in as they buy and sell assets in their quest to produce superior returns. The costs of running an index fund are, by contrast, very small since changes are made to an index fund's portfolio only on the rare occasions when the fund's underlying index changes. As a result, trading costs are low and there is no need to pay for a professional manager. The overall result is that while the largest and most popular index fund currently charges its investors only .18 percent per year for its services, the typical actively managed fund charges more than 1.5 percent per year.

So why are actively managed funds still in business? The answer may well be that index funds are boring. Because they are set up to mimic indexes that are in turn designed to show what average performance levels are, index funds are by definition stuck with average rates of return and absolutely no chance to exceed average rates of return. For investors who want to try to beat the average, actively managed funds are the only way to go.

buy more risk-free bonds, investors have to sell risky assets. This drives down their prices and—because prices and average expected rates of return are inversely related—causes their average expected rates of return to increase. The result is that asset A moves up vertically in Figure 34.4, its average expected rate of return increasing from Y_1 to Y_2 as investors reallocate their wealth from risky assets like asset A to risk-free bonds.

This process explains why investors are so sensitive to Federal Reserve policies. Any increase in the risk-free interest rate leads to a decrease in asset prices that directly reduces investors' wealth. This reduction obviously hurts investors personally but it also may have broader implications. As was pointed out in Chapter 29, the reduction of wealth caused by falling asset prices may lead to a reverse wealth effect, the result of which could be less spending by consumers. Thus, increases in interest rates matter greatly for the economy as a whole. They not only tend to cause direct reductions in investment spending and interest-sensitive consumption spending (the main intent of restrictive monetary policy), but they also may reduce aggregate demand indirectly through their impact on asset prices.

The underlying reason that the Federal Reserve has so much power to manipulate asset prices by shifting the SML is because the SML defines all of the investment options available in the financial markets. As we pointed out previously, arbitrage will force every investment to lie on the SML. This means that when investors think about investing their limited wealth, all of their options will lie on the SML and they will be forced to select a portfolio that best suits their personal preferences about risk and returns from the limited options defined by the SML. The Federal Reserve's power to change asset prices stems entirely from the fact that when it shifts the SML, it totally redefines the investment opportunities available in the economy. As the set of options changes, investors modify their portfolios in order to obtain the best possible combination of risk and returns from the new set of investment options. In doing so, they engage in massive amounts of buying and selling in order to get rid of assets they no longer want and acquire assets that they now desire. These massive changes in supply and demand for financial assets are what cause their prices to change so drastically when the Federal Reserve alters the risk-free interest rate.

Summary

1. The compound interest formula shows how quickly a given amount of money will grow if interest is paid not only on the amount initially invested but also on any interest payments previously paid. It states that if X dollars is invested today at interest rate i and allowed to grow for t years, it will become $(1 + i)^t X$ dollars in t years.

2. The present value model rearranges the compound interest formula to make it easy to determine the present value (that is, the current number of dollars) that you would have to invest today in order to receive X dollars in t years. The present value formula says that you would have to invest $X/(1 + i)^t$ dollars today at interest rate i in order for it to grow into X dollars in t years.

3. An extremely wide variety of financial assets is available to investors, but it is possible to study them all under a unified framework because they have a common characteristic: In exchange for a certain price today they all promise to make one or more payments in the future. A risk-free investment's proper current price is simply equal to the sum of the present values of each of the investment's expected future payments.

4. The three most popular investments are stocks, bonds, and mutual funds. Stocks are ownership shares in corporations. They have value because they give shareholders the right to share in any future profits that the corporations may generate. Their primary risk is that future profits are unpredictable and that companies may go bankrupt. Bonds are a type of loan contract. They are valuable because they give bondholders the right to receive a fixed stream of future payments that serve to repay the loan. They are risky because of the possibility that the corporations or government bodies that issued the bonds may default on them, or not make the promised payments. Mutual funds are investment companies that pool the money of many investors in order to buy a portfolio (or collection) of assets. They are valuable to investors because any returns generated by that portfolio belong to fund investors. Their risks reflect the risks of the stocks and bonds that they hold in their portfolios. Some funds are actively managed, with portfolio managers constantly trying to buy and sell stocks to maximize returns, whereas others are passively managed index funds whose portfolios are determined by the indexes that they mimic.

5. Investors evaluate the possible future returns to risky projects using average expected rates of return, which give higher weight to outcomes that are more likely to happen.

6. Average expected rates of return are inversely related to an asset's current price. When the price goes up, the average expected rate of return goes down.

7. Arbitrage is the process whereby investors equalize the average expected rates of return generated by identical or nearly identical assets. If two identical assets have different rates of return, investors will sell the asset with the lower rate of return in order to buy the asset with the higher rate of return. Because average expected rates of return are inversely related to asset prices, this will cause the rates of return to converge: As investors buy the asset with the higher rate of return, its price will be driven up, causing its average expected rate of return to fall. At the same time, as investors sell the asset with the lower rate of return, its price will fall, causing its average expected rate of return to rise. The process will continue until the two assets have equal average expected rates of return.

8. In finance, an asset is risky if its future payments are uncertain. Under this definition of risk, what matters is not whether the payments are big or small, positive or negative, or good or bad—only that they are not guaranteed ahead of time.

9. Diversification is an investment strategy that seeks to reduce the overall risk facing an investment portfolio by selecting a group of assets whose risks offset—so that when bad things are happening to some of the assets, good things are happening to others. Risks that can be canceled out by diversification are called diversifiable risks. Risks that cannot be canceled out by diversification are called nondiversifiable risks. Nondiversifiable risks include things like recessions, which affect all investments in the same direction simultaneously so that selecting assets that offset each other is not possible.

10. Beta is a statistic that measures the nondiversifiable risk of an asset or portfolio relative to the amount of nondiversifiable risk facing the market portfolio. By definition, the market portfolio has a beta of 1.0, so that if an asset has a beta of 0.5, it has half as much nondiversifiable risk as the market portfolio. Since the market portfolio is the portfolio that contains every asset trading in the financial markets, it is as diversified as possible and consequently has eliminated all of its diversifiable risk—meaning that the only risk to which it is exposed is nondiversifiable risk. Consequently, it is the perfect standard against which to measure levels of nondiversifiable risk.

11. Because investors dislike risk, they demand compensation for bearing risk. The compensation comes in the form of higher average expected rates of return. The riskier the asset, the higher its average expected rate of return will be. Notice, however, that we always assume that an asset is part of a well-diversified portfolio—meaning that all of its diversifiable risk has been eliminated. As a result, investors will need to be compensated only for the asset's level of nondiversifiable risk as measured by beta.

12. Average expected rates of return also must compensate for time preference and the fact that, all other things being equal, most people prefer to consume sooner rather than later. Consequently, an asset's average expected rate of return will be the sum of the rate of return that compensates for time preference plus the rate of return that compensates for the asset's level of nondiversifiable risk as measured by beta. Note that because all investment activities involve delaying consumption, the rate of return that compensates for time preference will be the same for all assets regardless of how risky they are.

13. The rate of return that compensates for time preference is assumed to be equal to the rate of interest generated by short-term U.S. government bonds. This is true because these bonds are considered to be risk-free, meaning that their rate of return must be purely compensation for time preference since they have no risk to compensate for. Indeed, the interest rate that these bonds generate is often called the risk-free interest rate, partly to remind people that the bonds are risk-free and partly to remind them that, because they are risk-free, their interest rate must be solely to compensate for time preference. The Federal Reserve has the power to manipulate this interest rate and thereby affect what the economywide compensation for time preference will be.

14. The Security Market Line (SML) is a straight line that plots how the average expected rates of return on assets and portfolios in the economy must vary with their respective levels of nondiversifiable risk as measured by beta. Arbitrage ensures that every asset in the economy should plot onto the SML. The slope of the SML indicates how much investors dislike risk. If investors greatly dislike risk, then the SML will be very steep, indicating that investors demand a great amount of compensation in terms of higher average expected rates of return for bearing increasingly large amounts of nondiversifiable risk. If investors are more comfortable with risk, then the SML will be flatter, indicating that that they require only moderately higher average expected rates of return to compensate them for higher levels of nondiversifiable risk.

15. The SML takes account of time preference and the fact that investors must be compensated for delaying consumption. Since the compensation for time preference is the risk-free interest rate on short-term U.S. government bonds, which is controlled by the Federal Reserve, the Federal Reserve can shift the entire SML by changing risk-free interest rates and the compensation for time preference that must be paid to investors in all assets regardless of their risk level. When the SML shifts, the average expected rate of return on all assets changes. This is very important because, since average expected rates of return are inversely related to asset prices, the shift in the SML also will change asset prices. Consequently, the Federal Reserve's power to shift short-run interest rates also gives it the power to shift asset prices throughout the economy.

Terms and Concepts

economic investment	default	diversifiable risk
financial investment	mutual funds	nondiversifiable risk
compound interest	portfolios	average expected rate of return
present value	index funds	probability weighted average
stocks	actively managed funds	beta
bankrupt	passively managed funds	market portfolio
limited liability rule	percentage rate of return	time preference
capital gains	arbitrage	risk-free interest rate
dividends	risk	Security Market Line
bonds	diversification	risk premium

Study Questions

1. Suppose that the city of New York issues bonds to raise money to pay for a new tunnel linking New Jersey and Manhattan. An investor named Susan buys one of the bonds on the same day that the city of New York pays a contractor for completing the first stage of construction. Is Susan making an economic or a financial investment? What about the city of New York? **LO1**

2. Suppose that a risk-free investment will make three future payments of $100 in one year, $100 in two years, and $100 in three years. If the Federal Reserve has set the risk-free interest rate at 8 percent, what is the proper current price of this investment? What if the Federal Reserve raises the risk-free interest rate to 10 percent? **LO1**

3. How do stocks and bonds differ in terms of the future payments that they are expected to make? Which type of investment (stocks or bonds) is considered to be more risky? Given what you know, which investment (stocks or bonds) do you think commonly goes by the nickname "fixed income"? **LO2**

4. Mutual funds are very popular. What do they do? What different types of mutual funds are there? And why do you think they are so popular with investors? **LO2**

5. Consider an asset that costs $120 today. You are going to hold it for 1 year and then sell it. Suppose that there is a 25 percent chance that it will be worth $100 in a year, a 25 percent chance that it will be worth $115 in a year, and a 50 percent chance that it will be worth $140 in a year. What is its average expected rate of return? Next, figure out what the investment's average expected rate of return would be if its current price were $130 today. Does the increase in the current price increase or decrease the asset's average expected rate of return? At what price would the asset have a zero rate of return? **LO3**

6. **KEY QUESTION** Corporations often distribute profits to their shareholders in the form of dividends, which are simply checks mailed out to shareholders. Suppose that you have the chance to buy a share in a fashion company called Rogue Designs for $35 and that the company will pay dividends of $2 per year on that share every year. What is the annual percentage rate of return? Next, suppose that you and other investors could get a 12 percent per year rate of return by owning the stocks of other very similar fashion companies. If investors care only about rates of return, what should happen to the share price of Rogue Designs? (Hint: This is an arbitrage situation.) **LO3**

7. This question will compare two different arbitrage situations. Recall that arbitrage should equalize rates of return. We want to explore what this implies about equalizing prices. In the first situation, two assets, A and B, will each make a single guaranteed payment of $100 in 1 year. But asset A has a current price of $80 while asset B has a current price of $90. **LO3**

   a. Which asset has the higher expected rate of return at current prices? Given their rates of return, which asset should investors be buying and which asset should they be selling?

   b. Assume that arbitrage continues until A and B have the same expected rate of return. When arbitrage ceases, will A and B have the same price?

   Next, consider another pair of assets, C and D. Asset C will make a single payment of $150 in one year while D will make a single payment of $200 in one year. Assume that the current price of C is $120 and that the current price of D is $180.

   c. Which asset has the higher expected rate of return at current prices? Given their rates of return, which asset should investors be buying and which asset should they be selling?

   d. Assume that arbitrage continues until C and D have the same expected rate of return. When arbitrage ceases, will C and D have the same price?

   Compare your answers to questions *a* through *d* before answering question *e*.

e. We know that arbitrage will equalize rates of return. Does it also guarantee to equalize prices? In what situations will it also equalize prices?

8. **KEY QUESTION** Why is it reasonable to ignore diversifiable risk and care only about nondiversifiable risk? What about an investor who puts all of his money into only a single risky stock? Can he properly ignore diversifiable risk? **LO4**

9. **KEY QUESTION** If we compare the betas of various investment opportunities, why do the assets that have higher betas also have higher average expected rates of return? **LO5**

10. In this chapter we discussed short-term U.S. government bonds. But the U.S. government also issues longer-term bonds with horizons of up to 30 years. Why do 20-year bonds issued by the U.S. government have lower rates of return than 20-year bonds issued by corporations? And which would you consider more likely, that longer-term U.S. government bonds have a higher interest rate than short-term U.S. government bonds, or vice versa? Explain. **LO5**

11. **KEY QUESTION** Consider the Security Market Line (SML). What determines its vertical intercept? What determines its slope? And what will happen to an asset's price if it initially plots onto a point above the SML? **LO3**

12. Suppose that the Federal Reserve wants to increase stock prices. What should it do to interest rates? **LO3**

13. Consider another situation involving the SML. Suppose that the risk-free interest rate stays the same, but that investors' dislike of risk grows more intense. Given this change, will average expected rates of return rise or fall? Next, compare what will happen to the rates of return on low-risk and high-risk investments. Which will have a larger increase in average expected rates of return, investments with high betas or investments with low betas? And will high-beta or low-beta investments show larger percentage changes in their prices? **LO5**

14. **LAST WORD** Why is it so hard for actively managed funds to generate higher rates of return than passively managed index funds having similar levels of risk? Is there a simple way for an actively managed fund to increase its average expected rate of return?

Web-Based Questions

1. **CALCULATING PRESENT VALUES USING CURRENT INTEREST RATES** To see the current interest rates ("yields") on bonds issued by the U.S. government, please go to **www.bloomberg.com/markets/rates/index.html** and scroll down to the section labeled U.S. Treasuries. By tradition, U.S. government bonds with maturities of less than 1 year are called bills, while those with longer maturities are referred to as either notes or bonds. The notes have maturities of 1 to 10 years, while the bonds have maturities exceeding 10 years. What are the current yields on 2-year notes and 30-year bonds? Use the current yield for the 2-year note to calculate the present value of an investment that will make a single payment of $95,000 in 2 years. Use the current yield on the 30-year bond to calculate the present value of an investment that will make a single payment of $95,000 in 30 years. To assist your computations, you can try out the present value calculator available at **www.timevalue.com/tools.html.** (When you go to that page, click on the Investment Calculators menu and then select "What is my future value worth today?" That will get you to the present value calculator.) Why the large difference in present values in the two situations?

2. **EVALUATING THE RISK LEVELS OF TOP MUTUAL FUNDS** The Security Market Line tells us that assets and portfolios that deliver high average expected rates of return should also have high levels of risk as measured by beta. Let us see if this appears to hold true for mutual fund portfolios. Go to the Mutual Fund Center at Yahoo Finance at **http://finance.yahoo.com/funds,** click on Top Performers, and then click on Overall Top Performers. This will give you lists of funds with the 10 best rates of return over various time periods. Click on each of the 10 funds listed under Top Performers—1 Year and find each fund's beta by clicking on the link labeled Risk. Do any of the funds have a beta less than 1.0? Do these results make sense given what you have learned? Should you be impressed that funds with risky portfolios generate high returns?

PART NINE

Extensions and Issues

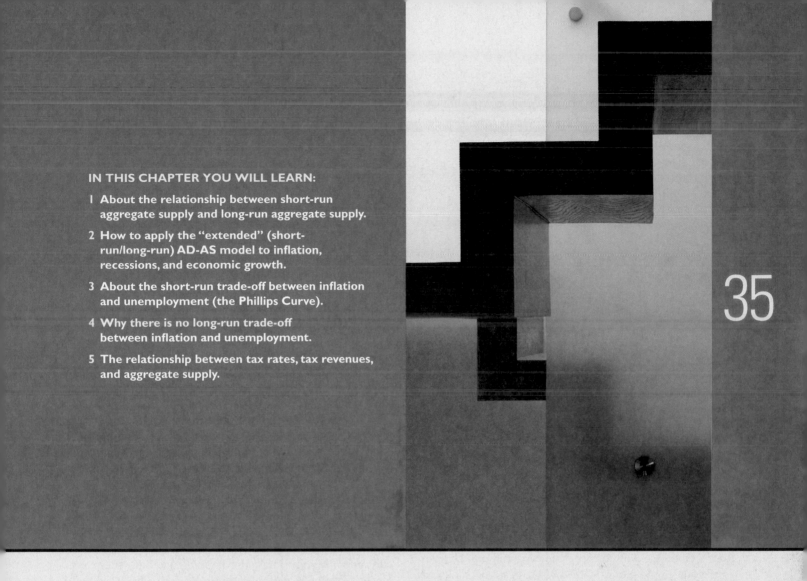

35

Extending the Analysis of Aggregate Supply

During the early years of the Great Depression, many economists suggested that the economy would correct itself in the *long run* without government intervention. To this line of thinking, economist John Maynard Keynes remarked, "In the long run we are all dead!"

For several decades following the Great Depression, macroeconomic economists understandably focused on refining fiscal policy and monetary policy to smooth business cycles and address the problems of unemployment and inflation. The main emphasis was on short-run problems and policies associated with the business cycle.

But over people's lifetimes, and from generation to generation, the long run is tremendously important for economic well-being. For that reason, macroeconomists have refocused attention on long-run macroeconomic adjustments, processes, and outcomes. The renewed emphasis on the long run has produced significant insights about aggregate supply, economic growth, and economic development. We will also see in the next chapter that it has renewed historical debates over the causes of macro instability and the effectiveness of stabilization policy.

Our goals in this chapter are to extend the analysis of aggregate supply to the long run, examine the inflation-unemployment relationship, and evaluate the effect of taxes on aggregate supply. The latter is a key concern of so-called *supply-side economics*.

From Short Run to Long Run

In Chapter 29, we noted that in macroeconomics the difference between the **short run** and the **long run** has to do with the flexibility of input prices. Input prices are inflexible or even totally fixed in the short run but fully flexible in the long run. (By contrast, output prices are assumed under these definitions to be fully flexible in both the short run and the long run.)

The assumption that input prices are flexible only in the long run leads to large differences in the shape and position of the short-run aggregate supply curve and the long-run aggregate supply curve. As explained in Chapter 29, the short-run aggregate supply curve is an upward-sloping line, whereas the long-run aggregate supply curve is a vertical line situated directly above the economy's full-employment output level, Q_f.

We will begin this chapter by studying how aggregate supply transitions *from* the short run *to* the long run. Once that is done, we will combine the long-run and short-run aggregate supply curves with the aggregate demand curve in order to form a single model that can give us insights into how the economy adjusts to both economic shocks as well as changes in monetary and fiscal policy in both the short run as well as the long run. That, in turn will lead us to discuss how long-run aggregate supply is affected by economic growth as well as how inflation and aggregate supply are related in both the long run and the short run. We will conclude with a discussion of economic policies that may help to increase aggregate supply in both the short run as well as the long run.

Short-Run Aggregate Supply

Our first objective is to demonstrate the relationship between short-run aggregate supply and long-run aggregate supply. We begin by briefly reviewing short-run aggregate supply.

Consider the short-run aggregate supply curve AS_1 in Figure 35.1a. This curve is based on three assumptions: (1) The initial price level is P_1, (2) firms and workers have established nominal wages on the expectation that this price level will persist, and (3) the price level is flexible both upward and downward. Observe from point a_1 that at price level P_1 the economy is operating at its full-employment output Q_f. This output is the real production forthcoming when the economy is operating at its natural rate of unemployment (or potential output).

Now let's review the short-run effects of changes in the price level, say, from P_1 to P_2 in Figure 35.1a. The higher prices associated with price level P_2 increase firms' revenues, and because their nominal wages and other input prices remain unchanged, their profits rise. Those higher profits lead firms to increase their output from Q_f to Q_2, and the economy moves from a_1 to a_2 on aggregate supply AS_1. At output Q_2 the economy is operating beyond its full-employment output. The firms make this possible by extending the work hours of part-time and full-time workers, enticing new workers such as homemakers and retirees into the labor force, and hiring and training the structurally unemployed. Thus, the nation's unemployment rate declines below its natural rate.

How will the firms respond when the price level *falls*, say, from P_1 to P_3 in Figure 35.1a? Because the prices they receive for their products are lower while the nominal wages they pay workers remain unchanged, firms discover that their revenues and profits have diminished or disappeared. So they reduce their production and employment, and, as shown by the movement from a_1 to a_3, real output falls to Q_3. Increased unemployment and a higher unemployment rate accompany the decline in real output. At output Q_3 the unemployment rate is greater than the natural rate of unemployment associated with output Q_f.

Long-Run Aggregate Supply

The outcomes are different in the long run. To see why, we need to extend the analysis of aggregate supply to account for changes in nominal wages that occur in response to changes in the price level. That will enable us to derive the economy's long-run aggregate supply curve.

FIGURE 35.1 Short-run and long-run aggregate supply. (a) In the short run, nominal wages and other input prices do not respond to price-level changes and are based on the expectation that price level P_1 will continue. An increase in the price level from P_1 to P_2 increases profits and output, moving the economy from a_1 to a_2; a decrease in the price level from P_1 to P_3 reduces profits and real output, moving the economy from a_1 to a_3. The short-run aggregate supply curve therefore slopes upward. (b) In the long run, a rise in the price level results in higher nominal wages and other input prices and thus shifts the short-run aggregate supply curve to the left. Conversely, a decrease in the price level reduces nominal wages and shifts the short-run aggregate supply curve to the right. After such adjustments, the economy obtains equilibrium of points such as b_1 and c_1. Thus, the long-run aggregate supply curve is vertical at the full-employment output.

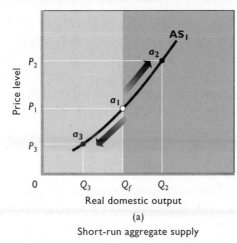

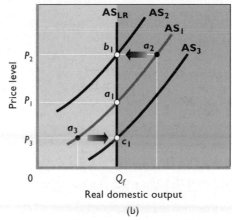

(a)

Short-run aggregate supply

(b)

Long-run aggregate supply

We illustrate the implications for aggregate supply in Figure 35.1b. Again, suppose that the economy is initially at point a_1 (P_1 and Q_f). As we just demonstrated, an increase in the price level from P_1 to P_2 will move the economy from point a_1 to a_2 along the short-run aggregate supply curve AS_1. At a_2, the economy is producing at more than its potential output. This implies very high demand for productive inputs, so that input prices will begin to rise. In particular, the high demand for labor will drive up nominal wages. Because nominal wages are one of the determinants of aggregate supply (see Figure 29.6), the short-run supply curve then shifts leftward from AS_1 to AS_2, which now reflects the higher price level P_2 and the new expectation that P_2, not P_1, will continue. The leftward shift in the short-run aggregate supply curve to AS_2 moves the economy from a_2 to b_1. Real output falls back to its full-employment level Q_f, and the unemployment rate rises to its natural rate.

What is the long-run outcome of a *decrease* in the price level? Assuming eventual downward wage flexibility, a decline in the price level from P_1 to P_3 in Figure 35.1b works in the opposite way from a price-level increase. At first the economy moves from point a_1 to a_3 on AS_1. Profits are squeezed or eliminated because prices have fallen and nominal wages have not. But this movement along AS_1 is the short-run supply response that results only while input prices remain constant. As time passes, input prices will

begin to fall because the economy is producing at below its full-employment output level. With so little output being produced, the demand for inputs will be low and their prices will begin to decline. In particular, the low demand for labor will drive down nominal wages. Lower nominal wages shift the short-run aggregate supply curve rightward from AS_1 to AS_3, and real output returns to its full-employment level of Q_f at point c_1.

By tracing a line between the long-run equilibrium points b_1, a_1, and c_1, we obtain a long-run aggregate supply curve. Observe that it is vertical at the full-employment level of real GDP. After long-run adjustments in nominal wages and other nominal input prices, real output is Q_f regardless of the specific price level. **(Key Question 3)**

Long-Run Equilibrium in the AD-AS Model

Figure 35.2 helps us understand the long-run equilibrium in the AD-AS model, now extended to include the distinction between short-run and long-run aggregate supply. (Hereafter, we will refer to this model as the extended AD-AS model, with "extended" referring to the inclusion of both the short-run and the long-run aggregate supply curves.)

In the short run, equilibrium occurs wherever the downsloping aggregate demand curve and upsloping short-run aggregate supply curve intersect. This can be at

FIGURE 35.2 Equilibrium in the extended AD-AS model. The long-run equilibrium price level P_1 and level of real output Q_f occur at the intersection of the aggregate demand curve AD_1, the long-run aggregate supply curve AS_{LR}, and the short-run aggregate supply curve AS_1.

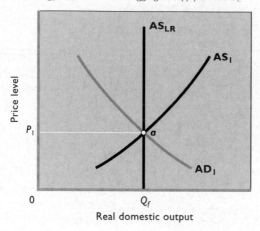

Real domestic output

any level of output, not simply the full-employment level. Either a negative GDP gap or a positive GDP gap is possible in the short run.

INTERACTIVE GRAPHS

G 35.1

Extended AD-AS model

But in the long run, the short-run aggregate supply curve adjusts as we just described. After those adjustments, long-run equilibrium occurs where the aggregate demand curve, vertical long-run aggregate supply curve, and short-run aggregate supply curve all intersect. Figure 35.2 shows the long-run outcome. Equilibrium occurs at point a, where AD_1 intersects both AS_{LR} and AS_1, and the economy achieves its full-employment (or potential) output, Q_f. At long-run equilibrium price level P_1 and output level Q_f, there is neither a negative GDP gap nor a positive GDP gap.

QUICK REVIEW 35.1

- The short-run aggregate supply curve has a positive slope because nominal wages and other input prices are fixed while output prices change.
- The long-run aggregate supply curve is vertical because input prices eventually rise in response to changes in output prices.
- The long-run equilibrium GDP and price level occur at the intersection of the aggregate demand curve, the long-run aggregate supply curve, and the short-run aggregate supply curve.

Applying the Extended AD-AS Model

The extended AD-AS model helps clarify the long-run aspects of demand-pull inflation, cost-push inflation, and recession.

Demand-Pull Inflation in the Extended AD-AS Model

Recall that demand-pull inflation occurs when an increase in aggregate demand pulls up the price level. Earlier, we depicted this inflation by shifting an aggregate demand curve rightward along a stable aggregate supply curve (see Figure 29.8).

In our more complex version of aggregate supply, however, an increase in the price level eventually leads to an increase in nominal wages and thus a leftward shift of the short-run aggregate supply curve. This is shown in Figure 35.3, where we initially suppose the price level is P_1 at the intersection of aggregate demand curve AD_1, short-run supply curve AS_1, and long-run aggregate supply curve AS_{LR}. Observe that the economy is achieving its full-employment real output Q_f at point a.

Now consider the effects of an increase in aggregate demand as represented by the rightward shift from AD_1 to AD_2. This shift might result from any one of a number of factors, including an increase in investment spending or a rise in net exports. Whatever its cause, the increase in aggregate demand boosts the price level from P_1 to P_2 and expands real output from Q_f to Q_2 at point b. There, a positive GDP gap of $Q_2 - Q_f$ occurs.

So far, none of this is new to you. But now the distinction between short-run aggregate supply and long-run aggregate supply becomes important. With the economy producing above potential output, inputs will be in high demand. Input prices including nominal wages will rise. As they do, the short-run aggregate supply curve will ultimately shift leftward such that it intersects long-run aggregate supply at point c.[1] There, the economy has reestablished long-run equilibrium, with the price level and real output now P_3 and Q_f, respectively. Only at point c does the new aggregate demand curve

---

[1]We say "ultimately" because the initial leftward shift in short-run aggregate supply will intersect the long-run aggregate supply curve AS_{LR} at price level P_2 (review Figure 35.1b). But the intersection of AD_2 and this new short-run aggregate supply curve (that is not shown in Figure 35.3) will produce a price level above P_2. (You may want to pencil this in to make sure that you understand this point.) Again nominal wages will rise, shifting the short-run aggregate supply curve farther leftward. The process will continue until the economy moves to point c, where the short-run aggregate supply curve is AS_2, the price level is P_3, and real output is Q_f.

FIGURE 35.3 Demand-pull inflation in the extended AD-AS model. An increase in aggregate demand from AD_1 to AD_2 drives up the price level and increases real output in the short run. But in the long run, nominal wages rise and the short-run aggregate supply curve shifts leftward, as from AS_1 to AS_2. Real output then returns to its prior level, and the price level rises even more. In this scenario, the economy moves from a to b and then eventually to c.

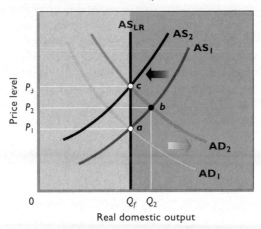

FIGURE 35.4 Cost-push inflation in the extended AD-AS model. Cost-push inflation occurs when the short-run aggregate supply curve shifts leftward, as from AS_1 to AS_2. If government counters the decline in real output by increasing aggregate demand to the broken line, the price level rises even more. That is, the economy moves in steps from a to b to c. In contrast, if government allows a recession to occur, nominal wages eventually fall and the aggregate supply curve shifts back rightward to its original location. The economy moves from a to b and eventually back to a.

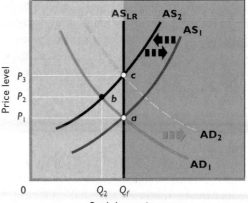

AD_2 intersect both the short-run aggregate supply curve AS_2 and the long-run aggregate supply curve AS_{LR}.

In the short run, demand-pull inflation drives up the price level and increases real output; in the long run, only the price level rises. In the long run, the initial increase in aggregate demand moves the economy along its vertical aggregate supply curve AS_{LR}. For a while, an economy can operate beyond its full-employment level of output. But the demand-pull inflation eventually causes adjustments of nominal wages that return the economy to its full-employment output Q_f.

Cost-Push Inflation in the Extended AD-AS Model

Cost-push inflation arises from factors that increase the cost of production at each price level, shifting the aggregate supply curve leftward and raising the equilibrium price level. Previously (Figure 29.10), we considered cost-push inflation using only the short-run aggregate supply curve. Now we want to analyze that type of inflation in its long-run context.

Analysis Look at Figure 35.4, in which we again assume that the economy is initially operating at price level P_1 and output level Q_f (point a). Suppose that international oil producers agree to reduce the supply of oil to boost its price by, say, 100 percent. As a result, the per-unit production cost of producing and transporting goods and services rises substantially in the economy represented by Figure 35.4. This increase in per-unit production costs shifts the

short-run aggregate supply curve to the left, as from AS_1 to AS_2, and the price level rises from P_1 to P_2 (as seen by comparing points a and b). In this case, the leftward shift of the aggregate supply curve is *not a response* to a price-level increase, as it was in our previous discussions of demand-pull inflation; it is the *initiating cause* of the price-level increase.

Policy Dilemma Cost-push inflation creates a dilemma for policymakers. Without some expansionary stabilization policy, aggregate demand in Figure 35.4 remains in place at AD_1 and real output declines from Q_f to Q_2. Government can counter this recession, negative GDP gap, and attendant high unemployment by using fiscal policy and monetary policy to increase aggregate demand to AD_2. But there is a potential policy trap here: An increase in aggregate demand to AD_2 will further raise inflation by increasing the price level from P_2 to P_3 (a move from point b to point c).

Suppose the government recognizes this policy trap and decides not to increase aggregate demand from AD_1 to AD_2 (you can now disregard the dashed AD_2 curve) and instead decides to allow a cost-push-created recession to run its course. How will that happen? Widespread layoffs, plant shutdowns, and business failures eventually occur. At some point the demand for oil, labor, and other inputs will decline so much that oil prices and nominal wages will decline. When that happens, the initial leftward shift of the short-run aggregate supply curve will reverse itself. That is, the declining per-unit production costs caused by the recession will shift the short-run aggregate supply curve rightward from AS_2 to AS_1. The price level will return to P_1, and the full-employment level of output will be restored at Q_f (point a on the long-run aggregate supply curve AS_{LR}).

This analysis yields two generalizations:

- If the government attempts to maintain full employment when there is cost-push inflation, even more inflation will occur.
- If the government takes a hands-off approach to cost-push inflation, the recession will linger. Although falling input prices will eventually undo the initial rise in per-unit production costs, the economy in the meantime will experience high unemployment and a loss of real output.

Recession and the Extended AD-AS Model

By far the most controversial application of the extended AD-AS model is its application to recession (or depression) caused by decreases in aggregate demand. We will look at this controversy in detail in Chapter 36; here we simply identify the key point of contention.

Suppose in Figure 35.5 that aggregate demand initially is AD_1 and that the short-run and long-run aggregate supply curves are AS_1 and AS_{LR}, respectively. Therefore, as shown by point a, the price level is P_1 and output is Q_f. Now suppose that investment spending declines dramatically, reducing aggregate demand to AD_2. Observe that real output declines from Q_f to Q_1, indicating that

FIGURE 35.5 Recession in the extended AD-AS model. A recession occurs when aggregate demand shifts leftward, as from AD_1 to AD_2. If prices and wages are downwardly flexible, the price level falls from P_1 to P_2 as the economy moves from point a to point b. With the economy in recession at point b, wages eventually fall, shifting the aggregate supply curve from AS_1 to AS_2. The price level declines to P_3, and real output returns to Q_f. The economy moves from a to b to c.

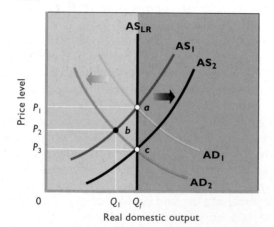

a recession has occurred. But if we make the controversial assumption that prices and wages are flexible downward, the price level falls from P_1 to P_2. With the economy producing below potential output at point b, demand for inputs will be low. Eventually, nominal wages themselves fall to restore the previous real wage; when that happens, the short-run aggregate supply curve shifts rightward from AS_1 to AS_2. The negative GDP gap evaporates without the need for expansionary fiscal or monetary policy since real output expands from Q_1 (point b) back to Q_f (point c). The economy is again located on its long-run aggregate supply curve AS_{LR}, but now at lower price level P_3.

There is much disagreement about this hypothetical scenario. The key point of dispute revolves around the degree to which both input and output prices may be downwardly inflexible and how long it would take in the real world for the necessary downward price and wage adjustments to occur to regain the full-employment level of output. For now, suffice it to say that most economists believe that if such adjustments are forthcoming, they will occur only after the economy has experienced a relatively long-lasting recession with its accompanying high unemployment and large loss of output. Therefore, economists recommend active monetary policy, and perhaps fiscal policy, to counteract recessions. **(Key Question 4)**

Ongoing Inflation in the Extended AD-AS Model

In our analysis so far, we have seen how demand and supply shocks can cause, respectively, demand-push inflation and cost-push inflation. But in all the cases analyzed up to now, the extent of the inflation was *finite* because the size of the initial movement in either the AD curve or the AS curve was *limited*. For instance, in Figure 35.3, the aggregate demand curve shifts right by a limited amount, from AD_1 to AD_2. As the economy's equilibrium moves from a, to b, to c, the price level rises from P_1, to P_2, to P_3. During this transition, inflation obviously occurs since the price level is rising. But once the economy reaches its new equilibrium at point c, the price level remains constant at P_3 and there is no further inflation. That is, the limited movement in aggregate demand causes a limited amount of inflation that ends when the economy returns to full employment.

This fact is crucial to understanding why modern economies experience ongoing positive rates of inflation. Simply put, there must be ongoing shifts in either the aggregate demand or aggregate supply curves since any single, finite shift in either curve will only cause an inflation of limited duration. In this section, we explore this idea, pointing out two facts. First, ongoing economic growth causes continuous rightward shifts of the aggregate supply curve that, by

FIGURE 35.6 Production possibilities and long-run aggregate supply. (a) Economic growth driven by supply factors (such as improved technologies or the use of more or better resources) shifts an economy's production possibilities curve outward, as from AB to CD. (b) The same factors shift the economy's long-run aggregate supply curve to the right, as from AS_{LR1} to AS_{LR2}.

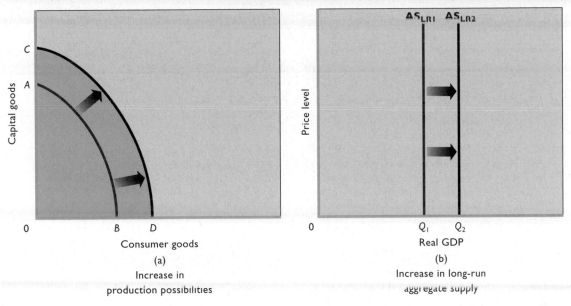

Increase in
production possibilities
(a)

Increase in long-run
aggregate supply
(b)

themselves, would tend to cause ongoing deflation. But, at the same time, central banks engineer ongoing increases in the money supply in order to cause slightly faster continuous rightward shifts of the aggregate demand curve. Taken alone, these rightward shifts in aggregate demand are inflationary. And because the central banks cause the inflationary rightward shifts of the aggregate demand curve to proceed just a little faster than the deflationary rightward shifts of the aggregate supply curve that are caused by economic growth, the net effect is (usually) a small positive rate of inflation. (We say "usually" because unexpected shocks to either aggregate demand or aggregate supply may cause inflation to be either a bit higher or a bit lower than the small positive rate that the central banks are attempting to engineer.)

Economic Growth and Aggregate Supply

As discussed in Chapter 25, economic growth is driven by supply factors such as improved technologies and access to more or better resources. Economic growth can be illustrated either as an outward shift of an economy's production possibilities curve or as a rightward shift of its long-run aggregate supply curve. As shown in Figure 35.6, the outward shift of the production possibilities curve from AB to CD in graph (a) is equivalent to the rightward shift of the economy's long-run aggregate supply curve from AS_{LR1} to AS_{LR2} in graph (b).

Economic Growth in the Extended AD-AS Model In Figure 35.7 we use the extended aggregate

demand–aggregate supply model to depict economic growth in the United States.

Suppose the economy's aggregate demand curve, long-run aggregate supply curve, and short-run aggregate supply curve initially are AD_1, AS_{LR1}, and AS_1, as shown. The equilibrium price level and level of real output are P_1 and Q_1.

Now let's assume that economic growth driven by changes in supply factors (quantity and quality of resources and technology) shifts the long-run aggregate supply curve rightward from AS_{LR1} to AS_{LR2}. The economy's potential output has increased, as reflected by the expansion of available real output from Q_1 to Q_2.

With no change in aggregate demand, the increase in long-run aggregate supply from AS_{LR1} to AS_{LR2} in Figure 35.7 would expand real GDP and lower the price level. Put plainly, economic growth is deflationary, other things equal. But declines in the price level are not a part of the U.S. growth experience. The reason? The Federal Reserve has expanded the nation's money supply over the years such that increases in aggregate demand have more than matched the increases in aggregate supply. We show this increase in aggregate demand as the shift from AD_1 to AD_2.

The increases of aggregate supply and aggregate demand in Figure 35.7 have increased real output from Q_1 to Q_2 and have boosted the price level from P_1 to P_2. At the higher price level P_2, the economy confronts a new short-run aggregate supply curve AS_2. The changes shown in Figure 35.7 describe the actual U.S. experience: economic growth, accompanied by mild inflation.

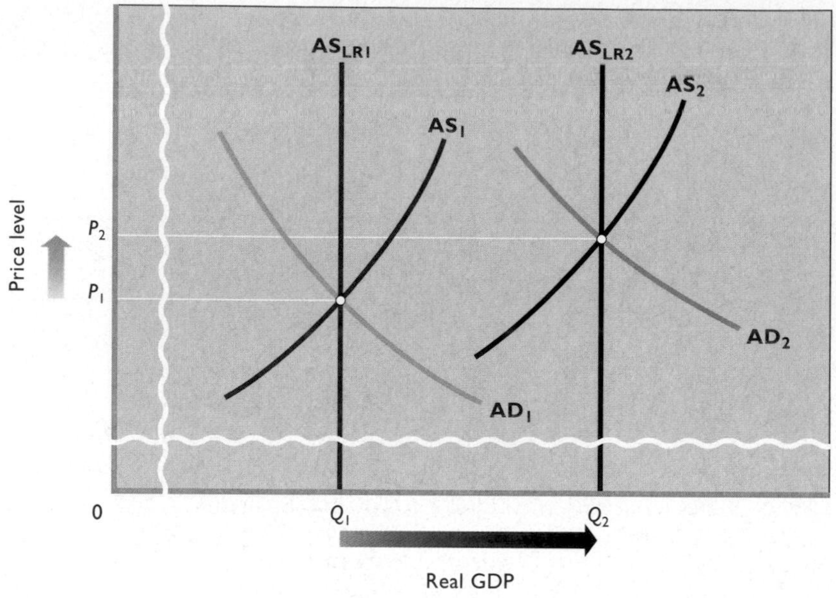

FIGURE 35.7 **Depicting U.S. growth via the extended AD-AS model.** Long-run aggregate supply and short-run aggregate supply have increased over time, as from AS_{LR1} to AS_{LR2} and AS_1 to AS_2. Simultaneously, aggregate demand has shifted rightward, as from AD_1 to AD_2. The actual outcome of these combined shifts has been economic growth, shown as the increase in real output from Q_1 to Q_2, accompanied by mild inflation, shown as the rise in the price level from P_1 to P_2.

In brief, economic growth causes increases in long-run aggregate supply. Whether deflation, zero inflation, mild inflation, or rapid inflation accompanies growth depends on the extent to which aggregate demand increases relative to aggregate supply. Any inflation that occurs is the result of the growth of aggregate demand. It is not the result of the growth of real GDP. **(Key Question 5)**

QUICK REVIEW 35.2

- In the short run, demand-pull inflation raises both the price level and real output; in the long run, nominal wages rise, the short-run aggregate supply curve shifts to the left, and only the price level increases.

- Cost-push inflation creates a policy dilemma for the government: If it engages in an expansionary policy to increase output, additional inflation will occur; if it does nothing, the recession will linger until input prices have fallen by enough to return the economy to producing at potential output.

- In the short run, a decline in aggregate demand reduces real output (creates a recession); in the long run, prices and nominal wages presumably fall, the short-run aggregate supply curve shifts to the right, and real output returns to its full-employment level.

- The economy has ongoing inflation because the Fed uses monetary policy to shift the AD curve to the right faster than economic growth shifts the AS curve to the right.

The Inflation-Unemployment Relationship

We have just seen that the Fed can determine how much inflation occurs in the economy by how much it causes aggregate demand to shift relative to aggregate supply. Given that low inflation and low unemployment rates are the Fed's major economic goals, its ability to control inflation brings up at least two interesting policy questions: Are low unemployment and low inflation compatible goals or conflicting goals? What explains situations in which high unemployment and high inflation coexist?

The extended AD-AS model supports three significant generalizations relating to these questions:

- Under normal circumstances, there is a short-run trade-off between the rate of inflation and the rate of unemployment.

- Aggregate supply shocks can cause both higher rates of inflation and higher rates of unemployment.

- There is no significant trade-off between inflation and unemployment over long periods of time.

Let's examine each of these generalizations.

The Phillips Curve

We can demonstrate the short-run trade-off between the rate of inflation and the rate of unemployment through the **Phillips Curve,** named after A. W. Phillips, who developed the idea in Great Britain. This curve, generalized

FIGURE 35.8 **The Phillips Curve: concept and empirical data.** (a) The Phillips Curve relates annual rates of inflation and annual rates of unemployment for a series of years. Because this is an inverse relationship, there presumably is a trade-off between unemployment and inflation. (b) Data points for the 1960s seemed to confirm the Phillips Curve concept. (Note: The unemployment rates are annual averages and the inflation rates are on a December-to-December basis.)

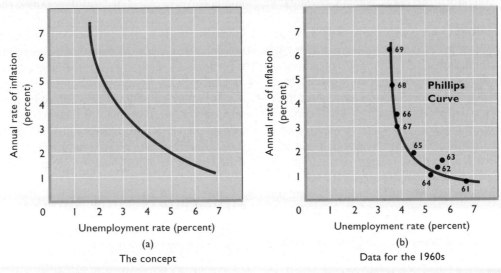

(a)

The concept

(b)

Data for the 1960s

Source: Bureau of Labor Statistics, **www.bls.gov.**

ORIGIN OF THE IDEA

O 35.1

Phillips Curve

in Figure 35.8a, suggests an inverse relationship between the rate of inflation and the rate of unemployment. Lower unemployment rates (measured as leftward movements on the horizontal axis) are associated with higher rates of inflation (measured as upward movements on the vertical axis).

The underlying rationale of the Phillips Curve becomes apparent when we view the short-run aggregate supply curve in Figure 35.9 and perform a simple mental experiment. Suppose that in some short-run period aggregate demand expands from AD_0 to AD_2, either because firms decided to buy more capital goods or the government decided to increase its expenditures. Whatever the cause, in the short run the price level rises from P_0 to P_2 and real output rises from Q_0 to Q_2. As real output rises, the unemployment rate falls.

Now let's compare what would have happened if the increase in aggregate demand had been larger, say, from AD_0 to AD_3. The new equilibrium tells us that the amount of inflation and the growth of real output would both have been greater (and that the unemployment rate would have been lower). Similarly, suppose aggregate demand during the year had increased only modestly, from AD_0 to AD_1. Compared with our shift from AD_0 to AD_2, the amount of inflation and the growth of real output would have been smaller (and the unemployment rate higher).

FIGURE 35.9 **The short-run effect of changes in aggregate demand on real output and the price level.** Comparing the effects of various possible increases in aggregate demand leads to the conclusion that the larger the increase in aggregate demand, the higher the rate of inflation and the greater the increase in real output. Because real output and the unemployment rate move in opposite directions, we can generalize that, given short-run aggregate supply, high rates of inflation should be accompanied by low rates of unemployment.

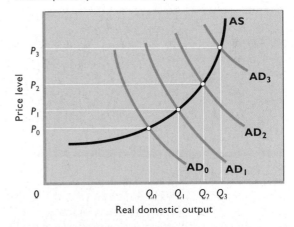

The generalization we draw from this mental experiment is this: *Assuming a constant short-run aggregate supply curve,* high rates of inflation are accompanied by low rates of unemployment, and low rates of inflation are accompanied by high rates of unemployment. Other things equal, the expected relationship should look something like Figure 35.8a.

Figure 35.8b reveals that the facts for the 1960s nicely fit the theory. On the basis of that evidence and evidence from other countries, most economists working at the end of the 1960s concluded there was a stable, predictable trade-off between unemployment and inflation. Moreover, U.S. economic policy was built on that supposed trade-off. According to this thinking, it was impossible to achieve "full employment without inflation": Manipulation of aggregate demand through fiscal and monetary measures would simply move the economy along the Phillips Curve. An expansionary fiscal and monetary policy that boosted aggregate demand and lowered the unemployment rate would simultaneously increase inflation. A restrictive fiscal and monetary policy could be used to reduce the rate of inflation but only at the cost of a higher unemployment rate and more forgone production. Society had to choose between the incompatible goals of price stability and full employment; it had to decide where to locate on its Phillips Curve.

For reasons we will soon see, today's economists reject the idea of a stable, predictable Phillips Curve. Nevertheless, they agree there is a short-run trade-off between unemployment and inflation. *Given short-run aggregate supply*, increases in aggregate demand increase real output and reduce the unemployment rate. As the unemployment rate falls and dips below the natural rate, the excessive spending produces demand-pull inflation. Conversely, when recession sets in and the unemployment rate increases, the weak aggregate demand that caused the recession also leads to lower inflation rates.

Periods of exceptionally low unemployment rates and inflation rates do occur, but only under special sets of economic circumstances. One such period was the late 1990s, when faster productivity growth increased aggregate supply and fully blunted the inflationary impact of rapidly rising aggregate demand (review Figure 29.11).

Aggregate Supply Shocks and the Phillips Curve

The unemployment-inflation experience of the 1970s and early 1980s demolished the idea of an always-stable Phillips Curve. In Figure 35.10 we show the Phillips

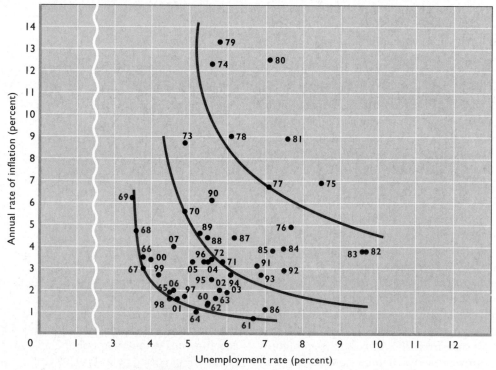

FIGURE 35.10 Inflation rates and unemployment rates, 1960–2007. A series of aggregate supply shocks in the 1970s resulted in higher rates of inflation *and* higher rates of unemployment. So data points for the 1970s and 1980s tended to be above and to the right of the Phillips Curve for the 1960s. In the 1990s the inflation-unemployment data points slowly moved back toward the original Phillips Curve. Points for the late 1990s and 2000s are similar to those from the earlier era. (Note: The unemployment rates are annual averages and the inflation rates are on a December-to-December basis.)

Source: Bureau of Labor Statistics, **www.bls.gov.**

Curve for the 1960s in blue and then add the data points for 1970 through 2007. Observe that in most of the years of the 1970s and early 1980s the economy experienced both higher inflation rates and higher unemployment rates than it did in the 1960s. In fact, inflation and unemployment rose simultaneously in some of those years. This condition is called **stagflation**—a media term that combines the words "stagnation" and "inflation." If there still was any such thing as a Phillips Curve, it had clearly shifted outward, perhaps as shown.

Adverse Aggregate Supply Shocks

The data points for the 1970s and early 1980s support our second generalization: Aggregate supply shocks can cause both higher rates of inflation and higher rates of unemployment. A series of adverse **aggregate supply shocks**—sudden, large increases in resource costs that jolt an economy's short-run aggregate supply curve leftward—hit the economy in the 1970s and early 1980s. The most significant of these shocks was a quadrupling of oil prices by the Organization of Petroleum Exporting Countries (OPEC). Consequently, the cost of producing and distributing virtually every product and service rose rapidly. (Other factors working to increase U.S. costs during this period included major agricultural shortfalls, a greatly depreciated dollar, wage hikes previously held down by wage-price controls, and slower rates of productivity growth.)

These shocks shifted the aggregate supply curve to the left and distorted the usual inflation-unemployment relationship. Remember that we derived the inverse relationship between the rate of inflation and the unemployment rate shown in Figure 35.8a by shifting the aggregate demand curve along a stable short-run aggregate supply curve (Figure 35.9). But the cost-push inflation model shown in Figure 35.4 tells us that a *leftward shift* of the short-run aggregate supply curve increases the price level and reduces real output (and increases the unemployment rate). This, say most economists, is what happened in two periods in the 1970s. The U.S. unemployment rate shot up from 4.9 percent in 1973 to 8.5 percent in 1975, contributing to a significant decline in real GDP. In the same period, the U.S. price level rose by 21 percent. The stagflation scenario recurred in 1978, when OPEC increased oil prices by more than 100 percent. The U.S. price level rose by 26 percent over the 1978–1980 period, while unemployment increased from 6.1 to 7.1 percent.

Stagflation's Demise

Another look at Figure 35.10 reveals a generally inward movement of the inflation-unemployment points between 1982 and 1989. By 1989 the lingering effects of the earlier period had subsided. One

precursor to this favorable trend was the deep recession of 1981–1982, largely caused by a restrictive monetary policy aimed at reducing double-digit inflation. The recession upped the unemployment rate to 9.5 percent in 1982. With so many workers unemployed, those who were working accepted smaller increases in their nominal wages—or, in some cases, wage reductions—in order to preserve their jobs. Firms, in turn, restrained their price increases to try to retain their relative shares of a greatly diminished market.

Other factors were at work. Foreign competition throughout this period held down wage and price hikes in several basic industries such as automobiles and steel. Deregulation of the airline and trucking industries also resulted in wage reductions or so-called wage givebacks. A significant decline in OPEC's monopoly power and a greatly reduced reliance on oil in the production process produced a stunning fall in the price of oil and its derivative products, such as gasoline.

All these factors combined to reduce per-unit production costs and to shift the short-run aggregate supply curve rightward (as from AS₂ to AS₁ in Figure 35.4). Employment and output expanded, and the unemployment rate fell from 9.6 percent in 1983 to 5.3 percent in 1989. Figure 35.10

GLOBAL PERSPECTIVE 35.1

The Misery Index, Selected Nations, 1997–2007

The misery index adds together a nation's unemployment rate and its inflation rate to get a measure of national economic discomfort. For example, a nation with a 5 percent rate of unemployment and a 5 percent inflation rate would have a misery index number of 10, as would a nation with an **8 percent** unemployment rate and a **2 percent** inflation rate.

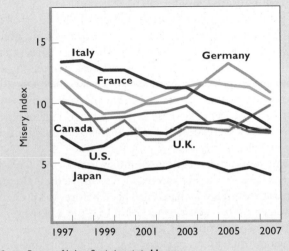

Source: Bureau of Labor Statistics, **stats.bls.gov.**

reveals that the inflation-unemployment points for recent years are closer to the points associated with the Phillips Curve of the 1960s than to the points in the late 1970s and early 1980s. The points for 1997–2007, in fact, are very close to points on the 1960s curve. (The very low inflation and unemployment rates in this latter period produced an exceptionally low value of the so-called *misery index*, as shown in Global Perspective 35.1.)

The Long-Run Phillips Curve

The overall set of data points in Figure 35.10 supports our third generalization relating to the inflation-unemployment relationship: There is no apparent *long-run* trade-off between inflation and unemployment. Economists point out that when decades as opposed to a few years are considered, any rate of inflation is consistent with the natural rate of unemployment prevailing at that time. We know from Chapter 26 that the natural rate of unemployment is the unemployment rate that occurs when cyclical unemployment is zero; it is the full-employment rate of unemployment, or the rate of unemployment when the economy achieves its potential output.

How can there be a short-run inflation-unemployment trade-off but not a long-run trade-off? Figure 35.11 provides the answer.

Short-Run Phillips Curve

Consider Phillips Curve PC$_1$ in Figure 35.11. Suppose the economy initially is experiencing a 3 percent rate of inflation and a 5 percent natural rate of unemployment. Such short-term curves as PC$_1$, PC$_2$, and PC$_3$ (drawn as straight lines for simplicity) exist because the actual rate of inflation is not always the same as the expected rate.

Establishing an additional point on Phillips Curve PC$_1$ will clarify this. We begin at a_1, where we assume nominal wages are set on the assumption that the 3 percent rate of inflation will continue. That is, because workers expect output prices to rise by 3 percent per year, they negotiate wage contracts that feature 3 percent per year increases in nominal wages so that these nominal wage increases will exactly offset the expected rise in prices and thereby keep their real wages the same.

But suppose that the rate of inflation rises to 6 percent, perhaps because the Fed has decided to move the AD curve to the right even faster than it had been before. With a nominal wage rate set on the expectation that the 3 percent rate of inflation will continue, the higher product prices raise business profits. Firms respond to the higher profits by hiring more workers and increasing output. In the short run, the economy moves to b_1, which, in contrast to a_1, involves

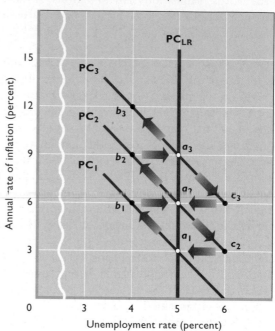

FIGURE 35.11 The long-run vertical Phillips Curve. Increases in aggregate demand beyond those consistent with full-employment output may temporarily boost profits, output, and employment (as from a_1 to b_1). But nominal wages eventually will catch up so as to sustain real wages. When they do, profits will fall, negating the previous short-run stimulus to production and employment (the economy now moves from b_1 to a_2). Consequently, there is no trade-off between the rates of inflation and unemployment in the long run; that is, the long-run Phillips Curve is roughly a vertical line at the economy's natural rate of unemployment.

a lower rate of unemployment (4 percent) and a higher rate of inflation (6 percent). The move from a_1 to b_1 is consistent both with an upward-sloping aggregate supply curve and with the inflation-unemployment trade-off implied by the Phillips Curve analysis. But this short-run Phillips Curve simply is a manifestation of the following principle: *When the actual rate of inflation is higher than expected, profits temporarily rise and the unemployment rate temporarily falls.*

Long-Run Vertical Phillips Curve

But point b_1 is not a stable equilibrium. Workers will recognize that their nominal wages have not increased as fast as inflation and will therefore renegotiate their labor contracts so that they feature faster increases in nominal wages. These faster increases in nominal wages make up for the higher rate of inflation and restore the workers' lost purchasing power. As these new labor contracts kick in, business profits will fall to their prior level. The reduction in profits means that the original motivation to employ more workers and increase output has disappeared.

Unemployment then returns to its natural level at point a_2. Note, however, that the economy now faces a higher actual and expected rate of inflation—6 percent rather than 3 percent. This happens because the new labor contracts feature 6 percent per year increases in wages to make up for the 6 percent per year inflation rate. Because wages are a production cost, this faster increase in wage rates will imply faster future increases in output prices as firms are forced to raise prices more rapidly to make up for the faster future rate of wage growth. Stated a bit differently, the initial increase in inflation will become *persistent* because it leads to renegotiated labor contracts that will perpetuate the higher rate of inflation. In addition, because the new labor contracts are public, it will also be the case that the higher rates of inflation that they will cause will be *expected* by everyone rather than being a surprise.

In view of the higher 6 percent expected rate of inflation, the short-run Phillips Curve shifts upward from PC_1 to PC_2 in Figure 35.11. An "along-the-Phillips-Curve" kind of move from a_1 to b_1 on PC_1 is merely a short-run or transient occurrence. In the long run, after nominal wage contracts catch up with increases in the inflation rate, unemployment returns to its natural rate at a_2, and there is a new short-run Phillips Curve PC_2 at the higher expected rate of inflation.

The scenario repeats if aggregate demand continues to increase. Prices rise momentarily ahead of nominal wages, profits expand, and employment and output increase (as implied by the move from a_2 to b_2). But, in time, nominal wages increase so as to restore real wages. Profits then fall to their original level, pushing employment back to the normal rate at a_3. The economy's "reward" for lowering the unemployment rate below the natural rate is a still higher (9 percent) rate of inflation.

Movements along the short-run Phillips curve (a_1 to b_1 on PC_1) cause the curve to shift to a less favorable position (PC_2, then PC_3, and so on). A stable Phillips Curve with the dependable series of unemployment-rate–inflation-rate trade-offs simply does not exist in the long run. The economy is characterized by a **long-run vertical Phillips Curve.**

The vertical line through a_1, a_2, and a_3 shows the long-run relationship between unemployment and inflation. Any rate of inflation is consistent with the 5 percent natural rate of unemployment. So, in this view, society ought to choose a low rate of inflation rather than a high one.

ORIGIN OF THE IDEA

O 35.2

Long-run vertical
Phillips Curve

Disinflation

The distinction between the short-run Phillips Curve and the long-run Phillips Curve also helps explain **disinflation**—reductions in the inflation rate from year to year. Suppose that in Figure 35.11 the economy is at a_3, where the inflation rate is 9 percent. And suppose that a

decline in the rate at which aggregate demand shifts to the right faster than aggregate supply (as happened during the 1981–1982 recession) reduces inflation below the 9 percent expected rate, say, to 6 percent. Business profits fall because prices are rising less rapidly than wages. The nominal wage increases, remember, were set on the assumption that the 9 percent rate of inflation would continue. In response to the decline in profits, firms reduce their employment and consequently the unemployment rate rises. The economy temporarily slides downward from point a_3 to c_3 along the short-run Phillips Curve PC_3. *When the actual rate of inflation is lower than the expected rate, profits temporarily fall and the unemployment rate temporarily rises.*

Firms and workers eventually adjust their expectations to the new 6 percent rate of inflation, and thus newly negotiated wage increases decline. Profits are restored, employment rises, and the unemployment rate falls back to its natural rate of 5 percent at a_2. Because the expected rate of inflation is now 6 percent, the short-run Phillips Curve PC_3 shifts leftward to PC_2.

If the rate at which aggregate demand shifts to the right faster than aggregate supply declines even more, the scenario will continue. Inflation declines from 6 percent to, say, 3 percent, moving the economy from a_2 to c_2 along PC_2. The lower-than-expected rate of inflation (lower prices) squeezes profits and reduces employment. But, in the long run, firms respond to the lower profits by reducing their nominal wage increases. Profits are restored and unemployment returns to its natural rate at a_1 as the short-run Phillips Curve moves from PC_2 to PC_1. Once again, the long-run Phillips Curve is vertical at the 5 percent natural rate of unemployment. **(Key Question 7)**

QUICK REVIEW 35.3

- As implied by the upward-sloping short-run aggregate supply curve, there may be a short-run trade-off between the rate of inflation and the rate of unemployment. This trade-off is reflected in the Phillips Curve, which shows that lower rates of inflation are associated with higher rates of unemployment.

- Aggregate supply shocks that produce severe cost-push inflation can cause stagflation—simultaneous increases in the inflation rate and the unemployment rate. Such stagflation occurred from 1973 to 1975 and recurred from 1978 to 1980, producing Phillips Curve data points above and to the right of the Phillips Curve for the 1960s.

- After all nominal wage adjustments to increases and decreases in the rate of inflation have occurred, the economy ends up back at its full-employment level of output and its natural rate of unemployment. The long-run Phillips Curve therefore is vertical at the natural rate of unemployment.

Taxation and Aggregate Supply

A final topic in our discussion of aggregate supply is taxation, a key aspect of **supply-side economics**. "Supply-side economists" or "supply-siders" stress that changes in aggregate supply are an active force in determining the levels of inflation, unemployment, and economic growth. Government policies can either impede or promote rightward shifts of the short-run and long-run aggregate supply curves shown in Figure 35.2. One such policy is taxation.

These economists say that the enlargement of the U.S. tax system has impaired incentives to work, save, and invest. In this view, high tax rates impede productivity growth and hence slow the expansion of long-run aggregate supply. By reducing the after-tax rewards of workers and producers, high tax rates reduce the financial attractiveness of working, saving, and investing.

Supply-siders focus their attention on *marginal tax rates*—the rates on extra dollars of income—because those rates affect the benefits from working, saving, or investing more. In 2008 the marginal tax rates varied from 10 to 35 percent in the United States. (See Table 4.1 for details.)

Taxes and Incentives to Work

Supply-siders believe that how long and how hard people work depends on the amounts of additional after-tax earnings they derive from their efforts. They say that lower marginal tax rates on earned incomes induce more work, and therefore increase aggregate inputs of labor. Lower marginal tax rates increase the after-tax wage rate and make leisure more expensive and work more attractive. The higher opportunity cost of leisure encourages people to substitute work for leisure. This increase in productive effort is achieved in many ways: by increasing the number of hours worked per day or week, by encouraging workers to postpone retirement, by inducing more people to enter the labor force, by motivating people to work harder, and by avoiding long periods of unemployment.

Incentives to Save and Invest

High marginal tax rates also reduce the rewards for saving and investing. For example, suppose that Tony saves $10,000 at 8 percent interest, bringing him $800 of interest per year. If his marginal tax rate is 40 percent, his after-tax interest earnings will be $480, not $800, and his after-tax interest rate will fall to 4.8 percent. While Tony might be willing to save (forgo current consumption) for an 8 percent return on his saving, he might rather consume when the return is only 4.8 percent.

Saving, remember, is the prerequisite of investment. Thus, supply-side economists recommend lower marginal tax rates on interest earned from saving. They also call for lower taxes on income from capital to ensure that there are ready investment outlets for the economy's enhanced pool of saving. A critical determinant of investment spending is the expected *after-tax* return on that spending.

To summarize: Lower marginal tax rates encourage saving and investing. Workers therefore find themselves equipped with more and technologically superior machinery and equipment. Labor productivity rises, and that expands long-run aggregate supply and economic growth, which in turn keeps unemployment rates and inflation low.

The Laffer Curve

In the supply-side view, reductions in marginal tax rates increase the nation's aggregate supply and can leave the nation's tax revenues unchanged or even enlarge them. Thus, supply-side tax cuts need not produce Federal budget deficits.

This idea is based on the **Laffer Curve**, named after Arthur Laffer, who popularized it. As Figure 35.12 shows, the Laffer Curve depicts the relationship between tax rates and tax revenues. As tax rates increase from 0 to 100 percent, tax revenues increase from zero to some maximum level (at m) and then fall to zero. Tax revenues decline beyond some point because higher tax rates discourage economic activity, thereby shrinking the tax base (domestic output and income). This is easiest to see at the extreme, where the tax rate is 100 percent. Tax revenues here are, in theory, reduced to zero because the 100 percent confiscatory tax rate has halted production. A 100 percent tax rate applied to a tax base of zero yields no revenue.

FIGURE 35.12 The Laffer Curve. The Laffer Curve suggests that up to point m higher tax rates will result in larger tax revenues. But tax rates higher than m will adversely affect incentives to work and produce, reducing the size of the tax base (output and income) to the extent that tax revenues will decline. It follows that if tax rates are above m, reductions in tax rates will produce increases in tax revenues.

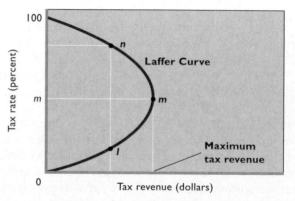

In the early 1980s, Laffer suggested that the United States was at a point such as *n* on the curve in Figure 35.12. There, tax rates are so high that production is discouraged to the extent that tax revenues are below the maximum at *m*. If the economy is at *n*, then lower tax rates can either increase tax revenues or leave them unchanged. For example, lowering the tax rate from point *n* to point *l* would bolster the economy such that the government would bring in the same total amount of tax revenue as before.

Laffer's reasoning was that lower tax rates stimulate incentives to work, save and invest, innovate, and accept business risks, thus triggering an expansion of real output and income. That enlarged tax base sustains tax revenues even though tax rates are lowered. Indeed, between *n* and *m* lower tax rates result in *increased* tax revenue.

Also, when taxes are lowered, tax avoidance (which is legal) and tax evasion (which is not) decline. High marginal tax rates prompt taxpayers to avoid taxes through various tax shelters, such as buying municipal bonds, on which the interest earned is tax-free. High rates also encourage some taxpayers to conceal income from the Internal Revenue Service. Lower tax rates reduce the inclination to engage in either tax avoidance or tax evasion. **(Key Question 9)**

Criticisms of the Laffer Curve
The Laffer Curve and its supply-side implications have been subject to severe criticism.

Taxes, Incentives, and Time
A fundamental criticism relates to the degree to which economic incentives are sensitive to changes in tax rates. Skeptics say ample empirical evidence shows that the impact of a tax cut on incentives is small, of uncertain direction, and relatively slow to emerge. For example, with respect to work incentives, studies indicate that decreases in tax rates lead some people to work more but lead others to work less. Those who work more are enticed by the higher after-tax pay; they substitute work for leisure because the opportunity cost of leisure has increased. But other people work less because the higher after-tax pay enables them to "buy more leisure." With the tax cut, they can earn the same level of after-tax income as before with fewer work hours.

Inflation or Higher Real Interest Rates
Most economists think that the demand-side effects of a tax cut are more immediate and certain than longer-term supply-side effects. Thus, tax cuts undertaken when the economy is at or near full employment may produce increases in aggregate demand that overwhelm any increase in aggregate

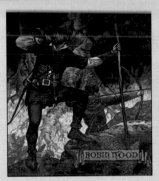

CONSIDER THIS . . .

Sherwood Forest

The popularization of the idea that tax-rate reductions will increase tax revenues owed much to Arthur Laffer's ability to present his ideas simply. In explaining his thoughts to a *Wall Street Journal* editor over lunch, Laffer reportedly took out his pen and drew the curve on a napkin. The editor retained the napkin and later reproduced the curve in an editorial in *The Wall Street Journal*. The Laffer Curve was born. The idea it portrayed became the centerpiece of economic policy under the Reagan administration (1981–1989), which cut tax rates on personal income by 25 percent over a 3-year period.

Laffer illustrated his supply-side views with a story relating to Robin Hood, who, you may recall, stole from the rich to give to the poor. Laffer likened people traveling through Sherwood Forest to taxpayers, whereas Robin Hood and his band of merry men were government. As taxpayers passed through the forest, Robin Hood and his men intercepted them and forced them to hand over their money. Laffer asked audiences, "Do you think that travelers continued to go through Sherwood Forest?"

The answer he sought and got, of course, was "no." Taxpayers will avoid Sherwood Forest to the greatest extent possible. They will lower their taxable income by reducing work hours, retiring earlier, saving less, and engaging in tax avoidance and tax evasion activities. Robin Hood and his men may end up with less revenue than if they collected a relatively small "tax" from each traveler for passage through the forest.

supply. The likely result is inflation or restrictive monetary policy to prevent it. If the latter, real interest rates will rise and investment will decline. This will defeat the purpose of the supply-side tax cuts.

Position on the Curve
Skeptics say that the Laffer Curve is merely a logical proposition and assert that there must be some level of tax rates between 0 and 100 percent at which tax revenues will be at their maximum. Economists of all persuasions can agree with this. But the issue of where a particular economy is located on its Laffer Curve is an empirical question. If we assume that we are at point *n* in Figure 35.12, then tax cuts will increase tax revenues. But if the economy is at any point below *m* on the curve, tax-rate reductions will reduce tax revenues.

Do Tax Increases Reduce Real GDP?*

Determining the Relationship Between Changes in Taxes and Permanent Changes in Real GDP is Fraught with Complexities and Difficulties. University of California-Berkeley Economists Christina Romer and David Romer have Recently Devised a Novel New Way to Approach the Topic. Their Findings Suggest That Tax Increases Reduce Real GDP.[†]

How do changes in the level of taxation affect the level of economic activity? The simple correlation between taxation and economic activity shows that, on average, when economic activity rises more rapidly, tax revenues also are rising more rapidly. But this correlation almost surely does not reflect a positive effect of tax increases on output. Rather, under our tax system, any positive shock to output raises tax revenues by increasing income.

In "The Macroeconomic Effects of Tax Changes: Estimates Based on a New Measure of Fiscal Shocks," authors Cristina Romer and David Romer observe that this difficulty is just one of many manifestations of a more general problem. Changes in taxes occur for many reasons. And, because the factors that give rise to tax changes often are correlated with other developments in the economy, disentangling the effects of the tax changes from the other effects of these underlying factors is inherently difficult.

To address this problem, Romer and Romer use the narrative record—Presidential speeches, executive branch documents, Congressional reports, and so on—to identify the size, timing, and principal motivation for all major tax policy actions in the post-World War II United States. This narrative analysis allows them to separate revenue changes resulting from legislation from changes occurring for other reasons. It also allows them to classify legislated changes according to their primary motivation.

Romer and Romer find that despite the complexity of the legislative process, most significant tax changes have been motivated by one of four factors: counteracting other influences

in the economy; paying for increases in government spending (or lowering taxes in conjunction with reductions in spending); addressing an inherited budget deficit; and promoting long-run growth. They observe that legislated tax changes taken to counteract other influences on the economy, or to pay for increases in government spending, are very likely to be correlated with other factors affecting the economy. As a result these observations are likely to lead to unreliable estimates of the effect of tax changes.

Tax changes that are made to promote long-run growth, or to reduce an inherited budget deficit, in contrast, are undertaken for reasons essentially unrelated to other factors influencing output. Thus, examining the behavior of output following these tax changes is likely to provide more reliable estimates of the output effects of tax changes. *The results of this more reliable test indicate that tax changes have very large effects: a tax increase of 1 percent of GDP lowers real GDP by roughly 2 to 3 percent.*

These output effects are highly persistent. The behavior of inflation and unemployment suggests that this persistence reflects long-lasting departures of output from previous levels. Romer and Romer also find that output effects of tax changes are much more closely tied to the actual changes in taxes than news about future changes, and that investment falls sharply in response to tax changes. Indeed, the strong response of investment helps to explain why the output consequences of tax increases are so large.

Romer and Romer find suggestive evidence that tax increases to reduce an inherited budget deficit have much smaller output costs than other tax increases. This is consistent with the idea that deficit-driven tax increases may have important expansionary effects through [improved] expectations and [lower] longterm interest rates, or through [enhanced] confidence.

*Abridged from Les Picker, "Tax Increases Reduce GDP," *The NBER Digest*, February/March 2008. The *Digest* provides synopses of research papers in progress by economists affiliated with the National Bureau of Economic Research (NBER).

[†]Cristina Romer and David Romer, "The Macroeconomic Effects of Tax Changes: Estimates Based on a New Measure of Fiscal Shocks," National Bureau of Economic Research Working Paper No. 13264, 2007.

Rebuttal and Evaluation

Supply-side advocates respond to the skeptics by contending that the Reagan tax cuts in the 1980s worked as Laffer predicted. Although the top marginal income tax rates on earned income were cut from 50 to 28 percent in that decade, real GDP and tax revenues were substantially higher at the end of the 1990s than at the beginning.

But the general view among economists is that the Reagan tax cuts, coming at a time of severe recession, helped boost aggregate demand and return real GDP to its full-employment output and normal growth path. As the economy expanded, so did tax revenues despite the lower tax rates. The rise in tax revenues caused by economic growth swamped the declines in revenues from lower tax rates. In essence, the Laffer Curve shown in Figure 35.12 stretched rightward, increasing net tax revenues. But the tax-rate cuts did not produce extraordinary rightward shifts of the long-run aggregate supply curve. Indeed, saving fell as a percentage of personal income during the period, productivity growth was sluggish, and real GDP growth was not extraordinarily strong.

Because government expenditures rose more rapidly than tax revenues in the 1980s, large budget deficits occurred. In 1993 the Clinton administration increased the top marginal tax rates from 31 to 39.6 percent to address these deficits. The economy boomed in the last half of the 1990s, and by the end of the decade tax revenues were so high relative to government expenditures that budget surpluses emerged. In 2001, the Bush administration reduced marginal tax rates over a series of years partially "to return excess revenues to taxpayers." In 2003 the top marginal tax rate fell to 35 percent. Also, the income tax rates on capital gains and dividends were reduced to 15 percent. Economists generally agree that the Bush tax cuts, along with a highly expansionary monetary policy, helped revive and expand the economy following the recession of 2001. Strong growth of output and income in 2004 and 2005 produced large increases in tax revenues, although large budget deficits remained because spending also increased rapidly. The 2004 deficit was $413 billion and the 2005 deficit was $318 billion. The deficit fell over the next two years, to $162 billion in 2007, but with the economy slowing in late 2007 and threatening to slip into recession in 2008, official forecasts predicted budget deficits of over $400 billion for both 2008 and 2009.

Today, there is general agreement that the U.S. economy is operating at a point below *m*—rather than above *m*—on the Laffer Curve in Figure 35.12. In this zone, the overall effect is that personal tax-rate increases raise tax revenues while personal tax-rate decreases reduce tax revenues. But, at the same time, economists recognize that, other things equal, cuts in tax rates reduce tax revenues in percentage terms by less than the tax-rate reductions. Similarly, tax-rate increases do not raise tax revenues by as much in percentage terms as the tax-rate increases. This is true because changes in marginal tax rates alter taxpayer behavior and thus affect taxable income. Although these effects seem to be relatively modest, they need to be considered in designing tax policy—and, in fact, the Federal government's Office of Tax Policy created a special division in 2007 devoted to estimating the magnitude of such effects when it comes to proposed changes in U.S. tax laws. Thus, supply-side economics has contributed to how economists and policymakers design and implement fiscal policy.

Summary

1. In macroeconomics, the short run is a period in which nominal wages do not respond to changes in the price level. In contrast, the long run is a period in which nominal wages fully respond to changes in the price level.

2. The short-run aggregate supply curve is upsloping. Because nominal wages are unresponsive to price-level changes, increases in the price level (prices received by firms) increase profits and real output. Conversely, decreases in the price level reduce profits and real output. However, the long-run aggregate supply curve is vertical. With sufficient time for adjustment, nominal wages rise and fall with the price level, moving the economy along a vertical aggregate supply curve at the economy's full-employment output.

3. In the short run, demand-pull inflation raises the price level and real output. Once nominal wages rise to match the increase in the price level, the temporary increase in real output is reversed.

4. In the short run, cost-push inflation raises the price level and lowers real output. Unless the government expands aggregate demand, nominal wages eventually will decline under conditions of recession and the short-run aggregate supply curve will shift back to its initial location. Prices and real output will eventually return to their original levels.

5. If prices and wages are flexible downward, a decline in aggregate demand will lower output and the price level. The decline in the price level will eventually lower nominal

wages and shift the short-run aggregate supply curve right-ward. Full-employment output will thus be restored.

6. One-time shifts in the AD and AS curves can only cause limited bouts of inflation. Ongoing mild inflation is caused by the Fed purposely shifting AD to the right a bit faster than the AS curve shifts to the right (due to economic growth.)

7. Assuming a stable, upsloping short-run aggregate supply curve, rightward shifts of the aggregate demand curve of various sizes yield the generalization that high rates of inflation are associated with low rates of unemployment, and vice versa. This inverse relationship is known as the Phillips Curve, and empirical data for the 1960s seemed to be consistent with it.

8. In the 1970s and early 1980s the Phillips Curve apparently shifted rightward, reflecting stagflation—simultaneously rising inflation rates and unemployment rates. The higher unemployment rates and inflation rates resulted mainly from huge oil price increases that caused large leftward shifts in the short-run aggregate supply curve (so-called aggregate supply shocks). The Phillips Curve shifted inward toward its original position in the 1980s. By 1989 stagflation had subsided, and

the data points for the late 1990s and first half of the first decade of the 2000s were similar to those of the 1960s.

9. Although there is a short-run trade-off between inflation and unemployment, there is no long-run trade-off. Workers will adapt their expectations to new inflation realities, and when they do, the unemployment rate will return to the natural rate. So the long-run Phillips Curve is vertical at the natural rate, meaning that higher rates of inflation do not permanently "buy" the economy less unemployment.

10. Supply-side economists focus attention on government policies such as high taxation that impede the expansion of aggregate supply. The Laffer Curve relates tax rates to levels of tax revenue and suggests that, under some circumstances, cuts in tax rates will expand the tax base (output and income) and increase tax revenues. Most economists, however, believe that the United States is currently operating in the range of the Laffer Curve where tax rates and tax revenues move in the same, not opposite, directions.

11. Today's economists recognize the importance of considering supply-side effects in designing optimal fiscal policy.

Terms and Concepts

short run	stagflation	disinflation
long run	aggregate supply shocks	supply-side economics
Phillips Curve	long-run vertical Phillips Curve	Laffer Curve

Study Questions  |ECONOMICS

1. Distinguish between the short run and the long run as they relate to macroeconomics. Why is the distinction important? **LO1**

2. Which of the following statements are true? Which are false? Explain why the false statements are untrue. **LO1**
   a. Short-run aggregate supply curves reflect an inverse relationship between the price level and the level of real output.
   b. The long-run aggregate supply curve assumes that nominal wages are fixed.
   c. In the long run, an increase in the price level will result in an increase in nominal wages.

3. **KEY QUESTION** Suppose the full-employment level of real output (Q) for a hypothetical economy is $250 and the price level (P) initially is 100. Use the short-run aggregate supply schedules below to answer the questions that follow: **LO1**

AS (P_{100})		AS (P_{125})		AS (P_{75})	
P	Q	P	Q	P	Q
125	$280	125	$250	125	$310
100	250	100	220	100	280
75	220	75	190	75	250

a. What will be the level of real output in the short run if the price level unexpectedly rises from 100 to 125 because of an increase in aggregate demand? What if the price level unexpectedly falls from 100 to 75 because of a decrease in aggregate demand? Explain each situation, using figures from the table.

b. What will be the level of real output in the long run when the price level rises from 100 to 125? When it falls from 100 to 75? Explain each situation.

c. Show the circumstances described in parts *a* and *b* on graph paper, and derive the long-run aggregate supply curve.

4. **KEY QUESTION** Use graphical analysis to show how each of the following would affect the economy first in the short run and then in the long run. Assume that the United States is initially operating at its full-employment level of output, that prices and wages are eventually flexible both upward and downward, and that there is no counteracting fiscal or monetary policy. **LO2**
   a. Because of a war abroad, the oil supply to the United States is disrupted, sending oil prices rocketing upward.

b. Construction spending on new homes rises dramatically, greatly increasing total U.S. investment spending.

c. Economic recession occurs abroad, significantly reducing foreign purchases of U.S. exports.

5. **KEY QUESTION** Between 1990 and 2007, the U.S. price level rose by about 61 percent while real output increased by about 63 percent. Use the aggregate demand–aggregate supply model to illustrate these outcomes graphically. **LO2**

6. Assume there is a particular short-run aggregate supply curve for an economy and the curve is relevant for several years. Use the AD-AS analysis to show graphically why higher rates of inflation over this period would be associated with lower rates of unemployment, and vice versa. What is this inverse relationship called? **LO3**

7. **KEY QUESTION** Suppose the government misjudges the natural rate of unemployment to be much lower than it actually is, and thus undertakes expansionary fiscal and monetary policies to try to achieve the lower rate. Use the concept of the short-run Phillips Curve to explain why these policies might at first succeed. Use the concept of the long-run Phillips Curve to explain the long-run outcome of these policies. **LO4**

8. What do the distinctions between short-run aggregate supply and long-run aggregate supply have in common with the distinction between the short-run Phillips Curve and the long-run Phillips Curve? Explain. **LO4**

9. **KEY QUESTION** What is the Laffer Curve, and how does it relate to supply-side economics? Why is determining the economy's location on the curve so important in assessing tax policy? **LO5**

10. Why might one person work more, earn more, and pay more income tax when his or her tax rate is cut, while another person will work less, earn less, and pay less income tax under the same circumstance? **LO5**

11. **LAST WORD** On average, does an increase in taxes raise or lower real GDP? If taxes as a percent of GDP go up 1 percent, by how much does real GDP change? Are the decreases in real GDP caused by tax increases temporary or permanent? Does the intention of a tax increase matter?

Web-Based Questions

1. **THE LAFFER CURVE—DOES IT STRETCH?** Congress did not substantially change Federal income tax rates between 1993 and 2000. Visit the Bureau of Economic Analysis Web site, **www.bea.gov.** Under Publications, click on Interactive Data Tables. On that page, click on National Income and Product Accounts, and then on the next page click on "list of All NIPA Tables." On the page that comes up, find Table 3.2 on Federal government current receipts and expeditures. Find the annual revenues from the Federal income tax from 1993 to 2000. What happened to those revenues over those years? Given constant tax rates, what do the changes in tax revenues suggest about changes in the *shape* of the Laffer Curve? If lower (or higher) tax rates do not explain the changes in tax revenues, what do you think does?

2. **DYNAMIC TAX SCORING—WHAT IS IT, AND WHO WANTS IT?** Go to **www.google.com** and search for information on "dynamic tax scoring." What is it? How does it relate to supply-side economics? Which political groups support this approach, and why? What groups oppose it, and why?

FURTHER TEST YOUR KNOWLEDGE AT
www.mcconnell18e.com

IN THIS CHAPTER YOU WILL LEARN:

1 About alternative perspectives on the causes of macroeconomic instability, including the views of mainstream economists, monetarists, real-business cycle advocates, and proponents of coordination failures.

2 What the equation of exchange is and how it relates to "monetarism."

3 Why new classical economists believe the economy will "self-correct" from aggregate demand and aggregate supply shocks.

4 The variations of the debate over "rules" versus "discretion" in conducting stabilization policy.

36

Current Issues in Macro Theory and Policy

As any academic discipline evolves, it naturally evokes a number of internal disagreements. Economics is no exception. In this chapter we examine a few alternative perspectives on macro theory and policy. We focus on the disagreements that various economists have about the answers to three interrelated questions: (1) What causes instability in the economy? (2) Is the economy self-correcting? (3) Should government adhere to *rules* or use *discretion* in setting economic policy?

What Causes Macro Instability?

As earlier chapters have indicated, capitalist economies experienced considerable instability during the twentieth century. The United States, for example, experienced the Great Depression, numerous recessions, and periods of inflation. Since the early 1980s, this instability has greatly moderated. Nevertheless, it remains a concern, and contemporary economists have different perspectives about why instability occurs.

Mainstream View

For simplicity, we will use the term "mainstream view" to characterize the prevailing macroeconomic perspective of the majority of economists. According to that view instability in the economy arises from two sources: (1) price stickiness and (2) unexpected shocks to either aggregate demand or aggregate supply.

As we explained in detail in Chapter 35, in the long run, when both input and output prices are fully flexible and have time to adjust to any changes in aggregate demand or short-run aggregate supply, the economy will always return to producing at potential output. In the shorter run, however, stickiness in either input or output prices will mean that any shock to either aggregate demand or aggregate supply will result in changes in output and employment. Although they are not new to you, let's quickly review shocks to aggregate demand and aggregate supply.

Changes in Aggregate Demand

Mainstream macroeconomics focuses on aggregate spending and its components. Recall that the basic equation underlying aggregate expenditures is

$$C_a + I_g + X_n + G = \text{GDP}$$

That is, the aggregate amount of after-tax consumption, gross investment, net exports, and government spending determines the total amount of goods and services produced and sold. In equilibrium, $C_a + I_g + X_n + G$ (aggregate expenditures) is equal to GDP (real output). A decrease in the price level increases equilibrium GDP and thus allows us to trace out a downsloping aggregate demand curve for the economy (see the appendix to Chapter 29). Any change in one of the spending components in the aggregate expenditures equation shifts the aggregate demand curve. This, in turn, changes equilibrium real output, the price level, or both.

Investment spending, in particular, is subject to wide "booms" and "busts." Significant increases in investment spending are multiplied into even greater increases in aggregate demand and thus can produce demand-pull inflation. In contrast, significant declines in investment spending are multiplied into even greater decreases in aggregate demand and thus can cause recessions.

Adverse Aggregate Supply Shocks

In the mainstream view, the second source of macroeconomic instability arises on the supply side. Occasionally, such external events as wars or an artificial supply restriction of a key resource can boost resource prices and significantly raise per-unit production costs. The result is a sizable decline in a nation's aggregate supply, which destabilizes the economy by simultaneously causing cost-push inflation and recession.

Monetarist View

Monetarism (1) focuses on the money supply, (2) holds that markets are highly competitive, and (3) says that a competitive market system gives the economy a high degree of macroeconomic stability. Monetarists argue that the price and wage flexibility provided by competitive markets should cause fluctuations in aggregate demand to alter product and resource prices rather than output and employment. Thus, the market system would provide substantial macroeconomic stability *were it not for government interference in the economy.*

ORIGIN OF THE IDEA
O 36.1
Monetarism

The problem, as monetarists see it, is that government has promoted downward wage inflexibility through the minimum-wage law, pro-union legislation, guaranteed prices for certain farm products, pro-business monopoly legislation, and so forth. The free-market system is capable of providing macroeconomic stability, but, despite good intentions, government interference has undermined that capability. Moreover, monetarists say that government has contributed to the economy's business cycles through its clumsy and mistaken attempts to achieve greater stability through its monetary policies.

Equation of Exchange

The fundamental equation of monetarism is the **equation of exchange:**

$$MV = PQ$$

where M is the supply of money; V is the **velocity** of money, that is, the average number of times per year a dollar is spent on final goods and services; P is the price level or, more specifically, the average price at which each unit of physical output is sold; and Q is the physical volume of all goods and services produced.

The left side of the equation of exchange, MV, represents the total amount spent by purchasers of output, while the right side, PQ, represents the total amount received by sellers of that output.

ORIGIN OF THE IDEA

O 36.2

Equation of exchange

The nation's money supply (M) multiplied by the number of times it is spent each year (V) must equal the nation's nominal GDP (= $P \times Q$). The dollar value of total spending has to equal the dollar value of total output.

Stable Velocity Monetarists say that velocity, V, in the equation of exchange is relatively stable. To them, "stable" is not synonymous with "constant," however. Monetarists are aware that velocity is higher today than it was several decades ago. Shorter pay periods, widespread use of credit cards, and faster means of making payments enable people to hold less money and to turn it over more rapidly than was possible in earlier times. These factors have enabled people to reduce their holdings of cash and checkbook money relative to the size of the nation's nominal GDP.

When monetarists say that velocity is stable, they mean that the factors altering velocity change gradually and predictably and that changes in velocity from one year to the next can be readily anticipated. Moreover, they hold that velocity does not change in response to changes in the money supply itself. Instead, people have a stable desire to hold money relative to holding other financial assets, holding real assets, and buying current output. The factors that determine the amount of money the public wants to hold depend mainly on the level of nominal GDP.

Example: Assume that when the level of nominal GDP is $400 billion, the public desires $100 billion of money to purchase that output. That means that V is 4 (= $400 billion of nominal GDP/$100 billion of money). If we further assume that the actual supply of money is $100 billion, the economy is in equilibrium with respect to money; the actual amount of money supplied equals the amount the public wants to hold.

If velocity is stable, the equation of exchange suggests that there is a predictable relationship between the money supply and nominal GDP (= PQ). An increase in the money supply of, say, $10 billion would upset equilibrium in our example since the public would find itself holding more money or liquidity than it wants. That is, the actual amount of money held ($110 billion) would exceed the amount of holdings desired ($100 billion). In that case, the reaction of the public (households and businesses) is to restore its desired balance of money relative to other items, such as stocks and bonds, factories and equipment,

houses and automobiles, and clothing and toys. But the spending of money by individual households and businesses would leave more cash in the checkable deposits or billfolds of other households and firms. And they too would try to "spend down" their excess cash balances. But, overall, the $110 billion supply of money cannot be spent down because a dollar spent is a dollar received.

Instead, the collective attempt to reduce cash balances increases aggregate demand, thereby boosting nominal GDP. Because velocity in our example is 4—that is, the dollar is spent, on average, four times per year—nominal GDP rises from $400 billion to $440 billion. At that higher nominal GDP, the money supply of $110 billion equals the amount of money desired ($440 billion/4 = $110 billion), and equilibrium is reestablished.

The $10 billion increase in the money supply thus eventually increases nominal GDP by $40 billion. Spending on goods, services, and assets expands until nominal GDP has gone up enough to restore the original 4-to-1 equilibrium relationship between nominal GDP and the money supply.

Note that the relationship GDP/M defines V. A stable relationship between nominal GDP and M means a stable V. And a change in M causes a proportionate change in nominal GDP. Thus, changes in the money supply allegedly have a predictable effect on nominal GDP (= $P \times Q$). An increase in M increases P or Q, or some combination of both; a decrease in M reduces P or Q, or some combination of both. **(Key Question 4)**

WORKED PROBLEMS

W 36.1

Equation of exchange

Monetary Causes of Instability Monetarists say that inappropriate monetary policy is the single most important cause of macroeconomic instability. An increase in the money supply directly increases aggregate demand. Under conditions of full employment, that rise in aggregate demand raises the price level. For a time, higher prices cause firms to increase their real output, and the rate of unemployment falls below its natural rate. But once nominal wages rise to reflect the higher prices and thus to restore real wages, real output moves back to its full-employment level and the unemployment rate returns to its natural rate. The inappropriate increase in the money supply leads to inflation, together with instability of real output and employment.

Conversely, a decrease in the money supply reduces aggregate demand. Real output temporarily falls, and the unemployment rate rises above its natural rate. Eventually, nominal wages fall and real output returns to its full-employment level. The inappropriate decline in the money supply leads to deflation, together with instability of real GDP and employment.

The contrast between mainstream macroeconomics and monetarism on the causes of instability thus comes into sharp focus. Mainstream economists view the instability of investment as the main cause of the economy's instability. They see monetary policy as a stabilizing factor. Changes in the money supply raise or lower interest rates as needed, smooth out swings in investment, and thus reduce macroeconomic instability. In contrast, monetarists view changes in the money supply as the main cause of instability in the economy. For example, they say that the Great Depression occurred largely because the Fed allowed the money supply to fall by roughly one-third during that period. According to Milton Friedman, a prominent monetarist,

> And [the money supply] fell not because there were no willing borrowers—not because the horse would not drink. It fell because the Federal Reserve System forced or permitted a sharp reduction in the [money supply], because it failed to exercise the responsibilities assigned to it in the Federal Reserve Act to provide liquidity to the banking system. The Great Contraction is tragic testimony to the power of monetary policy—not, as Keynes and so many of his contemporaries believed, evidence of its impotence.[1]

Real-Business-Cycle View

A third modern view of the cause of macroeconomic instability is that business cycles are caused by real factors that affect aggregate supply rather than by monetary, or spending, factors that cause fluctuations in aggregate demand. In the **real-business-cycle theory**, business fluctuations result from significant changes in technology and resource availability. Those changes affect productivity and thus the long-run growth trend of aggregate supply.

An example focusing on recession will clarify this thinking. Suppose productivity (output per worker) declines sharply because of a large increase in oil prices, which makes it prohibitively expensive to operate certain types of machinery. That decline in productivity implies a reduction in the economy's ability to produce real output. The result would be a decrease in the economy's long-run aggregate supply curve, as represented by the leftward shift from AS_{LR1} to AS_{LR2} in Figure 36.1.

As real output falls from Q_1 to Q_2, the public needs less money to buy the reduced volume of goods and services. So the demand for money falls. Moreover, the slowdown in business activity means that businesses need to borrow less from banks, reducing the part of the money supply

[1]Milton Friedman, *The Optimum Quantity of Money and Other Essays* (Chicago: Aldine, 1969), p. 97.

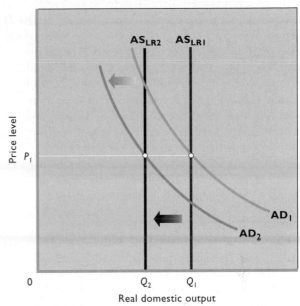

FIGURE 36.1 The real-business-cycle theory. In the real-business-cycle theory, a decline in resource availability shifts the nation's long-run aggregate supply curve to the left from AS_{LR1} to AS_{LR2}. The decline in real output from Q_1 to Q_2, in turn, reduces money demand (less is needed) and money supply (fewer loans are taken out) such that aggregate demand shifts leftward from AD_1 to AD_2. The result is a recession in which the price level remains constant.

created by banks through their lending. Thus, the supply of money also falls. In this controversial scenario, changes in the supply of money respond to changes in the demand for money. The decline in the money supply then reduces aggregate demand, as from AD_1 to AD_2 in Figure 36.1. The outcome is a decline in real output from Q_1 to Q_2, with no change in the price level.

Conversely, a large increase in aggregate supply (not shown) caused by, say, major innovations in the production process would shift the long-run aggregate supply curve rightward. Real output would increase, and money demand and money supply would both increase. Aggregate demand would shift rightward by an amount equal to the rightward shift of long-run aggregate supply. Real output would increase, without driving up the price level.

Conclusion: In the real-business-cycle theory, macro instability arises on the aggregate supply side of the economy, not on the aggregate demand side, as mainstream economists and monetarists usually claim.

Coordination Failures

A fourth and final modern view of macroeconomic instability relates to so-called **coordination failures.** Such failures occur when people fail to reach a mutually beneficial equilibrium because they lack a way to coordinate their actions.

Noneconomic Example Consider first a noneconomic example. Suppose you hear that some people might be getting together at the last minute for an informal party at a nearby beach. But because of a chance of rain, there is some doubt about whether people will actually come out. You make a cell phone call or two to try to get a read on what others are thinking, and then base your decision on that limited information. If you expect others to be there, you will decide to go. If you expect that others will not go, you will decide to stay home. There are several possible equilibrium outcomes, depending on the mix of people's expectations. Let's consider just two. If each person assumes that all the others will be at the party, all will go. The party will occur and presumably everyone will have a good time. But if each person assumes that everyone else will stay home, all will stay home and there will be no party. When the party does not take place, even though all would be better off if it did take place, a coordination failure has occurred.

Macroeconomic Example Now let's apply this example to macroeconomic instability, specifically recession. Suppose that individual firms and households expect other firms and consumers to cut back their investment and consumption spending. As a result, each firm and household will anticipate a reduction of aggregate demand. Firms therefore will cut back their own investment spending since they will anticipate that their future production capacity will be excessive. Households will also reduce their own spending (increase their saving) because they anticipate that they will experience reduced work hours, possible layoffs, and falling incomes in the future.

Aggregate demand will indeed decline and the economy will indeed experience a recession in response to what amounts to a self-fulfilling prophecy. Moreover, the economy will stay at a below-full-employment level of output because, once there, producers and households have no individual incentive to increase spending. If all producers and households would agree to increase their investment and consumption spending simultaneously, then aggregate demand would rise, and real output and real income would increase. Each producer and each consumer would be better off. However, this outcome does not occur because there is no mechanism for firms and households to agree on such a joint spending increase.

In this case, the economy is stuck in an *unemployment equilibrium* because of a coordination failure. With a different set of expectations, a coordination failure might leave the economy in an *inflation equilibrium*. In this view, the economy has a number of such potential equilibrium positions, some good and some bad, depending on people's mix of expectations. Macroeconomic instability, then,

reflects the movement of the economy from one such equilibrium position to another as expectations change.

> ### QUICK REVIEW 36.1
>
> - Mainstream economists say that macroeconomic instability usually stems from swings in investment spending and, occasionally, from adverse aggregate supply shocks.
> - Monetarists view the economy through the equation of exchange ($MV = PQ$). If velocity V is stable, changes in the money supply M lead directly to changes in nominal GDP ($P \times Q$). For monetarists, changes in M caused by inappropriate monetary policy are the single most important cause of macroeconomic instability.
> - In the real-business-cycle theory, significant changes in "real" factors such as technology, resource availability, and productivity change the economy's long-run aggregate supply, causing macroeconomic instability.
> - Macroeconomic instability can result from coordination failures—less-than-optimal equilibrium positions that occur because businesses and households lack a way to coordinate their actions.

Does the Economy "Self-Correct"?

Just as there are disputes over the causes of macroeconomic instability, there are disputes over whether or not the economy will correct itself when instability does occur. And economists also disagree on how long it will take for any such self-correction to take place.

New Classical View of Self-Correction

New classical economists tend to be either monetarists or adherents of **rational expectations theory:** the idea that businesses, consumers, and workers expect changes in policies or circumstances to have certain effects on the economy and, in pursuing their own self-interest, take actions to make sure those changes affect them as little as possible. The **new classical economics** holds that when the economy occasionally diverges from its full-employment output, internal mechanisms within the economy will auto-

> ### ORIGIN OF THE IDEA
> **O 36.3**
> Rational expectations theory

matically move it back to that output. Policymakers should stand back and let the automatic correction occur, rather than engaging in active fiscal and monetary policy. This perspective is often associated with the vertical long-run

Phillips Curve, which we discussed in Chapter 35. But we will analyze it here using the extended AD-AS model that was also developed in Chapter 35.

Graphical Analysis

Figure 36.2a relates the new classical analysis to the question of self-correction. Specifically, an increase in aggregate demand, say, from AD_1 to AD_2, moves the economy upward along its short-run aggregate supply curve AS_1 from a to b. The price level rises and real output increases. With the economy producing beyond potential output, high resource demand drives up the prices of labor and other productive inputs. Per-unit production costs increase and the short-run aggregate supply curve shifts leftward, eventually from AS_1 to AS_2. The economy moves from b to c, and real output returns to its full-employment level, Q_1. This level of output is dictated by the economy's vertical long-run aggregate supply curve, AS_{LR}.

Conversely, a decrease in aggregate demand from AD_1 to AD_3 in Figure 36.2b first moves the economy downward along its short-run aggregate supply curve AS_1 from point a to d. The price level declines, as does the level of real output. With the economy producing below potential output, low resource demand drives down the prices of labor and other productive inputs. When that happens, per-unit production costs decline and the short-run aggregate supply curve shifts to the right, eventually from AS_1 to AS_3. The economy moves to e, where it again achieves its full-employment level, Q_1. As in Figure 36.2a, the economy in Figure 36.2b has automatically self-corrected to its full-employment output and its natural rate of unemployment.

Speed of Adjustment

There is some disagreement among new classical economists on how long it will take for self-correction to occur. Monetarists usually hold the *adaptive expectations* view that people form their expectations on the basis of present realities and only gradually change their expectations as experience unfolds. This means that the shifts in the short-run aggregate supply curves shown in Figure 36.2 may not occur for 2 or 3 years or even longer. Other new classical economists, however, accept the rational expectations assumption that workers anticipate some future outcomes before they occur. When price-level changes are fully anticipated, adjustments of nominal wages are very quick or even instantaneous. Let's see why.

Although several new theories incorporate rational expectations, our interest here is the new classical version of the rational expectations theory (hereafter, RET). RET is based on two assumptions:

* People behave rationally, gathering and intelligently processing information to form expectations about things that are economically important to them. They adjust those expectations quickly as new developments affecting future economic outcomes occur. Where there is adequate information, people's beliefs about future economic outcomes accurately reflect the likelihood that those outcomes will occur. For example, if

FIGURE 36.2 New classical view of self-correction. (a) An unanticipated increase in aggregate demand from AD_1 to AD_2 first moves the economy from a to b. The economy then self-corrects to c. An anticipated increase in aggregate demand moves the economy directly from a to c. (b) An unanticipated decrease in aggregate demand from AD_1 to AD_3 moves the economy from a to d. The economy then self-corrects to e. An anticipated decrease in aggregate demand moves the economy directly from a to e. (Mainstream economists, however, say that if the price level remains at P_1, the economy will move from a to f, and even if the price level falls to P_4, the economy may remain at d because of downward wage inflexibility.)

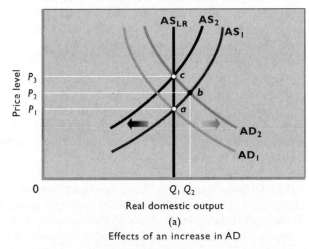

(a)

Effects of an increase in AD

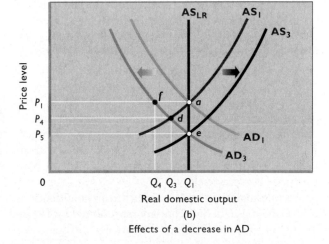

(b)

Effects of a decrease in AD

it is clear that a certain policy will cause inflation, people will recognize that fact and adjust their economic behavior in anticipation of inflation.

- RET economists assume that all product and resource markets are highly competitive and that prices and wages are flexible both upward and downward. But the RET economists go further, assuming that new information is quickly (in some cases, instantaneously) taken into account in the demand and supply curves of such markets. The upshot is that equilibrium prices and quantities adjust rapidly to unforeseen events—say, technological change or aggregate supply shocks. They adjust instantaneously to events that have known outcomes—for example, changes in fiscal or monetary policy.

Unanticipated Price-Level Changes The implication of RET is not only that the economy is self-correcting but that self-correction occurs quickly. In this thinking, unanticipated changes in the price level so-called **price-level surprises**—do cause temporary changes in real output. Suppose, for example, that an unanticipated increase in foreign demand for U.S. goods increases U.S. aggregate demand from AD_1 to AD_2 in Figure 36.2a. The immediate result is an unexpected increase in the price level from P_1 to P_2.

But now an interesting question arises. If wages and prices are flexible, as assumed in RET, why doesn't the higher price level immediately cause wages and other input prices to rise, such that there is no increase in real output at all? Why does the economy temporarily move from point a to b along AS_1? In RET, firms increase output from Q_1 to Q_2 because of misperceptions about rising prices of their own products relative to the prices of other products (and to the prices of labor). They mistakenly think the higher prices of their own products have resulted from increased demand for those products relative to the demands for other products. Expecting higher profits, they increase their own production. But in fact *all* prices, including the price of labor (nominal wages), are rising because of the general increase in aggregate demand. Once firms see that *all* prices and wages are rising, they decrease their production to previous levels.

In terms of Figure 36.2a, the increase in nominal wages shifts the short-run aggregate supply curve leftward, ultimately from AS_1 to AS_2, and the economy moves from b to c. Thus, the increase in real output caused by the price-level surprise corrects itself.

The same analysis in reverse applies to an unanticipated price-level decrease. In the economy represented by Figure 36.2b, firms misperceive that the prices of their own

products are falling due to decreases in the demand for those products relative to other products. They incorrectly anticipate declines in profit and cut production. As a result of their collective actions, real output in the economy falls. Once firms see what is really happening—that *all* prices and wages are dropping—they increase their output to prior levels. The short-run aggregate supply curve in Figure 36.2b shifts rightward from AS_1 to AS_3, and the economy "self-corrects" by moving from d to e.

Fully Anticipated Price-Level Changes In RET, fully *anticipated* price-level changes do not change real output, even for short periods. In Figure 36.2a, again consider the increase in aggregate demand from AD_1 to AD_2. Businesses immediately recognize that the higher prices being paid for their products are part of the inflation they had anticipated. They understand that the same forces that are causing the inflation result in higher nominal wages, leaving their profits unchanged. The economy therefore moves directly from a to c. The price level rises as expected, and output remains at its full-employment level Q_1.

Similarly, a fully *anticipated* price-level decrease will leave real output unchanged. Firms conclude that nominal wages are declining by the same percentage amount as the declining price level, leaving profits unchanged. The economy represented by Figure 36.2b therefore moves directly from a to e. Deflation occurs, but the economy continues to produce its full-employment output Q_1. The anticipated decline in aggregate demand causes no change in real output.

Mainstream View of Self-Correction

Almost all economists acknowledge that the new classical economists have made significant contributions to the theory of aggregate supply. In fact, mainstream economists have incorporated some aspects of RET into their own models. However, most economists strongly disagree with RET on the question of downward price and wage flexibility. While the stock market, foreign exchange market, and certain commodity markets experience day-to-day or minute-to-minute price changes, including price declines, that is not true of many product markets and most labor markets. There is ample evidence, say mainstream economists, that many prices and wages are inflexible downward for long periods. As a result, it may take years for the economy to move from recession back to full-employment output, unless it gets help from fiscal and monetary policy.

Graphical Analysis To understand this mainstream view, again examine Figure 36.2b. Suppose aggregate demand declines from AD_1 to AD_3 because of a significant decline in investment spending. If the price level is stuck at P_1, the economy will not move from a to d to e, as suggested by RET. Instead, the economy will move from a to f, as if it were moving along a horizontal aggregate supply curve between those two points. Real output will decline from its full-employment level, Q_1, to the recessionary level, Q_4.

But let's assume that large amounts of unsold inventories eventually cause the price level to fall to P_4. Will this lead to the decline in nominal wages needed to shift aggregate supply from AS_1 to AS_3, as suggested by the new classical economists? "Highly unlikely" say mainstream economists. Even more so than prices, nominal wages tend to be inflexible downward. If nominal wages do not decline in response to the decline in the price level, then the short-run aggregate supply curve will not shift rightward. The self-correction mechanism assumed by RET and new classical economists will break down. Instead, the economy will remain at d, experiencing less-than-full-employment output and a high rate of unemployment.

> **INTERACTIVE GRAPHS**
>
> **G 36.1**
>
> Self-correction

Downward Wage Inflexibility

In Chapter 29 we discussed several reasons why firms may not be able to, or may not want to, lower nominal wages. Firms may not be able to cut wages because of wage contracts and the legal minimum wage. And firms may not want to lower wages if they fear potential problems with morale, effort, and efficiency.

While contracts are thought to be the main cause of wage rigidity, so-called efficiency wages and insider-outsider relationships also may play a role. Let's explore both.

Efficiency Wage Theory

Recall from Chapter 29 that an **efficiency wage** is a wage that minimizes the firm's labor cost per unit of output. Normally, we would think that the market wage is the efficiency wage since it is the lowest wage at which a firm can obtain a particular type of labor. But where the cost of supervising workers is high or where worker turnover is great, firms may discover that paying a wage that is higher than the market wage will lower their wage cost per unit of output.

Example: Suppose a firm's workers, on average, produce 8 units of output at a $9 market wage but 10 units of output at a $10 above-market wage. The efficiency wage is $10, not the $9 market wage. At the $10 wage, the labor cost per unit of output is only $1 (= $10 wage/ 10 units of output), compared with $1.12 (= $9 wage/ 8 units of output) at the $9 wage.

How can a higher wage result in greater efficiency?

- *Greater work effort* The above-market wage, in effect, raises the cost to workers of losing their jobs as a result of poor performance. Because workers have a strong incentive to retain their relatively high-paying jobs, they are more likely to provide greater work effort. Looked at differently, workers are more reluctant to shirk (neglect or avoid work) because the higher wage makes job loss more costly to them. Consequently, the above-market wage can be the efficient wage; it can enhance worker productivity so much that the higher wage more than pays for itself.

- *Lower supervision costs* With less incentive among workers to shirk, the firm needs fewer supervisory personnel to monitor work performance. This, too, can lower the firm's overall wage cost per unit of output.

- *Reduced job turnover* The above-market pay discourages workers from voluntarily leaving their jobs. The lower turnover rate reduces the firm's cost of hiring and training workers. It also gives the firm a more experienced, more productive workforce.

The key implication for macroeconomic instability is that efficiency wages add to the downward inflexibility of wages.

> **ORIGIN OF THE IDEA**
>
> **O 36.4**
>
> Efficiency wages

Firms that pay efficiency wages will be reluctant to cut wages when aggregate demand declines, since such cuts may encourage shirking, require more supervisory personnel, and increase turnover. In other words, wage cuts that reduce productivity and raise per-unit labor costs are self-defeating.

Insider-Outsider Relationships

Other economists theorize that downward wage inflexibility may relate to relationships between "insiders" and "outsiders." Insiders are workers who retain employment even during recession. Outsiders are workers who have been laid off from a firm and unemployed workers who would like to work at that firm.

When recession produces layoffs and widespread unemployment, we might expect outsiders to offer to work for less than the current wage rate, in effect, bidding down wage rates. We also might expect firms to hire such workers in order to reduce their costs. But, according to the **insider-outsider theory,** outsiders may not be able to underbid existing wages because employers may view the nonwage cost of hiring them to be prohibitive. Employers might fear that insiders would view acceptance of such underbidding as undermining years of effort to increase wages or, worse, as "stealing" jobs. So insiders may refuse to cooperate with new workers who have undercut their pay. Where teamwork is critical for production, such lack of cooperation will reduce overall productivity and thereby lower the firms' profits.

Even if firms are willing to employ outsiders at less than the current wage, those workers might refuse to work for less than the existing wage. To do so might invite harassment from the insiders whose pay they have undercut. Thus, outsiders may remain unemployed, relying on past saving, unemployment compensation, and other social programs to make ends meet.

As in the efficiency wage theory, the insider-outsider theory implies that wages will be inflexible downward when aggregate demand declines. Self-correction may eventually occur but not nearly as rapidly as the new classical economists contend. **(Key Question 7)**

QUICK REVIEW 36.2

- New classical economists believe that the economy "self-corrects" when unanticipated events divert it from its full-employment level of real output.

- In RET, unanticipated price-level changes cause changes in real output in the short run but not in the long run.

- According to RET, market participants immediately change their actions in response to anticipated price-level changes such that no change in real output occurs.

- Mainstream economists say that the economy can get mired in recession for several months or more because of downward price and wage inflexibility.

- Sources of downward wage inflexibility include contracts, efficiency wages, and insider-outsider relationships.

Rules or Discretion?

These different views on the causes of instability and on the speed of self-correction have led to vigorous debate on macro policy. Should the government adhere to policy rules that prohibit it from causing instability in an economy that is otherwise stable? Or should it use discretionary fiscal and monetary policy, when needed, to stabilize a sometimes-unstable economy?

In Support of Policy Rules

Monetarists and other new classical economists believe policy rules would reduce instability in the economy. They believe that such rules would prevent government from trying to "manage" aggregate demand. That would be a desirable trend because, in their view, such management is misguided and thus is likely to *cause* more instability than it cures.

Monetary Rule Since inappropriate monetary policy is the major source of macroeconomic instability, say

CONSIDER THIS . . .

On the Road Again

Economist Abba Lerner (1903–1982) likened the economy to an automobile traveling down a road that had traffic barriers on each side. The problem was that the car had no steering wheel. It would hit one barrier, causing the car to veer to the opposite side of the road. There it would hit the other barrier, which in turn would send it careening to the opposite side. To avoid such careening in the form of business cycles, said Lerner, society must equip the economy with a steering wheel. Discretionary fiscal and monetary policy would enable government to steer the economy safely between the problems of recession and demand-pull inflation.

Economist Milton Friedman (1912–2006) modified Lerner's analogy, giving it a different meaning. He said that the economy does not need a skillful driver of the economic vehicle who is continuously turning the wheel to adjust to the unexpected irregularities of the route. Instead, the economy needs a way to prohibit the monetary passenger in the back seat from occasionally leaning over and giving the steering wheel a jerk that sends the car off the road. According to Friedman, the car will travel down the road just fine unless the Federal Reserve destabilizes it.

Lerner's analogy implies an internally unstable economy that needs steering through discretionary government stabilization policy. Friedman's modification of the analogy implies a generally stable economy that is destabilized by inappropriate monetary policy by the Federal Reserve. For Lerner, stability requires active use of fiscal and monetary policy. For Friedman, macroeconomic stability requires a monetary rule forcing the Federal Reserve to increase the money supply at a set, steady annual rate.*

---

*In his later years, Friedman softened his call for a monetary rule, acknowledging that the Fed had become much more skillful at keeping the rate of inflation in check through prudent monetary policy.

monetarists, the enactment of a **monetary rule** would make sense. One such rule would be a requirement that the Fed expand the money supply each year at the same annual rate as the typical growth of the economy's production capacity. That fixed-rate expansion of the money supply would occur whatever the state of the economy. The Fed's sole monetary role would be to use its tools (open-market operations, the discount rate, the term auction facility, and

FIGURE 36.3 Rationale for a monetary rule. A monetary rule that required the Fed to increase the money supply at an annual rate linked to the long-run increase in potential GDP would shift aggregate demand rightward, as from AD_1 to AD_2, at the same pace as the shift in long-run aggregate supply, here AS_{LR1} to AS_{LR2}. Thus the economy would experience growth without inflation or deflation.

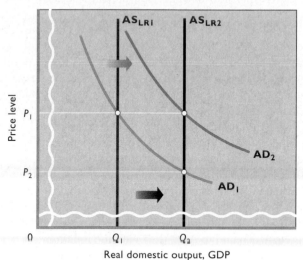

reserve requirements) to ensure that the nation's money supply grew steadily by, say, 3 to 5 percent a year. According to Milton Friedman,

> Such a rule ... would eliminate ... the major cause of instability in the economy—the capricious and unpredictable impact of countercyclical monetary policy. As long as the money supply grows at a constant rate each year, be it 3, 4, or 5 percent, any decline into recession will be temporary. The liquidity provided by a constantly growing money supply will cause aggregate demand to expand. Similarly, if the supply of money does not rise at a more than average rate, any inflationary increase in spending will burn itself out for lack of fuel.[2]

Figure 36.3 illustrates the rationale for a monetary rule. Suppose the economy represented there is operating at its full-employment real output, Q_1. Also suppose the nation's long-run aggregate supply curve shifts rightward, as from AS_{LR1} to AS_{LR2}, each year, signifying the average annual increase in potential real output. As you saw in earlier chapters, such annual increases in "potential GDP" result from added resources, improved resources, and improved technology.

Monetarists argue that a monetary rule would tie increases in the money supply to the typical rightward shift of long-run aggregate supply. In view of the direct link between changes in the money supply and aggregate demand, this would ensure that the AD curve would shift

rightward, as from AD_1 to AD_2, each year. As a result, while GDP increases from Q_1 to Q_2, the price level would remain constant at P_1. A monetary rule, then, would promote steady growth of real output along with price stability.

Generally, rational expectations economists also support a monetary rule. They conclude that an expansionary or restrictive monetary policy would alter the rate of inflation but not real output. Suppose, for example, the Fed implements an easy money policy to reduce interest rates, expand investment spending, and boost real GDP. On the basis of past experience and economic knowledge, the public would anticipate that this policy is inflationary and would take protective actions. Workers would press for higher nominal wages; firms would raise their product prices; and lenders would lift their nominal interest rates on loans.

All these responses are designed to prevent inflation from having adverse effects on the real income of workers, businesses, and lenders. But collectively they would immediately raise wage and price levels. So the increase in aggregate demand brought about by the expansionary monetary policy would be completely dissipated in higher prices and wages. Real output and employment would not be increased by the easy money policy.

In this view, the combination of rational expectations and instantaneous market adjustments dooms discretionary monetary policy to ineffectiveness. If discretionary monetary policy produces only inflation (or deflation), say the RET economists, then it makes sense to limit the Fed's discretion and to require that Congress enact a monetary rule consistent with price stability at all times.

In recent decades, the call for a Friedman-type monetary rule has faded. Some economists who tend to favor monetary rules have advocated **inflation targeting**, under which the Fed would be required to announce a targeted band of inflation rates, say, 1 to 2 percent, for some future period such as the following 2 years. It would then be expected to use its monetary policy tools to keep inflation rates within that range. If it did not hit the inflation target, it would have to explain why it failed.

Strictly interpreted, inflation targeting would focus the Fed's attention nearly exclusively on controlling inflation and deflation, rather than on counteracting business fluctuations. Proponents of inflation targeting generally believe the economy will have fewer, shorter, and less severe business cycles if the Fed adheres to the rule "Set a known inflation goal and achieve it."

We discussed another modern monetary rule—the Taylor rule—in Chapter 33 on monetary policy. This rule specifies how the Fed should alter the Federal funds rate under differing economic circumstances. We discuss this rule in more depth in this chapter's Last Word.

---

[2] As quoted in Lawrence S. Ritter and William L. Silber, *Money*, 5th ed. (New York: Basic Books, 1984), pp. 141–142.

Balanced Budget Monetarists and new classical economists question the effectiveness of fiscal policy. At the extreme, a few of them favor a constitutional amendment requiring that the Federal government balance its budget annually. Others simply suggest that government be "passive" in its fiscal policy, not intentionally creating budget deficits or surpluses. They believe that deficits and surpluses caused by recession or inflationary expansion will eventually correct themselves as the economy self-corrects to its full-employment output.

Monetarists are particularly strong in their opposition to expansionary fiscal policy. They believe that the deficit spending accompanying such a policy has a strong tendency to "crowd out" private investment. Suppose government runs a budget deficit by printing and selling U.S. securities—that is, by borrowing from the public. By engaging in such borrowing, the government is competing with private businesses for funds. The borrowing increases the demand for money, which then raises the interest rate and crowds out a substantial amount of private investment that would otherwise have been profitable. The net effect of a budget deficit on aggregate demand therefore is unpredictable and, at best, modest.

RET economists reject discretionary fiscal policy for the same reason they reject active monetary policy: They don't think it works. Business and labor will immediately adjust their behavior in anticipation of the price-level effects of a change in fiscal policy. The economy will move directly to the anticipated new price level. Like monetary policy, say the RET theorists, fiscal policy can move the economy along its vertical long-run aggregate supply curve. But because its effects on inflation are fully anticipated, fiscal policy cannot alter real GDP even in the short run. The best course of action for government is to balance its budget.

In Defense of Discretionary Stabilization Policy

Mainstream economists oppose both a strict monetary rule and a balanced-budget requirement. They believe that monetary policy and fiscal policy are important tools for achieving and maintaining full employment, price stability, and economic growth.

Discretionary Monetary Policy In supporting discretionary monetary policy, mainstream economists argue that the rationale for the Friedman monetary rule is flawed. While there is indeed a close relationship between the money supply and nominal GDP over long periods, in shorter periods this relationship breaks down. The reason is that the velocity of money has proved to be more variable and unpredictable than monetarists contend. Arguing that velocity is variable both cyclically and over time,

mainstream economists contend that a constant annual rate of increase in the money supply might not eliminate fluctuations in aggregate demand. In terms of the equation of exchange, a steady rise of M does not guarantee a steady expansion of aggregate demand because V—the rate at which money is spent—can change.

Look again at Figure 36.3, in which we demonstrated the monetary rule: Expand the money supply annually by a fixed percentage, regardless of the state of the economy. During the period in question, optimistic business expectations might create a boom in investment spending and thus shift the aggregate demand curve to some location to the right of AD_2. (You may want to pencil in a new AD curve, labeling it AD_3.) The price level would then rise above P_1; that is, demand-pull inflation would occur. In this case, the monetary rule will not accomplish its goal of maintaining price stability. Mainstream economists say that the Fed can use a restrictive monetary policy to reduce the excessive investment spending and thereby hold the rightward shift of aggregate demand to AD_2, thus avoiding inflation.

Similarly, suppose instead that investment declines because of pessimistic business expectations. Aggregate demand will then increase by some amount less than the increase from AD_1 to AD_2 in Figure 36.3. Again, the monetary rule fails the stability test: The price level sinks below P_1 (deflation occurs). Or if the price level is inflexible downward at P_1, the economy will not achieve its full-employment output (unemployment rises). An expansionary monetary policy can help avoid each outcome.

Mainstream economists quip that the trouble with the monetary rule is that it tells the policymaker, "Don't do something, just stand there."

Discretionary Fiscal Policy Mainstream economists support the use of fiscal policy to keep recessions from deepening or to keep mild inflation from becoming severe inflation. They recognize the possibility of crowding out but do not think it is a serious problem when business borrowing is depressed, as is usually the case in recession. Because politicians can abuse fiscal policy, most economists feel that it should be held in reserve for situations where monetary policy appears to be ineffective or working too slowly.

As indicated earlier, mainstream economists oppose requirements to balance the budget annually. Tax revenues fall sharply during recessions and rise briskly during periods of demand-pull inflation. Therefore, a law or a constitutional amendment mandating an annually balanced budget would require that the government increase tax rates and reduce government spending during recession and reduce tax rates and increase government spending during economic booms. The first set of actions would worsen recession, and the second set would fuel inflation.

Increased Macro Stability

Finally, mainstream economists point out that the U.S. economy has been much more stable in the last half-century than it had been in earlier periods. It is not a coincidence, they say, that use of discretionary fiscal and monetary policies characterized the latter period but not the former. These policies have helped tame the business cycle. Moreover, mainstream economists point out several specific policy successes in the past three decades:

- A tight money policy dropped inflation from 13.5 percent in 1980 to 3.2 percent in 1983.
- An expansionary fiscal policy reduced the unemployment rate from 9.7 percent in 1982 to 5.5 percent in 1988.
- An easy money policy helped the economy recover from the 1990–1991 recession.
- Judicious tightening of monetary policy in the mid-1990s, and then again in the late 1990s, helped the economy remain on a noninflationary, full-employment growth path.
- In late 2001 and 2002, expansionary fiscal and monetary policy helped the economy recover from a series of economic blows, including the collapse of numerous Internet start-up firms, a severe decline in investment spending, the impacts of the terrorist attacks of September 11, 2001, and a precipitous decline in stock values.

- In 2004 and 2005 the Fed tempered continued expansionary fiscal policy by increasing the Federal funds rate in $\frac{1}{4}$ percentage-point increments from 1 percent to 4.25 percent. The economy expanded briskly in those years, while inflation stayed in check. The mild inflation was particularly impressive because the average price of a barrel of crude oil rose from $24 in 2002 to $55 in 2005. The Fed's further increases in interest rates to 5.25 percent in 2006 also kept inflation mild that year and the next despite continued strong growth and oil reaching $99 per barrel in late 2007.
- In 2007, the Fed vigorously responded to a crisis in the mortgage market to ensure monetary liquidity in the banking system. Besides aggressively lowering the Federal funds rate from 5.25 percent in the summer of 2007 to just 2 percent in April 2008, the Fed greatly increased the reserves of the banking system through the creation and use of the term auction facility. The Fed's actions helped to soften the negative impact of the crisis on the broader economy.

Summary of Alternative Views

In Table 36.1 we summarize the fundamental ideas and policy implications of three macroeconomic theories: mainstream macroeconomics, monetarism, and rational

TABLE 36.1 Summary of Alternative Macroeconomic Views

Issue	Mainstream Macroeconomics	New Classical Economics	
		Monetarism	Rational Expectations
View of the private economy	Potentially unstable	Stable in long run at natural rate of unemployment	Stable in long run at natural rate of unemployment
Cause of the observed instability of the private economy	Investment plans unequal to saving plans (changes in AD); AS shocks	Inappropriate monetary policy	Unanticipated AD and AS shocks in the short run
Assumptions about short-run price and wage stickiness	Both prices and wages stuck in the immediate short run; in the short run, wages sticky while prices inflexible downward but flexible upward.	Prices flexible upward and downward in the short run; wages sticky in the short run	Prices and wages flexible both upward and downward in the short run
Appropriate macro policies	Active fiscal and monetary policy	Monetary rule	Monetary rule
How changes in the money supply affect the economy	By changing the interest rate, which changes investment and real GDP	By directly changing AD, which changes GDP	No effect on output because price-level changes are anticipated
View of the velocity of money	Unstable	Stable	No consensus
How fiscal policy affects the economy	Changes AD and GDP via the multiplier process	No effect unless money supply changes	No effect because price-level changes are anticipated
View of cost-push inflation	Possible (AS shock)	Impossible in the long run in the absence of excessive money supply growth	Impossible in the long run in the absence of excessive money supply growth

The Taylor Rule: Could a Robot Replace Ben Bernanke?

Macroeconomist John Taylor of Stanford University Calls for a New Monetary Rule That Would Institutionalize Appropriate Fed Policy Responses to Changes in Real Output and Inflation.

In our discussion of rules versus discretion, "rules" were associated with a *passive* monetary policy—one in which the monetary rule required that the Fed expand the money supply at a fixed annual rate regardless of the state of the economy. "Discretion," on the other hand, was associated with an *active* monetary policy in which the Fed changed interest rates in response to actual or anticipated changes in the economy.

Economist John Taylor has put a new twist on the rules-versus-discretion debate by suggesting a hybrid policy rule that dictates the precise active monetary actions the Fed should take when changes in the economy occur. You first encountered this Taylor rule in our discussion of monetary policy in Chapter 33. The **Taylor rule** combines traditional monetarism, with its emphasis on a monetary rule, and the more mainstream view that active monetary policy is a useful tool for taming inflation and limiting recession. Unlike the Friedman monetary rule, the Taylor rule holds, for example, that monetary policy should respond to changes in both real GDP and inflation, not simply inflation. The key adjustment instrument is the interest rate, not the money supply.

The Taylor rule builds on the belief held by many economists that central banks are willing to tolerate a small positive rate of inflation if doing so will help the economy to produce at potential output. The Taylor rule assumes that the Fed has a 2 percent "target rate of inflation" that it is willing to tolerate and that the Fed follows three rules when setting its target for the Federal funds rate (the rate of interest that commercial banks with excess reserves charge on overnight loans to banks that wish to borrow reserves in order to meet their reserve requirements). The three rules are

- When real GDP equals potential GDP and inflation is at its target rate of 2 percent, the Federal funds target rate should be 4 percent, implying a *real* Federal funds rate of 2 percent (= 4 percent nominal Federal funds rate—2 percent inflation rate).

- For each 1 percent increase of real GDP above potential GDP, the Fed should raise the *real* Federal funds rate by ½ percentage point.

- For each 1 percent increase in the inflation rate above its 2 percent target rate, the Fed should raise the *real* Federal funds rate by ½ percentage point.[*]

Taylor has neither suggested nor implied that a robot, programmed with the Taylor rule, should replace Ben Bernanke, chairman of the Federal Reserve System. The Fed's discretion to override the rule (or "contingency plan for policy") would be retained, but the Fed would have to explain why its policies diverged from the rule. So the rule would remove the "mystery" associated with monetary policy and increase the Fed's accountability. Also, says Taylor, if used consistently, the rule would enable market participants to predict Fed behavior, and this would increase Fed credibility and reduce uncertainty.

Critics of the Taylor rule acknowledge that it is more in tune with countercyclical Fed policy than with Friedman's simple monetary rule. And they concede that the Fed's recent monetary policy closely mimics the rule. But they see no reason to limit the Fed's future discretion in adjusting interest rates as it sees fit to achieve stabilization and growth. Monetary policy must consider all risks to the economy and react accordingly. The critics also point out that the Fed has done a good job of promoting price stability, full employment, and economic growth over the past two decades. In view of this success, they conclude that a mechanical monetary rule is unnecessary and potentially detrimental.

---

[*]John Taylor, *Inflation, Unemployment, and Monetary Policy* (Cambridge, Mass.: MIT Press, 1998), pp. 44–47.

expectations theory. Note that we have broadly defined new classical economics to include both monetarism and the rational expectations theory since both adhere to the view that the economy tends automatically to achieve equilibrium at its full-employment output.

These different perspectives have obliged mainstream economists to rethink some of their fundamental principles and to revise many of their positions. Although considerable disagreement remains, mainstream macroeconomists agree with monetarists that "money matters" and that excessive growth of the money supply is the major cause of long-lasting, rapid inflation. They also agree with RET proponents and theorists of coordination failures that expectations matter. If government can create expectations of price stability, full employment, and economic growth, households and firms will tend to act in ways to make them happen. In short, thanks to ongoing challenges to conventional wisdom, macroeconomics continues to evolve. **(Key Question 13)**

Summary

1. The mainstream view is that macro instability is caused by a combination of price stickiness and shocks to aggregate demand or aggregate supply. With prices inflexible in the shorter run, changes in aggregate demand or short-run aggregate supply result in changes in output and employment. In the long run when both input and output prices are fully flexible, the economy will produce at potential output.

2. Monetarism focuses on the equation of exchange: $MV = PQ$. Because velocity is thought to be stable, changes in M create changes in nominal GDP ($= PQ$). Monetarists believe that the most significant cause of macroeconomic instability has been inappropriate monetary policy. Rapid increases in M cause inflation; insufficient growth of M causes recession. In this view, a major cause of the Great Depression was inappropriate monetary policy, which allowed the money supply to decline by roughly one-third.

3. Real-business-cycle theory views changes in resource availability and technology (real factors), which alter productivity, as the main causes of macroeconomic instability. In this theory, shifts of the economy's long-run aggregate supply curve change real output. In turn, money demand and money supply change, shifting the aggregate demand curve in the same direction as the initial change in long-run aggregate supply. Real output thus can change without a change in the price level.

4. A coordination failure is said to occur when people lack a way to coordinate their actions in order to achieve a mutually beneficial equilibrium. Depending on people's expectations, the economy can come to rest at either a good equilibrium (noninflationary full-employment output) or a bad equilibrium (less-than-full-employment output or demand-pull inflation). A bad equilibrium is a result of a coordination failure.

5. The rational expectations theory rests on two assumptions: (1) With sufficient information, people's beliefs about future economic outcomes accurately reflect the likelihood that those outcomes will occur; and (2) markets are highly competitive, and prices and wages are flexible both upward and downward.

6. New classical economists (monetarists and rational expectations theorists) see the economy as automatically correcting itself when disturbed from its full-employment level of real output. In RET, unanticipated changes in aggregate demand change the price level, and in the short run this leads firms to change output. But once the firms realize that all prices are changing (including nominal wages) as part of general inflation or deflation, they restore their output to the previous level. Anticipated changes in aggregate demand produce only changes in the price level, not changes in real output.

7. Mainstream economists reject the new classical view that all prices and wages are flexible downward. They contend that nominal wages, in particular, are inflexible downward because of several factors, including labor contracts, efficiency wages, and insider-outsider relationships. This means that declines in aggregate demand lower real output, not only wages and prices.

8. Monetarist and rational expectations economists say the Fed should adhere to some form of policy rule, rather than rely exclusively on discretion. The Friedman rule would direct the Fed to increase the money supply at a fixed annual rate equal to the long-run growth of potential GDP. An alternative approach—inflation targeting—would direct the Fed to establish a targeted range of inflation rates, say, 1 to 2 percent, and focus monetary policy on meeting that goal. They also support maintaining a "neutral" fiscal policy, as opposed to using discretionary fiscal policy to create budget deficits or budget surpluses. A few monetarists and rational expectations economists favor a constitutional amendment requiring that the Federal government balance its budget annually.

9. Mainstream economists oppose strict monetary rules and a balanced-budget requirement, and defend discretionary monetary and fiscal policies. They say that both theory and evidence suggest that such policies are helpful in achieving full employment, price stability, and economic growth.

Terms and Concepts

monetarism	rational expectations theory	insider-outsider theory
equation of exchange	new classical economics	monetary rule
velocity	price-level surprises	inflation targeting
real-business-cycle theory	efficiency wage	Taylor rule
coordination failures		

Study Questions

1. The mainstream view of macroeconomic instability empha-sizes sticky prices. To answer the following questions, modify the aggregate supply curve in the extended AD-AS model introduced in Chapter 35. First, imagine that both input and output prices are fixed. What does the aggregate supply curve look like? If AD decreases in this situation, what will happen to equilibrium output and the price level? Next, imagine that input prices are fixed, but output prices are flexible. What does the aggregate supply curve look like? In this case, if AD decreases, what will happen to equilibrium output and the price level? Finally, if both input and output prices are fully flexible, what does the aggregate supply curve look like? In this case, if AD decreases, what will hap-pen to equilibrium output and the price level? (Hint: If you are having trouble drawing these three aggregate supply curves, review the immediate-short-run aggregate supply curve and the short-run aggregate supply curve introduced in Chapter 29 as well as the long-run aggregate supply curve introduced in Chapter 35.) **LO1**

2. According to mainstream economists, what is the usual cause of macroeconomic instability? What role does the spending-income multiplier play in creating instability? How might adverse aggregate supply factors cause instabil-ity, according to mainstream economists? **LO1**

3. State and explain the basic equation of monetarism. What is the major cause of macroeconomic instability, as viewed by monetarists? **LO2**

4. **KEY QUESTION** Suppose that the money supply and the nominal GDP for a hypothetical economy are $96 billion and $336 billion, respectively. What is the velocity of money? How will households and businesses react if the central bank reduces the money supply by $20 billion? By how much will nominal GDP have to fall to restore equilib-rium, according to the monetarist perspective? **LO2**

5. Briefly describe the difference between a so-called real business cycle and a more traditional "spending" business cycle. **LO1**

6. Craig and Kris were walking directly toward each other in a congested store aisle. Craig moved to his left to avoid Kris, and at the same time Kris moved to his right to avoid Craig. They bumped into each other. What concept does this

example illustrate? How does this idea relate to macroeco-nomic instability? **LO1**

7. **KEY QUESTION** Use an AD-AS graph to demonstrate and explain the price-level and real-output outcome of an an-ticipated decline in aggregate demand, as viewed by RET economists. (Assume that the economy initially is operating at its full-employment level of output.) Then demonstrate and explain on the same graph the outcome as viewed by mainstream economists. **LO1**

8. What is an efficiency wage? How might payment of an above-market wage reduce shirking by employees and reduce worker turnover? How might efficiency wages contribute to downward wage inflexibility, at least for a time, when aggregate demand declines? **LO1**

9. How might relationships between so-called insiders and outsiders contribute to downward wage inflexibility? **LO1**

10. Use the equation of exchange to explain the rationale for a monetary rule. Why will such a rule run into trouble if V unexpectedly falls because of, say, a drop in investment spending by businesses? **LO2**

11. Answer parts *a* and *b*, below, on the basis of the following information for a hypothetical economy in year 1: money supply = $400 billion; long-term annual growth of potential GDP = 3 percent; velocity = 4. Assume that the banking system initially has no excess reserves and that the reserve requirement is 10 percent. Also assume that velocity is con-stant and that the economy initially is operating at its full-employment real output. **LO2**
    a. What is the level of nominal GDP in year 1?
    b. Suppose the Fed adheres to a monetary rule through open-market operations. What amount of U.S. securities will it have to sell to, or buy from, banks or the public between years 1 and 2 to meet its monetary rule?

12. Explain the difference between "active" discretionary fiscal policy advocated by mainstream economists and "passive" fiscal policy advocated by new classical economists. Explain: "The problem with a balanced-budget amendment is that it would, in a sense, require active fiscal policy—but in the wrong direction—as the economy slides into recession." **LO4**

13. **KEY QUESTION** Place "MON," "RET," or "MAIN" beside the statements that most closely reflect monetarist, rational expectations, or mainstream views, respectively: **LO1**
    a. Anticipated changes in aggregate demand affect only the price level; they have no effect on real output.
    b. Downward wage inflexibility means that declines in aggregate demand can cause long-lasting recession.
    c. Changes in the money supply M increase PQ; at first only Q rises because nominal wages are fixed, but once workers adapt their expectations to new realities, P rises and Q returns to its former level.
    d. Fiscal and monetary policies smooth out the business cycle.
    e. The Fed should increase the money supply at a fixed annual rate.

14. You have just been elected president of the United States, and the present chairperson of the Federal Reserve Board has resigned. You need to appoint a new person to this position, as well as a person to chair your Council of Economic Advisers. Using Table 36.1 and your knowledge of macroeconomics, identify the views on macro theory and policy you would want your appointees to hold. Remember, the economic health of the entire nation—and your chances for reelection—may depend on your selections. **LO1**

15. **LAST WORD** Compare and contrast the Taylor rule for monetary policy with the older, simpler monetary rule advocated by Milton Friedman.

Web-Based Question

1. **THE EQUATION OF EXCHANGE—WHAT IS THE CURRENT VELOCITY OF MONEY?** In the equation of exchange, $MV = PQ$, the velocity of money, V, is found by dividing nominal GDP ($= PQ$) by M, the money supply. Calculate the velocity of money for the past 4 years. How stable was V during that period? Is V increasing or decreasing? Get current-dollar GDP data from the Gross Domestic Product section at the Bureau of Economic Analysis Web site, **www.bea.gov.** Find $M1$ money supply data (seasonally adjusted) at the Fed's Web site, **www.federalreserve.gov,** by selecting, in sequence, Economic Research and Data, Statistical Releases and Historical Data, and Money Stock Measures—H6, then Historical Data.

FURTHER TEST YOUR KNOWLEDGE AT
www.mcconnell18e.com

PART TEN

International Economics

37

International Trade

The WTO, trade deficits, dumping. Exchange rates, the current account, the G8 nations. The IMF, official reserves, currency interventions. This is some of the language of international economics, the subject of Part 10. To understand the increasingly integrated world economy, we need to learn more about this language and the ideas that it conveys.

In this chapter we build on Chapter 5 by providing both a deeper analysis of the benefits of international trade and a fuller appraisal of the arguments for protectionism. Then in Chapter 38 we examine the U.S. balance of payments, exchange rates, and U.S. trade deficits.

Some Key Facts

In Chapter 5, we provided an abundance of statistical information about U.S. international trade. The following "executive summary" reviews the most important of those facts:

- A *trade deficit* occurs when imports exceed exports. The United States has a trade deficit in goods. In 2007, U.S. imports of goods exceeded U.S. exports of goods by $816 billion.
- A *trade surplus* occurs when exports exceed imports. The United States has a trade surplus in services (such as air transportation services and financial services). In 2007, U.S. exports of services exceeded U.S. imports of services by $107 billion.
- Principal U.S. exports include chemicals, agricultural products, consumer durables, semiconductors, and aircraft; principal imports include petroleum, automobiles, metals, household appliances, and computers.
- Like other advanced industrial nations, the United States imports some of the same categories of goods that it exports. Examples: automobiles, computers, chemicals, semiconductors, and telecommunications equipment.
- Canada is the United States' most important trading partner quantitatively. In 2007, about 22 percent of U.S. exported goods were sold to Canadians, who in turn provided 16 percent of the U.S. imports of goods.
- The United States has a sizable trade deficit with China. In 2007, it was $257 billion.
- The U.S. dependence on foreign oil is reflected in its trade with members of OPEC. In 2007, the United States imported $174 billion of goods (mainly oil) from OPEC members, while exporting $49 billion of goods to those countries.
- The United States leads the world in the combined volume of exports and imports, as measured in dollars. Germany, the United States, China, Japan, and France are the top five exporters by dollar volume (see Global Perspective 5.1, p. 95). Currently, the United States provides about 9 percent of the world's exports (see Global Perspective 37.1).
- Exports of goods and services (on a national income account basis) make up about 12 percent of total U.S. output. That percentage is much lower than the percentage in many other nations, including Canada, Italy, France, and the United Kingdom (see Table 5.1, p. 93).
- China has become a major international trader, with an estimated $1.2 trillion of exports in 2007. Other

GLOBAL PERSPECTIVE 37.1

Shares of World Exports, Selected Nations

Germany has the largest share of world exports, followed by the United States and China. The eight largest export nations account for nearly 50 percent of world exports.

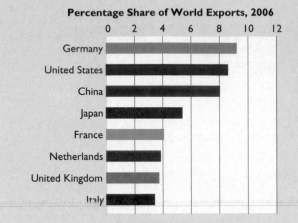

Percentage Share of World Exports, 2006

Source: World Trade Organization, **www.wto.org.** Used by permission.

Asian economies—including South Korea, Taiwan, and Singapore—are also active in international trade. Their combined exports exceed those of France, Britain, or Italy.

- International trade (and finance) links world economies (review Figure 5.1, p. 92). Through trade, changes in economic conditions in one place on the globe can quickly affect other places.
- International trade is often at the center of debates over economic policy, both within the United States and internationally.

With this information in mind, let's look more closely at the economics of international trade.

The Economic Basis for Trade

Chapter 5 revealed that international trade enables nations to specialize their production, enhance their resource productivity, and acquire more goods and services. Sovereign nations, like individuals and the regions of a nation, can gain by specializing in the products they can produce with greatest relative efficiency and by trading for the goods they cannot produce as efficiently. A more complete answer to the question "Why do nations trade?" hinges on three facts:

- The distribution of natural, human, and capital resources among nations is uneven; nations differ in their endowments of economic resources.

- Efficient production of various goods requires different technologies or combinations of resources.
- Products are differentiated as to quality and other nonprice attributes. A few or many people may prefer certain imported goods to similar goods made domestically.

To recognize the character and interaction of these three facts, think of Japan, for example, which has a large, well-educated labor force and abundant, and therefore inexpensive, skilled labor. As a result, Japan can produce efficiently (at low cost) a variety of **labor-intensive goods** such as digital cameras, video game players, and DVD players whose design and production require much skilled labor.

In contrast, Australia has vast amounts of land and can inexpensively produce such **land-intensive goods** as wheat, wool, and meat. Brazil has the soil, tropical climate, rainfall, and ready supply of unskilled labor that are needed for the efficient, low-cost production of coffee.

Industrially advanced economies with relatively large amounts of capital can inexpensively produce goods whose production requires much capital, including such **capital-intensive goods** as automobiles, agricultural equipment, machinery, and chemicals.

All nations, regardless of their labor, land, or capital intensity, can find special niches for individual products that are in demand worldwide because of their special qualities. Examples: fashions from Italy, luxury automobiles from Germany, software from the United States, and watches from Switzerland.

The distribution of resources, technology, and product distinctiveness among nations, however, is not forever fixed. When that distribution changes, the relative efficiency and success with which nations produce and sell goods also changes. For example, in the past few decades South Korea has upgraded the quality of its labor force and has greatly expanded its stock of capital. Although South Korea was primarily an exporter of agricultural products and raw materials a half-century ago, it now exports large quantities of manufactured goods. Similarly, the new technologies that gave us synthetic fibers and synthetic rubber drastically altered the resource mix needed to produce these goods and changed the relative efficiency of nations in manufacturing them.

As national economies evolve, the size and quality of their labor forces may change, the volume and composition of their capital stocks may shift, new technologies may develop, and even the quality of land and the quantity of natural resources may be altered. As such changes occur, the relative efficiency with which a nation can produce specific goods also will change.

Comparative Advantage: Graphical Analysis

Implicit in what we have been saying is the principle of comparative advantage, described through production possibilities tables in Chapter 5. Let's look again at that idea, now using graphical analysis.

Two Isolated Nations

Suppose the world economy is composed of just two nations: the United States and Brazil. Also for simplicity, suppose that the labor forces in the United States and Brazil are of equal size. Each nation can produce both wheat and coffee, but at different levels of economic efficiency. Suppose the U.S. and Brazilian domestic production possibilities curves for coffee and wheat are as shown in Figure 37.1a and 37.1b. Note especially three realities relating to these production possibilities curves:

- *Constant costs* The "curves" are drawn as straight lines, in contrast to the bowed-outward production possibilities frontiers we examined in Chapter 1. This means that we have replaced the law of increasing opportunity costs with the assumption of constant costs. This substitution simplifies our discussion but does not impair the validity of our analysis and conclusions. Later we will consider the effects of increasing opportunity costs.
- *Different costs* The production possibilities curves of the United States and Brazil reflect different resource mixes and differing levels of technological progress. Specifically, the differing slopes of the two curves tell us that the opportunity costs of producing wheat and coffee differ between the two nations.
- *U.S. absolute advantage in both* In view of our assumption that the U.S. and Brazilian labor forces are of equal size, the two production possibilities curves show that the United States has an *absolute advantage* in producing both products. If the United States and Brazil use their entire (equal-size) labor forces to produce either coffee or wheat, the United States can produce more of either than Brazil. The United States, using the same number of workers as Brazil, has greater production possibilities. So output per worker—labor productivity—in the United States exceeds that in Brazil in producing both products.

United States In Figure 37.1a, with full employment, the United States will operate on its production possibilities curve. On that curve, it can increase its output of wheat from 0 tons to 30 tons by forgoing 30 tons of coffee

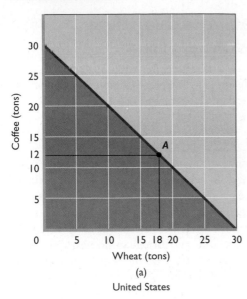

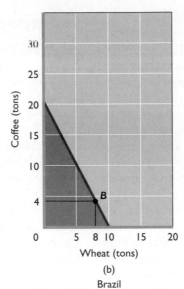

(a)
United States

(b)
Brazil

FIGURE 37.1 Production possibilities for the United States and Brazil. The two production possibilities curves show the combinations of coffee and wheat that (a) the United States and (b) Brazil can produce domestically. The curves for both countries are straight lines because we are assuming constant opportunity costs. The different cost ratios, 1 coffee ≡ 1 wheat for the United States, and 2 coffee ≡ 1 wheat for Brazil, are reflected in the different slopes of the two lines.

output. This means that the slope of the production possibilities curve is −1 (= −30 coffee/+30 wheat), implying that 1 ton of coffee must be sacrificed for each extra ton of wheat. In the United States the domestic exchange ratio or **opportunity-cost ratio** for the two products is 1 ton of coffee for 1 ton of wheat, or $1C \equiv 1W$. (As in Chapter 5, the "≡" sign simply means "equivalent to.") Within its borders, the United States can "exchange" a ton of coffee for a ton of wheat. Our constant-cost assumption means that this exchange or opportunity-cost equation prevails for all possible moves from one point to another along the U.S. production possibilities curve.

Brazil Brazil's production possibilities curve in Figure 37.1b represents a different full-employment opportunity-cost ratio. In Brazil, 20 tons of coffee must be given up to get 10 tons of wheat. The slope of the production possibilities curve is −2 (= −20 coffee/+10 wheat). This means that in Brazil the opportunity-cost ratio for the two goods is 2 tons of coffee for 1 ton of wheat, or $2C \equiv 1W$.

Self-Sufficiency Output Mix If the United States and Brazil are isolated and are to be self-sufficient, then each country must choose some output mix on its production possibilities curve. It will choose the mix that provides the greatest total utility, or satisfaction. Assume that point A in Figure 37.1a is the optimal mix in the United States; that is, society deems the combination of 18 tons of wheat and 12 tons of coffee preferable to any other combination of the goods available along the production possibilities curve. Suppose Brazil's optimal product mix is 8 tons of wheat and 4 tons of coffee, indicated by point B in Figure 37.1b. These choices are reflected in column 1 of Table 37.1.

Specializing Based on Comparative Advantage

Although the United States has an absolute advantage in producing both goods, gains from specialization and trade are possible. Specialization and trade are mutually

TABLE 37.1 International Specialization According to Comparative Advantage and the Gains from Trade

Country	(1) Outputs before Specialization	(2) Outputs after Specialization	(3) Amounts Exported (−) and Imported (+)	(4) Outputs Available after Trade	(5) Gains from Specialization and Trade (4) − (1)
United States	18 wheat 12 coffee	30 wheat 0 coffee	−10 wheat +15 coffee	20 wheat 15 coffee	2 wheat 3 coffee
Brazil	8 wheat 4 coffee	0 wheat 20 coffee	+10 wheat −15 coffee	10 wheat 5 coffee	2 wheat 1 coffee

beneficial, or profitable, to the two nations if the *comparative* opportunity costs of producing the two products within the two nations differ, as they do in this example. The **principle of comparative advantage** *says that total output will be greatest when each good is produced by the nation that has the lowest domestic opportunity cost for that good.* In our two-nation illustration, the United States has the lower domestic opportunity cost for wheat; the United States need

ORIGIN OF THE IDEA
O 37.1
Comparative advantage

forgo only 1 ton of coffee to produce 1 ton of wheat, whereas Brazil must forgo 2 tons of coffee for 1 ton of wheat. The United States has a comparative (cost) advantage in wheat and should specialize in wheat production. The "world" (that is, the United States and Brazil) in our example would clearly not be economizing in the use of its resources if a high-cost producer (Brazil) produced a specific product (wheat) when a low-cost producer (the United States) could have produced it. Having Brazil produce wheat would mean that the world economy would have to give up more coffee than is necessary to obtain a ton of wheat.

Brazil has the lower domestic opportunity cost for coffee; it must sacrifice only $\frac{1}{2}$ ton of wheat in producing 1 ton of coffee, while the United States must forgo 1 ton of wheat in producing a ton of coffee. Brazil has a comparative advantage in coffee and should specialize in coffee production. Again, the world would not be employing its resources economically if coffee were produced by a high-cost producer (the United States) rather than by a low-cost producer (Brazil). If the United States produced coffee, the world would be giving up more wheat than necessary to obtain each ton of coffee. Economizing requires that any particular good be produced by the nation having the lowest domestic opportunity cost, or the comparative advantage for that good. The United States should produce wheat and Brazil should produce coffee.

In column 2 of Table 37.1 we verify that specialized production enables the world to get more output from its fixed amount of resources. By specializing completely in wheat, the United States can produce 30 tons of wheat and no coffee. Brazil, by specializing completely in coffee, can produce 20 tons of coffee and no wheat. The world ends up with 4 more tons of wheat (30 tons compared with 26) *and* 4 more tons of coffee (20 tons compared with 16) than it would if there were self-sufficiency or unspecialized production.

Terms of Trade

But consumers of each nation want both wheat *and* coffee. They can have both if the two nations trade the two products. But what will be the **terms of trade?** At what

exchange ratio will the United States and Brazil trade wheat and coffee?

Because $1W \equiv 1C$ in the United States, the United States must get *more than* 1 ton of coffee for each ton of wheat exported; otherwise, it will not benefit from exporting wheat in exchange for Brazilian coffee. The United States must get a better "price" (more coffee) for its wheat in the world market than it can get domestically; otherwise, there is no gain from trade and it will not occur.

Similarly, because $1W \equiv 2C$ in Brazil, Brazil must get 1 ton of wheat by exporting some amount *less than* 2 tons of coffee. Brazil must be able to pay a lower "price" for wheat in the world market than it must pay domestically, or else it will not want to trade. The international exchange ratio or terms of trade must lie somewhere between

$$1W \equiv 1C \text{ (United States' cost conditions)}$$

and

$$1W \equiv 2C \text{ (Brazil's cost conditions)}$$

But where between these limits will the world exchange ratio fall? The United States will prefer a rate close to $1W \equiv 2C$, say, $1W \equiv 1\frac{3}{4}C$. The United States wants to get as much coffee as possible for each ton of wheat it exports. Similarly, Brazil wants a rate near $1W \equiv 1C$, say, $1W \equiv 1\frac{1}{4}C$. Brazil wants to export as little coffee as possible for each ton of wheat it receives in exchange. The exchange ratio or terms of trade determine how the gains from international specialization and trade are divided between the two nations.

The actual exchange ratio depends on world supply and demand for the two products. If overall world demand for coffee is weak relative to its supply and if the demand for wheat is strong relative to its supply, the price of coffee will be lower and the price of wheat higher. The exchange ratio will settle nearer the $1W \equiv 2C$ figure the United States prefers. If overall world demand for coffee is great relative to its supply and if the demand for wheat is weak relative to its supply, the ratio will settle nearer the $1W \equiv 1C$ level favorable to Brazil. (We discuss equilibrium world prices later in this chapter.)

Gains from Trade

Suppose the international terms of trade are $1W \equiv 1\frac{1}{2}C$. The possibility of trading on these terms permits each nation to supplement its domestic production possibilities curve with a **trading possibilities line** (or curve), as shown in **Figure 37.2 (Key Graph).** Just as a production possibilities curve shows the amounts of these products a full-employment economy can obtain by shifting resources from one to the other, a trading possibilities line shows the amounts of two products a nation can obtain by specializing

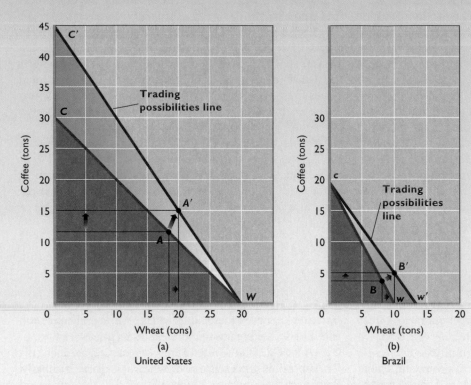

FIGURE 37.2 Trading possibilities lines and the gains from trade. As a result of specialization and trade, both the United States and Brazil can have higher levels of output than the levels attainable on their domestic production possibilities curves. (a) The United States can move from point A on its domestic production possibilities curve to, say, A' on its trading possibilities line. (b) Brazil can move from B to B'.

QUICK QUIZ FOR FIGURE 37.2

1. The production possibilities curves in graphs (a) and (b) imply:
   a. increasing domestic opportunity costs.
   b. decreasing domestic opportunity costs.
   c. constant domestic opportunity costs.
   d. first decreasing, then increasing, domestic opportunity costs.

2. Before specialization, the domestic opportunity cost of producing 1 unit of wheat is:
   a. 1 unit of coffee in both the United States and Brazil.
   b. 1 unit of coffee in the United States and 2 units of coffee in Brazil.
   c. 2 units of coffee in the United States and 1 unit of coffee in Brazil.
   d. 1 unit of coffee in the United States and $\frac{1}{2}$ unit of coffee in Brazil.

3. After specialization and international trade, the world output of wheat and coffee is:
   a. 20 tons of wheat and 20 tons of coffee.
   b. 45 tons of wheat and 15 tons of coffee.
   c. 30 tons of wheat and 20 tons of coffee.
   d. 10 tons of wheat and 30 tons of coffee.

4. After specialization and international trade:
   a. the United States can obtain units of coffee at less cost than it could before trade.
   b. Brazil can obtain more than 20 tons of coffee, if it so chooses.
   c. the United States no longer has a comparative advantage in producing wheat.
   d. Brazil can benefit by prohibiting coffee imports from the United States.

Answers: 1. c; 2. b; 3. c; 4. a

in one product and trading for the other. The trading possibilities lines in Figure 37.2 reflect the assumption that both nations specialize on the basis of comparative advantage: The United States specializes completely in wheat (at point *W* in Figure 37.2a), and Brazil specializes completely in coffee (at point *c* in Figure 37.2b).

Improved Options Now the United States is not constrained by its domestic production possibilities line,

which requires it to give up 1 ton of wheat for every ton of coffee it wants as it moves up its domestic production possibilities line from, say, point *W*. Instead, the United States, through trade with Brazil, can get $1\frac{1}{2}$ tons of coffee for every ton of wheat it exports to Brazil, as long as Brazil has coffee to export. Trading possibilities line *WC'* thus represents the $1W \equiv 1\frac{1}{2}C$ trading ratio.

Similarly, Brazil, starting at, say, point *c*, no longer has to move down its domestic production possibilities curve, giving up 2 tons of coffee for each ton of wheat it wants. It can now export just $1\frac{1}{2}$ tons of coffee for each ton of wheat it wants by moving down its trading possibilities line cw'.

Specialization and trade create a new exchange ratio between wheat and coffee, reflected in each nation's trading possibilities line. This exchange ratio is superior for both nations to the unspecialized exchange ratio embodied in their production possibilities curves. By specializing in wheat and trading for Brazil's coffee, the United States can obtain more than 1 ton of coffee for 1 ton of wheat. By specializing in coffee and trading for U.S. wheat, Brazil can get 1 ton of wheat for less than 2 tons of coffee. In both cases, self-sufficiency is undesirable.

Added Output
By specializing on the basis of comparative advantage and by trading for goods that are produced in the nation with greater domestic efficiency, the United States and Brazil can realize combinations of wheat and coffee beyond their production possibilities curves. Specialization according to comparative advantage results in a more efficient allocation of world resources, and larger outputs of both products are therefore available to both nations.

Suppose that at the $1W \equiv 1\frac{1}{2}C$ terms of trade, the United States exports 10 tons of wheat to Brazil and in return Brazil exports 15 tons of coffee to the United States. How do the new quantities of wheat and coffee available to the two nations compare with the optimal product mixes that existed before specialization and trade? Point A in Figure 37.2a reminds us that the United States chose 18 tons of wheat and 12 tons of coffee originally. But by producing 30 tons of wheat and no coffee and by trading 10 tons of wheat for 15 tons of coffee, the United States can obtain 20 tons of wheat and 15 tons of coffee. This new, superior combination of wheat and coffee is indicated by point A' in Figure 37.2a. Compared with the no-trade amounts of 18 tons of wheat and 12 tons of coffee, the United States' **gains from trade** are 2 tons of wheat and 3 tons of coffee.

Similarly, recall that Brazil's optimal product mix was 4 tons of coffee and 8 tons of wheat (point B) before specialization and trade. Now, after specializing in coffee and trading, Brazil can have 5 tons of coffee and 10 tons of wheat. It accomplishes that by producing 20 tons of coffee and no wheat and exporting 15 tons of its coffee in exchange for 10 tons of American wheat. This new position is indicated by point B' in Figure 37.2b. Brazil's gains from trade are 1 ton of coffee and 2 tons of wheat.

As a result of specialization and trade, both countries have more of both products. Table 37.1, which summarizes the transactions and outcomes, merits careful study.

The fact that points A' and B' are economic positions superior to A and B is enormously important. We know that

a nation can expand its production possibilities boundary by (1) expanding the quantity and improving the quality of its resources or (2) realizing technological progress. We have now established that international trade can enable a nation to circumvent the output constraint illustrated by its production possibilities curve. The outcome of international specialization and trade is equivalent to having more and better resources or discovering improved production techniques.

INTERACTIVE GRAPHS

G 37.1

Comparative Advantage

WORKED PROBLEMS

W 37.1

Gains from trade

Trade with Increasing Costs

To explain the basic principles underlying international trade, we simplified our analysis in several ways. For example, we limited discussion to two products and two nations. But multiproduct and multinational analysis yields the same conclusions. We also assumed constant opportunity costs (linear production possibilities curves), which is a more substantive simplification. Let's consider the effect of allowing increasing opportunity costs (concave-to-the-origin production possibilities curves) to enter the picture.

Suppose that the United States and Brazil initially are at positions on their concave production possibilities curves where their domestic cost ratios are $1W \equiv 1C$ and $1W \equiv 2C$, as they were in our constant-cost analysis. As before, comparative advantage indicates that the United States should specialize in wheat and Brazil in coffee. But now, as the United States begins to expand wheat production, its cost of wheat will rise; it will have to sacrifice more than 1 ton of coffee to get 1 additional ton of wheat. Resources are no longer perfectly substitutable between alternative uses, as the constant-cost assumption implied. Resources less and less suitable to wheat production must be allocated to the U.S. wheat industry in expanding wheat output, and that means increasing costs—the sacrifice of larger and larger amounts of coffee for each additional ton of wheat.

Similarly, Brazil, starting from its $1W \equiv 2C$ cost ratio position, expands coffee production. But as it does, it will find that its $1W \equiv 2C$ cost ratio begins to rise. Sacrificing a ton of wheat will free resources that are capable of producing only something less than 2 tons of coffee because those transferred resources are less suitable to coffee production.

As the U.S. cost ratio falls from $1W \equiv 1C$ and the Brazilian ratio rises from $1W \equiv 2C$, a point will be reached where the cost ratios are equal in the two nations, perhaps at $1W \equiv 1\frac{3}{4}C$. At this point the underlying basis for further specialization and trade—differing cost ratios—has disappeared, and further specialization is therefore uneconomical. And, most important, this point of equal cost ratios may be reached while the United States is still producing some coffee along with its wheat and Brazil is producing some wheat along with its coffee. The primary effect of increasing opportunity costs is less-than-complete specialization. For this reason, we often find domestically produced products competing directly against identical or similar imported products within a particular economy. (Key Question 4)

The Case for Free Trade

The case for free trade reduces to one compelling argument: Through free trade based on the principle of comparative advantage, the world economy can achieve a more efficient allocation of resources and a higher level of material well-being than it can without free trade.

Since the resource mixes and technological knowledge of the world's nations are all somewhat different, each nation can produce particular commodities at different real costs. Each nation should produce goods for which its domestic opportunity costs are lower than the domestic opportunity costs of other nations and exchange those goods for products for which its domestic opportunity costs are high relative to those of other nations. If each nation does this, the world will realize the advantages of geographic and human specialization. The world and each free-trading nation can obtain a larger real income from the fixed supplies of resources available to it.

Government trade barriers lessen or eliminate gains from specialization. If nations cannot trade freely, they must shift resources from efficient (low-cost) to inefficient (high-cost) uses in order to satisfy their diverse wants. A recent study suggests that the elimination of trade barriers since the Second World War has increased the income of the average U.S. household by at least $7000 and perhaps by as much as $13,000. These income gains are recurring; they happen year after year.[1]

One side benefit of free trade is that it promotes competition and deters monopoly. The increased competition from foreign firms forces domestic firms to find and use the lowest-cost production techniques. It also compels them to be innovative with respect to both product quality and production methods, thereby contributing to economic growth. And free trade gives consumers a wider range of product choices. The reasons to favor free trade are the same as the reasons to endorse competition.

---

[1]Scott C. Bradford, Paul L. E. Grieco, and Gary C. Hufbauer, "The Payoff to American from Globalization," *The World Economy*, July 2006, pp. 893–916.

A second side benefit of free trade is that it links national interests and breaks down national animosities. Confronted with political disagreements, trading partners tend to negotiate rather than make war.

QUICK REVIEW 37.1

- International trade enables nations to specialize, increase productivity, and increase output available for consumption.
- Comparative advantage means total world output will be greatest when each good is produced by the nation that has the lowest domestic opportunity cost.
- Specialization is less than complete among nations because opportunity costs normally rise as any given nation produces more of a particular good.

Supply and Demand Analysis of Exports and Imports

Supply and demand analysis reveals how equilibrium prices and quantities of exports and imports are determined. The amount of a good or a service a nation will export or import depends on differences between the equilibrium world price and the equilibrium domestic price. The interaction of *world* supply and demand determines the equilibrium **world price**—the price that equates the quantities supplied and demanded globally. *Domestic* supply and demand determine the equilibrium **domestic price**—the price that would prevail in a closed economy that does not engage in international trade. The domestic price equates quantity supplied and quantity demanded domestically.

In the absence of trade, the domestic prices in a closed economy may or may not equal the world equilibrium prices. When economies are opened for international trade, differences between world and domestic prices encourage exports or imports. To see how, consider the international effects of such price differences in a simple two-nation world, consisting of the United States and Canada, that are both producing aluminum. We assume there are no trade barriers, such as tariffs and quotas, and no international transportation costs.

Supply and Demand in the United States

Figure 37.3a shows the domestic supply curve S_d and the domestic demand curve D_d for aluminum in the United States, which for now is a closed economy. The intersection of S_d and D_d determines the equilibrium domestic price of $1 per pound and the equilibrium domestic

FIGURE 37.3 U.S. export supply and import demand. (a) Domestic supply S_d and demand D_d set the domestic equilibrium price of aluminum at $1 per pound. At world prices above $1 there are domestic surpluses of aluminum. At prices below $1 there are domestic shortages. (b) Surpluses are exported (top curve), and shortages are met by importing aluminum (lower curve). The export supply curve shows the direct relationship between world prices and U.S. exports; the import demand curve portrays the inverse relationship between world prices and U.S. imports.

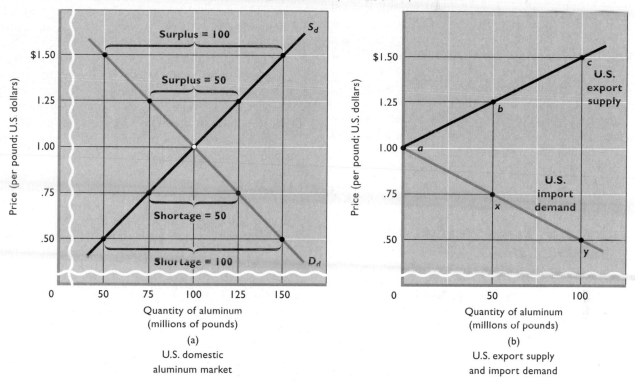

Quantity of aluminum
(millions of pounds)
(a)
U.S. domestic
aluminum market

Quantity of aluminum
(millions of pounds)
(b)
U.S. export supply
and import demand

quantity of 100 million pounds. Domestic suppliers produce 100 million pounds and sell them all at $1 a pound. So there are no domestic surpluses or shortages of aluminum.

But what if the U.S. economy were opened to trade and the world price of aluminum were above or below this $1 domestic price?

U.S. Export Supply
If the aluminum price in the rest of the world (that is, Canada) exceeds $1, U.S. firms will produce more than 100 million pounds and will export the excess domestic output. First, consider a world price of $1.25. We see from the supply curve S_d that U.S. aluminum firms will produce 125 million pounds of aluminum at that price. The demand curve D_d tells us that the United States will purchase only 75 million pounds at $1.25. The outcome is a domestic surplus of 50 million pounds of aluminum. U.S. producers will export those 50 million pounds at the $1.25 world price.

What if the world price were $1.50? The supply curve shows that U.S. firms will produce 150 million pounds of aluminum, while the demand curve tells us that U.S. consumers will buy only 50 million pounds. So U.S. producers will export the domestic surplus of 100 million pounds.

Toward the top of Figure 37.3b we plot the domestic surpluses—the U.S. exports—that occur at world prices above the $1 domestic equilibrium price. When the world and domestic prices are equal (= $1), the quantity of exports supplied is zero (point a). There is no surplus of domestic output to export. But when the world price is $1.25, U.S. firms export 50 million pounds of surplus aluminum (point b). At a $1.50 world price, the domestic surplus of 100 million pounds is exported (point c).

The U.S. **export supply curve,** found by connecting points a, b, and c, shows the amount of aluminum U.S. producers will export at each world price above $1. This curve *slopes upward,* indicating a direct or positive relationship between the world price and the amount of U.S. exports. As world prices increase relative to domestic prices, U.S. exports rise.

U.S. Import Demand
If the world price is below the domestic $1 price, the United States will import aluminum. Consider a $.75 world price. The supply curve in Figure 37.3a reveals that at that price U.S. firms produce only 75 million pounds of aluminum. But the demand curve shows that the United States wants to buy 125 million

pounds at that price. The result is a domestic shortage of 50 million pounds. To satisfy that shortage, the United States will import 50 million pounds of aluminum.

At an even lower world price, $.50, U.S. producers will supply only 50 million pounds. Because U.S. consumers want to buy 150 million pounds at that price, there is a domestic shortage of 100 million pounds. Imports will flow to the United States to make up the difference. That is, at a $.50 world price U.S. firms will supply 50 million pounds and 100 million pounds will be imported.

In Figure 37.3b we plot the U.S. **import demand curve** from these data. This *downsloping curve* shows the amounts of aluminum that will be imported at world prices below the $1 U.S. domestic price. The relationship between world prices and imported amounts is inverse or negative. At a world price of $1, domestic output will satisfy U.S. demand; imports will be zero (point *a*). But at $.75 the United States will import 50 million pounds of aluminum (point *x*); at $.50, the United States will import 100 million pounds (point *y*). Connecting points *a*, *x*, and *y* yields the *downsloping* U.S. import demand curve. It reveals that as world prices fall relative to U.S. domestic prices, U.S. imports increase.

Supply and Demand in Canada

We repeat our analysis in Figure 37.4, this time from the viewpoint of Canada. (We have converted Canadian dollar prices to U.S. dollar prices via the exchange rate.) Note that the domestic supply curve S_d and the domestic demand curve D_d for aluminum in Canada yield a domestic price of $.75, which is $.25 lower than the $1 U.S. domestic price.

The analysis proceeds exactly as above except that the domestic price is now the Canadian price. If the world price is $.75, Canadians will neither export nor import aluminum (giving us point *q* in Figure 37.4b). At world prices above $.75, Canadian firms will produce more aluminum than Canadian consumers will buy. Canadian firms will export the surplus. At a $1 world price, Figure 37.4b tells us that Canada will have and export a domestic surplus of 50 million pounds (yielding point *r*). At $1.25, it will have and will export a domestic surplus of 100 million pounds (point *s*). Connecting these points yields the upsloping Canadian export supply curve, which reflects the domestic surpluses (and hence the exports) that occur when the world price exceeds the $.75 Canadian domestic price.

FIGURE 37.4 Canadian export supply and import demand. (a) At world prices above the $.75 domestic price, production in Canada exceeds domestic consumption. At world prices below $.75, domestic shortages occur. (b) Surpluses result in exports, and shortages result in imports. The Canadian export supply curve and import demand curve depict the relationships between world prices and exports or imports.

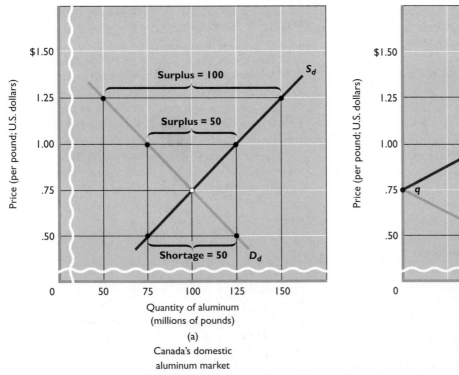

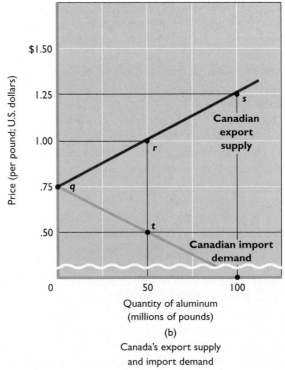

(a)
Canada's domestic
aluminum market

(b)
Canada's export supply
and import demand

At world prices below $.75, domestic shortages occur in Canada. At a $.50 world price, Figure 37.4a shows that Canadian consumers want to buy 125 million pounds of aluminum but Canadian firms will produce only 75 million pounds. The shortage will bring 50 million pounds of imports to Canada (point *t* in Figure 37.4b). The Canadian import demand curve in that figure shows the Canadian imports that will occur at all world aluminum prices below the $.75 Canadian domestic price.

Equilibrium World Price, Exports, and Imports

We now have the tools for determining the **equilibrium world price** of aluminum and the equilibrium world levels of exports and imports when the world is opened to trade. Figure 37.5 combines the U.S. export supply curve and import demand curve in Figure 37.3b and the Canadian export supply curve and import demand curve in Figure 37.4b. The two U.S. curves proceed rightward from the $1 U.S. domestic price; the two Canadian curves proceed rightward from the $.75 Canadian domestic price.

International equilibrium occurs in this two-nation model where one nation's import demand curve intersects another nation's export supply curve. In this case the U.S.

FIGURE 37.5 Equilibrium world price and quantity of exports and imports. In a two-nation world, the equilibrium world price (= $.88) is determined by the intersection of one nation's export supply curve and the other nation's import demand curve. This intersection also decides the equilibrium volume of exports and imports. Here, Canada exports 25 million pounds of aluminum to the United States.

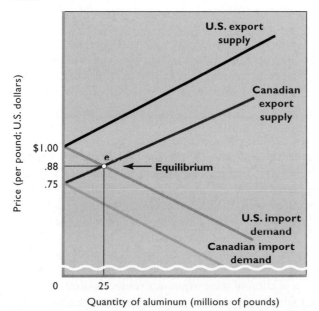

Quantity of aluminum (millions of pounds)

import demand curve intersects Canada's export supply curve at *e*. There, the world price of aluminum is $.88. The Canadian export supply curve indicates that Canada will export 25 million pounds of aluminum at this price. Also at this price the United States will import 25 million pounds from Canada, indicated by the U.S. import demand curve. The $.88 world price equates the quantity of imports demanded and the quantity of exports supplied (25 million pounds). Thus, there will be world trade of 25 million pounds of aluminum at $.88 per pound.

Note that after trade, the single $.88 world price will prevail in both Canada and the United States. Only one price for a standardized commodity can persist in a highly competitive world market. With trade, all consumers can buy a pound of aluminum for $.88, and all producers can sell it for that price. This world price means that Canadians will pay more for aluminum with trade ($.88) than without it ($.75). The increased Canadian output caused by trade raises Canadian per-unit production costs and therefore raises the price of aluminum in Canada. The United States, however, pays less for aluminum with trade ($.88) than without it ($1). The U.S. gain comes from Canada's comparative cost advantage in producing aluminum.

Why would Canada willingly send 25 million pounds of its aluminum output to the United States for U.S. consumption? After all, producing this output uses up scarce Canadian resources and drives up the price of aluminum for Canadians. Canadians are willing to export aluminum to the United States because Canadians gain the means— the U.S. dollars—to import other goods, say, computer software, from the United States. Canadian exports enable Canadians to acquire imports that have greater value to Canadians than the exported aluminum. Canadian exports to the United States finance Canadian imports from the United States. **(Key Question 6)**

Trade Barriers

No matter how compelling the case for free trade, barriers to free trade *do* exist. Let's expand Chapter 5's discussion of trade barriers.

Excise taxes on imported goods are called **tariffs;** they may be imposed to obtain revenue or to protect domestic firms. A **revenue tariff** is usually applied to a product that is not being produced domestically, for example, tin, coffee, or bananas in the case of the United States. Rates on revenue tariffs are modest; their purpose is to provide the Federal government with revenue. A **protective tariff** is designed to shield domestic producers from foreign competition. Although protective tariffs are usually not high enough to stop the importation of foreign goods, they put foreign producers at a competitive disadvantage in selling in domestic markets.

An **import quota** specifies the maximum amount of a commodity that may be imported in any period. Import quotas can more effectively retard international commerce than tariffs. A product might be imported in large quantities despite high tariffs; low import quotas completely prohibit imports once quotas have been filled.

A **nontariff barrier (NTB)** refers either to a licensing requirement that specifies unreasonable standards pertaining to product quality and safety, or to unnecessary bureaucratic red tape that is used to restrict imports. Japan and the European countries frequently require that their domestic importers of foreign goods obtain licenses. By restricting the issuance of licenses, imports can be restricted. The United Kingdom uses this barrier to bar the importation of coal.

A **voluntary export restriction (VER)** is a trade barrier by which foreign firms "voluntarily" limit the amount of their exports to a particular country. VERs, which have the effect of import quotas, are agreed to by exporters in the hope of avoiding more stringent trade barriers. In the late 1990s, for example, Canadian producers of softwood lumber (fir, spruce, cedar, pine) agreed to a VER on exports to the United States under the threat of a permanently higher U.S. tariff. Later in this chapter we will consider the arguments and appeals that are made to justify protection.

> **ORIGIN OF THE IDEA**
>
> **O 37.2**
>
> Mercantilism

Economic Impact of Tariffs

Once again we turn to supply and demand analysis—now to examine the economic effects of protective tariffs. Curves D_d and S_d in Figure 37.6 show domestic demand and supply for a product in which a nation, say, the United States, has a comparative disadvantage—for example, digital versatile

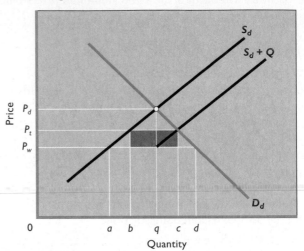

FIGURE 37.6 The economic effects of a protective tariff or an import quota. A tariff that increases the price of a good from P_w to P_t will reduce domestic consumption from d to c. Domestic producers will be able to sell more output (b rather than a) at a higher price (P_t rather than P_w). Foreign exporters are injured because they sell less output (bc rather than ad). The brown area indicates the amount of tariff paid by domestic consumers. An import quota of bc units has the same effect as the tariff, with one exception: The amount represented by the brown area will go to foreign producers rather than to the domestic government.

disk (DVD) players. (Disregard curve $S_d + Q$ for now.) Without world trade, the domestic price and output would be P_d and q, respectively.

Assume now that the domestic economy is opened to world trade and that the Japanese, who have a comparative advantage in DVD players, begin to sell their players in the United States. We assume that with free trade the domestic price cannot differ from the world price, which here is P_w. At P_w domestic consumption is d and domestic production is a. The horizontal distance between the domestic supply and demand curves at P_w represents imports of ad. Thus far, our analysis is similar to the analysis of world prices in Figure 37.3.

Direct Effects

Suppose now that the United States imposes a tariff on each imported DVD player. The tariff, which raises the price of imported players from P_w to P_t, has four effects:

- *Decline in consumption* Consumption of DVD players in the United States declines from d to c as the higher price moves buyers up and to the left along their demand curve. The tariff prompts consumers to buy fewer players, and reallocate a portion of their expenditures to less desired substitute products. U.S. consumers are clearly injured by the tariff, since they pay P_wP_t more for each of the c units they buy at price P_t.

- **Increased domestic production** U.S. producers—who are not subject to the tariff—receive the higher price P_t per unit. Because this new price is higher than the pretariff world price P_w, the domestic DVD-player industry moves up and to the right along its supply curve S_d, increasing domestic output from a to b. Domestic producers thus enjoy both a higher price and expanded sales; this explains why domestic producers lobby for protective tariffs. But from a social point of view, the greater domestic production from a to b means that the tariff permits domestic producers of players to bid resources away from other, more efficient, U.S. industries.

- **Decline in imports** Japanese producers are hurt. Although the sales price of each player is higher by P_wP_t, that amount accrues to the U.S. government, not to Japanese producers. The after-tariff world price, or the per-unit revenue to Japanese producers, remains at P_w, but the volume of U.S. imports (Japanese exports) falls from ad to bc.

- **Tariff revenue** The brown rectangle represents the amount of revenue the tariff yields. Total revenue from the tariff is determined by multiplying the tariff, P_wP_t per unit, by the number of players imported, bc. This tariff revenue is a transfer of income from consumers to government and does not represent any net change in the nation's economic well-being. The result is that government gains this portion of what consumers lose by paying more for DVD players.

Indirect Effect Tariffs have a subtle effect beyond what our supply and demand diagram can show. Because Japan sells fewer DVD players in the United States, it earns fewer dollars and so must buy fewer U.S. exports. U.S. export industries must then cut production and release resources. These are highly efficient industries, as we know from their comparative advantage and their ability to sell goods in world markets.

Tariffs directly promote the expansion of inefficient industries that do not have a comparative advantage; they also indirectly cause the contraction of relatively efficient industries that do have a comparative advantage. Put bluntly, tariffs cause resources to be shifted in the wrong direction—and that is not surprising. We know that specialization and world trade lead to more efficient use of world resources and greater world output. But protective tariffs reduce world trade. Therefore, tariffs also reduce efficiency and the world's real output.

Economic Impact of Quotas

We noted earlier that an import quota is a legal limit placed on the amount of some product that can be imported in a given year. Quotas have the same economic impact as a tariff, with one big difference: While tariffs generate revenue for the domestic government, a quota transfers that revenue to foreign producers.

Suppose in Figure 37.6 that, instead of imposing a tariff, the United States prohibits any imports of Japanese DVD players in excess of bc units. In other words, an import quota of bc players is imposed on Japan. We deliberately chose the size of this quota to be the same amount as imports would be under a P_wP_t tariff so that we can compare "equivalent" situations. As a consequence of the quota, the supply of players is $S_d + Q$ in the United States. This supply consists of the domestic supply plus the fixed amount $bc (= Q)$ that importers will provide at each domestic price. The supply curve $S_d + Q$ does not extend below price P_w because Japanese producers would not export players to the United States at any price below P_w; instead, they would sell them to other countries at the world market price of P_w.

Most of the economic results are the same as those with a tariff. Prices of DVD players are higher (P_t instead of P_w) because imports have been reduced from ad to bc. Domestic consumption of DVD players is down from d to c. U.S. producers enjoy both a higher price (P_t rather than P_w) and increased sales (b rather than a).

The difference is that the price increase of P_wP_t paid by U.S. consumers on imports of bc—the brown area—no longer goes to the U.S. Treasury as tariff (tax) revenue but flows to the Japanese firms that have acquired the quota rights to sell DVD players in the United States. For consumers in the United States, a tariff produces a better economic outcome than a quota, other things being the same. A tariff generates government revenue that can be used to cut other taxes or to finance public goods and services that benefit the United States. In contrast, the higher price created by quotas results in additional revenue for foreign producers. **(Key Question 7)**

Net Costs of Tariffs and Quotas

Figure 37.6 shows that tariffs and quotas impose costs on domestic consumers but provide gains to domestic producers and, in the case of tariffs, revenue to the Federal government. The consumer costs of trade restrictions are calculated by determining the effect the restrictions have on consumer prices. Protection raises the price of a product in three ways: (1) The price of the imported product goes up; (2) the higher price of imports causes some consumers to shift their purchases to higher-priced domestically produced goods; and (3) the prices of domestically produced goods rise because import competition has declined.

Study after study finds that the costs to consumers substantially exceed the gains to producers and government. A sizable net cost or efficiency loss to society arises from trade protection. Furthermore, industries employ large amounts of economic resources to influence Congress to pass and retain protectionist laws. Because these rent-seeking efforts divert resources away from more socially desirable purposes, trade restrictions impose these additional costs on society as well.

Conclusion: The gains that U.S. trade barriers create for protected industries and their workers come at the expense of much greater losses for the entire economy. The result is economic inefficiency, reduced consumption, and lower standards of living.

The Case for Protection: A Critical Review

Despite the logic of specialization and trade, there are still protectionists in some union halls, corporate boardrooms, and congressional conference rooms. What arguments do protectionists make to justify trade barriers? How valid are those arguments?

Military Self-Sufficiency Argument

The argument here is not economic but political-military: Protective tariffs are needed to preserve or strengthen industries that produce the materials essential for national defense. In an uncertain world, the political-military objectives (self-sufficiency) sometimes must take precedence over economic goals (efficiency in the use of world resources).

Unfortunately, it is difficult to measure and compare the benefit of increased national security against the cost of economic inefficiency when protective tariffs are imposed. The economist can only point out that when a nation levies tariffs to increase military self-sufficiency it incurs economic costs.

All people in the United States would agree that relying on hostile nations for necessary military equipment is not a good idea, yet the self-sufficiency argument is open to serious abuse. Nearly every industry can claim that it makes direct or indirect contributions to national security and hence deserves protection from imports.

Are there not better ways than tariffs to provide needed strength in strategic industries? When it is achieved through tariffs, this self-sufficiency increases the domestic prices of the products of the protected industry. Thus only those consumers who buy the industry's products shoulder the cost of greater military security. A direct subsidy to strategic industries, financed out of general tax revenues, would distribute those costs more equitably.

CONSIDER THIS . . .

Shooting Yourself in the Foot

In the lore of the Wild West, a gunslinger on occasion would accidentally pull the trigger on his pistol while retrieving it from its holster, shooting himself in the foot. Since then, the phrase "shooting yourself in the foot" implies doing damage to yourself rather than the intended party.

That is precisely how economist Paul Krugman sees a trade war:

> A trade war in which countries restrict each other's exports in pursuit of some illusory advantage is not much like a real war. On the one hand, nobody gets killed. On the other, unlike real wars, it is almost impossible for anybody to win, since the main losers when a country imposes barriers to trade are not foreign exporters but domestic residents. In effect, a trade war is a conflict in which each country uses most of its ammunition to shoot itself in the foot.*

The same analysis is applicable to trade boycotts between major trading partners. Such a boycott was encouraged by some American commentators against French imports because of the opposition of France to the U.S.- and British-led war in Iraq. But the decline of exports to the United States would leave the French with fewer U.S. dollars to buy American exports. So the unintended effect would be a decline in U.S. exports to France and reduced employment in U.S. export industries. Moreover, such a trade boycott, if effective, might lead French consumers to retaliate against American imports. As with a "tariff war," a "boycott war" typically harms oneself as much as the other party.

---

*Paul Krugman, *Peddling Prosperity* (New York: Norton, 1994), p. 287.

Diversification-for-Stability Argument

Highly specialized economies such as Saudi Arabia (based on oil) and Cuba (based on sugar) are dependent on international markets for their income. In these economies, wars, international political developments, recessions abroad, and random fluctuations in world supply and demand for one or two particular goods can cause deep declines in export revenues and therefore in domestic income. Tariff and quota protection are allegedly needed in such nations to enable greater industrial diversification. That way, these economies will not be so dependent on exporting one or two products to obtain the other goods they need. Such goods will be available domestically, thereby providing greater domestic stability.

There is some truth in this diversification-for-stability argument. But the argument has little or no relevance to the United States and other advanced economies. Also, the economic costs of diversification may be great; for example, one-crop economies may be highly inefficient at manufacturing.

Infant Industry Argument

The infant industry argument contends that protective tariffs are needed to allow new domestic industries to establish themselves. Temporarily shielding young domestic firms from the severe competition of more mature and more efficient foreign firms will give infant industries a chance to develop and become efficient producers.

This argument for protection rests on an alleged exception to the case for free trade. The exception is that young industries have not had, and if they face mature foreign competition will never have, the chance to make the long-run adjustments needed for larger scale and greater efficiency in production. In this view, tariff protection for such infant industries will correct a misallocation of world resources perpetuated by historically different levels of economic development between domestic and foreign industries.

Counterarguments There are some logical problems with the infant industry argument. In the developing nations it is difficult to determine which industries are the infants that are capable of achieving economic maturity and therefore deserving protection. Also, protective tariffs may persist even after industrial maturity has been realized.

Most economists feel that if infant industries are to be subsidized, there are better means than tariffs for doing so. Direct subsidies, for example, have the advantage of making explicit which industries are being aided and to what degree.

Strategic Trade Policy In recent years the infant industry argument has taken a modified form in advanced economies. Now proponents contend that government should use trade barriers to reduce the risk of investing in product development by domestic firms, particularly where advanced technology is involved. Firms protected from foreign competition can grow more rapidly and achieve greater economies of scale than unprotected foreign competitors. The protected firms can eventually dominate world markets because of their lower costs. Supposedly, dominance of world markets will enable the domestic firms to return high profits to the home nation. These profits will exceed the domestic sacrifices caused by

trade barriers. Also, advances in high-technology industries are deemed beneficial because the advances achieved in one domestic industry often can be transferred to other domestic industries.

Japan and South Korea, in particular, have been accused of using this form of **strategic trade policy.** The problem with this strategy and therefore with this argument for tariffs is that the nations put at a disadvantage by strategic trade policies tend to retaliate with tariffs of their own. The outcome may be higher tariffs worldwide, reduction of world trade, and the loss of potential gains from technological advances.

Protection-against-Dumping Argument

The protection-against-dumping argument contends that tariffs are needed to protect domestic firms from "dumping" by foreign producers. **Dumping** is the sale of a product in a foreign country at prices either below cost or below the prices commonly charged at home.

Economists cite two plausible reasons for this behavior. First, with regard to below-cost dumping, firms in country A may dump goods at below cost into country B in an attempt to drive their competitors in country B out of business. If the firms in country A succeed in driving their competitors in country B out of business, they will enjoy monopoly power and monopoly prices and profits on the goods they subsequently sell in country B. Their hope is that the longer-term monopoly profits will more than offset the losses from below-cost sales that must take place while they are attempting to drive their competitors in country B out of business.

Second, dumping that involves selling abroad at a price that is below the price commonly charged in the home country (but that is still at or above production costs) may be a form of price discrimination, which is charging different prices to different customers. As an example, a foreign seller that has a monopoly in its home market may find that it can maximize its overall profit by charging a high price in its monopolized domestic market while charging a lower price in the United States, where it must compete with U.S. producers. Curiously, it may pursue this strategy even if it makes no profit at all from its sales in the United States, where it must charge the competitive price. So why bother selling in the United States? Because the increase in overall production that comes about by exporting to the United States may allow the firm to obtain the per-unit cost savings often associated with large-scale production. These cost savings imply even higher profits in the monopolized domestic market.

Because dumping is an "unfair trade practice," most nations prohibit it. For example, where dumping is shown to injure U.S. firms, the Federal government imposes tariffs called *antidumping duties* on the goods in question. But relatively few documented cases of dumping occur each year, and specific instances of unfair trade do not justify widespread, permanent tariffs. Moreover, antidumping duties can be abused. Often, what appears to be dumping is simply comparative advantage at work.

Increased Domestic Employment Argument

Arguing for a tariff to "save U.S. jobs" becomes fashionable when the economy encounters a recession or experiences slow job growth during a recovery (as in the early 2000s in the United States). In an economy that engages in international trade, exports involve spending on domestic output and imports reflect spending to obtain part of another nation's output. So, in this argument, reducing imports will divert spending on another nation's output to spending on domestic output. Thus, domestic output and employment will rise. But this argument has several shortcomings.

While imports may eliminate some U.S. jobs, they create others. Imports may have eliminated the jobs of some U.S. steel and textile workers in recent years, but other workers have gained jobs unloading ships, flying imported aircraft, and selling imported electronic equipment. Import restrictions alter the composition of employment, but they may have little or no effect on the volume of employment.

The *fallacy of composition*—the false idea that what is true for the part is necessarily true for the whole—is also present in this rationale for tariffs. All nations cannot simultaneously succeed in restricting imports while maintaining their exports; what is true for one nation is not true for all nations. The exports of one nation must be the imports of another nation. To the extent that one country is able to expand its economy through an excess of exports over imports, the resulting excess of imports over exports worsens another economy's unemployment problem. It is no wonder that tariffs and import quotas meant to achieve domestic full employment are called "beggar my neighbor" policies: They achieve short-run domestic goals by making trading partners poorer.

Moreover, nations adversely affected by tariffs and quotas are likely to retaliate, causing a "trade war" (more precisely, a *trade barrier war*) that will choke off trade and make all nations worse off. The **Smoot-Hawley Tariff Act** of 1930 is a classic example. Although that act was meant to reduce imports and stimulate U.S. production, the high tariffs it authorized prompted adversely affected nations to retaliate with tariffs equally high. International trade fell, lowering the output and income of all nations. Economic historians generally agree that the Smoot-Hawley Tariff Act was a contributing cause of the Great Depression.

Finally, forcing an excess of exports over imports cannot succeed in raising domestic employment over the long run. It is through U.S. imports that foreign nations earn dollars for buying U.S. exports. In the long run, a nation must import in order to export. The long-run impact of tariffs is not an increase in domestic employment but, at best, a reallocation of workers away from export industries and to protected domestic industries. This shift implies a less efficient allocation of resources.

Cheap Foreign Labor Argument

The cheap foreign labor argument says that domestic firms and workers must be shielded from the ruinous competition of countries where wages are low. If protection is not provided, cheap imports will flood U.S. markets and the prices of U.S. goods—along with the wages of U.S. workers—will be pulled down. That is, domestic living standards in the United States will be reduced.

This argument can be rebutted at several levels. The logic of the argument suggests that it is not mutually beneficial for rich and poor persons to trade with one another. However, that is not the case. A low-income farmworker may pick lettuce or tomatoes for a rich landowner, and both may benefit from the transaction. And both U.S. consumers and Chinese workers gain when they "trade" a pair of athletic shoes priced at $30 as opposed to U.S. consumers being restricted to buying a similar shoe made in the United States for $60.

Also, recall that gains from trade are based on comparative advantage, not on absolute advantage. Look back at Figure 37.1, where we supposed that the United States and Brazil had labor forces of exactly the same size. Noting the positions of the production possibilities curves, observe that U.S. labor can produce more of either good. Thus, it is more productive. Because of this greater productivity, we can expect wages and living standards to be higher for U.S. labor. Brazil's less productive labor will receive lower wages.

The cheap foreign labor argument suggests that, to maintain its standard of living, the United States should not trade with low-wage Brazil. What if it does not trade with Brazil? Will wages and living standards rise in the United States as a result? No. To obtain coffee, the United States will have to reallocate a portion of its labor from its efficient wheat industry to its inefficient coffee industry. As a result, the average productivity of U.S. labor will fall, as will real wages and living standards. The labor forces of both countries will have diminished standards of living because without specialization and trade they will have less output available to them. Compare column 4 with column 1 in Table 37.1 or points A' and B' with A and B in Figure 37.2 to confirm this point.

Another problem with the cheap foreign labor argument is that its proponents incorrectly focus on labor costs per hour when what really matters is labor costs per unit. As an example, suppose that a U.S. factory pays its workers $20 per hour while a factory in a developing country pays its workers $4 per hour. The proponents of the cheap foreign labor argument look at these numbers and conclude—incorrectly—that it is impossible for the U.S. factory to compete with the factory in the developing country. But this conclusion fails to take into account two crucial facts:

- What actually matters is labor costs per *unit*, not labor costs per *hour*.
- Differences in productivity typically mean that labor costs per unit are often nearly identical despite huge differences in labor costs per hour.

To see why these points matter so much, let's take into account how productive the two factories are. Because the U.S. factory uses much more sophisticated technology, better trained workers, and a lot more capital per worker, one worker in one hour can produce 20 units of output. Since the U.S. workers get paid $20 per hour, this means the U.S. factory's labor cost *per unit of output* is $1. The factory in the developing country is much less productive since it uses less efficient technology and its relatively untrained workers have a lot less machinery and equipment to work with. A worker there produces only 4 units per hour. Given the foreign wage of $4 per hour, this means that the labor cost per unit of output at the factory in the developing country is also $1.

As you can see, the lower wage rate per hour at the factory in the developing country does not translate into lower labor costs per unit—meaning that it won't be able to undersell its U.S. competitor just because its workers get paid lower wages per hour.

Proponents of the cheap foreign labor argument tend to focus exclusively on the large international differences that exist in labor costs per hour. They typically fail to mention that these differences in labor costs per hour are mostly the result of tremendously large differences in productivity and that these large differences in productivity serve to equalize labor costs per unit of output. As a result, firms in developing countries only *sometimes* have an advantage in terms of labor costs per unit of output. Whether they do in any specific situation will vary by industry and firm and will depend upon differences in productivity as well as differences in labor costs per hour. For many goods, labor productivity in high-wage countries like the United States is so much higher than labor productivity in low-wage countries that it is actually cheaper *per unit of output* to manufacture those goods in high-wage countries. That is why, for instance, Intel still makes microchips in the United States and why most automobiles are still produced in the United States, Japan, and Europe rather than in low-wage countries.

QUICK REVIEW 37.3

- A tariff on a product increases its price, reduces its consumption, increases its domestic production, reduces its imports, and generates tariff revenue for government; an import quota does the same, except a quota generates revenue for foreign producers rather than for the government imposing the quota.
- Most rationales for trade protections are special-interest requests that, if followed, would create gains for protected industries and their workers at the expense of greater losses for the economy.

The World Trade Organization

As indicated in Chapter 5, the Uruguay Round of 1993 established the **World Trade Organization (WTO)**. In 2008, the WTO, which oversees trade agreements and rules on disputes relating to them, had 153 member nations. It also provides forums for further rounds of trade negotiations. The ninth and latest round of negotiations—the **Doha Round**—was launched in Doha, Qatar, in late 2001. (The trade rounds occur over several years in several geographic venues and are named after the city or country of origination.) The negotiations are aimed at further reducing tariffs and quotas, as well as agricultural subsidies that distort trade. One of this chapter's questions asks you to update the progress of the Doha Round (or, alternatively, the Doha Development Agenda) via an Internet search.

Along those same lines, you also may want to review the sections in Chapter 5 dealing with offshoring and trade adjustment assistance. Offshoring is the practice of shifting work previously done by American workers to workers located overseas. It is a natural consequence of the reduced trade barriers and increased global trade promoted by the WTO. While offshoring helps to increase overall economic efficiency and raises average living standards both at home and abroad, it does create severe economic hardship for those American workers who lose their jobs. The government takes this problem seriously and has developed trade adjustment assistance programs to help those workers who have lost their jobs to offshoring. Chapter 5 provides the details.

Petition of the Candlemakers, 1845

French Economist Frédéric Bastiat (1801–1850) Devastated the Proponents of Protectionism by Satirically Extending Their Reasoning to Its Logical and Absurd Conclusions.

Petition of the Manufacturers of Candles, Waxlights, Lamps, Candlesticks, Street Lamps, Snuffers, Extinguishers, and of the Producers of Oil Tallow, Rosin, Alcohol, and, Generally, of Everything Connected with Lighting.

TO MESSIEURS THE MEMBERS OF THE CHAMBER OF DEPUTIES.

Gentlemen—You are on the right road. You reject abstract theories, and have little consideration for cheapness and plenty. Your chief care is the interest of the producer. You desire to emancipate him from external competition, and reserve the national market for national industry.

We are about to offer you an admirable opportunity of applying your—what shall we call it? your theory? No; nothing is more deceptive than theory; your doctrine? your system? your principle? but you dislike doctrines, you abhor systems, and as for principles, you deny that there are any in social economy: we shall say, then, your practice, your practice without theory and without principle.

We are suffering from the intolerable competition of a foreign rival, placed, it would seem, in a condition so far superior to ours for the production of light, that he absolutely inundates our national market with it at a price fabulously reduced. The moment he shows himself, our trade leaves us—all consumers apply to him; and a branch of native industry, having countless ramifications, is all at once rendered completely stagnant. This rival . . . is no other than the Sun.

What we pray for is, that it may please you to pass a law ordering the shutting up of all windows, skylights, dormer windows, outside and inside shutters, curtains, blinds, bull's-eyes; in a word, of all openings, holes, chinks, clefts, and fissures, by or through which the light of the sun has been in use to enter houses, to the prejudice of the meritorious manufacturers with which we flatter ourselves we have accommodated our country,—a country which, in gratitude, ought not to abandon us now to a strife so unequal.

If you shut up as much as possible all access to natural light, and create a demand for artificial light, which of our French manufacturers will not be encouraged by it? If more tallow is consumed, then there must be more oxen and sheep; and, consequently, we shall behold the multiplication of artificial meadows, meat, wool, hides, and, above all, manure, which is the basis and foundation of all agricultural wealth.

The same remark applies to navigation. Thousands of vessels will proceed to the whale fishery; and, in a short time, we shall possess a navy capable of maintaining the honor of France, and gratifying the patriotic aspirations of your petitioners, the undersigned candlemakers and others.

Only have the goodness to reflect, Gentlemen, and you will be convinced that there is, perhaps, no Frenchman, from the wealthy coalmaster to the humblest vender of lucifer matches, whose lot will not be ameliorated by the success of this our petition.

Source: Frédéric Bastiat, *Economic Sophisms* (Edinburgh: Oliver and Boyd, Tweeddale Court, 1873), pp. 49–53, abridged.

Summary

1. The United States leads the world in the combined volume of exports and imports. Other major trading nations are Germany, Japan, the western European nations, and the Asian economies of China, South Korea, Taiwan, and Singapore. The United States' principal exports include chemicals, agricultural products, consumer durables, semiconductors, and aircraft; principal imports include petroleum, automobiles, metals, household appliances, and computers.

2. World trade is based on three considerations: the uneven distribution of economic resources among nations, the fact that efficient production of various goods requires particular techniques or combinations of resources, and the differentiated products produced among nations.

3. Mutually advantageous specialization and trade are possible between any two nations if they have different domestic opportunity-cost ratios for any two products. By specializing on the basis of comparative advantage, nations can obtain larger real incomes with fixed amounts of resources. The terms of trade determine how this increase in world output is shared by the trading nations. Increasing (rather than constant) opportunity costs limit specialization and trade.

4. A nation's export supply curve shows the quantities of a product the nation will export at world prices that exceed the domestic price (the price in a closed, no-international-trade economy). A nation's import demand curve reveals the quantities of a product it will import at world prices below the domestic price.

5. In a two-nation model, the equilibrium world price and the equilibrium quantities of exports and imports occur where one nation's export supply curve intersects the other nation's import demand curve. A nation will export a particular product if the world price exceeds the domestic price; it will import the product if the world price is less than the domestic price. The country with the lower costs of production will be the exporter and the country with the higher costs of production will be the importer.

6. Trade barriers take the form of protective tariffs, quotas, nontariff barriers, and "voluntary" export restrictions. Supply and demand analysis reveals that protective tariffs and quotas increase the prices and reduce the quantities demanded of the affected goods. Sales by foreign exporters diminish; domestic producers, however, gain higher prices and enlarged sales. Consumer losses from trade restrictions greatly exceed producer and government gains, creating an efficiency loss to society.

7. The strongest arguments for protection are the infant industry and military self-sufficiency arguments. Most other arguments for protection are interest-group appeals or reasoning fallacies that emphasize producer interests over consumer interests or stress the immediate effects of trade barriers while ignoring long-run consequences.

8. The cheap foreign labor argument for protection fails because it focuses on labor costs per hour rather than on what really matters, labor costs per unit of output. Due to higher productivity, firms in high-wage countries like the United States can have lower wage costs per unit of output than competitors in low-wage countries. Whether they do will depend on how their particular wage and productivity levels compare with those of their competitors in low-wage countries.

9. In 2008 the World Trade Organization (WTO) consisted of 153 member nations. The WTO oversees trade agreements among the members, resolves disputes over the rules, and periodically meets to discuss and negotiate further trade liberalization. In 2001 the WTO initiated a new round of trade negotiations in Doha, Qatar. By 2008 the Doha Round (or Doha Development Agenda) was still in progress.

Terms and Concepts

labor-intensive goods

land-intensive goods

capital-intensive goods

opportunity-cost ratio

principle of comparative advantage

terms of trade

trading possibilities line

gains from trade

world price

domestic price

export supply curve

import demand curve

equilibrium world price

tariffs

revenue tariff

protective tariff

import quota

nontariff barrier (NTB)

voluntary export restriction (VER)

strategic trade policy

dumping

Smoot-Hawley Tariff Act

World Trade Organization (WTO)

Doha Round

Study Questions

1. Quantitatively, how important is international trade to the United States relative to other nations? **LO2**

2. Distinguish among land-, labor-, and capital-intensive commodities, citing one nontextbook example of each. What role do these distinctions play in explaining international trade? What role do distinctive products, unrelated to cost advantages, play in international trade? **LO1**

3. Suppose nation A can produce 80 units of X by using all its resources to produce X or 60 units of Y by devoting all its resources to Y. Comparable figures for nation B are 60 units of X and 60 units of Y. Assuming constant costs, in which product should each nation specialize? Why? What are the limits of the terms of trade? **LO1**

4. **KEY QUESTION** To the right are hypothetical production possibilities tables for New Zealand and Spain. Each country can produce apples and plums.

   Plot the production possibilities data for each of the two countries separately. Referring to your graphs, answer the following: **LO1**
   a. What is each country's cost ratio of producing plums and apples.
   b. Which nation should specialize in which product?

New Zealand's Production Possibilities Table
(Millions of Bushels)

Product	Production Alternatives			
	A	**B**	**C**	**D**
Apples	0	20	40	60
Plums	15	10	5	0

Spain's Production Possibilities Table
(Millions of Bushels)

Product	Production Alternatives			
	R	**S**	**T**	**U**
Apples	0	20	40	60
Plums	60	40	20	0

   c. Show the trading possibilities lines for each nation if the actual terms of trade are 1 plum for 2 apples. (Plot these lines on your graph.)
   d. Suppose the optimum product mixes before specialization and trade were alternative B in New Zealand and alternative S in Spain. What would be the gains from specialization and trade?

5. "The United States can produce X more efficiently than can Great Britain. Yet we import X from Great Britain." Explain. **LO1**

6. **KEY QUESTION** Refer to Figure 3.6, page 55. Assume that the graph depicts the U.S. domestic market for corn. How many bushels of corn, if any, will the United States export or import at a world price of $1, $2, $3, $4, and $5? Use this information to construct the U.S. export supply curve and import demand curve for corn. Suppose the only other corn-producing nation is France, where the domestic price is $4. Which country will export corn; which will import it? **LO2**

7. **KEY QUESTION** Draw a domestic supply and demand diagram for a product in which the United States does not have a comparative advantage. What impact do foreign imports have on domestic price and quantity? On your diagram show a protective tariff that eliminates approximately one-half of the assumed imports. What are the price-quantity effects of this tariff on (a) domestic consumers, (b) domestic producers, and (c) foreign exporters? How would the effects of a quota that creates the same amount of imports differ? **LO3**

8. "The potentially valid arguments for tariff protection are also the most easily abused." What are those arguments? Why are they susceptible to abuse? Evaluate the use of artificial trade barriers, such as tariffs and import quotas, as a means of achieving and maintaining full employment. **LO3**

9. Evaluate the following statements: **LO4**
   a. Protective tariffs reduce both the imports and the exports of the nation that levies tariffs.
   b. The extensive application of protective tariffs destroys the ability of the international market system to allocate resources efficiently.
   c. Unemployment in some industries can often be reduced through tariff protection, but by the same token inefficiency typically increases.
   d. Foreign firms that "dump" their products onto the U.S. market are in effect providing bargains to the country's citizens.
   e. In view of the rapidity with which technological advance is dispersed around the world, free trade will inevitably yield structural maladjustments, unemployment, and balance-of-payments problems for industrially advanced nations.
   f. Free trade can improve the composition and efficiency of domestic output. Competition from Volkswagen, Toyota, and Honda forced Detroit to make a compact car, and foreign imports of bottled water forced American firms to offer that product.
   g. In the long run, foreign trade is neutral with respect to total employment.

10. Suppose Japan agreed to a voluntary export restriction (VER) that reduced U.S. imports of Japanese steel by 10 percent. What would be the likely short-run effects of that VER on the U.S. and Japanese steel industries? If this restriction were permanent, what would be its long-run effects in the two nations on (a) the allocation of resources, (b) the volume of employment, (c) the price level, and (d) the standard of living? **LO3**

11. In 2005, manufacturing workers in the United States earned an average wage of $23.65 per hour. That same year, manufacturing workers in Mexico earned an average wage of $2.63 per hour. How can U.S. manufacturers possibly compete? Why isn't all manufacturing done in Mexico and other low-wage countries? **LO4**

12. What is the WTO and how does it relate to international trade? How many nations belong to the WTO? (Update the number given in this book at **www.wto.org**.) What did the Uruguay Round (1994) of WTO trade negotiations accomplish? What is the name of the current WTO round of trade negotiations? **LO4**

13. **LAST WORD** What point is Bastiat trying to make in his imaginary petition of the candlemakers?

Web-Based Questions

1. **TRADE LIBERALIZATION—THE WTO** Go to the Web site of the World Trade Organization (**www.wto.org**) to retrieve the latest news from the WTO. List and summarize three recent news items relating to the WTO.

2. **THE U.S. INTERNATIONAL TRADE COMMISSION—WHAT IS IT AND WHAT DOES IT DO?** Go to **www.usitc.gov** to determine the duties of the U.S. International Trade Commission (USITC). How does this organization differ from the World Trade Organization (question 12)? Go to the Information Center and find News Releases. Identify and briefly describe three USITC "determinations" relating to charges of unfair international trade practices that harm U.S. producers.

FURTHER TEST YOUR KNOWLEDGE AT
www.mcconnell18e.com

IN THIS CHAPTER YOU WILL LEARN:

1 How currencies of different nations are exchanged when international transactions take place.

2 About the balance sheet the United States uses to account for the international payments it makes and receives.

3 How exchange rates are determined in currency markets.

4 The difference between flexible exchange rates and fixed exchange rates.

5 The causes and consequences of recent record-high U.S. trade deficits.

The Balance of Payments, Exchange Rates, and Trade Deficits

If you take a U.S. dollar to the bank and ask to exchange it for U.S. currency, you will get a puzzled look. If you persist, you may get a dollar's worth of change: One U.S. dollar can buy exactly one U.S. dollar. But on March 20, 2008, for example, 1 U.S. dollar could buy 2362 Colombian pesos, 1.12 Australian dollars, .50 British pound, 1.03 Canadian dollars, .65 European euro, 98.79 Japanese yen, or 10.72 Mexican pesos. What explains this seemingly haphazard array of exchange rates?

In Chapter 37 we examined comparative advantage as the underlying economic basis of world trade and discussed the effects of barriers to free trade. Now we introduce the highly important monetary or financial aspects of international trade.

International Financial Transactions

This chapter focuses on international financial transactions, the vast majority of which fall into two broad categories: international trade and international asset transactions. International trade involves either purchasing or selling currently produced goods or services across an international border. Examples include an Egyptian firm exporting cotton to the United States and an American company hiring an Indian call center to answer its phones. International asset transactions involve the transfer of the property rights to either real or financial assets between the citizens of one country and the citizens of another country. It includes activities like buying foreign stocks or selling your house to a foreigner.

These two categories of international financial transactions reflect the fact that whether they are from different countries or the same country, individuals and firms can only exchange two things with each other: currently produced goods and services or preexisting assets. With regard to assets, however, money is by far the most commonly exchanged asset. Only rarely would you ever find a barter situation in which people directly exchanged other assets—such as trading a car for 500 shares of Microsoft stock or a cow for 30 chickens and a tank of diesel fuel.

As a result, there are two basic types of transactions:
- People trading either goods or services for money.
- People trading assets for money.

In either case, money flows from the buyers of the goods, services, or assets to the sellers of the goods, services, or assets.

When the people engaged in any such transactions are both from places that use the same currency, what type of money to use is not an issue. Americans from California and Wisconsin will use their common currency, the dollar. People from France and Germany will use their common currency, the euro. However, when the people involved in an exchange are from places that use different currencies, an intermediate asset transaction has to take place: the buyer must convert her type of money into the currency that the seller uses and accepts.

As an example, consider the case of an English software design company that wants to buy a supercomputer made by an American company. The American company sells these high-powered machines for $300,000. To pay for the machine, the English company has to convert some of the money it has (British pounds sterling) into the money that the American company will accept (U.S. dollars). This process is not difficult. As we will soon explain in detail, there are many easy-to-use foreign exchange markets in which those who wish to sell pounds and buy dollars can interact with others who wish to sell dollars and buy pounds. The demand and supply created by these two groups determine the equilibrium exchange rate, which, in turn, determines how many pounds our English company will have to convert in order to pay for the supercomputer. If, for instance, the exchange rate is $2 = £1$, then the English company will have to convert £150,000 in order to obtain the $300,000 necessary to purchase the computer. **(Key Question 2)**

The Balance of Payments

A nation's **balance of payments** is the sum of all the financial transactions that take place between its residents and the residents of foreign nations. The large majority of these transactions fall into the two main categories that we have just discussed: international trade and international asset transactions. As a result, the majority of the items included in the balance of payments are things like exports and imports of goods, exports and imports of services, and international purchases and sales of financial and real assets. But the balance of payments also includes international transactions that fall outside of these main categories—things such as tourist expenditures, interest and dividends received or paid abroad, debt forgiveness, and remittances made by immigrants to their relatives back home.

The U.S. Commerce Department's Bureau of Economic Analysis compiles a balance-of-payments statement each year. This statement summarizes all of the millions of payments that individuals and firms in the United States receive from foreigners as well as all of the millions of payments that individuals and firms in the United States make to foreigners. It shows "flows" of inpayments of money *to* the United States and outpayments of money *from* the United States. For convenience, all of these money payments are given in terms of dollars. This is true despite the fact that some of them actually may have been made using foreign currencies—as when, for instance, an American company converts dollars into euros to buy something from an Italian company. When including this outpayment of money from the United States, the accountants who compile the balance of payments statement use the number of dollars the American company converted—rather than the number of euros that were actually used to make the purchase.

Table 38.1 is a simplified balance-of-payments statement for the United States in 2007. Because the vast majority of international financial transactions fall into

TABLE 38.1 The U.S. Balance of Payments, 2007 (in Billions)

Current account		
(1) U.S. goods exports	$+1149	
(2) U.S. goods imports	−1965	
(3) *Balance on goods*		$−816
(4) U.S. exports of services	+479	
(5) U.S. imports of services	−372	
(6) *Balance on services*		+107
(7) *Balance on goods and services*		−709
(8) Net investment income	+74*	
(9) Net transfers	−104	
(10) **Balance on current account**		**−739**
Capital and financial account		
Capital account		
(11) *Balance on capital account*		−2
Financial account		
(12) Foreign purchases of assets in the United States	+1905†	
(13) U.S. purchases of assets abroad	−1164†	
(14) *Balance on financial account*		+741
(15) **Balance on capital and financial account**		**+739**
		$ 0

*includes other, less significant, categories of income.
†Includes one-half of an $84 billion statistical discrepancy that is listed in the capital account.

Source: U.S. Department of Commerce, Bureau of Economic Analysis, **www.bea.gov.** Preliminary 2007 data. The export and import data are on a "balance-of-payment basis," and usually vary from the data on exports and imports reported in the National Income and Product Accounts.

only two categories—international trade and international asset exchanges—the balance of payments statement is organized into two broad categories. *The current account* given at the top of the table mostly deals with international trade. *The capital and financial account* at the bottom of the table mostly deals with international asset exchanges.

Current Account

The top portion of Table 38.1 that mostly summarizes U.S. trade in currently produced goods and services is called the **current account.** Items 1 and 2 show U.S. exports and imports of goods (merchandise) in 2007. U.S. exports have a *plus* (+) sign because they are a *credit*; they generate flows of money toward the United States. U.S. imports have a *minus* (−) sign because they are a *debit*; they cause flows of money out of the United States.

Balance on Goods Items 1 and 2 in Table 38.1 reveal that in 2007 U.S. goods exports of $1149 billion were less than U.S. goods imports of $1965 billion. A country's *balance of trade on goods* is the difference between its exports and its imports of goods. If exports

exceed imports, the result is a surplus on the balance of goods. If imports exceed exports, there is a trade deficit on the balance of goods. We note in item 3 that in 2007 the United States incurred a trade deficit on goods of $816 billion.

Balance on Services The United States exports not only goods, such as airplanes and computer software, but also services, such as insurance, consulting, travel, and investment advice, to residents of foreign nations. Item 4 in Table 38.1 shows that these service "exports" totaled $479 billion in 2007. Since they generate flows of money toward the United States, they are a credit (thus the + sign). Item 5 indicates that the United States "imports" similar services from foreigners. Those service imports were $372 billion in 2007 and since they generate flows of money out of the United States, they are a debit (thus the − sign). Summed together, items 4 and 5 indicate that the balance on services (item 6) in 2007 was $107 billion. The **balance on goods and services** shown as item 7 is the difference between U.S. exports of goods and services (items 1 and 4) and U.S. imports of goods and services (items 2 and 5). In 2007,

U.S. imports of goods and services exceeded U.S. exports of goods and services by $709 billion. So a **trade deficit** occurred. In contrast, a **trade surplus** occurs when exports of goods and services exceed imports of goods and services. (Global Perspective 38.1 shows U.S. trade deficits and surpluses with selected nations.)

Balance on Current Account Items 8 and 9 do not have to do with international trade in goods and services. But they are listed as part of the current account (which is mostly about international trade in goods and services) because they can be thought of as dealing with international financial flows that in some sense compensate for things that can be conceptualized as being *like* international trade in either goods or services. For instance, item 8, *net investment income*, represents the difference between (1) the interest and dividend payments foreigners paid U.S. citizens and companies for the services provided by U.S. capital invested abroad ("exported" capital) and (2) the interest and dividends the U.S. citizens and companies paid for the services provided by foreign capital invested here ("imported" capital). Observe that in 2007 U.S. net investment income was a positive $74 billion.

GLOBAL PERSPECTIVE 38.1

U.S. Trade Balances in Goods and Services, Selected Nations, 2007

The United States has large trade deficits in goods and services with several nations, in particular, China, Japan, and Canada.

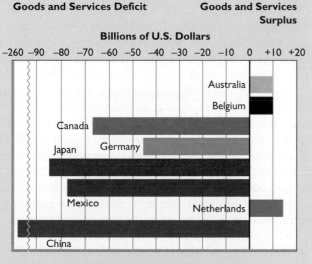

Source: Bureau of Economic Analysis, **www.bea.gov.**

Item 9 shows net transfers, both public and private, between the United States and the rest of the world. Included here is foreign aid, pensions paid to U.S. citizens living abroad, and remittances by immigrants to relatives abroad. These $104 billion of transfers are net U.S. outpayments (and therefore listed as a negative number in Table 38.1). They are listed as part of the current account because they can be thought of as the financial flows that accompany the exporting of goodwill and the importing of "thank you notes."

By adding all transactions in the current account, we obtain the **balance on current account** shown in item 10. In 2007 the United States had a current account deficit of $739 billion. This means that the U.S. current account transactions created outpayments from the United States greater than inpayments to the United States.

Capital and Financial Account

The bottom portion of the current account statement summarizes U.S. international asset transactions. It is called the **capital and financial account** and consists of two separate accounts: the *capital account* and the *financial account*.

Capital Account The capital account mainly measures debt forgiveness—which is an asset transaction because the person forgiving a debt essentially hands the IOU back to the borrower. It is a "net" account (one that can be either + or −). The −$2 billion listed in line 11 tells us that in 2007 Americans forgave $2 billion more of debt owed to them by foreigners than foreigners forgave debt owed to them by Americans. The − sign indicates a debit; it is an "on-paper" outpayment (asset transfer) by the net amount of debt forgiven.

Financial Account The financial account summarizes international asset transactions having to do with international purchases and sales of real or financial assets. Line 12 lists the amount of foreign purchases of assets in the United States. It has a + sign because any purchase of an American-owned asset by a foreigner generates a flow of money toward the American who sells the asset. Line 13 lists U.S. purchases of assets abroad. These have a − sign because such purchases generate a flow of money from the Americans who buy foreign assets toward the foreigners who sell them those assets.

Items 11 and 12 combined yielded a $741 billion balance on the financial account for 2007 (line 14). In 2007 the United States "exported" $1905 billion of ownership of its real and financial assets and "imported" $1164 billion. Thought of differently, this surplus in the financial account brought in income of $741 billion to the United States.

The **balance on the capital and financial account** (line 15) is $739 billion. It is the sum of the $2 billion deficit on the capital account and the $741 billion surplus on the financial account. Observe that this $739 billion surplus in the capital and financial account equals the $739 billion deficit in the current account. This is not an accident. The two numbers always equal—or "balance." The next section explains why.

Why the Balance of Payments Balances

The balance on the current account and the balance on the capital and financial account must always sum to zero because any deficit or surplus in the current account automatically creates an offsetting entry in the capital and financial account. This happens because, as we keep emphasizing, people can only trade one of two things with each other: currently produced goods and services or preexisting assets. An important result of this fact is that if trading partners have an imbalance in their trade of currently produced goods and services, the only way to make up for that imbalance is with a net transfer of assets from one party to the other.

To see why this is true, let's use an example that involves trade between individuals rather than countries. Suppose that John makes shoes and Henri makes watches and that they only trade with each other. In addition, each of them begins the year with assets worth $1000. To keep things simple, these assets are all in the form of money: each of them has $1000 in the bank at the beginning of the year. Next, suppose that John sells (exports) $300 worth of shoes to Henri this year while buying (importing) $500 worth of watches from Henri this year. The result is that John ends the year with a $200 trade deficit with Henri.

This trade deficit implies that there will be an *automatic and unavoidable* asset transfer from John to Henri. This happens because each goods transaction is paid for using an asset—money. When John exports shoes to Henri, Henri pays for them by transferring $300 of money to John. Shoes flow from John to Henri and $300 of money flows from Henri to John. Similarly, when John imports watches from Henri, John pays for them by transferring $500 of money to Henri. Watches flow from Henri to John and $500 of money flows from John to Henri.

Now consider what these transfers of assets do to their respective total asset holdings. In our simple example, each starts out the year with initial assets consisting of $1000 of money. But at the end of the year, John will have only $800 of money while Henri will have $1200 of money.

In John's case, he started out with $1000, received an inflow of $300 for exporting shoes to Henri, and then made an outflow of $500 when importing watches from Henri. Adding these up shows that John ends the year with $800 (= $1000 + $300 − $500). A similar calculation shows how Henri ends up with $1200.

Thus, the $200 trade deficit that John has with Henri automatically causes $200 worth of John's initial asset holdings of $1000 to be transferred to Henri. This is unavoidable. Because John's exports only generate an inflow of cash worth $300, the only way for him to pay for his $500 worth of imports is to dip into his initial asset holdings. Put slightly differently, the $300 he makes from his exports only pays for the first $300 of his $500 worth of imports. The only way for him to pay for the remaining $200 worth of imports is for him to give up some of his initial asset holdings. Thus, $200 of John's initial asset holdings get transferred to Henri.

This automatic asset transfer is why the current account and the capital and financial account always sum to zero. Consider John's balance of payments statement. His $200 trade deficit would go into the current account at the top of the statement as a −$200 entry because the current account deals with flows of money related to currently produced goods and services and his trade deficit creates a $200 flow of money from John to his foreign trading partner (Henri). At the same time, that $200 flow of money is also recognized as an asset transfer from John to Henry in the capital and financial account at the bottom of the statement. The only confusing part is that it goes in as a +$200 entry under "foreign purchases of assets." Why there? Because we can think of what happened this year as Henri using $200 worth of currently produced goods to purchase $200 worth of John's initial holding of assets. John didn't give those assets to Henri for nothing. Henri had to purchase them by giving $200 worth of watches to John. The +$200 entry under "foreign purchases of assets" recognizes this fact.

Thus, the balance of payments always balances because any current account deficit or surplus in the top half of the statement automatically generates an offsetting international asset transfer that shows up in the capital and financial account in the bottom half of the statement. More specifically, current account deficits automatically generate transfers of assets *to* foreigners while current account surpluses automatically generate transfers of assets *from* foreigners.

Payments, Deficits, and Surpluses

Although the balance of payments must always sum to zero, as in Table 38.1, economists and policymakers sometimes speak of **balance-of-payments deficits and surpluses.** The central banks of nations hold quantities of **official reserves,** consisting of foreign currencies, reserves held with the International Monetary Fund, and stocks of gold. These reserves are drawn on—or replenished—to make up any net deficit or surplus that otherwise would occur in the balance-of-payment account. (This is much as you would draw on your savings or add to your savings as a way to balance your annual income and spending.) In some years, a nation must make an inpayment of official reserves to its capital and financial account in order to balance it with the current account. In these years, a *balance-of-payments deficit* is said to occur.

In other years, an outpayment of official reserves from the capital and financial account must occur to balance that account with the current account. The outpayment adds to the stock of official reserves. A *balance-of-payments surplus* is said to exist in these years.

A balance-of-payments deficit is not necessarily bad, just as a balance-of-payments surplus is not necessarily good. Both simply happen. However, any nation's official reserves are limited. Persistent payments deficits, which must be financed by drawing down those reserves, would ultimately deplete the reserves. That nation would have to adopt policies to correct its balance of payments. Such policies might require painful macroeconomic adjustments, trade barriers and similar restrictions, or a major depreciation of its currency. For this reason, nations strive for payments balance, at least over several-year periods.

The United States held $71 billion of official reserves in 2007. The typical annual depletion or addition of official reserves is not of major concern, particularly because withdrawals and deposits roughly balance over time. For example, the stock of official U.S. reserves rose from $68 billion in 2000 to $86 billion in 2004. It fell to $65 billion in 2005 before climbing back up over the next two years to $71 billion in 2007.

The historically large current account deficits that the United States has been running over the past several years are of more concern than annual balance-of-payment deficits or surpluses. The current account deficits need to be financed by equally large surpluses in the capital and financial account. Thus far, that has not been a problem. Later in this chapter, we will examine the causes and potential consequences of large current account deficits. **(Key Question 3)**

WORKED PROBLEMS

W 38.1

Balance of payments

- A nation's balance of payments statement summarizes all of the international financial transactions that take place between its residents and the residents of all foreign nations. It includes the current account balance and the capital and financial account balance.

- The current account balance is a nation's exports of goods and services less its imports of goods and services plus its net investment income and net transfers.

- The capital and financial account balance includes the net amount of the nation's debt forgiveness as well as the nation's sale of real and financial assets to people living abroad less its purchases of real and financial assets from foreigners.

- The current account balance and the capital and financial account balance always sum to zero because any current account imbalance automatically generates an offsetting international asset transfer.

Flexible Exchange Rates

Both the size and the persistence of a nation's balance-of-payments deficits and surpluses and the adjustments it must make to correct those imbalances depend on the system of exchange rates being used. There are two "pure" types of exchange-rate systems:

- A **flexible- or floating-exchange-rate system** through which demand and supply determine exchange rates and in which no government intervention occurs.

- A **fixed-exchange-rate system** through which governments determine exchange rates and make necessary adjustments in their economies to maintain those rates.

We begin by looking at flexible exchange rates. Let's examine the rate, or price, at which U.S. dollars might be exchanged for British pounds. In **Figure 38.1 (Key Graph)** we show demand D_1 and supply S_1 of pounds in the currency market.

INTERACTIVE GRAPHS

G 38.1

Flexible exchange rates

The *demand-for-pounds curve* is downward-sloping because all British goods and services will be cheaper to the United States if pounds become less expensive to the United States. That is, at lower dollar prices for pounds, the United States can obtain more pounds and therefore more British goods and services per dollar. To buy those cheaper British goods, U.S. consumers will increase the quantity of pounds they demand.

keygraph

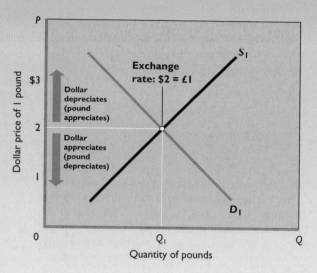

FIGURE 30.1 The market for foreign currency (pounds). The intersection of the demand-for-pounds curve D_1 and the supply-of-pounds curve S_1 determines the equilibrium dollar price of pounds, here, $2. That means that the exchange rate is $2 = £1. The upward green arrow is a reminder that a higher dollar price of pounds (say, $3 = £1, caused by a shift in either the demand or the supply curve) means that the dollar has depreciated (the pound has appreciated). The downward green arrow tells us that a lower dollar price of pounds (say, $1 = £1, again caused by a shift in either the demand or the supply curve) means that the dollar has appreciated (the pound has depreciated).

QUICK QUIZ FOR FIGURE 38.1

1. Which of the following statements is true?
   a. The quantity of pounds demanded falls when the dollar appreciates.
   b. The quantity of pounds supplied declines as the dollar price of the pound rises.
   c. At the equilibrium exchange rate, the pound price of $1 is £$\frac{1}{2}$.
   d. The dollar appreciates if the demand for pounds increases.

2. At the price of $2 for £1 in this figure:
   a. the dollar-pound exchange rate is unstable.
   b. the quantity of pounds supplied equals the quantity demanded.
   c. the dollar price of £1 equals the pound price of $1.
   d. U.S. goods exports to Britain must equal U.S. goods imports from Britain.

3. Other things equal, a leftward shift of the demand curve in this figure:
   a. would depreciate the dollar.

   b. would create a shortage of pounds at the previous price of $2 for £1.
   c. might be caused by a major recession in the United States.
   d. might be caused by a significant rise of real interest rates in Britain.

4. Other things equal, a rightward shift of the supply curve in this figure would:
   a. depreciate the dollar and might be caused by a significant rise of real interest rates in Britain.
   b. depreciate the dollar and might be caused by a significant fall of real interest rates in Britain.
   c. appreciate the dollar and might be caused by a significant rise of real interest rates in the United States.
   d. appreciate the dollar and might be caused by a significant fall of interest rates in the United States.

Answers: 1. c; 2. b; 3. c; 4. c

The *supply-of-pounds curve* is upward-sloping because the British will purchase more U.S. goods when the dollar price of pounds rises (that is, as the pound price of dollars falls). When the British buy more U.S. goods, they supply a greater quantity of pounds to the foreign exchange market. In other words, they must exchange pounds for dollars to purchase U.S. goods. So, when the dollar price of pounds rises, the quantity of pounds supplied goes up.

The intersection of the supply curve and the demand curve will determine the dollar price of pounds. Here, that price (exchange rate) is $2 for £1.

Depreciation and Appreciation

An exchange rate determined by market forces can, and often does, change daily like stock and bond prices. When the dollar price of pounds *rises*, for example, from $2 = £1 to $3 = £1, the dollar has *depreciated* relative to the pound (and the pound has appreciated relative to the dollar). When a currency depreciates, more units of it (dollars) are needed to buy a single unit of some other currency (a pound).

When the dollar price of pounds *falls*, for example, from $2 = £1 to $1 = £1, the dollar has *appreciated* relative to the pound. When a currency appreciates, fewer units of it (dollars) are needed to buy a single unit of some other currency (pounds).

In our U.S.-Britain illustrations, depreciation of the dollar means an appreciation of the pound, and vice versa. When the dollar price of a pound jumps from $2 = £1 to $3 = £1, the pound has appreciated relative to the dollar because it takes fewer pounds to buy $1. At $2 = £1, it took £$\frac{1}{2}$ to buy $1; at $3 = £1, it takes only £$\frac{1}{3}$ to buy $1. Conversely, when the dollar appreciated relative to the pound, the pound depreciated relative to the dollar. More pounds were needed to buy a dollar.

Determinants of Exchange Rates

What factors would cause a nation's currency to appreciate or depreciate in the market for foreign exchange? Here are three generalizations:

- If the demand for a nation's currency increases (all else equal), that currency will appreciate; if the demand declines, that currency will depreciate.
- If the supply of a nation's currency increases, that currency will depreciate; if the supply decreases, that currency will appreciate.
- If a nation's currency appreciates, some foreign currency depreciates relative to it.

With these generalizations in mind, let's examine the determinants of exchange rates—the factors that shift the demand or supply curve for a certain currency. As we do so, keep in mind that the other-things-equal assumption is always in force. Also note that we are discussing factors *that change the exchange rate*, not things that change *as a result of* a change in the exchange rate.

Changes in Tastes Any change in consumer tastes or preferences for the products of a foreign country may alter the demand for that nation's currency and change its exchange rate. If technological advances in U.S. wireless phones make them more attractive to British consumers and businesses, then the British will supply more pounds in the exchange market in order to purchase more U.S. wireless phones. The supply-of-pounds curve will shift to the right, causing the pound to depreciate and the dollar to appreciate.

In contrast, the U.S. demand-for-pounds curve will shift to the right if British woolen apparel becomes more fashionable in the United States. So the pound will appreciate and the dollar will depreciate.

Relative Income Changes A nation's currency is likely to depreciate if its growth of national income is more rapid than that of other countries. Here's why: A country's imports vary directly with its income level. As total income rises in the United States, people there buy both more domestic goods and more foreign goods. If the U.S. economy is expanding rapidly and the British economy is stagnant, U.S. imports of British goods, and therefore U.S. demands for pounds, will increase. The dollar price of pounds will rise, so the dollar will depreciate.

Relative Price-Level Changes Changes in the relative price levels of two nations may change the demand and supply of currencies and alter the exchange rate between the two nations' currencies.

The **purchasing-power-parity theory** holds that exchange rates equate the purchasing power of various currencies. That is, the exchange rates among national currencies adjust to match the ratios of the nations' price levels: If a certain market basket of goods costs $10,000 in the United States and £5000 in Great Britain, according to this theory the exchange rate will be $2 = £1. That way, a dollar spent in the United States will buy exactly as much output as it would if it were first converted to pounds (at the $2 = 1£ exchange rate) and used to buy output in Great Britain.

In practice, however, exchange rates depart from purchasing power parity, even over long periods. Nevertheless, changes in relative price levels are a determinant of exchange rates. If, for example, the domestic price level rises rapidly in the United States and remains constant in Great Britain, U.S. consumers will seek out low-priced British goods, increasing the demand for pounds. The British will purchase fewer U.S. goods, reducing the supply of pounds. This combination of demand and supply changes will cause the pound to appreciate and the dollar to depreciate.

Relative Interest Rates Changes in relative interest rates between two countries may alter their exchange rate. Suppose that real interest rates rise in the United States but stay constant in Great Britain. British citizens will then find the United States a more attractive place in which to loan money directly or loan money indirectly by buying bonds. To make these loans, they will have to supply pounds in the foreign exchange market to obtain dollars. The increase in the supply of pounds results in depreciation of the pound and appreciation of the dollar.

Changes in Relative Expected Returns on Stocks, Real Estate, and Production Facilities
International investing extends beyond buying foreign bonds. It includes international investments in stocks

CONSIDER THIS . . .

The Big Mac Index

The purchasing-power-parity (PPP) theory says that exchange rates will adjust such that a given broad market basket of goods and services will cost the same in all countries. If the market basket costs $1000 in the United States and 100,000 yen in Japan, then the exchange rate will be $1 = ¥100 (= 1000/100,000). If instead the exchange rate is $1 = ¥110, we can expect the dollar to depreciate and the yen to appreciate such that the exchange rate moves to the purchasing-power-parity rate of $1 = ¥100. Similarly, if the exchange rate is $1 = ¥90, we can expect the dollar to appreciate and the yen to depreciate.

Instead of using a market basket of goods and services, *The Economist* magazine has offered a light-hearted test of the purchasing-power-parity theory through its *Big Mac index*. It uses the exchange rates of 100 countries to convert the domestic currency price of a Big Mac into U.S. dollar prices. If the converted dollar price in, say, Britain exceeds the dollar price in the United States, the *Economist* concludes (with a wink) that the pound is overvalued relative to the dollar. On the other hand, if the adjusted dollar price of a Big Mac in Britain is less than the dollar price in the United States, then the pound is undervalued relative to the dollar.

The *Economist* finds wide divergences in actual dollar prices across the globe and thus little support for the purchasing-power-parity theory. Yet it humorously trumpets any predictive success it can muster (or is that "mustard"?):

Some readers find our Big Mac index hard to swallow. This year (1999), however, has been one to relish. When the euro was launched at the start of the year most forecasters expected it to rise. The Big Mac index, however, suggested the euro was overvalued against the dollar—and indeed it has fallen [13 percent]. . . . Our correspondents have once again been munching their way around the globe . . . [and] experience suggests that investors ignore burgernomics at their peril.*

Maybe so—bad puns and all. Economist Robert Cumby examined the Big Mac index for 14 countries for 10 years.[†] Among his findings:

- A 10 percent undervaluation, according to the Big Mac standard, in one year is associated with a 3.5 percent appreciation of that currency over the following year.

- When the U.S. dollar price of a Big Mac is high in a country, the relative local currency price of a Big Mac in that country generally declines during the following year. Hmm. Not bad.

*"Big MacCurrencies," *The Economist,* Apr. 3, 1999; "Mcparity," *The Economist,* Dec. 11, 1999.

[†]Robert Cumby, "Forecasting Exchange Rates and Relative Prices with the Hamburger Standard: Is What You Want What You Get with Mcparity?" National Bureau of Economic Research, January 1997.

and real estate as well as foreign purchases of factories and production facilities. Other things equal, the extent of this foreign investment depends on relative expected returns. To make the investments, investors in one country must sell their currencies to purchase the foreign currencies needed for the foreign investments.

For instance, suppose that investing in England suddenly becomes more popular due to a more positive outlook regarding expected returns on stocks, real estate, and production facilities there. U.S. investors therefore will sell U.S. assets to buy more assets in England. The U.S. assets will be sold for dollars, which will then be brought to the foreign exchange market and exchanged for pounds, which will in turn be used to purchase British assets. The increased demand for pounds in the foreign exchange market will cause the pound to appreciate and therefore the dollar to depreciate relative to the pound.

Speculation Currency speculators are people who buy and sell currencies with an eye toward reselling or repurchasing them at a profit. Suppose speculators expect the U.S. economy to (1) grow more rapidly than the British economy and (2) experience a more rapid rise in its price level than will Britain. These expectations translate into an anticipation that the pound will appreciate and the dollar will depreciate. Speculators who are holding dollars will therefore try to convert them into pounds. This effort will increase the demand for pounds and cause the dollar price of pounds to rise (that is, cause the dollar to depreciate). A self-fulfilling prophecy occurs: The pound appreciates and the dollar depreciates because speculators act on the belief that these changes will in fact take place. In this way, speculation can cause changes in exchange rates. (We deal with currency speculation in more detail in this chapter's Last Word.)

Table 38.2 has more illustrations of the determinants of exchange rates; the table is worth careful study.

TABLE 38.2 Determinants of Exchange Rates: Factors That Change the Demand for or the Supply of a Particular Currency and Thus Alter the Exchange Rate

Determinant	Examples
Change in tastes	Japanese electronic equipment declines in popularity in the United States (Japanese yen depreciates; U.S. dollar appreciates).
	European tourists reduce visits to the United States (U.S. dollar depreciates; European euro appreciates).
Change in relative incomes	England encounters a recession, reducing its imports, while U.S. real output and real income surge, increasing U.S. imports (British pound appreciates; U.S. dollar depreciates).
Change in relative prices	Switzerland experiences a 3% inflation rate compared to Canada's 10% rate (Swiss franc appreciates; Canadian dollar depreciates).
Change in relative real interest rates	The Federal Reserve drives up interest rates in the United States, while the Bank of England takes no such action (U.S. dollar appreciates; British pound depreciates).
Changes in relative expected returns on stocks, real estate, or production facilities	Corporate tax cuts in the United States raise expected after-tax investment returns in the United States relative to those in Europe (U.S. dollar appreciates; the euro depreciates)
Speculation	Currency traders believe South Korea will have much greater inflation than Taiwan (South Korean won depreciates; Taiwan dollar appreciates).
	Currency traders think Norway's interest rates will plummet relative to Denmark's rates (Norway's krone depreciates; Denmark's krone appreciates).

Flexible Rates and the Balance of Payments

Proponents of flexible exchange rates say they have an important feature: They automatically adjust and eventually eliminate balance-of-payments deficits or surpluses. We can explain this idea through Figure 38.2, in which S_1 and D_1 are the supply and demand curves for pounds from Figure 38.1. The equilibrium exchange rate of $2 = £1 means that there is no balance-of-payments deficit or surplus between the United States and Britain. At that exchange rate, the quantity of pounds demanded by U.S. consumers to import British goods, buy British transportation and insurance services, and pay interest and dividends on British investments in the United States equals the amount of pounds supplied by the British in buying U.S. exports, purchasing services from the United States, and making interest and dividend payments on U.S. investments in Britain. The United States would have no need to either draw down or build up its official reserves to balance its payments.

Suppose tastes change and U.S. consumers buy more British automobiles; the U.S. price level increases relative to Britain's; or interest rates fall in the United States compared to those in Britain. Any or all of these changes will increase the U.S. demand for British pounds, for example, from D_1 to D_2 in Figure 38.2.

If the exchange rate remains at the initial $2 = £1, a U.S. balance-of-payments deficit will occur in the amount of *ab*. At the $2 = £1 rate, U.S. consumers will demand the quantity of pounds shown by point *b*, but

Britain will supply only the amount shown by *a*. There will be a shortage of pounds. But this shortage will not last because this is a competitive market. Instead, the dollar price of pounds will rise (the dollar will depreciate) until the balance-of-payments deficit is eliminated.

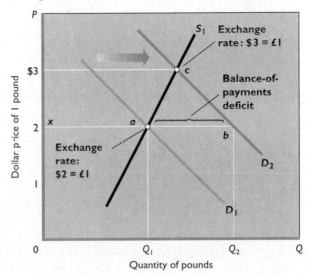

FIGURE 38.2 Adjustments under flexible exchange rates and fixed exchange rates. Under flexible exchange rates, a shift in the demand for pounds from D_1 to D_2, other things equal, would cause a U.S. balance-of-payments deficit *ab*. That deficit would be corrected by a change in the exchange rate from $2 = £1 to $3 = £1. Under fixed exchange rates, the United States would cover the shortage of pounds *ab* by using international monetary reserves, restricting trade, implementing exchange controls, or enacting a contractionary stabilization policy.

That occurs at the new equilibrium exchange rate of $3 = £1, where the quantities of pounds demanded and supplied are again equal.

To explain why this occurred, we reemphasize that the exchange rate links all domestic (U.S.) prices with all foreign (British) prices. The dollar price of a foreign good is found by multiplying the foreign price by the exchange rate (in dollars per unit of the foreign currency). At an exchange rate of $2 = £1, a British automobile priced at £15,000 will cost a U.S. consumer $30,000 (= 15,000 × $2).

A change in the exchange rate alters the prices of all British goods to U.S. consumers and all U.S. goods to British buyers. The shift in the exchange rate (here from $2 = £1 to $3 = £1) changes the relative attractiveness of U.S. imports and exports and restores equilibrium in the U.S. (and British) balance of payments. From the U.S. view, as the dollar price of pounds changes from $2 to $3, the British auto priced at £15,000, which formerly cost a U.S. consumer $30,000, now costs $45,000 (= 15,000 × $3). Other British goods will also cost U.S. consumers more, so that U.S. imports of British goods will decline. A movement from point *b* toward point *c* in Figure 38.2 graphically illustrates this concept.

From Britain's standpoint, the exchange rate (the pound price of dollars) has fallen (from $£\frac{1}{2}$ to $£\frac{1}{3}$ for $1). The international value of the pound has appreciated. The British previously got only $2 for £1; now they get $3 for £1. U.S. goods are therefore cheaper to the British, and U.S. exports to Britain will rise. In Figure 38.2, this is shown by a movement from point *a* toward point *c*.

The two adjustments—a decrease in U.S. imports from Britain and an increase in U.S. exports to Britain—are just what are needed to correct the U.S. balance-of-payments deficit. These changes end when, at point *c*, the quantities of British pounds demanded and supplied are equal. **(Key Questions 7 and 10)**

Disadvantages of Flexible Exchange Rates

Even though flexible exchange rates automatically work to eliminate payment imbalances, they may cause several significant problems. These are all realted to the fact that flexible exchange rates are often volatile and can change by a large amount in just a few weeks or months. In addition, they often take substantial swings that can last several years or more. This can be seen in Figure 38.3, which plots the dollar-pound exchange rate from 1970 through 2007. (You can track other exchange rates, for example, the dollar-euro or dollar-yen rate, by going to the Federal Reserve Web site, **www.federalreserve.gov**, selecting Economic Research and Data, Statistical Releases and Historical Data, and finally Exchange Rates and International Data.)

Uncertainty and Diminished Trade The risks and uncertainties associated with flexible exchange rates may discourage the flow of trade. Suppose a U.S. automobile dealer contracts to purchase 10 British cars for £150,000. At the current exchange rate of, say, $2

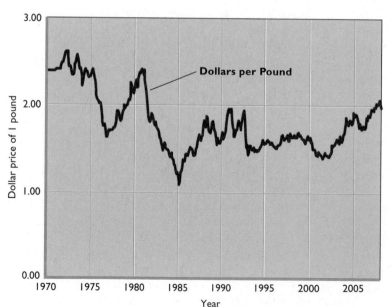

FIGURE 38.3 The dollar-pound exchange rate, 1970–2007. Before January 1971, the dollar-pound exchange rate was fixed at $2.40 = £1. Since that time, its value has been determined almost entirely by market forces, with only occasional government interventions. Under these mostly flexible conditions, the dollar-pound exchange rate has varied considerably. For instance, in January 1981, it took $2.40 to buy a pound. But by February 1985 it took only $1.09 to buy a pound. The dollar during that time period also showed a similarly massive apprecation against other major currencies. In contrast, since 2002 the U.S. dollar has generally depreciated, as indicated by the rising dollar price of pounds.

for £1, the U.S. importer expects to pay $300,000 for these automobiles. But if during the 3-month delivery period the rate of exchange shifts to $3 for £1, the £150,000 payment contracted by the U.S. importer will be $450,000.

That increase in the dollar price of pounds may thus turn the U.S. importer's anticipated profit into a substantial loss. Aware of the possibility of an adverse change in the exchange rate, the U.S. importer may not be willing to assume the risks involved. The U.S. firm may confine its operations to domestic automobiles, so international trade in this product will not occur.

The same thing can happen with investments. Assume that when the exchange rate is $3 to £1, a U.S. firm invests $30,000 (or £10,000) in a British enterprise. It estimates a return of 10 percent; that is, it anticipates annual earnings of $3000 or £1000. Suppose these expectations prove correct in that the British firm earns £1000 in the first year on the £10,000 investment. But suppose that during the year, the value of the dollar appreciates to $2 = £1. The absolute return is now only $2000 (rather than $3000), and the rate of return falls from the anticipated 10 percent to only $6\frac{2}{3}$ percent (= $2000/$30,000). Investment is risky in any case. The added risk of changing exchange rates may persuade the U.S. investor not to venture overseas.[1]

Terms-of-Trade Changes
A decline in the international value of its currency will worsen a nation's terms of trade. For example, an increase in the dollar price of a pound will mean that the United States must export more goods and services to finance a specific level of imports from Britain.

Instability
Flexible exchange rates may destabilize the domestic economy because wide fluctuations stimulate and then depress industries producing exported goods. If the U.S. economy is operating at full employment and its currency depreciates, as in our illustration, the results will be inflationary, for two reasons. (1) Foreign demand for U.S. goods may rise, increasing total spending and pulling up U.S. prices. Also, the prices of all U.S. imports will increase. (2) Conversely, appreciation of the dollar will lower U.S. exports and increase imports, possibly causing unemployment.

---

[1]You will see in this chapter's Last Word, however, that a trader can circumvent part of the risk of unfavorable exchange-rate fluctuations by "hedging" in the "futures market" or "forward market" for foreign exchange.

Flexible or floating exchange rates also may complicate the use of domestic stabilization policies in seeking full employment and price stability. This is especially true for nations whose exports and imports are large relative to their total domestic output.

Fixed Exchange Rates

To circumvent the disadvantages of flexible exchange rates, at times nations have fixed or "pegged" their exchange rates. For our analysis of fixed exchange rates, we assume that the United States and Britain agree to maintain a $2 = £1 exchange rate.

The problem is that such a government agreement cannot keep from changing the demand for and the supply of pounds. With the rate fixed, a shift in demand or supply will threaten the fixed-exchange-rate system, and government must intervene to ensure that the exchange rate is maintained.

In Figure 38.2, suppose the U.S. demand for pounds increases from D_1 to D_2 and a U.S. payment deficit ab arises. Now, the new equilibrium exchange rate ($3 = £1) is above the fixed exchange rate ($2 = £1). How can the United States prevent the shortage of pounds from driving the exchange rate up to the new equilibrium level? How can it maintain the fixed exchange rate? The answer is by altering market demand or market supply or both so that they will intersect at the $2 = £1 rate. There are several ways to do this.

Use of Reserves

One way to maintain a fixed exchange rate is to engage in **currency interventions.** These are situations in which governments manipulate an exchange rate through the use of official reserves. For instance, by selling some of its reserves of pounds, the U.S. government could increase the supply of pounds, shifting supply curve S_1 to the right so that it intersects D_2 at b in Figure 38.2, thereby maintaining the exchange rate at $2 = £1.

Notice that when the U.S. government sells some of its reserves of pounds, it is transferring assets to foreigners (since they gain ownership of the pounds). In terms of the balance of payments statement shown in Table 38.1, this transfer of assets enters positively on line (12), "Foreign purchases of assets in the United States." This positive entry is what offsets the balance of payments deficit caused by the fixed exchange rate and ensures that the U.S. balance of payments does in fact balance.

How do official reserves originate? Perhaps a balance-of-payments surplus occurred in the past. The U.S. government would have purchased that surplus. That is, at some earlier time, the U.S. government may have spent tax dollars to buy the surplus pounds that were threatening to reduce the exchange rate to below the $2 = £1$ fixed rate. Those purchases would have bolstered the U.S. official reserves of pounds.

Nations also have used gold as "international money" to obtain official reserves. In our example, the U.S. government could sell some of its gold to Britain to obtain pounds. It could then sell pounds for dollars. That would shift the supply-of-pounds curve to the right, and the $2 = £1$ exchange rate could be maintained.

It is critical that the amount of reserves and gold be enough to accomplish the required increase in the supply of pounds. There is no problem if deficits and surpluses occur more or less randomly and are of similar size. Then, last year's balance-of-payments surplus with Britain will increase the U.S. reserve of pounds, and that reserve can be used to "finance" this year's deficit. But if the United States encounters persistent and sizable deficits for an extended period, it may exhaust its reserves, and thus be forced to abandon fixed exchange rates. Or, at the least, a nation whose reserves are inadequate must use less-appealing options to maintain exchange rates. Let's consider some of those options.

Trade Policies

To maintain fixed exchange rates, a nation can try to control the flow of trade and finance directly. The United States could try to maintain the $2 = £1$ exchange rate in the face of a shortage of pounds by discouraging imports (thereby reducing the demand for pounds) and encouraging exports (thus increasing the supply of pounds). Imports could be reduced by means of new tariffs or import quotas; special taxes could be levied on the interest and dividends U.S. financial investors receive from foreign investments. Also, the U.S. government could subsidize certain U.S. exports to increase the supply of pounds.

The fundamental problem is that these policies reduce the volume of world trade and change its makeup from what is economically desirable. When nations impose tariffs, quotas, and the like, they lose some of the economic benefits of a free flow of world trade. That loss should not be underestimated: Trade barriers by one nation lead to retaliatory responses from other nations, multiplying the loss.

Exchange Controls and Rationing

Another option is to adopt exchange controls and rationing. Under **exchange controls** the U.S. government could handle the problem of a pound shortage by requiring that all pounds obtained by U.S. exporters be sold to the Federal government. Then the government would allocate or ration this short supply of pounds (represented by xa in Figure 38.2) among various U.S. importers, who demand the quantity xb. This policy would restrict the value of U.S. imports to the amount of foreign exchange earned by U.S. exports. Assuming balance in the capital and financial account, there would then be no balance-of-payments deficit. U.S. demand for British imports with the value ab would simply not be fulfilled.

There are major objections to exchange controls:

- **Distorted trade** Like tariffs, quotas, and export subsidies (trade controls), exchange controls would distort the pattern of international trade away from the pattern suggested by comparative advantage.
- **Favoritism** The process of rationing scarce foreign exchange might lead to government favoritism toward selected importers (big contributors to reelection campaigns, for example).
- **Restricted choice** Controls would limit freedom of consumer choice. The U.S. consumers who prefer Volkswagens might have to buy Chevrolets. The business opportunities for some U.S. importers might be impaired if the government were to limit imports.
- **Black markets** Enforcement problems are likely under exchange controls. U.S. importers might want foreign exchange badly enough to pay more than the $2 = £1$ official rate, setting the stage for black-market dealings between importers and illegal sellers of foreign exchange.

Domestic Macroeconomic Adjustments

A final way to maintain a fixed exchange rate would be to use domestic stabilization policies (monetary policy and fiscal policy) to eliminate the shortage of foreign currency. Tax hikes, reductions in government spending, and a high-interest-rate policy would reduce total spending in the U.S. economy and, consequently, domestic income. Because the volume of imports varies directly with domestic income, demand for British goods, and therefore for pounds, would be restrained.

If these "contractionary" policies served to reduce the domestic price level relative to Britain's, U.S. buyers of consumer and capital goods would divert their demands from British goods to U.S. goods, reducing the demand for pounds. Moreover, the high-interest-rate policy would lift U.S. interest rates relative to those in Britain.

Lower prices on U.S. goods and higher U.S. interest rates would increase British imports of U.S. goods and would increase British financial investment in the United States. Both developments would increase the supply of pounds. The combination of a decrease in the demand for and an increase in the supply of pounds would reduce or eliminate the original U.S. balance-of-payments deficit. In Figure 38.2 the new supply and demand curves would intersect at some new equilibrium point on line *ab*, where the exchange rate remains at $2 = £1.

Maintaining fixed exchange rates by such means is hardly appealing. The "price" of exchange-rate stability for the United States would be a decline in output, employment, and price levels—in other words, a recession. Eliminating a balance-of-payments deficit and achieving domestic stability are both important national economic goals, but to sacrifice stability to balance payments would be to let the tail wag the dog.

QUICK REVIEW 38.2

- In a system in which exchange rates are flexible (meaning that they are free to float), the rates are determined by the demand for and supply of individual national currencies in the foreign exchange market.

- Determinants of flexible exchange rates (factors that shift currency supply and demand curves) include changes in (a) tastes; (b) relative national incomes; (c) relative price levels, (d) real interest rates; (e) relative expected returns on stocks; real estate, and production facilities; and (f) speculation.

- Under a system of fixed exchange rates, nations set their exchange rates and then maintain them by buying or selling reserves of currencies, establishing trade barriers, employing exchange controls, or incurring inflation or recession.

The Current Exchange Rate System: The Managed Float

Over the past 130 years, the world's nations have used three different exchange-rate systems. From 1879 to 1934, most nations used a gold standard, which implicitly created fixed exchange rates. From 1944 to 1971, most countries participated in the Bretton Woods system, which was a fixed-exchange-rate system indirectly tied to gold. And since 1971, most have used managed floating exchange rates, which mix mostly flexible exchange rates with occasional currency interventions. Naturally, our focus here is on the current exchange rate system. However, the history of the previous systems and why they broke down is highly fascinating. For that reason, we have included information about them at the book's Web site along with other Chapter 38 materials.

The current international exchange-rate system (1971–present) is an "almost" flexible system called **managed floating exchange rates.** Exchange rates among major currencies are free to float to their equilibrium market levels, but nations occasionally use currency interventions in the foreign exchange market to stabilize or alter market exchange rates.

Normally, the major trading nations allow their exchange rates to float up or down to equilibrium levels based on supply and demand in the foreign exchange market. They recognize that changing economic conditions among nations require continuing changes in equilibrium exchange rates to avoid persistent payments deficits or surpluses. They rely on freely operating foreign exchange markets to accomplish the necessary adjustments. The result has been considerably more volatile exchange rates than those during the Bretton Woods era.

But nations also recognize that certain trends in the movement of equilibrium exchange rates may be at odds with national or international objectives. On occasion, nations therefore intervene in the foreign exchange market by buying or selling large amounts of specific currencies. This way, they can "manage" or stabilize exchange rates by influencing currency demand and supply.

The leaders of the *G8 nations* (Canada, France, Germany, Italy, Japan, Russia, United Kingdom, and United States) meet regularly to discuss economic issues and try to coordinate economic policies. At times they have collectively intervened to try to stabilize currencies. For example, in 2000 they sold dollars and bought euros in an effort to stabilize the falling value of the euro relative to the dollar. In the previous year the euro (€) had depreciated from €1 = $1.17 to €1 = $.87.

The current exchange-rate system is thus an "almost" flexible exchange-rate system. The "almost" refers mainly to the periodic currency interventions by governments; it also refers to the fact that the actual system is more complicated than described. While the major currencies such as dollars, euros, pounds, and yen fluctuate in response to changing supply and demand, some developing nations peg their currencies to the dollar and allow their currencies to fluctuate with it against other currencies. Also, some nations peg the value of their currencies to a "basket" or group of other currencies.

How well has the managed float worked? It has both proponents and critics. **(Key Question 11)**

In Support of the Managed Float

Proponents of the managed-float system argue that it has functioned far better than many experts anticipated. Skeptics had predicted that fluctuating exchange rates would reduce world trade and finance. But in real terms world trade under the managed float has grown tremendously over the past several decades. Moreover, as supporters are quick to point out, currency crises such as those in Mexico and southeast Asia in the last half of the 1990s were not the result of the floating-exchange-rate system itself. Rather, the abrupt currency devaluations and depreciations resulted from internal problems in those nations, in conjunction with the nations' tendency to peg their currencies to the dollar or to a basket of currencies. In some cases, flexible exchange rates would have made these adjustments far more gradual.

Proponents also point out that the managed float has weathered severe economic turbulence that might have caused a fixed-rate system to break down. Such events as extraordinary oil price increases in 1973–1974 and again in 1981–1983, inflationary recessions in several nations in the mid-1970s, major national recessions in the early 1980s, and large U.S. budget deficits in the 1980s and the first half of the 1990s all caused substantial imbalances in international trade and finance, as did the large U.S. budget deficits and soaring world oil prices that occurred in the middle of the first decade of the 2000s. Flexible rates enabled the system to adjust to all these events, whereas the same events would have put unbearable pressures on a fixed-rate system.

Concerns with the Managed Float

There is still much sentiment in favor of greater exchange-rate stability. Those favoring more stable exchange rates see problems with the current system. They argue that the excessive volatility of exchange rates under the managed float threatens the prosperity of economies that rely heavily on exports. Several financial crises in individual nations (for example, Mexico, South Korea, Indonesia, Thailand, Russia, and Brazil) have resulted from abrupt changes in exchange rates. These crises have led to massive "bailouts" of those economies via loans from the International Monetary (IMF). The IMF bailouts, in turn, may encourage nations to undertake risky and inappropriate economic policies since they know that, if need be, the IMF will come to the rescue. Moreover, some exchange-rate volatility has occurred even when underlying economic and financial conditions were relatively stable, suggesting that speculation plays too large a role in determining exchange rates.

Skeptics say the managed float is basically a "nonsystem"; the guidelines concerning what each nation may or may not do with its exchange rates are not specific enough to keep the system working in the long run. Nations inevitably will be tempted to intervene in the foreign exchange market, not merely to smooth out short-term fluctuations in exchange rates but to prop up their currency if it is chronically weak or to manipulate the exchange rate to achieve domestic stabilization goals.

So what are we to conclude? Flexible exchange rates have not worked perfectly, but they have not failed miserably. Thus far they have survived, and no doubt have eased, several major shocks to the international trading system. Meanwhile, the "managed" part of the float has given nations some sense of control over their collective economic destinies. On balance, most economists favor continuation of the present system of "almost" flexible exchange rates.

QUICK REVIEW 38.3

- The managed floating system of exchange rates (1971–present) relies on foreign exchange markets to establish equilibrium exchange rates.
- The system permits nations to buy and sell foreign currency to stabilize short-term changes in exchange rates or to correct exchange-rate imbalances that are negatively affecting the world economy.
- Proponents point out that international trade and investment have grown tremendously under the system. Critics say that it is a "nonsystem" and argue that the exchange rate volatility allowed under the managed float discourages international trade and investment. That is, trade and investment would be even larger if exchange rates were more stable.

Recent U.S. Trade Deficits

As indicated in Figure 38.4a, the United States has experienced large and persistent trade deficits over the past several years. These deficits increased tremendously from 1999 through 2007. The only two years during which the deficits declined were 2001 when the U.S. economy was in recession and 2007 when a substantial decline in the value of the U.S. dollar relative to foreign currencies caused U.S. exports to increase faster than U.S. imports. In 2007, the trade deficit on goods was $816 billion and the trade deficit on goods and services was $709 billion. The current account deficit (Figure 38.4b) reached a record $811 billion in 2006. It rose from 3.3 percent of GDP in 1999 to 6.2 percent of GDP in 2006 before declining to 5.3 percent of GDP in 2007. Large trade deficits are expected to continue for many years, in both absolute and relative terms.

FIGURE 38.4 U.S. trade deficits, 1999–2007. (a) The United States experienced large deficits in *goods* and in *goods and services* between 1999 and 2007. (b) The U.S. current account, generally reflecting the goods and services deficit, was also in substantial deficit. These deficits are expected to continue throughout the current decade.

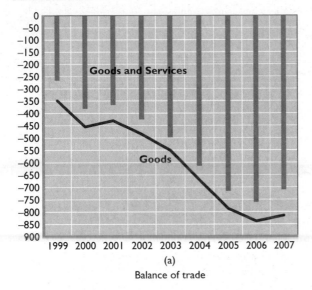

Billions of Dollars

(a)
Balance of trade

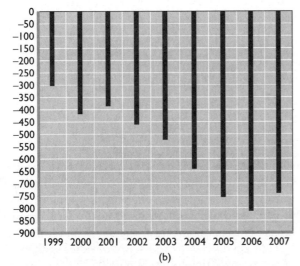

Billions of Dollars

(b)
Balance on current account

Source: Bureau of Economic Analysis, **www.bea.gov.**

Causes of the Trade Deficits

Several reasons account for these large trade deficits. First, between 1999 and 2000, and again between 2003 and 2007, the U.S. economy grew more rapidly than the economies of several of its major trading partners. That strong growth of U.S. income enabled Americans to buy more imported goods. In contrast, Japan and some European nations either suffered recession or experienced slower income growth. So their purchases of U.S. exports did not keep pace with the growing U.S. imports.

Also, large trade deficits with China have emerged, reaching $257 billion in 2007. This amount is even greater than the U.S. trade imbalance with Japan ($85 billion in 2007). The United States is China's largest export market, and although China has increased its imports from the United States, its standard of living has not yet increased enough for its citizens to afford large quantities of U.S. goods and services. Adding to the problem, China has fixed the exchange rate of it currency, the yuan, to a basket of currencies that includes the dollar. Therefore, its large trade surplus with the United States has not caused the yuan to appreciate by much relative to the U.S. dollar. Greater appreciation would make Chinese goods more expensive in the United States and reduce U.S. imports of Chinese goods. In China a stronger yuan would reduce the dollar price of U.S. goods and increase Chinese purchases of U.S. exports. Reduced U.S. imports from China and increased U.S. exports to China would reduce the large U.S. trade deficit.

Another factor causing the large U.S. trade deficits has been the rapid rise of the price of oil. Because the United States imports a large percentage of its oil, rising prices tend to aggravate trade deficits. For example, in 2007 the United States had a $125 billion trade deficit with the OPEC countries.

Finally, a declining U.S. saving rate (= saving/total income) also has contributed to U.S. trade deficits. In recent years, the saving rate has declined while the investment rate (= investment/total income) has remained stable or even increased. The gap has been met through foreign purchases of U.S. real and financial assets, creating a large capital and financial account surplus. Because foreign savers are willingly financing a larger part of U.S. investment, Americans are able to save less than otherwise and consume more. Part of that added consumption spending is on imported goods. Also, many foreigners view U.S. assets favorably because of the relatively high risk-adjusted rates of return they generate. The purchase of those assets provides foreign currency to Americans to finance their strong appetite for imported goods.

The point is that the capital account surplus may be a partial cause of the trade deficits, not just a result of those deficits.

Implications of U.S. Trade Deficits

The recent U.S. trade deficits are the largest ever run by a major industrial nation. Whether the large trade deficits

Are Speculators a Negative or a Positive Influence in Currency Markets and International Trade?

Most people buy foreign currency to facilitate the purchase of goods, services, or assets from another country. A U.S. importer buys Japanese yen to purchase Japanese autos. A Hong Kong financial investor purchases Australian dollars to invest in the Australian stock market. But there is another group of participants in the currency market—speculators—that buys and sells foreign currencies in the hope of reselling or rebuying them later at a profit.

Contributing to Exchange-Rate Fluctuations Speculators were much in the news in late 1997 and 1998 when they were widely accused of driving down the values of the South Korean won, Thailand baht, Malaysian ringgit, and Indonesian rupiah. The value of these currencies fell by as much as 50 percent within 1 month, and speculators undoubtedly contributed to the swiftness of those declines. The expectation of currency depreciation (or appreciation) can be self-fulfilling. If speculators, for example, expect the Indonesian rupiah to be devalued or to depreciate, they quickly sell rupiah and buy currencies that they think will increase in relative value. The sharp increase in the supply of rupiah indeed reduces its value; this reduction then may trigger further selling of rupiah in expectation of further declines in its value.

But changed economic realities, not speculation, are normally the underlying causes of changes in currency values. That was largely the case with the southeast Asian countries in which actual and threatened bankruptcies in the financial and manufacturing sectors undermined confidence in the strength of the currencies. Anticipating the eventual declines in currency values, speculators simply hastened those declines. That is, the declines in value probably would have occurred with or without speculators.

Moreover, on a daily basis, speculation clearly has positive effects in foreign exchange markets.

Smoothing Out Short-Term Fluctuations in Currency Prices When temporarily weak demand or strong supply reduces a currency's value, speculators quickly buy the currency, adding to its demand and strengthening its value. When temporarily strong demand or weak supply increases a currency's value, speculators sell the currency. That selling increases the supply of the currency and reduces its value. In this way speculators smooth out supply and demand, and thus exchange rates, over short time periods. This day-to-day exchange-rate stabilization aids international trade.

Absorbing Risk Speculators also absorb risk that others do not want to bear. Because of potential adverse changes in exchange rates, international transactions are riskier than domestic

should be of significant concern to the United States and the rest of the world is debatable. Most economists see both benefits and costs to trade deficits.

Increased Current Consumption

At the time a trade deficit or a current account deficit is occurring, American consumers benefit. A trade deficit means that the United States is receiving more goods and services as imports from abroad than it is sending out as exports. Taken alone, a trade deficit allows the United States to consume outside its production possibilities curve. It augments the domestic standard of living. But here is a catch: The gain in present consumption may come at the expense of reduced future consumption. When and if the current account deficit declines, Americans may have to consume less than before and perhaps even less than they produce.

Increased U.S. Indebtedness

A trade deficit is considered unfavorable because it must be financed by borrowing from the rest of the world, selling off assets, or dipping into official reserves. Recall that current account deficits are financed primarily by net inpayments of foreign currencies to the United States. When U.S. exports are insufficient to finance U.S. imports, the United States increases both its debt to people abroad and the value of foreign claims against assets in the United States. Financing of the U.S. trade deficit has resulted in a larger foreign accumulation of claims against U.S. financial and real assets than the U.S. claim against foreign assets. In 2006, foreigners owned about $2.5 trillion more of U.S. assets (corporations, land, stocks, bonds, loan notes) than U.S. citizens and institutions owned in foreign assets.

transactions. Suppose AnyTime, a hypothetical retailer, signs a contract with a Swiss manufacturer to buy 10,000 Swatch watches to be delivered in 3 months. The stipulated price is 75 Swiss francs per watch, which in dollars is $50 per watch at the present exchange rate of, say, $1 = 1.5 francs. AnyTime's total bill for the 10,000 watches will be $500,000 (= 750,000 francs).

But if the Swiss franc were to appreciate, say, to $1 = 1 franc, the dollar price per watch would rise from $50 to $75 and AnyTime would owe $750,000 for the watches (= 750,000 francs). AnyTime may reduce the risk of such an unfavorable exchange-rate fluctuation by hedging in the futures market. Hedging is an action by a buyer or a seller to protect against a change in future prices. The futures market is a market in which currencies are bought and sold at prices fixed now, for delivery at a specified date in the future.

AnyTime can purchase the needed 750,000 francs at the current $1 = 1.5 francs exchange rate, but with delivery in 3 months when the Swiss watches are delivered. And here is where speculators come in. For a price determined in the futures market, they agree to deliver the 750,000 francs to AnyTime in 3 months at the $1 = 1.5 francs exchange rate, regardless of the exchange rate then. The speculators need not

own francs when the agreement is made. If the Swiss franc depreciates to, say, $1 = 2 francs in this period, the speculators profit. They can buy the 750,000 francs stipulated in the contract for $375,000, pocketing the difference between that amount and the $500,000 AnyTime has agreed to pay for the 750,000 francs. If the Swiss franc appreciates, the speculators, but not AnyTime, suffer a loss.

The amount AnyTime must pay for this "exchange-rate insurance" will depend on how the market views the likelihood of the franc depreciating, appreciating, or staying constant over the 3-month period. As in all competitive markets, supply and demand determine the price of the futures contract.

The futures market thus eliminates much of the exchange-rate risk associated with buying foreign goods for future delivery. Without it, AnyTime might have decided against importing Swiss watches. But the futures market and currency speculators greatly increase the likelihood that the transaction will occur. Operating through the futures market, speculation promotes international trade.

In short, although speculators in currency markets occasionally contribute to swings in exchange rates, on a day-to-day basis they play a positive role in currency markets.

If the United States wants to regain ownership of these domestic assets, at some future time it will have to export more than it imports. At that time, domestic consumption will be lower because the United States will need to send more of its output abroad than it receives as imports. Therefore, the current consumption gains delivered by U.S. current account deficits may mean permanent debt, permanent foreign ownership, or large sacrifices of future consumption.

We say "may mean" above because the foreign lending to U.S. firms and foreign investment in the United States increases the U.S. capital stock. U.S. production capacity therefore might increase more rapidly than otherwise because of a large surplus on the capital and financial account. Faster increases in production capacity and real GDP enhance the economy's ability to service foreign debt and buy back real capital, if that is desired.

In short, trade deficits are a mixed blessing. The long-term impacts of the record-high U.S. trade deficits are largely unknown. That "unknown" worries some economists, who are concerned that foreigners will lose financial confidence in the United States. If that happens, they would restrict their lending to American households and businesses and also reduce their purchases of U.S. assets. Both actions would decrease the demand for U.S. dollars in the foreign exchange market and cause the U.S. dollar to depreciate. A sudden, large depreciation of the U.S. dollar might disrupt world trade and negatively affect economic growth worldwide. Other economists, however, downplay this scenario. Because any decline in the U.S. capital and financial account surplus is automatically met with a decline in the current account deficit, U.S. net exports would rise and the overall impact on the American economy would be slight.

Summary

1. International financial transactions involve trade either in currently produced goods and services or in preexisting assets. Exports of goods, services, and assets create inflows of money, while imports cause outflows of money. If buyers and sellers use different currencies, then foreign exchange transactions take place so that the exporter can be paid in his or her own currency.

2. The balance of payments records all international trade and financial transactions taking place between a given nation and the rest of the world. The balance on goods and services (the trade balance) compares exports and imports of both goods and services. The current account balance includes not only goods and services transactions but also net investment income and net transfers.

3. The capital and financial account includes (a) the net amount of the nation's debt forgiveness and (b) the nation's sale of real and financial assets to people living abroad less its purchases of real and financial assets from foreigners.

4. The current account and the capital and financial account always sum to zero. A deficit in the current account is always offset by a surplus in the capital and financial account. Conversely, a surplus in the current account is always offset by a deficit in the capital and financial account.

5. A balance-of-payments deficit is said to occur when a nation must draw down its official reserves, making inpayments to its balance of payments, in order to balance the capital and financial account with the current account. A balance-of-payments surplus occurs when a nation must increase its official reserves, making outpayments from its balance of payments, to balance the two accounts. The desirability of a balance-of-payments deficit or surplus depends on its size and its persistence.

6. Flexible or floating exchange rates between international currencies are determined by the demand for and supply of those currencies. Under flexible rates, a currency will depreciate or appreciate as a result of changes in tastes, relative income changes, relative price changes, relative changes in real interest rates, and speculation.

7. The maintenance of fixed exchange rates requires adequate reserves to accommodate periodic payments deficits. If reserves are inadequate, nations must invoke protectionist trade policies, engage in exchange controls, or endure undesirable domestic macroeconomic adjustments.

8. Since 1971 the world's major nations have used a system of managed floating exchange rates. Market forces generally set rates, although governments intervene with varying frequency to alter their exchange rates.

9. Between 1997 and 2007, the United States had large and rising trade deficits, which are projected to last well into the future. Causes of the trade deficits include (a) more rapid income growth in the United States than in Japan and some European nations, resulting in expanding U.S. imports relative to exports, (b) the emergence of a large trade deficit with China, (c) rising prices of imported oil, and (d) a large surplus in the capital and financial account, which enabled Americans to reduce their saving and buy more imports.

10. U.S. trade deficits have produced current increases in the living standards of U.S. consumers. The accompanying surpluses on the capital and financial account have increased U.S. debt to the rest of the world and increased foreign ownership of assets in the United States. This greater foreign investment in the United States, however, has undoubtedly increased U.S. production possibilities.

Terms and Concepts

balance of payments

current account

balance on goods and services

trade deficit

trade surplus

balance on current account

capital and financial account

balance on capital and financial account

balance-of-payments deficits and surpluses

official reserves

flexible- or floating-exchange-rate system

fixed-exchange-rate system

purchasing-power-parity theory

currency interventions

exchange controls

managed floating exchange rates

Study Questions

1. Do all international financial transactions involve exchanging one currency for another? Could a nation that neither imports nor exports goods and services still engage in international financial transactions? Explain: "U.S. exports earn supplies of foreign currencies that Americans can use to finance imports." **LO1**

2. **KEY QUESTION** Indicate whether each of the following creates a demand for or a supply of European euros in foreign exchange markets: **LO1**
   a. A U.S. airline firm purchases several Airbus planes assembled in France.
   b. A German automobile firm decides to build an assembly plant in South Carolina.
   c. A U.S. college student decides to spend a year studying at the Sorbonne in Paris.
   d. An Italian manufacturer ships machinery from one Italian port to another on a Liberian freighter.
   e. The U.S. economy grows faster than the French economy.
   f. A U.S. government bond held by a Spanish citizen matures, and the loan amount is paid back to that person.
   g. It is widely believed that the euro will depreciate in the near future.

3. **KEY QUESTION** Alpha's balance-of-payments data for 2008 are shown below. All figures are in billions of dollars. What are the (*a*) balance on goods, (*b*) balance on goods and services, (*c*) balance on current account, and (*d*) balance on capital and financial account? Suppose Alpha needed to deposit $10 billion of official reserves into the capital and financial account to balance it against the current account. Does Alpha have a balance-of-payments deficit or surplus? Explain. **LO2**

Goods exports	$+40
Goods imports	−30
Service exports	+15
Service imports	−10
Net investment income	−5
Net transfers	+10
Balance on capital account	0
Foreign purchases of Alpha assets	+20
Alpha purchases of assets abroad	−40

4. China had a $372 billion overall current account surplus in 2007. Assuming that China's net debt forgiveness was zero in 2007 (its capital account balance was zero), what can you specifically conclude about the relationship of Chinese purchases of financial and real assets abroad versus foreign purchases of Chinese financial and real assets? Explain. **LO2**

5. "A rise in the dollar price of yen necessarily means a fall in the yen price of dollars." Do you agree? Illustrate and elaborate: "The critical thing about exchange rates is that they provide a direct link between the prices of goods and services produced in all trading nations of the world." Explain the purchasing-power-parity theory of exchange rates. **LO3**

6. Suppose that a Swiss watchmaker imports watch components from Sweden and exports watches to the United States. Also suppose the dollar depreciates, and the Swedish krona appreciates, relative to the Swiss franc. Speculate as to how each would hurt the Swiss watchmaker. **LO3**

7. **KEY QUESTION** Explain why the U.S. demand for Mexican pesos is downward-sloping and the supply of pesos to Americans is upward-sloping. Assuming a system of flexible exchange rates between Mexico and the United States, indicate whether each of the following would cause the Mexican peso to appreciate or depreciate: **LO3**
   a. The United States unilaterally reduces tariffs on Mexican products.
   b. Mexico encounters severe inflation.
   c. Deteriorating political relations reduce American tourism in Mexico.
   d. The U.S. economy moves into a severe recession.
   e. The United States engages in a high-interest-rate monetary policy.
   f. Mexican products become more fashionable to U.S. consumers.
   g. The Mexican government encourages U.S. firms to invest in Mexican oil fields.
   h. The rate of productivity growth in the United States diminishes sharply.

8. Explain why you agree or disagree with the following statements: **LO3**
   a. A country that grows faster than its major trading partners can expect the international value of its currency to depreciate.
   b. A nation whose interest rate is rising more rapidly than interest rates in other nations can expect the international value of its currency to appreciate.
   c. A country's currency will appreciate if its inflation rate is less than that of the rest of the world.

9. "Exports pay for imports. Yet in 2007 the nations of the world exported about $709 billion more worth of goods and services to the United States than they imported from the United States." Resolve the apparent inconsistency of these two statements. **LO2**

10. **KEY QUESTION** Diagram a market in which the equilibrium dollar price of 1 unit of fictitious currency zee (Z) is $5 (the exchange rate is $5 = Z1). Then show on your diagram a decline in the demand for zee. **LO4**
    a. Referring to your diagram, discuss the adjustment options the United States would have in maintaining the exchange rate at $5 = Z1 under a fixed-exchange-rate system.
    b. How would the U.S. balance-of-payments surplus that is created (by the decline in demand) get resolved under a system of flexible exchange rates?

11. **KEY QUESTION** Suppose that a country follows a managed-float policy but that its exchange rate is currently floating freely. In addition, suppose that it currently has a massive current account deficit. Does it also have a balance of payments deficit? If it decides to engage in a currency manipulation in order to reduce the size of its current account deficit, will it buy or sell its own currency? As it does so, what will happen to its official reserves of foreign currencies? Will they get larger or smaller? And, finally, will the

country have a balance of payments deficit while it is manipulating the exchange rate? **LO4**

12. What have been the major causes of the large U.S. trade deficits since 1999? What are the major benefits and costs associated with trade deficits? Explain: "A trade deficit means that a nation is receiving more goods and services from abroad than it is sending abroad." How can that be called "unfavorable"? **LO5**

13. **LAST WORD** Suppose Super D'Hiver—a hypothetical French snowboard retailer—wants to order 5000 snowboards made in the United States. The price per board is $200, the present exchange rate is 1 euro = $1, and payment is due in dollars when the boards are delivered in 3 months. Use a numerical example to explain why exchange-rate risk might make the French retailer hesitant to place the order. How might speculators absorb some of Super D'Hiver's risk?

Web-Based Questions

1. **THE U.S. BALANCE ON GOODS AND SERVICES—WHAT ARE THE LATEST FIGURES?** The U.S. Census Bureau reports the latest data on U.S. trade in goods and services at its Web site, **www.census.gov/indicator/www/ustrade.html.** In the latest month, did the trade balance in goods and services improve (that is, yield a smaller deficit or a larger surplus) or deteriorate? Was the relative trade strength of the United States compared to the rest of the world in goods or in services? Which product groups had the largest increases in exports? Which had the largest increases in imports?

2. **THE YEN-DOLLAR EXCHANGE RATE** The Federal Reserve Board of Governors provides exchange rates for various currencies for the last decade at **www.federalreserve.gov/ releases** (Under the heading Exchange Rates and International Data, notice the subheading Foreign Exchange Rates. Click on the Annual link. You will find links to annual releases of exchange rate information. Use the most current and previous ones to answer the following question.) Has the dollar appreciated, depreciated, or remained constant relative to the Canadian dollar, the European euro, the Japanese yen, the Swedish krona, and the Swiss franc since 2000?

SUPPLEMENTAL WEB CONTENT FOR
CHAPTER 38: THE BALANCE OF PAYMENTS,
EXCHANGE RATES, AND TRADE DEFICITS

Previous International Exchange-Rate Systems

Chapter 38 discusses the current system of managed floating exchange rates in some detail. But before this system began in 1971, the world had previously used two other exchange rate systems: the gold standard, which implicitly created fixed exchange rates, and the Bretton Woods system, which was an explicit fixed-rate system indirectly tied to gold. Because the features and problems of these two systems help explain why we have the current system, they are well-worth knowing more about.

The Economics of Developing Countries

Chapter 39 Web is a bonus chapter found at the book's Web site, **www.mcconnell18e.com**. It extends the analysis of Part 10, International Economics, by examining the special problems of developing countries. It may, or may not, be assigned by your instructor.

Note: Terms set in *italic* type are defined separately in this glossary.

ability-to-pay principle The idea that those who have greater *income* (or *wealth*) should pay a greater proportion of it as taxes than those who have less income (or wealth).

acreage allotments A pre-1996 government program that determined the total number of acres to be used in producing (reduced amounts of) various food and fiber products and allocated these acres among individual farmers. These farmers had to limit their plantings to the allotted number of acres to obtain *price supports* for their crops.

actively managed funds *Mutual funds* that have portfolio managers who constantly buy and sell *assets* in an attempt to generate higher returns than some benchmark rate of return for similar *portfolios*.

actual investment The amount that *firms* invest; equal to *planned investment* plus *unplanned investment*.

actual reserves The funds that a bank has on deposit at the *Federal Reserve Bank* of its district (plus its *vault cash*).

adverse selection problem A problem arising when information known to one party to a contract or agreement is not known to the other party, causing the latter to incur major costs. Example: Individuals who have the poorest health are most likely to buy health insurance.

advertising A seller's activities in communicating its message about its product to potential buyers.

AFL-CIO An acronym for the American Federation of Labor–Congress of Industrial Organizations; the largest federation of *labor unions* in the United States.

agency shop A place of employment where the employer may hire either *labor union* members or nonmembers but where those who do not join the union must either pay union dues or donate an equivalent amount of money to a charity.

aggregate A collection of specific economic units treated as if they were one. For example, all prices of individual goods and services are combined into a *price level*, or all units of output are aggregated into *gross domestic product*.

aggregate demand A schedule or curve that shows the total quantity of goods and services demanded (purchased) at different *price levels*.

aggregate demand–aggregate supply (AD-AS) model The macroeconomic model that uses *aggregate demand* and *aggregate supply* to determine and explain the *price level* and the real *domestic output*.

aggregate expenditures The total amount spent for final goods and services in an economy.

aggregate expenditures–domestic output approach Determination of the equilibrium *gross domestic product* by finding the real GDP at which *aggregate expenditures* equal *domestic output*.

aggregate expenditures schedule A schedule or curve showing the total amount spent for final goods and services at different levels of *real GDP*.

aggregate supply A schedule or curve showing the total quantity of goods and services supplied (produced) at different *price levels*.

aggregate supply shocks Sudden, large changes in resource costs that shift an economy's aggregate supply curve.

agribusiness The portion of the agricultural and food product industries that is dominated by large corporations.

Alcoa case A 1945 case in which the courts ruled that the possession of monopoly power, no matter how reasonably that power had been used, was a violation of the antitrust laws; temporarily overturned the *rule of reason* applied in the *U.S. Steel case*.

allocative efficiency The apportionment of resources among firms and industries to obtain the production of the products most wanted by society (consumers); the output of each product at which its *marginal cost* and *price* or *marginal benefit* are equal, and at which the sum of *consumer surplus* and *producer surplus* is maximized.

anticipated inflation Increases in the price level (*inflation*) that occur at the expected rate.

antitrust laws Legislation (including the *Sherman Act* and *Clayton Act*) that prohibits anticompetitive business activities such as *price fixing*, bid rigging, monopolization, and *tying contracts*.

antitrust policy The use of the *antitrust laws* to promote *competition* and economic efficiency.

appreciation (of the dollar) An increase in the value of the dollar relative to the currency of another nation, so a dollar buys a larger amount of the foreign currency and thus of foreign goods.

arbitrage The activity of selling one *asset* and buying an identical or nearly identical asset to benefit from temporary differences in prices or rates of return; the practice that equalizes prices or returns on similar financial instruments and thus eliminates further opportunities for riskless financial gains.

asset Anything of monetary value owned by a firm or individual.

asset demand for money The amount of *money* people want to hold as a *store of value*; this amount varies inversely with the *interest rate*.

asymmetric information A situation where one party to a market transaction has much more information about a product or service than the other. The result may be an under- or overallocation of resources.

average expected rate of return The *probability weighted average* of an investment's possible future returns.

average fixed cost (AFC) A firm's total *fixed cost* divided by output (the quantity of product produced).

average product (AP) The total output produced per unit of a *resource* employed (*total product* divided by the quantity of that employed resource).

average propensity to consume Fraction (or percentage) of *disposable income* that households plan to spend for consumer goods and services; consumption divided by *disposable income*.

average propensity to save (APS) Fraction (or percentage) of *disposable income* that households save; *saving* divided by *disposable income*.

average revenue Total revenue from the sale of a product divided by the quantity of the product sold (demanded); equal to the price at which the product is sold when all units of the product are sold at the same price.

average tax rate Total tax paid divided by total (taxable) income, as a percentage.

average total cost (ATC) A firm's *total cost* divided by output (the quantity of product produced); equal to *average fixed cost* plus *average variable cost*.

average variable cost (AVC) A firm's total *variable cost* divided by output (the quantity of product produced).

backflows The return of workers to the countries from which they originally migrated.

balance of payments (See *international balance of payments*.)

balance-of-payments deficit The amount by which *inpayments* from a nation's stock of *official reserves* are required to balance that nation's *capital and financial account* with its *current account* (in its *balance of payments*).

balance-of-payments surplus The amount by which *outpayments* to a nation's stock of *official reserves* are required to balance that nation's *capital and financial account* with its *current account* (in its *international balance of payments*).

balance on capital and financial account The sum of the *capital account balance* and the *financial account balance*.

balance on current account The exports of goods and services of a nation less its imports of goods and services plus its *net investment income* and *net transfers* in a year.

balance on goods and services The exports of goods and services of a nation less its imports of goods and services in a year.

balance sheet A statement of the *assets*, *liabilities*, and *net worth* of a firm or individual at some given time.

bank deposits The deposits that individuals or firms have at banks (or thrifts) or that banks have at the *Federal Reserve Banks*.

bankers' bank A bank that accepts the deposits of and makes loans to *depository institutions*; in the United States, a *Federal Reserve Bank*.

bank reserves The deposits of commercial banks and thrifts at *Federal Reserve Banks* plus bank and thrift *vault cash*.

bankrupt A legal situation in which an individual or *firm* finds that it cannot make timely interest payments on money it has borrowed. In such cases, a bankruptcy judge can order the individual or firm to liquidate (turn into cash) its assets in order to pay lenders at least some portion of the amount they are owed.

barrier to entry Anything that artificially prevents the entry of firms into an industry.

barter The exchange of one good or service for another good or service.

base year The year with which other years are compared when an index is constructed; for example, the base year for a *price index*.

beaten paths Migration routes taken previously by family, relatives, friends, and other migrants.

benefits-received principle The idea that those who receive the benefits of goods and services provided by government should pay the taxes required to finance them.

beta A relative measure of *nondiversifiable risk* that measures how the nondiversifiable risk of a given *asset* or *portfolio* compares with that of the *market portfolio* (the portfolio that contains every asset available in the financial markets).

bilateral monopoly A market in which there is a single seller (*monopoly*) and a single buyer (*monopsony*).

Board of Governors The seven-member group that supervises and controls the money and banking system of the United States; the Board of Governors of the Federal Reserve System; the Federal Reserve Board.

bond A financial device through which a borrower (a firm or government) is obligated to pay the principal and interest on a loan at a specific date in the future.

brain drains The exit or *emigration* of highly educated, highly skilled workers from a country.

break-even income The level of *disposable income* at which *households* plan to consume (spend) all their income and to save none of it.

break-even output Any output at which a (competitive) firm's *total cost* and *total revenue* are equal; an output at which a firm has neither an *economic profit* nor a loss, at which it earns only a *normal profit*.

break-even point An output at which a firm makes a *normal profit* (total revenue = total cost) but not an *economic profit*.

British thermal unit (BTU) The amount of energy required to raise the temperature of 1 pound of water by 1 degree Fahrenheit.

budget constraint The limit that the size of a consumer's income (and the prices that must be paid for goods and services) imposes on the ability of that consumer to obtain goods and services.

budget deficit The amount by which the expenditures of the Federal government exceed its revenues in any year.

budget line A line that shows the different combinations of two products a consumer can purchase with a specific money income, given the products' prices.

budget surplus The amount by which the revenues of the Federal government exceed its expenditures in any year.

built-in stabilizer A mechanism that increases government's budget deficit (or reduces its surplus) during a recession and increases government's budget surplus (or reduces its deficit) during an expansion without any action by policymakers. The tax system is one such mechanism.

Bureau of Economic Analysis (BEA) An agency of the U.S. Department of Commerce that compiles the national income and product accounts.

business cycle Recurring increases and decreases in the level of economic activity over periods of years; consists of peak, recession, trough, and expansion phases.

business firm (See *firm*.)

cap-and-trade program A government strategy for reducing harmful emissions or discharges by placing a limit on their total amounts and then allowing firms to buy and sell the rights to emit or discharge specific amounts within the total limits.

capital Human-made resources (buildings, machinery, and equipment) used to produce goods and services; goods that do not directly satisfy human wants; also called capital goods.

capital and financial account The section of a nation's *international balance of payments* that records (1) debt forgiveness by and to foreigners and (2) foreign purchases of assets in the United States and U.S. purchases of assets abroad.

capital and financial account deficit A negative balance on its *capital and financial account* in a country's *international balance of payments*.

capital and financial account surplus A positive balance on its *capital and financial account* in a country's *international balance of payments*.

capital flight (Web chapter) The transfer of savings from *developing countries* to *industrially advanced countries* to avoid government expropriation, taxation, higher rates of inflation, or simply to realize greater returns on *financial investments*.

capital gain The gain realized when securities or properties are sold for a price greater than the price paid for them.

capital goods (See *capital*.)

capital-intensive goods Products that require relatively large amounts of *capital* to produce.

capitalism An economic system in which property resources are privately owned and markets and prices are used to direct and coordinate economic activities.

capital-saving technology (Web chapter) An improvement in *technology* that permits a greater quantity of a product to be produced with a specific amount of *capital* (or permits the same amount of the product to be produced with a smaller amount of capital).

capital stock The total available *capital* in a nation.

capital-using technology (Web chapter) An improvement in *technology* that requires the use of a greater amount of *capital* to produce a specific quantity of a product.

capricious-universe view (Web chapter) The view held by some people that fate and outside events, rather than hard work and enterprise, will determine their economic destinies.

cardinal utility Satisfaction (*utility*) that can be measured via cardinal numbers (1, 2, 3…), with all the mathematical properties of those numbers such as addition, subtraction, multiplication, and division being applicable.

cartel A formal agreement among firms (or countries) in an industry to set the price of a product and establish the outputs of the individual firms (or countries) or to divide the market for the product geographically.

causation A relationship in which the occurrence of one or more events brings about another event.

CEA (See *Council of Economic Advisers*.)

cease-and-desist order An order from a court or government agency to a corporation or individual to stop engaging in a specified practice.

ceiling price (See *price ceiling*.)

Celler-Kefauver Act The Federal act of 1950 that amended the *Clayton Act* by prohibiting the acquisition of the assets of one firm by another firm when the effect would be less competition.

central bank A bank whose chief function is the control of the nation's *money supply*; in the United States, the Federal Reserve System.

central economic planning Government determination of the objectives of the economy and how resources will be directed to attain those goals.

ceteris paribus assumption (See *other-things-equal assumption*.)

change in demand A change in the *quantity demanded* of a good or service at every price; a shift of the *demand curve* to the left or right.

change in quantity demanded A change in the amount of a product that consumers are willing and able to purchase because of a change in the product's price.

change in quantity supplied A change in the amount of a product that producers offer for sale because of a change in the product's price.

change in supply A change in the *quantity supplied* of a good or service at every price; a shift of the *supply curve* to the left or right.

Change to Win A loose federation of American unions that includes the Service Workers and Teamsters and has a total membership of 6 million workers.

checkable deposit Any deposit in a *commercial bank* or *thrift institution* against which a check may be written.

checkable-deposit multiplier (See *monetary multiplier*.)

check clearing The process by which funds are transferred from the checking accounts of the writers of checks to the checking accounts of the recipients of the checks.

checking account A *checkable deposit* in a *commercial bank* or *thrift institution*.

circular flow diagram An illustration showing the flow of resources from *households* to *firms* and of products from firms to households. These flows are accompanied by reverse flows of money from firms to households and from households to firms.

Clayton Act The Federal antitrust act of 1914 that strengthened the *Sherman Act* by making it illegal for firms to engage in certain specified practices.

climate-change problem The problem of rising world temperatures that most climate experts believe are caused at least in part by increased carbon dioxide and other greenhouse gases generated as by-products of human economic activities.

closed economy An economy that neither exports nor imports goods and services.

closed shop A place of employment where only workers who are already members of a labor union may be hired.

Coase theorem The idea, first stated by economist Ronald Coase, that some *externalities* can be resolved through private negotiations of the affected parties.

coincidence of wants A situation in which the good or service that one trader desires to obtain is the same as that which another trader desires to give up and an item that the second trader wishes to acquire is the same as that which the first trader desires to surrender.

COLA (See *cost-of-living adjustment.*)

collective bargaining The negotiation of labor contracts between *labor unions* and *firms* or government entities.

collective voice The function a *labor union* performs for its members as a group when it communicates their problems and grievances to management and presses management for a satisfactory resolution.

collusion A situation in which firms act together and in agreement (collude) to fix prices, divide a market, or otherwise restrict competition.

command system A method of organizing an economy in which property resources are publicly owned and government uses *central economic planning* to direct and coordinate economic activities; command economy; communism.

commercial bank A firm that engages in the business of banking (accepts deposits, offers checking accounts, and makes loans).

commercial banking system All *commercial banks* and *thrift institutions* as a group.

communism (See *command system.*)

comparative advantage A situation in which a person or country can produce a specific product at a lower opportunity cost than some other person or country; the basis for specialization and trade.

compensating differences Differences in the *wages* received by workers in different jobs to compensate for nonmonetary differences in the jobs.

compensating wage differential (See *compensating differences.*)

compensation to employees *Wages* and salaries plus wage and salary supplements paid by employers to workers.

competition The presence in a market of independent buyers and sellers competing with one another along with the freedom of buyers and sellers to enter and leave the market.

competitive industry's short-run supply curve The horizontal summation of the short-run supply curves of the *firms* in a purely competitive industry (see *pure competition*); a curve that shows the total quantities offered for sale at various prices by the firms in an industry in the short run.

competitive labor market A resource market in which a large

number of (noncolluding) employers demand a particular type of labor supplied by a large number of nonunion workers.

complementary goods Products and services that are used together. When the price of one falls, the demand for the other increases (and conversely).

complementary resources Productive inputs that are used jointly with other inputs in the production process; resources for which a decrease in the price of one leads to an increase in the demand for the other.

compound interest The accumulation of money that builds over time in an investment or interest-bearing account as new interest is earned on previous interest that is not withdrawn.

concentration ratio The percentage of the total sales of an industry made by the four (or some other number) largest sellers in the industry.

conflict diamonds Diamonds that are mined and sold by combatants in war zones in Africa as a way to provide the currency needed to finance their military activities.

conglomerate merger The merger of a *firm* in one *industry* with a firm in another industry (with a firm that is not a supplier, customer, or competitor).

conglomerates Firms that produce goods and services in two or more separate industries.

constant-cost industry An industry in which expansion by the entry of new firms has no effect on the prices firms in the industry must pay for resources and thus no effect on production costs.

constant opportunity cost An *opportunity cost* that remains the same for each additional unit as a consumer (or society) shifts purchases (production) from one product to another along a straight-line *budget line* (*production possibilities curve*).

constant returns to scale Unchanging *average total cost* of producing a product as the firm expands the size of its plant (its output) in the *long run.*

consumer equilibrium In marginal utility theory, the combination of goods purchased based on *marginal utility* (MU) and *price* (P) that maximizes *total utility*; the combination for goods X and Y at which $MU_x/P_x = MU_y/P_y$. In indifference curve analysis, the combination of goods purchased that maximize *total utility* by enabling the consumer to reach the highest *indifference curve*, given the consumer's *budget line* (or *budget constraint*).

consumer goods Products and services that satisfy human wants directly.

Consumer Price Index (CPI) An index that measures the prices of a fixed "market basket" of some 300 goods and services bought by a "typical" consumer.

consumer sovereignty Determination by consumers of the types and quantities of goods and services that will be produced with the scarce resources of the economy; consumers' direction of production through their *dollar votes.*

consumer surplus The difference between the maximum price a consumer is (or consumers are) willing to pay for an additional unit of a product and its market price; the triangular area below the demand curve and above the market price.

consumption of fixed capital An estimate of the amount of *capital* worn out or used up (consumed) in producing the *gross domestic product;* also called depreciation.

consumption schedule A schedule showing the amounts *households* plan to spend for *consumer goods* at different levels of *disposable income.*

contractionary fiscal policy A decrease in *government purchases* for goods and services, an increase in *net taxes,* or some combination of the two, for the purpose of decreasing *aggregate demand* and thus controlling inflation.

coordination failure A situation in which people do not reach a mutually beneficial outcome because they lack some way to jointly coordinate their actions; a possible cause of macroeconomic instability.

copayment The percentage of (say, health care) costs that an insured individual pays while the insurer pays the remainder.

copyright A legal protection provided to developers and publishers of books, computer software, videos, and musical compositions against the copying of their works by others.

corporate income tax A tax levied on the net income (accounting profit) of corporations.

corporation A legal entity ("person") chartered by a state or the Federal government that is distinct and separate from the individuals who own it.

correlation A systematic and dependable association between two sets of data (two kinds of events); does not necessarily indicate causation.

corruption (Web chapter) The misuse of government power, with which one has been entrusted or assigned, to obtain private gain; includes payments from individuals or companies to secure advantages in obtaining government contracts, avoiding government regulations, or obtaining inside knowledge about forthcoming policy changes.

cost-benefit analysis A comparison of the *marginal costs* of a government project or program with the *marginal benefits* to decide whether or not to employ resources in that project or program and to what extent.

cost-of-living adjustment (COLA) An automatic increase in the incomes (wages) of workers when inflation occurs; guaranteed by a collective bargaining contract between firms and workers.

cost-push inflation Increases in the price level (inflation) resulting from an increase in resource costs (for example, raw-material prices) and hence in *per-unit production costs;* inflation caused by reductions in *aggregate supply.*

Council of Economic Advisers (CEA) A group of three persons that advises and assists the president of the United States on economic matters (including the preparation of the annual *Economic Report of the President*).

countercyclical payments (CCPs) Cash *subsidies* paid to farmers when market prices for certain crops drop below targeted prices. Payments are based on previous production and are received regardless of the current crop grown.

craft union A labor union that limits its membership to workers with a particular skill (craft).

creative destruction The hypothesis that the creation of new products and production methods simultaneously destroys the market power of existing monopolies.

credible threat In *game theory,* a statement of harmful intent by one party that the other party views as believable; often issued in conditional terms of "if you do this; we will do that."

credit An accounting item that increases the value of an asset (such as the foreign money owned by the residents of a nation).

credit union An association of persons who have a common tie (such as being employees of the same firm or members of the same labor union) that sells shares to (accepts deposits from) its members and makes loans to them.

cross elasticity of demand The ratio of the percentage change in *quantity demanded* of one good to the percentage change in the price of some other good. A positive coefficient indicates the two products are *substitute goods;* a negative coefficient indicates they are *complementary goods.*

crowding model of occupational discrimination A model of labor markets suggesting that *occupational discrimination* has kept many women and minorities out of high-paying occupations and forced them into a limited number of low-paying occupations.

crowding-out effect A rise in interest rates and a resulting decrease in *planned investment* caused by the Federal government's increased borrowing to finance budget deficits and refinance debt.

currency Coins and paper money.

currency appreciation (See *exchange-rate appreciation.*)

currency depreciation (See *exchange-rate depreciation.*)

currency intervention A government's buying and selling of its own currency or foreign currencies to alter international exchange rates.

current account The section in a nation's *international balance of payments* that records its exports and imports of goods and services, its net *investment income,* and its *net transfers.*

cyclical asymmetry The idea that *monetary policy* may be more successful in slowing expansions and controlling *inflation* than in extracting the economy from severe recession.

cyclical deficit A Federal *budget deficit* that is caused by a recession and the consequent decline in tax revenues.

cyclical unemployment A type of *unemployment* caused by insufficient total spending (or by insufficient *aggregate demand*).

deadweight loss (See *efficiency loss.*)

debit An accounting item that decreases the value of an asset (such as the foreign money owned by the residents of a nation).

declining industry An industry in which *economic profits* are negative (losses are incurred) and that will, therefore, decrease its output as firms leave it.

decreasing-cost industry An industry in which expansion through the entry of firms lowers the prices that firms in the industry must pay for resources and therefore decreases their production costs.

deductible The dollar sum of (for example, health care) costs that an insured individual must pay before the insurer begins to pay.

defaults Situations in which borrowers stop making loan payments or do not pay back loans that they took out and are now due.

defensive medicine The recommendation by physicians of more tests and procedures than are warranted medically or economically as a way of protecting themselves against later malpractice suits.

deflating Finding the *real gross domestic product* by decreasing the dollar value of the GDP for a year in which prices were higher than in the *base year*.

deflation A decline in the economy's *price level*.

demand A schedule showing the amounts of a good or service that buyers (or a buyer) wish to purchase at various prices during some time period.

demand curve A curve illustrating *demand*.

demand factor (in growth) The increase in the level of *aggregate demand* that brings about the *economic growth* made possible by an increase in the production potential of the economy.

demand management The use of *fiscal policy* and *monetary policy* to increase or decrease *aggregate demand*.

demand-pull inflation Increases in the price level (inflation) resulting from an excess of demand over output at the existing price level, caused by an increase in *aggregate demand*.

demand schedule (See *demand*.)

demographers Scientists who study the characteristics of human populations.

demographic transition (Web chapter) The idea that population growth slows once a developing country achieves higher standards of living because the perceived marginal cost of additional children begins to exceed the perceived marginal benefit.

demand shocks Sudden, unexpected changes in demand.

dependent variable A variable that changes as a consequence of a change in some other (independent) variable; the "effect" or outcome.

depository institutions Firms that accept deposits of *money* from the public (businesses and persons); *commercial banks, savings and loan associations, mutual savings banks*, and *credit unions*.

depreciation (See *consumption of fixed capital*.)

depreciation (of the dollar) A decrease in the value of the dollar relative to another currency, so a dollar buys a smaller amount of the foreign currency and therefore of foreign goods.

derived demand The demand for a resource that depends on the demand for the products it helps to produce.

determinants of aggregate demand Factors such as consumption spending, *investment*, government spending, and *net exports* that, if they change, shift the aggregate demand curve.

determinants of aggregate supply Factors such as input prices, *productivity*, and the legal-institutional environment that, if they change, shift the aggregate supply curve.

determinants of demand Factors other than price that determine the quantities demanded of a good or service.

determinants of supply Factors other than price that determine the quantities supplied of a good or service.

developing countries Many countries of Africa, Asia, and Latin America that are characterized by lack of capital goods, use of nonadvanced technologies, low literacy rates, high unemployment, rapid population growth, and labor forces heavily committed to agriculture.

diagnosis-related group (DRG) system Payments to doctors and hospitals under *Medicare* based on which of hundreds of carefully detailed diagnostic categories best characterize the patient's condition and needs.

differentiated oligopoly An *oligopoly* in which the firms produce a *differentiated product*.

differentiated product A product that differs physically or in some other way from the similar products produced by other firms; a product such that buyers are not indifferent to the seller when the price charged by all sellers is the same.

diffusion (Web chapter) The spread of an *innovation* through its widespread imitation.

dilemma of regulation The tradeoff faced by a *regulatory agency* in setting the maximum legal price a monopolist may charge: The *socially optimal price* is below *average total cost* (and either bankrupts the *firm* or requires that it be subsidized), while the higher, *fair-return price* does not produce *allocative efficiency*.

diminishing marginal returns (See *law of diminishing returns*.)

diminishing marginal utility (See *law of diminishing marginal utility*.)

direct foreign investment (See *foreign direct investment*.)

direct payments Cash subsidies paid to farmers based on past production levels; unaffected by current crop prices and current production.

direct relationship The relationship between two variables that change in the same direction, for example, product price and quantity supplied; positive relationship.

discount rate The interest rate that the *Federal Reserve Banks* charge on the loans they make to *commercial banks* and *thrift institutions*.

discouraged workers Employees who have left the *labor force* because they have not been able to find employment.

discretionary fiscal policy Deliberate changes in taxes (tax rates) and government spending by Congress to promote full employment, price stability, and economic growth.

discrimination The practice of according individuals or groups inferior treatment in hiring, occupational access, education and training, promotion, wage rates, or working conditions even though they have the same abilities, education, skills, and work experience as other workers.

discrimination coefficient A measure of the cost or disutility of prejudice; the monetary amount an employer is willing to pay to hire a preferred worker rather than a nonpreferred worker.

diseconomies of scale Increases in the *average total cost* of producing a product as the *firm* expands the size of its *plant* (its output) in the *long run*.

disinflation A reduction in the rate of *inflation*.

disposable income (DI) *Personal income* less personal taxes; income available for *personal consumption expenditures* and *personal saving*.

dissaving Spending for consumer goods and services in excess of *disposable income*; the amount by which *personal consumption expenditures* exceed disposable income.

diversifiable risk Investment *risk* that investors can reduce via *diversification*; also called idiosyncratic risk.

diversification The strategy of investing in a large number of investments in order to reduce the overall risk to an entire investment *portfolio*.

dividends Payments by a corporation of all or part of its profit to its stockholders (the corporate owners).

division of labor The separation of the work required to produce a product into a number of different tasks that are performed by different workers; *specialization* of workers.

Doha Round The latest, uncompleted (as of fall 2008) sequence of trade negotiations by members of the *World Trade Organization*; named after Doha, Qatar, where the set of negotiations began.

dollar votes The "votes" that consumers and entrepreneurs cast for the production of consumer and capital goods, respectively, when they purchase those goods in product and resource markets.

domestic capital formation The process of adding to a nation's stock of *capital* by saving and investing part of its own domestic output.

domestic output *Gross* (or net) *domestic product*; the total output of final goods and services produced in the economy.

domestic price The price of a good or service within a country, determined by domestic demand and supply.

dominant strategy In *game theory*, an option that is better than any other alternative option regardless of what the other firm does.

dumping The sale of a product in a foreign country at prices either below cost or below the prices commonly charged at home.

DuPont cellophane case The antitrust case brought against DuPont in which the U.S. Supreme Court ruled (in 1956) that while DuPont had a monopoly in the narrowly defined market for cellophane, it did not monopolize the more broadly defined market for flexible packaging materials. It was thus not guilty of violating the *Sherman Act*.

durable good A consumer good with an expected life (use) of 3 or more years.

earmarks Narrow, specially designated spending authorizations placed in broad legislation by Senators and representatives for the purpose of providing benefits to firms and organizations within their constituencies without undergoing the usual evaluation process or competitive bidding.

earned-income tax credit (EITC) A refundable Federal tax credit for low-income working people designed to reduce poverty and encourage labor-force participation.

earnings The money income received by a worker; equal to the *wage* (rate) multiplied by the amount of time worked.

economic concentration A description or measure of the degree to which an industry is dominated by one or a handful of firms or is characterized by many firms. (See *concentration ratio*.)

economic cost A payment that must be made to obtain and retain the services of a *resource*; the income a firm must provide to a resource supplier to attract the resource away from an alternative use; equal to the quantity of other products that cannot be produced when resources are instead used to make a particular product.

economic efficiency The use of the minimum necessary resources to obtain the socially optimal amounts of goods and services; entails both *productive efficiency* and *allocative efficiency*.

economic growth (1) An outward shift in the *production possibilities curve* that results from an increase in resource supplies or quality or an improvement in *technology*; (2) an increase of real output (*gross domestic product*) or real output per capita.

economic immigrants International migrants who have moved to a country from another to obtain economic gains such as better employment opportunities.

economic investment (See *investment*.)

economic law An *economic principle* that has been tested and retested and has stood the test of time.

economic model A simplified picture of economic reality; an abstract generalization.

economic perspective A viewpoint that envisions individuals and institutions making rational decisions by comparing the marginal benefits and marginal costs associated with their actions.

economic policy A course of action intended to correct or avoid a problem.

economic principle A widely accepted generalization about the economic behavior of individuals or institutions.

economic profit The *total revenue* of a firm less its *economic costs* (which include both *explicit costs* and *implicit costs*); also called "pure profit" and "above-normal profit."

economic regulation (See *industrial regulation* and *social regulation*.)

economic rent The price paid for the use of land and other natural resources, the supply of which is fixed (*perfectly inelastic*).

economic resources The *land*, *labor*, *capital*, and *entrepreneurial ability* that are used in the production of goods and services; productive agents; factors of production.

economics The social science concerned with how individuals, institutions, and society make optimal (best) choices under conditions of scarcity.

economic system A particular set of institutional arrangements and a coordinating mechanism for solving the economizing problem; a method of organizing an economy, of which the *market system* and the *command system* are the two general types.

economic theory A statement of a cause-effect relationship; when accepted by all or nearly all economists, an *economic principle*.

economies of scale Reductions in the *average total cost* of producing a product as the firm expands the size of plant (its output) in the *long run*; the economies of mass production.

economizing problem The choices necessitated because society's economic wants for goods and services are unlimited but the resources available to satisfy these wants are limited (scarce).

efficiency factors (in growth) The capacity of an economy to combine resources effectively to achieve growth of real output that the *supply factors* (of growth) make possible.

efficiency gains from migration Additions to output from *immigration* in the destination nation that exceeds the loss of output from *emigration* from the origin nation.

efficiency loss Reductions in combined consumer and producer surplus caused by an underallocation or overallocation of resources to the production of a good or service. Also called deadweight loss.

efficiency loss of a tax The loss of net benefits to society because a tax reduces the production and consumption of a taxed good below the level of *allocative efficiency*. Also called the deadweight loss of the tax.

efficiency wage A wage that minimizes wage costs per unit of output by encouraging greater effort or reducing turnover.

efficient allocation of resources That allocation of an economy's resources among the production of different products that leads to the maximum satisfaction of consumers' wants, thus producing the socially optimal mix of output with society's scarce resources.

elastic demand Product or resource demand whose *price elasticity* is greater than 1. This means the resulting change in *quantity demanded* is greater than the percentage change in *price*.

elasticity coefficient The number obtained when the percentage change in *quantity demanded* (or supplied) is divided by the percentage change in the *price* of the commodity.

elasticity formula (See *price elasticity of demand*.)

elasticity of resource demand A measure of the responsiveness of firms to a change in the price of a particular *resource* they employ or use; the percentage change in the quantity of the resource demanded divided by the percentage change in its price.

elastic supply Product or resource supply whose price elasticity is greater than 1. This means the resulting change in quantity supplied is greater than the percentage change in price.

electronic payments Purchases made by transferring funds electronically. Examples: Fedwire transfers, automated clearinghouse transactions (ACHs), payments via the PayPal system, and payments made through stored-value cards.

emigration The exit (outflow) of residents from a country to reside in foreign countries.

employment rate The percentage of the *labor force* employed at any time.

empty threat In *game theory*, a statement of harmful intent that is easily dismissed by the second party because the threat is not viewed as being believable; compare to *credible threat*.

entitlement programs Government programs such as *social insurance*, *food stamps*, *Medicare*, and *Medicaid* that guarantee particular levels of transfer payments or noncash benefits to all who fit the programs' criteria.

entrepreneurial ability The human resource that combines the other resources to produce a product, makes nonroutine decisions, innovates, and bears risks.

equality-efficiency trade-off The decrease in *economic efficiency* that may accompany a decrease in *income inequality*; the presumption that some income inequality is required to achieve economic efficiency.

equation of exchange $MV = PQ$, in which M is the supply of money, V is the *velocity* of money, P is the *price level*, and Q is the physical volume of *final goods and services* produced.

equilibrium GDP (See *equilibrium real domestic output*.)

equilibrium position In the indifference curve model, the combination of two goods at which a consumer maximizes his or her *utility* (reaches the highest attainable *indifference curve*), given a limited amount to spend (a *budget constraint*).

equilibrium price The *price* in a competitive market at which the *quantity demanded* and the *quantity supplied* are equal, there is neither a shortage nor a surplus, and there is no tendency for price to rise or fall.

equilibrium price level The price level at which the aggregate demand curve intersects the aggregate supply curve.

equilibrium quantity (1) The quantity demanded and supplied at the equilibrium price in a competitive market; (2) the profit-maximizing output of a firm.

equilibrium real domestic output The *gross domestic product* at which the total quantity of final goods and services purchased *(aggregate expenditures)* is equal to the total quantity of final goods and services produced (the real domestic output); the real domestic output at which the aggregate demand curve intersects the aggregate supply curve.

equilibrium real output (See *equilibrium real domestic output*)

equilibrium world price The price of an internationally traded product that equates the quantity of the product demanded by importers with the quantity of the product supplied by exporters; the price determined at the intersection of the export supply curve and the import demand curve.

euro The common currency unit used by 15 European nations (as of 2008) in the Euro zone, which consists of Austria, Belgium, Cyprus, Finland, France, Germany, Greece, Ireland, Italy, Luxembourg, Malta, the Netherlands, Portugal, Slovenia, and Spain.

European Union (EU) An association of 27 European nations (as of 2008) that has eliminated tariffs and quotas among them, established common tariffs for imported goods from outside the member nations, eliminated barriers to the free movement of capital, and created other common economic policies.

excess capacity Plant resources that are underused when imperfectly competitive firms produce less output than that associated with achieving minimum average total cost.

excess reserves The amount by which a bank's or thrift's *actual reserves* exceed its *required reserves*; actual reserves minus required reserves.

exchange controls (See *foreign exchange controls.*)

exchange rate The *rate of exchange* of one nation's currency for another nation's currency.

exchange-rate appreciation An increase in the value of a nation's currency in foreign exchange markets; an increase in the *rate of exchange* for foreign currencies.

exchange-rate depreciation A decrease in the value of a nation's currency in foreign exchange markets; a decrease in the *rate of exchange* for foreign currencies.

exchange-rate determinant Any factor other than the *rate of exchange* that determines a currency's demand and supply in the *foreign exchange market.*

excise tax A tax levied on the production of a specific product or on the quantity of the product purchased.

exclusive unionism The practice of a *labor union* of restricting the supply of skilled union labor to increase the wages received by union members; the policies typically employed by a *craft union.*

exhaustive expenditure An expenditure by government resulting directly in the employment of *economic resources* and in the absorption by government of the goods and services those resources produce; a *government purchase.*

exit mechanism The process of leaving a job and searching for another one as a means of improving one's working conditions.

expanding industry An industry whose firms earn *economic profits* and for which an increase in output occurs as new firms enter the industry.

expansion A phase of the *business cycle* in which *real GDP, income,* and employment rise.

expansionary fiscal policy An increase in *government purchases* of goods and services, a decrease in *net taxes,* or some combination of the two for the purpose of increasing *aggregate demand* and expanding real output.

expansionary monetary policy Federal Reserve system actions to increase the *money supply,* lower *interest rates,* and expand *real GDP*; an easy money policy.

expectations The anticipations of consumers, firms, and others about future economic conditions.

expected rate of return The increase in profit a firm anticipates it will obtain by purchasing capital (or engaging in research and development); expressed as a percentage of the total cost of the investment (or R&D) activity.

expected-rate-of return curve (Web chapter) As it relates to research and development (*R&D*), a curve showing the anticipated gain in *profit,* as a percentage of R&D expenditure, from an additional dollar spent on R&D.

expenditures approach The method that adds all expenditures made for *final goods and services* to measure the *gross domestic product.*

expenditures-output approach (See *aggregate expenditures–domestic output approach.*)

explicit cost The monetary payment a *firm* must make to an outsider to obtain a *resource.*

exports Goods and services produced in a nation and sold to buyers in other nations.

export subsidies Government payments to domestic producers to enable them to reduce the *price* of a good or service to foreign buyers.

export supply curve An upward-sloping curve that shows the amount of a product that domestic firms will export at each *world price* that is above the *domestic price.*

export transaction A sale of a good or service that increases the amount of foreign currency flowing to a nation's citizens, firms, and government.

external benefit (See *positive externality.*)

external cost (See *negative externality.*)

external debt Private or public debt owed to foreign citizens, firms, and institutions.

externality A cost or benefit from production or consumption, accruing without compensation to someone other than the buyers and sellers of the product (see *negative externality* and *positive externality*) .

external public debt The portion of the public debt owed to foreign citizens, firms, and institutions.

extraction cost All costs associated with extracting a natural resource and readying it for sale.

face value The dollar or cents value placed on a U.S. coin or piece of paper money.

fair-trade movement The efforts by groups in high-income nations to get growers of agricultural crops in low-income nations to adhere to certain wage and workplace standards in exchange for their goods being promoted as "fair-trade goods" to consumers in the high-income nations, and the efforts by the groups to convince those consumers to buy these goods instead of otherwise close substitutes.

factors of production *Economic resources: land, capital, labor,* and *entrepreneurial ability.*

fair-return price The price of a product that enables its producer to obtain a *normal profit* and that is equal to the *average total cost* of producing it.

fallacy of composition The false notion that what is true for the individual (or part) is necessarily true for the group (or whole).

farm commodities Agricultural products such as grains, milk, cattle, fruits, and vegetables that are usually sold to processors, who use the products as inputs in creating *food products.*

fast-second strategy (Web chapter) An approach by a dominant firm in which it allows other firms in its industry to bear the risk of innovation and then quickly becomes the second firm to offer any successful new product or adopt any improved production process.

FDIC (See *Federal Deposit Insurance Corporation.*)

Federal Deposit Insurance Corporation (FDIC) The federally chartered corporation that insures deposit liabilities (up to $100,000 per account) of *commercial banks* and *thrift institutions* (excluding *credit unions*, whose deposits are insured by the *National Credit Union Administration*).

Federal funds rate The interest rate banks and other depository institutions charge one another on overnight loans made out of their *excess reserves*.

Federal government The government of the United States, as distinct from the state and local governments.

Federal Open Market Committee (FOMC) The 12-member group that determines the purchase and sale policies of the *Federal Reserve Banks* in the market for U.S. government securities.

Federal Reserve Banks The 12 banks chartered by the U.S. government to control the *money supply* and perform other functions. (See *central bank*, *quasi-public bank*, and *bankers' bank*.)

Federal Reserve Note Paper money issued by the *Federal Reserve Banks*.

Federal Reserve System The U.S. central bank, consisting of the *Board of Governors* of the Federal Reserve and the 12 *Federal Reserve Banks*, which controls the lending activity of the nation's banks and thrifts and thus the *money supply*; commonly referred to as the "Fed."

Federal Trade Commission (FTC) The commission of five members established by the *Federal Trade Commission Act* of 1914 to investigate unfair competitive practices of firms, to hold hearings on the complaints of such practices, and to issue *cease-and-desist orders* when firms were found to engage in such practices.

Federal Trade Commission Act The Federal act of 1914 that established the *Federal Trade Commission*.

fee for service In the health care industry, payment to physicians for each visit made or procedure performed rather than payment as an annual salary.

fiat money Anything that is *money* because government has decreed it to be money.

final goods and services Goods and services that have been purchased for final use and not for resale or further processing or manufacturing.

financial capital (See *money capital.*)

financial investment The purchase of a financial asset (such as a *stock*, *bond*, or *mutual fund*) or real asset (such as a house, land, or factories) or the building of such assets in the expectation of financial gain.

financial services industry The broad category of firms that provide financial products and services to help households and businesses earn *interest*, receive *dividends*, obtain *capital gains*, insure against losses, and plan for retirement. Includes *commercial banks*, *thrifts*, insurance companies, mutual fund companies, pension funds, investment banks, and securities firms.

firm An organization that employs resources to produce a good or service for profit and owns and operates one or more *plants*.

first-mover advantage In *game theory*, the benefit obtained by the party that moves first in a *sequential game*.

fiscal policy Changes in government spending and tax collections designed to achieve a full-employment and noninflationary domestic output; also called *discretionary fiscal policy*.

fishery A stock of fish or other marine animal that is composed of a distinct group, for example New England cod, Pacific tuna, or Alaskan crab.

fishery collapse A rapid decline in a fishery's population because the fish are being harvested faster than they can reproduce.

fixed cost Any cost that in total does not change when the *firm* changes its output; the cost of *fixed resources*.

fixed exchange rate A *rate of exchange* that is set in some way and therefore prevented from rising or falling with changes in currency supply and demand.

fixed resource Any resource whose quantity cannot be changed by a firm in the *short run*.

flexible exchange rate A *rate of exchange* determined by the international demand for and supply of a nation's money; a rate free to rise or fall (to float).

flexible prices Product prices that freely move upward or downward when product demand or supply changes.

floating exchange rate (See *flexible exchange rate.*)

follower countries As it relates to *economic growth*, countries that adopt advanced technologies that previously were developed and used by *leader countries*.

Food, Conservation, and Energy Act of 2008 Farm legislation that continued and extended previous agricultural subsides of three basic kinds: *direct payments*, *countercyclical payments*, and *marketing loans*.

food products Processed agricultural commodities sold through grocery stores and restaurants. Examples: bread, meat, fish, chicken, pork, lettuce, peanut butter, and breakfast cereal.

food-stamp program A program permitting low-income persons to purchase for less than their retail value, or to obtain without cost, coupons that can be exchanged for food items at retail stores.

foreign competition (See *import competition.*)

foreign direct investment Financial investments made to obtain a lasting ownership interest in firms operating outside the economy of the investor; may involve purchasing existing assets or building new production facilities.

foreign exchange control The control a government may exercise over the quantity of foreign currency demanded by its citizens and firms and over the *rates of exchange* in order to limit its *outpayments* to its *inpayments* (to eliminate a *payments deficit*).

foreign exchange market A market in which the money (currency) of one nation can be used to purchase (can be exchanged for) the money of another nation; currency market.

foreign exchange rate (See *rate of exchange.*)

foreign purchase effect The inverse relationship between the *net exports* of an economy and its price level relative to foreign price levels.

45° line A line along which the value of *GDP* (measured horizontally) is equal to the value of *aggregate expenditures* (measured vertically).

four-firm concentration ratio The percentage of total industry sales accounted for by the top four firms in the industry.

fractional reserve banking system A *reserve requirement* that is less than 100 percent of the checkable-deposit liabilities of a *commercial bank* or *thrift institution.*

freedom of choice The freedom of owners of property resources to employ or dispose of them as they see fit, of workers to enter any line of work for which they are qualified, and of consumers to spend their incomes in a manner that they think is appropriate.

freedom of enterprise The freedom of *firms* to obtain economic resources, to use those resources to produce products of the firm's own choosing, and to sell their products in markets of their choice.

Freedom to Farm Act A law passed in 1996 that revamped 60 years of U.S. farm policy by ending *price supports* and *acreage allotments* for wheat, corn, barley, oats, sorghum, rye, cotton, and rice.

free-rider problem The inability of potential providers of an economically desirable good or service to obtain payment from those who benefit, because of *nonexcludability.*

free trade The absence of artificial (government-imposed) barriers to trade among individuals and firms in different nations.

frictional unemployment A type of unemployment caused by workers voluntarily changing jobs and by temporary layoffs; unemployed workers between jobs.

fringe benefits The rewards other than *wages* that employees receive from their employers and that include pensions, medical and dental insurance, paid vacations, and sick leaves.

full employment (1) The use of all available resources to produce want-satisfying goods and services; (2) the situation in which the *unemployment rate* is equal to the *full-employment unemployment rate* and where *frictional* and *structural* unemployment occur but not *cyclical unemployment* (and the *real GDP* of the economy equals *potential output*).

full-employment unemployment rate The *unemployment rate* at which there is no *cyclical unemployment* of the *labor force;* equal to between 4 and 5 percent in the United States because some *frictional* and *structural unemployment* is unavoidable.

functional distribution of income The manner in which *national income* is divided among the functions performed to earn it (or the kinds of resources provided to earn it); the division of national income into wages and salaries, proprietors' income, corporate profits, interest, and rent.

future value The amount to which some current amount of money will grow if the interest earned on the amount is left to compound over time. (See *compound interest.*)

gains from trade The extra output that trading partners obtain through specialization of production and exchange of goods and services.

game theory A means of analyzing the business behavior of oligopolists that uses the theory of strategy associated with games such as chess and bridge.

GDP (See *gross domestic product.*)

GDP gap Actual *gross domestic product* minus potential output; may be either a positive amount (a *positive GDP gap*) or a negative amount (a *negative GDP gap*).

GDP price index A *price index* for all the goods and services that make up the *gross domestic product;* the price index used to adjust *nominal gross domestic product* to *real gross domestic product.*

G8 nations A group of eight major nations (Canada, France, Germany, Italy, Japan, Russia, United Kingdom, and United States) whose leaders meet regularly to discuss common economic problems and try to coordinate economic policies.

General Agreement on Tariffs and Trade (GATT) The international agreement reached in 1947 in which 23 nations agreed to give equal and nondiscriminatory treatment to one another, to reduce tariff rates by multinational negotiations, and to eliminate *import quotas.* It now includes most nations and has become the *World Trade Organization.*

generalization Statement of the nature of the relationship between two or more sets of facts.

Gini ratio A numerical measure of the overall dispersion of income among households, families, or individuals; found graphically by dividing the area between the diagonal line and the *Lorenz curve* by the entire area below the diagonal line.

gold standard A historical system of fixed exchange rates in which nations defined their currencies in terms of gold, maintained a fixed relationship between their stocks of gold and their money supplies, and allowed gold to be freely exported and imported.

government failure Inefficiencies in resource allocation caused by problems in the operation of the public sector (government), specifically, rent-seeking pressure by special-interest groups, shortsighted political behavior, limited and bundled choices, and bureaucratic inefficiencies.

government purchases (G) Expenditures by government for goods and services that government consumes in providing public goods and for public capital that has a long lifetime; the expenditures of all governments in the economy for those *final goods and services.*

government transfer payment The disbursement of money (or goods and services) by government for which government receives no currently produced good or service in return.

grievance procedure The method used by a *labor union* and a *firm* to settle disputes that arise during the life of the collective bargaining agreement between them.

gross domestic product (GDP) The total market value of all *final goods and services* produced annually within the boundaries of the United States, whether by U.S.- or foreign-supplied resources.

gross private domestic investment (I_g) Expenditures for newly produced *capital goods* (such as machinery, equipment, tools, and buildings) and for additions to inventories.

growth accounting The bookkeeping of the supply-side elements such as productivity and labor inputs that contribute to changes in *real GDP* over some specific time period.

guiding function of prices The ability of price changes to bring about changes in the quantities of products and resources demanded and supplied.

H1-B provision A provision of the U.S. immigration law that allows the annual entry of 65,000 high-skilled workers in "specialty occupations" such as science, R&D, and computer programming to work legally and continuously in the United States for six years.

health maintenance organizations (HMOs) Health care providers that contract with employers, insurance companies, labor unions, or government units to provide health care for their workers or others who are insured.

health savings accounts (HSAs) Accounts into which people with high-deductible health insurance plans can place tax-free funds each year and then draw on these funds to pay out-of-pocket medical expenses such as *deductibles* and *copayments*. Unused funds accumulate from year to year and later can be used to supplement *Medicare*.

Herfindahl index A measure of the concentration and competitiveness of an industry; calculated as the sum of the squared percentage market shares of the individual firms in the industry.

homogeneous oligopoly An *oligopoly* in which the firms produce a *standardized product*.

horizontal axis The "left-right" or "west-east" measurement line on graph or grid.

horizontal merger The merger into a single *firm* of two firms producing the same product and selling it in the same geographic market.

household An economic unit (of one or more persons) that provides the economy with resources and uses the income received to purchase goods and services that satisfy economic wants.

human capital The knowledge and skills that make a person productive.

human capital investment Any expenditure undertaken to improve the education, skills, health, or mobility of workers, with an expectation of greater productivity and thus a positive return on the investment.

hyperinflation A very rapid rise in the price level; an extremely high rate of inflation.

hypothesis A tentative explanation of cause and effect that requires testing.

illegal immigrants People who have entered a country unlawfully to reside there; also called unauthorized immigrants.

IMF (See *International Monetary Fund*.)

imitation problem (Web chapter) The potential for a firm's rivals to produce a close variation of (imitate) a firm's new product or process, greatly reducing the originator's profit from *R&D* and *innovation*.

immediate short-run aggregate supply curve An aggregate supply curve for which real output, but not the price level, changes when the aggregate demand curves shifts; a horizontal aggregate supply curve that implies an inflexible price level.

immigration The inflow of people into a country from another country. The immigrants may be either *legal immigrants* or *illegal immigrants*.

immobility The inability or unwillingness of a worker to move from one geographic area or occupation to another or from a lower-paying job to a higher-paying job.

imperfect competition All market structures except *pure competition*; includes *monopoly*, *monopolistic competition*, and *oligopoly*.

implicit cost The monetary income a *firm* sacrifices when it uses a resource it owns rather than supplying the resource in the market; equal to what the resource could have earned in the best-paying alternative employment; includes a *normal profit*.

import competition The competition that domestic firms encounter from the products and services of foreign producers.

import demand curve A downsloping curve showing the amount of a product that an economy will import at each *world price* below the *domestic price*.

import quota A limit imposed by a nation on the quantity (or total value) of a good that may be imported during some period of time.

imports Spending by individuals, *firms*, and governments for goods and services produced in foreign nations.

import transaction The purchase of a good or service that decreases the amount of foreign money held by citizens, firms, and governments of a nation.

incentive function of price The inducement that an increase in the price of a commodity gives to sellers to make more of it available (and conversely for a decrease in price), and the inducement that an increase in price offers to buyers to purchase smaller quantities (and conversely for a decrease in price).

incentive pay plan A compensation structure that ties worker pay directly to performance. Such plans include piece rates, bonuses, *stock options*, commissions, and *profit sharing*.

inclusive unionism The practice of a labor union of including as members all workers employed in an industry.

income A flow of dollars (or purchasing power) per unit of time derived from the use of human or property resources.

income approach The method that adds all the income generated by the production of *final goods and services* to measure the *gross domestic product*.

income effect A change in the quantity demanded of a product that results from the change in *real income (purchasing power)* caused by a change in the product's price.

income elasticity of demand The ratio of the percentage change in the *quantity demanded* of a good to a percentage change in consumer income; measures the responsiveness of consumer purchases to income changes.

income inequality The unequal distribution of an economy's total income among households or families.

income-maintenance system A group of government programs designed to eliminate poverty and reduce inequality in the distribution of income.

income mobility The extent to which income receivers move from one part of the income distribution to another over some period of time.

increase in demand An increase in the *quantity demanded* of a good or service at every price; a shift of the *demand curve* to the right.

increase in supply An increase in the *quantity supplied* of a good or service at every price; a shift of the *supply curve* to the right.

increasing-cost industry An *industry* in which expansion through the entry of new firms raises the prices *firms* in the industry must pay for resources and therefore increases their production costs.

increasing marginal returns An increase in the *marginal product* of a resource as successive units of the resource are employed.

increasing returns An increase in a firm's output by a larger percentage than the percentage increase in its inputs.

independent goods Products or services for which there is little or no relationship between the price of one and the demand for the other. When the price of one rises or falls, the demand for the other tends to remain constant.

independent unions U.S. unions that are not affiliated with the *AFL-CIO*.

independent variable The variable causing a change in some other (dependent) variable.

index funds *Mutual funds* that select stock or bond *portfolios* to exactly match a stock or bond index (a collection of stocks or bonds meant to capture the overall behavior of a particular category of investments) such as the Standard & Poor's 500 Index or the Russell 3000 Index.

indifference curve A curve showing the different combinations of two products that yield the same satisfaction or *utility* to a consumer.

indifference map A set of *indifference curves*, each representing a different level of *utility*, that together show the preferences of a consumer.

individual demand The demand schedule or *demand curve* of a single buyer.

individual supply The supply schedule or *supply curve* of a single seller.

individual transferable quotas A limit by a government or a fisheries commission on the total number or total weight of a species that an individual fisher can harvest during some particular time period; fishers holding the quota right can sell all or part of it to other fishers.

industrially advanced countries High-income countries such as the United States, Canada, Japan, and the nations of western Europe that have highly developed *market economies* based on large stocks of technologically advanced capital goods and skilled labor forces.

industrial regulation The older and more traditional type of regulation in which government is concerned with the prices charged and the services provided to the public in specific industries, in contrast to *social regulation*.

industrial union A *labor union* that accepts as members all workers employed in a particular industry (or by a particular firm).

industry A group of (one or more) *firms* that produce identical or similar products.

inelastic demand Product or resource demand for which the *elasticity coefficient* for price is less than 1. This means the resulting percentage change in *quantity demanded* is less than the percentage change in *price*.

inelastic supply Product or resource supply for which the price elasticity coefficient is less than 1. The percentage change in *quantity supplied* is less than the percentage change in *price*.

inferior good A good or service whose consumption declines as income rises, prices held constant.

inflating Determining *real gross domestic product* by increasing the dollar value of the *nominal gross domestic product* produced in a year in which prices are lower than those in a *base year*.

inflation A rise in the general level of prices in an economy.

inflationary expectations The belief of workers, firms, and consumers about future rates of inflation.

inflationary expenditure gap The amount by which the *aggregate expenditures schedule* must shift downward to decrease the *nominal GDP* to its full-employment noninflationary level.

inflation premium The component of the *nominal interest rate* that reflects anticipated inflation.

inflation targeting The annual statement by a *central bank* of a goal for a specific range of inflation in a future year, coupled with monetary policy designed to achieve the goal.

inflexible prices Product prices that remain in place (at least for a while) even though supply or demand has changed; stuck prices or sticky prices.

information technology New and more efficient methods of delivering and receiving information through use of computers, fax machines, wireless phones, and the Internet.

infrastructure The capital goods usually provided by the *public sector* for the use of its citizens and firms (for example, highways, bridges, transit systems, wastewater treatment facilities, municipal water systems, and airports).

injection An addition of spending to the income-expenditure stream: *investment*, *government purchases*, and *net exports*.

injunction A court order directing a person or organization not to perform a certain act because the act would do irreparable damage to some other person or persons; a restraining order.

in-kind transfer The distribution by government of goods and services to individuals for which the government receives no currently produced good or service in return; a *government transfer payment* made in goods or services rather than in money; also called a noncash transfer.

innovation The first commercially successful introduction of a new product, the use of a new method of production, or the creation of a new form of business organization.

inpayments The receipts of domestic or foreign money that individuals, firms, and governments of one nation obtain from the sale of goods and services abroad, as investment income and remittances, and from foreign purchases of domestic assets.

insider-outsider theory The hypothesis that nominal wages are inflexible downward because firms are aware that workers ("insiders") who retain employment during recession may refuse to work cooperatively with previously unemployed workers ("outsiders") who offer to work for less than the current wage.

insurable risk An event that would result in a loss but whose frequency of occurrence can be estimated with considerable accuracy. Insurance companies are willing to sell insurance against such losses.

interest The payment made for the use of money (of borrowed funds).

interest income Payments of income to those who supply the economy with *capital*.

interest rate The annual rate at which interest is paid; a percentage of the borrowed amount.

interest-rate-cost-of-funds curve (Web chapter) As it relates to research and development (*R&D*), a curve showing the *interest rate* the firm must pay to obtain any particular amount of funds to finance R&D.

interest-rate effect The tendency for increases in the *price level* to increase the demand for money, raise interest rates, and, as a result, reduce total spending and real output in the economy (and the reverse for price-level decreases).

interindustry competition The competition for sales between the products of one industry and the products of another industry.

interlocking directorate A situation where one or more members of the board of directors of a *corporation* are also on the board of directors of a competing corporation; illegal under the *Clayton Act*.

intermediate goods Products that are purchased for resale or further processing or manufacturing.

internally held public debt *Public debt* owed to citizens, firms, and institutions of the same nation that issued the debt.

international balance of payments A summary of all the transactions that took place between the individuals, firms, and government units of one nation and those of all other nations during a year.

international balance-of-payments deficit (See *balance-of-payments deficit*.)

international balance-of-payments surplus (See *balance-of-payments surplus*.)

international gold standard (See *gold standard*.)

International Monetary Fund (IMF) The international association of nations that was formed after the Second World War to make loans of foreign monies to nations with temporary *pay-ments deficits* and, until the early 1970s, to administer the *adjustable pegs*. It now mainly makes loans to nations facing possible defaults on private and government loans.

international monetary reserves The foreign currencies and other assets such as gold that a nation can use to settle a *balance-of-payments deficit*.

international value of the dollar The price that must be paid in foreign currency (money) to obtain one U.S. dollar.

intertemporal choice Choices between benefits obtainable in one time period and benefits achievable in a later time period; comparisons that individuals and society must make between the reductions in current consumption that are necessary to fund current investments and the higher levels of future consumption that those current investments can produce.

intrinsic value The market value of the metal within a coin.

invention (Web chapter) The first discovery of a product or process through the use of imagination, ingenious thinking, and experimentation and the first proof that it will work.

inventories Goods that have been produced but remain unsold.

inverse relationship The relationship between two variables that change in opposite directions, for example, product price and quantity demanded; negative relationship.

inverted-U theory (Web chapter) The idea that, other things equal, *R&D* expenditures as a percentage of sales rise with industry concentration, reach a peak at a four-firm *concentration ratio* of about 50 percent, and then fall as the ratio further increases.

investment In economics, spending for the production and accumulation of *capital* and additions to inventories. (For contrast, see *financial investment*.)

investment banks Firms that help corporations and government raise money by selling stocks and bonds; they also offer advisory services for corporate mergers and acquisitions in addition to providing brokerage services and advice.

investment demand curve A curve that shows the amounts of *investment* demanded by an economy at a series of *real interest rates*.

investment goods Same as *capital* or capital goods.

investment in human capital (See *human capital investment*.)

investment schedule A curve or schedule that shows the amounts firms plan to invest at various possible values of *real gross domestic product*.

"invisible hand" The tendency of firms and resource suppliers that seek to further their own self-interests in competitive markets to also promote the interests of society.

Joint Economic Committee (JEC) Committee of senators and representatives that investigates economic problems of national interest.

Keynesianism The philosophical, ideological, and analytical views pertaining to *Keynesian economics*.

kinked-demand curve The demand curve for a noncollusive oligopolist, which is based on the assumption that rivals will match a price decrease and will ignore a price increase.

labor People's physical and mental talents and efforts that are used to help produce goods and services.

labor force Persons 16 years of age and older who are not in institutions and who are employed or are unemployed and seeking work.

labor-force participation rate The percentage of the working-age population that is actually in the *labor force*.

labor-intensive goods Products requiring relatively large amounts of *labor* to produce.

labor productivity Total output divided by the quantity of labor employed to produce it; the *average product* of labor or output per hour of work.

labor union A group of workers organized to advance the interests of the group (to increase wages, shorten the hours worked, improve working conditions, and so on).

Laffer Curve A curve relating government tax rates and tax revenues and on which a particular tax rate (between zero and 100 percent) maximizes tax revenues.

laissez-faire capitalism (See *capitalism*.)

land Natural resources ("free gifts of nature") used to produce goods and services.

land-intensive goods Products requiring relatively large amounts of *land* to produce.

land reform (Web chapter) A set of policies designed to create more efficient distribution of land ownership in developing countries; policies vary country to country and can involve everything from government purchasing large land estates and dividing the land into smaller farms to consolidating tiny plots of land into larger, more efficient private farms.

law of demand The principle that, other things equal, an increase in a product's price will reduce the quantity of it demanded, and conversely for a decrease in price.

law of diminishing marginal utility The principle that as a consumer increases the consumption of a good or service, the *marginal utility* obtained from each additional unit of the good or service decreases.

law of diminishing returns The principle that as successive increments of a variable resource are added to a fixed resource, the *marginal product* of the variable resource will eventually decrease.

law of increasing opportunity costs The principle that as the production of a good increases, the *opportunity cost* of producing an additional unit rises.

law of supply The principle that, other things equal, an increase in the price of a product will increase the quantity of it supplied, and conversely for a price decrease.

leader countries As it relates to *economic growth*, countries that develop and use advanced technologies, which then become available to *follower countries*.

leakage (1) A withdrawal of potential spending from the income-expenditures stream via *saving*, tax payments, or *imports*; (2) a withdrawal that reduces the lending potential of the banking system.

learning by doing Achieving greater *productivity* and lower *average total cost* through gains in knowledge and skill that accompany repetition of a task; a source of *economies of scale*.

least-cost combination of resources The quantity of each resource a firm must employ in order to produce a particular output at the lowest total cost; the combination at which the ratio of the *marginal product* of a resource to its *marginal resource cost* (to its *price* if the resource is employed in a competitive market) is the same for the last dollar spent on each of the resources employed.

legal cartel theory of regulation The hypothesis that some industries seek regulation or want to maintain regulation so that they may form or maintain a legal *cartel*.

legal immigrant A person who lawfully enters a country for the purpose of residing there.

legal tender A legal designation of a nation's official currency (bills and coins). Payment of debts must be accepted in this monetary unit, but creditors can specify the form of payment, for example, "cash only" or "check or credit card only."

lending potential of an individual commercial bank The amount by which a single bank can safely increase the *money supply* by making new loans to (or buying securities from) the public; equal to the bank's excess reserves.

lending potential of the banking system The amount by which the banking system can increase the *money supply* by making new loans to (or buying securities from) the public; equal to the *excess reserves* of the banking system multiplied by the *monetary multiplier*.

liability A debt with a monetary value; an amount owed by a firm or an individual.

limited liability Restriction of the maximum loss to a predetermined amount for the owners (stockholders) of a *corporation*. The maximum loss is the amount they paid for their shares of stock.

liquidity The ease with which an asset can be converted quickly into cash with little or no loss of purchasing power. Money is said to be perfectly liquid, whereas other assets have a lesser degree of liquidity.

loanable funds *Money* available for lending and borrowing.

loanable funds theory of interest The concept that the supply of and demand for *loanable funds* determine the equilibrium rate of interest.

lockout An action by a firm that forbids workers to return to work until a new collective bargaining contract is signed; a means of imposing costs (lost wages) on union workers in a collective bargaining dispute.

logrolling The trading of votes by legislators to secure favorable outcomes on decisions concerning the provision of *public goods* and *quasi-public goods*.

long run (1) In *microeconomics*, a period of time long enough to enable producers of a product to change the quantities of all the resources they employ; period in which all resources and costs are variable and no resources or costs are fixed. (2) In *macroeconomics*, a period sufficiently long for *nominal wages* and other input prices to change in response to a change in the nation's *price level*.

long-run aggregate supply curve The aggregate supply curve associated with a time period in which input prices (especially *nominal wages*) are fully responsive to changes in the *price level*.

long-run competitive equilibrium The price at which firms in *pure competition* neither obtain *economic profit* nor suffer losses in the *long run* and the total quantity demanded and supplied are equal; a price equal to the *marginal cost* and the minimum long-run *average total cost* of producing the product.

long-run supply curve As it applies to macroeconomics, a supply curve for which price, but not real output, changes when the demand curves shifts; a vertical supply curve that implies fully flexible prices.

long-run supply In *microeconomics*, a shedule or curve showing the prices at which a purely competitive industry will make various quantities of the product available in the *long run*.

long-run vertical Phillips Curve The *Phillips Curve* after all nominal wages have adjusted to changes in the rate of inflation; a line emanating straight upward at the economy's *natural rate of unemployment*.

Lorenz curve A curve showing the distribution of income in an economy. The cumulated percentage of families (income receivers) is measured along the horizontal axis and cumulated percentage of income is measured along the vertical axis.

lump-sum tax A tax that is a constant amount (the tax revenue of government is the same) at all levels of GDP.

M1 The most narrowly defined *money supply*, equal to *currency* in the hands of the public and the *checkable deposits* of commercial banks and thrift institutions.

M2 A more broadly defined *money supply*, equal to *M1* plus *noncheckable savings accounts* (including *money market deposit accounts*), small *time deposits* (deposits of less than $100,000), and individual *money market mutual fund* balances.

macroeconomics The part of economics concerned with the economy as a whole; with such major aggregates as the household, business, and government sectors; and with measures of the total economy.

managed floating exchange rate An *exchange rate* that is allowed to change (float) as a result of changes in currency supply and demand but at times is altered (managed) by governments via their buying and selling of particular currencies.

managerial prerogatives The decisions that a firm's management has the sole right to make; often enumerated in the labor contract (work agreement) between a *labor union* and a *firm*.

marginal analysis The comparison of marginal ("extra" or "additional") benefits and marginal costs, usually for decision making.

marginal benefit The extra (additional) benefit of consuming 1 more unit of some good or service; the change in total benefit when 1 more unit is consumed.

marginal cost (MC) The extra (additional) cost of producing 1 more unit of output; equal to the change in *total cost* divided by the change in output (and, in the short run, to the change in total *variable cost* divided by the change in output).

marginal cost–marginal benefit rule As it applies to *cost-benefit analysis*, the tenet that a government project or program should be expanded to the point where the *marginal cost* and *marginal benefit* of additional expenditures are equal.

marginal product (MP) The additional output produced when 1 additional unit of a resource is employed (the quantity of all other resources employed remaining constant); equal to the change in *total product* divided by the change in the quantity of a resource employed.

marginal productivity theory of income distribution The contention that the distribution of income is equitable when each unit of each resource receives a money payment equal to its marginal contribution to the firm's revenue (its *marginal revenue product*).

marginal propensity to consume (MPC) The fraction of any change in *disposable income* spent for *consumer goods*; equal to the change in consumption divided by the change in disposable income.

marginal propensity to save (MPS) The fraction of any change in *disposable income* that households save; equal to the change in *saving* divided by the change in disposable income.

marginal rate of substitution (MRS) The rate at which a consumer is willing to substitute one good for another (from a given combination of goods) and remain equally satisfied (have the same *total utility*); equal to the slope of a consumer's *indifference curve* at each point on the curve.

marginal resource cost (MRC) The amount the total cost of employing a *resource* increases when a firm employs 1 additional unit of the resource (the quantity of all other resources employed remaining constant); equal to the change in the *total cost* of the resource divided by the change in the quantity of the resource employed.

marginal revenue The change in *total revenue* that results from the sale of 1 additional unit of a firm's product; equal to the change in total revenue divided by the change in the quantity of the product sold.

marginal-revenue–marginal-cost approach A method of determining the total output where *economic profit* is a maximum (or losses are a minimum) by comparing the *marginal revenue* and the *marginal cost* of each additional unit of output.

marginal revenue product (MRP) The change in a firm's *total revenue* when it employs 1 additional unit of a resource (the quantity of all other resources employed remaining constant); equal to the change in total revenue divided by the change in the quantity of the resource employed.

marginal revenue productivity (*See marginal revenue product.*)

marginal tax rate The tax rate paid on an additional dollar of income.

marginal utility The extra *utility* a consumer obtains from the consumption of 1 additional unit of a good or service; equal to the change in total utility divided by the change in the quantity consumed.

market Any institution or mechanism that brings together buyers (demanders) and sellers (suppliers) of a particular good or service.

market demand (See *total demand.*)

market economy An economy in which the private decisions of consumers, resource suppliers, and firms determine how resources are allocated; the *market system.*

market failure The inability of a market to bring about the allocation of resources that best satisfies the wants of society; in particular, the overallocation or underallocation of resources to the production of a particular good or service because of *externalities* or informational problems or because markets do not provide desired *public goods.*

market for externality rights A market in which firms can buy rights to discharge pollutants. The price of such rights is determined by the demand for the right to discharge pollutants and a *perfectly inelastic supply* of such rights (the latter determined by the quantity of discharges that the environment can assimilate).

market period A period in which producers of a product are unable to change the quantity produced in response to a change in its price and in which there is a *perfectly inelastic supply.*

market portfolio The portfolio consisting of every financial asset (including every *stock* and *bond*) traded in the financial markets. The market portfolio is used to calculate *beta* (a measure of the degree of riskiness) for specific stocks, bonds, and mutual funds.

market system All the product and resource markets of a *market economy* and the relationships among them; a method that allows the prices determined in those markets to allocate the economy's scarce resources and to communicate and coordinate the decisions made by consumers, firms, and resource suppliers.

marketing loan program A Federal farm subsidy under which certain farmers can receive a loan (on a per-unit-of-output basis) from a government lender and then, depending on the price of the crop, either pay back the loan with interest or keep the loan proceeds while forfeiting their harvested crop to the lender.

median-voter model The theory that under majority rule the median (middle) voter will be in the dominant position to determine the outcome of an election.

Medicaid A Federal program that helps finance the medical expenses of individuals covered by the *Supplemental Security Income (SSI)* and *Temporary Assistance for Needy Families (TANF)* programs.

Medicare A Federal program that is financed by *payroll taxes* and provides for (1) compulsory hospital insurance for senior citizens, (2) low-cost voluntary insurance to help older Americans pay physicians' fees, and (3) subsidized insurance to buy prescription drugs.

Medicare Part D The portion of Medicare that enables enrollees to shop among private health insurance companies to buy highly subsidized insurance to help reduce the out-of-pocket expense of prescription drugs.

medium of exchange Any item sellers generally accept and buyers generally use to pay for a good or service; *money;* a convenient means of exchanging goods and services without engaging in *barter.*

menu costs The reluctance of firms to cut prices during recessions (that they think will be short lived) because of the costs of altering and communicating their price reductions; named after the cost associated with printing new menus at restaurants.

merger The combination of two (or more) firms into a single firm.

microeconomics The part of economics concerned with decision making by individual units such as a *household,* a *firm,* or an *industry* and with individual markets, specific goods and services, and product and resource prices.

Microsoft case A 2002 antitrust case in which Microsoft was found guilty of violating the *Sherman Act* by engaging in a series of unlawful activities designed to maintain its monopoly in operating systems for personal computers; as a remedy the company was prohibited from engaging in a set of specific anticompetitive business practices.

midpoint formula A method for calculating *price elasticity of demand* or *price elasticity of supply* that averages the two prices and two quantities as the reference points for computing percentages.

minimum efficient scale (MES) The lowest level of output at which a firm can minimize long-run *average total cost.*

minimum wage The lowest *wage* that employers may legally pay for an hour of work.

modern economic growth The historically recent phenomenon in which nations for the first time have experienced sustained increases in *real GDP per capita.*

monetarism The macroeconomic view that the main cause of changes in aggregate output and *price level* is fluctuations in the *money supply;* espoused by advocates of a *monetary rule.*

monetary multiplier The multiple of its *excess reserves* by which the banking system can expand *checkable deposits* and thus the *money supply* by making new loans (or buying securities); equal to 1 divided by the *reserve requirement.*

monetary policy A central bank's changing of the *money supply* to influence interest rates and assist the economy in achieving price stability, full employment, and economic growth.

monetary rule The rule suggested by *monetarism.* As traditionally formulated, the rule says that the *money supply* should be expanded each year at the same annual rate as the potential rate of growth of the *real gross domestic product;* the supply of money should be increased steadily between 3 and 5 percent per year. (Also see *Taylor rule.*)

money Any item that is generally acceptable to sellers in exchange for goods and services.

money capital Money available to purchase *capital;* simply *money,* as defined by economists.

money income (See *nominal income.*)

money market The market in which the demand for and the supply of money determine the *interest rate* (or the level of interest rates) in the economy.

money market deposit accounts (MMDAs) Bank- and thrift-provided interest-bearing accounts that contain a variety of short-term securities; such accounts have minimum balance requirements and limits on the frequency of withdrawals.

money market mutual funds (MMMFs) Interest-bearing accounts offered by investment companies, which pool depositors' funds for the purchase of short-term securities. Depositors can write checks in minimum amounts or more against their accounts.

money supply Narrowly defined, *M1*; more broadly defined, *M2*. (See *M1* and *M2*)

monopolistic competition A market structure in which many firms sell a *differentiated product*, into which entry is relatively easy, in which the firm has some control over its product price, and in which there is considerable *nonprice competition*.

monopoly A market structure in which the number of sellers is so small that each seller is able to influence the total supply and the price of the good or service. (Also see *pure monopoly*.)

monopsony A market structure in which there is only a single buyer of a good, service, or resource.

moral hazard problem The possibility that individuals or institutions will change their behavior as the result of a contract or agreement. Example: A bank whose deposits are insured against losses may make riskier loans and investments.

mortgage debt crisis The period beginning in late 2007 when thousands of homeowners defaulted on mortgage loans when they experienced a combination of higher mortgage interest rates and falling home prices.

most-favored-nation (MFN) status An agreement by the United States to allow some other nation's *exports* into the United States at the lowest tariff level levied by the United States. Now referred to as *normal-trade-relations status*.

MR = MC rule The principle that a firm will maximize its profit (or minimize its losses) by producing the output at which *marginal revenue* and *marginal cost* are equal, provided product price is equal to or greater than *average variable cost*.

MRP = MRC rule The principle that to maximize profit (or minimize losses), a firm should employ the quantity of a resource at which its *marginal revenue product* (MRP) is equal to its *marginal resource cost* (MRC), the latter being the wage rate in a purely competitive labor market.

multinational corporations Firms that own production facilities in two or more countries and produce and sell their products globally.

multiple counting Wrongly including the value of *intermediate goods* in the *gross domestic product*; counting the same good or service more than once.

multiplier The ratio of a change in the equilibrium GDP to the change in *investment* or in any other component of *aggregate expenditures* or *aggregate demand*; the number by which a change in any such component must be multiplied to find the resulting change in the equilibrium GDP.

multiplier effect The effect on equilibrium GDP of a change in *aggregate expenditures* or *aggregate demand* (caused by a change in the *consumption schedule*, *investment*, government expenditures, or *net exports*).

mutual funds *Portfolios* of *stocks* and *bonds* selected and purchased by mutual fund companies, which finance the purchases by pooling money from thousands of individual fund investors; includes both *index funds* as well as *actively managed funds*. Fund returns (profits or losses) pass through to the individual fund investors who invest in the funds.

mutual interdependence A situation in which a change in price strategy (or in some other strategy) by one firm will affect the sales and profits of another firm (or other firms). Any firm that makes such a change can expect the other rivals to react to the change.

Nash equilibrium In *game theory*, an outcome from which neither firm wants to deviate; the outcome that once achieved is stable and therefore lasting.

national bank A *commercial bank* authorized to operate by the U.S. government.

National Credit Union Administration (NCUA) The federally chartered agency that insures deposit liabilities (up to $100,000 per account) in *credit unions*.

national health insurance (NHI) A proposed program in which the Federal government would provide a basic package of health care to all citizens at no direct charge or at a low cost-sharing level. Financing would be out of general tax revenues.

national income Total income earned by resource suppliers for their contributions to *gross domestic product* plus *taxes on production and imports*; the sum of wages and salaries, *rent, interest, profit, proprietors' income*, and such taxes.

national income accounting The techniques used to measure the overall production of the economy and other related variables for the nation as a whole.

National Labor Relations Act (Wagner Act of 1935) As amended, the basic labor-relations law in the United States; defines the legal rights of unions and management and identifies unfair union and management labor practices; established the *National Labor Relations Board*.

National Labor Relations Board (NLRB) The board established by the *National Labor Relations Act* of 1935 to investigate unfair labor practices, issue *cease-and-desist orders*, and conduct elections among employees to determine if they wish to be represented by a *labor union*.

natural monopoly An industry in which *economies of scale* are so great that a single firm can produce the product at a lower average total cost than would be possible if more than one firm produced the product.

natural rate of unemployment (NRU) The *full-employment unemployment rate*; the unemployment rate occurring when there is no cyclical unemployment and the economy is achieving its potential output; the unemployment rate at which actual inflation equals expected inflation.

near-money Financial assets, the most important of which are *noncheckable savings accounts, time deposits,* and U.S. short-term securities and savings bonds, which are not a medium of exchange but can be readily converted into money.

negative externality A cost imposed without compensation on third parties by the production or consumption of sellers or buyers. Example: A manufacturer dumps toxic chemicals into a river, killing the fish sought by sports fishers; an external cost or a spillover cost.

negative GDP gap A situation in which actual *gross domestic product* is less than *potential output.* Also known as a recessionary output gap.

negative relationship (See *inverse relationship.*)

negative self-selection As it relates to international *migration,* the idea that those who choose to move to another country have poorer wage opportunities in the origin country than those with similar skills who choose not to *emigrate.*

negative-sum game In *game theory,* a game in which the gains (+) and losses (−) add up to some amount less than zero; one party's losses exceed the other party's gains.

net benefits The total benefits of some activity or policy less the total costs of that activity or policy.

net domestic product *Gross domestic product* less the part of the year's output that is needed to replace the *capital goods* worn out in producing the output; the nation's total output available for consumption or additions to the *capital stock.*

net exports (X_n) *Exports* minus *imports.*

net foreign factor income Receipts of resource income from the rest of the world minus payments of resource income to the rest of the world.

net investment income The interest and dividend income received by the residents of a nation from residents of other nations less the interest and dividend payments made by the residents of that nation to the residents of other nations.

net private domestic investment *Gross private domestic investment* less *consumption of fixed capital;* the addition to the nation's stock of *capital* during a year.

net taxes The taxes collected by government less *government transfer payments.*

net transfers The personal and government transfer payments made by one nation to residents of foreign nations less the personal and government transfer payments received from residents of foreign nations.

network effects Increases in the value of a product to each user, including existing users, as the total number of users rises.

net worth The total *assets* less the total *liabilities* of a firm or an individual; for a firm, the claims of the owners against the firm's total assets; for an individual, his or her wealth.

new classical economics The theory that, although unanticipated price-level changes may create macroeconomic instability in the short run, the economy is stable at the full-employment level of domestic output in the long run because prices and wages adjust automatically to correct movements away from the full-employment, noninflationary output.

NLRB (See *National Labor Relations Board.*)

nominal gross domestic product (GDP) The *GDP* measured in terms of the price level at the time of measurement (unadjusted for *inflation*).

nominal income The number of dollars received by an individual or group for its resources during some period of time.

nominal interest rate The interest rate expressed in terms of annual amounts currently charged for interest and not adjusted for inflation.

nominal wage The amount of money received by a worker per unit of time (hour, day, etc.); money wage.

noncash transfer A *government transfer payment* in the form of goods and services rather than money, for example, food stamps, housing assistance, and job training; also called in-kind transfers.

noncollusive oligopoly An *oligopoly* in which the firms do not act together and in agreement to determine the price of the product and the output that each firm will produce.

noncompeting groups Collections of workers in the economy who do not compete with each other for employment because the skill and training of the workers in one group are substantially different from those of the workers in other groups.

nondiscretionary fiscal policy (See *built-in stabilizer.*)

nondiversifiable risk Investment *risk* that investors are unable to reduce via *diversification;* also called systemic risk.

nondurable good A *consumer good* with an expected life (use) of less than 3 years.

nonexcludability The inability to keep nonpayers (free riders) from obtaining benefits from a certain good; a *public good* characteristic.

nonexhaustive expenditure An expenditure by government that does not result directly in the employment of economic resources or the production of goods and services; see *government transfer payment.*

nonincome determinants of consumption and saving All influences on consumption and saving other than the level of *GDP.*

noninterest determinants of investment All influences on the level of investment spending other than the *interest rate.*

noninvestment transaction An expenditure for stocks, bonds, or secondhand *capital goods.*

nonmarket transactions The value of the goods and services that are not included in the *gross domestic product* because they are not bought and sold.

nonprice competition Competition based on distinguishing one's product by means of *product differentiation* and then *advertising* the distinguished product to consumers.

nonproduction transaction The purchase and sale of any item that is not a currently produced good or service.

nonrenewable natural resource Things such as oil, natural gas, and metals, which are either in actual fixed supply or which renew so slowly as to be in virtual fixed supply when viewed from a human time perspective.

nonrivalry The idea that one person's benefit from a certain good does not reduce the benefit available to others; a *public good* characteristic.

nontariff barriers (NTBs) All barriers other than *protective tariffs* that nations erect to impede international trade, including *import quotas*, licensing requirements, unreasonable product-quality standards, unnecessary bureaucratic detail in customs procedures, and so on.

normal good A good or service whose consumption increases when income increases and falls when income decreases, price remaining constant.

normal profit The payment made by a firm to obtain and retain *entrepreneurial ability*; the minimum income entrepreneurial ability must receive to induce it to perform entrepreneurial functions for a firm.

normal-trade-relation (NTR) status A designation for countries that are allowed to export goods and services into the United States at the lowest tariff rates available to any other country allowed to export those goods to the United States; until recently called *most-favored-nation status*.

normative economics The part of economics involving value judgments about what the economy should be like; focused on which economic goals and policies should be implemented; policy economics.

North American Free Trade Agreement (NAFTA) A 1993 agreement establishing, over a 15-year period, a free-trade zone composed of Canada, Mexico, and the United States.

occupation A category of activities or tasks performed by a set of workers for pay, independent of employer or industry. Examples are managers, nurses, farmers, and cooks.

occupational licensure The laws of state or local governments that require that a worker satisfy certain specified requirements and obtain a license from a licensing board before engaging in a particular occupation.

occupational segregation The crowding of women or minorities into less desirable, lower-paying occupations.

official reserves Foreign currencies owned by the central bank of a nation.

offshoring The practice of shifting work previously done by American workers to workers located abroad.

Okun's law The generalization that any 1-percentage-point rise in the *unemployment rate* above the *full-employment unemployment rate* is associated with a rise in the negative *GDP gap* by 2 percent of *potential output* (potential GDP).

oligopoly A market structure in which a few firms sell either a *standardized* or *differentiated product*, into which entry is difficult, in which the firm has limited control over product price because of *mutual interdependence* (except when there is collusion among firms), and in which there is typically *nonprice competition*.

one-time game In *game theory*, a game in which the parties select their optimal strategies in a single time period without regard to possible interaction in subsequent time periods.

OPEC (See *Organization of Petroleum Exporting Countries*.)

open economy An economy that exports and imports goods and services.

open-market operations The buying and selling of U.S. government securities by the *Federal Reserve Banks* for purposes of carrying out *monetary policy*.

open shop A place of employment in which the employer may hire nonunion workers and the workers need not become members of a *labor union*.

opportunity cost The amount of other products that must be forgone or sacrificed to produce a unit of a product.

opportunity-cost ratio An equivalency showing the number of units of two products that can be produced with the same resources; the cost 1 corn ≡ 3 olives shows that the resources required to produce 3 units of olives must be shifted to corn production to produce 1 unit of corn.

optimal amount of R&D (Web chapter) The level of *R&D* at which the *marginal benefit* and *marginal cost* of R&D expenditures are equal.

optimal reduction of an externality The reduction of a *negative externality* such as pollution to the level at which the *marginal benefit* and *marginal cost* of reduction are equal.

ordinal utility Satisfaction that is measured by having consumers compare and rank products (or combinations of products) as to preference, without asking them to specify the absolute amount of satisfaction provided by the product.

Organization of Petroleum Exporting Countries (OPEC) A cartel of 13 oil-producing countries (Algeria, Angola, Ecuador, Indonesia, Iran, Iraq, Kuwait, Libya, Nigeria, Qatar, Saudi Arabia, Venezuela, and the UAE) that attempts to control the quantity and price of crude oil exported by its members and that accounts for a large percentage of the world's export of oil.

other-things-equal assumption The assumption that factors other than those being considered are held constant; *ceteris paribus* assumption.

outpayments The expenditures of domestic or foreign currency that the individuals, firms, and governments of one nation make to purchase goods and services, for remittances, to pay investment income, and for purchases of foreign assets.

output effect The situation in which an increase in the price of one input will increase a firm's production costs and reduce its level of output, thus reducing the demand for other inputs; conversely for a decrease in the price of the input.

paper money Pieces of paper used as a *medium of exchange*; in the United States, *Federal Reserve Notes*.

paradox of voting A situation where paired-choice voting by majority rule fails to provide a consistent ranking of society's preferences for *public goods* or *services*.

parity concept The idea that year after year a specific output of a farm product should enable a farmer to acquire a constant amount of nonagricultural goods and services.

parity ratio The ratio of the price received by farmers from the sale of an agricultural commodity to the prices of other goods paid by them; usually expressed as a percentage; used as a rationale for *price supports*.

partnership An unincorporated firm owned and operated by two or more persons.

passively managed funds *Mutual funds* whose *portfolios* are not regularly updated by a fund manager attempting to generate high returns. Rather, once an initial portfolio is selected, it is left unchanged so that investors receive whatever return that unchanging portfolio subsequently generates. *Index funds* are a type of passively managed fund.

patent An exclusive right given to inventors to produce and sell a new product or machine for 20 years from the time of patent application.

payments deficit (See *balance-of-payments deficit*.)

payments surplus (See *balance-of-payments surplus*.)

payroll tax A tax levied on employers of labor equal to a percentage of all or part of the wages and salaries paid by them and on employees equal to a percentage of all or part of the wages and salaries received by them.

P = MC rule The principle that a purely competitive firm will maximize its profit or minimize its loss by producing that output at which the *price* of the product is equal to *marginal cost*, provided that price is equal to or greater than *average variable cost* in the short run and equal to or greater than *average total cost* in the long run.

peak The point in a business cycle at which business activity has reached a temporary maximum; the economy is near or at full employment and the level of real output is at or very close to the economy's capacity.

per capita GDP *Gross domestic product* (GDP) per person; the average GDP of a population.

per capita income A nation's total income per person; the average income of a population.

percentage rate of return The percentage gain or loss, relative to the buying price, of an *economic investment* or *financial investment* over some period of time.

perfectly elastic demand Product or resource demand in which *quantity demanded* can be of any amount at a particular product *price*; graphs as a horizontal *demand curve*.

perfectly elastic supply Product or resource supply in which *quantity supplied* can be of any amount at a particular product or resource *price*; graphs as a horizontal *supply curve*.

perfectly inelastic demand Product or resource demand in which *price* can be of any amount at a particular quantity of the product or resource demanded; *quantity demanded* does not respond to a change in price; graphs as a vertical *demand curve*.

perfectly inelastic supply Product or resource supply in which *price* can be of any amount at a particular quantity of the product or resource demanded; *quantity supplied* does not respond to a change in price; graphs as a vertical *supply curve*.

per se violations Collusive actions, such as attempts by firms to fix prices or divide a market, that are violations of the *antitrust laws*, even if the actions themselves are unsuccessful.

personal consumption expenditures The expenditures of *households* for *durable* and *nondurable consumer goods* and *services*.

personal distribution of income The manner in which the economy's *personal* or *disposable income* is divided among different income classes or different households or families.

personal income (PI) The earned and unearned income available to resource suppliers and others before the payment of personal taxes.

personal income tax A tax levied on the taxable income of individuals, households, and unincorporated firms.

personal saving The *personal income* of households less personal taxes and *personal consumption expenditures*; *disposable income* not spent for *consumer goods*.

per-unit production cost The average production cost of a particular level of output; total input cost divided by units of output.

Phillips Curve A curve showing the relationship between the *unemployment rate* (on the horizontal axis) and the annual rate of increase in the *price level* (on the vertical axis).

planned investment The amount that *firms* plan or intend to invest.

plant A physical establishment that performs one or more functions in the production, fabrication, and distribution of goods and services.

"play or pay" A means of expanding health insurance coverage by requiring that employers either provide insurance for their workers or pay a special *payroll tax* to finance insurance for noncovered workers.

policy economics The formulation of courses of action to bring about desired economic outcomes or to prevent undesired occurrences.

political business cycle The alleged tendency of Congress to destabilize the economy by reducing taxes and increasing government expenditures before elections and to raise taxes and lower expenditures after elections.

portfolio A specific collection of *stocks*, *bonds*, or other *financial investments* held by an individual or a *mutual fund*.

positive economics The analysis of facts or data to establish scientific generalizations about economic behavior.

positive externality A benefit obtained without compensation by third parties from the production or consumption of sellers or buyers. Example: A beekeeper benefits when a neighboring farmer plants clover. An *external benefit* or a spillover benefit.

positive GDP gap A situation in which actual *gross domestic product* exceeds *potential output*. Also known as an inflationary output gap.

positive relationship (See *direct relationship*.)

positive sum game In *game theory*, a game in which the gains (+) and losses (−) add up to more than zero; one party's gains exceeds the other party's losses.

post hoc, ergo propter hoc fallacy The false belief that when one event precedes another, the first event must have caused the second event.

potential competition The new competitors that may be induced to enter an industry if firms now in that industry are receiving large *economic profits*.

potential output The real output *(GDP)* an economy can produce when it fully employs its available resources.

poverty A situation in which the basic needs of an individual or family exceed the means to satisfy them.

poverty rate The percentage of the population with incomes below the official poverty income levels that are established by the Federal government.

preferred provider organization (PPO) An arrangement in which doctors and hospitals agree to provide health care to insured individuals at rates negotiated with an insurer.

present value Today's value of some amount of money that is to be received sometime in the future.

price The amount of money needed to buy a particular good, service, or resource.

price ceiling A legally established maximum price for a good or service.

price discrimination The selling of a product to different buyers at different prices when the price differences are not justified by differences in cost.

price elasticity of demand The ratio of the percentage change in *quantity demanded* of a product or resource to the percentage change in its *price*; a measure of the responsiveness of buyers to a change in the price of a product or resource.

price elasticity of supply The ratio of the percentage change in *quantity supplied* of a product or resource to the percentage change in its *price*; a measure of the responsiveness of producers to a change in the price of a product or resource.

price fixing The conspiring by two or more firms to set the price of their products; an illegal practice under the *Sherman Act*.

price floor A legally determined minimum price above the *equilibrium price*.

price index An index number that shows how the weighted-average price of a "market basket" of goods changes over time.

price leadership An informal method that firms in an *oligopoly* may employ to set the price of their product: One firm (the leader) is the first to announce a change in price, and the other firms (the followers) soon announce identical or similar changes.

price level The weighted average of the prices of all the final goods and services produced in an economy.

price-level stability A steadiness of the price level from one period to the next; zero or low annual inflation; also called "price stability."

price-level surprises Unanticipated changes in the price level.

price maker A seller (or buyer) that is able to affect the product or resource price by changing the amount it sells (or buys).

price support A minimum price that government allows sellers to receive for a good or service; a legally established or maintained minimum price.

price taker A seller (or buyer) that is unable to affect the price at which a product or resource sells by changing the amount it sells (or buys).

price war Successive and continued decreases in the prices charged by firms in an oligopolistic industry. Each firm lowers its price below rivals' prices, hoping to increase its sales and revenues at its rivals' expense.

prime interest rate The benchmark *interest rate* that banks use as a reference point for a wide range of loans to businesses and individuals.

principal-agent problem A conflict of interest that occurs when agents (workers or managers) pursue their own objectives to the detriment of the principals' (stockholders') goals.

principle of comparative advantage The proposition that an individual, region, or nation will benefit if it specializes in producing goods for which its own *opportunity costs* are lower than the opportunity costs of a trading partner, and then exchanging some of the products in which it specializes for other desired products produced by others.

private good A good or service that is individually consumed and that can be profitably provided by privately owned firms because they can exclude nonpayers from receiving the benefits.

private property The right of private persons and firms to obtain, own, control, employ, dispose of, and bequeath *land*, *capital*, and other property.

private sector The *households* and business *firms* of the economy.

probability weighted average Each of the possible future rates of return from an investment multiplied by its respective probability (expressed as a decimal) of happening.

process innovation (Web chapter) The development and use of new or improved production or distribution methods.

producer surplus The difference between the actual price a producer receives (or producers receive) and the minimum acceptable price; the triangular area above the supply curve and below the market price.

product differentiation A strategy in which one firm's product is distinguished from competing products by means of its design, related services, quality, location, or other attributes (except price).

product innovation (Web chapter) The development and sale of a new or improved product (or service).

production possibilities curve A curve showing the different combinations of two goods or services that can be produced in a *full-employment, full-production* economy where the available supplies of resources and technology are fixed.

productive efficiency The production of a good in the least costly way; occurs when production takes place at the output at which *average total cost* is a minimum and *marginal product* per dollar's worth of input is the same for all inputs.

productivity A measure of average output or real output per unit of input. For example, the productivity of labor is determined by dividing real output by hours of work.

productivity growth The increase in *productivity* from one period to another.

product market A market in which products are sold by *firms* and bought by *households*.

profit The return to the resource *entrepreneurial ability* (see *normal profit*); *total revenue* minus *total cost* (see *economic profit*).

profit-maximizing combination of resources The quantity of each resource a firm must employ to maximize its profit or minimize its loss; the combination in which the *marginal revenue product* of each resource is equal to its *marginal resource cost* (to its *price* if the resource is employed in a competitive market).

profit sharing plan A compensation device through which workers receive part of their pay in the form of a share of their employer's profit (if any).

progressive tax A tax whose *average tax rate* increases as the taxpayer's income increases and decreases as the taxpayer's income decreases.

property tax A tax on the value of property (*capital, land, stocks* and *bonds*, and other *assets*) owned by *firms* and *households*.

proportional tax A tax whose *average tax rate* remains constant as the taxpayer's income increases or decreases.

proprietor's income The net income of the owners of unincorporated firms (proprietorships and partnerships).

protective tariff A *tariff* designed to shield domestic producers of a good or service from the competition of foreign producers.

public assistance programs Government programs that pay benefits to those who are unable to earn income (because of permanent disabilities or because they have very low income and dependent children); financed by general tax revenues and viewed as public charity (rather than earned rights).

public choice theory The economic analysis of government decision making, politics, and elections.

public debt The total amount owed by the Federal government to the owners of government securities; equal to the sum of past government *budget deficits* less government *budget surpluses*.

public good A good or service that is characterized by *nonrivalry* and *nonexcludability*; a good or service with these characteristics provided by government.

public interest theory of regulation The presumption that the purpose of the regulation of an *industry* is to protect the public (consumers) from abuse of the power possessed by *natural monopolies*.

public investments Government expenditures on public capital (such as roads, highways, bridges, mass-transit systems, and elec-

tric power facilities) and on *human capital* (such as education, training, and health).

public sector The part of the economy that contains all government entities; government.

public utility A firm that produces an essential good or service, has obtained from a government the right to be the sole supplier of the good or service in the area, and is regulated by that government to prevent the abuse of its monopoly power.

purchasing power The amount of goods and services that a monetary unit of income can buy.

purchasing power parity The idea that exchange rates between nations equate the purchasing power of various currencies. Exchange rates between any two nations adjust to reflect the price-level differences between the countries.

pure competition A market structure in which a very large number of firms sells a *standardized product*, into which entry is very easy, in which the individual seller has no control over the product price, and in which there is no nonprice competition; a market characterized by a very large number of buyers and sellers.

purely competitive labor market A *resource market* in which many firms compete with one another in hiring a specific kind of labor, numerous equally qualified workers supply that labor, and no one controls the market wage rate.

pure monopoly A market structure in which one firm sells a unique product, into which entry is blocked, in which the single firm has considerable control over product price, and in which *nonprice competition* may or may not be found.

pure profit (See *economic profit*.)

pure rate of interest An essentially risk-free, long-term interest rate that is free of the influence of market imperfections.

quantity demanded The amount of a good or service that buyers (or a buyer) desire to purchase at a particular price during some period.

quantity supplied The amount of a good or service that producers (or a producer) offer to sell at a particular price during some period.

quasi-public bank A bank that is privately owned but governmentally (publicly) controlled; each of the U.S. *Federal Reserve Banks*.

quasi-public good A good or service to which excludability could apply but that has such a large *positive externality* that government sponsors its production to prevent an underallocation of resources.

R&D Research and development activities undertaken to bring about *technological advance*.

rate of exchange The price paid in one's own money to acquire 1 unit of a foreign currency; the rate at which the money of one nation is exchanged for the money of another nation.

rate of return The gain in net revenue divided by the cost of an investment or an *R&D* expenditure; expressed as a percentage.

rational behavior Human behavior based on comparison of marginal costs and marginal benefits; behavior designed to maximize total utility.

rational expectations theory The hypothesis that firms and households expect monetary and fiscal policies to have certain effects on the economy and (in pursuit of their own self-interests) take actions that make these policies ineffective.

rationing function of prices The ability of market forces in competitive markets to equalize *quantity demanded* and *quantity supplied* and to eliminate shortages and surpluses via changes in prices.

real-balances effect The tendency for increases in the *price level* to lower the real value (or purchasing power) of financial assets with fixed money value and, as a result, to reduce total spending and real output, and conversely for decreases in the price level.

real-business-cycle theory A theory that *business cycles* result from changes in technology and resource availability, which affect *productivity* and thus increase or decrease long-run aggregate supply.

real capital (See *capital*.)

real GDP (See *real gross domestic product*.)

real GDP per capita *Inflation*-adjusted output per person; *real GDP*/population.

real gross domestic product (GDP) *Gross domestic product* adjusted for inflation; gross domestic product in a year divided by the GDP *price index* for that year, the index expressed as a decimal.

real income The amount of goods and services that can be purchased with *nominal income* during some period of time; nominal income adjusted for inflation.

real interest rate The interest rate expressed in dollars of constant value (adjusted for *inflation*) and equal to the *nominal interest rate* less the expected rate of inflation.

real wage The amount of goods and services a worker can purchase with his or her *nominal wage*; the purchasing power of the nominal wage.

recession A period of declining real GDP, accompanied by lower real income and higher unemployment.

recessionary expenditure gap The amount by which the *aggregate expenditures schedule* must shift upward to increase the real GDP to its full-employment, noninflationary level.

Reciprocal Trade Agreements Act A 1934 Federal law that authorized the president to negotiate up to 50 percent lower tariffs with foreign nations that agreed to reduce their tariffs on U.S. goods. (Such agreements incorporated the *most-favored-nation* clause.)

refinancing the public debt Selling new government securities to owners of expiring securities or paying them money gained from the sale of new securities to others.

regressive tax A tax whose *average tax rate* decreases as the taxpayer's income increases and increases as the taxpayer's income decreases.

regulatory agency An agency, commission, or board established by the Federal government or a state government to control the prices charged and the services offered by a *natural monopoly*.

remittances Payments by *immigrants* to family members and others located in the origin countries of the immigrants.

rental income The payments (income) received by those who supply *land* to the economy.

renewable natural resources Things such as forests, water in reservoirs, and wildlife that are capable of growing back or building back up (renewing themselves) if they are harvested at moderate rates.

rent-seeking behavior The actions by persons, firms, or unions to gain special benefits from government at the taxpayers' or someone else's expense.

repeated game In *game theory*, a game that is played again sometime after the previous game ends.

replacement rate The birthrate necessary to offset deaths in a country and therefore to keep the size of its population constant (without relying on immigration). For most countries, the replacement rate is about 2.1 births per woman per lifetime.

required reserves The funds that banks and thrifts must deposit with the *Federal Reserve Bank* (or hold as *vault cash*) to meet the legal *reserve requirement*; a fixed percentage of the bank's or thrift's checkable deposits.

reserve ratio The fraction of *checkable deposits* that a bank must hold as reserves in a *Federal Reserve Bank* or in its own bank vault; also called the *reserve requirement*.

reserve requirement The specified minimum percentage of its checkable deposits that a bank or thrift must keep on deposit at the Federal Reserve Bank in its district or hold as *vault cash*.

resource A natural, human, or manufactured item that helps produce goods and services; a productive agent or factor of production.

resource market A market in which *households* sell and *firms* buy resources or the services of resources.

restrictive monetary policy Federal Reserve system actions to reduce the *money supply*, increase *interest rates*, and reduce *inflation*; a tight money policy.

revenue tariff A *tariff* designed to produce income for the Federal government.

right-to-work law A state law (in about 22 states) that makes it illegal to require that a worker join a *labor union* in order to retain his or her job; laws that make *union shops* and *agency shops* illegal.

risk The uncertainty as to the actual future returns of a particular *financial investment* or *economic investment*.

risk-free interest rate The *interest rate* earned on short-term U.S. government bonds.

risk premium The *interest rate* above the *risk-free* interest rate that must be paid and received to compensate the lender or investor for *risk*.

rule of reason The rule stated and applied in the *U.S. Steel case* that only combinations and contracts unreasonably restraining trade are subject to actions under the antitrust laws and that size and possession of monopoly power are not illegal.

rule of 70 A method for determining the number of years it will take for some measure to double, given its annual percentage increase. Example: To determine the number of years it will take for the *price level* to double, divide 70 by the annual rate of *inflation*.

sales and excise taxes (See *sales tax*; see *excise tax*.)

sales tax A tax levied on the cost (at retail) of a broad group of products.

saving Disposable income not spent for consumer goods; equal to *disposable income* minus *personal consumption expenditures*.

savings The accumulation of funds that results when people in an economy spend less (consume less) than their incomes during a given time period.

savings account A deposit in a *commercial bank* or *thrift institution* on which interest payments are received; generally used for saving rather than daily transactions; a component of the *M2* money supply.

savings and loan association (S&L) A firm that accepts deposits primarily from small individual savers and lends primarily to individuals to finance purchases such as autos and homes; now nearly indistinguishable from a *commercial bank*.

saving schedule A schedule that shows the amounts *households* plan to save (plan not to spend for *consumer goods*), at different levels of *disposable income*.

savings deposit A deposit that is interest-bearing and that the depositor can normally withdraw at any time.

savings institution (See *thrift institution*.)

Say's law The largely discredited macroeconomic generalization that the production of goods and services (supply) creates an equal *demand* for those goods and services.

scarce resources The limited quantities of *land*, *capital*, *labor*, and *entrepreneurial ability* that are never sufficient to satisfy people's virtually unlimited economic wants.

scientific method The procedure for the systematic pursuit of knowledge involving the observation of facts and the formulation and testing of hypotheses to obtain theories, principles, and laws.

secular trend A long-term tendency; a change in some variable over a very long period of years.

Security Market Line (SML) A line that shows the average expected rate of return of all financial investments at each level of *nondiversifiable risk*, the latter measured by *beta*.

self-interest That which each firm, property owner, worker, and consumer believes is best for itself and seeks to obtain.

seniority The length of time a worker has been employed absolutely or relative to other workers; may be used to determine which workers will be laid off when there is insufficient work for them all and who will be rehired when more work becomes available.

self-selection As it relates to international migration, the idea that those who choose to move tend to have greater motivation for economic gain or greater willingness to sacrifice current consumption for future consumption than those with similar skills who choose to remain at home.

separation of ownership and control The fact that different groups of people own a *corporation* (the stockholders) and manage it (the directors and officers).

sequential game In *game theory*, a game in which the parties make their moves in turn, with one party making the first move, followed by the other party making the next move, and so on.

service An (intangible) act or use for which a consumer, firm, or government is willing to pay.

Sherman Act The Federal antitrust act of 1890 that makes monopoly and conspiracies to restrain trade criminal offenses.

shirking Workers' neglecting or evading work to increase their *utility* or well-being.

shocks Sudden, unexpected changes in *demand* (or *aggregate demand*) or supply (or *aggregate supply*).

shortage The amount by which the *quantity demanded* of a product exceeds the *quantity supplied* at a particular (below-equilibrium) price.

short run (1) In microeconomics, a period of time in which producers are able to change the quantities of some but not all of the resources they employ; a period in which some resources (usually plant) are fixed and some are variable. (2) In macroeconomics, a period in which nominal wages and other input prices do not change in response to a change in the price level.

short-run aggregate supply curve An aggregate supply curve relevant to a time period in which input prices (particularly *nominal wages*) do not change in response to changes in the *price level*.

short-run competitive equilibrium The price at which the total quantity of a product supplied in the *short run* in a purely competitive industry equals the total quantity of the product demanded and that is equal to or greater than *average variable cost*.

short-run supply curve A supply curve that shows the quantity of a product a firm in a purely competitive industry will offer to sell at various prices in the *short run*; the portion of the firm's short-run marginal cost curve that lies above its *average-variable-cost* curve.

shutdown case The circumstance in which a firm would experience a loss greater than its total *fixed cost* if it were to produce any output greater than zero; alternatively, a situation in which a firm would cease to operate when the *price* at which it can sell its product is less than its *average variable cost*.

simple multiplier The *multiplier* in any economy in which government collects no *net taxes*, there are no *imports*, and *investment* is independent of the level of income; equal to 1 divided by the *marginal propensity to save*.

simultaneous consumption The same-time derivation of *utility* from some product by a large number of consumers.

simultaneous game In *game theory*, a game in which both parties choose their strategies and execute them at the same time.

single-tax movement The political efforts by followers of Henry George (1839-1897) to impose a single tax on the value of land and eliminate all other taxes.

skill transferability The ease to which people can shift their work talents from one job, region, or country to another job, region, or country.

slope of a straight line The ratio of the vertical change (the rise or fall) to the horizontal change (the run) between any two points on a line. The slope of an upward-sloping line is positive, reflecting a direct relationship between two variables; the slope of a downward-sloping line is negative, reflecting an inverse relationship between two variables.

Smoot-Hawley Tariff Act Legislation passed in 1930 that established very high tariffs. Its objective was to reduce imports and stimulate the domestic economy, but it resulted only in retaliatory tariffs by other nations.

social insurance programs Programs that replace the earnings lost when people retire or are temporarily unemployed, that are financed by payroll taxes, and that are viewed as earned rights (rather than charity).

socially optimal price The price of a product that results in the most efficient allocation of an economy's resources and that is equal to the *marginal cost* of the product.

social regulation Regulation in which government is concerned with the conditions under which goods and services are produced, their physical characteristics, and the impact of their production on society; in contrast to *industrial regulation*.

Social Security The social insurance program in the United States financed by Federal payroll taxes on employers and employees and designed to replace a portion of the earnings lost when workers become disabled, retire, or die.

Social Security trust fund A Federal fund that saves excessive Social Security tax revenues received in one year to meet Social Security benefit obligations that exceed Social Security tax revenues in some subsequent year.

sole proprietorship An unincorporated *firm* owned and operated by one person.

special-interest effect Any result of government promotion of the interests (goals) of a small group at the expense of a much larger group.

specialization The use of the resources of an individual, a firm, a region, or a nation to concentrate production on one or a small number of goods and services.

speculation The activity of buying or selling with the motive of later reselling or rebuying for profit.

SSI (See *Supplemental Security Income*.)

stagflation Inflation accompanied by stagnation in the rate of growth of output and an increase in unemployment in the economy; simultaneous increases in the *inflation rate* and the *unemployment rate*.

standardized budget A comparison of the government expenditures and tax collections that would occur if the economy operated at *full employment* throughout the year; the full-employment budget.

standardized product A product whose buyers are indifferent to the seller from whom they purchase it as long as the price charged by all sellers is the same; a product all units of which are identical and thus are perfect substitutes for each other.

Standard Oil case A 1911 antitrust case in which Standard Oil was found guilty of violating the *Sherman Act* by illegally monopolizing the petroleum industry. As a remedy the company was divided into several competing firms.

start-up (firm) A new firm focused on creating and introducing a particular new product or employing a specific new production or distribution method.

state bank A *commercial bank* authorized by a state government to engage in the business of banking.

static economy A hypothetical economy in which the basic forces such as resource supplies, technological knowledge, and consumer tastes are constant and unchanging.

statistical discrimination The practice of judging an individual on the basis of the average characteristic of the group to which he or she belongs rather than on his or her own personal characteristics.

sticky prices (See *inflexible prices*.)

stock (corporate) An ownership share in a corporation.

stock options Contracts that enable executives or other key employees to buy shares of their employers' stock at fixed, lower prices even when the market price subsequently rises.

store of value An *asset* set aside for future use; one of the three functions of *money*.

strategic behavior Self-interested economic actions that take into account the expected reactions of others.

strategic trade policy The use of trade barriers to reduce the risk inherent in product development by domestic firms, particularly that involving advanced technology.

strike The withholding of labor services by an organized group of workers (a *labor union*).

structural unemployment Unemployment of workers whose skills are not demanded by employers, who lack sufficient skill to obtain employment, or who cannot easily move to locations where jobs are available.

subprime mortgage loans High-interest rate loans to home buyers with above-average credit risk.

subsidy A payment of funds (or goods and services) by a government, firm, or household for which it receives no good or service in return. When made by a government, it is a *government transfer payment*.

substitute goods Products or services that can be used in place of each other. When the price of one falls, the demand for the other product falls; conversely, when the price of one product rises, the demand for the other product rises.

substitute resources Productive inputs that can be used instead of other inputs in the production process; resources for which an increase in the price of one leads to an increase in the demand for the other.

substitution effect (1) A change in the quantity demanded of a *consumer good* that results from a change in its relative expensiveness caused by a change in the product's price; (2) the effect of a change in the price of a *resource* on the quantity of the resource employed by a firm, assuming no change in its output.

sunk cost A cost that has been incurred and cannot be recovered.

Supplemental Security Income (SSI) A federally financed and administered program that provides a uniform nationwide minimum income for the aged, blind, and disabled who do not qualify for benefits under *Social Security* in the United States.

supply A schedule showing the amounts of a good or service that sellers (or a seller) will offer at various prices during some period.

supply curve A curve illustrating *supply*.

supply factor (in growth) An increase in the availability of a resource, an improvement in its quality, or an expansion of technological knowledge that makes it possible for an economy to produce a greater output of goods and services.

supply schedule (See *supply*.)

supply shocks Sudden, unexpected changes in *aggregate supply*.

supply-side economics A view of macroeconomics that emphasizes the role of costs and *aggregate supply* in explaining *inflation*, *unemployment*, and *economic growth*.

surplus The amount by which the *quantity supplied* of a product exceeds the *quantity demanded* at a specific (above-equilibrium) price.

surplus payment A payment to a resource that is not required to ensure its availability in the production process; for example, land rent.

tacit understanding An unspoken, unwritten agreement by an oligopolist to set prices and outputs that does not involve outright (or overt) *collusion*. *Price leadership* is a frequent example.

TANF (See *Temporary Assistance for Needy Families*.)

tariff A tax imposed by a nation on an imported good.

taste-for-discrimination model A theory that views discrimination as a preference for which an employer is willing to pay.

tax An involuntary payment of money (or goods and services) to a government by a *household* or *firm* for which the household or firm receives no good or service directly in return.

taxes on production and imports A *national income accounting* category that includes such taxes as *sales*, *excise*, business property taxes, and *tariffs* which firms treat as costs of producing a product and pass on (in whole or in part) to buyers by charging a higher price.

tax incidence The person or group that ends up paying a tax.

tax subsidy A grant in the form of reduced taxes through favorable tax treatment. For example, employer-paid health insurance is exempt from Federal income and payroll taxes.

tax-transfer disincentives Decreases in the incentives to work, save, invest, innovate, and take risks that result from high *marginal tax rates* and *transfer payments*.

Taylor rule A modern monetary rule proposed by economist John Taylor that would stipulate exactly how much the Federal Reserve should change real interest rates in response to divergences of real GDP from potential GDP and divergences of actual rates of inflation from a target rate of inflation.

technological advance New and better goods and services and new and better ways of producing or distributing them.

technology The body of knowledge and techniques that can be used to combine *economic resources* to produce goods and services.

Temporary Assistance for Needy Families (TANF) A state-administered and partly federally funded program in the United States that provides financial aid to poor families; the basic welfare program for low-income families in the United States; contains time limits and work requirements.

term auction facility The *monetary policy* procedure used by the Federal Reserve, in which commercial banks anonymously bid to obtain loans being made available by the Fed as a way to expand reserves in the banking system.

terms of trade The rate at which units of one product can be exchanged for units of another product; the price of a good or service; the amount of one good or service that must be given up to obtain 1 unit of another good or service.

theoretical economics The process of deriving and applying economic theories and principles.

theory of human capital The generalization that *wage differentials* are the result of differences in the amount of *human capital investment* and that the incomes of lower-paid workers are raised by increasing the amount of such investment.

thrift institution A *savings and loan association*, *mutual savings bank*, or *credit union*.

till money (See *vault cash*.)

time deposit An interest-earning deposit in a *commercial bank* or *thrift institution* that the depositor can withdraw without penalty after the end of a specified period.

time preference The human tendency for people, because of impatience, to prefer to spend and consume in the present rather than save and wait to spend and consume in the future; this inclination varies in strength among individuals.

time-value of money The idea that a specific amount of money is more valuable to a person the sooner it is received because the money can be placed in a financial account or investment and earn *compound interest* over time; the *opportunity cost* of receiving a sum of money later rather than earlier.

token money Bills or coins for which the amount printed on the *currency* bears no relationship to the value of the paper or metal embodied within it; for currency still circulating, money for which the face value exceeds the commodity value.

total allowable catch A limit set by government or a fisheries commission on the total number of fish or tonnage of fish that fishers collectively can harvest during some particular time period.

total cost The sum of *fixed cost* and *variable cost*.

total demand The demand schedule or the *demand curve* of all buyers of a good or service; also called market demand.

total demand for money The sum of the *transactions demand for money* and the *asset demand for money*.

total fertility rate The average total number of children that a woman is expected to have during her lifetime.

total product (TP) The total output of a particular good or service produced by a firm (or a group of firms or the entire economy).

total revenue (TR) The total number of dollars received by a firm (or firms) from the sale of a product; equal to the total expenditures for the product produced by the firm (or firms); equal to the quantity sold (demanded) multiplied by the price at which it is sold.

total-revenue test A test to determine elasticity of *demand* between any two prices: Demand is elastic if *total revenue* moves in the opposite direction from price; it is inelastic when it moves in the same direction as price; and it is of unitary elasticity when it does not change when price changes.

total spending The total amount that buyers of goods and services spend or plan to spend; also called *aggregate expenditures*.

total supply The supply schedule or the *supply curve* of all sellers of a good or service; also called market supply.

total utility The total amount of satisfaction derived from the consumption of a single product or a combination of products.

Trade Adjustment Assistance Act A U.S. law passed in 2002 that provides cash assistance, education and training benefits, health care subsidies, and wage subsidies (for persons age 50 or older) to workers displaced by imports or relocations of U.S. plants to other countries.

trade balance The export of goods (or goods and services) of a nation less its imports of goods (or goods and services).

trade bloc A group of nations that lower or abolish trade barriers among members. Examples include the *European Union* and the nations of the *North American Free Trade Agreement*.

trade controls *Tariffs, export subsidies, import quotas,* and other means a nation may employ to reduce *imports* and expand *exports*.

trade deficit The amount by which a nation's *imports* of goods (or goods and services) exceed its *exports* of goods (or goods and services).

trademark A legal protection that gives the originators of a product an exclusive right to use the brand name.

trade-off The sacrifice of some or all of one economic goal, good, or service to achieve some other goal, good, or service.

trade surplus The amount by which a nation's *exports* of goods (or goods and services) exceed its *imports* of goods (or goods and services).

trading possibilities line A line that shows the different combinations of two products that an economy is able to obtain (consume) when it specializes in the production of one product and trades (exports) it to obtain the other product.

tragedy of the commons The tendency for commonly owned *natural resources* to be overused, neglected, or degraded because their common ownership gives nobody an incentive to maintain or improve them.

transactions demand for money The amount of money people want to hold for use as a *medium of exchange* (to make payments); varies directly with *nominal GDP*.

transfer payment A payment of *money* (or goods and services) by a government to a *household* or *firm* for which the payer receives no good or service directly in return.

trough The point in a *business cycle* at which business activity has reached a temporary minimum; the point at which a *recession* has ended and an expansion (recovery) begins.

tying contract A requirement imposed by a seller that a buyer purchase another (or other) of its products as a condition for buying a desired product; a practice forbidden by the *Clayton Act*.

unanticipated inflation Increases in the price level (*inflation*) at a rate greater than expected.

underemployment A situation in which workers are employed in positions requiring less education and skill than they have.

undistributed corporate profits After-tax corporate profits not distributed as dividends to stockholders; corporate or business saving; also called retained earnings.

unemployment The failure to use all available *economic resources* to produce desired goods and services; the failure of the economy to fully employ its *labor force*.

unemployment compensation (See *unemployment insurance*).

unemployment insurance The social insurance program that in the United States is financed by state *payroll taxes* on employers and makes income available to workers who become unemployed and are unable to find jobs.

unemployment rate The percentage of the *labor force* unemployed at any time.

unfulfilled expectations Situations in which households and businesses were expecting one thing to happen but instead find that something else has happened; unrealized anticipations or plans relating to future economic conditions and outcomes.

uninsurable risk An event that would result in a loss and whose occurrence is uncontrollable and unpredictable. Insurance companies are not willing to sell insurance against such a loss.

union (See *labor union*.)

unionization rate The percentage of a particular population of workers that belongs to *labor unions;* alternatively, the percentage of the population of workers whom unions represent in *collective bargaining*.

union shop A place of employment where the employer may hire either *labor union* members or nonmembers but where nonmembers must become members within a specified period of time or lose their jobs.

unit elasticity Demand or supply for which the *elasticity coefficient* is equal to 1, means that the percentage change in the quantity demanded or supplied is equal to the percentage change in price.

unit labor cost Labor cost per unit of output; total labor cost divided by total output; also equal to the *nominal wage* rate divided by the *average product* of labor.

unit of account A standard unit in which prices can be stated and the value of goods and services can be compared; one of the three functions of *money*.

unlimited liability Absence of any limits on the maximum amount that an individual (usually a business owner) may become legally required to pay.

unlimited wants The insatiable desire of consumers for goods and services that will give them satisfaction or *utility*.

unplanned changes in inventories Changes in inventories that firms did not anticipate; changes in inventories that occur because of unexpected increases or decreases of aggregate spending (or of *aggregate expenditures*).

unplanned investment Actual investment less *planned investment*; increases or decreases in the *inventories* of firms resulting from production greater than sales.

Uruguay Round A 1995 trade agreement (fully implemented in 2005) that established the *World Trade Organization (WTO)*, liberalized trade in goods and services, provided added protection to intellectual property (for example, *patents* and *copyrights*), and reduced farm subsidies.

user cost The *opportunity* cost of extracting and selling a nonrenewable resource today rather than waiting to extract and sell the resource in the future; the *present value* of the decline in future revenue that will occur because a nonrenewable resource is extracted and sold today rather than being extracted and sold in the future.

U.S. securities U.S. Treasury bills, notes, and bonds used to finance *budget deficits*; the components of the *public debt*.

U.S. Steel case The antitrust action brought by the Federal government against the U.S. Steel Corporation in which the courts ruled (in 1920) that only unreasonable restraints of trade were illegal and that size and the possession of monopoly power were not violations of the antitrust laws.

usury laws State laws that specify the maximum legal interest rate at which loans can be made.

utility The want-satisfying power of a good or service; the satisfaction or pleasure a consumer obtains from the consumption of a good or service (or from the consumption of a collection of goods and services).

utility-maximizing rule The principle that to obtain the greatest *utility*, the consumer should allocate *money income* so that the last dollar spent on each good or service yields the same marginal utility.

value added The value of the product sold by a *firm* less the value of the products (materials) purchased and used by the firm to produce the product.

value-added tax A tax imposed on the difference between the value of the product sold by a firm and the value of the goods purchased from other firms to produce the product; used in several European countries.

value judgment Opinion of what is desirable or undesirable; belief regarding what ought or ought not to be (regarding what is right (or just) or wrong (or unjust)).

value of money The quantity of goods and services for which a unit of money (a dollar) can be exchanged; the purchasing power of a unit of money; the reciprocal of the *price index*.

variable cost A cost that in total increases when the firm increases its output and decreases when the firm reduces its output.

VAT (See *value-added tax*.)

vault cash The *currency* a bank has in its vault and cash drawers.

velocity The number of times per year that the average dollar in the *money supply* is spent for *final goods and services;* nominal GDP divided by the money supply.

venture capital (Web chapter) That part of household saving used to finance high-risk business enterprises in exchange for shares of the profit if the enterprise succeeds.

vertical axis The "up-down" or "north-south" measurement line on a graph or grid.

vertical integration A group of *plants* engaged in different stages of the production of a final product and owned by a single *firm*.

vertical intercept The point at which a line meets the vertical axis of a graph.

vertical merger The merger of one or more *firms* engaged in different stages of the production of a final product.

very long run A period in which *technology* can change and in which *firms* can introduce new products.

vicious circle of poverty (Web chapter) A problem common in some *developing countries* in which their low *per capita incomes* are an obstacle to realizing the levels of saving and investment needed to achieve rates of growth of output that exceed their rates of population growth.

voice mechanism Communication by workers through their union to resolve grievances with an employer.

voluntary export restrictions (VER) Voluntary limitations by countries or firms of their exports to a particular foreign nation to avoid enactment of formal trade barriers by that nation.

wage The price paid for the use or services of *labor* per unit of time (per hour, per day, and so on).

wage differential The difference between the *wage* received by one worker or group of workers and that received by another worker or group of workers.

wage rate (See *wage*.)

wages The income of those who supply the economy with *labor*.

wealth Anything that has value because it produces income or could produce income. Wealth is a stock; *income* is a flow. Assets less liabilities; net worth.

wealth effect The tendency for people to increase their consumption spending when the value of their financial and real assets rises and to decrease their consumption spending when the value of those assets falls.

welfare programs (See *public assistance programs*.)

Wheeler-Lea Act The Federal act of 1938 that amended the *Federal Trade Commission Act* by prohibiting and giving the commission power to investigate unfair and deceptive acts or practices of commerce (such as false and misleading advertising and the misrepresentation of products).

"will to develop" (Web chapter) The state of wanting *economic growth* strongly enough to change from old to new ways of doing things.

World Bank A bank that lends (and guarantees loans) to developing nations to assist them in increasing their *capital stock* and thus in achieving *economic growth*.

world price The international market price of a good or service, determined by world demand and supply.

World Trade Organization (WTO) An organization of 153 nations (as of fall 2008) that oversees the provisions of the current world trade agreement, resolves trade disputes stemming from it, and holds forums for further rounds of trade negotiations.

WTO (See *World Trade Organization*.)

X-inefficiency The production of output, whatever its level, at a higher average (and total) cost than is necessary for producing that level of output.

zero-sum game In *game theory*, a game in which the gains (+) and losses (−) add up to zero; one party's gain equals the other party's loss.

Selected Economics Statistics for Various Years, 1903–2007

Statistics in rows 1–5 are in billions of dollars in the year specified. Details may not add to totals because of rounding

GDP AND INCOME DATA	1983	1984	1985	1986	1987	1988	1989	1990	1991	1992	1993
1 Gross domestic product	3536.7	3933.2	4220.3	4462.8	4739.5	5103.8	5484.4	5803.1	5995.9	6337.7	6657.4
1A Personal consumption expenditures	2290.6	2503.3	2720.3	2899.7	3100.2	3353.6	3598.5	3839.9	3986.1	4235.3	4477.9
1B Gross private domestic investment	564.3	735.6	736.2	746.5	785.0	821.6	874.9	861.0	802.9	864.8	953.4
1C Government purchases	733.5	797.0	879.0	949.3	999.5	1039.0	1099.1	1180.2	1234.4	1271.0	1291.2
1D Net exports	−51.7	−102.7	−115.2	−132.7	−145.2	−110.4	−88.2	−78.0	−27.5	−33.2	−65.0
2 Net domestic product	3092.9	3460.6	3713.5	3931.5	4177.5	4506.2	4840.1	5120.6	5270.0	5585.8	5881.0
3 National income	3084.2	3482.3	3723.4	3902.3	4173.7	4549.4	4826.6	5089.1	5227.9	5512.8	5773.4
3A Wages and salaries	2042.6	2255.6	2424.7	2570.1	2750.2	2967.2	3145.2	3338.2	3445.2	3635.4	3801.4
3B Rent	37.8	40.2	41.9	33.5	33.5	40.6	43.1	50.7	60.3	78.0	95.6
3C Interest	285.3	327.1	341.3	366.8	366.4	385.3	432.1	442.2	418.2	388.5	365.7
3D Profits	264.2	318.6	330.3	319.5	368.8	432.6	426.6	437.8	451.2	479.3	541.9
3E Proprietor's income	192.5	243.3	262.3	275.7	302.2	341.6	363.3	380.6	377.1	427.6	453.8
3F Taxes on production and imports*	261.9	297.4	322.8	336.8	352.7	440.8	416.2	439.7	475.8	503.9	514.9
4 Personal income	2960.7	3289.5	3526.7	3722.4	3947.4	4253.7	4587.8	4878.6	5051.0	5362.0	5558.5
5 Disposable income	2608.4	2912.0	3109.3	3285.1	3458.3	3748.7	4021.7	4285.8	4464.3	4751.4	4911.9
6 Disposable income per capita	11,131.0	12,319.0	13,037.0	13,649.0	12,241.0	15,297.0	16,237.0	17,131.0	17,609.0	18,494.0	18,872.0
7 Personal saving as percent of DI	9.0	10.8	9.0	8.2	7.0	7.3	7.1	7.0	7.3	7.7	5.8

OTHER STATISTICS	1983	1984	1985	1986	1987	1988	1989	1990	1991	1992	1993
8 Real GDP (billions of 2000 dollars)	5423.8	5813.6	6053.7	6263.6	6475.1	6742.7	6981.4	7112.5	7100.5	7336.6	7532.7
9 Economic growth rate (change in real GDP)	4.5	7.2	4.1	3.5	3.4	4.1	3.5	1.9	−0.2	3.3	2.7
10 Consumer Price Index (1982–1984 = 100)	99.6	103.9	107.6	109.6	113.6	118.3	124.0	130.7	136.2	140.3	144.5
11 Rate of inflation (percent change in CPI)	3.2	4.3	3.6	1.9	3.6	4.1	4.8	5.4	4.2	3.0	3.0
12 Money supply, M1 (billions of $)	521.4	551.6	619.8	724.7	750.2	786.7	792.9	824.7	897	1024.9	1129.6
13 Federal funds interest rate (%)	9.09	10.23	8.1	6.8	6.66	7.57	9.21	8.1	5.69	3.52	3.02
14 Prime interest rate (%)	10.79	12.04	9.93	8.33	8.21	9.32	10.87	10.01	8.46	6.25	6.0
15 Population (millions)	234.3	236.3	238.5	240.7	242.8	245.0	247.3	250.1	253.5	256.9	260.3
16 Civilian labor force (millions)	111.6	113.5	115.5	117.8	119.9	121.7	123.9	125.8	126.3	128.1	129.2
16A Employment (millions)	100.8	105.0	107.1	109.6	112.4	115.0	117.3	118.8	117.7	118.5	120.3
16B Unemployment (millions)	10.7	8.5	8.3	8.2	7.4	6.7	6.5	7.0	8.6	9.6	8.9
17 Unemployment rate (%)	9.6	7.5	7.2	7.0	6.2	5.5	5.3	5.6	6.8	7.5	6.9
18 Productivity growth, business sector (%)	3.6	2.7	2.3	3.0	0.6	1.5	1.0	2.0	1.5	4.3	0.4
19 After-tax manufacturing profit per dollar of sales (cents)	4.1	4.6	3.8	3.7	4.9	5.9	4.9	3.9	2.4	0.8	2.8
20 Price of crude oil (U.S. average, dollars per barrel)	29.08	28.75	26.92	14.44	17.75	14.87	18.33	23.19	20.2	19.25	16.75
21 Federal budget surplus (+) or deficit (−) (billions of dollars)	−207.8	−185.4	−212.3	−221.2	−149.7	−155.2	−152.6	−221.0	−269.2	−290.3	−255.1
22 Public debt (billions of dollars)	1371.7	1564.7	1817.5	2120.6	2346.1	2601.3	2868.0	3206.6	3598.5	4002.1	4351.4
23 Trade balance on current account (billions of dollars)	−38.7	−94.3	−118.2	−147.2	−160.7	−121.1	−99.5	−79.0	2.9	−50.1	−84.8

*includes a statistical discrepancy.